THE PAST
FOREIGN COUNTRY · REVISITED

The past is past, but survives in and all around us, indispensable and inescapable. Three decades after his classic *The Past Is a Foreign Country*, David Lowenthal re-examines why we love or loathe what seems old or familiar. His new book reveals how we know and remember the past, and the myriad ways – nostalgia or amnesia, restoration, replay, chauvinist celebration or remorseful contrition – we use and misuse it. We transform the past to serve present needs and future hopes, alike in preserving and in discarding what nature and our ancestors have handed down.

Whether treasured boon or traumatic bane, the past is the prime source of personal and collective identity. Hence its relics and reminders evoke intense rivalry. Resurgent conflicts over history, memory, and heritage pervade every facet of public culture, making the foreign country of the past ever more our domesticated own.

The past in the Internet age has become more intimate yet more remote, readily found but rapidly forgotten. Its range today is stupendous, embracing not just the human but the terrestrial and even the cosmic saga. And it is seen and touched and smelled as well as heard and read about. Traumatic recollection and empathetic re-enactment demote traditional history. A clear-cut chronicle certified by experts has become a fragmented congeries of contested relics, remnants and reminiscences. New insights into history and memory, bias and objectivity, artefacts and monuments, identity and authenticity, and remorse and contrition, make Lowenthal's new book an essential key to the past that we inherit, reshape, and bequeath to the future.

David Lowenthal is Emeritus Professor of Geography and Honorary Research Fellow at University College London. He is a medallist of the Royal Geographical, the Royal Scottish Geographical and the American Geographical Societies, a Fellow of the British Academy and honorary D.Litt. Memorial University of Newfoundland. In 2010 he was awarded the Forbes Lecture Prize by the International Institute for Conservation. His books include *West Indian Societies* (1972), *The Past Is a Foreign Country* (1985), *The Heritage Crusade and the Spoils of History* (1998), and *George Perkins Marsh, Prophet of Conservation* (2000).

THE PAST IS A
FOREIGN COUNTRY –
REVISITED

David Lowenthal

CAMBRIDGE
UNIVERSITY PRESS

CAMBRIDGE
UNIVERSITY PRESS

University Printing House, Cambridge CB2 8BS, United Kingdom

One Liberty Plaza, 20th Floor, New York, NY 10006, USA

477 Williamstown Road, Port Melbourne, VIC 3207, Australia

4843/24, 2nd Floor, Ansari Road, Daryaganj, Delhi - 110002, India

79 Anson Road, #06-04/06, Singapore 079906

Cambridge University Press is part of the University of Cambridge.

It furthers the University's mission by disseminating knowledge in the pursuit of education, learning and research at the highest international levels of excellence.

www.cambridge.org
Information on this title: www.cambridge.org/9780521616850

© David Lowenthal 2015

A catalogue record for this publication is available from the British Library

Library of Congress Cataloging in Publication data
Lowenthal, David.
The past is a foreign country - revisited / David Lowenthal.
pages   cm
Includes bibliographical references and index.
ISBN 978-0-521-85142-8 (Hardback) – ISBN 978-0-521-61685-0 (Paperback)
1. History–Philosophy.   2. History.   I. Title.
D16.8.L52 2013
901–dc23   2013000789

ISBN 978-0-521-85142-8 Hardback
ISBN 978-0-521-61685-0 Paperback

TABLE OF CONTENTS

ILLUSTRATIONS

PERMISSIONS

ACKNOWLEDGEMENTS

I am grateful to many institutions for fruitful discourse: UNESCO, ICCROM, ICOMOS, International Institute for Conservation, Council of Europe, European Heritage Association, Getty Conservation Institute, Association of American Geographers, British Academy, British Museum, Australian, UK, and US National Trusts; Norway's Rijksantikvaran and Academy of Sciences; Australian Museums Council; Philosophy of History Research Seminars (London); Landscape Research Group (UK); Institute of Art & Law (UK); Browning Society; the Universities of Cambridge, Dundee, Edinburgh, St Mary's (Strawberry Hill), Strathclyde, and York (UK); California–Berkeley and Santa Barbara, Georgia, Massachusetts–Amherst, North Carolina, Vermont, Wisconsin–Madison (US); Massachusetts and Stevens Institutes of Technology, and Middlebury, Smith, Vassar, Wellesley, and Williams colleges; Huizinga Instituut (Amsterdam); European University Institute and Gabinetto Vieusseux (Florence), Lausanne and Zurich Universities; Alnarp, Linnaeus, Stockholm Universities and the Swedish Royal Institute of Technology; Université de Savoie; Memorial University Newfoundland.

Thanks for guidance, stimulus, generous assistance, and crucial material to Walter Alvarez, Robert Anderson, Ana-Lucia Araujo, Godfrey Baldacchino, Gilles Barbey, Gillian Beer, Francesca Bewer, Lester Borley, Richard Bosworth, Max Bourke, Carl Bray, Peter Brimblecombe, Michael F. Brown, Gillian Cowlishaw, †Kenneth Craik, William Cronon, Carole Crumley, Michael Daley, Jeremy Davies, Graeme Davison, Veronica Della Dora, Dydia DeLyser, †Greg Dening, Lisa Dolling, Gary Dunbar, John Elder, Karen Fields, Ruth Finnegan, Stephen Frith, Daniel Gade, Dario Gamboni, Richard Gaskin, †Peter Gathercole, Christina Gillis, David Glassberg, Alex Govorunov, Marcus Hall, Stephen Harrison, Cornelius Holtorf, Valerie Johnson, Gwyneira Isaac, Y Raj Isar, Michael Jones, †Michael Kammen, †Roger Kennedy, Piotr Kwiatkowski, Marc Laenen, Rob van der Laarse, John Latschar, Alan Liu, James Loewen, Scott Magelssen, Sabina Magliocco, Mandy Martin, Alistair McCapra, Tracy Metz, Nanouschka Myrberg Burstrom, Adam Nicolson, Pierre Nora, Richard Norgaard, Shane O'Dea, Onora O'Neill, Jorge Otero-Pailos, Sven Ouzman, Max Page, Norman Palmer, Mark Salber Phillips, Ann Plane, Gerald Pocius, Jerry Podany, Jeremy Popkin, Susannah Radstone, Alison Richmond, Ann Rigney, Adam Roberts, Dolores Root, Henry Rousso, Martin Rudwick, Bruce Ryan, Karin Sanders, Roger Sandilands, Fabio Sani, Marya Schechtman, Peter Seixas, Neil Asher Silberman, Per Kristian Skulberg, Edward Slingerland, Anthony Smith, Beverley Southgate, Sverker Sörlin, Randall Stephens, Henry and Diura Thoden Van Velzen Stobart, Lauren Talalay, Janna Thompson, Karen Till, John Torpey, Claudio Vita Finzi, Harald Welzer, Ernst van der Wetering, †Michael Williams, Justin Winkler, Gordon Wood, Izaly Zemtsovski, and Michael Zuckerman.

Enduring camaraderie, provocative discussion, and meticulous chapter critiques came from Stephen Brown, Peter Burke, †Denis Cosgrove, Simon Ditchfield, Jan Dizard, Anthony Grafton, Sally Greene, Tom Griffiths, Anthony Pace, Bernard Richards, Alessandro Scafi, and Samuel Wineburg, to which gifts were added unlimited hospitality from Michael Bell, Christina Gillis, Rolf Diamant, †David Hooson, Sheila and †Peter Lindenbaum, John Henry Merryman, Nora Mitchell, John T. Noonan Jr., Patrick O'Keefe, Karen and Kenneth Olwig, Lyndel Prott, Peter and Luisa Quartermaine, and Libby Robin. I am indebted to John Gillis and Cariadne Margaret Mackenzie Hooson for enduring the entire text, and to Mary Alice Lowenthal for unflagging expertise in domesticating this perversely foreign country.

Lynx-eyed readers have spared me manifold errors. 'I know by now to the full how many mistakes I have made', the late great Nikolaus Pevsner launched the final volume of his *Buildings of England*. I echo Pevsner's mortification but cannot claim his faith in revision: 'The first editions are only *ballons d'essai* [trial balloons]; it is the second editions which count.'[1]

---

[1] Nikolaus Pevsner, *Staffordshire* (Penguin, 1974), 17–18.

ABBREVIATIONS

Newspapers [*Times, Guardian, Independent, Evening Standard, Telegraph*, etc.]
all London

AASLH	American Association for State and Local History (Nashville, Tennessee)
AHA	American Historical Association
AHR	*American Historical Review*
CPW	Freud, *Complete Psychological Works*
CW	*Collected/Complete Works/Writings*
EH	English Heritage
ELH	*English Literary History*
GPO	Government Printing Office, Washington, DC
ICOMOS	International Council on Monuments and Sites
IHT	*International Herald Tribune*
IJCP	*International Journal of Cultural Property*
JHI	*Journal of the History of Ideas*
MIT	Massachusetts Institute of Technology
MLA	Modern Language Association
MLN	*Modern Language Notes*
NPS	National Park Service, US Department of Interior
NYRB	*New York Review of Books*
NYT	*New York Times*
PMLA	Publications of the Modern Language Association
SF	science fiction
SUNY	State University of New York Press, Albany, NY
TLS	*Times Literary Supplement*
USM&DR	*United States Magazine and Democratic Review*

Introduction

The past is everywhere. All around us lie features with more or less familiar antecedents. Relics, histories, memories suffuse human experience. Most past traces ultimately perish, and all that remain are altered. But they are collectively enduring. Noticed or ignored, cherished or spurned, the past is omnipresent. 'What is once done can never be undone ... Everything remains forever', wrote Václav Havel, 'somewhere *here*'.[1] The past is not simply what has been saved; it 'lives and breathes ... in every corner of the world', adds a historian.[2] A mass of memories and records, of relics and replicas, of monuments and memorabilia, sustains our being. We efface traces of tradition to assert our autonomy and expunge our errors, but the past inheres in all we do and think. Residues of bygone lives and locales ceaselessly enrich and inhibit our own. Awareness of things past comes less from fact finding than from feeling time's impact on traits and traces, words and deeds of both our precursors and ourselves. To know we are ephemeral lessees of age-old hopes and dreams that have animated generations of endeavour secures our place – now to rejoice, now to regret – in the scheme of things.

Ever more of the past, from the exceptional to the ordinary, from remote antiquity to barely yesterday, from the collective to the personal, is nowadays filtered by self-conscious appropriation. Such all-embracing heritage is scarcely distinguishable from past totality. It includes not only what we like or admire but also what we fear or abominate. Besides its conscious legacies, the past's manifold residues are embedded in our minds and muscles, our genes and genres de vie. Of passionate concern to all, the 'goodly heritage' of Psalm 16 becomes 'the cuckoo in the historian's nest', purloining the progeny of Clio, the muse of history.[3]

None of the past definitively eludes our intense involvement. What we are now indifferent to once meant much or may later do so. That being so, I survey the past not only through lenses of memory and history but also through present-day perspectives – impassioned views of right and wrong, good and evil, ownership and alienation, identity and entitlement. We descry the past both for its sake and for our sake. Neither historian nor layman is ever aloof or detached from it. To know is to care, to care is to use, to use is to transform the past. Continually refashioned, the remade past continuously remoulds us.

Embraced or rejected, lauded or lamented, remembered or forgotten, the whole past is always with us. No one has not 'said things, or lived a life, the memory of which is so unpleasant to him that he would gladly expunge it'. And yet one learns wisdom only by

---

[1] Václav Havel, *To the Castle and Back*, (Knopf, 2007), 330 (my emphasis).
[2] Constantin Fasolt, *The Limits of History* (Chicago, 2004), 16.
[3] Graeme Davison, *The Uses and Abuses of the Past* (Allen & Unwin, 2000), 9–14, 110–30.

passing through 'all the fatuous or unwholesome incarnations', says Proust's painter Elstir. 'The picture of what we were ... may not be recognisable and cannot, certainly, be pleasing to contemplate in later life. But we must not repudiate it, for it is a proof that we have really lived.' Indeed, however you try, 'you can't put the past behind you', concludes a scion of slavery. 'It's buried in you; it's turned your flesh into its own cupboard.'[4] We inherit a legacy no less inalienable when obscure or obnoxious. To be is to have been, and to project our messy, malleable past into our unknown future.

An authorial credo

Relations with the past can neither be prescribed nor proscribed, for they infuse all our ideas and institutions. Asked to add to a batch of historical manifestos, I demurred that 'historians should disdain manifestos; they are contradictions in terms. To issue proclamations and thunder denunciations is the duty of prelates and politicos. Our calling is not to moralise or preach but to discern and reveal – to make manifest (from the Italian *manifestare*) what deserves being evident'.[5] But I could not resist the urge to pontificate, avowing concern for the communal past and deploring its evisceration and domestication.

Having previously vilified populist history, I was accused of 'weeping in [my] beard' for lost academic felicity. For my faith in empirical objectivity I was taken to task as a 'bittersweet' nostalgist.[6] I do affirm the existence of historical truth and laud its disclosure. I do regret the modernist and postmodern breach with classical and biblical legacies. Like Mary Beard, I hold these legacies inextricably integral to Western culture, its horrors along with its glories.[7] I do share Gordon Wood's cheer that most historians still adhere to coherent and causally related narrative.[8] But I also consider invented heritage, no less than revealed history, both inescapable and indispensable. In fabricating the past 'we tell ourselves who we are, where we came from, and to what we belong'.[9]

I have not exhaustively studied most of the topics this book surveys. Instead I have sought to fashion a plausible synthesis out of extremely heterogeneous materials. Trespassing beyond my own expertise, I am bound often to have misinterpreted the art and architectural historians, psychologists and psychoanalysts, archaeologists and theologians, medievalists and Renaissance scholars on whose research I rely. For this I beg their pardon and readers' forbearance. Apart from a few realms – nineteenth-century American history, landscape perceptions, science fiction, historic preservation – my citations reflect no comprehensive sampling, but selections whose aptness authorities generally attest.

---

[4] Marcel Proust, *Remembrance of Things Past* (1913–27; Penguin, 1983), 1: 923–4; Claudia Rankine, *Citizen: An American Lyric* (Minneapolis, MN, Graywolf 2014).

[5] See my 'The past of the future: from the foreign to the undiscovered country', in Keith Jenkins et al., eds., *Manifestos for History* (Routledge, 2007), 205–19 at 205.

[6] David Harlan, 'Historical fiction and the future of academic history', 108–30 at 120, and Hayden White, 'Afterword: manifesto time', 220–31 at 231, both in Jenkins et al., eds., *Manifestos for History*.

[7] Mary Beard, 'Do the classics have a future?' *NYRB*, 12 Jan. 2012: 54.

[8] Gordon S. Wood, *The Purpose of the Past: Reflections on the Uses of History* (Penguin, 2008), 40–61.

[9] David Lowenthal, *The Heritage Crusade and the Spoils of History* (Cambridge, 1998), xvii.

Reversion to original sources reflects my well-founded suspicion of secondary sources, need to reconcile variant readings, and efforts to ensure contextual accuracy.[10]

My syntheses tap the collective takes on the past of many disciplines. Save for unlettered antiquity and recent popular culture, such insights are heavily weighted towards literate elites who troubled to record their views and were most inclined to speculate about the past. 'The wisest men in every age ... possess and profit by the constantly increasing accumulation of the ideas of all ages', noted John Stuart Mill, 'but the multitude ... have the ideas of their own age, and no others'.[11] My own conclusions inevitably rely mainly on that influential minority, present and past. It is this knowledgeable fraction to whom my 'we' and 'our' generally refers.

Present attitudes and those of our immediate forebears dominate this study, but exploring them often led me back to ancient times. Quality of evidence, confidence in sources, and comprehension of alien realms and cultures decline as the past recedes, but I perforce move back and forth across centuries with what may seem casual disregard for such differences. Spatially and culturally my conclusions are also parochial. Although I focus broadly on Western culture and rely on pan-European classical and subsequent scholarship, notably French, German, and Italian, I rely most heavily on anglophone literature. For non-European cultures equivalent studies would reach radically different conclusions.

A final caveat: I adduce such heterogeneous evidence – fiction, religious tracts, psychological treatises, interviews, autobiographies, heritage marketing, the history of ideas, polemics on preservation and restoration – as to seem wantonly eclectic or absurdly disparate. I do so not because I suppose all these sources analogous or of equal evidential value, but to make cogent what otherwise goes unnoted. Gleaned from things recalled and culled over a lifetime, my trove resembles Henry James's grab-bag of memory more than J. H. Hexter's coherence of history.[12]

How my past became foreign

'The past is a foreign country', begins L. P. Hartley's *The Go-Between;* 'they do things differently there'. From his 1950s' memory of 1900, he sought to convey the 'illusion of stability ... the confidence in life, the belief that all's well with the world'. That seemingly pervasive belief would soon be shattered by slaughter in the trenches and tumultuous change in civil society.[13]

That they did indeed do things differently is a quite recent perception. During most of history scholars scarcely differentiated past from present, referring even to remote events,

---

[10] See my 'The frailty of historical truth: learning why historians inevitably err', AHA *Perspectives on History* 51:3 (March 2013): 25–6.

[11] John Stuart Mill, 'The spirit of the age, I', *Examiner,* Jan.–May 1831, nos. I, IV, in *CW* (Toronto, 1963–91), 22: 227–34 at 234.

[12] Henry James, *The American Scene* (1907; Indiana, 1968), 410; J. H. Hexter, 'The rhetoric of history', *International Encyclopedia of the Social Sciences* (Macmillan, 1968), 6: 368–94.

[13] L. P. Hartley, *The Go-Between* (1953; NYRB Classics, 1962, repr. 2002), 17, and 'Author's introduction' (1962 edn), 7–15 at 8–10.

if at all, as though just then occurring. Up to the nineteenth century the historical past was generally thought much like the present. To be sure, history recorded major changes of life and landscape, gains and losses, but human nature supposedly remained constant, events actuated by unchanging passions and prejudices. Even when ennobled by nostalgia or deprecated by partisans of progress, the past seemed not a foreign country but part of their own. And chroniclers portrayed bygone times with an immediacy and intimacy that reflected the supposed likeness.[14]

This outlook had two particular consequences. Past departures from present standards were praised as virtuous or condemned as depraved. And since past circumstances seemed comparable and hence relevant to present concerns, history served as a source of useful exemplars. A past explained in terms similar to the present also suited common views of *why* things happened as they had. Whether unfolding in accordance with the Creator's grand design or with nature's cyclical laws, towards decline or towards progress, history's pattern was immutable and universal.

From time to time, prescient observers realized that historical change made present unlike past circumstances. But awareness of anachronism ran counter to prevailing needs and perspectives. Only in the late eighteenth century did Europeans begin to conceive the past as different, not just another country but a congeries of foreign lands shaped by unique histories and personalities. This new past gradually ceased to provide comparative lessons. Instead it became cherished for validating and exalting the present. This aroused urges to preserve and restore monuments and memories as emblems of communal identity, continuity, and aspiration.

During early-modern times archetypes of antiquity had dominated learning and law, informed the arts, and suffused European culture. Antiquity was exemplary, beneficial, and beautiful. Yet its physical remains were in the main neglected or demolished. Architects and sculptors were more apt to mine classical vestiges for their own works than to protect them against pillage and loss; patrons gave less thought to collecting antique fragments than to commissioning new works modelled on their virtues. Only in the nineteenth century did preservation evolve from an antiquarian, quirky, personal pursuit into sustained national programmes. Only in the late twentieth did every country seek to secure its own heritage against despoliation and decay.

Recognizing the past's difference promoted its preservation; the act of preserving accentuated that difference. Venerated as a fount of communal identity, cherished as an endangered legacy, yesterday became less and less like today. Yet its relics and residues are increasingly stamped with today's lineaments. We fancy an exotic past by contrast with a humdrum or unhappy present, but we forge it with modern tools. The past is a foreign country reshaped by today, its strangeness domesticated by our own modes of caring for its vestiges.

The past also accrues intentional new evocations. When I conceived this book's precursor in the 1970s the American scene was already steeped in pastness – mansarded and half-timbered shopping plazas, exposed brick and butcher-block historic precincts,

---

[14] Erwin Panofsky, *Renaissance and Renascences in Western Art* (1960; Paladin, 1970), 108–13; Zachary Sayre Schiffman, *The Birth of the Past* (Johns Hopkins, 2011).

heritage villages, urban preservation. Previously confined to a handful of museums and antique shops, the trappings of history festooned the whole country. All memorabilia were cherished, from relics of the Revolution to teacups from the *Titanic*. Antiques embraced even yesterday's ephemera. Genealogical zeal ranged from Alex Haley's *Roots* to the retrospective conversion of Mormon ancestors. Newly unsure of the future, Americans *en masse* took comfort in looking back. Historic villages and districts became familiar and reassuring home towns.

As an American then transplanted to Britain I espied similar trends in a nation more secure in its older collective identity. While disdaining a Disneyfied history, British conservationists mounted guard on everything from old churches to hoary hedgerows, deplored the drain of heritage across the Atlantic, and solaced present discontents with past glories. Presaging the 2010s TV series *Downton Abbey*, the quasi-feudal country house remained an icon of national identity even as death duties impoverished its chatelains. 'Millions knew who they were by reference to it. Hundreds of thousands look back to it, and not only grieve for its passing but still depend on it . . . to tell them who they are', wrote Nigel Dennis. 'Thousands who never knew it . . . cherish its memory.'[15] When the European Parliament suggested renaming Waterloo Station, then Eurostar's rail terminus, because it perpetuated divisive memories of the Napoleonic Wars, Britons retorted that it was 'salutary for the French to be constantly reminded of Wellington's great victory'.[16] Fashions for old films, old clothes, old music, old recipes were ubiquitous; revivals dominated architecture and the arts; schoolchildren delved into local history and grandparental recollections; historical romances and tales of olden days deluged the media. Bygones of every kind were salvaged with 'techniques of preservation that would have dumbfounded our forefathers', commented Dennis's fictional nostalgist. So expert was our 'taxidermy that there is now virtually nothing that is not considerably more lively after death than it was before'.[17]

Finding the foreign country

This book has multiple points of departure and destination. The past bewitches all historians. My enthrallment stems from a study, begun in 1949, of the American polymath George Perkins Marsh (1801–82), who chronicled landscape history from the debris of nature and the relics of human impact. Paralleling recent deforestation in his native Vermont with earlier Mediterranean denudation and subsequent erosion by Alpine torrents, Marsh gained unique insight into how humans had deranged – largely unintentionally, often disastrously – the habitable Earth. Marsh's apocalyptic warning that 'another era of equal human crime and human improvidence' would so impoverish the Earth 'as to threaten the depravation, barbarism, and perhaps even extinction of the species', made his 1864 *Man and Nature* the fountainhead of the conservation movement.[18]

---

[15] Nigel Dennis, *Cards of Identity* (1955; Weidenfeld & Nicolson, 1974), 119.
[16] John de Courcy Ling quoted in 'British refighting Battle of Waterloo', *IHT*, 29–30 Sept. 1984: 1.
[17] Dennis, *Cards of Identity*, 136.
[18] George P. Marsh, *Man and Nature* (1864; Harvard, 1965), 43. See my *George Perkins Marsh: Versatile Vermonter* (Columbia, 1958) and *George Perkins Marsh: Prophet of Conservation* (Washington, 2000).

Marsh sought to protect history as well as nature, to preserve artefacts of everyday life along with great monuments of antiquity. Not the accoutrements of princes and prelates, but the tools of field and workshop, the household implements and customary trappings of their own forebears, would remind Americans of their antecedents. Linked with the Romantic nationalism rooted in folklore and vernacular languages, Marsh's concern with common material vestiges bore fruition a generation later in Artur Hazelius's Skansen in Sweden, precursor of today's farm and industrial museums.[19] Marsh's stress on the workaday past prefigured today's heritage populism.

Moving between the New World and the Old in the 1960s, I saw how differently peoples depicted and reshaped communal legacies. English locales seemed permeated by fondness for the old and traditional. All the arts and the whole built environment reflected this bias. Delight in continuity and cumulation was integral to English appreciation of *genius loci*, the enduring idiosyncrasies that lend places their essential identity.[20] For Americans the past seemed both less intimate and less consequential. Far from venerating inherited vestiges, they traditionally derogated them as reminders of decadence and dependency. Admired relic features were either safely distant in Europe, sanitized by patriotic purpose as at Mount Vernon and Williamsburg, or debased by hucksters. Only a handful of wistful WASPs esteemed ancestry and antiques; to most Americans the past was musty, irrelevant, corrupt.[21]

The early 1970s turned attention to historical preservation on both sides of the Atlantic. The erosion of older city cores by urban redevelopment, the surge of nostalgia in the wake of post-war social and ecological debacles, the mounting pillage of antiquities for rapacious collectors led me to postulate that these trends had common roots and common outcomes. Present needs reshaped tangible remains in ways strikingly analogous to revisions of memory and history, as in Freud's archaeological metaphors for psychoanalytic excavation (Chapter 7 below).

Celebration of ethnic and national roots next engaged me. In the mid-1970s American bicentennial memorabilia and re-enactments reshaped the Revolutionary past to present desires. I traced the ways appreciation and protection transformed valued relics and locales. I studied how and why age and wear affected viewers in ways unlike historical antiquity. Dwelling abroad led me to compare Caribbean and Australian orientations with North American. Each of these New World realms had shaped diverse ways of defining, vaunting, and rejecting their various pasts.

Historic preservation, now a popular calling, next drew my attention. Sojourns among preservation programmes in Vermont, Kansas, and Tennessee revealed the primacy of architectural salvage and ensuing problems of gentrification. To learn what people cared

---

[19] Edward P. Alexander, *Museum Masters: Their Museums, and Their Influence* (AASLH, 1983), 239–75; Karin Belent et al., eds., *Skansen* (Stockholm: Sandvikens Tryckeri, 2002).

[20] David Lowenthal and Hugh C. Prince, 'The English landscape' and 'English landscape tastes', *Geographical Review* 54 (1964): 309–46 and 55 (1965): 186–222.

[21] See my 'The American scene', *Geographical Review* 58 (1968): 61–88.

to save, Marcus Binney of SAVE Britain's Heritage and I held a London symposium in 1979, followed by an Anglo-American conference on heritage management and legislation. Practitioners joined academics in discussing motives for saving everything from heirlooms to hatpins and related problems of provenance, stewardship, public entitlement, and the corrosive effects of popularity on fabric and ambience.[22]

The rage for time-travel fantasy led me to review imaginative journeys in science fiction, folklore, and children's literature. Their venturers yearned for and coped with visits to remote or recent pasts. Not unlike time travellers, legacy-seeking nations craved relics and records of fancied pasts. Formerly subjugated peoples deprived of precious patrimony highlighted issues of ownership, restitution, safety, conservation, and exhibition. The Elgin Marbles conflict was a prime instance of political passions aroused. A 1981 lecture of mine on heritage restitution figured in the confrontation between Greek culture minister Melina Mercouri and the British Museum over the return of the Parthenon frieze.

National efforts to fashion praiseworthy pasts resembled individual needs to construct viable life histories. Students of nationalism, psychoanalysis, and literature realized that states like persons confront competing pulls of dependence and autonomy, tradition and innovation. Similar metaphors for managing both supportive and burdensome pasts resounded across manifold disciplines and epochs. Attitudes towards the past, and reasons for preserving and altering its residues, reflected predispositions common to history, to memory, and to relics.

Publication of *The Past Is a Foreign Country* in 1985 led me to address curatorial dilemmas among archaeologists and art historians at the British, the Victoria and Albert, the Science, and Ironbridge Gorge museums. The historian Peter Burke and I led three years of seminars on 'The Uses of the Past' at the Warburg Institute and University College London. Growing concern over heritage authenticity and legitimacy was central to the British Museum's 1990 exhibition 'Fake? The Art of Deception', which I helped Mark Jones to curate. And as post-imperial critique began to query Western domination in archaeology, with Peter Ucko, Peter Gathercole, and others I helped mount the First World Archaeology Congress in Southampton in 1986.

Growing global participation likewise broadened UNESCO's World Heritage Site designations, while cosmopolitanism spurred revision of the canonical 1964 Venice Charter. That document had accorded prime value to western Europe's surviving marble monuments and stone and brick buildings. Less durable wooden architecture predominant in Norway and Japan led conservators to focus on rebuilt form rather than original substance; I joined the 1990s Bergen workshop and the Nara conference that rewrote criteria of authenticity accordingly. A decade later other cultural differences in heritage fuelled a similar drive to celebrate and protect intangible heritage. Where structures and artefacts soon decayed or were customarily replaced by new creations, what truly mattered was the maintenance of traditional skills and crafts, arts, and genres de vie.

---

[22] David Lowenthal and Marcus Binney, eds., *Our Past before Us: Why Do We Save It?* (Temple Smith, 1981); David Lowenthal, 'Conserving the heritage: Anglo-American comparisons', in John Patten, ed., *The Expanding City: Essays in Honour of Jean Gottmann* (Academic Press, 1983), 225–76.

Publication of my earlier book intensified my own involvement in challenging new approaches to history and heritage. In unifying Europe, felt needs for a consensual historical memory coexisted uneasily with resurgent national and regional identities. I addressed these history and heritage conflicts in advisory roles at the Council of Europe and Europa Nostra and in Poland, Finland, Sweden, Norway, Italy, Germany, Switzerland, and France. Pierre Nora, whose *Lieux de mémoire* began to appear at the same time as my book, and I held discussions at French universities on cultural and linguistic impediments to trans-national understanding of the past.

Growing globalization of history texts, heritage concerns, antiquities' issues and cultural tourism animated efforts to understand the past on a sounder philosophical basis. History remained overwhelmingly nationalistic, heritage traditionally crisis driven, its concerns dormant until activated by actual or threatened loss or damage. Various academic initiatives – at UNESCO, ICCROM, the Getty Conservation Institute, and elsewhere – foundered for want of institutional support, in a budgetary climate that confined past-related benefits to immediate economic payoffs.

The dawn of the new millennium saw the erosion of heritage enterprise, including my own teaching programmes at West Dean and Strawberry Hill, England. Meanwhile, rising tribal and subaltern demands to return human remains and artefacts beleaguered museums, nation-states, and international agencies. Restitution and repatriation concerns and mounting antiquities theft and plunder made management of the past a moral and legal minefield. Meanwhile the surge of traumatic memory and reconciliation issues in the wake of the Holocaust, apartheid, and other crimes against humanity transformed how the past was understood, blamed, and atoned for. This impelled my own return to consequences of slavery and racism that had been my Caribbean concerns half a century earlier. Together with the US National Park Service and colleagues in Norway, Italy, Malta, Greece, and Turkey I sought to bridge stewardship of past and future, nature and culture, protection and restoration in history, landscape, the arts and politics.

Frequenting the foreign country

'Your book is twenty years old. Update it!' my editor bade me in 2004. The idea was alluring. I'd recently revised my nearly fifty-year-old biography *George Perkins Marsh: Versatile Vermonter*. Two decades seemed a comparative snap.

Rereading sapped my euphoria. It's one thing to update a life, especially one long gone. It is quite another to modernize a book dealing with views of the past. Where to begin and end? In 2002 my Russian translator asked me what certain early '80s news items meant. For many I could recall nothing. Should ancient trivia be ditched for fresh ephemera? Some illustrations – notably the cartoons – seemed bizarrely outdated. Nothing fades faster than humour.

Updating, moreover, demanded more than replacing old anecdotes and not-so-current events. It meant recasting the book entirely, given the spate of recent work on history and memory, bias and objectivity, artefacts and monuments, facts and fakes, identity and authenticity, remorse and contrition. Much had changed in how the past was envisioned. Previously I had dealt with postmodernism only in its architectural context, with restitution and repatriation hardly at all, and was wholly unprepared for the ensuing spurt in everyday-memory studies and concomitant apologies for past crimes and evils. Other newly salient stances towards the past included the shift from written to visual portrayal, the rise of multi-vocal, reflexive narrative, polychronic flashbacks, Internet and website effects, online quests for genetic, personal, family, and tribal pasts. A properly comprehensive revision threatened to take the rest of my life. Ten years on, it has almost done so.

Updating also risked surfeit. *The Past Is a Foreign Country* struck some as all too much like the past itself – messy, inchoate, 'just one damned thing after another'. One reviewer faintly praised it as 'a fantastic treasure-house, a Calke Abbey of a book' – referring to the English National Trust mansion acquired from Sir Harpur Vauncey-Crewe, who had filled room after room with stuffed birds, seashells, rocks, swords, butterflies, baubles, and gewgaws. My verbally inflated cabinet of curiosities resembled the Derbyshire baronet's obsessive amassing. 'What could be alien' to Lowenthal? my critic wondered. 'Ballet? Brewing? Bionics? Bee-keeping?'[23]

I had already penned a book that took off from where *The Past Is a Foreign Country* ended.[24] In it I distinguished the rising cult of heritage – partisan manipulations of the past – from historians' impartial and consensual efforts to understand it. Appropriating the past for *parti pris* purposes, heritage purged its foreignness. The past's growing domestication now threatened to subvert this book's premise. I weighed retitling in the past tense. But *The Past Was a Foreign Country* lacked felicity. 'What a great title', said many – often implying they had read no further. Yet for all the renown of Hartley's riveting phrase, it is often mangled. Reviewers with the book in their hands misnamed it *The Past Is Another*, a *Distant, Different, Strange, Lonely*, even a *Weird Country*.

'Well, Emmeline, what's new?' Tobey's interlocutor asks her bygones-burdened hostess in the 1976 cartoon (Fig.1). 'We can be certain', wrote one of my reviewers, 'that the 1980s will come to be seen as the "good old days"'. The 1980s don't yet have the appeal of the 1950s, which 'the extreme reaches of the Right, confirmed bachelors of a certain vintage, drag queens and couturiers … wish had never ended'.[25]

So what else is new? Like nostalgia, the past ain't what it used to be. Thirty years have scuppered many previous outlooks. Mere passage of time made this inevitable. The '80s now moulder in the graveyard of the long-ago. What then seemed portentous or fateful, helter-skelter or baffling, today seems obvious or trivial, blinkered and blind-sided. Yesteryear's consuming concern – the Cold War – is now passé, overtaken by events and succeeded by anxieties then undreamt.

Many witnesses to that earlier past are now gone, and its survivors are a lot older: age renders some forgetful, others more sceptical, less sanguine. The lengthened recollections of retired baby-boomers merge with the collectively chronicled stream, memory

[23] A. H. Halsey, 'Past perfect?' *History Today* (Mar. 1986): 54; Colin Welch, 'Gone before but not lost', *Spectator*, 23 Nov. 1985: 27; Martin Drury, 'The restoration of Calke Abbey', *Journal of the Royal Society of Arts* 136 (1988): 490–9.

[24] David Lowenthal, *The Heritage Crusade and the Spoils of History*, (Cambridge, 1998).

[25] Lincoln Allison, 'Spirit of the eighties', *New Society*, 25 Apr. 1986: 24; Lisa Armstrong, 'Goodbye hippie chic as Galliano turns hourglass back to the 50s', *Times*, 7 July 2004.

"Well, Emmeline, what's new?"

Figure 1 The past all-pervasive: 'Well, Emmeline, what's new?'
(Barney Tobey, New Yorker, 25/10/1976, p. 37)

dovetailing into a longer personal history.[26] Meanwhile, oldsters confront the bizarre takes on the past of youngsters not even born when this book's precursor came out. Their sense of history, like their memories, often seems to their elders trivial, curtailed, amnesiac; History Channel viewers ask for 'younger historians, with better hair'.[27]

Additionally, calendric happenstance imposes a *fin-de-siècle* sense of change – we are no longer twentieth- but twenty-first-century people, denizens even of a new millennium. Like post-French Revolutionaries of the early 1800s and *fin-de-siècle* survivors in the early 1900s, we feel marooned in fearsome novelty. The past is not simply foreign but utterly estranged, as if on some remote planet. Our exile from it seems total, lasting, irrevocable. 'The worst thing about being a child of the 20th century is that you end up an adult of the 21st', remarked a caustic columnist. 'It was natural to be nineteenth century in the nineteenth century, and anyone could do it, but in the twentieth it takes quite a lot of toil', wrote English observers of 1960s America.[28] In the twenty-first century being nineteenth century seems appealing but impossible.

Irrelevant and irretrievable as the past may seem, it is by no means simply sloughed off. To assuage the grief of loss, the pain of rupture, the distress of obsolescence, we cling avidly to all manner of pasts, however alien or fragmentary. We also add to them in ways evident and extraordinary. Newly augmented and embellished pasts cannot replace the traditional 'world we have lost'.[29] But they comprise a complex of histories and memories, relics and traces, roots and reinterpretations, quite unlike our legacy a third of a century back.

Self-evident is the past's lengthening by the accretion of some thirty years. Every quarter-century seems especially earth-shaking to eyewitnesses; recent years commonly feel most momentous. It is a common fallacy to deem one's own epoch singularly significant or dire. Early theologians divined in contemporary annals portents of imminent apocalypse; palaeontologists discerned from fossil sequences the anatomical perfection reached in their own time; moderns consider their era critical because millennial.[30] Every present is specially salient to its self-centred denizens.

To be sure, recent decades have been eventful: the collapse of the Berlin Wall and the Soviet Union, the end of the Cold War and of apartheid, the disintegration of Yugoslavia, genocide in Bosnia and Rwanda, global warming, 9/11 and faith-based suicidal terrorism, the decline of American hegemony, revolutions in electronic data and communications, the spread of AIDS and Ebola, the demographic ageing of the West and the economic rise of the East, Chinese and Indian growth, Mideast turmoil and the failed Arab Spring – such events, sanguine or ominous, engender histories that no prognosis foresaw.

The last three decades were not uniquely dislocating – compare Revolutionary and Napoleonic 1790–1815, or World Wars and Holocaust 1914–45. But they were *differently* disruptive. Events spawned media persistently catastrophic in theme and tone, warning of

---

[26] Andrew Sanders, *In the Olden Time: Victorians and the British Past* (Yale, 2013), 312.

[27] Jim Rutenberg, 'Media talk', *NYT*, 5 Aug. 2002.

[28] Alan Coren, 'How I found myself in the wrong century', *Times*, 10 Aug. 2004; Malcolm Bradbury and Michael Oursler, 'Department of amplification', *New Yorker*, 2 July 1960: 58–62 at 59.

[29] Peter Laslett, *The World We Have Lost: England before the Industrial Age* (Methuen, 1965).

[30] Stephen Jay Gould, *Wonderful Life: The Burgess Shale and the Nature of History* (Norton, 1989), 43–5.

the end of history, the end of humanity, the end of nature, the end of everything. Millennial prospects in 2000 were lacklustre and downbeat; Y2K seemed a portent of worse to come. Not even post-Hiroshima omens of nuclear annihilation unleashed such pervasive glum foreboding. Today's angst reflects unexampled loss of faith in progress: fears that our children will be worse off than ourselves, doubts that neither government nor industry, science nor technology, can set things right.

The past has lengthened backwards far more than towards the present. Science shines new light on events ever longer ago in human, hominid, terrestrial, and cosmic time, to the first nanoseconds 13.7 billion years ago. Non-recurrent contingencies that have long informed geological history now enliven astronomy and biology. History's sweep came to include galaxies, stars, comets, and atoms, the universe evolving like living beings and human societies. All nature – plants, animals, continents, planets, stars, and galaxies – is now historicized. Cyclical regularity and enduring equilibria no longer set natural history apart from human annals. Genes, cells, organs, and organisms all change historically.[31] Narrative awareness is integral to modern biology. 'We cannot foretell a biosphere', instead, we 'tell the stories as it unfolds'. Hence 'biospheres demand their Shakespeares as well as their Newtons'.[32]

Intentionality aside, biological and stellar histories rival human annals in unpredictability. Cyclical regularity yields to chaotic temporal drift. Nature is seen to share humanity's turbulent, capricious career; geologists and biologists conjure like historians with opposing forces of friction (custom or tradition) and of stress (innovation or revolution). The episodic flows and fractures of the Earth's crust are as contingent as human history: nothing ever precisely repeats. In sum, 'cosmic history. natural history, and human history have come together in a single fabric'.[33] The segregation of prehistoric from historical archaeology, once de rigueur, is now virtually expunged, timeless prehistory becoming eventful history. Biology, neurology, pharmacology, and linguistics combine in tracing preliterate hominid and human annals.[34]

Mirroring mishaps of the recent past are disasters now shown to have punctuated previous aeons. The newly enlarged and convoluted past arouses fears similar to those unleashed by the nineteenth-century expansion of time. Then, Earth's demonstrably awesome antiquity cast disturbing doubts on Scriptural history. Today, ecological insights dismay those once comforted by nature's presumed constancy and regularity. Used to an Earth undisturbed by remote cosmic events, they took heart in the benign succession of seasons and in supposedly stable ecological equilibrium. But proof of episodic mass

---

[31] Fred Spier, *The Structure of Big History: From the Big Bang until Today* (Amsterdam University Press, 1996); Fred Spier, 'Big history', *Interdisciplinary Science Reviews* 33:2 (2008): 141–52; David Christian, *Maps of Time* (California, 2004); David Christian, 'A single historical continuum', *Cliodynamics* 2 (2011): 6–26; Harlow Shapley, *Beyond the Observatory* (Scribner's, 1967), 15–16; Immanuel Maurice Wallerstein, *The Uncertainties of Knowledge* (Temple, 2004), 23, 115–16; Martin J. S. Rudwick, *Bursting the Limits of Time* (Chicago, 2005), 188–93, 642–51.

[32] Stuart A. Kauffman, *Investigations* (Oxford, 2000), 22.

[33] William H. McNeill, 'Passing strange: the convergence of evolutionary science with scientific history', *History and Theory* 44:1 (2001): 1–15 at 5.

[34] Daniel Lord Smail, *On Deep History and the Brain* (California, 2008); Andrew Shryock and Daniel Lord Smail, eds., *Deep History: The Architecture of Past and Present* (California, 2011).

extinctions, sudden reversals of oceanic currents and climatic regimes, now leaves nothing safe or certain, revealing natural history imbued with a ferocity more ominous than any biblical harbingers.

Concurrently, human history is amalgamated into the extended terrestrial saga. No longer mere prologue, ongoing natural history informs thought and action over the whole of human history. As the biosphere ever alters our environs, so humanity's ecological impacts unfurl ever further back, disclosing Earth anciently humanized. Genetics link human evolution with other species extinct and extant. Climate, soils, plants and animals, including billions of symbiotic micro-organisms within us, incessantly remould and in turn reflect human destiny. Everything human bears nature's stamp; all nature now is anthropogenic.

That human action has long irreversibly transformed the Earth, and now does so with mounting intensity, is well known to environmental scientists and historians. But it newly alarms the general public. With an Earth made fruitful by divine fiat, people felt at home; an Earth despoiled and ruined alienates. That our unintended (let alone deliberate) impacts could be lethal for life for aeons to come seems intolerable. 'It is a kind providence that has withheld a sense of history from the thousands of species of plants and animals that have exterminated each other to build the present world', noted Aldo Leopold after Hiroshima. 'The same kind providence now withholds it from us.'[35]

Oral accounts dwelt mainly on distant origins and recent events, only sketchily referring to what happened in between, in the 'hourglass' pattern of the past described by Jan Vansina.[36] Recency and antiquity are again stressed at the expense of intermediate eras. This makes the past in its entirety harder to grasp. Starts and ends are mythic, befuddled, inscrutable. What comes first and last is literally unhinged – nothing prior attaches to the primordial, nothing links beyond the latest, which is soon engulfed in the present. At one end we are obsessed by primordial origins, for knowing how something began seems to explain all. At the other end, we are engrossed in personal recall. Electronic media privilege up-to-the-minute data, yesterday, not yesteryear. Historical learning follows suit: twentieth-century events, notably the adrenalin-pumping Second World War and the Holocaust, dominate curricula.

Ancient and recent alike are sexy, accessible – and murky. Great antiquity charms *because* it is little known; the veriest tiro freely opines on prehistory. To write about 'the distant past' (before the First World War), contends the novelist Hilary Mantel, is 'to flee to a world blurry enough so that men can behave like Vikings and not seem ridiculous, and ladies can be ladies without being pathetic'.[37] And any ignoramus can assert knowledge of yesterday simply by virtue of being around when it happened. Yet sheer recency leaves it incoherent. Hindsight cannot assimilate what has just happened into a properly mulled chronicle. To sift and evaluate require the test of time. Hence we delay nominating to halls of fame, designating historic sites, erecting memorials and

---

[35] Aldo Leopold, *A Sand County Almanac* (1949; Oxford, 1966), 50.
[36] Jan Vansina, *Oral Tradition as History* (Wisconsin, 1985), 23, 168–9; Schiffman, *Birth of the Past*, 33–4.
[37] Larissa MacFarquhar, 'The dead are real: Hilary Mantel's imagination', *New Yorker*, 15 Oct. 2012: 46–57 at 46.

monuments. It takes two or three generations to sieve a trustworthy collective past from the muddled trauma and trivia of living memory, the nostalgia or amnesia of immediate heirs. Emphasizing the very recent elevates fleeting fad and fashion over enduring culture.

Just as the past lengthens, so it expands in locale, in content, and in controversy. Once commonly confined to 'Western Civilization', history now at least sketchily includes all cultures everywhere. Once limited to the annals of kingship and conquest and the deeds of great men, it now dwells on the everyday lives and aspirations of 'people without history' – previously unsung women, children, workers, the poor, the enslaved, the unlettered. Every facet of life is now historicized: a vast panoply of players, a multiform narrative embracing annals of child-rearing, cookery, commemorating, tattooing, funerary practices, music-making. Such history deploys kinds of evidence and modes of analysis undreamt of by our precursors. But these accretions tend to occlude what history previously promised – ordered coherence, causal continuity, consensual assurance, contextual clarity. The new bloated past is often too inchoate to absorb. History's consumers are fascinated by relics and remembrances, caught up in bygone splendours and horrors. But they cheer or jeer at pasts they understand less and less. Our collective legacy is more bewildering than enlightening.

New habits of seeing and thinking accompany the past's temporal and topical enlargement. It is perceived with more of our senses, apprehended in alternative ways, self-consciously memorialized, re-enacted, and empathized with. Since the late 1980s the visual past has become all-pervasive. Pictures are not merely a sexy adjunct but a preferred way of encountering the past. More and more, the public believe and children are taught that the past is what they *see*, often contrary to the past they read or are told about.

The visual turn in history popularizes the past in general. History seen rather than read does not have to be translated into the mind's eye or thought about in the context of previous learning; it is immediately accessible to anyone, however unschooled. From a past in large measure seamless, univocal, canonical, certified by experts, and reliant on written texts, we nowadays confront a fragmented, dubious, ambiguous past open to any and all interpreters. Historians still strive for unbiased consensual understanding. But history is merely one among many versions of the past, and to most no more veracious than any other. In common with all takes on the past, history is seen as moulded to myriad personal and collective ends. Hence today's public is encouraged to privilege its own view of the past. Postmodernists preach that historians like all of us are partial and selective; we should dismiss academics all the more for claiming to be above the fray. All past views are biased. This is not altogether distressing; however defective, all pasts are equally deserving of attention. Your past, my past, so-and-so's past all have the populist merit of being *someone's* past. In this sense, the collective past is a collage, the crazy quilt of humanity's myriad individual memories.

But 'truth' in the old sense – a veridical account of the past based on consensually agreed evidence – has become passé. A past that feels appropriate, that suits any ephemeral personal need, is accorded validity. Even frankly fictitious concoctions are respected as some narrator's historical happenstance. Non-judgemental today, we extend permissiveness to yesterday. Just as anything goes now, anything likewise went back then: no version of the past is too far-fetched to ignore, too fantastic to lack insight. Since all pasts are constructed to be self-serving, the more avowedly self-interested they are the more honest and insightful we judge their narrators.

Precisely because such wannabe pasts as *The Da Vinci Code* are delectably persuasive, these self-avowed fictions are denounced for purveying spurious facts. And the line between fact and fiction does indeed blur. The contriver no less than the consumer of historical fiction comes to believe his invented past to be what actually happened. 'You know that firefight in Chapter 9, where you and a wounded [Navy] SEAL hold off 100 insurgents for a week?' says Garry Trudeau's cartoon character. 'Well, that was *me. I* was that wounded SEAL!' 'Dude, I made it all up', the author responds. 'Oh . . . Are you sure? It seemed so real.'[38]

Finally, the past is more and more bitterly contested, a prime arena of envious rivalry.[39] Clamour over purloined paintings, antiquities smuggling, tomb rifling, the opening of archives and the closing of libraries, demands for national and tribal restitution, court trials over repressed and false memories, quarrels over memorials and monuments, wills and bequests, make the past the world's largest – and most costly – legal arena. Who in the 1970s dreamed that nations would spend millions in bribes to accredit – or discredit – UNESCO World Heritage Sites? That tribal spokesmen would need to mandate that previous incarnation as an American Indian did not entitle one to tribal membership today? That Israel would do battle with the Church of Jesus Christ of the Latter-Day Saints over the posthumous conversion to Mormonism of hundreds of thousands of Holocaust victims? 'If you can't get them while they're alive, you'll get them while they're dead.'[40] Memory, history, and relics are no less spectacularly divisive today than when Crusaders torched Constantinople or Napoleon sacked Rome.

Themes and structure

This book comprises four broad themes: wanting, disputing, knowing, and remaking the past. Part I reviews how the past enriches and impoverishes us, and why we embrace or shun it. Part II surveys competing viewpoints about things past and present, old and new. How we become aware of and learn about the past, and how we respond to such knowledge, occupies part III. Part IV considers how we save and change the received past; why its vestiges are salvaged or contrived; and how these alterations affect the past and ourselves. I show how the past, once virtually indistinguishable from the present, became ever more foreign, yet increasingly suffused by present hopes and habits.

Chapters 1 and 2 explore age-old dreams of recovering or returning to the past. Nostalgia (Chapter 1) transcends yearnings for lost childhoods and scenes of early life, embracing imagined pasts never experienced. From an often fatal ailment nostalgia

---

[38] 'Doonesbury', *IHT*, 1 Dec. 2011: 12.
[39] J. E. Tunbridge and G. J. Ashworth, *Dissonant Heritage* (Wiley, 1996); Helaine Silverman, ed., *Contested Cultural Heritage: Religion, Nationalism, Erasure, and Exclusion* (Springer, 2011).
[40] Rabbi Moshe Waldoks quoted in Mark Oppenheimer, 'A twist on posthumous baptisms leaves Jews miffed at Mormon rite', *NYT*, 2 Mar. 2012: A12.

became a benign and even healing response to dislocation, absence, and loss. Recent disillusionments have expanded nostalgia's remit over time, space and topic, but also have provoked critical backlash against its regressive follies. Today unfeigned longing for childhood or homelands or Golden Ages gives way to retro irony and retro product marketing.

Faith in reincarnation and past-life regressions seems unquenchable. Fanciful returns to bygone days allure millions of 'Back to the Future' fans. Surveys show widespread desire to visit or relive some past period, recent or remote. The impossibility of doing so deters few imaginative voyagers. To some, such returns promise power, wealth, or immortality, to others a chance to undo errors or right wrongs, to still others an escape from present woes. Would-be time travellers' aims, surveyed in Chapter 2, shed light on the conflicting goals commonly sought in bygone realms. Some strive to remake the past what it should have been, others to protect past reality against perversion. Like these time travellers, we all seek to profit from the past while avoiding its trammels.

Chapter 3 surveys the benefits the past supplies and the fears its influence arouses. Thanks to the past we recognize familiar faces and places, reaffirm beliefs held and actions taken. The past provides exemplary guidance and personal and communal identity. It lets us commune with admired precursors; enriches present-day experience; and offers respites or escapes from the pace and pressure of the here and now. These merits all stem from qualities uniquely past, not present or future. Our awareness of antiquity, sequence, continuity, accretion, and above all termination decisively differentiates the past from the present. Because the past is *over*, it can be summarized and recapitulated as the present cannot. Nor is it subject to change as is the present.

Against these benefits must be set the past's grievous, stifling, and menacing drawbacks. We commonly seek but seldom manage to forget traumatic memory and to obliterate malign or tragic history. Alternatively, bygone glory may sap present endeavour. Time-honored tradition may seem onerous even to worshipful inheritors. Collective efforts to cope with a heritage at once revered and resented parallel individual needs both to follow and to reject parental precepts. Perennial debates pit imitation against innovation, ancient against modern prowess. Every inheritance is alike beneficial and baneful; each society reweighing the balance.

How the past has judged achievements and deficiencies in four epochs – the Renaissance; early-modern England and France; Victorian Britain; Revolutionary and national America – is reviewed in Chapter 4. In each of these epochs, the rival claims of past and present elicited quite different passionate debates.

Humanist reverence for classical antiquity did not mean humanists judged the past superior. Rather, it fostered Renaissance confidence that moderns might surpass ancient greatness. Antiquity's scattered and dismembered vestiges served as exemplars by being resuscitated and made whole. Translating classical works into vernacular tongues, readapting pagan motifs to Christian credos and iconography, reworking Greek and Roman architectural principles, scholars drew sustenance from the distant past while avoiding servile indebtedness. Yet doubts about emulative rivalry preoccupied humanists from Dante and Petrarch to Erasmus, du Bellay, and Montaigne. They were well aware that changing times and new audiences demanded new ideas and approaches. But the heretical disrepute of novelty led them to hide their innovations even from themselves, under the guise of reviving or restoring classical and patristic precedents.

The seventeenth- and eighteenth-century quarrel between the Ancients and the Moderns polarized past–present tensions. The relative worth of modern and antique achievements hinged on several issues: the decline of culture presumed by the doctrine of universal decay; the concept that moderns saw further only because they were 'dwarves on the shoulders of giants';[41] the felt contrast between science's cumulative achievements and art's unique but isolated creations. Aided by the printing-press, multiple variant texts enabled critical comparative analysis of now dubious past evidence. The triumphs of experimental science and the new worlds discovered by the telescope, the microscope, and geographical exploration magnified knowledge while calling into question sacred verities. By the Enlightenment, the classical tradition ceased to be the *ne plus ultra* in science but remained authoritative in the arts – a daunting legacy now aggravated by the feats of recent as well as remote precursors.

Victorian Britain deployed past decorum as a refuge from a progressive but cheerless present. Changes set in train by the French and Industrial Revolutions radically sundered today from yesterday; pride in material advance mingled with dismay at its sordid and brutal concomitants. Classical and medieval manners and mores were accorded the pastoral, chivalric, and hierarchical pieties violated by modernity. Immersion in antiquity and skilful replication spurred self-conscious eclectic revivalism but discouraged stylistic innovation. Nostalgic sentiment revived pre-industrial ideals in the Arts and Crafts movement, vernacular building, neo-Greek and Gothic architecture. Traditions backdated to time immemorial sanctified all that was anciently best. Whig history invested constitutional law and liberties with an Anglo-Saxon aura. But obeisance to old times, old practices, old forms also begot efforts to shed a heritage lampooned as anachronistic and irrelevant – iconoclastic impulses that exploded in *fin-de-siècle* despair and anti-historical modernism.

Americans' break from Britain generated parental and filial metaphors, both sides citing the bonds and reciprocal duties of parents and offspring. A revolution in child-rearing practices lent sanction to rebellions throughout the Americas that condemned all past authority: the present generation must be sovereign, free from parental tyranny. Taught to disdain inherited precepts, later generations were then torn between antipathy towards authority and reverence for the Founding Fathers' legacy. To emulate their forebears they should throw off the shackles of the past; but to safeguard their inheritance they must preserve, not create anew. These ideals were plainly incompatible. And the lingering fondness of some Americans for Old World hierarchal order offended the populist ethos that smelled evil and autocracy in such vestiges. The Civil War ultimately resolved the dilemma over preserving or creating, but national unity was regained at the cost of an amnesiac fiction of past amity. Tensions between progress and filial piety

---

[41] Robert K. Merton, *On the Shoulders of Giants* (Harcourt Brace Jovanovich, 1965).

thereafter shifted to WASP anxieties over immigration and urbanization, engendering nostalgia both for British and for colonial forms and fashions.

Those in each of these four epochs thus confronted their inheritance with mingled appreciation and resentment. Each sought in different ways to compromise or to choose between reverence and rejection. And each invented past traditions that reflected these painful dilemmas.

Chapters 5 and 6 explore responses to ageing, decay, and marks of use and wear, as distinct from indicators of a historical past. Artefacts and institutions are commonly assigned lifespans analogous to our own, their ageing likened to human old age – a condition usually dismayingly repellent, as shown in Chapter 5. Decay suggests not only enfeeblement and incipient demise, but corruption and evil, caricatured in venomous portrayals of senile impotent geezers and withered witch-like crones. Although medical advance has multiplied the numbers and political clout of the elderly, age-averse stereo- types and nursing-home horrors show geriatric animus unabated. Bias against the fact and look of age extends from humans to other creatures, natural features, nations and states, and most artefacts. Almost all are beautiful and virtuous when young, ugly and depraved when aged and decrepit.

Ageism is far from universal, however. Chapter 6 details how marks of age are felt to enhance the beauty and value of certain artefacts – notably buildings and paintings. Long ago admired in China and Japan, wear and tear became widely prized in Europe in the sixteenth century, first for confirming and authenticating antiquity, then as attractive in their own right. Monumental ruin and decay first acclaimed as *memento mori* later betokened picturesque aesthetic. Age appreciation earlier progressed from long-buried Chinese bronzes and neo-Romantic fondness for fragmented sculpture to time-softened varnished paintings. Today it includes Cor-Ten structures and sculptures meant to rust, artworks admired as they evanesce, and corroding industrial and military ruins. But the public in general shuns the appearance of age. Teddy bears and retro pubs aside, most old things should look new-made. But impassioned differences between friends and foes of the patina of age surface in continuing controversy over cleaning buildings and restoring paintings.

Chapters 7 through 9 survey how we become aware of and informed about the past. The past itself is gone – all that survives are our memories, accounts by its denizens, and a small fraction of its material residues. Such evidence can tell us nothing with absolute certainty. For the past's survivals on the ground, in texts, and in our heads are selectively preserved from the start and continually altered by the passage of time. These remnants conform too well with one another and with the known present to be denied all validity, yet the past's reality remains in doubt. There can be no certainty that the past ever existed, let alone in the form we now conceive it. But sanity and security require us to believe that it did exist, as its overwhelmingly accordant records and relics indeed suggest.

Access to the past via memory, history, and relics exhibit important resemblances and differences. Memory, by its nature personal, and hence largely unverifiable, extends back only to childhood, although we do accrete to our own recollections those told us by forebears. By contrast, history is longer, more public, durable, and confirmable. History extends back to or beyond earliest records Death extinguishes countless memories, whereas recorded history is potentially immortal. Yet all history depends on memory, and much recall incorporates history. And both are distorted by selective perception, intervening circumstance, and hindsight.

The uses and misuses of memory (Chapter 7) are integral to human existence. The remembered past endows us with habits and recognitions essential to present functions and future anticipations. Various types of memory – bodily, semantic, episodic, autobiographical, eidetic – combine to differently access the past, linking personal recall with collective memory. Together they construct awareness of enduring identity. Yet the passage of time continually alters old and creates new memories. Contrary to common belief, no original memory survives in its initial form. Recording techniques from writing to film and tape progressively displace or transform recollection. Forgetting is likewise essential, lest a surfeit of often conflicting memory overwhelm us. Hence memory is necessarily selective and continually sieved. Yet much of what we remember turns out to be at best partly true, and sometimes entirely experientially false. The ease with which false memories can be induced, with unhappy consequences for the deluded and for the sake of justice, has become well understood as the result of several traumatic inquiries into reported cases of fantasized abuse.

Psychological understanding of everyday and autobiographical memory has made huge strides over the last quarter century. And public interest in memory is evident in the proliferation (and problematic veracity) of memoirs; in traumatic accounts of the Holocaust and other mass horrors; and in growing doubts about memory accuracy in judicial proceedings. Indeed, memory bids fair to replace history as a more immediate, personal, empathetic, and visceral response to the past.

Historical knowledge (Chapter 8) seems on a firmer footing than what is known from memory alone, because it is consensually reached and shared, and to a large degree verifiable. Yet history is shaped – and misshaped – by subjectivity, by hindsight, and by an insurmountable gulf between the actual past and any account of it. Every chronicle is both more and less than what happened – less because no account incorporates any entire past, however exhaustive the records, more because later narrators are privy to subsequent outcomes. While hindsight adds to our understanding of the past, it distances us from its denizens.

Historians necessarily narrate the past from the standpoint of the present, rearranging data and revising conclusions in a modern manner. Shifting needs of narrators and audiences shape history's substance and rhetoric. So do changing notions of chronology and narrative. Diverse Classical, Judaeo-Christian, and humanist perspectives on relations between past and present, time and eternity, chance and fate, divine and human agency permeate Western history's own complex history. Growing doubts about the repetitive constancy of human affairs, growing acceptance of the inevitability of change, and growing faith that change meant progress led to Eurocentric awareness of the past as different from the present – a foreign country. Today as fiction and film trump academic history, that foreign past seems increasingly multifaceted, discordant, and debatable. Hence it gets domesticated.

Memory and history both derive and gain authority from physical remains (Chapter 9). Tangible survivals' vivid immediacy helps assure us there really was a past. Physical remains have limited evidentiary worth: themselves mute, they require interpretation. Moreover, differing rates of erosion and demolition skew the material record. But however depleted by time and use, relics crucially bridge then and now. They confirm or deny what we think of the past, symbolize or memorialize communal links among generations, and provide archaeological metaphors that illumine history and memory. Locales and relics are objects of curiosity or beauty, historical evidence, and talismans of continuity reified by visceral contact with the past. However ill-informed our responses, they bespeak our concern with what has been. All knowledge of the past requires caring about it – feeling pleasure or disgust, awe or disdain, hope or despair about its legacies.

Surviving relics and recollections undergo ceaseless change, much of it of our own making. Even when we strive to save bygone things and thoughts intact, we cannot avoid altering them. Some changes are made unconsciously, others reluctantly, still others deliberately. Chapters 10 to 12 examine how and why we transform the past, and how such changes affect our environs and ourselves.

Simply to identify something as 'past' affects its ambience: recognition entails marking, protecting, and enhancing relics to make them more accessible, secure, or attractive. Preserving things (Chapter 10) inevitably transforms them, often in unintended and undesired ways. Appreciation if not survival may require moving relics from original locales. Enshrined in historical precincts yet immersed in the trappings of present-day management, vestiges of the past seem newly contrived. Present choices – whether to retain relics *in situ* or to shift them, to leave them fragmented or to make them whole again – vitally affect how the past is experienced.

Imitations, fakes, and new works inspired by earlier prototypes extend and alter auras of antiquity. The fame or scarcity of originals begets replicas that copy, emulate, or echo the old. Creations that hark back to or reflect some attribute of a bygone era have for two millennia dominated the cultural landscape of the Western world. Modern awareness of classical architecture derives from an amalgam of Hellenistic, Renaissance, Enlightenment, Romantic, and Victorian works, in which extant Greek and Roman remains are sparse. Frequently mistaken for originals, copies and replicas may be preferred to them for their completeness, their freshness, or their accordance with modern taste and expectations. Originals often seem less 'authentic' than current views of what things past should have been.

When the past is gone beyond recovery, we often recall or re-enact its events and lineaments. Chapter 11 discusses two pervasive modes of recapitulation. One is to restore what is gone. An innate urge to restore is pervasive in every aspect of life. Restoration takes different forms and confronts different dilemmas in politics and poetics, dentistry and gerontology, architecture and painting, theology and ecology. Yet practitioners in each of these realms borrow one another's metaphors and methods. Time's irreversible arrow makes restoration an ultimately impossible ideal. But this is a stark reality that restorers habitually deny or wish away, as seen especially in efforts to recover 'original' works of art and 'natural' landscapes.

Another common mode of recall is re-enactment, an ancient sacred practice now a highly popular mode of secular commemoration. At historic sites and in battle replays, in experimental archaeology and in cinema, re-enacting serves pedagogic, patriotic, and recreational purposes. Those eager to relive the past, either by adopting its personae and lifestyles or by engaging with others who enact it, strive to slough off their present selves. But literal re-enactment would require unawareness of today's circumstances as well as now unendurable deprivations. Sailors who replay Captain Bligh's voyages are not flogged; soldiers who restage Civil War battles do not undergo unanaesthesized amputations, let alone die on the battlefield. All re-enactments are to some degree inauthentic, just as no restorations are complete.

Chapter 12 surveys deliberate alterations of the past. We remould it to maximize the benefits outlined in part I. Patriotic zeal or private pride conforms past remnants to present needs and expectations. Accentuating past virtues enhances our self-esteem and advances our interests. Hence we antiquate antiquity, contrive missing continuities, invent ancestral prerogatives and achievements, ignore ignominy, and avenge defeat.

Many falsify past events and fabricate things that never happened. Most fakes and hoaxes, however, aim not to deceive but to improve. We especially reshape the past to make it our own, individually or collectively. As abstract entity the past has little merit; as our own possession it provides identity, precedent, patrimonial pride. We manipulate the legacy given us to secure it as heritage, hyped improvements sanctifying it in our eyes and distinguishing it from others.

Revising, enlarging, and commemorating each lend the past a host of improved new lineaments. We embellish and amplify on the one hand, conceal and expurgate on the other, or nowadays deplore and denigrate disapproved pasts. We also anachronize the past, antiquating to claim precedence and justify possession, modernizing to make it more exemplary. These ahistorical perversions are widely accepted by the general public and in large measure unavoidable.

To be sure, knowing that we alter the past renders dubious our esteemed fixed and stable heritage and undermines trust in our prospective role as faithful stewards. Yet to be aware that we improve what we inherit has its compensations. Realizing that the past is not just what happened back then but also what we and others have made of it, we discard the mystique of an inflexible legacy. Remaking that legacy is not only inevitable but salutary. Historically informed knowledge of our fabrication – both conceiving *and* deceiving – enables groups like individuals to achieve a realistic, liberating, and self-respecting past.[42]

The Epilogue appraises current views of bygone things and times. The lengthened and deepened past has become almost omnipresent, engulfing the media and personal memory. Yet at the same time collective memories have withered away. While historians know more and more about the past, the public at large knows less and less, and what is commonly known is increasingly recent, trivial, and ephemeral. Both in private proliferation and public demise, the past comes to resemble the present. Domesticated into today, it is ever less a foreign country. Memory overwhelms history, and authoritative understanding succumbs to untutored surmise. Cynical doubts assail the entire corpus of

---

[42] Albert J. Solnit, 'Memory as preparation: developmental and psychoanalytic perspectives' (1984), in Joseph Sandler, ed., *Dimensions of Psychoanalysis* (London: Karnac, 1989), 193–218 at 218.

the past. 'Just about everybody who was actually there is dead now, so who knows which author got it right? If any of them did. It's all a lot of bullshit'.[43]

A corollary of conflating the past within the present is failure to realize that bygone people lived according to other codes, their modes of thought as well as *genres de vie* alien to our own. Unable to conjure with inexplicably different norms, they blame ancestral precursors for not thinking and behaving like themselves. But we are simultaneously enjoined to make amends for precursors' misbehaviour – injunctions rarely obeyed. All the same rationales for historical accountability, from Erasmus and Burke to modern jurists and philosophers, seem to me invaluable. Linking the living, the dead, and those to come as a continuing community, we become responsible for the past in its entirety. Informed tolerance toward our total legacy is a necessary condition of enhancing the present and enabling the future.

---

[43] Seventeen-year old in Sylvi Lewis, *Beautiful Decay* (Philadelphia: Running Press Teens, 2013), 107.

PART I

WANTING THE PAST

The poetry of history lies in the quasi-miraculous fact that once, on this earth, on this familiar spot of ground, walked other men and women, as actual as we are today, thinking their own thoughts, swayed by their own passions, but now all gone, one generation vanishing after another, gone as utterly as we ourselves shall shortly be gone.
                                                George Macaulay Trevelyan, 1949[1]

There is only the past. The future hasn't come into being yet, and the present is a hairline thinner than the thinnest imaginable hair ... Let us glory in having added more and more to the past.
                                                Anthony Burgess, 1983[2]

Someone asks a Greek cartoonist whether the country has a future. Well, he said, 'we have a past. You can't have everything.'
                                                Patricia Storace, 1997[3]

The miracle of life is cruelly circumscribed by birth and death. Of the immense aeons, the abyss of years before and after our own brief lives, we directly experience nothing. Consciousness that blesses humans with knowledge of a past also curses us with awareness of time's awesome duration beyond our own evanescence. Why, asked Arthur Schopenhauer, should we lament our future non-existence any more than our absence from pre-natal eras?[4] Some indeed do mourn both: viewing home movies filmed a few weeks before his birth, Vladimir Nabokov was appalled by the rich reality of this past he had not shared and where nobody had missed him. A brand-new empty baby carriage had 'the smug, encroaching air of a coffin ... as if, in the reverse order of things, his very bones had disintegrated'. Defying the prison of time present, he strove 'to steal into realms that existed before I was conceived'.[5]

Past and future are alike inaccessible. But though beyond physical reach, they are integral to our imagination. Reminiscence and expectation suffuse every present moment. Yet they attract – and repel – differently. Times ahead are fearsomely uncertain. We depict desired futures but cannot foretell the outcomes of our own acts, let alone the fate of posterity. And we do well to be careful what we crave. Future wishes are famously subverted.

---

[1] George Macaulay Trevelyan, 'Autobiography of an historian', in *An Autobiography & Other Essays* (Longmans, Green, 1949), 1–64 at 13.
[2] Anthony Burgess, *End of the World News* (McGraw-Hill, 1983), 216.
[3] Patricia Storace, *Dinner with Persephone: Travels in Greece* (Granta, 1997), 159.
[4] Arthur Schopenhauer, *Parerga and Paralipomena* (1851), in *Short Philosophical Essays* (Oxford, 1974), 2: 268.
[5] Vladimir Nabokov, *Speak, Memory: An Autobiography Revisited* (1951; Putnam, 1966), 19–20. See Brian Boyd, 'Nabokov, time, and timelessness', *New Literary History* 37 (2006): 469–78.

A Faustian yearning for posthumous fame (long condemned as diabolical) led Max
Beerbohm's Enoch Soames, a *fin-de-siècle* poet deservedly neglected in his own day, to
sell his soul to the devil so that he could learn what posterity would think of him.
A century later Soames returns to the British Library, to find only one catalogue entry
under his name: "'an immajnari karrakter . . . a thurd-rate poit hoo beleevz imself a grate
jeneus" in a story by Max Beerbohm'.[6] In another Faustian deal, the devil will make a
writer the best of his generation, nay, of the century, the millennium. 'Your glory will
endure forever. All you have to do is sell me your grandmother, your mother, your wife,
your kids, your dog and your soul'. 'Sure, where do I sign?' Then he hesitates. 'Just a
minute. What's the catch?'[7]

Memorial prospects once seemed more secure, poetic perpetuity likely. Horace would
be 'continually . . . renewed in the praises of posterity'. Robert Herrick would never
'forgotten lie / [for his] eternal poetry / . . . / Unto the thirtieth thousand year, / When
all the dead shall reappear'. Literary creation vanquished mortality for Samuel Daniel,
confident 'That when our days do end, they are not done, / And though we die, we shall
not perish quite, / But live two lives where others have but one'.[8] Creative immortality
enriched sacred and then secular memorialization, through benefactions to churches,
hospitals, museums, and universities.[9]

Downsizing today – from your name on a building to just one brick, from a concert
hall to a single seat, from a library to a mere shelf – enables anyone to live on in future
memory for a paltry sum. In practice, however, even the most lavish donors are
soon shuffled off. For his $20 million gift Leon Levy would be memorialized at the
Metropolitan Museum of Art's new Greek and Roman wing 'in perpetuity'. 'How long is
that?' he asked. 'For you, fifty years', said director Philippe de Montebello. 'For 20
million', Levy countered, 'make it seventy-five years'.[10] Forever ends ever sooner. But
ever more sites and cornerstones, podiums and professorships, are nowadays embellished with the names of wannabe immortals. Whatever their heavenly afterlife, the
deceased linger ever longer on earth, whether cryogenically or in copyright, cinematic

---

[6] Max Beerbohm, 'Enoch Soames', in *Seven Men and Two Others* (1919; Oxford, 1966), 36. Soames devotees
witnessed his return to the reading room on 3 June 1997 ([Raymond Joseph] Teller, 'A Memory of the
nineteen-nineties', *Atlantic Monthly* 280:5 (Nov. 1997): 48–53). See David Colvin and Edward Maggs, eds.,
Enoch Soames (London: Maggs, 2001); on diabolical vainglory, Piero Boitani, '*Those who will call this time
ancient*: the futures of prophecy and piety', in J. A. Burrow and Ian P. Wei, eds., *Medieval Futures* (Boydell,
2000), 51–65 at 62.

[7] Margaret Atwood, *Negotiating with the Dead: A Writer on Writing* (Cambridge, 2002), 101–2.

[8] Horace, *Works*, (c. 23 BC; Cambridge, 1821), Ode 30, 1: 221; Robert Herrick, 'Poetry perpetuates the
poet' (1648), in *Hesperides and Noble Numbers* (New York, 1898), 82; Samuel Daniel, 'Musophilus'
(1599), in *A Selection from the Poetry of Samuel Daniel & Michael Drayton*, ed. H. C. Beeching (London,
1899), 38.

[9] Robert Jay Lifton and Eric Olson, 'Symbolic immortality' (1974), in Antonius C. G. M. Robben, ed., *Death,
Mourning and Burial* (Wiley-Blackwell, 2004), 32–9. See John Kotre, *Outliving the Self* (Johns Hopkins,
1984), expanded in his *Make It Count: How to Generate a Legacy That Gives Meaning to Your Life* (Free
Press, 1999).

[10] Andrew Stark, 'Forever or not?' *Wilson Quarterly* 30:1 (Winter 2006): 58–61; Leon Levy with Eugene
Linden, *The Mind of Wall Street* (New York: Public Affairs, 2002), 190.

voiceovers, and commercial endorsements. Elvis Presley and John Lennon today rival the Pharaohs in accrued post-mortem wealth.[11]

Utopian planners in the Modernist 1920s and 1930s envisaged the future as 'another country, which one might visit like Italy, or even try to re-create in replica', recalled an architectural historian. Futurism was 'a period style, a neo-gothic of the Machine Age ... a city of gleaming, tightly clustered towers, with helicopters fluttering about their heads and monorails snaking around their feet ... under a vast transparent dome'.[12] Post-war hubris canonized 'every new technology from nuclear power to plastic flowers. [Soon] we would be inhabiting plexiglass bubbles and living on protein pills.'[13] But that fancied future faded in the 1960s with hippie flower children peddling '*hand-lettered* posters [with] pictures of windmills'. The technological utopia became a wistful memory; what lay ahead seemed ever less promising if not downright menacing. High-rise tower blocks were 'no longer the exciting future but the evil past'; Modernist architecture gave way to postmodern retro pastiche.[14]

Every facet of life fled the failed future for some consoling past. Le Corbusier's avant-garde machine for living was forsaken for the blue remembered hills of Housman's heritage-worthy land of lost content. Historical city cores came to resemble open-air museums, their restored facades offering 'the illusion we are still living in the eighteenth century', carps a Dutch conservator, 'embalmed like a mummy' to meet banal tourist expectations.[15] Heritage engulfed not just the built legacy but film and fiction. Memory obsession flooded autobiography, memoir, and retro styles of every epoch, recalling times when the future still beckoned.

Unlike the scant and scary contours of times ahead, the past is densely delineated. Countless vestiges in landscape and memory reflect what we and our precursors have done and felt. More familiar than the geographically remote, the richly elaborated past feels firmer than the present, for the here and now lacks the structured finality of what time has filtered and ordered. The past is less disconcerting than the present because its measure has already been taken.

Moreover, we feel quite sure that the past really happened, that its traces and memories reflect irrefutable scenes and acts. The flimsy future may never arrive: man or nature may destroy all; time may terminate. But the securely tangible past is seemingly fixed, indelible, unalterable. 'How much nicer to go back', exclaims a fictional modern visitor to the world of 1820; 'the past was safe!'[16] We are at home in it because it *is* our home – the past is where we come from. Few have not wished, at least in fancy, to return to an earlier time. The past is 'Paris' in a Russian's lament, 'I wish I were in Paris again.' 'But

---

[11] Michael A. Kearl, 'The proliferation of postselves in American civic and popular culture', *Mortality* 15 (2010): 47–63.

[12] Reyner Banham, 'Come in 2001 ...', *New Society*, 8 Jan. 1976: 62–3.

[13] Hannah Lewi, 'Paradoxes in the conservation of the modern movement', in Hans-Hubert Henket and Hilde Heynen, eds., *Back from Utopia* (Rotterdam: 010, 2002), 350–7 at 357.

[14] Banham, 'Come in 2001'; Simon Jenkins, 'Why reel life now depends on fantasy', *Times*, 21 Dec. 2001.

[15] A. E. Housman, *A Shropshire Lad* (1896; London, 1956); Wim Denslagen, *Romantic Modernism: Nostalgia in the World of Conservation* (Amsterdam University Press, 2009), 9.

[16] Brian W. Aldiss, *Frankenstein Unbound* (Jonathan Cape, 1973), 26.

you've never been to Paris', says his friend. 'No, but I've wished I was in Paris before.' The revisited past does not always satisfy, but it seldom disappoints so cruelly as the future did poor Enoch Soames.

Yet we can no more slip back to the past than spring ahead to the future. Except in imagined reconstruction, yesterday is closed; all we have of prior experience are attenuated memories, dubious chronicles, fragmented and degraded relics. We dream of escaping the confines of today, often to prefer it again when it becomes yesterday. Such, wrote a friend, was the nostalgic torment of Tennyson, 'always discontented with the present till it has become the Past, and then he yearns towards it, and worships it'.[17] In recent decades such nostalgic yearning, like the cult of preservation, became pervasive and addictive.

Present absorption with the past transcends partisan purposes. Popular history, biography, autobiography, and historical fiction deluge the media. Re-enactments retrieve the immediacy of all bygone aspects, mythic or mundane, heroic or quotidian. 'Calendars so full of memorial days for the remarkable events of the past [leave] almost no room . . . for anything more to happen in the future'.[18] DNA elevates genealogy from elite pursuit to populist passion. Oral archives celebrate the annals of hitherto unsung masses, local histories their most humdrum details, the narrator a 'beachcomber among the casually washed-up detritus of the past', in Simon Schama's phrase.[19] Unexceptional memoirs by ordinary people are 'disgorged by virtually everyone who has ever had cancer, been anorexic, battled depression, lost weight . . . Owned a dog. Run a marathon. Found religion. Held a job.'[20] We furnish our homes with things that consciously evoke the past, adorn walls with family photos and mantels with memorabilia, convert city streets into 'Memory Lanes', archive personal memories. The Internet flogs digital retention of total recall from cradle to grave, every Facebook twitterer his own autobiographer.

Vestiges of the past, whole, dismembered, or discernible only in traces, lie everywhere around us, yet until recently these remnants were seldom prized. Taking decay for granted, people let antiquity disappear as the laws of nature and the whims of culture dictated. Ancient Egypt entombed artefacts only for dead elites; early Christendom treasured few survivals other than sacred relics. More oddities than antiquities filled Renaissance cabinets of curiosities. Seventeenth-century cognoscenti admired archaeological finds but took few trophies. Victorian devotees of Walter Scott's historical novels and George Gilbert Scott's historical architecture acquired tangible mementoes of previous epochs, but no past patron rivalled the magpie hoards of such modern accumulators as William Randolph Hearst.

Saving the tangible, and lately the intangible, past is today a global enterprise. Nations like individuals salvage things in greater quantity and variety than ever before, albeit often

[17] James Spedding quoted in Philipp Wolf, *Modernization and the Crisis of Memory* (Amsterdam: Rodopi, 2002), 100–1.

[18] Tzvetan Todorov, *Hope and Memory* (Princeton, 2003), 159.

[19] Simon Schama, 'The Monte Lupo story', *London Review of Books*, 18 Sept. 1980: 23.

[20] Neil Genzlinger, 'The problem with memoirs', *NYT Book Review*, 28 Jan. 2011.

vicariously, as in BBC TV's *Restoration* (2003–). To be sure, preservation is an age-old enterprise. Mortal remains, religious relics, emblems of power and of endurance are perennially cherished. But to retain a substantial portion of the past is signally a latter-day goal. As recently as 1996 a heritage authority held culture 'not really an active or primary interest to the majority of people anywhere'.[21] Only with the nineteenth century were European nations defined by their material heritage; only in the twentieth were concerted efforts made to protect it. Global programmes to ward off destruction and decay stem from the past six decades.

That saving the past is of universal concern is now widely assumed. To possess the tangible (and today the intangible) corpus of heritage is a sine qua non of collective identity and well-being, as vital a nutriment as food and drink. 'The marvels of humanity's past, and the issues we face in understanding and conserving them' are held to be 'topics of concern as never before'.[22]

Buildings – prominent, durable, seemingly intrinsic to their surroundings – are a major catalyst of collective historical identity. Disgust with modernism fuelled historic preservation from the 1960s. Before, 'old buildings were universally understood to be less valuable than new. Now', said Stewart Brand of America in 1994, 'it is almost universally understood that old buildings are more valuable than new'. Most Britons, too, preferred old houses to new, widely viewed as featureless, mean, and lifeless.[23] 'A new building is rarely anything like as good as an old one because it is unique'; a London developer extols the neoclassical white stucco 'Regency facade', with copied pillars and cornices, dear to foreign tycoons.[24]

But preservation also embraces manuscripts and motor cars, silent films and steam engines. The valued past ranges from great monuments to trifling memorabilia, from durable remains to mere traces. Virtually any old thing which would once have been junked is now enshrined in popular memory and collectors' hearts. Diverse motives animate lovers of architectural relics, archaeological sites, ancient landscapes, antiques and collectables. But the results have much in common.[25] Relics saved confirm identity and shed glory on nations, neighbourhoods, and individuals. Refuges from bewildering novelty, historical sites and antique objects spell security, ancient bricks and mortar assure stability. Like photo-laden mantels and antique parlours, hoary villages are havens imbued with fond remembrance of *some* past. To halt demolition and stave off erosion furthers a virtual immortality that defies the devouring tooth of time.

Preservation is also stridently collective. Every state strives to safeguard its historical monuments. Antiquities are prized whether ancient and abundant, scarce or recent.

---

[21] Peter Groote and Tialde Haartsen, 'The communication of heritage', in Brian Graham and Peter Howard, eds., *The Ashgate Research Companion to Heritage and Identity* (Ashgate, 2008), 181–94 at 183–9; Jeanette Greenfield, *The Return of Cultural Treasures* (1989; 2nd edn Cambridge, 1996), 299.

[22] Martin Filler, 'Smash it: who cares?' *NYRB*, 8 Nov. 2012: 24; John H. Stubbs, *Time Honored: A Global View of Architectural Conservation* (Wiley, 2009), and John H. Stubbs and Emily G. Makaš, *Architectural Conservation in Europe and the Americas* (Wiley, 2011), document such concerns.

[23] Stewart Brand, *How Buildings Learn* (Penguin, 1994), 88, 109.

[24] Ben Rogers, 'The home of bad design', *Prospect*, Dec. 2010: 38–42; Richard Holledge, 'Modern conveniences behind traditional facades', *IHT*, 19 Nov. 2010: 14.

[25] Mihaly Csikszentmihalyi and Eugene Rochberg-Halton, *The Meaning of Things: Domestic Symbols and the Self* (1981; Cambridge, 2002), 62–96.

Myriad agencies – the International Council of Museums (ICOM), the International Council on Monuments and Sites (ICOMOS), the International Centre for the Study of the Preservation and the Restoration of Cultural Property (ICCROM), the International Institute for Conservation of Historic and Artistic Works (IIC), UNESCO's World Heritage Convention – enlist global preservation concern.

The urge to preserve is triggered by the pace of evanescence. Amid wholesale change we cling to familiar vestiges. Things no longer useful are admired as obsolete. Saving discarded objects gives them a genealogy, lends them temporal depth, makes up for the longevity that casting them off foreclosed. Interest in each remnant mounts as it threatens to disappear – steam engines, thatched roofs, pottery ovens inspire affection seldom elicited when still plentiful. Nothing so quickens preservative action as foreboding of imminent extinction, whether of a bird, a building, or a folkway.

Global warfare, technological innovation, rapid obsolescence, radical modernization, massive migration, and increased longevity leave us in ever less familiar surroundings, estranged even from our recent pasts. 'Every man is a traveler from another time', said the publisher William Jovanovich, 'and if the journey is long he ends up as a stranger'.[26] Attachment to buildings that were here before us reflects a rational hunger for permanence. 'The more rapidly society changes, the less readily should we abandon anything familiar which can still be made to serve a purpose', advised a sociologist. However efficient or handsome the new, abrupt discontinuity inflicts intolerable stress.[27]

Aerial bombing and deliberate destruction destroyed up to half the urban heritage of Europe and Japan. Historic buildings and traditional scenes in Britain and Italy succumbed en masse to post-war developmental pressures. Losses in war-torn Afghanistan, Iraq, and Syria are no less horrific.[28] Iconoclasm and theft, fire and flood decimate antiquities and archives the world over. The past generation is said to have destroyed more prehistory than was previously known to exist. 'The tempo of destruction is presently so great', warned Karl Meyer in 1973, 'that by the end of the century most remaining important archaeological sites may well be plundered or paved over'.[29] The four decades since have aggravated damage. In China as in Italy bulldozers and tomb-robbers imperil ever-more-valued antiquities; thieves 'know what they want, and they destroy the rest'. Despite a twelve-fold increase in policing since 2005, archaeologists find 95 per cent of newly discovered tombs already emptied by a hundred thousand thieves. A recently excavated pre-Inca complex in Peru was hailed as the first *unlooted* site found. Beset by tourists as well as thieves, Third World global heritage sites face irreversible loss and damage.[30]

[26] Quoted in Henry Beetle Hough, *Soundings at Sea Level* (Houghton Mifflin, 1980), 206.

[27] Peter Marris, *Loss and Change* (1974; rev. edn. Routledge, 1986), 150.

[28] Francesco Siravo, 'Historic cities and their survival in a globalized world', *Change over Time* 1 (Spring 2011): 110–28 at 116.

[29] Karl E. Meyer, *The Plundered Past* (Atheneum, 1973), xv.

[30] Asif Efrat, 'Protecting against plunder: the United States and the international efforts against looting of antiquities', Cornell Law Faculty Working Paper 47 (2009); Jim Yardley, 'Bulldozers and thieves imperil Chinese relics', *IHT*, 6 Feb. 2007; Tania Branigan, 'China's tomb raiders laying waste to

Such destruction is far from new. A Victorian antiquary noted the 'rapid disappearance and exhaustion' of Celtic skulls and vases owing to 'agricultural improvements, and the ill-conducted pillage of idle curiosity'. Ancient monuments were 'increasingly the prey of the ignorant sightseer on the one hand or the needy owner of the soil on the other', and antiquaries were said to do more damage than the owners.[31] But destruction has accelerated. Modern machinery can metamorphose a city or a landscape virtually at a stroke; urban skylines are transformed unrecognizably every few years, street scenes altered in the blink of an eye. Trees are felled, hedgerows uprooted, buildings obliterated unremarked, or vandalized to forestall an impending preservation order. Modern pollution erases masterpieces that have withstood centuries of travail. To safeguard the Acropolis and *The Last Supper* against atmospheric sulphur would require ridding Athens and Milan of automobiles and industry.

Military technology augments the toll. Bombs enable iconoclasts to expunge any detested legacy. Popularity also speeds the past's destruction. Mass tourism aggravates theft and erosion at historical sites. Visitors no longer carry away slivers of Shakespeare's supposed chair at Stratford or hire hammers to chip keepsakes from Stonehenge,[32] but these gains in decorum are small compared with modern losses. Tourist footwear wore out the turf around the Stonehenge sarsens; cathedral sightseers rub inscriptions to illegibility; collectors promote illicit traffic that devastates ancient sites: Mayan temples are hacked to pieces for clandestine export. Growing appreciation threatens survival *in situ*; thieves posing as preservation officers pilfer old chimneypieces and banisters. The high cost of protecting sites and relics speeds their doom. Effective safeguards are expensive or onerous. Modern fire rules call for insulation and escape routes that historical sites can ill afford. In applying height, lighting, and staircase rules mandated for new structures to old buildings, England's public-health officers habitually destroyed their historic character. Insurance can bankrupt museums and galleries and is hence often forgone, as with Edvard Munch's *The Scream*, one version stolen in 1994 and another in 2004 from museums in Oslo.

Threatened by technology, pollution, and popularity, surviving vestiges command protective attention as never before. The expertise that speeds demolition also locates and salvages history hitherto hidden under the ground, beneath the sea, behind the varnish of a painting. And new techniques mend old materials once beyond hope of

---

thousands of years of history', *Guardian*, 1 Jan. 2012; Heather Pringle, 'First unlooted royal tomb of its kind unearthed in Peru', *National Geographic Daily News*, 27 June 2013; Global Heritage Fund, *Save Our Vanishing Heritage: Safeguarding Endangered Cultural Heritage Sites in the Developing World* (Palo Alto, 2010).

[31] Thomas Bateman, *Ten Years' Diggings in Celtic and Saxon Grave Hills* (London, 1861), v–vi; 'Archæologia', *Edinburgh Review* 154 (1881): 101–21 at 120–1; Simon Thurley, *Men from the Ministry* (Yale, 2013), 40.

[32] 'We cutt off a Chip according to the Custom' (John Adams, 'Notes on a tour of English country seats, &c., with Thomas Jefferson', in *Diary and Autobiography*, 4–10 Apr. 1786 (Harvard, 1961), 3: 185). A piece broken off Plymouth Rock by a descendant of Pilgrim founder William Bradford features in a 2013 museum display (William L. Bird, Jr., *Souvenir Nation: Relics, Keepsakes and Curios from the Smithsonian's National Museum of American History* (Princeton Architectural Press, 2013), 45–7. Svetlana Boym, *The Future of Nostalgia* (Basic Books, 2001), xvi.

repair. Alternatively, what is gone stimulates devotion to its history and fondness for its memories. Like a newcomer to an old town who seeks to acquire local roots, we become nostalgically attached to the scenes and the songs, the things and the tastes, even the turmoils and the traumas, of the pasts we once or even never had. However beyond return our lost homeland, however irrecoverable our vanished past, today's massive uprooting and fearsome change, suggests Svetlana Boym, seats nostalgia 'at the very core of the modern condition'.[33]

---

[33] Svetlana Boym, *The Future of Nastalgia*, (Basic Books, 2002), xvi.

1

Nostalgia: dreams and nightmares

> There once was a place where neighbors greeted neighbors in the quiet of summer twilight. Where children chased fireflies. And porch swings provided easy refuge ... Remember that place? Perhaps from your childhood ... That place is here again, in a new town called Celebration ... that takes you back to that time of innocence ... A place of caramel custard and cotton candy, secret forts and hopscotch on the streets ... A whole new kind of lifestyle that's not new at all – just lost for a while. That fellow who said you can't go home again? He was wrong. Now you can come home.
>
> Disney brochures, 1995[1]

> Nostalgia is like a grammar lesson. You find the present tense, but the past perfect.[2]

> Everything is nostalgia. Everyone wants to live in the past. The present has no style. The present is ugly. The present is gross ... It's part of the human condition to look to the past, because if you look to the future you have to look forward to your own death ... So the past is where we all want to be.   Jonathan Ames, 2005[3]

Nostalgia is today's favoured mode of looking back. It saturates the press, serves as advertising bait, merits sociological study, expresses modern malaise. Obsolescence confers instant bygone status – no sooner is the fire engine retired than it becomes a precious relic. 'Bring back proper kiosks', yearned an English nostalgist. 'Bring back trolley-buses ... Bring back cars with starting handles.' A Britain addicted to Victorian chivalry, neo-Gothic architecture, and the film *Excalibur*, surmised a 1981 critic, would 'soon be appointing a Curator instead of a Prime Minister'.[4] British curators are treasures in their own right, their heritage expertise exported worldwide, while at home *Brideshead Revisited* redux became *Downton Abbey*, today's Edwardian triumph. Nostalgia 'harks back to some rose-tinted past, of Marmite and *The Magic Roundabout* [1965–77], when kids played in the street, it was summer all year round, and Edrich was always 103 not out'.[5] And before

---

[1] Quoted in Andrew Ross, *The Celebration Chronicles: Life, Liberty, and the Pursuit of Property Value in Disney's New Town* (Ballantine, 1999), 18; and Stephen Brown, *Marketing: The Retro Revolution* (Sage, 2001), 185–6; Thomas Wolfe, *You Can't Go Home Again* (Harper & Row, 1934).
[2] Attributed to radio historian Owens Lee Pomeroy or speechwriter Robert Orben.
[3] Jonathan Ames, '"Snobs": the nonworking class', *NYT Book Review*, 13 Mar. 2005.
[4] Paul Jennings in *Sunday Telegraph*, 4 Feb. 1979: 16; J. Mordaunt Crook, 'Honour and its enemies', *TLS*, 25 Sept. 1981: 1102.
[5] 'Heritage skills are worth billions', *Times*, 18 Oct. 2004: 29; Patrick Foster, 'Downton: you ain't seen nothing yet', *Times*, 10 Nov. 2010: Arts 13–14; Ben Macintyre, 'In with the bulldozers! Away with nostalgia!' *Times*, 19 Nov. 2009: 35. John Edrich was a famed English cricketer.

Britain's imperial decline. 'We're going back to the past', James Bond tells M in *Skyfall*, 'where we have the advantage.'[6]

But nostalgia is by no means uniquely British. America's Nostalgia Book Club 'put you years behind the times – by choice'. *Good Old Days*, the 'Magazine that Remembers the Best', fondly recalls porches, cedar buckets, hitching posts, woodsheds, showboats, 'Casey at the Bat', Bonnie & Clyde, The Lone Ranger, the Second World War; subscribers collect Zane Grey books, Sears Roebuck catalogues, McGuffey Readers, old sheet music.[7] *Looking Back* offers 'heartwarming wartime romances, old-time advertising. 'Return to the loveliness of yesteryear, an era of timeless charm, enduring quality, beauty and elegance … a breath of relief from this fast paced world', urges *Victoria Magazine*, while *Martha Stewart Living*'s 'Summer Supper' provides 'memories rich enough to last 1001 nights'.[8]

At the new millennium's eve a critic moaned that 'America has no now. Our culture is composed of sequels, reruns, remakes, revivals, reissues, … recreations, re-enactments, adaptations, anniversaries, memorabilia, oldies radio, and nostalgia record collections.' His plaint itself echoed the 1980s, the founding decade of 'replay, recycle, recall, retrieve, reprocess, and rerun' from more creative times.[9] A recent paean to the vanished past conveys its nostalgic appeal:

Before texts and tweets, when there was time. Before apps, when there were attention spans. Before social media, when we were social. Before celebrities, when there were stars. Before identity theft, when nobody could steal you. Before the Greens, when we faced the Reds. Before movies-on-demand, when movies were demanding. Before dystopia, when utopia beckoned. Before Facebook, when there was Camelot. Before reality shows, when things were real. Before attitude, when there was apathy. Before YouTube, when there was you and me. … we managed just the same, without passwords, even in black and white.[10]

Indeed, Britons now suggest that Americans are *more* nostalgic. In Britain, the Past Times retro-themed chain of shops went broke in 2012. 'We lost interest in its historically themed knick-knacks. It could no longer flog us Henry VIII duvet covers, Black Death vitamin pills and King Canute Lilos … We don't want the past any more.' Whereas Americans adore everything retro. 'Over there, everyone's drinking tea and hiring butlers.'

To us, *Downton Abbey* is old news. It's so 2011. We're over it … *Downton* was, of course, popular here too. But we watched it giggling. We knew it was a nonsensical confection of invented past. We knew its tale of happy, cap-doffing plebs, slimy middle classes and angelic toffs … was a Henry VIII duvet cover of a programme … Americans, however not only believe that England was just like that in 1916, they think it's like that *now*.[11]

---

[6] Ben Macintyre, '007's latest mission: restoring Britain's pride', *Times*, 2 Nov. 2012: 35.
[7] Richard Stenhouse, ed., *Live It Again: 1942* (Berne, IN: DRG, 2010).
[8] 1991 ads quoted in Barbara B. Stern, 'Historical and personal nostalgia in advertising text', *Journal of Advertising* 21:4 (1992): 1–22 at 15, 18.
[9] George Carlin, *Brain Droppings* (Hyperion, 1997), 110; Tom Shales, 'The re decade', *Esquire* (Mar. 1986): 67–70.
[10] Roger Cohen, 'Change or perish', *NYT*, 5 Oct. 2010 (excerpted).
[11] Victoria Coren, 'Nostalgia is such old hat', *Observer*, 22 Jan. 2012.

Once the solace or menace of the few, nostalgia now attracts and afflicts all. Myriad ancestor-hunters scour archives; millions throng to historic houses; antiques engross hoi polloi; every childhood past is souvenired. Reversing earlier ill-repute, nostalgia is promoted as therapeutic, an aid to self esteem, a crutch for personal continuity, a defence against reminders of mortality.[12] A London hospital's 1940s/50s Nostalgia Room encourages elderly patients to reminisce while sipping tea from real china cups. Handling heritage objects loaned by museums proved therapeutic for home-care residents.[13] In the BBC's *The Young Ones* (2010), six geriatric celebrities were 'rejuvenated' by five days immured in the 1975 trappings – decor, food, TV – of their heyday; the show sparked a surge in retro furnishings among elderly viewers.[14]

Restaurants lead the nostalgia boom. Several Greenwich Village hostelries offer visions of bohemian Old New York's aspirational intimacy. Like 'an old townhouse passed down through generations without anyone throwing anything away', 'The Lion' parades a faux-past enhanced by photos of Al Capone, Babe Ruth, and Frank Sinatra, with a Duke Ellington, Andrews Sisters, and 1960s Barbra Streisand soundtrack.[15] Retro-1950s English teashops artfully scatter old 'Ordnance Survey maps [with] pipe-smoking ramblers on their covers over the kind of three-mirror dressing table that Celia Johnson might have used to primp her hair' in *Brief Encounter* (1945).[16] In loving memory of the Hard Rock Café and Planet Hollywood, the House of Blues Southern juke-joint themed restaurants/nightclubs are 'shellacked with layer upon layer of fake authenticity. The windows weep with fake water damage; ersatz graffiti confronts you in the toilet; pretend tobacco stains dot the ceilings'.[17]

Nostalgia fuelled the nascent film industry and suffuses modern cinema. Movies are especially 'vulnerable to fears of obsolescence', suggests critic A. O. Scott, because 'film is so much younger than the other great art forms'. Born at the very onset of modernism, movies exemplify its fleeting fragility. 'We sense – and sorrow – that back then ... the stars were more glamorous, the writing sharper, the stories more cogent'. What 'we used to love is going away, or already gone'. Digitization dooms even cinema's

old material hallmarks – the grainy swirl of emulsion as light passes through the stock, the occasional shudder of sprockets sliding into place, the whirr and click of the projector ...

---

[12] Constantine Sedikides et al., 'Nostalgia as enabler of self-continuity', in Fabio Sani, ed., *Self-Continuity* (New York: Psychology Press, 2008), 227–39; Clay Routledge et al., 'Finding meaning in the past: nostalgia as an existential resource', in Keith D. Markman et al., *The Psychology of Meaning* (Washington, DC: American Psychological Association, 2013), 297–316; John Tierney, 'A stroll down memory lane has benefits', *IHT*, 10 July 2013: 8.

[13] Jackie O'Sullivan, 'See, touch and enjoy Newham University Hospital's nostalgia room', in Helen Chatterjee, ed., *Touch in Museums* (Oxford: Berg, 2008), 224–30; Healing Heritage exhibition, University College London, July 2011.

[14] *Times*, 14 Sept. 2010: 57. The show repeated Harvard psychologist Ellen J. Langer's 1979 study; she had a group of elderly men in a retrofitted 1959 setting pretend for a week they were twenty-two years younger (Ellen J. Langer, *Counterclockwise* (Ballantine, 2009), 5–10).

[15] Diane Cardwell, 'In the Village, restaurants offer a vision of the city as it once was', *NYT*, 20 May 2010: 21–2.

[16] Ian Jack, 'Sugar coats this hunger for the past', *Guardian*, 17 July 2010: 15.

[17] Joshua Glenn, 'Fake authenticity: an introduction', *Hermenaut* 15 (22 Dec. 1999).

Nostalgia . . . is built into moviegoing, which is why moviegoing itself has been, almost from the beginning, the object of nostalgia.[18]

Not by chance, cinema's quintessential locales are the Wild West and the Effete East. As the death of the West coincided with the birth of the movies, the archetypal Western was saturated from the start with nostalgia for 'an older, rougher, simpler society'. Heroes and villains knew they were 'living not just in the West but also in a Western', soon global in locale, American cowboys morphing into samurai and spaghetti personae, at length feminist, kung-fu and wallaby Westerns.[19] Counterpoised to Hollywood's savage saloon shoot-outs are Britain's snobbish Bridesheads and Downton Abbeys.

Revivals from ten, thirty, seventy years ago out-sell new shows and songs. In Hollywood 'the hottest thing today is yesterday'.[20] Since *any* recognition sells, sequels are made to films that bombed. Hence forgettable remakes such as *Cheaper by the Dozen* (1950/2003), *The In-Laws* (1979/2003), *Stepford Wives* (1975/2004), *All the King's Men* (1949/2006), *Poseidon* (1972/2006), *When a Stranger Calls* (1979/2006), *The Bad News Bears* (1976/2006), *Prom Night* (1980/2008). Familiarity breeds contentment: with the top box-office hits all sequels, a critic wondered 'whether Hollywood should bother to have an original thought'.[21]

Not only films are retro; recycling pervades theatre too. On Broadway, 'the unfamiliar tends to be as welcome as a bedbug', so most shows are 'revamped, reinterpreted and, forever and ever, revived'.[22] Set in the 1960s, John Waters's 'Hairspray in Concert' (2013) – 'a stage show of a movie of a stage show of a movie' – is 'a revival of a revival of a revival', notes marketing historian Stephen Brown.[23] Meanwhile, new films treat the past as a storehouse of problems resolved, including 'films about boys who do not want to grow up, ever, ever, ever'.[24]

Extreme nostalgic attachments are pathological. Some addicts suffocate in bygones, unable to relinquish anything – the carefully husbanded 'Pieces of string too short to use', the man who hoarded thousands of jars of his own excrement, the reliquary phials of an old love affair, labelled 'Dust from dress of R. Dust by bed of R. Dust near door of R's room', the artist Ilya Kabakov's dust archive in 'The Man Who Never Threw

---

[18] A. O. Scott, 'Do movies matter? Right now they feel especially perishable'. *IHT*, 18 Nov. 2011: 10–11.

[19] A. O. Scott, 'How the Western was won', *NYT Magazine*, 11 Sept. 2007: 55–8; John Exshaw, 'Bury my heart in Hill Valley', in Sorcha Ní Fhlainn, ed., *The Worlds of Back to the Future* (London: McFarland, 2010), 91–111 at 97.

[20] Andy Pemberton quoted in Chris Nelson, 'The old days never looked so good', *NYT*, 11 Sept. 2002: B1, 3.

[21] Brian Tallerico, 'The top ten remakes nobody asked for', Movieretriever.com, 13 Mar. 2009; A. O. Scott, 'Blockbuster 4: the same but worse', *NYT*, 9 June 2010; Michael Cieply, 'Familiarity breeds Hollywood sequels', *NYT*, 28 Dec. 2011; Katrina Onstad, 'The case of cinematic déjà vu', *NYT*, 14 Dec. 2012.

[22] Ben Brantley, 'Think you've seen it all? You have', *NYT*, 12 Sept. 2010, Theater; Ben Brantley, 'Revivals are nice, but revel in the new', *NYT*, 20 Feb. 2011: AR6. See Simon Reynolds, *Retromania: Pop Culture's Addiction to its own Past* (Faber & Faber, 2011).

[23] Stephen Brown, 'Retro from the Get-go: reactionary reflections on marketing's yester-mania' *Journal of Historical Research in Marketing* 5:4 (2013): 521–36, at 526.

[24] Joe Queenan, 'The worst movie year ever?' *Wall Street Journal*, 28 July 2010; A. O. Scott, 'What's ahead: more movies that look back', *NYT*, 12 Sept. 2005.

Figure 2 Rubbish into 'Antiques': Coventry, Vermont

Anything Away'. Forced by health inspectors to clean the dust-cocooned wishbones dangling over his bar, the proprietor of McSorley's Old Ale House in New York reverently preserved the sacred dust.[25]

To Nigel Dennis's fictional 'spiritual recapitulation' pub throng devotees of

medieval calligraphy, puzzling the postmen with their renascent addresses ... Some wore small, curved bowler hats [and] drank their beer out of old moustache-cups. Many were gardeners, and would grow only roses which had not been seen for some centuries [The pub] covered all periods from Thomist to Edwardian, and rejected nothing but the malaise of the present.[26]

Dennis's anachronistic haunt became reality in 1982 at Blists Hill Open Air Museum in Ironbridge Gorge. To nearby 'All Nations' pub came museum guides 'in sub-Victorian garb; heavy hobnail boots, plain serge trousers, and mock Halifax corduroy gathered at the waist with binder twine ... Decrepit old jackets open to reveal grubby collarless

[25] Bette Pesetsky, 'The hobbyist', in *Stories up to a Point* (Bodley Head, 1982), 35–43 at 42; Ilya Kabakov, 'The man who never threw anything away' (c. 1977), in Charles Merewether, ed., *The Archive* (MIT Press, 2006), 32–7; Ilya Kabakov, *The Garbage Man* (1995), Museum of Contemporary Art, Oslo; Dan Barry, 'Dust is gone above the bar, but a legend still dangles', *NYT*, 7 Apr. 2011: A19. See Randy O. Frost and Gail Steketee, *Stuff: Compulsive Hoarding and the Meaning of Things* (Harcourt, 2010). The artist Piero Manzoni sealed, dated, numbered, and signed ninety cans of his own excrement (Jonathan Glancey, 'Merde d'artiste', *Guardian*, 13 June 2007; Dave Praeger, *Poop Culture* (Los Angeles: Feral House, 2007), 151–9).

[26] Nigel Dennis, *Cards of Identity* (1955; Weidenfeld & Nicolson, 1974), 133.

workingmen's shirts ... These phantoms of the past-present quaff real ale, ... liquid history bearing silent witness against the present'.[27]

Present woes are drowned in Irish theme pubs, 'commodifications of the Celtic Revival of the late nineteenth century ... itself a politically-motivated commodification ... of half-baked Irish pre-history'. Sheffield, England, hosts, a 'Celtic-twilighted composite of little people-peopled, faux fairyland-filigreed and peat-briquetted, begorrah-bespoken, bejabbers-bejases' adorned with pseudo shillelaghs, sham o'shanters, and plastic paddy paraphernalia outfitted from kits made in Essex. For ersatz rustic ethnicity – 'leather tankards dip from the beamed ceiling, [and] a scythe balanced precariously on two (rusty) nails threatens to guillotine you' – the pub's minstrelled conviviality fosters bleary-eyed déjà vus among foreign students, summoning up homeland haunts in China, India, Greece or Peru.[28]

Present malaise and future mistrust fuelled nostalgia from the 1970s, when threats of resource exhaustion, of ecological collapse, of nuclear Armageddon made the past a haven from millennial angst. 'The past looks like a keel to many people', noted a journalist, 'so they're trying to get a hook into it, pull it alongside, and fix it in place'. Against dismays of Suez and Vietnam, oil and inflation, bygone times promised 'that life was once liveable and, yes, yes, if we looked long and hard enough at some right thing in our past, it would be right again'.[29] Against the killings of the Kennedys and Martin Luther King, the crimes of Richard Nixon, and the impotence of Jimmy Carter, the imperial presidency of Ronald Reagan, Hollywood's 'grand architect of time itself', restored 'morning again in America'. In sync with Margaret Thatcher's resurgent Victorianism, Reagan revived mythic 1950s American family values and upbeat optimism, like the country's surrogate father Doc Brown in *Back to the Future*, a Reagan icon.[30]

'I can read your future', offers a palmist, 'or, as so many seem to prefer these days, I can reminisce nostalgically about your past'.[31] Until the 1970s, nostalgia trips were 'surreptitious and ambivalent, because we didn't want to relinquish our hold on the present'. But as the present grew woeful, modernity lost its charm. The phrase 'they don't make them like that any more' shed its ironic edge and became a true lament.[32] So prevalent became the backward glance that a British critic termed nostalgia

[27] Bob West, 'The making of the English working past: a critical view of Ironbridge Gorge Museum', in Robert Lumley, ed., *The Museum Time-Machine* (Routledge, 1988), 36–62 at 36–7.

[28] Anthony Patterson and Stephen Brown, 'Knick-knack Paddy-whack, give the pub a theme', *Journal of Marketing Management* 16 (2000): 647–62 at 656; Anthony Patterson and Stephen Brown, 'Comeback for the *Craic*: a literary pub crawl', 75–93 at 76, 81, and Stephen Brown, 'No then there', 3–18 at 8, all in Stephen Brown and John F. Sherry, Jr., eds., *Time, Space, and the Market* (Armonk, NY: M. E. Sharpe, 2003).

[29] Eric Sevareid, 'On times past', *Preservation News* 14:10 (1974): 5; Richard Hasbany, '*Irene*: considering the nostalgic sensibility', *Journal of Popular Culture* 9 (1976): 816–26 at 819.

[30] Susan Jeffords, *Hard Bodies* (Rutgers, 1994); Sorcha Ní Fhlainn, 'Introduction: it's about time', in her *Worlds of Back to the Future*, 6–8.

[31] Ed Fisher, cartoon, *New Yorker*, 15 Mar. 1976: 39.

[32] Michael Wood, 'Nostalgia or never: you can't go home again', *New Society*, 7 Nov. 1974: 343–6; Gaby Porter, 'Putting your house in order: representations of women and domestic life', in Lumley, ed., *Museum Time-Machine*, 101–26 at 101–2.

'a sickness that has reached fever point', and an American feared 'a future in which people may again die of nostalgia'.[33]

Instead of death came rejuvenation. As a visitable realm of solace, nostalgia made the past 'the foreign country with the healthiest tourist trade of all'. Sepia photos of bygone premises festooned bars and pubs, shops and schools. Offering 'acres of nostalgia', Beamish Open Air Museum won the 1987 European Museum of the Year Award. Realtors touted proximity to pasts however ersatz, from the Sussex monument to the fraudulent Piltdown Man, to Ian Fleming's *Goldeneye* in Jamaica.[34] If some grumble at being 'a quaint romantic bygone in the local souvenir shop', heritage tourism brings the UK some 253,000 jobs and 30 billion pounds a year.[35] Nostalgia's 105 million Google hits as of June 2013 plug everything from medieval battle games to dune buggies, handmade goats'-milk soap to Andrei Tarkovsky's 1983 film *Nostalgia*.

Personal links market nostalgia. Frith's sepia-toned *fin-de-siècle* scenes are 'Your village, your town, your roots … your own personal piece of nostalgia'. The 'Imperial Tankard' commemorated for Britons 'the Empire they never knew, perhaps, but also the Empire they should not be allowed to forget'. Most lucrative are celebrity collectables – an O. J. Simpson glove, Buckingham Palace toilet paper, a glass shard from Princess Diana's fatal crash, jelly beans from Ronald Reagan's desk, Sylvester Stallone's urine, Miss America's saliva.[36] Like saintly bones, hair and fingernails, and milk of the Virgin Mary, physical remnants of modern celebrities command the highest prices, strands of Marilyn Monroe's locks fetching $400. Auctioned Jimi Hendrix memorabilia included a lavatory seat used by Elvis Presley and a piece of toast half eaten by Beatle George Harrison. Floridian Diana Duyser's decade-old, miraculously mould-free 'Virgin Mary Grilled Cheese Sandwich' – after taking a bite, she saw 'Virgin Mary staring back at me' – fetched $28,000 at auction.[37]

Such was 1970s' lust for the past that a satirist foresaw an eco-nostalgic shortage, with past resources and revivals strictly rationed. So voracious were 1990s retro consumers that 'we may run entirely out of past as soon as 2005'.[38] Happily, digital technology and the Internet now ensure we will never be short of past, nostalgia endlessly fed by instant access to an infinitely recyclable archive. We are promised digital scanning of 3.5 trillion old photos.[39]

[33] Robert Hewison, *The Heritage Industry: Britain in a Climate of Decline* (Methuen, 1987), 10; Jay Anderson quoted in *History News* 38:12 (1983): 11.

[34] Sheridan Morley, 'There's no business like old business', *Punch*, 29 Nov. 1972: 777; David Kirby, 'Escapes', *NYT*, 26 July 2002.

[35] Libby Purves, 'In Moore's America, we aren't even worth a joke', *Times*, 6 July 2004; Kareen El Beyrouty and Andrew Tessler, *The Economic Impact of the UK Heritage Tourism Economy*, Oxford Economics, May 2013, and English Heritage, *Heritage Counts 2014*.

[36] Barton Lidice Beneš, *Curiosa: Celebrity Relics, Historical Fossils, & Other Metamorphic Rubbish* (Abrams, 2002).

[37] David Sinclair, 'Nostalgia? It's gonna cost you', *Times*, 20 Nov. 2004; George E. Newman et al., 'Celebrity contagion and the value of objects', *Journal of Consumer Research* 38 (2011): 215–28; Peter Stiff, 'How much would you pay for one strand of Justin Bieber's hair?' *Times*, 6 Aug. 2011: 42.

[38] Sheridan Morley, 'There's no business like old business', *Punch*, 29 Nov. 1972: 777; 'U.S. Dept. of Retro warns: "We may be running out of Past"', *Onion* 32:14 (4 Nov. 1997).

[39] Mitch Goldstone, 'Nostalgia, what's old is new again at CES', *Scan.my.photos.com*, 2 Jan. 2009.

People even plan ahead nostalgically. Like Kierkegaard, they look back in the midst of enjoyment to recapture it for memory. One young woman imagined herself as a grandmother recalling the infancy of her yet unborn daughters.[40] 'Just such a honey-suckle filtered, sunny conversational afternoon', a Margaret Drabble character subse-quently remembered, would later cause 'the most sad and exquisite nostalgia. She was sad in advance, yet at the same time all the happier . . . creating for herself a past.'[41] The BBC producer of the 2000 reading of the first Harry Potter novel wanted 'there to be children now who say to each other in their twenties, "You remember that Christmas when we all listened to Harry Potter on the radio?"'[42] A nostalgia guru swooned over a Hollywood designer's antiques-and-retro-laden loft: 'It was the kind of place I wish I would be able to look back on having lived in. . . . I want to have lived in [it], when I'm 85. I want this to be part of my future – but only in memory, I sort of skipped over actually experiencing it.'[43] Her nostalgia is more for past thoughts than past things, 'like thinking we loved the books of our youth, when all we love is the thought of ourselves young, reading them'.[44]

Nostalgia is worldwide. *The Country Diary of an Edwardian Lady* and *Brideshead Revisited* tapped global markets. Old oak beams from East Anglia (or glass-fibre copies) solace homeowners in Helsinki and Osaka; Peter Rabbit lures hordes of Japanese pilgrims to Beatrix Potter's Hilltop Farm in the Lake District. Russian nostalgia for pre-Revolutionary troikas, furs, and family samovars, epitomized in the Romanov-era novels of Boris Akunin, coexists with wistful memories of imagined idealism and heroic sacrifice in Stalinist times; Orthodox dreams of chaste civilization mingle with Art-Deco-cum-fascist 'Stalin Empire'-style interiors and the iconic sausage and fermenting sauerkraut of sparse communist fare. 'Russians are rushing backward because they see nothing good in the future. . . . Only in the past, as in the womb, is it warm and safe; only in the past are there symbols and victories that people can understand'.[45] East German arts and artefacts alike celebrate pre-unification culture. An 'Ostalgia' exhibition recalls pre-perestroika eastern Europe, dire or dour memories fuelled by Blushing Babushka, Siberian Sipper, and Kanon Kremlin vodka cocktails.[46] Parisians prefer keeping their city a decaying museum. Greeks' mythicized classical past buttresses claims for heritage restitution.[47] Shanghai's 'time-honoured' (2010) shopping mall peddles exclusively

---

[40] Søren Kierkegaard, *Either/Or* (1843; Oxford, 1944), I: 240–1; Fred Davis, *Yearning for Yesterday* (Free Press, 1979), 12.

[41] Margaret Drabble, *Jerusalem the Golden* (Penguin, 1969), 93.

[42] Quoted in Stephen Brown, 'Marketing for muggles: Harry Potter and the retro revolution', *Journal of Marketing Management* 17:5/6 (2001): 463–79 at 468.

[43] Eva Hagberg in Eryn Loeb, 'Rooms with a view to the past: Eva Hagberg's "Dark Nostalgia"', *TheFasterTimes.com.nostalgia*, 29 Sept. 2009.

[44] Amanda Cross, *Poetic Justice* (New York: Avon, 1979), 140.

[45] Victor Erofeyev, 'Imperial crutches', *IHT*, 20 Nov. 2009: 6; Jerome de Groot, *The Historical Novel* (Routledge, 2010), 94–5; Andrew E. Kramer, 'Back to the ('30s) U.S.S.R.', *NYT*, 30 May 2013: D1, 6–7; Anya von Bremen, *Mastering the Art of Soviet Cooking* (Crown, 2013).

[46] Anthony Enns, 'Politics of *Ostalgie*: post-socialist nostalgia in recent German film', *Screen* 48 (2007): 475–91; Holland Cotter, 'Out of the rust of the Iron Curtain', *IHT*, 25 July 2011.

[47] 'Parisians prefer city as a "museum"', *IHT*, 24 Sept. 2004; John Boardman, *The Archaeology of Nostalgia: How the Greeks Re-created Their Mythical Past* (Thames & Hudson, 2003).

pre-Revolutionary clothing and cosmetics. The Japanese popular song genre *enka*, recreated to sound timelessly old, yearns for the past as lost home, as mother, as national identity. In the *enka* Japan becomes 'Japan', much as the Isle of Wight exemplifies Olde England in Julian Barnes's *England, England*.[48] In sum, nostalgic remembrance is a burgeoning enterprise everywhere, and almost any era will do.

Nostalgia far and near

> It's never safe to be nostalgic about something until you're absolutely certain there's
> no chance of its coming back.   Bill Vaughn, 1975

Times beyond our ken can be as nostalgically comforting as times actually experienced. Few who flock to Bogart films, enjoy Glenn Miller music, or throw 1960s parties are old enough to recall them. Douglas Coupland deplores 'forcing people to have memories they don't actually possess' as 'legislated nostalgia'. But longing for Depression-era or wartime 'hardiness in the face of austerity' today appeals to young and old alike.[49] Web-guests to Lisa's Nostalgia Café enjoy 'good old days' from the 1910s to the 1990s. London Transport's 1980s Vintage Time Machine bus invited patrons to 1925, 'when every day seemed like high summer'. It was 'summer all year round' for an American longing to 'take a Sunday walk the way we used to, with your silk parasol and your long dress whishing along, and sit on those wire-legged stools at the soda parlor'.[50]

Old codgers remember 'when beer was cheaper ... and people had more respect'; the Courage ale slogan 'Fings *are* wot they used to be' endeared the grubby 1930s. No matter if those days were in fact wretched: 'life was lovely back in the 1900s', asserted elderly Irish women raised in rural destitution.[51] An American mutes Depression hardships and wartime privations with memories of 'the smell of new-mown hay and honeysuckle wafting on the breezes'.[52]

Even horrendous memories can evoke nostalgia. A 1970s Londoner recalled wartime bombing as 'pure, flawless happiness'; seventieth anniversary Blitz parties in mock air-raid shelters let period-garbed nostalgists 'escape the drab safety of the modern world for a time when Londoners defied Hitler's Luftwaffe bombers from behind the blackout curtains'.[53] Britain's current austerity drive fuels nostalgia for the moral fibre and

[48] Jonna Dagliden, 'Retro Chinese brands', *LifeStyle News*, 17 Jan. 2011; Christine R. Yano, *Tears of Longing: Nostalgia and the Nation in Japanese Popular Song* (Harvard Asian Center, 2000), 8, 14–17, 178–9; Julian Barnes, *England, England* (Jonathan Cape, 1998).

[49] Douglas Coupland, *Generation X* (St Martin's Press, 1991), 41; Owen Hatherley, 'Austerity nostalgia', blog, 5 Feb. 2009; Dan Fox, 'The bad old days. Again. And again ...', *frieze Magazine*, 6 Feb. 2009, website.

[50] Ray Bradbury, 'A scent of sarsaparilla' (1953), in *The Day It Rained Forever* (Penguin, 1963), 192–8 at 193.

[51] Michael Wood, 'Nostalgia or never: you can't go home again', *New Society*, 7 Nov. 1974: 343; Richard Milner, 'Courage cockneys tap taste for nostalgia', *Sunday Times*, 25 Apr. 1982: 49; Grant Woodward, 'Fings *are* wot they used to be!' *Yorkshire Evening Post*, 6 Sept. 2005; Mary Kenny, 'When the going was bad', *Sunday Telegraph*, 19 Aug. 1979.

[52] Frank C. Newby, *His Name Was Amy Mable: A Lifetime of Memories* (iUniverse, 2007), jacket.

[53] Tom Harrisson, *Living through the Blitz* (Collins, 1976), 325, 1; 'London partygoers reliving spirit of the Blitz', *Reuters.com*, 8 June. 2010. See Lara Feigel, *The Love-Charm of Bombs: Restless Lives in the Second World War* (Bloomsbury, 2013).

make-and-mend mentality of ration-book powdered eggs and suet, beet-juice lipstick, and Bisto bronzer. The home front's dourest hour 'has definitely got to come back', says diet guru Jamie Oliver. 'Things weren't so jolly back then, and by god, they shouldn't be too fun now, if only to ensure historical accuracy.'[54]

We all know the past was not really like our nostalgic memories. Back then seems brighter partly because we lived more vividly and hopefully when young. Now less able to savour intensely, we mourn a lost immediacy, even as spectators. A website cheers the 'monochrome glory' of 1950s TV, as 'everyone feels nostalgia for the television they watched when very young'.[55] Nostalgia excises the obnoxious and the awkward. Childhood thus recalled excludes the family quarrels, the boredom, the waiting in queues for grubby loos; it is memory with the pain removed, the past's evils and failures forgotten. We look back misty-eyed at a time 'when doctors prescribed Camels, Radium was on every wrist'.[56] Nostalgists aim 'to get out of modernity without leaving it altogether; we want to relive those thrilling days of yesteryear, but only because we are absolutely assured that those days are out of reach'.[57]

Nostalgia nowadays engulfs the whole past. Billy Collins's 'Nostalgia' conveys the temporal sweep:

> Remember the 1340s? We were doing a dance called the Catapult.
> You always wore brown, the color craze of the decade . . .
> Everything was hand-lettered then, not like today. . . .
> Where has the summer of 1572 gone? Brocade sonnet marathons were the rage. . . .
> The 1790s will never come again Childhood was big.
> People would take walks to the very tops of hills and
>   write down what they saw in their journals without speaking.
> Our collars were high and our hats were extremely soft.
> We would surprise each other with alphabets made of twigs.
> It was a wonderful time to be alive, or even dead. . . .
> I am very fond of the period between 1815 and 1821.
> Europe trembled while we sat still for our portraits.
> And I would love to return to 1901 if only for a moment,
> time enough to wind up a music box and do a few dance steps,
> or shoot me back to 1922 or 1941, or at least let me
> recapture the serenity of last month . . .
> Even this morning would be an improvement over the present . . .[58]

'History', observed art-historian Bevis Hillier in 1975, got 'recycled as nostalgia almost as soon as it happened': just eight years later his own book had become a nostalgic memory.[59]

---

[54] Quoted in Mireille Silcoff, 'Austerity chic in the U.K.', NYT, 11 Mar. 2011; Mireille Silcoff, 'Pig swill and bones and bottle caps and wire!' NYT Magazine, 13 Mar. 2011: 41–2.

[55] 1950s British TV nostalgia, whirligig-tv.co.uk.

[56] Roger Cohen, 'Change or perish', IHT, 5 Oct. 2010: 8.

[57] Roger Rosenblatt, 'Look back in sentiment', NYT, 28 July 1973: 23.

[58] Billy Collins, 'Nostalgia', in Questions about Angels (Morrow, 1991), 104–5.

[59] Bevis Hillier, Austerity Binge: The Decorative Arts of the Forties and Fifties (London: Studio Vista, 1975), 187–9, 195; Bevis Hillier, The Style of the Century: 1900–1980 (London: Herbert, 1983).

Nostalgia for the very recent past began with the return to prelapsarian 1962 in George Lucas's iconic film *American Graffiti* (1973). By 1975 'the student anti-war demonstrations of the late 1960s [were] already being sentimentalized as some great turbulent but glorious phenomenon of a dead long-ago'. Russell Baker found Americans focused on 'a past so recent that only an 11-year-old could possibly view it as past'.[60] In 1997 the US Retro Clock stood at 1990, 'an alarming 74% closer to the present' than a decade earlier. Life becomes heritage almost before it has a chance to be lived.'[61]

Recent absence gladdens the heart. 'Welcome to the 90s', offers a website. 'Why 90's nostalgia already? As the lifespan of fads gets shorter and shorter, looking back gets easier. ... Rather than wait for the memory to fade, the best time to immortalize the decade is now!'[62] A British observer concurs. 'The big business now is decade nostalgia for decades which have scarcely passed.' Outworn by 2004 were the polyester '70s, the shoulder-padded '80s, the materialist '90s; the new rage was the Botox '00s. 'We love the Zeros', was a 2004 forecast for 2010. Ironists project nostalgia for today thirty years hence, digital retro parties featuring primitive iPhones.[63] Since the Noughties turned naughty, 'nostalgia for events which have yet to occur' takes their place.[64] Instant retro swamps the Old World too. With the wheel of fashion revolving ever faster, 'the interval between creation and revival' drops from centuries to seconds; past collapses into present.[65]

Once a grandparental privilege, nostalgia is now peddled to teenagers. *Antiques Roadshow* attracts youngsters like the legacy-besotted thirteen-year-old who bought a Degas.[66] When nineteen-year-old footballer Wayne Rooney opted for a £3.5 million Queen Anne-style mansion with 'rusticated quoins', he was lauded for 'finding comfort in echoes of the past'. Adolescent tastes for the clothes, hairstyle, music, cars, and home decor of ten or fifteen years before one's own birth persist in adult retro fancies. Hence today's '40s to '60s cults.[67]

Nostalgia evokes better-off as well as better times. 'Take a magical step back in time', Goodwood Revival in 2013 lured visitors to join motor-racing toffs in tweeds and trilbies; 'leave the modern world behind and immerse yourself in a bygone age of elegance and sophistication'. A Maharaja-style trip around Rajasthan in saloon cars with porters in period dress 'brings back to life the vintage splendours'. One need hardly leave home; a 'Venice–Simplon' train trip through Kent earns 'an Orient Express Certificate to

---

[60] Russell Baker, 'Shock of things past', *IHT*, 2 May 1975: 14.
[61] 'U.S. Dept. of Retro warns: "We may be running out of Past"', *Onion* 32:14 (4 Nov. 1997); Barbara Kirschenblatt-Gimblett, 'Intangible heritage as multicultural production', *Museum International*, special issue, Intangible Cultural Heritage, 56:1–2 (May 2004): 52–65 at 56.
[62] www.inthe90s.com website.
[63] Rod Liddle, 'Rolling back the years', *Times*, 10 July 2004; Joe Moran, 'Decoding the decade', *Guardian*, 14 Nov. 2009: 30.
[64] 'U.S. Dept. of Retro warns: "We may be running out of Past"', *Onion* 32:14 (4 Nov. 1997).
[65] Gavin Stamp, 'The art of keeping one jump ahead: conservation societies in the twentieth century', in Michael Hunter, ed., *Preserving the Past: The Rise of Heritage in Modern Britain* (Stroud: Sutton, 1996), 76–98 at 98.
[66] Peter N. Carroll, *Keeping Time: Memory, Nostalgia, and the Art of History* (Georgia, 1990), 179; Peta Bee, 'The Peter Pan generation', *Times* 2, 12 Nov. 2003: 6–7; Ralph Gardner, Jr., 'Curators from the cradle', *NYT*, 13 May 2004: House&Home 1, 8.
[67] Simon Jenkins, 'Rooney shows true taste', *Times*, 26 Nov. 2004; Christina Goulding, 'Exploratory study of age-related vicarious nostalgia and aesthetic consumption', *Advances in Consumer Research* 29 (2002): 542–6.

remember your nostalgic journey into the opulent past'. If not rich, the yearned-for past is rustic, the urban countryman kitted out in 'clothes worn back when we were horny-handed sons of toil (bakers' jackets, whalebone cord, hessian)', tailored for young nobs who've 'handled nothing rougher than facial exfoliant'.[68] Miners' and labourers' back-to-back terraces, knickknacks and worn utensils are all part of the National Trust's newly aspic'd past.[69]

Descendants of serfs who now tour one-time masters' stately mansions feed on a nostalgia for visible social differences when 'people knew where they stood, classes were classes'.[70] 'Bring back Edwardian Britain', mocked a journalist, 'the lower classes doing as they were bloody well bidden'. In the Royal Enclosure at Ascot hoi polloi fantasize 'that they are part of some vanished leisure class, that the world they mourn and admire and pretend they would have belonged to if it still existed . . . is alive and well and living near Windsor'. So wrote Julian Fellowes, who six years later reified that fantasy. A *Downton Abbey* critic 'can't move for bumping into women in proto-flapper drop-waist shifts and cloche hats, quadrilling out of a brougham after an afternoon shoot'.[71]

Cults of nobility, real and fake, flourish anew. Lord Nicholas Windsor wed a Croatian princess whose aristocratic 'Frankopan' title the *Almanach de Gotha* adjudged 'more aspirational' than inherited.[72] Alongside ethno-nostalgia for bygone tribal ways, Americans like Europeans look back longingly at vanished imperial patrician chic. 'People are longing for things they don't get out of the republic', says a Hohenzollern promoter, 'looking for little princes and princesses'. Gilded Age Victorian dandyism is all the rage, fedoras, derbies, and bowlers, brass-buttoned military coats, tweedy vests and knee-britches recalling moustachioed macho blue-bloods sporting muzzle-loading rifles. The elegance of aristocrats suffuses haute couture nostalgia for an era when 'women trotted through dressage, riding side-saddle, looking crisp but sensual under top hats'. The allure of the past saturates luxury fashions, 'heritage' the buzzword in menswear.[73]

Looking back to Europe

In the absence of history one succumbs easily to its mutant form – nostalgia.

Peter N. Carroll, 1990[74]

---

[68] Luke Leitch, 'Country kit is everywhere – but don't cross the line between sheep farmer and sheep', *Times*, 10 Nov. 2010: Arts 11.

[69] A. A. Gill, *The Angry Island: Hunting the English* (London: Phoenix, 2006), 215.

[70] Raphael Samuel, *Patriotism: The Making and Unmaking of British National Identity*, vol. I: *History and Politics* (Routledge, 1989), xlix. On nostalgic fascination with servants' quarters, see Lucy Delap, *Knowing Their Place: Domestic Service in Twentieth-Century Britain* (Oxford, 2011), 206–34.

[71] Rod Liddle, 'Rolling back the years', *Times*, 10 July 2004; Julian Fellowes, *Snobs* (Weidenfeld & Nicolson, 2004), 17–18; Caitlin Moran, 'Christmas TV', *Times* SatRev, 31 Dec. 2011: 10.

[72] John Kennedy quoted in David Brown et al., 'Royal match that really is a fairytale', *Times*, 30 Sept. 2006.

[73] Rolf Seelmann-Eggebert quoted in Allan Hall, 'It's another royal wedding – then back to the day job', *IHT*, 27 Aug. 2011: 49; David Colman, 'This just in from the 1890s', *NYT*, 11 Nov. 2009; Christine Haughney, 'Getting the royal treatment', *NYT*, 25 Apr. 2010: 22; Suzy Menkes, 'Dior: Hand of history', *IHT*, 26 Jan. 2010: 10 (dressage); Suzy Menkes, 'Heritage luxury: past becomes the future', *IHT*, 9 Nov. 2010: 9–12; Eric Wilson, 'Heritage shouldn't reek of mothballs', *NYT*, 14 Feb. 2011: D8 ('buzzword').

[74] Carroll, *Keeping Time*, 179.

As first portrayed, in the *Odyssey*, nostalgia combined physical pain and mental grief with the prospect of redemptive recovery. Despite the seductive beauty of his captors Nausicaa and Calypso, Odysseus yearned to return home to Penelope: 'he's left to pine on an island, racked with grief / ... he has no way to voyage home [*nostós*] to his own native land ... / Wrenching his heart with sobs and groans and anguish [*alghós*]'.[75] Two millennia later in Rome the poet Joachim du Bellay penned a classic Homerian reprise in sonnets yearning for French childhood scenes.[76] Later New World voyagers and migrants pined for native lands. Homesickness brought back more than half the Italian and one in three Danish overseas emigrants of the 1870–1914 exodus to America. Expressions of nostalgia dominated Scandinavian-American writing.[77] For a Romanian immigrant only 'the thought that some day I would go back ... kept me alive'; but he had dreamed of it so long that 'the craving had come to seem more agreeable than the realization'.[78] Just as Homer's successors made Europe classical, so being European now means being 'nostalgic for Europe' – not today's high-tech, fractious continent, but 'good old Europe', recalls a Latvian, when people spent 'a lot of time sitting and talking with each other, writing letters, doing things with their own hands'.[79]

Old Europe's nostalgic cue came from the heroic and pastoral pasts of Virgil's *Aeneid*. The fourteenth-century humanist Petrarch sought classical refuge from his own 'wretched' and 'worthless' age.

I have dwelt especially upon antiquity, for our own age has always repelled me ... Had it not been for the love of those dear to me, I should have preferred to have been born in any other period than our own. In order to forget my own time, I have constantly striven to place myself in spirit in other ages.[80]

A bittersweet Arcadian past suffused early modern poetry and the canvases of Claude and Poussin. Oliver Goldsmith's *Deserted Village* charmed Goethe as a classically elegiac lost paradise featuring schoolchildren, churchyards, and ruins.[81]

[75] Homer, *The Odyssey*, (Penguin, 1996), 153–5, 169–74; Constantina Nadia Seremetakis, ed., *The Senses Still* (Westview, 1994), 4.
[76] Joachim du Bellay, 'The Regrets', in *Three Latin Elegies* (1558; PennPress, 2006); George Hugo Tucker, *Poet's Odyssey: Du Bellay* (Oxford, 1990).
[77] Andreea Deciu Rítívoi, *Yesterday's Self: Nostalgia and the Immigrant Identity* (Rowman & Littlefield, 2002), 102–7; Hildor Arnold Barton, *A Folk Divided: Homeland Swedes and Swedish Americans, 1840–1940* (Southern Illinois, 1994), xi, 87, 189–96; Susan J. Matt, *Homesickness: An American History* (Oxford, 2011), 141–75; Dorothy Burton Skårdal, *The Divided Heart: Scandinavian Immigrant Experience through Literary Sources* (Nebraska, 1974), 264.
[78] Marcus Eli Ravage (1923) quoted in Matt, *Homesickness*, 170.
[79] Milan Kundera, *The Art of the Novel* (1986; HarperCollins, 2000), 63; Alvis Hermanis with Bonnie Marranca, 'Poetry of things past', *PAJ* 32 (Jan. 2010): 23–35 at 32.
[80] Erik Gray, 'Nostalgia, the classics, and the intimations ode: Wordsworth's forgotten education', *Philological Quarterly* 80 (2001): 187–204; Petrarch to Livy, 22 Feb. 1349(?), in *Petrarch's Letters to Classical Authors* (Chicago, 1910), 101–2, and 'Letter to posterity' (c. 1372), in *Petrarch: ... A Selection from His Correspondence* (New York, 1898), 64.
[81] Oliver Goldsmith, *The Deserted Village* (London, 1770); Johann Wolfgang von Goethe, *Dichtung und Wahrheit* (1821; Leipzig, 1881), 123. See Aaron Santesso, *A Careful Longing: The Poetics and Problems of Nostalgia* (Delaware, 2006), 11, 19.

Romantic poets followed Virgil in mourning lost childhood along with childhood scenes. Wordsworth's evocations of Grasmere moved millions to lament irrecoverable youth, Housman's 'land of lost content, / I see it shining plain, / The happy highways where I went / And cannot come again'. Aged thirty, the historian James Anthony Froude yearned 'but for one week of my old child's faith, to go back to calm and peace again'.[82]

Radical upheaval linked nostalgia with national chauvinism. The French Revolution sundered past from present; after the guillotine and Napoleon, the previous world, above all the lost homeland, seemed irretrievably remote, hence doubly dear. 'Those who have not lived in the eighteenth century before the Revolution', grieved the monarchist Talleyrand, 'know nothing of the sweetness of life.'[83] Industrialization along with conflict uprooted millions of Europeans into alien locales. People 'who had only ever owned hand-crafted objects', daunted by mass-produced factory wares, took comfort in Wedgwood's and furniture makers' familiar historical replicas. Exiles and romantics solaced devastating change with half-remembered, half-invented bygone images. Crumbling mythic pasts featured in Isidore Taylor and Charles Nodier's twenty-three-volume *Voyages pittoresques et romantiques dans l'ancienne France* (1820–78). From the nostalgists in Samuel Palmer's 'Arcadian' Shoreham, to 'medieval' knights jousting at Eglinton, to railway travellers regret-ting stagecoach days, Victorians hallowed the lost past.[84] City dwellers mourned departed rural life. Laments by 'An Old Inhabitant' and 'Glimpses from the Past' filled the press. Even 'the huddles of wooden shacks, the ancient "dwellings of the labouring poor"' in London's Kentish Town 'were seen, once they had been swept away, with a sentimental eye'.[85]

At the turn of the twentieth century all Britain seemed bent on nostalgic quest. 'Let us live again in the past', urged one celebrant, and 'surround ourselves with the treasures of past ages'.[86] Poet Laureate Alfred Austin sought out 'old England's washing days, home-made jams, lavender bags', and took pride in uttering 'none but the very oldest and most out-of-fashion ideas'.[87] Luxuriating in 'Sussex medievalism', Kipling banned the tele-phone at Bateman's, his seventeenth-century home. Ottoline Morrell's ramshackle Tudor Garsington Manor tempted D. H. Lawrence 'to lapse back into its peaceful beauty of bygone things, to live in pure recollection'.[88]

---

[82] Virgil, *Georgics* (29 BC), 3. 66–8; Housman, *Shropshire Lad*, Poem XL; Christopher Clausen, 'Tintern Abbey to Little Gidding: the past recaptured', *Sewanee Review* 84 (1976): 405–24 at 417; James Anthony Froude, *The Nemesis of Faith*, 2nd edn (London, 1849), 28.

[83] Charles-Maurice de Talleyrand-Périgord, *La Confession de Talleyrand* (1891; abridged, Hamburg: Tredition, 2012), 47. See also François Guizot, *Mémoires pour servir à l'histoire de mon temps* (Paris, 1858), 1: 2.

[84] Alice Rawsthorn, 'Looking ahead by looking back', *IHT* 6 Feb. 2012: 7; Steven Adams, 'Space, politics and desire: configuring the landscape in post-Revolutionary France', *Landscape Research* 35 (2010): 487–509 at 506–7; Mark Girouard, *The Return to Camelot: Chivalry and the English Gentleman* (Yale, 1981).

[85] Gillian Tindall, *The Fields Beneath: The History of One London Village* (1977; Weidenfeld & Nicolson, 2002), 174–5.

[86] P. H. Ditchfield, *The Story of Our English Towns* (London, 1897), 34; but, he adds, 'no wise man will wish to bring back that past'.

[87] Alfred Austin, *Haunts of Ancient Peace* (Macmillan, 1902), 18–19.

[88] W. Thurston Hopkins, *Rudyard Kipling's World* (London, 1925), 11; D. H. Lawrence to Cynthia Asquith, 3 Dec. 1915, in *The Letters of D. H. Lawrence* (Viking, 1932), 283. See Martin J. Wiener, *English Culture and the Decline of the Industrial Spirit, 1850–1980* (1981; Cambridge, 2004), 45, 57, 62, 76.

Chivalric romance lured Americans 'to leave the present, so weighted with cumbersome enigmas and ineffectual activity, and go back' to simpler times of straightforward aims.[89] Evoking Wordsworth's *Intimations of Immortality* (1807), Henry Adams rued the lost childlike innocence of the twelfth century.[90] New England, left behind for greener western pastures, re-emerged as nostalgic retreat, its scenery and surviving oldsters redolent of cherished bygone ways. Half a century later, Americans looked back to the early twentieth century as a Golden Age. In revisiting the 1900s, as the 1900s had the 1800s, visitors to Main Street, U.S.A. at Disneyland and other theme parks escaped 'unnatural present-day cares … and become more *like themselves*'[91] – that is, the authentic selves they fancied would emerge in the reborn past.

'Olde English' vernacular buildings catered for such nostalgia. Like Tudorbethan for late Victorians, Mock Tudor was the favoured interwar style. Praised as 'quaint' and 'old-fashioned; to be up-to-date now meant to look as old as possible'. The BBC's immensely popular 'Our Bill' lauded England's ancient churches and wayside inns where one could 'step aside into some small pool of history, to be lapped awhile in the healing peace of a rich, still-living past'.[92] To sate his Tudor nostalgia, Gloucestershire architect Charles Wade at Snowshill Manor worked with period tools, ate in an antique kitchen, and slept in a cupboard bed (Fig. 3).[93] Why not be comforted by some past? 'In England we may choose from any of a dozen different centuries to live in', said Kenneth Grahame; 'and who would select the twentieth?'[94]

Nostalgia was no less widespread in Europe. Goethe and the Grimm brothers summoned up lost pasts in Germany, Victor Hugo and Viollet-le-Duc in France. Severance from forebears' worlds fuelled longing for manifold retrievals.[95] French medievalist nostalgia peaked after the defeat by German forces and the Paris Commune debacle of 1870–1. As a refuge from social fragmentation, labour anarchy, and church–state feuds, the Middle Ages became a time of unity, social cohesion, purity of faith. And medievalism restored French pride: 'Look, children', enthused Léon Gautier, promoting the classic *Chanson de Roland*, 'how impressive France already was then and how much she was loved eight centuries ago'. The Middle Ages permeated architecture, art, literature, and consumer goods. Pierre Loti hosted fifteenth-century parties in his medieval dining hall; Émile Zola and Anatole France reclined on heraldically emblazoned Gothic

[89] Agnes Repplier, 'Old wine and new', *Atlantic Monthly* 77 (1896): 686–96 at 696.

[90] Henry Adams, *Mont-Saint-Michel and Chartres* (1912; Constable, 1950), 2.

[91] Edward Harwood, 'Rhetoric, authenticity, and reception: the eighteenth-century landscape garden, the modern theme park, and their audiences', in Terence Young and Robert Riley, eds., *Theme Park Landscapes* (Dumbarton Oaks, 2002), 49–68 at 59–61; Dona Brown, *Inventing New England: Regional Tourism in the Nineteenth Century* (Smithsonian Institution, 1995), ch. 5; John M. Findlay, *Magic Lands: Western Cityscapes and American Culture after 1940* (California, 1992), 70.

[92] Wiener, *English Culture*, 64–6, 74–6; Mark Girouard, *Sweetness and Light: The 'Queen Anne' Movement, 1860–1900* (Clarendon Press, 1977), 5, 25–7, 60–2; Andrew Ballantine and Andrew Law, *Tudoresque* (Reaktion, 2011).

[93] H. D. Molesworth, 'A note on the collection', *Snowshill Manor* (London: National Trust, 1995; brochure), 30–1; Charles Wade, *Haphazard Notes* (National Trust, 1979).

[94] Kenneth Grahame, *First Whisper of 'The Wind in the Willows'* (Lippincott, 1945), 26.

[95] Peter Fritzsche, *Stranded in the Present: Modern Time and the Melancholy of History* (Harvard, 2004), 154.

Figure 3 Tudor nostalgia: Charles Wade's Snowshill Manor, Gloucestershire

thrones. Joan of Arc dolls, souvenir dinner plates, cheese, chocolates, and toothpaste linked *fin-de-siècle* consumers to feudal decor. Later epochs also figured; a 1900 *Figaro* ad offered 'historically accurate' Henri II (1547–59) dining rooms and Louis XV (1715–74) bedrooms.[96]

Medical homesickness

In the seventeenth century Odysseus' nostalgia became a medical ailment with dire and often lethal symptoms. Diagnosed in 1688 by a Swiss physician, it affected 'fibers of the middle brain in which the impressed traces of ideas of the Fatherland still

---

[96] Elizabeth Emery and Laura Morowitz, *Consuming the Past: The Medieval Revival in Fin-de-Siècle France* (Ashgate, 2003), 209–12, 7–8.

cling'.[97] Erasmus Darwin defined nostalgia as 'an unconquerable desire of returning to one's native country, frequent in long voyages'. He termed it a 'disease of volition', like excessive family pride.[98] Enforced emigrants and soldiers abroad lapsed from 'melancholy indifference toward everything [to] the near impossibility of getting out of bed, ... the rejection of food and drink; emaciation, marasmus and death'. To leave home for long was fraught with peril. 'I suffer homesickness', wrote Balzac, away from Paris in Milan; 'if I remained this way for two weeks, I should die'. A young Swiss who left Berne to study in Basel barely 40 miles away soon succumbed there.[99]

Swiss mercenary soldiers were nostalgia's chief victims, especially in lowlands far from their beloved Alps, their exile thought aggravated by change in air pressure.[100] To hear a familiar herder's tune aggravated illness.

> The intrepid Swiss, that guards a foreign shore,
> Condemn'd to climb his mountain-cliffs no more,
> If chance he hears the song so sweetly wild
> Which on those cliffs his infant hours beguil'd,
> Melts at the long-lost scenes that round him rise,
> And sinks a martyr to repentant sighs.[101]

Because the melody haunted hearers with heartbreaking childhood memories, Swiss soldiers abroad were forbidden to play, sing, or whistle alpine tunes.[102]

Medication included leeches, purges, emetics, blood-letting, 'hypnotic emulsions', and opium. A Russian general in 1733 found terror efficacious: when soldiers laid up by nostalgia were buried alive, homesickness soon subsided.[103] But repatriation was the only effective cure until Friedrich Schiller, a medical student before he became a poet, cured a colleague in 1780 with a regimen of moderate exercise and poetry reading in a peaceful rustic milieu. The notion of nature as therapy stemmed from Bernard de Fontenelle's praise of pastoral life and literary evocations of rural childhood. It initiated nostalgia's transition from malignant pathological trauma to pleasurable therapy. But

[97] Johannes Hofer, 'Medical dissertation on nostalgia' (1688), *Bulletin of the Institute of the History of Medicine* (Aug. 1934): 376–91 at 384.

[98] Erasmus Darwin, *Zoomania; or the Laws of Organic Life* (1794; 3rd edn, London, 1801), 1: 82.

[99] François Gabriel Boisseau and Philippe Pinel, 'Nostalgie' (1821), Leopold Auenbrugger, *Inventum novum* (1761), and Honoré de Balzac to Eveline Hanska, 23 May 1838, in Jean Starobinski, 'The idea of nostalgia', *Diogenes* 54 (June 1966): 81–103 at 97–8, 86; Hofer, 'Medical dissertation on nostalgia', 382. See Nicole Mozet, *Balzac et le temps* (Saint-Cyr-sur-Loire: Pirot, 2005).

[100] Johann Jakob Scheuchzer, 'Von dem Heimwehe' (1705), in George Rosen, 'Nostalgia: a forgotten psychological disorder', *Clio Medica* 10 (1975): 28–51 at 33–4; Andreas Schmidt, 'Heimweh und Heimkehr: zur Gefühlskultur in einer komplexen Welt', in Silke Göttsch and Christel Köhle-Hezinger, eds., *Komplexe Welt* (Münster: Waxmann, 2003), 36–48 at 39–40.

[101] Samuel Rogers, *Pleasures of Memory* (1792; London, 1802), 26. See William Wordsworth, 'On hearing the "ranz des vaches" on the top of the pass of St. Gothard' (1820), in *Poetical Works* (Clarendon Press, 1940–66), 3: 178.

[102] Starobinski, 'The idea of nostalgia', 93; Davis, *Yearning for Yesterday*, 3, 73. But this frequently reported prohibition is seldom documented (Guy S. Métraux, *Le Ranz des vaches* (Lausanne: 24 Heures, 1984), 53–7).

[103] Hofer, 'Medical dissertation', 389; Starobinski, 'Idea of nostalgia', 95–6.

malign malady and curative aesthetics continued to commingle, as exemplified in Emily Brontë's sufferings and recourse to wild nature.[104]

Nostalgia lingered on as ailment. Said to kill as many as yellow fever in post-Revolutionary wars, it decimated French prisoners in Germany after 1870.[105] Homesickness was a major cause of desertion among American Revolutionary soldiers, and it was seen as a disabling debility among immigrant frontiersmen and slaves sold down the river.[106] In the American Civil War nostalgia was calamitous. With over five thousand certified Union Army cases, 'homesickness, the most pitiless monster that ever hung about a human heart', wrote a soldier, 'killed as many ... as did the bullets of the enemy'.[107] Whether 'the *cause*, or the *result*', of endemic diarrhoea, dysentery and typhoid, nostalgia was 'dreaded as the most serious [ailment] that could befall the patient'.[108] So popular was John Howard Payne's 'Home, Sweet Home' that, as with the Swiss 'Ranz des vaches', troops on both sides were forbidden to play it for fear of mass desertion.[109] As late as the Second World War the US Surgeon General termed nostalgia a contagion that might 'spread with the speed of an epidemic'. An eminent social scientist held homesickness a possibly fatal 'psycho-physiological' complaint.[110] Homesickness is still a common ailment said to afflict most boarding-school and university students.[111]

But the malady was becoming mental rather than physical, its locus less in lost place than in lost time, a longing more for childhood than for homeland. From fatal illness nostalgia morphed into remedial recall. The transition in Jane Austen's *Sense and Sensibility* (1811) is stunning. Felled by a wasting regret at leaving home, Marianne Dashwood is ultimately cured, exclaiming, 'I love to be reminded of the past ... Whether it be melancholy or gay, I love to recall it.' No longer crippling, nostalgia becomes a cure. Unlike Lady Catherine in *Pride and Prejudice* (1813), who indulges in unpleasant recollections, Elizabeth deploys the selective amnesia of subsequent Victorian nostalgia, eliminating negative or disturbing memory. 'Every unpleasant circumstance ... ought to be forgotten', she tells Darcy; 'think only of the past as its remembrance gives you

---

[104] Linda M. Austin, *Nostalgia in Transition, 1780–1917* (Virginia, 2007), 7–11, 29–45.

[105] Fernand Papillon, 'Nostalgia' (1874), cited in Nauman Naqvi, *The Nostalgic Subject*, ... (Messina: Università degli Studi, 2007), 15–16.

[106] Matt, *Homesickness*, 21–3, 75–7, 94–102, 275.

[107] Donald L. and Godfrey T. Anderson, 'Nostalgia and malingering in the military during the Civil War', *Perspectives in Biology and Medicine* 28 (1984): 156–66 at 157; Matt, *Homesickness*, 77–101; Eric T. Dean, *Shook over Hell: Post-Traumatic Stress, Vietnam, and the Civil War* (Harvard, 1997), 129.

[108] J. Theodore Calhoun, 'Nostalgia, as a disease of field service', *Medical and Surgical Reporter* 11 (27 Feb. 1864): 130–2; Frances Clarke, 'So lonesome I could die: nostalgia and debates over emotional control in the Civil War North', *Journal of Social History* 41 (2007): 253–82 at 257.

[109] Ernest L. Abe, '"Home, Sweet Home": a Civil War soldier's favorite song', *America's Civil War*, 9:2 (May 1996), historynet.com.

[110] David J. Flicker and Paul Weiss, 'Nostalgia and its military implications', *War Medicine* 4 (1943): 380–7 at 386–7; Beardsley Ruml, 'Some notes on nostalgia', *Saturday Review of Literature*, 29 (22 June 1946): 7–9.

[111] Linzee Kull McCray, 'Not home sick', University of Iowa *ParentTimes* online, 47:3 (Spring 2004); 'Homesickness can affect anyone', National Union of Students [UK], website; Christopher A. Thurber and Edward Walton, 'Preventing and treating homesickness', *Pediatrics* 119 (Jan. 2007): 192–201; and their 'Homesickness and adjustment in university students', *Journal of American College Health* 60:5 (July 2011): 1–5; Matt, *Homesickness*, 251–5.

pleasure'. Her percept echoes on in the pop lyric 'Don't let the past remind us of what we are not now.'[112] Photography encouraged Victorians to recapture beloved images for memory. Enchanted by daguerreotype portraits, Elizabeth Barrett Browning longs 'to have such a memorial of every Being dear to me in the world'.[113]

Mortal malady lingered in France in the troubled wake of the Revolution. But by mid-century social advance reduced homesickness; 'we cling [less] to the tombs of our ancestors and to the soil on which we were born'.[114] An 1879 authority predicted that '*mal de pays*, already rare in our time, is destined to disappear before the progress of hygiene and civilization'.[115] But nostalgia endured in backward Auvergne and Brittany and resurged among their migrants to urban centres; the ailment seemed rife among the feeble-minded. The psychiatrist Karl Jaspers asserted that nostalgic despair drove semi-savage rural servant girls to arson and infanticide.[116]

Still sometimes seen as a social crime, the illness mainly lingers on as fictional surmise; Anthony Powell's Hugh Moreland wondered whether nostalgia would suffocate him. 'I can see the headline: MUSICIAN DIES OF NOSTALGIA, a malady to which he had been a martyr for many years.' But he would die not of grief, but of pleasure.[117] For most nostalgia is no longer affliction but affection for a rose-coloured past whose loss is assuaged by bittersweet remembrance. And because that past, like Odysseus', feels ultimately recoverable, 'the bitter is less potent than the sweet'.[118]

Sentimental longing to retro irony

> May we all be preserved from nostalgia, and still more from nostalgia for nostalgia.
> Francis Hope, 1973[119]

> The hipster is our archetype of ironic living. . . . Manifesting a nostalgia for times he
> never lived himself, this contemporary urban harlequin appropriates outmoded

[112] Jane Austen, *Sense and Sensibility* (1811; London: Signet, 1997), 91; Jane Austen, *Pride and Prejudice* (1813; New York: Scholastic, 2000), 221, 384; Nicholas Dames, *Amnesiac Selves: Forgetting, Nostalgia, and British Fiction, 1810–1870* (Oxford, 2001), 5–26; Stephen Stills, 'Suite: Judy Blue Eyes' (1969).

[113] To Mary Russell Mitford, 7 Dec. 1843, quoted in Helen Groth, *Victorian Photography and Literary Nostalgia* (Oxford, 2003).

[114] Demais-Eugène Pilet, 'De la nostalgie considérée chez l'homme de guerre' (1844), quoted in Michael S. Roth, 'Dying of the past: medical studies of nostalgia in nineteenth-century France' (1991), 23–38 at 32, and 'Remembering forgetting: *Maladies de la mémoire* in nineteenth-century France' (1989), 3–22, both in his *Memory, Trauma, and History: Essays on Living with the Past* (Columbia, 2011). See Alice Bullard, 'Self-representation in the arms of defeat: fatal nostalgia and surviving comrades in French New Caledonia, 1871–1880', *Cultural Anthropology* 12:2 (1997): 179–212.

[115] V. Widal, 'Nostalgie' (1879), quoted in Roth, 'Dying of the past', 35.

[116] Karl Jaspers, 'Heimweh und Verbrechen' (1909), and Hans Gross, *Criminal Psychology* (1911), in Naqvi, *Nostalgic Subject*, 33–9.

[117] Anthony Powell, *Temporary Kings* (Heinemann, 1973), 229–30; Nicholas Dames, 'Nostalgia and its disciplines: a response', *Memory Studies* 3 (2010): 269–75 at 271.

[118] Erica G. Hepper et al., 'Odyssey's end: lay conceptions of nostalgia reflect its original Homeric meaning', *Emotion* 12 (2012): 102–19 at 113–16.

[119] Francis Hope, 'My grandfather's house', *New Statesman*, 1 June 1973: 807.

fashions (the mustache, the tiny shorts), mechanisms (fixed-gear bicycles, portable record players) and hobbies (home brewing, playing trombone).

Christy Walpole, 2012[120]

As nostalgia shifted from place to past – 'Odysseus longs for home; Proust is in search of lost time'[121] – it went from medical malaise to chronic angst. How could anyone be cured of the past? One can return to a place, but never to a past. But though time is lost for good, Proust celebrates its *vicarious* recovery. And we now retrieve the past as virtual reality at the click of a computer key. Reduplicated products and replicated processes supply desired memories on instant demand. Surrogate images of home solace distant émigrés and voyagers. Global sameness familiarizes remote locales. People will soon 'no longer need to ... yearn for their yesterdays, because wherever they are they'll see the landscape of their youths', suggests a psychologist. 'When they remember the Starbucks where they met the one they married or the Gap where they lost the one they didn't, they'll be marinating in memories that happened everywhere ... Let us revel in our nostalgia, and long for the days when longing was easy', back in the 1970s.[122]

Remember nostalgia? Remember when you remembered the 1950s? Remember remembering your first kiss? Remember remembering your first prom? Remember remembering your first name? ... Yes, those were the '70s – *innocent* days ... *simpler* days, when all you had to do for a good time was sit back and remember malt shops, doubledips, ponytails ... You cherish the memory of remembering these memories ... Yes, you remembered it all in the '70s, the Golden Age of Nostalgia, ... the most treasured memories you remember remembering ... And now here's your own grandmother to tell you how to order.[123]

Like film remakes, 'state of the art reproductions of past state of the art reproductions of the past' revive or reproduce products that traded on nostalgia to start with, such as Laura Ashley's remake of William Morris's fabric and wallpaper patterns.[124]

Ironic putdown of nostalgia as the 'most fashionable of palliatives for the spiritually deprived' long predates postmodern mockery.[125] Don Quixote's chivalric nostalgia confused ideal for reality. *Tristram Shandy*'s Toby and Trim obsessively restaged old military sieges.[126] Thomas Love Peacock scoffed at poets who adored bygone 'barbarous manners, obsolete customs and exploded superstitions'.[127] Thomas Hardy pitied villagers expected 'to remain stagnant & old-fashioned for the pleasure of romantic spectators'.[128] Appalled

---

[120] Christy Walpole, 'How to live without irony', *NYT*, 17 Nov. 2012.

[121] James Phillips, 'Distance, absence, and nostalgia', in Don Ihde and Hugh J. Silverman, eds., *Descriptions* (SUNY Press, 1985), 64–75 at 65.

[122] Daniel Gilbert, 'Times to remember, places to forget', *NYT*, 31 Dec. 2009: A25.

[123] George W. S. Trow, 'Bobby Bison's big memory offer', *New Yorker*, 30 Dec. 1974: 27.

[124] Brown, *Marketing*, 6–8; Stephen Brown, 'Once upon a marketplace', in Brown and Sherry, eds., *Time, Space, and the Market*, 293–312 at 307.

[125] Barry Humphries, 'Up memory creek', *TLS*, 9 Apr. 1976: 418.

[126] Laurence Sterne, *The Life and Opinions of Tristram Shandy* (1759; Penguin, 2003), 184–90, 510–11.

[127] Thomas Love Peacock, 'The four ages of poetry' (1820), in H. F. Brett-Smith, ed., *Peacock's Four Ages of Poetry; Shelley's Defence of Poetry* (Blackwell, 1921), 1–19 at 16.

[128] Thomas Hardy, 'The Dorsetshire labourer' (1883), in *Thomas Hardy's Public Voice* (Oxford, 2001), 37–56 at 49.

in 1919 by new-found fondness for early Victorian times, the critic Roger Fry assailed the 'optimism of memory' that built an 'earthly paradise out of the boredoms, the snobberies, the cruel repressions, the mean calculations and rapacious speculations of the mid-nineteenth century'. *Punch* foretold future nostalgia for wartime hardship: 'In about thirty years' time', says a woman in an interminable shopping queue, 'people will insist on describing this as the good old days'.[129] Seventy years after its wartime fame, Vera Lynn's 'We'll Meet Again' topped the charts in 2009.

But as baby-boomers gave way to Generation X, retro fashion irony mocked the past it copied, trivializing while exploiting it. Whereas Victorian revivals adulated bygone deeds and lifestyles, and postwar nostalgists evinced unalloyed affection, retro recall lampooned the past's failings and ridiculed its absurdities.[130] 'Did you people actually listen to the same decade I did?' 'scoffed a 1980s hater two decades later. 'You had eight years of Reagan. There was cocaine everywhere. There were yuppies.' Marketing fostered 'arm-chair nostalgia' devoid of historical memory.[131] The postmodern Proustian madeleine still evoked a flood of memories, but they now tasted more sour than bittersweet. Against baby-boomer wistfulness, Generation X swore off nostalgia.[132]

Nostalgia ceased to be benign. No longer prized as precious memory or dismissed as diverting jest, in post-Thatcher Britain it became a term of abuse. Diatribe upon diatribe dismissed nostalgia as reactionary, regressive, ridiculous, a 'spurious ... uncreative miasma'. In America it became a political insult. Fearing the future and denying the truth about the past, nostalgists were as pathologically warped as earlier melancholics. In sum, nostalgia was vulgar, demeaning, inauthentic, retrograde, fraudulent, sinister, morbid.[133]

Nostalgic pop culture spawned paranoid, even criminal, fantasy. Obsession with the Beatles was held responsible for Charles Manson's Sharon Tate massacre, with *Taxi Driver* for John Hinckley's assault on Reagan, with *Dallas* for the murder of 'Bobby Ewing's' parents – showbiz pasts more real than present reality. Revulsion against the cult of heritage sparked nostophobic rants.[134] Detractors exposed the downside of nostalgized pasts. In the 'good old days' of 1947 ('even the coffee tasted better back then'), 'polio was epidemic, Jim Crow was thriving, Europe was rubble and Hiroshima was a scorch mark on the map'.[135] Harold Macmillan's 1957, when Britons famously 'never had it so good', was a 'law-abiding and trusting age ... But boy, was it ever dull ... dreary, smoggy, deferential and prim ... an authoritarian, illiberal, puritanical society ... like today, in the

---

[129] Douglas Lionel Mays, cartoon, *Punch*, 4 Oct. 1944: 295.

[130] Elizabeth F. Guffey, *Retro: The Culture of Revival* (Reaktion, 2006), 10–14, 162–4.

[131] Jeff Leeds, 'We hate the 80's', *NYT*, 13 Feb. 2005; Arjun Appadurai, *Modernity at Large* (Minnesota, 1996), 77–8.

[132] Carl Wilson, 'My so-called adulthood', *NYT*, 4 Aug. 2011.

[133] Christopher Lasch, 'The politics of nostalgia', *Harper's Magazine* 269 (Nov. 1984): 65–70; Christopher Lasch, *The True and Only Heaven: Progress and Its Critics* (Norton, 1991), 112–19; David Lowenthal, 'Nostalgia tells it like it wasn't', in Christopher Shaw and Malcolm Chase, eds., *The Imagined Past: History and Nostalgia* (Manchester, 1989), 18–32 at 20.

[134] Hewison, *Heritage Industry*; Sven Birkerts, 'American nostalgias', in *Readings* (St Paul, MN, 1999), 22–41; Austin, *Nostalgia in Transition*, 201.

[135] Bob Garfield, 'Maxwell House 1892 ad brews up bad memories', *Advertising Age* 62:25 (17 June 1991): 50.

grip of an all-consuming but sterile nostalgia.'[136] 'You can praise times past', mocks a critic of the Swinging '60s. 'But do you really want to relive them, with Vietnam, class warfare, strikes, Hula Hoops, beehive hairdos and pelmet skirts? And what about the lousy food?'[137] Deriding Margaret Thatcher's Victorian values, Labourites shunned highbrow classical arts; 'in the public realm, nostalgia was nasty and the baggage of history unwanted'. Being nostalgic meant being out of touch.[138]

Besides nostalgia's starry-eyed view of wretched times, falsified history, kitschy commerce, and regressive elitism, it is faulted for foolish faith that issues were faced, action taken, crises averted, and problems solved better and faster in the past. Americans wax 'nostalgic for an era when presidents had big, bold, risky ideas that mostly worked out OK' (the New Deal), 'when actual weapons of mass destruction were removed without resort to actual invasion' (Cuban missile crisis), 'when Middle East wars lasted less than a week' (Iraq invasion 2003), and other 'wars ended in less than three months and only involved the British' (Falklands).[139]

Unfazed by such critiques, manufacturers mine memories, touting new products to nostalgic tunes that conform to the rosy view of former times consumers are supposed to want.[140] Volkswagen marketed its New Beetle – 'the engine's in the front, but its heart's in the same place' – as a return to rugged individualism. In line with the free-spirited past consumers are promised that 'As long as liberty is alive, Maxwell House coffee will always be good to the last drop'.[141] Nostalgia adverts redoubled in the wake of 9/11. Because 'America today is looking for institutions it can trust', Sears peddled century-old vignettes. People asked, 'Where can I get a plow for the spring planting? . . . a radio to listen to the game? . . . a new electric washing machine? . . . my wife a wig?' At Sears: 'it was true then, and it's true now'.[142]

Economic collapse in 2008 reinforced views that 'tough times call for familiarity', as evinced in pitches for things past at Super Bowl XLIV: Cheap Trick and Kiss (1970s rock bands) for Audi and Dr Pepper, toys such as 1930s sock monkeys, a teddy bear for the 2011 Kia Motors Sorrento; Budweiser's venerable Clydesdales. And these 'were pikers' compared with memory-bank raiders at Super Bowl XLV.[143] Across the Atlantic Notting Hill publican Jesse Dunford Wood plugged '70s muck – chicken Kiev, deep-fried brie ('for the full nostalgic rush, use cheap supermarket brie'), Arctic Rolls, soup in battered old mugs. Rampant cupcake nostalgia caps the regressive craze

---

[136] David Kynaston, *Family Britain 1951–1957* (Bloomsbury, 2009), 529–31, 538–44.

[137] 'A la recherche: nostalgia for the retro glamour of a previous generation', *Times*, 17 Nov. 2006: 2.3.

[138] Libby Purves, 'Old Britannia has survived the war on nostalgia', *Times*, 10 Aug. 2010: 17; John J. Su, *Ethics and Nostalgia in the Contemporary Novel* (Cambridge, 2005), 2, 122. Despite mainly left-wing critiques, radicals professed (or repressed) nostalgic yearning for lost working-class and anti-imperialist solidarity (Alastair Bonnett, *Left in the Past* (Continuum, 2010)).

[139] Bruce Handy, 'Looking forward to looking back', *NYT*, 5 Jan. 2007.

[140] Motti Neiger et al., eds., *On Media Memory* (Palgrave Macmillan. 2011), 9.

[141] Oren Meyers, '"The engine's in the front, but its heart's in the same place": advertising, nostalgia, and the construction of commodities as realms of memory', *Journal of Popular Culture* 42 (2009): 733–55.

[142] Stuart Elliott, 'Sears, riding wave of nostalgia, emphasizes heritage in campaign', *NYT*, 23 Aug 2002: C1, 4.

[143] Stuart Elliott, 'In Super Bowl commercials, the nostalgia bowl', *NYT*, 7 Feb. 2010: B3; Stuart Elliott, 'Between the touchdowns, ads go for nostalgia', *NYT*, 7 Feb. 2011: B4.

for old infantile comfort foods.[144] Likewise the scents of yesteryear are nostalgically recalled by deodorized modernity.[145]

Remember that perfume you were crazy about in college, or on your honeymoon in Tunisia, or when still married to your madcap first husband? Did you really love your mother's Odalisque and wish you could inhale it again? You can reach back in time to inhale fragrances from the past through www.longlostperfume.com ... lovingly concocted for anyone with a fragrance nostalgia that won't go away.[146]

Promising elusive permanence, electronic goods avidly embrace retro design. Artificial shutter-snaps on digital cameras, USB keyboards masquerading as typewriters, iPod docks dressed as juke boxes, iPod cases distressed to look like literary collectables. No one has yet said, 'It's a nice Ferrari, but it would be cooler if it looked like a covered wagon'.[147] To overcome reluctance to surrender tried-and-true devices, nostalgia segues into sagas of progress. Today's Beetle and Nike sports shoes are both old fashioned and newfangled, retro and techno. They combine unique, new, and exclusive performance with old familiar appearance.[148] But digital change comes faster than customers can bond nostalgically.[149] Citroen's anti-retro campaign oxymoronically attributes 'never look back for inspiration' to Marilyn Monroe ('I don't know why so many people live in the past ... Nostalgia isn't glamorous') and John Lennon ('why all this nostalgia?').[150]

Loss of faith in progress transmutes space-age retro-future nostalgia from swashbuckling optimism to wistful escapism for uncertain times ahead. By contrast, interior designers conceal modern efficiency behind '60s and '70s cosy naturalness in 'high-tech rustic' wooden floors and furniture, terracotta dishes, folkloric decor.[151] The bygone clutter of taxidermy and antlers (candlesticks, coat hooks, chandeliers), combines Tory chic with wilderness machismo.[152]

Debacles of the past decade – 9/11, Iraq, financial meltdown – evoke nostalgia akin to the 1970s celebration of 1930s economic adversity and fascist threat. We yearn for a time of purpose and a modicum of success.[153] Once again past times are hauled back into nostalgic consumption, not for their actual faith in the future, but for film and fashion

---

[144] Tony Turnbull, 'Anyone for Arctic Roll?', *Times Mag.*, 16 July 2011: 75, 77; Kathe Newman, 'Tour de cupcake: mapping the gentrification frontier, deliciously', cake*spy*.com, 14 July 2009.

[145] Constance Classen et al., *Aroma: The Cultural History of Smell* (Routledge, 1994, 2003), 84, 87–8.

[146] Bonnie Kimberly Taylor, 'Reincarnating the beloved lost perfume', *BeautyNewsNYC.com.*, Mar. 2005.

[147] Roy Furchgott, 'High-tech electronics dressed up to look old', *NYT*, 22 Dec. 2010; Joshua Brustein, 'Why innovation doffs an old hat', *NYT*, 18 Feb. 2011.

[148] Stephen Brown, et al., 'Teaching old brands new tricks', *Journal of Marketing* 67 (July 2003): 19–33; Brown, 'Retro from the get-go'.

[149] Janelle Wilson, *Nostalgia* (Bucknell, 2005); Vivian Sobchack, 'Nostalgia for a digital object: regrets on the quickening of quicktime', *Millennium Film Journal*, no. 34 (Fall 1999): 4–23.

[150] Tara Hanks, 'Anti-retro and the "new" Marilyn', *tarahanks.com.* 20 Feb. 2010.

[151] Ruth La Ferla, 'They're out of this world', *NYT*, 25 Mar. 2009; Kasia Maciejowska, 'New year, new nostalgia', *Times*, 8 Jan. 2010: Bricks&Mortar 4.

[152] Eric Wilson, 'If there's a buck in it somewhere', *NYT*, 26 Apr. 2007; 'The new taxidermy', 4 Sept. 2009, *ravishingbeasts.com/domestic.adornments*; Penelope Green, 'The new antiquarians', *NYT*, 29 July 2009: Gardens; Eva Hagberg, *Dark Nostalgia* (New York: Monacelli, 2009).

[153] Robert Nisbet, *History of the Idea of Progress* (Basic Books, 1980), 298–9.

trappings from science fiction and space exploration. Like Disney's Tomorrowland, the phenomenal popularity of *The Sims* – 175 million copies of the interactive game sold by 2013 – is a relic of what the future used to hold. The only desirable past the public today seem able to conceive simply rehashes an imagined 1950s of burgeoning barbecues, pearly picket fences, happy-clappy nuclear families, and bright new tomorrows.[154]

No wonder sophisticates scoff. Who 'does not repudiate nostalgia?' asks a reviewer of a neoconservative plea for bygone virtues. Yet 'who does not end up, yearning, even so, for various Golden Ages of yore?'[155] Even Generation X succumbs to the lure of its childhood, as its formative years merge into retro revivalism.

At first I shut my eyes to the slow reappearance of jean jackets, floral-print dresses, lace shirts and platform wedges. . . . But denial waves a white flag when . . . this summer includes Third Eye Blind, Limp Bizkit, Alice in Chains, Faith No More and the Stone Temple Pilots. . . . Meanwhile MTV is exhuming 'Beavis and Butthead' and 'Pop-Up Video', while Nickelodeon is offering a 1990s-themed block of . . . shows like 'The Adventures of Pete & Pete', presumably to help herbally-sautéed 20-somethings regress in giggly reminiscence.

Even Generation X sentimentalizes its youth. So how 'can an anti-nostalgic generation honor its past without becoming the thing it hated?' asks a critic. Only by keeping in mind 'that the time in question was hell as much as heaven'. And to be 'nostalgic for a time when we were not nostalgic', warns Svetlana Boym, is to mistake longing for belonging, and to fantasize 'a phantom homeland' – a past subject to our wildest desires. To that wishful fancy I now turn. [156]

---

[154] Russell W. Belk, 'The Sims and the retro future', in Brown and Sherry, eds., *Time, Space, and the Market*, 35–53.

[155] Paul Berman, 'Irving Kristol's brute reason', *NYT Book Review*, 27 Jan. 2011.

[156] Carl Wilson, 'My so-called adulthood', *NYT*, 4 Aug. 2011; Svetlana Boym, *The Future of Nostalgia* (Basic Books, 2002), xv–xvi, 355.

2

Time travelling

Is it not possible ... that things we have felt with great intensity ... have an existence independent of our minds; are in fact still in existence? And if so, will it not be possible, in time, that some device will be invented by which we can tap them? ... Instead of remembering here a scene and there a sound, I shall fit a plug into the wall; and listen in to the past ... Strong emotion must leave its trace; and it is only a question of discovering how we can get ourselves again attached to it, so that we shall be able to live our lives through from the start.   Virginia Woolf, 1938[1]

What if you could live your life over again? and again? and again? and again? Most of us would die for a chance to replay.   Ken Grimwood, 1988[2]

When he awoke, the dinosaur was still there.   Augusto Monterroso, 1959[3]

The pull of the past transcends nostalgic longing for a fanciful or surrogate yesteryear. Revisiting some actual past has long been a fond desire. Many would pay handsomely to relive a year of their personal lives, most to retrieve a day or an hour, especially from youth.[4] 'O for one hour of youthful joy! / Give me back my twentieth spring! ... / One moment let my life-blood stream / From boyhood's fount of flame!'[5]

The allure of time travel mirrors that of reincarnation. That the past should be irrevocably lost seems unbearable. We crave its recovery. Is there no way to recapture, re-experience, relive it? Some agency, some mechanism, some faith must let us know, see, sense the past. We will feel afresh the daily life of our grandparents, the rural sounds of yesteryear, the deeds of the Founding Fathers, the creations of Michelangelo, the glory that was Greece.

Woolf's longing surmise, penned just before her own death, involves two linked conjectures: that all memories survive, and that they can be retrieved. For things to be brought back they have first to be preserved. Those who yearn to view the past often conflate the two processes. A lengthy tradition of memory's permanence, even immortality, buttresses such hopes.

Many cite William Faulkner's famed line that 'the past is never dead. It's not even past.'[6] It carries on an active afterlife, quickening objects that receive its echoes, entering minds attuned to it. 'We live in ... the past, because it is itself alive',

---

[1] Virginia Woolf, 'A sketch of the past', in *Moments of Being* (Chatto & Windus, 1976), 61–139 at 74.
[2] Ken Grimwood, *Replay* (New York: Arbor House, 1988), jacket blurb.
[3] Augusto Monterroso, 'El Dinosaurio', in *Complete Works and Other Stories* (Texas 1995), 42.
[4] Thomas J. Cottle, *Perceiving Time: A Psychological Investigation with Men and Women* (Wiley, 1976), 222–4.
[5] Oliver Wendell Holmes, Sr., 'The old man dreams' (1854), in *The Autocrat of the Breakfast-Table* (Boston, 1859), 76.
[6] William Faulkner, *Requiem for a Nun* (Random House, 1951), 92.

Ivy Compton-Burnett's fictional daughter cautions her father, who seeks to shed it. 'Nothing ever dies.'[7] Searching sources, a biographer can't believe 'the historic past was extinguished, gone; surely it must simply be somewhere else, shunted into another plane of existence, still peopled and active and available if only one could reach it'.[8] Charismatic figures and iconic relics persuade us that the past not only survives but resurfaces. Mormon prophet Joseph Smith convinced disciples he had lived long ago, describing ancient peoples and folkways 'with as much ease . . . as if he had spent his whole life with them'.[9] The forger Tom Keating thought 'the spirits of the old masters came down and took over his work'; those who watched Alceo Dossena counterfeit classical paintings felt he truly reincarnated the spirit of antiquity.[10]

Hopeful belief in memory retrieval is venerable and persistent. But the retention and ultimate recovery of the *historical* past, in the mind or the cosmos, gained broad credence only two centuries ago. Scientists and poets concurred that the past endured and might somehow be resurrected. 'Once an event has happened', Thomas Hardy echoed Stoic philosophy, it 'enters a spacious realm containing all times where it goes on happening over and over again forever'.[11]

Scholars postulated cosmic storage. Since all physical residues survived somewhere, future science might open access to the whole historical record. The mathematician Charles Babbage presumed that every past event reordered atomic matter, leaving 'an ineffaceable, imperishable record, just as tree rings revealed bygone climates. 'No motion impressed by natural causes, or by human agency, is ever obliterated . . . The air itself is one vast library, on whose pages are forever written all that man has ever said . . . and the more solid materials of the globe, bear equally enduring testimony of the acts we have committed.' Even unspoken thoughts must survive in the cosmic ether, where 'stand for ever recorded, vows unredeemed, promises unfulfilled, an ineffaceable, imperishable record . . . from the birth of our first parent to the final extinction of our race; so that the physical traces of our most secret sins shall last until time shall be merged in . . . eternity'[12] – a truly Judgemental archive. Since 'a shadow never falls upon a wall without leaving thereupon a permanent trace', added an acolyte, 'vestiges of all our acts, silhouettes of whatever we have done', remain ineffaceable.[13]

---

[7] Richard Matheson, *Somewhere in Time* (London: Sphere, 1980), 37; Ivy Compton-Burnett, *A Father and His Fate* (Gollancz, 1957), 164.

[8] Penelope Lively, *According to Mark* (Heinemann, 1984), 110.

[9] Joseph Smith to his mother, c. 1823–4, quoted in David Persuitte, *Joseph Smith and the Origins of The Book of Mormon*, 2nd edn (Jefferson, NC: McFarland, 2000), 17.

[10] Guy Rais, 'Old Masters' spirits took over, says Tom Keating', *Telegraph*, 2 Feb. 1979; Donald MacGillivray, 'When is a fake not a fake? When it's a genuine forgery', *Guardian*, 2 July 2005; Frank Arnau, *Three Thousand Years of Deception in Art and Antiques* (Jonathan Cape, 1961), 223–5.

[11] J. Hillis Miller, 'History as repetition in Thomas Hardy's poetry: the example of "Wessex Heights"' (1972), in *Tropes, Parables, Performatives* (Duke, 1991), 107–34 at 127. See Georges Poulet, *Studies in Human Time* (1949; Johns Hopkins, 1956), 185–200.

[12] Charles Babbage, *The Ninth Bridgewater Treatise*, 2nd edn (1838), in *Works* (NYU Press, 1989), 9: 36–8, elaborated in George Perkins Marsh, *Man and Nature* (1864; Harvard, 1965), 464–5n.

[13] John William Draper, *History of the Conflict between Science and Religion* (1873; Cambridge, 2009), 111.

A century later, Walter Benjamin echoed Babbage: 'Nothing that has ever happened should be regarded as lost for history, [but] only a redeemed mankind receives the fullness of its past.' Each lived moment is reanimated on Judgement Day.[14] Yet the resurrectional promise also embodied a Tristram Shandean menace. For 'as we pass eternally on, we shall have more and more to remember, and finally shall have gathered in more ... than is now contained in all the libraries of the world', worried a Congregational minister. Without divine mercy, overflowing memory would 'drown all our other faculties', and the souls of the saved 'would virtually cease to be any thing more than registers of the past'.[15]

Science and science fiction recurrently renew promises of recovery. Relativity theory revivified faith in an accessible past. Since memory survives the loss of cerebral matter during life, held the astronomer Gustaf Strömberg, it might survive the dissolution of brain cells after death, to 'become an eternal part of the cosmos'.[16] Indeed, in the distant cosmos we actually see a more or less remote past *instead of* the present. Because ancient terrestrial events are only now 'visible' in galaxies light years away and will later be manifest still farther off, Earth's history can in theory be seen somewhere over and over again.

In a great many fields, researchers would give their eyeteeth to have an unfettered, direct glimpse of the past. Instead, they ... have to piece together a view of remote conditions [using] remnants — weathered fossils, decaying parchments or mummified remains. Cosmology ... is the one field in which we can actually witness history.[17]

'Every detail of life – and all other events – remains recorded in the matrix of space-time', held a hopeful scholar, and was potentially retrievable.[18] H. G. Wells foresaw a day when 'recovered memories may grow as vivid as if we ... shared the thrill & the fear of those primordial days, ... when we shall walk again in vanished scenes, stretch painted limbs we thought were dust, and feel again the sunshine of a million years ago'.[19] The philosopher Ervin Laszlo posits a cosmic memory field that retains all human experiences.[20] Arthur C. Clarke forecast the storage of present thoughts 'for eternity in frozen lattices of light'.[21] Envisioned 'reruns, repeats, reproductions of every recorded fact and feat in any time, [where] deceased stars perform with living ones' already proliferate.[22] Today's e-memory revolution promises – or threatens – total recall. 'Even our phobia of

[14] Walter Benjamin, 'Theses on the philosophy of history' (1940), in *Illuminations* (New York: Schocken, 1969), 253–64 at 254.
[15] Horace Bushnell, 'The power of an endless life' (Heb. 7.16), in *Sermons for the New Life* (New York, 1858), 304–25 at 310–11.
[16] Gustaf Strömberg, *The Soul of the Universe* (1938; Philadelphia, 1948), 188–92; Stephen Kern, *The Culture of Time and Space 1880–1918* (1983; Harvard, 2003), 41–2. The belief is immortalized in Bram Stoker's *Dracula* (1897).
[17] Brian Greene, *The Hidden Reality: Parallel Universes and the Deep Lives of the Cosmos* (Knopf, 2011), 48.
[18] Michael Kirsch quoted in Peter Laurie, 'About mortality in amber', *New Scientist*, 3 Apr. 1975: 37.
[19] H. G. Wells, 'The grisly folk' (1921), in *Selected Short Stories* (Penguin, 1979), 279–98 at 297–8.
[20] Ervin Laszlo, *Science and the Akashic Field* (Rochester, VT: Inner Traditions, 2004).
[21] Arthur C. Clarke, *2001: A Space Odyssey* (1968; New American Library, 1999), 185.
[22] Gary Kern, 'News vs. fiction: reflections on prognostication', in George E. Slusser et al., eds., *Storm Warnings: Science Fiction Faces the Future* (Southern Illinois, 1987), 211–31 at 229.

forgetting cannot be forgotten. Even if we wished to forget, we couldn't, as somewhere in the cyberspace cloud engulfing us, the engrams of our old fears will live for eternity.'[23]

Memory is the undying past's traditional receptacle. The 'natural and mighty palimpsest' of the brain piled up 'everlasting layers of ideas, images, feelings', in Thomas De Quincey's words. 'Each succession has seemed to bury all that went before. And yet, in reality, not one has been extinguished.'[24] To recall childhood excursions, William Hazlitt had only to 'unlock the casket of memory, and draw back the warders of the brain; and there this scene of my infant wandering still lives unfaded, or with fresher dyes'.[25] Seemingly forgotten early childhood memories must still survive.

Even foetal memories were sought. Shelley startled a mother by begging her weeks-old baby to describe life in the womb; surely a newborn had not already forgotten it![26] Swedenborg like opium-aided Coleridge and De Quincey retrieved vividly detailed pasts. Fever heightened perception: in a delirium, George Gissing conjured up the thronged processions, sepulchral marbles, and great vases of Calabria's ancient Croton two millennia before, reconstructing 'to the last perfection . . . a world known to me only in ruined fragments'.[27]

Belief in total memory retention underlay Freudian insight. 'Impressions are preserved, not only in the same form in which they were first received, but also in all their subsequent altered forms', Freud maintained. 'Theoretically every earlier state of mnemonic content could thus be restored to memory again.' Although many of Freud's views on memory changed, he consistently deemed it recoverable. 'Not only *some* but *all* of what is essential from childhood has been retained . . . It is simply a question of knowing how to extract it.'[28] Psychoanalysis confirmed that recollections never perished. 'Integral conservation of the past', wrote Henri Bergson, was verified by Freud's disciples.[29] Proust, Joyce, and Mann made the storehouse of unconscious memory a stock literary theme. 'Every action, every thought, every creative breath, . . . every shovelful of mud, every motion that cleared a brick from the ruins' had been recorded; from the novelist Danilo Kis's Borgesian archive one might retrieve memories of every moment in one's life.[30]

Seeming confirmation came from 1950s neurosurgery. Through electrical stimuli, Wilder Penfield claimed to locate patients' complete and authentic memory: 'A permanent record of the stream of consciousness within the brain . . . is preserved in amazing

[23] Yadin Dudai, 'To forget or not to forget', *New Scientist*, 24 Oct. 2009: 48–9. See Gordon Bell and Jim Gemmell, *Total Recall: How the E-Memory Revolution Will Change Everything* (Boston: Dutton, 2009).

[24] Thomas de Quincey, *Suspira de Profundis* (1845–54; Constable, 1927), 246–7.

[25] William Hazlitt, 'Why distant objects please' (1821), in *CW* (Dent, 1930–4), 8: 255–64 at 257.

[26] Thomas Jefferson Hogg, *The Life of Percy Bysshe Shelley* (London, 1858), 1: 239–40.

[27] George Gissing, *By the Ionian Sea* (1901; London: Richards, 1956), 82–4. See Georges Poulet, 'Timelessness and romanticism', *JHI* 15 (1954): 3–22.

[28] Sigmund Freud, *The Psychopathology of Everyday Life* (1901; Benn, 1966), 275; Sigmund Freud, 'Remembering, repeating and working-through' (1914), in *CPW* (Hogarth Press, 1966–74), 12: 148.

[29] Henri Bergson, *La Pensée et le mouvant* (1907), in *Oeuvres*, 3rd edn (Presses Universitaires de France, 1970), 1316.

[30] Danilo Kis, *Encyclopedia of the Dead* (1983; Faber & Faber, 1989), 56–7.

detail. No man can, by voluntary effort, call this detail back to memory. But, hidden in ...
the temporal lobes, there is a key to the mechanism that unlocks the past.' And 'the
original record seems to be available ... as long as a man may live and keep his wits.
Nothing is lost ... the record of each man's experience is complete'.[31] Subsequent
research refuted Penfield. But his vivid image of memory's quasi-immortal completeness
nonetheless endures. Well into the 1980s most psychologists still believed all memories
potentially retrievable. So does the general public to this day.[32]

Scientists speculated that memories persisted not only in individuals but in species,
even in stars. Freud attributed patients' 'primal fantasies' to genetically inherited experience. Genetic affinities might transfer memory from a past to a present mind, suggested
J. B. S. Haldane.[33] Such conjectures lent time travel scientific credibility. 'The life
experiences of our not-too-distant ancestors are inherited in certain cells of the brain,
just as their physical characteristics are duplicated in our bodies', supposed a 1930s
fantasist; hypnotism might induce one to relive ancestral experience.[34] Daphne du
Maurier's fictional biophysicist surmises that some drug might 'enable us to see, hear,
become cognisant of things that happened in the past' by reviving archaic brain
patterns.[35] 'Every time a user recalls a memory, he is not only remembering it', suggests
a sci-fi author, 'but also, from an electrochemical perspective, literally re-creating the
experience'.[36]

Reincarnation, a normative belief in Western culture although banned as heretical in
AD 553, is again increasingly popular, offering hope that death is not the end to those
lacking belief in a heavenly hereafter.[37] From Pythagoras and Empedocles on, many have
'remembered' previous lives. The Irish poet Æ 'recalled' his past personae sailing in
galleys over the antique ocean, living in tents and palaces, lying in Egyptian crypts;
Salvador Dali 'remembered' being St John of the Cross in his monastery.[38] As a child, the
archaeologist Dorothy Eady 'recognized' a picture of her ancient Abydos temple home
and ultimately returned to Egypt as Om Seti, the Nineteenth-Dynasty temple waif she
had once been. 'Sometimes I wake up in the morning', she told a visitor, 'and can't

---

[31] Wilder Penfield, 'Some mechanisms of consciousness discovered during electrical stimulation of the brain',
Proceedings of the National Academy of Sciences 44:2 (15 Feb. 1958): 51–66 at 65; Wilder Penfield, 'The
permanent record of the stream of consciousness', *Acta Psychologica* 11 (1955): 47–69 at 67, 69. See Alison
Winter, *Memory: Fragments of a Modern History* (Chicago, 2012), 75–102.
[32] Elizabeth F. and Geoffrey R. Loftus, 'On the permanence of stored information in the human brain',
American Psychologist 35 (1980): 409–20 at 410; Winter, *Memory*, 75–102. See Chapter 7.
[33] Sigmund Freud, *Totem and Taboo* (1913), in *CPW*, 13: 1–161; J. B. S. Haldane, *The Man with Two
Memories* (London: Merlin, 1976), 137–9.
[34] Amelia R. Long, 'Reverse phylogeny' (1937), in Groff Conklin, ed., *Science Fiction Adventures in Dimension*
(London, 1955), 31–43 at 33.
[35] Daphne du Maurier, *The House on the Strand* (1969; London: Pan, 1979), 196.
[36] Charles Yu, *How to Live Safely in a Science Fictional Universe* (Pantheon, 2010), 149.
[37] Richard J. McNally, 'Explaining "memories" of space alien abduction and past lives', *Journal of
Experimental Psychopathology* 3:1 (2012): 2–16.
[38] Æ, *The Candle of Vision* (Macmillan, 1918), 56–65, 143–7; Ben Martin, 'Dali greets the world' (1960),
quoted in Joseph Head and S. L. Cranston, eds., *Reincarnation* (1968; New York: Aeon, 1999), 102. The
vision inspired Dali's *Christ of St John of the Cross* (1951; Glasgow, Kelvingrove Museum).

remember whether it's B.C. or A.D'.[39] A graduate student of mine, convinced he had been a seventeenth-century Romanian, made Bucharest his doctoral topic and married a Romanian girl to forge links with his past (the dissertation never materialized, the marriage collapsed).

Intimate details of past-life regressions stimulated public appetites: Joan Grant's 'far memory' of Egypt's First Dynasty, of the Nomarch of Oryx, of Rameses II; Arthur Guirdham's previous selves in ancient Rome, Celtic Cumberland, Napoleon's navy; L. Ron Hubbard's 'rediscovered' life as a Carthaginian sailor – Hubbard's Scientologists do not 'recall' but 'relive' previous existences.[40] Accounts of past lives are fondly offered as genealogical evidence. Hence American Indian tribes, swamped by applications for inclusion, issue caveats that having been Indian in a previous incarnation is not a valid ground of entitlement.

Hypnotism is a regular route to past-life retrieval. Memories unlocked by hypnotic regression are persuasive because subjects remain unaware of the pastness of the events they recount; to them they are happening *now*. The 'previous life histories' elicited by Helen Wambach or by Virginia Tighe's *alter ego* Bridey Murphy seem to yield historical knowledge and behaviour unknown to their subjects when conscious.[41] But all such accounts are riddled with anachronisms that betray recent origins – origins disclosed when subjects are 'regressed' to the occasions they first read or heard about the remote past they have unwittingly absorbed. Thus, Jane Evans's hypnotically induced 'memories' of Roman times and twelfth-century York embody Jean Plaidy's *Katharine, the Virgin Widow* (1961) and Louis de Wohl's *The Living Wood* (1959).[42] Hypnotists' own suggestions also taint the memories. 'Hypnosis makes you more confident – and more inaccurate', psychologists conclude. Yet, folk belief that hypnosis can recover repressed memories persists, sustained by numerous professional therapists who 'retrieve' memories back as far as birth.[43]

Retrieving the past was from the start a major concern of science fiction (hereafter SF).[44] From H. G. Wells to *Doctor Who*, sojourners in bygone times have riveted time-

---

[39] Christopher S. Wren, 'The double life of Om Seti', *IHT*, 26 Apr. 1979: 14; Lawrence Lancina, 'Watch on the Nile', *IHT*, 5–6 May 1979: 4. See Nicole B. Hansen, ed., *Omm Sety's Living Egypt* (Chicago: Glyphdoctors, 2008).

[40] Joan Grant with Denys Kelsey, *Many Lifetimes* (1974); Arthur W. Guirdham, *The Lake and the Castle* and *The Cathars and Reincarnation* (1991); Peter Moss with Joe Keeton, *Encounters with the Past* (1981); L. Ron Hubbard, *Have You Lived before This Life?* (1960), *Mission into Time* (1973), and *Dianetics: The Modern Science of Mental Health* (Los Angeles, 1950).

[41] Helen Wambach, *Reliving Past Lives*, (Bantam, 1979); Morey Bernstein, *Search for Bridey Murphy* (1956; Doubleday, 1989); Jeffrey Iverson, *More Lives Than One?* (Warner, 1977); Ian Stevenson, *Children Who Remember Previous Lives*, rev. edn (Jefferson, NC, McFarland, 2002); Ian Stevenson, *Where Reincarnation and Biology Intersect* (Praeger, 1997); Winter, *Memory*, 103–24.

[42] Ian Wilson, *Reincarnation? The Claims Investigated* (Penguin, 1983), 233–43, and *Past Lives* (Cassell, 2005); Paul Edwards, *Reincarnation* (Buffalo, NY: Prometheus, 1996); Winter, *Memory*, 103–24.

[43] Nicholas P. Spanos, *Multiple Identities and False Memories* (American Psychological Association, 1996), 135–40; Marcia K. Johnson et al., 'The cognitive neuroscience of true and false memories', in Robert F. Belli, ed., *True and False Recovered Memories* (Springer, 2012), 15–52 at 24.

[44] The Science Fiction Library, until 1995 at North East London Polytechnic, was an invaluable resource. Peter Nicholls's *Encyclopedia of Science Fiction* (Granada, 1979; rev. edn with John Clute, Orbit, 1993):

travel aficionados. Few SF authors think actual time travel possible. Most accept the logician Kurt Gödel's view that 'if it is possible, then time itself is impossible. A past that can be revisited has not really passed.'[45] But SF visions of what it would be like to see or live in bygone times, of how to get back there, of the consequences of such visits cater for widespread fascination with the promises and perils of a visitable past.

Besides SF tales explicitly set in the past, many that are future oriented feature nostalgic or ironically retro themes, the futures themselves often primitive or pastoral. The huge popularity of time travel in recent film and fiction reflects heightened distress about a present felt depraved, debauched, done for. SF writers and fans look 'ever more wistfully toward the past', not least SF's own '30s to '60s Golden Age. As with much nostalgia, the archaic and the antique are replacing high-tech futuristic SF.[46]

SF tales offer invaluable clues to our preoccupations with the past. They yield insights into desires no less compelling for being impossible to consummate. Precisely because unbridled by practicality, these fantasies bring passions for the past into sharp relief. Time-travel metaphors transcend SF to denote all manner of bygone entertainment. Heritage tourists 'time trip' back through the centuries. 'My pupils were transported directly into Tudor times', an English teacher lauded a historic-house theatrical. 'They bridged 400 years or so almost as though they were time travellers.' Time-travel terminology saturates the museum world.[47]

'Not a thing in the past', an H. G. Wells figure remarks, 'has not left its memories about us. Some day we may learn to gather in that forgotten gossamer, we may learn to weave its strands together again, until the whole past is restored to us.'[48] The wish was father to the thought for H. Rider Haggard's protagonist, whose imagination 'shot its swift shuttle back across the ages, weaving a picture on their blackness so real and vivid ... that I could almost for a moment think that I had triumphed o'er the Past, and that my spirit's eyes had pierced the mystery of Time'.[49]

Ears as well as eyes transport us back in time. In the empty wastes of the Frozen Sea, Rabelais's Pantagruel hears cannon booming, bullets whistling, the clang of armour, the thud of battle axes, horses neighing, warriors shouting and groaning – battle sounds that had frozen in the air the previous winter were now tumbling noisily down, melting into audibility.[50] Munchausen's winter is so cold that a postilion's tune

'Adam and Eve', 'Alternative worlds', 'Origin of man', 'Reincarnation' (Brian Stableford); 'Atlantis', 'Pastoral' (David Pringle); 'History in science fiction' (Tom Shippey); 'Mythology' (Peter Nicholls); 'Time paradoxes', 'Time travel' (Malcolm J. Edwards).

[45] Quoted in Jim Holt, 'Time bandits: what were Einstein and Gödel talking about?' in Donald Goldsmith and Marcia Bartusiac, eds., $E = Einstein$ (New York: Sterling, 2006), 250.

[46] Adam Roberts, *The History of Science Fiction* (Palgrave Macmillan, 2006), 195–218; Darren Harris-Fain, *Understanding Contemporary American Science Fiction* (South Carolina, 2005), 109.

[47] Quoted in Lawrence Rich, 'Ten thousand children in need of a sponsor', *National Trust Magazine*, no. 35 (1981): 8–9; Robert Lumley, ed., *Museum Time-Machine* (Routledge, 1988), 6, 17, 143.

[48] H. G. Wells, *The Dream* (Collins, 1929), 236.

[49] H. Rider Haggard, *She* (1887; London: Macdonald, 1948), 199.

[50] François Rabelais, *The Five Books of Gargantua and Pantagruel* (1535; Modern Library, 1944), bk IV, ch. 56 (649–51).

freezes in his horn, emerging after thaw as audible notes.[51] Mystic identification with past cultures enables Hermann Hesse's itinerant minstrels 'to perform the music of earlier epochs with perfect ancient purity'.[52] In a museum Thomas Hardy sees 'the mould of a musical bird long passed from light, / Which over the earth before men came was winging', and fancies that 'the coo of this ancient bird / Has perished not, but is blent, or will be blending ... / In the full-fugued song of the universe unending'.[53]

Occultists promote such surmises. 'The faintest sound produces an eternal echo', Mme Blavatsky told her followers; 'a disturbance is created on the invisible waves of the shoreless ocean of space, and the vibration ... will live for ever'.[54] Old sounds linger until vacuumed up by J. G. Ballard's 'Sound-Sweep', walls and furniture throbbing for days with resonating residues. To retrieve 'the mating-cries of mammoths, the recitations of Homer, first performances of the master-works of music', a light beam reflects back sound that left Earth thousands of years before. One might record Stone Age sonic history in reverse by slowly evaporating stalactites in once-inhabited caves.[55] To recover valued past scenes a writer envisages 'delay-glass' through which light takes years to pass; beautiful past views hide the hideous or humdrum here and now.[56] At the Derbyshire house whence Mary Queen of Scots vainly tried an escape, Alison Uttley's time traveller senses 'the vibrant ether had held the thoughts of the perilous ruinous adventure, so that the walls ... were quickened by them, the place itself alive with the memory of things once seen and heard'.[57]

SF not only retrieves past sights and sounds but returns people bodily to previous times. 'We can't see the past, back in the bends and curves behind us. But it's there', says Jack Finney's physicist. Unified field theory ought somehow allow us to 'walk back to one of the bends ... If Albert Einstein is right ... the summer of 1894 *still exists*. That silent empty apartment exists back in that summer precisely as it exists in the summer that is coming.' A time traveller could make his way 'out of that unchanged apartment and into that other summer'.[58]

Getting into the past is imaginatively achieved in myriad ways – drugs, dreams, knocks on the head, pacts with the devil, lightning bolts, thunderclaps, and in the wake of H. G. Wells and quantum theory, time machines, Tipler cylinders, black holes, Gödel rockets, cosmic strings, space–time wormholes, and warp drives.[59] As with memory, evocative relics – votive axes, remnants of crosses, heirloom fans – trigger transit to the past. A fossilized sword awakens ancestral memories in a Francis Ashton hero who

[51] K. F. H. von Munchausen, *Travels and Adventures of Baron Munchausen* (1785; London, 1941), 36–7.
[52] Hermann Hesse, *The Glass Bead Game* (1943; Penguin, 1972), 28.
[53] Thomas Hardy, 'In a museum', in *Collected Poems* (Macmillan, 1948), 404.
[54] Helena Petrovna Blavatsky, *Isis Unveiled* (New York, 1877), 1: 114.
[55] J. G. Ballard, 'The sound-sweep' (1960), in *The Complete Stories* (Norton, 2009), 106–36; Ariadne, *New Scientist*, 25 Mar. 1975: 816; 26 Jan. 1978: 264.
[56] Bob Shaw, *Other Eyes, Other Days* (Gollancz, 1972), 48.
[57] Alison Uttley, *A Traveller in Time* (1939; Puffin, 1978), 106. That 'objects retain something of the eyes which have looked at them' Proust adopted as emotional truth (*Remembrance of Things Past*, 3: 920).
[58] Jack Finney, *Time and Again* (Simon & Schuster, 1970), 52, 63.
[59] Paul J. Nahin, *Time Machines: Time Travel in Physics, Metaphysics, and Science Fiction*, 2nd edn (Springer, 1999), 110–23; Kip Thorne, *Black Holes and Time Warps* (Norton, 1994).

'recognizes' it was long ago his own; a Celtic sword hilt found off the coast of Maine transports Betty Levin's twentieth-century children to Iron Age Ireland and early Christian Orkney; a painted shield lures Penelope Lively's fourteen-year-old back to the New Guinea tribe that gave it to her ethnologist great-grandfather. In an old house battered by time and use, a young visitor finds things that had long remained hidden. Places, like clocks, can be made to stop 'so that a moment goes on, as it were, forever', letting one see into other people's time. To hold a Bronze Age aurochs's vertebra gave ecologist George Monbiot 'an electric jolt of recognition' that revived 'a genetic memory' evolutionary past.[60]

To thus relive the past demands wholehearted immersion. Empathetic bonds, detailed knowledge, profound familiarity with the chosen epoch are prerequisites. Time travellers must avoid antagonizing – even perplexing – people they meet in the past. John Dickson Carr's historian knows the minutiae of seventeenth-century life well enough to seamlessly return to it. Finney's trainee time travellers live for months in simulated pasts that reproduce the sights, sounds, and smells of their destinations, wearing the clothes, eating the food, speaking the dialect of the time to make sure they will feel entirely at home back then.[61]

Such difficulties seldom deter the past-entranced whose craving is unassuaged by memory, history, and relics. Memories are partial and fleeting, history is prosaic, physical remains are decayed or hard to reach or interpret; historical enclaves, whether actual backwaters or contrived reconstructions, seem tame and false. True addicts require journeys that unlock gates to the past, let them see or roam there at will, and enjoy full-blooded bygone communion.

Goals in the revisited past

If time came adrift . . . there's no reason why everyone shouldn't see things happen the way they want them to . . . set free to live their lives to their deepest desires.

Peter Hunt, 1983[62]

Sometimes I wish . . . the years could go the other way and you could end up knowing all your dead relatives, like your grandmother, then your great-grandmother, then your great-great-grandmother, and so on.   Doreen Grainger, late 1970s[63]

Time travel's temptations are manifold: to enjoy exotic antiquity, to inhabit a happier age, to know what actually happened, to commune with forebears, to reap the rewards of being modern among ancients, to correct the past or to improve the present. Some want simply to relive past times, others to annul past errors.[64] SF fantasies highlight the hopes

---

[60] Francis Ashton, *The Breaking of the Seals* (London, 1946), 26; Betty Levin, *The Sword of Culann* (Macmillan, 1973), and *A Griffon's Nest* (Macmillan, 1975); Penelope Lively, *The House in Norham Gardens* (Pan, 1977), and *A Stitch in Time* (Pan, 1978), 104; George Monbiot, *Feral: Rewilding the Land, the Sea, and Human Life* (Penguin, 2013), 33–34, 207, and 'Our ecological boredom', *NYT* 18 Jan. 2015.

[61] John Dickson Carr, *The Devil in Velvet* (Penguin, 1957), 9; Finney, *Time and Again*, 48, 65.

[62] Peter Hunt, *The Maps of Time* (London: MacRae, 1983), 91, 123.

[63] Quoted in *Intimate Appraisals: The Social Writings of Thomas J. Cottle* (UPNE, 2002), 66.

[64] Jennifer Harwood-Smith and Francis Ludlow, '"Doing it in style": the narrative rules of the Back to the Future trilogy', in Sorcha Ní Fhlainn, ed., *Worlds of Back to the Future* (London: McFarland, 2010), 232–54.

and dreams evoked by the past but thwarted by its felt inaccessibility. The time-travel desiderata surveyed below illumine the polarized reactions to tradition and innovation that the following chapters survey.

Impassioned feeling features in both the goals sought and the sacrifices time travellers seem willing to endure. Like Faust or Enoch Soames, some would traffic with the devil to go back. 'The urge to see, to listen, to move amongst' fourteenth-century folk was so intense that du Maurier's hero risks health and even life for his excursions back in time.[65] 'To know that just by turning a few dials you can see and watch anything, anybody, anywhere, that has ever happened' makes a time-viewer 'feel like a god'. To be his seventeenth-century namesake at the court of Charles II, John Dickson Carr's hero would sell his soul.[66]

Fancied involvement ranges from glimpsing history in the safety of the present, to entry unseen by the past's inhabitants, to mutual contact, to meddling in past lives and events, to 'becoming' some past personage. Du Maurier's protagonist sees, hears, and smells fourteenth-century Cornwall, but cannot interfere; 'whatever happened I could do nothing to prevent it'.[67] An entrepreneur peddles tours to 'daily life in ancient Rome, or Michelangelo sculpting the Pietà, or Napoleon leading the charge at Marengo'; time travellers can visit Helen of Troy in her bath or sit in on 'Cleopatra's summit conference with Caesar'. In Gregory Benford's future 'Society for Dissipative Anachronisms', a Beatles-besotted nostalgist 'lived increasingly in the Golden Age of the '60s, imagining himself playing side man along with Paul or George or John'. Tourists to prehistory seek ever earlier epochs; they find the Cretaceous overcrowded, the safari-hunter Jurassic 'more like a fair ground every year', even the Devonian too popular.[68]

Explaining the past

To know how and why things happened is a compelling lure. 'Most historians', avers one, 'would give a great deal to [be] actually present at . . . events they have described'. To verify accounts of the Battle of Hastings, to hear Greek as spoken by Homer and Plato drew Wells's protagonists. Much scholarly trouble would be spared 'if you could actually *see* what took place in the past, without having to infer it' from fragmentary records and traces.[69] But SF chroniclers mainly seek new data to solve old dilemmas. Envisaging 'all the treasure houses of history waiting to be opened, explored, catalogued', Wilson Tucker's historian wants 'to stand on the city wall of Ur and watch the Euphrates flood

---

[65] Du Maurier, *House on the Strand*, 241.

[66] Thomas L. Sherred, 'E for effort', *Astounding Science Fiction*, 39:3 (1947): 119–62 at 123; Carr, *Devil in Velvet*, 13–14.

[67] Du Maurier, *House on the Strand*, 40.

[68] Keith Laumer, *The Great Time Machine Hoax* (Grosset & Dunlap, 1963), 35; Gregory Benford, 'Doing Lennon' (1975), in David G. Hartwell and Milton T. Wolf, eds., *Visions of Wonder* (New York: Tor, 1996), 253–62 at 255; Brian W. Aldiss, *An Age* (Faber & Faber, 1967), 18.

[69] Pardon E. Tillinghast, *The Specious Past: Historians and Others* (Reading, MA: Addison-Wesley, 1972), 171; H. G. Wells, *The Time Machine* (1895; Signet, 2002), 6; Arthur C. Clarke, 'Time's arrow' (1950), in *Reach for Tomorrow* (Corgi, 1976), 132–48 at 139. See Nahin, *Time Machines*, 35–7.

... to know how *that* story got into Genesis'. To reveal history's secrets 'back to the dawn of time' inspires Arthur C. Clarke's and Philip José Farmer's venturers.

Think of the historical mysteries and questions you could clear up! You could talk to John Wilkes Booth and find out if Secretary of War Stanton was really behind the Lincoln assassination. You might ferret out the identity of Jack the Ripper ... Interview Lucrezia Borgia and those who knew her and determine if she was the poisoning bitch most people think she was. Learn the identity of the assassins of the two little princes in the Tower.[70]

To ascertain Mark Antony's birth date, photograph paintings in Correggio's studio, and record 'the sonorous voice of Sophocles reading aloud from his own dramas' are another histronaut's ambitions. Fred Hoyle's historian opts to visit classical Greece 'to settle all the controversy and arguments about ancient music'. Isaac Asimov's 'chronoscope' inventor yearns to disprove the slander that the Carthaginians immolated children as sacrificial victims. Many trust the actual past will refute conventional histories.[71]

Origins obsess time travellers as they do scholars. Darwin's *On the Origin of Species* engenders many fictional visits to the dawn of mankind. Others search the inception of fire, of agriculture, of Indo-European languages, motives for Alexander's conquests or Columbus's voyages. A visitor seeks out an immortal world's oldest inhabitants, for 'if the first of them are still alive then they might know their origin! They would know how it began!'[72]

Personal curiosity actuates return to some key episode or figure in one's own background. Clifford Simak's genealogical clients interrogate ancient forebears. Like Shelley, Scientology prods converts to recall foetal experience, even conception.[73] Incestuous fancy prompts many: Ward Moore's time traveller confesses 'a notion to court my grandmother and wind up as my own grandfather', but Marty McFly in *Back to the Future* prudently fends off his flirtatious future mother.[74]

To revisit the past would vastly improve history. If historians 'could go back in time and see what happened and talk to people who were living then', Simak's character conjectures, 'they would understand it better'. Combining immediacy and hindsight, Moore's observer who knew how events turned out could 'write history as no one ever did before, with the detachment of the present and the accuracy of an eyewitness knowing specifically what to look for'.[75] But most time travellers are historically naive. They assume the past is known only from what is observed as things happen and dismiss

---

[70] Wilson Tucker, *The Year of the Quiet Sun* (1970; Boston: Gregg, 1979), 107; Philip José Farmer, *To Your Scattered Bodies Go* (1971; Boston: Gregg, 1980), 44. See Nahin, *Time Machines*, 35–37; Clarke, 'Time's arrow', 143.

[71] Wilson Tucker, *The Lincoln Hunters* (Hodder & Stoughton, 1979), 112; Fred Hoyle, *October the First Is Too Late* (Penguin, 1968), 96; Isaac Asimov, 'The dead past' (1956), in *Earth is Room Enough* (Doubleday, 1957), 9–50 at 25. See Paul Seabury, 'Histronaut', *Columbia University Forum* 4:3 (1961): 4–8.

[72] R. A. Lafferty, *Nine Hundred Grandmothers* (New York: Ace, 1970), 7–19 at 10.

[73] Clifford D. Simak, *Catface* (1973; Methuen, 1978), 163; Hubbard, *Dianetics*, 266–8.

[74] Ward Moore, *Bring the Jubilee* (1955; London, 1976), 164; Andrew Shail and Robin Stoate, *Back to the Future* (Palgrave Macmillan, 2010), 85–7.

[75] Simak, *Catface*, 54; Moore, *Bring the Jubilee*, 159–60, 169.

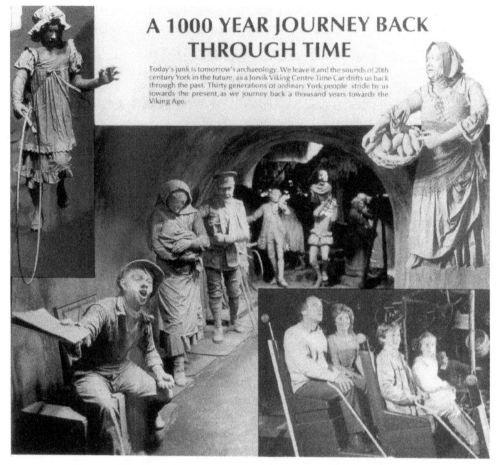

A 1000 YEAR JOURNEY BACK THROUGH TIME

Today's junk is tomorrow's archaeology. We leave it and the sounds of 20th century York in the future, as a Jorvik Viking Centre Time Car drifts us back through the past. Thirty generations of ordinary York people stride by us towards the present, as we journey back a thousand years towards the Viking Age.

Figure 4 The lure of time travel: Jorvik Viking Centre 'Time Car', York

subsequent insight as of little moment. They ignore the value of retrospection and see the past simply as another present.

Searching for the Golden Age

Forget six counties overhung with smoke
The snorting steam and piston stroke,
Forget the spreading of the hideous town;
Think rather of the pack-horse on the down,
And dream of London, small, and white, and clean,
The clear Thames bordered by its gardens green   William Morris, 1868[76]

That the past was better is SF's usual leitmotiv. Often pseudo-medieval, pastoral charms reflect Luddite anguish. Some admire all epochs, finding any previous period 'vastly

---

[76] William Morris, *The Earthly Paradise* (London, 1868), 3.

preferable to [our] own regimented day'.[77] Greens fancy a lush, unpolluted, pre-industrial planet only lightly tenanted – America 'before the white men came', or better yet, 'before there were any men at all', says a Simak character. 'Give us the Miocene; we want another chance', cry today's cramped slum-dwellers. Prehistoric 15,000 BC was paradise for Farmer's explorer: 'damned few humans, and an abundance of wild life; ... this is the way a world should be'.[78] Psychedelic mystic Terence McKenna concurred:

Every time a culture gets into trouble it casts itself back into the past looking for the last sane moment it ever knew. And the last sane moment we ever knew was on the plains of Africa 15,000 years ago ... before history, before standing armies, before slavery and property, before warfare and phonetic alphabets and monotheism, before, before, before.[79]

Environmental guru Edward Abbey found his 'true ancestral home' in America's south-western desert. Eager 'to flex Paleolithic muscles', Earth First! founder Dave Foreman bade followers 'restore the Pleistocene', when 'humans knew their rightful place ... as natural people'. To assuage Monbiot's craving for a richer, rawer, wilder life than 'ecologically boring' modernity, he yearns to go wild in a thrilling primeval landscape.[80]

Others choose their unspoiled childhood era. Mary McCarthy's 1940s utopian commune went back to 'the magical moment of their average birth-date' and favoured stage of mechanization (carpet sweepers not vacuum cleaners, ice boxes instead of refrigerators). The 1910 buildings and furnishings 'took them back to the age of their innocence'.[81] But not to austerity. 'The quiet fifties [are] as early as I dare go without sacrificing the cultural comforts I desire', said a 1970s past-seeker.[82] *Back to the Future* leaves despoiled 1985 (graffiti, homeless drunks in littered parks, terrorists stalking mean streets) for pristine, prelapsarian 1955. Many 1980s time-travel films portrayed the present as 'dehumanized, diseased, out of control, and perhaps doomed'.[83] Stephen King's visitor to 1958 'saw people helping people', an everyday altruism unimaginable in 2011. King's 'Land of Ago' had 'a lot less paperwork and a hell of a lot more trust'.[84]

Others prefer less recent pastoral pasts. Marking out on old maps areas that became industrial slums – Dagenham, north Cardiff, much of Manchester – Peter Hunt's 1980s protagonist rubs away the 'filth and squalor' to restore the 'pure, clean' 1860s countryside. America in the 1880s was far from perfect, realizes Finney's hero, but 'the air was still

[77] Alfred Bester, 'Hobson's choice' (1952), in *Starburst* (New York: Signet, 1958), 133–48 at 147–8; 43. Wilson Tucker, *The Lincoln Hunters* (Hodder & Stoughton, 1979).

[78] Simak, *Catface*, 54, 241; Philip José Farmer, *Time's Last Gift* (Ballantine, 1972), 79, 137.

[79] Terence McKenna, *The Archaic Revival* (Harper & Row, 1992), and his Alien Dreamtime, *deoxy.org/t_adt. htm*.

[80] Edward Abbey in Eric Temple, *A Voice in the Wilderness* (documentary, Canyon Productions, 1993); Dave Foreman, *Confessions of an Eco-Warrior* (New York: Harmony Books, 1991), 63; Dave Foreman (1984) quoted in Martha Frances Lee, *Earth First! Environmental Apocalypse* (Syracuse, 1995), 84; Monbiot, *Feral*, xiii, 6, 8, 106, 139, 256.

[81] Mary McCarthy, *The Oasis* (Random House, 1949), 42–3.

[82] David Gerrold, *The Man Who Folded Himself* (Random House, 1973), 122.

[83] Andrew Gordon, '*Back to the Future*: Oedipus as time traveller' (1987), in Ní Fhlainn, ed., *Worlds of Back to the Future*, 29–48 at 34, 30.

[84] Stephen King, *11.22.63: A Novel* (Scribner, 2011), 247, 368.

clean. The rivers flowed fresh, as they had since time began. And the first of the terrible corrupting wars still lay decades ahead.' In the play *Berkeley Square*, the quiet streets, petrol-free air, and sedan chairs of 1784 London make taxi-laden, bustling 1928 noisome and ugly.[85]

Recent or remote, the desired past is natural and simple, yet also vivid and exciting. 'The old, gray, modern existence' had little to offer Robin Carson's hero after 'the new, colorful opulence' of Renaissance Venice. A visitor who 'becomes' Cyrus in ancient Persia finds early warfare more tolerable than modern foxholes. The fourteenth century was 'cruel, hard, and very often bloody', learns du Maurier's protagonist, but it 'held a fascination ... lacking in my own world of today'.[86] Early Romans seldom lived long, admits a returnee from antiquity, 'but while they lived, they *lived*'. Old England's 'rough plenty' and 'sauntering life' compensated William Morris for 'its cool acceptance of rudeness and violence'.[87] At first appalled by nauseous medieval squalor and casual brutality, Ford Madox Ford's Edwardian protagonist becomes besotted with its ways (and women): 'I thought the fourteenth century was the only bearable time in the history of the world [and] when I came back ... the modern world seemed to me a horribly mean and dirty sort of place – worthless, useless, disgusting. I wonder now that I could ever have lived in it. It appears little and grey and cold and unimportant.'[88]

Today's faces seem 'much more alike and much less alive' to Finney's time traveller. 'There was also an *excitement* in the streets of New York in 1882 that is gone'. Back then people 'carried with them a sense of purpose ... They weren't *bored* ... Those men moved through their lives in unquestioned certainty that there was a reason for being ... Faces don't have that look now.' The grave and experienced faces carved in a medieval cloister struck Stephen Spender as 'more significantly alive' than those of his own time. Today's time-travel fiction – Douglas Coupland's Translit – discerns 'a spirituality lacking in the modern world that can only be squeezed out of other, more authentic eras'.[89]

SF golden ages little resemble any time that ever was, of course. Like nostalgists, time travellers fantasize childhoods divested of sorrow and privation, glamour-drenched histories devoid of squalor, and Edenic landscapes invested with all they feel missing in modernity.

Self-aggrandizement

Visitors to the past often fancy that technology and foreknowledge give them an unbeatable lead; modern know-how will make them powerful, famous, or rich back then. Mark Twain's Connecticut Yankee in medieval England expects to 'boss the whole

[85] Peter Hunt, *Maps of Time* (1983), 58, 123; Finney, *Time and Again*, 398; John L. Balderston with J. C. Squire, *Berkeley Square* (Longmans, Green, 1929), 37–8.

[86] Robin Carson, *Pawn of Time* (Holt, 1957), 437; Poul Anderson, *Guardians of Time* (Pan, 1977), 68; Du Maurier, *House on the Strand*, 267.

[87] Sam Merwin, Jr., *Three Faces of Time* (New York: Ace, 1955), 33; William Morris, 'Hopes of civilisation' (1885), in *CW* (Longmans, Green, 1910–15), 23: 59–80 at 62.

[88] Ford Madox Ford, *Ladies Whose Bright Eyes* (Constable, 1911), 96, 150, 107.

[89] Finney, *Time and Again*, 218–19; Stephen Spender, *Love-Hate Relations: A Study of Anglo-American Sensibilities* (Hamish Hamilton, 1974), 191; Douglas Coupland, 'Convergences', *NYT Book Review*, 11 Mar. 2012: 10.

country inside of three months; for . . . I would have the start of the best-educated man in the kingdom by . . . thirteen hundred years'. Being in the sixth century magnifies his prospects:

I wouldn't have traded it for the twentieth. Look at the opportunities here for a man of knowledge, brains, pluck, and enterprise to sail in and grow up with the country. The grandest field that ever was; and all my own . . . ; not a man who wasn't a baby to me in acquirements and capacities; whereas, what would I amount to in the twentieth century? I should be foreman of a factory, that is about all.[90]

Like Robert Reed's modern hero playing god in pre-Columbian Mesoamerica, myriad SF venturers follow in the Yankee's triumphal wake. 'All the treasures of the past would fall to one man with a submachine gun. Cleopatra and Helen of Troy might share his bed, if bribed with a trunkful of modern cosmetics'.[91] *Goodnight Sweetheart*'s (BBC, 1993–9) Gary Sparrow moves back and forth from wartime London, selling past artefacts as antiques in today's world, bringing modern luxuries to his 1940s lover.

Foreknowledge uniquely privileges modern visitors to finished pasts. Unlike the insecure present, the past is safely mapped, its pleasures tried and tested, its perils located and confined. The time traveller acts in a play whose outcome he alone knows. 'Watching old-timers' jaws drop in amazement while people who are 40 years ahead of them toy with them and give them the know-it-all treatment', Russell Baker comments, 'you are like a person playing poker with a stacked deck'.[92] Histronauts gain prestige at the expense of the past's true denizens. Their modern benefits resemble those of historians, for whom hindsight is both inescapable and insightful. But the historian properly eschews anachronistic judgement, whereas the judgemental time traveller may be fatally tempted to alter history's outcomes.

Changing the past

The past as known is partly a product of the present, for we continually reshape memory, rewrite history, refashion relics. The nature of and motives for such changes are discussed in part IV. But to alter what actually did happen, as distinct from reinterpreting it, is impossible.[93] Yet how ardently we often wish we could change the past! More persuasively than counter-factual history, SF offers imaginative release from the obdurate fixity of the past.

Three main motives impel time travellers to tamper with history: to improve the past; to undo its resultant evils; and to protect or restore historical stability against malign interference.

---

[90] Mark Twain, *A Connecticut Yankee in King Arthur's Court* (1889; California, 1983), 17, 62–3.

[91] Robert Reed, 'Two Sams', *Asimov's SF*, May 2000; Larry Niven, 'The theory and practice of time travel', in *All the Myriad Ways* (Ballantine, 1971), 123.

[92] Russell Baker, 'Time-warped power', *IHT*, 30 Oct. 1981: 16.

[93] Few theologians disputed Aristotle's view that 'not even God can make undone what has been done'. (*Nichomachean Ethics*, c. 340 BC (Chicago, 2011), 117.

Faith in progress is implicit in most efforts to improve the past. Arthurian England's ignorance and superstition, illiteracy and fecklessness appal Twain's archetypal improver, convinced scientific technology will make life safer, happier, longer. His civilizing mission envisions 'the destruction of the throne, nobility abolished, every member of it bound out to some useful trade, universal suffrage instituted, and the whole government placed in the hands of the men and women of the nation'. Within three years England is democratic and prosperous: 'Schools everywhere, and several colleges; a number of pretty good newspapers ... Slavery was dead and gone; all men were equal before the law ... The telegraph, the telephone, the phonograph, the type-writer, the sewing machine, and all the thousand willing and handy servants of steam and electricity were working their way into favor.'[94]

Avant-garde novelties work wonders in most past epochs. Rider Haggard's prehistoric venturers save their tribe from starvation by inventing fire; Manly Wade Wellman brings antiseptics and electricity to Lorenzo de' Medici's Florence. But modernizing often fails or boomerangs. Trying to avert the fall of the Roman Empire, William Golding's prescient envoy gives Caesar a steamship, gunpowder, and the printing-press, but the only modern appliance the gourmet ruler adopts is a pressure cooker. Sprague de Camp's reformer imports Arabic numbers, newspapers, telegraphy, distillation, double-entry book-keeping, and horse collars into sixth-century Italy in a vain effort to save Europe from medieval retrogression.[95]

To accord bygone authors deserved homage is Benford's historian's aim. He goes back to tell great writers, just before their death, how the future will esteem their works. But this revivifies them; they recover and continue to write, thus changing literary history. Ian Watson plans to 'yank past geniuses out of time, ... honor them so that they would know their lives had been worthwhile in the eyes of the future. But then ... tell them – oh so kindly – where they had gone wrong or fallen short. And how much more we knew nowadays.'[96]

Others aid the past by intervening at critical moments. To avoid the 'mistakes' that destroyed Rome and corrupted the barbarians, Poul Anderson's time traveller unites fifth-century Saxons and Romans in a Christian faith 'which will educate and civilize men without shackling their minds'. Preventing the ambush of Charlemagne's forces at Roncesvalles in 778, R. A. Lafferty's characters forestall the breach with Spanish Islam and thus spare Christian Europe centuries of cultural isolation. Aghast at the impending fate of Mary Queen of Scots, Uttley's heroine strives to 'put back the clock of time and save her'.[97] Such interventions are seldom solely altruistic; in ameliorating past conditions, time travellers also better their own lot. One teaches Stone Age people 'fishing – so

[94] Twain, *Connecticut Yankee*, 300, 397–8.

[95] H. Rider Haggard, *Allan and the Ice-Gods* (London, 1927); Manly Wade Wellman, *Twice in Time* (New York: Galaxy, 1958); William Golding, 'Envoy extraordinary' (1956), in *The Scorpion God* (Faber & Faber, 1971), 115–78; L. Sprague de Camp, *Lest Darkness Fall* (1939; London: Sphere, 1979).

[96] Gregory Benford, 'Not of an age' (1994), cited in Nahin, *Time Machines*, 266; Ian Watson, 'Ghost lecturer' (1984), in Gardner R. Dozois, ed., *Time Travelers* (New York: Ace, 1989), 155–74.

[97] Anderson, *Guardians of Time*, 46; R. A. Lafferty, 'Thus we frustrate Charlemagne' (1967), in *Nine Hundred Grandmothers*, 171–84 at 172–3; Uttley, *Traveller in Time*, 108.

I could eat fish; raising beef, so I could eat steak – and, later on, painting pictures that I could look at and making music for me to hear'. Another, nauseated by the slaughter of ancient Rome, replaces sanguinary gladiatorial games with football.[98]

The most compelling motive for altering the past is to change the present and the future – to make one's own fame or fortune, impose a hegemony, right a wrong, avert a personal tragedy, prevent global catastrophe. One time traveller retrospectively rescues his fiancée from a bombing raid, another eliminates a modern rival by having seventeenth-century buccaneers take him prisoner.[99] Others preclude the birth of enemies or invest for millionaire futures. 'Just think!! One might invest all one's money, leave it to accumulate at interest, and hurry on ahead!'[100] Broader concerns animate some. Sherred's 'time-view' inventor publicizes nationalist evils and hence averts nuclear war, by filming history's wicked tyrants.[101]

The futility of trying to avert past catastrophe features the best-intentioned interventions. To snuff out Soviet Communism at its inception, Paul Seabury's Cold Warrior goes back to assassinate Lenin in 1917. He succeeds – but returns to 1968 to find Washington occupied by Nazis. Stephen Fry's scientist precludes Hitler's existence by killing his grandparents; but the Axis powers win the Second World War. Stephen King's hero stops Oswald from assassinating Kennedy in 1963, triggering global nuclear war, radiation poisoning, and earthquakes that threaten the whole planet.[102] Other time travellers find that while they cannot change the past, they have already affected it, usually for the worse. Visiting from the twenty-fifth century, G. C. Edmondson's 'Misfit' not only fails to prevent the plague in 562 Rome or the Black Death in medieval Europe, but his visit proves to be the cause of both.[103]

Others defend the present by preventing villains from warping the past. Poul Anderson's Kublai Khan threatens to alter the course of history by conquering America in the thirteenth century; 'our own world wouldn't exist, wouldn't ever have existed'. Anderson's 'time patrol' absorbs the invaders without a trace into Eskimo and Indian populations, thus conserving the present as we know it.[104] The hero of the NBC series *Quantum Leap* (1989–1993), 'driven by an unknown force to change history for the better', inhabits different people of the recent past to 'put right what once went wrong' – saving young Heimlich from choking and inspiring his medical career, preventing Oswald from killing Jackie along with JFK, delaying Marilyn Monroe's death so she could film *The Misfits*.[105] Henry Harrison's status-quo protector returns to the 1850s to forestall a Southerner's deployment of modern weaponry that would reverse the outcome of the Civil War.

---

[98] Laumer, *Great Time Machine Hoax*, 198; Merwin, *Three Faces of Time*, 140.

[99] Anderson, *Guardians of Time*, 41–5; Carr, *Devil in Velvet*; L. Ron Hubbard, *Typewriter in the Sky* (1940; London: Fantasy, 1952).

[100] Wells, *Time Machine*, 6. See Mack Reynolds, 'Compounded interest' (1956), in Judith Merril, ed., *SF: The Best of the Best* (New York: Dell, 1967), 199–213; Henry Harrison, *A Rebel in Time* (New York: Tor, 1983).

[101] Thomas L. Sherred, 'E for effort', *Astounding Science Fiction*, 39:3 (1947): 119–62.

[102] Seabury, 'Histronaut'; Stephen Fry, *Making History* (Hutchinson, 1996); King, *11.22.63*, 709–14.

[103] G. C. Edmondson, 'The misfit' (1959), in *Stranger Than You Think* (New York: Ace, 1965).

[104] Anderson, *Guardians of Time*, 102, 120–60.

[105] Robert Hanke, '*Quantum Leap*: the postmodern challenge of television as history', in Gary R, Edgerton, and P. C. Rollins, eds., *Television Histories* (Kentucky, 2001), 59–78 at 65–72.

To validate the New Testament, Michael Moorcock's modern witness at the Crucifixion takes on the Messiah's role when he realizes the actual Jesus will fail to do so. Simak's fundamentalists seek to embargo visits to the time of Jesus, lest 'probing back . . . destroy the faith that has been built up through the ages'.[106] Such fears reflect a wider apprehension, as we shall see, that what lies undisclosed in the graveyard of the past had best remain buried there.

To change the past is nonetheless a revealing ambition. It sharply contrasts the only outcomes we can have with those we might prefer. We rely on the fixed irrevocability of what has transpired; but often wish it might have been otherwise. The desire to alter what has happened is a recurrent reaction to our discomfiting awareness of happenstance: past events determined the world and ourselves as we are; yet we know that these events were not preordained but simply contingent, that matters might easily have turned out otherwise. From that might-have-been we fantasize reaching back to make it so.

All these time-travel motives bear on actual attachments to the past discussed in the next chapter. But just as time travellers' desires are intense, the attendant dangers are grave, involving risks not only to themselves but to all of us, if not to the cosmos.

Risks of revisiting the past

Devotion to the past [is] one of the more disastrous forms of unrequited love.
Susan Sontag, 1977[107]

Living in the past was a little like living underwater and breathing though a tube.
Stephen King, 2011[108]

Suppose you *could* go back? How would it feel? What would be the consequences? Even those seduced by time travel are dubious about its outcomes, fearful that the past's dangers and griefs may outweigh its gains. They may be disappointed with the past they find, unable to cope with its conditions, concerned lest they be forever marooned back then, or appalled lest they imperil the actual fabric of history. Such surmises mirror widespread feelings about risks inherent in favouring the past.

The past disappoints

History and memory so routinely glamorize the past that it is little wonder to find the reality disillusioning. 'I saw enough of the Depression', says the embittered inventor of a time machine that conveys him to the 1930s; 'I don't want to spend my old age watching people sell apples.' Such returns can betray fond memories. A nostalgic visit to New York's Lower East Side miserably dispirits former residents, some because they

---

[106] Henry Harrison, *Rebel in Time* (1983); Michael Moorcock, *Behold the Man* (Fontana/Collins, 1980), 37; Simak, *Catface*, 190.

[107] Susan Sontag, 'Unguided tour', *New Yorker*, 31 Oct. 1977: 40–5 at 40.

[108] King, *11.22.63*, 100.

recognized too little, others too much.[109] A day in Plimoth Plantation's cramped, dung-splattered 1627 pioneer village leaves tourists happy for modern hygiene. The recent past can be a sorry eye-opener. 'I have returned to the Sixties', said a visitor of the solstice-rite hippie encampment at Stonehenge, 'and it stinks'.[110]

That the past literally stinks dismays many time travellers. Connie Willis's histronaut is told to cauterize her nose against incapacitating medieval stenches. A modern disgusted by the late Roman Empire complains that nothing prepared him for 'all the dirt and disease, the insults and altercations' of the past.[111] A bedraggled seventeenth-century village convinces Robert Westall's hero he is in the actual, not a re-enacted, past: 'Forget Merrie England ... These houses straggled down a mud track, and they not only had no telly-aerials on the chimneys – most of them had no chimneys ... The thatch looked old black and mouldy, the half timber was sagging and rotten, and the people ... were all bloody midgets'.[112]

Encounters with famed historical figures likewise disillusion, their aura dispelled by humdrum proximity. Lafferty's time travellers are revolted by Aristotle's barbarous Greek and Tristan and Isolde's bear-grease pomade; they find Voltaire's wit a 'cackle' and Nell Gwynn 'completely tasteless'; hearing Sappho, they think it lucky 'that so few of her words have survived'.[113] In ill-fitting breeches, a rust-speckled chain-mail shirt, and moth-eaten fur cloak, Keith Laumer's paunchy William the Conqueror yawns and belches at news of the Battle of Hastings.[114]

Moderns in the past miss the comforts of their own time. Fame and fortune in Renaissance Venice do not quench a visitor's fierce nostalgia that came 'with a snatch of remembered music, with the desire for a cigarette, and in his memory of women of his era'. An English girl back in ancient Rome is chagrined at the thought of waiting fifteen centuries for a cup of tea.[115] Henry James's Ralph Pendrel, at first in love with the past, ends by straining back to 'all the wonders and splendours' of his own once-disdained Edwardian world, 'of which he now sees only the ripeness, richness, attraction and civilisation', the virtually flawless perfection.[116] Voyeuristic slum-goers to time-frozen diners, industrial sites, and rural villages are relieved to return to the present. Yearning for a life with meaning, Douglas Coupland's rootless Craig is shunted back to become a thirteenth-century peasant: 'You'll love it there! ... You've

---

[109] Marion Gross, 'The good provider' (1952), in Groff Conklin, ed., *Science Fiction Adventures in Dimension* (London, 1955), 167–71 at 170; Richard F. Shepard, 'About New York: old neighborhoods visited mainly in memory', *NYT*, 18 Aug. 1977: B15.

[110] Jay Anderson, *Time Machines: The World of Living History* (AASLH, 1984), 52; Stanley Reynolds, 'Stoned henge', *Sunday Times*, 28 June 1981: 35.

[111] Connie Willis, *Doomsday Book* (Bantam, 1992), 10; L. Sprague de Camp, *Lest Darkness Fall* 1979, 13–14. The pong of the medieval past is a literary byword (Mark Jenner, 'Following your nose?' *AHR* 116 (2011): 339–40).

[112] Robert Westall, *The Devil on the Road* (Macmillan, 1978), 156.

[113] R. A. Lafferty, 'Through other eyes' (1960), in *Nine Hundred Grandmothers*, 282–96 at 282–4.

[114] Laumer, *Great Time Machine Hoax*, 36–7.

[115] Robin Carson, *Pawn of Time* (Holt, 1957), 57; Merwin, *Three Faces of Time*, 13.

[116] Henry James, *The Sense of the Past* (Scribners, 1917), 337–8.

got a role to fulfill! Just be sure to worship and defend whoever owns you! ... We crippled you a bit so you'll fit in better.'[117]

Truly reliving the past comes at the cost of its accumulated agonies. The gruesome evils of the slave trade led Babbage to muse on ineradicable memory that 'irrevocably chained' the criminal 'to the testimony of his crime'.[118] Memory is 'in the atoms somewhere, and even if we're blown apart, that memory stays', worries Willis's time traveller. 'What if we do get burned up by the sun and we still remember? What if we go on burning and burning and remembering and remembering?'[119] The gift of seeing the past is 'how wisdom comes, and how we shape our future', says the Receiver of Memory in Lois Lowry's dystopian refuge. Yet, to re-witness the whole world's memories – the grief and anguish, the horrors and terrors, of endless aeons of strife and suffering – proves unbearably painful.[120]

Inability to cope with the past

Modern know-how might prove a handicap rather than a royal road to success in the past. Lack of temporal nous and practical prowess would make today's technology useless, if one 'can't get the tools to make the tools to make the tools'. Few moderns could quickly master the arcane skills of an earlier era, even if they escaped cholera, smallpox, the gallows, and slavery. Poul Anderson's 'Man who came early' lacks the practical savvy needed for survival in tenth-century Iceland; Richard Cowper's visitor to 1665 London dies of the plague before he can repair his damaged time machine; Twain's Yankee succumbs to his own electrical ingenuity.[121] Up-to-date notions may prove heretically fatal: 'people of most historic communities would fear and suspect us, imprison and interrogate us, perhaps even put us to death'. Laumer's visitor to Llandudno in 1723 is burned as a witch for sponsoring birth control, evolution, and psychoanalysis. Anachronistic suspicion is now almost instant. 'If you had mentioned food combining or wheat intolerance back in 1992', notes a visitor from 2005, 'they might have thrown you into a pond to see if you floated'.[122]

Unbridgeable disparities aggravate the risks of being in the past. 'How much can you learn in a totally strange environment', asks Poul Anderson, 'when you can barely speak a word and are liable to be arrested on suspicion before you can swop for a suit of

---

[117] Douglas Coupland, *Generation X* (St Martin's, 1991), 11, and *Generation A* (London: Windmill, 2010), 268.

[118] Babbage, *Ninth Bridgewater Treatise*, 38–9.

[119] Connie Willis, *Fire Watch* (Bantam, 1985), 198.

[120] Lois Lowry, *The Giver* (1993; HarperCollins, 2003), 99, 131.

[121] Poul Anderson, 'The man who came early' (1956), in *The Horn of Time* (Boston: Gregg, 1968), 68–90; Richard Cowper, 'Hertford manuscript', *Fantasy and SF* 51:4 (1976): 6–37; Twain, *Connecticut Yankee*; Bud Foote, *The Connecticut Yankee in the Twentieth Century: Travel to the Past in Science Fiction* (Greenwood, 1991).

[122] Stacy F. Roth, *Past into Present: Effective Techniques for First-Person Historical Interpretation* (North Carolina, 1998), 67; Keith Laumer, *Dinosaur Beach* (New York: Daw, 1971), 100; Billy Frolick, '1992 house', *New Yorker*, 17 Jan. 2005: 49.

contemporary clothes?'[123] The most scrupulous schooling in bygone customs cannot make up for the absence of myriad shared recollections. Back in 1820, James's Ralph Pendrel is caught out again and again for lacking memory of family and neighbourly details. His knowledge, '*almost* as right as possible for the "period" ... and yet so intimately and secretly wrong', can never match that of 1820s natives; anything he does or says, even opening his mouth to reveal well-cared-for teeth 'that undentisted age can't have known the like of', is liable to betray him. It is 'one thing to "live in the Past" *with* ... the whole candour of confidence and confidence of candour, that he would then have naturally had', concludes James, 'and a totally different thing to find himself living in it without ... those preponderant right instincts'.[124]

The mere hope of moving back through time might prove lethal, were fantasy made real. Communing with a sixteenth-century man through a ouija board, a twentieth-century English woman became so besotted with him that she killed herself, 'so that we can go back to live as we used to'. Given all the threats, concludes a time-travel scholar, 'it would take a brave soul to do much more, while in the past, than just stand still and breathe'.[125]

Problems of returning to the present

Perhaps the visited past's worst peril is to be forever stranded there. Terror at being unable to return, the horror ... of 'being *in* the past to stay, heart-breakingly to stay and never know his own precious Present again', corrodes Ralph Pendrel's pleasure in 1820 and sours his sojourn there.[126] Hubbard's film-writer fails to escape from the diabolical clatter of the deceased author's typewriter imprisoning him in the seventeenth century.[127] Marghanita Laski's tubercular protagonist, trapped back in 1864, is unable to return to medically enlightened modernity.[128] Blackadder can't remember how to reset his time machine to return to 1999 from the Cretaceous. He ends up instead at the court of Elizabeth I, to whom his gift of a Polo mint – which she finds 'the tastiest thing in the history of the world' – saves him from beheading.[129] Few are so fortunate as to travel back 'with vaccinations, a wad of cash and a clean set of ruling-class garb'. Only with Translit – novels that 'cross history without being historical' – do 'we visit multiple pasts safe in the knowledge that we'll get off the ride intact'.[130]

Getting stuck in the past seems a just desert for trifling with its denizens. After returning Madame Bovary to her own time and place, Woody Allen's professor's time-machine misfires and plants him in a old textbook of remedial Spanish, pursued by a

---

[123] Poul Anderson, *There Will Be Time* (Sphere, 1979), 46.
[124] James, *Sense of the Past*, 295–6, 301.
[125] 'Mother killed by train "was obsessed"', *Times*, 24 Apr. 1981: 4; Nahin, *Time Machines*, 51.
[126] James, *Sense of the Past*, 294; William Righter, *American Memory in Henry James* (Ashgate, 2004), 201–5.
[127] Hubbard, *Typewriter in the Sky*, 70, 75, 95.
[128] Marghanita Laski, *The Victorian Chaise-longue* (Ballantine, 1953).
[129] Richard Curtis and Ben Elton, *Blackadder: Back & Forth* (Penguin, 2000).
[130] Douglas Coupland, 'Convergences', *NYT Book Review*, 11 Mar. 2012: 10.

large and hairy irregular verb.[131] Each night, René Clair's dispirited protagonist in *Les Belles de Nuit* (1952) dreams that an old man tells him 'It was much better in my day.' So he goes back another generation, only to repeat the same dream over and over, ending up in the Stone Age still longing for the 'good old days'.[132] While some crooks seek time-travel sanctuaries, incorrigible criminals may be permanently exiled to a prison-house of the past. 'Off to the reptiles' a hundred million years back, 'no one to talk with, boredom, and in the end ... an afternoon snack to a tyrannosaurus'.[133]

Others return to feel that sojourn in the past misfits them for present existence or to find today unliveable. The intensity of fourteenth-century life alienates du Maurier's protagonist from the drab present. A stay in sixteenth-century Venice unfits Carson's hero for modern America; coming back 'with a skull full of maddening memories ... I couldn't even qualify as an assistant professor of Renaissance history'. Disgust with the present spurs enervating addiction to visitable pasts; Aldiss's future nostalgists seek only to escape their advanced but dreary time.[134] Alfred Bester's disgruntled 'time stiffs' keep 'bumming through the centuries ... looking for the Golden Age'. Visitors from Finney's foredoomed twenty-first century elect to stay in the past, scattering back over the preceding three millennia.[135] But as Descartes warned, too much time spent frequenting past centuries leaves one ignorant of one's own.[136]

Endangering the temporal fabric

Subsequent interference imperils the past itself. Like historical restoration, an SF scholar surmises, time travel makes the past thin and artificial and may one day wear it out altogether. 'Every operation leaves reality a bit cruder, a bit uglier, a bit more makeshift, and a whole lot less rich in those details and feelings that are our heritage'. Stephen King's time traveller goes back to undo his changes lest their dire consequences destroy 'reality itself'.[137]

Indeed, the slightest alteration of the past – a grain of dust misplaced – could jeopardize all that follows. 'The stomp of your foot, on one mouse, could start an earthquake, the effects of which could shake our earth and destinies down through Time', warns a safari leader to the Jurassic. In that tale, crushing a butterfly 65 million years back results in the election of the 'wrong' US president in 2055.[138] Efforts to improve the past

[131] Woody Allen, 'The Kugelmass episode' (1978), in *Side Effects* (Random House, 1980), 59–78.

[132] Alwyn Eades, 'Dream On', *New Scientist*, 22 Sept. 2007: 25.

[133] Sever Gansovsky, 'Vincent Van Gogh' (1970), in Boris and Arkady Strugatsky, eds., *Aliens, Travelers, and Strangers: The Best of Soviet SF* (Macmillan, 1984), 51–118 at 100–1.

[134] Du Maurier, *House on the Strand*, 267; Carson, *Pawn of Time*, 433; Aldiss, *An Age*.

[135] Bester, 'Hobson's choice', 146; Jack Finney, 'Such interesting neighbors' (1951), in *The Clock of Time* (London: Panther, 1961), 5–20 at 16–18.

[136] René Descartes, *Discours de la méthode* (1637; Paris, 1947), 5–6; Anthony T. Grafton, *Bring Out Your Dead: The Past as Revelation* (Harvard, 2001), 194.

[137] Fritz Leiber, *The Big Time* (1957; New York: Ace, 1961), 57; King, *11.22.63*, 698–9.

[138] Ray Bradbury, 'A sound of thunder' (1952), in *R Is for Rocket* (Pan, 1972), 73–86 at 77. The butterfly effect is ascribed to chaos theory pioneer Edward Lorenz in 1963 (Robert C. Hilborn, 'Sea gulls, butterflies, and grasshoppers', *American Journal of Physics* 72:3 (Apr. 2004): 425–7).

usually backfire. Owing to a time traveller's antibiotics and anaesthesia in ancient Rome, by the sixth century the city grows lethally overpopulated.[139]

One even risks erasing one's future self. Undoing some previous act courts self-annihilation if an ancestor perishes in the process. 'If we once start doubling back to tinker with our personal pasts, we'd soon get so tangled up that none of us would exist.'[140] To minimize risks of interference, some time travellers go only to remote prehistory: Sprague de Camp's visitors to times before 100,000 BC; Simak's to epochs ancient enough to preclude meeting early humans.[141]

Others deny that any impacts could significantly alter the past. Time is a river into which billions of events are dropped; no individual can affect their collective course. 'You can't erase the conquests of Alexander by nudging a neolithic pebble', reasons Fritz Leiber, or 'extirpate America by pulling up a shoot of Sumerian grain'. Similarly, 'if I went back to … the Middle Ages and shot one of FDR's Dutch forebears, he'd still be born in the late nineteenth century – because he and his genes resulted from the entire world of his ancestors'.[142] With all his twentieth-century resources and foreknowledge, Carr's hero still cannot change the past; he 'might alter a small and trifling detail, [but] the ultimate result would be just the same'. In fact, you can't change anything, insists Larry Niven. 'You can't kill your grandfather because you *didn't*. You'll kill the wrong man if you try it; or your gun won't fire.'[143]

Still others suggest that the known present includes the effects of previous temporal interventions. 'If time travel was going to make any changes, it had already done so', asserts a Farmer character. 'Whatever he was to do had been done, and events and lives had been determined before he was born even if he had helped determine them.' The firm fixity of the past frustrates a husband's retrospective revenge against his unfaithful wife. Going back to kill her grandparents, he returns to the present to find her still in his rival's embrace. He alters history more radically, annihilating George Washington, Columbus, Mohammed – all to no avail.[144]

'If a thing has happened, it has happened' philosophers agree, and 'you cannot make it not to have happened.'[145] Were it alterable, no aspect of the past could be depended upon. Any revisited past would be irreparably marooned. 'Lacking a past in the past, and having memories of the future', Ralph Pendrel thereby destroys the past he so intensely

[139] Frederik Pohl, 'The deadly mission of Phineas Snodgrass' (1962), in *The Gold at the Starbow's End* (Ballantine, 1972). See Foote, *Connecticut Yankee*, 101.

[140] Anderson, *Guardians of Time*, 52.

[141] L. Sprague de Camp, 'Gun for dinosaur', in *Best of L. Sprague de Camp* (Ballantine, 1978), 272–302; Simak, *Catface*, 241–51.

[142] Fritz Leiber, 'Try and change the past' (1958), in Robert Silverberg, ed., *Trips in Time* (Nelson, 1977), 93–101 at 94; Anderson, *Guardians of Time*, 130.

[143] Carr, *Devil in Velvet*, 15; Niven, 'The theory and practice of time travel', in *All the Myriad Ways* (1971), 120.

[144] Farmer, *Time's Last Gift*, 12, 20; Alfred Bester, 'The men who murdered Mohammed' (1958), in *The Light Fantastic* (Gollancz, 1977), 113–29.

[145] Michael Dummett, 'Bringing about the past', *Philosophical Review* 73 (1964): 338–59 at 341. 'Just to visit the Past would be to change the Past, and this cannot be' (Arthur C. Danto, 'Narrative sentences', *History and Theory* 2 (1962–3): 146–79 at 160). See Nicholas J. J. Smith, 'Bananas enough for time travel?' *British Journal for the Philosophy of Science* 48 (1997): 363–89 at 374.

desires to belong to.[146] In seeking to assimilate its details, he detaches its own inhabitants from their moorings; his 'very care had somehow annihilated them', his uncanny understanding turning them 'to stone or wood or wax'. As a horrified eighteenth-century lady tells her intrusive twentieth-century suitor, 'You have been thinking of me in the past tense, talking about me as though I were already dead!'[147]

Ancestor-worshippers fear forebears' reprisals if their graves are neglected or mistreated. Time travellers similarly fear history will punish any interference with the past. Hence they eventually abstain. 'We shall never make the best of our present world', concludes a histronaut after a spell in the Middle Ages, 'until we realize how false it is to hanker after the ideals of a dead past'. Enthralled by medieval architecture, he was appalled by much else in those days and returned 'strengthened to the common routine of life in our own soulless century'.[148]

People are normally aware that the actual past is irrecoverable. Yet memory and history, relic and replica, leave impressions so concretely vivid that we feel nonetheless deprived. Surely routes so enticing and well mapped should be open to us in reality! The hopes and fears aroused by the past are heightened by the conflict between knowing it is beyond reach yet craving it anyhow.

We feel the present alone inadequate, not least because it is continuously dislodged to further enlarge the past. Disenchantment with an ever-dismembered today impels yesterday's recovery. That quest takes many forms: hallowing memories, cherishing tradition, devotion to relics, treasuring antiques and souvenirs, simply valuing what is old, rejecting change. These reactions lack the fantasy of time travel but reflect the same yearning for bygone times.

It is easy to see what is amiss with such craving. 'Through the vistas of the years every age but our own seems glamorous and golden', concludes Bester. 'We yearn for the yesterdays and tomorrows, never realizing . . . that today, bitter or sweet, anxious or calm, is the only day for us. The dream of time is the traitor, and we are all accomplices to the betrayal of ourselves.'[149] Yet the enduring if quixotic quest to relive the past at least brings history and memory vividly to mind, setting in sharp relief both the defects and the merits of the present.

To live again in the past lends fullness and duration to the present. Coexistence in past and present convinces du Maurier's protagonist that 'there was no past, no present, no future. Everything living is part of the whole. We are all bound, one to the other, through time and eternity.' The vivid reality of fourteenth-century Cornwall 'proved that the past was living still, that we were all participants, all witnesses'. And temporal conjunction made us more truly ourselves.[150]

---

[146] Allan W. Bellringer, 'Henry James's *The Sense of the Past*', *Forum for Modern Language Studies* 17 (1981): 201–16 at 210; J. Hillis Miller, 'The "Quasi-Turn-of-Screw effect" . . . : *The Sense of the Past*', in *Literature as Conduct: Speech Acts in Henry James* (Fordham, 2005), 291–326.

[147] James, *Sense of the Past*, 213; Balderston, *Berkeley Square*, 80.

[148] George Gordon Coulton, *Friar's Lantern* (1906; London, 1948), 227, 34.

[149] Bester, 'Hobson's choice', 148.

[150] Du Maurier, *House on the Strand*, 169–70.

The dreams and nightmares of revisiting the past are no less instructive for being unlikely. They offer clues to what of the past we truly need and can accept or should avoid and reject. And they throw light on deep-seated stances towards tradition and change. Both sides in Britain's 2010 election deployed the BBC's *Ashes to Ashes*, whose wounded protagonist reawakens in 1981. Depicting David Cameron lolling against the film's luxury Audi Quattro (then new), Labour warned against a return to the Thatcherian past – 'Don't let him take Britain back to the 1980s!'. 'Fire up the Quattro. It's time for change', Tory posters countered. 'Millions of people … wish it was the 1980s'.[151] Passionate pursuit of the past is less debilitating than to lack concern for the past altogether.

---

[151] Patrick Hennessy, 'Labour's Ashes to Ashes poster scores own goal', *Telegraph*, 3 Apr. 2010.

3

Benefits and burdens of the past

Only a good-for-nothing is not interested in his past.   Sigmund Freud[1]

Dwell on the past and you'll lose an eye; forget the past and you'll lose both eyes.
                                                                 Russian proverb

The future is dark, the present burdensome; only the past, dead and finished, bears
contemplation. Those who look upon it have survived it; they are its products and its
victors.   Geoffrey Elton, 1967[2]

We want to live in history, where all our ancestors and all our brethren live and die in
common ... But we also desire to escape from history ...We want to be chained in
history but we also want to be unlinked   Alan Liu, 2008[3]

Is the past a burden and a trap? Or an anchor and a springboard?
                                                          Penelope Green, 2010[4]

Why do we need the past? What do we want it for? What risks does regard for it entail?
Does fondness for things past match the yearnings of nostalgia and time-travel fiction?
How we engage with our heritage is more consequential, yet the dilemmas that ensue
have much in common with those revealed in previous chapters. Here I survey attitudes
towards the past in general, the benefits it supplies, the burdens it entails, and the traits
that make it desirable or reprehensible.

   We live in the present and see only what currently exists. What is to come is of obvious
moment; we are programmed to care about the future we'll inhabit. But why be concerned
with things over and done with? Modernity threatens to strip the past of two hallowed values:
enlightenment and empowerment. Yet bygone times command attention and affection as
strongly as ever. An anthropologist finds 'perduring belief in both the importance and
knowability of the past' from the traces it has left – human remains, documents, artefacts,
psychic memories, genetic mutations.[5]

   The past was once an indispensable guide. Only by studying former lives and learning
history could people understand present selves and circumstances and prepare for times
to come. The past was a fount of precepts for further use. Faith in its guidance rested on

[1] Quoted in Suzanne Cassirer Bernfeld, 'Freud and archeology', *American Imago* 8 (1951): 107–28 at 111.
[2] Geoffrey R. Elton, *The Practice of History* (1967; rev. edn Blackwell, 2002), 1.
[3] Alan Liu, 'Escaping history', in *Local Transcendence* (Chicago, 2008), 258.
[4] Penelope Green, 'In a crumbling estate, creativity and history meet', *NYT*, 21 July 2010.
[5] Nadia Abu El-Haj, *The Genealogical Science* (Chicago, 2012), 221.

three assumptions: that the past was knowable and the future ordained; that change was gradual, cyclical, or inconsequential; and that human nature was the same in all times and places.

Because these certitudes are no more, the past has lost much of its pedagogic function. Fears of repeating former errors remain widespread, but past knowledge now foretells little about the future. Faith in a knowable past is likewise in tatters. Although research continually throws new light on history, the actual past eludes us: all we have is partial accounts of it, based on all-too-fallible memories, and fragments of its much-altered residues – topics reviewed in part III. And the pasts constructed as proxies for that lost realm are anything but fixed and solid: they vary from viewer to viewer and year to year, as recent events crowd our chronological canvas, and later perspectives supersede earlier.

The past was once of special import to those privileged by antiquity and precedence. Ancient lineage and hallowed tradition conferred power, property, and prestige. But today's professedly egalitarian societies no longer license past-based privilege, save for indigenous 'first' peoples. The rise of the proletariat and the waning of social hierarchy extinguish prerogatives of lineage. 'Ancestors are to be counted as a valuable asset', exclaims a pioneering Western heroine, 'but not as working capital'.[6] The past as a fount of profit and power, like the pedagogic past, is becoming *passé*.

Yet loss of the past's exemplary guidance and patronage of privilege has not diminished attachments to it. Many seem more than ever devoted to *some* past, of individual or family, community or creed, village or nation. Past-based passions embrace every aspect of existence: natural objects and living beings, artefacts and archives, folkways and philosophies. And they spur campaigns to salvage rare or representative specimens of past forms and features against accelerating decay and disappearance.

Reactions to the past are innately contrarian. Avowals of admiration or disdain conceal their opposites; reverence for tradition incites iconoclasm; nostalgic retrieval foments modernist clean sweeps. Revolutionaries exorcise recent evils with primordial exemplars and end by reviving what they first rejected. Once avid to extirpate *anciens régimes*, Russians and Chinese later waxed wistful for pre-Revolutionary customs and artefacts – succeeded in turn by Stalinist and Maoist nostalgia.[7] Diktats for and against the past reflect vested interests; antiquity bolsters some claims, innovation others. Renaissance chroniclers denigrated the recent past to exalt present patrons, whereas antiquarians magnified past feats to present detriment. While museum curators safeguard outmoded relics, sanitary engineers discard antiquated fittings.

With these caveats, I turn first to the past's felt merits.

---

[6] Harold Bell Wright, *The Winning of Barbara Worth* (Chicago, 1911), 131.
[7] Andrew E. Kramer, 'Back in the ('30s) U.S.S.R.', *NYT*, 30 May 2013: D1, 6–7, Nikolay Koposov, '"The armored train of memory": the politics of history in post-Soviet Russia', *AHA Perspectives on History*, Jan. 2011: 236; Ban Wang, *Illuminations from the Past: Trauma, Memory, and History in Modern China* (Stanford, 2004), 212–13; Daniel Leese, *Mao Cult* (Cambridge, 2011).

Benefits

The past for Poets; the Present for Pigs.   Samuel Palmer, 1862[8]

It is a universal article of faith that the past was golden. Men were more manly, women were faithful, ministers were godly, society was harmonious, whereas in the present day ... the wrong people have all the luck and nobody has good manners.
                                                                                        Hilary Mantel, 2009[9]

Growing up here, you can't help being obsessed with the past. Nothing ever dies in this town. It's like a bottle of wine, it just gets older and better.
                                    Jamie Westendorff, Charleston, South Carolina, c. 1997[10]

The time I would really beg for ... would be *time in the past*, time in which to comfort, to complete and to repair – time wasted before I knew how quickly it would slip by.   Iris Origo, 1970[11]

The past's desiderata far exceed nostalgia. 'The most Polite part of Mankind', wrote architect–playwright John Vanbrugh three centuries ago, agree 'in the Value they have ever set upon the Remains of distant times'.[12] Today the plebs share the penchant of the polite. A taste so widespread may be a necessity. But why is the past necessary? And what qualities make it so?

Reasons advanced for admiring the past are usually imprecise; its desirability is simply taken for granted. The 'charm of the past is that it is the past', says Oscar Wilde's Henry Wotton.[13] Victorians prized the past less for specific traits than for general ambience. Today we are likewise all-embracing: almost anything old, olde, or old-fashioned may be desirable. 'I love anything old, it's so proper', says a barrister of his clothes. Many who wear vintage, asserts a vendor, 'want to look back to another era altogether'.[14] So eclectic a past includes whatever is wanted. The newest things soon seem 'immemorial', like Andrew Meikle's threshing machine (1784) within a few years of its appearance in England. 'Remember', says a stroller on a street lined with fitness studios, 'when all this was yoga centers?'[15]

Equally ineffable is the medley of beloved national pasts. British heritage embodies 'certain sights and sounds ... a morning mist on the Tweed at Dryburgh where the magic of Turner and the romance of Scott both come fleetingly to life ... a celebration of the

[8] To Laura Richmond (1862), in A. H. Palmer, *Life and Letters of Samuel Palmer, Painter & Etcher* (London, 1892), 249.
[9] Hilary Mantel, 'Dreams and duels of England', *NYRB*, 22 Oct. 2009: 8–12 at 12.
[10] Quoted in Tony Horwitz, *Confederates in the Attic* (Pantheon, 1998), 61.
[11] Iris Origo, *Images and Shadows* (Boston: Godine, 1999), 258.
[12] To the Duchess of Marlborough, 11 June 1709, in John Vanbrugh, *CW* (London: Nonesuch, 1925–8), 4: 29.
[13] Oscar Wilde, *The Picture of Dorian Gray* (1891; London: Dent, 1930), 153.
[14] John Hilton quoted in Sally Brampton, 'Their strongest suits', *Observer Magazine*, 18 Apr. 1982; Graham Cassie quoted in Tom Bottomley, 'Old, obscure objects of desire', *Times2*: 25 Oct. 2004.
[15] Richard Jefferies, *The Life of the Fields* (1884; London, 1948), 151; David Sipress, cartoon, *New Yorker* 14/21 Feb. 2011: 38.

Eucharist in a quiet Norfolk church with the medieval glass filtering colours'. And in a prime minister's pastoral idyll, 'long shadows on county [cricket] grounds, warm beer . . . and, as George Orwell said, "old maids cycling to holy communion through the morning mist", and Shakespeare'.[16] The authors of England's 1983 National Heritage Act 'could no more define [it] than we could define, say, beauty or art . . . So we decided to let the national heritage define itself'. It was not just the Tower of London but agricultural vestiges visible only in air photos, 'not only the duke's castle and possessions but . . . the duke himself'.[17] Ensuing decades make it still more miscellaneous. After the first dozen icons of Englishness – Stonehenge, the King James Bible, the Spitfire, the anthem 'Jerusalem', Hans Holbein's *Henry VIII*, Punch and Judy, Antony Gormley's *Angel of the North*, the Routemaster bus, SS *Empire Windrush*, a cup of tea, the FA Cup, *Alice in Wonderland* – others enthroned by a 2006 online survey included Morris dancing, pubs, Big Ben, cricket, the St George flag, HMS *Victory*, the Domesday Book, Hadrian's Wall, Blackpool Tower, *Pride and Prejudice*, *The Origin of Species*, the Globe Theatre, and Constable's *Hay Wain*. Respondents in 2008 added fish and chips, *Dr Who*, the Glastonbury Festival, black cabs, Land Rovers, chicken tikka masala, and queuing.[18]

Americans are little less besotted by their indiscriminate collective legacy. *American Heritage* magazine celebrates 4,000 places and 140,000 artefacts, from flags and muskets to naval paintings, swords, quilts, uniforms, and spittoons. A typical issue featured the Civil Rights movement, Mark Twain's board games, Abraham Lincoln, the 1876 Battle of Little Big Horn, the Pony Express, Benjamin Franklin, Satchel Paige, the Second World War, the Mexican War, and historical sites in Colorado; the sixtieth anniversary issue added Lincoln, Martin Luther King, and FDR to Emanuel Leutze's iconic 1851 painting *Washington Crossing the Delaware*.[19]

Treasured pasts transcend national legacies. Childhood memories, chats with grandma, seaside souvenirs, family photographs, family trees, old trees, old money are prized everywhere. The World Soundscape Project has recorded a vanishing sonic legacy that includes the ring of cash registers, washboard scrubbing, butter-churning, razor stropping, a hissing kerosene lamp, the squeak of leather saddlebags, hand coffee-grinders, milk cans rattling on horse-drawn vehicles, heavy doors clanked shut and bolted, school hand bells, rocking-chairs on wooden floors.[20]

What endears depends on who and where one is. Some live in patently ancient countries, others in lands with newer lineaments. The latter seek out the former:

[16] Patrick Cormack, *Heritage in Danger* (Quartet, 1978), 14; John Major, speech, 22 Apr. 1993, misquoting George Orwell, *The Lion and the Unicorn* (1941), in *The Collected Essays, Journalism and Letters*, 4 vols. (Secker & Warburg, 1968), 2: 56–109.

[17] Lord Charteris of Amisfield, 'The work of the National Heritage Memorial Fund', *Journal of the Royal Society of Arts* 132 (1984): 325–38 at 327; J. P. Carswell, 'Lost for words on "the heritage"', *Times*, 8 Sept. 1983: 11.

[18] 'New icons of Englishness unveiled', BBC News, 27 Apr. 2006; Robert Henderson, 'English icons – an exercise in Anglophobic NuLabour propaganda', *englandcalling.wordpress.com.*, 21 Nov. 2010; Georgi Gyton, 'Icons – a portrait of England reveals the next instalment', 1 Apr. 2008, *culture24.org.uk/history*.

[19] *American Heritage* 60:1 (Spring 2010): cover; 59:4 (Winter 2010).

[20] R. Murray Schafer, *The Soundscape: Our Sonic Environment and the Tuning of the World* (Rochester, VT: Inner Traditions, 1993), 209.

Americans come to Europe to feel at home in time. Or they dwell on other aspects of heritage, antiques or arrowheads or ancestral locales. 'Where newness and brevity of tenure are the common substance of life', Henry James wrote of nineteenth-century New England, 'the fact of one's ancestors having lived for a hundred and seventy years in a single spot ... become[s] an element of one's morality'.[21]

Massive migration and the loss of tangible relics intensify appetites for ancestors. 'The more the ancient landmarks are destroyed, the more many of us hunger for a firm anchorage in time and place', held England's Herald of Arms half a century ago. 'Through genealogy the transient flat-dweller of the cities can join himself to the peasant rooted in ancestral soil', for his lineage stems from that older world. 'Cut off from his roots by profound changes in ways of living, by migration from home and by loss of contact with his kindred, modern man seeks ... to reconstruct human links.'[22]

The rising appeal of roots is phenomenal. 'In the early 1960s there would be a *handful* of people looking through the census returns at the Public Record Office', recalled the then Rouge Dragon Pursuivant. 'Now they've got a special search room with 100 microfilm readers, and in the summer there's a big queue.' Today the queue is much longer. Most want to know more about their ancestors; family-tree websites promise access to billions of records.[23] *Who Do You Think You Are, You Don't Know You're Born, Faces of America,* and *Ancestors in the Attic* are among TV's most popular series. The English National Trust's 4.2 million members evince 'unprecedented appetite for [the] cultural and natural heritage; ... all looking for our enduring roots'. Genetic tracing potentially back to 'Mitochondrial Eve' and 'Y-Chromosomal Adam' makes personal archaeology the world's fastest-growing hobby, myriad DNA kits at the ready.[24]

'Not long ago genealogy was a hobby for aristocrats, maiden aunts, and eccentrics', noted a 1988 survey, and 'most Europeans would have stared blankly if asked to give their great-grandmother's name'. With humble origins newly chic, all forebears become ancestral worthies.[25] 'When I was a boy at Harrow School in the 1920s', the architectural historian Sir John Summerson told me sixty years later, 'I did all I could to prevent *any*one finding out my grandfather was a common labourer. Today I'd make sure *every*one knew.' No longer content with 'simple, honest, law-abiding' forebears, many roots-seekers now relish ancestral rogues.[26] Jonathan Raban relates his Anglican vicar father's switch from genteel to rougher roots. His 1950s 'antique truffle hunt [for] an unbroken arc of ... Anglo-Saxons in mead halls' down through army officers and minor gentry gave way in the 1980s to digging up 'our criminal past'. Ancestors 'engaged in

[21] Henry James, *Hawthorne* (Macmillan, 1879), 14.

[22] Anthony Richard Wagner, *English Genealogy* (1960), 3, and *English Ancestry* (Oxford, 1961), 6.

[23] Patric Dickinson quoted in Martyn Harris, 'Mark the heralds', *New Society*, 9 Feb. 1984: 198.

[24] Fiona Reynolds, *National Trust Annual Review 2002/2004*: 1; Chris Johnston, 'Forget dark, silent archives and an academic elite – this is a global internet phenomenon', *Times*, 26 July 2010: 37; Jennifer Alsever, 'DNA kits aim to link you to the here and then', *NYT*, 5 Feb. 2006: BusinessSec5; Jerome de Groot, *Consuming History: Historians and Heritage in Contemporary Popular Culture* (Routledge, 2009), 73–87.

[25] 'Europe's genealogy craze', *Newsweek*, 7 Mar. 1988, 58–9. See André Burguière, 'La généalogie', in Pierre Nora, comp., *Les Lieux de mémoire* (Paris: Gallimard, 1984–92), III.3: 18–51 at 20.

[26] Carol Shields, *The Stone Diaries* (Random House of Canada, 1993), 166.

smuggling, privateering and the slave trade', showed that 'rapine, plunder, fiddling the books and dealing under the counter ran in our blood'. Convict forebears who once disgraced Australian descendants now lend them racy chic.[27]

Access to ancestors fosters visceral connection with previously unknown or shadowy pasts, although often, as with Sebastian Coe's discovery of slavery and illegitimacy, an emotional rollercoaster. Scores of Internet firms – '23andMe', 'Mygenome', 'Mycellf' – promote identity quests. These purely mitochondrial and y-chromosomal ancestries are misleadingly fragmentary, however, for they identify only two of a thousand forebears ten generations back.[28] But those bereft of ancestry – 'branches without roots', like many descendants of slaves – feel that 'even knowing some tiny part of your history is better than knowing zero'.[29] Biology certifies desirable identities. Awareness of genetic relationship 'not only tells us who we really are', claims a genealogical determinist, but 'requires that one actively embrace' that knowledge, 'transforming ancestry into identity'.[30]

Eagerly adopted, these biologically certified identities are variously desirable. 'I'm born of Songhai – queen, artist, warrior and wise', exults an African American. 'I've never felt more Irish', crows an Irish-American testee; 'my next tattoo is going to incorporate the Red Hand of Ulster in honor of my O'Neill kin'. Others glory in descent from famed ancestors, 'ascrib[ing] greatness to themselves because it's inscribed in their genes'.[31] Many fondly boast royal antecedents, unaware that practically everyone is 'descended from one royal personage or another'. The African-American producer of 'Faces in America' is chuffed to find that 'we are all mulattos'.[32] Going way way back, suggested an astronomer, we might 'get in touch with our cosmic roots'. Since most atoms in our bodies stem from ancient supernovae, 'we are, in a very real sense, children of the stars'.[33]

Many lovers of the past focus on its physical or spiritual retention, seeking enclaves for anachronistic remnants and traditions. Lacking roots of their own, newcomers to old villages spearhead militant defence of ancient landmarks against bulldozers usually manned by unsentimental old-timers. Others adopt yesteryear's forms and styles in

[27] Jonathan Raban, *Coasting* (CollinsHarvill, 1986), 152, 172; Graeme Davison, *The Use and Abuse of Australian History* (Allen & Unwin, 2000), 80-109; Christopher Koch, 'Archival days', in Gillian Winter, ed., *Tasmanian Insights* (Hobart: State Library of Tasmania, 1992), 227–31; Tom Griffiths, *Hunters and Collectors* (Cambridge, 1996), 223–5.
[28] Sebastian Coe, 'There's no running away from your past', *Times2*, 24 Aug. 2011: 11; Anders Nordgren and Eric T. Juengst, 'Can genomics tell me who I am?' *New Genetics & Society* 28 (2009): 157–72 at 162.
[29] Zora Neale Thurston, *Their Eyes Were Watching God* (1937; HarperCollins 1991), 21; Gina Paige quoted in Jennifer Marshall, 'Genes, money and the American quest for identity', *New Scientist*, 11 Mar. 2006: 10–11.
[30] El-Haj, *Genealogical Science*, 114.
[31] Kimberly Elise, *Africanancestry.com/testimonials*; Larry Slavens quoted in Amy Harmon, 'Love you, K2a2a, whoever you are', *NYT*, 22 Jan. 2006; Amy Harmon, 'Greatness in your genes?', *NYT*, 11 June 2006. See Henry T. Greely, 'Genetic genealogy', in Barbara A. Koenig et al., eds., *Revisiting Race in a Genomic Age* (Rutgers, 2008), 215–34 at 225; Eviatar Zerubavel, *Ancestors and Relatives: Genealogy, Identity, and Community* (Oxford, 2012), 6, 71.
[32] Matt Crenson, 'Genealogists discover royal roots for all', *Washington Post*, 1 July 2006. See Richard Tutton, 'They want to know where they came from', *New Genetics & Society* 23:1 (2004): 105–29.
[33] Frank Winkler, 'Stardust memories', *NYT*, 5 May 2006. See Daniel R. Altschuler, *Children of the Stars* (Cambridge, 2002).

revival architecture and reproduction furniture, or connect with remoter antiquity at archaeological digs. Colonial American sites attract a hundred million visitors a year, drawn by nostalgia for organic community, artisanal relics and recipes, and intimacy with nature and neighbours.[34]

Below I group past fulfilments under the terms familiarity; guidance; communion; affirmation; identity; possession; enhancement; and escape. No boundaries delimit these desiderata, and their benefits often dovetail. A sense of identity also enriches; familiarity provides guidance. Revival-style building simultaneously justifies the present and suggests a refuge from it. Tradition sanctified such 1970s innovations as pedestrian shopping enclaves, high-rise condos, 'heritage' villages, gated communities (said to derive from Puritan settlements), Southern plantations, Western missions, pioneer encampments. Yet, like Disney's Celebration and the Prince of Wales's Poundbury, retro heritage also panders to dreams of escape from the soulless stress of modern milieus.

Familiarity

Attachment to the past is inescapable. Dependence on recognition is universal. Concern with what has been is built into our bones and embedded in our genes. Sheer survival calls for facility of habit and faculty of memory; without them we could neither learn nor long endure. Habit lets us repeat actions without conscious effort; memory recalls known features, negotiates familiar routes, and harks back to familiar experience. Recall and repetition dominate daily life.

The past renders the present recognizable. Its traces on the ground and in our minds let us make sense of current scenes. Without past experience, no sight or sound would mean anything; we perceive only what we are accustomed to. Features and patterns become such because we share their history. Every object, every grouping, every view is made intelligible by previous encounters, tales heard, texts read, pictures seen. Habituation unveils what lies around us. 'If you saw a slab of chocolate for the first time, you might think it was for mending shoes, lighting the fire, or building houses.'[35] Perceived identity stems from past acts and involvements. In Hannah Arendt's words, 'the reality and reliability of the human world rest primarily on the fact that we are surrounded by things more permanent than the activity by which they were produced'.[36]

Things that lack familiar elements or configurations remain incomprehensible. On C. S. Lewis's fictional planet a newcomer at first perceives 'nothing but colours – colours that refused to form themselves into things', because 'he knew nothing yet well enough to see it'.[37] No terrestrial scene, however, is totally novel except to a newborn infant: a life-long urbanite dropped into a tropical jungle would still find day predictably alternating with night, rain with sunshine; would recognize trees, sky, earth, and water, and respond

---

[34] James C. Makens, 'The importance of U.S. historic sites as visitor attractions', *Journal of Travel Research* 25 (Winter 1987): 8–12; Catherine M Cameron and John B. Gatewood, 'Excursions into the un-remembered past: what people want from visits to historic sites', *Public Historian* 22:3 (2000): 107–27.

[35] John Wyndham, 'Pillar to post' (1971), in *The Seeds of Time* (Penguin, 1975), 140–69 at 148.

[36] Hannah Arendt, *The Human Condition* (Chicago, 1958; 2nd edn 1998), 95–6.

[37] C. S. Lewis, *Out of the Silent Planet* (1938; Scribner, 2003), 43.

to up and down, back and forth much as on city streets. Every earthly locale connects at least marginally with everybody's experienced past.

Not only is the past recalled in what we see; it is incarnate in what we create. Familiarity endears surroundings; hence we keep memorabilia and favour new things whose decor evokes the old. Electric fireplaces simulate Victorian coal or Tudor burning-log effects; plastic cabinets and vinyl-tile floors come with a wood-grain look; leaded lights painted on windows feign ancient cosiness; electric fixtures recall candles. Such embrace of the past is often subconscious. Designers intend the anachronism of concrete hearth logs or candle-drip light bulbs, non-functional spokes on car wheels, analogue features on digital devices, book-like Kindles – 'you just make it look like what was there before' – but for customers these skeuomorphs (material metaphors) seldom evoke memories of the prototypes that lend them familiar charm.[38] Obsolete artefacts live on unobserved in parlance: newsmen make up pages 'on the stone' though that technology is long defunct; horsepower applied to steam engines continues in cars; we still 'dial' numbers on cell phones; tarmac-flattening machines are 'steamrollers', graphite sticks 'lead pencils', computer printouts 'manuscripts'. Few users are aware of computer 'worms' and 'viruses' biological antecedents.

Surrogate and second-hand experiences further infuse present perception: we conceive of things not only as currently seen but as heard and read about before. My image of London is a composite of personal exploration, recent media, and historical vignettes from Hogarth and Turner, Pepys and Dickens. Despite the initial novelty of the English scene, the American Charles Eliot Norton felt on arrival that an 'old world look' gave 'those old world things ... a deeper familiarity than the very things that have lain before our eyes since we were born'.[39] Past imprints that suffuse a place occlude first-hand impressions. Constable's Suffolk has become 'the countryside' for us all, even if we have a quite different landscape outside our windows', notes an art historian. 'We have grown up ... with jigsaws and illustrated biscuit tins showing that little boy on a pony beside the river with the mill in the distance ... England was like that, [and] we convince ourselves that his country is ... still surviving today'.[40] Hardy's Wessex, Wordsworth's Lake District, Samuel Palmer's North Downs, 'ghost features kept in existence by nostalgia', take over the actual landscapes, imposing 'a vanished past over a palpable present'. Monet so 'shaped our notion of the Ile de France' as to remain its 'complete, definitive and everlasting' rendition.[41]

Not just habituation leaves such impressions enduring. Hindsight makes better sense of past scenes than the incoherent present; yesterday's comprehensible perceptions outlast today's kaleidoscopic images. But the past we depend on to fathom the present is mostly recent; it relies mainly on our own few earthly years. The farther back in time,

---

[38] Bill Moggridge quoted in Joshua Brustein, 'Why innovation doffs an old hat', *NYT*, 18 Feb. 2011: WeekRev.2. See Bill Moggridge, *Designing Interactions* (MIT Press, 2006); Nicholas Gessler, 'Skeuomorphs and cultural algorithms', in V. W. Porto et al., eds., *Evolutionary Programming* (Springer, 1998), 229–38.

[39] To James Russell Lowell, 30 Aug. 1868, in *Letters of Charles Eliot Norton* (London, 1913), 1: 306.

[40] Nicholas Penny, 'Constable: an English heritage abroad', *Sunday Times*, 11 Nov. 1984: 43.

[41] Hugh Prince, 'Reality stranger than fiction', *Bloomsbury Geographer* 6 (1973): 2–22 at 16; John Russell, 'In the mythical Ile de France', *IHT*, 15 July 1983: 9.

the fewer the surviving traces, the more they have altered, and the less they anchor contemporary reality.

Familiarity thrives on continuity in our selves and surroundings. Habit and memory are effective and efficient only if things around us are stable enough to recognize and act on with expectable results. Rare cataclysms aside, most aspects of the natural scene – skies, seas, terrain, plants, animals – commonly endure little altered, changing slowly enough to remain indubitably themselves. Thus, the 'ancient permanence' of his Dorset Egdon Heath as 'it always had been' comforted Thomas Hardy:

> Ever since the beginning of vegetation its soil had worn the same antique brown dress [varied only by] an aged highway, and a still more aged barrow ... themselves almost crystallized to natural products by long continuance ... To know that everything around and underneath had been from prehistoric times as unaltered as the stars overhead, gave ballast to the mind adrift on change, and harassed by the irrepressible New.[42]

Even urban routes and facades generally persist in identifiable form. Nowadays, however, novelty in things built and made comes on apace. And longevity and emigration leave ever fewer in the locales, let alone the houses, of birth or youth. With so much perforce left behind, what surrounds us in later life is seldom what we grew up with. But biology ill equips us to cope with continually unfamiliar scenes. Stranded by swift and massive displacement and seeking anchorage in some familiar sanctuary, we cling to whatever survives from or reminds us of the past. We indulge habit and memory not simply out of nostalgic yearning, but from a vital need for security in perilously novel milieus.

In short, attachment to the past is both innate and essential. Amnesiacs unable to recognize or retrieve memories, residents of realms transformed beyond recognition, and refugees ejected from life-long locales are grievously bereft of cherished linkages – cherished because familiar, and familiar because cherished. And those dispossessed seek out substitute pasts.

Guidance

Faith that past instructs present dates to the dawn of history and animates much of it. For Greeks history was useful because the rhythm of its changes promised ongoing repetition. Study of the past might foretell, though not forestall, the future. Past example showed sufferers how to bear cruel fate.[43]

The timeless truths of medieval and Renaissance historians taught morals, manners, prudence, patriotism, statecraft, virtue, piety. Classical sources illumined present concerns. A Carolingian historian summarized the Roman emperors' deeds so that Charles II

---

[42] Thomas Hardy, *The Return of the Native* (1878; London, 1912), 6–7.

[43] R. G. Collingwood, *The Idea of History* (Oxford, 1946), 24, 35–6; Charles William Fornara, *The Nature of History in Ancient Greece and Rome* (California, 1983), 106–15; John Marincola, *Greek Historians* (Oxford, 2001).

of France might 'readily observe from their actions what you should imitate or what you should avoid'.[44] Knowing the classical past enhanced humanist confidence in the relevance of its lessons. In early-modern England 'knowledge of history helped one to rise in the world, and knowledge of God's providence in history solaced adversity'.[45] Such guidance was morally elevating. Like pilgrimages to sacred sites, the study of history improved character and inspired fealty.

The past's exemplary power and purpose remained an Enlightenment certitude:

The usefulness of history ... is a truth too generally receiv'd to stand in need of proof ... The theatre of the world supplies only a limited number of scenes, which follow one another in perpetual succession. In seeing the same mistakes to be regularly follow'd by the same misfortunes, 'tis reasonable to imagine, that if the former had been known, the latter would have been avoided.[46]

Knowing the follies of the past, one might predict and perhaps avert those to come. Scholars who found history exemplary likened all past and present. 'Mankind are so much the same, in all times and places, that history informs us of nothing new or strange', stated David Hume. 'Its chief use is only to discover the constant and universal principles of human nature.'[47]

This authoritative aim suffused Western thought well into the nineteenth century. But the kind of guidance the past provided was now quite different. Earlier scholars had assumed that classical models exemplified eternal virtues: they saw antiquity's honour, patriotism, stoicism, and tribulations mirrored in their own times. But even in the seventeenth century, some were showing pasts unlike one another, undermining history's utility as guide; viewing the past historically scuttled its timeless truths.[48] Growing distance from antiquity and awareness of its diversity severely tempered its authority. For Victorians history ceased to provide explicit precedents or moral exemplars. Instead, parallels with past circumstances alternated with past–present contrasts as instructive lessons. History was about change as well as stasis.

Despite postmodern scepticism, the past is still invoked as cautionary lesson, on the hoary maxim that those who forget history are doomed to repeat it.[49] Popular history continues to deploy past wisdom for present perplexities. The advice of legendary heroes is eagerly solicited; pundits ever asked what Lincoln or Washington or Henry Ford would do today. 'How to be boss – learn from a past master' extols management maxims of Moses, Elizabeth I, Attila the Hun, and Machiavelli. Jesus is consulted on everything from

[44] Lupus of Ferrières to Charles the Bold (844), quoted in Rosamond McKitterick, *History and Memory in the Carolingian World* (Cambridge, 2004), 275–6.
[45] F. Smith Fussner, *The Historical Revolution: English Historical Writing and Thought 1580–1640* (Routledge, 1962), 59. See Myron P. Gilmore, *Humanists and Jurists* (Harvard, 1963), 37; Paulina Kewes, 'History and its uses', 1–30, and Daniel Woolf, 'From hystories to the historical', 31–68, both in Paulina Kewes, ed., *The Uses of History in Early Modern England* (California, 2006).
[46] Charles Duclos, *History of Louis XI* (Paris, 1745), 1: ii. I pruned Duclos's translation.
[47] David Hume, *An Enquiry Concerning Human Understanding* (1748), in *The Philosophical Works* (repr. edn 1886; Aalen: Scientia, 1964), 4: 3–135 at 68.
[48] Anthony T. Grafton, *What Was History? The Art of History in Early Modern Europe* (Cambridge, 2007).
[49] George Santayana, *The Life of Reason or the Phases of Human Progress* (London, 1905), 1: 284.

the rectitude of invading Iraq to Sarah Palin's presidential candidacy.[50] Popular films depicted modern Chinese going back to gain insights from historical figures, until in 2011 the government, vexed that this implied a superior past, banned time travel for fomenting fatalism, feudalism, and reincarnation.[51]

Even a postmodernist contends that history provides 'moral lessons'. Not the old lessons, however. 'The past really is sometimes, past', warns an anthropologist; 'after a while it runs out of lessons to teach us'. Yet to 'effectively inhabit' the present one must 'learn how the past made it what it is', holds a littérateur.[52] If no longer a model, it remains a guide; if it cannot tell us what we should do, it tells us what we might do; ominous or auspicious, it prefigures the present.

Communion

Empathy with precursors reanimates exemplary pasts. Archetypal is communion of the living with the dead in the eucharistic consumption of Christ's body and blood. Communion expressed in re-enactment is popular in secular like sacred ceremony, as detailed in Chapter 11.

Anachronistic rapport used to be literally evoked: 'Alexander walked in the footsteps of Miltiades', and Caesar 'took Alexander as his prototype'.[53] Renaissance and Enlightenment worthies engaged in intimate converse with classical poets and philosophers. Petrarch felt himself among Roman authors as he read them: 'It is with these men that I live at such times and not with the thievish company of today', he 'told' Livy.[54] Exiled Machiavelli relished the past's immediacy. He spent evenings in 'the ancient courts of ancient men, where, being lovingly received I . . . speak with them . . . and they courteously answer me. For hours . . . I give myself completely over to the ancients.'[55] A later Vatican curator talked to his classical statues 'as if they were living', reported John Evelyn, 'kissing & embracing them'.[56]

This love was at best symbolically requited. Intimate converse with ancient Romans was incompatible with their historical distance, of which the ancients' failure to respond kept humanists poignantly aware. Their felt empathy with great classical authors was not reciprocated. The beloved ancients 'maintained a marble or a bronze repose that could break hearts', in Thomas Greene's phrase. 'The pathos of this incomplete embrace' left humanist adoration unrequited.[57]

Eighteenth-century *philosophes* wrapped themselves in the togas of Cicero and Lucretius to re-enact ancient converse. 'Continuously preoccupied with Rome and Athens', wrote Rousseau while reading Plutarch, 'living . . . with their great men, . . . I pictured

[50] Stanley Bing, *What Would Machiavelli Do?* (HarperCollins, 2002); Adam Cohen, 'Consulting Jesus on tax policies', *IHT*, 11 June 2003: 9.
[51] Ian Johnson, 'Studio city', New Yorker, 22 Apr. 2013: 48–55 at 53.
[52] Alan Munslow, *The New History* (Longman, 2003), 177; Clifford Geertz, 'Morality tale', *NYRB*, 7 Oct. 2004: 4–6; Edward Mendelson, 'Post-modern vanguard', *London Review of Books*, 3 Sept. 1981: 10.
[53] Thomas Mann, 'Freud and the future' (1936), in *Essays of Three Decades* (Knopf, 1947), 411–28 at 424.
[54] 22 Feb. 1349 (?) in *Petrarch's Letters to Classical Authors*, 101–2.
[55] To Francesco Vettori, 10 Dec. 1513, quoted in Zachary Sayre Schiffman, *The Birth of the Past* (Johns Hopkins, 2011), 8–9.
[56] *Diary of John Evelyn*, 27 Feb. 1644 (1818; Oxford, 1959), 150, referring to Hippolito Vitellesco.
[57] Thomas M. Greene, *The Light in Troy: Imitation and Discovery in Renaissance Poetry* (Yale, 1982), 43.

myself as a Greek or a Roman.'[58] The philosopher Baron d'Holbach was days on end enthralled by 'the ever-charming conversation of Horace, Virgil, Homer and all our noble friends of the Elysian fields'.[59] Ancient heroes permeated Enlightenment consciousness. 'He has all the eloquence of Cicero, the benevolence of Pliny, and the wisdom of Agrippa', wrote Frederick the Great in 1740 after meeting Voltaire, who retorted that Frederick 'talked in as friendly a manner to me as Scipio to Terence'.[60] Napoleon identified first with Alexander, then with Charlemagne – not that he was *like* Charlemagne or that '"My situation is like Charlemagne's"', but quite simply: '"I am he."'[61]

In Anne-Louis Girodet's 1801 canvas, ghosts of Ossian's characters welcome Napoleon and other French heroes in an Elysium, spirits of dead 'in inspirational and amicable cohabitation with the living'.[62] At Victor Hugo's 1850s seances, his guest-list

included Cain, Jacob, Moses, Isaiah, Sappho, Socrates, Jesus, Judas, Mohammed, Joan of Arc, Luther, Galileo, Molière, the Marquis de Sade, ... Mozart, Walter Scott, some angels, Androcles' Lion, Balaam's Ass ... The language was mid-nineteenth-century French, though ... Hannibal spoke in Latin, and Androcles' Lion ... a few words of lion language.

Hugo was pleased to find that all the great minds of the past spoke more or less like himself.[63]

Fantasized communion lingered into modernity. Bartold Georg Niebuhr meant his history of Rome to shed such a light that the Romans would stand before his readers' eyes, 'distinct, intelligible, familiar as contemporaries, with their institutions and the vicissitudes of their destiny, living and moving'.[64] Colloquies among classical heroes animate Walter Savage Landor's *Imaginary Conversations* (1824–36): 'To-day there came to visit us ... Thucydides ... Sophocles left me about an hour ago ... Euripedes was with us at the time.' His 'conversations' involved figures who could never have met, conflating centuries in the fashion Gibbon had mocked.[65] 'How much instruction has been conveyed to us in the form of conversations at banquets, by Plato and Xenophon and Plutarch', exclaims Thomas Love Peacock's Dr Opimiam.[66] Fancying himself an ancient, many a Victorian had an insistent 'urge to buttonhole one of those old Greeks and Romans and tell him what the future had in store'.[67] But retrospective prophecy did not spare them humanist pathos; as Hazlitt wistfully put it, 'We are always talking of the Greeks and Romans; – *they* never said any thing of us.'[68]

[58] Jean-Jacques Rousseau, *Confessions* (1781; Penguin, 1973), 20.
[59] To John Wilkes, 3 Dec. 1746, in Max Pearson Cushing, *Baron d'Holbach* (New York, 1914), 9–10.
[60] Wayne Andrews, *Voltaire* (New York: New Directions, 1981), 42, 47.
[61] Mann, 'Freud and the future', 424.
[62] Girodet painting, *L'Apothéose des héros français mort pour la Patrie pendant la guerre de la Liberté* (1802); Simon During, 'Mimic toil', *Rethinking History* 11 (2007): 318.
[63] Graham Robb, *Victor Hugo: A Biography* (Norton, 1999), 334; Robert Douglas-Fairhurst, *Victorian Afterlives: The Shaping of Influence in Nineteenth-Century Literature* (Oxford, 2002), 246–7.
[64] Bartold Georg Niebuhr, *The History of Rome* (1811–12; Cambridge, 1831), 1: 5.
[65] Walter Savage Landor, *Pericles and Aspasia* (1836; London, 1890), letters 141, 145, 154, 2: 28, 36, 53; Edward Gibbon, *Index Expurgatorius* (c. 1768–9), No. 30, in *The Miscellaneous Works* (London, 1814), 5: 566.
[66] Thomas Love Peacock, *Gryll Grange* (London, 1861), 168.
[67] Richard Jenkyns, *The Victorians and Ancient Greece* (Blackwell, 1980), 52.
[68] William Hazlitt, 'Schlegel on the drama' (1816), in *CW* (Dent, 1930–4), 16: 57–99 at 66.

Communing with great figures from the past remains a popular lure. PBS's *Meeting of Minds* (1977–81) welcomed the 'historically illiterate' to hear the bygone famed – Plato, Socrates, Aristotle, Cleopatra, Aquinas, Luther, Bacon, Shakespeare (and some of his characters), Voltaire, Marie Antoinette, Tom Paine, Jefferson, Karl Marx, Florence Nightingale – talk with producer Steve Allen 'in their own words' (mostly). 'Newton, Cromwell, Byron, Milton, Tennyson, Pepys, Darwin: You ought to try living with them some time', tempts American students to come to Cambridge. 'Sit under the same apple tree that gave Sir Isaac Newton a headache – and the world the theory of gravitation. Stroll through the courts, quads, and pathways that inspired Milton, Pepys and Tennyson.'[69] Hearing late twentieth-century Virginians talking as though Thomas Jefferson 'might, at any moment, train his telescope on them from Monticello', a British historian realized that, for Americans, long-dead precursors were their heirs' and successors' still living property.[70]

A few moderns still claim actual contact with precursors. Wilmarth Lewis, who spent most of his life immortalizing Horace Walpole, at times felt literally in touch with him.[71] But such empathy is much rarer nowadays. Few are steeped enough in the classics to claim Horace or Livy or Homer as intimates. And historical relativism distances even the most admired exemplars. Only reincarnates and unschooled naives now achieve whole-hearted communion with folk from any past.

Affirmation

More than rapport, the present seeks reaffirmation. The past endorses present views and acts, showing their descent from or likeness to former ones. Previous usage sanctions today's. Precedent legitimates current practice as traditional: 'This is how it's always been done.' What has been should continue to be or become again.

Validation often dates from time immemorial. Traditionalists presume that things are or should be the way they always have been. Oral transmission readjusts the past to fit its idealized fixity. Literate peoples less easily sustain that fiction, for written records reveal pasts *unlike* the present; archives expose traditions eroded by time and corrupted by novelty, anything but faithfully adhered to. Yet societies nonetheless invoke supposedly timeless values and unbroken lineages. French rulers recurrently identify with the Gallic hero Vercingetorix, Napoleon to stress continuity with ancient Rome, Pétain to legitimize the Vichy regime, Mitterrand to proclaim French parentage of the European Union. Glorying in, yet greater than, previous Caesars, Mussolini favoured a celestial trinity: 'Homer, the divine in Art, Jesus, the divine in Life, and Mussolini, the divine in Action'.[72] Whig historians claimed Victorian Britain as the heir of legal and political forms essentially faithful to medieval origins. Fundamentalist Christians cite biblical authority

---

[69] University of California, Los Angeles, advertisement, *NYRB*, 22 Jan. 1981, 20.

[70] J. R. Pole, 'The American past: is it still usable?' *Journal of American Studies* 1 (1967): 63–78 at 63.

[71] Geoffrey Hellman, 'The age of Wilmarth Lewis', *New Yorker*, 15 Sept. 1975, 104–11.

[72] Michael Dietler, 'Tale of three sites', *World Archaeology* 30 (1998): 85, and 'Our ancestors the Gauls', *American Anthropologist* 96 (1994): 584–605; Asvero Gravelli, *Uno e molti: interpretazione spirituali di Mussolini* (1938), quoted in R. J. B. Bosworth, *Whispering City: Rome and Its Histories* (Yale, 2011), 195.

for perdurable creeds and values. Modern Greeks look back to Hellenic precursors for grandeur not only Greek but globally classical.[73]

Recovering lost or subverted institutions legitimates the present order against subsequent mishap or corruption. Renaissance humanists looked behind dark ages of evil and oblivion to descry classical glories. Revolutionary innovators, noted Marx, evoke ancient exemplars:

In creating something that has never yet existed, ... they anxiously conjure up the spirits of the past ... and borrow from them names, battle cries and costumes in order to present the new scene of world history in this time-honoured disguise and this borrowed language. Thus Luther donned the mask of Apostle Paul, the Revolution of 1789 to 1814 draped itself alternately as the Roman republic and the Roman empire.[74]

So did the Pre-Raphaelites invoke 'pure' Gothic, Tea Party libertarians the Founding Fathers. Whig historians' claims of unbroken continuity alternated with adjurations to restore traditions interrupted by 'foreign' innovations.[75]

Endlessly salutary, Founding Fathers remain uplift fixtures. 'His humanness will fit you like a glove', the History Channel touted its *Benjamin Franklin*. 'You'll be reminded of the best that's in you ... The man who inspired a revolution in 1776, will leave you inspired – in 2004 – by your own personal revolution.' More mundane, or earthy, is the Elvis Presley link promised purchasers of 'a few *precious* drops of Elvis's perspiration ... Elvis poured out his soul for you, and NOW you can let his PERSPIRATION be your INSPIRATION.'[76]

A past improved on betokens advance from dear but dread times. Those who surmount a deprived youth enjoy looking back to measure their progress, like The Five Little Peppers whose 'dear old things' at the beloved little house in Badgertown confirm their rise from rags to riches.[77] We cherish the bad old days as proof of our improvement, conserving its remnants as evidence 'that life was really awful for our ancestors', hence a lot better for us.[78] But improvers, no less than traditionalists, revere organic roots. The former reject 'the narrative of nostalgia [that] looks longingly to a past presumed to be simpler and better than ... the present'; the latter regret 'the narrative of progress ... that has removed us from it'.[79] Moderns for whom antiquity or childhood validates either tradition or progress neither *envy* the past's felicities nor *scorn* its deficiencies; instead, they *identify* with people of the past.

---

[73] P. B. M. Blaas, *Continuity and Anachronism* (The Hague: Nijhoff, 1978); J. W. Burrow, *A Liberal Descent: Victorian Historians and the English Past* (Cambridge, 1981); Herbert Butterfield, *The Whig Interpretation of History* (London, 1931); Yannis Hamilakis, *The Nation and Its Ruins: Antiquity, Archaeology, and National Imagination in Greece* (Oxford, 2007).

[74] Karl Marx, *The Eighteenth Brumaire of Louis Napoleon* (1852; New York, 1972), 245–6.

[75] J. G. A. Pocock, *Politics, Language and Time* (Methuen, 1972), 245–60.

[76] History Channel ad, *NYT*, 5 Dec. 2004; 1985 greeting card; John Windsor, 'Identity parades', in John Elsner and Roger Cardinal, eds., *Cultures of Collecting* (Reaktion, 1994), 49–67 at 56.

[77] Margaret Sidney, *Five Little Peppers Midway* (Boston, 1890), 148; Betty Levin, 'Peppers' progress', *Horn Book Magazine* 57 (1981): 161–73 at 170.

[78] Dave Barry, 'Why I like old things', *Historic Preservation* 35:1 (1983): 49.

[79] Richard Handler and Eric Gable, *The New History in an Old Museum: Creating the Past at Colonial Williamsburg* (Duke, 1997), 99, 130.

In short, the past is a route to self-realization; through it we become more our selves, *better* selves, reinvigorated by our appreciation of it. The healing power of popular history – especially film – makes the past 'a source of reflection and recuperation about ways of perception, habits of thought and ways of being that, could we but recover them and hold them in memory, might help us to become the kind of people we have always wished to be'.[80]

Identity

The past is integral to our sense of self, 'I was' requisite to being sure that 'I am'. Ancient Greeks equated individual existence with what was memorable; Renaissance humanists found the past essential to personality. Rousseau's *Confessions* and Wordsworth's lyrics inaugurated modern consciousness of cumulative identity. Even painful memories remain essential emotional history. Constructing a coherent self-narrative, as discussed in Chapter 7, is widely held crucial to personal integrity and psychic well-being.

Many maintain touch with their past in natal or long-inhabited locales. Places need not be magnificent to be memorable. The genius of the place is identifiable 'more by the tenacity of its users than by its architecture', wrote an English architect-planner. 'It may even be ugly, will generally be shabby, will invariably be overcrowded ... Civic societies passionately defend its every cobblestone', but they guard 'more than bricks and mortar; it is the need for ... rootedness'.[81] In London's mundane Kentish Town, a chronicler time and again noticed how important to residents were memories of their physical habitat.[82] Helen Santmyer's childhood Ohio town, 'shabby, worn, and unpicturesque', was cherished nonetheless.

The unfastidious heart makes up its magpie hoard, heedless of the protesting intelligence. Valentines in a drugstore window, the smell of roasting coffee, sawdust on the butcher's floor–these are as good to have known and remembered ... as fair streets and singing towers and classic arcades.[83]

As Adam Nicolson writes of his childhood Sissinghurst, 'a place consists of everything that has happened there; it is a reservoir of memories and ... a menu of possibilities ... Any place that people have loved is ... drenched both in belonging and in longing to belong.'[84]

Some need the tangible feel of native soil; for others the faintest emanations suffice. The endurance even of unseen relics can sustain identity. 'Many symbolic and historic locations in a city are rarely visited by its inhabitants', noted planner Kevin Lynch, but 'the survival of these unvisited, hearsay settings conveys a sense of security and continuity'.[85] Those bereft of ancestral locales forge identities through other pasts. 'Of all the bewildering things about a new country, the absence of human landmarks' struck

---

[80] David Harlan quoted in Robert A. Rosenstone, 'The reel Joan of Arc: reflections on the theory and practice of the historical film', *Public Historian* 25:3 (Summer 2003): 61–77 at 70.

[81] Lionel Brett, *Parameters and Images: Architecture in a Crowded World* (Weidenfeld & Nicolson, 1970), 143.

[82] Gillian Tindall, *The Fields Beneath* (1977; Weidenfeld & Nicolson, 2002), 212.

[83] Helen Santmyer, *Ohio Town* (1962; Harper & Row, 1984), 307, 50.

[84] Adam Nicolson, *Sissinghurst* (Harper, 2008), 73.

[85] Kevin Lynch, *What Time Is This Place?* (MIT Press, 1972), 40.

Willa Cather as 'the most depressing and disheartening'.[86] Lack of links in new lands leads many emigrants to romanticize remote homelands. Emotional ties with Wallace Stegner's ancestral but never-visited Norway mitigated his history-starved boyhood on a New World frontier prairie.[87]

Portable emblems lend needed continuity. For exiled Jews after the destruction of the Jerusalem Temple it was the Torah, Heinrich Heine's 'portable Fatherland'. Forced out of their ancient homeland, the East African Masai 'took with them the names of their hills, plains and rivers and gave them to the hills, plains and rivers in the new country, carrying their cut roots with them as a medicine'.[88] Many who sunder home ties furnish new landscapes with replicas of scenes left behind. Azoreans in Toronto reproduced the flagstoned patios, wine cellars, and household saints of their island homes; English suburb and High Street features embellish towns in Australia and Ontario, Benares and Barbados. An Indian's homesickness in London is solaced by familiar street furniture – the imperial British having previously brought it to India to palliate their own homesickness.[89]

Keepsakes substitute for surrendered sites. Loading jalopies for the trek to California, Steinbeck's uprooted Okies are told there is no room for such souvenirs as old hats and china dogs, but cannot bear to leave them behind – 'How will we know it's us without our past?'[90] The elderly need mementoes and memories to assuage the loss of long-loved places. Hoarding visual reminders, some are harder hit by the loss of family photos than of money or jewellery. Keepsakes anchor precious memories. Jean Paul's schoolteacher devoted an hour daily to recalling his childhood. He kept things from each stage of youth – a taffeta baby bonnet, a gold sequined whip, a tin finger ring, a box with old booklets, a grandfather clock, a perch for finches – and on his deathbed surrounded himself with these souvenirs.[91]

In China, reminders of vanished sites and structures are apt to be poetic rather than pictorial, the past treasured less in things than in words. Revering ancestral memory and calligraphy, the Chinese traditionally held the past's material traces in small regard. Memory of art, not its physical persistence, suffused consciousness and spurred new creations.[92] China lacks such ruins as the Roman Forum or Angkor Wat, not for want of skills 'but because of a different attitude about how to achieve an enduring monument'. Ancient cities became sites of heritage through 'a past of words, not of stones'. Suzhou's Tang dynasty Maple Bridge is famed as a locus, not for its looks. No poem describes the stones forming the span: what mattered was their literary associations. The city's essential legacy was 'a past of the mind'. Memory is prized less in perishable monuments than

---

[86] Willa Cather, O Pioneers! (1913; Houghton Mifflin, 1941), 19.

[87] Wallace Stegner, Wolf Willow (1962; Penguin, 2000), 112.

[88] Heinrich Heine, On the History of Religion and Philosophy in Germany and Other Writings, ed. Terry Pinkard (1833-5), xix, 213; Isak Dinesen [Karen Blixen], Out of Africa (Putnam, 1937), 402.

[89] Deryck Holdsworth, 'Landscapes and archives as texts', in Paul Groth and Todd Bressi, eds., Understanding Ordinary Landscapes (Yale, 1997), 44–55 at 54; Lynch, What Time Is This Place?, 39.

[90] John Steinbeck, The Grapes of Wrath (Heinemann, 1939), 76, 79.

[91] Jean Paul Friedrich [Richter], Leben des vergnügten Schulmeisterlein Maria Wuz in Auenthal (1790; Munich: Goldmann, 1966).

[92] Wang Gungwu, 'Loving the ancient in China', in Isabel McBryde, ed., Who Owns the Past? (Melbourne: Oxford University Press, 1985), 175–95; Pierre Ryckmans, 'The Chinese attitude towards the past' (1986), in [as Simon Leys], The Hall of Uselessness (NYRB, 2013), 285–301.

in imperishable words that recall a vanished past.[93] Only lately has wholesale demolition sparked efforts to salvage venerated sites and replicate structures, just as wealthy Chinese pay astronomical sums to repatriate ancient treasures. Sales in China's art auctions rose ten-fold between 2003 and 2012.[94]

Prized pasts legitimate tribes and nations. 'A collectivity has its roots in the past', wrote Simone Weil. 'We possess no other life, no other living sap, than the treasures stored up from the past and digested, assimilated, and created afresh by us.'[95] Rootless groups are like orphaned children. In Iceland family and communal lore make the past all-pervasive, equating history with identity.[96] Parallels between personal and national identity, a powerful stimulus to nineteenth-century nationalism, likened family icons and heirlooms to national monuments.[97] 'Antiquity stands … revealed before our eyes' exulted Danish archaeologist Jens Worsaae.

We see our forefathers … We hold in our hands the swords with which they made the Danish name respected and feared … The remains of antiquity thus bind us more firmly to our native land; hills and vales, fields and meadows become connected with us … Their barrows and antiquities constantly remind us that our forefathers lived in this country, from time immemorial.[98]

Reverence for the collective patrimony suffused nineteenth-century French identity. Clovis, Charlemagne, Joan of Arc, pilgrimages, and cathedrals figured like stained glass in fictive reconstructions. Bygone spirituality, chivalry, and troubadour traditions embodied pre-industrial, faith-based folkways against urbanization, migration, dialect degeneration. Pilgrims and *primitifs* preserved relics, mounted neo-medieval festivals, embellished today with yesteryear. 'The men of these ancient times are really our fathers', declared medievalist Gaston Paris. 'Nothing touches me more than knowing what my faraway ancestors were like.'[99]

The recovery of things past allays present loss. Subjugated peoples enshrine historical comforts. The neglect of Welsh history 'hath eclipsed our Power, and corrupted our Language, and almost blotted us out of the Books of Records', lamented a chronicler; to

---

[93] F. W. Mote, 'A millennium of Chinese urban history: form, time, and space concepts in Soochow', *Rice University Studies* 59:4 (1973): 35–66 at 49–53; Zongjie Wu, 'Let fragments speak for themselves: vernacular heritage, emptiness, and Confucian discourse of narrating the past', *International Journal of Heritage Studies* 20 (2014): 851–65.

[94] Paola Demattè, 'After the flood: cultural heritage and cultural politics in Chongong municipality and the Three Gorges areas, China', *Future Anterior* 9:1 (Summer 2012): 49–64; Ian Buruma, 'The man who got it right', *NYRB*, 12 Aug. 2013: 68–72 at 72; Madeleine O'Dea, 'How China went from art-market afterthought to world auction superpower', *Art & Auction*, May 2012; David Barboza and Amanda Cox, 'Art and fraud in China', *NYT*, 28 Oct. 2013: 1, 3–4.

[95] Simone Weil, *The Need for Roots* (1949; Harper, 1971), 8, 51.

[96] Kirsten Hastrup, 'Uchronia and the two histories of Iceland, 1400–1800', in her *Other Histories* (Routledge, 1992), 102–20 at 114–17.

[97] Max Dvořák, *Katechismus der Denkmalpflege* (Vienna, 1916).

[98] J. J. A. Worsaae, *The Primeval Antiquities of Denmark* (1843; London, 1849), 149–50.

[99] Anne-Marie Thiesse, *Ils apprenaient la France: L'exaltation des régions dans le discours patriotique* (Paris: Maison des sciences de l'homme, 1997); Gaston Paris, *La Poésie du Moyen Age* (1885), quoted in Elizabeth Emery and Laura Morowitz, *Consuming the Past: The Medieval Revival in Fin-de-Siècle France* (Ashgate, 2003), 218–19.

Figure 5 Securing a national symbol: Market Square, Old Town, Warsaw,
after Nazi destruction, 1944

Figure 6 Securing a national symbol: Market Square, Old Town, Warsaw,
after Polish reconstruction, 1970

mitigate these calamities, scribes and antiquaries salvaged and magnified family lore –
giving rise to Vanbrugh's portrayal of Wales as 'a realm where every Man is born a
Gentleman, and a Genealogist'.[100] Nineteenth-century Irish glorified iconic artefacts –
cross, harp, brooch, round tower – against English aspersions of primitive savagery.
Governor-General Lord Durham's 1839 slur that French Canadians were 'a people
with no history, and no literature' roused Québécois militancy. Twentieth-century
Turks reconfigured their Ottoman past to reflect their title to present greatness.[101]
Beleaguered states guard unto death legacies that embody their communal spirit.
Rather than see their city destroyed, Carthaginians beseeched Roman conquerors to
kill them all.[102] Hence iconoclasts – Saracen, Tudor, Communard, Nazi, Taliban –
uproot tangible emblems of foes' identity. The Nazis sacked historic Warsaw to cripple
the will of the Poles, who quickly rebuilt the old centre (Figs. 5 and 6). 'It was our
duty to resuscitate it.' 'We wanted the Warsaw of our day and that of the future to
continue the ancient tradition.'[103] Many states today nationalize their tangible past,
outlawing pillage or excavation by foreign archaeologists and demanding the return of
antiquities previously taken as booty, sold, or stolen. 'Whatever is Greek, wherever
in the world', asserts a Greek culture minister, 'we want it back'. 'Whoever took our
stuff', echoes a Peruvian culture minister, 'we want it back because it is here where it
belongs.'[104]

Like pilfered antiquities, lost or stolen identities are coveted by those deprived of them.
Yearning for ancient connections marks current retrievals of long-hidden Jewish ancestry
by Africans, as Israel's lost tribes, and by Latin Americans, as descendants of *conversos*
expelled from Iberia in the fifteenth and sixteenth centuries. Many reconvert to Judaism.
Myriad clues manifest the 'inescapable' ancestral pull.

There were the grandparents who wouldn't eat pork, the fragments of a Jewish tongue from
medieval Spain that spiced up the language, and puzzling family rituals such as the lighting of
candles on Friday nights. 'The Jewish spark was never quenched, and … they are taking
back the Jewish identity that was so brutally stolen from their forefathers.' They felt history
coursing through their veins as they … put together pieces of a puzzle that pointed to a Jewish
ancestry.[105]

[100] Thomas Jones, *The British Language in Its Lustre* (1688; Scolar Press 1972); John Vanbrugh, *Aesop* (1697),
     in *CW*, 2: 1–65 at 33.
[101] Jeanne Sheehy, *The Rediscovery of Ireland's Past: The Celtic Revival 1830–1930* (Thames & Hudson, 1980);
     Richard Handler, *Nationalism and the Politics of Culture in Quebec* (Wisconsin, 1988), 19–20; Tekin Alp,
     'The restoration of Turkish history', in Elie Kedourie, ed., *Nationalism in Asia and Africa* (Weidenfeld &
     Nicolson, 1971), 207–24 at 211.
[102] 'Punic Wars', in *Appian's Roman History* (before AD 165) (Harvard, 1912), bk. 8, pt. I, ch. 12, 1: 545.
[103] Stanislaw Lorentz, 'Reconstruction of the old town centers of Poland', *Historic Preservation Today* (1966),
     43–72 at 46–7.
[104] Giorgios Voulgarakis quoted in Helena Smith, 'Greece demands return of stolen heritage', *Guardian*, 10
     July 2006; Luis Jaime Castillo Butters quoted in Rachel Donadio, 'Vision of home: returned antiquities',
     NYT, 20 Apr. 2014: AR 21.
[105] Juan Forero, 'Colombian evangelical Christians convert to Judaism, embracing hidden past', *Washington
     Post*, 24 Nov. 2012, quoting Michael Freund of Shavei Israel.

Even lacking clues to any linkage, 'many Jews by choice are descendants of Jews', drawn by 'subconscious historical memory', contends an advocate.[106] 'It was like our souls had memory', said a Colombian evangelical pastor who led dozens of his flock back to Judaism.[107]

Possession

Proclaiming ownership greatly augments the past's benefits. Possession enhances self-possession. 'Everyone loves his country, his manners, his language, his wife, his children, not because they are the best in the world', held Herder, 'but because they are absolutely his own, and loves himself and his labors in them'. Posthumous control over children, memory, fame feeds craving for virtual immortality.[108]

Whether personal goal or collective cause, possessing the past is self-interested. 'When the child begins to say, "Mine!" it is to state that it is not yours'. What's mine is thereby endeared. Similarly selfish is the collective legacy. 'All heritage is someone's heritage and therefore logically not someone else's.' And because it is ours, adds a philosopher, 'stories of *our* past' carry more weight 'than stories of other people's pasts'.[109] As Yigael Yadin exhorted Israeli army recruits at the fabled Dead Sea fortress of Masada, 'When Napoleon stood among his troops next to the pyramids of Egypt, he declared: "Four thousand years of history look down upon you." But what would he not have given to be able to say: "Four thousand years of *your own* history look down upon you."'[110] The prior 'Minoan' past contrived for Cretans by Arthur Evans enabled them to view Hellenes 'from a position of superiority, as the direct descendants and thus rightful owners of the past'.[111] Such claims – usually invented or exaggerated, as discussed in Chapter 12 – buttress ruling elites everywhere.[112]

Ownership links heirloom possessors to original makers and intervening owners, augmenting self-worth. An American in John Cheever's story gloats over his inherited antique lowboy 'as a kind of family crest . . . that would vouch for the richness of his past

[106] Jonina Duker, 'Genealogy on a grand scale', in Karen Primack, ed., *Jews in Places You Never Thought of* (Hoboken, NJ: KTAV, 1998), 273–5 at 275.

[107] Juan Carlos Villegas quoted in Juan Forero, 'Colombian evangelical Christians convert to Judaism', *Washington Post*, 24 Nov. 2012.

[108] Johann Gottfried von Herder, *Ideen zur Philosophie der Geschichte der Menschkeit* (1784–91), quoted in Maurizio Viroli, *For Love of Country* (Clarendon Press, 1995), 122; Steffen Huck et al., 'Learning to like what you have', *Economic Journal* 115 (2005): 689–702; Jerome C. Wakefield, 'Immortality and the externalization of self: Plato's unrecognized theory of generativity', in Don P. McAdams and Ed de St Aubin, eds., *Generativity and Adult Development: How and Why We Care for the Next Generation* (American Psychological Association, 1999), 133–74 at 166–7.

[109] J. E. Tunbridge and Gregory J. Ashworth, *Dissonant Heritage* (Wiley, 1996), 20–1; Jeffrey Blustein, *The Moral Demands of Memory* (Cambridge, 2008), 196–7.

[110] Quoted in Amos Elon, *The Israelis: Founders and Sons* (Penguin, 1971), 288.

[111] Yannis Hamilakis, 'The colonial, the national, and the local: legacies of the "Minoan" past', in Yannis Hamilakis and Nicoletta Momigliano, eds., *Archaeology and European Modernity: Producing and Consuming the 'Minoans'*, Creta Antica 7 (Padua: Bottego d'Erasmo, 2006), 145–62 at 158–9.

[112] J. H. Plumb, *The Death of the Past* (1969; Penguin, 1973), 26.

and authenticate his descent from the most aristocratic of the seventeenth-century settlers'.[113] Others' legacies incite covetous lust. Collectors annex exotic relics without compunction and soon convince themselves they are rightfully their own. From the ruins of Palmyra, Robert Wood 'carried off the marbles wherever it was possible', complaining that 'the avarice or superstition of the inhabitants made that task difficult – sometimes impracticable'.[114] Taking fragments of Melrose Abbey for his own 'Gothic shrine', Walter Scott exulted in 'that glorious old pile [as] a famous place for antiquarian plunder. [With] rich bits of old-time sculpture for the architect, and old-time story for the poet, there is as rare picking in it as in a Stilton cheese, and in the same taste, – the mouldier the better'.[115] Digging for antiquities at Saqqara in the 1870s, Amelia Edwards felt remorse at being a party to plunder, but

soon became quite hardened to such sights, and learned to rummage among dusty sepulchres with no more compunction than would have befitted a gang of professional body-snatchers ... So infectious is the universal callousness, and so overmastering is the passion for relic-hunting, that I do not doubt we should again do the same things under the same circumstances.[116]

A psychiatrist termed the craving for relics 'a passion so violent that it is inferior to love or ambition only in the pettiness of its aims'. Accumulation afflicts us all. 'Life is about acquiring STUFF, acquiring more STUFF, ... storing STUFF, acquiring even more STUFF', notes a journalist, 'and then you die with STUFF all'.[117] As Sartre's Antoine Roquentin asserts, 'You don't put your past in your pocket; you have to have a house. The past is a landlord's luxury.'[118] Cumulation nourishes the collector's sense of self. '"I am what I own", whether cattle or coin, concubines or Canalettos, has been the guiding principle of the technically ignorant throughout the ages'.[119] And of the knowledgeable as well. 'A man's Self is the sum total of all that he CAN call his', wrote William James, including 'his wife and children, his ancestors and friends, his reputation and works, his lands and horses, and yacht and bank-account'.[120]

Historians commonly deny the charge that their expertise entitles them to own the past.[121] Yet they not uncommonly covet the archives they research, though few match the callous greed of a Connecticut chronicler who culled what he wanted from his town's oldest newspapers and then burned the rest. 'The history of the Town of Bethel is my own

---

[113] 'The lowboy', in *The Stories of John Cheever* (Knopf, 1978), 404–12 at 406.

[114] Robert Wood, *The Ruins of Palmyra, Otherwise Tedmore, in the Desart* (1753; London, 1773), 2.

[115] Quoted in Washington Irving, *Abbotsford and Newstead Abbey* (London, 1835), 54. Scott's rape of Melrose incurred John Ruskin's rebuke that he loved Gothic only because it was old, dark, picturesque, and ruinous (*Modern Painters* (1856), pt. IV, ch. 16, para 22 (New York, 1886), 3:265).

[116] Amelia Edwards, *A Thousand Miles up the Nile* (1877; London: Century, 1982), 51.

[117] Henri Codet, *Esssai sur le collectionnisme* (1921), quoted in Brian M. Fagan, *The Rape of the Nile* (1977; 3rd edn. Westview, 2004), 154; Martin Kelner, 'The importance of STUFF', *Independent*, 15 May 1993.

[118] Jean-Paul Sartre, *Nausea* (1938; New York: New Directions, 1959), 91.

[119] John Windsor, 'Identity parades', in Elsner and Cardinal, *Cultures of Collecting*, 62. 'I am what I own I know 'cause I saw the commercial. / I am what I owe I signed and I made it official' (Rob Szabo, 'That cold hard sell', *Life & Limb* CD Album, 2008).

[120] William James, *The Principles of Psychology* (New York, 1890), 1: 291.

[121] James B. Gardner, 'History, museums, and the public', *Public Historian* 26:4 (Fall 2004): 11–21 at 14.

personal business', he rebuked residents seeking data for the bicentenary. 'It's all mine now. Why should I tell you or anybody else? A man has a right to what is his.'[122]

Having a piece of the past fructifies connection with it. 'My own fierce joy on acquiring a Roman coin at the age of 15, and my frenzied researches into the dim, fourth-century emperor portrayed on it', recalled Auberon Waugh, 'served a far more useful purpose than it would in the county museum'.[123] Honorary curator of one such museum, John Fowles defended public access to Dorset's fossiliferous cliffs against 'vigilante fossil wardens. What [people] pick up and take home and think about from time to time is a little bit of the poetry of evolution.'[124] The 2013 Grand National Relic Shootout at Virginia's Flowerdew Hundred Plantation, one of many advertised on television's 'Dig Wars', netted nine thousand pre-1865 artefacts, rewarding fascination with the (lucrative) past. Avowedly salted sites, such as Paul's Famous Fossil Dig at Wisconsin Dells, 'where artifacts from all over the world can be unearthed for free', likewise reward acquisitive curiosity.[125]

Far from being free, much of the past is in costly conflict, its treasured remains contested by rival states, tribes, creeds, and kinfolk. Paris auctions of Hopi masks in 2013 violated tribal sanctity. Yet even those spiritually attached to their past may choose to sell it. Defying national heritage diktats, Tuscan tomb-robbers claim communion with and sanction from Etruscan forebears who tell them when and where to dig. They then market their finds to Swiss dealers. *Tombaroli* skills, along with proceeds from smuggled antiquities, are passed on to communal and family descendants.[126]

Newly cherished is our specific genetic legacy. Genes accrue the awe once accorded immortal souls, An invisible yet real substance, the genome – like the True Cross – can replicate without being depleted. The Human Genome Project is both Scripture and Holy Grail; finding DNA in *E.T.*'s dying hero was likened to finding the King James Bible in a Martian spaceship.[127]

The germ-plasm notion of identity that defined and exalted nationhood from 1800 on became racist anathema in the post-Nazi world, but remains potent in popular consciousness. Half a century after Hitler's *Blut und Boden* ideology, an official German spokesman insisted that all that really mattered were 'aspects of culture you are born with', an English writer extolled the 'mystical, atavistic' rural Arcadia embedded 'in our genetic memory bank', and Americans were charged with having 'a misanthropic gene' ingrained in their DNA code.[128]

Ancestor-hunting genetic tool-kits reinforce the mystique of inherited ethnic and national traits. Despite stressing that 'race' is a myth and that we are all mixed, geneticists

[122] 'Chief has corner on town history', *NYT*, 18 July 1958: 4.
[123] Auberon Waugh, 'A matter of judgment', *New Statesman*, 17 Aug. 1973: 220.
[124] 'Fowles defends fossil collectors', *Times*, 10 Sept. 1982: 6.
[125] Taft Kiser, 'Open season on history', *NYT*, 3 Aug. 2013; Aedh Aherne, 'Travels in retroreality', in Brown and Sherry, eds., *Time, Space, and the Market*, 158–70 at 162.
[126] Diura Thoden van Velzen, 'The world of Tuscan tomb robbers', *IJCP* 5 (1996): 111–26.
[127] Dorohty Nelkin and M. Susan Lindee, *The DNA Mystique* (1995; 2nd ed., Michigan, 2004), 38–42, 50, 57.
[128] Jane Kramer, 'Neo-Nazis: a chaos in the head', *New Yorker*, 14 June 1993, 52–70 at 67; Auberon Waugh, 'It is often a mistake for exiles to return', *Spectator*, 29 Oct. 1994; Andrew Kohut quoted in *IHT*, 2 May 1995; David Lowenthal, *The Heritage Crusade and the Spoils of History* (Cambridge, 1998), 192–206.

reinforce stereotypes of genetic determinism. Aimed at distinguishing origins of and regional differences among manifold components of early Britons, the People of the British Isles project excludes recent migrant strains on the implicit assumption that 'the history and heritage of Britain belongs to ... British people of native descent and that other people – 'ethnic minorities' – have their own equally valid but different heritages'. In short, culture is a biologically inherited group possession. Hence 'the ancient and early history of Britain is naturally only of interest to those of native descent ... a heritage that belongs to them. Other people have their own stories and heritages', but we have no interest in theirs, nor they in ours. Commonality and ownership derive from a group's genetic ancestry.[129]

Yet the legacy that moulds us is not only our own but the whole of the past, exotic as well as domestic, alien along with familiar. Awareness of legacies and histories beyond the confines of our own kinfolk, our own community, our own country, enlarges empathetic understanding. Through foreign pasts we view our own past – indeed, our own being – in comparative context. We learn that how we used to be, and became what we are, were contingent on myriad external happenstances. Ecumenical concern with the memories and relics of others mitigates the narrow chauvinism that typically adulates – or execrates – our own heritage.

Indeed, awareness of the past as realms distinct from the present promotes comparative stock-taking. Having conquered almost the whole of the world then known to them, ancient Romans were said to have found distinctive differences not in geography but in history, notably in admired Greek precursors. In a sense, the past was their *only* foreign country. Romans were the first avid collectors of another culture, whose relics served as poetic metaphors and material insignia of their own power and connoisseurship.[130] Renaissance humanists augmented the Roman tradition of collecting with Roman reliquary and literary riches. Subsequent European booty from the Levant, the Far East, and pre-Columbian America brought manifold pasts into patrons' and then public view, educating and enlivening the Western present.[131]

The popularity of museums and historical sites, of biography and autobiography, of historical romance and sagas of former lives, betokens growing interest in pasts beyond our own purlieus. Other's relics and ruins lubricate cultural tourism, far-flung pasts illumining awareness of our own. Indeed, just as our own past is never solely our own, so in myriad ways do we share the pasts of others. But such pasts must be seen to belong to somebody, suggests a Haitian anthropologist; they cannot be unclaimed or forsaken. 'History did not need to be mine in order to engage me. It just needed to relate to someone, anyone. It could not just be The Past. It had to be *someone*'s past.'[132] But whether *someone*'s past can also be everyone's remains, as discussed in Chapter 12, highly problematic.

---

[129] Catherine Nash, 'Genome geographies: mapping national ancestry and diversity in human population genetics', *Transactions of the Institute of British Geographers* 38 (2013): 193–206 at 203–4.
[130] Alexandra Bounia, *The Nature of Classical Collecting* (Ashgate, 2004), 58–64, 310–12.
[131] Susan Pearce and Rosemary Flanders, eds., *The Collector's Voice*, vol. 3: *Imperial Voices* (Ashgate, 2002).
[132] Michel-Rolph Trouillot, *Silencing the Past: Power and the Production of History* (Beacon, 1997), 142.

Enhancement

Boundless time enriches thin quotidian life. 'The present when backed by the past is a thousand times deeper than the present when it presses so close that you can feel nothing else', held Virginia Woolf.[133] The past lengthens life's reach by linking us with scenes, events, and people former to ourselves, as well as to our prior selves. William Morris likened ancient buildings to family heirlooms, both keys to personal memories vital for passionate engagement with life.[134] We transcend the brevity of our own span and gain surrogate longevity by reading history, inhabiting an old house, communing with antiquities, wandering in an ancient city.

Stretching present feelings back in time also augments the immediate moment. Benjamin Constant's lovers strengthen mutual devotion in asserting they have *always* loved each other.[135] Projecting present experience back magnifies it; recalling the past absorbs it into a magnified present. The contemplation of her cherished antiques assures Henry James's Mrs Gereth to feel that

everything was in the air – every history of every find, every circumstance of every struggle . . . The old golds and brasses, old ivories and bronzes, the fresh old tapestries and deep old damasks threw out a radiance in which the poor woman saw in solution all her old loves and patiences, all her old tricks and triumphs.[136]

Treasuring his recollections, Proust's Marcel likens himself 'to an abandoned quarry . . . from which memory, selecting here and there, can, like some Greek sculptor, extract innumerable different statues'.[137]

Past treasures enrich literally as well. Preservatives made mummies merchandise; Chinese bronzes, made potent by age, ward off evil spirits. Antiques become investments, ancient creations modern riches. From Troy to the *Titanic* divers rifle shipwrecks. *The Da Vinci Code*'s hidden cache made Rennes-le-Château a two-million-dollar bonanza, hundreds of thousands of tourists viewing medieval sites while munching Crusty Christ and Papal Pepperoni pizzas.[138] Past profits dominate heritage television: five antiques shows – *Flog It!, Cash in the Attic, Bargain Hunt, Antiques Road Show*, and *Car Booty* – accounted for 61 per cent of Britain's 13,000 heritage programmes' nine million annual viewing hours in 2005–6.[139]

The Old World's uplifting past became a stock trope among New World visitors who at home felt nothing but the present. 'The soil of American perception is a poor barren

---

[133] Virginia Woolf, *Moments of Being* (Chatto & Windus, 1976), 98.

[134] Chris Miele, 'Morris and conservation', in his, ed. *From William Morris: Building Conservation and the Arts and Crafts Cult of Authenticity, 1877–1939* (Yale, 2005), 30–65 at 59–61.

[135] Benjamin Constant, *Adolphe* (1816; London, 1924), 64–5. See Georges Poulet, *Studies in Human Time* (1949; Johns Hopkins, 1956), 205–22.

[136] Henry James, *The Spoils of Poynton* (1897; Penguin, 1963), 43.

[137] Marcel Proust, *Remembrance of Things Past* (1913–27; Penguin, 1983), 3: 921.

[138] '"Da Vinci Code" fans besiege French village in quest', *IHT*, 29 Oct. 2004; Christiane Amiel, 'L'abîme au trésor, ou l'or fantôme de Rennes-le-Château', in Claudie Voisenat, ed., *Imaginaires archéologiques* (Paris: Maison des sciences de l'homme, 2008), 61–86.

[139] Angela Piccini, *A Survey of Heritage Television Viewing Figures*, Council for British Archaeology *Research Bulletin* 1 (2007): 4.

artificial deposit', exclaims Henry James's expatriate artist in Florence. 'Our silent past, our deafening present [are] void of all that nourishes and prompts and inspires.'[140] For John Ruskin, landscape came to life only amid ancient architecture, which 'we may live without, but we cannot remember without'. He thought America a cultural void, its denizens blind to the past. 'The charm of romantic association can be felt only by the European. It rises ... out of the contrast of the beautiful past with the frightful and monotonous present; and it depends ... on the existence of ruins and traditions, on the remains of architecture, the traces of battlefields, and the precursorship of eventful history. The instinct to which it appeals can hardly be felt in America.'[141]

In fact, some Americans felt they alone truly savoured Olde England. So indifferent to antiquity seemed the English that Nathaniel Hawthorne proposed exiling them 'to some convenient wilderness' and replacing them with awestruck Yankees.[142] Henry James adored English palimpsests dense with pastness, even the socially regressive squire and parson and ancient almshouses and asylums 'so quaint and venerable that they almost make ... poverty delectable ... Written in the hedgerows and in the verdant acres ... imperturbable British Toryism' deepens the very colour of the air.[143] Unlike American soil, 'not humanized enough' to interest Oliver Wendell Holmes, 'in England so much of it has been trodden by feet' as to thoroughly civilize it.[144] Even ghosts 'took their place by the family hearth', wrote Hawthorne while American consul at Liverpool, 'making this life now passing more dense ... by adding all the substance of their own to it'.[145] A day in a thirteenth-century English house, his own tread hollowing the floors and his own touch polishing the oak, let James share its six living centuries.[146] Deploring the dearth of ancestral homes in America, Charles Eliot Norton likened their merits to time-enhanced tones of antique instruments. 'As the vibrations of the music constrain the fibres of the violin till, year by year, it gives forth a fuller and deeper tone, so the vibrations of life as generations go by shape the walls of a home ... The older it is the sweeter and richer garden does it become.'[147]

The English continue to exalt their past, alike for tourists and themselves. England's 'quiet villages, peaceful homes and pleasing prospects' are praised for 'the stamp of centuries of ... builders, farmers, gardeners, the village blacksmith, the rich wool merchant, the parson, the squire and the yeoman'.[148] Adam Nicolson felt Sissinghurst's past 'everywhere around me, co-existent with present and future, soaked into this soil, ...

---

[140] Henry James, *The Madonna of the Future* (1879; London, 1883), 7.
[141] John Ruskin, *The Seven Lamps of Architecture* (1848), ch. VI, sec. I (New York: Noonday, 1961), 167–9; Ruskin, *Modern Painters*, pt 4, ch. 17, para. 21, 3: 292.
[142] Nathaniel Hawthorne, 'Leamington spa' (1862), in *Works* (Ohio State, 1962–80), 5:41–64 at 64.
[143] Henry James, 'In Warwickshire' (1877), in *English Hours* (Heinemann, 1905), 197–223 at 210.
[144] Oliver Wendell Holmes, Sr, *Our Hundred Days in Europe* (Boston, 1887), 288–9.
[145] Nathaniel Hawthorne, *Doctor Grimshawe's Secret* (Houghton Mifflin, 1883), 230.
[146] Henry James, 'Abbeys and castles' (1877), in *English Hours*, 225–43 at 235.
[147] Charles Eliot Norton, 'Waste', *Nation* 2 (8 Mar. 1866): 301–2, and 'The lack of old homes in America', *Scribner's Magazine* 5 (May 1889): 638–40 at 638. See James M. Lindgren, *Preserving Historic New England* (Oxford, 1995), 15–25.
[148] Reg Gammon, *One Man's Furrow: Ninety Years of Country Living* (Exeter: Webb & Bower, 1990), 176.

in a bobbled scurf of things, the embedded quirk, the wrinkle in a face'. He saw fellow grandees, likewise bereft of National-Trusted ancestral domains, as 'inheritance consultants, ... experts in buried meaning, in the unfolding of the past into the management of the future.'[149] And these patricians ascribed supreme worth to their familial 'order in *time*', as their chronicler recounts.

The walls of their houses were adorned with ancestral paintings; the pages of Burke and Debrett catalogued and chronicled their forebears; their homes were usually in the style of an earlier period. They planted trees that only their descendants would see in full splendour; they granted building leases for ninety-nine years in the confident hope that their grandchildren would enjoy the reversion; and they entailed their estates so as to safeguard them for as long as possible.[150]

The enveloping past most enriches those ancestrally familiar. Australian Aborigines 'feel the spirits of generations of the dead in the surrounding land' as European settlers cannot. The saturations of time made rooted Gaelic Ireland far more cherished than the English Pale, perched in a thin and isolated present that disregarded the Celtic past. 'Those O'Connells, O'Connors, O'Callaghans, O'Donoghues ... were one ... with the very landscape itself', wrote their chronicler.

To run off the family names ... was to call to vision certain districts – hills, rivers and plains; ... to recollect the place-names in certain regions was to remember the ancient tribes and their memorable deeds. How different it was with the [English] Planters. ... For them, all that Gaelic background of myth, literature and history had no existence ... The landscape they looked upon was indeed but rocks and stones and trees.[151]

Family history similarly suffuses rural Normandy; every field and path recalling some event. Lacking such memories, newcomers inhabit merely a meagre, monochrome present.[152]

Escape

Rather than enhance the here and now, the past may replace the intolerable present altogether. When 'we cannot bear to face today's news', suggests a reporter, 'we want to believe the past is another, more respectable country'. What we miss today we find in yesterday – a time for which we have no responsibility and when no one can answer back. 'The way out is back.' The true faith of the twentieth century was not modernism, exulted California mystic Terence McKenna, but 'nostalgia for the archaic' pervading 'body piercing, abstract expressionism, surrealism, jazz, rock-n-roll, and catastrophe theory'. *Cavemanforum.com* rejects couch-potato modernity for Stone Age hunter-gatherer

---

[149] Nicolson, *Sissinghurst*, 328, 318, 161.

[150] David Cannadine, *The Decline and Fall of the British Aristocracy* (Yale, 1990), 24.

[151] Howard Morphy, 'Landscape and the reproduction of the ancestral past', in Eric Hirsch and Michael O'Hanlon, eds., *The Anthropology of Landscape* (Clarendon Press, 1995), 184–209 at 185–6; Daniel Corkery, *The Hidden Ireland* (1924; Dublin, 1970), 64–6.

[152] Lucien Bernot and René Blanchard, *Nouville, un village français* (Paris: Institut d'Ethnologie, 1953).

barefoot sprinting, berries and raw meat, and a Paleo domestic lifestyle.[153] To escape the tyranny of today's lock-step, high-tech world and regain a sense of purpose, weekend warriors re-enact medieval revels or Civil War encampments (Chapter 11). SF nostalgists rhapsodize 'reconstructing the old cultures, the old languages, even the old troubles' against today's oppressive regimens.[154]

Preference for the past is age-old. 'Many would have thought it a happiness to have had their lot of life in . . . ages past', noted Sir Thomas Browne in the seventeenth century, and 'he that hath . . . rightly calculated the degenerate state of this age, is not likely to envy those that shall live in the next'.[155] Reading the Greek classics while composing *Lohengrin* in dreary Dresden, Richard Wagner felt himself 'more truly at home in ancient Athens than in any conditions which the modern world has to offer'.[156] Some would decamp permanently to the past. Revulsion against the present grew apace after the Second World War. 'Never before', wrote a novelist, 'have I heard so many people wish that they lived "at the turn of the century," or "when life was simpler," or "worth living," or simply "in the good old days."'[157]

Longing for the past was a widespread postwar refrain. From hippie American communes to austerity-rationed Britain to communist-ridden Poland, many were desperate to leave the present.[158] 'I hate the guts of the modern world', grumbled Elizabethan scholar A. L. Rowse, 'everything about it, even its good points'. He reiterated the architect Edwin Lutyens's moan that 'the old was good, the new could but be worse'. The plaint continues to resound. 'The best is all behind us', laments a British critic. 'We will never be able to live as marvellously as our ancestors.' Many dreamt 'of wishing you were a dead person, from a dead time, because it would be better than living now'.[159] Demonized in the media, today's drawbacks seem omnipresent. 'Given all that you hear now in the news', says a German schoolgirl, 'I would rather have been on the earth during a former age.'[160] People long to treat 'history as though it were geography', wrote Stephen Spender, 'themselves as though they could step out of the present into the past of their choice'.[161]

But whatever its allure, the past offers permanent escape only for committed reincarnates. Although his 'heart and mind were fixated on a shifting and fugitive past', a recent

[153] Charles Isherwood, 'Theatrical stumbles of historic proportions', *NYT*, 10 Dec. 2010; Terence McKenna, *Archaic Revival* (Harper & Row, 1992), and Alien Dreamtime, *deoxy.org/t_adt.htm*. Marlene Zuk, *Paleofantasy* (Norton, 2013) confutes this primitivist fallacy.

[154] Jay Anderson, *Time Machines* (AASLH, 1984), 183–5; Cordwainer Smith, 'Alpha Ralpha Boulevard' (1961), in Robert Silverberg, ed., *The Ends of Time* (Gillette, NJ: Wildside, 1970), 1–40 at 2.

[155] 'A letter to a friend on the death of his intimate friend' (1656), in *Miscellaneous Works of Sir Thomas Browne* (Cambridge, 1831), 233–70 at 257.

[156] Richard Wagner, *My Life* [1870s] (New York, 1911), 416.

[157] Jack Finney, 'I'm scared' (1951), in *Clock of Time* (London: Panther, 1961), 24–37 at 36–7.

[158] Barbara Szacka, 'Two kinds of past-time orientation', *Polish Sociological Bulletin* 1–2 (1972): 63–75 at 66.

[159] *The Diaries of A. L. Rowse*, ed. Richard Ollard (Allen Lane, 2003), 368; Robert Lutyens, *Sir Edwin Lutyens* (Country Life, 1942), 31; A. A. Gill, *The Angry Island* (Phoenix, 2006), 214–15.

[160] Cornelius J. Holtorf, *From Stonehenge to Las Vegas: Archaeology as Popular Culture* (AltaMira, 2005), 110.

[161] Stephen Spender, *Love–Hate Relations: A Study of Anglo-American Sensibilities* (Hamish Hamilton, 1974), 121.

American Historical Association president knew himself doomed 'to live in the all too obtrusive present'.[162] Most settle for occasional escape. Even if today is tolerable and the past no golden age, immersion in history can alleviate contemporary stress. 'Come to Williamsburg ... Spend some time in gaol', a brochure depicts tourists grinning in eighteenth-century stocks: 'it will set you free' – free from workaday cares. 'Step into our village and watch something magical happen', offers Historic Naperville, Illinois. 'Your pulse slows. You breathe ... easier. The hassles of everyday life are forgotten.'[163] Cades Cove National Park, in Tennessee's Great Smoky Mountains, lured visitors to a past century when life 'proceeded at a pace rarely faster than a walk ... This allowed time to see and hear the world one lived in. Cowbells in the pasture ... the wind coming up and the sun going down. A decent "howdy" while walking past a neighbor's house', and natural beauty stemming from a deeply felt partnership with nature. (This idyllic community was in fact uprooted to establish the park.)[164]

In disheartened 1970s Britain, some saw the country's future as an enclave of the past, going from making to curating history. 'Shudder as we may, perhaps the creation of a living history book in this clutch of islands is not so bad a prospect', said Labour politician Andrew Faulds. He envisioned Britain as 'a sort of Switzerland with monuments in place of mountains ... to provide the haven, heavy with history, for those millions ... who will come seeking peace in a place away from the pulsating pressures and the grit and grievances of their own industrial societies'.[165] By the late 1980s, groaned heritage critics, Britain had indeed become 'an escapist theme park that stretches all the way from Dover to John o' Groats'.[166]

Arcadian longing has classical and Renaissance antecedents, but became de rigueur in the early nineteenth century. As revolutionary change distanced customary tradition, yearning for the past lovingly depicted by novelists and painters, historians and architects suffused European imagination. Poet–historian Robert Southey (1774–1843) 'found in the past, in the study of huge folios and long dead chroniclers', the peace denied him in the shifting present.[167] In art and rural scenes many like Walter Pater sought relic epochs sequestered from modern progress. Places that lagged behind the modern maelstrom, half-forgotten enclaves of bygone worlds, kept the flavour of Thomas Hardy's 'street for a medievalist to revel in, [where] smells direct from the sixteenth century hung in the air in all their original integrity and without a modern taint'.[168] That taint was hard to avoid

---

[162] Jonathan Spence, 'Fugitive thoughts', AHA *Perspectives*, Jan. 2004: 5.

[163] Naper Settlement web site. See Stephen Gapps, 'Mobile monuments', *Rethinking History* 13 (2009): 395–409 at 402.

[164] NPS, *Cades Cove Auto Tour* (1972), quoted in Terence Young, 'Virtue and irony in a U.S. national park', in Terence Young and Robert Riley, eds., *Theme Park Landscapes* (Dunbarton Oaks, 2002), 157–81 at 172–5.

[165] Andrew Faulds, 'The ancient assets that may be our salvation', *Times*, 19 Jan. 1976: 12.

[166] Stephen Pile, 'Waving a white flag at nostalgia's army', *Sunday Times*, 27 Aug. 1989: A10.

[167] Thomas Preston Peardon, *The Transition in English Historical Writing, 1760–1830* (Columbia, 1933), 243–4 .

[168] Walter Pater, *Marius the Epicurean*, 2nd edn (London, 1885), 1: 109; Thomas Hardy, *A Laodicean* (1881; London, 1912), 444.

even in Venice, Ruskin grumbled. 'Modern work has set its plague spot everywhere – the moment you begin to feel' that you have truly escaped to the past, 'some gaspipe business forces itself upon the eye, and you are thrust into the 19th century; . . . your very gondola has become a steamer'.[169]

Gas pipes and steamers notwithstanding, islands of the past still serve as refuges from modernity. Antiquated Australians conjure up gnarled codgers in Victorian numbers of *Punch*; 'these delightful dodos, extinct in England, are still extant in the former colonies'. Singapore preserves Edwardian dress and demeanour in retro-fitted Raffles Hotel. Spa retreats revert to *Last Year at Marienbad*, Alain Resnais's 1961 evocation of aristocratic pre-war Europe, itself narrated wholly in the past tense.[170]

The charm of such anachronistic places – and their fidelity to the past whose aura they convey – requires unawareness. Their denizens are not moderns being quaint, but locals leading normal lives. Were their datedness deliberate, such places would become period stage sets knowingly purveying the past. 'Fifteen years ago I could go into any muddy village in the Near East and step backward in time', remarked an art curator in 1970; 'today, in the tiniest Turkish town, you walk into the local merchant's and see tacked to the wall a list of Auction prices current issued by Sotheby's'.[171] Forty-five years on, that town may be self-consciously neo-Ottoman.

Even a contrived past, however, may alleviate present dismay. As 'refuges for those bewildered by the normal pace of change', a planner suggested retarding certain 'backward regions' by banning modern improvements.[172] Rest cures in time-frozen Amish or simulated colonial villages might be antidotes to the frenzy of modern life, proposed Alvin Toffler. 'The communities must be consciously encapsulated . . . Men and women who want a slower life, might actually make a career out of "being" Shakespeare or Ben Franklin or Napoleon – not merely acting out their parts on stage, but living, eating, sleeping, as they did.'[173]

Enclaves that sooth exhausted moderns may enable their descendants' sheer survival. Like genetic stocks of endangered plants and animals, 'banks' of bygone folkways might 'increase the chances that someone will be there to pick up the pieces in case of massive calamities'. Robert Graves's fictional Scottish islanders and Catalans reproduce Bronze and early Iron Age life in a new 'ancient' community in Crete, sealed off for three generations from the misguided post-apocalyptic world.[174]

Classical Greece and medieval Britain were the main loci of Victorian imaginative escape, Celtic and medieval times of the French. Today's escapist pasts are more often

---

[169] John Ruskin, 14 Sept. 1845, in *Ruskin in Italy: Letters to His Parents* (Clarendon Press, 1972), 201.

[170] Peregrine Worsthorne, 'Home thoughts from Down Under', *Sunday Telegraph*, 25 Feb. 1979: 8–9; Daniel P. S. Goh, 'Capital and the transfiguring monumentality of Raffles Hotel', *Mobilities* 5:2 (May 2010): 177–95; Thomas Beltzer, '*Last Year at Marienbad*': *Senses of Cinema*, issue 10 (Nov. 2000); Richard Brody, 'Last Year at Marienbad', *New Yorker*, 21 Mar. 2011, blog; Marguerite Valentine, 'Time, space and memory in *Last Year in Marienbad*', *International Journal of Psychoanalysis* 93 (2012): 1045–57.

[171] Cornelius Clarkson Vermuele III quoted in Karl E. Meyer, *The Plundered Past* (Atheneum, 1973), 57.

[172] Lynch, *What Time Is This Place?*, 77–8.

[173] Alvin Toffler, *Future Shock* (Pan, 1971), 353–4.

[174] Robert Graves, *Seven Days in New Crete* (Cassell, 1949), 41–2.

grandparental or great-grandparental, 'far enough away to seem a strange country', explained *American Heritage*'s founder-editor, 'yet close enough ... to bring a tear to the eye'.[175] Much historical fiction re-creates eras sixty to a hundred years back, beyond memory's reach but intimately linked with people and places still held dear. Reconstructed Stonefield, Wisconsin, was set up to remain always seventy-five years old, in a time 'which hasn't yet become dim'.[176]

One lure of that vintage is that it barely antedates ourselves. 'The time just before our own entrance into the world is bound to be peculiarly fascinating to us; if we could understand it, we might be able to explain our parents, and hence come closer to know[ing] why we are here.' In contrast, the nearer past can often seem too close for comfort. Parental pasts often still impinge as irksomely admonitory, or embarrass us as out of date, whereas grandparents are *supposed* to be *passé*: their world survives less in our mental sets than in their mementoes. That is why it often seems quaintly anachronistic – a touching, unthreatening past beyond our purview. Parents are not 'quaint; more like *so last year!*'[177]

James Laver's dress-style terms corroborate preference for the not-too-recent past. Clothes a year old are 'dowdy', those 10 and 20 years back 'hideous' or 'ridiculous'. Fashions are 'amusing' at 30, 'quaint' at 50, 'charming' at 70, 'romantic' at 100, 'beautiful' 150 years after their time. Before most old stuff can be properly admired, it has to outlive a 'black patch of bad taste' associated with parental times.[178] Nostalgia for the '90s still elicits hesitant approval at most.

Past benefits vary with epoch, culture, individual, and stage of life. Different pasts – classical or medieval, national, or ethnic – suit different purposes. Once morally edifying, the past has become more a source of sensate pleasure than of educational or ethical instruction. But all the benefits discussed above remain viable in some context. More than for any functional use, we treasure old things, old thoughts, old ways of being for the pastness inherent in them; they reflect ancestral inheritance, recall former friends and occasions, and vivify remembrance.[179] Fondness for the past feels innate.

We read history for the same reason we listen to old songs: we all believe in yesterday. That we might not learn anything from them doesn't alter our taste for old music. Life is a long slide down, and the plateau just passed is easier to love than the one coming up. The long look back is part of the long ride home.[180]

---

[175] Oliver Jensen, comp., *America's Yesterdays: Images of Our Lost Past Discovered in the Photographic Archives of the Library of Congress* (New York: American Heritage, 1978), 11.

[176] Ray S. Sivesind, 'Historic interiors in Wisconsin', *Historic Preservation* 20:2 (1968): 74–7.

[177] Robert B. Shaw, 'The world in a very small space', *Nation*, 23 Dec. 1978: 706; Jervis Anderson, 'Sources', *New Yorker*, 14 Feb. 1977: 112–23; Andy Borowitz, 'Real-estate note', *New Yorker*, 24/31 Jan. 2005: 48.

[178] James Laver, *Taste and Fashion from the French Revolution to the Present Day* (1937; Harrap, 1945), 202–8.

[179] Mihaly Csikszentmihalyi and Eugene Rochberg-Halton, *The Meaning of Things* (1981; Cambridge, 2002); Edmund Sherman and Joan Dacher, 'Cherished objects and the home', in Graham D. Rowles and Habib Chaudhury, eds., *Home and Identity in Late Life* (Springer, 2005), 63–80.

[180] Adam Gopnik, 'Decline, fall, rinse, repeat', *New Yorker*, 12 Sept. 2011: 40–7 at 47 (phrasing reordered).

Valued attributes

> We are divided of course between liking to feel the past strange and liking to feel it
> familiar.   Henry James, 1888[181]

> Just wait until now becomes then. You'll see how happy we were.
>   Susan Sontag, 1977[182]

> People in olden times drank too much, had wild sex, got naked and wrestled in the
> streets, and on special days dressed up as barnyard animals and summoned the god of
> hellfire. Now, we sit at work all day looking at stuff on the internet, then go home and
> look at stuff on the internet. This is called 'progress'.
>   Alex von Tunzelmann, 2010[183]

> The past is obviously much easier to turn into good telly than the present, because the
> cars were prettier, the clothes were better, there was no boring climate change and we
> know how everything turned out.   Giles Coren, 2011[184]

What traits make the past beneficial? What aspects of bygone times help us confirm and enhance identity, acquire and sustain roots, enrich life and environment, validate a pleasing or escape a repugnant present? Inheritors value the same legacies in various ways. Enumerating the benefits of classical antiquity, George Steiner notes that the Greeks were

to Cicero and his successors . . . the incomparable begetters of philosophy, of the plastic arts, of the cultivation of poetic and speculative speech; . . . to the Florentine Renaissance . . . the abiding model of spiritual, aesthetic, and even political excellence and experience; [to] the Enlightenment . . . the architecture of Monticello and of the porticoes of our public edifices, . . . the canonic source of beauty itself; [to] the modern imagination . . . the archaic, the Dionysian Hellas, with its ecstatic immediacy, [and Freud's] mapping of the unconscious.[185]

This list of particulars is not, however, translatable into general traits – traits that would reckon also with the perceived virtues of Rome, the Middle Ages, the Renaissance, and every epoch's later devotees the world over, and with the numbing diversity of individual as well as collective heritages. Perhaps the plethora of historical, cultural, and personal variables nullify any effort to classify the past's valued traits. But for the sake of discussion I subsume them below under antiquity (being old), continuity (seeming unbroken), accretion (the past as cumulation), sequence (being ordered over time), and termination (being over).

---

[181] Henry James, *The Aspern Papers* (1888; Scribners, 1936), Preface, x.
[182] Susan Sontag, 'Unguided tour', *New Yorker*, 31 Oct. 1977: 40–5 at 42.
[183] Alex von Tunzelmann, 'Becoming Jane: a novel take but still lost in Austen', *Guardian*, 20 May 2010.
[184] Giles Coren, 'Wicked stovepipe hat you've got there, bruv', *Times*, 8 Jan. 2011: 26.
[185] George Steiner, 'Where burning Sappho loved and sung', *New Yorker*, 9 Feb. 1981: 115–18 at 115.

Antiquity

'I just love history: it's . . . it's so *old*', enthuses an American tourist in Olde England.[186] Antiquity roots credentials in the past; ancestral possession makes things our own, valorizing claims to power, prestige, property, propriety. Antecedence lends authority to things that precede us. 'These trees are older than I am and I can't help feeling that makes them wiser', wrote England's New Forest chronicler.[187] Knossos as reconstructed by Arthur Evans gave Cretans welcome proof of 'the most ancient social regime of law and order in Europe'.[188]

Those with shallower roots envy Old World ancientness. A Philadelphian in 1837 held it useless to preserve American relics because 'our *antiquities* are too *modern* to excite veneration'.[189] English patina still humbles Americans. 'Is this college pre-war?' asks a tourist. 'Ma'am', says the Cambridge porter, 'it's pre-American'. When a British journalist interviewed on American TV called his monarchy obsolete, Barbara Walters was shocked: 'Mr Hitchens, how can you say such an awful thing in that lovely old English accent?' The American who tells his aide, 'I'm off to Britain on Friday; remind me to turn my watch back 500 years', terms British fealty to the past 'a virtually genetic trait'.[190] The absence of such fealty in Australia animated a Slovene migrant to guide me around Victorian neo-Gothic Melbourne. 'I'm from Europe', she explained. 'The Australians are new. Only we Europeans *appreciate* the past.'

Antiquity comprises at least four distinct notions: precedence (being first); remoteness (being far back in time); primordiality (being the source); and primitiveness (being unspoilt by modern 'progress'). Claims of priority suffuse every realm of life. People fervently insist that their lineages, languages, faiths, fossils, even rivers and rocks are previous to those of others. Why is being first so ardently claimed and, when lacking, invented? 'First come, first served' sounds impartially just. It is also a law of nature: like early birds, first-comers feed best. Precedence is legendary in legacies. Double portions were allotted Old Testament firstborn sons; primogeniture gave the eldest all.

Not every firstborn legacy is enviable. Old Testament readiness to sacrifice eldest sons won those sons a reward in heaven, but on earth the second-born took over. The first in line have been at grave risk since Jehovah smote the eldest sons of Egypt and took unto himself all Israel's firstborn. (Spared the trap, the second mouse gets the cheese.) But precedence generally implies superiority and confers supremacy. Matthew's (20:16) 'the first shall be last, and the last shall be first' quixotically inverts near-universal experience.

Priority's benefits colour every use of first. First fruits, first class, first prize, first violin, first of all, first and foremost, primate, prime minister are expressions so customary we forget their ordinal implications. The first blow is half the battle. Caesar would rather be

[186] Michael Thompson, *Rubbish Theory: The Creation and Destruction of Value* (Oxford, 1979), 57.
[187] Peter Tate, *The New Forest: 900 Years After* (Macdonald & Jane's, 1979), 14.
[188] Stephanos Xanthoudides (1904) quoted in Hamilakis, 'The colonial, the national, and the local', 149.
[189] Philadelphia *Public Ledger* (1837) quoted in Michael Kammen, *Mystic Chords of Memory* (Knopf, 1991), 53.
[190] Thomas J. Colin, 'Heroic efforts', *Historic Preservation* (Nov.–Dec. 1989): 4. See Christopher Hitchens, *The Monarchy* (Chatto & Windus, 1990).

first in a village than second at Rome.[191] Metaphors of priority pervade patriotic maxims. 'First in war, first in peace, first in the hearts of his countrymen' was Washington's archetypal accolade. Where you initially come from, says Oliver Goldsmith's *Traveller*, is what finally counts: 'The patriot's boast, where'er we roam, / His first, best country, ever is at home'.[192] In myriad *Books of Firsts* precedence is the spur. The first to find a cure or a continent, to detect hidden treasure, to walk on the moon, to cry 'Bingo!' inherit fame or fortune; few note who came next. As Alfred Russel Wallace and next-at-the-patent-office telephone and auto-assembly inventors found to their cost, Darwin, Bell, and Ford alone got the kudos. Monuments and memorial albums in American towns commemorate the first couple to marry there, the first child locally born, the first funeral. North America's initial (1979) World Heritage sites were chosen as primordial: Canada's L'Anse aux Meadows for the 'first' European structures in the New World, Mesa Verde as the 'earliest' surviving Indian dwelling.

Precedence evokes pride and proves title. 'The most important point about English history', crowed an eminent Victorian, 'is that the English were the first people who formed for themselves a national character at all'.[193] A cult of Gaulish antiquity exalts France as 'the oldest of the mature European nations'. Descent from 'first peoples' certifies tribal rights in Anglo-America and the Antipodes. Ethnic French in Manitoba demand autonomy because 'we were here as a nation before there was a Manitoba'.[194]

Pre-Trojan origins, held Alfonso de Cartagena at the Council of Basle in 1434, entitled the Spanish monarch to ceremonial precedence over England's king. Czech, Hungarian, and Balkan students in Vienna each scoured medieval charters to prove their people's prime antiquity; 'no nation within the [Habsburg] monarchy wanted to have a younger history than its neighbour'.[195] Ulster Protestant vie with Catholic antiquity claims: 'British Israelites' contend that the prophet Jeremiah carried the Ark of the Covenant to County Antrim and liken the siege of Derry to Jericho and Marathon; Orangemen term seventeenth-century Scots-Irish the rightful heirs of original Britons ousted by Gaelic intruders.[196] When told that African rock art dated back thirty to forty thousand years, Tanzanian children joyfully hugged the archaeologist for finding their culture older than the British. The British had earlier embraced their own ancient geology, naming the oldest strata then known 'Silurian', after a local tribe famed for resisting Roman

---

[191] Plutarch, *Parallel Lives: Life of Alexander/Life of Caesar*, c. AD 75 (Harvard, 1919), 469.

[192] Henry Lee, *George Washington! A Funeral Oration on His Death*, 26 Dec. 1799 (London, 1800); Oliver Goldsmith, *The Traveller* (1764; London, 1868), 10.

[193] Mandell Creighton, *The English National Character* (London, 1896), 8.

[194] Pierre Chaunu, *La France* (1982), quoted in Peter Burke, 'French historians and their cultural identities', in Elizabeth Tonkin et al., eds., *History and Ethnicity* (Routledge, 1989), 157–67 at 162; Gilberte Proteau quoted in Michael T. Kaufman, 'Ethnic French give Manitoba a language test', *IHT*, 3 Nov. 1982: 4. See Raymond M. Hébert, *Manitoba's French Language Crisis* (McGill–Queen's Press, 2004), 3–8.

[195] Sabine MacCormack, 'History, memory and time in Golden Age Spain', *History & Memory* 4:2 (1992): 38–68 at 49; Walter E. Leitsch, 'East Europeans studying history in Vienna (1855–1918)', in Dennis Deletant and Harry Hanak, eds., *Historians as Nation-Builders* (Macmillan, 1988), 139–56 at 145.

[196] T. B. Macaulay, *The History of England from the Accession of James II* (London, 1848), 3: 256; Anthony Buckley, '"We're trying to find our identity": uses of history among Ulster Protestants', in Tonkin et al., eds., *History and Ethnicity*, 183–97.

invaders.[197] The 1995 Chinese quarry fossil find of *Eosimias sinensis*, the 'first' proto-human, launched Peking's proud claim to anthropoid primacy, much as the 1920s discovery of Peking Man made China the cradle of all humanity.[198]

Claims to priority derogate rivals. Early Christians deployed the Old Testament to antedate upstart pagans' claims; 'the antiquity of these writings ensures their trustworthiness, for they are more ancient than your oldest records'. And Moses surpassed in antiquity all other gods and oracles by several centuries.[199] Subsequent replacement of Roman by Judaeo-Christian forebears made the Holy Roman Empire more holy than Roman.[200] 'Jerusalem *was* Israel's capital a thousand years before the birth of Christianity', retorted Prime Minister David Ben-Gurion in 1950 when the Vatican rebuked Israel for declaring Jerusalem its capital.[201] 'What other nation', bragged a Japanese educator, 'can point to an Imperial family of one unbroken lineage reigning over the land for twenty-five centuries?'[202] The English preen themselves on royal antiquity: unlike other lands' 'Mickey Mouse leaders, "our" monarchs have biological lines stretching back in their purity to the dawn of history'. Whereas 'some guy' in Spain just 'set himself up as King, ours can look right back to Ethelred the Unready'.[203] 'The most noticeable thing about our history is that we have more of it than any other country', says an English columnist. 'Rome is older, but Italy is a nineteenth-century upstart. The length of time, the depth and richness of our island story, gives us ... pre-eminence.' Touting Stonehenge, Dover Castle, and Hadrian's Wall, English Heritage gloated that 'it will take another 3000 years before America can run an ad like this'.[204] When America is disparaged as 'new', encomiasts retort that the United States is the world's oldest extant republic, with the oldest written constitution.

Since in the mists of time men were ruled by gods, ancient priority signalled divine intercession. A fifteenth-century papal nuncio assured the French they were 'the first to be planted on earth by God'. Divine royal attributes promised myriad peoples they were God's elect nation. Puritans saw England as a second Israel succoured by Jehovah against

[197] Emmanuel Anati, 'Parks and museums at rock art and archeological sites', in *International Perspectives on Cultural Parks* (Washington, DC: US NPS, 1989), 107–14 at 107–9; Robert A. Stafford, 'Annexing the landscapes of the past: British imperial geology in the nineteenth century', in John M. MacKenzie, ed., *Imperialism and the Natural World* (Manchester, 1990), 67–89 at 71–6.

[198] K. Christopher Beard, *Hunt for the Dawn Monkey* (California, 2004), 11, 79, 193; Sigrid Schmalzer, *The People's Peking Man: Popular Science and Human Identity in Twentieth-Century China* (Chicago, 2009), 17ff., 207, 249–56.

[199] Tertullian, *The Apology of Tertullian for the Christians* (c. AD 208; London, 1890), 61–3. See Arnaldo D. Momigliano, 'Pagan and Christian historiography in the fourth century A.D.', in his, ed., *The Conflict between Paganism and Christianity in the Fourth Century* (Clarendon Press, 1963), 79–99 at 83, 85, 91.

[200] Matthew Innes, 'Teutons or Trojans? The Carolingians and the Germanic past', in Yitzhak Hen and Matthew Innes, eds., *The Uses of the Past in the Early Middle Ages* (Cambridge, 2000), 227–49; Hayden White, 'What is a historical system?' (1972), in *The Fiction of Narrative* (Johns Hopkins, 2010), 126–35.

[201] Quoted in Amos Elon, *Jerusalem* (Little, Brown, 1989), 242.

[202] Baron Dairoku Kikuchi, 'The claim of Japan, by a Japanese statesman', *Encyclopaedia Britannica*, 11th edn (1910–11), 5: 273. See George Macklin Wilson, 'Time and history in Japan', *AHR* 85 (1980): 557–71.

[203] Security guard quoted in Michael Billig, *Talking of the Royal Family* (1992; Routledge, 1998), 51–2.

[204] Bernard Levin, 'Shakespeare – the history man', *Times*, 18 Sept. 1989: 16; EH ad, *Times*, 24 June 2004.

its foes; that God first revealed His new great age to 'his English-men' was the message of Foxe's *Martyrs* (1563).[205]

'Antique is above ancient, and ancient above old', judged a French medievalist; he put the old at one hundred, the ancient at two hundred, the antique as more than a thousand years back. The more ancient the more admirable a lineage. Sheer age lends romance to times gone by, and 'the more remote were these times', held Chateaubriand, 'the more magical they appeared'.[206] Wordsworth's 'secrets older than the flood' and Shelley's 'thrilling secrets of the birth of time' express fascination with hidden distance.[207] Distance purges the past of personal attachments and makes it venerable, lending the remote majesty and dignity. That 'our ancestors and elders speak to us in the wisdom of thousands of generations' gives Cree indigeneity a primordial imprimatur. The same mystique promotes tourism. 'I am ancient', beckons a Mexican 'Mayan' maiden, '*I was born thousands of years ago*'.[208]

Being ancient makes things precious by proximity to beginnings. After a Knesset hullabaloo over aspersions against King David and the accuracy of Exodus, Israelis bragged that theirs was the only 'state where events of three thousand years ago can cause such a heated controversy'.[209] Defending his choice of the Maison Carré in Nîmes as the model for Virginia's Capitol in Richmond, Jefferson argued that 'it has obtained the approbation of fifteen or sixteen centuries, and is, therefore, preferable to any design which might be newly contrived'.[210]

Divine nature, ancient in preceding history, is much acclaimed as *fons et origo*. 'The first men, having the unsullied purity of Nature for their guide', declaimed Giorgio Vasari, perfected the arts of design.[211] 'New' countries like the United States and Australia compensate for civic recency by celebrating primordial nature. Florida's shores struck Henry James as older than the Nile, *previous* to any other scene.[212] Yellowstone deserved World Heritage status for 'ancient volcanic remnants . . . going back to Eocene time'.[213] Nature's ancientness solaces Australians for their shallow European past. The

[205] Liah Greenfield, *Nationalism* (Harvard, 1992), 94, 76; J. G. A. Pocock, 'England', in Orest Ranum, ed., *National Consciousness, History, and Political Culture in Early-Modern Europe* (Johns Hopkins, 1975), 98–117 at 105–10.

[206] J.-B. de la Curne de Ste-Palaye, *Dictionnaire des antiquités françaises* (c. 1756), quoted in Jacques Le Goff, *History and Memory* (1977; Columbia, 1992), 25; François-René de Chateaubriand, *The Genius of Christianity* (1802; Baltimore, 1871), 385.

[207] William Wordsworth, 'To enterprise' (1832), variant l. 84, in *Poetical Works* (Clarendon Press, 1940–66), 2: 280–6 at 283; Percy Bysshe Shelley, *Alastor* (1815), l. 128, in *Complete Poetical Works* (Clarendon Press, 1972–5), 2: 43–64 at 48.

[208] Ronald Niezen, *The Origins of Indigenism* (California, 2003), 175–6; Mexican Mundo Maya ad, in Traci Ardren, 'Where are the Maya in ancient Maya archaeological tourism?' in Yorke Rowan and Uzi Baram, *Marketing Heritage* (AltaMira, 2004), 103–13 at 111. See Alejandro J. Figueroa et al., 'Mayanizing tourism on Roatán island, Honduras', in Sarah M. Lyon and A. J. Figueroa, eds., *Global Tourism* (AltaMira, 2012), 43–60.

[209] Magen Broshi, 'Religion, ideology and politics and their impact on Palestinian archaeology' (1987), in *Bread, Wine and Scrolls* (Sheffield: Academic Press, 2003), 14–38 at 33.

[210] To James Madison, 1 Sept. 1785, in *The Writings of Thomas Jefferson* (Washington, DC, 1907), 5: 110.

[211] Giorgio Vasari, *The Lives of the Most Eminent Painters, Sculptors, and Architects* (1550/1568; London, 1850), 1: 15–16.

[212] Henry James, *The American Scene* (1907; Indiana, 1968), 462.

[213] 'World Heritage List established', *Parks*, 3:3 (1978), 14.

1994 find of Jurassic-era pine trees revealed awesome Aussie antiquity. That living fossil, the ginkgo, offers a 'glimpse of Father Time as a boy'. The common horsetail (*Equisetum arvense*) is 'Nature's living ancient monument, whose primeval patina … is so much more exciting than the heap of stuff up on [Salisbury] Plain', Stonehenge, built only yesterday.[214] Purveyors of Victorian nostrums cribbed fictitious origins from the timeless wisdom of Mother Nature or of native ancients – 'Indian root pills', snake-oil liniment.

Especially worthy are indigenous legacies still rooted in ancestral locales. To be sure, all ancestral roots are ultimately of equal age. Welsh and French, Polish and Romanian heritages hark back to Celtic and Gaulish, Sarmatian and Dacian 'first nations'. The phrase 'our ancestors the Gauls' transmutes primitive ethnicity into French legend. But the charisma of prehistoric occupance endorses Maori, Aboriginal, Native American, Inuit, and other 'First Nation' claims. Ancestral occupance makes modern Hopis and Navajos rightful stewards of their tribal lands. This mythic stability ignores the tribal upheavals and environmental changes that have utterly transformed them. Mistaken for unchanged ancestors, Hopis and Navajos are venerated by themselves and others as hoary traditionalists whose 'customary law dates back to the tribe's very origin'.[215]

Once a stigma of backwardness, indigenous antiquity is now hijacked by post-Columbian newcomers. Traces of extinct Arawaks become Creole heritage emblems in West Indian nations. North Americans discover a usable past in Indian relict landscapes. Midwesterners now can 'walk out along Main Street and look about and say, "Oh, that's two thousand years old. That's as old as the Emperor Augustus."'[216] Aboriginal 'Dreamtime' legacies similarly deepen white Australian roots.

Emigrants likewise appropriate mystiques of native antiquity. Relative newcomers to modern Israel, Yemenites are accorded ancestral status. Initially patronized as exotic primitives, they gained acceptance as custodians of ancient Jewish dress and dance. They became seen as the authorized source of basic dance steps 'directly descended from the most ancient prayer movements'. 'Israel is a Biblical land, so … its dance company should be Yemenite', argued a dancer. 'The Yemenites are a Biblical people. We even dressed Biblically in Yemen.'[217]

Antiquity varies in age according to ancestry, to materials, to construction, to style, or to traditional usage. An 'ancient' stone labyrinth on Stora Makholmen, western Sweden, was revealed in 2001 to have been built by two eleven-year-old boys in the 1970s. By law, Swedish ancient monuments had to be the product of 'human activity in olden times'. Yet the labyrinth was authentically ancient, archaeologists argued, 'the latest expression of

[214] Angela Milne, 'Ancient monuments', *Punch*, 8 Aug. 1962; Peter Crane, *Ginko: Tree That Time Forgot* (Yale, 2012).

[215] Kristen A. Carpenter et al., 'Clarifying cultural property: a response', *IJCP* 17 (2010): 581–98 at 587.

[216] Jane Brown Gillette, 'A conversation with Roger Kennedy', *Historic Preservation* (Nov.–Dec. 1994): 49–51; Roger G. Kennedy, *Hidden Cities* (Simon & Schuster, 1994); Howard Creamer, 'Aboriginal perceptions of the past', in Peter Gathercole and David Lowenthal, eds., *The Politics of the Past* (Unwin Hyman, 1990), 130–40.

[217] Quoted in Shalom Staub, 'Folklore and authenticity', in Burt Feintuch, ed., *The Conservation of Culture* (Kentucky, 1988), 166–79 at 175–6.

thousands of years of tradition'. So it remains displayed as a reflection of 'customs of old times'.[218] Even material remoteness is, after all, only relative. Household goods that date back a mere two generations are treasured for longevity. A cup's survival attests care against the tooth of time: 'My grandmother brought it back from Newfoundland ... 65–70 years ago. That's how long I've had it, and it's not even cracked. It's so old [I'm] proud that I've still got it'.[219]

What's *primitive* is admired for innocence and purity uncorrupted by sophistication. It takes many forms: preference for untouched wilderness over human occupance; for pre-industrial Arcadian pastoral scenes over cities and factories; for tribal cultures and folkways over civilized artifice. Green nostalgia in England conjures up warm, wooded, well-watered Neolithic harmony seven millennia back. Americans found divine primordial nature morally superior to degenerate Old World history. 'What is the echo of roofs that a few centuries since rung with barbaric revels ... to the silence which has reigned in these dim groves since the first Creation?'[220] Most fantasize some equable past, 'a time when everything about us – body, mind, and behaviour – was in sync with the environment'.[221]

Convinced that modern technical skills cheapened and corrupted art, eighteenth-century European *primitifs* abjured architecture after the Doric, literature later than Homer, sculpture beyond Phidias, as mannered, false, ignoble. Pre-Raphaelites expunged subsequent artifice by reverting to the quattrocento's 'primitive' and 'natural honesty'.[222] Modernists exalted archaic art for its elemental unconsciousness. Primeval nature and prehistory inspired artists at odds with high technology. Affinity with contemporary art validated ancient artefacts' archetypal appeal: displaying them as works of art implies that they are beautiful *because* primitive.[223] So too in the jewellery shop: Garrard, 'the oldest jeweller in the world', touted stone arrowheads, blades, awls, and microliths from the Sahara, 'relics of man's remotest past', as 'mute testimony of the dawn of man's striving to derive aesthetic pleasure from his own handiwork ... each painstakingly formed with a lost expertise'. Here converge all the virtues of antiquity: great age, uniqueness, scarcity, ancient irrecoverable skills, and assumptions that primitive man lived in harmony with nature and conjoined utility with beauty.

---

[218] Nanouschka Myrberg, 'False monuments? On antiquity and authenticity', *Public Archaeology* 3 (2004): 151–61.

[219] Csikszentmihalyi and Rochberg-Halton, *Meaning of Things*, 60, 82.

[220] Charles Fenno Hoffman, *A Winter in the West* (New York, 1835), 1: 195–6.

[221] Zuk, *Paleofantasy*, 270. No such moment ever existed; we've 'always lurched along in evolutionary time ... always facing new environments, and always shackled by genes from the past' (270, 227).

[222] Ernst Gombrich, 'The dread of corruption', *Listener*, 15 Feb. 1979: 242–5; Michael Greenhalgh, *The Classical Tradition in Art* (Duckworth, 1978), 214; Robert Rosenblum, *Transformations in Late Eighteenth Century Art* (Princeton, 1967), 140–60.

[223] Lucy C. Lippard, *Overlay: Contemporary Art and the Art of Prehistory* (Pantheon, 1983); Frances S. Connolly, *The Sleep of Reason: Primitivism in Modern European Art and Aesthetics* (PennPress, 1995); Robert Goldwater, *Primitivism in Modern Art* (Harvard, 2003); Christopher Green and Jens M. Daehner, eds., *Modern Antiquity* (Los Angeles: J. Paul Getty Museum, 2011).

Figure 7 Lure of the primitive: Joseph-Benoit Suvée, The Invention of Drawing, 1791

Continuity

The worth of many things past is weighed by their durability. Endurance shows that a heritage is no ephemeral fancy but a rooted verity. Personal continuity is psychically rewarding, providing certitude and agency; social continuity extends mortal lives into the communal past and future. 'It's lasted that long', Prince Philip defended Britain's thousand-year-old monarchy, 'it can't be all that bad'.[224] Nor need it be especially good. Like Thomas Hardy's Paula Power, we display 'veneration for things old, not because of any merit in them, but because of their long continuance'.[225]

---

[224] Philip quoted in Stephen Robson, 'Instalment 512 of the British soap opera', *GLW* [GreenLeft], issue 64, 26 Oct. 1994; John Darnton, 'A new royal squabble: Charles vs. father', *NYT*, 18 Oct. 1994.

[225] Thomas Hardy, *A Laodicean* (London, 1881), 305.

Figure 8 Lure of the primitive: John Flaxman, 'Agamemnon and Cassandra',
Compositions from the Tragedies of Aeschylus, 1795

Pride inheres in perpetuity – unbroken connections, permanent traits and institutions. Maintaining such links reaffirms their lasting reliability. Since any breach in a lineage might jeopardize a legacy's transmission and a people's loyalty, stewards exalt unbroken linkage. The late Roman Empire deployed names of ancient illustrious families as credentials of imperial continuity.[226] Perpetuation of royal blood from Franks to Valois lent prestige to the French monarchy. Seamless apostolic tradition, 'neither broken nor interrupted but continuous', held a Vatican historian, preserved 'the visible monarchy of the Catholic Church' forever.[227] Duty to founders 'whose principles we inherit' required Americans to leave 'no gaps in the record'.[228] Proof of continuity is crucial to today's tribal Indians: to secure federal benefits and claim ancestral lands, tribes must show identity unbroken since European contact – a daunting task, given that tribal identity was long ruthlessly expunged.

Boasts that eighty-seven generations of collective experience sustain two millennia of German history merge longevity with continuity. The French claim to be uniquely unabridged: 'all other history is mutilated, ours alone complete', held historian Jules Michelet; 'Italy lacks the last centuries, the Germans and the English lack the first'.

---

[226] Patrick J. Geary, *The Myth of Nations: The Medieval Origins of Europe* (Princeton, 2002), 118–19.

[227] Cesare Baronio, *Annales Ecclesiastici* (1588–1607), quoted in Simon Ditchfield, *Liturgy, Sanctity and History in Tridentine Italy* (Cambridge, 1995), 283.

[228] Southern Historical Society (1873) quoted in Kammen, *Mystic Chords of Memory*, 111.

The Revolution was no breach but a bridge from regal protector of Christendom to champion of secular liberty.[229] France remained for Mitterrand culturally peerless. 'From the time that our ancestors the Gauls, so fond of lively colours and sonorous words, were initiated into ... Greco-Roman culture', summed up an art historian. 'Practice of the visual or literary arts has scarcely been interrupted in this country'.[230] A Lascaux cave painting in a 1995 France Telecom ad joins persistence to priority: '20,000 years ago we were on the cutting edge of communications. And we've been there ever since.' The French got there first and are still the best.

Inconvenient breaches are ignored or passed off as 'anomalous discontinuities', such as Czech eras of autocracy, or unnatural parentheses in republican continuity, as in repressive Vichy and fascist Italian regimes. Turning a blind eye to lengthy Byzantine and Ottoman lacunae, Greeks claim unbroken continuity of demotic modern Greek with classical forebears. Whig celebrants of 'enduring' Anglo-Saxon virtues resurgent in the seventeenth century minimized lamentable intervening centuries as a now-healed lapse in continuity. The inter-war revival of English folk music, little sung for many centuries, aimed to assert 'that the vital rhythms of English music had been continuous across the ages'. Since marks of any breach may imperil accustomed loyalties, states like churches become bastions of constancy in the midst of turbulent upheaval.[231] The 1941 slaughter of Jews at Jedwabne was termed an aberrant 'moment' in long-standing amity said to have made Poland a 'paradise for Jews'.[232] Slavery was 'a 4,000-year-old African institution that affected us [Americans] a mere couple of hundred years'.[233] The reunification of Germany revived ideals of historical continuity that required much forgetting both of Nazism and of East German communism.[234]

---

[229] Alexander Kluge (1983) cited in Anton Kaes, *From Hitler to Heimat: The Return of History as Film* (Harvard, 1989), 133–4; Jules Michelet, *Le peuple*, 3rd edn (Paris, 1846), 327.

[230] François Mitterrand (1989) cited in Robert Gildea, *The Past in French History* (Yale, 1994), 112; Georges Lafenestre, *Les primitifs* (1904) quoted in Emery and Morowitz, *Consuming the Past*, 12. See Suzanne Citron, *Mythe national: L'histoire de France en question revisitée*, rev. edn (Paris: L'Atelier, 2008); Pierre Nora, 'Lavisse, instituteur national, 1: 247–89, and 'L'Histoire de France de Lavisse', II.1: 317–75, both in Nora, *Lieux de mémoire*.

[231] Ladislav Holy, *The Little Czech and the Great Czech Nation* (Cambridge, 1996), 84, 120–4; De Gaulle and Mitterrand cited in W. James Booth, *Communities of Memory* (Cornell, 2006), 150, 54; Eric Conan and Henry Rousso, *Un passé qui ne passe pas* (Paris: Fayard, 1994); Bosworth, *Whispering City*, 229; Peter Mackridge, *Language and National Identity in Greece, 1766–1976* (Oxford, 2009), 73, 104–7, 145, 330–4. See Ditchfield, *Liturgy, Sanctity and History*, 345–56; Christophe Charle, 'Les grands corps', in Nora, *Lieux de mémoires*, III.2: 194–235 at 230.

[232] Lucy S. Davidowicz, *The Golden Tradition: Jewish Life and Thought in Eastern Europe* (1967; Syracuse, 1996), 268; David Engel, 'On reconciling the histories of two chosen peoples', *AHR* 114 (2009): 914–29 at 926–7. Debates over Jedwabne have reminded Poles of the darker aspects of Polish-Jewish relations (Antony Polonsky and Joanna Beata Michlic, eds., *The Neighbors Respond: The Controversy over the Jedwabne Massacre in Poland* (Princeton, 2004); J. B. Michlic and Malgorzata Melchior, 'The memory of the Holocaust in post-1989 Poland', in John-Paul Himka and J. B. Michlic, eds., *Bringing the Dark Past to Light: The Reception of the Holocaust in Postcommunist Europe* (Nebraska, 2013), 402–50 at 424–35.

[233] Said to Campbell Robertson, 'Making a stand for the Confederacy, 150 years later', *NYT*, 21 Mar. 2011.

[234] Michael Petzet, 'Der neue Denkmalkultus am Ende des 20. Jahrhunderts', *Die Denkmalpflege* 52:1 (1994): 22–32 at 31; Michael Petzet, *International Principles of Preservation* (Paris: ICOMOS, 2009); Rudy

Britons laud their malleably steadfast living history. 'Almost uniquely among European nations, we are at ease with our past', boasted a Tory Cabinet minister in 1994. 'We have not had to tear down our royal palaces or convert them to soulless museums. We have not had to bulldoze our great churches or convert them into warehouses. We have not had some great constitutional rupture in our affairs [like] the French, Germans and Italians ... Here is a nation proud of its past.'[235] Perpetual linkage is the ritual refrain. 'No existing institution or right or claim can be explained without going back a long way', Bishop Mandell Creighton averred, 'no [other] nation has carried its whole past so completely into its present'. Herbert Butterfield felt such continuity comforting. 'Because we in England have maintained the threads between past and present we do not, like some younger states, have to go hunting for our own personalities.' English Heritage reasserts this 'sense of entity and continuity, of evolution as a nation over more than ten centuries'.[236]

English stability is enshrined in landscapes that bear the stamp, its champions fondly say, of centuries of countrymen and women – even of surviving aboriginal cattle. Hardy's Casterbridge is haunted by ghosts 'from the latest far back to those old Roman hosts / Whose remains one yet sees, / Who loved, laughed, and fought, hailed their friends, drank their toasts / At their meeting-times here, just as these!'[237] A Tory environment chief lauded stewardship that left much of rural England 'as she was: changeless in our fast-changing world'.[238] Reassurance that 'some things remain stable, permanent and enduring', a sociologist contends, is a rural desideratum. Rurality sanctions the status quo. Exalting rustic roots, Prime Minister Stanley Baldwin wanted 'the tinkle of the hammer on the anvil in the country smithy' to continue to ring in English ears. He conjured up

the last load at night of hay being drawn down a lane as twilight comes on, ... and above all, most subtle, most penetrating and most moving, the smell of wood smoke coming up in the autumn evening, ... the wood smoke that our ancestors, tens of thousands of years ago, must have caught on the air when they were coming home from a day's forage.

These were the 'eternal values and eternal traditions from which we must never allow ourselves to be separated'. Baldwin's countryside atavism made him not 'the man in the street ... but a man in a field-path, a much simpler person steeped in tradition and impervious to new ideas'.[239]

J. Koshar, 'On cults and cultists: German historic preservation in the twentieth century', in Max Page and Randall Mason, eds., *Giving Preservation a History* (Routledge, 2004), 45–78 at 74–5.

[235] John Redwood, 'Why Jack Straw should be reading King Lear', *Times*, 12 Dec. 1994: 7.

[236] Creighton, *English National Character*, 14–15; Herbert Butterfield, *The Englishman and His History* (Cambridge, 1944), 113–14; 'All our yesterdays', *EH Magazine*, 3 (Oct. 1988): 3.

[237] Harriet Ritvo, 'Race, breed, and myths of origin' (1992), in *Noble Cows and Hybrid Zebras: Essays on Animals and History* (Virginia, 2010)), 132–56 at 144; Thomas Hardy, 'At Casterbridge Fair' (1902), in *Collected Poems*, 4th edn (Macmillan, 1948), 223–6 at 226.

[238] Michael Heseltine, 'Wales, and a yard-square blaze of colour long ago', *Field* 272 (May 1990): 78–9; Howard Newby, 'Revitalizing the countryside', *Journal of the Royal Society of Arts* 138 (1990): 630–6.

[239] Stanley Baldwin, 'On England' (1926), 1–10 at 7, and 'The Classics' (1926), 99–118 at 101, in *On England* (1927; London, 1971); and his 'The love of country things' (1931), in *The Torch of Freedom* (London, 1935), 120.

Obdurate adhesion to precedent is immortalized in Francis Cornford's satire of Cambridge academic life, making the past a rock on which all novelty should founder. Any proposed change could be rejected as having been tried and found wanting, needing revisions for which the time was not yet ripe, or exciting demands for further reform. From this it followed that 'Every public action which is not customary, either is wrong, or, if it is right, is a dangerous precedent. It follows that nothing should ever be done for the first time.'[240]

The English still cleave to Cornford's precept. To keep Her Majesty's Stationery Office just as it is, a Tory MP in 1996 hailed the hoary dictum that 'if it is not necessary to change, it is necessary not to change'.[241] In the Codrington Library of All Souls College, Oxford, I was shown Sir Christopher Codrington's will. 'By the by', asked the librarian, 'have you used our library before?' 'No', I said, 'I haven't.' 'Oh, then I'm afraid you can't use it now.' (An All Souls Fellow was torn away from afternoon tea to vouch for me.)

The sense of enduring succession is manifest in storied locales. Looking out from a Saxon boundary bank, W. G. Hoskins found it immensely satisfying

to know which of these farms is recorded in Domesday Book, and which came ... in the great colonisation movement of the thirteenth century; to see on the opposite slopes, with its Georgian stucco shining in the afternoon sun, the house of some impoverished squire whose ancestors settled on that hillside in the time of King John ... ; to know that behind one there lies an ancient estate of a long-vanished abbey where St Boniface had his earliest schooling, and that in front stretches the demesne farm of Anglo-Saxon and Norman kings; to be ... part of an immense unbroken stream that has flowed over this scene for more than a thousand years.[242]

The unbroken stream is a peculiarly English virtue. Community of descent connects earliest folk with later, first with latest artefacts and surviving traces of intervening epochs. British Teutonic settlement became 'more of a living thing' to E. A. Freeman when he found 'that the boundary of the land which Ceawlin won from the Briton abides, after thirteen hundred years, [as] the boundary of his own parish and his own fields'.[243] Hardly another country, claimed a celebrant of British royal tradition in 1937, had so continually adapted its medieval institutions 'as to avoid their complete overthrow or their entire reconstruction'.[244]

Rejoicing in our own continuity, we delight in espying it elsewhere. 'Faces are facts', declared a 1925 English visitor to St Peter's in Rome, 'and the true Middle Ages arrive with ... the countenances of the princes, prelates, priests and monks of the Church. For these faces do not change ... There is not one ... that one has not seen before, in this picture or that'.[245] Photo captions assure *National Geographic* readers that 'though kingdoms rise and fall, these Kurdish fishermen carry on' (1938), and that 'across the gulf of countless generations, the Minoan love of dance still finds

[240] Francis M. Cornford, *Microcosmographia Academica* (1908; Cambridge, 1953), 15.
[241] Patrick Cormack, House of Commons, 18 Mar. 1996, *Hansard*, pt. 31, column 107.
[242] W. G. Hoskins, *Provincial England* (Macmillan, 1963), 228.
[243] Edward A. Freeman, *The History of the Norman Conquest of England* (Oxford, 1867–79), 5: ix–x.
[244] Percy Ernest Schramm, *The History of the English Coronation* (Clarendon Press, 1937), 105.
[245] E. V. Lucas, *A Wanderer in Rome* (1926; 3rd edn Methuen, 1930), 40–2.

expression in Crete' (1978). Galilee fishermen are posed in postures evoking Jesus as fisher of men.[246] Continuity is extolled as organic tradition in our own culture but perceived as quaintly changeless abroad.

Accretion

Each year and every generation add their own traces to the scene, giving the past a sense of cumulative creation. Time's accretions generally surpass its dissolutions. No single member of 'the obscure generations of my own obscure family ... has left a token of himself behind', muses Virginia Woolf's Orlando in the ancestral hall, 'yet all, working together with their spades and their needles, their love-making and their child-bearing, have left ... this vast, yet ordered building'.[247] Residues of successive generations betoken partnership, harmony, and order. Accumulation enriches.

Accretions of enduring occupance enchant those from lands that lack them. Hawthorne's American visitor admired an English estate because 'the life of each successive dweller there was eked out with the lives of all who had hitherto lived there'; the past lent 'length, fulness, body, substance'.[248] In his ancestral London house James's American enjoys 'items of duration and evidence, all smoothed with service and charged with accumulated messages'; permeated with antiquity, the very air seemed 'to have filtered through the bed of history'.[249]

A single generation may suffice. Back in her birthplace, Santmyer found it 'immeasurably richer than when I was a child. It is the added years that make it so ... the town is richer by the life of a generation. Since I last stood here with a sled rope in my hand there has been that accretion: the roofs of the town have sheltered an added half-century ... Humdrum daily life ... has given to the scene that weight and density.'[250]

Indeed, mere contiguity of two distinct pasts may convey accretion, like the medieval tithe barn athwart Avebury's prehistoric stone circle (Fig. 10) or the seventeenth-century dwellings hollowed into the west front of Bury St Edmunds medieval abbey church (Fig. 9). A Trevelyan family display at Wallington adds 'a distinct nineteenth-century chapter to a seventeenth-century house with an eighteenth-century interior'.[251] Roman and medieval walls link on to twentieth-century terraces in many English towns, merging past traces with one another and the present in diachronic proximity (Fig. 11). Sixteen centuries of classical and Gothic adaptation and revival, consciously drawing on the forms and motifs of antiquity, give European landscapes an organic density unmatched in

[246] Catherine A. Lutz and Jane L. Collins, *Reading National Geographic* (Chicago, 1993), 56; Joan Gero and Dolores Root, 'Public presentations and private concerns: archaeology in the pages of *National Geographic*', in Gathercole and Lowenthal, eds., *Politics of the Past*, 19–37 at 31.

[247] Virginia Woolf, *Orlando* (1928; New American Library, 1960), 69.

[248] Hawthorne, *Doctor Grimshawe's Secret*, 229.

[249] Henry James, *The Sense of the Past* (Scribners, 1917), 64–5.

[250] Santmyer, *Ohio Town*, 309.

[251] Robin Fedden, 'Problems of conservation: the Trust and its buildings', *Apollo* 81 (1965): 376–9; John Cornforth, 'Some problems of decoration and display', *National Trust Newsletter*, no. 4 (Feb. 1969): 6; Brian Edwards, 'Avebury and other not-so-ancient places', in Hilda Kean et al., eds., *Seeing History in Britain Now* (London: Boutle, 2000), 65–79.

Figure 9 Charms of continuity: Bury St Edmunds, dwellings set into the medieval abbey front

lands where an ancient past nakedly jostles a modern present. Thus in Egypt 'stand pharaonic temples and concrete apartment houses, and nothing links them', observed a Cairo lecturer. 'What is missed and missing is the middle distance … Saladin is juxtaposed to cinemas, and To-day, having no ancestry, is uncertain of itself.'[252]

Continuity expresses the conjunction of various pasts, accretion their continuance into the present. 'The flitting moment, existing in the antique shell of an age gone by', felt Hawthorne in Rome, 'has a fascination which we do not find in either the past or present, taken by themselves'.[253] For Cardinal Wiseman, Rome exhibited 'no distinction of past and present. Ancient Rome lives yet in modern Rome, so as to appear indestructible; and modern Rome is so interlaced with ancient Rome, as justly to seem primeval' – a classical–clerical amalgam of old and new that later morphed into imperial–fascist.[254] Could we but 'join … our past and present selves with all their objects', wrote art critic Adrian Stokes, 'we would feel continually at home'.[255]

[252] Robin Fedden, 'An anatomy of exile', in his ed., *Personal Landscape* (London: Editions Poetry, 1945), 9–10.

[253] Nathaniel Hawthorne, *The Marble Faun* (1859), in *Works*, 4: 229.

[254] Nicholas Wiseman, *The Perception of Natural Beauty by the Ancients and the Moderns: Rome, Ancient and Modern* (London, 1856), 38.

[255] Adrian Stokes, *The Invitation in Art* (London: Tavistock, 1965), 61.

Figure 10 Charms of continuity: Avebury, medieval tithe barn athwart prehistoric stone circle

Figure 11 Decor of diachrony: Roman wall and interwar house, near Southampton

Intimate bonds of recall permeated William Maxwell's boyhood home:

There were traces everywhere of human occupation: the remains of a teaparty on the wicker teacart in the moss-green and white living room, building blocks or lead soldiers in the middle of the library floor, a book lying face down on the window seat, an unfinished game of solitaire, a piece of cross-stitching with a threaded needle stuck in it, a paintbox and beside it a drinking glass full of cloudy water, flowers in cut-glass vases, fires in both fireplaces in the wintertime, lights left burning in empty rooms because somebody meant to come right back. Traces of being warm, being comfortable, being cozy together. Traces of us.[256]

Du Maurier's 'Manderley' drawing room bore similar 'witness to our presence. The little heap of library books marked ready to return, and the discarded copy of *The Times*. Ash-trays, with a stub of a cigarette; cushions, with the imprint of our heads upon them, lolling in the chairs; the charred embers of our log fires still smouldering'. We want animate shelter, not 'a desolate shell ... with no whisper of the past about its staring walls'.[257] Love lavished on inherited relics bespeaks needs for a living past. Daily tending her long-dead husband's shaving kit and watering her long-gone daughter's hanging plants, an elderly widow keeps her past warmly alive.[258]

Commemorative rites commingle past with present. A talismanic shield confers symbolic immortality on a New Guinea tribesman: 'Accepting death, and yet denying it, he is not separated from his grandfather or his great-grandfather. They live on, protective and influential, represented by objects.'[259] Each stone or wooden *churinga* worked by the Aranda of central Australia 'represents the physical body of a definite ancestor and generation after generation, it is formally conferred on the living person believed to be this ancestor's reincarnation'. To Lévi-Strauss 'the churinga furnishes the tangible proof that the ancestor and his living descendant are of one flesh'. He likens them to archival papers whose loss would be 'an irreparable injury that strikes to the core of our being'. And he likens the initiation pilgrimages of Australian Aborigines, escorted by their sages, to conducted tours to the homes of famous men.[260]

Accretive continuity enhances the whole lifespan; we see people not only as they are but also as they were, layer atop previous layer. 'We are none of us "the young", or the "middle-aged", or "the old"', comments Penelope Lively. 'We are all of these things.'[261] Growing up, maturing, ageing accompany awareness that the present develops from an inherent past. 'Maturity means cultivating that past, integrating former experiences – previous ways of being – into the ongoing psychic activity.' Household goods and memen-toes quicken temporal awareness. 'We have my great grandparents' bed which my daughter sleeps on', recounted an old woman. 'It's very small for a double bed and it amazes me that 3 sets of parents slept in it and conceived children in it!' Such links with ancestors

---

[256] William Maxwell, *Ancestors* (Knopf, 1971), 191.

[257] Daphne du Maurier, *Rebecca* (1938; Pan, 1975), 7.

[258] Csikszentmihalyi and Rochberg-Halton, *Meaning of Things*, 103–4.

[259] Penelope Lively, *The House in Norham Gardens* (Pan, 1977), 51.

[260] Claude Lévi-Strauss, *The Savage Mind* (1962; Weidenfeld & Nicolson, 1966), 238–44. See T. G. H. Strehlow, *Aranda Traditions* (Melbourne University Press, 1947), 16–18, 55–6, 84–6, 132–7, 172.

[261] Penelope Lively, 'Children and memory', *Horn Book Magazine* 49 (1973): 400–7 at 404.

and descendants mitigate mortality, much as vitrifying the dead in commemorative medallions once lent permanence to transient lives and instilled ancestral memories in descendants.[262]

The ultimate in diachronic accretion was Jeremy Bentham's proposal for landscaping the dead (his own clothed cadaver is permanently displayed at University College London): 'If a country gentleman had rows of trees leading to his dwelling, the Auto-Icons [embalmed bodies] of his family might alternate with the trees.' With 'their robes on their back – their coronets on their head, ... so now may *every man be his own statue*'.[263] A later benefactor, to 'be of some use again one day', more modestly asked that his cremated ashes go into an egg-timer.[264]

Celebrating accretion, as distinct from antiquity, is implicitly progressive. The past is appreciated not just for its own sake but as the portal to the present, its cumulations culminating in our own time.[265] The accretive palimpsest is a living past bound up with the present, not one exotically different or obsolete.

The virtues of continuity often conflict with those of antiquity. Preservation and restoration are similarly opposed. Those who hold antiquity supreme would excise subsequent additions and alterations to restore 'original' conditions; those devoted to continuity would preserve all time's accretions as witnesses to their entire history.[266]

Sequence

The present is an indivisible fleeting instant, whereas whatever duration we assign the past, it is a *length* of time. Length lets us order and segment the past and hence begin to explain it. The histories of all things start in some past and go on until they cease to exist or to be remembered. Sequential order gives everything that has happened a temporal place, assigns the past a shape, and sets our own brief lifetime memories into the lengthier historical saga.

As commonly experienced, sequential awareness involves four temporal properties: diachrony, recurrence, novelty, and duration. Time is felt as a series of events that precede or follow each other; the past is a multitude of happenings, some earlier, others later, though many overlap. Their relation is one of potential cause and effect: what happens first may affect what happens later, but never vice versa. Diachronic consciousness has inestimable value: to recognize that certain things happened before and others after enables us to shape memory, secure identity, generate tradition, and prepare for the future.

---

[262] Quoted in Csikszentmihalyi and Rochberg-Halton, *Meaning of Things*, 100, 215–16; Philippe Ariès, *The Hour of Our Death* (1977; Penguin, 1983), 513–16.

[263] C. F. A. Marmoy, 'The "auto-icon" of Jeremy Bentham at University College London', *Medical History* 2:2 (1958): 1–10; Jeremy Bentham, 'Auto-Icon: or, Farther Uses of the Dead to the Living' (1817), quoted in Martin A. Kayman, 'A memorial for Jeremy Bentham', *Law and Critique* 15 (2004): 207–29.

[264] Tom Gribble quoted in 'Old timer', *Times*, 3 June 1983: 3.

[265] Francis Haskell, 'The manufacture of the past in nineteenth-century painting', *Past & Present*, no. 53 (1971): 109–20 at 112, 118.

[266] See Chapters 10 and 11.

Recurrence involves the repetition of events within which life is lived: the waxing and waning, ebbing and flowing of diurnal, lunar, and seasonal rhythms; our own breathing and heartbeats, sleeping and waking. Along with these cyclic happenings we experience others that are singular, unique, unrepeatable – the flow of individual careers and collective histories. These two modes of being are known as time's circle and time's arrow.

Time's arrow flies only once from the irrecoverable past towards the unmapped future, never again the same. The targets of time's arrow are the contingent events and sporadic vagaries of human and natural history, a temporal dimension distinct from natural law's recurrent clockwork time. The interplay of circle and arrow continually shapes our lives. Habitual customs – law-like, regular, predictable – interact with the uncertainties of history's directional events.[267]

Awareness of duration lets us measure time into comparable lengths. Standardized seconds and minutes and hours, weeks and months and years, pattern our routines, tasks, and relationships. Agreed chronologies let us segment the past into equal or unequal intervals, analyse events across cultural and geographical divides, and calculate paces of change. We celebrate anniversaries, count up days since important dates, and base expectations on calendric regularities. Duration places things in temporal context, points up past resemblances and differences, and fixes bygone events within firm temporal grids. Links between chronology and history are explored in Chapter 8.

Termination

The past is cherished in no small measure because it is over; what happened has happened. Termination gives it an aura of completion, of stability, of permanence lacking in the ongoing present. Back then 'tensions and contradictions were ultimately reconciled ... Everybody knew what to do and what to believe'.[268] Nothing more can happen to the past; it is safe from the unexpected and the untoward, from accident or betrayal. Nothing in the past can now go wrong; said a Henry James character, 'the past is the one thing beyond all spoiling'.[269] Some feel it cleansed of evil and peril because no longer active, now impotent. To Carlyle all the dead were holy, even those who had been 'base and wicked when alive'.[270]

Being completed also makes the past comprehensible; we see things more clearly after their consequences emerge. To be sure, the past has new consequences for each successive generation and so must be endlessly reinterpreted. But these interpretations all benefit from hindsight available only for the past. We are able to sum up yesterday far better than today. The benefits and burdens of hindsight are discussed in Chapter 8.

Because it is over, the past can be arranged and domesticated, given a coherence foreign to the chaotic, ever-shifting present. Each age looks back enviously at the

[267] Stephen Jay Gould, *Time's Arrow, Time's Cycle* (Harvard, 1987), 196–8.
[268] Holtorf, *From Stonehenge to Las Vegas*, 109.
[269] Henry James, *The Awkward Age* (1899; Penguin, 1966), 150.
[270] Thomas Carlyle, 'Biography' (1832), in *Critical and Miscellaneous Essays* (London, 1888), 2: 245–60 at 256.

fancied quiet integrity and comforting certainties of the past, the Victorians to medieval times as more stable and coherent than their own, modern nostalgists to Victorian times for the same virtues.[271] 'Men had fixed beliefs in those days', wrote the historian J. A. Froude. 'Over the pool of uncertainties in which our generation is floundering there was then a crust of undisturbed conviction on which they could plant their feet and step out like men.'[272] This Victorian encomium to the eighteenth century echoes in every succeeding era. The relative simplicity and transparency of bygone things and processes makes them seem easier to comprehend. Yesteryear's forms and functions were integral to our youth when we learned how things worked, whereas today's innovations are baffling save to computer nerds and eight-year-olds. Hence the appeal of old tools and machinery: the steam engine is more intelligible than the computer chip not only because its working parts are visible, but because it fits into an order of things familiar from childhood.[273]

Childhood remembered shares this sense of pastness: in contrast to life's later stages it is finished, completed, summed up. Unlike our present incoherent mess, childhood is framed by a beginning and an end. Its saga has the shape of fable: 'once upon a time', it starts, and formulaically ends 'happily ever after'.[274]

A past too well ordered or understood loses some of its appeal, however. Hence we prefer survivals (and revivals) to seem haphazard and organic, like the architect Blunden Shadbolt's rambling, 'wibbly-wobbly' neo-Tudor dwellings.[275] To feel secure from present control or interference, the past should feel both completed *and* uncontrived.

The cherished traits I ascribe to the past are seldom consciously identified. Nonetheless, each of these attributes – antiquity, continuity, accretion, sequence, termination – is an experienced reality. Together they give the past a character that shapes both its inestimable benefits and its inescapable burdens. To the latter I now turn.

Threats and evils

Every past is worth condemning.   Friedrich Nietzsche, 1874[276]

In the Past is no hope ... the Past is the text-book of tyrants.
                                                        Herman Melville, 1850[277]

The past is useless. That explains why it is past.   Wright Morris, 1963[278]

---

[271] Raymond Chapman, *The Sense of the Past in Victorian Literature* (London: Croom Helm, 1986), 13.

[272] J. A. Froude, 'Reminiscences of the High Church revival', *Good Words* 1 (1881): 18–23 at 21.

[273] Many mourn machines that can be seen, heard, and felt – steam locomotives, gramophones, and typewriters (Rosecrans Baldwin, 'The digital ramble: machinery nostalgia', *NYT*, 19 June 2008; Tom Hanks, 'I am TOM. I like to TYPE. Hear that?' *IHT*, 8 Aug. 2013: 7).

[274] See my 'The past is a childlike country', in *Travellers in Time* (Histon, Cambridge: Green Bay, 1990), 75–82.

[275] Donald Campbell, 'Blunden Shadbolt', *Thirties Society Journal*, no. 3 (1982): 17–24; Clive Aslet, 'Let's stop mocking the neo-Tudor', *Times*, 11 June 1983: 8; Dan Carrier, 'Calls to protect "wibbly-wobbly" Shadbolt home', *Camden New Journal* [London], 2 Dec. 2010.

[276] Friedrich Nietzsche, *The Use and Abuse of History* (1874; Bobbs-Merrill, 1957), 21.

[277] Herman Melville, *White-Jacket* (1850; Northwestern, 1970), 150.

[278] Wright Morris, *Cause for Wonder* (Atheneum, 1963), 53.

Forget history. Now is all that matters.   Nissan car ad, 2010[279]

We should build a monument to Amnesia and forget where we put it.
     Edna Longley (at 26th Bloody Sunday anniversary, Londonderry, 1998)[280]

The past not only aids and delights; it also saddens and threatens. All its advantages have drawbacks, all its benefits subsume risks. This section reviews the evils felt to inhere in the past and the burdens it imposes, and shows how such pasts are exorcized or neutralized.

Traditionally, the past was as much feared as revered – indeed, feared *because* revered. Fateful events and tragic victims dominated its doom-laden teachings. Following St Augustine, medieval scholars viewed Adam's fall as the origin of history, the record of human alienation from God, a litany of sins and tribulations, and a morally contagious malady.[281] Like nostalgia, the past as communicable illness is a recurrent metaphor. Walt Whitman warned Americans heading for the Old World that 'there were germs hovering above this corpse. Bend down to take a whiff of it, and you might catch the disease of historic nostalgia for Europe'.[282] The sorry past still lingers on to endanger the present, its influence malign, its relics corrupting. 'Where men have lived a long time', J. B. Priestley surmised, 'the very stones are saturated in evil memories'.[283] The evils are threefold: the concomitant griefs that the grievous past saddles on the present; the burdensome weight of the past's duration and unmatchable achievements; and the menace of its continuing potency.

The grievous past

The problem with the olden days ... is that life was so unimaginably vile ... Mud. Hens. Huge facial sores. Women getting raped. Children falling down wells. Hot mercury poured into open wounds. Horses having their heads cut off on battlefields. Rain for 500 years, non-stop, leading to whole countries getting wiped out by mildew. And everyone stinking of lard, pigs, urine and weasel.   Caitlin Moran, 2010[284]

History is quintessentially seen largely as a recapitulation of crimes and calamities, as for Robert Browning:

I saw no use in the past: only a scene
Of degradation, ugliness and tears

---

[279] *New Scientist*, 14 Aug. 2010, inside front cover.
[280] Edna Longley, 'Northern Ireland: commemoration, clergy, forgetting', in Ian McBride, ed., *History and Memory in Modern Ireland* (Cambridge, 2001), 223–53 at 230–1.
[281] Robert K. Markus, 'History', in Allan D. Fitzgerald, ed., *Augustine through the Ages* (Eerdmans, 1999), 432–6 at 433.
[282] Walt Whitman, *Democratic Vistas* (1871; Iowa, 2010), 72, paraphrased in Spender, *Love–Hate Relations*, xi.
[283] J. B. Priestley, *I Have Been Here Before* (London: Samuel French, 1939), 41.
[284] Caitlin Moran, 'It's like Grand Designs, but with witches and Ian McShane in a Betty Boo wig', *Times*, 23 Oct. 2010: SatRev., 14.

> The record of disgraces best forgotten
> A sullen page in human chronicles
> Fit to erase.[285]

Observers looked back aghast at countless evils and errors. 'In the five progressive centuries that preceded' presidential historian Edward Eggleston's nineteenth, 'there was never a bad, that was not preceded by a worse'. The past's 'fixed essences and hierarchies', agreed a successor a century later, make it 'a world we are fortunate to have lost and properly continue to flee'.[286] Often enough, the more we learn about it the less we like it. Miseries of recent pasts overwhelm previously lauded glories. 'The past which haunts us is not a golden age', observes a historian of twentieth-century modernity, 'but rather an iron age, one of fire and blood'. It is the memory of Auschwitz.[287]

Indiscriminate admirers of the past mistake changes in themselves for changes in the world, their own ageing ills for those of society in general. 'Commending ... those times their younger years have heard their fathers condemn, and condemning those times the gray heads of their posterity shall commend', misanthropic oldsters 'extol the days of their forefathers and declaim against the wickedness of times present', wrote Thomas Browne.[288] Nostalgic Luddites forget that every generation has lamented the loss of bygone felicity, morality, seemliness, argues psychologist Steven Pinker. '"What is the world coming to?" they ask when a terrorist bomb explodes, a sniper runs amok, an errant drone kills an innocent'.

The world in the past was much worse. The medieval rate of homicide was 35 times the rate of today, and the rate of death in tribal warfare 15 times higher than that. ... The Crusades, the slave trade, the wars of religion, and the colonisation of the Americas had death tolls which ... rival or exceed those of world wars. In earlier centuries ... a seven-year old could be hanged for stealing a petticoat, a witch could be sawn in half, and a sailor ... flogged to a bloody pulp.[289]

A résumé of life in bygone Britain presents a picture 'so painful that it instantly improves the present. We all know that the Middle Ages were frightful, dirty, smelly and danger-ous, but it comes as a surprise how awful the 17th, 18th and 19th centuries were.'[290] Power cuts in the wake of Hurricane Sandy (2012) left a New York historian dirty, cold, frustrated by candlelight reading, and vowing 'to spend more time in the present and a little less time wishing I was living at some time in the past'.[291]

Once-subjugated peoples claim uniquely parlous pasts. Centuries of Irish bards have keened 'agony the most vivid, the most prolonged, of any recorded on the blotted page of

---

[285] Robert Browning, 'Paracelsus' (1835), pt. 5, ll. 814–16, in *CW* (Ohio, 1969–81), 1: 59–266 at 261–2.
[286] Edward Eggleston, 'The new history', in *Annual Report of the AHA* (Washington, DC, 1901), 1: 35–47 at 47; Steven E. Ozment, *Ancestors* (Harvard, 2001), 1.
[287] Henry Rousso, *The Haunting Past* (1998; PennPress, 2002), 17.
[288] Thomas Browne, *Pseudodoxia epidemica* (1646), in *Miscellaneous Works*, 271–304 at 274–5.
[289] Steven Pinker, 'If I ruled the world', *Prospect* Nov. 2011: 9. See Steven Pinker, *Better Angels of Our Nature* (Viking, 2011).
[290] Leslie Geddes-Brown, review of David N. Durant, *Living in the Past*, *Sunday Times*, 29 May 1988: G11.
[291] Susan Ferber, 'Falling out of love with living in the past', AHA *Perspectives on History* 51:3 (Mar. 2013): 26–7.

human suffering'. A. M. Sullivan's canonical *Story of Ireland* (1867) showed it 'like no other country in the world . . . in cruelties of oppression endured'.[292] The Irish Free State long continued to MOPE, as the 'Most Oppressed People Ever'.[293] The poet Adam Mickiewicz personified Poland as 'the Christ among nations', crucified for others' sins. Stripped of autonomy, scarred by dismemberment, and plundered of cherished heritage, Poles keep a calendar of grievous reminders: Polish National Day mourns the stillborn eighteenth-century constitution.[294] 'There is only one nation of victims', an Israeli journalist contends. 'If somebody else wants to claim this crown of thorns for himself, we will bash his head in.'[295] Other claimants to that crown include the United States, Germany, Ulster, and Colombia.[296] A recent study finds Britain a 'nation of victims', because 73 per cent of all Britons – the disabled, women, ethnic minorities, homosexuals – are officially oppressed, some (black lesbians, for example) trebly impaired.[297] At California history textbook hearings in 1987, group after group demanded that the curriculum show 'its forebears had suffered more than anyone else in history'.[298]

Stressing past misery has its benefits. Bunker Hill, Gallipoli, and Pearl Harbor reinforced losers' bonds more than their subsequent victories. 'Suffering in common unifies more than joy does', Renan consoled the French for their surrender to Prussia in 1870. In national memory 'griefs are of more value than triumphs, for they impose duties and require a common effort'.[299] The Chinese Communist Party deploys gory reminders of China's victimization in the 'century of humiliation' from the First Opium War (1839–42) through the 1945 Sino-Japanese War to reinforce patriotism.[300]

Yet evil pasts can devastate those constrained to recall their dreadfulness. The antique lowboy in Cheever's story mires its inheritor in a miserable yesteryear. Conjuring up the mishaps of the chest's previous owners and 'driven back upon his wretched childhood',

[292] A. M. Sullivan, *The Story of Ireland* (New York, 1892), 474, 563; Roy Foster, *The Story of Ireland* (Clarendon Press, 1995), 11; Declan Kiberd, 'The war against the past', in Audrey S. Eyler and Robert E. Garratt, eds., *Uses of the Past: Essays in Irish Culture* (Delaware, 1988), 24–54. See Roger Cohen, 'The suffering Olympics', *IHT*, 31 Jan. 2012: 6.

[293] Liam Kennedy, *Colonialism, Religion and Nationalism in Ireland* (Belfast: Institute of Irish Studies, 1996), 121.

[294] Adam Mickiewicz, *Books of the Polish Nation and of the Polish Pilgrims* (1832), quoted in Robert Bideleux and Ian Jeffries, *A History of Eastern Europe* (Routledge, 2007), 298; Ladis K. D. Kristof, 'The image and the vision of the Fatherland: the case of Poland in comparative perspective', in David Hooson, ed., *Geography and National Identity* (Blackwell, 1994), 221–32; Norman Davies, 'Poland's dreams of past glories', *History Today*, 32:11 (Nov. 1982): 23–30.

[295] Uri Avnery, 'Mourning becomes Israel: the role of victimhood in the Jewish psyche', *Washington Report on Middle East Affairs* 23:3 (Apr. 2004): 16–17.

[296] Charles J. Sykes, *A Nation of Victims: The Decay of the American Character* (St Martin's Press, 1992); Reanna Brooks, 'A nation of victims', *Nation*, 22 June 2003; Helmut Schmitz, ed., *A Nation of Victims? Representations of German Wartime Suffering from 1945 to the Present* (Rodopi, 2007); Brian Lennon, 'A nation of victims? Northern Ireland's two minorities', *Commonweal* 124:5 (14 Mar. 1997): 12–14; Clifford Krauss, 'An aimless war in Colombia creates a nation of victims', *NYT*, 10 Sept. 2000: A1.

[297] David G. Green, *We're (Nearly) All Victims Now!* (London: Civitas, 2006), 5–7.

[298] Diane Ravitch, 'History and the perils of pride', AHA *Perspectives*, Mar. 1991: 13.

[299] Ernest Renan, *Qu'est-ce qu'une nation?* ed. Philippe Forest (1882; Paris: Bordas, 1991), 38–9, 50.

[300] Zheng Wang, *Never Forget National Humiliation: Historical Memory in Chinese Politics and Foreign Relations* (Columbia, 2012).

he succumbs to the past's horrors.[301] Many a parent strives to spare children knowledge of family skeletons or bygone collective calamity. The global past in Lois Lowry's post-catastrophe Community is so demoralizing that its memory is banned, save for a solitary Receiver tasked to recall the whole of human history. 'The worst part of holding the memories [of] the deep and terrible suffering of the past ... is not the pain. It's the loneliness' – an anguished isolation endured by traumatized Holocaust survivors and shamed victims of sexual abuse.[302]

Old wounds still fester. Inherited pain persists. Ancient injuries sap the pride, shrink the purse, cripple the power, and constrain the will even of remote putative posterity, who 'too easily accept the story that they and their kind were always good for nothing', and blame themselves for their subordination. 'Grief is passed on genetically', a Lakota/Dakota Indian says of the legacy of trauma, shame, fear, and anger handed down to Native Americans. 'It has been paralyzing to us as a group.'[303] Endemic racism and accrued inequities hamper slave descendants to this day. Scarred by 'post-traumatic slave syndrome', some remain haunted by ancestral bondage. Ancient injustices are ingrained in the posterity of victims (and transgressors). 'Passed down to children almost with their mothers' milk', such mindsets endure for generations.[304] Persisting reminders of victim-hood enhance tribal and national identity at psychic and therapeutic cost.

The stifling past

> I am getting lost in my childhood memories like an old man ... I'm being devoured
> by the past.   Gustave Flaubert, 1875[305]

A past need not be evil or unhappy to poison the present. It is a common complaint that yesterday outshines today – a superiority that discourages creativity and makes the present mediocre. That each new generation is inferior to the last is a traditional truism.[306] A past too esteemed or closely embraced saps present purposes and engenders apathy. In adoring antiquity, warned Sir Thomas Browne, men 'impose a thraldom on their times, which the ingenuity of no age should endure'.[307] The forger Alceo Dossena's compulsion to imitate Renaissance masterpieces exemplified the burden of 'Rome's great and overwhelming past, at once a curse and a blessing' that could never be shaken off.[308]

---

[301] Cheever, 'Lowboy', 401–11.

[302] Lois Lowry, *The Giver* (1993; HarperCollins, 2003), 99, 131, 139, 190.

[303] Jeremy Waldron, 'Superseding historic injustice', *Ethics* 103 (1992): 4–28 at 6; Rebecca Tsosie, 'The BIA's apology to Native Americans', in Elazar Barkan and Alexander Karn, eds., *Taking Wrongs Seriously* (Stanford, 2006), 185–212 at 203.

[304] Joy DeGruy Leary, *Post Traumatic Slave Syndrome* (Milwaukie, OR: Uptone, 2005), 13–14; Leif Wenar, 'Reparations for the future', *Journal of Social Philosophy* 37 (2006): 396–405 at 404. See P. E. Digeser, *Political Forgiveness* (Cornell, 2001), 53.

[305] Shoshana Felman, 'Flaubert's signature' (1984), in *The Claims of Literature* (Fordham, 2007), 248–74 at 273.

[306] Eviatar Zerubavel, *Time Maps: Collective Memory and the Social Shape of the Past* (Chicago, 2004), 16–18.

[307] Browne, *Pseudodoxia epidemica*, in *Miscellaneous Works*, 273–4.

[308] Frank Arnau, *Three Thousand Years of Deception in Art and Antiques* (Jonathan Cape, 1961), 222.

The preservationist slogan 'They don't build them like they used to. And they never will again' presumes today's inherent mediocrity.

The sheer persistence of past routine can dim the present. It saddens a Hawthorne protagonist 'to think how the generations had succeeded one another' in a venerable English village, 'lying down among their fathers' dust, and forthwith getting up again, and recommencing the same meaningless round, and really bringing nothing to pass ... It seemed not worthwhile that more than one generation of them should have existed.'[309] Hardy's Tess rejects such history as self-demeaning: 'Finding out that there is set down in some old book somebody just like me, and to know that I shall only act her part' would deny her personal agency.[310]

Obsession with roots and relics, heirlooms and mementoes, pre-empts concern for the present. In Marx's phrase, 'the tradition of all past generations weighs like an alp upon the brain of the living'.[311] Pasts too revered inhibit change, embargo progress, dampen optimism, stifle creativity. 'Your worst enemy' is faith 'in a happy prehistoric time', wrote Cesare Pavese, when 'everything essential has already been said by the first thinkers'.[312]

The classic indictment is Nietzsche's. Men 'sick of the historical fever', dilettante spectators born old and grey, are 'withered shoots of a gladder and mightier stock' mired in lethargic retrospection. Nietzsche cites two retrogressive follies. One is 'hatred of present power and greatness masquerad[ing] as an extreme admiration of the past'. Despising the present without loving the past', the 'monumental' historian invokes past authority to ensure present failure, as if to say, 'Let the dead bury the living.' The other is indiscriminate antiquarianism, 'raking over all the dust heaps of the past'. Mummifying life with insatiable lust for everything old paralyzes the new.[313]

Antiquarian regress – and complaints about its stultifying effects – are perennial. Second-century self-contempt 'prostrated itself before Greek models, and educated Romans grew ecstatic over ruins', writes Peter Gay.[314] Classical authority 'transmitted with blind deference from one generation of disciples to another', in Gibbon's criticism, 'precluded every generous attempt to exercise the powers, or enlarge the limits, of the human mind'.[315]

Classical antiquity's monumental relics remain ubiquitous reminders of matchless virtues. Since the past stands for purity, the present is *ipso facto* polluted; ancient glory breeds modern decadence. In Kostas Mitropoulos's cartoons the classical past imprisons modern Greeks.[316] 'I woke with this marble head in my hands', wrote the

[309] Hawthorne, *Doctor Grimshawe's Secret*, 220.
[310] Thomas Hardy, *Tess of the d'Urbervilles* (1891; Penguin, 1978), 182.
[311] Marx, *Eighteenth Brumaire of Louis Napoleon*, 5.
[312] Cesare Pavese, *This Business of Living*, 25 Aug. 1942 (1952; London, 1961), 132.
[313] Nietzsche, *Use and Abuse of History*, 29, 48–51, 17–20.
[314] Peter Gay, *The Enlightenment* (Knopf, 1966), 1: 120.
[315] Edward Gibbon, *The History of the Decline and Fall of the Roman Empire* (1776–88; Allen Lane, 1994), 1: 51–2.
[316] Suzanne Saïd, 'The mirage of Greek continuity', in William V. Harris, ed., *Rethinking the Mediterranean* (Oxford, 2005), 268–93 at 277–89; Yannis Hamilakis, 'No laughing matter: antiquity in Greek political cartoons', *Public Archaeology* 1 (2000): 57–72.

poet Seferis; 'it exhausts my elbows and I don't know where to put it down'.[317] Curated hordes of fragmented statues bespeak the support exacted from the living to prop up the dead. 'For modern Greek artists', confesses one, 'the ancient forebears are a tough act to follow'.[318] The past is too grand to live up to. 'Greeks aren't what they used to be', concludes a survey, for the sense of national identity relies mainly on precursors two-and-a-half millennia ago. 'The most powerful individuals in this country', complains a curator, 'are the archaeologists'.[319]

Ancestral marvels demean modern heirs who cannot create but only husband and copy. Italian painters and draughtsmen – Panini, Piranesi – so immortalized Roman decay and dissolution that tourists closed their eyes on everything modern for defiling the aura of antiquity.[320] Romantic poets who flocked to Italy were besotted by its past and dismissive of its present. 'Rome is a city of the dead, or rather of those … puny generations which inhabit and pass over the spot … made sacred to eternity', wrote Shelley in 1818.[321] He echoed Petrarch's own regret, in recalling his wanderings there, that contemporary Romans were blind to the city's past – 'nowhere is Rome less known than in Rome' – and the Romanticist Ugo Foscoli's obsessive remembrances of the neglected dead. Lapped in sentimental adoration of Dante and Petrarch, the Brownings and their expatriate successors disparaged modern Italians as inept custodians of their ancient legacy.[322]

Casting off this demeaning heritage was the *cri de coeur* of Italian Futurists. The late nineteenth century left Italy deprived of all but its past. Faced with Risorgimento failures, Italians took refuge in harking back to imperial Rome. Scorning the past as a obstacle to progress, Futurists termed Italy 'the country of the dead', Rome and Venice mired in mouldy relics, Florence a graveyard of antiquarian rubbish for transalpine tourists, their inhabitants slavish lackeys purveying fake antiques. Why 'this eternal and futile worship of the past?' thundered Marinetti. He sought 'to free this land from its smelly gangrene of professors, archaeologists, *ciceroni* and antiquarians'. The real Italy lay in modern machine-age Milan and Turin, not the Baedekered, *dolce far niente*, fetid necropolises.[323]

[317] George Seferis, 'Mythistorema' (1935), in *Collected Poems 1925–1955* (Jonathan Cape, 1969), 1–59 at 7, 53.

[318] Quoted in John Carr, 'Modern Greece aims to step out of the shadow of its glorious past', *Times*, 23 May 2005: 47.

[319] Survey in *ekathimerini.com* 2005; Fani Palli-Petralia quoted in John Carr, 'Culture clash over cash for the arts', *Times*, 23 May 2005: 47; Argyro Loukaki, *Living Ruins, Value Conflicts* (Ashgate, 2008), 137, 142.

[320] Tarnya Cooper, 'Forgetting Rome and the voice of Piranesi's "speaking ruins"', in Adrian Forty and Susanne Küchler, eds., *The Art of Forgetting* (Berg, 1999), 107–8; Jonah Siegel, *Haunted Museum: Longing, Travel, and the Art-Romance Tradition* (Princeton, 2005), 2–4, 28.

[321] To Thomas Love Peacock, 22 Dec. 1818, in *Peacock's Memoirs of Shelley. With Shelley's Letters to Peacock* (London, 1909), 154.

[322] Petrarch to Giovanni Colonna, 20 Nov. 1341, in Ronald G. Musto, *Apocalypse in Rome* (California, 2003), 56; Joseph Luzzi, *Romantic Europe and the Ghost of Italy* (Yale, 2008), 3–9 [Foscoli], 16, 49, 53–76, 80–1; Roderick Cavaliero, *Italia Romantica: English Romantics and Italian Freedom* (I. B. Tauris, 2005), 207–23.

[323] Filippo Tommaso Marinetti, 'The founding and manifesto of Futurism' (1909), in Umbro Apollonio, comp., *Futurist Manifestos* (Viking, 1973), 19–23 at 22. See Clarence Rainey et al., eds., *Futurism* (Yale, 2009), 52, 63-4, 74, 105, 218, 260, 274.

Many Futurists soon morphed into fascists. Italians must 'quit living off ... the past', declared Mussolini, cease being 'degenerate and parasitic', and ensure 'past glories are surpassed by those of the future'.[324]

'For something genuinely new to begin', Mircea Eliade sums up zealots' root-and-branch cleansing of the past, 'the vestiges and ruins of the old cycle must be completely destroyed'. Cistercians, Puritans, Futurists, and Modernists all sought to remake a world that owed nothing to recent tradition.[325]

Adulation of the past inhibits the present not least because its cumulations engorge finite space and energy. Were the 'enormous hosts of the dead ... raised while the living slept', exclaims Dickens's 'Uncommercial Traveller', 'there would not be the space of a pin's point in all the streets and ways for the living, [and] the vast armies of the dead would overflow the hills and valleys far beyond the city'.[326] So too with their artefacts. 'As each generation leaves its fragments & potsherds behind', observed Hawthorne at the British Museum in 1855, 'the world is accumulating too many materials for knowledge'. Admiring the Parthenon frieze, the Elgin Marbles, Egyptian sarcophagi, he nonetheless feared their incapacitating impact:

The present is burthened too much with the past. We have not time ... to appreciate what is warm with life, and immediately around us; yet we heap up all these old shells, out of which human life has long emerged, casting them off forever. I do not see how future ages are to stagger under all this dead weight, with the additions that will continually be made to it.[327]

Like many Americans, Hawthorne was simultaneously fascinated and appalled by the European past. Roman antiquity left 'a perception of such weight and density in a by-gone life' as to press down or crowd out the present. Next to the massive Roman past 'all matters, that we handle or dream of, now-a-days, look evanescent'.[328]

More menacing than our museumized past is the discarded past, detritus that never truly disappears. In Italo Calvino's 'Leonia', everything is new-made daily, all the used artefacts, from sheets and soap to boilers and pianos, are consigned to garbage every night, to be dumped outside the urban walls.

But as yesterday's sweepings piled up on the sweepings of the day before, ... a fortress of indestructible leftovers surrounds Leonia, ... the scales of its past are soldered into a cuirass that cannot be removed. ... The greater its height grows, ... the more the danger of a landslide looms,

---

[324] Jan Nelis, 'Constructing fascist identity: Benito Mussolini and the myth of *romanità*', *Classical World* 100 (2007): 391–415 at 403, 409. See Claudia Lazzaro and Roger J. Crum, eds., *Donatello among the Blackshirts: History and Modernity in the Visual Culture of Fascist Italy* (Cornell, 2005); Bosworth, *Whispering City*, 166–7, 173; Borden Painter, *Mussolini's Rome* (Macmillan, 2005); Emilio Gentile, *Fascismo di pietra* (Rome: Laterza, 2007); John Agnew, '"Ghosts of Rome": the haunting of Fascist efforts to remake Rome as Italy's capital city', *Annali d'italianistica* 28 (2010): 179–98.

[325] Mircea Eliade, *Myth and Reality* (Allen & Unwin, 1964), 51; David Gross, *Lost Time: On Remembering and Forgetting in Late Modern Culture* (MIT Press, 2000), 101–4.

[326] Charles Dickens, 'Night walks' (1860), in *The Uncommercial Traveller* (Macmillan, 1925), 109–17 at 114.

[327] Nathaniel Hawthorne, *The English Notebooks*, 29 Sept. 1855 and 26 Mar. 1856 (New York: [P]MLA, 1941), 242, 294.

[328] Hawthorne, *Marble Faun*, 6.

... an avalanche of unmated shoes, calendars of bygone years, withered flowers, submerging the city in its own past.[329]

The menacing past

The past not only appals by its crimes or cripples by its grandeur; it threatens by its lasting potency. 'We live entirely in the past, nourished by dead thoughts, dead creeds, dead sciences', moaned Henry Miller. 'The past ... is engulfing us.'[330] As followers of Freud and Nietzsche are aware, 'the past is old stuff, and like depleted and worn out objects, it just clogs up our lives'. But though 'spent, banished, used up and made void, ... the threat of the uncanny' implacably persists.[331] James Fenimore Cooper's tale of the Swiss hereditary hangman who 'can neither inherit or transmit aught but disgrace' spells out the fearsome consequences of an inescapable legacy, the Roman *damnosa hereditas*.[332] 'Any normal child', concludes a biologist, 'hates what he inherits'. We must dispute the philosopher's dictum that 'we only dread the future, but not the past'.[333]

A miserable childhood and utopian Marxism turned the philosopher Ernst Bloch firmly against reminiscence. 'Nothing past should be sought so faithfully that one goes back, truly back. ... The desire for it is depraved, and one will pay for it too. ... The return disappoints; ... life then and life now have no connection, or merely one in melancholy', towards things dead or broken. 'Separating oneself from one's past is a test of one's adaptation to fate.'[334]

Previous others live on to haunt us. In cemetery and charnel house, song and story, the dead oppress and cajole the living, who cannot exorcise their ghosts. Sheer survival may mandate concealing or expunging ancestral remains. Transgressors' bodies were staked into bogs to make sure they would not rise from the dead to bedevil the living; Bronze Age burials were obliterated to expunge posthumous powers.[335] Academics 'who could slaughter their intellectual ancestors' are more apt to prosper than those who adored them.[336] As the progeny of past generations, Nietzsche reminded readers, 'we are also the products of their aberrations, passions, and errors, and indeed of their crimes'.[337] They

---

[329] Italo Calvino, *Invisible Cities* (1972; Vintage, 1997), 114–16.

[330] Henry Miller, *The Time of the Assassins: A Study of Rimbaud* (1946; New York: New Directions, 1956), x.

[331] John Scanlan, *On Garbage* (Reaktion, 2005), 162–3.

[332] James Fenimore Cooper, *The Headsman* (London, 1833), 2: 50.

[333] Midas Dekkers, *The Way of All Flesh* (1997; London: Harvill, 2000), 61; Craig Bourne, *A Future for Presentism* (Oxford, 2006), 17.

[334] Ernst Bloch, 'Reunion without connection', in *Traces* (1910–26; Stanford, 2006), 62–3.

[335] Allan A. Lund, *Mummificerede moselig* (2002), cited in Karin Sanders, *Bodies in the Bog and the Archaeological Imagination* (Chicago, 2009), 6–8, 238 n17; Sarah Semple, 'A fear of the past: the place of prehistoric burial mounds in the ideology of middle and later Anglo-Saxon England', *World Archaeology* 30:1 (1998): 109–26; Klavs Randborg, 'Impressions of the past: early material heritage in Scandinavia', *Acta Archaeologica* 70 (1999): 185–94.

[336] Anthony Grafton, *Bring Out Your Dead: The Past as Revelation* (Harvard, 2001), 293.

[337] Nietzsche, *Use and Abuse of History*, 102.

still threaten. 'Those who venture too close ... risk being pulled back into a past of fixed essences and hierarchies' ruled by princes and prelates.[338]

Japanese who find the weight of tradition unbearable break entirely with long-worshipped ancestors. Wretched inheritors of ancestral woes and misfortunes, they sever karmic bonds to escape forebears' malign grip.[339] Convinced that ancestral character resurfaces in descendants, a Yoruba villager seeks to erase a forebear's grievous life from collective tribal memory, lest inherited disgrace wreck his descendants' prospects.[340]

Like the ancestral past, inherited property can be a dubious blessing. Not every relic is seemly or desirable. Along with the 'the Old Master over the carved surround of the saloon fireplace' in the stately home comes 'the peeling wallpaper in the servant's bedroom'.[341] Adored survivals may be also detested. Among the cabbages, diesel six-wheelers, and theatre props in old Covent Garden, one's delight in 'this tight-packed, smelly, rakishly scruffy and vital corner of London is equalled by a deep conviction ... that the whole bloody lot ought to be bulldozed'.[342] Clinging to Lancashire's old industrial monuments was held sheer masochism, yet 'in fighting to remove the greyness of its economy, it would be a pity to tamper with its soul'. But even the soul may perish in such surroundings. Dank Mancunian greyness so depressed one lover of the past that she felt inclined to eradicate everything Victorian and Edwardian.[343]

Many strive to forget or banish baneful recall. To prevent sorrows being 'kept raw by the edge of repetitions', Thomas Browne termed it mercifully beneficial to be 'forgetful of evils past'.[344] Memory must be curtailed or obliterated, advised Nietzsche, lest the past become the gravedigger of the present. 'No artist will paint his picture, no general win his victory, no nation gain its freedom' without forgetting the past.[345] Zionist pioneers in Palestine 'cultivate[d] oblivion. We are proud of our short memory. The more rootless we see ourselves, the more we believe that we are more free, more sublime. It is roots that delay our upward growth.' After the Holocaust horror, some Jews wanted to consign Jewish history to oblivion.[346] Cambodia's prime minister urged his countrymen to 'dig a deep hole and bury the past'.[347]

---

[338] Ozment, *Ancestors*, 1.

[339] Karen Kerner, 'The malevolent ancestors: ancestral influence in a Japanese religious sect', 205–17, and Takie Sugiyama Lebra, 'Ancestral influence on the suffering of descendants in a Japanese cult', 219–30, in William H. Newell, ed., *Ancestors* (The Hague: Mouton, 1976).

[340] J. D. Y. Peel, 'Making history: the past in the Ijesha present', *Man* 19 (1984): 111–32 at 125.

[341] Patrick A. Faulkner, 'A philosophy for the preservation of our historic heritage', *Journal of the Royal Society of Arts* 126 (1978): 452–80 at 455.

[342] Tom Baistow, 'The Covent Garden to come', *New Statesman*, 19 Apr. 1968: 511.

[343] Dennis Johnson, 'Masochism in Lancashire', *New Statesman*, 1 Mar. 1968: 262; Anne Angus, 'What's wrong with the North?' *New Society*, 13 July 1967: 55.

[344] Thomas Browne, *Hydriotaphia: Urn Burial* (1658), in *Miscellaneous Works* (1852), 3: 1–50 at 45.

[345] Nietzsche, *Use and Abuse of History*, 9.

[346] Berl Katznelson quoted in Zerubavel, *Time Maps*, 93; Yosef Hayim Yerushalmi, *Zakhor: Jewish History and Jewish Memory* (1982; rev. edn Washington, 1996), 97.

[347] Hun Sen quoted in Seth Mydans, 'Cambodian leader resists punishing top Khmer Rouge', *NYT*, 29 Dec. 1998.

The need for exorcism impels Naipaul's post-colonial Africans:

We have to learn to trample on the past . . . to get rid of the old, to wipe out the memory of the intruder . . . There may be some parts of the world . . . where men can cherish the past and think of passing on furniture and china to their heirs . . . Some peasant department of France full of half-wits in châteaux; some crumbling Indian palace-city, or some dead colonial town in a hopeless South American country. Everywhere else . . . the past can only cause pain.

Naipaul was equally dismissive of the 'ecstatically contemplated . . . golden Indian past . . . a religious idea, clouding intellect and painful perception, numbing the stress in bad times'.[348] So too the Russian in Thomas Harris's *Archangel* warns that the past still menaces: 'this isn't England or America, the past isn't safely dead here. In Russia, the past carries razors and a pair of handcuffs'.[349]

   Demolition is the common fate of despised and dangerous legacies. As with distressing memories, out of sight, out of mind. Iconoclasts down the ages expunge detested reminders. Dreaded, oppressive, shameful pasts spawn iconoclastic frenzy. Each Chinese dynasty made an auto-da-fé of its predecessor's precious relics. Roman emperors regularly removed images of rivals, destroying or displacing portraits, razing or substituting new heads on statues.[350] During English monastic dissolution, Protestants aimed to wipe out every Catholic icon, to make 'utterly extinct and destroy all shrines', in a 1547 Tudor injunction, 'so that there remain no memory of the same'.[351] An Egyptian jihadist would demolish the pyramids and the Giza sphinx: 'All Muslims are charged . . . to remove such idols, as we did in Afghanistan when we destroyed the Buddha statues.'[352] The missionary founder of Berea College, Kentucky, Dr John Fee, so loathed slavery that he literally knifed out every Scriptural reference to servitude. Fee's mutilated Bible, on display in Berea's library, attests his faith that evil can be undone by being literally excised.[353]

   Oblivion is a parallel remedy: expunging all mention of the now-detested man or matter and enjoining amnesia. Two aims animate injunctions to forget: to doom a sinner by blotting out his name (Deuteronomy 29:20); to blot out the sin, 'forgive their iniquity and . . . remember their sins no more' (Jeremiah 31:34).[354] Forgetting is a common prelude to forgiving: amnesia facilitates amnesty. To restore amity after Odysseus' vengeance against Penelope's suitors, Zeus purges antagonists' 'memories of the bloody slaughter of their brothers and their sons'. To foster a myth of uninterrupted ancestral freedom, and to antiquate Solon's laws and thus make them unassailable, public amnesia

---

[348] V. S. Naipaul, *A Bend in the River* (Knopf, 1979), 152–53, 33; V. S. Naipaul, 'India: paradise lost', *NYRB*, 28 Oct. 1976: 10–16 at 15; V. S. Naipaul, *India: A Wounded Civilization* (Knopf, 1977).

[349] Thomas Harris, *Archangel* (Hutchinson, 1998), 167.

[350] Ryckmans, 'Chinese attitude towards the past', 285–301; Peter Stewart, *Statues in Roman Society* (Oxford, 2003), 261–99.

[351] Order in Council quoted in Martin S. Briggs, *Goths and Vandals: A Study of the Destruction, Neglect and Preservation of Historical Buildings in England* (Constable, 1952), 34–5. See Margaret Aston, *England's Iconoclasts* (Oxford, 1988), 2, 10, 256.

[352] Quoted in '"Destroy the idols", Egyptian jihadist calls for removal of Sphinx, Pyramids', *Al Arabiya*, 12 Nov. 2012.

[353] I saw Fee's Bible in the Berea College library in 1988.

[354] Avishai Margalit, *The Ethics of Memory* (Harvard, 2002), 188–90.

was decreed when Athens regained democracy in 403 BC. Citizens were forbidden to discuss recent sufferings or to seek revenge against traitors who had aided the oligarchs. Recall was forbidden precisely because the recent past was remembered all too well; it was put out of mind because dangerously painful.[355]

The ancient Athenian example proved serviceable in early-modern Europe, when religious conflicts imperilled social stability and state exchequers. To enable reconciliation, former foes had to forget past injuries. The 1598 Edict of Nantes required memory of quarrels 'be extinguished and put to rest'.[356] Ending the Thirty Years War, the Treaty of Westphalia (1648) imposed 'perpetual oblivion and amnesty' on all parties.[357] Mindful of Restoration England's festering sores, Thomas Hobbes pronounced forgetting the basis of a just state, amnesia the cornerstone of the social contract. Disregarding 'the evil past' for the sake of 'the good to follow', offences should be pardoned, not punished; wrongs forgotten, not avenged. Remedial oblivion became a vital tool of English statecraft, Civil War antagonists adjured to forget. 'Acts of Oblivion' in 1660 pardoned men who had borne arms against Charles II and in 1690 those who had opposed William III. Suppressing memory of grievances defanged enduring resentments.[358]

French revolutionaries decreed oblivion integral to freedom; écrasez l'infâme exhorted reformers to expunge all traces of the base past. After the Terror of 1794, citizens were ordered to 'forget the misfortunes inseparable from a great revolution'.[359] Amnesia was essential to the national heritage, taught Ernest Renan in 1882. 'Every French citizen has to have forgotten the massacre of St. Bartholomew, the massacres in the 13th century Midi': only by smothering such crimes could France flourish.[360] A century later the genocidal ruptures of Vichy France had in turn to be forgotten. 'Are we going to keep open the bleeding wounds of our national discords forever?' chided President Georges Pompidou in 1972; it was time 'to forget those times when the French didn't like each other'.[361] Selective amnesia also promoted Anglo-French amity. English consent to let Napoleon's corpse be taken from St Helena for reburial in Paris would 'wipe out all traces

---

[355] Homer, Odyssey, bk. 24, ll. 535–6, 483; Nicole Loraux, The Divided City: On Memory and Forgetting in Ancient Athens (New York: Zone Books, 2001), 40–1; Andrew Wolpert, Remembering Defeat: Civil War and Civic Memory in Ancient Athens (Johns Hopkins, 2002), 29–30, 118.

[356] Bernard Cottret, 1598 L'Édit de Nantes: pour en finir avec des guerres de religion (Paris: Perrin, 1997), 363; Tzvetan Todorov, Hope and Memory (Princeton, 2003), 163; Paul Ricoeur, Memory, History, Forgetting (Chicago, 2004), 454–5.

[357] Harald Weinrich, Lethe: The Art and Critique of Forgetting (1997; Cornell, 2004), 171–2; Jörg Fisch, Krieg und Frieden im Friedensvertrag (Stuttgart: Klett-Cotta, 1979).

[358] Thomas Hobbes, Leviathan (1651), ch. 15, 7th Law of Nature, 94. Thomas Hobbes, Dialogue between a Philosopher and a Student on the Common Laws of England (1681; Chicago, 1971), 26–7, 157–8; Georges de Scudéry, Curia Politiae: or, The Apologies of Severall Princes: justifying to the world their most eminent Actions (London, 1654), 98; Sheldon S. Wolin, The Presence of the Past (Johns Hopkins, 1989), 142. See my 'Memory and oblivion', Museum Management & Curatorship 12 (1993): 171–82 at 175.

[359] Citron, Mythe national, 183; Bertrand Barer de Vieira, 'Report by the Committee of Public Safety', An II [1794], quoted in Gildea, Past in French History, 32.

[360] Renan, Qu-est-ce qu'une nation? 38.

[361] Quoted in Ronald Koven, 'National memory', Society [New Brunswick] 32:6 (Sept.–Oct. 1995): 52–8, on 52, 55; Michael Curtis, Verdict on Vichy (Weidenfeld & Nicolson, 2002), 7.

of a sorrowful past', envisaged a French worthy.[362] Of Canada's bitter Anglo-French
battles Prime Minister Wilfrid Laurier in 1900 urged that 'the memory of those conflicts
of the last century be forever forgotten'.[363]

American colonists expunged from memory Old World evils to realize the blessings
of the New. Immigrants shed noxious European traditions to embrace American novelty.
'Forget your past, your customs, and your ideals' to speed Americanization, a Jewish
immigration guidebook advised in 1890. 'We had to try to obliterate centuries' worth of
memory', an Italian-American agreed, 'in just two or three generations'.[364] President
George H. W. Bush invoked the statute of limitations against the festering wounds of
Vietnam; Americans must forget it, for 'no great nation can long afford to be sundered
by a memory'.[365]

It may be true that 'some measure of neglect and even forgetting are the necessary
condition for civic health', as Tony Judt concluded. But 'a nation has first to have
remembered something before it can begin to forget it'. The French had to remember
Vichy as it was – not as they had misremembered it; so too the Poles with the Jews, Spain
with its Civil War.[366] Yet the hoary maxim that 'to know all is to forgive all' seems no
more valid in private than public affairs. Rather, as Ivy Compton-Burnett's discreet butler
observes, 'to forgive, it is best to know as little as possible'.[367] To exorcise corrupt
memory, once-cherished keepsakes are banished. 'Out they go – the Roman coins, the
sea horse from Venice, and the Chinese fan. Down with the stuffed owl in the upstairs
hall and the statue of Hermes on the newel post! ... Dismiss whatever molests us and
challenges our purpose.' Throwing out souvenirs, 'getting rid of all the physical and
emotional blockages in your home', promises to restore one's health.[368]

Neutralizing its relics tames the past. 'By displaying what had gone before and making
an ornament of it', writes Lively, 'you destroyed its potency. Less sophisticated societies
propitiate their ancestors; this one makes a display of them and renders them harmless.'[369] We subdue an overbearing past by sequestering it. Once memorialized, it loses
power to harm the present – as with Nabokov's narrator who 'transformed everything we
saw into monuments to our still nonexistent past ... so that subsequently when the past
really existed for us, we would know how to cope with it, and not perish under its
burden'.[370]

[362] Interior minister Charles, Comte de Rémusat (12 May 1840), quoted in Ida Minerva Tarbell, *A Life of Napoleon Bonaparte* (New York, 1901), 297.
[363] Wilfrid Laurier, speech, 20 Aug. 1900, quoted in B. A. Balcom et al., '1995 – a year of commemoration', *Heritage Notes* [Louisbourg], no. 4 (Feb. 1994).
[364] Michael Kammen, 'Some patterns and meanings of memory distortion in American history', in *In the Past Lane* (Oxford, 1997), 199–212 at 202, 333; Lowenthal, *Heritage Crusade*, 157.
[365] George H. W. Bush, inaugural address, 20 Jan. 1989.
[366] 'From the house of the dead', *NYRB*, 6 Oct. 2005: 12–16.
[367] Ivy Compton-Burnett, *A Heritage and Its History* (1959; Virago, 1992), 110.
[368] Cheever, 'Lowboy', 411–12; Dawna Walter and Mark Franks, *The Life Laundry: How to De-Junk Your Life* (BBC Books, 2002).
[369] Penelope Lively, *The Road to Lichfield* (Heinemann, 1977), 178.
[370] 'The Admiralty spire' (1933), in *The Stories of Vladimir Nabokov* (Vintage, 2006), 348–57 at 352.

Satire is another way to neuter the past. An SF tale portrayed Napoleon as obsessively touchy about being short and Robin Hood as a Mafia-type lout; thus made risible they ceased to be figures of dread.[371] A cartoonist's dialogue demystifies the autobiographical past:

> 'I almost drowned yesterday, and my whole life flashed in front of me!'
> 'That must have been exciting!'
> 'Not really; I'd seen it before.'[372]

The scholar confronts the past's evils is to understand it better. 'If the Past has been an obstacle and a burden', Lord Acton advised, 'knowledge of the Past is the safest and surest emancipation'.[373] History's emancipatory role is the main burden of J. H. Plumb's 1969 *The Death of the Past*. 'Nothing has been so corruptly used as concepts of the past' in ideologies designed mainly to justify ruling elites.

[But this] old past is dying, its force weakening, and ... the historian should speed it on its way, for it was compounded of bigotry, of national vanity, of class domination ... History has burrowed like a death-watch beetle in this great fabric of the past, honeycombing the timbers and making the structure ruinous ... This critical, destructive role is still necessary, [given persisting] illusions about the past ... and historians [must] cleanse ... those deceiving visions of a purposeful past.[374]

But Plumb's vision of the enlightened historian cleansing bygone times of delusive myths and errors, plumbing the past for its hidden unsavoury secrets, threatens both inquirer and the past. Zealous curiosity is traditionally feared as a danger to the fabric of the past. Equating the search for forbidden lore with greed for hidden treasure, Christianity blamed the Fall on impious lust for knowledge. Augustine held 'lust of the eyes' the besetting sin of pagan priests, philosophers, and heretics. Worse than the desire for riches was the quest for prideful renown that bred diseased craving for arcane secrets, notably the evil arts of astrology and alchemy. Beyond knowing God, all human knowledge was sheer vanity. Not until long after Francis Bacon did unfettered curiosity cease to be a diabolical vice.[375]

Efforts to divine the future were most anathematized, but inquiries into the past, especially the pagan past, were likewise censured. Medieval treasure hunters who craved the fabled riches of antiquity found their transgressions regularly thwarted. In William of Malmesbury's tale, the magically versed Gerbert of Aurillac (Pope Sylvester II, 999–1003) seeks Octavian's treasures in subterranean Rome, near a statue inscribed 'Strike Here'. Unlike previous seekers, Gerbert hits not the statue but the spot shadowed by its pointing finger – a trope taken from St Augustine's commentary on fathoming the subtext of Holy

[371] Charles Alverson, *Time Bandits* (London: Sparrow, 1981), 28–32, 44–6.
[372] Johnny Hart, 'B.C.', *IHT*, 12 July 1979.
[373] Lord Acton, 'Inaugural lecture on the study of history' (1895), in *Lectures on Modern History* (Macmillan, 1906), 1–30 at 4.
[374] Plumb, *Death of the Past*, 16, 83, 115.
[375] Peter Harrison, *The Fall of Man and the Foundations of Science* (Cambridge, 2007), 34–45; Roger Shattuck, *Forbidden Knowledge* (St Martin's Press, 1996), 64–75, 306–8.

Figure 12 The past neutralized as display: agricultural and other bygones, Woodstock, Vermont

Scripture. Digging discloses a golden king and queen dining off golden dishes in a vast golden palace. But they are beyond reach; when Gerbert tries to touch them 'all these images . . . leap into life and rush at the offender', plunging the whole scene into darkness; Gerbert barely extricates himself. The admonitory lesson is *nihil erat quod posset tangi etsi posset videri* – 'what is unveiled is only to be understood by the eyes, and is never to be transformed into tangible riches'.[376]

To penetrate the past is perilous. Dante's infernal underground brimmed with the glories of pagan antiquity, but its denizens were damned for all eternity – the past was 'the Devil's greatest whore', in Luther's phrase. While the future was known only to God, knowledge of the past was a mystique shared by Satan and his hybrid offspring, such as Merlin, who knew all things that had been said and done.[377]

[376] William of Malmesbury, *Gesta Regum Anglorum* (1125), cited in Monika Otter, 'Functions of fiction in historical writing', in Nancy Partner, ed., *Writing Medieval History* (Hodder Arnold, 2005), 109–30 at 116–17, and quoted in David Rollo, *Glamorous Sorcery: Magic and Literacy in the High Middle Ages* (Minnesota, 2000), 16, 18.

[377] Martin Luther, 'Last sermon in Wittenberg, Romans 12:3, 17 Jan. 1546', in *Werke* (Weimar, 1914), 51: 123–34 at 126; Jennifer Hockenbery Dragseth, ed., *The Devil's Whore: Reason and Philosophy in the Lutheran Tradition* (Minneapolis: Fortress, 2011); Robert de Boron (attrib.), *Merlin and the Grail: Joseph of Arimathea, Merlin, Perceval: The Trilogy of Arthurian Romances . . .* (Cambridge: Brewer, 2001), 45–114 at 55, 92; Stephen Knight, *Merlin: Knowledge and Power through the Ages* (Cornell, 2010). See Shattuck, *Forbidden Knowledge*, 1–47.

While both divination and retrospection were forbidden, the future was 'higher', the past 'lower', with the added opprobrium of pagan artifice.[378] Malmesbury's Gerbert is a stand-in for the historian-chronicler, announcing that what is surmised of the past never existed or, still worse, that those who seek possession destroy its very reality. Adjurations never to look back, as in the dire warnings addressed to Lot's wife and to Orpheus, apply to time as well as place. Insistence on knowing his past devastates Oedipus. 'The past is seen as a separate place, ... or ambiguously undead', writes a medieval historian. 'It is untouchable, sequestered' from the observer by mechanical and magical barriers, 'and utterly irretrievable'.[379]

Yet it is ever at risk of violation. Merely examining the past can be fatal to it. In archaeological excavation 'We murder to dissect'.[380] 'The antiquarians had felled the tree that they might learn its age by counting the rings in the trunk', commented a nineteenth-century observer in Rome. 'They had destroyed, that they might interrogate.'[381] The mummified head of Ottokar II of Bohemia rapidly disintegrated when his thirteenth-century tomb, in Prague's St Vitus Cathedral, was reopened to see what could be learned from it.[382] Reminiscent of Gerbert is Herbert Winlock's account of penetrating the Meket-Rē' tomb at Thebes in 1920. Turning on his flashlight, the explorer fancied that he momentarily glimpsed the little green men coming and going in uncanny silence – who then froze, motionless, forever. 'Winlock had looked into a cavity and seen the past in motion, and stilled it with his torch'.[383] The risk is more than fanciful: 'Shine a light bright enough to see an object', a conservator warns, 'and it will fall apart before your very eyes'. Assured that 'nothing will change' when the National Trust exhibits her beloved shabby stately home, Alan Bennett's chatelaine retorts, 'the *looking* will change it. Looking always does.'[384]

The evils attributed to the past are as manifold and complex as the benefits in whose wake they often follow. Malignant compulsions and coercive injunctions offset the past's attractions; excessive devotion to it dims confidence and thwarts enterprise. To deny the past is less usual than to rejoice in it, but its demerits are nonetheless consequential. The past's virtues may distress us no less than the vices. 'It is not just bad experiences we want to protect ourselves from but good experiences as well, and for some of the same reasons', notes a reporter. 'It scares us to turn over a rock and find some worm of history we thought dead still crawling about; it scares us too, though, to find the darkened present illuminated by some flickering light from the past.'[385]

---

[378] Carlo Ginzburg, 'High and low: the theme of forbidden knowledge in the sixteenth and seventeenth centuries', *Past & Present* 73 (1976): 28–41.

[379] Otter, 'Functions of fiction', 118. See Shattuck, *Forbidden Knowledge*, 329–32.

[380] William Wordsworth, 'The tables turned' (1798), l. 28, in *Poetical Works*, 4: 57.

[381] George Stillman Hillard, *Six Months in Italy* (Boston, 1853), 4: 299.

[382] Malcolm W. Browne, 'Prague protects its medieval architecture', *IHT*, 25 Jan. 1977: 3.

[383] Herbert Winlock, 'Digger's luck' (1921), in *Models of Daily Life in Ancient Egypt* (Harvard, 1955), 9–16. Loren Eiseley, *All the Strange Hours* (1975; Nebraska, 2000), 104.

[384] Jonathan Ashley-Smith, 'Conservation and information', lecture, Art Historians' conference, London, 26 Mar. 1983; Alan Bennett, *People* (Faber & Faber, 2012), 33.

[385] 'Notes and comment', *New Yorker*, 24 Sept. 1984: 39.

Only a past seen as truly over ceases to be a threat. While still alive, Henry James's cousin Minny Temple was both beloved and menacing, once dead 'a bright flame of memory' worshipped in complete safety.[386] At the Hangchow tomb of Sung dynasty hero Yueh Fei, kneeling effigies of his betrayers were traditionally stoned by tourists; they are now protected objects of historical worth. Images of pagan gods smashed by early Christians now shelter in the Vatican Museum, no longer dangerous rivals but historical curiosa of aesthetic merit.[387] A century after Culloden, Victoria trivialized the long-gone Stuart threat as masked-ball theatre, and with Albert at Balmoral danced the Highland Fling in tartan plaids.[388] But once-dead pasts may return to intimidate the present. A Confucian temple restored in China in 1965 was burnt two years later. 'When they had confidence in historical progress ... Communists could patronize their Chinese cultural past. But if the pastness of the past was not so certain, ... and regress was the spectre, crisis ... stripped the national cultural heritage of its protective historical color.'[389]

In sum, the past 'is a time bomb, and its fuse burns brightest in the half-light of competing versions' of founding myths of national identity. We inherit the obsessions of the dead, 'assume their burdens; carry on their causes; promote their mentalities, ideologies, and ... superstitions; and often we die trying to vindicate their humiliations', writes Robert Pogue Harrison. 'Why this servitude? We have no choice. Only the dead can grant us legitimacy.'[390]

---

[386] Leon Edel, *Henry James: The Untried Years, 1843–1870* (Lippincott, 1953), 325.

[387] Frederic E. Wakeman, Jr., 'Foreword', in Joseph R. Levenson, *Revolution and Cosmopolitanism: The Western Stage and the Chinese Stages* (California, 1971), i–xxxi at xiv–xvi.

[388] Andrew Sanders, *In the Olden Time* (Yale, 2013), 212–13.

[389] Levenson, *Revolution and Cosmopolitanism*, 53–4.

[390] Alan Cowell, 'The perils of history as politics', *IHT*, 31 Jan. 2012: 2; Robert Pogue Harrison, *The Dominion of the Dead* (Chicago, 2003), x.

PART II

DISPUTING THE PAST

Wanting the past is shadowed by doubts about whether its merits outweigh its flaws. The valued attributes that distinguish the past from the present often come at a heavy cost. The next three chapters survey the disputes that perennially embroil partisans of tradition versus innovation, youth versus age. Chapter 4 discusses the rival repute of past and present in four different epochs. Chapters 5 and 6 deal with pastness in terms of life-cycle analogies, first surveying well-nigh universal preferences for the new and young, then contrarian fondness for the old, the worn, and the decayed.

4

Ancients vs. Moderns: tradition and innovation

In spite of all the direct precepts of tradition, the son advances in his own way.
Aristotle was assiduous to distinguish himself from Plato, Epicurus from Zeno ... The
work of time proceeds to the good of the race by necessary opposition.

Johann Gottfried von Herder, 1784–91[1]

When I most want to be contemporary the Past keeps pushing in, and when I long for
the Past ... the Present cannot be pushed away.   Robertson Davies, 1981[2]

Speak of the Moderns without contempt, and of the Ancients without idolatry.

Lord Chesterfield, 1748[3]

'Tradition shouldn't be the enemy of innovation'. That maxim once graced a window of
the Chemical Bank of New York. I asked the bank's archivist what it meant. 'Oh', she
said, 'the Chemical has all this history and tradition, and they're saying that it doesn't
really interfere with doing new things fast, like computing your statement in two
seconds'. Yet tradition *is* a brake on progress. We may praise the virtues of yesteryear
and the benefits of relics and roots, but we also know the old has to give way, youth must
be served, new ideas need room to develop. The past ought not constrain the present.

Stability and change are alike essential. We cannot function without a familiar past, but
risk paralysis unless we update or replace received legacies. Yet coping amid change also
demands continuity. Survival requires an inherited culture to be stable as well as malleable. Tradition is alike conservative *and* flexible.

No nation or individual is wholly original. Since all depend on what previous generations have transmitted, creative activity is never 'purely innovative but rather modifies
the heritage', observed Wilhelm von Humboldt two centuries ago.[4] 'There is all this talk
about originality, but what does it amount to?' asked Goethe. 'As soon as we are born the
world begins to influence us, and this goes on till we die.'[5] Though notoriously contemp-
tuous of tradition, Emerson admitted that even 'the originals are not original. There is
imitation, model, and suggestion, to the very archangels, if we knew their history.'[6]

[1] Johann Gottfried von Herder, *Reflections on the Philosophy of the History of Mankind* (1784–91) (Chicago, 1968), 104.
[2] Robertson Davies, *The Rebel Angels* (Penguin, 1983), 124.
[3] Lord Chesterfield, *Letters ... to His Son, Philip Stanhope, Esq.*, 22 Feb. 1748 (London, 1774), 1: 262.
[4] Wilhelm von Humboldt, *Linguistic Variability & Intellectual Development* (1836; Miami, 1971), 28.
[5] Johann Wolfgang von Goethe, to Johann Peter Eckermann, 5 Dec. 1825, in *Goethe: Conversations and Encounters* (Regnery, 1966), 138–9.
[6] Ralph Waldo Emerson, 'Quotation and originality' (1859), in *The Portable Emerson* (Viking, 1946), 284–303 at 286.

All ideas are secondhand, consciously and unconsciously drawn from a million outside sources, and daily used by the garnerer with a pride and satisfaction born of the superstition that he originated them; whereas there is not a rag of originality about them ... except in the little discoloration they get from his mental and moral caliber and his temperament.[7]

Yet heritage is at the same time always transformed. The most faithful traditionalists cannot avoid innovating, for time's erosions and additions alter all original structures, outdate all previous meanings. Living in ever new configurations of nature and culture, we must think and act *de novo* even to survive; change is as inescapable as tradition.

Negative and positive responses to the past each entail their opposites. 'By perpetuating the past, by reproducing ritualistically its external features, we are actually exposing its pastness, pointing to its anachronism', reasons Renaissance scholar Thomas Greene. 'By ostensibly ridiculing the past, by exposing its inconsequence and parodying its rhetoric, we may be revealing how we depend on it, how necessary it is to us, how little free of it we are, how we really stem from it'.[8] Although Nietzsche urged 'calling the past into court, putting it under indictment, and finally condemning it', he knew this was futile counsel, for 'it is impossible to shake off this chain'.[9]

Every achievement in science and art 'either repeats or refutes *what someone else has done*', wrote Paul Valéry, 'refines or amplifies or simplifies it, or else rebuts, overturns, destroys, and denies it, but thereby assumes it and has invisibly used it'.[10] The more we think we escape the past the greater our indebtedness; an ignored forerunner becomes a giant of the imagination who never ceases to haunt us.[11] Instancing Rousseau and Baudelaire, Paul de Man argued that 'the more radical the rejection of anything that came before, the greater the dependence on the past'.[12] Every rebellion carries the renounced past on its back; 'the rejected predecessor comes also to be seen, somehow, as a precursor'.[13]

Unwanted indebtedness is exorcized in several ways. One is to minimize the influence by correcting or completing the work of exemplars held not to have gone far enough or to have swerved off the true creative path. A second is to repress the memory of influence, detaching oneself from the precursor or disclaiming his uniqueness, denying his origin-ality. A third is openly to fight the venerated dead, purging oneself of the endowment or disowning the ancestry. In making the past seem modelled on the present, great poets often usurp their precursors' immortality. So much had the poet John Ashbery taken over his predecessor Wallace Stevens that 'when I read [Stevens's] *Le Monocle de Mon Oncle* (1918) now', Harold Bloom felt 'compelled to hear Ashbery's voice, for this mode has been captured by him, inescapably and perhaps forever'. Browning, Dickinson, Yeats,

---

[7] Jonathan Lethem, 'The ecstasy of influence' (2007), in *The Ecstasy of Influence* (Random House, 2012), 93–124 at 111.

[8] Thomas Greene, *The Light in Troy: Imitation and Discovery in Renaissance Poetry* (Yale, 1982), 195.

[9] Friedrich Nietzsche, *The Use and Abuse of History* (1874; Bobbs Merrill, 1957), 21.

[10] Paul Valéry, 'Letter about Mallarmé' (1927), in *CW* (Routledge, 1971–5), 8: 240–53 at 241.

[11] Harold Bloom, *The Anxiety of Influence* (1975; 2nd edn Oxford, 1997), 107.

[12] Paul de Man, 'Literary history and literary modernity' (1970), in *Blindness and Insight*, 2nd edn (Methuen, 1983), 142–65 at 161.

[13] Murray Krieger, *Arts on the Level* (Tennessee, 1981), 37n.

Stevens likewise 'achieve[d] a style that captures and oddly retains priority over their precursors, so that the tyranny of time almost is overturned, and one can believe, for startled moments, that they are being *imitated by their ancestors*'.[14]

As in art, so in life. Those who reject the past's authority and those who crave its return become inseparable. The conservative manifests rigid allegiance to the *status quo ante*, imbuing it with traditionalist icons to be re-enthroned in a redemptive future; but such restoration is secure only if others also submit to it. The radical modernist rebels against the oppressive authority of his childhood, yet cannot escape embedded dependence on it. He repudiates the past with fervour out of subconscious fear of its influence. Maligning the past, the reformer nevertheless harks back to a golden age that shapes his future vision. Idealizing the past, the traditionalist seeks refuge in his ennobling heritage, but remains subconsciously attracted to the new influences he affects to despise.[15]

Such ambivalence is essential to our being. Children grow up immersed in ideas and artefacts that antedate their birth, of necessity copying and emulating their elders. Yet to become adult they must throw off these crutches and make their own way, denying or surpassing parental models. Those who fail to do so remain fixated on the past and never gain maturity, as Freud observed. Instead of recalling events as past, they treat childhood memories as contemporary experience; recollection as present reality.[16]

Growing up takes ever longer. Early adulthood was inevitable and routine when survival depended on physical strength, 'the old man must move over' a common rural adage. Generational succession was the natural order. But succession became uncertain when brute strength ceased to be essential. Unwilling to give way, the old viewed the young with suspicion and fear; the young remained unsure when or even if they would gain dominance.[17] Rebellion met resistance not only from parents but from offspring who internalized their roles as devoted and obedient children. To disown parental models, as maturation was said to require, dismayed old and young alike.

Generational conflicts reflect these quandaries. Some strive to remain dutiful followers; others relinquish that role at psychic cost; still others become ardent iconoclasts. While parents are assumed to warrant our homage, growing need for autonomy impels us to spurn their authority and example. But autonomy cannot be gained by amnesia. 'A father is a man's link with the past', declared a littérateur. 'To be rid of all trace and knowledge of him is to be left "free and unencumbered" – but also without identity.' Becoming an adult, writes a psychoanalyst, 'does not mean leaving the child in us behind', but rather accepting the child within us, letting us go back from time to time.[18] Maturity does not preclude dependence.

[14] Bloom, *Anxiety of Influence*, 141–4. See Harold Bloom, *John Ashbery* (New York: Infobase, 2004), 11–12.
[15] Robert Jay Lifton, 'Individual patterns in historical change', 369–83, and Frederick Wyatt, 'In quest of change: comments on R. J. Lifton', 384–92, both in *Comparative Studies in Society & History* 6 (1964).
[16] Sigmund Freud, *Beyond the Pleasure Principle* (1920), in *CPW*, 18: 1–64 at 18.
[17] Bruno Bettelheim, 'The problem of generations', *Daedalus* 91 (1962): 68–96 at 70–6; John Demos, 'Oedipus and America', *Annual of Psychoanalysis* 6 (1978): 23–39.
[18] Tony Tanner, *City of Words: American Fiction, 1950–1970* (Jonathan Cape, 1971), 245; Hans W. Loewald, *Psychoanalysis and the History of the Individual* (Yale, 1978), 22.

Parent–child analogies repeatedly underscore the rivalry of past and present. To blindly follow the footsteps of past masters was to remain forever a child; one should challenge and finally displace them. Inherited wisdom was a source of guidance and a fount of inspiration to be assimilated and then transformed, not simply venerated and reiterated. Precursors should not be slavishly copied, but reshaped to one's own purpose: 'Even if there shall appear in you a likeness to him who, by reason of your admiration, has left a deep impress upon you', Seneca exhorted his pupils, 'I would have you resemble him as a child resembles his father, and not as a picture resembles its original.' The filial relation, the family resemblance, brought a saving *un*likeness: The son bears the paternal impress, but maturity remoulds it into his own face.[19]

Collectivities confront analogous dilemmas. Nations and communities draw sustenance from their past, yet to fulfil ongoing needs must also put it behind them. Societies like individuals imitate the ancients and pay homage to precursors, yet also innovate and create for their present selves, hence break with tradition and reject inherited patterns. Whether avowedly traditional or defiantly iconoclastic, every generation requires a modus vivendi that at once embraces and abandons precedent. And filial metaphors denote ambivalent relations with precursors in every aspect of life.

Tensions between tradition and innovation surfaced when Romans copied Greeks and fought off the implication that copying was uncreative, and Roman law codified *damnosa hereditas* – the legacy one could not afford.[20] The benefits and drawbacks of heritage have been hotly debated ever since. Harking back to Rome, Charles Babbage deemed the worth of a distinguished family name eclipsed by its demerits, like a man 'inheriting a vast estate, so deeply mortgaged that he can never hope ... to redeem it'.[21]

The conflict sharpened during the early-modern Ancients–Moderns quarrel, the former insisting antique excellence unmatchable, the latter that observation and experiment unfettered by tradition transcended antiquity's insights. The arts of the past three centuries are replete with injunctions to admire but not to imitate past examples, to honour a rich but intimidating heritage without stultifying creativity. Burdened by venerated precursors both remote and near, eighteenth-century Augustan poets gave up trying to rival them. The classics of antiquity were hard enough to come to terms with; Elizabethan and Jacobean giants, notably Milton and Spenser, still more stifling.[22] In the shadow of that matchless past, later poets grew yet more downhearted, for Romantic premises now demanded originality and self-expression. Postmodern subjectivity

---

[19] Seneca, *Ad Lucilium epistulae morales* (*c.* AD 63–65) (Heinemann, 1920), 2: 381.

[20] Gaius, *Institutes of Roman Law* (*c.* AD 160), 6.2 (Oxford, 1881), 163; Jane F. Gardner, *Family and Familia in Roman Law and Life* (Clarendon Press, 1998), 42–3; Lord Cooke of Thorndon, 'Damnosa hereditas', in Mads Andenas and Duncan Fairgrieve, eds., *Judicial Review in International Perspective*, vol. 2 (Boston: Kluwer, 2000), 237–46.

[21] Charles Babbage, *Passages from the Life of a Philosopher* (London, 1864), 2, quoting Carlo Filangieri.

[22] Walter Jackson Bate, *The Burden of the Past and the English Poet* (1971; Harvard, 1991).

and reflexivity again lengthened precursors' shadows. Bloom termed moderns 'more desperate' about the 'terrible splendor' of cultural heritage than even 'the Milton-haunted eighteenth century, or the Wordsworth-haunted nineteenth'. Those who denied all canonical authority were deluded 'sufferers of the anxieties of Shakespeare's influence'.[23]

Nineteenth-century historical awareness triggered remarkable insights into the past but left many despairingly dominated or determined by it. Countering the past's determinative force, Modernists rebelled against collective heritage, while psychoanalysts sought to return memory from the hag-ridden present to the past where it belonged. It was not to conserve the archaic past that Freud aimed to explain its psychic consequences, but to render that past safely harmless.[24]

Education and example teach us to revere past achievements and absorb their canonical virtues. But we are then forbidden to resemble these exemplars – the double bind expressed in divine injunctions to 'Be like Me', but 'Do not presume to be too like Me'.[25] Art and architecture notably bid devotees to admire but not to follow too closely what they admire.

How to benefit from the past without being swamped or corrupted by it is a universal dilemma. All legacies need to be both revered and rejected. Rivalry between tradition and innovation engages every society. Any effort to balance inherited boons and burdens betokens conflicting needs to sustain and shed the past. Failure looms either way: if we follow admired exemplars we cannot resemble them; if we deny precursors' feats we cannot match them. Groups like individuals face this dilemma in manifold modes. Some look back with gratitude, others with regret. Some can scarcely imagine being parted from past exemplars, however burdensome, and are made inconsolable by their loss. Others, dazzled and daunted, are resigned to their own inferiority. Still others aim to outdo past achievements or deny them any exemplary role.

This chapter examines four epochs of Western history: the Renaissance; early-modern England and France; Victorian Britain; and post-Revolutionary America. My aim is to explore competing stances and common ambivalences towards things old versus new. Each era reveals distinctive ways of reacting to and coping with the stress and distress of ancestral inheritance. Disparate cultural issues, time spans and sources differentiate them. Renaissance confrontations with philosophical and artistic precursors involved small coteries of humanists who reshaped prevailing scholarly and aesthetic mindsets. By contrast, North American patrimonial tension was overwhelmingly political, and arguments over the past as guardian or tyrant touched most citizens. In Victorian Britain, competing claims of tradition and innovation in manifold realms – art and architecture, religion and morals, social and material conditions, the very role of the past – engaged both elites and laity.

---

[23] Bloom, *Anxiety of Influence*, 32; preface to 2nd edn, xix.

[24] Erik H. Erikson, *Life History and the Historical Moment* (Norton, 1975), 100; H. Stuart Hughes, *Consciousness and Society: The Reorientation of European Social Thought 1890–1930* (Knopf, 1958), 33–9.

[25] Bloom, *Anxiety of Influence*, 152.

The Renaissance and the Classical heritage

No one can ever swim well who does not dare to throw away the life preserver.

Erasmus, 1528[26]

The benefits and burdens of the past first came under sustained scrutiny in the Renaissance. To be sure, the promises and perils of imitating Greek forerunners were much debated in early imperial Rome.[27] But only in the fourteenth century, with Petrarch, did the rival merits of old and new become a major concern, first in Italy, then in France and England. That concern arose out of Renaissance rediscovery of the supreme merits of classical antiquity, in profound contrast to recent 'dark ages'. Humanist insights remain vital to this day; many subsequent treatments of prized precursors are variations on Renaissance themes.

From Roman forerunners, humanists borrowed not only classical forms and precepts, but also Roman modes of extolling ancient Greece. Admiration of classical antiquity stimulated humanists' own creativity. Indeed, reverence for antiquity reflected an over-riding concern with the present. *'The ideal often lay in the past but it was still the present which guided the individual's steps'*, concludes a philosopher.

However past-directed the thinking of Renaissance man may have been in some respects, in practice he lived entirely *in and for the present*. The past was the ideal, but keeping pace with the present was the true – and dynamic – motive of action. There have been few periods of history in which men gave themselves over so unconditionally to the present as they did during the Renaissance.[28]

Present efforts might match and should strive to surpass classical attainments. Renaissance achievers were the polar opposite of medieval churchmen who insisted, with Umberto Eco's Brother Jorge, that 'there is nothing further to say ... the last word had already resounded, and no "man shall add unto these things"'.[29]

Humanist views of ancients' and moderns' relative merits are hard to gauge because the topic was a rhetorical minefield. Statements about past or present superiority were often advanced solely as debating points. Florentine chancellor Benedetto Accolti paraded his virtuosity by upholding specious modernist claims. Thus he held ancient rhetoric vitiated by the decline of Roman oratory; praised such modern military innovations as the hiring of mercenaries, the arts of trickery and deceit, the invention of cannon, and the use of armour; defended Church opulence and excused the paucity of modern martyrs: 'if there were more martyrs in antiquity, that was because there was more persecution'.[30] These arguments thinly disguised assertions of ancient superiority.

---

[26] Erasmus, *Ciceronianus* (1528) quoted in G. W. Pigman III, 'Versions of imitation in the Renaissance', *Renaissance Quarterly* 33 (1980): 1–32 at 25.

[27] Alan Wardman, *Rome's Debt to Greece* (1976; Duckworth, 2002); Gordon Williams, *Change and Decline: Roman Literature in the Early Empire* (California, 1978).

[28] Agnes Heller, *Renaissance Man* (1967; Routledge, 1978), 193–4 (emphases in original).

[29] Umberto Eco, *The Name of the Rose* (1980; Harcourt, Brace, 1983), 399–400 (see Revelation 22.18–19).

[30] Benedetto Accolti, *Dialogue on the Preeminence of Men of His Own Time* (1462–3), paraphrased in Robert Black, *Benedetto Accolti and the Florentine Renaissance* (Cambridge, 1985), 199, 201–4, 293–4. See Robert

Others damned moderns with faint praise. Many felt truly ambivalent, now comparing their own epoch favourably with antiquity, now disparaging moderns as dwarfs compared with ancient giants, new work as mere dregs next to classical nectar.

Changing viewpoints further defy generalization. After the first flush of classical rediscovery, profligate and servile worship of the ancients crippled the initiative of Petrarch's immediate successors. Petrarch himself contemned his own dark times; his followers further disparaged the present and the recent past. Obsessive love of antiquity hobbled constructive enterprise. The humanist Niccolò Niccoli (1364–1437), who spent a fortune gathering ancient manuscripts and relics, felt it futile to compete with the classics and wrote practically nothing. So many regarded the ancients as unmatchable, complained Domenico da Prato in 1420, as to paralyse creative energy.[31]

By then, however, the creative tide was turning. If the classics immobilized Petrarch's early followers, later self-confident spokesmen viewed antiquity less as irrecoverable golden age than as exemplary model, encouraging moderns to rival classical languages, literature, arts, and statecraft. The Florentine scholar-statesman Leonardo Bruni exemplifies the transition: in 1408–9 he termed his contemporaries hapless dwarfs; in 1418 he proclaimed Florence the equal of antiquity.[32] Leon Battista Alberti, earlier dismissive of modern painting, in 1428 praised Brunelleschi, Donatello, and Masaccio as equals to ancient masters. The painting of Fra Filippo Lippi, Fra Angelico, Luca della Robbia, the writing of Bruni, the sculpture of Ghiberti, the architecture of Alberti rivalled ancient Greece. Moderns should defer less to antiquity; the Florentine Alamanno Rinuccini reproached craven antiquarians who 'decry the manners of their own time, condemn its talents, belittle its men and deplore their misfortune ... to be born in this century'.[33] Machiavelli likened those who over-praised antiquity to oldsters mourning their youth. His confrere Guicciardini, even while lamenting Italy's post-Renaissance decline, agreed that 'ancient times are not *always* to be preferred to the present'.[34]

Literary formalism imitative of Cicero sapped Italian creativity in the sixteenth century, and the classics were again seen as unmatchable. The canonical virtues ascribed to antique statues repressed creativity, complained Gianfranceso Pico in 1512: any sculpture 'of recent make, even if it excels those made in ancient times, is considered inferior'. Statues supposed ancient were profusely praised, 'but as soon as it turns out that they are more recent ... we get at once a thousand Aristarchuses [severe critics] ... disapproval'. A painting reputedly by Apelles (fourth century BC) cost twice a modern Raphael or

Black, 'Benedetto Accolti', in Christopher S. Celenza and Kenneth Gouwens, eds., *Humanism and Creativity* (Brill, 2005), 61–83.

[31] Petrarch, 'Epistle to Posterity' (1351), in *Letters from Petrarch* (Indiana, 1966), 7; Hans Baron, 'The *Querelle* of the Ancients and the Moderns as a problem for Renaissance scholarship', *JHI* 20 (1959): 3–22 at 17.

[32] Hans Baron, *The Crisis of the Early Italian Renaissance* (1955; rev. edn Princeton, 1966), 282–3; Jerrold E. Siegel, '"Civic humanism" or Ciceronian rhetoric?', *Past & Present*, no. 34 (1966): 3–48.

[33] Alberti, *Della pittura* (1436), and Rinuccini, 'Dedicatory epistle' (1473), in E. H. Gombrich, 'The Renaissance conception of artistic progress and its consequences' (1952), in *Norm and Form: Studies in the Art of the Renaissance* (Phaidon, 1966), 1–10 at 1–3.

[34] Mark Salber Phillips, *Francesco Guicciardini* (Manchester, 1977), 85–6, 107–8.

Tintoretto.[35] Self-confidence vis-à-vis the past moved across the Alps. 'If our ancestors during the past hundred years due to an indolent veneration for antiquity had not dared to try anything new', France would not have its present great literature, claimed Guillaume Budé.[36]

Three perspectives on the past – distance, imitation, and revival – dominated humanist thinking. A sense of distance connected them imaginatively with admired remote precursors. Classical theories of imitation were elaborated into emulative creativity. And concepts of revival and rebirth – literally, renaissance – ennobled acts of unearthing and resurrecting. Distance, imitation, and revival were not perspectives exclusive to the Renaissance, but they then most prominently mediated between past and present.

Distance

Most crucial to humanists was the classical past's sheer antiquity. Primordial remoteness distinguished it from intervening dark ages – the recent heritage the Renaissance disowned. Indeed, proximity to the original source of excellence, Divine creation, made classical greatness akin to the work of God Himself.[37]

Remoteness enabled humanists to engage more creatively with the venerated past than had Romans with their Greek precursors. Being more than a thousand years past lightened antiquity's burden. The veil of historical distance and dark-age discontinuity made antiquity both foreign and serviceable, for the temporal gulf required its translation into modern idiom. Scholars needed to reshape the classics in order to use them, and vernacular conversion transformed them radically. Reconstituting the past to make it their own, they became creative in their own right. Had the classical world still been alive it would not have needed reviving. It became 'the object of a passionate nostalgia', in Panofsky's famed conclusion. 'The Renaissance stood weeping at [antiquity's] grave and tried to resurrect its soul.'[38] Conscious of their exemplars' distance and well 'aware of the remoteness of the world they lovingly evoked', humanists were torn between making the ancient world live again or consigning the ancient texts back to their own time and culture.[39]

Distance also let them feel superior to ancients who had in certain respects – notably religion – come too soon. Dismayed that early Romans had been deprived of Christianity,

---

[35] Pico, *De imitatione* (1512), quoted in Ernst H. Gombrich, 'The worship of ancient sculpture' (1981), in *Reflections on the History of Art* (California, 1987), 97–105 at 101; Giovan Francesco Tinti, *La nobiltà di Verona* (1592), cited in Eric Cochrane, *Historians and Historiography in the Italian Renaissance* (Chicago, 1981), 441.

[36] Guillaume Budé, *De Asse et partibus ejus* (1514), quoted in Samuel Kinser, 'Ideas of temporal change and cultural process in France, 1470–1535', in Anthony Molho and John A. Tedeschi, eds., *Renaissance Studies in Honor of Hans Baron* (Northern Illinois, 1971), 713–55 at 738–9.

[37] Giorgio Vasari, *Lives of the Most Eminent Painters, Sculptors, and Architects* (1550/1568; London, 1850), 1: 15; Erwin Panofsky, 'Renaissance – self-definition or self-deception?' in *Renaissance and Renascences in Western Art* (1960; Paladin, 1970), 36–8.

[38] Erwin Panofsky, 'Renaissance and renascences' (1944), in *Renaissance and Renascences*, 113.

[39] Aldo Schiavone, *The End of the Past: Ancient Rome and the Modern West* (1996; Harvard, 2000), 31; Peter Burke, 'The sense of anachronism from Petrarch to Poussin', in Chris Humphrey and W. M. Ormrod, eds., *Time in the Medieval World* (York Medieval Press, 2001), 157–73.

Petrarch feared lest his own classical zeal taint him with paganism's barbarous beliefs. While classical mythology was a prime fount of Renaissance art and poetry, its heathen tone and content aroused anxiety.[40] Christian faith encouraged anachronistic updating. In discussing 'the mysteries of our religion', we should not 'use words as if [we] were writing in the times of Virgil and Ovid', warned Erasmus. Yet he himself made antiquity retrospectively Christian. 'He didn't speak like Cicero?' queries Erasmus's strict tradition-alist. 'No, he spoke as he probably would speak ... if he were alive now, that is, in a Christian manner on Christian topics.'[41]

But revision raised problems. Improving on antiquity meant that present and exem-plary past were unalike, implying that change was inherent in history. It was impossible to speak or write just like Cicero, for since his time 'religion, governmental power, magistracies, commonwealth, laws, customs, pursuits, the very appearance of men – really just about everything' was radically different. As 'the entire scene of human events has been turned upside down, who today can observe decorum [speak appropriately] unless he differs greatly from Cicero?'[42]

Historical change thus authorized departures from past models. But Erasmus's insight was long ignored or rejected because it threatened to subvert two canonical uses of the past: guidance and imitation. The purpose of history was to provide exemplary parallels; the purpose of imitation was to assimilate the best of the past. Were Erasmus right, history would lose its relevance and imitation become pointless. Deeming an exemplary past essential to present conduct, humanists repressed Erasmus's insight into the past's otherness or, like his Spanish confrère Joan Luis Vivès, reduced it to triviality. To be sure, ways of living, dress, lodging, waging war, and governing had changed since classical times and were still changing, but these changes were superficial, in Vivès's normative view. What really mattered was unaltered. 'Similar changes do not ever take place in the essential nature of human beings.' Indeed, nothing of the ancients cannot be adapted to our modes of life; the forms may differ, but the use remains the same. To save history's exemplary role, past–present differences were minimized.[43]

But to identify with classical precursors risked submerging humanists' own identities. Engaging antiquity in intimate dialogue, they had to respect its alien quality, deploying its outdated idioms and inflections while remaining men of their own time. Unable to overcome the sense of distance and difference, some humanists discounted the worth of ancient experience and precept; others sought 'to make the ancient world live again, assuming its undimmed relevance and unproblematic accessibility'.[44]

---

[40] Angelo Mazzocco, 'The antiquarianism of Francesco Petrarca', *Journal of Medieval and Renaissance Studies* 7 (1977): 203–24 at 223; Giuseppe Mazzotta, *The Worlds of Petrarch* (Duke, 1993), 152.

[41] Erasmus to John Maldonatus, 30 Mar. 1527, quoted in G. W. Pigman III, 'Imitation and the Renaissance sense of the past: the reception of Erasmus' *Ciceronianus*', *Journal of Medieval and Renaissance Studies* 9 (1979): 155–77 at 160; Desiderius Erasmus, *Dialogus Ciceronianus* (1528), in *CW* (Toronto, 1999), 28: 436; István Bejczy, *Erasmus and the Middle Ages: The Historical Consciousness of a Christian Humanist* (Brill, 2001), 165–8.

[42] Pigman, 'Imitation', 158; Bejczy, *Erasmus and the Middle Ages*, 165.

[43] Joan Luis Vivès, *On Education* [*De tradendis disciplinis*] (1531; Cambridge, 1913), 232–3.

[44] Anthony T. Grafton, *Defenders of the Text* (Princeton, 1991), 26–7; Burke, 'Sense of anachronism', 162.

Both confidence and anxiety vis-à-vis remote models mounted as vernacular tongues began to replace Latin. Rather than simply copying the ancients, vernacular advocates claimed to *act* like them; just as Greek glorified Athens, so Dante's Italian exalted Florence. Earlier humanists had created little, for Greek and Latin took so much of their time and effort. Rivalling antiquity required writing in the vernacular.[45] The poet Joachim du Bellay blamed French inferiority on excessive devotion to dead languages.[46] Modern imitators in Greek and Latin missed the antique essence because the ancient languages were not their native tongues. The very scarcity of classical antecedents encouraged French writers to borrow more eclectically. Less 'defiled by the deposit of ages' than Italian humanists, they could sift with impunity and restore with originality.[47]

Vernacular usage helped humanists to domesticate change, to accept the continual alteration of tradition and to admire their own achievements. Yet in eschewing Greek and Latin they gained a freedom that was isolated and risky, for unlike the great embalmed languages the vernaculars were unstable and localized. The discontinuity was distressing in France and Britain, lacking classicizing forerunners comparable to Dante, Petrarch, and Boccaccio. 'Perceiving an independence both daunting and liberating, writers in both countries ... had to begin the task of revival at the beginning.'[48] The classics were indispensable to Tasso, Montaigne, Shakespeare, and Cervantes, but their uses of them stressed the ambiguity and questioned the authority of antiquity.[49]

In sum, felt distance freed humanists from viewing classical antiquity as an unalterable, irreproachable forerunner. Finding revision desirable, even necessary, they thought themselves potentially equal or superior to the ancients. But they also feared lest their own achievements alienate them from antiquity, leaving them marooned between reactionary worship and lonely modernity.

Imitation and emulation

Distance helped explain the venerated past; imitation furthered its admiration. Renaissance imitation of classical antiquity embraced a spectrum of meanings wider than today's pejorative usage. The word *copy*, now confined to mere reproduction and repetition, then denoted copious eloquence.[50] Imitation taught Renaissance painters, sculptors, architects, and littérateurs how to both reanimate and improve on ancient models. Reuse

---

[45] Baron, *Crisis*, 452; Angelo Mazzocco, *Linguistic Theories in Dante and the Humanists* (Brill, 1993), 108–58.
[46] Joachim du Bellay, 'The Regrets, in *Three Latin Elegies* (1558; PennPress, 2006)'; Margaret Ferguson, 'The exile's defense: Du Bellay's *La Deffence et illustration de la langue francoyse*', *PMLA* 93 (1978): 275–89 at 288 n30.
[47] Budé, *De asse*, 740.
[48] Greene, *Light in Troy*, 32.
[49] Timothy Hampton, *Writing from History* (Cornell, 1990), 299–303.
[50] E. H. Gombrich, 'The style *all'antica*: imitation and assimilation' (1961), in *Norm and Form*, 122–8; Terence Cave, *The Cornucopian Text: Problems of Writing in the French Renaissance* (Clarendon Press, 1979), 4–5, 9; Leonard Barkan, *Unearthing the Past: Archaeology and Aesthetics in the Making of Renaissance Culture* (Yale, 1999), 273–89; Zachary Sayre Schiffman, *The Birth of the Past* (Johns Hopkins, 2011), 149ff.

ranged from faithful copying to fundamental transformation, roughly what humanists termed *translatio*, *imitatio*, and *aemulatio*.

Translatio meant to follow without deviation, reproducing an enshrined text or image with total fidelity. Exhorted to dig out ancient relics and hand them down unaltered, Petrarch's disciples gathered phrases, passages, and figures from classical literature and art. Poetic models become sacred exemplars. Copies celebrated the originals, as with Rubens's loving 1629 copy of Titian's 1562 *Rape of Europa*.[51] The poet or painter shunned his own time's style and vocabulary out of reverence for past exemplars.

Eclectic variation treated the past as a stockpile to draw upon at will. Humanist writers selectively excerpted classical phrases and allusions, redeployed 'a birth of one's intellect, not something begged and borrowed from elsewhere. ... To be successful in our imitation of Cicero, the first thing must be to conceal our imitation of Cicero', advised Erasmus.[52] Eclectic imitation in painting synthesized diverse traditions, like Annibale Carracci combining Lombard-Venetian *colore* with Tuscan-Roman *disegno*, or like Rubens freely adapting precursors. Excerpting from Raphael's *Baldassare Castiglione* and Elsheimer's *Il Contento*, Rubens infused the composite with his own lifelike style.[53] But to thus depart from originals was not to try to surpass them. Zeuxis, whose painting of Helen of Troy combined the best features of five beautiful models, epitomized limited refinements on past excellence.[54]

With openly innovative imitation, the painter or poet made clear his debts to classical sources while consciously distancing them, forcing viewer or reader to notice both allusions to and departures from the past. Petrarch spelled out the rationale:

A proper imitator should take care that what he writes resembles the original without reproducing it. The resemblance should not be that of a portrait to the sitter – in that case the closer the likeness is the better – but ... of a son to his father ... With a basis of similarity there should be many dissimilarities ... Thus we may use another man's conceptions and the color of his style, but not use his words. In the first case the resemblance is hidden deep; in the second it is glaring. The first procedure makes poets, the second makes apes.[55]

A poem's resemblance to its models should never be spelled out. 'Rather, one sub-reads, patiently and intuitively, the dim, elusive presence of the model in the modern composition.' Innovative imitators 'produced buildings and statues and poems that have to be scrutinized for subterranean outlines or emergent presences or ghostly reverberations'. We penetrate the 'visual or verbal surface to make out the vestigial form below'. Knowing Virgil's *Aeneid*, Petrarch's reader would 'perceive the Rome of [his epic poem] *Africa* as an archaeological construct ... He would superimpose present decay upon

[51] Jeffrey M. Muller, 'Rubens's theory and practice of the imitation of art', *Art Bulletin* 64 (1982): 229–47 at 239; Jeffrey M. Muller, *Rubens: The Artist as Collector* (Princeton, 1989).

[52] Erasmus, *Dialogus Ciceronianus*, 368.

[53] Giovanni Battista Agucchi, *Trattato della pittura* (1607–1615), and G. P. Lomazzo, *Trattato dell'arte della pittura scoltura ed architettura* (1584), cited in Donald Posner, *Annibale Carracci* (London: Phaidon, 1971), 77–92; Muller, 'Rubens's theory and practice', 239.

[54] Cicero, *De inventione* (c. 85 BC), II, ch. 1, para. 3 (London, 1909).

[55] To Giovanni Boccaccio, 28 Oct. 1366, in *Letters from Petrarch*, 198–9; Mazzotta, *Worlds of Petrarch*, 93–4. See Kenneth Gouwens, 'Erasmus', '"Apes of Cicero"', and conceptual blending', *JHI* 71 (2010): 523–45.

past glory.' As Greene notes, 'this habit of seeking out everywhere the latent vestiges of history is shared today by every tourist, but in Petrarch's century it was a momentous acquisition'.[56]

Innovative imitation embellished continuity with change: no longer bound fast to precursors, the practitioner resuscitated *and* re-created. The confluence of ancient source with modern voice showed off the distinctive timbre of both borrowed and newly made. Attuning admired exemplars to renewed perceptions and uses did more than preserve: it rehabilitated.

Frankly dialectical *aemulatio* confronted sources expressly to improve on them. Past models however inspiring were outmoded; the emulator gloried in using the ancients and abusing them, too. Rubens manipulated originals in just this way: scuttling Mantegna's rigidity and petrified effects, he depicted famed Roman sculptures – the *Farnese Hercules, Laocoön, Apollo Belvedere, Venus de' Medici* – with an inner luminosity absent in the marbles.[57] Not concealing indebtedness to past masters, emulation challenged comparison with them. To vie with exemplars combined zeal to surpass with scorn for servility. 'Better to do without a leader', wrote Petrarch, 'than to be forced to follow a leader through everything'.[58]

Contentious striving was emulation's hallmark – not just to equal but to best antiquity, held Erasmus. 'Aflame with a desire to compete with the ancients', said a poet of his confrères, 'they delight in vanquishing them by snatching from their hand even material which has long been their peculiar possession ... and improving it'.[59] Renaissance emulators relished challenging the past. 'No brilliant minds can make substantial progress unless they have an antagonist', asserted a Ferrarese polymath. Humanists must war against 'those who wrote in the past ... otherwise we will always be speechless children; it is not only disgraceful but also dangerous ... to stick always to another's footsteps'.[60]

Humanists thus treated their legacy with mingled confidence and anxiety. But two features steadily recur. One was commitment to creativity. However much indebted to classical models, most were intent on self-expression. 'I much prefer that my style be my own ... made to the measure of my mind, like a well-cut gown, rather than to use someone else's', wrote Petrarch: 'Each of us has naturally something individual and his own in his utterance and language as in his face and gesture. It is better and more rewarding for us to develop and train this quality.' Borrowing should be eclectic; several exemplars were preferable to just one. In painting, selective imitation formed personal style; Rubens absorbed myriad ancient sculptures to make his canvases the capstone of his own peerless genre.[61]

---

[56] Greene, *Light in Troy*, 93, 90–1, citing *Aeneid* 8: 347–8.

[57] Muller, 'Rubens's theory and practice', 236, 240–2.

[58] To Boccaccio, quoted in Pigman, 'Versions of imitation', 21.

[59] Erasmus, *Dialogus Ciceronianus*, 376, 379; Marco Girolamo Vida, *De arte poetica* (1527), bk. 3, ll. 228–30 (Columbia, 1976), 101.

[60] Celio Calcagnini quoted in Pigman, 'Versions of imitation', 17–18.

[61] Petrarch to Boccaccio (1359), in *Letters from Petrarch*, 183; Muller, 'Rubens's theory and practice', 235, 243–4. The argument for eclectic borrowing derives from Quintilian's *Institutio Oratoria* (c. AD 95).

But gnawing doubt about the rectitude of innovation was also a persistent refrain. At once subservient to and rebellious against the past, emulators both proclaimed and denied the desirability of invention. While ritualized repetition strengthened reverence for the classics, improvised emulation stimulated sacrilegious revolt. In du Bellay's championship of vernacular French, advice to be original alternates with exhortation to imitate; du Bellay cannot shed his innate assumption that the first were necessarily the best. Although the modern poet's task is to cultivate a young plant (French culture) rather than to rescue one old and dying (classical Greek), only continuous transfusion from original sources keeps the plant alive. Invention is by definition reserved to first-comers.[62]

Yet there was still hope for du Bellay's French. He lessened the debt to classical precursors by pointing out that these too had borrowed – Romans from Greeks, Greeks from India, Egypt, and the East. Since they themselves were not 'primary' inventors, modern imitators might equal them. But this demanded 'good imitation', not 'passive veneration'.[63] Ancient exemplars blocked modern artists' true source of inspiration, nature itself, warned Leonardo da Vinci. A painter who imitates another's manner 'will be called a grandson and not a son of Nature'.[64]

The potent classical past still daunted. Imitation had so enriched the French language, said du Bellay, that the French *almost* equalled the Greeks (they had not yet produced an epic). But the Greek heritage also impeded poetic powers. Imitation's polarized modes – reverential copying and iconoclastic transformation – were irreconcilable. The faithful follower sought to merge with the essential spirit of the exemplary model, but lacked its genius. The emulative contender sought to improve on rather than to join the past, but in so doing corrupted, devoured, or effaced the original. Du Bellay shunned both slavish imitation, which neither captured the spirit of the past nor rivalled its excellence, and revisionist innovation, which transformed, profaned, and finally extinguished the past. His gravest attacks on antiquity reflect underlying devotion to it. The same ambivalence echoes in Montaigne, who warned that exclusive reliance on the past stifled present efforts and lamented thraldom to memory, yet also venerated antiquity, chastised fallible moderns, and upheld tradition as essential to stability.[65]

Rubens felt a similar tension between creativity and adherence to tradition. Close study of ancient sculpture was essential to the modern artist, yet also dangerous, lest admiration annihilate art.[66] Imitative practice left humanists precariously perched between self-denying submergence in the past and self-regarding assault against it.

---

[62] Joachim du Bellay, *La Deffence et illustration de la langue francoyse* (1547), bk. I, chs. 4 and 8, 83, 93 (Geneva: Droz, 2001); Ferguson, 'Exile's defense', 280–1.

[63] Du Bellay, *La Deffence*, bk. 1, ch. 10, 102.

[64] Leonardo da Vinci, *On Painting: A Lost Book ('Libro A')* (1508–15; California, 1964), 32.

[65] Ferguson, 'Exile's defense', 283–6; Rodrigo Cacho Casal, 'The memory of ruins: Quevedo's *Silva* to "Roma antigua y moderna"', *Renaissance Quarterly* 62 (2009): 1167–2003; Ricardo J. Quinones, *The Renaissance Discovery of Time* (Harvard, 1972), 234–7. See Marc Fumaroli, 'La génie de la langue française', in Pierre Nora, comp., *Les Lieux de mémoire* (Gallimard, 1984–92), III.3: 911–93.

[66] Rubens, *De imitatione statuarum* (c. 1608), cited in Arnout Balis, 'Rubens and his studio', 30–51, and Tine Meganck, 'Rubens on the human figure', 52–65, both in Joost vander Auwera, ed., *Rubens: A Genius at Work* (Tielt, Belgium: Lannoo, 2007).

Revival as creation

Self-conscious re-enactment further shaped Renaissance relations with antiquity – the past reborn, the dead resurrected. The classical heritage seemed so remote, its remnants so reduced, that retrieval required extreme efforts. Distance and decay led to doubts that re-creations could be worthy of time-misted originals. But recovery was also intensely fulfilling.

Humanists conceived the revival of antiquity as *creative* obeisance, a proof of their own talents. The rescue of ancient texts was the high road to invention. 'An "inventor" was ... a person who found something which had been lost', in Keith Thomas's phrase, 'not one who devised a new solution unknown to previous generations'.[67] Of his ancient Roman coinage, Budé boasted that 'I am the first to have undertaken to restore this aspect of antiquity'.[68] But since innovation was frowned on as impious, humanists termed their own creative contributions simply restorations of ancient wisdom. Erasmus was clearly more bent on displacing the medieval Vulgate with elegant modern Latin than retrieving any original patristic text, in any case lost in a sea of variants. Yet when charged with introducing novelties into his New Testament, he responded that 'all I do is restore the old; I put forward nothing new'. Erasmus's strategy of disguise is the obverse of today's, suggests István Bejczy. 'In our age, which sets excessive store by originality, scholars often proclaim the novelty of their stale ideas.'[69]

Retrieving antiquity took on necromantic overtones of rebirth, resuscitation, reincarnation, even resurrection. Petrarch called lost and fragmented literary remains 'ruins'; in his canzone 'Spirto gentil' the Scipios, Brutus, and Fabricius rejoice at imminent release from their tombs; Petrarch himself was lauded for 'exhuming' the Latin language.[70] Recovering ancient texts deployed explicitly archaeological terms. Just as antiquaries pieced together long-vanished imperial Rome from surviving vestiges of temples and statuary, scholars who collated remnants of classical authors 'unearthed fragments'. To conjoin such fragments was a laudable act of healing. Poggio's rediscovery in 1446 of Quintilian's complete works, previously available only in 'a mangled and mutilated state', restored him 'to his original dress and dignity, ... and to a condition of sound health'. Echoing both the reintegration of Virgil's fragmented *Aeneid* and the return of Aeneas, Poggio likened himself to Aesculapius, who remade Hippolytus and returned a dispersed people from exile. Like Lycurgus, who had stitched up the scattered work of Homer, humanists were physicians restoring lacerated heroes – the ancient exiled texts – to honourable homes.[71] In

---

[67] Keith Thomas, *Religion and the Decline of Magic* (1973; Oxford, 1997), 430.
[68] Budé, *De asse*, 740.
[69] Bejczy, *Erasmus and the Middle Ages*, 131–41, 193.
[70] Petrarch, *The Canzoniere* (1327–68), no. 53 (Indiana, 1999), 87; Greene, *Light in Troy*, 92; Mazzotta, *Worlds of Petrarch*, 20–3, 78, 120–1.
[71] Poggio Bracciolini to Guarino of Verona, in, *Petrarch's Letters to Classical Authors* (Chicago, 1910), 93; A. Bartlett Giamatti, 'Hippolytus among the exiles', in *Exile and Change in Renaissance Literature* (Yale, 1984), 12–32.

his life-work of restoring theology, Erasmus, unwell, hoped the physician Paracelsus might 'restore me also'.[72]

Digging up crumbled remains to recover lost or buried antiquities led to a further act of healing: reconstructing a building, a text, or an ethos. Resurrected relics became nutriment for new metamorphoses. Metaphors of digestion, appropriation, arrogation, making things one's own, regained the past for present and future use. The restored work of illustrious ancients enriched restorers, too. Like Hippolytus, the healing humanist reassembled himself as well, reconstituting from fragments of his own past an identity that combined consciousness at once old and new. As a block of stone ceased to belong to nature when it became the sculptor's, so creative reuse consumed textual relics in reshaping them to living purpose.[73] Petrarch 'digested' the works of Virgil, Horace, Livy, and Cicero not only to fix them in memory but to absorb them into his very marrow, refashioning ancient literature in the honey of his own creations:

Take care that the honey does not remain in you in the same state as when you gathered it; bees would have no credit unless they transformed it into something different and better. Thus if you hit upon something worthy while reading or reflecting, change it into honey by means of your style.[74]

Such resurrection demanded not simply the past's rebirth but its replacement. 'The reader must devour his models, destroying their alien substance so that they may be regenerated ... as a product of his own essential nature', a scholar sums up the humanist enterprise. 'The dead must be devoured and digested before new life can ensue.' Creativity required both exemplars and their destruction. What merely degenerated could not be regenerated; as in Mircea Eliade's cycle of replacement, the old world had to be destroyed before it could be re-created.[75]

Yet resurrecting and appropriating the past disquieted many humanists. Were they not robbers dishonouring a heritage of whose very ruins they were unworthy? The poet groping for Latin quotations was as much a pillager as the builder pilfering marble from the Pantheon. Du Bellay likened his imitative verse to the plunder of Roman antiquities. 'The contemporary mason, collecting broken statuary for the foundations of a modern palazzo', in Greene's gloss, is the poet too, Renaissance man writ postmodern. But whether he gleaned ancient stones or ancient words he would 'sow no new seed, make no new design; ... true creation is denied him'.[76]

---

[72] Erasmus to Theophrastus Paracelsus, Mar. 1527, in Johan Huizinga, *Erasmus and the Age of Reformation* (1924; Harper & Row, 1957), 242–3.

[73] Greene, *Light in Troy*, 96–9, 187; Giamatti, 'Hippolytus among the exiles', in *Exile and Change*, 23–5.

[74] Petrarch quoted in Greene, *Light in Troy*, 99; Mazzotta, *Worlds of Petrarch*, 93–4. See Jonathan Woolfson, 'The Renaissance of bees', *Renaissance Quarterly* 24 (2010): 281–300.

[75] Cave, *Cornucopian Text*; Mircea Eliade, *Myth and Reality* (Allen & Unwin, 1964), 52.

[76] Greene, *Light in Troy*, 240–1; Joachim du Bellay, *Les Antiquités de Rome* (1558; Paris: Garnier-Flammarion, 1971), sonnets 19 and 32, 266–7, 278–9. See Margaret T. McGowan, *The Vision of Rome in Late Renaissance France* (Yale, 2000), 187–93, 211–18.

Renaissance attitudes remained complex and ambivalent. Multifariously involved with their heritage, humanist expositors were often of two or more minds and increasingly differentiated by creed and country. Yet the Renaissance is uniquely defined by humanists' relationship with the reborn past. The term 'renaissance' is ours, but the awareness was theirs too; they saw themselves shaped by recognizing, revering, and reviving precursors. Needing both to admire and to transcend, they did not simply oscillate between devotion and rejection, worship and sacrilege, preservation and transformation, but kept these contrarieties in balance.

Admiring antiquity also meant execrating the medieval past. Identification with Greece and Rome went hand in hand with disowning recent precursors, rubbishing the medieval while crediting the classical with every attainment but Christianity. The humanists were not the first or the last to prefer remote to proximate ancestors – imperial Rome and Revolutionary France are familiar examples – but the Renaissance preference was neither a self-pitying nostalgia nor a rationale for revolution; it was the core of self-awareness. Reviving a distant past for its own uses, the Renaissance was the first epoch viewed by its denizens as 'modern', as distinct from both the recent dark ages it discredited and the remote golden age it idolized.

The awareness of distance, the embrace of imitation, the implications of revival left humanists uncertain about their ability or even their right to assume the burdens of a past at first shouldered with crusading zeal. For such action ultimately risked dismembering or annihilating the touchstone of their identity. Yet confidence emerged that, wonderful as past accomplishments had been, moderns could rival and should aim to surpass them. Their own time's triumphs buttressed self-assurance. 'That I was born in this age, which produced countless numbers of men who so excelled in several arts and pursuits that they may well bear comparison with the ancients', lent Rinuccini reflected glory.[77] 'Since we see in our age letters restored to life', wrote Budé, 'what prevents us from expecting to see among us new Demosthenes, Platos, Thucydides, Ciceros?'[78] Moderns would surpass ancients, claimed Vivès, exalting progress as the essence of civilization.[79]

Growing material advance; dawning pride in nationality; the felt superiority of Christianity to paganism; the replacement of Latin by creative vernaculars; a conception of history that saw in antiquity exemplary parallels yet also standards for universal aspiration; the perfecting of vigorous and self-conscious emulation; faith in the supreme value of recovering antiquity, of resurrecting a long-buried past – these traits enabled Renaissance spokesmen to turn the past to advantage, to absorb its manifest benefits without being swamped by its manifold burdens.

[77] Alamanno Rinuccini, Preface to Philostratus' *Life of Apollonius* (1473) quoted in Gombrich, 'Renaissance conception', 2.

[78] *L'institution du prince* (1519), quoted in Donald R. Kelley, *Foundations of Modern Historical Scholarship: Language, Law, and History in the French Renaissance* (Columbia, 1970), 78. See Gilbert Gadoffre, *La Revolution culturelle dans la France des Humanistes: Guillaume Budé et François 1er* (Geneva: Droz, 1997).

[79] Joan Luis Vivès, *De disciplinis* (1531), cited in Baron, '*Querelle* of the Ancients and the Moderns', 13.

From *La querelle* to the Enlightenment

> In *Words*, as *Fashions*, the same Rule will hold;
> Alike Fantastick, if *too New*, or *Old*;
> Be not the *first* by whom the *New* are try'd,
> Nor yet the *last* to lay the *Old* aside.
>
> Alexander Pope, 1711[80]

> What do we care about a dispute about the ranking of ... epochs? Whether the man who sang more beautifully, conceived nobler edifices, created with greater dignity was named *la Chapelle* or *Anacreon*, *Perrault* or *Palladio*, *Phidias* or *Girardon*, what does it matter? Johann Gottfried von Herder, 1801[81]

The past's vices and virtues became sharply polarized in the legendary Ancients–Moderns *querelle*. Ancients stressed the enduring superiority of classical antiquity; Moderns claimed that they could or already did surpass the ancients, and deplored subservience. Few subscribed wholly to the past, none sought wholly to discard it, but the so-called Battle of the Books long embroiled antagonists. Disputing whether or not Athens and Rome remained 'the supreme models and standards for every sort of endeavor' grew into a rivalry 'more self-conscious and acrimonious with every passing year'.[82]

Why was the quarrel so virulent, and how was it finally dissipated? Four related causes bred its content and fuelled polemical fury: the supposed decay of all nature; new light thrown on the past by the proliferation of printed texts; empirical scientists' rising confidence; and political upheaval that challenged the social order and classical authorities.

Decay of nature

That decay seemed a universal law of nature led many to judge everything past better than anything present. Terrestrial degradation mirrored cultural and social degeneracy. Antiquity's 'golden' past made the present seem a 'stony' or an 'iron' age.[83] Some blamed social retrogression on nature, tottering to final dissolution; others faulted impious immorality. Decay as the daughter of depravity is discussed in Chapter 5.

Widespread conviction that former times were better – 'a group inferiority complex on a gigantic scale' – was made bearable by faith in ultimate redemption. Providential decay was a stock tenet from Francis Shakelton's *A Blazing Starre* (1580) through George

---

[80] Alexander Pope, 'An essay on criticism' (1711), ll. 333–6, in *Poems* (Psychology Press, 1966), 143–68 at 154.

[81] Johann Gottfried von Herder, 'Fine arts under Louis XIV' (1801), in *On World History: An Anthology*, ed. Hans Adler (Armonk, NY: M. E. Sharpe, 1997), 54.

[82] Joseph M. Levine, *Between the Ancients and the Moderns* (Yale, 1999), viii–x.

[83] Victor Harris, *All Coherence Gone: A Study of the Seventeenth Century Controversy over Disorder and Decay in the Universe* (Chicago, 1949), 135–6; George Williamson, 'Mutability, decay, and seventeenth-century melancholy', *ELH* 2 (1935): 121–50 at 135.

Goodman's *Fall of Man* (1616) to Thomas Burnet's *Sacred Theory of the Earth* (1684). 'What can we degenerates do in this wayward age?' asked Rubens; it seemed God's will that human talents should decay along with the ageing world.[84] Bred in nature's original perfection, unscathed by senescent corruption, ancient humanity had been stronger and wiser – the heroic figures depicted by classical sculptors and Renaissance painters. Modern landscape gardeners could never equal the Garden of Eden, for although 'God in later dayes has amply improved our knowledge', His original handiwork outdid anything human.[85]

Not all discerned decay or thought it inevitable. In some optimists' view, cosmic constancy ensured human progress, and nature's promised plenitude meant moderns would surpass ancients. Advances in religion, history, mathematics, science, and art were legion. Illusions of decay and antique superiority were errors of the elderly, 'so affection-ate to antiquitie, that they ... wish againe for the pleasures of youth', charged French humanists. The '*morosity* and crooked disposition of old men, alwais complaining of the hardnesse of the present times' and given to 'excessive admiration of *Antiquitie*' reflected their own senility, wrote the cleric George Hakewill. 'Men thinke the world is changed, whereas in truth the change is in themselves'.[86]

Milton's poem 'That Nature does not suffer from old age' (*c.* 1628) typified rising rebuttals to fated decline. 'Will nature's face sag, covered with furrowed wrinkles?' Never; 'The world's prime sphere ... rolls a steady daily route', its 'perpetual course in supreme order, [and] 'blooming Phoebus [the sun] gleams with his eternal youth'.[87] Far from decaying, declared William Wotton, the world had gone on, 'from Age to Age, improv-ing'. John Evelyn agreed: 'the gardening and husbandry of the antients ... had certainly nothing approaching the elegancy of the present age'.[88] No longer theologically or empirically justified, the corruption of nature ceased to be a serious argument for past superiority. Subsequent debates over decay were restricted to supposed declines in politics and the arts. In other spheres of life belief in progress increasingly held sway.

Effects of printing

From the late 1500s, the speedy spread of printed matter bred confidence in modern accomplishments. Print multiplied precious texts without laborious transcription;

[84] Gordon L. Davies, *The Earth in Decay* (London: Macdonald, 1969), 6; Rubens, *De imitatione statuarum* (*c.* 1608), quoted in Muller, 'Rubens's theory and practice', 231.

[85] John Beale to John Evelyn, quoted in Therese O'Malley and Joachim Wolschke-Bulmahn, *John Evelyn's 'Elysium Brittanicum' and European Gardening* (Dumbarton Oaks, 1998), 13, 18, 70–1.

[86] Louis Le Roy, *De la vicissitude, ou variété des choses en l'univers* (1576), quoted, and Jean Bodin, *Methodus ad facilem historiarum cognitionem* (1566), cited in Harris, *All Coherence Gone*, 100–1, 104; George Hakewill, *An Apologie* (1627), bk. I, ch. 3, sect. 5, (3rd edn Oxford, 1635), 1: 25.

[87] John Milton, 'Naturam non pati senium' (*c.* 1627), ll. 8–9, 12–14, 36–7, in *Complete Shorter Poems* (Wiley, 2009), 230–5. See Philip C. Almond, *Adam and Eve in Seventeenth-Century Thought* (Cambridge, 1999), 208.

[88] William Wotton, *Reflections upon Ancient and Modern Learning* (London, 1694), vi; John Evelyn to William Wotton, 28 Oct. 1696, in O'Malley and Wolschke-Bulmahn, *John Evelyn's 'Elysium Brittanicum'*, 75, 116, 27.

energies released from retrieval and preservation could be applied to creative tasks. When manuscripts were transcribed by hand, copying errors multiplied with distance from the original, so for accuracy the most ancient sources were necessarily the least inaccurate. Printing abolished that scribal distinction. Widespread dissemination also now enabled scholars to check conflicting variant texts, and comparison often faulted supposedly original ancient sources. Tradition could no longer be implicitly trusted. Thus printing undermined the past's authority. 'Veneration for the wisdom of the ages' dwindled as ancients formerly thought infallible were shown prone to error and to plagiarism. The exposure of myriad forgeries deepened mistrust of scribal texts. Ancient historians came to be seen as careless and biased, their works self-serving, their times undeserving of modern esteem.[89]

Printing not only disseminated past sources and exposed past errors, it added to newly cumulative stocks of knowledge. Since each present could now build on all preceding pasts, the accumulated legacy made moderns collectively superior, even if personally puny. 'We are like dwarfs standing on the shoulders of giants', a twelfth-century scholar had written; 'thanks to them, we see farther than they'.[90] The advent of print turned dwarves into printer's devils, revealing truths hidden from antiquity. Moderns not only built on the past's accumulated knowledge but benefited from its errors. 'We are under obligations to the ancients', was Bernard Fontenelle's backhanded compliment, 'for having exhausted almost all the false theories that could be formed'.[91]

Indeed, the passage of centuries was said to make moderns true ancients. 'Ancient times [were] the world's youth; its true antiquity is the present time' was Francis Bacon's dictum.[92] Time's cumulations, wrote Blaise Pascal, made progress inevitable:

How unwarranted is the deference we yield to the philosophers of antiquity ... Those whom we call the ancients really lived in the youth of the world, and the infancy of mankind; and as we have added to their knowledge the experience of the succeeding centuries, it is in ourselves that can be found the antiquity we revere in them.[93]

Inverting antiquity and modernity became a common trope for demoting the past. 'I honour antiquity, but that which is commonly called old time is young time', wrote Hobbes. 'By the longevity of their labours', said the poet Edward Young, moderns no longer subservient to the past 'might, one day became antients themselves'.[94]

---

[89] Elizabeth L. Eisenstein, *The Printing Press as an Agent of Change* (Cambridge, 1979; 3rd edn 1991), 289–90, 122; Arnaldo D. Momigliano, 'Ancient history and the antiquarian' (1950), in *Studies in Historiography* (Weidenfeld & Nicolson, 1966), 1–39 at 10–18.

[90] Peter of Blois to Reginald, Bishop of Bath, *Epistolae* 92 (1180), quoted in Robert Merton, *On the Shoulders of Giants* (Harcourt Brace Jovanovich, 1965), 216–17.

[91] Bernard Fontenelle, 'Digression sur les anciens et les modernes' (1688), in *Entretiens sur la pluralité des mondes & Digression* ... (Clarendon Press, 1955), 161–76 at 165.

[92] Francis Bacon, *The New Organon* (1620), I, Aphorism lxxxiv (Cambridge, 2000), 66; Francis Bacon, *The Advancement of Learning, Book I* (1605; Clarendon Press, 1885), 36.

[93] 'Fragment d'un traité du vide' (1651), in *Pensées de Pascal* (Paris, 1881), 2: 266–77 at 271.

[94] 'The answer of Mr. Hobbes to Sir William Davenant's preface before Gondibert' (1650), in *The English Works of Thomas Hobbes* (London, 1839–45), 4: 441–58 at 456; Edward Young, *Conjectures on Original Composition*, 2nd edn (1759; Manchester, 1918), 31–2.

As print weakened the past, its authoritative residues became less acceptable. Bygone models became millstones, each generation's legacy ever more burdensome: sheer accumulation inhibited efforts to rival precursors. 'The acquisition of knowledge occupies time that might be bestowed on invention', held the philosopher Adam Ferguson; prior occupation of 'every path of ingenuity' stymied new enterprise. 'We become students and admirers, instead of rivals; and substitute the knowledge of books, instead of the inquisitive or animated spirit in which they were written'.[95] Thus the past's too-durable literary store now undermined the confidence initially quickened by the printed word. Early-modern anxiety about excessive numbers of books heralds today's angst over Internet glut.[96] Facing predecessors' cumulative feats, Moderns had to confess their own inferiority or else reject the past entirely. This dilemma became a consuming post-Enlightenment poetic concern.

The new science

What most polarized the Ancients–Moderns conflict was the advent of a scientific spirit of inquiry. Sensory perception became revelation; current observations and experiments supplemented, corrected, even supplanted received wisdom. The physicist William Gilbert dedicated his *De magnete* (1600) to those 'who look for knowledge not only in books but in things themselves'. Indeed, why 'subject ourselves to the authority of the Ancients', added one such searcher, 'when our own experience can inform us better?'[97] Columbus had shown antiquity ignorant of geography, and Magellan's 1519–22 circumnavigation outdid all the ancients. Recent discoveries made clear that much was yet to be found. The ancients had known little of nature's principles. The past faithfully guided politics, philosophy, art, and law, where motives and means remained much the same, but in science and technology, declared Bacon, 'what has been done is not important. What is necessary is to see what can still be done.'[98] Scientific knowledge was present- and future-oriented.

Obeisance to precedent discredited discovery and discouraged invention. 'Too great Reverence borne to *Antiquity* is an error extremely prejudicial to the advancement of Science', wrote physician Noah Biggs, 'as if our Ancestours resting places, were to be like the *Hercules* pillars, inscrib'd with a *Ne Plus Ultra*'.[99] Bacon conceded the ancients great powers of abstract thought, but deplored their habit of generalizing from scant evidence. New discoveries must be sought from 'the light of nature', not fetched back out of 'the shadows of antiquity'. Neither Bacon nor his followers repudiated the past altogether.

---

[95] Adam Ferguson, *Essay on the History of Civil Society* (1767; Edinburgh, 1968), 217.

[96] Daniel Rosenberg, 'Early modern information overload', *JHI* 64 (2003): 1–9.

[97] William Gilbert, *On the Lodestone and Magnetic Bodies, and on the Great Magnet the Earth* (1600; New York, 1893), xlix; Jeremy Shakerly, *Anatomy of Urania Practica* (1649), quoted in Richard Foster Jones, *Ancients and Moderns*, 2nd edn (California, 1965), 123. See Ingrid D. Rowland, *The Culture of the High Renaissance: Ancients and Moderns in Sixteenth-Century Rome* (Cambridge, 1998).

[98] Quoted in Schiavone, *End of the Past*, 209–10. See Paolo Rossi, *The Birth of Modern Science and the Making of Europe* (Wiley-Blackwell, 2001), 41–3, 222.

[99] Noah Biggs, *Mataeotechnia medicinae praxeos* (1651), quoted in Jones, *Ancients and Moderns*, 132.

They depended on manifold previous observations as well as new instruments that magnified observations. To praise exclusively either the old or the new was self-defeating. 'Antiquity envies new improvements, and novelty is not content to add without defacing', warned Bacon against both extremes.[100]

By the late seventeenth century, however, reactionary response goaded some to reject certain classical tenets outright. Accused of forsaking time-hallowed verities for self-serving novelties, scientists retorted that they found in nature a previous higher truth; in dismissing bygone authorities they were discarding corrupt copies for true originals.[101] Nature's primordial antiquity became a stock defence against charges of sacrilege. When theologians condemned findings of Baltic shoreline change as contrary to Genesis, scientists replied that 'God had made both the Baltic and Genesis ... if there was any contradiction between the two works, the error must lie in the copies that we have of the book rather than in the Baltic Sea, of which we have the original'.[102]

Scientists were not alone in complaining that classical traditionalism hampered present-day needs. Growing vernacular literacy made Greek and Latin increasingly irrelevant. Inspirational when first rediscovered, magisterial classics began to dim into commonplace familiarity. Classical learning was enervating where veneration was com-pulsory, as with an Oxford statute that fined those 'who did not follow Aristotle faithfully ... five shillings for every point of divergence'.[103] Critics of the 'stupendous bulk of blinde learning' and 'shreds of *Latine*' accused scholars of perpetuating old errors to suppress new truths. 'Looking back, and prescribing Rules to ourselves from Antiquity, retards and lessens even our Appetite', charged the historian Clarendon. There was no worse 'Obstruction to the Investigation of Truth, or the Improvement of Knowledge, than ... to admire too much those who have gone before, and like Sheep to tread in their Steps'.[104]

Classicists in retort arraigned arrogant scientists for leaving 'the old beaten and known path, to find out wayes unknown, crooked and unpassable'. The old learning was an indispensable moral safeguard; science's contempt for antiquity might destroy religion, corrupt education, and brutalize society. To deny homage to the ancients was ungodly and seditious.[105] It was also disastrously hubristic, charged Giambattista Vico. Bacon's enthronement of scientific rationality masked unholy lust for power, a drive to conquer nature that ignored human fallibility. Those 'for whom the wisdom of the ages is inadequate, who in their pursuit of novelties enshrine the present, [and] hold that the

---

[100] Bacon, *New Organon*, Aphorism cxxii, cxxv, 94; Bacon, *Advancement of Learning*, 35.
[101] Thomas Sprat, *History of the Royal Society* (1667; St Louis: Washington University Studies, 1959), 371; Jones, *Ancients and Moderns*, 184–201, 237–40.
[102] Paul Philippe Gudin, *Aux mânes de Louis XV* (1777), quoted in Louis Ducros, *Les Encyclopédistes* (Paris, 1900; 1967), 123.
[103] James Lewis McIntyre, *Giordano Bruno* (Macmillan, 1903), 21.
[104] Biggs, *Mateotechnia*, and Francis Osborne, *Miscellany of Sundry Essayes* (1659), quoted in Jones, *Ancients and Moderns*, 100, 146; Edward Hyde, Earl of Clarendon, *Of the Reverence Due to Antiquity* (1670), in *A Collection of Several Tracts of ... Clarendon* (London, 1727), 218–40 at 218, 239.
[105] Alexander Ross, *Arcana microcosmi* (1652), quoted, and Meric Casaubon and Henry Stubbe cited, in Jones, *Ancients and Moderns*, 122, 241–62.

moderns are better than the ancients' seemed to Vico to 'mistake their own symbolic constructions ... for objective truths of nature'.[106]

The ultimate accolades to ancient learning were the baron de Longepierre's *Discours sur les anciens* (1687) (against Perrault), William Temple's *Essay on Ancient and Modern Learning* (1690) (against Fontenelle), and Jonathan Swift's 'Battle of the Books'. Since the ancients had 'perfected' all genres, wrote Longepierre, modern mastery required following exactly in their footsteps. Aesthetic canons were timeless. 'All people with good taste from all preceding ages have always felt the way we do.' Romans had admired Greeks, 'just as our fathers admired all of them, and just as we admire them ourselves'.[107] For Temple ancients in every way outshone moderns, who merely reflected received light. Swift assailed modern genius as egotistical folly. He likened the scientist to a spider, skilled in architecture and mathematics but spinning a poisonous web out of its own entrails. Swift's bees (Ancients) by contrast garnered from every good source, their honey and wax lending humanity sweetness and light.[108] But unlike the bees of Renaissance emulative practice, Swift's bees did not digest and transform what they ingested; they merely regurgitated it. For them the ancients' honey was no longer nutritious.

Science vs. Art

By 1700 few avid partisans remained on either side; most struck a balance between the triumphs and failings of past and present. 'Men are subject to errors', wrote Algernon Sidney, 'and it is the work of the best and wisest to discover and amend such as their ancestors may have committed', or to perfect their inventions.[109] Clarendon revered the ancient Church Fathers 'as great Lights which appeared in very dark Times; we admire their Learning and their Piety, and wonder how they arrived to either in Times of so much Barbarity and Ignorance. [But] the best way to preserve the Reverence that is due to Age', thought this Enlightenment precursor, was 'hoping and believing that the next Age may know more, and be better'.[110]

The eighteenth century left ancients and moderns opposed on principle but in practice dividing the honours. Science was seen as cumulative, a collective enterprise ceaselessly adding knowledge. Artistic endeavour was not additive; its merits came from individual effort alone. Goethe epitomized the difference: he made scientific but no poetic claims, for 'poets more excellent lived before me, but ... in the difficult science of colors ... I have a consciousness of superiority'.[111] For the modern poet or painter, architect, or composer, past achievements were as much burden as boon, precious but peerless

---

[106] Giambattista Vico, *On the Study Methods of Our Time* (1709), and *The New Science*, (1725), parsed in Giuseppe Mazzotta, *The New Map of the World: The Poetic Philosophy of Giambattista Vico* (Princeton, 1999), 56–7, 211.

[107] Joan DeJean, *Ancients against Moderns* (Chicago, 1997), 47–9.

[108] Sir William Temple, *Essays on Ancient and Modern Learning* (1690; Clarendon Press, 1909), 18; Jonathan Swift, 'The battle of the books' (1698), in *A Tale of the Tub and Other Satires* (Dent, 1975), 37–65.

[109] Algernon Sidney, *Discourses Concerning Government*, ch. 3, sect. 25 (1698; London, 1751), 364.

[110] Clarendon, *Of the Reverence Due to Antiquity*, 237, 224, 220.

[111] To Eckermann, 18 Feb. 1829, in *Conversations of Goethe with Eckermann and Soret* (London, 1871), 302.

creations. It seemed in the nature of science that moderns should win the day, and in the nature of the arts that they should lose.[112]

The distinction spurred scientific but deterred artistic effort. Acclaiming the progressive genius of science, Wotton attributed recent advances to enhanced observation made possible by the compass, navigation, and map-making. Far more was now known about landforms, stones, and minerals than in Pliny's day, for 'the Ancients were not sufficiently aware of the Treasures which the Earth contains within it. The Ancients did I say? hardly any of the Moderns, till within these last Thirty Years.'[113] The poet William Collins called poetry a retrograde exception to advances elsewhere:

> Each rising art by just gradation moves,
> Toil builds on toil, and age on age improves:
> The Muse alone unequal dealt her rage,
> And graced with noblest pomp her earliest stage.[114]

Joseph Priestley drew an analogous distinction: since science knew no bounds, Newton's outstanding genius had not discouraged but inspired further discoveries. But to artistic advance there were strict limits; past attainments precluded new prospects.[115]

Some arts seemed more progressive than others. If contemporary French epic, oratory, elegy, and satire fell short of the Augustan classics, as Charles Perrault averred, Nicolas Boileau claimed his own age the greatest for tragedy, philosophy, and lyric poetry.[116] Dryden's 'Eugenius' adores the Greeks and Romans but asserts that 'we equal the Ancients in most kinds of Poesie, and in some surpass them'.[117] Reliance on antiquity was most problematic in architecture, since archaeological inquiry revealed disturbing imperfections in classical and Palladian exemplars. Christopher Wren stressed authoritative classical perfection in architecture as in literature. But Wren's successors Hawksmoor and Vanbrugh shed many past shackles in their Baroque innovations.[118]

As science shook off the past, dependence on it more and more oppressed the arts. Eighteenth-century authors had to cope not only with classical precursors but with the closer eminence of Montaigne and Rabelais, Spenser and Milton. 'The virtues of their immediate predecessors' crippled the reigns of kingly successors, remarked Samuel

---

[112] Paul O. Kristeller, 'The modern system of the arts: a study in the history of aesthetics', *JHI* [I] 12 (1951): 496–527, [II] 13 (1952): 17–46; John D. Scheffer, 'The idea of decline in literature and the fine arts in eighteenth-century England', *Modern Philology* 34:2 (1936–7): 156–78; Joseph M. Levine, *The Battle of the Books* (Cornell, 1991); Marc Fumaroli, 'Les abeilles et les araignées', in Anne-Marie Lecoq, ed., *La Querelle des Anciens et des Modernes xviième–xviiième siècles* (Paris: Gallimard, 2001), 7–218; Ann Blair, 'Disciplinary distinctions before the "two cultures"', *The European Legacy* 13:5 (2008): 577–88.

[113] Wotton, *Reflections upon Ancient and Modern Learning*, 264–5; Joseph M. Levine, 'Natural history and the history of the scientific revolution' (1983), in *Re-enacting the Past* (Ashgate, 2004), 57–73 at 67.

[114] Collins, 'Epistle addressed to Sir Thomas Hanmer, on his edition of Shakespeare's Works' (1744), in *The Poems of Thomas Gray, William Collins, Oliver Goldsmith* (Longmans, Green, 1969), 389–400 at 391.

[115] Joseph Priestley, *Lectures on History, and General Policy* (Birmingham, 1788), 382.

[116] To Charles Perrault (1693), cited in Gilbert Highet, *The Classical Tradition* (Clarendon Press, 1949), 281.

[117] *Of Dramatick Poesie* (1668), in *The Works of John Dryden* (California, 1956–79), 17: 8.

[118] Joseph M. Levine, 'Christopher Wren and the quarrel between the Ancients and the Moderns', in *Between the Ancients and the Moderns*, 161–208 at 161–81.

Johnson, and 'he that succeeds a celebrated writer has the same difficulties to encounter'.[119] Recent glory 'extinguishes emulation, and sinks the ardour of the generous youth',
in Hume's phrase; a neophyte faced with countless models of eloquence 'naturally
compares his own juvenile exercises with these; and, ... is discouraged from any farther
attempts' to equal them. Yet to quell undue reverence rivalry was essential.[120]

Few felt the dilemma as keenly as Goethe. Towering figures – Raphael, Mozart,
Shakespeare – 'were so alluring that everyone emulates them and yet so great that no
one can equal them'.[121] So pernicious was their fame that no talented artist should keep
past exemplars at hand, advised Vico; those 'endowed with surpassing genius, should put
the masterpieces of their art out of their sight'.[122]

The very recognition of previous excellence condemned painters and poets to inferiority; past glory left them no role beyond imitation. 'Impossible', was the repeated lament.
'Nature being still the same', concluded the editor Richard Steele, 'it is impossible for any
modern writer to paint her otherwise than the ancients have done';[123] originality was
inconceivable. 'It is impossible for us, who live in the latter Ages of the World', wrote
Joseph Addison, 'to make Observations ... which have not been touched on by others'.[124]
Great precursors 'engross our attention, ... prejudice our judgment in favour of their
abilities, and so lessen the sense of our own', grieved the poet Edward Young. They
'intimidate us with the splendor of their renown, and thus under diffidence bury our
strength'.[125] Previous perfection inhibited modern sculptors, wrote the Scottish judge
Robert Cullen. 'Conscious of being unable to surpass the great models which he sees, the
artist is discouraged from making attempts. The posts of honour are already occupied;
superior praise and glory are not to be reached; and the ardour of the artist is checked by
perceiving that he cannot exceed' or perhaps even equal his predecessors.[126] Brooding at
the foot of a classical colossus, Fuseli's painter (Fig. 27) epitomized the artist at once
inspired and crushed by grandeur past.[127]

Even Enlightenment philosophes excluded the arts from the general march of progress.
'Almost all is imitation' held Voltaire. 'It is with books as with the fires in our grates;
everybody borrows a light from his neighbour to kindle his own.' Condillac believed

[119] The Rambler, no. 86, 12 Jan. 1751, in The Works of Samuel Johnson (Troy, NY, 1903), 4: 187–94 at 187.
[120] David Hume, 'Of the rise and progress of the arts and sciences' (1742), in The Philosophical Works
       (Aalen: Scientia, 1964), 3: 174–97 at 196. Hume blamed foreign imports: 'So many models of ITALIAN
       painting brought into ENGLAND, instead of exciting our artists, is the cause of their small progress.'
[121] Goethe to Eckermann, 6 Dec. 1829, in Goethe: Conversations and Encounters, 208.
[122] Vico, On the Study Methods of Our Time, 72.
[123] Richard Steele, 'On criticism, and the artifices of censorious critics', Guardian, no. 12, 25 Mar. 1713 (1814),
       60–4 at 62.
[124] Joseph Addison, 'On detraction among bad poets', Spectator no. 253, 20 Dec. 1711: 9. 'We fall short at
       present of the Ancients in ... all the noble Arts and Sciences which depend more upon Genius than
       Experience, but exceed them ... in Doggerel, ... Burlesque, and all the trivial Arts of Ridicule' ('Laughter
       and ridicule', Spectator no. 249, 15 Dec. 1711).
[125] Young, Conjectures on Original Composition, 9.
[126] Robert Cullen, 'On sculpture: causes of the superiority of the ancient over the modern', The Lounger
       [Edinburgh], no. 73, 24 June 1786 (London, 1804): 34–41 at 38.
[127] Henry Fuseli, The Artist in Despair before the Grandeur of Ancient Ruins (1778–9). See Jonah Siegel, Desire
       and Excess: The Nineteenth-Century Culture of Art (Princeton, 2000), 28–30.

imaginative decline made artistic exhaustion inevitable.[128] Precursors' superiority was bound to cripple successors. 'Michael Angelo, Raphael, Titian &c. are lofty oaks that keep down young plants in their neighbourhood, and intercept from them the sunshine of emulation.' Artistic like moral decline seemed a consequence of general *advance* in knowledge and civilization, impoverished imagination the sad price of scientific progress.[129] Material improvement deprived poets and painters of passion. Moreover, the atrophied creative impulse was censured as unseemly. Moderns 'invent new methods to please a capricious taste ... and turn aside from the beautiful simplicity of nature'.[130] The perfidious appeal of complexity and novelty Kames held a major cause of artistic decline. Since the modest despaired of attaining fame, only the conceited or the desperate would aim to improve on the past.[131]

How did the *querelle* shift allegiances between past and present? When Enlightenment scholars 'dropped the cult of antiquity', historians Paul Hazard and J. H. Plumb praised the liberating effects. Devotees of progress 'turned their backs on the past [as] inherently and inveterately deceptive' and untrustworthy. Thanks to the new science, 'the past, with all its mighty dead, was set at nought'.[132]

Philosophes were glad to be rid of the infamous past. Only those ignorant of history could regret the bad old days; no past had been as good as the present. 'What educated man would really wish he had lived in the barbarous and poetical time which Homer paints? ... Who regrets that he was not born at Sparta among those pretended heroes who ... practised theft, and gloried in the murder of a Helot; or at Carthage, the scene of human sacrifices, or at Rome ... under the rule of a Nero or a Caligula?' The sumptuous splendours of ancient empires had made their subjects neither wise nor happy. Scholars now scrutinized antiquity to find fault with it and laud modern progress.[133]

'The Past abandoned; the Present enthroned in its place!' was, however, by no means the universal temper.[134] New confidence in progress did not banish older doubts; many clung to a variety of pasts. John Locke judged the *querelle* prejudiced on both sides. To attribute 'all knowledge to the ancients alone, or to the moderns' was

---

[128] Voltaire, 'Prior, Butler, and Swift', in *A Philosophical Dictionary* (1764; London, 1824), 5: 322–3; Étienne Bonnot de Condillac, *Essay on the Origin of Human Knowledge* (1746), cited in Harold Mah, *Enlightenment Phantasies* (Cornell, 2004), 58. See Bate, *Burden of the Past*, 46.

[129] Kames, *Sketches of the History of Man*, 1: 300; Frank E. Manuel, *Shapes of Philosophical History* (Stanford, 1965), 67–8.

[130] James Marriott (1755) cited in Scheffer, 'Idea of decline', 162; Voltaire, 'An essay on taste' (1755), in Charles Harrison and Paul Wood, comps., *Art in Theory, 1648–1815* (Wiley-Blackwell, 2000), 531–2.

[131] Kames, *Sketches of the History of Man*, 1: 281–2, 296–7; Oliver Goldsmith, *Enquiry into the Present State of Polite Learning in Europe* (1759), in *CW* (Clarendon Press, 1966), 1: 243–341 at 260.

[132] Paul Hazard, *The European Mind* (1935; Yale, 1953), 29–30; Plumb, *Death of the Past*.

[133] François Jean de Chastellux, *An Essay on Public Happiness* (London, 1772); André Morellet, *Réflexions sur les avantages d'écrire et d'imprimer sur les matières d'administration* (1764), quoted in J. B. Bury, *The Idea of Progress* (1920; Dover, 1955), 192–3; Constantin-François, Comte de Volney, *The Ruins: or, A Survey of the Revolutions of Empire* (1789; 5th edn London, 1807), 49–61. See Carl L. Becker, *The Heavenly City of the Eighteenth-Century Philosophers* (Yale, 1932), 118; Dorothy Medlin, 'André Morellet and the idea of progress', *Studies on Voltaire and the Eighteenth Century*, no. 189 (1980): 239–46; Rosemary Sweet, *Antiquaries: The Discovery of the Past in Eighteenth-Century Britain* (Hambledon and London, 2004), 3.

[134] Hazard, *European Mind*, 30.

'fantastical'; one should 'get what helps he can from either'.[135] Antagonists agreed
more than they often admitted. Many intoxicated by visions of progress nonetheless
embraced the cultural legacy as an exemplary spur to future advance. Statues of
revered ancients in the Louvre would inspire viewers, and thus 'produce more Great
Men who will equal and perhaps surpass them'.[136] The ancients had shown what
poetry must *be*, declared Friedrich Schlegel; moderns taught what it should *become*.[137]
Improvement suffused not only science but, in some eyes, art as well. 'We look back on
the savage condition of our ancestors with the triumph of superiority [over] the feeble
efforts of remote ages', boasted an English panegyrist, and 'are pleased to mark the
steps by which we have been raised from rudeness to elegance'.[138]

The legacy of the *querelle* was truly an amalgam: confidence in science and material
progress, emulative traditionalism in the arts, ambivalence about the general uses of the
past. Contentious early issues – the prevalence of decay, the urge to unshackle science
from classical precedents, the role of vernacular tongues – were resolved or shelved; but
the *querelle*'s very vehemence generated new issues, setting past against present as
implacable rivals in both personal and national affairs.

Cumulative progress became the hallmark of scientific knowledge; but in the arts great
precursors inhibited prowess: novelty spelt not advance but decline. Spokesmen in both
realms acknowledged the power of the past for either good or evil, but science and
technology faced up to and overcame the past, whereas in the arts antiquity inspired but
also haunted inferior moderns. To follow precursors had been a creative option in the
Renaissance, but in the Enlightenment it betokened subservience. Imitation became
incompatible with innovation. Revolutionary and Romantic iconoclasm would openly
challenge the tyranny of the past.

Future horizons had previously been bounded by assumptions that nothing new could
arise and by the imminence of the Last Judgement. Secular science opened unlimited new
prospects, unpredictable in detail but predictably progressive, even divinely ordained, in
general. As a historian summed up the new mood, 'the future would be different from the
past, and better, to boot'.[139]

Victorian Britain

> The new things are based and supported on sturdy old things, and derive a massive
> strength from their deep and immemorial foundations, though with such limitations
> and impediments as only an Englishman could endure. But he likes to feel the weight
> of all the past upon his back; and, moreover, the antiquity that overburdens him has
> taken root in his being, and has grown to be rather a hump than a pack, so that there
> is no getting rid of it without tearing his whole structure to pieces . . . As he appears to

---

[135] John Locke, *The Conduct of the Understanding* (1706; London, 1825), 47–8.
[136] Maille Dussausoy, *Le citoyen désintéressé, ou diverse idées patriotiques* (1767), quoted in David A. Bell, *The Cult of the Nation in France* (Harvard, 2001), 116.
[137] Friedrich Schlegel, *On the Study of Greek Poetry* (1797; SUNY Press, 2001).
[138] Thomas Warton, *History of English Poetry*, vol. 1 (London, 1774).
[139] Reinhard Koselleck, *Futures Past: On the Semantics of Historical Time* (1979; Columbia, 2004), 267.

be sufficiently comfortable under the mouldy accretion, he had better stumble on with
it as long as he can.   Nathaniel Hawthorne, 1862[140]

Unprecedented change radically sundered the present from even the recent past in
nineteenth-century Europe and North America. Consciousness of that change magnified
both the virtues and vices of a heritage better known but more remote than ever before.
And revolutionary upheaval at both ends of the century unleashed iconoclastic rage that
aimed to render the past impotent if not wholly to efface it, but at the same time evoked
nostalgic longing for ways of life forever lost.

Innovation and retrospection

Ambivalence towards a past transcended and discarded, yet passionately yearned for, was
paramount in Victorian Britain. No people since the Renaissance combined such confidence in their own powers with antiquarian retrospection. But nineteenth-century Britain
was not fifteenth-century Italy. Echoes of humanist ambivalence still resonated, but
fundamental changes in material life, in modes of government, and in conceptions of
nature and history – Victorians saw the Renaissance as part of their own past – made for
tensions of a wholly different order.

Britain after 1815 (the defeat of Napoleon marked a more momentous divide than the
1837 accession of Victoria) left the political and material past behind, but clung to its
aesthetic and spiritual vestiges. After the French Revolution it seemed that nothing would
ever again be the same. Whether seen as the deserved downfall of a corrupt and frivolous
ruling class or as a demonic blood-bath under mob rule, the Revolution replaced the fall
of the Roman Empire as history's sternest moral lesson. The destruction of tradition
reverberated in later Continental uprisings: 1830, 1848, 1871. And the Hyde Park riots of
1866 seemed a harbinger of anarchy at home. Political flux threatened all past
authority.[141]

Yet evident material and social improvement led many to think their age a pinnacle of
progress. Reform movements of the 1820s and 1830s highlighted discontents analogous
to those across the Channel. Utilitarians and philanthropists condemned tradition,
precedent, prescriptive right, ancient privilege. But assaults against customary ways
provoked regressive defence of past tradition in medievalist fancies of the 1830s and
1840s.

Industrialization further spurred looking back. Manufacturing after Waterloo transformed British lives and landscapes almost beyond recognition – for many, beyond
redemption. Revulsion against industry was intense, notwithstanding or owing to the
immense wealth it created. Romantics and reactionaries blamed the brutal machinery of
change for mean and rootless modernity. Outworn pre-industrial relics were reverently

---

[140] Nathaniel Hawthorne, 'About Warwick' (1862), in *Works* 5: 65–89 at 70.
[141] Matthew Arnold, *Culture & Anarchy* (1869; Macmillan, 1938), 50–7, 171–4, 214–18; Walter E. Houghton,
Jr., *The Victorian Frame of Mind, 1830–1870* (Yale, 1957), 54–8; John D. Rosenberg, *Elegy for an Age: The
Presence of the Past in Victorian Literature* (London: Anthem, 2005).

cherished. Censure of the soulless, ugly, degrading present echoed into the twentieth century, for industrial and urban expansion made the six decades after 1840 as disorienting as the six decades before. Turn-of-the-century guides to go-ahead Manchester, Leeds, and Birmingham dwelt lovingly on their ancient origins, all but ignoring their modern growth. Anachronistic festivities – royal rituals, folkloristic pageants – became ever more popular.[142]

No other Old World society so embraced innovation or saw its surroundings so thoroughly altered. Nor did any view their past with such congratulatory gravitas or so earnestly reanimate it. Scott's historical novels, Gothic Revival architecture, neo-chivalric fashions in dress and deportment, pseudo-classical canons of beauty, successive passions for all things Roman, Greek, Egyptian, Chinese, early English – betokened a people besotted with almost any past. Too many of John Stuart Mill's countrymen, he quipped, 'carry their eyes in the back of their heads and can see no other portion of the destined track of humanity than that which it has already travelled'. Immersed in their fast-progressing world, they hankered after bygone backwardness.[143]

Medievalism and neoclassicism

The backward past paraded Old England's shared and ordered ways as an antidote to the tawdry, bustling present. Victorians found it 'salutary and refreshing to be taken back to men and times with whom we have so little in common'.[144] They now wished for, and consequently found, more in common. An Arthurian cult that peaked with Tennyson's 'Lady of Shalott' (1832) and *Idylls of the King* (1859) glorified a chivalric code of ethics and Pre-Raphaelite romanticism.[145] 'We *are* medievalists and rejoice in the name, wishing to do our work in the same simple but strong spirit which made the man of the thirteenth century so noble a creature', wrote the architect George Edmund Street.[146] Gothic Revival architect A. W. N. Pugin paired engravings of paradisaical fifteenth-century scenes with their Satanic modern counterparts – chantries replaced by toll houses, abbeys by prisons, almshouses by workhouses, church spires by smokestacks – a tactic textually adopted by Carlyle.[147] 'The Middle Ages are to me

---

[142] J. W. Burrow, 'The sense of the past', in Laurence Lerner, ed., *The Victorians* (Methuen, 1978), 120–38 at 125; Charles Dellheim, *The Face of the Past: The Preservation of the Medieval Inheritance in Victorian England* (Cambridge, 1982), 65–6; David Cannadine, 'Context, performance and meaning of ritual: the British monarchy', in Eric J. Hobsbawm and Terence Ranger, eds., *The Invention of Tradition* (Cambridge, 1983), 122, 138; Asa Briggs, *Victorian Cities* (1963; rev. edn California, 1993), 391–2.

[143] John Stuart Mill, 'The spirit of the age, I', in *CW*, 22: 229. See Peter J. Bowler, *The Invention of Progress* (Blackwell, 1989), 2–13; Andrew Sanders, *In Olden Time* (Yale, 2013).

[144] J. Beavington Atkinson in *Art-Journal* (1859) quoted in Francis Haskell, *Rediscoveries in Art*, 2nd edn (Phaidon, 1976), 106.

[145] Debra N. Mancoff, *The Return of King Arthur* (Abrams, 1995); *Arthuriana*, special issue, Victorian Arthuriana, 21:2 (Summer 2011): 3–124.

[146] George Edmund Street, in *Ecclesiologist* (1858), quoted in J. Mordaunt Crook, *William Burges and the High Victorian Dream* (London: Murray, 1981), 55.

[147] A. W. N. Pugin, *Contrasts; or a Parallel between the Noble Edifices of the Fourteenth and Fifteenth Centuries, and Similar Buildings of the Present Day; Shewing the Present Decay of Taste* (London, 1836); Thomas Carlyle, *Past and Present* (London, 1843). See Rosenberg, *Elegy for an Age*, 8, 16–21, 75, 222.

the only ages', declared Ruskin. 'That miracle-believing faith produced good fruit – the best yet in the world.'[148] Medieval builders' freehand drawings were crude, their perspective poor, their knowledge of mechanics and geometry nil, conceded William Burges – but they had crafted the cathedrals of Amiens, Westminster, Cologne, Beauvais. By contrast, modern architects' technical prowess lacked aesthetic merit.[149]

The architect Robert Kerr's fictional Georgius Oldhousen, a surrogate Burges, mocks the quintessential tone:

'We're standing in the ancient ways a great deal more than we used to … I hate things that are modern.'
'Just so … And do you really think the sixteenth century is ancient enough?'
'No', says Georgius, 'I don't … I wish I had been born in the thirteenth century!'

Georgius commends this as 'comfortable, cleanly, and economical, as well as logical, archaeological, artistic, and patriotic'.[150] Infatuated Victorians succumbed to the narcotic enchantment of medievalism even more than had Petrarch to antiquity. 'A pity 'tis I was not born in the Middle Ages', exclaimed the Pre-Raphaelite Edward Burne-Jones in 1897. 'People would then have known how to use me – now they don't know what on earth to do with me.'[151]

Medievalism was likewise potent in France, but there implied no denigration of the present. Rather, it reasserted the antiquity and continuance of Gaulish national virtues thought eternal, though now and then (as after the Prussian debacle of 1870) in need of shoring up. To admire cathedrals, pilgrims, chivalry, troubadour colours, and sonorous song was to extol the *modern* nation. 'Look, children, how impressive France already was and how much she was loved eight centuries ago', said Léon Gautier, reading aloud his translation of the *Chanson de Roland*. 'It's the past that makes the present worthwhile … it's in the past that we must live', declared medievalist Gaston Paris. His aim was not nostalgic reversion, though, but prideful emulation: 'in thinking fondly of our ancestors we think fondly of ourselves'.[152]

Gothicism notwithstanding, in Victorian Britain the classical past remained pre-eminent. Familiarity with the classics was the sine qua non of both politics and politesse; civilized Greeks and Romans were more acceptable role models than rude Gothic chieftains. Antiquity offered matchless models of 'moral grandeur' and 'spiritual health'. Deploring the fantastic 'caprice and eccentricity' of modern romantic excess, 'our

[148] John Ruskin to Charles Eliot Norton, 8 Jan. 1876, in Ruskin, *CW*, 37: 189.
[149] Crook, *William Burges*, 62–5.
[150] Robert Kerr, *His Excellency the Ambassador Extraordinary* (London, 1879), 1: 219, 330–1, 2:101.
[151] Georgiana Burne-Jones, *Memorials of Edward Burne-Jones* (Macmillan, 1904), 2: 318. See George P. Landow, '*Art-Journal*, 1850–1889: antiquarians, the medieval revival, and the reception of Pre-Raphaelitism', *Pre-Raphaelite Review* 2 (1979): 71–6.
[152] Léon Gautier, *Les Epopées françaises* (1892), and Gaston Paris, *La Poésie du Moyen Âge* (1885), quoted in Elizabeth Emery and Laura Morowitz, *Consuming the Past*, 12, 209, 218. See Krzysztof Pomian, 'Francs et Gaulois', in Nora, *Lieux de mémoire*, III.1: 40–105.

incredible vagaries in literature, in art, in religion, in morals', Matthew Arnold found 'the only sure guidance, the only solid footing, among the ancients'.[153]

Philhellene Britons thought themselves more Greek than the modern Greeks whose freedom they spearheaded in the 1820s (though not quite as Greek as the German who gibed that 'all the Greeks have to do in order to be what they used to be is to mimic the Germans').[154] Thomas Hardy fancied himself the Aeschylus of Wessex; Matthew Arnold's *Sohrab and Rustum* echoed Homer; Tennyson marked where *Idylls of the King* followed Homer and Pindar. Lord Leighton's self-portrait depicted an ancient Greek in *fin-de-siècle* London, confirming Henry James's 'odd impression [of Leighton] that we were speaking of the dead'.[155] Leighton's 'reputation was a kind of gilded obelisk, as if he had been buried beneath it; the body of legend and reminiscence of which he was to be the subject had crystallised in advance'.[156] These living time-capsules echoed the ghostly classical reverberations of Petrarch's texts. But nothing was less like Renaissance imitative strategies of openly contending against exemplars. Victorian modes of harking back were self-mockingly anachronistic. Walter Scott's 'romance and antiquarianism, his knighthood and monkery, are all false, and he knows them to be false, ... laughs at his own antiquarianism', charged Ruskin.[157] '"Let's pretend to be ancient Romans," the Pre-Raphaelites began by saying', and then '"Let's pretend to be Victorians pretending to be Romans."'[158]

Yet neither Goths nor Greeks and Romans outshone popular – and populist – nostalgia for Merrie England, a *mélange* of supposed Tudor and Stuart social harmony, egalitarianism, hospitality, philanthropy, and domesticity consonant with echt-Victorian values. This more accessible anachronism went hand in hand with an antiquarian shift, from elite devotion to property, genealogy, ecclesiastical relics and philology, to bourgeois fondness for vernacular buildings and folk customs.[159]

Dismay at thraldom to the past

Exalting the past outraged progressive Victorians. George Eliot regretted the loss of bygone folkways but felt 'better off for possessing Athenian life solely as an inodorous fragment of antiquity'. She was glad not to have lived 'when there were fewer reforms and plenty of highwaymen, fewer discoveries and more faces pitted with the small-pox'.

[153] Preface (1853), 1–17 at 14–15, 17, and 'Advertisement to the second edition' (1854), in *The Poems of Matthew Arnold, 1840 to 1867* (London, 1909).

[154] Georg Ludwig von Maurer, *Das griechische Volk* (1835–6), quoted in Stathis Gourgouris, *Dream Nation: Enlightenment, Colonization, and the Institution of Modern Greece* (Stanford, 1996), 255. See Simon Goldhill, *Victorian Culture and Classical Antiquity* (Princeton, 2011), 127–8.

[155] Henry James, 'The private life' (1893), in *Novels and Tales* (Scribners, 1908–9), 17: 215–66 at 226.

[156] Jenkyns, *Victorians and Ancient Greece*, 34–8, 309–10.

[157] John Ruskin, *Modern Painters* (1843–60; New York, 1886), pt. IV, ch. 16, sect. 32, 3: 265.

[158] Richard Jenkyns, *Dignity and Decadence: Victorian Art and the Classical Inheritance* (Harvard, 1991), 332–3. See Richard J. Ayres, *Classical Culture and the Idea of Rome in Eighteenth-Century England* (Cambridge, 1997).

[159] Sweet, *Antiquaries*, 338–42.

Praisers of the past preferred its selective idealized merits to the sordid trivialities of their entire vulgar present.

> Perhaps they would have had the same complaint to make about the age of Elizabeth, if, living then, they had ... sought refuge from ... the grating influences of its every-day meannesses ... in the contemplation of whatever suited their taste in a former age.[160]

Elizabeth Barrett Browning 'distrust[ed] the poet who discerns / no character or glory in his times, / but trundles back his soul five hundred years'. She scorned nostalgists who 'flinch from modern varnish' and 'Cry out for togas and the picturesque', decrying their own as 'an age of scum, spooned off the richer past'. So 'every age / Through being beheld too close, is ill-discerned'.[161]

Proud of progress, Dickens denounced the past, mocked its partisans, and hated 'hearing those infernal and damnably good old times extolled'. He named his shelf of dummy books 'The Wisdom of Our Ancestors' (a common trope of the time) and titled each 'Ignorance. Superstition. The Block. The Stake. The Rack. Dirt. Disease'.[162] Abominated alike by Jeremy Bentham and John Stuart Mill, ancestral wisdom sank from 'an expression of respect and homage' to a 'jibe of hatred and insult'.[163] All history revealed more to lament than to laud: a mean and corrupt classical world; medieval vice and cruelty. Only through selective blinkers could the past be loved. Walter Scott, the heroic past's supreme portrayer, himself lived very much in the present; for all its anachronistic trappings, his Abbotsford was Scotland's first gas-lit home.[164]

The general view that Victorians had improved on their past is epitomized in Gladstone's rebuttal of Tennyson's latter-day pessimism. The preceding age had had its glories – military, literary, artistic. But 'it brought our industrial arts to the lowest point of degradation ... a desert of universal ugliness ... It ground down the people by the Corn Law [1815–1846], and debased them by the Poor Law [amended 1834]'. Poverty and improvidence and prostitution still festered, but much mitigated by 'a vast general extension of benevolent and missionary means', with slavery abolished, Poor Law abuses swept away, patronage reduced, work conditions ameliorated, schooling expanded, suffrage extended, minority worship unshackled, cruel sports restricted, public profanity and duelling all but extinct, 'the duties of wealth to poverty, of strength to weakness' widely acknowledged – item for item almost what Twain's Connecticut Yankee would shortly accomplish.

---

[160] George Eliot, *Impressions of Theophrastus Such* (Edinburgh, 1879), 24, 27, and 'To the prosaic all things are prosaic', in her *Essays and Leaves from a Note-book* (Edinburgh, 1884), 304.

[161] Elizabeth Barrett Browning, *Aurora Leigh* (1856), ll. 161, 167–8, 207–8. See Margaret Gent, '"To flinch from modern varnish"', in Malcolm Bradbury and David Palmer, eds., *Victorian Poetry* (Edward Arnold, 1972), 11–35; Simon Dentith, *Epic and Empire in Nineteenth-Century Britain* (Cambridge, 2006), 85–7.

[162] Charles Dickens to Douglas Jerrold, 3 May 1843, in *The Letters of Charles Dickens, 1820–1870* (Clarendon Press, 1965–2002), 3: 481; Burrow, 'Sense of the past', 125. See Thomas Gaspey, *The Witch-Finder; or, The Wisdom of Our Ancestors* (London, 1824); Charles Dickens, *The Chimes* (London, 1844).

[163] Mill, 'Spirit of the age, I', 22: 228.

[164] David Daiches, 'Sir Walter Scott and history', *Études Anglaises* 24 (1971): 458–77 at 464.

Upon the whole ... we who lived fifty, sixty, seventy years back ... have lived into a gentler time; ... the public conscience has grown more tender; ... at sight of evils formerly regarded with indifference or even connivance, it now not only winces but rebels.[165]

The ill-effects of antiquarian longing were noted even by its addicts. Writers bemoaned their inability to match past achievements, their sense of inhabiting a lesser age. 'We are lost in wonder at what has been done', wrote Hazlitt, 'and dare not think of emulating it'.[166] Shelley termed the surviving fragments of Greek perfection 'the despair of modern art'. The weight of past greatness stifled modern poets; everything worth saying had already been said![167] 'Thrown into a state of humiliating passivity by the sight of the great things done in the far past', George Eliot felt 'so completely dwarfed by comparison that I should never have courage for more creation of my own'.[168]

The architectural legacy likewise intimidated. The daunting splendour of antique buildings frightened 'original talent ... into servile imitation', precluding inspiration. 'All that is excellent in art has been transmitted to us from past ages', was a typical refrain; and 'all the productions of modern skill are mere imitations of the ancient, far inferior to them in grandeur and beauty'. Progress was at an end; 'unable to improve upon the splendid individualities of the past, we are left to reclassify and re-employ them'.[169] Human imagination had run its course; 'the maturer age of the world' spurred no fresh creation. Moderns were fit only to remodel 'legacies from the superior intelligence of former ages'. Another critic almost wished 'the temples of Greece had long ago perished if the study of them is to supersede all invention on our part'.[170]

Socially progressive aesthetic reactionaries drew Ruskin's ire. 'While we ... act in accordance with the dullest modern principles of economy and utility, we look fondly back to the manners of the ages of chivalry, and delight in ... the fashions we pretend to despise, and the splendors we think it wise to abandon.' It was deplorable that 'the furniture and personages of our romance are sought ... in the centuries which we profess to have surpassed in everything', while present-day art 'is considered as both daring and degraded'. That said, Ruskin loathed almost everything modern, from cities and railways to 'improvements', 'selfishness', 'sins', 'smoke', and 'superciliousness'[171]

What undermined self-confidence was uncritical submission to the past's supposed superiority. The past was a burden too readily shouldered. 'Comparing one's own age

---

[165] William Ewart Gladstone, '"Lockskey Hall" and the Jubilee', *Nineteenth Century* 21:119 (Jan. 1887): 1–18 at 5, 8, 17.

[166] William Hazlitt, 'Schlegel on the drama', in *CW*, 16: 66.

[167] Percy Bysshe Shelley, *Hellas* (1822; London, 1886), Preface, ix; Jenkyns, *Victorians and Ancient Greece*, 23.

[168] To John Blackwood, 18 May 1860, in *The George Eliot Letters* (Yale, 1954–78), 3: 294.

[169] 'Public buildings of Edinburgh', *Blackwood's Edinburgh Magazine* 6 (1820): 370; Ebenezer Trotman, 'On the alleged degeneracy of modern architecture', and George Wightwick, 'A few observations on the reviving taste for pointed architecture', *Loudon's Architectural Magazine* 1 (June 1834): 148–54 at 148, and 2 (Aug. 1835): 342–8 at 344.

[170] *Athenaeum* (1829) and *Foreign Quarterly Review* (1830) quoted in Roger A. Kindler, 'Periodical criticism 1815–40: originality in architecture', *Architectural History* 17 (1974): 22–37 at 25.

[171] Ruskin, *Modern Painters*, pt IV (1856), ch. 16, sect. 15, 3: 255–6, and *CW* Index, 39: 352–3; Fiona Russell, 'John Ruskin, Herbert Read and the Englishness of British modernism', in David Peters Corbett et al., eds., *The Geographies of Englishness* (Yale, 2002), 303–21 at 303.

with former ages ... had occurred to philosophers' previously, observed Mill, 'but it never before was itself the dominant idea of any age'.[172] Hazlitt noted that 'constant reference to the best models of art necessarily tends to enervate the mind ... by a variety of unattainable excellence'.[173] Too close scrutiny of ancient masters deprived moderns of original genius; Constable chided artists 'intent only on the study of departed excellence'.[174]

Above all, Victorians feared lest anachronistic obeisance forfeit their own identity. 'A house may be adorned with towers and battlements, or pinnacles and flying buttresses', judged the connoisseur Richard Payne Knight, 'but it should still maintain the character of the age ... in which it is erected; and not pretend to be a fortress or monastery of a remote period'.[175] Growing knowledge of the past and skill in reproducing its forms threatened to deprive Victorians of any distinctive style of their own. Even some who doted on the past expressed strictures against its toils. The 'effect of working with this vivid *panorama* of the past placed constantly in our view', feared Gothic Revival champion George Gilbert Scott, 'is to induce a capricious eclecticism – building now in this style, now in that – content to pluck the flowers of history without cultivating any of our own'.[176]

Made abject by their borrowings, Victorians sought a self-respecting identity. But its very self-consciousness doomed the effort. No age had ever formed a style of its own by deliberately seeking it, held Scott; Greek and Renaissance creativity had flourished because 'no one thought much of the past, – each devoted his energies wholly to the present'. His own countrymen 'could look back upon a perfect history [of] the arts of the past', a marvel for 'amusement and erudition, but ... a hindrance rather than a help to us as artists'. Only by *forgetting* its predecessors could his epoch acquire its own éclat.[177] Nietzsche distilled Victorian angst: 'we moderns have nothing of our own'; heads were stuffed with 'an enormous mass of ideas, taken second hand from past times and peoples, not from immediate contact with life'.[178] The past encumbered because too well remembered.

Retrospection occluded past reality. Aesthetic revivals gleaned only the husk of exemplars; passionate attachment degenerated into academic trivia. Cathedrals like Amiens could no longer be built, thought Heinrich Heine, for 'the men of past times had convictions, we moderns have only opinions'.[179] Constable termed the Gothic Revival 'a vain endeavour to reanimate deceased Art'; it could only 'reproduce a body without a soul'.[180] The devout Gothicist Burges concluded in 1868 that he and his confrères had

---

[172]   Mill, 'Spirit of the age, I', in *CW*, 16: 228.
[173]   William Hazlitt, 'Fine arts, whether they are promoted by academies and public institutions' (1814), in *CW*, 18: 37–51 at 41.
[174]   John Constable, 'Various subjects of landscape characteristic of English scenery' (1833), in *John Constable's Discourses* (Suffolk Records Society, 1970), 7–27 at 10.
[175]   Richard Payne Knight, *An Analytical Inquiry into the Principles of Taste*, 3rd edn (London, 1805), 99.
[176]   George Gilbert Scott, *Remarks on Secular & Domestic Architecture* (1857), 26.
[177]   Ibid., 260.
[178]   Nietzsche, *Use and Abuse of History*, 24, 67.
[179]   Heinrich Heine, 'Über die französische Bühne: vertraute Briefe an August Lewald', 9th letter, (May 1837), in *Sämtliche Werke* (Munich: Kindler, 1964), 12: 229–90 at 279.
[180]   'Lecture on landscape' (1834–5), in *John Constable's Discourses*, 69–74 at 70.

'not been very successful, either in our copies or in our own efforts . . . [They] want spirit. They are dead bodies; they don't live.'[181]

The spirit of the age, 'amalgamati[ng] certain features in this or that style of each and every period', led to 'injudicious thraldom'. Aiming in vain for 'a distinct, individual, palpable style' of their own, Victorian architects laboriously mined a multitude of sources.[182] Eclecticism was worse than single-minded devotion to Greek or Gothic. 'We have all the centuries but our own', complained littérateur Alfred de Musset; 'unlike any other epoch, we take all that we find, this for its beauty, that for its commodity, the other for its antiquity, this other even for its ugliness; consequently we live only among debris'.[183] Spontaneity was dying. Fifty years later William Morris deplored all architectural revivals, from 'pedantic imitations of classical architecture of the most revolting ugliness' to 'ridiculous travesties of Gothic buildings', for bequeathing Britain an 'avowedly imitative', vulgar, insipid urban scene.[184]

Was it fruitless to borrow? Victorian artists and architects faced anew the dilemma of originality. They had two conflicting traditions: the classical, which stressed faithful following; and the Romantic, which stressed innovation. But for them, as for their humanist precursors, to innovate still meant reusing the legacy. The past was the creative architect's touchstone; 'the more richly he stores his mind with the ideas of others, the more likely will he be to bring forth new ideas of his own'. Invention for its own sake was abhorred; 'the continual attempt at *novelty*' had been the 'ruin' of modern Italian architecture.[185] But architects who pilfered and tacked together Palladian fragments in unthinking imitation were just as bad. The ideal was a mix of stylistic stability and change, a compromise between 'copyism' and 'originality', departure from, without rejecting, the past – a style both clearly new and at the same time clearly descended from the known and familiar.[186] In short, Victorians sought to swim on their own while visibly supported by Erasmus's life-preserver.

Whig history: reusing the past

That life-preserver also buoyed Whig historians, who retold the English past as an uplifting simulacrum of the present. Unlike nostalgic medievalists, Whig progressives fused their chosen Anglo-Saxons with modern times, stressing remote resemblances. 'The

[181] William Burges, 'Art and religion' (1868) quoted in Crook, *William Burges*, 127.

[182] T. L. Donaldson (1842) cited in Nikolaus Pevsner, *Some Architectural Writers of the Nineteenth Century* (Oxford, 1972), 82.

[183] Alfred de Musset, *Confession d'un enfant du siècle* (1836), in *Oeuvres complètes* (Gallimard, 1960), 3: 65–288 at 89. Lacking its own 'decisive color', echoed Austrian architect Ludwig von Förster, the nineteenth century borrowed visual idioms from every past (Carl Schorske, *Fin-de-siècle Vienna* (Random House, 1981), 36).

[184] William Morris, 'The revival of architecture', *Fortnightly Review* 3 (May 1888): 665–74 at 665, 673.

[185] [The Conductor], 'On the difference between common, or imitative, genius, and inventive, or original, genius, in architecture', *Loudon's Architectural Magazine* 1 (July 1834): 185–8; 'Restoration of the Parthenon in the National Monument', *Blackwood's Edinburgh Magazine* 6 (1819): 137–48 at 143.

[186] Pevsner, *Some Architectural Writers*, 222–37; W. J. Bray, *A History of English Critical Terms* (Boston, 1898), 211–12.

more one revered the ancients, the more exciting it was to find that one had something in common with them', in Jenkyns's summary.[187] Rather than praising the past at the expense of the present, they cherished but were not confined by their heritage; they coupled allegiance to continuity with faith in progress. Joining tradition and change was their leitmotiv: change within the confines of tradition, hence controllable; tradition made malleable by change, hence progressive. Sanctioned by presumed continuity, English institutions in fact assimilated all manner of novelties. Victorians knew the past should not, *could* not, be resurrected; adaptation not imitation was the right road. 'We are legislators, not antiquaries', asserted Thomas Babington Macaulay, who was both. To be truly 'worthy of their ancestors' was to adopt their principles and 'adapt them to the altered circumstances of the present day'.[188] A few sought the past to escape from the present; more aimed to embed bygone virtues in the present; most used the past as touchstone and inspiration.

Loss of faith in continuity cost later Victorians the security formerly found in the past. Too much was now known to sustain the old view that past and present were similar, history exemplary. The unlikeness of the past, the awareness of historical change that humanists had ignored or belittled, Vico's unbridgeable diversity of epochs and cultures each with its own, not *our* way, of looking at life – these insights could no longer be denied. The historian digging into distant and different epochs would find things foreign to himself. The past most evidently *was* a foreign country. Its contrasting differences might amuse, shock, or even instruct the present but could no longer sustain the past's admonitory role.[189] Tradition's intellectual collapse as much as its suffocating weight spawned the turn-of-the-century modernist revolt against past precepts, past artefacts, past modes of thought.

The Ancients–Moderns breach – forward-looking sciences, backward-looking arts – still beset Victorians. In engineering and manufacturing, Britain was the prototype of innovative self-confidence. In the arts, education, religion, and politics, ambivalence left the past alike a burden and a solace. The ills of industrialization hardened the revanchism roused by the French Revolution. Against the new order's rampant change and perilous innovations, Victorians took refuge in one or another past. These pasts were not simply preserved but lavishly recalled in architecture, art, and literature. But as the century wore on, familiarity made re-creation and revival more demanding and confining. 'How had the burden of precedent increased!' exclaimed Walter Pater's Marius of imperial Rome, similarly beholden. 'It was all around me – that smoothly built world of old classical taste, and accomplished fact, with an overwhelming authority on every point of the conduct of

---

[187] Jenkyns, *Victorians and Ancient Greece*, 81.

[188] T. B. Macaulay, 'Parliamentary reform', House of Commons speech, 2 Mar. 1831, *Hansard HC Deb*, ser. 3, 2:1189–2005 at 1194; Robert Grant, 'The Jews', House of Commons speech, 5 Apr. 1830, *Hansard* 23: 1287–1303 at 1297–8. See John Clive, 'The use of the past in Victorian England', *Salmagundi* 68/69 (1986): 48–65 at 60; J. W. Burrow, *Liberal Descent: Victorian Historians and the English Past* (Cambridge, 1981), 102–7; Robert E. Sullivan, *Macaulay* (Harvard, 2009), 66–74.

[189] P. B. M. Blaas, *Continuity and Anachronism* (The Hague: Nijhoff, 1978); Mazzotta, *New Map of the World*, 136–9.

Figure 13 The look of antiquity: seventeenth-century manor house,
Sibford Gower, Oxfordshire, remodelled 1915

Figure 14 The look of antiquity: Ernest Newton, design for Fouracre,
West Green, Hampshire, *c.* 1902

one's own work [and] no place left for novelty or originality.'[190] Espousing the entirety of past greatness fed an indiscriminate eclecticism. This hugger-mugger miscellany was at odds with both previous Romantic creative individuality and rising modernist impulse to dispense with the past altogether.

By the century's end, English nostalgia was principally for pre-industrial ways. With a technophobic fervour pilloried in Twain's *Connecticut Yankee*, chivalric trappings adorned the newly expanded knighthood and ceremonial monarchy. The concurrent births in the 1890s of the Ancient Monuments Act, *Country Life* magazine, the National Trust, and the Arts and Crafts movement showed the pervasive reach of rural recall. 'Old English' and 'Queen Anne' revivals felt as old as, if not older than, actual bygone cottages.[191] Anticipating Osbert Lancaster's 'Stockbroker's Tudor' by fifty years, H. G. Wells foresaw social and industrial progress spawning Arts-and-Crafts retro. The coming century would 'ransack the ages for becoming and alluring anachronisms', new houses 'tinted, even saturated, with the second-hand archaic ... sham chimneys ... "pictur-esque" mullions ... sham open fireplaces ... inglenooks about the sham glowing logs. The needlessly steep roofs will have a sham sag and sham timbered gables [with] forced lichens [for] a sham appearance of age.'[192]

New boarding schools exemplified the rival pulls of innovation and tradition. Catering for nouveaux riches manufacturers, they dignified social climbing by cloaking it in ancient garb – Gothic halls, pastoral landscapes, classical fixtures and features, cere-monies and curricula. Aristocratic traditions became emblems of acceptance for the rising rich. Domesticated into landed gentry, entrepreneurs learned to cherish the past's moral, cultural, and social traits, against the vulgar soulless present that had enriched them enough to spurn it.[193]

That past was not really alive, however. Indeed, being dead, and hence no longer a threat to the present, made its revival tolerable. 'Concern with the past did not conflict directly with the progress of modernization': an industrial tycoon might knowledgeably collect Roman coins; modern commerce in Bradford's Wool Exchange was unfettered by its neo-Gothic design. London's neo-Gothic parliament and courts of justice are redolent not of nostalgia but continuity; the murals of Manchester's Town Hall marry heraldic retrospect with radical tradition and mercantile progress. Conforming historical trap-pings with modern aspirations diminished the past's restrictive force. Largely confined to art, leisure, schooling, and imperial ritual, regressive nostalgia little impeded techno-logical advance. Not even Burges or Burne-Jones chose to live like medieval barons, and

---

[190] Walter Pater, *Marius the Epicurean*, 2nd edn (London, 1885), 1: 107.

[191] Mark Girouard, *Sweetness and Light: The 'Queen Anne' Movement, 1860–1900* (Clarendon Press, 1977); Martin J. Wiener, *English Culture and the Decline of the Industrial Spirit, 1850–1980* (1981; Cambridge, 2004), 44–70; Jan Marsh, *Back to the Land: The Pastoral Impulse in Victorian England* (London: Quartet, 1982); Melanie Hall, 'Affirming community life', in Chris Miele, ed., *From William Morris: Building Conservation and the Arts and Crafts Cult of Authenticity, 1877–1939* (Yale, 2005), 129–57; Sanders, *In the Olden Time*, 171–81.

[192] H. G. Wells, *Anticipations of the Reaction of Mechanical and Scientific Progress upon Human Life and Thought*, 4th edn (London, 1902), 115–17.

[193] Wiener, *English Culture*, 11–24.

few Victorians fancied being Tudor princes or eighteenth-century gentry. The past was not something to escape into, but to make over on their own terms, a malleable medium for the expression of modern taste and thought.[194]

Nor did love of ancient architecture demand adherence to its animating ideals. Late Victorians could safely steward medieval remnants because medieval times were gone for good. Conflicts between keeping the past and building the future were minimized by protecting specified monuments and – notwithstanding lip service to the whole – quietly forsaking the rest. Yet affection for things past profoundly influenced British institutions in general. An American historian's 1981 contention that Britons still found solace in obsolete modes of living and working, to the detriment of industrial innovation, roused a storm of outraged denial, followed by a calm of rueful recognition.[195]

Whatever the influence of attachment to things past in economic and social affairs, its importance in letters and landscape is beyond question. Well into post-war decline, the past was a burden willingly assumed by an elite who felt genuine alarm lest faceless modernity subvert English ethos and environment.

The England that we love is the England of old towns, tilled fields, little rivers, farms, churches and cottages. If by violently marring the fair country and vulgarizing the shy old buildings we obtain so much less to love, what shall it profit? Without an England to love we cannot remain stout of heart and enduring.[196]

The quintessential elegiac tone was James Lees-Milne's, peerless rescuer of rural mansions at risk, on the demise of the landed aristocracy. 'This evening the whole tragedy of England impressed itself upon me', he wrote in 1947 while negotiating the National Trust's acquisition of Brockhampton, Herefordshire. 'This small, not very important seat in the heart of our secluded country is now deprived of its last squire [John Talbot Lutley]. A whole social system has broken down. What will replace it beyond government by the masses, uncultivated, rancorous, savage, philistine, the enemies of all things beautiful?'[197] Sixty years on, mass media and masses alike acclaim Arcadian acres and stately homes kept in aristocratic aspic. Featuring royal connections spanning a thousand years, ducal chatelains of Wrotham Park in Hertfordshire, Cornbury Park in Oxfordshire, and Sudeley Castle in Gloucestershire bind present to past, regenerating ancient features and fabrics for the delectation of corporate clients, Sotheby sales, and Connoisseur Tourists.[198]

American Founding Fathers and sons

Whatever is old is corrupt, and the past turns to snakes. The reverence for the deeds of our ancestors is a treacherous sentiment.   Ralph Waldo Emerson, 1870[199]

---

[194] Sanders, *In the Olden Time*, 12, 180–5, 247, 315–16; Dellheim, *Face of the Past*, 179–81.
[195] Wiener, *English Culture*, 158–66.
[196] W. R. Lethaby, *Philip Webb and His Work* (1935), quoted in Peter Burman 'Defining a body of tradition', in Miele, ed., *From William Morris*, 67–99 at 97.
[197] James Lees-Milne, *Caves of Ice*, diary, 16 June 1947 (Chatto & Windus, 1983), 172.
[198] Melissa Knatchbull, 'To the manor born', *Country House*, June 2007: 31–4.
[199] Ralph Waldo Emerson, 'Works and days' (1870), in *CW* (Houghton Mifflin, 1904), 7: 155–85 at 177.

American deep ambivalence towards the past vividly recurs in metaphors of filial conflict. On the one hand, freedom from the crippling past was a defining creed of the Revolution and the new republic; on the other, Americans deplored the shallowness of their history and deified its Founding Fathers. Paternal devotion and laments for absent tradition flew in the face of the national mission to sweep away the past and look only forward.

The binding force of custom troubled New Englanders from the start. Recall of settler forebears who 'had all things to doe, as in the beginning of the world', transformed them 'into simplified figures of inimitable heroism. In this filial reduction of the parents to static exemplars of virtue', sons periodically cope with feeling small by exalting fathers and 'appointing themselves guardians of their patrimony'.[200] But volatile frontier conditions made it increasingly hard to follow patriarchal precepts. The idealized Puritan community – hierarchical, disciplined, austere, pious – was neither enforceable nor retrievable.

Each colonial generation cherished yet chafed at precursors' strictures. But post-Revolutionary cohorts faced a painful choice, because their revered exemplars were no longer religious and eternal, but political and personal: 'They could continue to idealize, and seek to perpetuate, the temper of the Founding Fathers; or they could try to adapt ... to drastic change', concluded Peter Gay. 'Rigid, they would turn themselves into anachronisms; flexible, they would betray their Puritanism.'[201]

Most troublesome was the legacy of English institutions and political thought. In severing imperial bonds, Americans discarded not only the mother country but many of its traditions. Three interrelated ideas justified such dismissal: faith in autonomy as the self-fashioning birthright of each successive generation; an organic analogy that assigned the New World a youthful position in world history; and divinely ordained exceptionalism that exempted America from Old World decay and decline.

Autonomy and generational freedom

Parent–child analogies obsessed American and British statesmen alike. Tories chided unruly colonial children for disobeying the mother country; rebels castigated Britain as tyrannical parent. The metaphors were common coin: family–state parallels pervaded English political debates over 'natural' freedom and social contract. Child-rearing was in flux, the traditional hierarchical household giving way to a more flexible family structure.[202]

Authoritarian views epitomized in Robert Filmer's *Patriarcha* (1680) aligned two precepts: a father's lifelong power over his offspring was absolute; a state's subjects owed their sovereign the same unqualified obedience. Against Filmer's patriarchal fiat, John Locke argued that no compact could forever bind posterity; sons when grown were

---

[200] Andrew Delbanco, *The Puritan Ordeal* (Harvard, 1989), 116, citing John Winthrop, Jr. (1640s), 224–5.

[201] Peter Gay, *A Loss of Mastery: Puritan Historians in Colonial America* (California, 1966), 110.

[202] Randolph Trumbach, *The Rise of the Egalitarian Family* (Academic Press, 1978); Jay Fliegelman, *Prodigals and Pilgrims: The American Revolution against Patriarchal Authority* (Cambridge, 1982).

by nature as free as their fathers. And against Filmer's regal divine right, Locke held that governmental trust required the consent of the governed; absolutism forfeited obedience.[203]

Punitive practices that kept offspring submissive gave way to Locke's precepts to instil obedience through example and tender guidance, lest 'children, when grown up, weary of you; and [ask] "When will you die, father?"'[204] Time set limits to childhood, agreed Rousseau. 'Children remain bound to their father only so long as they need him for their own self-preservation. The moment this need ceases, the natural bond is dissolved.'[205] To be sure, youth could be let go too soon. Whereas 'the last Age taught Mankind to believe that they were mere Children, and treated them as such, till they were near thirty Years old', an eighteenth-century theologian lamented that 'the present gives them Leave to fancy themselves complete Men and Women at twelve or fifteen ... and too often despise all Advice of their Elders'.[206]

That transition came apace across the Atlantic. Seventeenth-century colonists had kept adult sons dependent by curtailing access to land and money; eighteenth-century sons gained autonomy much younger, often taking adult roles by the age of thirteen. The Revolutionary epoch produced so many outstanding leaders, historians suggest, in part because family needs mandated youthful responsibility.[207] Yet Britain treated colonials as dependent offspring.

The colonies 'are yet Babes that cannot live without sucking the breasts of their Mother', wrote James Harrington in 1656, but they would wean themselves in time. A century later John Adams held the colonies 'nearer manhood than ever Harrington foresaw' in so short a time. 'You have been children long enough', lexicographer Noah Webster hectored his countrymen, 'subject to the control, and subservient to the interest of a haughty parent'.[208] Since parental Britain denied American maturity, George Washington became the indulgent Father who raised the 'infant country' to 'manhood and strength'. In line with Locke's dictum that a true parent not only begot but formed a

---

[203] Robert Filmer, *Patriarcha* [1680] *and Other Writings* (Cambridge, 1991), 1–68; John Locke, *Two Treatises of Government*, (1690; New York, 1947), 80, and chs. 6, 7, 15, 18; Gordon J. Schochet, *Patriarchalism in Political Thought: The Authoritarian Family and Political Speculation and Attitudes Especially in Seventeenth-Century England* (Blackwell, 1975), 273–6; Gordon S. Wood, *The Radicalism of the American Revolution* (Knopf, 1992), 110, 150.

[204] John Locke, *Some Thoughts Concerning Education* (1693; London: Scolar, 1970), 34.

[205] Jean-Jacques Rousseau, *The Social Contract* (1762), in *Political Writings* (Edinburgh: Nelson, 1953), 1–155 at 4.

[206] Isaac Watts, *A Discourse on the Education of Children and Youth* (1725), in *The Posthumous Works* (London, 1754), 100–236 at 205.

[207] Oscar and Mary F. Handlin, *Facing Life: Youth and Family in American History* (Little, Brown, 1971), 12–18; Kenneth S. Lynn, *A Divided People* (Greenwood, 1977), 68–9, 98–9. The speed and ease with which American boys achieved adulthood impressed Alexis de Tocqueville (*Democracy in America* (1835–40; Cambridge, MA, 1863), 2: 233–4; Demos, 'Oedipus and America', 35–6).

[208] James Harrington, *The Oceana* [1656] *and Other Works* (London, 1747), 33–27 at 44; John Adams, *Novanglus, or, a History of the Dispute with America* (1774), in *Works* (Boston, 1857), 4: 1–177 at 104; Noah Webster, Jr., 'On the education of youth in America' (1787–8), in *A Collection of Essays and Fugitive Writings* (Boston, 1790), 1–37 at 36.

child's mind, the childless Washington became Americans' father-surrogate. 'Americans! he had no child – but you, – and HE WAS ALL YOUR OWN.'[209]

Not all wanted to grow up. Revolutionary allegiances matched mode of upbringing. Most colonial Loyalists were raised by inflexible authoritarians who demanded prolonged filial fealty. Prominent American Patriots, by contrast, were reared along Lockean lines, their individuality respected, autonomy nurtured, libertarian spirit lauded.[210] 'To know whether it be the interest of the continent [America] to be independent', declared Paine, 'we need only ask this easy, simple question: Is it the interest of a man to be a boy all his life?'[211]

South American rebels similarly resented long-imposed infancy. Chilean separatist leaders inveighed against ageing imperial tyranny. Latin Americans owed no loyalty to Spanish rule that 'has kept us in a sort of permanent infancy'.[212] Canadians reproached England for disciplining them like adolescents.[213]

A doctrine of perpetual freedom of choice legitimized American rebellion. Proud of their rupture with the past, Americans assumed that their descendants would continue to slough off ancestral things and thoughts. Filial autonomy underlay Paine's and Jefferson's doctrine that every new generation was a sovereign nation that should replace inherited institutions with its own. 'The dead have no rights', wrote Jefferson. 'Our Creator made the world for the use of the living ... One generation of men cannot foreclose or burden its use to another.' Against English common-law rationale that rooted judicial precedent in the immemorial past, he held that the legal code ought to expire every nineteen years or so.[214]

---

[209] Josiah Dunham, *A Funeral Oration on George Washington* (1800), quoted in Fliegelman, *Prodigals and Pilgrims*, 203, 185; Gouverneur Morris, 'An oration upon the death of General Washington', in *Eulogies and Orations on ... George Washington ...* (Boston, 1800), 44–54 at 46–7. See Cynthia S. Jordan, '"Old words" in new circumstances: language and leadership in post-revolutionary America', *American Quarterly* 40 (1988): 491–513 at 507–10; Wood, *Radicalism of the American Revolution*, 149; François Furstenberg, *In the Name of the Father: Washington's Legacy ...* (Penguin, 2006), 75.

[210] Lynn, *Divided People*.

[211] Thomas Paine, 'The crisis No. III' (1777), in *The Political Writings of Thomas Paine* (New York: 1830), 1: 99–127 at 105.

[212] Simón Bolívar to Henry Cullen, 'Reply of a South American to a gentleman of this island [Jamaica]', 6 Sept. 1815, in *Selected Writings of Bolivar* (New York, 1951), 1: 103–22 at 111; Mary L. Felstiner, 'Family metaphors and the language of an independence revolution', *Comparative Studies in Society & History* 25 (1983): 154–80 at 167; John Lynch, *Simón Bolívar* (Yale, 2006), 93.

[213] John Eddy and Deryck Schreuder, eds., *The Rise of Colonial Nationalism* (Allen & Unwin, 1988), 47–8.

[214] Thomas Paine, 'Dissertations on government, &c' (1795), in *Political Writings*, 1: 365–414 at 393; Thomas Jefferson to John W. Eppes, 24 June 1813, to Samuel Kercheval, 12 July 1816, to Thomas Earle, 24 Sept. 1823, in *The Writings of Thomas Jefferson* (Washington, DC, 1907), 12: 260–1, 15: 42–3, 470. Jefferson had reason to detest inherited shackles; like many Virginia gentry, he was the legatee of indebtedness that made 'the planters a species of property annexed to certain mercantile houses in Britain' (Jefferson, 'Additional questions of M. de Meusnier, and answers' (1786), quoted in T. H. Breen, *Tobacco Culture: The Mentality of the Great Tidewater Planters on the Eve of Revolution* (1985; rev. edn Princeton, 2001), 141). See Robert W. Gordon, 'Paradoxical property', in John Brewer and Susan Staves, eds., *Early Modern Conceptions of Property* (Routledge, 1995), 95–110 at 99; Roscoe Pound, *The Formative Period of American Law* (Little, Brown, 1938), 7–8, 144–5; Allen Mendenhall, 'Jefferson's "Laws of Nature"', *Canadian Journal of Law and Jurisprudence* 23:2 (2010): 319–42.

The eternal youth of America

In the then common analogy, nations went from infancy and youth to maturity and old age, passing from innocence to strength and then to enfeebled corruption.[215] America epitomized the purity of youth; Bishop George Berkeley famously contrasted the virtuous New World with the degenerate Old:

> Not such as Europe breeds in her decay;
> Such as she bred when fresh and young . . .
> Westward the Course of Empire takes its Way;
> The four first Acts already past,
> A fifth shall close the Drama with the Day;
> Time's noblest Offspring is the last.[216]

America's early stage in the life cycle justified disregard of history. 'Youthful and vigorous nations [should] concern themselves with the present and the future rather than with the past', ran a typical screed. 'Not until the sun of their greatness . . . is beginning to decline [is] a spirit of antiquarian research' aroused.[217] The very lack of a long and glorious past augured a long and glorious future. 'It is for other nations to boast of what they have been, and like garrulous age, muse over the history of their youthful exploits, that only renders decrepitude more conspicuous', puffed one chauvinist. 'Ours is the more animating sentiment of hope, looking forward with prophetic eye.'[218] A New Yorker ascribed Europe's retrogression to its glut of relics: 'Did we live amidst ruins' and marks of 'present decay . . . we might be as little inclined as others, to look forward. But we delight in the promised sunshine of the future, and leave to those who . . . have passed their grand climacteric to console themselves with the splendors of the past.'[219]

Americans were not content, however, with youth that kept corrupt old age only temporarily at bay. They held their country immune from decay because *eternally* youthful. Newly forged by reason and virtue, America transcended temporal processes; Providence rescued it from history. Americans were God's chosen people, destined to restore a prelapsarian state of grace. Seed ripened in the New World would be spared worldly corruption in the promised millennium. America need never suffer the fate of Europe, long mature and now 'nearly rotten'; the Deity exempted the United States from the final period of ageing, even from death itself. 'If such is the youth of the Republic, what will be its old age?' asked a French statesman, and Senator Lewis Cass answered: 'Sir, it will have no old age.' All America resembled Michigan's Mackinac Island, a New World

[215] See Chapter 5.
[216] George Berkeley, 'America, or the Muse's refuge' (1726), in *The Works of George Berkeley* (London, 1848–57), 8: 153.
[217] George P. Marsh, *The Goths in New-England* (Middlebury, VT, 1843), 7. Marsh feared that lack of reverence for antiquity would cost Americans dear; see my *George Perkins Marsh: Prophet of Conservation* (Washington, 2000), 58–9, 96.
[218] James Kirke Paulding, 'Naval chronicle', *Analectic Magazine* 6 (1815): 231–57 at 249. See Ralph M. Aderman and Wayne R. Kime, *Advocate for America* (Susquehanna, 2003), 56–60.
[219] Cadwallader D. Colden, *Memoir, at the Celebration of the Completion of the New York Canals* (New York, 1825), 77–8.

Avalon or New Atlantis famed for near-immortal health; 'if people want to die, they can't die here – they're obliged to go elsewhere'.[220] Faith in the earthly paradise, Arnold Toynbee later found, mandated the belief that 'death is un-American'.[221]

Americans continued to depict their destiny in ahistorical terms of eternal vigour and youth. Secured against time's corrosion by divine covenant, the nation's stunning progress seemed a realization of God's purpose. Not until the 1890s was dispensation from decay seriously doubted. Well into the new millennium many Americans still speak as if exempt from secular history, while simultaneously becoming ever more perfect.[222] 'The road to Providence is uneven and unpredictable', ran the born-again president's 2005 State of the Union message, 'yet we know where it leads'. For George W. Bush, it led to freedom. He invoked Franklin Roosevelt's dream but his rhetoric echoed Adolf Hitler, after Germany's 1936 reoccupation of the Rhineland: 'I go the way that Providence dictates with the assurance of a sleepwalker.'[223]

The useless and crippling past

Inhabiting a new creation, Americans held aloof from history in general. 'We have no interest in the scenes of antiquity, only as lessons of avoidance of nearly all their examples', trumpeted the originator of American 'Manifest Destiny'.[224] History was just a record of errors. Paine thought it pointless 'to roam for information into the obscure field of antiquity', for 'the real volume, not of history but of facts, is directly before us, unmutilated by . . . the errors of tradition'.[225] Truth was the observable present, falsehood the hearsay past. Pleased to lack a past, Americans felt sorry for Europeans lumbered with one. 'A nation is much to be pitied that is weighed down by the past', says a James Fenimore Cooper character; 'its industry and enterprise are constantly impeded by. . . its recollections'.[226]

The sheer novelty of America made history irrelevant. 'With the Past we have literally nothing to do. Its lessons are lost and its tongue is silent', asserted a future Missouri governor. 'Precedents have lost their virtue and all their authority is gone'.[227] Envious Europeans echoed these accolades to the clean slate. In Goethe's lines:

[220] B. St V. [Jean Baptiste Bory de St Vincent to Constantine Rafinesque, 10 Aug. 1821], 'Fragments of correspondence, &c', Western Minerva 1 (1821): 70; Lewis Cass, 'The Mexican War: Speech', US Senate, 10 Feb. 1847, Congressional Globe, 29 Cong. 2nd sess., 1192; Frederick Marryat, Diary in America (1839; Indiana, 1960), 122.

[221] Arnold J. Toynbee, Man's Concern with Death (McGraw-Hill, 1969), 131.

[222] Ernest Lee Tuveson, Redeemer Nation (Chicago, 1968), 103–6, 110–11, 158–60, 213–14; Dorothy Ross, 'Historical consciousness in nineteenth-century America', AHR 89 (1984): 909–28 at 916, 921, 924; Thomas Bender, A Nation among Nations (Hill & Wang, 2006).

[223] George W. Bush, 2 Feb. 2005; Adolf Hitler, 15 Mar. 1936, quoted in Alan Bullock, Hitler (London: Oldhams Press, 1952), 375.

[224] John Louis O'Sullivan, 'The great nations of futurity', USM&DR 6 (1839): 427.

[225] Thomas Paine, Rights of Man (1791–2), in CW (Library of America, 1995), 433–664 at 572.

[226] James Fenimore Cooper, Home as Found (1849; New York, 1860), 34.

[227] Benjamin Gratz Brown (1850) quoted in Walter Agard, 'Classics on the Midwest frontier', in Walker D. Wyman and Clifton B. Kroeber, eds., The Frontier in Perspective (Wisconsin, 1965), 165–83 at 166.

> America, you are more fortunate
> Than our old continent,
> You have no ruined castles
> And no primordial stones.
> Your soul, your inner life,
> Remain untroubled by
> Useless memory . . .[228]

Europe's ivy-clad monuments and ancient ruins were seductive, but the charm was specious. Such relics betokened senile evils. 'It is said that *our* country has no past, no history, no monuments!' exclaims an American in an Emma Southworth best-seller, on seeing the decayed dungeons of an ancient British castle. 'I am glad of it! Better her past should be a blank page than be written over with such bloody hieroglyphics as these! When I . . . reflect upon the deeds of this crime-stained old land, I look upon our own young nation as an innocent child!'[229]

The nation shook off the historical past; its people threw off family legacies. The ideal American was 'emancipated from history, happily bereft of ancestry, untouched and undefiled by the usual inheritances of family and race; an individual standing alone, self-reliant and self-propelling', wrote a literary historian. While time and memory corrupted Europeans, Americans were Adam before the Fall. 'The national and hence the individual conscience was clear' because unsullied by time – America 'had no past'.[230]

Terming 'antiquity a humbug, precedent a sham', reformers repudiated the past. Our ancestors shall no longer be our master. We renounce all fealty to their antiquated notions. Henceforth to be old is to be questionable. We will hold nothing sacred which has long been worshipped, and nothing venerable which has long been venerated.'[231]

Renouncing the past meant rejecting elders' sway. 'I have lived some thirty years', Thoreau declared, 'and I have yet to hear the first syllable of valuable or even earnest advice from my seniors'.[232] Democracy made men forget their ancestors and 'imagine that their whole destiny is in their own hands', observed Tocqueville. In America, 'the tie which unites one generation to another is relaxed or broken; every man there readily loses all trace of the ideas of his forefathers, or takes no care about them'.[233]

Americans excised history from milieus as well as minds: the 'sovereignty of the present generation' applied no less to law than to landscape. Inherited property signalled the tyranny of forebears. Old houses were 'heaps of bricks and stones' that a man builds 'for himself to die in, and for his posterity to be miserable in'; the merit of America was that everything was periodically pulled down.[234] The reformer Holgrave in Hawthorne's

---

[228] Johann Wolfgang von Goethe, 'Die Vereinigten Staaten' (1812), in *Gedenkausgabe der Werke, Briefe, und Gespräche* (Zurich: Artemis, 1948–71), 2: 405–6.

[229] Emma Southworth, *Self-Raised; or, From the Depths* (1864; New York, 1884), 433–4.

[230] R. W. B. Lewis, *The American Adam* (Chicago, 1955), 5, 7. See Quentin Anderson, *The Imperial Self* (Knopf, 1971).

[231] Timothy Walker, *The Reform Spirit of the Day* (Cambridge, MA, 1850), 5.

[232] Henry David Thoreau, *Walden* (1854; Modern Library, 1937), 8.

[233] Tocqueville, *Democracy in America*, 2: 121, 2.

[234] Nathaniel Hawthorne, *The House of the Seven Gables* (1852), in *Works*, 2: 263.

House of the Seven Gables looked forward to 'when no man shall build his house for posterity'. He extolled the ephemeral:

Our public edifices – our capitols, state-houses, court-houses, city-halls and churches – ought [not] to be built of such permanent materials as stone or brick. It were better that they should crumble to ruin, once in twenty years, or thereabouts, as a hint to the people to examine into and reform the institutions which they symbolize.[235]

Thoreau proposed 'purifying destruction'. America must disown the habits of England, 'an old gentleman who is travelling with a great deal of baggage, trumpery ... accumulated from long housekeeping which he has not the courage to burn'.[236] The Old World notion 'that houses, like wines, improve with age [was] absurd'.[237]

Dislike of ancient premises extended to period revivals. 'Since they cannot live in real old houses, our lovers of antiquity ... imitate old barbarisms in their new structures', scoffed a critic. 'Building new houses to resemble old ones, is quite as ridiculous as it would be for a young man to affect the gait of his grandfather.'[238] Perhaps it was 'pardonable in Horace Walpole and Sir Walter Scott to build gingerbread houses in imitation of robber barons and Bluebeard chieftains, ... but there can be nothing more grotesque, more absurd, or more affected' than for an American 'who knows no more of the middle ages than they do of him, to erect for his family residence a gimcrack of a Gothic castle'. Gothicized churches and 'imitation mediaeval cathedrals' were likewise condemned: 'the gray moss of centuries, the clothing ivy, the irregular antique street, the humble hovel, the cloister pale, the stately palace, the dignity of age' were alien to the American scene and spirit.[239]

Oblivion was commended as foresight. 'Instead of moralising over magnificence in a process of decay', the European visiting America might marvel at marks of progress. Far better to consider 'bright futures and new speculations ... than to wander through the uncertain and questionable paths of antiquity, only to contemplate tottering ruins, demolished buildings, or the effects of devastating revolutions'.[240] Not palimpsests but *tabulae rasae* spurred American ambition:

> Though we boast no ancient towers,
> Where ivied streamers twine;
> The laurel lives upon our shores;
> The laurel, boy, is thine.[241]

[235] Ibid., 183–4. See Nathaniel Hawthorne, 'Earth's holocaust' (1844), in *Works*, 10: 381–95.
[236] Thoreau, *Walden*, 60–1. See C. Vann Woodward, 'The future of the past', *AHR* 75 (1970): 711–26 at 722–3.
[237] 'Our new homes', *USM&DR* 21 (1847): 392–5 at 392.
[238] Ibid., 392–3.
[239] Review (1846) of William H. Ranlett, *The American Architect*, quoted in Talbot Hamlin, *Greek Revival Architecture in America* (1944; Dover 1964), 325; 'Church architecture in New-York', *USM&DR* 20 (1847): 139–44.
[240] Laurence Oliphant, *Minnesota and the Far West* (Edinburgh, 1855), 1; J. Hector St John Crèvecoeur, *Journey into Northern Pennsylvania and the State of New York* (1801; Michigan, 1964), 456.
[241] Joseph Bartlett Burleigh, *The Thinker, a Moral Reader*, 6th edn (Philadelphia, 1852), lesson LXV, 122.

Faith in banishing the past and owing nothing to forebears, to tradition, to example, animated Americans up to the Civil War. An American Adam unencumbered by inherited ideas and habits was the Transcendental ideal. Countless pundits exhorted sloughing off all that was old.

Even the classical past, at first exempt from animus, at length fell into disfavour. In dismissing the British legacy, American colonials initially hailed remoter epochs whose merits mirrored their own. Like themselves, Plutarch and Livy, Cicero and Sallust had mourned lost innocence, deplored moral decline, contrasted present defects with a better past. Revolutionary Americans harked back to Roman virtues. Washington's fancied resemblance to Cincinnatus (also to Fabius, Lycurgus, and Solon) was one of myriad ancient parallels validating the new republic. Citations from Polybius and Cato lent classical authority to constitution makers.[242]

Like Roman claims to surpass Greece, however, Americans asserted superiority over antiquity. Classical veneration was soon muted, later largely relinquished. Pioneer settlers still lent the frontier culture and prestige with antique place-names and Greek Revival buildings, but by the mid-nineteenth century classical exemplars were 'a matter of curiosity, rather than of instruction'. Pompey and Caesar were names given slaves; Greek and Roman literature were 'heathen' tongues more to be avoided than imitated. Antebellum piety replaced the classics with the Bible.[243] The New World was beyond the farthest ken of classical authors; what could progressive Americans learn from them? The founders now supplanted the ancients: for ancestral advice and hero worship Cato and Cicero gave way to Washington and Jefferson. Evangelical faith, democratic populism, anti-intellectualism, and material progress variously made the classical past obsolete or derisory. Persuading President William Henry Harrison, bent on demonstrating learned nous, to delete classical references from his interminably (and lethally) lengthy 1841 inaugural address, Daniel Webster crowed he had 'killed *seventeen Roman proconsuls* as dead as smelts'.[244]

The demise of the Romans, now vilified as pagan and decadent, was immortalized in Lew Wallace's *Ben-Hur: The Tale of the Christ* (1880), the best-selling American novel

---

[242] Gilbert Chinard, 'Polybius and the American constitution', *JHI* 1 (1940): 38–58; Richard M. Gummere, *The American Colonial Mind and the Classical Tradition* (Harvard, 1963), 97–119; Bernard Bailyn, *The Ideological Origins of the American Revolution* (Harvard, 1967), 25–6; Garry Wills, *Cincinnatus* (Doubleday, 1984); Michael Meckler, ed., *Classical Antiquity and the Politics of America from George Washington to George W. Bush* (Baylor, 2006); Margaret Malamud, *Ancient Rome and Modern America* (Wiley-Blackwell, 2009), 133–44; Carl J. Richard, *The Founders and the Classics* (Harvard, 1994); Carl J. Richard, *Greeks and Romans Bearing Gifts: How the Ancients Inspired the Founding Fathers* (Rowman & Littlefield, 2008).

[243] The first paragraph of Thomas Smith Grimké's *Address on the Expediency and Duty of Adopting the Bible as a Text Book of Duty and Usefulness* ... (in his *Reflections on the Character and Objects of All Science and Literature* ... (New Haven, 1831), 59–109 at 61–2) is no. 116, 'The Bible the best of classics', in the famed *McGuffey's Fifth Eclectic Reader* (1843; Wiley, 1997), 350. See Shalom Goldman, *God's Sacred Tongue* (North Carolina, 2004), 165–6; Wilbur Zelinsky, 'Classical town names in the United States', *Geographical Review* 57 (1967): 463–95.

[244] Peter Harvey, *Reminiscences and Anecdotes of Daniel Webster* (Boston, 1877), 162–3. In President Harrison's tradition, Senator Richard Byrd interminably harangued his colleagues with hour-long Ciceronian 'Philippics' (Malamud, *Ancient Rome and Modern America*, 1–2).

until *Gone with the Wind*, and an enduring icon in film. Conceived while Wallace was governor of New Mexico, the novel portrayed the Judaeo-Christian hero's resistance to barbaric imperial Rome as a heroic precursor to civilized victory over Indian savagery.[245]

Ambivalence

But if Americans had truly shed the past, why continue to castigate it so vehemently? What made disavowals of tradition so strident? Why bother to flog a beaten rival? Why demand 'purifying destruction' of a heritage long forsworn? Clearly, the past still threatened. Assailing tradition, antiquity, heirlooms, inherited houses, as in *The House of the Seven Gables*, reveals that the past Americans claimed to have banished was a baneful living presence. Hawthorne himself was endlessly ambivalent. 'Let us thank God for having given us such ancestors', he wrote of Puritan forefathers; 'and let each successive generation thank him, not less fervently, for being one step further from them in the march of ages'. What alarmed Hawthorne about his revered forebears? 'The discipline which their gloomy energy of character had established' dispirited distant as well as immediate heirs; Americans had not yet 'thrown off all the unfavorable influences' bequeathed them.[246]

Emerson was equally of two minds. Demanding 'a poetry and philosophy of insight and not of tradition', the premier apostle of the present doubted that compatriots had put the past behind them. 'Our age is retrospective', he complained. 'It builds on the sepulchres of the fathers.' Like some anxious English Victorian, Emerson charged Americans with undue devotion to antiquity: Again and again he inveighed against 'this worship of the past', chiding one who dared not say, '"I think, I am," but quotes some saint or sage'.[247] Yet Emerson himself, fifteen years after scolding others for slavishly following the Founding Fathers, reversed course to blame fellow Americans for failing to live up to them. Hanging a Washington portrait in his dining-room, Emerson could not 'keep my eyes off of it'.[248] Why did the past he pressed others to abandon still mesmerize the Sage of Concord?

Paine and Jefferson had confirmed the sovereignty of each new generation. Why, fifty years on, should American children need urging to 'think "that they may be great themselves", instead of always subservient to dead men'? How could a scribe contend that upbringing made Americans worship the past and term obeisance to tradition an 'almost insurmountable obstacle ... against real advancement'?[249] How do laments over

[245] Blake Allmendinger, 'Toga! toga!', in Valerie J. and Blake Allmendinger, eds., *Over the Edge: Remapping the American West* (California, 1999), 32–49; Howard Miller, 'The charioteer and the Christ: *Ben-Hur* in America from the Gilded Age to the culture wars', *Indiana Magazine of History* 14:2 (2008): 153–75; Goldhill, *Victorian Culture and Classical Antiquity*, 215–18; Malamud, *Ancient Rome and Modern America*, 133–44.

[246] Nathaniel Hawthorne, 'Main-street' (1849), in *Works*, 11: 49–82 at 68.

[247] Ralph Waldo Emerson, 'Nature' (1836) and 'Self-Reliance' (1841), in *CW*, 1: 1–77 at 3; 2: 43–90 at 66–7.

[248] Ralph Waldo Emerson, 6 July 1852, in *Journals and Miscellaneous Notebooks* (Harvard, 1960–82), 13: 63.

[249] 'The East and the West', and [Lucius Alonso Hine], 'Daniel Webster: his political philosophy in 1820', *USM&DR* 22 (1848): 401–9 at 408; 129–38 at 130.

this 'retrospective age', this 'worship of the past', this 'subservience to dead men', square with a half century's self-congratulatory dismissals of the past? The American victory over the ancients left their revenants entrenched.

In fact, few Americans wholly rejected the past, and some embraced much of it. Opposing the 'party of Hope', in Emerson's phrase, a 'party of Memory' yearned for a storied past.[250] Many adopted both perspectives, at once embracing and rejecting history. Those who felt the pull of the past had the more strongly to resist it. Americans feared nostalgia's corrosive tug, but waxed nostalgic all the same.

Nostalgia for Old World antiquity

One cause of ambivalence was a dearth of cultural vestiges. Injunctions to throw off obeisance to antiquity alternated with laments about its absence – the lack of hoary relics, romantic ruins, reminders of continuity with remote forebears. 'I had never in my life seen an *old* building', Henry Ward Beecher explained his tears at Kenilworth Castle; 'I had never seen a ruin.' Old World ruins enthralled many. Longfellow termed the ruined Alhambra 'wonderful in its fallen greatness'; the Colosseum 'hoary with the years that have passed' enraptured Sophia Hawthorne. Piranesi's prints of Roman antiquities were widely popular.[251]

Europe's ruins spelt depravity against American natural purity, yet also served to make New World nature familiarly endearing. Landforms of the American West became ruin metaphors. 'The same processes that sheared fragments from the Pantheon fractured the canyon walls', felt explorers at Yellowstone's 'architectural' marvels. The very 'idea of the Gothic style of architecture', mused geologist Ferdinand V. Hayden, might have come 'from such carvings of Nature'.[252] Nebraska's bluffs and escarpments compelled comparison with ancient castle remnants; Oregon Trail landmark Chimney Rock seemed 'the ruins of some vast city erected by a race of giants, contemporaries of the Megatherii and Ichthyosaurii'.[253]

Raw wild America dismayed aesthetes who shared Mme de Staël's view that 'the most beautiful landscapes in the world, if they evoke no memory, if they bear no trace of any notable event, are uninteresting compared to historic landscapes'.[254] Past associations were prime attractions in painting and poetry, delineation of history the main aim of art. 'What are the most esteemed paintings?' asked an American schoolbook of 1806. The answer: 'Those representing historical events.'[255]

---

[250] Emerson, 'Historic notes of life and letters in New England' (1883), in *Portable Emerson*, 513–43 at 514.

[251] Henry Ward Beecher, *Star Papers; or, Experiences of Art and Nature* (1855; New York, 1873), 14; Henry Wadsworth Longfellow, *Outre-Mer* (1835), in *The Writings* (London, 1886–93), 1: 9–278 at 227; Sophia Hawthorne, *Notes on England and Italy* (New York, 1870), 407–8.

[252] Ferdinand V. Hayden, *Preliminary Report of the United States Geological Survey of Montana* (GPO, 1872), 79. See Roderick Nash, *Wilderness and the American Mind* (Yale, 1967; 4th edn 2001), 208–16.

[253] Samuel Parker, *Journal of an Exploring Tour beyond the Rocky Mountains* (Ithaca, NY, 1838), 60–1; Edwin Bryant, *What I Saw in California* (1847; Palo Alto, 1967), 102.

[254] Germaine Necker de Staël, *Corinne, ou l'Italie* (Paris, 1807), 1: 222.

[255] Charles Peirce, *The Arts and Sciences Abridged*, 2nd edn (Portsmouth, NH, 1811), 48.

The absence of a 'pictured, illuminated Past', wrote historian John Lothrop Motley in a typical moan of empty newness, gave America 'a naked and impoverished appearance'.[256] Lacking 'associations of tradition which are the soul and interest of scenery', America seemed to many 'a face without an expression'.[257] The brevity of American history had left ' but so thin and impalpable a deposit that we very soon touch the hard substratum of nature', wrote Henry James, 'and nature herself ... seem[s] rather crude and immature. The very air looks new and young ... Vegetation has the appearance of not having reached its majority. A large juvenility is stamped upon the face of things.'[258]

Europe's historical depth fulfilled needs unmet by American juvenility. The foremost celebrants of the new confessed the pull of the old. Thomas Cole's paintings famously enshrined the beauty of American nature, yet he also doted on the past; antique temples and towers festoon his Hudson River landscapes, re-creating the storied Rhine along the Hudson's wild shores.[259] 'He who stands on the mounds of the West [the Indian earthworks of the Mississippi Valley], the most venerable remains of American antiquity, *may* experience ... the sublimity of a shoreless ocean un-islanded by the recorded deeds of man', but 'he who stands on Mont Albano and looks down on ancient Rome, has his mind peopled with the gigantic associations of the storied past'.[260] James Fenimore Cooper scorned European ruins and celebrated wilderness virtues, but royalties from *Leatherstocking Tales* let him gothicize and castellate his family home and play at being an Old World country squire.[261] When not inveighing against antiquity's accumulated rubbish, Thoreau found it 'much more agreeable to sit in the midst of old furniture [which has] come down from other generations, than in that which was just brought from the cabinet-maker's and smells of varnish, like a coffin!'[262] Hawthorne wished 'the whole past might be swept away' and the burdensome Parthenon marbles 'burnt into lime', but found it hard to write about places devoid of antiquity: 'romance and poetry, like ivy, lichens, and wallflowers need ruin to make them grow'.[263]

Americans exaggerated both the charms of the past and its evils. As US consul at Liverpool, Hawthorne ridiculed visiting countrymen who sought ancestral links, yet confessed sharing 'this diseased American appetite for English soil'. He longed 'to find a gravestone in one of those old churchyards, with my own name upon it'. But his protagonist in *Doctor Grimshawe's Secret* renounces England's rich past for America's

[256] John Lothrop Motley, 'The polity of the Puritans', *North American Review* 69 (1849): 470–98 at 493–4.
[257] William Cullen Bryant, 'On poetry in its relation to our age and country' (1825), in *Prose Writings* (New York, 1884), 1: 24–35 at 24.
[258] Henry James, *Hawthorne* (Macmillan, 1879), 12–13.
[259] Louis Legrand Noble, *The Life and Works of Thomas Cole* (1853; Harvard, 1964), xxiii; Nash, *Wilderness and the American Mind*, 78–82.
[260] Thomas Cole, 'Essay on American scenery' (1835), *American Monthly Magazine* 1:2 (1836): 1–12 at 11.
[261] Van Wyck Brooks, *The World of Washington Irving* (Philadelphia, 1944), 421–5.
[262] Henry David Thoreau, 3 Oct. 1857, *Journal* (1906; Dover, 1962), 10: 59.
[263] Nathaniel Hawthorne, *The English Notebooks*, 29 Sept. 1855 and 27 Mar. 1856 (New York: [P]MLA, 1941), 243, 294; Nathaniel Hawthorne, *The Marble Faun* (1859), in *Works*, 4: 3.

'poor tents of a day, inns of a night'.[264] For Longfellow, Old World antique charms at length gave way to New World duty. Foreshadowing Henry James's time-travel angst, a character in Longfellow's *Hyperion* likens his preposterous nostalgia to 'falling in love with one's own grandmother'.[265]

Repelling nostalgia, Americans damned historical Europe as immoral, decadent, submissive, reeking of oppression and tyranny. 'The Atlantic is a Lethean stream', rejoiced Thoreau, enabling Americans 'to forget the Old World and its institutions'.[266] Nineteenth-century worthies repeatedly advised youth to shun European corruptions and seductions. 'Please don't get expatriated', entreated Longfellow; 'life is not all cathedrals or ruined castles, and other theatrical properties of the Old World'.[267] Disgusted by Italy's 'vast museum of magnificence and misery', Mark Twain mocked Yankees who gawked at ruins and castles.[268] Henry Greenough likened Italy to 'the skeleton of some mighty mastodon, among whose bones jackals, mice, and other vermin were prowling about'; American schoolbooks termed all Italy a 'horrid ruin'.[269]

Rome's beauty struck Hawthorne as sinister. In contrast to his *Marble Faun* sculptor's New World, where 'each generation has only its own sins and sorrows to bear, here, it seems as if all the weary and dreary Past were piled upon the back of the Present'. For an American to immortalize himself with a marble bust, 'leaving our features to be a dusty-white ghost among strangers of another generation', was outré. One should 'leave no more definite memorial than the grass'. The world 'will be fresher and better', says Hawthorne's Miriam, 'when it flings off this great burthen of stony memories' piled up by the pious ages.[270]

Perdurable English scenes captivated Americans. Hawthorne's mistrust of old houses, old institutions, and long lines of descent, declared his biographer Henry James, made him 'more American than many [who] have often a lurking esteem for things that show the marks of having lasted'.[271] The age-old Warwickshire village of Whitnash seemed to Hawthorne tediously moribund.

Rather than the monotony of sluggish ages, loitering on a village-green, toiling in hereditary fields, listening to the parson's drone lengthened through centuries in the gray Norman church, let us welcome whatever change may come – change of place, social customs, political institutions, modes of worship – trusting that ... they will but make room for better systems, and for a higher type of man to clothe his life in them, and to fling them off in turn.[272]

---

[264] Nathaniel Hawthorne, 'Consular experiences' (1863), in *Works*, 5: 6–40 at 20; Hawthorne letter in James T. Fields, *Yesterdays with Authors* (London, 1881), 74; Hawthorne, *Doctor Grimshawe's Secret* (Houghton Mifflin, 1883), 230.

[265] Henry Wadsworth Longfellow, *Hyperion* (1839), in *Writings*, 2: 13–285 at 137.

[266] Henry David Thoreau, 'Walking' (1861), in *The Writings* (Boston, 1893), 9: 251–304 at 263.

[267] Longfellow to Louise Chandler Moulton, in Edward Wagenknecht, *Henry Wadsworth Longfellow* (Longmans, Green, 1955), 195.

[268] Mark Twain, *The Innocents Abroad* (1869; New American Library, 1966), 182–5.

[269] Henry Greenough, *Ernest Carroll, or Artist-Life in Italy: A Novel* (Boston, 1858), 101; Ruth Miller Elson, *Guardians of Tradition: American Schoolbooks of the Nineteenth Century* (Nebrasks, 1964), 150.

[270] Hawthorne, *Marble Faun*, 301–2, 119.

[271] James, *Hawthorne*, 130.

[272] Nathaniel Hawthorne, 'Leamington Spa' (1862), in *Works*, 5: 41–64 at 60.

To be sure, there was 'something beautiful and touching in ... old manor houses and country halls ... where, age after age, the descendants of one family have lived, and loved, and suffered, and died ... sheltered by the same trees and guarded by the same walls', confessed landscape architect Andrew Jackson Downing. But for Americans such a heritage would not do: 'It is only an idyll, or only a delusion to us. ... It could only be reanimated at the sacrifice of the happiness of millions of free citizens.'[273]

No American felt the pull of the past more acutely and ambivalently than Henry James. London and Paris filled him with 'nostalgic poison' and a keen regret for the paucity of history in America.[274] James's *Sense of the Past* highlights the perils of historical charm for his protagonist, finding the scenes of his American youth 'deplorably lacking intensity'. Ralph Pendrel's old house in London comes alive as 'a conscious past, recognising no less than recognised', but permeated with evil. Mesmerized by its family portraits, Pendrel finds himself a century back as the lover of a long-dead collateral forebear – a victim of Longfellow's grandmother syndrome. A past too vividly evoked becomes an abode of nightmare, from which Pendrel barely extricates himself to return to his fiancée 'Aurora' in present-day America.[275] Succumbing to the seductive Old World past would exact a fatal cost.

Yet having lauded Hawthorne for eschewing England's 'sluggish ages', James goes on to regret all those items of civilized tradition absent from Hawthorne's youth in cold, thin, bleak New England:

No sovereign, no court, no personal loyalty, no aristocracy ... no country gentlemen, no palaces, no castles, nor manors, or old country-houses, nor parsonages, nor thatched cottages, nor ivied ruins; no cathedrals, nor abbeys, nor little Norman churches, nor great Universities. nor public schools – no Oxford, nor Eton, nor Harrow; no literature, no novels, no museums, no pictures ... nor Epsom nor Ascot![276]

The debt to the Founding Fathers

Conflicting moral imperatives left Americans confused about their past. Enjoined to be self-reliant and jettison tradition, they were at the same time exhorted to revere the Founding Fathers and protect their achievements. The Revolutionary generation had 'bequeathed to us almost all we have that is worth having', and 'it is our duty to preserve it for those who come after us'.[277] While the past in general was sloughed off, that precious legacy must be venerated and zealously safeguarded. But reverence and stewardship were not the same, and by and by the sons realized they could save the fathers' legacy only by *not* following their self-reliant example.

[273] Andrew Jackson Downing, *The Architecture of Country Houses* (1850; Dover, 1969), 268–9.
[274] Henry James, *The Reverberator* (1888), in *Novels and Tales*, 13: 1–211 at 195.
[275] James, *Sense of the Past*, 33, 65.
[276] James, *Hawthorne*, 48.
[277] 'Reminiscences of a walker round Boston', *USM&DR* 3 (1838): 79–87 at 80; 'The Missouri Compromise line', *Utica Daily Observer*, 7 Jan. 1861, in Howard Cecil Perkins, ed., *Northern Editorials on Secession* (New York: Appleton/AHA, 1942), 1: 298.

As during the break from 'mother' England, family metaphors dominated the republic's 'infancy'. The Founding Fathers were paternal models. 'So deeply rooted is the
principle of imitation in our nature and so ceaseless is our reverence for those who have
gone before us', wrote a journalist, 'that the habits and opinions of the people are almost
moulded after those of . . . the first founders'. The rising generation must remain devoted
offspring. 'As soon as he opens his lips', bade Noah Webster, every American child
should 'lisp the praise . . . of those illustrious heroes and statesmen, who have wrought a
revolution in [liberty's] favor'. Rufus Choate's fellow-countrymen imbibed patriotism
with their mothers' milk.[278] Filial adjurations long lived on. Sixteen months after
Lincoln's Emancipation Proclamation, a Connecticut senator nonetheless sought to
retain the original Fugitive Slave Act, enforcing the capture and return of runaway slaves,
on the ground that his precursors Roger Sherman and Oliver Ellsworth had voted for it in
1793, and 'who are we, that wisdom has come to us which was denied to them?' *Nation*
editor E. L. Godkin doubted that 'worship of ancestors has ever been carried much
further than this even in China'.[279]

The Constitution had become sacred scripture. Although Washington, Jefferson, and
Madison had expected and welcomed continual alteration, it was now so venerated that
amendment seemed sacrilege; none had been proposed since 1804. Abandoning the right
to revise struck Godkin as a 'degrading . . . confession of degeneracy'. Ignored was
Jefferson's warning against 'sanctimonious reverence ascrib[ing] to men of the preceding
age a wisdom more than human'; one might 'as well require a man to wear still the coat
which fitted him when a boy, as civilized society to remain ever under the regimen of
their barbarous ancestors'.[280]

The onset of the Civil War posed a dismaying dilemma. The sons could not resemble
the Founding Fathers without endangering their legacy, or preserve it without confessing
subordination. Persuading men 'to live by the will of dead fathers, and to do so *by their
own choice*' threatened to unman Americans.[281] Merely to save the legacy relegated them
to lasting inferiority, as heirs too impotent to act on their own. The fathers' greatness
made them inimitable; 'a hero cannot be a hero', in Hawthorne's words, 'unless in a
heroic world'. That world was now gone; as early as 1822 Emerson judged that his
country had moved from 'strength, to honour, . . . & at last to ennui'.[282] A generation
later American politics seemed 'no longer a contest of great minds for great ends, but a
pot-house squabble'. The present was condemned to a lesser role; 'it is for us to *preserve*,

---

[278] R.W., Jr., 'Machiavel's political discourses upon the first Decade of Livy', *Southern Literary Messenger* 5:12
(Dec. 1839): 819–26 at 820; Webster, 'On the education of youth in America', 23; Rufus Choate, 'American
nationality' (1858), in *The Political Writings of Rufus Choate* (Regnery, 2002), 373–94 at 386–7. See George
B. Forgie, *Patricide in the House Divided: A Psychological Interpretation of Lincoln and His Age* (Norton,
1979), 19–20; Michael Rogin, *Fathers and Children: Andrew Jackson and the Subjugation of the American
Indian* (Knopf, 1975), 36–54.

[279] Lafayette Foster, 'Repeal of fugitive slave law', 28 Cong., 1st sess., *Congressional Globe* (20 Apr. 1864),
1747; E. L. Godkin, 'The Constitution, and its defects', *North American Review* 99 (1864): 117–45 at 126.

[280] Godkin, 'Constitution', 127; Jefferson to Samuel Kercheval, 12 July 1816, in *Writings*, 12: 3–15.

[281] Furstenberg, *In the Name of the Father*, 231.

[282] Nathaniel Hawthorne, *The American Notebooks*, 7 May 1850, in *Works*, 8: 501; Ralph Waldo Emerson to
John Boynton Hill, 3 July 1822, in *Letters* (Columbia, 1939), 1: 120.

and not to create', concluded Charles Francis Adams.[283] 'We can win no laurels in a war for independence', admitted Daniel Webster. 'Earlier and worthier hands have gathered them all. Nor are there places for us by the side of Solon, and Alfred, and other founders of states. Our fathers have filled them.' Instead, Webster's contemporaries played subaltern roles, having to 'praise what we cannot equal, and celebrate actions which we were not born to perform'.[284] Amid encomiums to progress and prophecies of Manifest Destiny, Americans harked back incessantly to the republic's 'earlier and better days'. Their latter-day affluence was but 'the forcing-house of mediocrity', they themselves the second-rate progeny of superhuman forebears.[285]

Sons whose sacred duty was to preserve the inheritance could never match their fathers and thus never reap like rewards. The fathers would forever be remembered for what they had done; none would recall the sons, who merely shielded their legacy. The founders were justly famed; the stewards would be justly forgotten.

Several circumstances exacerbated this dilemma while inhibiting awareness of it. One was the longevity of many actual Fathers, living memorials to their own deeds half a century beyond the Revolution. For Americans in the 1820s the continuing presence of Adams and Jefferson suggested Revolutionary immortality. James Monroe, 'a living reminder of some past sufficiently distant for everyone to be proud of it', was long paraded in his old army uniform 'as if to ward off not the British, but time itself'.[286] History felt domestic and ageless as long as 'the heroes ... were still walking among the people'. These durable patriarchs buttressed the conceit that Americans were exempt from the running of time. Their continuing 'presence ... among us', noted Harvard president Edward Everett, bound following generations to the nation's momentous beginnings.[287] Many prized Revolutionary links; 'a *living history* was to be found in every family', recalled Abraham Lincoln, 'bearing the indubitable testimony of its own authenticity, in the limbs mangled, in the scars of wounds received, in the midst of the very scenes related'.[288] This intimate legacy impressed a Prussian visitor in 1845. Unlike Europeans who 'go back in sentiment through the twilight of ages', Americans' 'great, undoubted historical past lies near them; their *fathers* did great things, not their *great-great-grandfathers!*'[289]

[283] *Putnam's Monthly* (Nov. 1854) quoted in Forgie, *Patricide in the House Divided*, 67; Charles Francis Adams, 'Hutchinson's third volume', *North American Review* 38 (1834): 134–58 at 157.

[284] Daniel Webster, 'The Bunker Hill Monument' (1825), and 'The completion of the Bunker Hill Monument' (1843), in *The Writings and Speeches* (Boston, 1903), 1: 235–54 at 253–4, and 1: 259–83 at 262.

[285] James Russell Lowell, 'Self-possession *vs.* prepossession' (1861), in *CW* (Boston, 1904), 8: 761–9 at 763; Forgie, *Patricide in the House Divided*, 73, 173–4.

[286] Forgie, *Patricide in the House Divided*, 49; George Dangerfield, *The Awakening of American Nationalism, 1815–1828* (Harper, 1965), 22.

[287] 'Henry Clay as orator', *Putnam's Monthly* (1854), quoted in Forgie, *Patricide in the House Divided*, 10; Edward Everett in 'Circular' (1824), in George Washington Warren, *History of the Bunker Hill Monument Association* (Boston, 1877), 112.

[288] Abraham Lincoln, 'Address before the Young Men's Lyceum of Springfield, Illinois' (1838), in *Collected Works* (Rutgers, 1953), 1: 108–15 at 115.

[289] Frederick von Raumer, *America and the American People* (New York, 1846), 300.

Thraldom to these immortals persisted. But if the fathers never died, the sons could never assume power or patrimony. Some feared less that cords with Founding Fathers would snap than that the dead would strangle the living. Filial devotion was edged with resentment against perdurable fathers. Because 'the sire would live forever', a Hawthorne character observes, 'the heir [would] never come to his inheritance, and ... hate his own father, from the perception that he would never be out of his way'.[290] Hidden filial resentment suggests why monuments commemorating Founding Fathers were often opposed, their completion long delayed. And sons inflated fathers' antipathy to the past to justify their own. Needing to view the new nation as an orphan devoid of parental impress, they obscured Revolutionaries' acknowledged dependence on Anglo-Saxon precedent and portrayed them as out-and-out rebels.[291]

The beckoning frontier buoyed faith in future destiny unimpeded by ancestral debts. It also postponed a showdown between the duty to preserve and the urge to outdo the legacy. The ever-renewable West sustained the sense that the past was irrelevant, obviating need to rebel against it. Each new frontier, concluded historian Frederick Jackson Turner, furnished 'a new field of opportunity, a gate of escape from the bondage of the past'. Hence 'scorn of older society, impatience of its restraints and its ideas, and indifference to its lessons' marked the ever-renewed frontier mentality.[292]

Shifting needs made the parental legacy now a set of precepts to be faithfully followed, now a storehouse of icons to be plundered. Some admired fathers by exaggerating their severance of all past ties. Others rebelled against fathers by belittling their rebellious feats. Still others evaded the issue by repressing their own antipathy to the past – thus Hawthorne's Holgrave grudgingly accepts the inheritance he had inveighed against. 'Claiming simultaneously to be good sons of the fathers and to be adults unburdened by the past', in George Forgie's summary, 'they took their booty and moved into their fathers' house'.[293]

A few realized how ominous was the stress between veneration and aspiration, how dangerous any attempt to emulate the Founding Fathers. A man who now acted like Washington would be not a patriot but a tyrant, warned Virginia jurist Beverley Tucker.[294] Revolutionary behaviour today would not preserve the republic but subvert it. Lincoln expressed alarm lest frustrated ambition turn patricidal. 'This field of glory is harvested, and the crop is already appropriated. But new reapers will arise, and *they*, too, will seek a field.' Would ambition be satisfied simply 'in supporting and maintaining an edifice that has been erected by others? Most certainly ... not. Towering genius [that]

[290] Nathaniel Hawthorne, 'Septimius Felton' (1872), in *Works*, 13: 3–194 at 127.
[291] Forgie, *Patricide in the House Divided*, 92–3, 100–1; T. Trevor Colbourn, *The Lamp of Experience: Whig History and the Intellectual Origins of the American Revolution* (1965; Indianapolis: Liberty Fund, 1998), 190, 199; Nathan O. Hatch, *The Sacred Cause of Liberty: Republican Thought and the Millennium in Revolutionary New England* (Yale, 1977), 81–7.
[292] 'The significance of the frontier in American history' (1893), in *The Early Writings of Frederick Jackson Turner* (Wisconsin, 1938), 183–299 at 229. See Forgie, *Patricide in the House Divided*, 103–10.
[293] Stephen Bann, *The True Vine: On Visual Representation and the Western Tradition* (Cambridge, 1989), 193; Hawthorne, *House of the Seven Gables*; Forgie, *Patricide in the House Divided*, 122.
[294] Beverley Tucker, *A Discourse on the Genius of the Federative System of the United States* (Richmond, VA, 1839), 4, 14, 19.

scorns to tread in the footsteps of *any* predecessor' would not rest content with memorializing the fathers' fame; with nothing left to build, Lincoln feared they would 'set boldly
to the task of pulling down'.[295] Those born too late for a heroic age, a 'Procrustes'
agonized, might foment war to flaunt their own heroism.[296]

Anxiety mounted with sectional strife. Invective against blind obedience to the past
and 'the mouldering tombs of the eighteenth century' alternated with impassioned
appeals to restore original principles now subverted. 'It is the cant of the day to repudiate
the past', one reviewer complained; it became the counter-cant to lament that
repudiation.[297] Disregard of the past was deemed a besetting and perhaps fatal flaw
in the national character. Holding that no other generation 'made so little use of the
past as ours', critics termed compatriots too disposed 'to reject the experience and
authority of others', and deplored 'careless indifference to the associations and
memory of the past'.[298] The parlous state of Washington's homestead epitomized
the growing risk. Everett in 1858 urged Mount Vernon's rescue from threatened
despoliation as a token of national salvation. 'The Father of his country cries aloud
to us … to be faithful to the dear-bought inheritance which he did so much to secure
to us.' Pilgrimages to Washington's home and tomb, once restored, might mitigate
sectional animus.[299]

By then, such appeals aimed less to hang on than *return* to the past. The Republican
party's proclaimed mission was not to preserve but to rescue, to 'restore the government
to the policy of the fathers', in Lincoln's words. Their opponents *remembered* the
Revolution; Republicans would haul it back into the present. 'The dogmas of the quiet
past', which Lincoln had once thought unalterable, were not 'adequate to the stormy
present; as our case is new, so we must think anew, and act anew'.[300] Lincoln saw
himself as the republic's protector against those faithless sons whose parricide he had
prophesied.

The Civil War released Americans from a merely preservative piety towards patriarchs.
Crusading to restore the founders' edifice, they like them would earn descendants'
gratitude and deserve undying fame. The previous generation could only revere the
founders. Matching paternal deeds and valour, Unionists in the Civil War could also
criticize them. Regaining the legacy by their own sacrifices, they won freedom from
ancestor-worship. They themselves noted the end of that thraldom. 'The nation in its
childhood needed a paternal Washington, but now it has arrived at manhood'; need for a

---

[295] Lincoln, 'Address before the Young Men's Lyceum', in *CW*, 1: 114.

[296] Procrustes, 'Great men, a misfortune', *Southern Literary Messenger* 30:4 (1860): 308–14.

[297] News correspondent (1853) quoted in Forgie, *Patricide in the House Divided*, 97–8; Henry T. Tuckerman,
'American society', *North American Review* 81 (1855): 26–50 at 30.

[298] Andrew Preston Peabody, 'Arnold and Merivale: the History of Rome', *North American Review* 72 (1851):
442–66 at 443 (so little); 'Civilization: American and European', *American Whig Review* 4:1 (July 1846):
27–43 at 42 (reject); newspaper 1858 quoted in Forgie, *Patricide in the House Divided*, 175 (careless).

[299] Edward Everett, 'Washington at home and abroad' (1858), in *Orations and Speeches on Various Occasions*
(Boston, 1836–70), 3: 631–6 at 632. See Charles B. Hosmer, *Presence of the Past: A History of the
Preservation Movement in the United States before Williamsburg* (Putnam, 1965), 41–62.

[300] Abraham Lincoln, 'Speech at Edwardsville' (1858), in *CW*, 3: 91–6 at 93; Abraham Lincoln, 'Annual
Message to Congress', 1862, in *CW*, 5: 518–37 at 537.

father-figure was past.[301] But the rhetoric lingered on. The 1936 edition of David Savile Muzzey's *American History*, long the most popular school text, exhorted pupils to keep up the 'beautiful country estate' they had inherited. 'You would be ungrateful heirs indeed if you did not care to know who had bequeathed the estate to you, who had planned and built the house [and defended] it from marauders and burglars'.[302]

Centennial comforts of the colonial past

In the wake of Civil War carnage came a wave of nostalgia for earlier times. The sanguinary horrors of the recent past induced yearning for idealized colonial and Revolutionary epochs. Glorious early America in Currier & Ives prints helped avert eyes from Gilded Age tawdriness. Pictorial media and commemorative events hyped happier olden times. The 1876 Philadelphia Centennial Exhibition moved many to wistful retrospection. The youthful country looked fruitful, harmonious, wholly admirable. All had been progress: trans-Allegheny settlement, conquest of the wilderness, taming of the West, growing culture and prosperity. Later events had taken a sombre turn. Expansion aroused foreign jealousies, slavery inflamed sectional discord, manufacturing bred labour conflict. Initially virtuous and high-minded, America had become corrupt, acquisitive, imperialistic. Critics mourned the loss of past felicity.[303]

Industrialization, mass immigration, ever more noisome and odious cities heightened longings for an imagined Jeffersonian arcadia. Newcomers from southern and eastern Europe, alien in religion, language, customs, and temperament, seemed unassimilable threats to traditional mores. Old elites retreated defensively into historical myth. As an exclusive WASP heritage, relics of the colonial past offered a seemly escape.

But rebel rhetoric was turned on its head. The sons of Founding Fathers had felt themselves inheritors of the Glorious Revolution of 1688; the great-grandsons de-revolutionized them into conservative stewards of time-honoured tradition – suitable for teaching children and immigrants to respect WASP elites.[304] The British legacy was eagerly re-embraced: early America became an offshoot of Olde England, decorously Protestant and charmingly quaint, the Revolution just a temporary disruption of close fraternal bonds. The 1880s and 1890s saw the birth of scores of Sons, Daughters, and Dames societies, with Anglo-Saxon ancestry a sine qua non of membership. Native-born or not, Americans amassed fancied ancestral paraphernalia. Household decor copied supposed colonial patterns. When hunger for antiques outstripped resources, replicas filled the gap. Heroic homesteads and relics were refurbished, memorials erected, folkways reanimated in manias for historic pageantry.[305]

---

[301] John T. Trowbridge, 'We are a nation', *Atlantic Monthly*, 14 (1864): 769–75 at 773.

[302] Quoted in Frances FitzGerald, *America Revised: History Schoolbooks in the Twentieth Century* (Random House, 1980), 62.

[303] David D. Van Tassell, *Recording America's Past* (Chicago, 1960), 95–110; Russell Lynes, *The Tastemakers* (Grosset & Dunlap, 1954), 67–70; Elson, *Guardians of Tradition*, 27–8.

[304] Ray Raphael, *Founding Myths: Stories That Hide Our Patriotic Past* (New York: New Press, 2004), 259.

[305] Cushing Strout, *The American Image of the Old World* (Harper, 1963), 135–8; Samuel P. Hays, *The Response to Industrialism 1885–1914* (Chicago, 1957), 24–5, 40–3; T. J. Jackson Lears, *No Place of Grace:*

The swing from faith in progress to fervour for the past was no instant volte-face. Many near the century's end still looked forward. But the balance had shifted. Up to the centennial, most Americans were avowed modernists: they felt fortunate to have left the outmoded past behind. The 1880s and 1890s played another tune: the past had been *better* than the present. The party of Memory for the first time seriously rivalled Emerson's party of Hope.

Founding Fathers' sons had regretted filial inferiority; nostalgic great-grandsons felt that society as a whole had regressed. The ugliness of urban life, the savagery of industrial disputes, the alien subversion of immigration, and other marks of decline were not *their* fault. They cherished the past as a haven for traditional values that might, in time, restore their beloved America and would, meanwhile, shield them from the sordid present. Although they had lost the present, the past was theirs, in relics and pedigrees lovingly handed down.[306] Harping on old English ancestry, upbringing, and tradition, Harvard English professor Barrett Wendell epitomized such angst. Feeling that 'we Yankees are as much things of the past as any race can be', he consoled himself with his Portsmouth home's six generations of memorabilia, replacing the house's Victorian with colonial-revival features. A renowned restorer urged clients to 'approximat[e] the sane life of our Colonial forbears' in the 'old-time charm' of colonial-revival cottages with plumbing and electricity.[307]

Boston Brahmins, swamped and soon politically outdone by the Irish, liked 'to greet each new dawn with the word "old": old families, old names, old money. This, by entail, becomes the right schools and occupations, "antique" woods in the parlors, Canton china, and so on'.[308] As in late-Victorian and Edwardian England, 'old money' became a bulwark against crass and vulgar new. Alternatively, old faiths offered a sanctuary from impious Gilded Age materialism, as in Henry Adams's medievalist jeremiad against Manifest Destiny and secular progress:

> Crossing the hostile seas, our greedy band
> Saw ... our father's kingdom in the promised land
> – We seized it, and dethroned the father too
> And now we are the Father, with our brood,
> Ruling the infinite, not Three but One;
> We made our world and saw that it was good;
> Ourselves we worship, and we have no Son.[309]

The earlier dilemma had been how to protect the fruits of a revolution that enjoined perpetual change. Obedience to a past that denied its own legitimacy proved

Antimodernism and the Transformation of American Culture 1880–1920 (Pantheon, 1981), 5, 60–1, 159–66, 188–9; Richard Guy Wilson et al., eds., *Re-creating the American Past: Essays on the Colonial Revival* (Virginia, 2006); David Glassberg, *American Historical Pageantry* (North Carolina, 1990).
[306] Elizabeth Stillinger, *The Antiquers, 1850–1930* (Knopf, 1980), xiii; François Weil, *Family Trees: A History of Genealogy in America* (Harvard, 2013), 120–34.
[307] James M. Lindgren, *Preserving Historic New England* (Oxford, 1995), 18–19; Joseph Everett Chandler, *The Colonial House* (New York, 1916), 258, 33.
[308] Elizabeth Hardwick, 'Cheever, or the ambiguities', *NYRB*, 20 Dec. 1984: 3.
[309] Henry Adams, *Letters to a Niece and Prayer to the Virgin of Chartres* (c. 1900; Boston, 1920), 127.

an irksome legacy. Acutely aware of what they owed immediate forebears, post-Revolutionary Americans had to escape the self-denial and self-defeat that debt implied. To that end they denigrated the past in general almost as intensely as French or Russian revolutionaries. Americans had no truck with the imitative and emulative niceties of the Renaissance and Enlightenment. Nor did the ancients–moderns distinction between progressive science and perfected art seem pertinent; Americans thought *everything* they did improved on the past. Proud of their inventive bent, they were not inhibited by great precursors in any realm but statecraft.

The *fin-de-siècle* mantra of returning to 'what the republic used to be' lasted through the early decades of the twentieth century. 'Progressivism' was couched as 'rebirth' and 'reconstruction' harking back to great origins.[310] These pieties are again resurgent today. Increasingly enamoured of their own past, Americans add historical flavour to all things present. Every landscape and townscape advertises its heritage, every product boasts time-tested worth, every Tea Party politician trumpets devotion to the Founding Fathers.

The 'great awakening' to Americans' own heritage made it no longer 'necessary to travel abroad to see Europe's sultry castles and dusty cathedrals'.[311] Yet Americans keep on going back to Europe, partly to supplement the past at home. But heirs of Hawthorne and Henry James no longer feel half-guilty about being charmed by Old World heritage, perhaps because their own, too, now seems to them both more ancient and less innocent.

The periods reviewed above exhibited diverse feelings about forerunners. Some featured archaistic zeal that vilified the present in favour of a lost or revived past; others reluctantly accepted a dominating heritage. There were times of self-confident improvement on valued precursors; times of iconoclastic frenzy that scuttled the past to aggrandize the present; and times of hapless ambivalence. How the past was gauged vis-à-vis the present varied with matters at issue, the upbeat or gloomy mood of the moment, and observers' own stage in life.

To draw creative strength from the past without being overwhelmed by it is essential: any work of merit combines respect for tradition with self-respect. But a fine balance between things and thoughts once disparaged as novelties and those now disparaged as imitations is needed. Each epoch had to come to terms with a past seemingly more creative. The classical models Renaissance humanists admired seemed superior because allied by antecedence to that primordial original, Nature. Victorians despaired of rivalling the Greeks, whose glories they attributed to an unselfconsciousness no longer possible. Post-Revolutionary Americans believed that their own pedestrian and less demanding times condemned them to unheroic custodial roles. Like many sons of famous fathers, societies overshadowed by illustrious precursors are prone to resign themselves to the rubbish heap of history. Hence young Greeks today feel impotent in classical milieus that humiliate present effort.

---

[310] David Graham Phillips, *The Plum Tree* (New York, 1905), 232; Herbert Croly, *Progressive Democracy* (Macmillan, 1914), 19.
[311] Hans G. Egli, *Jim Thorpe (formerly Mauch Chunk) Guide/History* (Jim Thorpe, 1977).

When the venerated past is near rather than remote, parental rather than ancestral, despair may be still more debilitating. Two millennia distanced antiquity into a tolerable Renaissance precursor; the gulf in time made that past so alien it had to be translated into modern idiom. Having to reconstitute classical antiquity enabled Renaissance scholars to become creative in their own right. In contrast, eighteenth-century arts were thought to stagnate because more recent exemplars were accessible in unaltered form. These fore-runners were formidably enervating precisely because they were *not* dead and lost; they loomed over successors as active ingredients of the present. Resurrecting and assimilating a remote past made Renaissance humanism utterly different from confronting nearer precursors in Enlightenment Europe and post-Revolutionary America.

Conflict sharpened again at the start of the twentieth century, when the present's insistent claims clashed head-on with nostalgia. Italian Futurists railed against the cult of past splendours that had long paralysed their country's energies; shedding inherited burdens, Futurists denied past example any merit whatsoever. And Modernists did not bother to vie with tradition; concerned only with present deeds, they sought to expunge obeisance to precursors. Modern technology and social change demanded entirely new ideas, structures, artefacts, institutions. A self-reliant, forward-looking present had to reject the past, to liquidate history, to eliminate memory.[312] Art and architecture aban-doned history teaching and jettisoned cast models in symbolic riddance of past example. Authority and tradition were *ipso facto* evil. Recent decades have reversed the impulse; the present is now often deplored, the past harked back to, though less for its examples than its supposed psychic comforts.

Those who dismiss the past as demeaning never succeed in exorcizing it. However burdensome, it remains integral to our consciousness and to all of our works. Attempts to make moderns wholly autonomous left them haunted by ancestors no less powerful for being rejected. To be a modern, one must grant the ancients their place, for without ancients there can be no moderns. At the same time, admired antiquity needs modern alloys, not just allies. 'Come to the old country, see where your ancestors came from', travel ads lure Americans to 'old' Europe. 'Come to the new country, see what your descendants have created', is an apt rejoinder.[313]

---

[312] Pierre Boulez, *Conversations with Célestin Delìege* (1975; London: Eulenberg, 1976), 31–3; Stanley Rosen, *The Ancients and the Moderns* (Yale, 1989).

[313] Dave Dame, 'The role and responsibility of interpretation' (1982), in *International Perspectives on Cultural Parks* (Washington, DC: US NPS, 1989), 225–30 at 228.

5

The look of age: aversion

> How does the look of age come? ... Does it come of itself, unobserved, unrecorded, unmeasured? or do you woo it and set baits and traps for it, and watch it like the dawning brownness of a meerschaum pipe, and make it fast, when it appears, ... and give thanks to it daily? Or do you forbid it and fight it and resist it, and yet feel it settling and deepening about you, as irresistible as fate?   Henry James, 1871[1]

> O envious age! Thou dost destroy all things with the relentless teeth of old age, little by little in a slow death. Helen, when she looked in her mirror and saw the withered wrinkles made in her face by old age, wept and wondered why she had been twice ravished.   Leonardo da Vinci, 1508[2]

> I hope I die before I get old   Pete Townshend, 1965[3]

> That doesn't mean they're old, dear. Prunes are *supposed* to be wrinkled.
> 'Dennis the Menace', 1984[4]

Awareness of things past derives from two distinct but often conjoined traits: antiquity and decay. Antiquity involves cognizance of historical change, decay of biological or material change. The benefits and burdens of the past discussed in Chapters 3 and 4 mainly concerned age in its historical sense, though often couched in metaphors of youth and old age. This and the next chapter explore views about age in its biological sense.

Marks of age are quite distinct from manifestations of antiquity, such as historical residues and revivals or retro styles. Things seem biologically aged owing to erosion or accretion, altered colours or forms. Ageing is a worn chair, a wrinkled face, a corroded tin, an ivy-covered or mildewed wall; it is a house with sagging eaves, flaking paint, furnishings faded by time and use. Whatever their historical pedigree, objects that are weathered, decayed, or bear the marks of long use *look* aged and thus seem to stem from the past.

Wear and tear exhibit myriad forms: cracked varnish, scuffed shoes, gnarled trees, rubble-strewn demolition sites, river meanders and eroded peneplains. Sounds that seem worn or flawed strike the ear as products of decay: a scratchy recording, a cracked church bell, a wheezy car engine suggest near-terminal use. A quavering voice conveys agedness because we assume the speaker is old.

---

[1] Henry James, 'A passionate pilgrim' (1871), in *Novels and Tales* (Scribners, 1908–9), 13: 333–434 at 392.
[2] Leonardo da Vinci, 'Thoughts on life', no. 101, in *Thoughts on Art and Life* (Boston, 1906), 37 (paraphrasing Ovid, *Metamorphoses* XV (A D 8), 234–6).
[3] The Who, *My Generation*, album, 1965.
[4] Hank Ketcham cartoon, *IHT*, 10 Oct. 1984.

Such signs of decay betoken extinction, imminent or eventual. No product of man or nature endures forever. 'Men's Workes have an age like themselves', observed Thomas Browne, 'and though they out-live their Authors, yet they have a stint and period to their duration'.[5] As Antonio in John Webster's *Duchess of Malfi* remarks, 'all things have their end, / Churches and Cities (which have diseases like to men) / Must have like death that we have'.[6]

> Since brass, nor stone, nor earth, nor boundless sea,
> But sad mortality o'er-sways their power ...
> ... rocks impregnable are not so stout,
> Nor gates of steel so strong, but Time decays.[7]

Only the gods are immune from age and death, Oedipus reminds Theseus; 'All other things almighty Time disquiets. Earth wastes away; the body wastes away.'[8] The most timeless art is mortal; 'the Bust outlasts the throne, the Coin Tiberius', in Théophile Gautier's phrase,[9] but remnants of bust and coin finally commingle with the dust of those they commemorate. Knowing that nothing is exempt from time's ravages, conservators accept the ultimate mortality of all they strive to save. 'There are two ways for a painting to perish', remarked the philosopher Étienne Gilson: 'one is for it to be restored; the other is for it not to be restored'.[10] Most monuments are made to last; longevity is their *raison d'être*. But as Ausonius noted, even monumental inscriptions at length perish.[11]

Some contemplate all transience with equanimity. Sigmund Freud thought submission to the brevity of existence essential to well-being. But the poet Rainer Maria Rilke, walking with Freud in the Dolomites, could scarcely enjoy the exquisite vistas, knowing that their glory was transient. 'He was unable to forget that all this beauty was fated to extinction, that it would vanish ... like all human beauty and all the beauty and splendour that men have created.'[12] Aesthetes 'in thrall to beauty [are] especially aware of, and saddened by, its ephemeral character'.

Melancholic enthusiasm will see the moth hole beneath the curtain swatch and the ruin beneath the plan, [and cannot] walk into a freshly decorated house without feeling pre-emptively sad at the decay impatiently waiting to begin: how soon the walls will crack, the white cupboards will yellow and the carpets stain.

Shrinking from 'the slow disintegration of the objects of their love', they may refuse to buy a property, 'having realised that the house under offer, as well as the city and even civilisation itself, will soon enough be reduced to fragments of shattered brick'.[13]

---

[5] Thomas Browne, *Religio Medici* (1635), in *Works* (1852; London, 1928), 1: 9–93 at 35.
[6] John Webster, *The Duchess of Malfi*, V.iii (1614; Chatto & Windus, 1958), 124.
[7] William Shakespeare, Sonnet 65 (1609).
[8] Sophocles, *Oedipus at Colonus* (Harcourt Brace, 1941), ll. 609–10, 107.
[9] Théophile Gautier, 'L'Art' (1857), in *Émaux et Camées, Poésies complètes* (Paris, 1870), 3: 128–30 at 129.
[10] Étienne Gilson, *Painting and Reality* (Routledge, 1957), 99.
[11] Ausonius, *Epitaphs* (c. 385), bk. vi, no. 32, in *Works* (Harvard, 1919), 1: 159.
[12] Sigmund Freud, 'On transience' (1915), in *CPW*, 14: 303–7.
[13] Alain de Botton, *The Architecture of Happiness* (Penguin, 2007), 15–16.

Soon enough, but not necessarily all that soon. Some things endure for millennia, others only for moments; each species and kind of object ages at its own tempo. A cat may look old at seven years, a man at seventy, a cathedral at a thousand, a mountain in a hundred million. A car seems worn in a decade, a pair of shoes in a year, a sandcastle in ten minutes. Some fungi escape both senescence and death. The immortal jellyfish, *Turritopsis dohmii*, reverts to immaturity and continues ageing and rejuvenating indefinitely. Other species get stronger and less likely to die with age.[14] Durability varies among component parts. Blood, nerves, eyes, and skin wear out differently. The duration of discarded waste is as various as the lifespans of aardvarks and apples, vaccines and vehicles. Paper boxes disintegrate within weeks, glass bottles endure centuries, the half-life of some nuclear residues is millions of years.[15] Douglas Coupland finds solid plastic ski boots 'the worst. They'll be around till the sun goes supernova.'[16]

While conservation science preserves treasured heritage ever longer, modern technology shortens the lives of everything else. The brevity built into new houses, clothes, furniture, crockery, computers affects our surroundings no less than their outright destruction. More plentiful than ever, artefacts perish at an unprecedented pace. When materials were dear and labour cheap, much was made to last, handed down over generations. Today we replace rather than repair. Who now protects fabrics with dust covers? How many turn cuffs and collars or darn socks? It costs less to fashion whole new aggregates than to refurbish old structures. Since profits depend on high turnover, old goods become obsolete even when still serviceable. 'A machine less than ten years old can no longer be repaired because the design has been abandoned', wrote a critic a generation ago. '"They're not making them any more", and the machine becomes, literally, a museum piece.'[17]

Fast-fading colours, rotting paper, jerry-built houses distressed Ruskin back in 1857, when things lasted longer than now. Ephemeral materials invited careless craftsmanship, for no 'workman worthy the name will put his brains into a cup, or an urn, which he knows is to go to the melting-pot in half a score years'.[18] A Dürer could still be handled after two centuries, but contemporary engravings frayed badly within twenty years, and a

[14] Owen R. Jones et al., 'Diversity of ageing across the tree of life', *Nature* 505 (9 Jan. 2014): 169–73; Heinz D. Osiewacz, 'Genes, mitochondria and aging in filamentous fungi', *Ageing Research Reviews* 1 (2002): 425–42; I. Yu. Popov, 'Distribution of various aging patterns in the system of the animal world', *Advances in Gerontology* 2:1 (2012): 1–9; Shin Kubota, 'Repeating rejuvenation in *Turritopsis*, an immortal hydrozoan', *Biogeography* 13 (20 Sept. 2011): 101–3.

[15] Frank Kendig and Richard Hutton, *Life-Spans or How Long Things Last* (Holt, Rinehart & Winston, 1979); Merril Silverstein et al., eds., *Handbook of Theories of Aging*, 2nd edn (Springer, 2009), 63–86, 145–244.

[16] Douglas Coupland, *Generation X* (St Martins Press, 1991), 162. See Alan Weisman, *The World without Us* (Virgin, 2007), 126–8, 247.

[17] E. R. Chamberlin, *Preserving the Past* (Dent, 1979), 79. Economic recession has revived sock darning (Matt Richtel, 'Use it up, wear it out', *NYT*, 16 Feb. 2011: B1, 4); Jonnet Middleton, 'Long live the thing! Temporal ubiquity in a smart vintage wardrobe', *Ubiquity: The Journal of Pervasive Media* 1:1 (2012): 7–22.

[18] John Ruskin, 'The discovery and application of art', in *CW* 14: 15–56 at 45–6.

century reduced them to fragments. Nowadays paper decays sooner: impregnated with sulphuric acid to prevent the feathering of iron gall ink, modern books deteriorate faster than they can be preserved. The fugacity of books attests our acquiescence to obsolescence.[19]

Many synthetic materials erode or deliquesce ever faster. Film marvellously embalms human memory, but colour photographs and videos vanish in fifty years, cyanide dye in twenty-five. 'These are mortal objects, subject to creasing, fading and deterioration', notes a film curator. We fight 'a losing battle'. The life of electronic stuff ever dwindles. In the 'computer world any book printed more than two months ago is a campy nostalgia item'. As with cellulose-nitrate film and videotape, technical advance hastens the demise of digital data. Web-page lifespans become ever more transient; of extinct websites little or nothing remains.[20]

Countless objects rapidly made useless die out. 'Hitherto, the active life of almost any given class of artefact could be measured in centuries, if not millennia; there was little difference ... between a plough used by a Roman and one used by a nineteenth-century Dorset farmer. Now the cycle of invention, use and obsolescence [takes] a decade or less', wrote a 1970s observer.[21] Today what's modern is still more ephemeral: as the Futurists happily envisioned in 1911, most things we wear, use, and see around us are now shorter-lived than we are. 'Whereas in all previous civilisations it was the object and the monument that survived the generations ... today it is we who observe the birth and death of objects.'[22]

Cheap throwaways began replacing costly durables in the mid-nineteenth century, with paper for cloth in shirt fronts, collars, and cuffs. Machine-tool replicability and marketing hastened material demise: Henry Ford boasted that his Model T (1908) lasted forever, but competition then forced him to build cars replaceable every few years. General Motors' styling wizard's 'big job [was] to hasten obsolescence'. Between 1934 and 1955 he cut average car ownership span from five years to two. His goal was one year. 'Any article that refuses to wear out', warned silverware makers catering for newly-weds, was a commercial calamity.[23] During the Depression durable goods were seen to impede recovery; a popular tract urged that death warrants accompany all manufactures. The

[19] Nicola Jones, 'Monster ink', *New Scientist*, 14 Sept. 2002: 42–5. Richard Daniel Smith, 'Paper stability and collection risk', *Restaurator* 25 (2004): 199–219; Sarah Everts, 'Conservation at arm's length', *Chemical & Engineering News* 85:36 (3 Sept. 2007): 43–5.
[20] Russell Roberts quoted in Dalya Alberge, 'Artwork worth millions will just disappear into thin air', *Times*, 28 June 2003; Neal Stephenson, *Cryptonomicon* (Heinemann, 1999), 458; Brewster Kahle, in Margaret MacLean and Ben H. Davis, eds., *Time & Bits* (J. Paul Getty Trust, 1998), 39; Diane Vogt-O'Connor, 'Is the record of the 20th century at risk?' *Cultural Resource Management* 22:2 (1999): 21–4; Roy Rosenzweig, 'Scarcity or abundance? Preserving the past in a digital era', *AHR* 108 (2003): 735–62; Daniel J. Cohen, 'The future of preserving the past', *CRM: Journal of Heritage Stewardship* 2:2 (Summer 2005): 6–19 at 14–16; Bryan Bergeron, *Dark Ages II: When the Digital Data Die* (Pearson, 2001), 81–3, 139; Jonathan D. Wren, 'URL decay in MEDLINE', *Bioinformatics* 24:11 (1 June 2008): 1381–5: Jill Lepore, 'The cobweb: can the Internet be archived?' *New Yorker*, 26 Jan. 2015: 34–41.
[21] Chamberlin, *Preserving the Past*, 79.
[22] Paul Connerton, *How Modernity Forgets* (Cambridge, 2009), 122, 143.
[23] Jane Fisk Mitarachi, 'Harvey Earl and his product' (1955), quoted in David Gartman, *Auto Opium* (Routledge, 1994), 97; Giles Slade, *Made to Break* (Harvard, 2006), 32, 46, 53.

credo of disposability was satirized in Aldous Huxley's *Brave New World*: 'ending is better than mending ... more stitches less riches'.[24]

Cults of evanescence oust decay in artefacts just as cults of rejuvenation banish ageing in human beings. 'Things do not die of old age', notes a sociologist. 'They disappear long before they reach ... "natural death"; indeed, well before they begin to show signs of "senility" ... They could be infinitely durable, if we wished them to be. But we *do not wish* them to be.' Little is cherished lifelong. 'Forget about forever – nothing lasts a year', a 2010 analyst recalled wares already in the Great Technology Graveyard: Olympus M: Robe (2004), PocketPC (2002), MicroMV (2001), MSN Explorer (2002), Smart Display (2003). Accept obsolescence when you buy a gadget 'so you feel no sense of loss when it's discontinued'.[25]

Comparative experience reframes impressions of age. 'Everything in Liverpool is old', commented an 1850s American visitor, 'yet nothing is worn out'. By contrast, New York struck a British emigrant as 'an irregular collection of temporary buildings ... not meant to endure for any length of time'.[26] A modern English observer terms New York 'a very old city, indeed one of the oldest I have ever seen', so speedily did its cast-offs decay. 'That pot-hole became old as I watched it. The broken-down, burnt and charred remains of piers on the Hudson waterfront look as old as Roman remains.' Rather than repairing something old, Americans simply add 'a new face, even if that means leaving a lot of old faces around pending replacement. So for every glistening new Pepsodent-fresh landmark in New York, there are at least a couple of rotting black teeth.'[27]

Reactions to attrition are poorly understood. Romantic ruins aside, studies of relics indiscriminately lump biological with historical age. How museum-goers feel about wear and tear in displays is little known; public preferences are surmised, not surveyed. Yet 'whether a particular thing ought to appear old or new affects everything we look at', argued a museum director.[28] The look of age or youth arouses intense feeling.

What kind of relics best evoke the past? Those bright and clean, say many, with the sparkle of youth they had when new. Others feel marks of use and time crucial to living continuity. Pasts freshly made or revived and pasts scored by time and use answer different needs and elicit different outcomes. The youthful past's unblemished beauty and the elderly past's erosions and accretions variously enliven the present. The choice affects not only what we choose to recall and preserve, but also how we distinguish past from present.

Age and decay are comprehensively vilified. We prefer youth in both ourselves and our surroundings, including most of our own creations. Observers of urban scenes held to

[24] Bernard London, *Ending the Depression through Planned Obsolescence* (pamphlet, New York, 1932), available online; Aldous Huxley, *Brave New World* (Doubleday, 1932), 58, 142; Slade, *Made to Break*, 74–8. See Vance Packard, *The Waste Makers* (New York, 1960); Gilles Lipovetsky, *The Empire of Fashion* (Princeton, 1994), 137; Susan Strasser, *Waste and Want* (Holt, 1999), 267–78.

[25] Zygmunt Bauman, *Mortality, Immortality and Other Life Strategies* (Stanford, 1992), 188; David Pogue, 'The lessons of 10 years of talking tech', *NYT*, 24 Nov. 2010.

[26] William Wells Brown, *The American Fugitive in Europe* (Boston, 1855), 41; Frances Anne Kemble [Butler], *Journal of a Residence in America* (Paris, 1835), 97.

[27] Miles Kington, 'Moreover ...', *Times*, 2 Nov. 1982: 12.

[28] Roy Strong, 'Making things as good as new', *Times*, 16 Feb. 1985: 8.

be 'new' also thought them beautiful, clean, rich, and likeable, while locales felt to be 'old' were concomitantly ugly, dirty, poor, and disliked; youth and beauty, age and repellent traits are routinely linked. The Amazonian Nambikwara conflate 'young' and 'pretty' in one word, 'old' and 'ugly' in another.[29] The patina of age is sometimes admired. But in most cultures and epochs such admiration is the exception. Few old or long-used features exhibit 'pleasing decay'; wear and tear usually portends grievous or repugnant loss of function, senescence, imminent demise, posthumous decay. Relics are treasured more for being old-fashioned than old, youthful appearance extolled even in things prized for historical antiquity.

Of the *fin-de-siècle*'s polarized views about the marks of time, art historian Alois Riegl found 'on the one hand an adoration of the old for its own sake totally opposed to renovation, ... and on the other an adoration of the new for its own sake bent on uprooting every trace of age'. But the latter predominated: 'To the great majority, only the new and the whole are beautiful; the old, the fragmented, and the faded are ugly.'[30]

This chapter explores responses to ageing in people, nature, institutions, and artefacts. I begin by examining the organic analogy – parallels commonly drawn between our own lives and the careers of natural features, societies, and relics – and show how antipathy towards decaying objects and institutions reflects abhorrence of old age in humans. The next chapter reviews contrary preferences ascribing beauty and value to marks of age and wear. Finally I suggest what taste and distaste for age imply for other apprehensions of the past.

The organic analogy

Most talk of marks of age likens nature and artefacts to our ageing selves. Organic analogy transcends metaphor. Church and state, globe and cosmos were long considered mortal beings; scientists still write of planets being born, and 'baby' and 'senescent' stars and galaxies. Anthropomorphic analogies abound in Hellenic ideals of unity and propor-tion, Pauline doctrines of Christ's mystical body, humanism's man as the measure of all things, Renaissance notions of the body politic, *fin-de-siècle* fears of civilizational decay, today's Neoplatonic cults of Gaia. All things become metaphorically human – rocks as bones, soil as flesh, grass as hair, tides as pulse, sun and moon as eyes.[31]

We endow natural features and artefacts with organic stages of birth and growth, decay and death, lifespan similes. 'Infancy', 'youth', 'maturity', and 'old age' describe nations and neighbourhoods, arts and sciences, rocks and relics. 'The duration of the world'

[29] David Lowenthal and Marquita Riel, 'The nature of perceived and imagined environments', *Environment & Behavior* 4 (1972): 189–207 at 196–7, 204–5; Charles W. Perdue and Michael B. Gurtman, 'Evidence for the automaticity of ageism', *Journal of Experimental Social Psychology* 26 (1990): 199–216 at 203; Claude Lévi-Strauss, *Tristes tropiques* (1955; Hutchinson, 1961), 279.

[30] Alois Riegl, *Der moderne Denkmalkultus* (Vienna, 1903), 47–9. See Michael Gubser, *Time's Visible Surface: Alois Riegl and the Discourse on History and Temporality in Fin-de-Siècle Vienna* (Wayne State, 2006), 147–8.

[31] Walter Raleigh, *The History of the World*, bk. I, ch. 2, sect. 5 (London, 1614), 30; Yvonne Marshall and Chris Gosden, 'The cultural biography of objects', *World Archaeology* 31 (1999): 163–78.

mirrored human life, reasoned the early-modern scholar Charles Perrault. 'Man was a child in the childhood of the world, an adolescent in its adolescence, fully a man in the prime of its life, and now both are in their old age.'[32] Urban decay bred cadaver metaphors; 'so many corpses of cities lie thrown down', exclaimed Cicero's proconsul of Achaea in 45 BC; Poggio Bracciolini in 1431 descried ruined Rome as 'a giant putrescent corpse'.[33]

Painting restorers resemble urologists whose work nobody wants to discuss but everyone needs dermatologists' facial peels and Botox to obviate later facelifts, and above all, geriatricians.[34] Once 'going to the studio was almost like going to a morgue' for a postmortem. Today's paintings are treated as ... living, breathing patients.' Rubens's *Holy Family* altarpiece, previously 'a bleeding, desiccated corpse, [is] now a fragile senior with a few health problems'. But conservators are more cautious than doctors, whose fatal blunders are soon buried, whereas restorers' botched canvases remain on display for years.[35]

Such metaphors stress aversion to senescence. Since repugnance to human old age is well-nigh universal, likening 'old' artefacts and institutions and natural features to old people betokens antipathy to their similar 'senility'. To be sure, pristine is not preferred to antiquated solely because the one spells youth and the other age. But organic metaphors harden such biases, putting new and fresh in the best light, old and stale in the worst.

So sweeping is repugnance to old age that many shun the analogy's fated terminus. Few patristic philosophers or Renaissance humanists projected cosmos or state beyond maturity to degeneration or death. Gregory the Great's three ages of the Church stopped with youth and maturity; St Augustine's City of God was incompatible with old age. Decay need not necessarily portend death; 'all that totters does not fall', wrote Montaigne, relieved that certain ancient buildings endured despite decrepitude, their very hoariness a token of enduring strength.[36] Cherished features, institutions, and artefacts were likened not to mortal but to immortal beings.

Literal belief in the world as organism and society's 'body politic' dimmed in early-modern times; Montaigne derided those who inferred 'the decline and decrepitude of the world' from their own weakness and decay.[37] But the rhetoric endured, even, as shown in the previous chapter, intensified among fractious imperial 'fathers' and

---

[32] Charles Perrault, *Paralèlle* [sic] *des anciens et des modernes, en ce qui regarde les arts et les sciences* (Paris, 1693), 34.

[33] Cornelius J. Holtorf, 'The life-history of megaliths in Mecklenburg-Vorpommern (Germany)', *World Archaeology* 30 (1998): 23–38; Servius Sulpicius Rufus to Cicero, and Gian Francesco Poggio Bracciolini, *De varietatae fortune* (c. 1443), in Francesco Orlando, *Obsolete Objects in the Literary Imagination: Ruins, Relics, Rarities, Rubbish, Uninhabited Places, and Hidden Treasures* (1994; Yale, 2006), 67–8, 85.

[34] Rebecca Mead, 'The art doctor', *New Yorker*, 11 May 2009: 58–65 at 59.

[35] Scott Schaefer, 'Comment', 107, and Jørgen Wadum, 'Ravished images restored', 59–72 at 59, in Mark Leonard, ed., *Personal Viewpoints: Thoughts about Paintings Conservation* (Getty Conservation Institute, 2003).

[36] Garry W. Trompf, *The Idea of Historical Recurrence in Western Thought* (California, 1979), 214, 282; Erwin Panofsky, 'The first page of Giorgio Vasari's "Libro"' (1930), in *Meaning in the Visual Arts* (1955; Penguin, 1993), 169–224 at 216–20; Michel de Montaigne, 'Of vanitie' (1585–8), in *The Complete Essays* (Stanford, 1958), 721–65 at 733–4.

[37] Michel de Montaigne, 'Of coaches' (1585–8), in *Complete Essays*, 685–98 at 693.

colonial 'children'. Following Herder, historians compared institutions and nations at parallel times of organic growth and decline. Inspired by evolutionary biology, Herbert Spencer's *Principles of Sociology* (1876–96) revived organic political analogies. Nowadays culture is less, nature more often, limned as organisms, but both are cast in cradle-to-grave terms.[38]

Fondness for cultural and natural features reflects their place in supposed lifespans, beauty and goodness linked with youth, ugliness and evil with old age. 'New-born' is innocent and lovely, old decrepit and foul, alike in nations, artefacts, and the world as a whole. This bias arises from profound dismay about our ageing selves.

Antipathy to age in humans and other beings

> The woods decay, the woods decay and fall,
> The vapours weep their burthen to the ground,
> Man comes and tills the field and lies beneath,
> And after many a summer dies the swan.
> Me only cruel immortality
> Consumes: I wither slowly in thine arms . . .
> Immortal age beside immortal youth,
> And all I was in ashes
> Alfred, Lord Tennyson, 1833–59[39]

Old age is nothing but an inn of infirmities, the abode of melancholy and abominations, a never-ending vexation, an incurable sore, regret for things past, pain in the present, and . . . a near neighbor of death.   Fernando de Rojas, 1499[40]

Old age can be pitiful. First it was ignored. Then it was boosterized . . . This insistence on the joys of aging, the joy of menopause, the joy of late-life sex – this is all garbage.
Nora Ephron, 2007[41]

It gets worse and worse. You become shrivelled, you become decrepit, you lose your faculties, your peer group passes away, you sit up in your room, gumming your porridge.   Woody Allen, 2010[42]

---

[38] Francis W. Coker, *Organismic Theories of the State* (Columbia, 1910); David George Hale, *The Body Politic: A Political Metaphor in Renaissance English Literature* (Mouton, 1971), 135–7; Donald A. Schön, 'Generative metaphor', in Andrew Ortony, ed., *Metaphor and Thought*, 2nd edn (Cambridge, 1993), 137–64; Robert U. Ayres, 'Life cycle analysis', *Resources, Conservation and Recycling* 14 (1995): 190–233; Robert U. Ayres, 'On the life cycle metaphor', *Ecological Economics* 48:4 (2004): 425–38. Early-modern scholars (Leibniz, Fontenelle) repudiated metaphors of ageing as decline; 'decay' morphed from natural process to technological catastrophe (Reinhart Koselleck, '"Progress" and "Decline"', in *The Practice of Conceptual History* (Stanford, 2002), 218–35).

[39] Alfred, Lord Tennyson, 'Tithonus' (1833–59), ll. 1–6, in *The Poems* (London, 1969), 1114–17 at 1114.

[40] Fernando de Rojas, *The Celestina: A Novel in Dialogue* (California, 1955), 49.

[41] Nora Ephron, 'The older woman', *NYT Magazine*, 6 May 2007: 24.

[42] Ed Symkus, 'Woody Allen as himself', *MetroWest Daily News*, 3 Oct. 2010.

Thanks to B[ritish] P[etroleum], she's looking much better than her age.
BP ad re Henry Moore's *Recumbent Figure*, 1938, Tate Gallery, 2003.[43]

Longevity and rejuvenation are wistfully conjoined. 'Thou shalt not grow old', today's Eleventh Commandment, propels searches for cosmetic and surgical fountains of youth. People can now be old without looking old. But only if they are rich and fit. The rest, their decrepitude sad to behold, are shunted out of sight in nursing 'homes' and retirement 'communities'.

The modern West is not uniquely youth-loving. Antipathy towards old age is immemorial and pervasive. Even in traditionally respectful Japan, aged people as well as things are *furukusai* – decrepit, stale, old fashioned, unsightly. Negative traits linked to the elderly show ageism is pan-cultural.[44] We shrink from our own ageing, 'a foreign country with an unknown language to the young and even the middle-aged', held an elderly memoirist.[45] 'Old age looms ahead like a calamity', reflected Simone de Beauvoir. 'Almost no one ever foresees this state before it is upon him. We look at the image of our own future provided by the old and we do not believe it ... old age is something that only affects other people.' Elderly experience of loss and loneliness, diminished beauty and health are ominous harbingers of our fate.[46]

Children's classics routinely depict the elderly, especially old women, as evil, feckless, or mad – 'wicked old witch, selfish godmother, or demented hag'. To live 'happily ever after' implies eternally carefree Neverland youth.

> Cinderella and the prince
> lived, they say, happily ever after,
> Like two dolls in a museum case
> never bothered by diapers or dust, ...
> never telling the same story twice,
> never getting a middle-aged spread,
> their darling smiles pasted on for eternity.
> Regular Bobbsey Twins.[47]

Ageing has long been a misfortune, if not condign punishment, for living past one's prime. Adam is warned by Milton's archangel Michael that his beauty will wither, his pleasures dull, his wits wander.[48] Accursed by Christ, the Wandering Jew walks the earth until the Second Coming:

[43] *ArtWatch UK*, no. 18 (Spring–Summer 2003): 25.
[44] Marlene P. Soulsby, 'The sadness and beauty of aging in Murasaki and Kawabata', in M. P. Soulsby and J. T. Fraser, eds., *Time* (Greenwood, 2001), 19–30 at 20; Amy J. C. Cuddy et al., 'This old stereotype', *Journal of Social Issues* 61 (2005): 267–85 at 273–4.
[45] May Sarton, *As We Are Now* (Norton, 1973), 23.
[46] Simone de Beauvoir, *Old Age* (1970; Penguin, 1977), 10–13. See Sylvia Henneberg, *The Creative Crone* (Missouri, 2010), 2-4; Yiwei Chen et al., 'Counteracting age stereotypes', *Educational Gerontology* 36 (2010): 702–17.
[47] Sylvia Henneberg, 'Moms do badly, but grandmas do worse', *Journal of Aging Studies* 24 (2010): 125–39 at 128; Anne Sexton, 'Cinderella', in *Transformations* (Houghton Mifflin, 1971), 56–7.
[48] John Milton, *Paradise Lost* (1667; London, 1821), bk. 11, ll. 538–41.

> Unwilling witness of Life's hapless end,
> Stern matter's slow decay, and over Time
> Eternity's dread triumph, THE LAST MAN
> Now lived alone in all his quenchless pain ...
> Worn by his curse, and weary with old age,
> Furrow'd with care, Ahasuerus stood.[49]

'We all wish to prolong our life into old age', Abelard reiterated a medieval staple, but no one wants 'to be, or to be called, an old man'.[50] Fated to senile immortality, Jonathan Swift's Struldbrugs at ninety lacked teeth, eyesight, and memory.[51]

Worse yet, these ghastly oldsters would haunt us all, condemned to cohabit with undead revenants. 'We invest these remains – these wasted and torn bodies, these skeletons, these ashes – with special powers', writes a psychoanalyst. But however we seek 'to disgorge them, disperse them, or pacify them through ritual or revenge, we never finish burying them'.[52] Martin Amis is not alone in forecasting a *Logan's Run*-type chronological cleansing of the very old 'hogging the social services and stinking up the clinics and the hospitals'.[53]

In the Grimm tale, God originally set all creatures' lifespan at 30 years. Finding so long a life wearisome, the ass, dog, and monkey had theirs reduced by 18, 12, and 10 years respectively. Only man wished a longer life, adding to his previous span the 40 years other creatures had relinquished. He paid dearly for longevity. At 48 his condition became the ass's, carrying countless burdens; at 60 the dog's, growling toothlessly and dragging himself from corner to corner; at 70 the derisory, witless monkey's.[54] In line with the second childhood implied by the life cycle's rising and falling arc, 'Ages of man' stages-of-life charts labelled the '50s 'decline', the '60s 'decadence', the '70s 'decrepitude', and the '80s 'imbecility' (Fig. 15).[55] Erasmus's hugely popular *Praise of Folly* (1509), extolled the virtues of first infancy ('the merriest part of life') and then ironically of dotage, forgetfulness enabling men to 'wash away ... the perplexity of their minds, and so wax young again'.[56]

---

[49] [Robert Tyler], *Ahasuerus* (New York, 1842), 37.

[50] Peter Abelard, *Carmen ad Astralabium*, cited in Juanita Ruys, 'Medieval Latin meditations on old age', in Albrecht Classen, ed., *Old Age in the Middle Ages and the Renaissance* (De Gruyter, 2007), 171–200 at 189.

[51] Jonathan Swift, *Gulliver's Travels*, pt. III, ch. 10 (1726; Penguin, 1967), 257–60, and 'Thoughts on various subjects' (1727), in *The Prose Works of Jonathan Swift* (Blackwell, 1957–9), 4: 243–54 at 246. On endless ageing, see George Bernard Shaw, *Back to Methuselah* (Constable, 1921); Karel Capek, *The Makropoulos Secret* (Boston, 1923); Aldous Huxley, *After Many a Summer Dies the Swan* (Harper & Row, 1939).

[52] Roy Schafer, *Tragic Knots in Psychoanalysis* (London: Karnac, 2009), 26–7.

[53] Martin Amis, *The Pregnant Widow* (Knopf, 2010), 183; William F. Nolan and George Clayton, *Logan's Run* (New York, 1967).

[54] Jacob and Wilhelm Grimm, 'Die Lebenzeit' (1840), in *Kinder- und Hausmärchen*, no. 176 (Berlin, 1867).

[55] J. A. Burrow, *The Ages of Man* (Clarendon Press, 1986); Kathleen M. Woodward, *Aging and Its Discontents* (Indiana, 1991), 21; Pat Thane, ed., *The Long History of Old Age* (Thames & Hudson, 2005), 198; Anouk Janssen, 'The good, the bad, and the elderly', and Harry Peters, 'Jupiter and Saturn: medieval ideals of "Elde"', in Classen, *Old Age in the Middle Ages*, 437–83, 375–91.

[56] Desiderius Erasmus, *The Praise of Folly* (1509; Michigan, 1958), 18–19.

Figure 15 Elderly decrepitude: G.O. Wasenius, 'Ages of Man' 1831

Prolonged old age struck Edward Young (who lived to eighty-four) as grievous folly:

> For what live ever here? – With labouring step
> To tread our former footsteps? pace the round
> Eternal? ... to beat, and beat, / The beaten track? ...
> To taste the tasted, and at each return / Less tasteful?
>
> ********
>
> Ere man has measured half his weary stage, ...
> On cold-served repetitions he subsists,
> And in the tasteless present chews the past;
> Disgusted chews, and scarce can swallow down,
> Like lavish ancestors, his earlier years
> Have disinherited his future hours.[57]

Roger Bacon's alchemist followers and would-be centenarian Luigi Cornaro's hygienists apart, few fancied patriarchal let alone saintly longevity. And medical tenets increasingly linked old age with unavoidable, irreversible, often pathological decline. By the twentieth century senescence was firmly equated with senility.[58]

[57] Edward Young, *The Complaint: or, Night-Thoughts* (1742; London, 1813), 54.
[58] Gerald J. Gruman, *A History of Ideas about the Prolongation of Life* (1966; Springer, 2003);
Carole Haber, 'From senescence to senility', *International Journal of Aging and Human Development* 19

The aged and their stigmas are less demeaned in some societies and eras. Longevity in biblical annals was a divine attribute, hence uniquely exempt from decay and decline. Many Protestants held the long lived blessed, the pious elderly close to salvation, 'visible monuments of sovereign grace'. Puritans deferred to their elders, 'The hoary head is a crown of glory' (Proverbs 10:31) a New England commonplace. Old age betokened God's special favour. God's own face was older than time; the Puritan Christ, taken from the Book of Revelation, had hair white as snow. The god-like elderly gave valued advice: 'His hoary hairs, and grave aspect made way, / And all gave ear, to what he had to say', in Anne Bradstreet's lines.[59] Preachers enjoined the elderly to strive for biblically sanctioned health and social usefulness to the end, grandfather ticking on like an old clock up to 90. Distinguishing physical from spiritual ageing allowed them to see something more than decrepitude. Wrinkles evinced rectitude.[60]

Yet the old were honoured less in practice than in precept. 'To treat Aged Persons with disrespectful and disdainful language' was ungodly, but it was common to speak with contempt of '*Old Such An One*'.[61] John Stuart Mill thought deference for old age 'a conspicuous feature … of the ancient commonwealths'. But then, as now, ritualized deference was commonly mistaken for active respect.[62]

Elderly folk are more stigmatized when numerous, as in the last outbreak of the Black Death, which killed off more of the young and left society geriatrically burdened. Contrariwise, the rare octogenarian in seventeenth-century France was a legendary sage. But while a rich old man might be a venerated patriarch, the aged poor were cast out as coots and codgers, their miseries exacerbated by Poor Law incarceration.[63] Up to the 1940s old age assumed a 'most terrifying guise' in Ronald Blythe's rural England; 'the fate of the common labourer and his wife … was to be punished by society for

---

(1984): 41–5; Lucian Boia, *Forever Young* (Reaktion, 2004); David Boyd Haycock, *Mortal Coil: A Short History of Living Longer* (Yale, 2008).

[59] Nathanael Emmons, 'Piety, a peculiar ornament to the aged' (c. 1800), in *The Works of Nathanael Emmons, D.D.* (Boston, 1842), 2: 492–505 at 497–8; Anne Bradstreet, 'Of the four ages of man' (1678), ll. 49–50, in *The Works of Anne Bradstreet* (Harvard, 1967), 52. But she later deplored old age: 'My memory is bad, my brain is dry … My grinders are few, my sight doth fail / My skin is wrinkled' (ll. 416–20 at 63). See John Demos, 'Old age in early New England', in David D. Van Tassell, ed., *Aging, Death and Completion of Being* (PennPress, 1979), 115–64.

[60] Carole Haber and Brian Gratton, *Old Age and the Search for Security* (Indiana, 1994), 147–58.

[61] Increase Mather, *Dignity and Duty of Aged Servants of the Lord* (1716), quoted in David Hackett Fischer, *Growing Old in America* (Oxford, 1978), 59–60. See John R. Gillis, *A World of Their Own Making: Myth, Ritual, and the Quest for Family Values* (Basic Books, 1996), 54–7.

[62] John Stuart Mill, 'The spirit of the age, IV' (1831), in *CW*, 22: 289–95 at 293; Robert Kastenbaum and Barbara Ross, 'Historical perspectives on care', in John G. Howells, ed., *Modern Perspectives in the Psychiatry of Old Age* (New York: Brunner Mazel, 1975), 421–49.

[63] Marilyn Sandidge, 'Forty years of plague', in Classen, *Old Age in the Middle Ages*, 357–73 at 365–6; Pierre Goubert, *Louis XIV and Twenty Million Frenchmen* (Penguin, 1970), 21; George Rousseau, 'Towards a geriatric enlightenment', in Kevin L. Cope, ed., *1650–1850: Ideas, Aesthetics, and Inquiries in the Early Modern Era* (New York: AMS Press, 2001), 6: 3–44. Yet indigent rural elderly were not utterly cast out; 'they delivered messages, as well as babies. They nursed the sick, washed the dead, swept the church, and sometimes collected poor relief' (Lynn A. Botelho, *Old Age and the English Poor Law, 1500–1700* (Boydell, 2004), 153).

daring to grow old', so off they went to the workhouse to 'scrub and peel and chop their paths to the grave'.[64]

No longer in the workhouse, many today pine away in care facilities. Yet growing numbers win them political clout and economic security. America's Gray Panthers and Association of Retired People (AARP) form a formidable lobby; as in ageing Europe, no government dares pare pensioner perquisites. But longevity makes old people ever more burdensome to their juniors. And new technologies devalue inputs from the elderly, skills obsolete, counsel unsought. With the printing press, wise elders ceased to be exclusive repositories of wisdom; the Industrial Revolution reduced the value of long-inculcated craft skills. The British Company of Veteran Motorists renamed itself the Guild of Experienced Motorists lest it be thought a bunch of dodderers; 'veteran' now implying 'old', much as 'pensioner' suggests being put out to pasture.[65] Recession and baby-boomer retirement exacerbate ageism in America, afflicting even the middle aged. And the hapless very old, assailed by 'the most pejorative epithets the culture can devise', more and more hearken to Eskimo-on-an-ice-floe duty-to-die rhetoric.[66]

Increasingly, old age is stigmatized as presaging death. In the past working people aged early, as bent and withered at forty as today's centenarians. Few lived long enough to incur the geriatric ills that now afflict millions. The rare survivors to advanced age often kept fit until the end. Elderly ministers, teachers, statesmen seldom retired; patriarchs clung to power and office, Hawthorne's 'gray champions' to the last.[67] In former times, old people deprived of social roles soon perished; today's elderly often survive thirty or forty years beyond their ability to – or society's willingness to let them – contribute.

Old age today is more firmly linked with death because those who die of 'natural' causes are mainly the old. Death formerly struck with little warning at all ages, most frequently in infancy; indeed, those who survived early childhood not uncommonly lived into their fifties and sixties. But in lands where medical care now saves all but a few of the young, only the elderly seem mortal.[68] 'Old age is dreaded because it has become the only *normal* death-age.' Oldsters banish the thought by becoming Senior Citizens, but they die anyway. The old are avoided not only as hideous eyesores and helpless nuisances but as moribund harbingers.[69]

They are shunned even by those essential to their well-being. While the elderly become more numerous, geriatric specialists dwindle; their numbers in the United States fell by a third between 1998 and 2004. The reason is revulsion:

Mainstream doctors are turned off by geriatrics . . . The Old Crock is deaf. The Old Crock has poor vision, The Old Crock's memory might be somewhat impaired. With the Old Crock, you have to slow down, because he asks you to repeat . . . And the Old Crock doesn't have a chief complaint –

[64] Ronald Blythe, *The View in Winter: Reflections on Old Age* (Allen Lane, 1979), 52. See Charles Booth, *The Aged Poor in England and Wales* (London, 1894).
[65] 'Times diary', *Times*, 28 May 1983: 8; John Macnicol, *Age Discrimination* (Cambridge, 2006), 11.
[66] Margaret M. Gullette, *Agewise: Fighting the New Ageism in America* (Chicago, 2011), 14, 21–30, 221–2.
[67] Nathaniel Hawthorne, 'The gray champion' (1835), in *Works*, 9: 9–18.
[68] Joel T. Rosenthal, *Old Age in Late Medieval England* (PennPress, 1996); Albrecht Classen, 'Introduction', in Classen, ed., *Old Age in the Middle Ages*, 1–84 at 41–2.
[69] Blythe, *View in Winter*, 96; Greenberg et al., 'Ageism'.

the Old Crock has fifteen chief complaints . . . You're not going to cure something he's had for fifty years. He has high blood pressure, he has diabetes. He has arthritis. There's nothing glamorous about taking care of any of those things.[70]

The look of age seldom wins admiration even where it commands respect. Age-linked changes in stature, face, and voice connote weakness. Senescence sounds hoarse, crackly, squeaky, whiny, slurry, shrill, grumpy, feeble, blurred.[71] In ancient Greece only Cronos' first Golden Generation had lived like gods without 'dreadful old age'. Eos, the goddess of dawn, carried off the Trojan prince Tithonus, but forgot to ask Zeus to grant him eternal youth: when Tithonus turned gray she left his bed, and as 'savage old age' neared shut him up out of sight. The 'beautiful death' of Greek warriors in the full flower of youth saved them from the inexorable decay of ageing. Classical writers and orators decried old age as dismal and repugnant: Mimnermus hoped to die before he became an old man 'repulsive to young women'; Juvenal deplored 'doddering voices and limbs, bald heads, running noses'; Ovid warned a young woman that 'her fair face will be marred by the long years, and wrinkles of age' would ruin her beauty.[72] Merciless medieval descriptions and depictions of the old enlarged on the horror portrayed in Ecclesiastes and by Horace, Juvenal, and Martial.[73] The future Pope Innocent III's influential *De miseria humanae conditionis* (1195) gives an excoriating account of the evils of old age.

Scriptural annals likewise doted on the appearance of youth. Resurrected bodies would enjoy the beauty they 'should have attained in the flower of youth', promised St Augustine.[74] Icons celebrated Jesus only as a child and young man, St Irenaeus alone suggesting that had He lived to be old, He might have consecrated 'each stage of life by a likeness to himself, sanctifying the older men, and becoming an example to them also'.[75] Most felt, like St Thomas Aquinas, that Christ had chosen 'to commend the more His

[70] Felix Silverstone quoted in Atul Gawande, 'The way we age now', *New Yorker*, 30 Apr. 2007: 50–9 at 53; Atul Gawande, *Being Mortal* (Henry Holt, 2014), 36, 41, 52. See Todd D. Nelson, 'Ageism: prejudice against our feared future self', *Journal of Social Issues* 61:2 (2005): 207–21 at 211–13.

[71] Sue Ellen Linville, 'The sound of senescence', *Journal of Voice* 10:2 (1996): 190–200; Peter B. Mueller, 'Voice ageism', *Contemporary Issues in Communication Science and Disorders* 25 (Spring 1998): 62–4.

[72] Jean-Pierre Vernant, 'A "beautiful death" and the disfigured corpse in Homeric epic' (1982), in *Mortals and Immortals* (Princeton, 1991), 50–74; Hesiod, *Works and Days*, and *Homeric Hymns*, in Mary Lefkowitz, *Greek Gods, Human Lives* (Yale, 2003), 26, 38–9; Mimnermus, 'Censure of age' (*c.* 630–600 BC), in *Greek Lyric Poetry* (Schocken, 1972), 102–3; Juvenal, *The Satires* (early second century AD), no. 10, ll. 191–5 (Indiana, 1958), 128; Ovid, *Tristia* (after AD 8) bk. III, ch. 7, ll. 33–7 (Heinemann, 1924), 129. See Tim Parkin, *Old Age in the Roman World* (Johns Hopkins, 2003).

[73] Shulamith Shahar, *Growing Old in the Middle Ages* (Routledge, 1997), 47–51; Patrizia Bettella, *The Ugly Woman* (Toronto, 2005), 17–18; Erin J. Campbell, ed., *Growing Old in Early Modern Europe* (Ashgate, 2006); Umberto Eco, comp., *On Ugliness* (London: Harvill Secker, 2007), 160–7; Gretchen Mieszkowski, 'Old age and medieval misogyny', 299–320, Karen Pratt, '*De vetula*: the figure of the old woman in medieval French literature', 321–42, and Ruys, 'Medieval Latin meditations on old age', 172–3, all in Classen, *Old Age in the Middle Ages*.

[74] Augustine of Hippo, *The City of God* (413–26), bk. 22, ch. 20 (New York, 1886), 449.

[75] Irenaeus, *Adversus Haereses* (*c.*180), II, xxii, in *The Early Christian Fathers* (Oxford, 1956), 29–50; Shahar, *Growing Old in the Middle Ages*, 52–3.

love by giving up His life for us when He was in His most perfect state of life'.[76] In God's years 'there is no climacter', held Thomas Browne, lest 'long life be but a prolongation of death'.[77] In Renaissance art the young Son gained pictorial supremacy, the white-bearded Father seldom depicted. 'Ages of Man' sketches showed old men not as great warriors and wise rulers but as drowsy, senile invalids.

To charges that Michelangelo's painting of the Virgin made her look too young, Vasari retorted that spotless maidens long look youthful. Beauteous youth signified immortal sanctity, exempt saint-like from earthly decay.[78] Unblemished saints reflected popular distress at the putrescence and corruption of mortal remains. The damned in hell were portrayed as perpetually gnawed away and dismembered.[79] The Peter Pan syndrome, *puer aeternus*, links immaturity with eternal youth. Shunning adulthood as 'the first stage of death', SF guru Damon Knight's characters 'never mature . . . and that's why we don't die . . . We're the eternal adolescents of the universe.'[80]

Father Time came to symbolize decay and dissolution, his scythe, hourglass, and crutches linking old age with indigent decrepitude. Often a one-legged cripple or skeletal demon, he was a procurer of death who lurked among barren trees and ruinous buildings.[81] The transience of beauty and the inevitability of ugly old age obsessed Elizabethans.

> When I have seen by Time's fell hand defac'd
> The rich-proud cost of outworn buried age; . . .
> Ruin hath taught me thus to ruminate –
> That Time will come and take my love away.

'Time's injurious hand' and 'age's cruel knife' effaced comeliness along with youth.[82]

The old sisters in a Neapolitan fairy tale are 'the summary of all misfortunes, the register of all deformities, the ledger of all ugliness; to prevent even the Sun from [glimpsing] their hideous appearance, they stayed holed up' in a basement. The rejuvenation of ugly old crones, a Restoration trope, features a miller's promise to grind 'old, decrepit, wrinckled, blear-eyed, long nosed, blind, lame' women – even a 'Granny of ninety' – into handsome young wives.[83] Against ageing Thomas Hardy invoked oblivion:

> These market-dames, mid-aged, with lips thin-drawn,
> And tissues sere, are they the ones we loved in years agone,
> And courted here? . . .

---

[76] Thomas Aquinas, *Summa theologica* (1265–74), vol. 4, pt III, sect. 1 (New York: Cosimo, 2007), 2269.
[77] Browne, *Religio Medici*, in *Works* (1852), 1: 57.
[78] Giorgio Vasari, *Lives of the Most Eminent Painters, Sculptors, and Architects* (1550/1568; London, 1850), 4: 115. See Beauvoir, *Old Age*, 159–60; Philippe Ariès, *Hour of Our Death* (Penguin, 1983), 299.
[79] Caroline Walker Bynum, *The Resurrection of the Body in Western Christianity, 200–1336* (Columbia, 2005), 84, 104–8, 292.
[80] Damon Knight, 'Dio' (1957), in Frederik Pohl, ed., *The SFWA Grand Masters* (New York: Tor, 2000–1), 3: 209–43 at 230.
[81] Erwin Panofsky, 'Father Time' (1939), in *Studies in Iconology* (Harper & Row, 1972), 69–93.
[82] William Shakespeare, Sonnets, 64, 63 (1609).
[83] Giambattista Basile, 'The old woman who was skinned', in *The Tale of Tales* (1634; Wayne State, 2007), 115–25 at 115–16; John Dean, *The Dutch-Miller* (London, 1680).

> They must forget, forget! They cannot know
> What once they were, or memory would transfigure them, and show
> Them always fair.[84]

And Robert Frost feigned stoical resignation over transient beauty:

> The witch that came (the withered hag)
> To wash the step with pail and rag,
> Was once the beauty, Abishag . . .
>
> Die early and avoid the fate
> Or if predestined to die late,
> Make up your mind to die in state.
>
> Make the whole stock exchange your own!
> If need be occupy a throne,
> Where nobody can call *you* crone . . .
>
> No memory of having starred
> Atones for later disregard,
> Or keeps the end from being hard.[85]

Those who forgot or cloaked their age were ridiculed. Falstaff is reminded of his moist eye, dry hand, yellow cheek, white beard, and increasing belly. 'Is not your voice broken, your wind short, your chin double, your wit single, and every part about you blasted with antiquity?'[86] Dryden's Florimell resolved to 'look young till forty, and slip out of the world with the first wrinckle, and the reputation of five and twenty'.[87] Shuddering at ancient crones' 'baked apple ugliness', Gautier's maiden 'never looked at an old woman without horror . . . and I pray God that I may die young . . . Old women should . . . have enough respect for their imminent death to avoid rigging themselves out in . . . fripperies which beseem only the greenest youth. It is idle for them to coquet with life, for life has no more use for them.'[88]

Beauty is still limited to youth. 'They are old, *they are old*', an English boy of seventeen dismisses the elderly; 'they are ill and ugly and their life is over'. Or else ludicrous, like the Philip Larkin character whose 'eccentric appearance [harmonized] with the caricaturing onset of age'.[89] Film director Billy Wilder (who lived to ninety-six) hoped that 'maybe some day somebody will see beauty in gray hair and some sort of wisdom in experience, not just dirty old men and crazy old ladies in tennis shoes'. It is a forlorn hope. 'What

[84] Thomas Hardy, 'At Casterbridge Fair' (1902), in *Collected Poems* (Macmillan, 1948), 225.
[85] 'Provide, provide' (1934), in *The Poetry of Robert Frost* (Random House, 2001), 307.
[86] William Shakespeare, *Henry IV, Part 2* (1596–9), I.ii, ll. 206–10.
[87] John Dryden, *Secret Love, or, the Maiden Queen* (1668), III.i, in *Works*, 9: 123–203 at 160.
[88] Théophile Gautier, *Mademoiselle de Maupin* (1835; Folio Society, 1948), 208–9; Mary Russo, 'Aging and the scandal of anachronism', in Kathleen M. Woodward, ed., *Figuring Age: Women, Bodies, Generations* (Indiana, 1999), 20–33.
[89] Blythe, *View in Winter*, 120; Philip Larkin, *A Girl in Winter* (Faber & Faber, 1975), 192–3.

Figure 16 The evils of age: Pompeo Batoni, *Time orders Old Age to destroy Beauty*, 1746

would happen to the face-lift trade if our culture accepted the beauty of Rembrandt's mother as he painted her?'[90]

Computer-generated age-progression portraits of faces ten, twenty, or thirty years on, now deployed in searches for wanted criminals and missing children, arouse dismay.[91] A 'Face Aging' exhibition let viewers see their future selves at yearly intervals up to sixty-nine. As features sagged and wrinkled, pouched and rutted, and hair thinned and whitened, visiting schoolchildren were shaken and alienated; 'I don't want to get old' was the recurrent reaction as they fled, the show confirming stereotypes that 'aging is terrible'. Horrified by a withered old soul's marks of blight and death, a small boy tearfully asked his mother 'if that would happen to me too. The wrinkles, the blotched skin, the gnarled hands ... '.[92] When cosmetically 'aged' for film roles, admired young actors became repellent to TV viewers.[93]

Old people themselves shun the look of age. 'I really must not meet my image in a mirror', wrote André Gide at eighty – 'these bags under the eyes, these hollow cheeks, those drawn features'.[94] Yet age-segregation more and more consigns the elderly to locales where decrepitude is pervasive. 'You know what bugs me?' one Florida oldster says to another. 'Everybody I know is wizened.'[95]

Sexual pulchritude especially requires unblemished youth; a few wrinkles and a slight sag in the buttocks put Hugh Hefner's bunnies on the shelf at twenty-seven. Today 'the ideal age for feminine pulchritude is dropping toward thirteen'.[96] Like Shakespeare's 'Dark Lady' (Sonnet 130), a seventeenth-century traveller likened the ruins of Rome to fair ladies in old age, 'yet so comely, that they ravish still the beholders eye with their Beauties',[97] but they were clearly *more* beautiful when young. Benjamin Franklin commended older mistresses as grateful, knowing, and prudent but added that women 'study to be good' only when they 'cease to be handsome'.[98]

The ageing of formerly seductive women excites male revulsion as reminders of lost joys, dread of impotence, and harbingers of impending demise. When Rider Haggard's Ayesha starts to look her two thousand years, her lover sees on her withered face a 'stamp of unutterable age ... too hideous for words'.[99] Orwell's George Bowling can scarcely

---

[90] Mary Blume, 'Billy Wilder tackles the only taboo left', *IHT*, 3–4 Sept. 1977; Penelope Gilliatt, 'Study of a man under the axe', *New Yorker*, 13 Sept. 1976: 127–30 at 127.

[91] Michael L. Sand and Nancy Burton, *Seeing and Believing* (Santa Fe: Twin Palms, 2002); Maulin R. Gandhi, 'A Method for Automatic Synthesis of Aged Human Facial Features' (M.Sc.Eng. thesis, McGill University, 2004); S. J. Gibson et al., 'Computer assisted age progression', *Forensic Science, Medicine, and Pathology* 5:3 (Sept. 2009): 174–81.

[92] William Ian Miller, *Losing It: In Which an Aging Professor Laments His Shrinking Brain* (Yale, 2011), 17.

[93] Margaret Morganroth Gullette, *Aged by Culture* (Chicago, 2004), 3–8; Liz Gill, 'Older and wiser', *Times*, 10 Aug. 2004: 2:11.

[94] André Gide, *So Be It, or, the Chips Are Down* (1952; Knopf, 1959), 67.

[95] Stan Coren, *New Yorker*, 2 Dec. 1974: 56. Wizened Old Men, a classic Ontario rock-and-roll band (started 2002), deny being either wizened or old (nor are they all men).

[96] Gullette, *Aged by Culture*, 23.

[97] Richard Lassels, *The Voyage of Italy* (London, 1670), 120. The love of ugly old beauties was a mannerist trope exemplified in Robert Burton's *Anatomy of Melancholy* (Oxford, 1621); see Eco, *On Ugliness*, 170–3.

[98] 'Old mistresses apologue' (25 June 1745), in *The Papers of Benjamin Franklin*, (Yale, 1961), 3: 30–1.

[99] H. Rider Haggard, *She* (1887; London: Macdonald, 1948), 299.

credit the ravages that have transformed his long-lost girlfriend, then a comely wench of 22, into an old hag of 47.[100] Finding his former lover now a 'foul and rotted ancient woman', Carlos Fuentes's protagonist sees her wreckage as 'something worse than time', the work of disease and immeasurable evil.[101] Misogynist images have softened little since medieval portrayals of 'repulsive, toothless, stinking, ancient women' who are not only disgusting but 'crafty, dangerous, serving the devil' with poisonous post-menopausal toxins and vapours.[102]

But the archetype of age abhorrence is a male narcissist. Oscar Wilde's Dorian Gray dreads the 'day when his face would be wrinkled and wizen, his eyes dim and colourless, the grace of his figure broken and deformed ... He would become dreadful, hideous, and uncouth.' His portrait's conflation of age with evil, wickedness with decay, foretells the fearsome future:

It might escape the hideousness of sin, but the hideousness of age was in store for it. The cheeks would become hollow or flaccid. Yellow crow's feet would creep round the fading eyes and make them horrible. The hair would lose its brightness, the mouth would gape or droop, would be foolish or gross, as the mouths of old men are. There would be the wrinkled throat, the cold, blue-veined hands, the twisted body.[103]

He hides his picture because he cannot bear its signs of age, and perishes bearing them when he destroys it.

Concealing our own ravages of time is an ever-growing obsession. Fortunes are spent on facelifts, dyeing hair, smoothing wrinkles, firming flabby flesh. 'Golden Oldies' praises pop songs, not people. Other words cut worse: a teenager's father's generation are 'oldies', folk in their sixties 'wrinklies', great-grandma 'the crumblie'. The white locks, wrinkled cheeks, and shuffling gait of the elderly outcast in the film *Logan's Run* (1976) made him in youthful eyes not only weird but obscene. Not just wrinkles and varicose veins but ageing itself is now obsolete, 'a biological process that occurred before the advent of plastic surgery'.[104]

Antipathy to ageing even suffuses the lingo of developmental biology. Old age is routinely linked to deleterious decay and mortal decline. Scientists refer to 'weary old' molecules, 'ageing' proteins, 'retiring old' cells 'almost as if they had grey beards and used a zimmer frame to go and collect their pensions'.[105] Repugnance to old age extends to its accessories. 'Serviced with dentures, lenses, tiny loudspeakers, sticks, and hip-pins', noted

[100] George Orwell, *Coming Up for Air* (1939; Penguin, 1962), 205.
[101] Carlos Fuentes, *Terra Nostra* (1975; Farrar, Strauss & Giroux, 1976), 536–7.
[102] Mieszkowski, 'Old age and medieval misogyny', 299, 318–19. See Bettella, *Ugly Woman*, 71–2, 168. These female evils stem from Eve's corruption of nature, left 'defaced, disordered, mangled, and filthily spotted' (John Calvin, *Institutes of the Christian Religion* (1536), quoted in Naomi Baker, '"To make love to a deformity": praising ugliness in early modern England', *Renaissance Studies* 22 (2008): 86–109 at 87).
[103] Oscar Wilde, *The Picture of Dorian Gray* (1891; London: Dent, 1930), 91, 171.
[104] Anna Jane Grossman, *Obsolete: An Encyclopedia of Once-Famous Things Passing Us By* (Abrams, 2011), 21.
[105] John A. Vincent, 'The cultural construction of old age as a biological phenomenon', *Journal of Aging Studies* 22 (2008): 331–9 at 336.

Blythe, 'the flesh has become absurd'.[106] Russell Baker expressed dismay at such gifts as a rocking-chair, bifocal cleansers, pomade to conceal grey hair, a stair-rail lift, and – the ultimate indignity – a copy of *How to Avoid Probate*.[107]

Age is derogated in animals and plants as well. The old creature – spent, bedraggled, lame – is less attractive than the playful cub or virile adult; the faithful old dog is loved *despite* its odour of age. The long-lived tortoise is a curiosity, not a beauty. Decaying flowers have small allure; they 'wither like old and overly made-up dowagers, and they die ridiculously'.[108] Only old trees are partly exempt from such opprobrium. 'While animal decay is ugly', held an aesthete, 'vegetable decay is beautiful or tolerable'. Ancient trees, most appealing in old age, betoken beloved bonds.[109] England's gnarled oak, California's enduring redwood, the shade of the old apple tree, each is spared the woodman's axe for 'In youth it sheltered me, / And I'll protect it now'. Wordsworth bemoaned the loss of 'a brotherhood of venerable Trees' which, like Felicia Hemans's 'stately Homes of England ... amidst their tall ancestral trees', attested long continuity.[110] The 'quiet melancholy' of decaying patriarchal trees induced 'reverence for antiquity'.[111]

Even aged trees repel, however, where overabundant or moribund. Old age is odious if it is the only age in view. The gaunt massed remains of England's deciduous groves, some time-worn remnants of Parliamentary enclosures, others post-war victims of Dutch elm disease, evoke sorrow, even disgust. 'A certain amount of death and decay' is normal, but 'an excessive number of dying trees is a disagreeable symptom of a landscape out of balance'. While a few ancient trees in splendid health stimulate nostalgia for past glories, a plethora of degenerates become distressing reminders of loss.[112] The occasional dying tree connotes continuity, but wholesale extinction signals ruthless ruin. A regretful industrialist termed the 'dilapidated black and lifeless' skeletons among the blast furnaces of the polluted Midlands 'vegetable death in its saddest aspect'.[113] European copper and weeping beeches planted all at once, picturesque Gilded Age icons in elegant Newport, Rhode Island, are now ageing all at once, degenerating into unsightly, blighted, barkless skeletons.[114]

Products of plant decay have a certain charm. Slime moulds congeal into powdery grey or sulphur and crimson spores that allure a few. Stem decay yields the stunning intricacy of bird's-nest fungus. But gardeners usually link slime mould, rust, and fungi with disease and death; hence these excrescences, though essential adjuncts of the plants they infest,

---

[106] Blythe, *View in Winter*, 200.

[107] Russell Baker, 'Christmas orange', *IHT*, 21 Dec. 1979: 18.

[108] Georges Bataille, 'The language of flowers' (1929), in *Visions of Excess* (Minnesota, 1985), 10–14 at 12.

[109] Bernard Bosanquet, *A History of Aesthetic* (1932; rev. edn New York, 1957), 436. See Judith E. Schlanger, *Les Métaphores de l'organisme* (1971; Paris: L'Harmattan, 1995), 199–204.

[110] George Pope Morris, 'Oak', in *The Deserted Bride and Other Poems* (New York, 1838), 19; William Wordsworth, 'Degenerate Douglas', in *Poetical Works* (Clarendon Press, 1940–66), 3: 83; Felicia Hemans, 'The homes of England' (1827), in *Selected Poems, Prose and Letters* (Broadview, 2002), 334–6 at 334–5.

[111] John Ruskin, 'The poetry of architecture' (1838), in *CW*, 1: 1–172 at 76.

[112] Mary Powell, 'Variations on a theme of dying trees', *Landscape Research*, 6:1 (1981): 26–7.

[113] James Nasmyth, *Engineer: An Autobiography* (London, 1883), 163.

[114] Cornelia Dean, 'Next for Newport preservation: gilded-age beeches', *NYT*, 24 Oct. 2011.

to most seem inherently ugly. An essay lauding them is entitled 'The *sinister* beauty of smut'.[115]

The repugnant look of age in living beings colours attitudes towards natural features, nations and institutions, and man-made objects – in short, almost everything.

The decay of the world and its features

Long before James Lovelock dreamed up *Gaia*, Earth was seen as an animate being with a traceable life history. The world's birth, maturing, ageing, and prospective death suffuse Classical, Christian, and Renaissance texts. 'All things have their *birth*, their *growth*, *their flourishing*, *their failing*, their *fading*', wrote George Hakewill.[116] Humanist images of man as microcosm reinforced the organic analogy; the terrestrial life cycle mirrored the human. As astronomers discerned temporal change in the cosmos, earlier thought immutable, life-cycle metaphors spread to the sun, the stars, and, with the discovery of entropy, the whole universe. William Herschel's revelation that stars and galaxies grew and aged like plants led Erasmus Darwin to envision the entire cosmos as mortal.

> Flowers of the sky! Ye to age must yield . . .
> Suns sink on suns, and systems systems crush,
> Headlong, extinct, to one dark centre fall,
> And Death and Night and Chaos mingle all![117]

The material cosmos in terminal decay was long a Christian tenet. The City of Earth (as opposed to the City of God) was 'already failing and . . . drawing the last breath of extremist old age'. The world had passed through six stages of life into a final decrepit seventh, with 'an ende by putrefaction' imminent. Early-modern savants echoed this belief. 'The world hath had his infancie, next his youth, then his mans estate, & now he is in his old-age.'[118]

To Reformation theologians Earth's degeneration reflected original sin. Adam initiated not only the fall of man but the decay of nature, and as humanity's sins multiplied, nature further deteriorated. Earth's allotted six millennia were now almost spent, cumulative corruption foreshadowing the approaching end. In England, with sombre scenes of monastic decay, both Anglicans and Puritans held mankind to blame.

> Heaven's just displeasure & our unjust ways
> Change Natures course, bring plagues dearth and decays.
> This turns our lands to Dust, the skies to Brass,

---

[115] P. Gates, 'The sinister beauty of smut', *Independent on Sunday*, 2 June 1991: 70.

[116] George Hakewill, *Apologie*, bk. III, ch. 6, sect. 2, 1: 259. See Leonard Barkan, *Nature's Work of Art: The Human Body as Image of the World* (Yale, 1975).

[117] William Herschel, 'On the construction of the heavens' (1785; 1789), quoted in Richard Holmes, *The Age of Wonder* (Harper, 2008), 193–7; Erasmus Darwin, *The Botanic Garden, a Poem*, pt. I, canto IX, ll. 371, 374–5 (1791; 4th edn London, 1799), 213.

[118] Otto of Freising, *The Two Cities: A Chronicle of Universal History in the Year 1146 AD* (Columbia, 1928), 323; Polydore Vergil, *De inventoribus rerum* (1499), and Pierre de la Primaudaye, *L'Académie françoise* (1577–1618), quoted in Victor Harris, *All Coherence Gone* (Chicagt, 1949), 87, 197.

Makes old kind blessings into curses pass. . . .
The dregs and puddle of all ages now
Like Rivers near their fall, on us do flow.

Man 'drew the Curse upon the world', added Henry Vaughan, 'and Crackt / The whole frame with his fall'.[119] Nature's complicity in Adam's fall spread mortality everywhere. John Donne sensed 'decay and age in the whole frame of the world'.[120]

So foretold, impending death was seen in every falling leaf. Science confirmed scripture, showing the entire cosmos infected. 'The earth seems to grow grey with years, and . . . all the great animals of the universe perish like the small', wrote Giordano Bruno.[121] Yesterday 'on crutches', playwright Thomas Dekker's world was now 'bed-rid', declining into dotage.[122] The spotted and blemished sun 'waxeth weary' and 'shineth more dimly'; the moon grew paler, the stars 'weake & suspicious'.[123] Men too were smaller and weaker; giants, formerly common, were now seldom seen. 'As all things under the Sunne have . . . a youth and beautie, and then age and deformitie', wrote Raleigh, 'so Time itselfe . . . hath wasted and worne out . . . in Man, and Beasts, and Plants'.[124] Wheat mildewed, wood rotted, iron rusted ever faster. That all things diminish and decay was 'the received Opinion . . . from Antiquity down to our times', held naturalist John Ray.[125] 'Wrinkled o'er with wo', Time itself 'feebly went his slow, unmeasured round; / Dim was his glance, uncertain now his step, / And bent that form in olden days so proud; / Old age was stamped upon his hoary brow'.[126]

Eroded mountains, the 'bones of the world', were prime evidence of terrestrial decay. To Bishop Thomas Burnet, remnant 'Crags and Rocks and Cliffs' were the 'ruines of a broken World', the ragged Earth 'lying in its rubbish'. Earth before the Deluge, 'smooth, regular, and uniform . . . had the beauty of Youth . . . and not a wrinkle, scar or fracture in all its body'. But now in old age all was 'shapeless and ill-figur'd'.[127]

A Calvinist who termed the world decrepit found its 'crooked old age' repugnant. 'As a garment the older it waxeth, the lesse comely it is, the lesse able to warme him that weares it: so the materiall heavens by continuance of yeares decrease in beauty and vertue'.[128] Edmund Spenser lamented that the world 'being once amisse, growes daily wourse and

---

[119] Henry Vaughan, 'Daphnis' (1666), ll. 143–50, and 'Corruption' (1655), ll. 15–16, in *Works* (Clarendon Press, 1957), 676–80 at 679 and 387–545 at 440.

[120] John Donne, 'Devotions upon emergent occasions' (1624), in *Complete Poetry and Selected Prose* (London, 1929), 505–52 at 523.

[121] Giordano Bruno, *De l'infinito, universo et mondi* (1584), quoted in James Lewis McIntyre, *Giordano Bruno* (Macmillan, 1903), 221.

[122] Thomas Dekker, *Old Fortunatus* (1600; London, 1904), 33.

[123] John Dove, *A Confutation of Atheism* (1605), quoted in Harris, *All Coherence Gone*, 117.

[124] Raleigh, *The History of the World*, bk. I, ch. 5, sect. 5, 76–7.

[125] John Ray, *Miscellaneous Discourses concerning the Dissolution and Changes of the World* (London, 1692), 41.

[126] Tyler, *Ahasuerus*, 29.

[127] Thomas Burnet, *The Sacred Theory of the Earth* (Latin 1681–9; English 1684–90; Southern Illinois, 1965), 41, 53, 64, 91, 112, 115.

[128] Lambert Daneau, *The Wonderfull Workmanship of the World* (London, 1578); Samuel Rowlands, *Heavens Glory Seeke It &c* (1628; London, 1876), 18. See Philip C. Almond, *Adam and Eve in Seventeenth-Century Thought* (Cambridge, 1999), 206–8.

wourse'.[129] Earth's last age seemed its very dregs. Senescent analogies depicted a worn, limping world 'weake through age' decaying into an 'odious mass'.[130] Milton rejected as impious this prevision of 'loathsome old age', Earth stricken with 'the years' insatiable hunger, and filth, and rust'. The divine Creator would not have ordained the face of nature to 'wither away [to] foul old age'.[131] Terrestrial old age disgusted both believers in and deniers of universal decay.

Broken landscapes called to mind loathsome diseases, as in Charles Cotton's rant against England's Peak District: 'Like *Warts* and *Wens*, Hills on the one side swell / To all but *Natives* Inaccessible; / Th'other a blue scrofulus Scum defiles, / Flowing from th'earth's imposthumated boyles'.[132] Poets satirized the analogy: 'Swell'd with a dropsy, sickly Nature lies / And melting in a diabetes, dies'. Like decline, ugliness reflected continuing misdeeds. 'The gross irregularities of earth's surface, with its warts and pock-holes, were abiding evidence of the sin of man, [and] with each of man's major sins, the earth had grown increasingly ugly.'[133]

Terrestrial decay was denied by Bodin and Louis Le Roy in France and Hakewill and Wotton in England. Surely the Creator would not make a corruptible Earth; the world changed, but did not degenerate. Hakewill saw no loss of strength in living things: trees were as tall, herbs as potent as ever; sun and moon seemed more spotted only because telescopes showed greater detail. Biblical prophecy that 'the heavens shall wax old like a garment, doth not necessarily imply a *decay*', but only 'a *farther step*'. God's power and providence were manifest in nature's continuance, not decline. The discovery of a transatlantic world 'yet so new and so infantile' showed Montaigne the folly of inferring global 'decline and decrepitude ... from our own weakness and decay'.[134]

But allegories of terminal decay held sway long after geologists outdated Burnet. Awesome crags conjured up 'Revolutions of past Ages, the fleeting forms of Things, and the Decay even of this our Globe', wrote Shaftesbury. 'The wasted Mountains shew the World itself only as a noble Ruin'.[135] Even at the gentler 'friendly Hills' near Bath 'The shatter'd *Rocks* and *Strata* seem to say, / Nature is *old*, and tends to her *Decay*'. As late as 1810, Walter Scott unlovingly termed 'Crags, knolls, and mounds, confusedly hurl'd / The fragments of an earlier world'.[136]

Scholars and clerics had by then stripped terrestrial decay of credibility and emotional force – exempting parts of the cosmos, holding degradation completed,

[129] Edmund Spenser, *Faerie Queene*, bk. V, Prologue, stanza 1 (1590; Clarendon Press, 1909), 2: 159.
[130] William Alexander, *Doomes-Day* (1614), and Barnabe Rich, *The Honestie of the Age* (1614), in Harris, *All Coherence Gone*, 123, 135.
[131] John Milton, 'Naturam non pati senium' (c.1627), ll. 11–14, in *Complete Shorter Poems* (Wiley, 2009), 230.
[132] Charles Cotton, *The Wonders of the Peake*, 2nd edn (London, 1683), 1–2.
[133] John Gay, Alexander Pope, and John Abuthnot, *Three Hours after Marriage* (1717; Clark Library, UCLA, 1962), 142; Marjorie Hope Nicolson, *The Breaking of the Circle: Studies in the Effect of the 'New Science' upon Seventeenth-Century Poetry* (1950; rev. edn Columbia, 1960), 114.
[134] Hakewill, *Apologie*, bk. II, ch. 1, sect. 4, I: 84, bk. V, 2: 141; Montaigne, 'Of coaches' (1585–8), in *Complete Essays*, 693.
[135] Anthony Ashley Cooper, Third Earl Shaftesbury, *The Moralists*, pt. 3, sect. 1 (London, 1709), 201.
[136] Mary Chandler, *The Description of Bath*, ll. 85, 98–9 (1733; 6th edn London, 1744), 6–7; Walter Scott, *The Lady of the Lake* (1810), Canto I, sect. xiv, in *The Poetical Works* (Oxford, 1904), 207–312 at 211.

or ceasing to blame sinful humanity. Yet the analogy remained pervasive. The sparsely peopled Earth seemed proof that nature had 'lost the wonderful fruitfulness of the first ages'. Perhaps, thought Montesquieu, 'she is already old and fallen into decay'.[137] Marks of decline permeated daily life: the humbler scale of housekeeping, higher prices, scarcer coinage – even jaded palates: 'In the Infant Age of the World ... Mankind stood in no need of any additional Sauces, Ragoos, &c' required to stimulate appetites in the present elderly epoch.[138]

Life-cycle analogies long kept their appeal for earth scientists. A hydraulic engineer likened fluvial to human stages of development:

A river, from its source to the sea, depicts the different ages of man ... Its INFANCY is frolicsome and capricious; it turns mills and eddies playfully beneath the flowers. Its YOUTH is impetuous and hasty; it buffets, uproots and overturns. Its MIDDLE COURSE is serious and wise; it makes detours and yields to circumstances. In OLD AGE its step is measured, peaceful, majestic and silent; its tranquil waters roll softly and soon lose themselves in the immense ocean.[139]

A century later, Ruskin segmented Earth history into eras of youth (crystallization), strength (sculpturing), and, in his own day, decrepitude, with all mountains suffering deliquescent corrosion.[140] Of 'Ol' Man River', the Mississippi, a geologist wrote that 'the young river made an indenture in the sweep of the shores; the mature river filled it in'. Topographical 'youth' and 'old age' suffused geology texts: 'The degradation of the drift-less region [of Wisconsin] has passed beyond the time of youth. The ultimate result ... is old age declining again to the level of childhood.'[141]

Life-cycle geomorphology became iconic with Harvard's William Morris Davis. The smoothness and shallow lakes of uneroded landscapes were 'truly infantile features'; 'adolescent' rivers formed narrow courses; 'maturity' deepened valleys; finally the terrain is 'almost as low, flat and featureless' as at birth. 'This is simple old age, a second childhood in which infantile features are imitated.' Davisian streams passed from youth to senescence, when 'the flood-plains of maturity are carried down to the sea, and at last the river settles down to an old age of well-earned rest'. Elderly rivers showed a 'fading away of strength and variety ... Extreme old age or second childhood is, like the first childhood, characterized by imperfect work'.[142]

---

[137] Charles de Secondat de Montesquieu, *Persian Letters* (1718), no. 113 (Routledge, 1923), 250.

[138] Eliza Smith, *The Compleat Housewife: or, Accomplish'd Gentlewoman's Companion*, 9th edn (London, 1739), Preface.

[139] Pierre Louis George du Buat, *Principes d'hydraulique* (1779), quoted in Richard J. Chorley et al., *The History of the Study of Landforms* (Methuen, 1964–73), 1: 88.

[140] John Ruskin, 'The three aeras' (1875), in *CW*, 26: 115–23 at 117, 123. See Jerome Hamilton Buckley, *The Triumph of Time: A Study of Victorian Concepts of Time, History, Progress, and Decadence* (Harvard, 1967), 66–9.

[141] George Greenwood, *Rain and Rivers* (London, 1857), 185; T. C. Chamberlain and R. D. Salisbury, *The Driftless Area of the Upper Mississippi*, 6th Annual Report of the United States Geological Survey (Washington, DC: GPO, 1884–5). See Davies, *Earth in Decay*, 231–4.

[142] William Morris Davis, 'Geographic classification' (1885), quoted in Chorley et al., *History of the Study of Landforms*, 2: 165–6, 190; W. M. Davis, 'The rivers and valleys of Pennsylvania' (1889), 413–84 at 430–4, and 'Physical geography as a university study' (1894), 165–92 at 176–7, in *Geographical Essays* (Boston, 1909).

Thus, three centuries after the organic analogy's sacred birth, 'old age' was reborn as a secular metaphor for terrestrial degradation. Today it invokes even cosmic senescence. 'The stars we have are dying', say astronomers, 'and we're not making new ones the way we used to in the lusty primordial days when protogalaxies, all gas and spume, were . . . popping with blazing bright new stars'.[143] Like the immortal Struldbruggs in Jonathan Swift's Luggnagg, the Universe accretes senescent oldsters.

Natural features were, to be sure, adjudged beautiful or ugly for qualities besides presumed youth or age. Medieval folk feared mountains long before they thought them 'old', but the lifespan analogy reinforced prevailing antipathy. Uniformity, regularity, symmetry, and smoothness epitomized beauty long before Burnet linked them with Earth's innocent infancy, but the linkage strengthened bias against agedness. Only in the late eighteenth century, when roughness, irregularity, and asymmetry became 'sublime' or 'picturesque', did mountain forms, like ruins, gain favour.[144] But those who then adored mountains saw in them not terrestrial senescence, but glorious youth – God's original work. Just as ruined buildings symbolized nature's triumph over transient artifice, so wild and rugged scenes no longer signified the elderly but the primeval.

The superiority of youthful nations

Human institutions seem equally subject to the ravages of time. The recurrent demise of old and genesis of new states strikes many as an organic process. Polybius likened societies to living creatures: 'Every body, or polity [has] a natural stage of growth, zenith, and decay.' Like humans, states were vaunted in youth and belittled in old age. 'Everything in them is best at its zenith' and worst in decay.[145] Ever since, national old age has betokened corruption, decay, impotence. Denizens of ageing lands are ravaged, like Dorian Gray, by malice and debauchery.

Seneca linked Rome's infancy with Romulus, dated adolescence and 'manly strength' from Tarquinius' banishment to the end of the Punic Wars. Rome's old age, hastened by imperial expansion, ended in second childhood under Augustus. In the second century, Florus credited Trajan with averting old age and postponing senescence; in the fourth century Ammianus Marcellinus saw some good in the Eternal City's 'degeneration': though slack and declining, old Rome was peaceful and stable. Claudian depicted Rome as an ageing Amazon with withered cheeks and white hair, barely able to carry her shield.[146] The human lifespan cycle suffused Christian world history. St Augustine

[143] Dennis Overbye, 'Amid cosmic fatigue, scarcely a star is born', *NYT*, 19 Nov. 2012.

[144] Marjorie Hope Nicolson, *Mountain Gloom and Mountain Glory* (Cornell, 1959), 100–4, 269–323.

[145] Polybius, *The Histories* (after 146 BC; London, 1889), 1: 501, 507.

[146] Florus, *Epitome de T. Livio Bellorum*, cited in Trompf, *Idea of Historical Recurrence*, 188–91; Ammianus Marcellinus, *Res Gestae* (c. 390), cited in Michael Roberts, 'Rome personified, Rome epitomized', *American Journal of Philology* 122 (2001): 533–65 at 535; Claudian, *De bello Gildonico* (c. 398), cited in Cristina Sogno, 'Age and style in late antique epistolography', in Classen, *Old Age in the Middle Ages*, 85–102 at 89; Arnaldo Momigliano, 'Time in ancient historiography' (1966), in *Essays in Ancient and Modern Historiography* (Blackwell, 1977), 179–204.

termed the antediluvian 'day' mankind's infancy, that following the Flood its childhood, that after Abraham its adolescence, that from David its prime; a 'weakened and broken' old age stretched from Exile to Incarnation.[147]

The classical life cycle gained new currency in the Renaissance. Historians revived the Polybian framework, invoking biological explanations for states' growth, decay, and ruin.[148] So with elements of culture. Like human beings, wrote Vasari, painting and sculpture are born, mature, age and perish; like empires, added poet William Drummond, arts and sciences waned and died.[149] Revivified by the Hellenist Johann Winckelmann, the organic analogy permeated nineteenth-century rhetoric. Thomas Love Peacock termed poetry 'the mental rattle that awakened ... intellect in the infancy of civil society'; William Dyce discerned art's 'infancy', 'adolescence', and 'maturity' in Italy. Extending the analogy to whole cultures, Herder held their decay an inescapable corollary of their flowering.[150]

Political like geological metaphors of decay were pervasive. 'The affairs of all nations proceed in their rise, progress, mature state, decline and fall', wrote Vico, with terminal decay into senile impotence.[151] National ageing became an eighteenth-century obsession. 'Though they grow and improve for a time, ... the best constituted governments, like the best constituted animal bodies', wrote Bolingbroke, 'soon tend visibly to their dissolution'.[152] In Henry Fielding's *Amelia* every great kingdom declines into old age, 'enervated at home – becomes contemptible abroad; and such indeed is its Misery and Wretchedness, that it resembles a Man in the last decrepit Stage of life'.[153] States past maturity should accept their impending fate, advised Herder, 'lest the graves of ancient institutions ... rob the living of light, and narrow their habitations'.[154] Chateaubriand echoed that warning: 'The state follows the man ... infirm and corrupt in his old age ... sinking with decrepitude into despotism.'[155]

Only the rebel offshoot of Fielding's 'great kingdom' across the Atlantic used the analogy with unconcern. As noted in Chapter 4, Americans fancied their land in permanent vigorous youth, Europe in its dotage. 'Nations are often compared to individuals and to vegetables, in their progress from their origin to maturity and decay', stated Noah

---

[147] *On Genesis* (388–9) in *The Works of St. Augustine* (Hyde Park, NY: New City, 2002), 13: 62–5.

[148] Jean Bodin, *The Six Bookes of a Commonweale* (1576; London, 1601), 406; Trompf, *Idea of Historical Recurrence*, 276–82, 301–2.

[149] Vasari, *Lives of the Most Eminent Painters*, 'Introduction' 1: 32–3; William Drummond, 'A Cypresse Grove' (1623), in *The Poems of William Drummond of Hawthornden* (Edinburgh, 1832), 209–51 at 217.

[150] Johann Joachim Winckelmann, *Reflections on the Painting and Sculpture of the Greeks* (1755; Routledge, 1999); J. J. Winckelmann, *The History of Ancient Art among the Greeks* (1764; London: Scolar, 1972); Thomas Love Peacock, 'The four ages of poetry' (1820), in *Peacock's Four Ages of Poetry ...* (Blackwell, 1921), 18; William Dyce, *The National Gallery* (London 1853), 12; Johann Gottfried von Herder, *Reflections on the Philosophy of the History of Mankind* (1784–91; Chicago, 1968); J. G. von Herder, *On World History: An Anthology*, ed. Hans Adler (Armonk, NY: M.E. Sharpe, 1997), 110–15.

[151] Gianbattista Vico, *New Science* (3rd edn, 1774; Cornell, 1948), bk. I, para. 349, 93; Isaiah Berlin, *Vico and Herder* (Hogarth, 1976), 63–4.

[152] Henry St John Bolingbroke, *The Idea of a Patriot King* (London, c. 1740), 65. See Isaac Kramnick, *Bolingbroke and His Circle: The Politics of Nostalgia in the Age of Walpole* (Harvard, 1968), 35, 166–8.

[153] Henry Fielding, *Amelia* (1751; Clarendon Press, 1983), 461.

[154] Herder, *Reflections on the Philosophy of the History of Mankind*, 79.

[155] François-René de Chateaubriand, *The Genius of Christianity* (1802; Baltimore, 1871), 420.

Webster, and 'the resemblance is striking and just'.[156] Youth was preferable 'to complete manhood and old age, when we every day become less active, and less pleased' – and, others added, depraved and vicious. Nations already mature could look forward only to 'decline and mortification'.[157] Loyalists failed to refute the sorrows of seniority; when Alexander Hamilton scorned England as 'an old, wrinkled, withered, worn-out hag', Samuel Seabury lamely rejoined that though ancient, England was still a 'vigorous matron, just approaching a green old age, and with spirit and strength sufficient to chastise her undutiful and rebellious children'.[158]

National decay remained an Old World leitmotiv. Hegel, Schelling, Gobineau, and Marx consigned civilizations past creative prime to the dustbin of history. Oswald Spengler limited their lifespans to a thousand years. China and India had too long lingered as 'wornout giants of the primeval forest thrust[ing] their decaying branches towards the sky'; the West's 'metaphysically exhausted soil' betokened similar decline.[159] Futurists invoked organic analogy to condemn the 'smelly gangrene' of the poisoned past.[160]

Institutional and cultural decline is now thought historically contingent, not biologically ordained. Yet organic analogies linger on. Images of flowering, maturing, and fading refer to 'the birth of an art', the 'life of a style', the 'death of a school', even though we know that styles do not behave like people or plants. Long after the 'death agony of Byzantium', the Ottoman Empire became the 'sick man of Europe', a morbid state later assigned to Britain, Germany, Russia, Ireland, Italy, Spain, Greece, and today to the entire 'elderly and haggard' continent. Newly sovereign states contrast their youthful energies with the exhausted old West; references to 'the English disease' and the 'hardening of Britain's industrial arteries' saturated 1980s media.[161] US defense secretary Donald Rumsfeld's 2003 slur against sclerotic 'old' Europe touched a raw nerve, in line with a demographic warning that Europeans risked becoming 'old people in old houses with old ideas'.[162]

Rejection of age and wear in artefacts

We envision artefacts, even more than nations and nature, with lifespans ending in decay and dissolution. How things 'age' varies with substance, use, and wear; some moulder and

---

[156] Noah Webster, 'Remarks on the manners, government, and debt of the United States' (1787), in *Collection of Essays and Fugitive Writings* (Boston, 1970), 81–110 at 84. See V. P. Bynack, 'Noah Webster's linguistic thought and the idea of an American national culture', *JHI* 45 (1984): 99–114 at 103.

[157] Quoted in Stow Persons, *American Minds* (Holt, Rinehart & Winston, 1958), 122–5.

[158] 'A Westchester Farmer' [Samuel Seabury], *A View of the Controversy between Great-Britain and Her Colonies* (New York, 1774).

[159] Oswald Spengler, *The Decline of the West* (1918; Allen & Unwin, 1932), 106–7. See Frank E. Manuel, *Shapes of Philosophical History* (Stanford, 1965), 59, 122–7; Schlanger, *Métaphores de l'organisme*, 186–9.

[160] Filippo Tommaso Marinetti, 'Founding and manifesto of Futurism' (1909), in Umbro Apollonio, comp., *Futurist Manifestos* (Viking, 1973), 19–23.

[161] Martin J. Wiener, *English Culture and the Decline of the Industrial Spirit, 1850–1980* (Johns Hopkins, 1981). On subsequent recovery, David Edgerton, 'The decline of declinism', *Business History Review* 71 (1997): 201–6; *The New Sick Man of Europe: The European Union*, Pew Research Center, 13 May 2013. Pope Francis, 'Address to European Parliament', 25 Nov. 2014, Vatican Radio Newsletter.

[162] Alfred Sauvy, *Zero Growth* (1973; Blackwell, 1975), 49. See Henri Péquignot, *Vieillesses de demain: vieillir et être vieux* (Paris: Vrin, 1986); David Willetts, *Old Europe? Demographic Change and Pension Reform* (London: Centre for European Reform, 2003), 1.

erode, others discolour, deform, or shatter. Yet all decay invites metaphors of human frailty or illness – fatigue of metals, ageing of 'sick' glass, diseases of churches and cities. Technical terms such as 'tin pest' and 'weeping iron' equate metal corrosion with organic maladies. A conservator likens the 'deeply pitted and disfigured surface' effect of 'bronze disease' to 'the festering skin of a leper'.[163] Like invalids, ailing art objects require diagnosis and curative treatment.

Decay not only depreciates value but portends extinction, 'when like us in our old age', notes a furniture restorer, 'things start to fall off or wear out'.[164] The death of precious artefacts and artworks is so dismaying as to seem deviant, demanding our intervention to keep them alive forever, even at the cost of human life. 'I should certainly save [Raphael's] Dresden Madonna first', said an academic aficionado faced with a hypothetical choice. 'I can get another baby any day … but there is only one Dresden Madonna.' Harold Nicolson was 'prepared to be shot against a wall if … by such a sacrifice I could preserve the Giotto frescoes … nor should I hesitate for an instant … to save St. Mark's even if … by so doing I should bring death to my sons'.[165] The immortality of art elicits Henry James's heart-felt tribute, as his Nick Dormer views paintings at London's National Gallery:

The perfection of their survival often struck him as … the virtue that included all others, … the richest and most universal. Empires and systems and conquests had rolled over the globe and every kind of greatness had risen and passed away, but the beauty of the great pictures had known nothing of death or change, and the tragic centuries had only sweetened their freshness.[166]

Thus enraptured we try to keep them alive forever. But the search for miracle cures at length gives way to reluctant resignation, at least when terminal decay seems so unsightly as to require burial.

But would-be immortal treasures, like saintly relics, are exceptions to our indifference to, even pleasure in, the transience of the vast majority of things. Most ageing artefacts are jettisoned without compunction once useless. We piously preserve the Colosseum, remarked Le Corbusier, but merely endure the Roman aqueduct, and let the locomotive rust on the scrapheap.[167] Aqueducts and locomotives now join the Colosseum as cherished bygones, but the glut of unloved disposables overflows the scrapheaps. Shacks, caravans, and coaches seedy to begin with, in a 1930s critique, 'do not mellow with time', but linger on, 'patched and botched, into a decrepit and disreputable old age'.[168]

In artefacts made for common use any signs of decay repel: a rusting car, a corroded washing machine, a verminous mattress, peeling wallpaper. Obliterating decay enhances

---

[163] Elizabeth Pye, *Caring for the Past: Issues in Conservation for Archaeology and Museums* (London: James & James, 2001), 97; Glenn Wharton, *The Painted King* (Hawai'i, 2011), 6.
[164] Anne Jordan, 'Lamb dressed as mutton', *Interior Design* 17 (1977): 464–5.
[165] George Birdwood quoted in 'Madonna or baby?' *The Press* (Christchurch, N.Z.), 16 Nov. 1912; Harold Nicolson, 'Bombing works of art', *Spectator*, 25 Feb. 1944. See Edward Ford, 'The theory and practice of impermanence: the illusion of durability', *Harvard Design Magazine* 3 (1997): 12–18; Michael Shanks, 'The life of an artifact in an interpretive archaeology', *Fennoscandia Archaeologia* 15 (1998): 15–30 at 16–19; Ned Harris, *Building Lives: Constructing Rites and Passages* (Yale, 1999), 53, 135, 173.
[166] Henry James, *The Tragic Muse* (1890; London, 1921), 660.
[167] Le Corbusier *The City of Tomorrow and Its Planning* (1925; London: Rodker, 1929), 51.
[168] Patrick Abercrombie, *Town and Country Planning* (1933; Taylor & Francis, 2004), 289.

most old things. The used-car dealer expunges signs of wear. Old clothes are cleaned, fabrics renewed not just to conserve but to stop them seeming scruffy. Buildings are periodically repainted and repointed for looks as well as maintenance; an old house may charm, but not a tattered wreck. Many Modernist structures age hideously because, in the 1920s mindset that preferred expediency to permanence, they were not intended to last.[169] Modernist 'architectural masterpieces' of the 1960s likewise 'were never intended to last more than forty years. Like cheap motor-cars, they have obsolescence built into them.'[170]

However venerated an ancient relic, its decay is seldom admired. 'Antiquitie I unfainedly honour', wrote Hakewill, 'but why should I ... reverence the rust and refuse, the drosse and dregs, the warts and wenns thereof?'[171] Quests for constitutional precedents among 'rotten parchments under dripping and perishing Walls' struck Edmund Burke as unseemly and pointless; what mattered was not these precedents' material corpus but their living meaning. He treasured ancient memory but loathed the look of age.[172] Burke's revulsion was typical. Shakespeare's litany of time's corrosions –

> To ruinate proud buildings with thy hours,
> And smear with dust their glittering golden towers;
> To fill with worm-holes stately monuments,
> To feed Oblivion with the decay of things
> To spoil antiquities of hammered steel,
> And turn the giddy round of fortune's wheel

– is no mere rumination on decay's inevitability but a litany of its horrors.[173] Enumerating the perils of idolatry, an Anglican bishop condemned religious relics as 'old, stinking, ragged, rotten, filthy'. The 'rotten Foundations, ruinous Arches and Pillars, mouldering and tottering Walls' of mutilated English monasteries were widely abhorred before travellers began to find them picturesque.[174]

The picturesque apart, age and decay usually offended Western antiquarian taste. Most humanists viewed ruined structures as pathetic, if not hideous. Renaissance and Enlightenment critics deplored time's unsightly erosions. Classical art revived or emulated was bright, clean, new. Painters depicted antique structures newly built or in perfect repair.

---

[169] Hilde Heynen, 'Engaging modernism', in Hans-Hubert Henket and Hilde Heynen, eds., *Back from Utopia* (Rotterdam, 2002), 378–400; Mohsen Mostafavi and David Leatherbarrow, *On Weathering: The Life of Buildings in Time* (MIT Press, 1993); David N. Fixler, 'Repair of modern buildings', *Change over Time* 1 (Spring 2011): 80–108 at 82.

[170] Auberon Waugh, 'The way of the world', *Telegraph*, 27 Nov. 1995: 23, quoted in Gavin Stamp, 'The art of keeping one jump ahead', in Michael Hunter, ed., *Preserving the Past* (Stroud: Sutton, 1996), 98.

[171] Hakewill, *Apologie*, bk. V, 2: 133.

[172] To the Duke of Richmond, post-15 Nov. 1772, in *The Correspondence of Edmund Burke* (Cambridge, 1958–78), 2: 377.

[173] William Shakespeare, *The Rape of Lucrece* (1594), ll. 944–7, 951–2.

[174] Bishop Nicholas Shaxton of Salisbury (1530s) quoted in Charles Freeman, *Holy Bones, Holy Dust: How Relics Shaped the History of Medieval Europe* (Yale, 2011), 241; George Starkey, 'Epistolar discourse' (1665), quoted in Richard Foster Jones, *Ancients and Moderns* (California, 1965), 214.

Not even their ruins crumble: chipped or exfoliated stones exhibit clean breaks devoid of moss and ivy, later insignia of romantic age and wear. Neoclassicists decried 'deformed trees, ... crooked-bodied, old and rent, full of knots and hollowness, rough or ruined buildings with their parts lying up and down in confusion'.[175] Anticipating the Futurists, a burlesque tirade backed razing 'the sorry and barbarous Coliseum'.[176] Decay is the wreckage of antiquity. A tattered house – 'the walls are cracking, the foundation rotting, the doors worm-eaten, the furniture moldy' – is strewn with broken columns, shattered statues, and 'cauldrons full of ashes, labeled ... Corinth, Saguntum, Carthage, Troy, and a thousand other cities gone bad whose ashes are kept by Time in memory of his exploits'.[177]

Fondness for decay was felt perverse. The playwright Plautus ridiculed the miser who cherished even his cobwebs.[178] Addison mocked 'critics in Rust' devoted to tarnished medals, broken pottery, illegible manuscripts.[179] 'We are pleas'd in looking upon the Ruins of a Roman Amphitheater, or a triumphal Arch, tho' time may have defac'd its Beauty', argued Burnet, but while 'a Man may be pleas'd in looking upon a Monster, will you conclude therefore that he takes it for a Beauty?'[180]

Decay remained generally repugnant even after ruins gained favour. Dilapidation and obsolescence evoke horror in the Gothic tales of Ann Radcliffe and E. T. A. Hoffman. The putrescent evil of the worn-out past, a stock theme in Victorian literature, peaked in Bram Stoker's *Dracula* (1897) and Henry James's *Turn of the Screw* (1898). Thomas Hardy's Jude was appalled to find his long-dreamt-of Oxford colleges worn and rotten; the wounded, broken buildings seemed 'maimed, sentient beings'.[181] Victorian architects concurred: simply because softening tones enhanced old buildings did not justify age and decay.[182] Only crazed eccentrics cultivated dust and filth. As Le Corbusier put it, ordinary folk who wash their clothes and clean their houses rightly scorn the patina of age.[183]

Inveighing against restoration that exposed old paintings to unkind disclosure of decay, Louvre curator René Huyghe likened an old painting 'to a beauty, originally famous and admired, but upon whom the years have left their devastating mark. What we prize in her is the memory of her past splendour, not her present state of decay.' Avoid 'a glaring light that will accentuate her wrinkles', and veil time's injuries.[184]

---

[175] Gerard de Lairesse, *A Treatise on the Art of Painting* (1701; London, 1817), 286. See Thomas M. Greene, *The Light in Troy* (Yale, 1982), 147–70, 235.

[176] Marc-Antoine Girard de Saint-Amant, *La Rome Ridicule* (1643), stanza 13 (in Orlando, *Obsolete Objects*, 236).

[177] Giambattista Basile, 'The seven little doves', in *Tale of Tales*, 350–60 at 355–6.

[178] Plautus, *The Pot of Gold (Aulularia)* (c. 317–307 BC; Penguin, 1965), 15.

[179] Joseph Addison, *Dialogues upon the Usefulness of Ancient Medals* (1726), in *Works* (London, 1885), 1: 253–355 at 256. See Rosemary Sweet, *Antiquaries* (Hambledon and London, 2004), 4–5.

[180] Thomas Burnet, *Answer to the Exceptions Made by Mr. Erasmus Warren* ... (1690), in *Sacred Theory of the Earth*, 2: 295–370 at 314.

[181] Thomas Hardy, *Jude the Obscure* (1895; Oxford, 1998), 84.

[182] Stephan Tschudi-Madsen, *Restoration and Anti-Restoration*, 2nd edn (Oslo: Universitetsforlaget, 1976), 62.

[183] Le Corbusier, *When the Cathedrals Were White* (1937; McGraw-Hill, 1964), 46.

[184] René Huyghe, 'The Louvre Museum and the problem of cleaning old pictures', *Museum International* 3 (1950): 191–206 at 191.

Decay and wear generally detract from the appeal of antiquity. 'We love old buildings ... for what they stand for rather than for what they look like', John Piper disparaged post-war English taste. Restorers felt compelled to supplant worn medieval sculptures, scour and redecorate Elizabethan tomb figures, and 'tinker with every square inch of ancient surface', for originally all was new and bright and complete. Yet this stance conformed with common preference, and still does. Collectors' distaste for the look of age, complains an armour expert, fuels disastrous 'restoration' of medieval helmets and early modern flintlocks, expunging patina, buffing metal to a high shine.[185] Measures to arrest decay of the Sphinx's ancient stonework halted when over-zealous masons were found dismantling its left front paw. The workmen 'had all these nice, new limestone blocks', an Egyptologist explained; 'they would look better than the old, dirty ones'.[186]

For valued antiquities to look new is quintessential American practice. Colonial Williamsburg's restored and replica buildings, 'as neat and well painted as the houses in a new suburb', wrote a 1960 historian, 'never have the shabbiness that many of them must have shown in the colonial era'.[187] Despite lip-service to historical fidelity, a half-century later Colonial Williamsburg remains neat and well painted. Shabbiness seldom brings history to life; most feel the past 'real' only if its relics are in their prime.

An authentically worn and tattered artefact 'generally contradicts any feeling that it could possibly have been used by someone really alive'. The objects that train Jack Finney's time traveller to feel at home in 1882 New York are not actual survivals but freshly minted reconstructions. An 1880s dress from a museum, now faded and shrivelled, is rejected, for 'the women of the eighties ... were *living women*, and they would never have worn that rag!' Instead of mildewed books 'whose faded pages ... only a ghost could ever have read', bright new 'titles fresh-stamped in shining gold leaf, their pages pure white, the fresh black print still smelling of ink', bring olden times to life.[188]

Most who return to the past in imagination want it 'new' as they presume it was to its native denizens. To this end, wear and tear were banned from the Smithsonian Institution's 1976 bicentennial exhibition, which aimed to reproduce the Philadelphia centennial. Only the newest wares had been shown in 1876; faithfulness to the spirit of modernity required century-old objects in the 1976 show to look new. Originals too worn to rejuvenate were replaced by new replicas.[189]

Just as National Trust visitors some forty years ago lauded spotless and immaculate Clandon, found Knole 'tatty' and Chiddingstone village 'shabby', so they continue to

[185] John Piper, 'Pleasing decay' (1947), in *Buildings and Prospects* (London: Architectural Press, 1948), 89–116 at 90; John Schofield, 'Repair not restoration', in Marcus Binney and Peter Burman, eds., *Change and Decay: The Future of Our Churches* (London: Studio Vista, 1977), 153–6 at 154; David Edge, 'The armourer's craft: restoration or conservation?', in Andrew Oddy, ed., *Restoration: Is It Acceptable?* (British Museum Occasional Paper 99, 1994), 153–8.
[186] 'Near faux pas for the Great Sphinx', *IHT*, 6 Feb. 1980: 1.
[187] Daniel Boorstin, *America and the Image of Europe* (New York: Meridian, 1960), 93–4.
[188] Jack Finney, *Time and Again* (Simon & Schuster, 1970), 77–9.
[189] Robert C. Post, ed., *1876: A Centennial Exhibition* (Smithsonian, 1976), 25; Thomas J. Schlereth, *Artifacts and the American Past* (AASLH, 1980), 130–42.

prefer most historic houses fresh and sparkling. To film Kazuo Ishiguro's dystopian novel *Never Let Me Go*, the Trust briefly promoted signs of decay and neglect at Ham House, but made it sparkle again for its 400th birthday in 2010.[190] 'Even *pleasing* decay is not allowed by the officials who look after a ruined building', moaned Piper, 'because if they allowed it *people would think they were not looking after the building at all*'.[191] Visitors still see dust as neglect. 'The place was slightly dusty and the sunbeams gave it this ... wonderful evocative feeling of a building that was lived in', they say, but when asked what should now be done, then add, 'give it a decent mop and clean all the dust away'.[192]

Dust traditionally implied noxious disarray. The archetypal horror is Miss Havisham's sepulchral mouldering in Dickens's *Great Expectations* (1860), with every dust-strewn object dropping to pieces. Dust was the harbinger of Ruskin's ominous 'Storm-Cloud of the Nineteenth Century', 'a dry black veil partly diffused in feeble mist', a scraggy, filthy, mangy, malignant, loathsome, polluted plague-wind partly like two hundred furnace chimneys' poisonous smoke, but 'more as if made of dead men's souls'. The grim pall obscured cities days on end. As foretold in Revelation 6.12, 'the Empire of England, on which formerly the sun never set, has become one on which he never rises'.[193]

Ruskin adored ageing antiquity but excoriated suburban decay spawned by 'loathsome modern mechanisms' and symptomatic of moral and industrial degeneracy. He termed indescribable 'the forms of filth, and modes of ruin' around his childhood haunt in Dulwich. Revisiting Croxsted Lane in 1880, he found

mixed dust of every unclean thing that can crumble in drought, and mildew of every unclean thing that can rot or rust in damp: ashes and rags, beer-bottles and old shoes, battered pans, smashed crockery, shreds of nameless clothes, ... kitchen garbage, back-garden sewage, old iron, rotten timber jagged with out-torn nails, cigar-ends, ... cinders, bones and ordure,

along with remnants of posters and tabloids 'festering and flaunting out their last publicity in the pits of stinking dust and mortal slime'.[194]

Decay betokens failure. Holes in sleeves, cracks in walls, mould on the ceiling, weeds between paving stones, tumbledown houses evince distressing apathy. In Elizabeth Hardwick's desolating iconography of backwoods Maine squalor, worn-out household goods point to loss of hope and spirit.

Everywhere a crowd, a multitude of rust, breakage, iron, steel, and tin. Here, almost blocking the door, is the rusting wheel of an automobile ... A slide upside down, the ladder broken; a huge tin

[190] Martin Drury, National Trust, personal communication, 12 Sept. 1978; Sian Edwards, 'Role reversal', *National Trust Magazine*, no. 121 (Autumn 2010): 51–2.

[191] Piper, 'Pleasing decay', 96.

[192] Brian Dillon and Sina Najafi, 'Elementary particles: an interview with Peter Brimblecombe', *Cabinet Magazine*, issue 20, Ruins (Winter 2005/6).

[193] John Ruskin, 'The storm-cloud of the nineteenth century' (1884), in *CW*, 24: 7–80. See Michael Wheeler, ed., *Ruskin and the Environment* (Manchester, 1995); Brian Dillon, 'A dry black veil', *Cabinet Magazine*, issue 35, Dust (Fall 2009).

[194] John Ruskin, 'Discrimination in art teaching', in *CW*, 29: 559–60 at 560, and 'Fiction, fair and foul' (1880), in *CW*, 34: 265–397 at 266–7. See David Carroll, 'Pollution, defilement and the art of decomposition', in Wheeler, ed., *Ruskin and the Environment*, 58–75; John D. Rosenberg, *Elegy for an Age* (London: Anthem, 2005), 223, 235–7.

garbage pail, dented everywhere, as if from a thousand blows, its bottom a sieve. A battered baby stroller, clumps of wood, old chair legs, bed springs, a tarpaulin in which an old puddle of water nests. A sled, a barrel, rubber tires. All crowned by ... the car itself, leprously scarred ... What is an old appliance except a tomb of sorrow, a slab of disappointment?[195]

Some are so distressed by decay that they tolerate nothing old. 'Continually threatened by the presence in the house of piles of dying commodities', they permit possessions only at the start of life. 'No sooner have Christmas presents been unpacked from their wrappings than there is talk of "coping with the junk" ... There is always the fear that something or other may be on "its last legs".' They rigorously uproot all dying things, everything must be 'alive and purposeful and well'.[196] Neophiliac insistence on the fresh and pristine banishes the first signs of wear.

Decay is most dreadful when it seems our fault. Like theologians who blamed nature's corruption on mankind's sins, some fancy that desecration causes relics to wither. The novelist Brian Moore imagined Victorian memorabilia mysteriously resurrected, in pristine condition, in a California parking lot. But under the glare of publicity, the philistine gaze of tourist throngs, and the schemes of greedy entrepreneurs, these antiques degenerate 'like invalids suffering some wasting disease':

Machinery either warps or breaks down, the canvas cracks, the dolls' eyes no longer move, the damask and linen have brown stains, ... the statuary has developed cracks, even in the cast-iron pieces. The musical instruments all give out false notes, there are mysterious bare patches on the collection of sables and ermines, the Ross telescope lens is misted.

Everything becomes mouldy, mildewed, moth-eaten. Authenticity too is lost. 'The original materials now seem false; ... hallmarks have faded completely, so that I can't tell any more whether it's silver, or silver plate'; blocks of glass look like lucite; obvious imitations and blatant shams spoil the ambience of the remaining originals, which finally waste away entirely.[197]

Moore's spoiled antiquities recall the prescient foreboding of Hitler's architect Albert Speer, at the thousand-year Reich's Spandau conference site in 1934. Seeing structures already rusting, shuddering at centuries of neglect apt to come, Speer drew a future scene of fallen walls, collapsed pillars, and rampant ivy, reminiscent of ruined inscriptions, defaced statues, and mouldering triumphal arches that once celebrated the careers of Roman emperors or generals later fallen from favour.[198]

Admiration of decay remains atypical, often dismissed as an aberrant quirk. Chinese love of tarnished pottery, medals, and statues – 'the more eaten and consumed by time

[195] Elizabeth Hardwick, 'In Maine', NYRB, 7 Oct. 1971: 4, 6. See John Scanlan, On Garbage (Reaktion, 2005), 133–8.

[196] Laurie Taylor, 'Living with things', New Society, 5 Aug. 1976: 297–8. See Colin Campbell, 'The desire for the new', in Roger Silverstone and Eric Hirsch, eds., Consuming Technologies (Routledge, 1992), 44–58 at 50–2; Slade, Made to Break, 266–7.

[197] Brian Moore, The Great Victorian Collection (Jonathan Cape, 1975), 149, 203.

[198] Harald Welzer, 'Albert Speer's memories of the future', in Jürgen Straub, ed., Narration, Identity and Historical Consciousness (Berghahn, 2005), 244–55; Charles W. Hedrick, Jr., History and Silence (Texas, 2000), xiii.

Figure 17 The perils of age: François Perrier, *Time the Destroyer*, 1638

they are, the more they are judged to be noble' – seemed to a seventeenth-century Italian visitor to defy aesthetic logic.[199] In a Scottish garden, the Japanese novelist Natsume Sōseki (1867–1916) noted how thickly moss covered were the paths among trees. 'I offered a compliment, saying that these paths had magnificently acquired a look of age ... My host replied that he soon intended to get a gardener to scrape all this moss away.'[200] Conversely, Penelope Lively's young historian is hard put to justify English-ruin taste to Japanese tourists. 'Is all broken down. What a pity', they respond at Minster Lovell. 'Well, yes', he answers, 'but it's rather nice, all the same'. The English are fond of ruins, he adds lamely, 'we've got so many, we've had to make the best of them'.[201]

Taste for the appearance of youth is ubiquitous; almost every lifespan analogy deprecates old age. 'Aged' earth features are ugly; 'senescent' nations and institutions impotent and corrupt. Everything from ruins to 'elderly' rivers suffers disfiguring decay. Buildings, utensils, clothing, even antiquities look best when just fashioned. We constantly make fresh starts, new brooms sweep clean, youth is served. Age that comes before beauty sadly contrasts with it.

---

[199] Daniello Bartoli, *La Cina* (1663), quoted in Orlando, *Obsolete Objects*, 236.

[200] Matsui Sakuko, *Natsume Sōseki as a Critic of English Literature* (1975) quoted in Donald Keene, *The Pleasures of Japanese Literature* (Columbia, 1988), 21.

[201] Penelope Lively, *Treasures of Time* (Heinemann, 1979), 160.

Nonetheless marks of age at times provide comfort or pleasure. Above all they betoken wisdom, as with Spenser's 'old old man, halfe blind, / And all decrepid' with books 'all worme-eaten, and full of canker holes' in his ruinous library. 'Yet lively vigour rested in his mind ... Weake body well is chang'd for minds redoubled forse'.[202] When and how and by whom ruin and decay came to be admired, and how that taste affects awareness and treatment of the past in general are discussed in the next chapter.

[202] Spenser, *Faerie Queene*, bk II, canto 9, 2: 286.

6

The look of age: affection

Time truly works wonders. It sublimates wine; it sublimates fame; enriches and enlightens the mind; ripens cherries and young lips; festoons old ruins, and ivies old heads; ... smooths, levels, glosses, softens, melts, and meliorates all things ... All [is] the better for its antiquity, and the more to be revered ... Time hoared the old mountains, and balded their old summits, and spread the old prairies, and built the old forests, and molded the old vales. It is Time that has worn glorious old channels for the glorious old rivers.   Herman Melville, 1849[1]

'I mean to go in for letting the workmen have the use of all the rooms, with liberty to smudge them as much as they like, and so at the end we shall have a sort of antique effect.'
'They will be dirty.'
'You may call it dirt; I call it Art.'   Robert Kerr, 1879[2]

Arrest the actions of time, while preserving its effects.   Colin Jenner, 1994[3]

Everything oxidizes over the years, including us. But viewed from the right perspective, the marks of passing time have a beauty of their own.
                                        Costanza Algranti, designer, Livorno, 2010[4]

It is my absolute favorite thing to combine beautiful people with old, rusty, dirty settings.   Cassy Bartch, photographer, Alaska, 2009[5]

When the humanists opened their eyes to the glories of Greece and Rome, what they saw, beyond classical texts, were worn and mutilated remnants of antique architecture and sculpture. They admired these eroded fragments, not initially for their ruinous condition, but because their state of decay made them both intensely human and ripe for repair and embellishment. The classical past came to life most vividly in fresh re-creations. The time-worn fragments demanded to be to made whole again, in celebratory verse or in actual restoration. Not only did these tattered remnants inspire passion for the forms and ideas of antiquity, they enabled humanists to become co-creators, sculptors by restoring and replicating, architects by restaging in prime locales, poets and painters by portraying their trajectory from wholeness to ruin to resurrection. 'Fragmentariness was the most

---

[1] Herman Melville, *Mardi: and a Voyage Thither* (1849; Northwestern, 1970), 270–7.
[2] Robert Kerr, *His Excellency the Ambassador Extraordinary* (London, 1879), 3: 168.
[3] Colin Jenner, 'Giltwood restoration' in Andrew Oddy, ed., *Restoration* (British Museum Occasional Paper 99, 1994), 85–8 at 85.
[4] Quoted in Kate Singleton, 'Transforming trash into treasure', *IHT*, 27 July 2010.
[5] 'Connect with Cassy', Fairbanks photographer, *exposures-studio.com/blog/2009/03/31/beauty-grime/*.

crucial fact about rediscovered sculpture', writes Leonard Barkan of the newly found (1506) *Laocoön*. The 'physical incompleteness of so many ancient sculptures ... enabled both artists and viewers to enter into the works, ... to take part literally in the creation by restoring the objects'.[6]

The jumble of Roman ruins disfigured by time and neglect appealed to early-modern cognoscenti, as in Maerten van Heemskerck's depiction and Ulisse Aldrovandi's description of the headless and armless 'beautiful nude Bacchus' in the Palazzo Medici-Madama collection.[7] The Triumph of Time is personified in Hermannus Posthumus's sixteenth-century painting (this book's jacket), not by a decrepit scythe-bearing skeleton but by a sundial and rustic calendar. Posthumus playfully combines classical treasures – the Torlonia Vase, the Juno Ludovisi – already in Roman collections with ruinous structures that in his day were still whole. Against Ovid's 'Tempus edax rerum' – 'Ravenous Time, and you, envious Age, you destroy everything' – Posthumous celebrates acts to salvage, collect, depict and preserve. At almost the same moment, Pope Paul III deplored the precarious state of Roman monuments and urged their protection from neglect and theft.[8]

The ruins of Rome had enchanted Petrarch; Francesco Colonna rhapsodized over lovers walking among fallen columns, broken sculptures, dilapidated temples, overgrown pillars, and funerary vaults.[9] The poet Joachim du Bellay became ecstatic amid half-buried Rome's embedded memories. Ruined Rome seemed both alive and dead, its bygone greatness recalled in its monuments. Reconstruction, modern emulation, and poetic celebration would revive it, just as statues breathed new life and pruned trees regrew. Yet Rome was also a necropolis, a haunted wasteland, a 'bone-yard and a sink of corruption', modern Romans not restorers but robbers.[10]

Ruins roused reflections on the vainglorious new made decrepit, corrupt, degraded by the transience of men and deeds, the effects of depravity, the legacy of tyranny. As reminders of the evanescence of life and the futility of effort, ruins became a staple of later takes on the past. Initially valued as residues of bygone splendours and tokens of true antiquity, they were now lauded for their own look. The patina of age morphed from worthy sentiment to aesthetic canon. Time 'ripened' artefacts, marks of age enhanced art and architecture. Picturesque taste enshrined ruins as exemplars of the irregular, the accidental, and the natural; houses were made ruinous and new ruins

[6] Leonard Barkan, *Unearthing the Past* (Yale, 1999), 8–9.
[7] Ibid., 121.
[8] Ovid, *Metamorphoses* (c. AD 1), XV, ll 234–35; Ruth Olitsky Rubinstein, '"Tempus edax rerum": a newly discovered "Landscape with Roman Ruins" painting by Hermannus Posthumus', *Burlington Magazine* 127:988 (July, 1985): 425–36 at 425, citing 28 Nov. 1534 Papal brief, in Gaetano Marini, *Degli archiatri pontifici* (1784).
[9] Angelo Mazzocco, 'The antiquarianism of Francesco Petrarca', *Journal of Medieval and Renaissance Studies* 7 (1977): 203–24; Angelo Mazzocco, 'Petrarch: founder of Renaissance humanism?' in his ed., *Interpretations of Renaissance Humanism* (Brill, 2006), 215–42; Francesco Colonna, *Hypnerotomachia poliphili* (1499; Thames & Hudson, 2005).
[10] Richard Cooper, 'Poetry in ruins: the literary context of du Bellay's cycles on Rome', *Renaissance Studies* 3 (1989): 156–66 at 163; Joachim du Bellay, *'The Regrets'* (1558) ... (PennPress, 2006), 245–96.

manufactured. Spectacles of decay inspired sentimental travellers.[11] And antique sculpture became beautiful *as fragments*, mutilated torsos and heads preferred to intact originals.

Classical statuary epitomized the shift. Damaged remnants of archaic art had inspired Renaissance imagination but generally displeased its aesthetic taste. Humanists reassembled the mangled body of classical learning – Thomas Traherne's 'worthless shreds and Parcels' of fragmented relics – into an 'Intire piece'.[12] Like dismembered ancient texts, antiquities corroded by time were restored to the wholeness of lovely youth. In a famed sixteenth-century competition, sculptors invited to complete the *Laocoön* in replica vied with variant versions of the missing right arm.[13] Scattered fragments were reconstituted, pieces that did not fit forced into place, facsimiles forged of missing arms and legs, eyelids and ear-lobes. 'Antiquities thus restored were certainly more graceful than those mutilated trunks, those members without a head or … defective and maimed', in Giorgio Vasari's endorsement.

Through the eighteenth century restored statues fetched high prices, so shorn urns sprouted new ears and Venuses de Milo grew arms.[14] The sculptor Bertel Thorvaldsen added new heads and limbs to antique torsos so skilfully that he himself could not tell his own work from the original.[15] Wholeness long remained de rigueur at the Louvre, where restorers filled in missing pieces, concealed broken edges, and reglazed Etruscan vases. Bodily unity remains the popular norm.[16]

But the very incompleteness of antique ruins and sculptures began around 1500 to represent an antiquity 'as beautiful for its decay as for its absent grandeur', admired *as fragments*. The iconic *Belvedere Torso*, more powerful and beautiful in its effaced condition than were it whole, was deliberately left unrestored.[17] Over the next three centuries picturesque taste and the growing cachet of historical authenticity enthroned the charms of decay and injury. The emotional charge of a mutilated marble more than compensated for its lost formal unity. Just as they admired ruined buildings, connoisseurs

---

[11] Rosemary Sweet, *Antiquaries* (Hambledon and London, 2004), 316–19; Margaret T. McGowan, *The Vision of Rome in Late Renaissance France* (Yale, 2000), 187–93, 211–18, 345.

[12] Thomas Traherne, *Centuries of Meditation* (c. 1660s), 'Fourth Century', no. 54, in *Centuries, Poems, and Thanksgivings* (Clarendon Press, 1958), 1: 196.

[13] Barkan, *Unearthing the Past*, 9–11.

[14] Giorgio Vasari, *Lives of the Most Eminent Painters, Sculptors, and Architects* (1550/1568; London, 1850), 3: 152; Phoebe Dent Weil, 'Contribution toward a history of sculpture techniques', *Studies in Conservation* 12 (1967): 81–101 at 83; Jerry Podany, 'Restoring what wasn't there', in Oddy, *Restoration*, 9–16 at 13; Midas Dekkers, *The Way of All Flesh* (1997; London: Harvill, 2000), 96.

[15] Frank Arnau [Heinrich Schmitt], *Three Thousand Years of Deception in Art and Antiques* (Jonathan Cape, 1961), 301. See Jane Fejfer and Torben Melander, *Thorvaldsen's Ancient Sculptures* (Copenhagen: Thorvaldsen Museum, 2003).

[16] Jean Bousquet and Pierre Devambez, 'New methods in restoring ancient vases in the Louvre', *Museum International* 3 (1950): 177–80; David Willey, 'Italian PM "enhances" ancient Roman statues', *BBC News*, 18 Nov. 2010; Lauren E. Talalay, 'The past as commodity', *Public Archaeology* 3 (2004): 205–16 at 209.

[17] Barkan, *Unearthing the Past*, 187–206.

of the 'aesthetic of rupture' delighted in limbless torsos, scorning modern repairs that 'degraded' antique fragments.[18]

The Elgin Marbles helped spark the reversal in taste. Having acquired the Acropolis sculptures, Lord Elgin intended their repair in Rome, but Antonio Canova, the leading neoclassical sculptor, refused to restore them. Time and barbarism had sadly injured the statues, but they remained the unretouched 'work of the ablest artists the world had ever seen, and "it would be sacrilege in him or any man, to presume to touch them with a chisel"'. John Flaxman likewise declined, agreeing that 'the execution must be far inferior to the original parts. [Few] would set a higher value on a work of Phidias ... with a modern head and modern arms than they would in their present state'. Their fragmentation became a positive virtue, for Keats commingling 'Grecian grandeur with the rude Wasting of Old Time'.[19]

Preoccupation with ruin was not confined to crumbling buildings and fragmented sculpture. Mania for dismemberment spread from monumental remains to other art, old and new.[20] 'When the fragments of Sappho's poetry became known in the nineteenth century, their fragmentary condition was thought to improve them', and modern poets began to invent fragments of their own.[21] 'Many works of the ancients have become fragments', wrote Friedrich Schlegel; 'many modern works are fragments as soon as they are written'.[22] Literary creations like Goethe's *Faust* were advertised as 'Fragments'; many poets' own lives often seemed curtailed and cut off by premature demise.[23] Viewing the Elgin Marbles, Benjamin Haydon overheard this exchange:

> 'How broken down they are, a'ant they?'
> 'Yes, but how *like life*.'[24]

Fragmented works seemed more intensely alive than intact antiquities. 'It is not that we prefer time-worn bas-reliefs, or rusted statuettes as such', said André Malraux, 'but the sense of life they impart, from the evidence of their struggle with Time'.[25] Or alternatively from dismemberment and death, as in Théodore Géricault's macabre guillotined heads

---

[18] Edward Daniel Clarke, *Greek Marbles Brought from the Shores of the Euxine, Archipelago, and Mediterranean* (Cambridge, 1809), iii; Roland Mortier, *Le Poétique des ruines en France* (Geneva: Droz, 1974), 97–103.

[19] Canova in *Memorandum on the Subject of the Earl of Elgin's Pursuits in Greece* (1815), Flaxman in William Richard Hamilton to Elgin, 23 June 1807 and 8 Aug. 1802, quoted in Arthur Hamilton Smith, 'Lord Elgin and his collection', *Journal of Hellenic Studies* 36 (1916): 163–372 at 255, 297–8, 227; William St Clair, *Lord Elgin and the Marbles* (1967; 3rd edn Oxford, 1988), 149-50; John Keats, 'On seeing the Elgin Marbles' (1817), ll. 12–13, in *Poetical Works*, 2nd edn (Clarendon Press, 1958), 478.

[20] Georg Simmel, 'Die Ruine' (1907), in *Philosophische Kultur* (Berlin, 1983), 106–12.

[21] Peter Levi, 'Wondrous pleasures' *Times*, 5 Jan. 1984: 9.

[22] Friedrich von Schlegel, 'Athenaeum fragments' (1797–8), no. 24, in *Philosophical Fragments* (Minnesota, 1991), 18–93 at 21.

[23] Walter Kaufmann, *Time Is an Artist* (Reader's Digest Press, 1978), 61–3; Peter Fritzsche, *Stranded in the Present* (Harvard, 2004), 80.

[24] Benjamin Haydon, *Diary*, 28 May 1817 (Cambridge, 1960), 2: 120.

[25] André Malraux, *The Voices of Silence* (Doubleday, 1953), 635.; Millard Meiss, 'The aesthetic and historical aspects of the presentation of damaged pictures' (1963), in David Bomford and Mark Leonard, eds., *Issues in the Conservation of Paintings* (Getty, 2004), 370–90.

and severed limbs (1818), painted from fragments gathered from morgues and kept in his studio until the stench of decomposition became unbearable.[26] Classical fragments inspired art truncated to begin with, like William Rimmer's *Dying Centaur* (1869) and Arthur Lee's *Volupté* (*c.* 1912).[27]

Other attributes of decay likewise gained favour. The popularity of ruined castles, the price of patinated bronzes, the market for shabby-chic 'distressed' furniture attest the allure of divers marks of age. 'A spanking new coffee-table in brand new pine looked hideous, so we learned how to age things', says a distresser. Manufacturers were at first aghast. 'But once we had taken a hammer to their shiny new piece, they appreciated what we were after.'[28]

Corrosion not only enhances the aura of antiquity but is esteemed in its own right, precious because portending loss. Evanescence beautifies. Artists celebrate time with works intended to decay and perish. The worn and tattered state of cherished mementoes – battered jugs, stained cigarette packets, dog-eared theatre programmes – lends companionable charm. Aesthetic theorists ratify beauty in things 'irredeemably, and gloriously, shattered and broken'. Beautiful decay has become an 'internationally recognized design-driven lifestyle brand'.[29]

Disdaining durability, modern artists create ephemera *meant* to decay and perish. Picasso gave tiresome admirers signed *dédicaces*, gleefully aware that they would soon fade and ultimately vanish.[30] 'I love the way it's aged', said Cy Twombly of one of his works. 'I want a sign put on the back that says "Do not ever restore this painting."'[31]

Much auto-destructive art visibly disintegrates, fragments ejected, carbonized, pulverized, peeling off, liquefying, imploding, or shattering on impact. Bill Morrison's *Decasia: The State of Decay* (2001), a sixty-seven-minute montage of decomposing nitrate film, offered 'all the putrefaction you could ask for. Watch Master Narratives Crumble! Entropy Now.'[32] The aesthetic of revulsion is often didactic. 'Society is deteriorating. So is the sculpture', expounded Gustav Metzger. 'Auto-destructive art [is] a mirror image of reality.'[33] *Memento mori* was the message of Leopoldo Maler's self-sculpture in ice,

---

[26] Nina Athanassoglou-Kallmyer, 'Géricault's severed heads and limbs', *Art Bulletin* 74 (1992): 599–618; Linda Nochlin, *The Body in Pieces: The Fragment as a Metaphor of Modernity* (Thames & Hudson, 1995), 19–21. See 'Le corps en morceaux', *Terrain: revue d'ethnologie de l'Europe*, no. 18 (Mar. 1992).

[27] Milo M. Naeve, *The Classical Presence in American Art* (Art Institute of Chicago, 1978), 27. The taste for fragmentation waned until the recent revival of the aesthetic cult of incompleteness (Andrea Rothe, 'Croce e delizia', in Mark Leonard, ed., *Personal Viewpoints: Thoughts about Paintings Conservation* (Getty, 2003), 13–25 at 17).

[28] Brenda Polan, 'New aged interiors', *Sunday Times Magazine*, 8 Sept. 1991: 60–3.

[29] Guy Sircello, 'Beauty in shards and fragments', *Journal of Aesthetics and Art Criticism* 48 (1990): 21–35 at 34; Amir H. Fallah, beautifuldecay.com. See Robert Harbison, *The Built, the Unbuilt and the Unbuildable* (MIT Press, 1991), 122; Mélanie van der Hoorn, *Indispensable Eyesores* (Berghahn, 2009), 139–46.

[30] John Richardson, 'Crimes against the Cubists', *NYRB*, 16 June 1983: 32–4.

[31] Quoted in Leonard, ed., *Personal Viewpoints*, 112–15 (panel discussion). The iconoclastic intent is often postponed or altered. Man Ray's *Object to Be Destroyed* (1923) lasted 34 years until students smashed it (Janine Mileaf, 'Between you and me: Man Ray's *Object to Be Destroyed*', *Art Journal* 63:1 (2004): 4–23).

[32] Herb Muschamp, 'After the decay of decay, a new modernity', *NYT*, 7 Feb. 2004: 1, 23; Jonathan Jones, 'Ghost world', *Guardian*, 26 Sept. 2003.

[33] Gustav Metzger, *Auto-Destructive Art* (London: Architectural Association, 1965), 16, 18–19.

H₂OMBRE, melting in a New York gallery. 'Tomorrow it is not there anymore', said Maler, sipping tea made from *H₂OMBRE* melt-water, 'maybe like me'.[34] To stress the ephemeral, advised Martin Heidegger, the artist should use the most perishable material.[35] Earth art is overtly evanescent. Will Ashford's 'Mona Lisa', outlined by the selective spreading of fertilizer near Alamo, California, in 1979, reflected natural change. The picture 'grew' with the grass, matured with rain and sun, then wilted into invisibility.[36] Whether fugitive art gradually ages or speedily disintegrates, decay is integral to ongoing creative change, as in Dieter Roth's butterfat-and-chocolate and Sonja Alhäuser's chocolate–popcorn works, which expire when the chocolate crumbles.[37]

Artists' insistence that their work not be conserved, often mandated when sold or donated, upsets collectors and curators, museum-goers, and trustees, who regard works of art as permanent assets. To let them deliquesce or decay is culpable complicity in asset loss. Staff were appalled by the Philadelphia Museum of Art's 1998 purchase of Zoe Leonard's *Strange Fruit (for David)*, comprising sewn and zippered avocado, grapefruit, lemon, orange, and banana rinds and skins. Intentional evanescence violates curatorial mindsets: 'How can you give an acquisition number to something that won't always be there?' a curator ruefully reflected. Museums are dedicated to preserving not just individual works of art but 'the notion that works of art are fixed and immortal'.[38]

Art made to visibly decay entails a further irony. 'The more art aspires to the ephemeral nature of life, the more elaborate and indestructible its exoskeleton must be.' Indeed, the more transience is praised, the more things become permanent.[39] For Dan Flavin's fluorescent-light works, the look of decay requires regular replacement of the bulbs, thus rejuvenating their authentic patina. Now 'he's dead', declared a collector, 'dedicated acolytes [are] working to preserve what he left behind'. But like many ephemeral artists, Flavin himself moved from rejecting conservation ('permanence defies everything') in 1984 to ensuring, in 1998, that his art legacy would survive.[40] 'Good artists

---

[34] 'Artist delights in work's limited life', *NYT*, 10 May 1982.

[35] Martin Heidegger, 'The origin of the work of art' (1936), in *Basic Writings* (Harper, 1977), 171.

[36] Georg Gerster, 'Grow your own Mona Lisa', *Sunday Times Magazine*, 17 Feb. 1980: 26–8; Dolores Fox Ciardelli, 'Growing Mona Lisa', *Danville Express News*, 11 Jan. 2008.

[37] Carol Mancusi-Ungaro in 'Time and change: a discussion about the conservation of modern and contemporary art', *Conservation Perspectives* (Getty Conservation Institute) 17:3 (Fall 2002): 11–17 at 14; Randy Kennedy, 'Time, and moments that endure', *IHT* 19 Jan. 2013: 16, 18. See Heinz Althöfer, 'Fragmente und Ruine', *Kunstforum International* 19 (1977): 57–169 at 81, 162; Jackie Heuman, ed., *From Marble to Chocolate: The Conservation of Modern Sculpture* (London: Archetype, 1995); Ken Gewertz, 'Eat out', *Harvard Gazette*, 11 Oct. 2001. Roth insisted that his *Self Portrait at a Table* (chocolate, butter, collage, 1973–6), at the Tate Gallery, be allowed to deteriorate (interview, 25 Oct. 1977). See Heide Skowranek, 'Should we reproduce the beauty of decay? A *Museumsleben* in the work of Dieter Roth', *Tate Papers*, issue 8 (Autumn 2007).

[38] Ann Temkin, 'Strange fruit', in Miguel Angel Corzo, ed., *Mortality Immortality? The Legacy of 20th-Century Art* (Getty Conservation Institute 1999), 45–50; Sylvia Hochfield, 'Sticks and stones and lemon cough drops: from Joseph Beuys to Eva Hesse to Zoe Leonard', *ARTnews* 101 (2002): 116–23.

[39] Robert Storr, '"Immortalité provisoire"', 35–40 at 36, and Helen Escobedo, 'Work as process or work as product', 53–6 at 54, in Corzo, ed., *Mortality Immortality?*; Linda Sandino, 'Here today, gone tomorrow: transient materiality', *Journal of Design History* 17 (2004): 283–94.

[40] Greg Allen, 'The dark side of success', *NYT*, 2 Jan. 2005: AR 28. See Michael Govan et al., *Dan Flavin: The Complete Lights* (Dia Art/Yale, 2004); Gregory Williams and Christian Scheidemann, 'Conserving latex and liverwurst', *Cabinet Magazine*, 2 (Spring 2001): 103–7.

are incapable of destroying', concludes a reviewer. 'Some uncontrollable instinct for materials and mark-making condemns them to contribute to art's motley history even as they ... rage against its permanence.'[41]

Devotees of decay enjoy its successive stages. An aesthetic of ageing tempers preservation zeal with fondness for dissolution. Over the last two centuries, as factories poured out more and more goods, things used up, outworn, or obsolete were consigned to the rubbish heap. Decay and demolition were not only distressing tokens of mortality, but innate to ongoing life. Progressive change required prior decay. Were immortality an option, space would soon be exhausted. Moth and rust are indispensable. 'The world itself [is] a grave', said the poet Edward Young; 'Where is the dust that has not been alive? ... From human mould we reap our daily bread.'[42] Previously shunned as noxious, disgusting, sinister, or grotesque, the worn out and old fashioned were increasingly admired as venerable, memorable, and ornamental.

I discuss four aspects of fondness for the look of age: belief that old things ought to look old; faith in decay as a guarantor of antiquity; aesthetic delight in wear and tear; and reflections inspired by ruins and fragments.

Old things should look old

The Renaissance rediscovery of classical art made marks of age vital to the celebration of antiquity. The cult of the 'Old Master' – a venerable testimony from the past – spread throughout Europe. Collectors preferred paintings to look old; visible age conferred prestige on their possessors. 'By giving testimony to their antiquity', observed a connoisseur, the patina of time 'renders them proportionably beautiful'.[43]

A patina of age on ancestral heirlooms attested their owners' social status. 'Gentility is nothing but ancient riches', pronounced Queen Elizabeth's secretary of state. Furnishings battered by long use served, like family portraits, as tokens of lineage. Tarnish on silver lent assurance of ancestral possession, proof of things inherited, not recently bought. 'The greater the patina on certain objects, the longer the family ... had lived in a gentle manner for generations and therefore legitimately lived in that manner now.' Since heirlooms were rarely sold and their provenance was widely known, time-worn marks were effective guardians of status.[44]

The prestige of patina was ultimately eclipsed by the growing availability of manufactures, the fashion for novelty, and the declining import of inherited status. Heirlooms marked by wear and tear still carry cachet among a snobbish few, but social mobility and floods of facsimiles reduce former ancestral icons to quaint anachronisms. Patina's

[41] Roberta Smith, 'Walking on coffee, trying to get a fix on a master of impermanence', NYT, 3 Mar. 2006: B34.

[42] Edward Young, The Complaint: or, Night-Thoughts (1742; London, 1813), 272.

[43] Francesco Algarotti, An Essay on Painting (London, 1764), 56.

[44] William Cecil, Lord Burghley, 'Certain precepts for the well ordering of a man's life' (c. 1584), in Louis B. Wright, ed., Advice to a Son (Cornell, 1962), 7–14 at 10; Helen Clifford, 'The problem of patina', in Alison Bracker and Alison Richmond, eds., Conservation: Principles, Dilemmas, and Uncomfortable Truths (Elsevier, 2009), 125–8. See Grant McCracken, Culture and Consumption (Indiana, 1988), 33–8.

perquisites are now solely aesthetic. In centuries past, the sheen of age was admired as evidence of long use; today it is merely attractive, if at all, in its own right.

Patina embellishes manifold relics. Bruises and hard knocks commend antique wood fittings. 'Normal daily use imparts, merely by the touch of the human hand, the brush of a sleeve, and the stubbing with a leather-clad toe, the natural, not-too-perfect appearance that period furniture really should present'. Marks attesting long use – the hammer scarred from pulling out nails, its handle worn by the user's hand – lend tools personality.[45] 'Of all handmade things the dearest to me are the used ones', said Bertolt Brecht; 'the bruised copper containers … knives and forks worn by many hands … improve their appearance and become precious because often put to the test'.[46] Farm tools in museums convey history by signs of having done hard work.

An aura of antiquity justifies imperfections that would not pass muster in new work, such as rough-hewn floors and blackened timbers. Scratches in old recordings are treasured because 'worn' sounds powerfully evoke the past. Decay is electronically suggested by warp, echo, and phrasing; 'Pale tones irresolute / And traceries of old sounds / Blown from a rotted flute / Mingle with a noise of cymbals / Rouged with rust'. 'Hauntological' recordings simulate fuzzy and staticky effects of age, as if 'worn out or heard at a great distance through a grimy haze', on retro cassette tapes.[47]

Torn and twisted museum artefacts tell compelling tales. So do blood stains on a Boer War sword, Iron Age weapons ritually bent, the corroded hole in a long-buried bowl, foxing marks on paper. Sprinkling dirt on textiles, hammering dents in silverware, and installing woodworm to eat through historic timber helps to study processes of decay.[48] Ethnographic conservators honour hands-off tribal treatment of sacred fabrics as living beings with limited lifespans. Not embalmed in mortuary aspic, they finally succumb to insect infestation, initiating their journey into the afterworld. Since decay and dissolution are natural and inevitable, 'any bug should be collected along with any rug'.[49]

Wear and tear can seem endearing. It was a look of seamy conformability that James Agee admired in sharecroppers' softened and faded shabby clothes. Prolonged use gave each man's garment 'the shape and beauty of his induplicable body'; sun, sweat, and laundering rendering colour and texture 'ancient, veteran, composed, and patient';

---

[45] Peter Philp, 'Restoring furniture and clocks', *Antique Dealers and Collectors Guide* (Aug. 1978): 57–61 at 59. See Peter Philp and Gillian Walkling, *Antique Furniture Expert* (London: Century, 1991), 51, 82; Bill Viola, 'Permanent impermanence', in Corzo, ed., *Mortality Immortality?*, 85–94.

[46] Bertolt Brecht, *Gedichte und Lieder* (1981), quoted in Francesco Orlando, *Obsolete Objects in the Literary Imagination* (1994; Yale, 2006), 252.

[47] Mike Zwerin, 'The spirit moves with Oscar Sosa', *IHT*, 20 Oct. 2004: 10; 'Enoch Soames' poem, Andrew Porter letter, *Times*, 20 Mar. 1997; Carrie Clanton, 'Hauntology beyond the cinema', *manycinemas* issue 3 (2012): 66–76.

[48] Andrew Oddy, 'Does reversibility exist?', 1–5, and Jonathan Ashley-Smith, 'Restoration: politics and economics', 129–32 at 131, in Andrew Oddy and Sara Carroll, eds., *Reversibility: Does It Exist?* (British Museum Occasional Paper 135, 1999).

[49] Klavs Randborg, 'Plundered Bronze Age graves', *Acta Archaeologica* 69 (1998): 119–38 at 120; Helen Murdina Hughes, 'How greater knowledge of an object can affect an assessment of the restoration of previous treatments', 173–4 at 173, and Sergio Palazzi, 'Restoration', 175–8 at 177, in Oddy and Carroll, eds., *Reversibility*.

buttons 'blind as cataracts' slipping into worn holes; trouser legs as 'minutely wrinkled as the skin of aged faces'.[50] The grease-patch smocks, muck-corroded or mice-eaten gloves, and scuffed boots discarded in defunct factories enthralled Tim Edensor.[51] Progressive disintegration into nature fascinates visitors to an ancient car dump in Sweden. An old military site at Orford Ness in Suffolk is deliberately left to ruin; barbed wire and metal tank tracks corroding in the salty climate slowly revert to nature.[52]

The *fin-de-siècle* penchant for architectural decay went hand in hand with Anti-Scrape restoration precepts (see Chapter 11). Renovating time-battered buildings, charged William Morris, expunged 'the appearance of antiquity ... from such old parts of the fabric as are left'.[53] To an English architect anything 'spick and span and new ... requires an apology'. A French devotee of decay preferred 'the smallest village church as time has left it' to the Gothic church of St Ouen de Rouen as restored in the 1840s.[54] George Edmund Street decried 'irreverent hands' that threatened at Reims and Laon cathedrals to 'scrape off every weather stain, repair every damaged feature, and leave the whole as clean and new looking as it was when first built'.[55] Henry James deplored the self-conscious air of 'desperate clean freshness' in Salem's old colonial houses; antiquity needed 'musty secrets in the eaves'.[56] Agedness attested pre-industrial handcrafted honesty, as in the ponderous permanence of H. H. Richardson's American Romanesque buildings (Fig. 39), and in the burly primitivism of undressed rustication and penchant for rubble in Scottish and German castles.[57]

That old buildings should look old is a not uncommon view. Unlike people, 'buildings are expected to gain by the process of growing old'; we like 'their history written on their faces'. Victorians and moderns alike lauded the 'sooty dignity' of St Paul Cathedral's blackened grandeur. The velvety patina of soot provided 'visible evidence that the monument – like the nation – has weathered centuries of storm and crisis and come through battered but unbowed'. Sooty facades are reminders of 'London's foggy past ... a monument to the age of smoke ... as noble and meaningful as any other texture of history'.[58] That coal gas no longer pollutes urban England makes soot easier to enjoy,

[50] James Agee and Walker Evans, *Let Us Now Praise Famous Men* (1936; Houghton Mifflin, 1960), 267–9.

[51] Tim Edensor, *Industrial Ruins* (Berg, 2005).

[52] Mats Burström, 'Garbage or heritage: the existential dimension of a car cemetery', in Cornelius Holtorf and Angela Piccini, eds., *Contemporary Archaeologies* (Frankfurt am Main: Lang, 2008), 133–45; Deborah Mulhearn, 'A taste of space', *National Trust Magazine*, no. 101 (Spring 2004): 50–7. See Rachel Woodward, *Military Geographies* (Blackwell, 2004), 76–7, 148–9.

[53] William Morris, 'Manifesto of the Society for the Protection of Ancient Buildings' (1877), in Nicholas Stanley Price et al., eds., *Historical and Philosophical Issues in the Conservation of Cultural Heritage* (Getty, 1996), 319–21 at 320.

[54] Sidney Colvin (at SPAB, 1878) quoted in Martin J. Wiener, *English Culture and the Decline of the Industrial Spirit* (1981; Cambridge, 2004), 70; Eugène Delacroix, *Journal*, 29 Aug. 1857 (Paris, 1895), 3: 122.

[55] G. E. Street, 'Destructive restoration on the Continent', *Ecclesiologist* 18 (Dec. 1857): 342–5 at 342.

[56] Henry James, *The American Scene* (1907; Indiana, 1968), 268.

[57] James O'Gorman, *Living Architecture: A Biography of H. H. Richardson* (Simon & Schuster, 1997), 10, 108–9; Ranald MacInnes, '"Rubblemania"', *Journal of Design History* 9:3 (1996): 137–51.

[58] Augustus J. C. Hare, *Walks in London* (1878), 128–9; Andrew Sanders, *In the Olden Time* (Yale, 2013), 158–9; 'St Paul's: black or white?' *Architectural Review* 135 (1964): 243–5; Feliks Topolski, 'In praise of London grime', *Times*, 9 Nov. 1977.

since almost none of it is new. Indeed, as so little is left, soot is now saved as heritage. For 'aesthetic coherence', an architectural theorist preserves grime 'in the same pattern as it settled on the wall'.[59]

Decay is lauded for according with natural processes. 'It is no disgrace for a building ... to fall into ruin. ... It becomes a habitat for all wild things – nesting birds, bats, moulds, our own fertile imaginations.' Rotting tree stumps nurture new life; 'gnarled and verminous relics of the past contain useful nutrients ... It is natural to build on the rubble of the past, and let its dead trunks sprout new life.' We are urged to 'cherish the faltering trunks and fallen branches, whether in a monarchy, an art form, a university or a kitchen'.[60]

Likening a building to a living being ennobled its decay with 'some mysterious suggestion of what it had been, and of what it had lost'. Ruskin lauded an ancient Calais church tower as

useful still, going through its own daily work [though with] the record of its years written so visibly, ... its slates and tiles all shaken and rent, and yet not falling; its desert of brickwork full of bolts, and holes, and ugly fissures, and yet strong ... as some old fisherman beaten grey by storm, yet drawing his daily nets ... It completely expresses that agedness in the midst of active life which binds the old and the new into harmony.[61]

What endeared the tower was precisely what enfeebled it. By picturesque tenets, a broken stone had more charm than a whole one, a bent roof than a straight one; 'every excrescence or cleft involves some additional complexity of light and shade, and every stain of moss on eaves or wall adds to the delightfulness of color, [for] set in the deeper places of the heart [is] such affection for the signs of age that the eye is delighted even by injuries which are the work of time'.[62]

Many shared Ruskin's devotion to organic wear. John Soane sketched his buildings as they would look both when new and centuries later. 'Men should make buildings, as God made men, to be beautiful in age as in youth', felt John Piper, bearing in mind that 'some people will see it as an aged warrior or matron, not just as a brave baby'.[63]

Pleasure in diminished strength and function seemed perverse, however, when picturesque tenets required old-timers as well as old structures. The similarly irregular features of a parson's house and daughter led Uvedale Price to envisage the daughter grown even more picturesque 'when her cheeks were a little furrowed and weather-stained, and her teeth had got a slight incrustation'. But consistency mandated 'the same happy mixture of the irregular and picturesque ... through her limbs and person', responded Richard

---

[59] Andrew Goldstein, 'The ethics of dust: an interview with Venice Biennale artist Jorge Otero-Pailos', *ArtWeLove*, 5 Aug. 2009. Otero-Pailos was inspired by Ruskin's *The Ethics of Dust* (1866), in *CW*, 16, but Ruskin admired dust as incipient crystalline beauty, not as dirt.

[60] Katherine Swift, 'Gardens review', *Times*, 24 Aug. 2004: WR29; Libby Purves, 'Don't keep Britain too tidy', *Times2*, 26 Oct. 2004: 21.

[61] John Ruskin, *Modern Painters* (1859; New York, 1886), pt. 5, ch. 1, sect. 2–3, 4: 2–3.

[62] Ibid., pt. 5, para. 8: 6; I, pt. 2, sect. 1, ch. 7, para. 26, 4: 104.

[63] John Piper, 'Pleasing decay' (1947), in *Buildings and Prospects* (London: Architectural Press, 1948), 89–116 at 89.

Figure 18 The noble patina of soot: Robert Smirke, St Philip's, Salford, Manchester, 1825

Figure 19 Renewing the old: Canterbury Cathedral cloisters, 1978

Payne Knight; 'consequently she must have hobbled as well as squinted; and had hips and shoulders as irregular as her teeth, cheeks, and eyebrows'. And Price would 'hardly find any man fond enough of the picturesque' to marry a girl so deformed.

Price found thatched roofs most 'picturesque, when mossy, ragged, and sunk in among the rafters in decay', but 'the keenest lover of [ancient thatch] would rather see it on another's property than on his own'.[64] Although ancestral thatch was 'beautiful in youth, maturity & decay!' a later celebrant promoted modern copies, modelled on 'lines laid down for us by our forefathers', as healthier and 'more convenient'. But health stripped of antiquity seemed a sham: rather than unsightly new clinics with 'wards all spick and span and up to date', he preferred almshouses 'mellowed with age wherein men and women, on whom the snows of life have begun to fall thickly, may rest and recruit and take their ease before they start on the long, dark journey from which no traveller returns'.[65]

Ruskin deplored the heartless 'lower picturesque' delight in looking at an old labourer, 'pathetic in his grey hair, and withered arms, and sunburnt breast'. Amiens slum-dwellers were 'all exquisitely picturesque, and no less miserable ... Seeing the unhealthy face and melancholy mien ... I could not help feeling how many suffering persons must pay for my picturesque subject and happy walk.'[66] In America, Melville rebuked those with 'povertiresque' pictures in their drawing-rooms who shut their eyes to misery.[67] A fondness for 'plaster falling in blotches from the ancient brick-work' and other stains of time made Hawthorne 'suspect that a people are waning to decay and ruin, the moment that their life becomes fascinating either in the poet's imagination or in the painter's eye'.[68]

But few equated painting with reality. 'The most *beautiful* pictures may be produced by the most ugly and disgusting objects', held Price.[69] The mouldering abbey and the ancient cottage merited affection, agreed Humphry Repton, but nobody would suggest that a modern English gentleman should actually *live* in one. 'The antiquated cot' might be a proper home 'for squalid misery and want – but is affluence to be denied a suitable habitation – are we to banish all convenience' in deference to 'a prejudice against all that is neat and cleanly, or a ridiculous affectation of rural simplicity?'[70]

[64] Uvedale Price, *A Dialogue on the Distinct Characters of the Picturesque and of the Beautiful* (1801), and *Essay on Architecture and Buildings* (1794), in *Essays on the Picturesque* (London, 1810), 3: 181–400 at 292–3, 398 and 2: 171–370 at 340–1; Richard Payne Knight, *Analytical Inquiry into the Principles of Taste*, 3rd edn (London, 1895), 202–3.

[65] P. H. Ditchfield, *The Charm of the English Village* (London, 1905), 68; and *Vanishing England* (London, 1910), 329.

[66] Ruskin, *Modern Painters*, pt. 5, ch. 1, paras. 7 and 12n, 4: 5, 10n; John Ruskin, *The Diaries*, 12 May 1854 (Clarendon Press, 1956–9), 2: 493 (re Amiens). Unlike the 'lower picturesque', the 'noble picturesque' in J. M. W. Turner's and Samuel Prout's paintings showed sympathy 'of *suffering*, of *poverty*, or *decay* nobly endured' (Ruskin, *Modern Painters*, pt. v, ch. 1, para. 7, 4: 5; Robert Hewison, *John Ruskin: The Argument of the Eye* (Thames & Hudson, 1976), 48–60).

[67] Herman Melville, *Pierre: or, the Ambiguities* (1852; Northwestern, 1971), 276–7. See Gavin Jones, *American Hungers: The Problem of Poverty in U.S. Literature* (Princeton, 2008), 52–8, 67.

[68] Nathaniel Hawthorne, *The Marble Faun* (1859), in *Works* (Ohio State, 1962-80), 4: 296.

[69] Price, *Dialogue*, 3: 303.

[70] Humphry Repton, *Sketches and Hints on Landscape Gardening* (London, 1794), 61–4.

Neither the ravaged artefacts nor the raddled oldsters painters depicted were verisimilar. Fantasized decay gave relief from the humdrum present. The dilapidation of Hubert Robert's ruinous *Louvre* and Joseph Gandy's decrepit *Bank of England* abolished these buildings' prior workaday functions (Fig. 20).[71] Squalor repelled, but its depiction in a sufficiently distant past might be enjoyed. Pictures of human decay seem quaint if remote in time. Hence the present allure of Gustave Doré's sketches of the London poor (Fig. 21), of nineteenth-century pictures of slums and child labourers, and of Depression-era penury.[72]

Current fondness for decay reverses 1950s and '60s tidiness, with ruined abbeys and historic houses kept immaculate. Yet a heritage mentor finds Britain's museums still 'implausibly clean. The statues look as if nobody has knocked them over in decades ... Dust must settle and cobwebs form.'[73] Conjuring up 'dreams of yesteryear ... dust makes palpable the elusive passing of time; ... only after dust settles on an object do we begin to long for its lost splendor'.[74] A gardener chides English Heritage's spick-and-span conservators: 'A splendidly overgrown ruin [is given] the archaeologists' equivalent of Botox: tidied up, explained, made safe ... It gets sanitised and it loses all its atmosphere ... All that is left is a bare carcass and a sterile history lesson.'[75] In Amsterdam restoration is all the rage; anyone 'who wants to know what a church looked like in past centuries has nothing to learn from ... shiny polished Westerkerk and the restored-to-death ... Nieuwekerk. Only in the Nordenkerk do the floors still creak'.[76]

Regeneration that eliminates marks of age is increasingly deplored. 'We must be wary of becoming our own worst enemies', American neighbourhood gentrifiers were warned. 'A restoration could ruin the community's character, removing the patina of the years.'[77] The flavour of the past in Boston's restored Quincy Market comes not merely from the antique lettering on shopkeepers' signboards but from their flaking paintwork and decayed wood. Like former chophouses, themselves copies of historic British pubs, a reborn Greenwich Village restaurant features a damaged seventeenth-century oil painting, distressed repro lab stools, and carefully trimmed cobwebs.[78] East Berlin's tenement quarter restores 'saddlery' and 'coals for sale' signs in antiquated fonts. Protected with fresh transparent finish, this self-conscious new oldness restages a vanished durability.[79]

---

[71] Mortier, *Poétique des ruines*, 92; Christopher Hussey, *The Picturesque* (1927; London: Cass, 1967), 70–1, 202–3; Nina L. Dubin, *Futures & Ruins: Eighteenth-Century Paris* (Getty Research Institute, 2010), 152–3; Brian Lukacher, *Joseph Gandy* (Thames & Hudson, 2006); Christopher Woodward, *In Ruin* (Pantheon, 2001), 261–4; Mark Morris, 'Old before their time: artificial ruins', *frieze Magazine*, no. 79 (Nov.–Dec. 2003).

[72] Kathleen Pyne, 'Whistler and the politics of the urban picturesque', *American Art* 8:3–4 (1994): 60–77; Andrew Blaikie, 'Photography, childhood and urban poverty', *Visual Culture in Britain* 7:2 (2006): 47–68; Ann Whiston Spirn, *Daring to Look: Dorothea Lange's Photographs and Reports from the Field* (Chicago, 2008).

[73] Simon Jenkins, 'Let our curiosity kill the curator's catalogue', *Times*, 19 Dec. 2003.

[74] Celeste Olalquiaga, 'Museum of dust' (2007), in Brian G. Dillon, ed., *Ruins* (MIT Press, 2011), 32–5.

[75] Katherine Swift, 'Gardens review', *Times*, 24 Aug. 2004: WR29, re Witley Court, Worcestershire.

[76] Dekkers, *Way of All Flesh*, 118.

[77] 'The enemy within', *Preservation News* 16:10 (1976): 4.

[78] Diane Cardwell, 'In the Village, a vision of the city as it once was', *NYT*, 20 May 2010: 22–3.

[79] Florian Urban, 'From periodical obsolescence to eternal preservation', *Future Anterior* 3:1 (2006): 23–34.

Figure 20 Imagined decay: Joseph Michael Gandy, *Architectural Ruins: A Vision.
The Bank of England . . . 1832*

Newer still are Turkish carpets that fabricate careworn antiquity, retro traces of usage and age maturing a mantle of time. Decaying antiques in a ruined castle inspired the torn edges and faded colours of the 'Fragment' line. The craquelure in Bottticelli's *Birth of Venus* (1485) lends 'Patina' rugs their 'essential look of historicity', like pre-tattered jeans and 'pre-washed' digital photos. A Yale architect shaved down his neo-Gothic building steps to conjure up centuries of plodding students. Old cobblestoned streets in Brooklyn's Vinegar Hill, sacrificed for the safety of cyclists and pedestrians, will be replaced by 'old-looking' cobblestones, rounded and worn to simulate the effect of decades of rumbling vehicles.[80]

Decay demonstrates and secures antiquity

Wear and tear confirms antiquity, attesting both age and authenticity. The period furnishings in Théophile Gautier's Saint Germain mansion – 'the paintings, the gold ornaments, the damask, the brocade, were muted without being faded and did not grate on the eyes with the crude glare of newness. One felt that that richness was immemorial.'[81] Collectors assume that 'the more crude and gnarled and battered a piece

---

[80] 'Stepevi launched Patina, Fragment rug lines at London Design Festival', World Interior Design Network, 29 Sept. 2011; 'Patina & Fragment by Stepevi and Pudelskern', *COVER: Modern Carpets and Textile for Interiors*, 22 Aug. 2011 blog; Christy Walpole, 'How to live without irony', *NYT*, 17 Nov. 2012; Susan Ryan, 'The architecture of James Gamble Rogers at Yale University', *Perspecta* [Yale], 18 (1982): 25–42; Matt Flegenheimer, 'To replace old cobblestones, old-looking cobblestones', *NYT*, 30 Mar. 2013: 15.

[81] Théophile Gautier, *Spirite: nouvelle fastastique* (1865; Paris: Godefroy, 1982), 112.

Figure 21 Picturesque misery: Gustave Doré, 'Houndsditch', London, 1872

of furniture looks, the earlier it must be'; a piece in perfect condition cannot be genuine. The dearth of finish on a gilded chair imparts a sense of history.[82] When the Place de la Concorde's other mansions were cleaned in the 1960s, the Hôtel de Crillon's facade was left unwashed, the grime guaranteeing genuine age.[83] Peeling paint, cracked putty, corroded glazing bars on Kew Gardens' 1840s Palm House conferred a pastness absent in the stainless steel, plastic-coated 1980s replacements.[84] Much-worn lacquer on an old rocking-chair is a constant reminder of a departed mother's presence. The patina of dust on a museum's plaster casts of antique statues, friezes, cornices, and capitals accentuates their historicity.[85]

[82] C. K. Binns, 'Restored and unrestored pieces of early oak furniture', *Antiques Collector* 41 (1970): 184–90; Jenner, 'Giltwood restoration', in Oddy, *Restoration*, 85–8.

[83] Janet Flanner, 'Letter from Paris', *New Yorker*, 3 Feb. 1962: 84.

[84] Don Barker, 'Restoring Kew Gardens', *Architecture Week*, 30 Oct. 2002: C2.

[85] Anne Walker quoted in Elaine Louie, 'A blast from the past, courtesy of the Met', *NYT*, 10 Feb. 2005: D1,7.

Figure 22 Ruins made tidy: medieval remains, Yorkshire

Figure 23 Ruins left incomprehensible: medieval rubble, Bury St Edmunds, Suffolk

New copies of historic structures come complete with a requisite patina of age. Alongside Goethe's actual Garden House in Weimar a precise replica was given two centuries' wear and tear – 'scratches, the filling of crevices with dirt, and fly droppings, ... aged wooden furniture, green patina on the copper roof gutter, worn out steps'.[86]

Besides authenticating antiquity, erosion stimulates its study. To see and touch palpably aged documents brings the past to life. Handling old diaries and travel logs with 'some crinkle of antiquity' imparts the thrilling 'idea, however illusory, that some major discovery might be lurking in those yellowed pages'.[87]

Forgers have long fed on credulous faith in the aura of age. Roman fondness for Greek art led to 'weathered' copies. Faking marks of time became rife in the Renaissance and widespread thereafter. Lorenzo de' Medici persuaded Michelangelo to magnify the market value of his marble *Eros* by 'antiquing' it in acidic soil.[88] After 'smoking' a painting, Terenzio da Urbino gilded its decrepit shabby frame to 'look as though it were really old'.[89] Colours were tempered with chimney soot, canvases rolled up to induce minute fissures. Coins were 'aged' in a mixture of fatty broth and iron filings.[90] A few smoke-induced hours gave meerschaum pipes the honey warmth of years of smoking. In the 1960s Han van Meegeren passed off his 'Vermeers' by making his paint seem the product of centuries.[91] Artists 'age' their own work: James McNeill Whistler printed his lithographs on stained and foxed old paper.[92]

Fortunes are made in reproduction furniture by fabricating ancient wormholes and scratches, in clothing by feigning the scuff and fading of old jeans. Cohasset Colonials sells staining kits for 'that "200-year-old"' furniture look; 'wine dust' makes new bottles look (if not taste) old.[93] An artful use of old tiles and vegetation gave Port Grimaud, François Spoerry's 1960s 'Venetian' Riviera village, an immemorial air similar to Blunden Shadbolt's 1930s neo-Tudor structures that seemed to have been settling into the ground for centuries.[94] Modern neo-Georgian, mock-Tudor, demi-Gothic and all-purpose Edwardian houses are instantly aged; 'antique-effect garden fencing and quick-growing ... Virginia creeper ... accelerating the ravages of time'. 'Tumbling' and 'distressing' akin to stonewashed jeans technology simulates the colour, texture, and broken surfaces of old bricks. Mildewed, pock-marked, and soot-stained bricks are also available.[95] Dickens

---

[86] Cornelius Holtorf, 'On pastness: a reconsideration of materiality in archaeological object authenticity', *Anthropological Quarterly* 86 (2013): 427–44 at 438.

[87] John M. McKenna, 'Original historical manuscripts and the undergraduate', *AHA Newsletter*, 16:3 (1978): 6–7.

[88] Ascanio Condivi, *The Life of Michel-Angelo*, 2nd edn (1553; Penn State, 1999), 19.

[89] Giovanni Baglione, *Vite de' pittori* (1642), 157–8, trans. in Arnau, *Three Thousand Years of Deception*, 43.

[90] William Sanderson, *Graphice, or, The Use of Pen and Pensill* (London, 1658), 17; Adolf Rieth, *Archaeological Fakes* (London: Barrie & Jenkins, 1970), 24–5; Paul Craddock, *Scientific Investigation of Copies, Fakes and Forgeries* (Butterworth-Heinemann, 2009), 180.

[91] Arnau, *Three Thousand Years of Deception*, 101–2, 255–8; Craddock, *Scientific Investigation*, 307–11.

[92] Thea Burns, 'Preserving master drawings', *Paper Conservator* 25 (2001): 107–23 at 116.

[93] David Lee Murphy's 1995 'Dust on the bottle' country-music song lauded wine – and love – that gets sweeter with time. See Craddock, *Scientific Investigation*, on furniture, 37–9; on paint, ch. 12.

[94] François Spoerry, *L'Architecture douce de Port-Grimaud à Port-Liberté* (Paris: Laffont, 1991); Donald Campbell, 'Blunden Shadbolt', *Thirties Society Journal*, no. 3 (1982): 17–24.

[95] Stephen Brown, *Marketing: The Retro Revolution* (Sage, 2001), 187–9.

World, a Victorian London theme park in Chatham, Kent, uses soot, gas lamps, pick-pockets, and smells of offal and rotting cabbage to make 'new things look old, clean things look filthy ... solid things look rotten' far more realistically than actual Victorian-era brick back in London itself.[96]

Those gulled into mistaking decay for antiquity are much mocked. Hogarth's *Time Smoking a Picture* (1762) lampooned naive devotees of the antique (Fig. 24).[97] Mark Twain's 'Capitoline Venus' is a mediocre modern sculpture that accrues renown by being mutilated, buried, and dug up as an antiquity.[98] In Stephen Leacock's satire, a new clock artfully broken is 'hardly to be distinguished from a genuine *fractura*' found in clocks actually flung from Italian windows in the thirteenth century. But some old things 'rust and rot in a way you simply cannot imitate'; Leacock's collectors wax ecstatic over a ninth-century drinking horn 'all coated inside with the most beautiful green slime, absolutely impossible to reproduce'.[99]

Aesthetics aside, decay yields invaluable knowledge about past manufacture, function, and use. A ceramics curator welcomes old abrasion and 'eloquent scratches'.[100] Some patinas protect against further decay. 'Nothing contributes so much to the conservation of brass or copper coins', wrote an early authority, 'as that fine rust, appearing like varnish, which their lying in a particular soil occasions'.[101] The grime on Michelangelo's *David* actually protects 'an inferior piece of marble ... from more rapid decay'.[102] Conservation increasingly trumps aesthetics: corrosion crusts on glass, once removed to reveal the colourful iridescence of pitted translucent surfaces, are now retained to inhibit deterioration. A stable patina of blueing steel and anodizing aluminium checks erosion; burial in loam or dry earth lends tin-rich bronzes a protective coating. Metal corrosion can help preserve adjacent organic artefacts of wood, leather, and wool.[103]

Even destructive decay may be prized for the information it yields, the beauty it confers, and the ideas it suggests. Ageing adds 'something authentic or compelling about the passage of history' in works of art. Colour changes make Eva Hesse's embrittled resinous latex and fibreglass sculptures appealing.[104] Conservators today more readily

[96] Sam Anderson, 'Dickensian ghosts, past and present', *IHT*, 11 Feb. 2012: 23.

[97] Peter Wagner, 'Representation of time in Hogarth's paintings and engravings', in Frédéric Ogée et al., eds., *Hogarth* (Manchester, 2001), 102–24 at 109–12.

[98] Mark Twain, 'The legend of the Capitoline Venus', in *Sketches New and Old* (Hartford, CT, 1875), 285–92. Twain's story was inspired by the Cardiff Giant hoax (Chapter 12).

[99] Stephen Leacock, 'Old junk and new money' (1928), in *The Bodley Head Leacock* (London, 1957), 272–6.

[100] Amerimni Galanos and Yanna Doganis, 'Remnants of the epidermis on the Parthenon', *Studies in Conservation* 48 (2003): 3–16; Janet Chernela, 'In praise of the scratch: the importance of aboriginal abrasion on museum ceramic ware', *Curator* 12 (1969): 174–9.

[101] John Pinkerton, *An Essay on Metals* (London, 1808), 1: 202.

[102] Sven Ouzman, 'The beauty of letting go: fragmentary museums and archaeologies of archive', in Elizabeth Edwards et al., eds., *Sensible Objects* (Berg, 2006), 269–90 at 279.

[103] Sandra Smith, 'Opacity contrariwise: the restoration of deteriorated surfaces on vessel glass', in Oddy and Carroll, eds., *Reversibility*, 135–40; Elizabeth Pye, *Caring for the Past* (London: James & James, 2001), 91, 123, 137; David A. Scott, *Copper and Bronze in Art* (Getty, 2002).

[104] Jim Coddington, in 'Time and change', *Conservation Perspectives* (Getty Conservation Institute) 17:3 (Fall 2002): 11–17 at 14–15; 'Bronze', in *Grove Encyclopedia of Materials and Techniques in Art*, ed. Gerald W. R. Ward (Oxford, 2008), 64–72.

Figure 24 Age improves art: William Hogarth, *Time Smoking a Picture*, 1762

accept changes over the whole 'subsequent history' of works of art, embracing 'aging, deterioration, accident, repair, ... adaptation, reinterpretation'.[105]

The beauty of patina

A patina that confirms or protects antiquity is apt to be found attractive. Artists whose work gained esteem as it aged believed that time improved their pigments. Painters welcomed patina's harmonizing effect, sculptors encrustations on their bronzes, architects the mellowness of weathered stone. 'One of the greatest charms of old furniture is the change in colour and surface condition' wrought by 'hundreds of years' exposure to light and heat, dust and dirt, smoke from wood and coal fires, the application of beeswax and turpentine and the abrasion of countless polishing cloths'.[106]

Aesthetic patina is first recorded from ancient China. Ninth-century collectors delighted in the colours lent Shang and Chou bronze urns by centuries of burial, immersion, or simply being handed down. Once unearthed and cleaned, several years' smoothing and massaging perfected the desired brownish yellow or lustrous 'tea-dust' green. Artificial patinating was also practised, but Sung connoisseurs held that only great

[105] John Walsh, 'Comment', 29, and David Bomford, 'The conservator as narrator', 1–12 at 8, 12, in Leonard, ed., *Personal Viewpoints.*

[106] Phoebe Dent Weil, 'A review of the history and practice of patination', in Price et al., *Historical and Philosophical Issues*, 384–413 at 404–6; C. K. Binns, 'The importance of patina on old English furniture', *Antiques Collector* 42 (1971): 58–64 at 59.

age properly ripened bronzes. A twelfth-century text combines warnings against forgery with recipes for antiquing patina on bronzes. The continuing allure of the look of age employs an estimated 250,000 Chinese today in replicating the brush-strokes of revered masters, spinning clay into ancient forms, copying outlines of ancient patterns into pottery, and doctoring old sales catalogues to invent provenances.[107]

The lustre of antiquity in China and Japan comes from the oils that permeate a much-handled object. 'We do love things that bear the marks of grime, soot, and weather, and we love the colors and the sheen that call to mind the past that made them', a Japanese writer elucidated his countrymen's fondness for flaws and discolorations following the slow and graceful ageing of stone and wood.[108] Japanese fondness for the shabby rusted kettle, the cracked tea bowl, attributes a magical quality to long use and considers perishability integral to beauty. Western masterpieces designed to be indestructible seem aloof and stifling. 'The Sistine Chapel is magnificent, but it asks our admiration rather than our participation'; the irregular stones of the Zen Buddhist Ryōanji garden involve the spectator in its ongoing creation.[109]

In the West, by contrast, decay and other marks of age long remained generally repugnant. Nature had first to be subdued before its corrosive effects could be admired. The rise of picturesque taste, exemplified in depictions of ruins, heralded a revolutionary change that lent lustre to agedness. The stark, unsentimental realism of sixteenth-century pictorial decay (Hieronymus Cock, Hendrik van Cleve, Maerten van Heemskerck) gave way in the seventeenth to ruins as harmonious backdrops, in Poussin and Claude's Arcadian scenes; and in the eighteenth to crumbling structures half-reverting to nature. In Piranesi and Panini's mouldering landscapes, lilliputian figures meander among classical ruins decomposed by soggy mists, porous stone, and rampant underbrush (Fig. 25).[110] Lovers of the picturesque doted on literary locales such as John Dyer's *Grongar Hill* in Wales, where amid 'huge heaps of hoary mouldered walls ... the pois'nous adder breeds / Concealed in ruins, moss and weeds', and David Mallet's

> ... Place of Tombs
> Waste, desolate, where *Ruin* dreary dwells,
> Brooding o'er sightless Sculls and crumbling Bones
> ... the Column grey with Moss, the falling Bust
> The Time-shook Arch, the monumental Stone,
> Impair'd, effac'd, and hastening into Dust.[111]

---

[107] Ts'ao Chao, *Chinese Connoisseurship* (1388; Faber & Faber, 1971), 9; Brian Cockrell, 'Colourful corrosion: black bronze and its enigmatic patina', *Papers from the Institute of Archaeology* [UCL] 19 (2009): 85–90; Craig Clunas, 'Connoisseurs and aficionados: the real and the fake in Ming China', in Mark Jones, ed., *Why Fakes Matter* (British Museum Press, 1992), 151–6 at 152–3; David Barboza and Amanda Cook, 'Art and fraud in China', *NYT*, 28 Oct. 2013: 4.

[108] Junichiro Tanizaki, *In Praise of Shadows* (1933–4; Vintage, 2001), 18–20.

[109] Donald Keene, 'Japanese aesthetics' (1969), in *The Pleasures of Japanese Literature* (Columbia, 1988), 1–22 at 13, 19–20. See Alain de Botton, *The Architecture of Happiness* (Penguin, 2007), 235.

[110] Robert Rosenblum, *Transformations in Late Eighteenth Century Art* (Princeton, 1967), 113–15.

[111] John Dyer, *Grongar Hill*, ll. 80–3 (1761; Johns Hopkins, 1941), 90–1; David Mallet, *The Excursion* (London, 1728), 23. See James Stevens Curl, *The Victorian Celebration of Death* (Stroud: Sutton, 2000), 2–3.

At first only these depictions pleased, not the actual ruins. The sixteenth-century architect Sebastiano Serlio, who incorporated broken ruins into new buildings, was a rare picturesque precursor. Another praised Rome's decaying aqueducts as marvels of engineering full of romantic charm.[112] But unlike Piranesi's haunting engravings, actual Roman antiquities paled in interest for such archetypal observers as Goethe and John Flaxman. The desolate solitude of the Campagna horrified Charles Dickens; 'the resting-places of their Dead, have fallen like their Dead; and the broken hour-glass of Time is but a heap of idle dust!' Accounts and portrayals of ruins have pleased more than ruins themselves.[113]

Yet pictorial criteria that made ruins pleasingly ruinous more and more impinged on actual scenes, above all in the growing fashion for 'Sublime' mountains and 'Picturesque' landscape gardens. The cleric Thomas Burnet was an unconscious forerunner of Romantic taste for sublime wilderness. 'Theologically Burnet condemned mountains; actually he was obsessed by them.' Even while condemning 'the uncouth holes and hollows of a broken world', Burnet praised them for inspiring veneration, finding 'something august and stately' in mountains 'that inspires the mind with great thoughts and passions . . . and cast[s] it into a pleasing kind of stupor and admiration'.[114]

Time and weather made old trees and buildings picturesquely rough; moss, lichen, and other encrustations added tonal richness. Dead branches mingled with decaying Gothic turrets and pinnacles. Advanced decay beautified the long-abandoned cottage, whose 'weather-beaten thatch, bunchy and varied with moss – the mutilated chimney top – the fissures and crevices of the inclining wall – the roof of various angles and inclinations . . . and the unrepaired accidents of wind and rain' allured the eye.[115]

William Gilpin, the picturesque's chief exponent, rejoiced that at Tintern Abbey 'time has worn off all traces of the chissel . . . blunted the sharp edges of rule and compass, and broken the regularity' – though 'a mallet judiciously used . . . might be of service in fracturing' the too-regular remaining gable ends.[116] Gilpin's suggestion is ridiculed in Jane Austen's jest that Henry VIII had abolished the monasteries and left them to 'the ruinous depredations of Time' mainly to improve the English landscape. (She was unaware that Gilpin had praised Cromwell for having 'laid his iron hand' upon Raglan Castle and 'shattered it into ruin'.)[117] Piranesian taste for Roman ruins was reified in Rome by turning monks' cells into imaginary ruins, thus gaining the beauty of disorder without the inconvenience of actual decay. Apparent ancient instability – open roof,

---

[112] Sebastiano Serlio, *Tutte l'opere d'architettura et prospetiva* (1545), in *Sebastiano Serlio on Architecture*, (Yale, 1996–2001), vol. 1; Charles de Brosses, *L'Italie il y a cent ans* (Paris, 1836).

[113] Hugh Honour, *Neo-Classicism* (Penguin, 1968), 53; Charles Dickens, *Pictures from Italy* (London, 1846), 214; Robert Ginsberg, *The Aesthetics of Ruins* (Rodopi, 2004), xvii–xviii, 347–8.

[114] Marjorie Hope Nicolson, *Mountain Gloom and Mountain Glory* (Cornell, 1959), 213–15; Thomas Burnet, *The Sacred Theory of the Earth* (1684–90; Southern Illinois, 1965), 1: 6, 109–10, 115.

[115] John Thomas Smith, *Remarks on Rural Scenery . . . Relative to the Pictoresque* (London, 1797), 9. See Uvedale Price, *On the Picturesque, &c.* (1810), in *Essays on the Picturesque*, 1: 51–6; Price, *Dialogue*, 3: 200–3.

[116] William Gilpin, *Observations on the River Wye . . .* , 3rd edn (London, 1792), 47–8.

[117] Jane Austen, 'The history of England' (1791), in *Love and Freindship and Other Early Works & Lady Susan* (Penn State, 2007). 60–9 at 64; Gilpin, *Observations on the River Wye*, 89.

Figure 25 The grandeur of ruins: Giovanni Paolo Panini, *Capriccio with Belisarius*, 1730-5

Figure 26 The grandeur of ruins: John Constable, *Stonehenge*, 1835

Figure 27 Henry Fuseli, *The Artist Moved by the Grandeur of Ancient Ruins*, 1778-9

mouldering stone dense with moss and fern, walls patched with rags, windows pierced – masked dependable solidity in Charles-Louis Clérisseau's 1766 ruin-room at St Trinità dei Monti, Rome.[118]

But nature, not man, was the prime architect of pleasing decay. Rotten trees were 'capital sources of picturesque beauty'; hollow trunks made invaluable foregrounds, withered tops lent scenic diversity, and when 'ideas of wildness and desolation are required', what could beat 'the blasted oak, ragged, scathed, and leafless?' Ivy, mosses, lichens, maiden-hair, penny-leaf were 'ornaments of time that gave those full-blown tints, which add the richest finishing to a ruin'. These effects made Fountains Abbey,

---

[118] Harbison, *The Built, the Unbuilt and the Unbuildable*, 99–100; Sophie Thomas, *Romanticism and Visuality: Fragments, History, Spectacle* (Routledge, 2008), 44–5; John A. Pinto, *Speaking Ruins: Piranesi, Architects and Antiquity in Eighteenth-Century Rome* (Michigan, 2012).

'rooted for ages in the soil', to Gilpin a sacred place. 'The more broken, weather-stained, and decayed the stone and brickwork, the more the plants and creepers seem to have fastened and rooted in between their joints, the more picturesque' Price found Roman villas.[119] 'The rents, or fractures, or stains, or vegetation', agreed Ruskin a half century later, 'assimilate the architecture with the work of Nature', engendering 'universally beloved' forms and colours.[120]

To be sure, men furthered nature's efforts: Rousseau's coffin in Ermenonville, inspired by Hubert Robert and Piranesi's paintings of Nero's tomb, recreated 'in real leaf and stone ... the works of man slowly being absorbed by the organic forces of nature'.[121] But humans could not match nature's craft. No one could 'put stones together with that air of wild and magnificent disorder which they ... acquire by falling of their own accord', wrote William Cowper apropos ruins built by Henry Fox, Lord Holland, on the Isle of Thanet.[122] Lack of contrivance was essential both to the look and the very concept of ruins, Gilpin explained:

To give the stone its mouldering appearance – to make the widening chink run naturally through all the joints – to mutilate the ornaments – to peel the facing from the internal structure ... and to scatter heaps of ruin around with negligence and ease ... you must put your ruin at last into the hands of nature to adorn, and perfect it ... It is time alone, which meliorates the ruin; which gives it perfect beauty; and brings it ... to a state of nature.[123]

Nor could any artist adequately depict decay. George Crabbe's hapless painter of a ruined tower fails to match the effect of time:

> ... see how Nature's Work is done,
> How slowly true she lays her colours on; ...
> till in unnotic'd Years
> The stony Tower as gray with age appears;
> And wouldst thou, Artist! with thy Tints and Brush,
> Form Shades like these? Pretender, where thy Blush?
> In three short Hours shall thy presuming Hand
> Th' effect of three slow centuries command?[124]

As Anthony Trollope observed, 'no colourist that ever yet worked from a palette had ... come up to this rich colouring of years crowding themselves on years'. On Ullathorne's medieval walls ivy and creepers produced 'that delicious tawny hue which no stone can

---

[119] William Gilpin, *Remarks on Forest Scenery and Other Woodland Views* ... (London, 1794), 1: 8–14; Gilpin, *Observations on the River Wye*, 48; William Gilpin, *Observations, relative chiefly to Picturesque Beauty, on the Mountains, and Lakes of Cumberland, and Westmoreland* (London, 1796), 1: 188; Uvedale Price, *An Essay on Artificial Water* (1794), in *Essays on the Picturesque*, 2: 1–167 at 114.

[120] John Ruskin, *The Seven Lamps of Architecture* (1849; New York: Noonday, 1961), 160.

[121] James Stevens Curl, 'A short history of the cemetery movement in Europe', in Sandra Berresford, ed., *Italian Memorial Sculpture* (London: Frances Lincoln, 2004), 1–21 at 17–18; Blanche M. G. Linden, *Silent City on a Hill: Picturesque Landscapes of Memory* (1989; rev. edn Massachusetts, 2007), 56–9.

[122] To William Unwin, July 1779, in *The Correspondence of William Cowper* (London, 1904), 1: 155.

[123] Gilpin, *Observations ... Cumberland, and Westmoreland*, 1: 67–8.

[124] George Crabbe, *The Borough*, Letter 2 (1810; London, 1916), 16–17.

give, unless it has on it the vegetable richness of centuries'.[125] Of Florence's impending restoration, Bernard Berenson realized that 'for some years ... it will look a bit raw and the curves a trifle too geometrical. But so has every structure looked until time has caressed and licked away its asperities and relaxed the rigidity of its outlines'[126] The Paris ruins left by the 1871 Communards, notably of the Palais d'Orsay (1810), were at once admired as unconscious art; further eroded by wind and weather in the 1880s, their conversion from 'hideous barracks' to Piranesian etching delighted the reactionary Joris-Karl Huysmans, who proposed further embellishing Paris by burning down the Madeleine, the Opéra, and the Odéon, for the nineteenth-century architecture, 'so pitiful when it is raw, becomes imposing, almost splendid, when it is baked'.[127]

Such effusions conflate aged virtue with nature's temporal attritions. 'So gnawed by time', wrote Hawthorne, enraptured by Oxford's colleges, 'so crumbly, so blackened ... greatly enriching the Grecian columns, which look so cold when the outlines are hard and distinct'.[128] Nature paints better than man because infinitely older, gradual, gentle, and uncontrived. That two millennia had softened the *Venus de Milo* vastly enhanced its charm for Walter Pater.[129] But human interference dispelled ruins' hypnotic spell; 'if the archaeologists had arrived before Shelley' at the third-century Roman Baths of Caracalla, 'there would be no *Prometheus Unbound*', with its 'melancholy ruins ... huddled in gray annihilation'.[130]

Human erosive effects were laudable only in emulating nature. The more remote their vintage, the less they felt contrived. 'There is nothing marvellous in a temple' whose erection we ourselves have witnessed, wrote Chateaubriand. 'A monument is not venerable, unless a long history of the past ... be inscribed beneath its vaulted canopy, blackened with age.' Only the immemorially ancient became truly grand. Much as St Irenaeus posited the need for a venerable Christ, Chateaubriand argued that had God not created the world 'at the same time both young and old', the grandeur of age would have been missing from nature; 'every scene would have lost its wonders. Without this original antiquity. there would have been neither beauty nor magnificence in the work of the Almighty'.[131]

Patina's most celebrated – and most controversial – effects bear on paintings. That ageing beautifies, with time perfecting colours, early-modern connoisseurs commonly agreed. John Dryden lauded patina's ameliorative magic in portraiture:

> For Time shall with his ready Pencil stand;
> Retouch your Figures, with his ripening hand

[125] Anthony Trollope, *Barchester Towers* (1857; Oxford, 1925), 203. 'Ullathorne' reflected sixteenth-century Montacute House, Somerset.
[126] Bernard Berenson, 'On the reconstruction of Florence', in *Essays in Appreciation* (Chapman & Hall, 1958), 1–9 at 7–8.
[127] Louis Réau, *Histoire du Vandalisme* (1959; rev. edn Paris: Laffont, 1994), 802–3; J.-K. Huysmans (1886), quoted in Dario Gamboni, *The Destruction of Art* (Reaktion, 1997), 256.
[128] Nathaniel Hawthorne, *The English Notebooks* (New York: [P]MLA, 1941), 5 Sept. 1856, 412.
[129] Walter Pater, 'Luca della Robbia' (1872), in *The Renaissance: Studies in Art and Poetry*, 4th edn (Macmillan, 1917), 65–73 at 68.
[130] Woodward, *In Ruin*; Percy Bysshe Shelley, *Prometheus Unbound* (London, 1820), 4.4, ll. 288, 301.
[131] François-René de Chateaubriand, *The Genius of Christianity* (1802; 9th edn 1871), 385, 136–67.

> Mellow your Colours, and imbrown the Teint;
> Add every Grace, which Time alone can grant:
> To future Ages, shall your Fame convey;
> And give more Beauties, than he takes away.[132]

Painters assured clients that a few decades would soften what at first seemed glaring. As with new-killed meat and fruit just gathered, time sweetened pigments at first too sharp and strong, bestowing 'harmony upon the colours of a picture'.[133] Joseph Addison depicted Time as an ancient craftsman who 'wore off insensibly every little disagreeable Gloss', adding 'Mellowness that ... made every Picture appear more perfect than when it came fresh from the Master's Pencil'.[134] As age was generally thought to improve oil paintings, artists simulated time-darkened tones and other marks of age with amber varnish and other *sfumato* techniques.[135]

Patina in art became de rigueur in Victorian England. Sir George Beaumont, the National Gallery's founder and major patron, adored the subdued tints of heavily varnished old pictures. In reality, the 'subtle tonal unity' of Beaumont's Old Master paintings owed more to London fog, but admiration of the 'golden glow' of age led restorers to pile varnish everywhere.[136]

Much as fig leaves made classical nudes respectable, time tamed gaudy Mediterranean scenes. 'Several coats of dirt and dulled varnish made brightly coloured paintings, especially of the Italian and Spanish schools, seem more English, less foreign, less Catholic', a museologist observed. Victorians 'felt uneasy when the original picture was revealed, almost as if it had had its clothes taken off'.[137] Obscuring detail, patina helped viewers find in old paintings anything they sought. 'The romantic amateur loves the rust and haze of the varnish, [as] a veil behind which he can see whatever he desires'.[138]

The veil fell from favour a century later, restorers removing varnish and overpaint along with dirt. Decrying 'old master' patina, they aimed to return paintings to original freshness. Connoisseurs lamented the loss. Conflicts over patina fuelled the 1950s National Gallery cleaning controversy. The bright colours and flat tones of newly restored pictures shocked viewers used to dark old varnish.[139] Art historians termed varnish

---

[132] John Dryden, 'To Sir George Kneller' (1694), ll. 176–81, in *Works*, 4: 461–6 at 466.

[133] William Wotton, *Reflections upon Ancient and Modern Learning* (London, 1694), 76; Algarotti, *Essay on Painting*, 56–7.

[134] Joseph Addison, 'Dream of a picture gallery', *Spectator*, no. 83, 5 June 1711.

[135] E. H Gombrich, 'Blurred images and the unvarnished truth', *British Journal of Aesthetics* 2:2 (1962): 170–9; Mark Leonard et al., '"Amber varnish" and Orazio Gentileschi's "Lot and his Daughters"', *Burlington Magazine* 143 (2001): 4–10; Alessandra Melluco Vaccaro, 'The idea of patina', in Price et al., eds., *Historical and Philosophical Issues*, 366–71.

[136] Hussey, *Picturesque*, 262–3; Helmut Ruhemann, *The Cleaning of Paintings* (Faber & Faber, 1968), 228–9; Norman Brommelle, 'Material for a history of conservation: the 1850 and 1853 reports on the National Gallery', *Studies in Conservation* 2 (1956): 176–87.

[137] Kenneth Hudson, *A Social History of Museums: What the Visitors Thought* (Macmillan, 1975), 82.

[138] Simon Horsin-Déon, *De la conservation et de la restauration des tableaux* (1851), quoted in Ruhemann, *Cleaning of Paintings*, 85.

[139] Cesare Brandi, 'The cleaning of pictures, in relation to patina, varnish and glazes', *Burlington Magazine* 91 (1949): 183–8.

Figure 28 Pleasing decay: nature's work. Lichen at Montacute, Somerset

Figure 29 Pleasing decay: man's work. William Chambers, ruined arch, Kew Gardens, 1759-60

crucial to rectify time-altered pigments – Vermeer's green eclipsed, Poussin and Claude's blue aggressively glaring. A 'light patina masks the harshness of colour discords and restores the balance', argued René Huyghe, thereby 'covering up the injuries' of time. Over-cleaning wrecked that harmony.[140]

Radical restorers contended that the 'true' look of age was a painting's original fresh brilliance. But art historians held 'fresh brilliance' a modern not an ancient aim. 'The "restored" cathedrals of England, France, and Germany are sufficient reminders of what can happen when renowned experts claim to know the intentions of bygone ages', warned Ernst Gombrich. The restorer was bound to be 'influenced by his scale of values, his unconscious bias, and his conscious convictions'.[141] These now favoured bright colours and strong contrasts. The restorer boasted of 'clean[ing] a Rembrandt so successfully that its colours remind one now of Monet'. Aiming at 'the firm tones to which the modern eye is accustomed', in Huyghe's words, radical restoration contrived 'an altogether artificial youth'. Rejuvenated Old Masters were as discordant as old buildings restored to look new.[142]

Varieties and implications of aesthetic decay

Reactions to wear and tear vary with artefacts' ingredients and intended use. Decay blemishes most things made for utility, but enhances some made for ornament. We expect functional things to lose attraction as they age; we hope that works of art will remain fresh or accrue new charm. But distinctions between art and use founder in practice. Buildings are more generally improved by time's patina than paintings, even though buildings are 'useful' and paintings are not. Long exposure and use endear homely relics: dog-eared books, frayed curtains, pitted and stained spades bespeak intimacy with past labours. Yet when once-useful objects become functionally obsolete collectables, their marks of decay no longer signal loss of worth but lend allure.

Some substances age worse than others. Ruskin rejected iron in architecture 'as no builder has true command over … its modes of decay'.[143] Concrete gets uglier every passing year, greasy if smooth, squalid if rough; glass-fibre decays unhappily, as with the

[140] René Huyghe, 'The Louvre Museum and the problem of cleaning old pictures', *Museum International* 3 (1950): 191–206 at 191. See Otto Kurz, 'Time the painter' (1963), in *Selected Studies* (London: Pindar Press, 1982), 2: 169–75; Joyce Hill Stoner, 'Hell vs. Ruhemann, controversies about the cleaning of paintings', in Andrew Oddy and Sandra Smith, eds., *Past Practice – Future Prospects* (British Museum Occasional Paper 145, 2001), 109–14; Jo Hedley, 'Vigée Le Brun's newly conserved portrait of Mme Perregaux in the Wallace Collection', *Burlington Magazine* 146 (2004): 224–33.

[141] Ernst Gombrich, 'Dark varnishes', and 'Controversial methods and methods of controversy', *Burlington Magazine* 104 (1962): 51–5 at 55, and 105 (1963): 90–3 at 93. Gombrich continued to rail against over-cleaning and varnish removal ('Foreword', in Sarah Walden, *The Ravished Image* (1985; 2nd edn London: Gibson Square, 2004), 7; Dalya Alberghe, 'Gallery's zealous cleaning attacked from the grave', *Times*, 29 Oct. 2004).

[142] Otto Kurz, 'Varnishes, tinted varnishes, and patina' (1962), in *Selected Studies*, 2:159–62; Richard Boston, 'The lady varnishes', *Guardian*, 25 Sept. 1984: 11; Huyghe, 'Louvre Museum', 198; Charles Hope, 'The National Gallery cleaning controversy', *ArtWatch UK Journal* 28 (2012): 4–15 at 8, citing Cesare Brandi.

[143] Ruskin, *Seven Lamps of Architecture*, 42n16.

Brighton Pavilion's minaret replacements. The lustre of 'noble' patina beautifies oxidized copper and bronze, but most other metal corrosion elicits revulsion.[144] Albert Speer renounced steel along with concrete for lacking ruin value; it was 'inconceivable that a hunk of rusting metal could one day inspire heroic thoughts like the monuments of the past Hitler so admired'.[145] The philosopher Ernst Bloch loathed machine-age gadgets that 'cannot grow old, but only rot'. Discarded before they could gain a patina or merge into nature, American buildings often became unsightly ruins.[146] The architect Robert Smithson called abandoned highway construction in New Jersey 'ruins in reverse' – they 'don't fall into ruin after they are built but rather rise into ruin before they are built'.[147]

Old iron, however, can beautify. Except in buildings, rust for Ruskin gave iron the breath of life. Oxidized, iron 'falls into fruitful and beneficent dust ... It stains the great earth ... far and wide – it is the colouring substance appointed to colour the globe for the sight, as well as to subdue it to the service of man.'[148] Ruskinian rust was reified in Cor-Ten steel at Eero Saarinen's 1963 John Deere factory in Moline, Illinois. Once past salt contamination and run-off staining, Cor-Ten weathered into 'an attractive natural colour particularly pleasing in rural surroundings', said promoters. 'After one cleared one's mind of the nasty word *rust* ... it was a beautiful material such as only nature can produce.'[149] As with ruins, 'nature' endorsed ageing. Cor-Ten gained cachet in outdoor sculpture – Picasso's 1967 cubist statue in Chicago, Richard Serra's 1987 *Fulcrum* in London, a 2007 Serra retrospective at New York's Museum of Modern Art. Latterly, however, corrosion problems dim Cor-Ten's appeal in building facades.[150]

Stone remains the prime medium for time's patina. Seeing 'actual beauty' in its traces, Ruskin held that ageing always ennobled ornamental stonework:

The effect of time is such, that if the design be poor, it will enrich it; if overcharged, simplify it; if harsh and violent, soften it; if smooth and obscure, exhibit it; whatever faults it may have are rapidly disguised, whatever virtue it has still shines and steals out in the mellow light.

---

[144] B. Floyd Brown et al., eds., *Corrosion and Metal Artifacts* (1977; Nabu Press, 2012); Richard Hughes and Michael Rowe, *The Colouring, Bronzing and Patination of Metals* (New York: Watson-Guptill, 1991); Rutherford J. Gettens, 'Patina: noble and vile', in Suzannah Doeringer et al., eds., *Art and Technology: A Symposium on Classical Bronzes* (MIT Press, 1970), 57–72; Régis Bertholon, 'To get rid of the crust or not', in Oddy and Smith, eds., *Past Practice*, 5–11.

[145] Brian Dillon, 'Fragments from a history of ruin', *Cabinet Magazine*, issue 20: Ruins (Winter 2005/6).

[146] Quoted in Nick Yablon, *Untimely Ruins* (Chicago, 2010), 8.

[147] Robert Smithson, 'Tour of the monuments of Passaic, New Jersey' (1967), in *CW* (California, 1996), 68–74 at 72.

[148] John Ruskin, 'The work of iron, in nature, art, and policy' (1858), in *CW*, 16: 375–411 at 377–8. To natural (as opposed to the dirt, discomfort, and diseases of industrial) dust 'we owe much of the beauty, and perhaps even the very habitability, of the earth' (Alfred Russel Wallace, 'The importance of dust', in *The Wonderful Century* (New York, 1898), 69–85 at 80).

[149] British Steel Corporation, *Cor-Ten Steel* (1973), 4; John Dinkeloo, 'Steel will weather naturally' (1962), quoted in Alan Denney and Turloch O'Brien, 'An introduction to weathering steels', *Architects' Journal* 156 (1972): 959–79 at 966. See Reinhold Martin, 'What is a material?', in Eeva-Liisa Pelkonen and Donald Albrecht, eds., *Eero Saarinen* (Yale, 2006), 69–82 at 72–3.

[150] Michael Kimmelman, 'Man of steel', *NYT*, 1 June 2007, B21, 24; Kynaston McShine et al., *Richard Serra Sculpture* (New York: Museum of Modern Art, 2007); Linda Sandino, 'Here today, gone tomorrow: transient materiality', *Journal of Design History* 17 (2004): 283–94.

Figure 30 Fragments: the Elgin Marbles. Dione and Aphrodite (?), east pediment

Figure 31 Fragments: paintings and ruins

Every fine building was 'improved up to a certain period by all its signs of age, [no] building so ugly but that it may be made ... agreeable' by marks of antiquity. 'Few could have failed to admire the mouldering and peeled surface of the oolite limestone' of Queen's College, Oxford, wrote Ruskin, before it was hideously refaced.[151] William Morris's dictum that 'the natural weathering of the surface of a building is beautiful, and its loss disastrous' became a late Victorian maxim. Oxford's lichened colleges 'had done nothing but wait, and had become poetical', judged Thomas Hardy. 'How easy to the smallest building; how impossible to most men.'[152]

Stone corrosion is not always seemly. Structures that weather well in unpolluted or arid locales turn odious in sulphur-laden or humid air. Painted or plastered walls exposed to the elements look dilapidated and forlorn. Unsheltered stucco and frescoes are rapidly effaced. Were it left to 'the romantic visitor, who would prefer a discoloured wall overgrown with weeds to a painted wall protected by a roof', the art of ancient Pompeii would soon vanish, warned archaeologists – as much of it has anyway.[153]

How much decay enhances or detracts varies with the medium. Patina is bound to alter a painting's essential elements, admitted a leading restorer, but 'patina on a sculpture or a building adds something to them without substantially interfering with the main thing, their form'.[154] Objectivist paintings and drawings depict three-dimensional scenes on a flat surface; to keep them legible, injury and decay that interrupt the composition must be concealed or minimized. But sculpture, pottery, silver, ivory, buildings, gardens do not represent objects, they *are* objects; the observer's imagination corrects defects of erosion or accident. We admire a sculpted headless figure (Fig. 30) but view askance a decapitated painting (Fig. 31).

Decay's keenest devotees accept that beyond a point it no longer beautifies. Views differ about when that point is reached. British colleagues chided me for junking a frayed briefcase I found unsightly as well as unserviceable; they felt my new one more tolerable when I replaced its broken handle with an old rope. But even Ruskin allowed that after a 'certain period' decay negated the charm of weathering facades.[155]

Ruined ruins underscore the point. A structure may be more beautiful as a ruin than in its prime, but ruination in its later stages loses evocative power. At its best it seems just on the verge of dissolution. 'A building which has simply had its roof burnt and windows broken is usually perfectly uninteresting as a ruin; it demands to be reroofed', concluded

[151] Ruskin, *Seven Lamps of Architecture*, 178, 183; Ruskin, *Modern Painters*, pt .2, sect. 1, ch. 7, para. 26, 1: 104. See W. J. Arkell, *Oxford Stone* (Faber & Faber, 1947), 152, 168; H. A. Viles, '"Unswept stone, besmeer'd by sluttish time": air pollution and building stone decay in Oxford', *Environment and History* 2 (1996): 359–72; Christopher Andrew, 'Perception and aesthetics of weathered stone façades', in Richard Prikryl and Heather Viles, eds., *Understanding and Managing Stone Decay* (Prague: Karolinum, 2002), 331–9.

[152] William Morris, 'The beauty of life' (1880), in *CW*, 22: 51–80 at 69; Thomas Hardy, *Jude the Obscure* (1895; Oxford, 1998), 85.

[153] Amadeo Maiuri, 'Recent excavations at Pompeii', *Museum International* 3 (1950): 102–4. See Mary Beard, *Fires of Vesuvius: Pompeii Lost and Found* (Harvard, 2008); British School at Rome, 'Pompeii project' and 'Herculaneum conservation' (Rome: ICCROM, 2008/9).

[154] Ruhemann, *Cleaning of Paintings*, 218.

[155] Ruskin, *Modern Painters*, pt. 2, sect. 1, ch. 7, para. 26: 1: 105.

John Summerson. 'A building which has become a chaotic and meaningless heap of masonry is likewise valueless; it demands to be removed.' Walking under an arch is more enjoyable than walking over a pile of rubble.[156]

The decayed windows, broken banisters, crumbling kitchen, and faded wallpaper of Palladian Newhailes, acquired in 1997 by the National Trust of Scotland, lend it 'all-pervasive mellowness'; the weathered oak rail on the staircase 'has the extreme old age and weathered ancientness of a Japanese netsuke'. But restoration minimalism can go too far. Cracked window panes make Newhailes look 'disjointed', grey and black splotches on the exterior limewash leave a piebald effect, and steps to the front door, 'frozen at the moment of most extreme neglect with carefully preserved blistered black paint and naked rust', simply repel. 'Beauty and magic are not well served by preserving it at the bottom of the cycle of decay'.[157] Nor are they enhanced by prolonged neglect. Time's patina dignifies much sculpture, but runnels of soot and layers of lacquer and wax left Lee Lawrie's *Atlas*, the Art Deco bronze in New York's Rockefeller Center, neither wrinkled with age nor lined with wisdom, but dirty, darkened, and deadened, its details scabrously flaking, before cleaning in 2008.[158]

Attractive decay requires a delicate balance between neglect and intervention. But that balance must seem uncontrived: any sign that decay is deliberately arrested vitiates a ruin's appeal. 'We need ... the reassurance of accidental creation', adds Summerson. If it is a sham, we 'criticize it as a work of art; ... if it is known to be preserved the ruination seems no longer the work of pure accident'.[159]

Decay is inexorable, however; few ruins survive long unaided. The conserved ghost towns of the American West, whose brief, colourful lives ended with the mining booms that built them, exemplify the problem. To maintain sagging roofs and broken windows in a state of arrested decay and stabilize the fragile patina of age is no small task. It also poses an aesthetic conundrum,[160] for 'decay is not a stationary condition but a growing and continuing process', notes Piper. 'A building in which decay has been arrested smells ... of the museum; and in a few years it has the "dated" look of somebody or something that has outlived its time'.[161]

Yet Bodie, California, a meticulously preserved ghost town, attracts some 200,000 tourists a year by excluding the present – no interpretive signs, no guides, no hawkers of food or drink, no costumed actors, no current enterprise. Visitors see only the remains

---

[156] John Summerson, 'The past in the future' (1947), in *Heavenly Mansions* (Norton, 1963), 219–42 at 237; Kirk Varnedoe, in 'Time and change', *Conservation Perspectives* (Getty Conservation Institute) 17:3 (Fall 2002): 11–17 at 16.

[157] Una Richards, 'Newhailes', in Peter Burman, ed., *Celebrating Conservation* (York: The University, 2002), 70–1; Marcus Binney, 'Don't let preservation become an excuse for neglect', *Times*, 13 Oct. 2003; Peter Burman, 'Conservation philosophy in practice', *Architectural Heritage* 17 (2006): 15–42 at 30–2.

[158] John Bovey, 'Boats against the current', *Virginia Quarterly Review* 54 (1978): 577–600 at 577; David W. Dunlop, 'Bringing a smile (well, a shine) to a burdened statue of Atlas', *NYT*, 4 May 2008.

[159] Summerson, 'Past in the future', in *Heavenly Mansions*, 237.

[160] National Trust for Historic Preservation, *Ghost Towns and Mining Camps* (Preservation Press, 1977), 5–10, 25–8; Richard Francaviglia, 'Boomtowns and ghost towns', in Andrew Gulliford, ed., *Preserving Western History* (New Mexico, 2005), 348–64.

[161] Piper, 'Pleasing decay', 89, 91.

Figure 32 Ruin enlivens a landscape: Folly, Hodnet Hall, Shropshire, *c.* 1970

Figure 33 Unpleasing decay: former cement works, near Snelling, California

Figure 34 Abandoned decay: Vicksburg, Mississippi, 1933

Figure 35 Arrested decay: Calico Ghost Town, moved to Knott's Berry Farm,
Buena Park, California

of gold-rush Bodie, claims the self-guiding brochure, 'just as time, fire, and the elements have left it'. But the 'dated' look is temporally haphazard. Outside, rusted pick-up trucks and ancient gas pumps jostle remnants of horse-drawn wagons, all in ongoing decay. Inside, no 'taint of reconstruction' mars pervasive dilapidation, in haunted hostelries less evocative of miners' whores than of Dickens's Miss Havisham.[162]

Ideas evoked by decay

Decay's attractions go beyond its appearance. The sad, sinister, or violated air of ruins evoked Romantic musing. Dismay along with delight at the look of age prompted manifold reflections. 'No one of the least sentiment or imagination can look upon an old or ruined edifice without feeling sublime emotions', wrote a celebrant; 'a thousand ideas croud upon his mind, and fill him with awful astonishment'.[163]

The 'thousand ideas' elicited reflect diverse concerns. The veneer of age on paintings and objets d'art might betoken long-standing continuities, the dilapidation of ancestral mansions call to mind dreadful bygone deeds, crumbling ruins convey time's haunting remoteness. Retrospective awe was the stock Renaissance response – wonder felt not for existing remains but for original structures and sculptures. Monastic ruins in seventeenth-century England 'sett the thoughts a-worke to make out their magnificence, as they were when in perfection'.[164] Present attrition evokes memories of splendours past. Contrasting decay with former grandeur inspires countless poets and painters.

Decay was long an exemplary warning against sin and depravity; Bishop Hildebert of Le Mans in 1116 termed ruined ancient Rome heaven's rebuke for pagan splendour.[165] Ruins made manifest melancholy lessons. 'I could hardly keep back my tears faced with such mutations of time', lamented an antiquary at Rome's Colosseum.[166] The scars of monastic mutilation were cautionary: Canterbury's 'extreme povertie, nakedness, and decay' struck William Lambarde as divine retribution for the 'horrible crimes … of the Devil and the Pope'.[167] Ruins attested human retribution too; many who wreak martial devastation take 'joy in the contemplation of the ruinous results'.[168]

For Enlightenment viewers, ruins connoted nature repossessing culture, the frailty of social edifices, the transience of glory and the folly of pride. Viewing Hubert Robert's paintings of Roman ruins led Denis Diderot to 'anticipate the ravages of time on our own

---

[162] Dydia DeLyser, 'A walk through Old Bodie', in Stephen P. Hanna and Vincent J. Del Casino Jr., eds., *Mapping Tourism* (Minnesota, 2003), 79–106 at 88; Diana Strazdes, 'The display of ruins: lessons from the ghost town of Bodie', *Change over Time* 3 (2013): 222–43 at 236–7.

[163] 'On the pleasure arising from the sight of ruins or ancient structures', *European Magazine* (1795), quoted in Samuel H. Monk, *The Sublime* (1935; Michigan, 1960), 141. See Mortier, *Poétique des ruines*, 218–22; Ingrid G. Daemmrich, 'The ruins motif as artistic device in French literature', *Journal of Aesthetics and Art Criticism* 30 (1972): 449–57; 31 (1972): 30–41; Ginsberg, *Aesthetics of Ruins*.

[164] John Aubrey, *Wiltshire … 1659–70*, quoted in Margaret Aston, 'English ruins and English history: the Dissolution and the sense of the past', *Journal of the Warburg & Courtauld Institutes* 36 (1973): 231–55 at 251–2; Michael Hunter, *John Aubrey and the Realm of Learning* (Duckworth, 1975), 178–9, 234–5.

[165] Hildebert of Le Mans, *De Roma*, cited in Rose Macaulay, *The Pleasure of Ruins* (New York: Walker, 1953), 12.

[166] Arend van Buchell, *Iter Italicum* (1587), quoted in Mortier, *Poétique des ruines*, 43.

[167] William Lambarde, *A Perambulation of Kent* (1576; London, 1826), 268.

[168] Macaulay, *Pleasure of Ruins*, 1.

habitations ... Everything is annihilated, everything perishes ... Such is the first tenet of the poetics of ruins'.[169] Capitalizing on public fascination with demolition and catastrophe, Robert depicted scenes of cataclysmic destruction; in his *L'église des Feuillants en démolition* (1800) at Saint-Jean-en-Grève, onlookers marvel at the fourteenth-century monument's spectacular explosion, while three figures flee in terror.[170] But beyond death new life would emerge, ruination was part of a cyclical natural order not just destructive but also restorative and ameliorative.

Reformers saw ruins as emblems of tyranny overcome – fearsome rulers gone to just deserts, haughty mansions disintegrating into humble huts. 'The ruin of the palace enables it to acquire the virtues of the cottage', in Diderot's phrase.[171] Volney's *Ruins* (1791) delighted Americans to whom Old World castles spelt oppression, their decay symbolizing release from monastic and baronial subjugation.[172] Crumbling abbeys were picturesque proof that former 'abodes of tyranny and superstition are in ruin'.[173]

For exiles returning to post-Revolutionary France, however, ruins incarnated horrific and irremediable loss. In the wreckage of churches, abbeys, and chateaux they saw neither time's erosion nor nature's reclamation, but human 'annihilation, without any reparative power', held Chateaubriand. 'The effect of calamity, and not of years ... the destructions of man are ... much more violent and much more complete than those of time: the latter undermine, the former demolish'.[174] And the one charmed, the other repelled, as Victor Hugo said of lesions suffered by Notre-Dame: time, wind, and rain lent its stones a furrowed and roughened beauty, but the Revolutionary scars were hideous contusions and fractures. From 'a lifeless artifact of underdevelopment and superannuation', the ruin in France became 'a haunting relic ... of anguished memory'.[175]

Decay triggered mournful recollections. The mind is 'more taken with prospects of the ruinous kind', wrote Gilpin of England's monastic remnants, 'than with most smiling Views of Plenty and Prosperity'. The 'ruins of a noble tree ... speak to the imagination in a stile of eloquence, which the stripling cannot reach: they record the history of some storm, some blast of lightening ... which transfers its grand ideas to the landscape'.[176]

---

[169] Denis Diderot, *Ruines et paysages III: Salons de 1767* (Paris: Presses Internationales Polytechnique, 1995); D. Diderot, *Salons, critique d'art*, (1759–81; Clarendon Press, 1957–67), 3: 228.

[170] Nina Dubin, 'Robert des ruines', *Cabinet Magazine*, issue 20, 'Ruins' (Winter 2005/6).

[171] Diderot, *Salons, critique d'art*, 3: 246. See Anne Betty Weinshenker, 'Diderot's use of the ruin-image', *Diderot Studies* 16 (1973): 309–29.

[172] Constantin-François Volney, *The Ruins: or, A Survey of the Revolutions of Empire* (1789; 5th edn London, 1807); Marshall Davidson, 'Whither the course of empire?' *American Heritage* 8:6 (1957): 52–61 at 60.

[173] Uvedale Price, *Essay on Architecture and Buildings* (1794), in *Essays on the Picturesque* (London, 1810), 2: 171–370 at 264. See Stuart Piggott, *Ruins in a Landscape* (Edinburgh, 1976), 120.

[174] Chateaubriand, *Genius of Christianity*, 467–8, echoing Marcus Annaeus Lucan: 'it is not devouring time which has eroded and abandoned in decay these memorials of the past: it is the crime of civil war we see' (*De bello civili* (c. AD 62; Oxford, 1992), 139). See Rodrigo Cacho Casal, 'The memory of ruins', *Renaissance Quarterly* 62 (2009): 1167–1203.

[175] Victor Hugo, *Notre-Dame de Paris*, bk. 3, ch. 1 (1831; Paris, 1904), 85–91; Fritzsche, *Stranded in the Present*, 101–3, 107.

[176] William Gilpin, *A Dialogue upon the Gardens of the Right Honourable The Lord Viscount Cobham, at Stow in Buckinghamshire* (London, 1748), 5, and *Remarks on Forest Scenery* (London, 1794), 1: 9.

Ruins' manifest kinship with mortal beings incessantly evoke The End. Surrounded by decay, Ann Radcliffe's protagonist muses that in 'a few years ... I shall become like the mortals on whose relics I now gaze, and like them too, [become] the subject of meditation to a succeeding generation, which shall totter but a little while ... ere they also sink into dust'.[177] Others dwelt on transience ('all passes but God'), the futility of vanity ('A little rule, a little sway, / A sunbeam in a winter's day, / Is all the proud and mighty have / Between the cradle and the grave'), the brevity of human impress in perdurable nature ('what is my existence in comparison with this crumbling stone?').[178] On finishing his *Decline and Fall of the Roman Empire*, Gibbon ruefully reflected that man's 'monuments, like himself, are perishable and frail; and in the boundless annals of time his life and labours [but] a fleeting moment'.[179]

Painters depicted ruins and decay to stress the evanescence of man's works. Francesco Guardi's moist landscapes and mouldering buildings limn the decline of Venice; Piranesi and Hubert Robert depicted time and nature devouring antiquity. Viewing Italy's ruins, Thomas Cole conceived his last *Course of Empire* scene of desolation, 'ruined temples, broken bridges, fountains, sarcophagi [tolling] the funeral knell of departed greatness'.[180]

Morbid reaction varied with remnant epoch. To Kames, Gothic ruins exhibited 'the triumph of time over strength' (a melancholy thought), 'a Grecian ruin ... the triumph of barbarism over taste, a gloomy and discouraging thought'.[181] Whereas classical relics spurred the revival of antiquity towards modern progress, Gothic remains induced regressive nostalgia. Neoclassicists adored the past's suggestive vitality, encouraging finer material forms and social norms; Romantics adored the past's hypnotic pull, evoking reflections on transience and decline. Eschewing decay and ruin led classicizing modernists to appropriate antiquity for new programmes; venerating decay and ruin led gothicizing nostalgists to meditate on bygone felicities that could be neither restored nor matched. Those who enjoyed a bright new past presumed to reanimate it; those who hankered after a decayed and ruined past assumed it irretrievable. Whereas mouldering relics suggested a past beyond reach, new creations inspired by antiquity brought ancient ideals and forms again to life.[182]

Decay's overriding message is our own mortality. Marks of dissolution are *memento mori*, reminders of death's implacable imminence. 'As I am, so you shall be' is a customary forewarning epitaph. Ivy over a broken window, the sky glimpsed through a fallen roof 'moved to melancholy pleasure' romantics who 'dwelt gladly on the impermanence of human life and effort'. James Stevens Curl's childhood amid rural decay brought intense awareness of 'the nearness of death and of the dead'.[183] Such promptings

---

[177] Ann Radcliffe, *The Romance of the Forest* (1791; London, 1904), 21–2.
[178] Dyer, *Grongar Hill*, ll. 90–3.
[179] Edward Gibbon, *The History of the Decline and Fall of the Roman Empire* (1776–88; Allen Lane, 1994), 3: 863.
[180] William Gaunt, *Bandits in a Landscape* (London: Studio, 1937), 65; Cole to Luman Reed, 18 Sept. 1833, in Louis Legrand Noble, *The Life and Works of Thomas Cole* (1853; Harvard, 1964), 310.
[181] Henry Home, Lord Kames, *Elements of Criticism* (Edinburgh, 1762), 3: 313.
[182] Rosenblum, *Transformations in Late Eighteenth Century Art*, 107–45.
[183] Michael Sadleir, '"All horrid?": Jane Austen and the Gothic romance', in *Things Past* (Constable, 1944), 167–200 at 176; James Stevens Curl, *A Celebration of Death* (1980; Batsford, 1993), xxiv.

Figure 36 Skeletal death menaces its victim: Louis-François Roubiliac,
Tomb of Lady Elizabeth Nightingale, Westminster Abbey, 1761

Figure 37 Decay and resurrection: Girolamo della Robbia,
rejected *transi* of Catherine de Medici, 1566

were moral goads. Visiting England's ruined monasteries 'puts us in mind of our
mortality', wrote an antiquary, 'and consequently brings us to unfeigned repentance'.[184]

Images of mortal decay obsessed medieval Europeans beset by plague and famine.
Depictions of skeletal death menacing his victims were rife in the wake of the Black
Death. Sculptured effigies in splendid regalia lay above *transi* of decomposing corpses,
mocking evanescent pride with earthly decay. Such images, like the self-abasement of
flagellants, attested the deceased's contrition, lest eternal damnation punish worldly
arrogance. In an epoch given to extremes of debauchery and piety, *transi* denigrated
the flesh, hideous death following youthful beauty: 'after man, worms, and after worms,
stench and horror', as inscribed on the Avignon *transi* of schismatic Cardinal Jean de
Lagrange (d. 1402).[185]

---

[184] John Weever, *Antient Funerall Monuments* (1631; London, 1762), ix, xii, xli, cvi, 268.

[185] Bernard of Clairvaux quoted in Kathleen Cohen, *Metamorphosis of a Death Symbol: The Transi Tomb*
(California, 1973), 4–7, 21–8, 47–8; Rosemary Horrox, 'Purgatory, prayer and plague: 1150–1380', 90–118,
and Philip Morgan, 'Of worms and war: 1380–1588', 119–46, in Peter C. Jupp and Clare Gittings, eds.,
Death in England (Manchester, 1999). While verbal descriptions of plague victims were horrendously
graphic, artists seldom depicted putrefaction; they 'kept the dirt of life at a distance' (Rudolph Binion, *Past
Impersonal* (Northern Illinois, 2005), 130–5).

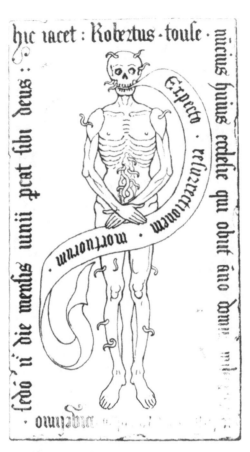

Figure 38 Death and resurrection: 'Expecto resurrectionem mortuorum': inscription
on slab tomb of Robert Touse, d. 1422

Transi are shrouded, emaciated, shrivelled, or putrescent. In a fresco at Campo Santo, Pisa (*c.* 1350), three hunters find their own decomposing corpses. A chapel memorial in the canton of Vaud shows François de la Sarra (d. 1363) as he might have looked after years of putrefaction, worms slithering in and out of the cadaver, toads covering eyes and genitals. A mouse, serpent, worm, frog, and beetle devour the Tewkesbury Abbey likeness of John Wakeman (*c.* 1539). Each creature conveyed a message: serpents Satanic temptation, frogs and toads sins, worms repentance or pangs of conscience.

The stench of death and decay permeated Renaissance locales of grief, like Juliet's 'charnel-house O'er-covered quite with dead men's rattling bones, with reeky shanks, and yellow chapless skulls' (*Romeo and Juliet* 4:1, ll. 81–3), a recurrent trope down to Edgar Allan Poe's *Fall of the House of Usher* (1839). Old iniquities overwhelm the Palladian mansion in County Kildare, where the Irish poet Michael Hartnett 'saw black figures dancing on the lawn, / Eviction, Droit de Seigneur, Broken Bones: / And heard the crack of ligaments being torn / and smelled the clinging blood upon the stones'.[186] Modern

---

[186] Michael Hartnett, 'Visit to Castletown House', in *Selected and New Poems* (Oldcastle, Co. Meath: Gallery, 1994), 5–6.

memento mori couple aesthetic angst with erotic kitsch. In the Chapman brothers' skeletal figures, worms, snails, and flies crawl in and out of every body orifice. The Venetian jeweller Codognato's *chef-d'oeuvre* is a coffin-shaped gold and jet ring, enclosing a skeleton with an erection.[187]

The less dolorous sixteenth century dimmed demands for *transi* and neutralized bodily decomposition. Save for saints, bodies were *meant* to decay, corruption a necessary prelude to resurrection. The cadaver likeness of René de Châlons (killed 1544) after three years' envisaged decay, his heart in his heaven-pointing hand, displays a corpse not feeding worms but affirming life eternal.[188] Like seventeenth-century tombstones and memorials, *vanitas* paintings combined *memento mori* – skulls, scythes, skeletons, hour-glasses, wilted flowers – with sleeping children to stress the transience of all joys.[189]

Delight in seeing mortality revived in the eighteenth century, as in the maudlin Methodist hymn:

> Ah! Lovely appearance of death!
> No sight upon earth is so fair:
> Not all the gay pageants that breathe
> Can with a dead body compare.[190]

As nightgown-like shrouds replaced winding sheets, the dead were prettified, perfumed, primped, and powdered, fitted with wigs and false teeth, pillowed for seemly sleep. Bereaved Victorians found comfort in death masks, photos of the deceased, notably babies in coffins, and portraits, both pre- and post-mortem. Ada Lovelace's husband had her portrait painted three months before her death from cancer in 1852, when she was 'wasted almost to a beautiful shadow', as her daughter said, 'like what I should imagine an angel to be'.[191] 'Beautiful death' – the pain-free smile on sighting the glory of heaven, as with Dickens's Little Nell – became a standard theme of art and fiction, exemplified in consumptive young women, from Samuel Richardson's *Clarissa* (1748) through Violetta in Verdi's *La Traviata* (1852) to Poe and the Pre-Raphaelites.[192]

---

[187] Jake and Dinos Chapman, *Flogging a Dead Horse* (Rizzoli, 2011); Heidi Ellison, 'The Codognato mystique', *NYT*, 17 June 2010: 11.

[188] Cohen, *Metamorphosis of a Death Symbol*, 103, 114–19, 171, 177–81; Erwin Panofsky, *Tomb Sculpture* (Thames & Hudson, 1964), 56–64, 80; T. S. R. Boase, *Death in the Middle Ages* (Thames & Hudson, 1972), 102.

[189] Dane Munro, '*Memento mori* and *vanitas* elements in the funerary art at St. John's Co-Cathedral', *Treasures of Malta* 11:1 (Dec. 2004); Dane Munro, *Memento Mori* (Valletta: MJ Publishers, 2005); Sarah Tarlow, 'Wormie clay and blessed sleep: death and disgust in later historic Britain', in Sarah Tarlow and Susie West, eds., *The Familiar Past* (Routledge, 1999), 183–98 at 187–8.

[190] Charles Wesley, 'On the corpse of a believer', in *Hymns on the Great Festivals* (London, 1746), 7–8.

[191] Tarlow, 'Wormie clay and blessed sleep', 194; Pat Jalland, 'Victorian death and its decline, 1850–1918', in Jupp and Gittings, eds., *Death in England*, 230–55 at 246–7. See Pat Jalland, *Death in the Victorian Family* (Oxford, 1996), 257–8, 289, 295, 378.

[192] Jalland, *Death in the Victorian Family*, 36–8; Charles Dickens, *The Old Curiosity Shop* (London, 1841), ch. 71; Elisabeth Bronfen, *Over Her Dead Body: Death, Femininity and the Aesthetic* (Manchester, 1992); Edgar Allen Poe, 'The death ... of a beautiful woman is ... the most poetical topic in the world' ('The philosophy of composition', *Graham's Magazine* 28:4 (April, 1846): 163–7 at 165). See Eric W. Carlson, ed., *A Companion to Poe Studies* (Westport, CT: Greenwood, 1996), 122, 287, 357, 388, 400; Philippe Ariès, *The Hour of Our Death* (1977; Penguin, 1983), 610–13.

Decay in general shed its aura of gloom. Watercolourists depicted ruined abbeys and castles in prosaic, even cheerful terms. Embroidered memorials festooned parlour and bedroom walls with maidens contemplating classical tombstones set among willows (sadness), withering oaks (transience), ships (departure), on the sea (tears). This iconography bespoke no recent bereavements. The pictures commemorated long-dead remote relatives, national heroes such as George Washington, or tragic Romantic figures such as Goethe's Werther. Constable's time-eroded sites and beings – Hadleigh Castle's sense of imminent destruction, Stonehenge's ancient decay, the gnarled stump set off by tender leaves in Leaping Horse – celebrate life amid death.[193]

The inevitability of biological decay was for many no cause for regret. Baudelaire welcomed ageing and death as concomitants of growth, putrefaction a prelude to regeneration; Ruskin and Morris insisted that buildings be left to age into ancient beauty and then perish. Decrepitude integral to organic existence celebrated universal evanescence. Transience, taught Alois Riegl, was innate in every human creation. The ageing of beloved memorabilia helps reconcile us to our own mortality and not to flinch from awareness of our own inexorable end.[194]

Degenerative decay can even seem like welcome accretion. Just as wear and tear reveals furniture's rich history, and faded fabric lends historic houses a lived-in feeling, so Russell Baker took 'comfort from an authentic life-hewn face, looking like a man who had made the usual excursions into life and been affected by them'. A full sense of being requires awareness of all life's stages: embryonic, nascent, penultimate, terminal. 'A life spent without any contemplation of death', writes a sepulchral historian, 'is a denial of life, since death is the logical and inevitable end for us all'.[195]

One can have too many such reminders, however. The young might relish the beauty of ruins, remarked the elderly Chateaubriand, but his ageing confrères faced more decay than they could bear. 'The old men of former times were less unfortunate and less isolated than those of the present day; if, when surviving, they lost their friends, little else was changed', but the Revolutionary exile 'has not only seen men die, but ideas also; principles, tastes, pleasures, pains, and sentiments; nothing bears any resemblance to what he has known'.[196]

The beauty of time-worn Venice was for Ruskin both a poignant testament to evanescence and, against overweening ambition, a warning, an example, and an instructive inspiration. Anent the three thrones of Tyre, Venice, and England,

Of the First of these great powers only the memory remains; of the Second, the ruin; the Third, which inherits their greatness, if it forget their example, may be led through prouder eminence to less pitied destruction . . . [Venice] in the final period of her decline [was] a ghost upon the sands

[193] LaVerne Muto, 'A feminist art: the American memorial picture', Art Journal 35 (1976): 352–8; Karl Kroeber, Romantic Landscape Vision (Wisconsin, 1975), 55, 113–15.

[194] D. G. Charlton, New Images of the Natural in France (Cambridge, 1984), 101–3; Alois Riegl, Der Moderne Denkmalkultus (Vienna, 1903), 23–7; Wolfdietrich Rasch, Die Literarische Decadence um 1900 (Munich: Beck, 1991).

[195] Russell Baker, 'Ageless idols', IHT, 21 Apr. 1978, 16; Curl, Celebration of Death, 1.

[196] François-René de Chateaubriand, Memoirs of Chateaubriand (1846), Journal Apr.–Sept. 1822 (London, 1849), 343.

of the sea, so weak – so quiet – and so bereft of all but her loveliness, that we might well doubt, as we watched her fine reflection in the mirage of the lagoon, which was the City, and which the Shadow.

Ruskin aimed 'to trace the lines of this image before it be for ever lost, and to record ... the warning ... uttered by every one of the fast-gaining waves, that beat, like passing bells, against the STONES OF VENICE'.[197]

Not marks of age but agonies of infirmity and dismemberment are cherished in Latin America, the heroic dead exalted, like early Christian martyrs, by stigmata of suffering and sacrifice. The mutilated bodies and severed limbs of military idols – Getúlio Vargas, Antonio López de Santa Ana, Álvaro Obregón – remain on reverential display. In Argentina Evita Perón is more often represented emaciated by terminal cancer than in glamorous youth.[198]

Imminent dissolution renders artefacts precious; and reminders of life's brevity enhance what remains of it. The miniature skeletons displayed on Roman banqueting tables were said to heighten diners' enjoyment, much as the lethal risk of consuming puffer fish lends spice to Japanese gourmands.[199] Venice's impending demise intensified that city's beauty for Ruskin. The ephemeral is most affecting: 'old toys, made for brief use, seemingly so fragile, associated with a passing and vulnerable phase of life, are much more emotive symbols than are permanent, serious memorials', noted city planner Kevin Lynch.[200] We love things because we know they will perish, as a Victorian poet put it:

> All beauteous things for which we live
> By laws of time and space decay.
> But oh, the very reason why
> I clasp them, is because they die.[201]

Portending life's end, marks of age lend it substance. 'Trying to preserve a century by keeping its relics up to date is like keeping a dying man alive by stimulants', protests F. Scott Fitzgerald's Gloria at Robert E. Lee's over-restored home. 'There's no beauty without poignancy and there's no poignancy without the feeling that it's going, men, names, books, houses – bound for dust – mortal.'[202] Scars of time are signs of life. It is 'all the infinite scratches, bumps, scars, and declivities, some the tricks of art, some the wear of fortune, which give such noble vitality' to the horses of San Marco, felt Jan Morris; putting them away in a museum to forestall corrosion denied them 'the slow dignified decline into age and dust which is the privilege of all living things'.[203]

---

[197] John Ruskin, *The Stones of Venice* (1851), in *CW*, 7: 1–2.

[198] Lyman L. Johnson, 'Why dead bodies talk', in his ed., *Death, Dismemberment, and Memory* (New Mexico, 2004), 1–26.

[199] Curl, *Celebration of Death*, 2; Norimitsu Onishi, 'If the fish liver can't kill, is it really a delicacy?' *NYT*, 4 May 2008.

[200] Kevin Lynch, *What Time Is This Place?* (MIT Press, 1972), 44.

[201] William Johnson Cory, 'Mimnermus in church' (1858), in *Ionica*, 3rd edn (London, 1905), 6.

[202] F. Scott Fitzgerald, *The Beautiful and the Damned* (1921; Penguin, 1966), 140.

[203] Jan Morris, 'The horses of San Marco', *Sunday Telegraph*, 2 Sept. 1979: 76–83. Morris was later reconciled to the 'dullard replicas' ('Venice changes – but for me it stays seductively, tantalisingly the same', *Guardian*, 25 Mar. 2010).

Statues that celebrate organic life undergo 'the equivalent of fatigue, age, and unhappiness', changing 'in the way time changes us', the hazards of history heightening their involuntary beauty. Shattered statues become new art forms, notes Marguerite Yourcenar: 'a torso which has no face to prevent us from loving it; ... a bust with eroded features, halfway between a portrait and a death's head'; works abandoned in the open acquiring 'the majesty or the languor of a tree or a plant'. Most striking are shipwrecked marble statues, resurfacing 'gnawed or eaten away, corroded, decorated with baroque volutes sculpted by the caprice of the tides, or encrusted with shells'.

The forms and gestures the sculptor gave them proved to be only a brief episode between their incalculable duration as rock in the bosom of the mountain and their long existence as stone lying at the bottom of the sea. They have passed through this decomposition without pain, through this loss without death, through this survival without resurrection.

Their 'sea-change / Into something rich and strange' recalls Ariel's' 'Full fathom five thy father lies; / Of his bones are coral made; / Those are pearls that were his eyes'.[204]

Time's erosions presage not just death but immortality. Byron saw ivy as 'The garland of eternity, where wave / The green leaves over all by time o'erthrown'.[205] Personal ageing and death intimate collective immortality. 'We are but the most recent lessees of similar bodies preceding ours and of similar ones to come after', mused Stephen Spender, 'the momentary organs of sensibility ... of the whole of human existence'.[206]

Yet contemplating briefer lifespans makes ours seem well-nigh infinite. 'Isn't it good to see the autumn come?' asks an insect in a fable. 'My reaction is different', replies another; 'my species is annual'. In human terms all 'these innumerable little lives quickly pass while ours endure ... The autumnal spectacle of the cessation of life on the earth, nature's yearly tragedy', wrote W. H. Hudson, 'multiplies our years and makes them so many that it is a practical immortality'.[207]

Decay makes domestic surroundings companionable, with mounting fondness for furnishings that grow old along with us. 'The joy of familiarity requires intimacy, wear, usage, and the accumulation of memories', home comfort 'nourished by mellowing and shabbiness'.[208] Marks of age consecrate enduring linkages with familiar things.

Beyond the familiar, however, decay can fearsomely alienate. The 'stump-pocked ... desolation ... of gaunt, staring, motionless wheels rising from mounds of brick rubble and ragged weeds lifting their rusting and unsmoking stacks' at a defunct sawmill was, for William Faulkner, nonetheless profoundly peaceful.[209] But no cloture mitigates the squalid chaos of Tim Edensor's abandoned Satanic mills. Part Gothic, part Piranesi, part

[204] Marguerite Yourcenar, 'That mighty sculptor, time' (1954), in *That Mighty Sculptor, Time* (1983; Macmillan, 1993), 57–62; William Shakespeare, *The Tempest* (c. 1611), I:2, ll. 560–4.
[205] Lord Byron, *Childe Harold's Pilgrimage* (1812–18), Canto IV. 99, ll. 888–9, in *Poetical Works* (Oxford, 1970), 179–252 at 240.
[206] Stephen Spender, *Love–Hate Relations* (Hamish Hamilton, 1974), 192.
[207] W. H. Hudson, *Nature in Downland* (Dent, 1900), 211.
[208] Henry Beetle Hough, *Soundings at Sea Level* (Houghton Mifflin, 1980), 98. See Robin Forster and Tim Whittaker, *The Well-Worn Interior* (Thames & Hudson, 2003).
[209] William Faulkner, *Light in August* (1932; Vintage, 2000), 6.

Lang's *Metropolis*, the befouled wastelands of bygone British enterprise are unrelieved by future prospect. Ruined workshops and warehouses, corroded sewers and pipes, the coagulated debris of residual shearings, filings, mouldering rags and begrimed receipts simply attest post-industrial demise.[210]

Yet even such decay, redolent of multiple malfunctions from New Jersey's Pulaski Skyway to Detroit, has Piranesian votaries. In postmodern art, architecture, and avant-garde cinema, para-aesthetic taste for the destructive uncanny – things faulty, disordered, chaotic, distressful, violated – bespeaks affection for degenerate nature.[211] The garbage recycling shed excites Don DeLillo's 'reverence for waste, for the redemptive qualities of the things we use and discard . . . the gut squalor of our lives', that 'come back to us with a kind of brave aging'.[212]

Musing over vestiges of the past has ceased to be conventional. Ruins move few sensitive souls to sublime and melancholy reflections about their own impending demise, the transience of life, the failure of memory, the futility of fame, or the irretrievable past. Diderot's reaction to Hubert Robert's paintings exemplifies the musings of his age – and underscores their remoteness from our own:

The ideas aroused in me by ruins are lofty . . . How old this world is! . . . Wherever I turn my eyes, the objects that surround me foretell an end and help me resign myself to the one that awaits me. What is my ephemeral existence compared to that of this stone collapsing with antiquity, of this deepening valley, of this forest tottering with age![213]

Traces of ruin taste survive in modern fondness for the fragmentary, the indistinct, the suggestively incomplete. But physical decay today spurs no contemplations like Diderot's, and his attendant sentimentality is even more outdated. We view the remnants of antiquity without the 'unutterable ecstasy' of the Pre-Raphaelite Edward Burne-Jones, who returned from an 1854 pilgrimage to ruined Godstow, Fair Rosamund's burial place, 'in a delirium of joy' induced by 'pictures of the old days, the abbey, and long processions of the faithful, banners of the cross, copes and crosiers, gay knights and ladies by the river bank, hawking parties and all the pageantry of the golden age'.[214] The pastoral melancholy of Wordsworth's 'Tintern Abbey' gave way to the mild nostalgic curiosity of 'some ruin-bibber, randy for antique', of Philip Larkin's 'Church Going'. Unlike Arnold, Hardy, or Eliot, Larkin finds the ancient church 'not in the least haunted . . . merely old'; he observes it not as a participant but as an 'anthropologist who has accidentally happened upon a minor shrine of a dead civilization'.[215] Our attachment to the wreckage of the past

[210] Edensor, *Industrial Ruins*, 38, 103–13, 166. See Dylan Trigg, *The Aesthetics of Decay* (New York: Peter Lang, 2006), 165–78.
[211] Harbison, *The Built, the Unbuilt and the Unbuildable*, 121; Dan Austin, *Lost Detroit* (Charleston, SC: History Press, 2010); Julia Hell and Andreas Schönle, eds., *Ruins of Modernity* (Duke, 2010).
[212] Don DeLillo, *Underworld* (Scribners, 1997), 809–10.
[213] Diderot, *Ruines et paysges III: Salon de 1767*, 228–9.
[214] Georgiana Burne-Jones, *Memorials of Edward Burne-Jones* (London: Macmillan, 1904), 1: 97. See M. W. Thompson, *Ruins* (Oxford, 1979), 95; Charles Jencks, ed., *Post-Modern Classicism*, special issue, *Architectural Design*, 50:5/6 (1980): 10–12.
[215] Philip Larkin, 'Church going', in *The Less Deceived* (London: Marvell, 1955), 28–9; Christopher Clausen, 'Tintern Abbey to Little Gidding', *Sewanee Review* 84 (1976): 405–24 at 422–4.

Figure 39 Romanesque monumentality for America: H. H. Richardson,
Cheney Building, Hartford, Connecticut, 1875

is now less personal, less emotional, altogether less involved. 'We have many accounts of people at mid-[nineteenth] century being moved to tears' by Thomas Cole's 'Desolation' in his 'Course of Empire' series, 'so great were its religious and philosophical associations. The same painting today is viewed with a dryer eye.'[216]

'Our age', ran a recent lament, 'is much too precise, too puritanical, and too impressed with its own power over nature, to enjoy ruins.'[217] Yet mounting fascination with ruins pervades both academe and popular culture. Unlike the Victorian craze for romantic ruins, however, today's ruin penchant imbues decaying buildings and artefacts with

---

[216] Daniel D. Reiff, 'Memorial Hall the splendor beneath the dust', *Harvard Bulletin*, 74:3 (1972): 29–42 at 40.
[217] Katherine Swift, 'Gardens review', *Times*, 24 Aug. 2004: WR29.

ecological angst.[218] Wrecks wasting back to nature are memory traces 'replete with loss and confusion' that reflect today's disenchantment with modernity.[219] 'You're walking on the ruins of these modernist buildings, just like in Rome or Greece', says an admirer of architectural disasters. 'This monument [Cyprien Gaillard's recycled concrete *Cenotaph* from a demolished Glasgow tower-block] is going to age so well. That is, so badly.' Fritz Koenig's sculpture *The Sphere* (1971), buried badly damaged under World Trade Center debris on 9/11, was re-erected unrestored in New York's Battery Park. 'It's amazing how it is now, ruined. It was never this beautiful before.'[220] Modernist Thamesmead (1967–80), a famed dystopian locale in *A Clockwork Orange* (1971) and in video shoots of urban anomie, emerges in the 'fierce beauty' of its current decay, the planners' logo inviting graffiti, mock-Tudor panels adorning the reinforced-concrete housing estates.[221]

But current obsession with haunted asylums, silent foundries, and vacant bunkers reflect less fondness for beauty than fascination with horror. The ruined towns in Cold War civil defence films of nuclear disaster trials, with mannequin victims in scorched and tattered clothing, and the urban wreckage of Hollywood disaster blockbusters depict destruction as essential to survival.[222] Here is no military-industrial sublime safely cocooned in *ville radieuse* memorial parks, as Le Corbusier intended, but repellent reminders of techno failure and foreboding.[223] Like the rawness of earlier American ruins, 'Brutalism is not so much ruined as dormant, derelict', writes a devotee. 'This rough beast might still charge towards a concrete New Jerusalem.' Indeed, it already does so in the sinister ruins of Anselm Kiefer's ash-strewn, desiccated wasteland, titled *New Year in Jerusalem*, and in architect–sculptor James Wines's vertiginous Vancouver ruin.[224]

Shorn of the poignant ideas decay once called to mind, its attractions dwindled. The look of age still has devotees, but many fanciers now find patina and 'pleasing decay' simply repugnant for making things less useful and betokening death. But ageing is implacable, death unavoidable. All things natural and man-made are worn by time and subject to incessant erosion. Finding some virtue in the marks of age enables devotees of decay to enhance present and future with an evanescent past.

The manifold ambiguities evoked by youth and age were memorably expressed by John Donne, Restoration master of the ugly–beauty genre, in an elegy addressed to fifty-year-old Magdalen Herbert. First he terms her peerless: 'No spring, nor summer beauty hath

---

[218] Tim Edensor, 'Comment' [on Gastón Gordillo, 'Ships stranded in the forest'], *Current Anthropology* 52:2 (2011): 162.

[219] Nick Gallent and Johan Andersson, 'Representing England's rural–urban fringe', *Landscape Research* 32 (2007): 1–21 at 18; Edensor, *Industrial Ruins*, 167–70. See Trigg, *Aesthetics of Decay*, 119–54; Anna Storm, *Hope and Rust: Reinterpreting the Industrial Place* (Stockholm: Royal Institute of Technology, 2008).

[220] Gaillard quoted in Joanna Fiduccia, 'Cyprien Gaillard: recycling the ruins', MAP #16 (Winter 2008); Fritz Koenig in Tara Mulholland, 'French artist looks for beauty in ruins' *IHT*, 16 June 2010: 13.

[221] Owen Hatherley, *Militant Modernism* (Ropley: 0 Books, 2008), 33–5.

[222] Dillon, 'Fragments from a history of ruin'; Joseph Masco, 'Fantastic city', *Cabinet Magazine* issue 20: Ruins (Winter 2005/6).

[223] Brian G. Dillon, 'Decline and fall', *frieze Magazine*, issue 130 (April 2010); Brian G. Dillon, 'The military-industrial sublime', in his ed., *Ruins*, 102–38. On literary dystopia, see Cecilia Enjuto Rangel, *Cities in Ruins* (Purdue, 2010).

[224] Hatherley, *Militant Modernism*, 42; Roberta Smith, 'Spectacle with a message', *NYT*, 19 Nov. 2010.

such grace / As I have seen in one autumnal face'. But then he tempers praise, contrasting evanescent youthful with enduring familiar beauty, initial hazardous ecstasy with ripe calm pleasure:

> Were her first years the Golden Age? that's true,
> But now they're gold oft tried, and ever new.
> That was her torrid and inflaming time;
> This is her tolerable tropic clime.
> Fair eyes; he who asks more heat than comes from hence,
> He in a fever wishes pestilence.

Next Donne strives to dismiss decay's link with death, poetic devices driving out demons of ageing: 'Call not these wrinkles, graves; if graves they were, / They were Love's graves, for else he is nowhere'. Mature love, poised neither at life's precarious start nor too near the end, brings serenity, a cumulative enduring virtue:

> Here, where evening is, not noon, nor night,
> Where no voluptuousness, yet all delight.
>
> This is love's timber; youth his underwood . . .
>
> If we love things long sought, age is a thing
> Which we are fifty years in compassing;
> If transitory things, which soon decay,
> Age must be loveliest at the latest day.

Yet to extol terminal beauty seems aesthetically perverse, Donne's revulsion against final ageing unsparing:

> But name not winter's faces, whose skin's slack,
> Lank as an unthrift's purse, but a soul's sack . . .
>
> Whose every tooth to a several place is gone,
> To vex their souls at Resurrection
> Name not these living death-heads unto me,
> For these, not ancient, but antiques be.

Donne at last resigns himself to the end, both of love's beauty and of his mortal self.

> I hate extremes; yet I had rather stay
> With tombs than cradles, to wear out a day . . .
>
> Not panting after growing beauties; so
> I shall ebb out with them who homeward go.[225]

---

[225] 'The Autumnall' (c.1607–20), in *Variorum Edition of the Poetry of John Donne*, vol 2: *The Elegies* (Indiana, 2000), 277–8 (spelling modernized); also 'Commentary', 2: 836–74. See Heather Dubrow, 'Donne's elegies and the ugly beauty tradition', in A. D. Cousins and Damian Grace, eds., *Donne and the Resources of Kind* (Fairleigh Dickinson, 2002), 59–70; Ramie Targoff, *John Donne* (Chicago, 2008). Italian poets from Petrarch on extolled grey-haired beloveds (Patrizia Bettella, *The Ugly Woman* (Toronto, 2005), 152–8, citing Torquato Tasso and Giuseppe Salomoni; Elizabeth M. A. Hodgson, *Gender and the Sacred Self in John Donne* (Delaware, 1999), 141–6).

PART III

KNOWING THE PAST

The past is an immense area of stony ground that many people would like to drive across as if it were a motorway, while others move patiently from stone to stone, lifting each one because they need to know what lies beneath.   José Saramago, 2010[1]

The way of history is not that of a billiard ball, which, once hit, moves in a straight line, but like drifting clouds, or the path of a man sauntering through the streets, diverted here by a shadow, there by a knot of bystanders or by a striking facade, until at last he arrives at a place he never knew of nor meant to go to. Inherent in the course of history is considerable deviation.   Robert Musil, 1930[2]

What we know of the past is mostly not worth knowing. What is worth knowing is mostly uncertain. Events in the past may be roughly divided into those which probably never happened and those which do not matter   William Ralph Inge, 1929[3]

In talking about the past we lie with every breath we draw.   William Maxwell, 1980[4]

The past is in myriad ways indispensable. 'What we know, do not know, can and cannot know, what we should and should not believe about the past', concludes a philosopher of history, vitally affects 'our temporal orientation, personal identity', and present conduct.[5] Previous chapters explored the range of our needs and desires; this section surveys the mechanisms that acquaint us with the past, as a precondition of meeting those needs.

How do we know about the past? How do we acquire this essential awareness? We remember things, read or hear stories and chronicles, and live among relics from previous times. The past surrounds and saturates us; every scene, every statement, every action is laden with its residues. All present awareness is grounded on past perceptions and acts; we recognize a person, a tree, a breakfast, an errand because we have sensed or done it before. Pastness is integral to our very being:

Everyman, as well as you and I, remembers things said and done, and must do so at every waking moment ... The memory of Mr. Everyman, when he awakens in the morning, reaches out into the country of the past ... and instantaneously ... pulls together ... things said and done in his yesterdays ... Without this historical knowledge, this memory of things said and done, his today would be aimless and his to-morrow without significance.[6]

---

[1] José Saramago, *The Elephant's Journey* (Harvill Secker, 2010), 18–19.
[2] Robert Musil, *Der Mann ohne Eigenschaften* (1930–42; Reinbek: Rowohlt, 1978), 1: 361.
[3] William Ralph Inge, 'Prognostications', in *Assessments and Anticipations* (Cassell, 1929), 104–5.
[4] William Maxwell, *So Long, See You Tomorrow* (Ballantine, 1980), 29.
[5] Aviezer Tucker, *Our Knowledge of the Past* (Cambridge, 2004), 262.
[6] Carl L. Becker, 'Everyman his own historian', *AHR* 37 (1932): 221–36 at 223.

Crucial to historical memory is not only what we but others before us said and did; our own experience is deeply dependent on those of precursors. 'Our everyday world is built upon millions and millions of events and decisions that occurred in the past', notes Michael Crichton's time traveller; most of what we have and do 'was decided hundreds of years ago'.[7] Not only are we produced by the past, we exist as palimpsests of long-accreted collective experience.

> We come into the world ... 'not in nakedness' but ... clothed far more completely than even Pythagoras supposed in a vesture of the past; ... in the language, which is more than one half of our thoughts; in the moral and mental habits, the customs, the literature, the very houses, which we did not make for ourselves; in the vesture of a past ... of the species.[8]

Echoing Walter Pater two decades later, Émile Durkheim stressed humanity's dependence on tradition. 'Each generation inherits a treasury of knowledge that it did not itself amass ... We speak a language we did not create; we use instruments we did not invent; we claim rights we did not establish.'[9]

Centuries of tradition inform every act of perception and creation, pervading not only artefacts and culture but the very cells of our bodies. Human cognition secretes events shaped by millions of years of genetic evolution, millennia of cultural history, and for every year of our lives, ten thousand hours of personal experience. Children explore and relate to the world around them 'through the mediating lenses of pre-existing human artifacts', embodying past makers' and users' views and aims.[10] Our minds and bodies are reservoirs of remnant ancestral relics: skeletal, behavioural, psychic, and linguistic. Dead but latent meanings 'lie buried in the roots and phonemes of our living words, where they carry on an active afterlife. Our psyches are the graveyards of impressions, traumas, desires, and archetypes that confound the law of obsolescence.'[11]

Seldom do we recognize that such residues stem from the past, or that camouflaged bygones continue to shape and direct our behaviour. The 'invisible rule of the past goes unquestioned', as unseen as the submerged dead coral sustaining a living coral island.[12] 'I must be modern: I live now', muses a Robertson Davies character. 'But ... I live in a muddle of eras, and some of my ideas belong to today, and some to an ancient past, and some to periods of time that seem more relevant to my parents than to me.'[13] The temporal *mélange* is taken for granted; it is the present's normal nature. Facets of the past that live on in words and gestures, rules and relics, appear to us as 'past' only when explicitly made known as such. Rarely aware of their provenance, we keep our noses to

---

[7] Michael Crichton, *Timeline* (Knopf, 1999), 323–4.

[8] Walter Pater, *Plato and Platonism* (1893; London, 1922), 72. 'Nakedness' refers to Wordsworth's 'Intimations of immortality from recollections of early childhood' (1807), in *Poetical Works*, 4: 279.

[9] Émile Durkheim, *The Elementary Forms of Religious Life* (1912; Free Press, 1995), 214. Pater thought men mistook these legacies as works of their 'own volition'; Durkheim that 'we know at least they are not of our own making'.

[10] Michael Tomasello, *The Cultural Origins of Human Cognition* (Harvard, 1999), 216, 202.

[11] Robert Pogue Harrison, *The Dominion of the Dead* (Chicago, 2003), 83.

[12] Crichton, *Timeline*, 33; Mircea Eliade, *Birth and Rebirth* (London: Harvill, 1958), 27.

[13] Robertson Davies, *The Rebel Angels* (Penguin, 1983), 124.

the grindstone, stay away in droves and roll in the hay, espy no spring chicken but a horse of a different colour, get things straight from the horse's mouth or dismiss them as hogwash from an idiot mad as a hatter.[14]

'How does the shadowy . . . past differ from the full-blown of the present?' wonders a philosopher, reviewing perennial debates between those who consider the past wholly unreal, real but dead, real only in momentary awareness, or permanent and lengthening.[15] To view the past as a distinct temporal realm, separate from and intrinsically unlike the present, is often held unique to modern Western consciousness: only in *our* historiography did the past become a foreign country.[16] Indeed, one historian contends that until the Enlightenment there was no such thing as *the* past, only multiple dissociated pasts. '"The past" has a history, and not until it came into being could we have ideas about it, ideas that gradually transformed it into . . . an intellectual entity that did not previously exist.'[17] Yet all humans save infants, the senile, and the brain-damaged are conscious of *some* past. At the very least, we remember what we repeat, recall there was a yesterday, and sense the growth and ageing, flowering and decay discussed in previous chapters. But fuller awareness demands alertness to processes begun and continued, recollections of things said and done, narratives of people and events – the core matter of memory and history.

Such awareness once arose from being introduced to antiquity. 'When a child begins to know there is a past . . . he attributes an overwhelming majesty to all recorded time', held a *fin-de-siècle* poet. 'He confers distance . . . bestows mystery. Remoteness is his. He assigns the Parthenon to a hill of ages, and the temples of Upper Egypt to sidereal time.' Adulthood redoubles remoteness, making infancy as distant as Parthenon and pyramids. 'Childhood is itself Antiquity.'[18]

'The past is never dead', in the classic phrase; 'it exists continuously in the minds of thinkers and men of imagination'.[19] Indeed, it pervades us all. We harbour not only our own previous thoughts and actions, but also those of others, directly witnessed or surmised. The slightest suggestion conjures up things past, noted the historian Herbert Butterfield:

The mind of every one of us holds a jumble of pictures and stories . . . that constitute what we have built up for ourselves of the Past, . . . called into play by a glimpse of some old ruin . . . or by a hint of the romantic . . . A cathedral bell, or the mention of Agincourt, or the very spelling of the word 'ycleped' may be enough to set the mind wandering into its own picture galleries of history.[20]

---

[14] Agnes Heller, *A Theory of History* (Routledge, 1982), 201; Jack Rosenthal, 'The progenitives live on', *IHT*, 17 July 2006: 7.

[15] Barry Dainton, 'Past, what past?' *TLS*, 8 Jan. 2010: 9–10; Peter Forrest, 'The real but dead past', *Analysis* 64 (2004): 358–62; Robin Le Poidevin, *The Images of Time* (Oxford, 2007).

[16] Donald R. Kelley, *Foundations of Modern Historical Scholarship* (Columbia, 1970), 3; Jörn Rüsen, ed., *Western Historical Thinking* (Berghahn, 2002). See Chapter 8 below.

[17] Zachary Sayre Schiffman, *The Birth of the Past* (Johns Hopkins, 2011), 277, 7.

[18] Alice Meynell, 'The illusion of historic time', in *The Colour of Life* (London, 1896), 89–93.

[19] Gilbert Highet, *The Classical Tradition: Greek and Roman Influences on Western Literature* (Clarendon Press, 1949), 447, although usually attributed to William Faulkner's *Requiem for a Nun* (1951).

[20] Herbert Butterfield, *The Historical Novel* (Cambridge, 1924), 1.

The past thus reanimated is simultaneously historical, memorial, and artefactual. Most of its scenes antedate ourselves, but what we read and hear and reiterate about even the remotest of times embeds them in our own memories as firmly as things directly experienced.

We discern the past as coexistent yet distinct from the present. What joins them is awareness of ongoing organic life; what sets them apart is self-conscious consideration of change. Deliberation distinguishes the here and now – doing tasks, forming ideas, taking steps – from bygone thoughts and events. 'The distinction between past and present [is] necessary for the very possibility of thinking about the past at all.' The present is here and malleable, the past absent and immutable.[21] But temporal severance is always in tension with temporal conflation; the past is felt *both* part of *and* separate from the present. We 'call the past ... into being by recollecting and by thinking historically', noted the historian R. G. Collingwood; 'but we do this by disentangling it out of the present in which it actually exists'.[22] Nor are they easily separable; 'the new and the old cannot in life be neatly distinguished', warns a historian of changing Catholicism, 'as the old slowly comes to fruition in the new'.[23] Temporal twining is the essence of musical experience, melodies perceived as continuous yet segmented wholes, each immediate note accompanied by a halo of retentions from the past and anticipated future notes.[24]

What the conscious past contains, why it is dwelt upon, how much it is felt a realm apart, all vary from culture to culture, person to person, era to era, even moment to moment. Some are so enlivened (or oppressed) by remembered pasts, real or imagined, as to wholly disregard the present; to others the past has little to say, the present pre-empting their attention. But whether meagre or copious, dead or alive, a realm apart or meshed with the present, the past comes into consciousness along similar routes much trodden by most peoples.

Three sources provide past knowledge: memory, history, and relics. Memory and history are processes of insight; each involves the other, with boundaries fluid and indistinct. Yet they are justly distinguishable: memory is inescapable and essential to existence, even when fallacious; history is contingent and accretive, but not a vital personal necessity. Unlike memory and history, relics are not processes but residues of processes, natural or cultural. Relics reveal the past both organically, through ageing and weathering, and historically, through forms and structures recognized as stemming from an earlier epoch.

Each route to the past – memory, history, relics – is a domain claimed by specialist disciplines: principally by psychology, by history, and by archaeology together with natural history. But knowing the past embraces wider perspectives than these disciplines normally treat, transcending academic expertise.

---

[21] Constantin Fasolt, *The Limits of History* (Chicago, 2004), 4.

[22] R. G. Collingwood, 'Some perplexities about time' (1926), in Charles M. Sherover, ed., *The Human Experience of Time* (1975; rev. edn Northwestern, 2001), 558–71 at 571.

[23] John T. Noonan, Jr., *A Church That Can and Cannot Change* (Notre Dame, 2005), 7.

[24] Edmund Husserl, *On the Phenomenology of the Consciousness of Internal Time* (1893–1917; Dordrecht: Kluwer, 1990), 21–75; Barry Dainton, *Stream of Consciousness* (Routledge, 2006), 124–8; John Butt, *Bach's Dialogue with Modernity* (Cambridge, 2010), 129–41.

Before reviewing how memory, history, and relics each bear on the past, I inquire into how the past is generally experienced and believed. The very fact that it is no longer present makes all knowledge of the past uncertain. Whether moments or millennia ago, the past can feel disconcertingly tenuous, its reality dubious. These doubts shadow all we supposedly know, turning the past into an elusive will-o'-the-wisp.

Reifying the chimerical past

All past events are more remote from our senses than the stars of the remotest galaxies, whose own light at least still reaches the telescopes. George Kubler, 1962[25]

Already a fictitious past occupies in our memories the place of another, a past of which we know nothing with certainty – not even that it is false.

Jorge Luis Borges, 1961[26]

Memory, history, and relics continually furnish awareness of the past. But how far do they reflect what actually happened? The past is gone, its parity with things now seen, recalled, or read about ever problematic. No statement about the past can be confirmed by examining the supposed facts. In a philosopher's summation, 'Only what can be observed can be known. Only what is present can be observed. Nothing past can be present. Therefore, nothing past can be known.'[27]

Because knowing occurs only in the present, cautioned C. I. Lewis, '*no* theoretically sufficient verification of any past fact can ever be hoped for'.[28] Neither observation nor experiment can authenticate it. Unlike geographically remote places that we could visit if we made the effort, the past is utterly beyond reach. Only metaphorically is the past a foreign country. Present facts known by hearsay or indirectly can perhaps be verified; past facts by their very nature cannot.

To name or to think of things past seems to imply their existence, but they do not exist; we have only present evidence of past circumstances. 'The past simply as past is wholly unknowable', concluded Collingwood; 'it is the past as residually preserved in the present that is alone knowable.' A persisting past would be a 'limbo, where events which have finished happening still go on'; it would imply 'a world where Galileo's weight is still falling, where the smoke of Nero's Rome still fills the intelligible air, and where interglacial man is still laboriously learning to chip flints'.[29]

From the past's absence two doubts ensue: that anything like the generally accepted past happened; and if it did, that it can ever be truly known. I treat these doubts in turn.

---

[25] George Kubler, *The Shape of Time* (1962; Yale, 2008), 72.
[26] Jorge Luis Borges, 'Tlön, Uqbar, Orbis Tertius' (1961), in *Labyrinths* (Penguin, 1970), 27–43 at 42–3.
[27] Edward J. Bond, 'The concept of the past', *Mind* 72 (1963): 533–44 at 535.
[28] Clarence Irving Lewis, *An Analysis of Knowledge and Valuation* (1946; Read Books, 1998), 200.
[29] R. G. Collingwood, 'The limits of historical knowledge', *Journal of Philosophical Studies* 3 (1928): 213–22 at 220–1.

Did events we believe took place actually happen? Perhaps a fictitious past occupies our memories, as Borges speculated. We may be deceived like L. Ron Hubbard's SF simulacra, who only '*thought* they remembered long pasts and ancestors'.[30] Historical records and memories may delude us into supposing a lengthy past. The planet could have been created five minutes ago, Bertrand Russell surmised, with a population that 'remembered' an illusory past.[31] A writer imagines a newspaper found in the fossilized jaws of a 70-million-year-old tyrannosaurus in Cretaceous strata, showing that 'the universe was in fact created at about five past nine this morning and whoever did it slipped up by leaving this copy of *The Times* lying around'.[32]

These hypothetical new-made worlds differ only in recency and brevity from sacred doctrine. Accomplished in six 'days', the Creation was calculated by Archbishop James Ussher to broad agreement on 23 October 4004 BC.[33] The six millennia usually allotted then sufficed all known events; geologically innocent seventeenth-century scholars felt no deficiency of previous time. Even today biblical literalists compress the known past into six millennia. They dismiss rock and fossil evidence of earlier existence as spurious and impious: seemingly antediluvian erosions and successions were part of the single act of Creation.

God '*doubtless did create the world with all the marks of antiquity and completeness which it now exhibits*', including 'both venerable forests and young plantations', and animals 'some full of days, others adorned with the graces of infancy', argued Chateaubriand. Why? Because 'if the world had not been at the same time young and old, the grand, the serious, the moral, would have been banished from the face of nature ... Every scene would have lost its wonders'.[34] But geology and palaeontology made the orthodox view increasingly hard to sustain; everywhere signs surfaced of a terrestrial past both far more ancient and far less familiar than Eden.[35]

In a famed defence of biblical chronology, naturalist Philip Henry Gosse contended that the newly created Adamic Earth displayed only *ostensible* pre-existence. Gosse's *Omphalos* (1857) was dismissed as risible.[36] But its argument prefigures Bertrand Russell's scepticism. Gosse admitted that the *historical* past had existed, for men who wrote about events they themselves had seen left direct witness of it. But *pre*history left no such accounts; no one was there to see and record it. Evidence from fossils, geological strata, and living tissues lacked eyewitness reliability.

No one ... declares he actually saw the living *Pterodactyle* flying about, or heard the winds sighing in the tops of the *Lepidodendra*. You will say, 'It is the same thing; we have seen the skeleton of the one, and the crushed trunk of the other, and therefore we are as sure of their past existence as if we

[30] L. Ron Hubbard, *Typewriter in the Sky* (1940; Fantasy, 1952), 60.
[31] Bertrand Russell, *The Analysis of Mind* (Allen & Unwin, 1921), 159.
[32] Karl Sabbagh, *New Statesman*, 11 Aug. 1967: 183.
[33] James Ussher, *Annales veteris testament, à primâ Mundi origine deducti* (London, 1650), 1.
[34] François-René de Chateaubriand, *The Genius of Christianity* (1802; Baltimore, 1871), 136.
[35] Martin J. S. Rudwick, *Bursting the Limits of Time* (Chicago, 2005), and *Worlds before Adam* (Chicago, 2008).
[36] Ann Thwaite, *Glimpses of the Wonderful: The Life of Philip Henry Gosse* (Faber & Faber, 2002), 222–3.

had been there at the time'. No, it is ... not quite the same thing [for] only by a process of reasoning [do] you infer they lived at all.[37]

By extension, 'the sequence of cause and effect ... would inevitably lead us to the eternity of all existing organic life'. And that would be nonsense. Everything including fossils, 'ancient' rock strata, and the apparent progenitors of all living things must at *some* point have been created.[38]

Every living thing evinced seeming pre-existence – the rings of trees, the human navel – which at the moment of Creation must have been 'false', reasoned Gosse. 'The "cuttle-bone" is an autographic record, indubitably genuine, of the Cuttlefish's history. Yes, it is certainly genuine; it is as certainly autographic: but it is *not true*. That Cuttle has been this day created.'[39] A deity who gave newly made creatures a factitious appearance of prior existence might be held perverse – 'God hid the fossils in the rocks in order to tempt geologists into infidelity' was the memorable gibe[40] – but it was not so, Gosse countered: 'Were the concentric timber-rings of a created tree formed merely to deceive? ... Was the navel of the created Man intended to deceive him into the persuasion that he had had a parent?' No, they were so made because the Creator decided to call the globe into existence 'exactly as it would have appeared at that moment of its history, if all the preceding eras of its history had been real'.[41]

Notwithstanding Gosse's faith in eyewitness accounts, his reasoning impeached the historical past as well. Had God chosen to create the world not in 4004 BC but in AD 1857 (Gosse's present), it would nonetheless appear full of 'evidence' of a past:

houses half-built; castles fallen into ruins; pictures on artists' easels just sketched in; wardrobes filled with half-worn garments; ships sailing over the sea; marks of birds' footsteps on the mud; skeletons whitening the desert sands; human bodies in every stage of decay in the burial grounds. These and millions of other traces of the past would be found, *because they are found in the world now* ... They are inseparable from the condition of the world at the selected moment of irruption into its history; ... they make it what it is.[42]

In short, the historical past was as illusory as the prehistoric.

Faith-based argument is untestable, hence irrefutable by observation. To deny the historical past, however, raises more formidable objections. A world created during supposedly historical times would falsify not just some but *all* chronicles, with dire implications for all credence. To disavow every account of the past, to doubt the veracity or the sanity of all who had painstakingly observed and documented *what had not happened* would discredit our own sanity and veracity as well. Russell's extension of

---

[37] Philip Henry Gosse, *Omphalos: An Attempt to Untie the Geological Knot* (London, 1857), 337, 104.
[38] Ibid., 338.
[39] Ibid., 239.
[40] Charles Kingsley to P. H. Gosse, 4 May 1858, paraphrased in Edmund Gosse, *Father and Son* (1907; Heinemann, 1964), 67, 105.
[41] Gosse, *Omphalos*, 347–8, 351. See Jorge Luis Borges, 'The Creation and P. H. Gosse' (1941), in *Other Inquisitions 1937–1952* (New York, 1966), 22–5; Thwaite, *Glimpses of the Wonderful*, 214–27; Geoffrey Cubitt, *History and Memory* (Manchester, 2007), 66–7.
[42] Gosse, *Omphalos*, 352–3.

Gosse's premise to a Creation just five minutes old posits the falsity not merely of all historical evidence, but also of our own memories; had the past begun only five minutes ago, all our recollections would be illusory.[43]

Would it make any difference had there been no past? Would we not behave just as we do anyway? 'What matters ... is not what my past actually was, or even whether I had one', argues a subjectivist; 'it is only the *memories* I have now which matter, be they false or true'.[44] But in fact nothing would be the same. Tradition would be farcical. None would heed the consequences of their actions. No one would apprehend wrongdoers were there no past when their crimes had been committed. Effects could not be traced back to causes, nor behaviour to motives. Nothing could be proved, for 'to doubt our sense of past experience as founded in actuality, would be to lose any criterion by which either the doubt itself or what is doubted could be corroborated; and to erase altogether the distinction between empirical fact and fantasy'.[45] Scepticism this extreme puts all reality in doubt, and ends in know-nothing solipsism.

Few are so sceptical. Nonetheless, the past's empirical absence leaves more than a grain of doubt. We 'take on faith the unproven events of unproven years', wrote Ray Bradbury. 'The reality, even of the immediate past, is irretrievable ... For all the reality of ruins and scrolls and tablets, we fear that much of what we read has been made up.'[46] Deluged by fabrications, we are dismayed by their increasing ease and ready acceptance in everything from memory and history to designer clothes and drugs.[47] False Memory Syndrome – insinuating invented memories of child abuse into the minds not only of alleged victims but of accused perpetrators – is discussed below. Prosthetic memories implanted from film, from virtual worlds, and from interactive museums compete with our own memories, and eventually become indistinguishable from them.[48] In the 1990 film *Total Recall*, a travel agency implants 'memories' of virtual trips to Mars.[49]

To expunge the real and implant a false past is a common despotic ruse. Two cautionary tales convey the ensuing sense of helpless unreality. Orwell's Big Brother rules the present by controlling the past. Since 'past events ... have no objective existence, but survive only in written records and in human memories', it follows that 'the past is whatever the records and the memories agree upon, [hence] whatever the Party chooses to make it ... Recreated in whatever shape is needed at the moment, ... this new version *is* the past, and no different past can ever have existed.' To secure the Party's infallibility, 'the past, starting from yesterday, has been actually abolished ... Nothing exists except an

[43] Stephen Jay Gould, 'Adam's navel' (1984), in *The Flamingo's Smile* (Norton, 1985), 99–113 at 110–11; Arthur C. Danto, *Analytical Philosophy of History* (Cambridge, 1965), 66–84; Russell, *Analysis of Mind*.
[44] Henry H. Price, *Thinking and Experience*, 2nd edn (London, 1969), 84.
[45] Lewis, *Analysis of Knowledge and Valuation*, 358.
[46] Ray Bradbury, 'The machine-tooled happyland: Disneyland', *Holiday* 38:4 (1965): 100–4 at 102.
[47] Tim Phillips, *Knockoff: The Deadly Trade in Counterfeit Goods* (Kogan Page, 2005); 'The spread of counterfeiting', *Economist*, 4 Mar. 2010.
[48] Alison Landsberg, *Prosthetic Memory* (Columbia, 2004), 28, 40–2.
[49] Based on Philip K. Dick, 'We can remember it for you wholesale' (1966), in *Collected Short Stories* (Gollancz, 2000), 5: 157–74.

endless present.' Orwell's inquisitor uses Gosse's reasoning to undermine Winston's faith in an ancient past:

'The earth is as old as we are, no older. How could it be older? Nothing exists except through human consciousness.'

'But the rocks are full of the bones of extinct animals – mammoths and mastodons and enormous reptiles which lived here long before man was ever heard of.'

'Have you ever seen those bones, Winston? Of course not. Nineteenth-century biologists invented them. Before man there was nothing.'[50]

Restoring a landscape to erase evidence of previous devastation is the theme of David Ely's 'Time out'. To ensure that no one will remember the Cold War nuclear accident that wiped out Britain decades earlier, an American–Soviet task force is recreating 'every stick and stone, ... every blade of grass, every hedge and bush, every mansion, palace, hut and hovel. *Everything*', along with archival and reliquary evidence of Britain's entire past – including events that would later have occurred had there been no catastrophe. Dragooned into helping build this fiction, the historian Gull objects that people are bound to find out what actually happened:

'What are they supposed to think when they see the construction squads putting up Blenheim Palace ... ?'

'They'll think like true-born Englishmen, Gull, because they'll have been reared that way. If the history books and the teachers tell them that Blenheim was completed in 1722, that is the date they will accept, regardless of the evidence of their eyes.'

'Brainwashing.'

'Possibly. But that's the way the young always have been brought up. You and I too, Gull. Why do we accept 1722 for Blenheim?'

'Because it's true ... or was true.'

'Because we've been trained to accept it.'

The completed re-creation leads Gull to wonder whether 'perhaps it had all happened before. Suppose this were the second time ... or the tenth? The England they were so diligently copying now, that might have been bogus too.'[51] Historical forgeries abound; could not the entire past be a contrivance?

For all our progress towards recovering and understanding the past, the doubts of Gosse and Orwell and Ely still haunt us. That history is dubious, indeed deeply counter-intuitive, is clear from schoolchildren's views of the past as unknowable. 'No-one knows', says ten-year-old Claire. 'Nobody alive today was there so nobody knows.'[52] 'Knowing the past', as Kubler says, 'is as astonishing a performance as knowing the stars'. It remains no less elusive when minutely documented. 'The past is a foreign country, but it is an unvisitable and unconquerable foreign country', concludes a historian.[53]

---

[50] George Orwell, *Nineteen Eighty-Four* (1948; Penguin, 1954), 179, 126–7, 213.

[51] David Ely, 'Time out', in *Time Out* (Secker & Warburg, 1968), 80–132 at 90, 104, 130–1.

[52] Peter Lee, 'Understanding history', in Peter Seixas, ed., *Theorizing Historical Consciousness* (Toronto, 2004), 129–64 at 135, 154.

[53] Kubler, *Shape of Time*, 17; Alan Megill, *Historical Knowledge, Historical Error* (Chicago, 2007), 213.

The past's existential uncertainty makes us all the more anxious to certify that things were as reputed. For assurance of yesteryear's knowability, we immerse ourselves among explicit bygone details, tangible affirmations of memory and history. Aficionados of the past like to suppose that those who lived back then wanted *us* to know how real it was. 'They took time to record their observations and feelings', viewers in 1978 were told of nineteenth-century Colorado pioneers' diaries, 'leaving us records of their most intimate thoughts'. They chronicled their lives for us to know them.

Yet all the while we suspect the past was not *quite* as real as the present, since it is not similarly knowable. The past *is* L. P. Hartley's foreign country, where they do things differently. Were the Victorians really like that? asks Virginia Woolf's Isa. 'I don't believe that there ever were such people', replies old Mrs Swithin, 'only you and me and William dressed differently'. William rightly retorts, 'You don't believe in history.'[54] History was far stranger than in dress alone. Against the habitual perception of early-modern grandees as '"just like us", with mentalities like modern Whitehall bureaucrats', a historical archaeologist finds that 'the more I think about who sixteenth-century people thought they were, the more alien their identities seem to me'.[55] Reproved for 'classing together, as subjects equally belonging to a past time, Oedipus and Macbeth', Matthew Arnold retorted that 'the European mind, since Voltaire, was as remote from the times of Macbeth [as from] those of Oedipus. As moderns … we have no longer any direct affinity with the circumstances and feelings of either … Alcestis or Joan of Arc, Charlemagne or Agamemnon – one of these is not really nearer to us now than another; each can be made present only by an act of poetic imagination.'[56]

Arnold's distress at the past's obscurity pales next to Carlyle's anguish at the utter obliteration of the age of Cromwell – an anguish compounded by the unsorted, unedited, unindexed fifty thousand Civil War pamphlets mouldering in the British Museum basement, memorable 'at the rate of perhaps one pennyweight per ton', and aggravated by modern agnosticism.

Overwhelmed under … the wreck and dead ashes of some six unbelieving generations, does the Age of Cromwell and his Puritans lie hidden from us. Our common spiritual notions … are fatal to a right understanding of the Seventeenth Century. The Christian Doctrines which then dwelt alive in every heart, have now … died out of all hearts … The Age of the Puritans is not extinct only and gone away from us; … it is grown unintelligible, what we may call incredible. Its earnest Purport awakens now no resonance in our frivolous hearts. … It seems delirious, delusive.

Such was indeed the case with every past. All history was

by very nature … a labyrinth and chaos, … a world-wide jungle, at once growing and dying. Under the green foliage and blossoming fruit-trees of Today there lie, rotting slower or faster, the

[54] L. P. Hartley, *The Go Between* (London, 1953); Virginia Woolf, *Between the Acts* (1941; Hogarth, 1965), 174–5.

[55] Matthew Johnson, 'Reconstructing castles and refashioning identities in Renaissance England', in Sarah Tarlow and Susie West, eds., *The Familiar Past* (Routledge, 1999), 69–86 at 84.

[56] Matthew Arnold, *The Poems of Matthew Arnold* (London, 1909), Preface, at 16–17.

forests of all other Years and Days. . . . All past centuries have rotted down, and gone confusedly dumb and quiet, even as that Seventeenth is now threatening to do.[57]

Moreover, what is now 'the past' was not what anyone ever experienced as 'the present'. In some respects we know it better than those who lived it; we sense 'the past in a way and to an extent which the past's awareness of itself cannot show', wrote T. S. Eliot.[58] We interpret the ongoing present while living through it, whereas we stand outside the past and view its finished operation – including its now known consequences for whatever was then the future. Old fen drainings become one phase in a series of successive reclamations; retrospective exhibitions show a painter's early work prefiguring his later; subsequent impacts on offspring, political heirs, scientific successors throw new light on careers long since ended.

Loss and bias make our capacity to perceive the past deeply deficient. The surviving residues of former thoughts and things represent a tiny fraction of previous generations' contemporary fabric. As participants in ongoing events, we are well aware 'that this event, as it will be inscribed in history, will be only a part of what it has been for us in the present'.[59] Empowered by hindsight, we remake people of the past into our own creations. Subjects of biographies seem 'miraculously sealed as in a magic tank', felt Woolf. 'They thought when they were alive that they could go where they liked. [But] look and listen and soon the little figures . . . will begin to move and to speak, and . . . we shall arrange them in all sorts of patterns of which they were ignorant.'[60] Our manipulation betrays their impotence. 'The past, because it is past, is only malleable where once it was flexible', in Jeanette Winterson's distinction. 'Once it could change its mind, now it can only undergo change.'[61] And the change is induced by us.

Memory feels as residual as history. However voluminous our recollections, they are mere fragmentary glimpses of what was a whole living realm. However vividly reproduced, the past becomes progressively shadowy, bereft of sensation, effaced by death. 'Recognition does not always give us back the warmth of the past', writes Simone de Beauvoir; 'we lived it in the present . . . and all that is left is a skeleton'. A long-ago scene recalled is 'like a butterfly pinned in a glass case: the characters no longer move in any direction. Their relationships are numbed, paralysed.' Beauvoir's own 'past is not a peaceful landscape lying there behind me, a country in which I can stroll wherever I please . . . As I was moving forward, so it was crumbling.' Time's erosion afflicts the memories she retains: 'The wreckage that can still be seen is colourless, distorted, frozen; its meaning escapes me.'[62]

[57] Thomas Carlyle, 'Introduction: anti-dryasdust', in *Oliver Cromwell's Letters and Speeches* (1845), in *The Works of Thomas Carlyle* (Cambridge, 2010), 6: 1–11.
[58] T. S. Eliot, 'Tradition and the individual talent' (1917), in *Selected Essays* (Faber & Faber, 1934), 13–22 at 16.
[59] Eugène Minkowski, *Lived Time* (1933; Northwestern University Press, 1970), 167.
[60] Virginia Woolf, 'I am Christina Rossetti' (1930), in *The Common Reader: Second Series* (Hogarth, 1932), 237–44 at 237.
[61] Jeanette Winterson, *Oranges Are Not the Only Fruit* (Grove, 1985), 95.
[62] Simone de Beauvoir, *Old Age* (1970; Penguin, 1977).

The certainty of today makes yesterday tenuous. 'The main reason why the past is so weak is the extraordinary strength of the present', suggests a classicist.

To try now to achieve a real 'sense of the past' is like looking out of a brilliantly lit room at dusk. There seems to be something out there in the garden, the uncertain forms of trees stirring in the breeze, the hint of a path, perhaps the glimmer of water. Or is there merely a picture painted on the window, like the Furies in Eliot's play? Is there nothing out there at all and is the lit room the only reality?[63]

Time occludes the known past. Reducing and corroding its residues, temporal distance leaves previous modes of perception likewise beyond reach. 'The participant understands and knows his culture with an [irrecoverable] immediacy and spontaneity', writes Michael Baxandall of the Italian Renaissance patron. 'He moves with ease and delicacy and flexibility within the rules of his culture ... learned, informally, since infancy.' The modern observer five centuries later 'has to spell out standards and rules, making them explicit and so ... also coarse, rigid and clumsy'. We like to feel we 'know' the past because many of its remains, especially beloved works of art, are familiar features of our mental landscapes. To grasp the historical disparity of this 'terrible carapace of false familiarity' we must realize how alien were the minds that made them.[64] It is the historian's task to 'destroy our false sense of proximity to people of the past ... The more we discover about [their] mental universe, the more we should be shocked by the cultural distance that separates us from them.'[65]

Linguistic survivals often mislead us into seeing a spurious likeness. The word 'artificial' is today a slur denoting the second-rate. But in 1610 a composer was praised as 'the most artificiall and famous Alfonso Ferrabosco'.[66] Time has reversed the meaning of artificial from 'full of deep skill and art' to 'shallow, contrived, and almost worthless'. We should be wary of *anything* from the past that appears familiar.

Painstaking retrievals and restorations further deceive us. We meticulously recreate past scenes and artefacts, even past sounds and smells – a stage set true to the Field of the Cloth of Gold in every sumptuous detail, the scratchy roughness of a linsey-woolsey garment, the exact hammer tone of an ancient anvil, the precise ingredients of twelfth-century food or sixteenth-century dung. But twenty-first-century sensory organs cannot see, feel, hear, taste, or smell old things as they first were. Time distances how the past is sensed as well as things sensed. The olfactory gulf between our deodorized world and richly scented antiquity, not to mention the medieval 'odour of sanctity', today makes unimaginable Antiphanes' Greek, his feet and legs anointed with Egyptian unguents, his jaws and breasts with palm oil, arms with mint extract, eyebrows and hair with marjoram,

[63] D. S. Carne-Ross, 'Scenario for a new year: 3. The sense of the past', *Arion: A Journal of the Humanities and the Classics* 8 (1969): 230–60 at 241. The vengeful Furies animate T. S. Eliot's *Family Reunion* (Faber & Faber, 1939).

[64] Michael Baxandall, *Patterns of Intention: On the Historical Explanation of Pictures* (Yale, 1985), 109, 115–16.

[65] Carlo Ginzburg interview, in Jonathan Kandell, 'Was the world made out of cheese?' *NYT Magazine*, 17 Nov. 1991: 47.

[66] John Dowland, *Varietie of Lute-lessons* (London, 1610), 39.

knees and neck with thyme.[67] 'What was rank and fetid to a 10th-century Viking's nostril is not recoverable today, not only because that world has evaporated' but because ten centuries of changing odours have denatured the modern nose.[68] 'How a lemon tastes is contingent on the tongue doing the licking.' Taste buds today jaded by extreme flavours – sugar cookies, Mexican chillies – can hardly savour subtle Georgian rose petals.[69]

Colonial Williamsburg's 'eighteenth-century sounds' are contaminated by the rumble of jet planes, the whooshing of highway traffic. Moreover, they are heard as novelties, not as accustomed noises. Music made centuries ago can never be experienced as it was initially: no ears that have heard a Verdi opera can hear a Monteverdi opera as did seventeenth-century auditors. No eyes that have seen Frank Gehry's buildings can ever see ancient or Renaissance architecture in the way anyone did when built, for subsequent scenes accustom us to other optics. We can glimpse something of past sensory worlds, but remain in the dark about how they were once felt.

Dubious owing to its very absence, inaccessible yet intimately known, the character of the past depends on how – and how much – it is consciously apprehended. How is such awareness acquired, and how does it shape our understanding?

---

[67] Constance Classen et al., *Aroma: The Cultural History of Smell* (Routledge, 1994; 2003), 5–6, 13, 17, citing Antiphanes' *Thoracians* (4th century BC).

[68] Rachel Herz, 'The influence of odors on mood and affective cognition', in Catherine Rouby et al., eds., *Olfaction, Taste and Cognition* (Cambridge, 2002), 160–77; Mark M. Smith, *Sensing the Past: Seeing, Hearing, Smelling, Tasting and Touching in History* (California, 2007), 120–5. See Mark S. R. Jenner, 'Follow your nose? Smell, smelling, and their histories', *AHR* 116 (2011): 335–51.

[69] Marc Meltonville (Historic Kitchens) cited in Lauren Collins, 'The king's meal', *New Yorker*, 21 Nov. 2011: 66–71 at 71. See Priscilla Parkhurst Ferguson, 'The senses of taste', *AHR* 116 (2011): 371–84 at 373.

7

Memory

The poor, short, lone fact dies at the birth: Memory snatches it up into her heaven, and bathes it in immortal waters. Then a thousand times over it lives and acts again, each time transfigured, ennobled.   Ralph Waldo Emerson, 1857[1]

The present ... is ever closely bound up with the past, and the cord which unites them is all woven of strands of memory... On the soundness of that cord we often hang honour, love, faith, justice, things more precious than life itself. Our reluctance to test its strength [is] as senseless as that of Alpine travellers who should refuse to try the rope ... to support them over the abyss.   Frances Power Cobbe, 1866[2]

When I was younger I could remember anything, whether it happened or not, but I am getting old, and soon I shall remember only the latter.   Mark Twain, c. 1908[3]

The past is what you remember, imagine you remember, convince yourself you remember, or pretend to remember.   Harold Pinter[4]

Memories are *forever*.   Lois Lowry, 1993[5]

All past awareness depends on memory. Recollection recovers consciousness of former events, distinguishes yesterday from today, and confirms that we have a past. Indeed, remembering objects, events, patterns, and people, concludes a developmental psychologist, 'is the sine qua non of cognition'.[6] And mnemonic effort – recalling people to be seen, things to be done, routes to be taken – secures the future via the past.[7]

Yet how memory works and gets verified, saved, and altered remains, after a century and a half of research, much misunderstood. Memory experts – neurologists, psychologists, teachers, trial lawyers, autobiographers, gerontologists – have only begun to converse with one another. Brain-storage areas and synapses that conduct memories, arts of memorizing, the sediment of emotional recall, the fallibility of eyewitnesses, amnesia's causes and consequences were each studied in virtual isolation.

---

[1] Ralph Waldo Emerson, 'Memory' (1857), in *CW*, 12: 63–82 at 71.
[2] Frances P. Cobbe, 'Fallacies of memory' (1866), in *Hours of Work and Play* (London, 1867), 87–113 at 88–9.
[3] Albert Bigelow Paine, 'Prefatory note', in *Mark Twain: A Biography* (Harper, 1912), 1: 1.
[4] Thomas P. Adler, 'Pinter's *Night*: a stroll down memory lane', *Modern Drama* 17 (1974): 461–5 at 462.
[5] Lois Lowry, *The Giver* (1993; HarperCollins, 2003), 177.
[6] Michael Tomasello, *The Cultural Origins of Human Cognition* (Harvard, 1999), 124.
[7] Judi A. Ells and Gillian Cohen, 'Memory for intentions, actions, and plans', in Gillian Cohen and Martin A. Conway, eds., *Memory in the Real World*, 3rd edn (Hove: Psychology, 2008), 141–72; D. L. Schacter et al., 'Remembering the past to imagine the future', *Nature Reviews Neuroscience* 8 (2008): 657–61; Dennis Hassabis et al., 'Imagine all the people: how the brain creates and uses personality models to predict behavior', *Cerebral Cortex* 23 (2013): 1726–31.

Until recent decades, everyday uses of memory went largely neglected. Short-term recall of the very recent past and of word and number tests – topics suited to replicable, value-free laboratory analysis – pre-empted psychologists' attention. So arcane was the discipline that Ulric Neisser, everyday memory pioneer, declared in 1978 that 'if X is an interesting or socially significant aspect of memory, then psychologists have hardly ever studied X'.[8] Virtually unchallenged, Neisser's charge stimulated major change, bridging academic and popular concerns.

What *does* interest people about memory is a congeries of topics: efforts to recall childhood, trouble remembering names or dates, reciting poetry by heart, how the old home has changed after thirty years' absence, discrepancies between one's own memory and other people's, the pleasure or sorrow of reminiscence, the malfunctions of computer recall, memory loss in old age. On such matters psychology up to the early 1980s was all but silent. Insight into memory's general uses came more from novelists, historians, and psychoanalysts.

Just when this book's precursor first appeared, public memory concerns began to spur relevant and accessible research. A mere decade after Neisser's charge of irrelevance, he reversed it: 'if X is an interesting or socially significant aspect of memory, some psychologist is probably trying to study it at this moment'. It had been hard to find enough pertinent material for the first edition of Neisser's path-breaking *Memory Observed*; for the second edition eighteen years later it was hard to choose among so many important essays.[9]

Yet public perceptions remain plagued by persisting false stereotypes. Memory is popularly seen as matter permanently stored in the mind and somehow retrievable. 'They can take away fifty feet of your intestines', says an elderly man, 'but they can't take away fifty seconds of your memory'.[10] That memories are permanent, immutable, accurate, and record like a video camera, as if events were imprinted or burned into one's brain, are media-perpetuated shibboleths.[11] A mass of evidence shows, on the contrary, that memory gets continually transformed. Far from being 'fossilized in some dusty forgotten corner of the brain', memory is 'a living network of understanding rather than a dormant warehouse of facts'.[12] Memory traces are stored in tissues and transmitted along synapses that change, grow, and decay.

---

[8] Ulric Neisser, 'Memory: what are the important questions?' (1978), in Ulric Neisser, ed., *Memory Observed: Remembering in Natural Contexts* (San Francisco: Freeman, 1982), 3–19 at 4–5.

[9] Ulric Neisser, 'New vistas in the study of memory', in his and Eugene Winograd, eds., *Remembering Reconsidered* (Cambridge, 1988), 1–10 at 2; Ulric Neisser, 'Preface', in his and Ira E. Hyman, eds., *Memory Observed*, 2nd edn (New York: Worth, 2000), xiii. See Ulric Neisser, 'A case of misplaced nostalgia' (1991), in Neisser and Hyman, *Memory Observed*, 28–40 at 28–32; Lia Kvavilashvili and Judi Ellis, 'Ecological validity and the real life/laboratory controversy in memory research', *History and Philosophy of Psychology* 6 (2004): 59–80; Charles Fernyhough, *Pieces of Light: The New Science of Memory* (London: Profile, 2012).

[10] Quoted in Thomas J. Cottle and Stephen L. Klineberg, *The Present of Things Future: Explorations of Time in Human Experience* (Free Press, 1974), 49.

[11] Daniel J. Simons and Christopher F. Chabris, 'What people believe about how memory works', *PloS One* 6 (8): e22757, 3 Aug. 2011, and 'Common (mis) beliefs about memory', *PloS One* 7(12): e51876, 18 Dec. 2012; Svein Magnussen et al., 'What do people believe about memory and how do they talk about memory?', in Svein Magnussen and Tore Helstrup, eds., *Everyday Memory* (New York: Psychology Press, 2007), 5–26. 'Instant expert memory', *New Scientist*, 3 Dec. 2011: cover and i–viii, confirms the myth.

[12] John McCrone, 'Not so total recall', *New Scientist*, 3 May 2003: 26–9.

That fixing a memory ensures its permanence and stability is a hoary enduring myth. 'Memory is neither an impression made, once for all ... nor yet safe for an hour from obliteration or modification', noted an essayist as early as 1866. Nothing like an engraved tablet, 'rather is memory a finger-mark traced on shifting sand'. Efforts to save it intact are doomed; in T. S. Eliot's doleful metaphor, 'there's no memory you can wrap in camphor but the moths will get in'.[13]

And recollection continually distances the original. Indeed, removal from short-term to long-term storage transforms memory's very nature. And every subsequent recall reconforms it to later experience and memories. Never faithful to the original trace, it departs from it ever further. 'Memory is not at all like a videotape recording' and retaining events. As Frederic C. Bartlett showed eighty years ago, 'it is more like a group of people playing Chinese whispers: each successive recall introduces new errors and distortions'.[14] Memory does not passively record the past but actively – and errantly – reconstructs it.

In sum, the recollected past departs ever further from the original experience, creative misremembering mounting with every recall. No scientist now accepts Henri Bergson's view that memory conserves the entire past, or Wilder Penfield's that every apprehended event can be reconstituted. On the contrary, time brings wholesale loss, increase, and change. Research confirms Jean Piaget and Barbël Inhelder's classic statement that 'throughout our life, we reorganize our memories and ideas of the past ... adding other elements' that change its meaning and significance.[15]

Habit, recall, memento, reverie

Recollection pervades life. We devote much of the present to getting or keeping in touch with things past. Few waking hours are devoid of recall; save among amnesiacs, only intense concentration on some immediate pursuit prevents the past coming unbidden to mind. Lacking memory, amnesiacs suffer vacancy. 'I felt nothing', a patient recalled years deprived of recollection; 'when you have no memory, you have no feelings'.[16] The loss destroys personality and voids life of meaning. Gabriel García Márquez's *One Hundred Years of Solitude* depicts an amnesiac's mounting plight: 'The recollection of his childhood began to be erased from his memory, then the name and notion of things, and finally the identity of people, and even the awareness of his own being ... until he sank

---

[13] Cobbe, 'Fallacies of memory', 104; T. S. Eliot, *The Cocktail Party* (Harcourt, Brace, 1950), 47.
[14] David R. Shanks quoted in Patrick Hosking, 'Memory expert attacks results in survey on L[egal] & G[eneral] customers', *Times*, 13 Oct. 2004; and Shanks to author, 18 Oct. 2008; Frederic C. Bartlett, *Remembering* (1932; Cambridge, 1995). See P. J. Eakin, 'Autobiography, identity, and the fictions of memory', in Daniel L. Schacter and Elaine Scarry, eds., *Memory, Brain, and Belief* (Harvard, 2000), 290–306 at 291; Eric R. Kandel, *In Search of Memory* (Norton, 2006), 132, 275–6.
[15] Henri Bergson, *Matter and Memory* (1896; Dover, 2004), 192–5; Wilder Penfield, see p. 59 above; Jean Piaget and Bärbel Inhelder, *Memory and Intelligence* (1968; Routledge, 1973), 381; Douwe Draaisma, *The Nostalgia Factory: Memory, Time and Ageing* (Yale, 2013), viii.
[16] Marjorie Wallace, 'The drug that gave this man his memory back', *Sunday Times*, 24 Apr. 1983: 13. The classic amnesiac is A. R. Luria, *The Mind of a Mnemonist* (Harvard, 1968) and *The Man with a Shattered World* (Harvard, 1972).

into a kind of idiocy that had no past.'[17] Deprived by the Muses even of sensory habit, in
Voltaire's cautionary fable, humans forget how to eat and excrete.[18]

Memories occupy a hierarchy of habit, recall, and memento. Habitual memory comprises all mental residues of past acts and thoughts, whether or not consciously remembered. Recall, less voluminous, involves awareness of past occurrences and states of being.
Mementoes are salvaged from the mass of recollections. Out of a vast array of potential
mnemonic aids we select a few reminders. Our working memory collection is in continual
flux, fresh keepsakes being added, old ones discarded, some newly surfacing to awareness,
others sinking beneath conscious note. Memories of all kinds accumulate with age. The
stock of things recallable grows as life lengthens and experiences multiply, until scatty
senescence sets in.

Memories are as multiform as a philosopher's compendium suggests:

I remember where – as a child – I used to swing, and I remember the feel of the air rushing by my
face. I remember who beat Napoleon at Waterloo, and I remember that 8 × 9 is 72. I haven't
forgotten how to swing a bat; and I remember – no, I feel it again in the weakness in my legs and
wrists and in the nausea in my stomach – the terror I felt when the captain made me a 'volunteer'
on the first search and destroy mission in the Ashau Valley. I remember the party we had when
I got married – the music, the friends, the food, the wine.[19]

Not all these memories offer insight into the past: we walk, write, brush our teeth,
swing a bat without recalling how or when we learned to do so. Visceral memories
embedded in habitual rituals – saluting, kneeling in prayer, applauding a performance –
reflect the past not by affirming its pastness but by continuing to perform it in the
present. What was learned becomes automatic and unconscious. In Marcel Proust's
phrase, 'our arms and legs are full of torpid memories'.[20] Recognizing a friend does not
summon up the former meetings that made recognition possible. Reciting a poem does
not remind me when or how I learned it. Semantic drill – memorizing multiplication
tables, lines of verse, structures of amino acids, national capitals, stores of words and
facts – sheds no light on the past. To be sure, many memorized facts are themselves
historical – British sovereigns, US presidents, sequences of significant dates. By fixing
events in time, memorizing helps us to know *about* the past, but knowing, say, that
Washington was president from 1791 to 1799 conveys no *sense* of the past per se.[21]

Sensing the past, however, requires conscious, often self-conscious, recall. Unlike
semantic, list-learning, and visceral memories, recollection concerns significant personal
events and episodes. The past is recalled as a congeries of distinctive occasions, different
enough from the present to know it as another time, similar enough to assure us it is our

---

[17] Gabriel García Márquez, *One Hundred Years of Solitude* (1967; Penguin, 1972), 46.
[18] Voltaire, *Aventure de la mémoire* (1773), in *Oeuvres complètes* (Paris, 1877–85), 21: 479–82.
[19] Paul Brockelman, 'Of memory and things past', *International Philosophical Quarterly* 15 (1975): 309–25
at 309. Americans suffered a disastrous Vietcong defeat in the A Shau valley in 1966.
[20] Marcel Proust, *Remembrance of Things Past* (1913–27; Penguin, 1983), 3: 716. See Paul Connerton, *How
Societies Remember* (Cambridge, 1989), 72–6, 83, 102.
[21] Endel Tulving, *Elements of Episodic Memory* (Oxford, 1982), and 'Episodic memory: from mind to brain',
Annual Review of Psychology 53 (2002): 1–25; Asher Koriat et al., 'Toward a psychology of memory
accuracy', *Annual Review of Psychology* 51 (2000): 481–537 at 510.

own. Such autobiographical memory extends back to periods that pre-date our conscious selves, embracing infantile episodes learned about second hand.

Intensity of recall varies with its purpose. Least evocative is instrumental memory – recalling a name, where we had dinner, when we paid the rent. This resurrects facts, not feelings: 'In what year was I an intern in Lariboisière Hospital? Let's see, it was two years after my sister died; that would be 1911' – how the writer felt about hospital or sister's death plays no part.[22] The past thus retrieved is a barren landscape. In the monolithic plain of past time, bleak calendric pinnacles, the sole survivors of locales once full of life, alone catch our attention. Scenes and events are recalled only for their order and location, as purposeful markers and grids. Such 'memory reflects life as a road with occasional signposts and milestones', in an analyst's metaphor, 'rather than as the landscape through which this road had led'.[23] Devoid of 'the concrete abundance of life', it is the GPS Satnav rather than the Ordnance Survey map. No longer an evocative 'travel over the old stone bridge – built in 1764! – until you see the brick library and Odd Fellows Hall on your right', but bluntly 'head NW on S Main St/MA 1A N .5 miles', a bland command shorn of history and memory.[24]

Children begin sensing and recalling what is there; adults increasingly see and hear what they are expected to and remember what they think they ought to. Maturity thrusts instrumental memory to the fore. That we can recall little of our earliest years in part reflects loss of recollections rarer after childhood. Adult memory schemata usually excise the smells, tastes, and other vivid sensations, along with the magical immediacy, of youth. Memorable impress gives way to 'automatic routine which we hardly note at all' as adults. 'All the days and weeks smooth themselves out', in William James's metaphor, 'and the years grow hollow and collapse'.[25]

Childhood like the past is irretrievable. 'We do not remember childhood – we imagine it. We search for it in vain through layers of obscuring dust, and recover some bedraggled shreds of what we think it was', writes Penelope Lively. Children inhabit 'a world we have lost and can never recover, a world of small unreachable alien creature[s] … with no knowledge of past or future'.[26] With maturity, memories once laden with feeling suffer attrition to become banal: Bartlett's adult subjects reduced the complex stories they were asked to recall to straightforward tales, to render them 'acceptable, understandable, comfortable, straightforward'.[27]

Reverie, by contrast, highlights remembered feelings. Contemplative musing elicits explicit but hazily dreamlike bygone scenes, as in Alain-Fournier's *Le Grand Meaulnes* (1913). To recover a lost impression, to see and feel again what was once vividly experienced, may require deliberate effort at the outset. Then reverie often becomes self-generating. Intense

---

[22] E. Pichon, 'Essai d'étude convergente des problèmes du temps' (1931), quoted in Eugène Minkowski, *Lived Time: Phenomenological and Psychopathological Studies* (1933; Northwestern, 1970), 152.

[23] Ernest G. Schachtel, *Metamorphosis* (New York: Basic Books, 1959), 287.

[24] Renée Loth, 'The first GPS', *IHT*, 20 Aug. 2010: 7.

[25] William James, *Principles of Psychology* (1890), 1: 625.

[26] Penelope Lively, *Moon Tiger* (Deutsch, 1987), 42–3. See Schachtel, *Metamorphosis*, 279–322; Piaget and Inhelder, *Memory and Intelligence*, 378–401.

[27] Bartlett, *Remembering*, 89.

affective memory reveals a past so entrancing – or horrific – it is virtually relived; closing his eyes, a reviewer did not 'remember' the film *Kagemusha* but 'saw it again'.[28] Recalling a youthful Venetian stay, a middle-aged man could 'see the buildings, I hear the talk, I feel the texture of the chair I sat on; . . . I smell the breeze from the bay, hear the cloud of pigeons at my feet; I feel the frustration I felt, and my heart constricts as I "re-await" the arrival of my lover . . . I can sit here in recall and almost lose myself, almost slip into the past'.[29] Summoning up a childhood summer, Brian Friel's protagonist in *Dancing at Lughnasa* finds everything simultaneously actual and illusory, itself and its echo.[30]

Chance reactivation of a forgotten touch or smell or taste or sound commonly yields heightened recollections. Like the Alpine melody for nostalgic Swiss soldiers, the village church bell was William Cowper's trigger:

> Clear and sonorous, as the gale comes on!
> With easy force it opens all the cells
> Where mem'ry slept. Wherever I have heard
> A kindred melody, the scene recurs,
> And with it all its pleasures and its pains.[31]

The 'ancient, unbearable recognition' of Wallace Stegner's prairie past came 'partly from the children and the footbridge and the river's quiet curve, but much more from the smell. For here, pungent and pervasive, is the smell that has always meant my childhood', the compound of water, mud, damp benches, burlap-tipped diving-board, that conjured up the poignant past.[32] The neurologist Oliver Sacks recounts the 'spontaneous, unsolicited rising [of] not merely memories, but frames of mind, thoughts, atmospheres, and passions' of his London boyhood during the Blitz. These intense recollections are involuntary, the more vivid the less open to deliberate retrieval. Desired or dreaded apparitions that come unbidden can devastate as well as delight, painfully re-evoking ancient agony.[33]

The past thus reborn haunts and hypnotizes the present. Thomas De Quincey wrote of a woman who combined total recall with temporal concurrence: 'In a moment, in the twinkling of an eye, every act, every design of her past life, lived again, arraying themselves not as a succession, but as parts of a coexistence.'[34] Like déjà vu (feeling we have already seen what we are seeing for the first time) and *déjà vécu* (feeling we have already done or lived it),

[28] Robert Hatch, 'Films', *Nation*, 15 Nov. 1980: 522.
[29] Brockelman, 'Of memory and things past', 321.
[30] Brian Friel, *Dancing at Lughnasa* (Faber & Faber, 1990). See James McConkey, *The Anatomy of Memory* (Oxford, 1996), 59.
[31] William Cowper, 'The Task' (1785), bk. VI, ll. 10–14, in *Poetical Works* (Oxford, 1934), 220.
[32] Wallace Stegner, *Wolf Willow* (1962; Penguin, 2000), 18. See Douwe Draaisma, *Why Life Speeds Up as You Get Older* (Cambridge, 2004), 31–44; Rachel Herz, 'Odor-evoked memory', in Jean Decety and John T. Cacioppo, eds., *The Oxford Handbook of Neuroscience* (Oxford, 2011), 265–76; Amanda N. Miles and Dorthe Berntsen, 'Odour-induced mental time travel into the past and future', *Memory* 19:8 (Nov. 2011): 930–40.; Chelsea A. Reid et al., 'Scent-evoked nostalgia', *Memory* 23:2 (2015): 157–66.
[33] Oliver Sacks, 'Speak, memory', *NYRB*, 21 Feb. 2013: 19–21. See Tore Helstrup et al., 'Memory pathways: involuntary and voluntary processes in retrieving personal memories', in Magnussen and Helstrup, eds., *Everyday Memory*, 291–316; John H. Mace, ed., *Involuntary Memory* (Blackwell, 2007).
[34] Thomas De Quincey, *Suspira de Profundis* (1845–54; London, 1927), 245.

paramnesia coalesces past and present. Obsessive, often opium-induced, time-collapse migrated from Rousseau to Coleridge, Byron, Blake, and Swedenborg to De Quincey, Baudelaire, and Proust. 'I sometimes seemed to have lived for 70 or 100 years in one night', reported De Quincey; swelling life's narrow span with as many memories as possible, he amplified lived time into an illusion of eternity.[35] Proust's *Recherche du temps perdu* similarly brought the past into the present as no mere 'echo or replica of a past sensation [but] that past sensation itself'.[36] To the poet Robert Lowell during bouts of insanity 'all history became a simultaneous event ... The distinctions of time vanished altogether, and the world was peopled by a series of tyrants and geniuses all jostling with one another.'[37]

Paramnesia conflates past with present – even life with death. Walking in an unfamiliar town in 1928, Borges conjectured his childhood existence there, and then 'the facile thought *I am in eighteen hundred and* ... ceased being a set of approximate words and deepened into a reality. I felt dead, I felt myself an abstract perceiver of the world', unable to separate 'one moment belonging to its apparent past from another belonging to its apparent present'.[38]

Likewise temporally unstuck, a spastic in time, is Kurt Vonnegut's Billy Pilgrim, who went 'to sleep a senile widower and awakened on his wedding day. ... He has seen his birth and death many times, ... and pays random visits to all the events in between ... with no control over where he is going next'. As for De Quincey, 'All moments, past, present and future, always have existed, always will exist'.[39]

Each type of recall supplies a different take on the past. Devoid of affect, instrumental memory's schematized past points towards the all-important present. Autobiographical memory retrieves a significant past lent cogency by what it omits, invents, elides, distorts, and simplifies. But repeated recall tends to transform autobiographical into instrumental memory, just as John Dean's rehearsed Watergate recollections became stable, unchanging, and divorced from sense of self. Reverie recalls particular feelings and evokes comparison of past with present states of being. Total recall immerses us willy-nilly in the past; the present is hag-ridden by previous events relived anew. Eugène Minkowski's wartime recollections exemplify these distinctions: 'Completely different attitudes toward the past are involved when we recount what we did during the war, when we try to relive what we experienced during that torment, and finally, when we feel it still present in the very fibers of our being ... a part of our present even more than the *actual* present.'[40]

---

[35] Thomas De Quincey, *Confessions of an English Opium-Eater* (1822; London: Constable, 1927), 115.

[36] Proust, *Remembrance of Things Past*, 3: 907. See Georges Poulet, 'Timelessness and romanticism', *JHI* 15 (1954): 3–22; Alan S. Brown, *The Déjà Vu Experience* (Psychology Press, 2004); Akira R. O'Conner et al., 'Novel insights into false recollection: a model of déjà vécu', *Cognitive Neuropsychiatry* 15 (2010): 118–44.

[37] Cited by Jonathan Miller (1980), in Ian Hamilton, *Robert Lowell* (Vintage, 1983), 314.

[38] Jorge Luis Borges, 'A new refutation of time' (1946), in *A Personal Anthology* (Jonathan Cape, 1967), 44–64 at 55. Borges's despair echoes Henry James's Pendrel in *The Sense of the Past* (Chapter 2).

[39] Kurt Vonnegut, *Slaughterhouse Five* (1969; Vintage, 2000), 17, 19.

[40] Ulric Neisser, 'John Dean's memory' (1981), in Neisser, ed., *Memory Observed*, 139–59; Minkowski, *Lived Time*, 153. See Helen L. Williams et al., 'Autobiographical memory', in Cohen and Conway, eds., *Memory in the Real World*, 21–90.

These memories are commonly cobbled together. From functional to autobiographical recall, through reverie, to virtual immersion in bygone time, awareness of the past is a multiform memorial continuum. Yet memory however protean seems a distinct category of experience. Remembering the feel of sand at the seashore is quite unlike recalling where we left the house keys or what we were told about life during the Great Depression, but we are conscious that all involve recollection. And they are experienced as an ensemble. Instrumental recall mingles with unbidden recollection; we daydream about last summer's holiday while trying to remember where we put those keys. Recall braids together these disparate threads of memory.

And they do have much in common. All memory transmutes experience, distils the past rather than simply reflecting it. We recall only a small fraction of what has impinged on us, let alone of all the world has displayed. And in the light of new memories and present needs, we select and rework what was initially recalled. Thus memory sifts and resifts what perception had already filtered, leaving amended and embellished fragments of the fragments of things once seen and now gone.

Personal and shared[41]

Memory is innately personal; it is always felt as having happened to *me*, even if, in actuality, it happened to someone else. 'Nothing is so uniquely personal to a man as his memories, and in guarding their privacy we seem almost to be protecting the very basis of our personality.' And our recollections remain private even if we aim to make them public. 'Though we speak of sharing our memories with others', notes a philosopher, 'we could no more share a memory than we could share a pain'.[42]

Innumerable childhood events and feelings remain uncommunicated. The secret language I invented, my fear of the man next door who disliked my dog, the pain of a bee sting, the trauma of breaking my arm are memories of my twelve-year-old self that no one else has. Violation of the private essence of a man's boyhood favourites – baseball star, opera singer, steamboat, ice-cream soda – is the leitmotif of Austin Wright's Michael Morley, whose intrusive doppelgänger reminds him of things Morley is certain he alone should be privy to.[43]

Memories become cherished possessions. Indeed, some prize personal pasts as sacred relics, congratulating themselves on having had the experience they recall. Some memoirists treat their birth 'like a piece of property that they would own in the country, or like a diploma', notes Philippe Lejeune. 'This grounds their entire narrative on an irrefutable

[41] A 'shared' memory is conveyed to or initiated jointly with other individuals, in contradistinction to Maurice Halbwachs's collective or cultural memory (*On Collective Memory*, 1925; Harper & Row, 1980). Personal and shared memories initiate past knowledge and awareness; collective or cultural memories function as aspects of intangible heritage, reshaping history as group myths, traditions, ideals, and *genres de vie*. I discuss these in Chapters 10 and 12.

[42] B. S. Benjamin, 'Remembering', *Mind* 65 (1956): 312–31 at 312.

[43] Austin M. Wright, *The Morley Mythology* (Harper & Row, 1977).

beginning.' Lejeune composed his own autobiography 'to regain control of my life, capture it at its roots, and reconstruct it'.[44]

Death extinguishes utterly personal memories, but those that have been transmitted linger for a time, such as Borges's 'doorway which survived so long as it was visited by a beggar and disappeared at his death' or John Kotre's reiterated recall of his grandfather's suede gloves.[45] The deceased who remain in Swahili memory become completely dead only when the last to have known of them are gone, and this memory may endure for four or five generations.[46]

Mirroring today's sped-up physical disposal of the dead by cremation, Western modernity truncates posthumous memories. 'Generations remain alive only in the flickering memory of a person whose own days are drawing to a close', writes a gerontologist of a lone elderly survivor 'Her mind is . . . the last preserve of all that gone on before in one branch of human existence.' Unable to pass on her inherited recollections, she is devastated by being the 'Last Leaf', for all that past will die with her.[47] Not all regret it, to be sure. Elderly Anna Freud could not bear to share her turmoiled past with the world, 'so I allow myself the privilege of taking it all with me'.[48] Taking memories to the grave safeguards them from sceptical scrutiny, for at the end 'there is no-one but me to say how true they are, and no-one but me to care'.[49]

Memoirs based on recall to which others lack access are not open to correction. A sole survivor is a uniquely privileged witness. Chided for omitting parts of a letter by his brother William from *Notes of a Son and Brother* (1914), Henry James explains that he 'instinctively regard[ed] it at last as all *my* truth, to do what I would with'. The brothers' letters were of '*our* old world, mine and his alone together', and James's truth not 'mere merciless transcript' but '*imaginative* record'.[50]

Thus keeping memory personal not only consigns it to extinction but flaws its integrity. Doubts assail recall that remains private. 'Because it is not shared, the memory seems fictitious', felt Stegner when, back in his boyhood prairie home, he found 'not a name that I went to school with, not a single person who would have shared' his own childhood experience. 'I have used those memories for years as if they really happened, I have made stories and novels of them. Now they seem uncorroborated and delusive . . .

---

[44] Philippe Lejeune, *On Autobiography* (Minnesota, 1989), 235, and 'The practice of the private journal (1986–1998)', in *On Diary* (Hawai'i, 2009), 29–50 at 29.

[45] Jorge Luis Borges, 'Tlön, Uqbar, Orbis Tertius' (1961), in *Labyrinths* (Penguin, 1970), 27–43 at 39; John Kotre, *White Gloves: How We Create Ourselves through Memory* (Free Press, 1995), 4–6, 10–14.

[46] Victor C. Uchendu, 'Ancestorcide! Are African ancestors dead?', in William H. Newell, ed., *Ancestors* (The Hague: Mouton, 1976), 283–96; Dorthe Refslund Christensen and Rane Willerslev, eds., *Taming Time, Timing Death: Social Technologies and Ritual* (Ashgate, 2013).

[47] Robert Kastenbaum, 'Memories of tomorrow', in Bernard S. Gorman and Alden E. Wessman, eds., *Personal Experience of Time* (New York: Plenum, 1977), 193–214 at 204.

[48] Anna Freud (1977) in Muriel Gardiner, 'Freud's brave daughter', *Observer*, 10 Oct. 1982: 31.

[49] Inga Clendinnen, *Tiger's Eye* (Melbourne: Text, 2000), 74.

[50] Henry James to Henry James III, 15–18 Nov. 1913, quoted in Adeline R. Tintner, 'Autobiography as "experimental" fiction' (1977), in *The Twentieth-Century World of Henry James* (Louisiana State, 2001), 121–42.

How little evidence I have that I myself have lived what I remember ... I half suspect that I am remembering not what happened but something I have written.'[51]

Personal pasts are affirmed, even confirmed, by being passed on to others. Sharing memories sharpens them and promotes their recall; events privy to us alone are more shakily evoked. In knitting our discontinuous recollections into narrative, we revise their personal components to fit the communally remembered past, and finally cease to distinguish the two. Oral discourse and reading aloud turns individual into collective pasts.[52] Speech was the 'first great victory over time', in Arthur C. Clarke's phrase. 'Now the knowledge of one generation could be handed on to the next, so that each age could profit from those that had gone before. Unlike animals, who knew only the present, Man has acquired a past.'[53] Language and memory obviate the need to reinvent the wheel; 'the vicarious experience of billions of people over thousands of generations' makes the cultural legacy a teaching storehouse for ourselves and our descendants.[54]

The origins like the reliability of recollections lie shrouded in doubt. It is hard to distinguish primary from secondary memories, remembering things from remembering remembering them – Wordsworth's 'naked recollection' as opposed to his 'after-meditation'.[55] Recalling childhood days in St Ives, Virginia Woolf felt she was 'watching things happen as if I were there ... My memory supplies what I had forgotten, so that it seems as if it were happening independently, though I am really making it happen.'[56] Moreover, other people's recollections masquerade as our own. 'Very often ... when I recall an event of my own past, I "see myself", which I obviously didn't do in the past', for example, 'I "see myself" getting out of bed' – a scene probably recounted by the writer's mother.[57] As Freud noted, 'our childhood memories show us our earliest years not as they were but as they appeared to us' in hindsight later on.[58]

Durable memory's late childhood onset, parental transference, and ongoing dialogue with older kin make recollection indubitably shared. We are never the first to know who we are; without kinship replay we would have to invent our early pasts. And elder siblings' like parents' memories partly preclude our own, notes the novelist Anne Tyler: 'Like most youngest children, he had trouble remembering his own past. The older ones

[51] Stegner, *Wolf Willow*, 14–17.
[52] Halbwachs, *On Collective Memory*, 23–5, 47–61, 75–8; Tomasello, *Cultural Origins of Human Cognition*, 69; Katherine Nelson, 'Self and social functions: individual autobiographical memory and collective narrative', *Memory* 11 (2003): 125–36.
[53] Arthur C. Clarke, *2001: A Space Odyssey* (1968; New American Library, 1999), 30.
[54] Daniel C. Dennett, 'Human nature', *New Scientist*, 24 May 2003: 40, and *Freedom Evolves* (Penguin, 2003).
[55] William Wordsworth, *The Prelude* (1805; Clarendon Press, 1959), 107.
[56] Virginia Woolf, 'A sketch of the past' (1938), in *Moments of Being* (Chatto & Windus, 1976), 61–139 at 67.
[57] Brockelman, 'Of memory and things past', 319.
[58] Sigmund Freud, 'Screen memories' (1899), in *CPW*, 3: 299–322 at 322. Children of two and three do recall events, but these memories fade away because not autobiographically tethered (Harlene Hayne and Fiona Jack, 'Childhood amnesia', *Wiley Interdisciplinary Reviews in Cognitive Science* 2:2 (2011): 126–45). See Patricia J. Bauer and Marina Larkina, 'The onset of childhood amnesia in childhood', *Memory* 22 (18 Nov. 2013), DOI: 10.1080/09658211.2013.854806; Patricia Bauer, 'The development of forgetting', in P. J. Bauer and Robyn Fivush, eds., *The Wiley Handbook on the Development of Children's Memories* (John Wiley, 2013), 513–4.

did it so well for him, why should he bother? They had built him a second-hand memory that included the years before he existed, even.'[59] To gain his very own past he must leave home or wait until his siblings depart.

Siblings, spouses, and other intimates often dispute not only memories' contents but their originators. 'I remember falling over and really hurting my elbow and knee when a wheel came off my roller skate', says a fifty-year-old. 'Well that actually happened to me', retorts his twin. 'What do you mean, it was me!' 'You skated home to get mum.' 'No, you skated home to get mum.' Contrariwise for shameful memories, 'each believe the other placed Monopoly money in a collection plate during a minister's talk in church, [and] each believe the other spilt a can of cola on a new cream carpet'.[60]

Many another childhood memory swims in seas of family saga and bears their stamp. 'There is for all of us a twilit zone of time, stretching back for a generation or two before we were born', notes Conor Cruise O'Brien. 'Our elders have talked their memories into our memories.' But elders' memory is no imprimatur of truth. '*There is no such thing as The Gospel According to Aunt Lizzie*', warn genealogists; 'family traditions are surrealistic images of the past, blurred by time, colored by emotion and imagination'. They are nonetheless invaluable. 'Every family's history is a collection of scandalous and amusing stories', none wholly veracious. But poet Charles Simic is 'ready to forgive every liar among my forebears' for 'marvelous tales … worth telling again and again'.[61] Family lore hails the 'maverick aura' of an uncle reputedly martyred in the 1916 Irish Easter Rising but who was in fact a British soldier killed in the Great War.[62]

How the children and grandchildren of Holocaust victims and perpetrators deal with original parental recall, searingly indelible yet unspeakably irrecoverable, transforms both legators and legacy. 'To grow up with such overwhelming inherited memories, to be dominated by narratives that preceded one's birth or one's consciousness', writes Marianne Hirsch of the 'postmemory' generation, 'is to risk having one's own stories and experiences displaced, even evacuated, by those of a previous generation'. Offspring of

---

[59] Anne Tyler, *The Clock Winder* (Random House, 1972), 293. See Tomasello, *Cultural Origins of Human Cognition*, 91, 133; Patricia J. Bauer et al., 'Working together to make sense of the past: mothers' and children's use of internal states language in conversations', *Journal of Cognition and Development* 6 (2005): 463–88; Katherine Nelson, 'Origins of autobiographical memory', in Neisser and Hyman, eds., *Memory Observed*, 309–18; Katherine Nelson, 'Self in time: emergence within a community of minds', 13–26, and Robyn Fivush et al., 'The intergenerational self', 131–44, in Fabio Sani, ed., *Self-Continuity* (Psychology Press, 2008); Robyn Fivush, 'Autobiography, time and history', in Nena Galanidou and Liv Helga Dommasnes, eds., *Telling Children about the Past* (Michigan, 2007), 42–58. Erasmus (*Copia: Foundations of the Abundant Style*, sect. 172 (1512), in *CW*, 24: 279–659 at 539–40) discriminated personal memories (*nostra aetate*), the older generation's (*nostra memoria*), and those transmitted from remoter forebears (*patrum memoria*).

[60] Mercedes Sheen et al., 'Disputes over memory ownership', *Genes, Brain and Behavior* 5(s1) (2006): 9–13. See Mercedes Sheen et al., 'Twins dispute memory ownership', *Memory & Cognition* 29 (2001): 779–88; Dorothy Rowe, *My Dearest Enemy, My Dangerous Friend: Making and Breaking Sibling Bonds* (Routledge, 2007), 210–52; Fernyhough, *Pieces of Light*, 110–36.

[61] Conor Cruise O'Brien, 'The Parnellism of Séan O'Faoláin' (1948), in *Maria Cross* (Oxford, 1952), 95–115 at 95; Gary B. Mills and Elizabeth Shown Mills, '*Roots* and the new "faction": a legitimate tool for Clio?', *Virginia Magazine of History and Biography* 89:1 (1981): 3–26 at 6; Charles Simic, 'Grass: the gold and the garbage', *NYRB* 24 Mar. 2011: 23.

[62] James Carroll, 'How family lore shapes character', *IHT*, 9 Oct 2012: 6.

survivors who remained mute absorbed an aura of overwhelming loss, often reified through photographs. 'Possessed by a history they had never lived' – the entire frame-work of European Jewish culture expunged along with the Jews – descendants strive to reactivate collective memory in poetry and painting, memoir and commemoration.[63]

Personal memory is also entwined with collective sagas, 'your own doings interwoven with the coarser and more indestructible fabric of history'.[64] Memory embeds public events in idiosyncratic experiences. Part and parcel of my New Deal recollections are my parents' partiality to Roosevelt, my grandparents' animus against him, my hoard of Hoover campaign buttons. Things we are bidden to remember give way to frivolous musings. 'The sight of an old textbook is much less likely to bring back the sequence of Presidents or the significance of the Smoot-Hawley Tariff Act than it is to evoke the scene of an eighth-grade classroom.'[65]

Yet we also cherish linkage with the larger past. People acutely recall their own actions and reactions at moments of public crisis, pleased to connect themselves with a meaningful cosmos. Those who later recalled Lincoln's and Kennedy's assassinations and the 9/11 attacks vividly remembered their own circumstances: how they heard, where they were, what they were doing.[66] To be sure, such recall is often as erroneous as it is vivid. Indeed, gross inaccuracy underscores the point: people are so eager to be part of 'history' that they falsely 'remember' their responses to, even having been present at, some momentous event.[67]

Communal commingling extends personal recall into past aeons. Conjoining memory of his father's death with the burning of the Reichstag, the Crucifixion, and awareness of the Palaeolithic, a writer felt his life 'stretched out infinitely ... he suddenly felt very old'.[68] Visiting a planetarium that scrolled the night sky as it was at his birth in January 1932, Umberto Eco joined his own beginning with that of the universe.[69]

The sources of collective memory range far beyond personal recall, but these sources too resist correction by others. Since we alone understand the legacy that is ours, we are

---

[63] Marianne Hirsch, *The Generation of Postmemory: Writing and Visual Culture after the Holocaust* (Columbia, 2012), 5, 33; Helen Epstein, *Children of the Holocaust* (Putnam, 1979), 14; Eva Hoffman, *After Such Knowledge: Memory, History, and the Legacy of the Holocaust* (New York: Public Affairs, 2004), 6, 9, 25, 187.

[64] Penelope Lively, *According to Mark* (Heinemann, 1984), 27.

[65] Frances FitzGerald, *America Revised; History Schoolbooks in the Twentieth Century* (Random House, 1980), 17.

[66] F. W. Colegrove, 'The day they heard about Lincoln' (1899), 41–8, and Roger Brown and James Kulik, 'Flashbulb memories' (1977), 50–65, in Neisser, ed., *Memory Observed*; Ulric Neisser and Nicole Harsch, 'Phantom flashbulbs: false recollections ...', 75–89, in Neisser and Hyman, eds., *Memory Observed*; Stephen R. Schmidt, 'Autobiographical memories for the September 11th attacks', *Memory* 12 (2004): 443–54; Olivier Luminet and Antonietta Curci, eds., *Flashbulb Memories* (New York: Psychology Press, 2008).

[67] Robert Buckhout, 'Eyewitness testimony' (1974), in Neisser, ed., *Memory Observed*, 116–24 at 119; Neisser et al., 'Remembering the earthquake: direct exposure vs. hearing the news', in Neisser and Hyman, eds., *Memory Observed*, 90–104; Kerry L. Pickel, 'When a lie becomes the truth: the effects of self-generated misinformation on eyewitness memory', *Memory* 12 (2004): 14–26.

[68] Cees Nooteboom, *Rituals* (1980; Louisiana State, 1983), 45–6.

[69] Umberto Eco, *Six Walks in the Fictional Woods* (Harvard, 1994), 131, 140.

free, or even bound, to construe it as we feel it ought to be. Those who share a communal legacy must accept some mutual notion of its nature. But each sharer treats that corporate bequest as his own; like personal memory, it remains barred to outsiders (see Chapter 12 below). In celebrating that legacy, we resemble those who validate memories by ever recounting them. 'By acting in a traditional way', writes an anthropologist, societies behave 'as if the past might be "proved true" if commemorated assiduously enough'.[70]

Confirmability

> We met at nine / *We met at eight* / I was on time / *No, you were late* . . .
> We dined with friends / *We dined alone* / A tenor sang / *A baritone* . . .
> That dazzling April moon! / *There was none that night*
> *And the month was June* / That's right. That's right.
> *It warms my heart to know that you remember still the way you do*
> Ah, yes, I remember it well
> Alan Jay Lerner, Honoré and Mamita in 'I Remember It Well', from *Gigi*, 1958

Since the past no longer exists, no memory of it can be confirmed with absolute certainty. 'It's easy to imagine that we ought to remember the past. But we do not remember the past. It is the present that we remember', a historian echoes C. I. Lewis.[71] We remember only what now remains. Yet this seems to defy both common sense, given that so many of us remember similarly, and physiology, given our elaborate apparatus for long-term memory recall.

Subjectivity makes memory in one sense a sure but in another a suspect guide. However mistaken it may be, it bears in some way on the past. A fantasy no less than an error recalls something; however distorted; no memory is totally delusive. Indeed, a false recollection firmly believed becomes a fact in its own right. 'Repeatedly retrieving, or repeatedly imagining, or being repeatedly exposed to false information, can all lead to remembering of events that never happened.'[72]

Eye-witnessing inspires faith in memories: we think them accurate because we were there. But DNA testing since the 1980s has exonerated hundreds jailed by eyewitness error. Witnesses traumatized by injury or loss are especially apt to be certain, and especially likely to be mistaken. 'The difference between false memories and true ones is the same as for jewels', in Salvador Dali's epigram; 'it is always the false ones that look the most real, the most brilliant'. Hence concerns about police suspect line-up procedures. 'Study after study revealed a troubling lack of reliability in eyewitness identifications', wrote New Jersey's chief

---

[70] James Fentress, '*Mafia* and the myth of Sicilian national identity', in James Fentress and Chris Wickham, *Social Memory* (Blackwell, 1992), ch. 5 at 198.

[71] Margus Laidre, 'Remembering the future', London, 23 Jan. 2008 (Estonian Ministry of Foreign Affairs, Välministeerium, *vm.ee/?=en/node/3670*).

[72] Henry L. Roediger III et al., 'Recovery of true and false memories', in Martin A. Conway, ed., *Recovered Memories and False Memories* (Oxford, 1997), 118–49 at 145. See Daniel L. Schacter, *The Seven Sins of Memory: How the Mind Forgets and Remembers* (Houghton Mifflin, 2001); Ayanna K. Thomas and Elizabeth Loftus, 'Creating bizarre memories through imagination', *Memory and Cognition* 30 (2002): 423–31; Juliana K. Leding, 'False memories and persuasion strategies', *Review of General Psychology*, 16 (2012): 256–68.

justice in a 2011 landmark decision. 'Indeed, . . . eyewitness misidentification is the leading cause of wrongful convictions.' Judges and juries alike mistake confidence for competence.[73]

Memory is also felt prima facie credible because consistent overall. Particular recall may be found flawed or contrived, but we remain confident about most of our memories because they are congruent; they hang together too well to be seriously doubted. Yet their consistency is in itself partly illusory. For the memories we retain and recall are those that best fit compatible mental frameworks. They are seamless because selectively sieved: we remember what accords with our world view and discount what contradicts it. Totally false but internally consistent memories seem more credible than inconsistent recall.[74]

No firm faith can confirm any particular memory. To remember at best credits a thing as probable. Present or future consequences may verify some memories, but they can be checked only against other recall of the past, never against the past itself.[75] Their personal origin bars corroboration. No one else can attest to our unique past experience. Memories proved wrong or inaccurate are not thereby dispelled; a false recollection can be as durable and potent as a true one, especially if it sustains a vital self-image.

Such was the case with Mary Antin's memory of the dahlias in her childhood garden in Belarus. On being told that her dahlias had in fact been common poppies, Antin clings to her memory.

> I must insist on my dahlias, if I am to preserve the garden at all. I have so long believed in them, that if I try to see *poppies* in those red masses over the wall, the whole garden crumbles away, and leaves me a gray blank. I have nothing against poppies. It is only that my illusion is more real to me than reality. And so do we often build our world on an error, and cry out that the universe is falling to pieces, if any one lift a finger to replace the error by truth.[76]

Unreliable recall is common experience. Plagued by erroneous copies of the Torah, Jewish lawmakers insisted that even legendarily mnemonic copyists should not transcribe a single letter without the text before their eyes.[77] Such cautionary rigour is rare; we mostly vest our own memories with unjustified confidence, seldom questioning their reliability. Yet we are well aware that *other* people often remember worse than they think, imagine what they profess to recall, and reshape their past to accord with present self-images.

Why do we trust our untrustworthy selves? 'We never remember that our remembrance is habitually not merely fallible, but faulty. We treat all mistakes as 'exceptional, rather than singular', wrote a Victorian critic. When we check records, we invariably find our recollection has exaggerated, misplaced, misjudged.

---

[73] *The Secret Life of Salvador Dali* (Dial Press, 1942), 38; Stuart J. Rabner decision, *State v. Larry R. Henderson*, 24 Aug. 2011, pp. 3–7. Brandon L. Garrett, *Convicting the Innocent* (Harvard, 2011), 45–83; Christopher Chabris and Daniel Simons, *The Invisible Gorilla* (HarperCollins, 2011), 231.

[74] C. D. B. Burt et al., 'Memory for true and false autobiographical event descriptions', *Memory* 12 (2004): 545–52.

[75] Lewis, *Analysis of Knowledge and Valuation*, 334–8, 353–62.

[76] Mary Antin, *The Promised Land* (Houghton Mifflin, 1912), 79. See Aleida Assmann, *Cultural Memory and Western Civilization: Functions, Media, Archives* (Cambridge, 2011), 242–3, 262–3.

[77] Birger Gerhardsson, *Memory and Manuscript: Oral Tradition and Written Transmission in Rabbinic Judaism and Early Christianity* (1961; Eerdmans, 1998), 43, 47, 65; George M. Stratton, 'Mnemonic feat of the "Shass Pollak"' (1917), in Neisser, ed., *Memory Observed*, 311–14.

Nevertheless, ... we remark complacently again and again: 'How strange that I should have mistaken such a fact! how singular that my memory (generally so accurate) should have made me fancy that house so much larger than it is!' ... We persist in attributing each freshly discovered error of memory ... to some singular chance ... So painful is the idea of fallaciousness ... that we prefer to encounter the consequences of endless mistakes rather than face the humiliating truth.

The main cause of such error, she concluded, was neither defective observation nor deliberate mendacity but a felt need to *improve* on memory. 'Diverging from literal truth, with the honest purpose of conveying a true meaning', we embellish our narrative with 'some touches not actually true, [but] believed to *explain* the truth'.[78] And we screen out recollections of which we are less certain.[79]

John Dean's Watergate testimony exemplifies the supposed infallibility of a detailed memory. The sheer specificity of Dean's recalled talks with Nixon and his henchmen persuaded senators of their accuracy. But tapes of the White House conversations revealed striking disparities between what Dean had said and heard and what he claimed to have said and heard. Although he conveyed the discussions' general gist, only where he had frequently rehearsed his own words did he give a near-verbatim account; elsewhere, hardly a single detail conformed with the facts. 'Dean's testimony described the meeting not as it was, but as it should have been'.[80]

Salman Rushdie's 'clear memory of having been in India during the China War' in 1962 shows the tenacity of delusive recall:

I 'remember' how frightened we all were, I 'recall' people making nervy little jokes about needing to buy themselves a Chinese phrase book ... I also know that I could not have been in India at that time. Yet *even after I found out that my memory was playing tricks* my brain simply refused to unscramble itself. It clung to the false memory, preferring it to ... literal happenstance. ... Its wrongness feels right.

So Rushdie's protagonist in *Midnight's Children* clings to known error. 'It is memory's truth, he insists, and only a madman would prefer someone else's version to his own.' Oliver Sacks's vivid memory of helping extinguish an incendiary bomb in London likewise lost no conviction when revealed as borrowed from a brother. 'Although I now know, intellectually, that this memory was "false," it still seems to me as real, as intensely my own, as before, ... as strongly embedded in my psyche ... as if it had been a genuine primary memory.'[81]

[78] Cobbe, 'Fallacies of memory', 87–8, 107.
[79] Asher Koriat and Tore Helstrup, 'Metacognitive aspects of memory', in Magnussen and Helstrup, eds., *Everyday Memory*, 251–74 at 266–7.
[80] Neisser, 'John Dean's memory'; W. Walter Menninger, 'Memory and history: what can you believe?', *Archival Issues* 21:2 (1996): 97–106 at 99.
[81] Salman Rushdie, 'Errata: or, unreliable narration in *Midnight's Children*' (1983), in *Imaginary Homelands* (Penguin, 1991), 22–5; Oliver Sacks, 'Speak, memory', *NYRB*, 21 Feb. 2013: 19–21 at 19. On the persistence of delusive self-memory, see William F. Brewer, 'What is autobiographical memory?' 25–49, and Craig R. Barclay, 'Schematization of autobiographical memory', 82–99, in David C. Rubin, ed., *Autobiographical Memory* (Cambridge, 1986); Sheen et al., 'Twins dispute memory ownership', 787.

Two inquests into Londonderry's Bloody Sunday of 1972, when fourteen unarmed Irish civilians were killed by British troops fearing an armed uprising, highlight the fragility and discrepancies of memory. The 1998–2005 Saville Inquiry aimed to repair the omissions of the first inquiry, which took no testimony from Irish eyewitnesses. Twenty-five years after the event, many memories these eyewitnesses recounted flatly contradicted their 1972 diaries and letters. Contemporary photographs in many cases disproved original accounts of where people said they were, who they were with, and what they did; in other cases they validated the later memories. Soldiers' testimonies were equally discrepant. The disparities highlight the fallibility of all memory.[82]

Forgetting

For memory to have meaning we must forget most of what we experience, lest we become like 'Funes, the Memorious':

> He remembered the shapes of the clouds in the south at dawn on the 30th of April of 1882, and he could compare them in his recollection with the marbled grain in the design of a leather-bound book which he had seen only once, and with the lines in the spray which an oar raised in the Río Negro on the eve of the battle of the Quebracho . . . Funes not only remembered every leaf on every tree of every wood, but even every one of the times he had perceived or imagined it . . . 'My memory, sir, is like a garbage disposal.'

The weight of unselective disjoined recollections proves intolerable. 'To think is to forget a difference, to generalize, to abstract. In the overly replete world of Funes there were nothing but details.'[83]

Memories must continually be discarded and conflated; only forgetting enables us to curb chaos and classify. 'We forget because we must, / And not because we will'. Like Henry James, we curtail recollection: 'The ragbag of memory hung on its nail in my closet, though I learnt with time to control the habit of bringing it forth.'[84] Memory too frequently resorted to inundates the present. Indeed, to remember more than a small fraction of our past would be fatal to enterprise. Tristram Shandy needed a year to recount just the first day of his life. 'It would take a life-time to record a life-time', notes a psychoanalyst, 'and since there is so much more of the past than there is of the present, and remembering it takes time and can itself be remembered, . . . anyone who attempted to write a blow-by-blow account of his life would get caught in an infinite regress, remembering oneself remembering oneself remembering'.[85]

---

[82] Graham Dawson, 'Remembering Bloody Sunday', in *Making Peace with the Past? Cultural Memory, Trauma, and the Irish Troubles* (Manchester, 2007), 87–206.

[83] Borges, 'Funes, the Memorious' (1942), in *Personal Anthology*, 35–43 at 40, 42–3. See Jill Price, *The Woman Who Can't Forget* (Free Press, 2008).

[84] Matthew Arnold, 'Switzerland: Absence' (1853), in *Poetical Works* (Oxford, 1945), 134–5 at 134; Henry James, *A Small Boy and Others* (1913), in *Autobiography* (London: W. H. Allen, 1956), 41.

[85] Laurence Sterne, *Life and Opinions of Tristram Shandy, Gentleman* (1759; Penguin, 2003), bk. 4, ch. 13; Jens Brockmeier, 'Remembering and forgetting: narrative as cultural memory', *Culture and Psychology* 8 (2002): 115–43 at 122–3. The computer engineer Gordon Bell's 'lifetime store of everything' is a hyper-Shandean enterprise (Alex Wilkinson, 'Remember this?', *New Yorker*, 28 May 2007: 38–44; Alan Liu, 'Escaping history', in

The most vividly remembered scenes and events are often those previously forgotten. "To be truly recognized ... an image or a sensation out of the past ... must be summoned back ... after a period of absence', Roger Shattuck elucidates Proust. 'The original experience or image must have been forgotten, completely forgotten ... True memory or recognition surges into being out of its opposite: *oubli.*' In Proust's own nostalgic passage:

As Habit weakens everything, what best reminds us of a person is precisely what we had forgotten. It is thanks to this oblivion alone that we can from time to time recover the person that we were, place ourselves in relation to things as he was placed ... Owing to the work of oblivion, the returning memory ... causes us to breathe a new air, an air which is new precisely because we have breathed it in the past ... since the true paradises are the paradises that we have lost.

Indeed, the convoluted length of *Remembrance of Things Past* ensures that the reader will forget what was read at the start, and recall it at the end with a shock of recognition. Creative reading and writing alike 'may require such forgettings', suggests Sacks, for ideas to be 'born again ... in new contexts and perspectives'.[86]

In this sense, Yerushalmi avers, 'all true knowledge is anamnesis, all true learning an effort to recall what has been forgotten'. He cites a Talmud passage anticipating Shelley on infantile amnesia (see p. 58): 'The fetus in the womb knows the entire Torah ... But at the very moment of birth an angel comes and slaps the infant on the mouth ... whereupon he immediately forgets everything and (alas) must learn the Torah anew.' The same sequence drives social history. 'Every "renaissance," every "reformation," reaches back into an often distant past to recover forgotten or neglected elements with which there is a sudden sympathetic vibration, a sense of empathy, of recognition. Inevitably, every such anamnesis also transforms the recovered past into something new; inexorably, it denigrates the immediate past as something that deserves to be forgotten.'[87]

Forgetting is not just necessary; it is normal. Repetitive events merge in recall: since each time I go to buy bread is much like every other, only one generic errand is remembered. Contrary to common belief, we forget most of our experiences; the greater part of what happens is soon irretrievably gone. Much of our past leaks away as inconsequential or inconvenient. 'I expect memories to be long-lasting because ... I can access a large number of very old memories', but the psychologist Marigold Linton found her expectation delusive. Periodic reviews of her diary, recording the outstanding events of each day, showed that memory grossly altered events two years old. After three or four years many diary items failed to trigger any recollection. Originally noteworthy details became fragments of nonsense, whole phrases unintelligible. Recall dwindled as time distanced items; after six years one-third of her recorded events had vanished from

Local Transcendence (Chicago, 2008), 255–8); Gordon Bell, 'Lifelogging; digital immortality available now', *New Scientist*, 16 Oct. 2010: 37.

[86] Roger Shattuck, *Proust's Binoculars: A Study of Memory, Time, and Recognition in 'A la recherche du temps perdu'* (Random House, 1963), 63, 100, 105; Proust, *Remembrance of Things Past*, 1: 692, 3: 903; Oliver Sacks, 'Speak, memory', *NYRB*, 21 Feb. 2013: 19–21 at 20.

[87] Yosef Hayim Yerushalmi, 'Postscript: reflections on forgetting' (1987), in *Zakhor* (1982; Washington, 1996), 105–16 at 113.

memory. She had been unaware of forgetting things precisely because she had forgotten them.[88] Later diarists confirm Linton's ongoing losses; as time outdates relevance, most everyday memories are schematized, fragmented, and forgotten.[89]

The very act of recounting or recording deforms or expunges memories. 'I am afraid of losing Venice, if I speak of it', says Italo Calvino's Marco Polo. 'Memory's images, once they are fixed in words, are erased.'[90] Wholesale loss reduces the remembered past to 'outcrops in a confused and layered landscape, like the random protrusions after a heavy snowfall, the telegraph pole and hump of farm machinery and buried wall', in Penelope Lively's image.[91] 'We relive our past years not in their continuous sequence, day by day', noted Proust, 'but in a memory focused upon the coolness or sunshine of some morning or afternoon'. Between these isolated moments lie 'vast stretches of oblivion'.[92]

Oblivion is the common fate of initially momentous events. Comparing Second World War experiences with memories thirty-five years later, Tom Harrisson found many Britons had forgotten things they could not imagine losing track of. For example, the writer Richard Fitter failed to remember having been to bomb-torn Coventry and 'could hardly believe his eyes when shown his hand-written accounts of a long visit to the place, including important conversations' with leading figures.[93] Ultimately everything is forgotten. 'The poet has his memorial in repetition, and the statesman in stone and bronze.' But human memory runs out, 'the wind and the sea wear the rocks away; and the cell-line runs to its limit, where meaning falls away from it and loses knowledge of its own nature'.[94]

Revising

Revision and elision complement oblivion. The remembered past is malleable and flexible; what seems to have happened undergoes continual change. Each time a memory is recalled, it is reprocessed. Subsequent experience and need reinterpret past events over and over. We select, distil, and distort, reshaping what we remember to suit present and prepare for future demands. One such need is intelligibility. 'Actual experience is a welter of sights, sounds, feelings, physical strains, expectations', notes a philosopher; memory simplifies and orders them. Ambiguous or inconsistent recall of diverse and disjointed

---

[88] Marigold Linton, 'Transformations of memory in everyday life' (1975), in Neisser, ed., *Memory Observed*, 77–91 at 86; Marigold Linton, 'Real-world memory after six years', in M. M. Gruneberg et al., eds., *Practical Aspects of Memory* (London: Academic Press, 1978), 69–76; Ulric Neisser, 'Memory day by day', in Neisser and Hyman, eds., *Memory Observed*, 119–24.

[89] Koriat et al., 'Toward a psychology of memory accuracy', 511. See C. B. D. Burt et al., 'What happens if you retest autobiographical memory after 10 years? *Memory & Cognition* 29 (2001): 127–36; Schacter, 'The sin of transience', in his *The Seven Sins of Memory*, 12–40.

[90] Italo Calvino, *Invisible Cities* (1972; Vintage, 1997), 87.

[91] Penelope Lively, *Going Back* (Heinemann, 1975), 11.

[92] Proust, *Remembrance of Things Past*, 2: 412–13.

[93] Tom Harrisson, *Living through the Blitz* (Collins, 1976), 327. See Lawrence J. Sanna et al., 'Accessibility experience and hindsight bias: I knew it all along vs. it never could have happened', *Memory and Cognition* 30 (2002): 1288–96.

[94] Hilary Mantel, *The Giant, O'Brien* (Holt, 1998), 188.

experience becomes clear, coherent, straightforward. Squeezing and truncating elapsed time, memory dwells disproportionately on the beginnings, the most intense moments, and end-point feelings of our experiences.[95]

Memory also improves the experienced past, refashioning it as what we later think it should have been, expunging unwanted episodes and whitewashing others (see chapter 12). Utter accuracy may matter in a courtroom, but is valued less in other contexts. For example, 'the aim of telling a joke ... is to tell it *effectively*; whether you tell it just as you heard it is of no consequence at all', notes Neisser. 'A singer of epic tales "repeats" a familiar story', not to reproduce it precisely, but 'to impress and entertain his present audience'.[96]

We are seldom aware that memory has altered original experience. Recall reshaped events about wartime Britain to conform with subsequent canons of behaviour. Playing the piano, a young girl in Stepney missed Prime Minister Neville Chamberlain's September 1939 broadcast and the siren alert; her diary records her mother shouting at her, her father's peremptory and futile warnings. Memory transformed it to a more seemly scene: 'We were gathered in our little living room ... all together for once', listening to the wireless and 'shaken to the roots' by the siren she in fact had not heard. For years she told this story, controverted by her candid original document, as a true account. And 'those who kept no records', comments Harrisson, 'would normally distort even more'.[97]

Similarly, associates of George Orwell claimed to have 'witnessed' incidents Orwell had in fact invented, and 'remembered' opinions of him they could have formed only subsequently. Orwell's sister had detested the little she knew of his work while he was alive; her familiarity and admiration came with his posthumous fame, lacing her memories with retrospective approval. For everyone, adds Orwell's biographer, 'the past is filtered through what one subsequently learns. ... Distinguished men of letters reread their early essays on Orwell just before being interviewed and then recounted them with commendable accuracy.'[98]

All recall, not just of facts but of feelings, is remoulded by subsequent need. Rousseau, one of the first to question his memory's credibility, thought he could at least be sure of how he had *felt* about things. 'I easily forget my misfortunes, but I cannot forget my faults, and still less my genuine feelings. ... I may omit or transpose facts, or make mistakes in dates, but I cannot go wrong in what I have felt'.[99] But Rousseau's feelings were no more faithful a guide than Harrisson's postwar interviewees' or Orwell's sister's. Unless traumatic, remembered feelings only *seem* unchanged.

However apparently regrettable, such memory revisions are universal and indeed necessary. Recollection must be ceaselessly revised, because at the time things happen

---

[95] Susanne K. Langer, *Feeling and Form* (London, 1953), 263; Daniel Kahneman, *Thinking, Fast and Slow* (Penguin, 2011), 385–7.

[96] Ulric Neisser, 'Remembering as doing', *Behavioral and Brain Sciences* 19 (1996): 203–4.

[97] Harrisson, *Living through the Blitz*, 325–6.

[98] Bernard Crick, 'Orwell and biography', *London Review of Books*, 7–20 Oct. 1982: 22–4. Orwell himself stressed the need 'to disentangle your real memories from their later accretions' (George Orwell, 'My country right or left' (1940), in *The Collected Essays* (Secker & Warburg, 1968), 1: 536–7).

[99] Jean-Jacques Rousseau, *Confessions* (1781; Penguin, 1953), 262.

we can never know what or how much they will later signify. Anti-Semitism that had been normative as well as compulsory under Hitler became horrific for most Germans in Holocaust hindsight. Families reshaped grandparental accounts of life under Nazism in conformity with postwar morality. Recast reminiscences of elderly Germans transformed complicity in persecution into courageous defence of Jews.[100]

Events recalled in hot passion or with express purpose magnify initial experience. Just as we forget or elide scenes that at first failed to strike us, we exaggerate those that did. A place may be wrongly remembered as uniformly icy and windswept by a single memorable blizzard; the memory of Cape Town's rare 1926 snowfall, photo-enshrined in many parlours, inscribes a durably false impression of that city's customary climate. We mask diversity and collapse countless earlier images into a few dominant memories, accentuating anything imposing and embellishing its splendour or horror.[101] Such emphases underpinned the classical art of memory. 'When we see in everyday life things that are petty, ordinary, and banal, we generally fail to remember them, because the mind is not being stirred by anything novel or marvellous', ran an early Roman text. 'But if we see or hear something exceptionally base, dishonourable, extraordinary, great, unbeliev-able, or laughable, that we are likely to remember a long time.'[102] Memory training thus concentrated on striking, vivid, even grotesque images.

Remembered places tend to converge unless highly distinctive, reducing a score of successive scenes to a single set of generic features. The newcomer's English memories syncretize Oxbridge colleges, transpose Exmoor to Dartmoor, conceive the South Downs and the North Downs as one. Memory reorders the calendar, shuffling the sequence of places visited, presenting episodes in an order more logical than actual. Unless calendrical precision is essential, remembered dates are vague or kaleidoscopic; 'long ago' or 'the other day' suffices. The recollected past is not an uninterrupted temporal sequence but a hotchpotch of discontinuous moments. We 'vividly recall certain events ... without being able to date them', noted the historian Siegfried Kracauer, and the more readily they come to mind the more they are misdated and dislocated.[103] People mainly

date things by events, they don't date them by years. They don't say 'that happened in 1930' or 'that happened in 1925'... They say 'that happened the year after the old mill burned down' or 'that happened after the lightning struck the big oak and killed Farmer James' or 'that was the year we had the polio epidemic'. ... The things they do remember don't go in any particular sequence ... There are just bits poking up here and there.[104]

Memory retrieval is hit and miss; rather than moving methodically forwards or backwards, it excavates the past as a welter of haphazardly juxtaposed fragments.[105]

---

[100] Harald Welzer, 'Re-narrations: how pasts change in conversational remembering', *Memory Studies* 3:1 (2009): 1–13.

[101] Ian M. L. Hunter, *Memory* (Penguin, 1964), 279.

[102] *Rhetorica ad Herennium* (c. 86–82 BC), bk. 3, sect. 22 (Harvard, 1954), 219.

[103] Siegfried Kracauer, 'Ahasuerus, or the riddle of time' (1963–6), in *History: The Last Things before the Last* (1969; rev. edn completed by Paul Osar Kristeller, Princeton: Markus Wiener, 1995), 139–63 at 149.

[104] Agatha Christie, *By the Pricking of My Thumbs* (London, 1968), 174.

[105] Eugenio Donato, 'The ruins of memory' (1978), in *The Script of Decadence* (Oxford, 1993), 168–90.

Each recall alters quality along with content. 'The very act of talking about the past tends to crystallize it', notes a psychoanalyst; once related as a story, the memory can never again be experienced as a vague Wordsworthian reverie.[106] After we consign our childhood to print, it is hard to remember it in any other way; the act of transcription fixes that account as our only memory and leads us, like John Dean after Watergate, to formulaic repetition. 'After you've written, you can no longer remember anything but the writing', reflects Annie Dillard. 'My memories – those elusive, fragmentary patches of color and feeling – are gone; they've been replaced by the work'.[107] To communicate a coherent narrative, we not only reshape the old but create a new past. And any auditor puts his own stamp on our past, reframing in his own mind and retelling in his own words a narrative shaped by interaction with us.

Maturing, ageing, and generational succession bring other memory changes. When we are children our parents seem wholly unlike our grandparents; as we grow up and our parents age they come to resemble them, and we our parents. 'My mother lives in my pockets and also in my face', writes a memoirist, finding in her own pockets similar crumpled-up tissues and candy remnants. 'In the mirror ... I steadily measure with her the spreading pores, the advancing crepe'.[108] After Proust's protagonist's grandmother died, his mother took on many of her traits, partly as a function of her own ageing, partly as a repository for grandmaternal memories. 'The dead annex the living who become their replicas and successors'.[109]

Ageing shifts the balance between our own and other people's memories. A world of seniors endowed with earlier and longer memories gives way to one of juniors who share only our recent years. Childhood memories were once corrected and amplified by seemingly omniscient elders, but as children in turn age they become the sole surviving eyewitnesses of their own earlier years; mortal attrition makes their early memories now incontestable. And recall of recent events markedly differs with age, the elderly more forgetful but supplying temporal depth.[110] Shifting attachments to various past times – memorial, custodial; consensual, contested – reshape the form, content, intensity, and veracity of recall.

Given that current experience continually remakes memory, how do we apprehend the past differently from the present and the future? For one thing, they excite different expectations. Present and future events are in some measure malleable. But the past is already enacted; no matter how skewed our recall, its events irrevocably remain what they

---

[106] Donald Spence, *Narrative Truth and Historical Truth: Meaning and Interpretation in Psychoanalysis* (Norton, 1982), 92, 173, 175.

[107] Annie Dillard, 'Coming of age in Pittsburgh: to fashion a text', *Wilson Quarterly* 12:1 (1988): 164–72 at 171.

[108] Nancy K. Miller, 'The marks of time' (1999), in *But Enough about Me: Why We Read Other People's Lives* (Columbia, 2002), 73–110 at 78, and *Bequest and Betrayal: Memoirs of a Parent's Death* (Oxford, 1996), 186.

[109] Proust, *Remembrance of Things Past*, 2: 796–7. See Habib Chaudhury and Graham D. Rowles, 'Between the shores of recollection and imagination: self, aging, and home', in G. D. Rowles and H. Chaudhury, eds., *Home and Identity in Late Life* (Springer, 2005), 3–18 at 11–12.

[110] Robert Kastenbaum, 'Time, death and ritual in old age', in J. T. Fraser and N. Lawrence, eds., *The Study of Time II* (Springer, 1975), 20–38 at 24–5; Robert Kastenbaum, *The Psychology of Death* (1972; Springer, 2000), 233–4.

were. Moreover, memory like history loads the past with hindsight. As Walter Benjamin put it, someone dead at thirty-five will be remembered 'at every point of his life [as] a man who dies at the age of thirty-five'; awareness of Mozart's untimely demise haunts what we know of his whole career.[111]

Memories revived by prior knowledge often disappoint. 'The images of the past that we recover are dated', felt Simone de Beauvoir. 'Our life escapes us – it was freshness, novelty and bloom. And now that freshness is out of date.'[112] Retrieval falls short of initial experience. Revisiting Tintern Abbey after five years, Wordsworth regretted his failure to recapture the immediacy of his first visit: 'An appetite; a feeling and a love, / That had no need of a remoter charm, / By thought supplied'.[113] Yet it was the second visit's reflections that animated the poem. If we *expect* an original experience to be duplicated, memory disappoints, but welcoming alteration can enhance it. Memory gained transcendent import for Proust by linking *then* dynamically with *now*. 'The remembered image is combined with a moment in the present affording a view of the same object. Like our eyes, our memories must see double; those two images then converge in our minds into a single heightened reality.'[114]

Memory, memoir, and identity

Memory of self is crucial for our sense of identity: knowing that we *were* confirms that we *are*. Personal continuity depends wholly on memory. Recalling past experiences links us with our earlier selves, however different we may have become. 'As memory alone acquaints us with the ... succession of perceptions', reasoned David Hume, it is 'the source of personal identity. Had we no memory, we never shou'd have any notion ... of that chain of causes and effects, which constitute our self or person.'[115] Extension over time also enhances selfhood. As Saul Bellow's Arthur Sammler put it, 'Everybody needs his memories. They keep the wolf of insignificance from the door.'[116]

We achieve identity not by calling up separate reminiscences, but, like Virginia Woolf's transgendered Orlando, by a unifying web of retrospect and prospect, memory and anticipation. Life conceived as a narrative augments present experience by interweaving with past and future. That story, holds Sacks, comes to define us. 'We *become* the autobiographical narratives' by which we tell our lives, concur other scholars. 'What happens to me is not interpreted as an isolated incident, but as part of an ongoing story' that creates and sustains life-long identity.[117]

---

[111] Walter Benjamin, 'The storyteller' (1936), in *Illuminations* (New York: Schocken, 1969), 83–109 at 100. See Piaget and Inhelder, *Memory and Intelligence*, 399–404; Anne S. Rasmussen and Dorthe Berntsen, 'The reality of the past versus the ideality of the future', *Memory & Cognition* 41:2 (2013): 187–200.

[112] Simone de Beauvoir, *Old Age* (Penguin, 1977), 407.

[113] William Wordsworth, 'Lines composed a few miles above Tintern Abbey' (1798), 2. 80–2, in *Poetical Works*, 2: 261.

[114] Shattuck, *Proust's Binoculars*, 47.

[115] David Hume, *A Treatise of Human Nature* (1739–40), in *Philosophical Works* (Aalen: Scientia, 1964), 1: 542.

[116] Saul Bellow, *Mr Sammler's Planet* (Viking, 1970), 190.

[117] Elizabeth M. Shore, 'Virginia Woolf, Proust, and *Orlando*', *Comparative Literature* 31 (1979): 232–45 at 242; Oliver Sacks, *The Man Who Mistook His Wife for a Hat* (Duckworth, 1985), 110; Jerome Bruner, 'Life

To secure identity, many convert memory into memoir. In writing *Father and Son* (1907), Edmund Gosse aimed to refashion his childhood from the corrective of maturity.[118] 'To write one's life is to live it twice', asserts a modern memoirist, 'and the second living' need not, indeed cannot, be wholly faithful to the first. 'Autobiographers are not telling lies but telling their lives', claims a historian of the genre, but lying may reveal a truth; the duplicity of memory is a royal route to self-revelation.[119] Even though an autobiography 'consists mainly of extinctions of the truth, shirkings of the truth, partial revealments of the truth', wrote Mark Twain, 'the remorseless truth *is* there between the lines, where the author-cat is raking dust up on it which hides neither it nor its smell'.[120] Twain's later autobiographical doubts were graver still:

What a wee little part of a person's life are his acts and his words! His real life is lived in his head, and is known to none but himself. . . . The mass of him is hidden – it and its volcanic fires that toss and boil . . . are his life, and they are not written, and cannot be written. . . . The man has yet to be born who could write the truth about himself.[121]

A proposal to pen his memoir appalled Freud, for a 'complete and honest confession . . . would require so much indiscretion . . . that it is simply out of the question'. Obligatory 'mendacity', he added, made 'all autobiographies worthless'.[122] No better were biographies (including his own), inevitably laden with 'lies, concealments, hypocrisy, flattery', and omniscient pretence, 'for biographical truth does not exist, and if it did we could not use it'.[123]

Life histories become coherent and credible only by continual revision and invention, often in defiance of known fact. They are validated not by being exactly true, but compellingly plausible. When ex-hostage Jackie Mann disavowed an anecdote in his memoir, his wife retorted: 'But darling, it's autobiography. You've got to give them a good story. They don't want truth'.[124] Nor does the writer himself. 'You do not even think of your own past as quite real', John Fowles muses, 'you dress it up, you gild it or blacken it, censor it, tinker with it . . . fictionalize it [into] your romanced autobiography.'[125]

as narrative', *Social Research* 54 (1987): 11–32 at 12; Marya Schechtman, 'Stories, lives, and basic survival', *Royal Institute of Philosophy* Supplement 60 (2007): 155–78 at 162.

[118] Edmund Gosse, *Father and Son* (1907; Heinemann, 1964), 227.

[119] Patricia Hampl, 'Memory and imagination' (1986), in *I Could Tell You Stories: Sojourns in the Land of Memory* (Norton, 1999), 21–37 at 35–7; Timothy Dow Adams, *Telling Lies in Modern American Autobiography* (North Carolina, 1990), 173, 31, 68–9.

[120] To William Dean Howells, 14 Mar. 1904, in *Mark Twain–Howells Letters* (Harvard, 1960), 2: 782. See Michael J. Kiskis, 'Dead man talking: Mark Twain's autobiographical deception', *American Literary Realism* 40:2 (2008): 95–113.

[121] Mark Twain, *Autobiography* (Harper, 1924), 1: vi; 'Mark Twain talks' (Curtis Brown interview, 30 July 1899), in *Mark Twain, the Complete Interviews*, ed. Gary Schornhorst (Alabama, 2006), 340–5 at 343.

[122] To Edward L. Bernays, 10 Aug. 1929, in *Letters of Sigmund Freud* (Basic Books, 1975), 391.

[123] To Arnold Zweig, 31 May 1936, in *The Letters of Sigmund Freud and Arnold Zweig* (Hogarth, 1970), 127. See Malcolm Bowie, 'Freud and the art of biography', in Peter France and William St Clair, eds., *Mapping Lives: The Uses of Biography* (Oxford, 2004), 177–92.

[124] Sunnie Mann quoted in *Observer*, 5 Apr. 1992: 26. See Jackie and Sunnie Mann, *Yours Till the End: Harrowing Life of a Beirut Hostage* (Heinemann, 1992).

[125] John Fowles, *The French Lieutenant's Woman* (1969; London: Picador, 1987), 84. See Jenna Campbell et al., 'Remembering all that and then some', *Memory* 19 (2011): 406–15.

The need to romance one's past is evident to every practitioner. While the historian strives to subdue subjectivity, the autobiographer exults in privileged self-perception. Like medieval annalists limning exemplary lives, memoirists render improving or redemptive versions of their careers. We 'remember mistakenly what we *need* to remember', comments a historian, to buttress precarious identities.[126] To flaunt the version of our life that 'thrills us, the one that happened to the people we really are, not to those we just happened to be once', argues André Aciman, memoirists use 'the conventions not of history, but of fiction'. And readers take invention for granted. 'If you write a novel, everyone assumes it's about real people, thinly disguised', asserts novelist–memoirist Margaret Atwood, 'but if you write an autobiography everyone assumes you're lying your head off'.[127]

Revisions vary with author and audience. Black Americans, noted Richard Wright, were *expected* to lie about themselves; if they told the truth, whites disbelieved them. Wright's own life story continually dissembles.[128] As every child knows, school and home events are often alien and incommunicable. The teacher who set Richard Rodriguez an essay on home life expected and got a fictional account: 'I never thought that nun *really* wanted me to write about my family life', nor could he. To depict family to any outsider is to falsify. 'Even when I quote them accurately, I profoundly distort my parents' words', adds Rodriguez, because 'I change what was said only to me' into something for public consumption.[129] Although a Tory MP posted a blog 'to enable my constituents to know me better and to reassure them of my commitment', she confessed at a sleaze inquiry that she 'relied heavily on poetic licence': the blog was '70 per cent fiction and 30 per cent fact'.[130]

'Maturation makes liars of us all': an analyst cites the 25-year-old who said he'd been third in his class; at 50 he recalled being second; at 75 he was sure he'd been first.[131] We tend to disparage our distant and laud our recent past selves. 'In piecing together a life story, the mind nudges moral lapses back in time and shunts good deeds forward', hatching 'a personal history that … makes us feel we're getting better and better'. From Puritan tracts to modern self-help manuals, from Jonathan Edwards to Newt Gingrich, the redeemed self is the thematic staple of American life-stories.[132] To see themselves as heroes of 'a life worth remembering, a drama worth having lived for', oldsters recast their

---

[126] Alphine W. Jefferson, 'Comment', in Jaclyn Jeffrey and Glenace Edwall, eds., *Memory and History* (University Press of America, 1994), 106 (comment on Karen E. Fields, 'What one cannot remember mistakenly', 89–104). See Mamie Garvin Fields with Karen Fields, *Lemon Swamp and Other Places: A Carolina Memoir* (Free Press, 1983).

[127] André Aciman, 'How memorists mold the truth', *NYT*, 7 Apr. 2013: 8; Margaret Atwood, 'Spotty-handed villainesses' (1994), in *Writing with Intent* (Carroll & Graf, 2005), 125–38 at 127–8.

[128] Richard Wright, *Black Boy* (Harper, 1945). See Adams, *Telling Lies*, 75–9.

[129] Richard Rodriguez, *Hunger of Memory* (Boston: Godine, 1981), 179, 186.

[130] Nadine Dorries quoted in Sam Coates, '"Hardworking" MP says blog was 70% fiction', *Times*, 22 Oct. 2010: 3.

[131] George E. Vaillant, *Adaptation to Life* (1977; Harvard, 1995), 197; W. Walter Menninger, 'Say, it isn't so', *History News* 40:12 (Dec. 1985): 10–13; Menninger, 'Memory and history', 102.

[132] Anne E. Wilson and Michael Ross, 'From chump to champ: people's appraisals of their earlier and present selves', *Journal of Personality and Social Psychology* 80 (2001): 572–84; Michael Ross and Anne E. Wilson, 'Autobiographical memory and conceptions of self: getting better all the time', *Current Directions in Psychological Science* 12 (2003): 66–9; Ralph Adolphs and Jessica R. Escobedo, 'Becoming a better person:

memories. Since 'the goal of their recollection is justification rather than insight and responsibility', the elderly slough off tarnished past selves to buttress coherent and progressive self-images: 'I am the same person as I was before – but better!'[133]

Or, increasingly nowadays, the same but worse. Manifold confessions reveal memories perverted and invented not to bolster favourable self-images but to demolish them, in line with accusations by others, whether our nearest and dearest or some bullying cult guru or legal prosecutor. Professed victims fabricate memories of sexual abuse either spontaneously or by suggestion. 'Inducing false memories in healthy young adults', say psychologists, 'appears almost trivially easy'.[134] And, like those accused of heresy or witchcraft, supposed perpetrators are brainwashed into fabricated confessions, assured, in Orwellian fashion, that they would remember the abuses they had committed once they admitted guilt. Even facing imprisonment, some find it less credible that a daughter could fantasize such monstrous acts than that they themselves had committed and then forgotten them.[135] Faith in others' malign memories requires self-abasing repudiation of one's own.

Religious conversion – a profound reversal of values – transforms the personal past: Augustine's *Confessions* and Newman's *Apologia pro vita sua* wholly reinterpret their authors' previous lives. So too with psychoanalytic revelation. Patients emerge 'as metamorphosed figures of the Freudian pantheon' to whom everything in the past only *now* makes sense.[136] The analyst serves as assistant autobiographer, in Charles Rycroft's phrase, editing out self-denigration or self-justification and retrieving the patient's 'own true voice' from a welter of 'learned imitations of ... ancestral voices'.[137] And our mutable pasts are felt to culminate in an immutable present that we fondly expect to persist for the rest of our lives, both because future change is hard to envisage and because it feels good to believe that we have finally become wholly admirable and 'having reached that exalted state' expect to stay that way.[138]

temporal remoteness biases memories for moral events', *Emotion* 10 (2010): 511–18; Dan P. McAdams, *The Redemptive Self* (Oxford, 2006).

[133] John-Raphael Staude quoted in Donald E. Polkinghorne, 'Narrative and self-concept', *Journal of Narrative and Life History* 1 (1991): 135–53 at 149; Kathleen Woodward, 'Reminiscence and the life review', in Thomas R. Cole and Sally Gadow, eds., *What Does It Mean to Grow Old?* (Duke, 1986), 135–62. See Jefferson A. Singer and Peter Salovey, *The Remembered Self* (Simon & Schuster, 1993), 143–57; Dan P. McAdams, 'Personality, modernity, and the storied self', *Psychological Inquiry* 7 (1996): 295–321; Anne E. Wilson and Michael Ross, 'The identity function of autobiographical memory', *Memory* 11:2 (2003): 137–50; Geoffrey Cubitt, *History and Memory* (Manchester, 2000), 107–8.

[134] Martin Conway, 'Introduction: what are memories?' in Conway, ed., *Recovered Memories and False Memories*, 1–22 at 1. See Richard Ofshe and Ethan Watters, *Making Monsters: False Memories, Psychotherapy, and Sexual Hysteria* (Scribners, 1994); Elizabeth F. Loftus, 'Planting misinformation in the human mind', *Learning & Memory* 12 (2005): 361–6; Gail S. Goodman et al., 'Memory illusions and false memories in the real world', in Magnussen and Helstrup, eds., *Everyday Memory*, 157–82.

[135] Lawrence Wright, *Remembering Satan: A Tragic Case of Recovered Memory* (London: Serpent's Tail, 1994); Elizabeth F. Loftus et al., 'The reality of illusory memories', in Schacter, ed., *Memory Distortion*, 47–68; Elizabeth F. Loftus, *Eyewitness Testimony* (1979; rev. edn Harvard, 1996); Daniel B. Wright and Elizabeth F. Loftus, 'Eyewitness memory', in Cohen and Conway, eds., *Memory in the Real World*, 91–105; Alison Winter, *Memory* (Chicago, 2012), 9–32; 225–56.

[136] Peter L. Berger, *Invitation to Sociology* (Penguin, 1966), 76–7.

[137] Charles Rycroft, 'Analysis and the autobiographer', *TLS*, 27 May 1983: 541.

[138] Jordi Quoidbach et al., 'The end of history illusion', *Science* 339:5115 (4 Jan. 2013): 96–8 at 98.

However inconsistent our recall, we rely on it as our very own. Even if we cannot wholly expunge what once shamed or vexed us, or it fails to fit what we now wish had happened, we tell our own tale best. 'It's an excellent biography of someone else', said Robertson Davies of Judith Skelton Grant's new life of him (1994). 'But I've really lived inside myself, and she can't get in there.'[139] A line in the song 'Killing Me Softly' (1973) runs 'Telling my whole life in his words'; but we really want to tell our life in our *own* words. The classic case is Thomas Hardy, who spent years ghost-writing his own official biography and had it passed off as his wife's memoir – an impersonation deserving to be called '*The Life and Work of Thomas Hardy by Florence Hardy*, by Thomas Hardy'.[140]

Many famous literary men and women who knew they were likely to be biographized have actively destroyed their records, or asked their heirs to destroy them, or have hurriedly written their own autobiographies, or commissioned friends to write their lives in predetermined ways ... to forestall, and to mitigate, the errors and misunderstandings ... intrinsic to ... biography.[141]

Would-be biographers are often thwarted and deceived; not being us, they are bound to get things wrong. Subjects even strive to ensure that biographers *do* get things wrong – impugning their motives like Freud, evading them altogether like Pyncheon and Salinger, like James crafting a canny memoir precluding alternative views of his early years, presenting partial and conflicting insights like Beckett and Nabokov, or, like Compton-Burnett, setting rival biographers at one another's throats.[142]

That memory moulds identity is a relatively recent insight. To be sure, memory mitigated the horror of oblivion for ancient Greeks and for medieval and Renaissance Europeans, but the memories so preserved were posthumous. Lives were conceived not in terms of continuities but constancies. Individual identity was fixed, consistent, and vested wholly in the present. Well into the eighteenth century reflective scholars viewed life as 'a discontinuous succession of sensory enjoyments', punctuated by unrelated 'chance events and momentary excesses', in Jean Starobinski's summary. 'Such lives had no distant goal, no finality beyond the limits of the imminent moment.' Identities limned in memoirs and fiction stayed the same over time; events did not remould character, but were simply fortuitous moments in preordained careers; no one waxed introspective about previous stages in their lives.[143]

---

[139] Quoted in Jim McCue, 'Far too young to be old', *Times*, 4 Apr. 1995.

[140] Michael Millgate, *Testamentary Acts: Browning, Tennyson, James, Hardy* (Clarendon Press, 1992), 127 (Hardy), 104–5 (James); Michael Millgate, 'Hardy as biographical subject', in Keith Wilson, ed., *A Companion to Thomas Hardy* (Wiley-Blackwell, 2009), 7–18.

[141] William St Clair, 'The biographer as archaeologist', in France and St Clair, eds., *Mapping Lives*, 219–34 at 227.

[142] Malcolm Bradbury, 'Telling life', in Eric Homberger and John Charmley, eds., *The Troubled Face of Biography* (St Martin's Press, 1988), 131–40; Paul Laity, 'A life in writing: Hilary Spurling', *Guardian*, 17 Apr. 2010 (Compton-Burnett); Miranda Seymour, 'Shaping the truth', in France and St Clair, eds., *Mapping Lives*, 253–66 (James).

[143] Jean Starobinski, *The Invention of Liberty* (Geneva: Skira, 1964), 207. See Georges Poulet, *Studies in Human Time* (1949; Johns Hopkins, 1956), 13–23; Ricardo J. Quinones, *The Renaissance Discovery of Time* (Harvard, 1972), 84–5, 232–3; Patricia Meyer Spacks, *Imagining a Self* (Harvard, 1976), 8–11, 284–5.

Even life-history novelists denied continuity with former selves. 'The same objects are before us – those inanimate things which we have gazed on in wayward infancy and impetuous youth, in anxious and scheming manhood – they are permanent and the same', says Walter Scott's Jonathan Oldbuck. 'But when we look upon them in cold, unfeeling old age, can we, changed in our temper, our pursuits, our feelings – changed in our form, our limbs, and our strength – can we ourselves be called the same? or do we not rather look back with a sort of wonder upon our former selves, as beings separate and distinct from what we now are?'[144] So too, as noted in chapter 1, did *Pride and Prejudice*'s Elizabeth become a different person. In Keats's antiquarian analogy, 'we are like the relict garments of a Saint, the same and not the same: for the careful Monks patch it and patch it till there's not a thread of the original garment left, and still they show it for St Anthony's shirt'.[145] The departure of the past makes the paradox patent. 'One now is what one is, because one no longer is what one was.' Yet we are irrevocably products of our past; like it or not, 'you cannot delete it and become somebody else, somebody who does not have *this* past'.[146]

Memory as a recognized key to self-development, securing and magnifying identity throughout life, derived, by way of biblical narrative, out of Enlightenment progress and Romantic organicism. The unfolding self remained itself despite change. 'We are ourselves, always ourselves, and not for one minute the same', held Denis Diderot.[147] And keeping identity over a lifetime confirmed the past's bona fides: since the self persisted despite change, the past must have been as real as the present.

Believing that childhood selves formed adult identities, followers of Rousseau and Wordsworth viewed life as an interconnected narrative. Acute memory stimulated intense self-consciousness, suffused with nostalgic narcissism and Romantic sensibility. Expanded personal histories fused with broader social pasts, interleaving individual with family and collective chronicles. 'The mind of the child became the archive in which parents invested their family traditions, even as they fostered the expectations of their children for a more promising future', concludes a historian of memory.[148]

'All normal persons in all societies view themselves as continuous entities ... from their earliest memories to the present, think about themselves in a chronological context', and aim at long-range cumulative goals, avers an anthropologist.[149] Psychologists concur that 'the majority of people, the majority of time', feel diachronic continuity, and that a major function of autobiographical memory is to assure us that we are the same person

[144] Walter Scott, *The Antiquary* (1816; London: Dent, 1907), 91.
[145] To George Keats, 17–27 Sept. 1819, in *The Letters of John Keats* (Oxford, 1931), 414.
[146] Frank Ankersmit, *Sublime Historical Experience* (Stanford, 2005), 332–3.
[147] Denis Diderot, *Réfutation suivie de l'ouvrage d'Helvétius intitulé 'L'Homme'* (1774), in *Oeuvres complètes* (Paris, 1975), 2: 275–456 at 373. See Robert Scholes and Robert Kellogg, *The Nature of Narrative* (1966; rev. edn Oxford, 2006), 123–65.
[148] Patrick H. Hutton, *History as an Art of Memory* (New England, 1993), 104. See Christopher Salvesen, *The Landscape of Memory* (Edward Arnold, 1965), 42–4; Karl J. Weintraub, 'Autobiography and historical consciousness', *Critical Inquiry* 1 (1974): 821–48, and *The Value of the Individual* (Chicago, 1978); Beth Lau, 'Wordsworth and current memory research', *Studies in English Literature, 1500–1900* 42 (2002): 675–92.
[149] Robert A. LeVine, 'Adulthood and aging in cross-cultural perspective', Social Science Research Council *Items*, 31/32:4/1 (1978): 1–5 at 2.

we have always been.[150] But self-continuity only lately became customary. 'When our
literature and whole conduct of life is unthinkable without a sense of time and of the past,
when practically no emotion can be felt without some reference of it to earlier experience
or to childhood', observes a Wordsworth scholar, it is easy to forget that this sense of
continuity was rare before the nineteenth century.[151] By that century's end, self-conscious
concern with the past became integral to psychoanalysis: as Wordsworth's *The Prelude*
had historicized personality, so Freud aimed to turn his patients into Wordsworths.[152]
'The adult ... selectively reconstruct[s] his past so that it seems to have planned him',
concluded an analyst, 'or better, he seems to have planned it'. The craving for retrospective consistency continually refashions lifelong memories.[153]

Today, however, many look back with less confidence in continuity. Both recent
history and our own prolonged lifespans feel increasingly discontinuous. 'During my life
so much has changed that it looks like a new world to me', a Dutch oldster puts it.
Impacted by sweeping change, we likewise reconceive our own identities.[154] Signal events
now recalled often seem confused and self-contradictory. All too aware that recall is
pliable and unreliable, we learn to mistrust our remembered past. Memories swiftly
updated and revised weaken coherent continuity. 'We go through life refashioning our
calendar of holy days, raising up and tearing down again the signposts that mark our
progress through time toward ever newly defined fulfilments', held a sociologist half a
century ago. Incessantly rejigged memories become too tenuous to support consistent
self-definition. 'Rather we stumble like drunkards over the sprawling canvas of our self-
conception, throwing a little paint here, erasing some lines there, never really stopping to
obtain a view of the likeness we have produced'.[155] A spate of deceptions has since further
undermined reliance on memory. Yet few are conscious of this deficiency; except for
those who glory in conversion, discrepancies between present and past self-images are
usually too painful to acknowledge.[156]

'No one lives comfortably with the knowledge that he or she cannot recall a continuous
past if *one wants to*', thought the Africanist Jan Vansina. But Vansina acknowledged that
not everyone wants to. Discontinuity is crucial in many creeds and a core part of some

[150] J. M. Lampinen et al., 'Diachronic disunity', in D. R. Beike et al., eds., *The Self in Memory* (Psychology
Press, 2004), 227–53 at 246; Susan Bluck et al., 'A tale of three functions: the self-reported uses of
autobiographical memory', *Social Cognition* 23 (2005): 91–117. See Michael J. Chandler, 'Surviving time:
the persistence of identity in this culture and that', *Culture and Psychology* 6 (2004): 209–31; Michael
J. Chandler and Travis Proulx, 'Personal persistence and persistent peoples', 213–26, Susan Bluck and
Nicole Alea, 'Remembering being me', 55–70, and Constantine Sedikides et al., 'Nostalgia as enabler of
self-continuity', 227–39, all in Sani, ed., *Self-Continuity.*
[151] Salvesen, *Landscape of Memory*, 172.
[152] Morse Peckham, 'Afterword: reflections on historical modes in the nineteenth century', in Malcolm
Bradbury and David Palmer, eds., *Victorian Poetry* (Edward Arnold, 1972), 277–300 at 279.
[153] Erik H. Erikson, *Young Man Luther* (Norton, 1958), 111–12. See Robert L. Rubinstein and Kate de
Medeiros, 'Home, self, and identity', in Rowles and Chaudhury, eds., *Home and Identity in Late Life*,
47–62.
[154] Gerben J. Westerhof, '"During my life so much has changed that it looks like a new world to me":
a narrative perspective on migrating in time', *Journal of Aging Studies* 24 (2010): 12–19.
[155] Berger, *Invitation to Sociology*, 72–3, 75.
[156] Burt et al., 'Memory for true and false autobiographical event descriptions'.

personalities.[157] Not everyone feels compelled to reshape memory for consistency with earlier selves, or to stress disparity simply to underscore new-found rectitude. Comfortable with episodic rather than diachronic selves, some feel no need to bring their past in line with their present. 'Let me lose *self* every hour, and be twenty successive selfs, or new selfs; 'tis all one to me', wrote Shaftesbury.[158] After two confessional memoirs, an essayist despairs of ever getting it right. Each seems 'a sin against the true story of my life, the one I can never tell and never know'.[159]

The lifelong narrative selfhood quest now fashionable strikes philosopher Galen Strawson as 'a gross hindrance to self-understanding ... Every studied conscious recall of past events brings an alteration ... The more you recall, retell, narrate yourself, the further you risk moving away from accurate self-understanding, from the truth of your being.'[160] Those emotionally cut off from past experiences and feelings are commonly said to live 'momentary, disjointed, fragmented lives'.[161] But those not diachronic by nature need no personal narrative to make their lives meaningful.

Strawson's sense of personal time is historical rather than memorial. While realizing that his past has formed him, he disowns attachment to it and resists autobiographical memory's bowdlerizing concealments and delusory comforts. 'I know perfectly well that I have a past', and he remembers it. 'Yet I have absolutely no sense of my life as a narrative.' A self-styled Episodic, he denies Diachronics' claim to narrative virtue. 'Narrative self-articulation is natural for some ... but in others it is highly unnatural and ruinous ... it almost always does more harm than good. ... The best lives almost never develop this kind of self-telling.'[162]

Yet those who disclaim continuity with past selves often continue to feel responsible for them. 'I think of the masterpiece in question', wrote Henry James in 1915 of one of his early novels, 'as the work of quite another person than myself'.[163] But James was nether alienated from nor indifferent to his past work. He had embarked, a decade before, on revising all his earlier novels, assuming, as the *same* person, the right and the duty to reshape past oeuvre in line with present principles. One may feel attached to, uninterested in, or estranged from one's past, but one cannot escape the 'unity of consciousness over time that constitutes personal survival' – not just remembering it but being profoundly influenced by that memory.[164]

---

[157] Jan Vansina, 'Memory and oral tradition', in Joseph C. Miller, ed., *The African Past Speaks: Essays on Oral Tradition and History* (Folkestone: Dawson, 1980), 262–79 at 266 (emphasis mine), 269.

[158] Anthony Ashley Cooper, Third Earl Shaftesbury, *Philosophical Regimen* (c. 1698), in Benjamin Rand, ed., *The Life, ... and Philosophical Regimen of Anthony, Earl of Shaftesbury* (London, 1900), 1–272 at 136. See Kenneth P. Winkler, '"All revolution is in us": personal identity in Shaftesbury and Hume', *Hume Studies* 26 (2000): 3–40 at 8; Dror Wahrman, *The Making of the Modern Self* (Yale, 2006), 166–96.

[159] Emily Fox Gordon, *Book of Days* (New York: Spiegel & Grau, 2010), 236.

[160] Galen Strawson, 'Against narrativity', in his, ed., *The Self?* (Blackwell, 2005), 63–86 at 82.

[161] Robert R. Ehman, 'Temporal self-identity', *Southern Journal of Philosophy* 12 (1974): 333–41 at 339.

[162] Strawson, 'Against narrativity', 69, 82, 73; Galen Strawson, *Selves: An Essay in Revisionary Metaphysics* (Oxford, 2009), 9, 93.

[163] Henry James to Rhoda Broughton, 3 Nov. 1915, in Philip Horne, *Henry James* (Allen Lane, 1999), 562–3.

[164] Schechtman, 'Stories, lives, and basic survival', 167. But see Andrew Lane, 'The narrative self-constitution view: why Marya Schechtman cannot require it for personhood', *Manchester Journal of Philosophy* 20 (2011): 100–15.

More than recapturing the past, recollection helps digest and comprehend it. Memories are selective reconstructions, remade by subsequent actions and perceptions, freshly envisioned by changing codes of knowledge. Memory does not preserve but adapts the past, to manage and enrich the present and anticipate the future; indeed, memory is as much the kernel of the future as the trace of the past.[165] Recollections alien to present thinking or of no current consequence are apt to vanish beyond recall. Nonetheless we remember far more than we need simply to cope with ongoing life. Memory steals 'fire / From the fountains of the past, / To glorify the present'.[166] It enables us not merely to follow but to build on previous efforts, not just to survive but to ornament our moments and days with a temporal tapestry that makes mortal humanity all but imperishable.

---

[165] Michael Lambek, 'The past imperfect', in Paul Antze and Michael Lambek, eds., *Tense Past: Cultural Essays in Trauma and Memory* (Routledge, 1996), 235–54 at 244; Ralph Hertwig et al., 'Hindsight bias', *Memory* 11 (2003): 357–77 at 375; Endel Tulving and Martin Lepage, 'Where in the brain is the awareness of one's past?' in Schacter and Scarry, eds., *Memory, Brain, and Belief*, 208–28 at 224.

[166] Alfred, Lord Tennyson, 'Ode to memory' (1830), ll. 12–13, in *The Poems* (London, 1969), 211–16 at 211. See James D. Kissane, 'Tennyson: passion of the past and the curse of time', *ELH* 32 (1965): 85–109.

8

History

Memory dictates, and history writes it down.   Pierre Nora, 1984[1]

The historian does simply not come in to replenish the gaps of memory. He constantly challenges even those memories that have survived intact.
                                                    Yosef Hayim Yerushalmi, 1982[2]

The study of memory teaches us that all historical sources are suffused by subjectivity right from the start.   Jan Vansina, 1980[3]

Experience is doubly defective; we are born too late to see the beginning, and we die too soon to see the end of many things. History supplies both these defects.
                                        Henry St John, Viscount Bolingbroke, c. 1735[4]

History is that certainty produced at the point where the imperfections of memory meet the inadequacies of documentation.   Julian Barnes, 2011[5]

History is protean. What it is, what people think it should be, and how it is told and heard vary with time, place, and person. Clio, the muse of history, was likened in America first to a social butterfly and then to a career woman, in the Soviet Union to a streetwalker or bureaucrat. Routed from her ivory tower, she is today an online dating site.[6] Equally diverse are estimates of her age: one in three Britons think history dates from a moment ago, another third think her ten to twenty years old, the rest date her back to the birth of time.[7] Americans often conflate history with today, terming yesterday antediluvian and tomorrow potentially hoary. 'I got married when I was 25', recalls a columnist; 'that was in the Mesozoic era, and we had no end of trouble keeping the stegosaurus away from the wedding cake'.[8] In line with the Los Angeles dictum that 'history is five years old', computer pioneer Steve Jobs sought to demolish his 1926

---

[1] Pierre Nora, 'Entre mémoire et histoire', in his, comp., *Lieux de mémoire* (Gallimard, 1984–92), 1: xv–xlii at xxxviii.

[2] Yosef Hayim Yerushalmi, *Zakhor: Jewish History and Jewish Memory* (1982; Washington, 1996), 94.

[3] Jan Vansina, 'Memory and oral tradition', in Joseph C. Miller, ed., *The African Past Speaks* (Folkstone: Dawson, 1980), 276.

[4] Henry St John Bolingbroke, *Letters on the Study and Use of History* (1735; rev. edn London, 1752), Letter II, 1: 35–6.

[5] Julian Barnes, *The Sense of an Ending* (Jonathan Cape, 2011), 17.

[6] Pendleton Herring, 'Political scientist considers the question' [do we need a new history], *Pennsylvania Magazine of History and Biography* 72 (1948): 118–38 at 126–27; *perfectmatch.com*; *loveawake.com*. On history as a whore, see Schopenhauer, below p. 336.

[7] 'History? It started a second ago', BBC *History Magazine*, Nov. 2009, poll of 1,900 readers.

[8] Gail Collins, 'Girls and boys together', *NYT*, 3 Mar. 2011: A23.

historic-register house. Jobs claimed 'I could build something far more historically interesting.'[9]

History extends and enriches, confirms and corrects memory through records and relics. It has come to comprise not only the annals of civilization but of aeons of so-called prehistory. The lack of written records does not mean that preliterates had no history nor does it preclude our inquiries into it. History is transmitted by vision and voice as well as by relics and texts. All manner of depictions – oral narratives, films, folkways, artworks – shed light on prehistoric as well as later times.

Wordless nature is historical too. 'Stones, trees, animals have a knowable past, but no history', thought Vico, because no conscious purposes animated that past.[10] Charles Kingsley drew a sharper line: 'History is the history of men and women, and of nothing else'.[11] Yet historical understanding now encompasses the past of non-human entities, from micro-organisms within us to stars and galaxies beyond. Annals of zoology, botany, geology, and astronomy lack the motivating agencies of human history, but their pasts, as discussed in my Introduction, are nonetheless historically contingent and intimately entwined with the career of humanity.[12]

The stuff and scope of historical awareness far surpass conventional history, calling on a wider range of sources and a more comprehensive notion of 'truth'. A total history, thought a French *Annales* pioneer, should 'embrace all the studies concerned with man and time'.[13] It increasingly does so. But our sense of the historical past comes less from texts and teachers than from everyday things seen and done since infancy. As opposed to academic 'humdrummery', as Bertie Rodgers recalled his 1920s Belfast childhood,

> History isn't handed down,
> It's handed up . . .
> History is in the bounce of a ball,
> In the flick of a skipping-rope.[14]

Just as myriad diverse memories merge in our minds, so does a host of heterogeneous historical data. Carl Becker's 1931 AHA presidential address told how 'Everyman' patterns history out of a thousand unremarked and unrelated sources:

From things learned at home and in school, from knowledge gained in business or profession, from newspapers glanced at, from books (yes, even history books) read or heard of, from remembered scraps of newsreels or educational films or *ex cathedra* utterances of presidents and kings, from

---

[9] Durs Grünbein, 'Aus der Hauptstadt des Vergessens Aufzeichnungen aus einem Solarium', *Frankfurter Allgemeine Zeiting*, 7 Mar. 1998: 1; Steve Jobs quoted in Patricia Leigh Brown, 'Free to a good home: a captain of industry's rejected mansion', *NYT*, 2 Jan. 2005.

[10] Isaiah Berlin, *Vico and Herder* (Hogarth, 1976), 29.

[11] Charles Kingsley, *The Limits of Exact Science as Applied to History* (Cambridge, 1860), 4.

[12] David Christian, 'A single historical continuum', *Cliodynamics* 2 (2011): 6–26 at 13–18, 21–4; Eric J. Chaisson, *Epic of Evolution* (Columbia, 2005); Daniel Lord Smail, *On Deep History and the Brain* (California, 2008); Richard Dawkins, *The Ancestor's Tale* (Houghton Mifflin, 2004).

[13] Jacques Le Goff, *La Nouvelle Histoire* (Paris: Retz-CEPL, 1978), 11.

[14] Darcy O'Brien, *W. R. Rodgers* (Bucknell, 1970), 16–17; W. R. Rodgers, *The Return Room* (BBC radio play, 1955), quoted in Michael Moss, 'Choreographed encounter', *Archives* 31:116 (2007): 1–17 at 9.

fifteen-minute discourses on the history of civilization broadcast by the courtesy . . . of Pepsodent, the Bulova Watch Company, or the Shepard Stores [closed 1937].

And beyond events personally experienced, Everyman embroiders 'a more dimly seen pattern . . . of things reputed to have been said and done in past times which he has not known . . . Out of the most diverse threads of information, picked up in the most casual way, from the most unrelated sources . . . he somehow manages, undeliberately for the most part, to fashion a history.'[15]

Everyman's history is broader ranging even than professional historians' increasingly inclusive reach. For all academe's manifold retrievals, history remains 'an odd, semi-fictional subject, part fact, part myth, and guesswork', notes a novelist. Everyman's history is 'an engaging blend of fact and fancy', dominated by data 'that seem best suited to his interests or promise most in the way of emotional satisfaction'.[16]

A near century on, Everyman's pastiches of the past arise from materials no less diverse and idiosyncratic than those of Becker. A British journalist's *mélange* is drawn from

ill-remembered lessons, what father did in the war, television documentaries with half the instalments missed, bodice-ripper historical novels, fragments of local folklore . . . what that French man seemed to be saying on the train, what we saw of Edinburgh Castle before the wee boy got sick, several jokes about Henry VIII and that oil painting of the king lying dead on the battlefield with his face all green.[17]

Formal history is overlain and undermined by myriad exotic arenas of apprehension.

Yet bizarrely adventitious insights infuse historians' intuitions too, often through some novel awareness that 'gradually makes sense of a whole large area of the past'. And it is 'more important that the initial perception should be sharp and vivid than that it should be true', counselled medievalist R. W. Southern. 'Truth comes from error more easily than from confusion'. Only a vivid perception can impel an energetic search.[18]

Historical knowledge depends on oft-disdained mythology. 'A myth is a once valid but now discarded version of the human story', noted Becker, 'as our now valid versions will in due course be relegated to the category of discarded myths'.[19] Perceptions of India's past supply 'no criteria for differentiating between myth and history', held a philosopher. 'What the Westerner considers as history in the West, he would regard as myth in India . . . what he calls history in his own world is experienced by Indians as myth', or nowadays as collective memory.[20]

---

[15] Carl L. Becker, 'Everyman his own historian', *AHR* 37 (1932): 221–36 at 229.

[16] Rosemary Harris, 'How to enjoy the first lessons in developing a sense of the past', *Times*, 31 Jan. 1973: 10; Becker, 'Everyman his own historian', 229–30.

[17] Neal Ascherson, *Games with Shadows* (London: Radius, 1988), 12.

[18] R. W. Southern, 'The historical experience' (1977), in *History and Historians* (Blackwell, 2004), 104–6.

[19] Becker, 'Everyman his own historian', 231.

[20] Raimundo Panikkar, 'Time and history in the tradition of India', in Louis Gardet et al., *Cultures and Time* (Paris: UNESCO, 1976), 63–88 at 76. See Dipesh Chakrabarty, 'The public life of history: an argument out of India', *Public Culture* 20:1 (2008): 147–68.

Soothsayers and priests, storytellers and minstrels are historians too, just as historians themselves are preachers. Modern 'historical accounts are only in the second place designed for the sake of knowledge about the past. In the first place they are a sacred ritual ... embod[ying] a religious faith: the view that humans are' bound neither by nature, by custom, nor by divine providence, but are 'free and independent agents with the ability to shape their fate, the obligation to act on that ability, and responsibility for the consequences'.[21] Lauding 'metaphorical' history, Nietzsche devalued factual explanation in favour of mythic insight from drama and fable.[22] As later work supplants their facts and sources, historical classics acquire the poetic, universalizing aura of myth. Gibbon is no longer read as authoritative Roman history, but rather as an eloquent meditation on imperial fate.[23]

Historical knowledge, academic and Everyman's alike, in many ways falls short of, in others transcends, the past itself. I treat each in turn.

History is less than the past

Even if all that has come down to us by report from the past should be true and known by someone, it would be less than nothing compared with what is unknown ... How puny and limited is the knowledge of even the most curious!

Michel de Montaigne, 1585–8[24]

A limited form of knowledge, history only scrapes the surface of the past.

Constantin Fasolt, 2004[25]

Only a tiny fraction of all that has happened can ever be recovered and recounted. Nor is any historical account the same as any actual past. These deficiencies lead some to dismiss history altogether, for besides being incomplete, in Arthur Schopenhauer's reproach, history 'is as permeated with lies and falsehood as is a common prostitute with syphilis'.[26] Three constraints limit what can be known: the immensity of the past; the gulf between past events and accounts of those events; and inescapable bias.

First, no historical inquiry can retrieve the virtually infinite sum total of past events. Arduous detailed retrieval recoups only a minute fraction of even the most accessible past. Most that has happened was never recorded, most of the rest fleeting, 'lost without recovery' in Thomas Carlyle's 'dark untenanted places of the Past'.[27] Thomas Browne found 'no antidote against the opium of time ... The iniquity of oblivion blindly scattereth her poppy, and deals with the memory of men without distinction to merit

[21] Constantin Fasolt, *The Limits of History* (Chicago, 2004), 230–1, xvi.

[22] Friedrich Nietzsche, *The Use and Abuse of History* (1874; Bobbs-Merrill, 1957), 39–42.

[23] Northrop Frye, *The Great Code: The Bible and Literature* (Routledge, 1983), 46–7.

[24] Michel de Montaigne, 'Of coaches', in *The Complete Essays* (Stanford, 1958), 692.

[25] Fasolt, *Limits of History*, 39–40.

[26] Arthur Schopenhauer, *Parerga and Paralipomena* (1851), in *Short Philosophical Essays* (Oxford, 1974), 2: 447.

[27] Thomas Carlyle, 'On history' (1830), in *Critical and Miscellaneous Essays* (London, 1888), 2: 221.

of perpetuity ... The greater part must be content to be as though they had not been, to be found in the register of God, not in the record of man.'[28]

That most things are transitory elucidates Herbert Butterfield's 'tremendous truth – the impossibility of history':

The ploughman whom Gray saw, plodding his weary way, the rank and file of Monmouth's rebel crowd – every man of them a world in himself, a mystery of personality ... – these have left no memorial and all that we know about them is just enough to set us guessing and wondering. Things by which we remember an old friend – his peculiar laugh, his way of drawing his hand through his hair, his whistle in the street, his humour – we cannot hope to recapture in history [just as we] cannot hope to read the hearts of half-forgotten kings. The Memory of the world is not a bright, shining crystal, but a heap of broken fragments, a few fine flashes of light that break through the darkness.[29]

In Flaubert's phrase, 'writing history is like drinking an ocean and pissing a cupful'.[30]

Second, no account can recover any actual past, for no past was a mere account; it was a set of situations and events. As the past no longer exists, descriptions can never be checked against it, but only against other versions of that past; veracity is judged by correspondence with other reports, not with events themselves. The historian selects not from the totality of what has happened (*res gestae*), but from other accounts of what happened (*historia rerum gestarum*); in this respect, so-called primary sources approximate past reality little better than derivative chronicles.[31] No hard evidence refutes Peter Munz's claim that 'any particular event ... can be said to have occurred only because somebody thought it did', or Claude Lévi-Strauss's that 'historical fact ... only exists as ... retrospective reconstruction'.[32] As Becker insisted:

Left to themselves, the facts do not speak; left to themselves they do not exist; ... there is no fact until someone affirms it. ... Since history is not part of the external material world, but an imaginative reconstruction of vanished events, the form and substance of historical facts ... vary with the words employed to convey them.[33]

This is not to deny that historical consensus provides real knowledge. Indeed, 'without genuinely knowable past experience there could be no answer to any question, nor any question to be answered, because there could be no such thing as fact and no intelligible

---

[28] Thomas Browne, *Hydriotaphia: Urn Burial* (1658), in *Works* (1852; London, 1928), 3: 1–50 at 43–4.

[29] Herbert Butterfield, *The Historical Novel* (Cambridge, 1924), 14–15.

[30] Gustave Flaubert quoted in Denis Shemilt, 'Drinking an ocean and pissing a cupful: how adolescents make sense of history', in Linda Symcox and Arie Wilschut, eds., *National History Standards* (Charlotte, NC: Information Age, 2007), 141–209 at 142.

[31] Confusing the past itself with accounts of it bedevils Anglophone thought because in English 'history' means both (German distinguishes *Gegenwart* from *Geschichte*, French *passé* from *histoire*, Italian *passato* from *storia*). Only context reveals that the dismissive 'He's history' and the laudatory 'Barnsley Council will make history today' refer to the past itself, not to a text (John Davis, 'The social relations of the production of history', in Elizabeth Tonkin et al., eds., *History and Ethnicity* (Routledge, 1989), 104–20 at 104).

[32] Peter Munz, *The Shapes of Time* (Wesleyan, 1977), 184–5, 209, 186 (quoting Lévi-Strauss (1965)). On retrospective reconstruction see Lawrence D. Walker, 'A note on historical linguistics', *History and Theory* 19:2 (1980): 154–64.

[33] Becker, 'Everyman his own historian', 233.

discourse', concluded C. I. Lewis.[34] But just as memories never strictly correspond with original events, neither can historical accounts. As Umberto Eco says of translation, 'there is a way things go, independent of the way our languages make them go', so there is a way things were, independent of how we chronicle them.[35]

Third, historical knowledge, no matter how consensually verified, is necessarily shaped by both narrator and audience. Imparting and imbibing history depends on precursors' vision and voice, recipients' eyes and ears: interpreters and receivers stage manage our apprehension of past events. To be sure, narrators' spin is potentially corrigible by access to written and other sources. When original observers' own words are available, we are not entirely dependent on traditions retwisted by storytellers. But for the most part we remain at historians' mercy. And to 'explain' the past, they are bound to go beyond the actual record, couching it in contemporary modes of thought and speech. Selecting data from a chosen era, synthesizing later commentaries, the historian reaches conclusions of his own bent. 'Not one but a hundred generations', wrote the sociologist W. Lloyd Warner, 'are now sending their own delayed interpretations' of history.[36] But whether narrators are single and recent or multivocal from many epochs, we cannot escape the frameworks they impose. In clarifying the past, these inevitably distance its naked actuality.

Nor can we escape our own frames of reference. Narrators' perspectives and predilections shape their accounts, our own determine what we make of them. The past we construe is contingent on our background, our outlook, our own present. We are products of the past, but the known past is an artefact of our own making. However immersed in antiquity, no perceiver can divest himself of his own experience and assumptions, or 'recall past events without in some subtle fashion relating them to what he needs or desires to do'.[37] The disinterested historian concerned with the past entirely for its own sake had little in common, in Michael Oakeshott's view, with 'non-historical', 'practical' people who use the past to understand, sustain, or reform the present.[38] But these polar opposites are unreal: the practical man's past is seldom exclusively operational; the historian is unavoidably present minded. 'We are all in some measure both seekers of true knowledge and purposive manipulators of the past', observes Jörn Rüsen; 'no historian can leave his or her time and dive into the depths of otherness. He or she always takes him or herself along into the encounter with historical difference.'[39] Our own hopes and fears, expertise and expectations reshape the historical no less than the

[34] Clarence Irving Lewis, *An Analysis of Knowledge and Valuation* (1946; Read Books, 1998), 361–2. See C. Behan McCullagh, *The Truth of History* (Routledge, 1998), chs. 2, 4.

[35] Umberto Eco, *Mouse or Rat: Translation as Negotiation* (London: Phoenix, 2004), 182.

[36] W. Lloyd Warner, *The Living and the Dead* (Yale, 1959), 217.

[37] Becker, 'Everyman his own historian', 227.

[38] Michael Oakeshott, 'The activity of being an historian' (1955), in *Rationalism in Politics and Other Essays* (Methuen, 1967), 151–83 at 165–6; Michael Oakeshott, *On History and Other Essays* (Blackwell, 1983), 35–9, 43. See Stuart Isaacs, *The Politics and Philosophy of Michael Oakeshott* (Routledge, 2006), 109–21; A. L. Macfie, 'Oakeshott's answer', *Rethinking History* 14 (2010): 521–30.

[39] Jörn Rüsen, 'The horror of ethnocentrism', *History and Theory* 47 (2008): 261–9 at 268.

remembered past. To be sure, such predilections are creative as well as limiting, but in either case they distort.

Beyond personal bents, the passage of time that outdates bygone things continually alters our knowledge. Everything we know filters through present-day mental lenses. Newfangled premises and modes of discourse constrain historians' ability to convey the past to a later age. 'We are moderns and our words and thoughts can not but be modern', noted the legal historian Frederic W. Maitland, 'it is too late for us to be early English'; we cannot see the past with their eyes.[40] 'No recipe exists from which to concoct the thoughts, values, and emotions of people who lived in the past', cautions a chronicler. 'Even having steeped ourselves in the literature of the period, worn its clothes, and slept on its beds, we never shed [today's] perspectives and values.'[41]

Today's perspective cumulatively misinterprets the past, as lengthened remoteness multiplies its anachronisms and interposes the outlooks of ever more intervening epochs. Discussing William Morris's take on ancient Greece, Walter Pater showed how our contact with Hellenism is mediated through Roman, medieval, Renaissance, and subsequent prisms, enriching yet estranging our understanding. We cannot expunge our composite inherited experience of all subsequent ages to come directly face to face with the ancient Greeks, any more than we could 'become a little child, or . . . be born' again.[42]

The language of history also reconfigures the past. Historians' impressions are conveyed in words, converted into mental images by reader or auditor – but the images differ from historians' originals. Any distance – in time, in space, in culture, in point of view – widens the gulf between narrator and audience. And every language imposes its own conventions, deforming understanding of the original record.

Dispute over biblical revision points up dilemmas of obsolescence. Rhetorical force and liturgical tradition make the King James version a much-loved classic. But four centuries leave many of its archaisms incomprehensible; errors of translation and omission continually surface. King Solomon sounds splendid with peacocks, but once one knows the 1611 translators erred, the peacocks (1 Kings 10.22) get replaced by monkeys (more correctly baboons). Confusion clouds Ezekiel 13:18's misogynist prophecy, 'woe to the women that sew pillows to all armholes'.[43] Anachronistic unintelligibility is the fate not only of fixed written texts but also of faithful oral accounts, gobbledegook even to narrators deploying obsolete words or alluding to customs now extinct.

To be sure, hindsight also gives us knowledge that people of bygone times could not have had. But at the same time it blinds us to their awareness of that past, for them the present. Hindsight's falsification of perspective troubled W. G. Sebald. 'We, the survivors, see everything from above, see everything at once, and still we do not know how it was', he wrote of the carnage of war.[44] 'Can we really be fair to men of the past', asked a historian of Tudor England, 'knowing what they could not know? Can we, indeed,

---

[40] Frederic William Maitland, *Township and Borough* (1898; Cambridge, 2010), 22.
[41] Marcella Sherfy, 'The craft of history', *In Touch* [NPS], no. 13 (1976): 4–7 at 5.
[42] Walter Pater, 'Poems by William Morris', *Westminster Review* (Oct. 1868): 300–12 at 307.
[43] Christopher Howse, 'The global phenomenon that will never be lost in translation', *Daily Telegraph*, 14 Dec. 2010; Gordon Campbell, *The Bible: The Story of the King James Version 1611–2011* (Oxford, 2011).
[44] W. G. Sebald, *Rings of Saturn* (Harvill, 1998), 106–17, 125, 145, 176.

understand them at all ... with our minds prepossessed by a knowledge of the result?'[45] But as 'knowledge of the result' suggests, hindsight bias not only occludes the past, it also enlarges it. To these additions I now turn.

History is more than the past

> All things are engaged in writing their history ... In nature ... the narrative is the print of the seal. It neither exceeds nor comes short of the fact. But ... in man, the report is something more than print of the seal. It is a new and finer form of the original ... in a new order. The facts which transpired do not lie in it inert; but some subside, and others shine; so that soon we have a new picture.
>
> Ralph Waldo Emerson, 1850[46]

Anachronism misinterprets history; hindsight reinterprets it. To explain the past to the present demands taking into account not only changed viewpoints and values, but also what has happened since the period under study. We are bound to see the Second World War differently in 2015 from in 1945, not merely because new evidence has come to light, but also because the ensuing decades unfolded further consequences: the Bomb, decolonization, the Cold War, and much more.

Revisiting old sources with modern tools, deploying data newly emergent, the historian discovers both what had been forgotten and things never before known. 'People and societies are caught up in processes which can be perceived and described only in hindsight; documents are ripped out of their original context ... to illustrate a pattern [unknown] to any of their authors.'[47] No denizens knew they were living in 'classical antiquity' or the 'Renaissance', both subsequent constructions. Terms of our own which did not exist back then help us understand what happened.[48]

But they also reconfigure how what happened is understood. History informed by hindsight not only adds to what could be known at the time, it makes the reconstructed past more comprehensible than when it happened, endowing it with retrospective plausibility. 'What we recognize as the Roman Empire was a series of disconnected experiences for the generations who made it up', writes a medievalist. 'It is we who give them coherence'. Because we commonly view bygone scholars as more consistent than they usually were, we fabricate 'a history of thoughts which no one ever actually' thought, in Quentin Skinner's derisive phrase, 'at a level of coherence which no one ever actually attained'.[49] Driven to 'see the world as more tidy, simple, predictable, and coherent than

[45] Albert Frederick Pollard, 'Historical criticism', *History* 5 (1920): 21–9 at 29.
[46] Ralph Waldo Emerson, 'Goethe: or, the writer', in *CW* (Houghton Mifflin, 1904–12), 4: 259–90 at 261–2.
[47] R. Stephen Humphreys, 'The historian, his documents, and the elementary modes of historical thought', *History and Theory* 19 (1980): 1–20 at 12.
[48] Munz, *Shapes of Time*, 80, 93.
[49] Gordon Leff, *History and Social Theory* (Doubleday, 1971), 105; Quentin Skinner, 'Meaning and understanding in the history of ideas', *JHI* 8 (1969): 3–53 at 18.

it really is', concludes a psychologist, we impose causal order on the past, making it more explicable than its usual happenstance.[50]

Historical insight, in Wilhelm von Humboldt's persuasive analogy, is 'like the clouds which take shape for the eye only at a distance'.[51] In the near view, the clouds are simply fog. Just as maturity puts childhood in perspective, so is historical truth the daughter of time.[52] Following Humboldt, historians left recent times to journalists and social scientists, disowning modern history as an oxymoron. Friedrich Schleiermacher in the 1820s famously refused to lecture on post-1648 Europe; Johan Huizinga in 1931 chose to teach the eighteenth century rather than 'the imperfect and unreliable' recent past.[53] Erwin Panofsky in the 1950s judged that art history required a distance of sixty to eighty years.[54] Citing a widely accepted twenty-year rule, an American historian in the 1990s noted colleagues' discomfort in 'trying to make sense of events close to their own lifetimes'.[55]

Knowing the future of the past forces historians to transcend past immediacy, by taking into account how things later came out. The narrator's tempo and structure reflect this retrospective knowledge; being cognizant of the upshot of relevant events, he cannot avoid using what he knows in telling his story.[56] How hindsight awareness helped make the past a foreign country is explored later in this chapter.

An intelligible past demands inventive retelling. History no less than memory conflates, exaggerates, abridges; what is crucial or unique is made to stand out, uniformities and minutiae fade away. 'Time is foreshortened, details selected and highlighted, action concentrated, relations simplified', notes a literary historian, 'not to alter or distort the actors and events but to bring them to life and to give them meaning'.[57] For us, as for Henry James, 'history is never, in any rich sense, the immediate crudity of what "happens," but the much finer complexity of what we read into it'. We make sense of the past by communicating it allegorically, enriching its actors and actions with subsequent imagination.[58]

---

[50] Daniel Kahneman, *Thinking, Fast and Slow* (Penguin, 2011), 182, 202–4, 218. See Nassim Taleb, *The Black Swan* (Allen Lane, 2007), 10–12, 70.

[51] Wilhelm von Humboldt, 'On the historian's task' (1822), *History and Theory* 6 (1967): 57–71 at 58.

[52] Mark Salber Phillips, *On Historical Distance* (Yale, 2013), 1–2. '*Veritas filia temporis*' (Aulus Gellius (c. 130–180), *Noctes Atticae*), 'Truth the daughter of time', became Francis Bacon's Aphorism 84 (*New Organon* (1620; Cambridge, 2000), 69).

[53] Jaap den Hollander et al., 'The metaphor of historical distance', *History and Theory* 50:4 (2011): 1–10 at 2–3.

[54] Erwin Panofsky, 'Three decades of art history in the United States' (1953), in *Meaning in the Visual Arts* (1955; Penguin, 1993), 321–46 at 329.

[55] James T. Patterson, 'Americans and the writing of twentieth-century United States history', in Anthony Molho and Gordon S. Wood, eds., *Imagined Histories* (Princeton, 1998), 185–204 at 190.

[56] J. H. Hexter, 'The rhetoric of history', in *International Encyclopedia of the Social Sciences* (Macmillan, 1968), 6: 368–94 at 378. See Allan Megill and Donald N. McCloskey, 'The rhetoric of history', in John S. Nelson et al., eds., *The Rhetoric of the Human Sciences* (Wisconsin, 1987), 221–38.

[57] R. F. Arragon, 'History's changing image', *American Scholar* 33 (1964): 222–33 at 230.

[58] Henry James, *The American Scene* (1907; Indiana, 1968), 182. See Hayden White, 'The question of narrative in contemporary historical theory' (1984), in *The Content of the Form: Narrative Discourse and Historical Representation* (Johns Hopkins, 1987), 26–57.

The past's formless miscellanies become intelligible only when shaped into stories. The medieval *Annals of St Gall*'s bare listing of a sequence of years, some left blank, others annotated with discrete, unrelated events – '710. Hard year and deficient in crops . . . 712. Flood everywhere . . . 720. Charles fought against the Saracens . . . 722. Great crops . . . 725. Saracens came for the first time' – provides neither meaning nor continuity. It implies things about the past – that farming mattered, that the Saracens raided – but it lacks fullness, structure, and discourse.[59] Likewise random and disconnected is the *Anglo-Saxon Chronicle*: '776. In this year a red cross appeared in the sky after sunset. And that year the Mercians and the people of Kent fought at Otford. And marvellous adders were seen in Sussex.'[60]

Chronicles lend chronology meaning but lack closure and summing up: they simply end, leaving the plot unfinished, the past provisional. Historical narrative adds moral meaning and overview to facts about the past. It is not a faithful portrait of what happened but a story about it. History 'may well be one damned thing after another', argues Munz, 'but it cannot possibly *appear* as such', for that would void it of meaning.[61] A story 'confers both shape and meaning on events: it records not one thing *after* another . . . but one thing *because* of another'.[62] And because most stories stress causal explanation over chance and accident, history imparted to and known by us appears less muddled, more foreseeable, than the past ever was when present.

Thus Bede's life of St Cuthbert (721) wins 'favour with modern historians because of its satisfyingly coherent narrative with its emphasis on chronology and causation', notes Catherine Cubitt. 'Yet it is precisely these qualities that should make the modern scholar wary. Narrative is essentially an artifice, a literary device . . . to create the illusion of actuality and to endow fragmented and disconnected events with meaning', in Bede's case to provide a model of spiritual progress by converting Cuthbert's miracles into 'lessons for aspiring monks'.[63]

History bereft of shape and conviction would not be understood or attended to. Partiality and empathy warp knowledge, but distortion is essential to its conveyance – even to its very existence. Indeed, the more salient the historian's bias, the more believable his account. Early-modern scholars argued that well-informed history could not be impartial, since only those intimately involved with its shaping knew the reasons for their acts.[64] History is made credible because it is organized by and filtered through

---

[59] Hayden White, 'The value of narrativity in the representation of reality' (1980), in *Content of the Form*, 1–25 at 6–7.

[60] Sarah Foot, 'Finding the meaning of form: narrative in annals and chronicle', in Nancy Partner, ed., *Writing Medieval History* (Hodder Arnold, 2005), 88–108 at 89. See Elizabeth M. Tyler and Ross Balzaretti, eds., *Narrative and History in the Early Medieval West* (Turnhout: Brepols, 2006), 2.

[61] Munz, *Shapes of Time*, 239.

[62] Foot, 'Finding the meaning of form', 90–1. See Donald E. Polkinghorne, 'Narrative psychology and historical consciousness', in Jürgen Straub, ed., *Narration, Identity and Historical Consciousness* (Berghahn, 2005), 3–22 at 15.

[63] Catherine Cubitt, 'Memory and narrative in the cult of the early Anglo-Saxon saints', in Yitzhak Hen and Matthew Innes, eds., *The Uses of the Past in the Early Middle Ages* (Cambridge, 2000), 29–66 at 46–9.

[64] Anthony T. Grafton, *What Was History* (Cambridge, 2007), 130–2, citing Francesco Patrizi. Fear or ambition led all to err, thought an early-modern sceptic who declared most medieval historians forgers

subjective minds, not despite that fact; impassioned interpretation gives it life and meaning. 'Rhetoric is ordinarily deemed icing on the cake of history', but historiographer J. H. Hexter found it 'mixed right into the batter. It affects not merely the outward appearance of history ... but its inward character, its essential function – its capacity to convey knowledge of the past.' Emotional involvement enables the historian to communicate; without it his account is disjointed, insipid, unread.[65]

Hexter showed how quotations and lists of names serve rhetorical needs. Quotations – veritable vestiges of the past – make the reader not simply respond 'Yes', but exclaim 'Yes, indeed!' Lists lend conviction by sonorous allusion:

The Christian Revival, that intensification of religious sentiment and concern, ... in its full span had room for Cardinal Ximenes and Girolamo Savonarola, Martin Luther and Ignatius Loyola, the Reformed churches and the Jesuits, John of Leiden and Paul IV, Thomas Cranmer and Edmund Campion and Michael Servetus.

The reader is deliberately *not* told who they are, but by implication, to 'draw on the reservoir of your knowledge of the times in which these men lived to give meaning to this list'. Greater specificity would have signalled: 'Stop drawing on ... your knowledge. I have already told you how I want you to think about these men', thus stifling imagination. In gambling that readers would know enough to make sense of the names, the historian may have erred. But historians always have to gauge how much their audience already knows, whether to hint rather than be precise, when to sacrifice fact for evocative force. In translating past into present, they always juggle competing needs for literal faithfulness, allusive recognition, literary quality, sense of period, degree of archaism, subsequent interpretations, and consonance with today's mindset.[66] To do so capably 'gives us, not the familiar remembered things, but the glittering intensity of the summoned-up hallucination'.[67] Conveyed as mirage, the historian's message revivifies the past.

Confirmability

The unprovable belief that pasts actually existed gives historians the confidence to collect and order evidence, bringing them 'closer to knowing the truth', argues Gordon Wood, 'even if the full and complete truth about the past will always remain beyond their grasp'. Only such faith distinguishes history from fiction.[68]

Yet scholarly 'truth' is a relatively recent and still uncommon criterion for evaluating histories. Earlier folk gauged accounts more by narrators' repute than by fidelity to known facts. The true past was what was worthy of belief or whatever ancestral spokesmen declared to be true, even about events well known not to have happened. Hence scholars accommodated mutually incompatible faiths – both 'divine immutability and

(Anthony T. Grafton, 'Jean Hardouin: the antiquary as pariah', *Journal of the Warburg & Courtauld Institutes* 62 (1999): 241–67; Anthony T. Grafton, *Bring Out Your Dead* (Harvard, 2001), 193–4).
[65] Hexter, 'Rhetoric of history', 390, 380–1.
[66] Ibid. 386–9; Eco, *Mouse or Rat.*
[67] Frye, *Great Code*, 227.
[68] Gordon Wood, 'Writing history', *NYRB*, 16 Dec. 1982: 59.

historical change, the truth of Jewish sacrifices ... as well as of the Christian sacraments that had superseded them'. We still comfortably embrace contradictory testimonies, even conflicting accounts by the same informant.[69]

History has always served functions other than 'truth', often at cross-purposes with it – to secure the pedigrees of existing or would-be rulers, to promote patriotic zeal, to sanction religious causes or revolutionary reform, to venerate or derogate the dead. Expressly concerned to keep records 'lest age or oblivion destroy the memory of modern events', medieval chroniclers nonetheless conveyed a deliberately contrived and selected version of them. 'Truth' in medieval and early-modern culture meant not literal accuracy but a plausible exposition of virtues and vices and cognizance of what *ought* to have happened.[70]

History's great truths were received and eternal; the historian's mission was not to find but to buttress preconceived conclusions such as the existence of God or, with the Enlightenment, the inevitability of progress. Examples chosen as illustrative were by definition true, and those rejected false; the end purified the means. A true chronicle of a revered ruler was not the events of his life but an exposition of his virtues. And some still elide secular annals with sacred faith. 'In listening to the voice of history', declaimed an American historian in 1893, 'we well recognize the voice of God'.[71] That the history of America reflects divine will remains the avowed credo of many if not most of its elected leaders.

Only since the Enlightenment did knowing the past as it actually was become some historians' holy grail. Purged of precursors' prejudices, successive generations of scholars fancied themselves free of bias. Montesquieu thought himself unprejudiced; exposing Montesquieu's prejudices, the Jacobin Jean-Paul Marat believed he himself had none.[72] Few recognized their own fallibility. 'Our ancestors ... thought themselves as little under the influence of prejudice and idle fancy, as we may deem ourselves', wrote an eighteenth-century sceptic. 'The time may arrive, when this age also may be denominated dark; and we' chastised as *'credulous'*.[73] Alert to bias in others, nineteenth-century historians preened themselves on being rational and impartial.

As faith in received truth dwindled, historians' own judgements gained weight. Critical comparison of sources made chronicler bias more apparent and less pardonable; it began to seem wrong to slant history for partisan purpose. The ideal historian became 'a man of science, ascetic, levelheaded and detached', who renounced precursors' 'impassioned writing' and 'unabashed partisanship'. Keeping an aloof distance, the historian shed bias.[74] In 1883 Pope Leo XIII assailed secular historians for twisting evidence and called

[69] Carlo Ginzburg, 'Distance and perspective', in *Wooden Eyes: Nine Reflections on Distance* (Columbia, 2001), 139–56 at 148; Thomas L. Haskell, 'Objectivity', *History and Theory* 43 (2004): 321–59 at 343–4.
[70] Matthew Paris, *Chronica majora* (c. 1250), quoted in Michael Clanchy, *From Memory to Written Record* (Harvard, 1979), 118–20, 147. See Janet Coleman, *Ancient and Medieval Memories* (Cambridge, 1992), 294–9; Ruth Morse, *Truth and Convention in the Middle Ages* (Cambridge, 1991), 86–91, 113–38.
[71] William Wirt Henry quoted in Michael Kammen, *Mystic Chords of Memory* (Knopf, 1991), 195; Dorothy Ross, 'Grand narrative in historical writing', *AHR* 100 (1995): 651–77 at 655.
[72] Lionel Gossman, *Medievalism and Ideologies of the Enlightenment* (Johns Hopkins, 1968), 350–1.
[73] Joseph Berington, *History of the Lives of Abeillard and Eloisa*, 2nd edn (Basle, 1793), 1: li–lii.
[74] Jo Tollebeek and Ilaria Porciani, 'Institutions, networks and communities in a European perspective', in Ilaria Porciani and Jo Tollebeek, eds., *Setting the Standards: Institutions, Networks and Communities of National Historiography* (Palgrave Macmillan, 2012), 3–26 at 7.

for history 'written by men looking for truth and not for weapons ... true history, better history, impartial history'. Leo was certain that opening the papal archives would vindicate veracious papal annalists.[75] Reproving nationalist historiography, in 1896 Lord Acton exhorted *Cambridge Modern History* authors to lofty impartiality: 'Our Waterloo must be one that satisfies French and English, Germans and Dutch alike.' Historians sought disinterested objectivity, 'that noble dream'.[76] Today testable truth is history's hallmark, veracious history truth's ultimate arbiter. Queries such as 'How will history judge Nixon?' imply that we are all bound, in the end, to get our just due. (Nixon himself believed that 'history will treat me fairly', though 'historians probably won't'.[77])

Historians' credibility depends on their sources being open to general scrutiny. A trustworthy history must conform to accessible evidence. But it must also be largely consonant with other accepted chronicles. Not even Everyman's self-made personal history can overstep limits set by his fellows; living with others whose affairs Everyman intimately shares 'has taught him the expediency of recalling certain events with much exactness'.[78]

The history we consensually inherit is not all equally certain, but much of it is exceedingly sure and stable: it has survived the test of time and the vicissitudes of rival views. 'Nowadays, historians love to talk about invented pasts' as an antidote to positivist assumptions that history simply reflects past realities, a medievalist comments. But creative medieval accounts of early Lombard history could not be totally fabricated.

The war between the Lombards and the Longobards reported by [Piacenza notary Johannes] Codagnellus [*Liber Rerum Gestarum*, 1222] is invented to a considerable degree. But even to him, the distant Lombard past was not infinitely malleable. Medieval historiographers mostly dealt with truths that were already there. ... Even invented pasts could not be invented freely, they had to be likely enough to have come to pass.

Unlike the 'happy' fictional ending of the 1961 film *Rosamunda e Alboino* [*Sword of the Conquerer*], 'whoever wrote histories in the Middle Ages, even *historiae fabulosae*, could not have made the Gepids win'. They could have tweaked the personae or the order of tribal settlement. But 'the Lombards had to win, for ... Italy was a Lombard not a Gepid kingdom, and the region around Milan and Pavia was called Lombardy. After all, people knew what their past had led to.'[79]

---

[75] Owen Chadwick, *Catholicism and History: The Opening of the Vatican Archives* (Cambridge, 1978), 100–2.

[76] Lord Acton, 'Letter to contributors for *Cambridge Modern History*, 12 Mar. 1898', in *Lectures on Modern History*, 315–18; Gordon S. Wood, 'A century of writing early American history', *AHR* 100 (1995): 678–96 at 684; Peter Novick, *That Noble Dream: The 'Objectivity Question' and the American Historical Profession* (Cambridge, 1988), 71–2, 259.

[77] Michael Schudson, *Watergate in American Memory* (New York: Basic Books, 1992), 216.

[78] Becker, 'Everyman his own historian', 228. Everyman's coal bill is flagrantly exaggerated, suggesting a Becker spoof (Laurel Thatcher Ulrich, 'Mr Everyman buys coal', AHA *Perspectives on History* (Sept. 2009): 3–4).

[79] Walter Pohl, 'Memory, identity and power in Lombard Italy', in Hen and Innes, eds., *Uses of the Past in the Early Middle Ages*, 9–28 at 27–8. Because the Carolingian past had largely been forgotten, Verona scholars could invent a largely fictitious one (Cristina La Rocca, 'A man for all seasons: Pacificus of Verona and the creation of a local Carolingian past', in Hen and Innes, eds., *Uses of the Past*, 250–79).

We may be uncertain just who killed Caesar, but to doubt that Caesar was assassinated at all, we would have to reject 'an enormous range of other implicated facts, both about Caesar and about Roman history ... in general'. To jettison all this would soon make it difficult to believe *anything* about the past, Leon Pompa points out. If so much accepted history were dubious, we would be forced to distrust all extant historical and indeed contemporary thought.[80]

No absolute truth lies waiting to be found; however assiduous and fair-minded, the historian can no more relate the past 'as it really was' than can our memories. But history is not thereby invalidated. We rightly feel it casts *some* light on the past, contains a core of truth. Future insights are bound to reveal present error and falsify present surmise, but evidence now at hand proves that some things certainly did happen while others did not. No opaque curtain cordons off historians from the past; they peer into bygone tableaux, confident that their perceptions and accounts are not just mental figments but at least approximate bygone reality.

Yet most generally received history stems neither from direct empirical knowledge nor rational inference; it reflects a cumulative consensus among those who have sought to know the past. We find it credible not because we ourselves have seen documentary proof, but because we inherit confidence in the repute of those who have. History is verified as much by collegial trust as by its canonical contents; 'we agree to regard each other – at least some others – as bearers of truth', concludes a folklorist, and accept what they tell us as reasonably close to what must have happened.[81] To be sure, countless historical impostures have deceived the credulous, but unfolding evidence progressively corrects errors and exposes mendacities.

The prospect of public exposure makes sourced historical knowledge, even of remote and obscure events, more reliable than eyewitness recall, even of the recent and accessible past. Underlying our trust is faith that previous chroniclers, however naive or self-interested, were, on the whole, honest and assiduous. 'Were not the memory tenacious to a certain degree; had not men commonly an inclination to truth and a principle of probity; were they not sensible to shame when discovered in a falsehood', reasoned David Hume, 'we should never repose the least confidence in human testimony.'[82] We accredit historical accounts that conform with other trusted accounts. And because consensual, histories can be more rigorously verified or falsified than most memories.

Such confidence is challenged by critics of many stamps, from religious zealots to postmodern nihilists. A classic precursor was Archbishop Richard Whately's anti-Napoleonic satire. Whately argued that those who disbelieved Christian miracles must by the same token doubt Napoleon's existence, for most 'who talk about Buonaparte do not even pretend to speak from their own authority, but merely ... repeat what they have casually heard'. Professed eyewitnesses had been conned into believing the man they saw

[80] Leon Pompa, *Human Nature and Historical Knowledge* (Cambridge, 1990), 197–205, 222. On historical consensus, see Aviezer Tucker, *Our Knowledge of the Past* (Cambridge, 2004) , 23–45.

[81] Sam Schrager, 'What is social in social history?' *International Journal of Oral History* 4 (1983): 76–98 at 78.

[82] David Hume, 'Of Miracles', in *An Enquiry Concerning Human Understanding* (1748), in *Philosophical Works* (Aalen: Scientia, 1964), 4: 3–135 at, 127.

was Napoleon. Yet only tales in lying or duped newspapers attested his exploits. Their 'grossly contradictory' accounts made them all dubious, but

the story told by any one of them ... carries an air of fiction and romance on the very face of it. All the events are great, and splendid, and marvellous: great armies, great victories, great frosts, great reverses, 'hairbreadth 'scapes', empires subverted in a few days; ... everything upon that grand scale so common in Epic Poetry, so rare in real life; and thus calculated to strike the imagination of the vulgar, – and to remind the sober-thinking few of the Arabian Nights. Every event, too, has that *roundness* and completeness which is so characteristic of fiction; nothing is done by halves; we have *complete* victories, – *total* overthrows, – *entire* subversion of empires, – *perfect* re-establishments of them, – crowded upon us in rapid succession ... The improbabilities ... would fill volumes.

Only one 'ignorant of history and of human nature' could find it 'conformable to *Experience*, our best and only sure guide. In vain will he seek in history for something similar to this wonderful Buonaparte.'[83]

Postmodern sceptics' aim was the opposite of Whately's: not to reaffirm faith in seemingly incredible sources, but to demonstrate that *all* sources are fatally tarnished, hence unreliable. Such doubts begin to corrode public confidence in history, as discussed in my final chapters. But they are still very much the exception.

Few caveats subvert historical faith instilled in school. Children are 'taught history as they were taught math – as a finite subject with definite right or wrong answers', fretted a museum director. Most history texts are 'written as if their authors did not exist, as if they were simply instruments of a divine intelligence transcribing official truths'. Their veracity goes unquestioned. 'All the information is written down', students say; 'you've just got to find the answers in the book'. Textbook certitude makes it hard for teachers to deal with doubt and controversy; saying 'I don't know' violates the authoritarian norm of classroom certitude. Hence history teachers adopt the omniscient tone of their texts. Students ignore historical actors diverse motives; taking for granted that texts and teachers simply report known facts is less effort and earns higher marks.[84]

Older folk learned history as Simone de Beauvoir recalled of her 1920s schooling, 'never dreaming there might be more than one view of past events'.[85] Today contrary

---

[83] Richard Whately, *Historic Doubts Relative to Napoleon Buonaparte* (1819; 7th edn London, 1841), 12–18, 25–30. Whately scoffed at the 'abundance of busts and prints of this great being; all striking likenesses – of one another' (54). When Napoleon's remarkably preserved corpse was exhumed in 1840 to be reburied in Paris, Whately suggested duplicate remains to compensate St Helena, instancing the several skulls of Oliver Cromwell (55–6). Three years after Cromwell's death in 1658, his disinterred remains were hanged at Tyburn, the head falling off. Three skulls were later claimed as Cromwell's ('Cromwell's head riddle', *Oxford Times*, 3 Mar. 1988: 1).

[84] Indianapolis Children's Museum director Peter Sterling quoted in George Gonis, 'History in the making', *History News* 40:7 (July 1985): 12–15. See Samuel S. Wineburg, 'Probing the depths of students' historical knowledge', AHA *Perspectives* 30:3 (Mar. 1992): 19–24; Samuel S. Wineburg, 'On the reading of historical texts' (1991), in *Historical Thinking and Other Unnatural Acts* (Temple, 2001), 63–88 at 76–7, and vii–viii; James W. Loewen, *Lies My Teacher Told Me: Everything Your American History Textbook Got Wrong* (New York: New Press, 1995), 280–1.

[85] Simone de Beauvoir, *Memoirs of a Dutiful Daughter* (1958; London, 1963), 127.

views may be posed, but alternatives are only good or bad, right or wrong; honest differences of opinion are seldom an option. Asked to decide between two versions of a historical event, a student says, 'It was cool to hear both sides of the story and choose who you think was telling the truth.'[86] Both sides! Truth! History becomes a courtroom: every story has just two sides, and whoever was wrong must have lied. Historians scrutinize documents like prosecutors; students take them as literally as jurors.

In school texts, history remains one-dimensional even where controversy is rampant. The antiquity of Native American settlement is nowadays keenly disputed, but textbook readers would never know this; most texts portray either the 'early' or the 'late' arrival version as undisputed fact. Loose ends are avoided lest they unravel faith. Everything in school history was 'presented as if it were the full picture', recalled a student in 1991, 'so I never thought to doubt that it was'. Few historians try to explain that there may be more than one 'accurate' version of the same event.[87]

To show children 'that history and the way we interpret it is not carved in granite ... that the past can never be totally reconstructed', the museum director cited above stressed how provisional history is:

We're not saying, 'This is the past. Believe it!' ... We're saying, 'Given what we know, this is our best interpretation.' [Children] find out we're constantly finding out things that change our perception of the past. They'll learn that what we know about the past today is not what we'll know [tomorrow]. They'll also learn that there are some things we can never find out.[88]

But this laudable lesson is seldom learned, for it is rarely taught. Many children do, however, learn to mistrust textbooks, either as politically sanctioned or test-worthy diktats. Two generations of Soviet-dominated Estonians imbibed party-line history curricula while scorning it. Anglo-American students learn to regurgitate textbook history for good grades. Asked to monitor his eleven-year-old daughter's history lessons, a historical novelist is horrified by their preposterous perversions. 'Oh, poppy! this is for an exam; this is not the truth. I know better than this.'[89]

But rubbishing received history has its own hazards. Conflicting versions of what caused the Jamestown colony's 'starving time' (1609–10) led students to reject all accounts of the past as constructed by people who 'regularly and intentionally distorted the truth, ... just made things up or were simply lying'. Was it wise, asks their teacher, for 10-year-olds to abandon 'sublime trust in the veracity of history textbooks' for 'intrigue-filled but overgeneralized suspicion?' To dismiss history as bogus 'because historical agents are all lying' presupposes an ideal of unattainable probity. 'If only they were to

[86] Judy P. Hohmann, 'Discovering documents', *History News* (Sept.–Oct. 1993): 13–16. See Denis J. Shemilt, 'Adolescent ideas about evidence and methodology in history', in Christopher Portal, ed., *The History Curriculum for Teachers* (Lewes: Falmer, 1988), 39–61 at 41–3.

[87] Loewen, *Lies My Teacher Told Me*, 92–3, 5 [student]; Eric Foner and John Sayles, 'A conversation', in Mark C. Carnes, ed., *Past Imperfect: History According to the Movies* (New York: Henry Holt, 1995), 11–29 at 25.

[88] Peter Sterling quoted in Gonis, 'History in the making', 12–15.

[89] Robert Penn Warren in Ralph Ellison et al., 'The uses of history in fiction', *Southern Literary Journal* 1:2 (Spring 1969): 57–90 at 70.

tell the truth, then we could get to ... what really happened'. But absent an impeccable witness, all chroniclers were dishonest, all chronicles alike untrustworthy.[90]

The historian's often declared task is to provide society with a discriminating memory.[91] Yet to do so the historian must likewise discriminate. Only by selectively reshaping selected sources can any chronicler, whether academic scholar or spinner of romance, memorably recount the past. But the gulf between historians' discriminating memory and the fables of the popular media widens all the time. More about the past is known than ever before, yet is less shared. The 'Progressive' synthesis that marked American history writing up to half a century ago, for example, gave way to congeries of fragments. Among the general public, burgeoning historical fiction and retro fancies contrast starkly with the growing neglect of history in school, decline in academe, and professional historians' diminishing role in purveying the past.[92]

Thirty years ago I attributed the gulf mainly to the enormous expansion of historical knowledge. Widespread literacy and the preservative powers of print allowed everything known about the past to accumulate, and formal history had broadened to include the past of non-European cultures and of a host of new phenomena. As a result, no individual could take in more than a tiny fraction of it.[93] We were already all specialists, the football fanatic who knew every team's past scores no less than the expert on the lives of saints or the history of majolica. Historians perforce remain ignorant of most aspects of things past. Many blamed historians' increasingly narrow remits, forbidding technical paraphernalia, disregard of the wider public: 'fragmentation and overspecialization have stultified ... much of the profession'.[94]

Plaints continue to be made that 'academic history ... is in danger of becoming a priestly caste', marooned in historians' 'cobwebbed studies' and 'the bilious world of the intellectuals'.[95] 'Historians are more and more specialized, experts on single decades or single subjects, and still they cannot keep up with the profusion of monographs. Most now make no pretence of writing for the educated public. They write for each other, and with all their scientific paraphernalia ... they can sometimes count their readers on their hands', noted Gordon Wood in 1982. A quarter-century later the ongoing loss of readers and history course enrolment led Wood to renew his criticism; postmodern theory had made 'academic history writing almost as esoteric and inward directed as th[at] of literary scholars'.[96]

---

[90] Bruce A. VanSledright, 'Confronting history's interpretive paradox while teaching fifth graders to interpret the past', *American Educational Research Journal* 39:4 (2002): 1089–115 at 1103–5, and *The Challenge of Rethinking History Education* (Routledge, 2011), ch. 4.

[91] Michael Kammen, 'Vanitas and the historian's vocation', *Reviews in American History* 10:4 (1982): 1–27 at 19–20.

[92] John Lukacs, 'Obsolete historians', *Harper's Magazine* 261 (Nov. 1980): 80–4.

[93] *The Past Is a Foreign Country* (Cambridge, 1985), xxiv–xxv.

[94] E. Bradford Burns, 'Teaching history: a changing clientele', AHA *Perspectives* 21:1 (1983): 19–21.

[95] David Harlan, 'Historical fiction and the future of academic history', in Keith Jenkins et al., *Manifestos for History* (Routledge, 2007), 108–30 at 120; Ivo Dawnay, 'History matters', *National Trust Magazine*, no. 108 (Summer 2006): 20–2.

[96] Gordon S. Wood, 'Star-spangled history', *NYRB*, 12 Aug. 1982: 4; Gordon S. Wood, *Purpose of the Past* (Penguin, 2008), 3–6.

With few exceptions historians continue to eschew neologisms and jargon for ordinary language, in work more accessible to the general public than that of most other scholars. Yet growing specialization makes historical dialogue 'ever more technical and selfreferential', in AHA president William Cronon's recent charge, hence 'dry, dead, and boring' for non-professionals.[97] Indeed, academic historians agree that their work, long on analysis and short on synthesis, 'is not meant to be accessible'. And their concentration on specialized knowledge leaves students with an absence of connective tissue.[98]

Today's populist Zeitgeist likewise encourages the public to privilege its own take on the past without deferring to expert views. Postmodernists preach that historians like all of us are partial, selective, above the fray; we should mistrust self-interested professionals all the more for claiming expertise. But students taught 'that every historical source is biased . . . often dismiss all sources as unreliable and give up on the possibility of knowing anything about the past'.[99] But if all pasts are dubious, they are also equally deserving of attention. Your past, my past, so-and-so's past all differ, but each has the high populist merit of being someone's past. The collective past thus becomes the ungraded crazy quilt of humanity's individual memories. In this anti-elitist *mélange* 'everything is presumed as equally important, since any . . . emphasis would suggest [the politically incorrect view] that certain ideas, cultures, or individuals are worthier of interest than others'.[100]

How the learned imbibe history also sets them more apart. Sources now seem 'impenetrable, irreducible, resistant to our efforts to exploit them for information and meaning; instead of reading through them as if they were windows onto the past, historians now treat them . . . as mysterious body parts of the vanished past'.[101] But while professionals increasingly recognize history as 'an unnatural act', the public at large, bemused by simplified visual displays and by ready Internet access to 'facts', tends to view the past as transparently easy to fathom, graspable without effort let alone doubt. 'Accepting false information as truth is an everyday classroom occurrence', notes Sam Wineburg. Asked 'how they "know" that our president was born in Kenya or that the Mossad (or George Bush himself) plotted 9/11, students . . . blithely respond, "I found it on the Internet"'.[102]

Not those who query sources but those who swallow them whole feel Mircea Eliade's 'terror of history', softened by Charles Schulz in 'Peanuts' into something 'that should always be studied in the morning, before anything else can happen'.[103]

[97] William Cronon, 'Professional boredom', AHA *Perspectives on History* (Mar. 2012): 5–6.
[98] Johann N. Neem, 'Taking historical fundamentalism seriously', *Historically Speaking* 12:5 (2011): 2–5 at 4. See Gordon S. Wood, 'In defense of academic history writing', AHA *Perspectives* (Apr. 2011): 19–20.
[99] Keith C. Barton, 'Research on students' historical thinking and learning', AHA *Perspectives* (Oct. 2004): 19–21.
[100] Paula Marantz Cohen, 'Make mine a vixen' *TLS*, 17 Sept. 2004: 7–8.
[101] Lionel Gossman, 'Voices of silence', *History and Theory* 43 (2004): 272–7 at 274. See Ann Rigney, *Imperfect Histories: The Elusive Past and the Legacy of Romantic Historicism* (Cornell, 2001).
[102] Sam Wineburg, 'Changing the teaching of history, one byte at a time', *Edutopia: Education Trends*, 14 Nov., 2013 edutopia.org. Digital con artists dupe textbook authors as well as students. The falsehood that 'thousands' of slaves fought for the Confederacy in the Civil War (Joy Masoff, *Our Virginia: Past and Present* (Five Ponds Press, 2010)) came from a Sons of Confederate Veterans website.
[103] Mircea Eliade, *The Myth of the Eternal Return* (1949; Princeton, 1994), 139–62.

Western and other histories

History has long been seen – notably by Western historians – as a preponderantly Western enterprise. Other peoples' interest in their pasts was a far cry from the *historical* awareness that emerged in the European Renaissance. Some further held that only Europe *had* history: non-Europeans were historically unconscious because they had no history to be conscious of, until contact with (and the usual sequel, conquest by) Europeans.[104]

Scholars of many stripes confined history to modern Western civilization. Karl Marx thought non-Europeans unreachable by revolutionary change because outside the stream of history.[105] 'The Caucasians form the only truly *historical* race', intoned a popular 1870s schoolbook. 'Civilization is the product of the brain of this race'.[106] Up to 1950, a canonical architectural text dismissed non-Western (Asian and Saracenic) building styles as 'Non-Historical'.[107] 'The history of the world, for the last five centuries, in so far as it has significance, has been European history', declared the English historian Hugh Trevor-Roper in 1965. 'Perhaps, in the future, there will be some African history. But at present, there is none: there is only the history of Europeans in Africa. The rest is largely, like . . . pre-Columbian America, darkness.'[108]

Eurocentrism embraced overseas settlers of European stock. 'The only population of America that has counted in history has been of European origin', held a respected 1904 text.[109] California high school students in the 1970s, white and black alike, agreed that 'if Africa had had a history worth learning about, we would have had it last year in Western Civ'. To this day, 'the world outside Europe, except for the United States, hardly exists in European school history'.[110] Non-Western history concerns only 16 percent of British historians, Asia and sub-Saharan Africa barely 13 percent of Anglo-Americans' historical research.[111]

The supposed absence of history elsewhere reflected Enlightenment views that equated history with progressive change, long limited to the 'civilized' West. For Hegel Africa was 'unhistorical, undeveloped, . . . mere nature'. Consigning non-Europeans to static time-lessness accorded with their own reiterated claims of hewing to ancestral practice.

---

[104] Eric R. Wolf, *Europe and the People without History* (California, 1982), is the classic statement.
[105] Samir Amin, *L'eurocentrisme* (Paris: Anthropos, 1988); Kevin B. Anderson, *Marx at the Margins* (Chicago, 2010).
[106] William Swinton, *Outlines of the World's History* (New York, 1874), 2. See Peter Munz, *Our Knowledge of the Growth of Knowledge* (Routledge, 1985), 314.
[107] Banister Fletcher, *A History of Architecture on the Comparative Method*, 15th edn (Batsford, 1950), 888.
[108] Hugh Trevor-Roper, *The Rise of Christian Europe* (Thames & Hudson, 1965), 11, reiterated in his 'The past and the present: history and sociology', *Past & Present* 42 (1969): 3–17. See Finn Fuglestad, 'The Trevor-Roper trap', *History in Africa* 19 (1992): 309–26; Finn Fuglestad, *The Ambiguities of History: The Problem of Ethnocentrism in Historical Writing* (Oslo: Academic Press, 2005), 10–11, 16, 64–5, 75.
[109] Edward Potts Cheyney, *European Background of American History, 1300–1600* (New York, 1904), xxvii.
[110] Martha Doerr Toppin, 'I know who's going with me: reflections on the fellowship of history', *Social Education* 44 (1980): 456–60; Joke van der Leeuw-Roord, 'Beyond the doorstep: the nature of history teaching across Europe', in Semih Aktekin et al., eds., *Teaching History and Social Studies for Multicultural Europe* (Ankara: Harf, 2009), 155–76 at 169. See Joke van der Leeuw-Roord, 'Yearning for yesterday', in Symcox and Wilschut, eds., *National History Standards*, 73–95 at 91n20.
[111] Luke Clossey and Nicholas Guyatt, 'It's a small world over all: the wider world in historians' peripheral vision', AHA *Perspectives on History* 51:5 (May 2013): 24–7.

Anthropologists recorded the immutable traditionalism of backward peasants and tribal primitives, resistant to change until impacted by Western dynamism.[112] Whether seen as rural idiots or, later, as noble savages, such folk had no history. It was to counter this demeaning depiction that Chinua Achebe's historical novels aimed to teach Nigerians 'that their past – with all its imperfections – was not one long night of savagery from which the first Europeans acting on God's behalf delivered them'.[113]

The Western fallacy was to mistake mystiques of changelessness for actuality, to assume that 'a society can be subject to the gaze of history only when the society itself' is historically self-conscious.[114] 'History is *conscious*', asserted Oswald Spengler, '*making*' history as opposed to merely passive 'endurance of fate'.[115] Peoples 'without history' were not devoid of interest in the past or unaware that it differed from the present, although, like most Europeans until recently, they deeply regretted change. All peoples claim to cleave to ancestral tradition despite overwhelming contrary evidence. To palliate dismaying change inherent in all societies, continuity is stressed and mutable history denied.

The view that Westerners are especially historically-*minded* has more merit. To be sure, diurnal, seasonal, and generational regularities still dominate quotidian life in the West as elsewhere. But biblical concepts of linear and unrepeatable history superimposed a divinely ordained narrative in which events happened once and only once. A sacred chronology beginning in Creation and ending in Resurrection made secular time finite and irreversible. The datable life and death of Jesus ordained historical consciousness, secular as well as sacred. As discussed in Chapter 5, the course of individual human lives became a template for the history of nations, Earth, and cosmos.[116]

Yet Christians, no less than polytheists, long denied fundamental change beyond the scripturally ordained. Only with the Renaissance and the Reformation did new perspectives on time and causality begin to direct Western thought. Briefly, these are a linear view of past and future, reliance on written texts, awareness of anachronism, belief in growth if not progress, focus on collective agency, search for causal explanation, and zeal for objectivity. Together, they comprise 'specifically historical interest in the past' as opposed to stress on memory and tradition.[117] Barely nascent for fifteen centuries, such historicism is by no means universal today; cyclic modes of consciousness persist

---

[112] G. W. F. Hegel, *The Philosophy of History* (1830–1; Dover, 1956), 99; Marshall Sahlins, *Islands of History* (Chicago, 1985); Edmund Leach, 'Tribal ethnography', in Tonkin et al., eds., *History and Ethnicity*, 37–47 at 37–40.

[113] Chinua Achebe, 'The novelist as teacher' (1965), in *Morning Yet on Creation Day* (Heinemann, 1975), 42–8 at 45. Jack Goody (*The Theft of History* (Cambridge, 2006), 1–7, 23, 186–92), rebuts Trevor-Roper and Fernand Braudel's claims of European inventive uniqueness versus static 'others'.

[114] Smail, *On Deep History and the Brain*, 50.

[115] Oswald Spengler, *Aphorisms* (Regnery, 1967), 46.

[116] Johan Galtung, 'Western deep thinking and Western historical thinking', in Jörn Rüsen, ed., *Western Historical Thinking* (Berghahn, 2002, 85–100 at 87–91.

[117] Peter Burke, 'Western historical thinking in a global perspective', 15–30, and Hayden White, 'The Westernization of world history', 111–118 at 112, both in Rüsen, ed., *Western Historical Thinking*. To be sure, other cultures exhibit or claim some of these traits: Chinese devotion to textual analysis, Korean to impartial objectivity, Indian to progress within cyclical determinism. See Ming-ke Wang, 'What continued in history?', in Chun-Chieh Huang and John B. Henderson, eds., *Notions of Time in Chinese Historical Thinking* (Hong Kong: Chinese University Press, 2006), 185–9.

alongside them. But by and large they distinguish Western historical philosophy, if not practice, today, and, with globalization, increasingly that of the rest of the world.

Chronology and narrative

Narratives sequences, dates, and chronologies so suffuse Western history as to seem attributes of the past itself. But they are not; our precursors put them there. From classical times to the Renaissance, chronology was a valued scholarly enterprise.[118] Ordering events by universally accepted dates is much more recent and far from unanimous practice. Even today, the past remains for many chaotically episodic, a hotchpotch of chronologically muddled figures and events. In this heaving and formless sea stand a few islands of measured fixity, on which unlettered moderns huddle for temporal security.

Facts about the past are timeless and discontinuous unless woven together in stories. We do not experience a flow of time, only a succession of situations and events. To many, historical awareness remains as temporally untethered as memory. Calendric vagueness is the rule in oral societies, temporal distance ignored or smudged by narrators and auditors alike. Without dates or records to consult, neither the duration nor the order of past events is fixed; they are telescoped, expanded, and reordered in line with their ascribed significance. Brief moments of perceived change typically punctuate long periods of stasis; significant events are consigned either to a mythic time of origin or to recent living memory. Dynastic founders get credit both for their own deeds and for their successors', whose own agency is forgotten. The repetitive regularity of the orally transmitted past fits the mantra that 'nothing happened' between the beginning and recent times. In contrast, historians reliant on written sources dwell on incremental change over the whole span of time; their history never stands still.[119]

Oral temporal habits persisted well into Europe's scribal age, when chronicles were still mainly read aloud. Medieval audiences shuffled Caesar, Charlemagne, Alexander, David, and other ancients like playing cards, viewing each as prototypes; thus Alexander walked in Miltiades' footsteps. Caesar took Alexander as his model, Charlemagne became Caesar. It took two centuries of printing to accustom literate Europeans to look back via ordered sequences of epochs. Even after writing made dating easier, few but tax collectors and census-takers were impelled to divide time into calendrically equivalent segments.[120]

Temporal order was instead segmented by dynasty, chronologies dated by consular or regnal epochs, starting with the first year and ending with the ruler's last. Calendric tables stressed distance from Adam or Abraham, Noah or Aeneas, Romulus and Remus. Nascent efforts to universalize time in the Roman Empire foundered with its fall. Chronologies based on noble lineages grounded medieval time in procreation and

---

[118] Daniel Rosenberg and Anthony Grafton, *Cartographies of Time* (Princeton Architectural Press, 2010), 10.

[119] Louis O. Mink, 'History and fiction as modes of comprehension', *New Literary History* 1 (1970): 541–58 at 545–6; David P. Henige, *The Chronology of Oral Tradition* (Clarendon Press, 1974), 2–9; Joseph C. Miller, 'Listening for the African past', in his, ed., *African Past Speaks* (Folkestone: Dawson, 1980), 1–59 at 16, 37.

[120] Paul Connerton, *How Societies Remember* (Cambridge, 1989), 62; Elizabeth L. Eisenstein, 'Clio and Chronos: an essay on the making and breaking of history-book time', *History and Theory*, 6 (1966): 36–64.

filiation.[121] But these dynastic histories were disconnected. Separate temporal frameworks precluded comparative analysis.

The need for an agreed sacred calendar, manifest in fixing dates for Easter, at length unified Western chronology. Fully accepted only a millennium on, the sixth-century Christian calendar overcame the insularity of dynastic narrative. Annalistic replaced event-dominated accounts; year-by-year frameworks overshadowed the episodes they framed. Specific happenings – a plague, a coronation, an eclipse, a royal birth – were assigned to various years in these annuaries, with other years simply left blank: it was the enumeration itself that mattered. Showing the years of our Lord unfolding from known beginning towards promised end, this agreed chronology, from the Incarnation to the impending Resurrection, possessed God-given fullness and continuity.[122] But growing disparities between Christian and scientific history made the commingling of sacred with secular calendars, of mythical with verifiable events, first futile and then dispensable. Few now know – and some who do complain – that BC means before Christ, AD in the year of our Lord.[123]

The start and end of millennia, centuries, and decades spawn recurrent mystiques. From millennial forebodings preceding the year 1000, decimal determinism ascribed reality to epochs demarcated by century, with *fin-de-siècle* malaise around 1700, 1800, 1900, and 2000. Decades became clotheshorses for calendric fashion – the Gay '90s, the Stylish '30s, the Swinging '60s, the Naughty '00s. What began as nominal shorthand – fifth-century Athens, seventeenth-century England – became frames for fleeting Zeitgeists. Like such synthesizing constructs as 'the Middle Ages' or 'the Depression', calendar stereotypes harden and reify thought about the past: the nineteenth century or the 1930s become a 'thing' like a battle or a birthplace, and causal agents in their own right.[124]

These excesses aside, we owe much to the chronologists: clock, calendar, and numbered page habituated us to sequential order. But only the printing press and the spread of literacy secured its acceptance and universality. And centuries of painstaking

---

[121] Denis Feeney, *Caesar's Calendar* (California, 2007); Gabrielle M. Spiegel, 'History, historicism, and the social logic of the text in the Middle Ages', *Speculum* 65 (1990): 59–86 at 78–80; Deborah Mauskopf Deliyannis, 'Year-dates in the early Middle Ages', in Chris Humphrey and W. M. Ormrod, eds., *Time in the Medieval World* (York Medieval Press, 2001), 5–22.

[122] Denys Hay, *Annalists and Historians* (Methuen, 1977), 22–7, 38–42; Mink, 'Everyman his or her own annalist', 233–4; Rosenberg and Grafton, *Cartographies of Time*, 11–12; Rosamond McKitterick, *History and Memory in the Carolingian World* (Cambridge, 2009), 86–100, 277. Deeds and charters were long dated by regnal years rather than *anno Domini*; the king's coronation was more recent and publicly remembered (Clanchy, *From Memory to Written Record*, 240).

[123] Eisenstein, 'Clio and Chronos', 43; E. G. Richards, *Mapping Time: The Calendar and Its History* (Oxford, 2000); Lynn Hunt, *Measuring Time, Making History* (Budapest: Central European University Press, 2008). BC also stands for Before Columbus, Bar Code, Birth Control, and Bacon Cheeseburger, AD for After Death, American Dream, and Alzheimer's Disease, among others.

[124] Frank Kermode, *The Sense of an Ending* (Oxford, 1968), 96–8; Herbert Butterfield, *Man on His Past* (Cambridge, 1969), 136; Roger Bromley, *Lost Narratives* (Routledge 1988), 102–3; Hillel Schwartz, *Century's End* (Doubleday, 1989); Mikuláš Teich and Roy Porter, eds., *Fin de Siècle and Its Legacy* (Cambridge, 1990); Walter Laqueur, 'Fin de siècle', *Journal of Contemporary History* 31 (1996): 5–47; Joan DeJean, *Ancients against Moderns* (Chicago, 1997), 19–20, 23; Sally Ledger and Roger Luckhurst, eds., *The Fin de Siècle* (Oxford, 2001).

correlation from myriad sources were needed for the securely timed and dated series on which we now rely.[125]

Chronology or 'history-book time' accustomed the schooled to view the past as an all-inclusive narrative. Above all, the printing press enabled each 'to sort out and arrange almost any portion of the past he encounters, to find his ancestors or to "find himself"'. A sequence of familiar monarchs made Britain the fortunate possessor, a historian recalled, of 'a national time scale immediately understandable to any English child'. A novelist's 1950s Oxford course 'began at the beginning of English history' and went 'on in a nice straight line without any gaps, [shaping] an orderly, chronological image . . . a nice, linear, uninterrupted memory'.[126]

Offshoots of Joseph Priestley's charts, my own 1940s Harvard history chronologies mapped Western Civilization from the Egyptians and Babylonians to 1815.[127] Some epochs in this continuum I barely recognized, but being charted made them seem retrievable. Aligning pharaohs and kings and presidents in one chronological column, battles and conquests in another, discoveries and inventions, poets and painters in a third bolstered faith that all history was knowable and interrelated *because* datable. Reliance on chronology was often rigid or simplistic, to be sure. It envisioned history as an interlinked process of growing complexity and improvement. 'Western Civilization' curricula revealed history as an unfolding panorama of progress.

Along with progress, dates and chronology are now out of fashion. Censured as constricting and simplistic, they give way to flashbacks and fast-forwards in history as in fiction. History today follows not one Eurocentric line but those of many diverse cultures, impossible (and politically incorrect) to lump within a common sequence. As historians discovered both the Third World and the West's previously voiceless 'minorities' – women, children, peasants, blacks – 'Western Civ' gave way along with the ethnocentrism that made it canonically pre-eminent.[128]

Emphasizing economic, social, and intellectual history further vitiated chronological relevance: cultures and ideologies proved less datable than kings and conquests. Newfound aspects of the past 'impinge on the modern consciousness from so many directions', observed an historian in 1966, 'that they tax the capacity of the human intelligence to order them coherently'.[129] Half a century on, many abandon coherent order as

---

[125] James William Johnson, 'Chronological writing', *History and Theory* 2 (1962): 124–45; Anthony Grafton, 'Joseph Scaliger and historical chronology', *History and Theory* 14 (1975): 156–85; Donald J. Wilcox, *The Measure of Times Past* (Chicago, 1987).

[126] Richard Cobb, 'Becoming a historian', in *A Sense of Place* (Duckworth, 1975), 7–48 at 21–2; Penelope Lively, 'Children and the art of memory', *Horn Book Magazine* 54 (1978): 17–23, 197–203 at 200.

[127] Joseph Priestley, *A New Chart of History* (London, 1769); Robert E. Schofield, *The Enlightenment of Joseph Priestley* (PennPress, 1997), 128–31.

[128] Gilbert Allardyce, 'The rise and fall of the Western Civilization course', *AHR* 87 (1982): 695–725, and Morris Rossabi, 'Comment' on Allardyce, *AHR* 87 (1982): 729–32; Eugen Weber, 'Western Civilization', in Molho and Wood, eds., *Imagined Histories*, 206–20. See William H. McNeill, 'What we mean by the West', *American Educator* 24 (2000): 10–15; Daniel A. Segal, '"Western Civ" and the staging of history in American higher education', *AHR* 105 (2000): 770–805; Glenn Ricketts et al., *The Vanishing West 1964–2010: The Disappearance of Western Civilization from the American Undergraduate Curriculum* (Princeton: National Association of Scholars, 2011).

[129] Eisenstein, 'Clio and Chronos', 63.

chimerical. The common response to the dilemma is to scrap chronology entirely, as Penelope Lively's fictional headmaster urged a history teacher:

'Children under fifteen just aren't ready for a chronological approach to history. And yet here we are teaching them history as narrative, one thing after another.'

'That's what it is. One thing does happen after another.'

'Yes, but that's a very sophisticated concept . . . children can't grasp it. So you give it to them in nice digestible chunks, as themes or projects. You teach them about revolutions, or civil wars, or whatever.'[130]

The dating of events, not long ago the sine qua non of historical knowledge, is so passé that most French schoolchildren were said to know neither that the French Revolution began in 1789 nor what century that year was in. 'They ask me a question, 16-year-olds', says an English history teacher, 'the Hundred Years' War, was that in 1914–18?' Another fifteen-year-old located the Battle of Hastings 'sometime between Robin Hood and when Alfred burned the cakes'.[131] Many American schoolchildren know only two dates, 1492 and the 4th of July, and not what happened at either.[132] Children turned off by chronology seem incapable of conceiving continuity. 'You know the 18th century?' Jenny Diski's sixteen-year-old asks her teacher. 'Was it before or after the war?' She had never connected the two; in her world-view 'there was only either pure narrative or disembodied detail'.[133]

Temporal order is terra incognita to youngsters unmoored in the twenty-first century. Few have any sense of a datable past, virtually none of time before their grandparents' day. As one youngster said when told a building was 400 years old, not 100 as he had thought, 'Old is old, it doesn't matter how old.'[134] Lack of a chronological frame of reference deprives children today of the 'arc of connectedness' set by traditional time-lines.[135] 'Our [own] sense of chronology is so deeply ingrained', say British history teachers, 'that we can hardly grasp the difficulties encountered by those who do not have it'. They have been robbed, charges an American archivist, not only of knowledge about the past but of the ability to *sense* the past.[136]

In forsaking dates much is lost; events are jumbled into a grab-bag of epochs and empires, significant figures and social movements cut adrift from context. 'In the minds of modern illiterates . . . who know how to read and write and even teach in schools and

---

[130] Penelope Lively, *The Road to Lichfield* (Heinemann, 1977), 87, 188. I conflate the exchange with the subsequent retelling.

[131] Thomas Kamm, 'French debate teaching of history', *IHT*, 11 Apr. 1980: 6; Brian Moynahan, 'Teaching: it's trendy to be trad', *Sunday Times* 10 Feb. 1985: 15; Shemilt, 'Drinking an ocean and pissing a cupfull', in Symcox and Wilschut, eds., *National History Standards*.

[132] Rosenberg and Grafton, *Cartographies of Time*, 197.

[133] Jenny Diski, 'On the existence of Mount Rushmore and other improbabilities' (1993), in *The Vanishing Princess* (Weidenfeld & Nicolson, 1995), 169–77. See Simon Schama, 'Fine-cutting Clio', *Public Historian* 25:3 (2003): 15–25 at 17.

[134] Reid Bishop, 'The Perception and Importance of Time in Architecture' (Ph.D. thesis, University of Surrey, 1982), 149, 190.

[135] Harry Belafonte interview in Mary Willis, 'Daylight come', *Modern Maturity* 45:3 (May–June 2000): 87.

[136] Historical Association, *History 14–19: Report and Recommendations* (London, 2005), sec. 5.4.12; Richard J. Cox, *No Innocent Deposits: Forming Archives by Rethinking Appraisal* (Scarecrow Press, 2003), 210.

at universities, history is present but blurred, in a state of strange confusion', charged Nobelist Czeslaw Milosz. 'Molière becomes a contemporary of Napoleon, Voltaire a contemporary of Lenin.'[137] So-called thematic history – 'Revolutions' that lump the Puritan with the French, the American, the Russian, the Cuban – scants the obdurate reality that people at *each* of these times lived lives, acted from motives, and fashioned milieux distinctively their own.

Understanding the past demands awareness of temporal location. To clarify things in context, to capture the essential individuality of past events, requires a chronological framework. History taught as 'glittering pearls of Romans, cavemen, the battles of the First World War, medieval monks, and Stonehenge, suspended in temporal, non-causative isolation, hardly enhance[s] appreciation of the necklace of time'.[138] The pearls of history accrue value not merely from being many and lustrous, but from being sequentially strung; the narrative confers a conformity that ennobles the necklace.

To be sure, the linear narrative constrains historical understanding, forcing the auditor or reader to stay on a single track from start to finish. *Awareness* of the past involves far more than linear movement. Myriad social and cultural circumstances defy or complicate a narrative in continual flux with histories of other peoples, other institutions, other ideas. The past is too multiform and reflexive to be wholly conveyed in one-dimensional story lines. History hence increasingly ditches the straightforward, unilinear, annalistic frame-work. Lucidity may favour not recounting past acts at particular times, but scanting or coalescing many events, continually violating temporal sequence.

Such 'polychronicity' captures historical realities missed by old-style sequential simpli-city. The new history attracts 'because its mode of cognition approximates the reality of everyday life; most readers view the past in the same manner as they comprehend their own existence' – an interwoven, overlapping set of stories.[139] Just as we think back and cast ahead in recapitulating memories, so do historical narratives backtrack to clarify (or else undermine) causality and amplify hindsight. So doing, however, risks confusing past events with accounts of those events.

Historians latterly rediscovered the virtues of narrative. But they mainly eschew the once-popular broad sweep over entire cultures and epochs, now condemned as simplis-tically univocal. Instead, emulating the comprehensive details and narrative sweep that make Tolstoy's *War and Peace* so forcefully gripping, they scrutinize particular events and arenas circumscribed in time and space and personae – George R. Stewart's *Pickett's Charge* (1959), Emmanuel Le Roy Ladurie's handful of Pyrenean peasants in fourteenth-century *Montaillou* (1976), Carlo Ginzburg's deluded miller in *The Cheese and the Worms* (1980), Natalie Zemon Davis's *The Return of Martin Guerre* (1983), Robert Darnton's *The Great Cat Massacre* (1984), Laura Thatcher Ulrich's *The Midwife's Tale* (1990), Davis's seventeenth-century women of divers faiths and fortunes (*Women on the*

---

[137] Czeslaw Milosz, 'Nobel lecture, 1980', *NYRB*, 5 Mar. 1981: 12.
[138] Peter J. Fowler, 'Archaeology, the public and the sense of the past', in David Lowenthal and Marcus Binney, eds., *Our Past before Us* (London: Temple Smith, 1981), 56–68 at 67.
[139] James Henretta, 'Social history as lived and written', *AHR* 84 (1979): 1293–1322 at 1318–19. See Munz, *Shapes of Time*, 28–43.

Margins, 1995), Jonathan Spence's late Ming dynasty aesthete and chronicler (*Return to Dragon Mountain*, 2007).

Dwelling on the lives and loves of the poor and previously obscure, often unknown, armed with sources and insights derived from art and fiction and symbolism, micro-history sheds light on the psyches of past peoples, the hidden dynamics of past communities, the interplay between beliefs and values and social relations.[140] But narrowed focus may make such case studies eccentric rather than characteristic. The 'sheer interest and intensity of their particular stories overwhelm their larger significance', suggests Gordon Wood, 'turning them into little trees in search of a forest'.[141] Seldom relating the particular lives and events they treat to larger trends, they fragment awareness of the past, lending it an anachronistic likeness to an exoticized present.

These trends – multivocality, polychronicity, abandonment of grand narrative – share postmodern history's relativistic dubiety about all knowledge, and hence its aversion to causal judgement. Given the multiform shifting ground of history's manifold actors and interpreters, it becomes safer and humbler to avoid inquiry into motives and aims, along with their temporal contexts. But to so confine history deprives it of its true significance: what events meant to people then and afterward.

Past vs. present: emergence of the foreign country

This book's title declared the past an alien land; back then, L. P. Hartley's *Go-Between* told us, people did things differently. The remembered past seems less a foreign than a neighbourly realm supporting present hopes and dreams, aims and plans. And belief that the historical past is distinct from the present is not innate; it is acquired, and often uncertain, incomplete, or wholly absent. Hartley's view is recurrently contested. Some, like Virginia Woolf's Mrs Swithin, feel past–present differences trivial. Others attribute a common humanity to people past and present but, like English teenage history students, dismiss pre-moderns in primitive surroundings as 'closer to monkeys in them days', their weird beliefs and practices explained by moral and intellectual inferiority.[142]

Where knowledge is transmitted only by voice or gesture, no records exist, and no relics survive or are seen as such, awareness of bygone times depends on present accounts. Whatever may have in fact changed, past and present are not differentiated. In Anglo-Saxon England 'remembered truth was flexible and up to date, because no ancient custom could be proved older than the memory of the oldest living wise man',

---

[140] Lawrence Stone, 'The revival of narrative' (1979), in *The Past and the Present Revisited* (Routledge, 1987), 74–96; Carlo Ginzburg, 'Microhistory', *Critical Inquiry* 20 (1993): 10–35; Mark Salber Phillips, *On Historical Distance* (Yale, 2013), ix–xi, 187–9, 197–201.

[141] Wood, *The Purpose of the Past*, 129.

[142] Hartley, *The Go-Between*; 174–5; Woolf, *Between the Acts*; Denis Shemilt, 'Beauty and the philosopher: empathy in history and classroom', in A. K. Dickinson et al., eds., *Learning History* (Heinemann, 1984), 39–84 at 49; Peter Lee, 'Fused horizons? UK research into students' second-order ideas in history', in Holger Thünemann et al., eds., *History of Researching History Education* (Schwalbach, Germany: Wochenschau, 2013).

writes Michael Clanchy; 'hence there was no conflict between past and present practice'.[143] Some oral societies consider the present merely a continuation of an all-
encompassing past; in others the present pre-empts attention and the past vanishes
unremarked. Neither truly distinguish past from present. The past 'is not felt as an
itemized terrain', concluded Walter Ong. 'It is the domain of the ancestors, a resonant
source for renewing awareness of present existence.'[144] Absent textual relics, oral communities rely on present-day narrators to convey that ancestral domain, or indeed any
past prior to living memory.

Unlike oral myth and memory, historical understanding rests on *past* accounts in the
form of eyewitness testimonies or subsequent chronicles. Such accounts need be neither
accurate or impartial (and seldom are); their historical salience inheres in coming from
earlier times and voices. 'What is handed down ... in a text is transmitted like nothing
else that comes down to us from the past':[145] the written word is uniquely durable,
portable, and replicable. 'The pastness of the past depends upon a historical sensibility
that can hardly begin to operate without permanent written records'.[146] Yet not even such
records assure that sensibility.

Although durable records make patent the distinction between past and present,
Western savants long resolutely denied it. 'Any linear ... history, irreversible and
cumulative', asserts a Norwegian polymath, 'will leave the past irrevocably behind, more
and more "foreign"'.[147] But for medieval scholars past otherness was heresy. Scripture
was sacred truth valid for all time. Allegedly ancient textual evidence of difference must
have been misread or fabricated to instil diabolical error. Gospel certitudes delayed
historical insights in Christendom for nearly two millennia.[148]

Medieval historians largely ignored or anachronized the past's strangeness to
reassure themselves that nothing fundamental had really changed. Yet they were
intermittently aware of (and even deliberately perpetrated) anachronisms to shore
up some patron's or monastic order's claim to nobility or priority. For example,
the twelfth-century Abbot Wibald veered between atemporal rhetoric and sophisticated time-twisting; for him 'the past was truly like a foreign country', but only in
Douglas Adams's sense that 'they do things exactly the same there'.[149]

Common to medieval and early-modern devotees was detestation of change, which
either had not or ought not to have occurred. All change was degradation. Reformation
divines and Renaissance savants appalled by medieval changes sought to return to
original biblical and patristic purity. Absent the sainted men and holy wonders of

---

[143] Clanchy, *From Memory to Written Record*, 233.
[144] Walter J. Ong, *Orality and Literacy* (1982; Routledge, 2002), 97.
[145] Connerton, *How Societies Remember*, 96.
[146] Goody and Watt, 'Consequences of literacy', 34.
[147] Galtung, 'Western deep thinking', 96.
[148] Magne Sæbø, ed., *Hebrew Bible/Old Testament: The History of Its Interpretation*, vol. 2: *From the Renaissance to the Enlightenment* (Göttingen: Vandenhoeck & Ruprecht, 2008).
[149] Jean Dunbabin, 'Discovering a past for the French aristocracy', 1–14, and Timothy Reuter, 'Past, present and no future in the *regnum Teutonicum*', 15–36 at 36, in Paul Magdalino, ed., *Perception of the Past in Twelfth-Century Europe* (Hambledon Press, 1992); Douglas Adams, *Life, the Universe, and Everything* (1982; Del Rey, 1985), 85.

distant antiquity, wrote the twelfth-century monk Ordericus Vitalis, moral decay
mounted, and as the world neared its end 'all the historian can do is record crimes
and more crimes'.[150]

Christianity brought sacred history into secular annals. But rather than secular time
thereby becoming historical, it got swallowed up within eternal, immutable, and changeless sacred time. Transcendent import made Christ's life, death, and resurrection ritually
ever present. Scriptural rhetoric denied and cancelled change over time; Jerome's Vulgate
(c. 400) was esteemed because fathers and grandfathers had read and spoken the same
words.[151] Even when too archaic to comprehend, its durability ensured to posterity the
necessary signs of salvation.[152] 'What was remembered was a universal truth, not the
sensual particulars of the disordered and meaningless past.' History was purged (blanched,
the Cistercians put it) of all but Scripture's universal experiences. Abolishing historical or
mutable time united the believer with the time of direct revelation. Christian history
anticipated and portended sacred eternity.[153]

Temporal uniformity had to be avowed lest neologisms unravel the fabric of faith.
Time's sacred chain led from Christ to the Elders who knew him, to those who knew the
Apostles, to the literal texts of their words and deeds, to a consensual Vulgate, and to the
martyrs and their relics. That chain ensured the sacred past's total survival. Hence
historicity was denied, any seeming novelty declared an original truth. The divinely
completed past, insisted Bernard of Clairvaux (c. 1140), made any new doctrine or
practice *ipso facto* wrong, any innovation presumptuous.[154] History was a unified Christian drama intolerant of secular temporal change.

Thus, secular history was effectively annulled. To the Spanish priest Orosius, Alaric's
sack of Rome and subsequent Goth incursions were trivial events, for the miseries of all
peoples in all ages were essentially the same. In medieval eyes the Roman Empire endured
in essence in the Holy Roman Empire; the Corpus Christianum was metaphysically 'one
single world in which past, present and future were effectively co-existent'.[155]

'The men of those ages had no past', concluded a Victorian chronicler. Apart from
family lineage, Le Roy Ladurie's French peasants 'lived in a kind of "island in time", even
more cut off from the past than from the future'. As Raymond de l'Aire of Tignac put it in
the early fourteenth century, 'There is no other age than ours.'[156] As late as 1521, that

---

[150] Ordericus Vitalis, *Historia Ecclesiastica* (1140), quoted in Aron J. Gurevitch, *Categories of Medieval Culture* (1972; Routledge, 1985), 123.

[151] Anthony Kemp, *The Estrangement of the Past: A Study in the Origins of Modern Historical Consciousness* (Oxford, 1991), 9; Connerton, *How Societies Remember*, 97.

[152] M. T. Clanchy, 'Reading the signs at Durham Cathedral', in Karen Schousboe and Mogens Trolle Larsen, eds., *Literacy and Society* (Copenhagen: Akademisk, 1989), 171–82 at 171.

[153] Coleman, *Ancient and Medieval Memories*, 324, 186; Jean-Claude Schmitt, 'Appropriating the future', in A. J. Burrow and Ian P. Wei, eds., *Medieval Futures* (Boydell, 2000), 3–18 at 16.

[154] 'To the Canons of Lyons, on the conception of Mary', in *Some Letters of Saint Bernard* (London, 1904), 307, and 'Sermons on *The Song of Songs*', in *Bernard of Clairvaux: Selected Works* (Mahwah, NJ: Paulist Press, 1987), 207–78 at 262.

[155] Paulus Orosius, *Historiarum adversus paganos, The Anglo-Saxon Version* (c. 417; London, 1773), 49–52, 85, 238; Kemp, *Estrangement of the Past*, 33. See Gurevitch, *Categories of Medieval Culture*, 100–1.

[156] E. A. Freeman, *The Preservation and Restoration of Ancient Monuments* (Oxford, 1852), 16–17; Emmanuel Le Roy Ladurie, *Montaillou* (1975; London: Braziller, 2008), 284.

future wholesale innovator Henry VIII asserted that no true novelty was possible.[157] Anachronisms later derogated as implausible were highly regarded by medieval scholars. Showing 'a Jesus not of a distant, foreign past, but of an eternal present', they reinforced the conceit of a Christ who had died not just in His own, but in *their* own world and time. In the medieval view only eternal substances were true and worth knowing. Thus, tradition accumulated by denying its accumulations, and declaring its innovations ancient and original.[158]

Yet early-modern like medieval authors routinely modernized biblical and Roman materials. English humanists recognized classical texts as products of another culture, but one to which they felt such close affinity that they lacked 'any sense of the past as a foreign country', concludes Quentin Skinner. 'Having dusted down the ancient texts they exhibit almost no interest' in trying to understand them in the context of their times. 'On the contrary, they approach them as if they are contemporary documents with an almost wholly unproblematic relevance to their own circumstances.'[159]

The Reformation and the Renaissance continued to detest change, but instead of pretending it was absent, found its corruptions ubiquitous. 'Where medieval history condemned innovation and denied it had occurred, Luther condemned innovation and saw it everywhere.'[160] For humanists (Chapter 4), the evil novelty was the retrogression that cost the Dark Ages the classical legacy. For religious reformers, the evil novelty was the Satanic corruption that destroyed Christianity's original innocence. Both evils must be expunged to retrieve the pure source of inspiration, Christ and the classics, after which nothing would ever change again.

Humanist historians who rebelled against the divine authority of the papacy and the Holy Roman Empire – both pope and emperor claimed communion with changeless eternity – were deemed sacrilegious. But they contended, and for the most part even believed, that 'far from breaking with the past, they were reviving it', writes Constantin Fasolt.

They were doing nothing but telling the truth, except to tell it better. ... Maintaining that their interpretation of the texts was merely a better understanding of the same ancient sources on which the authorities relied (only more of them, and in more authentic form), they were oblivious to the charge of heresy. The continuity with ancient truths in which they saw themselves confirmed them in the good conscience that they were right.

The self-deception was crucial alike to their physical survival and their persuasive certitude. But 'fear of authority thus contaminated history with a subliminal degree of dishonesty', concludes Fasolt, 'that has never been altogether shed' and lingers on in the illusion of objectivity.[161]

For Catholic theologians, secular history since the Apostles had changed nothing; for Protestant reformers, intervening centuries marked a dreadful fall from grace. This

[157] Henry VIII, *Defence of the Seven Sacraments* (1521; New York, 1908).
[158] Kemp, *Estrangement of the Past*, 50, 79.
[159] Quentin Skinner, *Reason and Rhetoric in the Philosophy of Hobbes* (Cambridge, 1996), 40.
[160] Kemp, *Estrangement of the Past*, 82.
[161] Fasolt, *Limits of History*, 17–23.

narrowed reformers' range of historical empathy. Whereas the medieval mind could identify intellectually with all past Christian generations, Protestants could identify with none but the earliest; all since the Apostles had been in error. 'A person of the 14th century could experience complete intellectual communion with the past ... a person of the 17th felt that all who had come before had lived in ignorance.' Only the primitive and the classical were esteemed.[162]

The new shape of time thus estranged all but the distant past. Restoring the Golden Age – the primitive church, the classical vision – was Protestants' and humanists' parallel and often conjoined aim; 'to awake all antiquity', as Francis Bacon put it, required rediscovering 'the ancient authors, both in divinity and in humanity'.[163] But the new history was still anti-historical in essence. Truth was eternal and unchanging, innovation diabolical, reform simply reversion to original timeless perfection.

The Pilgrims who fled the Old World to escape the sinful present epitomized such sacred return. Plymouth founder William Bradford saw the past as a human invention, history as idolatry; recovering gospel purity required complete severance from history.[164] Subsequent sages, religious and secular alike, reiterated the longing for divinely inspired truth freed from the woeful annals of humanity. 'Foregoing generations perceived God and nature face to face; we, through their eyes', grieved Emerson; the occluding past was oppressive and crippling.[165] Restorationists from Millerites through Mormons and beyond posited a blessed primitive church providentially reanimated in their own latter-day sects. Most sheltered in the sacred fixity of their chosen Scripture. In a common statement of faith, the Authorized Version 'preserves the very words of God in the form in which He wished them to be represented in the universal language of these last days: English'. Not content with anathematizing historical change in the past, Baptists rule out changes to come: 'The King James Bible supersedes any extant Greek or Hebrew text, including any texts *that may be discovered in the future.*'[166]

Awareness of antiquity as another time separated from their own was a paramount insight for Petrarch and Erasmus. Renaissance humanists saw the classical past as *another* country, but one they sought to make less foreign, usefully illustrative of enduring virtues and vices. As noted in Chapter 4, many humanists denied or ignored Erasmus's perception of historical change. Yet the more clearly they perceived antiquity, the less it resembled their own world. And when Enlightenment *philosophes* again rediscovered the classical world, they realized how remote it was, how unattainable the model of

[162] Kemp, *Estrangement of the Past*, 82, 104.
[163] Francis Bacon, *The Advancement of Learning, Book I* (1605; Clarendon Press, 1885), iv, 28.
[164] William Bradford, *Of Plymouth Plantation*, (Xlibris, 2006), bk 1 (1630; 1856), 27–124; bk 2 (1647–50; Boston, 1912), 125–429. Bradford always contended there was 'no new thing under the sun' ('First Dialogue' (1648), quoted in Mark L. Sargent, 'William Bradford's "Dialogue" with history', *New England Quarterly* 65 (1992): 389–421 at 416). But Book II (1647–50) moves from viewing history as fixed and preordained to circumstantial and contingent, 'so uncertain are the mutable things of this unstable world' (*Of Plymouth Plantation*, 170). See Walter P. Wenska, 'Bradford's two histories', *Early American Literature* 13 (1978): 151–64 at 158–9.
[165] Ralph Waldo Emerson, 'Nature', in *CW*, 1:3.
[166] 'The King James Bible: the authorized version', *av1611godsword.yuku.com/topic/1258.*

antique harmony. Though its relics abounded, the iconic past became truly irrecoverable.[167] And the conjoint impact of the French and the Industrial Revolutions made more recent pasts likewise irrecoverable. Thus, slowly and with much angst, came about 'the complex, paradoxical, and drawn-out process by which humanity gradually learned that the past is a foreign country'.[168]

That perception was a plant of slow growth nurtured by secularism, comparative scrutiny of sources, and dawning awareness of anachronism. Munz calls it 'one of the greatest changes which have come over our view of the world'.[169] Yet influential school texts such as Johannes Buno's *Idea historiae universalis* (Lüneburg 1672) left past and present wholly undifferentiated.[170] Even beyond the eighteenth century, the past remained for many a seamless whole scarcely distinguishable from the present, human motivations the same in all epochs. 'Instead of having a history, [people] regarded themselves as having an unchanging nature or essence.'[171] English Whig historians stressed the familiarity and continuity of pasts they found exemplary. The immemorial open-air gatherings of Swiss cantons vividly conjoined past and present for Freeman; Macaulay witnessed the passage of the 1831 Reform Bill as 'like seeing Caesar stabbed in the Senate House, or seeing Oliver Cromwell taking the mace from the table'; late-Victorian classicists found Homer's world a mirror image of their own, and fondly ascribed their own thoughts to Plato and Aristotle.[172] Organic metaphor stressed such analogies: the seeds of the present seemed immanent in the past, past effects everywhere evident. Today's obsession with roots and DNA, ancestors foreshadowing descendants, family traits forever ingrained, reflects similar essentialist premises.

Countering cults of continuity and recurrence, however, comparative insights revealed the extraordinary diversity of historical experience. Herder and his followers assigned every epoch as well as each culture its own unique character. Uniformity over time came to seem a hoary error, the present of necessity unlike any past. The Romantic imagination delighted less in antiquity's parallels than in its exotic remoteness.[173] The past really was dead, noted the Victorian littérateur James Anthony Froude; not intimacy but inaccessibility made medieval and even early-modern England poignant:

In the alteration of our own character, we have lost the key which would interpret the characters of our fathers, and the great men even of our own English history before the Reformation seem to us almost like the fossil skeletons of another order of beings ... Now it is all gone; ... and between

[167] Myron P. Gilmore, *Humanists and Jurists* (Harvard, 1963), 14, 95–6, 101, 109; Jean Starobinski, *1789: The Emblems of Reason* (Virginia, 1982), 272.

[168] Grafton, *Bring Out Your Dead*, 279.

[169] Munz, *Our Knowledge of the Growth of Knowledge*, ix–x.

[170] John Butt, *Bach's Dialogue with Modernity* (Cambridge, 2010), 118–19.

[171] Zachary Sayre Schiffman, *The Birth of the Past* (Johns Hopkins, 2011), 272.

[172] Edward A. Freeman, *The Growth of the English Constitution from the Earliest Times* (London, 1872), 1–8; T. B. Macaulay to Thomas Flower Ellis, 30 Mar. 1831, in *The Letters of Thomas Babington Macaulay* (Cambridge, 1974), 2: 9; Frank M. Turner, *The Greek Heritage in Victorian Britain* (Yale, 1981), 175–86, 418–27. See Pompa, *Human Nature and Historical Knowledge*, 42–9, 192, 223.

[173] Berlin, *Vico and Herder*, 145; Hugh Honour, *Romanticism* (Penguin, 1981), 175–84, 197ff.; Mark Girouard, *The Return to Camelot* (Yale, 1981); Robert Harbison, *Deliberate Regression* (Knopf, 1980), 139–40.

us and the old English there lies a gulf of mystery which the prose of the historian will never adequately bridge. They cannot come to us, and our imagination can but feebly penetrate to them.[174]

The pace of visible change made the past not just remote but fearsomely different. History diversified also grew ephemeral: views of the past were now in flux. 'Time has now become so fluidly rapid. It is not possible to keep up', remarked the novelist Dorothea Schlegel in 1809; between one day and the next 'lies an entire historical epoch'. Goethe concurred: 'In the same town one will hear in the evening an account of a significant event different from that heard in the morning.'[175] A particularly poignant gulf alienated the present from the *ancien régime*. The speed with which everything – landscape, customs, manners, fortunes, loyalties, allegiances – seemed to change left survivors of the French Revolution and its aftermath adrift, aware that the world of their forebears was forever gone. Trying to make historical sense of the times, Chateaubriand in 1797 realized that whatever he had written during the day was by night already overtaken by events; the French Revolution had no previous example.[176] 'Never before in a period of ten years', wrote a German observer in 1799, 'have such a large number of important and intertwined events, such a rapid sequence of transformations and restless movement, and such piled-up revolutions taken place'.[177]

The dissolution of religious orders, abrupt endings of the French monarchy and the Holy Roman Empire, Napoleonic incursions into Europe and beyond, the rise of new sovereign states, brought ordinary people into the flow of history and severed them from the traditional timeless past, many as hapless refugees. Before, daily and annual rounds of time's cycle had conserved the rural past pretty much intact; from 1789 and 1815 on, time's arrow flew. 'The past was conceived more and more as something bygone and lost, and also strange and mysterious, and though partly accessible, always remote.' And people of the 1820s and 1830s, added Tocqueville, 'do not resemble their fathers, – nay they perpetually differ from themselves, for they live in a state of incessant change of place, feeling, and fortunes'.[178]

The frenzy of material novelty left George Eliot breathless.

Those old leisurely times, when the boat, gliding sleepily along the canal, was the newest locomotive wonder, [are] gone – gone where the spinning-wheels are gone, and the pack-horses, and the slow wagons ... [They tell you] the steam-engine is to create leisure for mankind. Do not believe them; it only creates a vacuum for eager thought to rush in. Even idleness is eager for amusement;

[174] James Anthony Froude, *History of England from the Fall of Wolsey to the Defeat of the Spanish Armada* (1856; rev. edn. London, 1893), 1: 3, 62.
[175] Dorothea Schlegel to Sulpiz Boisserée, quoted in Peter Fritzsche, *Stranded in the Present* (Harvard, 2004), 93; Goethe to Ludwig I of Bayern, 17 Dec. 1829, quoted in Reinhart Koselleck, *Futures Past* (1979; Columbia, 2004), 208.
[176] François-René de Chateaubriand, *Essai historique, politique et moral sur les révolutions anciennes et modernes* (1797; Paris, 1861), 249. See François Furet, 'L'ancien régime et la révolution', in Nora, *Lieux de mémoire* (1992), III, 1: 107–39.
[177] Friedrich von Gentz, *Politische Paradoxien* (1799), quoted in Fritzsche, *Stranded in the Present*, 27.
[178] Fritzsche, *Stranded in the Present*, 27–9, 5; Alexis de Tocqueville, *Democracy in America* (1834–40; Cambridge, MA, 1863), 2: 69.

prone to excursion-trains ... and cursory peeps through microscopes. ... Old Leisure was quite a different personage ... contemplative ... quiet ... sauntering ... sheltering.[179]

Accelerating change fuelled fears of society spinning out of control. 'The series of events comes swifter and swifter', wrote Carlyle, 'velocity increasing as the square of time', foreboding a fearsome future.[180] Writers from Tennyson and Ruskin and Hardy to Spengler and Wells likened the decline of the West to the death of the universe. *Fin-de-siècle* forecasts of universal winter, reprieved by Rutherford's 1904 discovery of the sun's radioactive energy, later resurfaced as fiery fate by nuclear fission. The Bomb and its dread progeny have since made doom-laden prognoses common coin.[181]

Thus, in the span of a single century the past ceased to be familiar and omnipresent, becoming remote and lost in nostalgic mists. History was more and more seen as a relentless, often painful alienation from the past. By the end of the nineteenth century objectively minded historians had erected a 'Chinese wall between past and present', in Raphael Samuel's phrase. And 'a progressively widening and deepening knowledge of antiquity increasingly rendered it dead and buried'.[182]

Regarding the past as a foreign country came at a steep cost. Distanced and differentiated, it ceased to be a valuable source of lessons and became a midden of anachronisms. Many historians were at a loss to discern its causal links to the present. 'To live in any period of the past', as a medievalist thought a historian should aim to do, 'is to be so overwhelmed with the sense of difference as to confess oneself unable to conceive how the present has become what it is'.[183]

Against this alien past's reduced relevance, compensatory benefits emerged. With the loss of its exemplary role, the past ceased to exert so crippling an influence. To bring about the 'death of the past' and thus relieve the present of its burden became an avowed historical aim.[184] 'Explaining, and therefore lightening, the pressure that the past must exercise upon the present' was for Maitland the duty of historical research. 'Today we study the day before yesterday, in order that yesterday may not paralyze today, and today may not paralyze tomorrow.' Benedetto Croce concurred: history liberated humanity from slavery to the past.[185]

Recognizing the past as foreign also enhanced appreciation of hindsight. The past as depicted in history becomes more definitive and magisterial than the present, for hindsight clarifies yesterday as it cannot clarify today. The consequences of the past are at least partly

---

[179] George Eliot, *Adam Bede* (1859; Chicago, 1888), 461–2.
[180] Thomas Carlyle, 'Shooting Niagara: and after?' (1867), in *Critical and Miscellaneous Essays* (London, 1888), 4: 586–627 at 590.
[181] Jerome H. Buckley, *The Triumph of Time* (Harvard, 1967), 55–70; Gillian Beer, '"The death of the sun": Victorian solar physics and solar myth', in J. B. Bullen, ed., *The Sun Is God* (Clarendon Press, 1989), 159–80 at 171–3.
[182] Raphael Samuel, 'On the methods of the History Workshop', *History Workshop* 9 (1980): 162–76 at 168; Schiffman, *Birth of the Past*, 273.
[183] V. H. Galbraith, 'Historical research and the preservation of the past', *History*, n.s. 22 (1938): 303–14 at 312.
[184] J. H. Plumb, *The Death of the Past* (1969; Penguin, 1973).
[185] F. W. Maitland, 'A survey of the century' (1901), in *The Collected Papers* (Cambridge, 1911), 3: 432–9 at 439; Benedetto Croce, *History as the Story of Liberty* (London, 1941), 44.

worked out and revealed; the results of present acts are yet to be seen. Unlike current accounts, those that 'history presents to us, both of men and of events, are generally complete', wrote the prescient Bolingbroke. 'We see [men] at their whole length in history ... through a medium less partial ... than that of [immediate] experience.'[186]

No past is ever entirely over and done with, of course; whatever our present retrospective wisdom, new insights ever unfold. But any degree of hindsight makes the past more definitively known than the present, as the Victorian writer Elizabeth Gaskell ironically observed:

> In looking back to the last century, it appears curious to see how little our ancestors had the power of putting two things together, and perceiving either the discord or the harmony thus produced. Is it because we are farther off from those times, and have, consequently, a greater range of vision? Will our descendants have a wonder about us, such as we have about the inconsistency of our forefathers, or a surprise about our blindness? ... Such discrepancies ran through good men's lives in those days. It is well for us that we live at the present time, when everybody is logical and consistent.[187]

Even more than memory, history clarifies, tidies, and elucidates. This is the point of Lewis Namier's paradox that historians 'imagine the past and remember the future':[188] They explain what has happened through the lens of subsequent events, events that lay in that past's future.

That the passage of time clarifies the past for us but not for those who lived in it often goes unrecognized. 'Man proceeds in the fog. But when he looks back to judge people of the past, he sees no fog on their path', observed Milan Kundera.

> From his present, which was their faraway future, their path looks perfectly clear to him, good visibility all the way. Looking back, he sees the path, he sees the people proceeding, he sees their mistakes, but not the fog ... Who is more blind? Mayakovsky, who as he wrote his poem on Lenin did not know where Leninism would lead? Or we, who judge him decades later and do not see the fog that enveloped him? Mayakovsky's blindness is part of the general human condition. But for us not to see the fog on Mayakovsky's path is to forget what man is, forget what we ourselves are.[189]

Narrative needs magnify temporal disparities. To make history intelligible, the historian can hardly resist giving the illusory impression that things had to happen more or less as they did. Knowing something of the past's outcome, the historian uses that knowledge to give a sense of fullness and completion. Only apocalyptic prophets describe the present in this way. Hence the authoritative flavour common in biographies. The biographer's revelatory hindsight yields an ordered clarity in marked contrast with the felt chaos of the biographee's actual life, as the imprecision of our own unfinished lives well corroborates.[190]

---

[186] Bolingbroke, *Letters on the Study and Use of History*, Letter II, I: 32.

[187] Elizabeth Gaskell, *Sylvia's Lovers* (1863; London, 1964), 58–9.

[188] Lewis Namier, *Conflicts: Studies in Contemporary History* (Macmillan, 1942), 70.

[189] Milan Kundera, *Testaments Betrayed* (1992; HarperCollins, 1996), 238. Vladimir Mayakovski's 'Lenin lived! Lenin lives! Lenin will live forever!' (1924) was constantly recited in Soviet schools.

[190] Helen Vendler, 'All too real', *NYRB*, 17 Dec. 1981: 32; Bromley, *Lost Narratives*, 60.

Yet hindsight merges past with present as well as differentiating them. To understand now what happened then, as distinct from what people in the past thought or wanted others to think was happening, requires our own current thinking. And just as present thoughts shape knowing of the past, so awareness of the past suffuses the present. A literary historian writes 'not merely with his own generation in his bones', in T. S. Eliot's phrase, 'but with a feeling that the whole of the literature of Europe from Homer ... has a simultaneous existence and composes a simultaneous order'.[191]

Eliot's sense of past–present synchrony, however, resonates less and less nowadays among historians for whom the past remains a foreign country, and who feel it their mission to convey that alien strangeness to a public that prefers to deny it and is bent on domesticating the past. 'The truly great historians lived in times ... where the present ... was so different from the past and so surprising that someone had to ... sit down and puzzle out some sense from it all', suggests historian-turned-novelist Philippa Gregory.[192]

History, fiction, and faction

> I cannot help but be a story-teller, it is my way of describing the world; but I have
> learned to be a historian, it is my way of understanding the world.
>   Philippa Gregory, 2005[193]

The most pellucid pearls of historical narrative are formed in fiction's shells. Ever since Scott and Dumas, historical romance has trumped history texts in memorably conveying the past.[194] Novelists use history as a theatre for made-up people, fictionalize real lives, insert imaginary episodes among actual events. To give 'as complete an illusion as possible of having lived in the past', Hervey Allen felt the novelist 'under obligation to alter facts, circumstances, people, and even dates'.[195] Some fictional pasts seem faithful depictions of former times, others exotically unlike them. Either way, novelists commonly outdo historians in making readers aware of the past. And the fictional past has another advantage: because it is contrived, it *must* make sense. Contrariwise, history must in part baffle. 'Fiction makes us feel more metaphysically comfortable', notes Eco, because 'in fiction every secret message can be deciphered', since created by authorial intent.[196] Victorians portrayed fictional life as 'a coherent tale, summarizable, pointed, and finally moralizable'. Paradoxically, it is only in the fictional narrative that we can be absolutely certain about something. In actual history we wonder, with Eco, 'whether there is a message and, if so, whether [it] makes sense'.[197]

---

[191] T. S. Eliot, 'Tradition and the individual talent', in *Selected Essays* (Faber and Faber, 1934), 13–22 at 14.
[192] Philippa Gregory, 'Born a writer', *History Workshop Journal* 59:1 (Spring 2005): 237–42 at 239.
[193] Gregory, 'Born a writer: forged as a historian', 242.
[194] Scott's star has faded from 'the most popular and influential author on the planet' to the 'Great Unread' (Alan Taylor, 'Did Walter Scott invent Scotland?' *TLS*, 8 Dec. 2010; Kathryn Sutherland, 'Factory settings', *TLS*, 27 Sept. 2013: 3–5).
[195] Hervey Allen, 'History and the novel', *Atlantic Monthly*, 173:2 (Feb. 1944): 119–20.
[196] Umberto Eco, *The Book of Legendary Lands* (Maclehose, 2013), 440, and *Six Walks in the Fictional Woods* (Harvard, 1994), 116.
[197] Nicholas Dames, *Amnesiac Selves* (Oxford, 2001), 7; Eco, *Six Walks in the Fictional Woods*, 116.

Conversing with the past points up a cognate distinction between history and fiction. Desire for intense personal contact with bygone times animates practitioners of both, was 'what drew us in the first place to the books we chose to read ... the lives we chose to live'. And literary historians 'seized with the conviction that someone we do not know is addressing us personally with urgency and eloquence' continue to pursue that dream despite knowing that the dead cannot really hear or speak.[198] Even when 'all I could hear was my own voice', recalled Stephen Greenblatt, 'even then I did not abandon my desire'.

My own voice was the voice of the dead, for the dead, [many] uncannily full of the will to be heard, had contrived to leave textual traces of themselves ... in the voices of the living ... It is paradoxical, of course, to seek the living will of the dead in fictions, ... where there was no bodily being to begin with. But those who love literature tend to find more intensity in simulations, [for they self-consciously] anticipate and compensate for the vanishing of the actual life that has empowered them.[199]

Crucial to the discipline of history, however, is 'the assumption of an absolute distinction between past and present, a kind of primal rupture that turns the dead not into conversational partners so much as ever-elusive objects of desire', writes David Harlan. The dead are not reincarnated but given 'scriptural entombment'. And historians fear that literary enthusiasts 'who throw themselves into their own narrative ... silence the dead by domesticating them ... forc[ing] them to speak in our voices rather than their own'.[200]

In according fabrication parity with truth, the fictional analogy troubles many historians. To be sure, they themselves cannot avoid rhetorical invention. Like novelists tellers of tales, they nonetheless distance themselves as *truthful* chroniclers. Open to critical peer scrutiny, historians must cleave scrupulously to past realities; writers of fiction can be largely heedless of such constraints. The reader of a history of the French Revolution expects conformity with and confirmation by well-attested sources; the reader of Dickens's *A Tale of Two Cities* has few such demanding expectations.[201]

Both the opposition and historians' dismay are recent, however. In former epochs, history and fiction often coalesced or were mutually supportive. Classical writers did distinguish *historia* (true narrative) from *fabula* (untrue), but fictive works such as the *Aeneid* and Aesop's fables were canonically admired. Indeed, fiction, which told what *might* have happened (and explained how), was deemed superior to history, prosaically limited to what *had* happened. Instancing Homer's *Iliad*, Erasmus praised pagan historians' fictional dialogues, 'for everyone accepts that they are allowed to put speeches into the mouths of their characters' (Erasmus allowed Christian historians less inventive scope). Style and language outranked factual fidelity; much history mattered less for *what* it said about the past than *how* it was said.[202]

[198] Stephen Greenblatt, '"Stay, illusion": on receiving messages from the dead', PMLA 118:3 (2003): 417–26 at 419, 414.
[199] Stephen Greenblatt, *Shakespearean Negotiations* (California, 1988), 1.
[200] David Harlan, 'Reading, writing, and the art of history', AHA *Perspectives on History*, Nov. 2010: 37–8.
[201] Monika Otter, 'Functions of fiction in historical writing', in Partner, *Writing Medieval History*, 114–15.
[202] Charles William Fornara, *The Nature of History in Ancient Greece and Rome* (California, 1983), 94–5, 135, 163–5; Desiderius Erasmus, *Copia* (1512), in CW, 24: 279–656 at 649; Eric Cochrane, *Historians and Historiography in the Italian Renaissance* (Chicago, 1981), 488–90.

Medieval theorists saw the history/fiction distinction as linguistic. 'Connoting clerical and scholarly seriousness of purpose, not to mention divine sanction', the use of Latin was suggestive of historical truth, whereas vernacular writing could be more openly and even playfully inventive. But many Latin histories were famously fictitious, and many vernacular writers claimed historicity. Moreover, in bracketing sober factual elements with saintly miracles and monstrous hybrid creatures, fiction no less than history might allegorically portray deeper moral or theological truths.[203] 'The poetic lyre strikes a false note on the superficial rind of the letter', wrote the theologian Alain de Lille, 'but on a more profound level communicates . . . a secret of higher understanding . . . and sweeter kernel of truth'.[204]

The divorce of history from fiction followed early-modern concern with source accuracy. The two genres diverged into 'history' (actual events open to scrutiny from manifold sources) and 'poetry' or 'romance' (eschewing pretence to historical fidelity). Prose became the preferred genre of historical fact, poetry of fiction. 'The poet may say or sing things, not as they were but as they ought to have been', remarks *Don Quixote*'s Samson, whereas 'the historian must write things . . . as they have been, without adding or taking aught from the truth'.[205] For William Godwin 'true history consists in a delineation of consistent, human character', which the historian could not know; hence 'the writer of real history' was the imaginative romantic novelist.[206] Restricted to known facts, historians abdicated bardic omniscience. And as history retreated to the arid confines of empirical rigour, fiction pre-empted the colourful and fanciful that historians relinquished. 'To make the past present, to bring the distant near . . . to invest with the reality of human flesh and blood . . . to call up our ancestors before us with all their peculiarities of language, manners, and garb, to show us over their houses, to seat us at their tables, to rummage their old-fashioned wardrobes', wrote Macaulay, 'these parts of the duty which properly belongs to the historian, have been appropriated by the historical novelist'.[207]

As history's handmaid, nineteenth-century fiction gained wide acclaim. Scott's imaginative empathy endeared the past; he showed 'bygone ages . . . actually filled by living men . . . with colour in their cheeks, with passions in their stomach', extolled Carlyle, 'not by protocols, state-papers, controversies and abstractions'.[208] The novelist recreated a vivified past. 'Out of the fictitious book I get the expression of the life of the time – the old times live again', attested Thackeray. 'Can the heaviest historian do more

---

[203] Otter, 'Functions of fiction', 112–16.

[204] Alain de Lille, *De Planctu Naturae* (1160/1180) quoted in David Rollo, 'William of Malmesbury, Gerbert of Aurillac and the excavation of the Campus Martius', in Renate Blumenfeld-Kosinski et al., eds., *Translatio Studii* (Rodopi, 2000), 261–86 at 262.

[205] Gabrielle M. Spiegel, *The Past as Text: The Theory and Practice of Medieval Historiography* (Johns Hopkins, 1997), xvi, 182, 191–2; Miguel de Cervantes, *History of Don Quixote de la Mancha* (1615; London, 1923), 2: 21. Historical truth, however, was deliberately slanted, a partisan record 'serving particular group interests' (Spiegel, *The Past as Text*, 193).

[206] William Godwin, 'Of history and romance' (1797), appendix to *Things as They Are* (1794; Penguin, 1988), 359–74 at 372.

[207] Thomas Babington Macaulay, 'Hallam' (1828), in *Critical and Historical Essays Contributed to the Edinburgh Review* (London, 1903), 1: 115–202 at 115.

[208] Thomas Carlyle, 'Sir Walter Scott' (1838), in *Critical and Miscellaneous Essays*, 3: 165–223 at 214.

for me?' Fiction went beyond history's momentous episodes to vibrant everyday life. His Henry Esmond 'would have History familiar rather than heroic'.[209]

No wonder the Marxist critic Georg Lukács commended Scott. The awakening of ordinary folk caught up in great events mattered more than the events themselves; in the humble annals of the poor, readers saw how past masses thought, felt, and acted. In quotidian lives 'great events' were rightly crowded out, wrote a reviewer of Scott, for 'a greater part of the time of the greater part of the people is spent in making love and money'.[210] Fiction not history expressed a people's true unique essence devoid of dross. Like landscape gardeners, novelists smoothed away history's rough contours and unified past incongruities.

Scholars turned novelist the better to convey the past. 'We write novels like history, and history like novels', in Disraeli's Mr Sievers's summation; 'all our facts are fancy, and all our imagination reality'. As priests Kingsley, Wiseman, and Newman penned historical fiction to impart spiritual lessons – the holiness of the medieval church, the need to revive it again – to the widest public. In means if not ends they saw eye to eye with Heine and Hegel, who praised novels for making the past accessible to the unlearned. Fiction was a virtue, the novelist's past more vital than the historian's *because* partly made up.[211]

Historical fiction's great champion was the historian Butterfield. 'The past as it exists for all of us is history synthesised by the imagination, and fixed into a picture by ... fiction.' The historical novel let readers *feel* the past as formal history could not:

> The life that fills the street with bustle, that makes every corner of a slum a place of wonder and interest, the life that is a sad and gay, weary and thrilling thing in every hillside cottage, is a dim blurred picture in a history. Because of this, history cannot come so near to human hearts and human passions as a good novel can; its very fidelity to facts takes it ... farther away from the heart of things ... To make a bygone age live again, history must not merely be eked out by fiction ... it must be turned into a novel.[212]

Not content to let the past tell its own tale, the hindsight-encumbered historian hauled it 'into relationships with the whole of subsequent development'. Barred from immersion in the past, the reader of history 'stands aside to compare it with the present'. Seeing from a distance a world finished and ended forcibly reminds him that he is *not* in the past. Conversely, fiction allied readers with people of the past, who could not know what was coming next.

---

[209] William Makepeace Thackeray, *The English Humourists of the Eighteenth Century* (New York, 1853), 94; W. M. Thackeray, *The History of Henry Esmond* (1852; Penguin, 1970), 46.

[210] Georg Lukács, *The Historical Novel* (1937; Penguin, 1981), 44; 'Francis Jeffrey, Tales of my landlord', *Edinburgh Review* (Mar. 1817): 528–35 at 533. See Rigney, *Imperfect Histories*, 31–7.

[211] Benjamin Disraeli, *Vivian Grey* (1827; Teddington: Echo, 2007), 323; Andrew Sanders, *The Victorian Historical Novel 1840–1880* (Macmillan, 1978), 15, 120–47, citing Charles Kingsley's *Hypatia* (1852–3), Nicholas Wiseman's *Fabiola* (1854), and John Henry Newman's *Callista* (1855); Heine and Hegel cited in Lukács, *Historical Novel*, 57–61; Morse Peckham, *The Triumph of Romanticism* (South Carolina, 1970), 141.

[212] Butterfield, *Historical Novel*, 22, 18, 23.

It is not enough to know that Napoleon won a certain battle; if history is to come back to us as a human thing we must see him on the eve of battle eagerly looking to see which way the dice will fall ... The victory that is achieved on one day must not be regarded as being inevitable the night before ... To the men of 1807 the year 1808 was a mystery and an unexplored tract; ... to study the year 1807 remembering all the time what happened in 1808 ... is to miss the adventure and the great uncertainties and the element of gamble in their lives; where we cannot help seeing the certainty of a desired issue, the men of the time were all suspense ... History does not always give us [these] irrecoverable personal things; but we know they existed.

These 'are the very touches that are needed to turn history into a story'. Unlike history, fictional narrative could forget or transcend hindsight.[213]

But never entirely. Butterfield to the contrary, historical fiction exhibits certain hindsight needs, not just to make the past intelligible but to reveal *some* matters not available to original eyewitnesses. Like historians, novelists cannot avoid portraying the past in present-day terms. 'To all situations one brings a modern spirit', in Goethe's words, 'for only in this way can we understand them and, indeed, bear to see them'.[214] Scott was frank about his modernizing. 'It is necessary, for exciting interest of any kind, that the subject [be] translated into the manners as well as the language of the age we live in.'[215] His Anglo-Saxon and Norman characters not only spoke pretty much the English of Scott's grandparents' day, they explained history far more clearly than medieval folk could have done. But Scott did not confuse the twelfth with the sixteenth century', his anachronistic jumble of Elizabethan with medieval sources was deliberate.[216] Temporal juggling in historical fiction is not only desirable; it is unavoidable.

Butterfield assigned history and fiction clearly defined roles: 'To the historian the past is the whole process of development that leads up to the present; to the novelist it is a strange world to tell tales about.'[217] But as the ideal of scientific objectivity took hold in the late nineteenth century, professional historians faulted fiction. Initially inspired to explore the past by Walter Scott, Leopold von Ranke later renounced historical romance because he was dismayed by Scott's deliberately false portrayals of Charles the Bold and Louis XI in *Quentin Durward*.[218] Rebuking littérateurs for preferring fable to fact, *fin-de-siècle* historians denounced booming sales of popular historical narrative as vulgar fabrication. The 'noble dream' of objectivity divorced scholarly history from fiction.[219] And their subsequent reconciliation, fuelled by relativist disavowal of all historical truth and by historians' re-embrace of narrative, remains frail and flimsy, disconfiting to both.

[213] Ibid., 22–6.
[214] Johann Wolfgang von Goethe, 'Teilnahme Goethes aus Manzoni' (1827), in *Gedenkausgabe der Werke* (1948–71), 14: 812–44 at 838.
[215] Walter Scott, 'Dedicatory epistle to the Rev. Dr. Dryasdust, F.A.S'. (1817), in *Ivanhoe* (1820; Boston, 1834), 3–15 at 8.
[216] Lukács, *Historical Novel*, 63; Michael Alexander, *Medievalism: The Middle Ages in Modern England* (California, 2007), 131.
[217] Butterfield, *Historical Novel*, 113.
[218] C. Veronica Wedgwood, 'The sense of the past' (1957), in *Truth and Opinion* (Collins, 1960), 27–8.
[219] Gregory M. Pfitzer, *Popular History and the Literary Marketplace* (Mississippi, 2006), 9–16, 64–7, 332–4; Novick, *That Noble Dream*.

Yet both history and fiction now claim to disown Butterfield's distinction. Each encroaches on the other's domain; history grows more like fiction, fiction more like history. And both restructure the past more profoundly than ever. Flashbacks, streams of consciousness, duplicitous narrators, and multiple endings decompose temporal flow. While *The French Lieutenant's Woman* is saturated with history, John Fowles let readers choose their preferred ending.[220] The 1982 Booker prize for fiction went to Thomas Keneally's *Schindler's Ark*, which the author termed a 'true history'; as the prize chairman temporized at the ensuing controversy, 'history is always a kind of fiction'.[221] Novelists enjoy confounding the two. 'There's no more fiction or nonfiction now, there's only narrative', asserted E. L. Doctorow, who called his novel *Ragtime* 'a false document'.[222] Novelists glory in overcoming 'inconsequential' distinctions between fact and fiction.

Convergence led compilers of historical fiction to term it 'more truthful than history itself', for history often pretends to be true but is false, while novelists simply say much of their past is 'true to life and much fictional'.[223] Arrogating the past's 'inner' truths to themselves, some novelists deprecate historians' insights. 'Fiction is truer than history, because it goes beyond the evidence, and each of us knows from his own experience that there is something beyond the evidence', argued E. M. Forster.[224] 'The novelist's 'imaginative truth ... transcends ... what the historian can give you', William Styron enlarged on Butterfield. 'An historian can tell you just what happened at Borodino, but only Tolstoy, often dispensing with facts, can tell you what it really was to be a soldier at Borodino.' Unlike the astute novelist who tells it like it really was, the historian is merely a shallow chronicler.[225] A literary scholar lauds fiction as 'the higher reality, not limiting and arbitrary like historical truth'. Most dismissive is Gore Vidal's narrator: 'There is no history, only fictions of varying degrees of plausibility. What we think to be history is nothing but fiction.'[226]

Now inclined to doubt that history could ever achieve a wholly faithful account, some historians began to think it wrong even to try. They themselves constructed the past, charged postmodern relativists. 'Historical explanations are crafted forms', and

the most illuminating works of history are those governed by the most imaginative and capacious regulative fictions. ... The blurring of lines between history and fiction ought to humble historians, reminding them how fragmentary and oblique their view of the past must always be ... They might even acknowledge the truth-telling power of literary fictions.

[220] Cushing Strout, *The Veracious Imagination:* (Wesleyan, 1981), 10, 18; Tony E. Jackson, 'Charles and the hopeful monster: postmodern evolutionary theory in "The French Lieutenant's Woman"', *Twentieth Century Literature* 43:2 (1997): 221–43.

[221] John Carey quoted in Michael Hulse, 'Virtue and the philosophic innocent: the British reception of *Schindler's Ark*', *Critical Quarterly* 25:4 (Dec. 1983): 43–52.

[222] E. R. Doctorow quoted in Barbara Foley, 'From *U.S.A.* to *Ragtime*: notes on the forms of historical consciousness in modern fiction', *American Literature* 50 (1978): 85–105 at 102, 99.

[223] Daniel D. McGarry and Sarah H. White, *World Historical Fiction Guide* (Metuchen, NJ: Swallow Press, 1973), xx.

[224] E. M. Forster, *Aspects of the Novel* (New York, 1927), 98. See Nancy Partner, 'Historicity in an age of reality fictions', in Frank Ankersmit and Hans Kellner, eds., *A New Philosophy of History* (Chicago, 1995), 21–39.

[225] William Styron in Ellison et al., 'Uses of history in fiction', 76.

[226] Larzer Ziff quoted in Edwin McDowell, 'Fiction: often more real than fact', *NYT*, 16 July 1981: C21; Gore Vidal, *1876* (Heinemann, 1976), 196–7, 194.

For example, García Márquez's *One Hundred Years of Solitude* 'devastates positivist assumptions about linear causality and historical truth ... but it also tells some profound historical truths about the "modernization" of a colonial society'.[227]

Being seen as 'higher' history, however, hobbles fiction's ability to retrieve the spirit of the past. In modernizing Edwardian notables, *Ragtime* subverts racial confrontations both back then and in Doctorow's 1960s. Anachronistic modern sensibilities in *The Sot-Weed Factor*'s (1960) picaresque seventeenth-century world suggest that John Barth 'does not believe in such a thing as history even while his narrative pretends to evoke it'.[228] Much recent historical fiction sets out not to clarify but to scarify, making the past fearsomely unfamiliar. By showing us how little we know the past, they further estrange us. Toni Morrison's *Beloved* (1987), Cormac McCarthy's *Blood Meridian* (1985), Richard Flanagan's *Gould's Book of Fish* (2001), Bernice Morgan's *Cloud of Bone* (2007) serve up histories so brutally inhumane as to be not only unrecognizable but unknowable, too agonizing to absorb.[229]

All histories are partly invented; all storytelling distorts. At the same time, all fiction is partly true to the past; a wholly fictitious story cannot be imagined, for no one could understand it. True history is not the only truth about the past; every tale is true in countless ways, more anchored to past actualities in history, more imaginatively veracious in fiction. If fiction belittles history in cannibalizing it, history derogates fiction while borrowing fictional insights and techniques. New sources and devices enable historians to do what Victorians thought only fiction could do – chronicle the everyday past in hallucinatory detail. And historians increasingly accept that fictive rhetoric is both unavoidable, as Hayden White shows, and essential, as Hexter argued.[230]

Some go further, avowing error and invention as integral to historical validity. Alex Haley thus defended *Roots* when much of his eighteenth-century African setting was disclosed as invented. Elusive actual facts mattered less, Haley retorted, than his fictionalized symbolic past, with which millions of black Americans had come to identify. The Juffure he described had never existed, but was a justifiable composite likeness of Gambian villages of the time. Haley's Juffure in fact amalgamated West Africa with Avalon, Eden, and idealized small-town America in a Club Med-cum-Platonic city-state. Indeed, only such anachronisms let black Americans identify *their* past with this remote unlikely place; had Haley depicted Juffure as it actually was, his picture would have been not just disbelieved but ignored. Factuality was jettisoned for a serviceable past. And that past triumphed, tourist fame transforming Juffure into a facsimile of Haley's idealization.[231]

---

[227] T. J. Jackson Lears, in 'Writing history', *NYRB*, 16 Dec. 1982: 58–9.

[228] Tony Tanner, *City of Words: American Fiction 1950–1970* (Jonathan Cape, 1971), 245.

[229] Viktor Shklovsky, 'Art as technique' (1917), in David Lodge, ed., *Modern Criticism and Theory* (Longman, 1988), 16–30; Jess Row, 'Styron's choice', *NYT Book Review*, 5 Sept. 2008.

[230] Hayden White, 'The historical text as literary artifact', in *Tropics of Discourse* (Johns Hopkins, 1978), 81–100, and 'Historical fiction, fictional history, and historical reality', *Rethinking History* 9 (2005): 147–57; Hexter, 'Rhetoric of history'.

[231] Gary B. Mills and Elizabeth Shown Mills, '*Roots* and the new "faction"', *Virginia Magazine of History and Biography* 89:1 (Jan. 1981): 3–26; Philip Nobile, 'Uncovering Roots', *Village Voice* [NY], 2 Feb. 1993: 31–8; Tina Susman, 'Bitter "Roots": Kunta Kinte's village bashes Alex Haley', *Seattle Times*, 1 Apr. 1995.

Historians who claim unique fidelity to the past, and writers of fiction who claim total exemption from such fidelity, are equally mistaken. The difference between history and fiction is more one of purpose than of content. Whatever rhetorical devices the historian deploys, tenets of the craft forbid deliberate invention or concealment. In terming their work a history, they opt to have it judged for accuracy, internal consistency, and congruence with surviving evidence. And they dare not fabricate characters, ascribe unknown traits or incidents to real ones, or ignore incompatible evidence to make their tale more gripping or intelligible. Such perversions cannot be hidden from others with access to the record, nor condoned when found out.[232]

By contrast, the historical novelist is bound to invent either characters and events, or imaginary thoughts and actions for real people in the past. The constraints the historian willingly embraces are intolerable to the writer of fiction, as John Updike found when gathering materials for a life of President James Buchanan. Suffocated by the stubborn facticity of history, Updike could not leap the divide from fiction. 'Researched details failed to act like remembered ones, they had no palpable medium of the half-remembered in which to swim; my imagination was frozen by the theoretical discoverability of *everything*. An actual man, Buchanan, had done this and this, exactly so, once; and no other way. There was no air.'[233]

History and fiction are neither mutually exclusive nor wholly congruent routes to the past. Combining them does not, however, condone performance that claims the merits of both but abides by the strictures of neither. 'Factional' docudrama follows postmodernist fashion in smudging distinctions between history and fiction, but its pretended omniscience glosses over the past's profound otherness.

Similar anachronisms in nineteenth-century fiction went undetected or unregretted. Novelists feigned 'a bogus sense of intimacy with Pompeii' by flattering readers with 'a special knowledge denied to pedants and professors'.[234] Verisimilitude made their romances seem authentic, but it denied, tamed, and leached away the past's true strangeness. Anachronism became decoration, residues too rough to digest were hidden or bowdlerized. Those who painstakingly verified every detail forgot that readers craved not accuracy but intimate immediacy. By the time of the Pre-Raphaelite Brotherhood, authenticity had become a tedious bane; 'now that history provided a museum of styles, none seemed authentic'. Pastiche and parody permeated historical painting as they did historical fiction, in striking harbingers of postmodern aesthetics.[235]

All such recreations, Henry James objected (anent Sarah Orne Jewett's 1901 *Tory Lover*), sought in vain to represent 'the old *consciousness*, the soul, the sense, the horizon, the vision of individuals in whose minds half the things that make . . . the modern world, were non-existent, [and] whose own thinking was intensely otherwise conditioned. You

[232] J. H. Hexter, *The History Primer* (Basic Books, 1971), 289–90.
[233] John Updike, *Buchanan Dying* (Knopf, 1974), 'Afterword', 259.
[234] Richard Jenkyns, *The Victorians and Ancient Greece* (Blackwell, 1980), 83–6.
[235] Alexander, *Medievalism*, 27, 119, 162, 208. See Rigney, *Imperfect Histories*, 33–4; Frederic Jameson, 'Postmodernism and consumer society', in John Belton, ed., *Movies and Mass Culture* (Rutgers, 1996), 185–202.

may multiply the little facts that can be got from pictures and documents, relics and prints as much as you like – the *real* thing is almost impossible to do.'[236]

Factional portrayals wish away that impossibility. TV docudramas like historical novels readily abandon fact for fiction. But in continuing to claim factual fidelity, they let go of the anchor while pretending still to be grasping it. Deceptive authenticity has bedevilled documentary filmmaking at least since Robert Flaherty's *Nanook of the North* (1922).[237] 'This is how it was' heralds faction, not 'It may have been something like this'. All-knowing certitude, cloaked in authoritative anonymity, lends such sagas a stamp of revealed truth. Hence the TV past is readily mistaken for gospel truth. Viewers take shows that confessedly commingle fact and fiction as veracious accounts of what actually happened and what life was really like.

In written histories, the author's voice alerts us at the outset to authorial perspective. Television eliminates authorial specificity and responsibility, lending documentaries an aura of unassailable expertise enhanced by compelling visual images more convincing than written accounts. 'In the good old days, people believed things they read', said a critic. But faith in the invariable veracity of books and newspapers gave way to the belief that 'the camera never lies ... You can actually see it, so it must be true.'[238] Producers themselves share this faith. Those who made *The Birth of a Nation* (1914), along with most who saw it, felt it literally true. 'You will see what actually has happened', said director D. W. Griffith, 'there will be no opinions expressed. You will merely be present at the making of history ... The film could not be anything but the truth.'[239]

Griffith's credulity persists. John Sturges's *The Great Escape* (1963) began with the blunt assertion 'This is a true story', though no Stalag Luft III 1944 escapees had leapt the barbed wire like Steve McQueen (on a motorcycle built twenty years later). Hollywood still claims adherence to naked truths. 'I've shown this movie to world-class historians who have said it's amazing', exclaimed Zack Snyder of his Battle of Thermopylae box-office hit *300* (2007). 'They can't believe it's as accurate as it is. ... This stuff really happened! Well, most of it, anyway. ... The events are 90% accurate', for his narrator, 'knows how not to wreck a good story with truth'.

Indeed, directors deride historical doubt as fuddy-duddy claptrap. 'Historians from England will say I'm a liar!' intones the voiceover in *Braveheart*, an England-bashing film that makes a horrendous haggis of Scottish heritage; 'but history is written by those who have hanged heroes!'[240] Even more dismissive of historians is Roland Emmerich, whose film *Anonymous* (2011) claims that the Earl of Oxford authored Shakespeare. 'You have

---

[236] To Sarah Orne Jewett, 5 Oct. 1901, in *Selected Letters of Henry James* (London, 1956), 234–5.

[237] Angela Piccini, 'Faking it: why the truth is so important for TV archaeology', in Timothy Clack and Marcus Brittain, eds., *Archaeology and the Media* (Left Coast Press 2009), 221–36 at 223.

[238] Patrick Brogan, 'America's history being rewritten on TV by confusing fact–fiction serials', *Times*, 11 Oct. 1977.

[239] Griffith quoted in Pierre Sorlin, *The Film in History* (Blackwell, 1980), viii–ix; Griffith, 'Five dollar "movies" prophesied' (1915), quoted in Robert Lang, ed., *The Birth of a Nation* (Rutgers, 1994), 4.

[240] Snyder quoted in Josh Horowitz, '"300" trivia', 13 Mar. 2007, *mtv.com*; Alex von Tunzelmann, 'Braveheart: dancing peasants, gleaming teeth and a cameo from Fabio', *The Guardian*, 31 July 2008.

to be careful of history books, because they are old scholars, basing their stuff on errors, and often writing within a totalitarian state.'[241]

Paying lip-service to history before ignoring or butchering it was said to peak with *Pearl Harbor*'s (2001) anachronistic wartime America blessedly free of smoking and segregation. 'Playing fast and loose with the past is no longer acceptable in film', avers a British critic. Given 'a historically literate audience ... , film-makers now feel an obligation to reflect the past as accurately as possible within the demands of the art'. Yet four of *Time* magazine's Top 10 Historically Misleading Films postdate 2006 (*300*, *Robin Hood*, *The King's Speech*, and *10,000 BC*, in which woolly mammoths help build the pyramids). Hollywood turned Aztecs into Mayans who succumb to the Spanish six centuries too soon in *Apocalypto* (2006); slandered Spartans as quasi-democratic Athenians, Persians (to Iranian anger) as demonic barbarian monsters in *300* (2007); and credited *Robin Hood* (2010) with Magna Carta.[242]

However revamped, the past must still *seem* authentic. Grossly anachronistic portrayals are papered over with painstakingly genuine antiquity. *Brideshead Revisited*'s 1981 TV producers secured Evelyn Waugh's actual 1920s rooms at Oxford, speckled pullet eggs to simulate the novel's plovers' eggs, and (echoing Vanbrugh and Hawksmoor) garnished Castle Howard with faux-marble columns and Felix Kelly murals. Yet it was a post-war fantasy of England's aristo past that entranced viewers. In filmed versions of E. M. Forster's *Maurice* (1987), Waugh's *A Handful of Dust* (1987), Julian Mitchell's *Another Country* (1984), and the Merchant-Ivory production of *A Passage to India* (1984), as in the current (2011–) *Downton Abbey* series, the splendour of the settings overwhelms the ironic or sardonic intent of the narratives, put-downs of pomp and privilege smothered in the surfeit of period detail.[243] British antiquity in film is constructed 'in our own image of it ... the Iron Age is always already as we know it', combining today's anti-hegemonic stance with yesterday's denigration of 'the Celtic fringes as backward and unchanging'.[244]

Film and TV history is not, for all its 'meticulous scholarship', what historians normally term history. Rather it is a semi-fictitious saga of impassioned valour and villainy. *Mutiny on the Bounty* portrayed Captain Bligh as a sadist for the sake of 'a closeknit, strong, and more comprehensive' portrayal; the actuality might have 'confused the issue'.[245] Indeed, 'getting [things] wrong is quicker, simpler, and usually makes a better story than getting them right', explained an apologist for Disney's 1995 *Pocahontas*.[246]

[241] Caroline Frost, '"Anonymous" asks the right questions of Shakespeare's work, says director Roland Emmerich', *Huffington Post*, 26 Oct. 2011.

[242] Ben Macintyre, 'At last Hollywood history is no longer bunk', *Times*, 18 Jan. 2011: 21; *Time Magazine*, 26 Jan. 2011; Alex von Tunzelmann, 'Pearl Harbor: no smoking, no racism, no clue', 18 Sept. 2008; 'Apocalypto and the end of the wrong civilisation', 6 Nov. 2008; 'Snyder's 300 is an epic fail', 9 Oct. 2008; 'Reel history special: Ridley Scott's Robin Hood – wide of the mark?' 23 Sept. 2010; Robert Tait, 'Spartans film is psychological war, says Iran', 15 Mar. 2007, all in *Guardian*.

[243] Andrew Higson, *English Heritage, English Cinema* (Oxford, 2003), 80–4.

[244] Angela Piccini, 'Filming through the mists of time', *Current Anthropology* 37 (1996): s87–s111 at s88.

[245] Film teaching manual quoted in Greg Dening, *Mr Bligh's Bad Language* (Cambridge, 1992), 158; Greg Dening, 'Hollywood makes history' (1993), in *Performances* (Melbourne University Press, 1996), 168–90 at 179–80.

[246] Hanay Geiogamah quoted in 'Disney assailed for Pocahontas portrayal', *IHT*, 27–28 May 1995.

In *Lincoln*'s (2012) counterfactual climatic scene, Connecticut congressmen vote to keep rather than abolish slavery as they actually did. Screenwriter Tony Kushner cited a 'time-honored' justification for the blatant canard: when history failed to follow 'the rules of drama', the film must 'manipulate a small detail in the service of a greater historical truth'. And director Steven Spielberg privileged cinema's portrayal of 'impossible places' off limits to historians – the past's undocumented unknowns. Transcending historical evidence, filmmakers 'enlist the imagination ... to bring the dead back to life [and] form our collective memory of all that has passed [in] perfect and complete recall'.[247]

To be sure, fictional pasts have been peddled as true to the spirit if not the facts of history at least since Walter Scott, if not Shakespeare. But today fiction is the principal, often the sole, source of public understanding of remote as well as recent times. Given little history at school, youngsters turn to film and TV, especially for knowledge of the twentieth century. 'They learn of the Great War from *Birdsong* and of the Holocaust from *Schindler's List*. For Normandy, they watch *The Longest Day* and *Saving Private Ryan*. For Vietnam they go to *The Deerhunter* and *Apocalypse Now*. For the death of Kennedy, Heaven help them, they rely on *JFK*.'[248] They learn about biblical times from *The Da Vinci Code* (which doesn't pretend to be true) and terrorist history from *Fahrenheit 9/11* (which does).

Purported documentaries are likewise congeries of truth and 'truthiness'. 'There was a time when TV documentaries were broadly fact-based', recalls a critic; 'now they always embed truth within story'.[249] And their 'uninflected capture of actual life' more and more brazenly manipulates subjects and feelings to stress argument, advocacy, prosecutorial zeal. Fact and faction become indistinguishable.

When we say 'like a documentary' do we really mean 'like one of those sitcoms pretending to be a documentary', in which characters glance at and sometimes speak directly into the camera? 'Like reality television?' 'Like the evening news?' ... Do we mean something that tries to make us forget we're watching a movie, by giving us what seems like raw, unmediated access to characters and their stories? Or do we mean the opposite: a film that reminds us with every awkward cut and jolting camera movement that what we are watching is not the literal truth?[250]

The confusion has become endemic. Fiction is not the opposite of fact but its complement. To 'locate our own private stories within a larger collective narrative' we embrace 'true' lies, credible falsehoods.[251] That myths may be batty and irrational does not negate their influence. Camelot and the Holy Grail lack historical credibility but convey psychological authority; rooted mythologies lend cosmic meaning to our own lifetime quests.

[247] Tony Kushner to Joseph Courtney, 7 Feb. 2013, quoted in Maureen Dowd, 'The Oscar for best fabrication', *NYT*, 17 Feb. 2013: 11; Steven Spielberg, 'Speech for the 149th anniversary of Lincoln's Gettysburg Address', Gettysburg, 19 Nov. 2012, *lincolnfellowship.org*.

[248] Simon Jenkins, 'History is not bunk, but most historians are', *Times*, 5 July 2002.

[249] Tony Whittaker, 'The National Trust and its plans for a younger generation', *Times*, 20 Oct. 2010 (letter).

[250] A. O. Scott, 'As documentaries pour forth, the word has lost its meaning', *IHT*, 15 Oct. 2010: 10–11; A. O. Scott, 'How real does it feel?' *NYT*, 9 Dec. 2010.

[251] George Lipsitz, *Time Passages: Collective Memory and American Popular Culture* (Minnesota, 1990), 163.

Said the presenter of Alex Haley's flagrantly anachronistic *Roots*, 'There you have it ... some of it fact, and some of it fiction, but all of it true, in the true meaning of the word'.[252]

History and memory

Appraising these two routes to the past through the same lens distresses historians who feel 'history to be hard work while recollection seems passive, noninferential, and unverified'.[253] In academe, memory engages only a minority of psychologists, but history is historians' fundamental enterprise. And while most psychologists usually deal with lab-test recall remote from everyday memory, historians' central remit is pasts familiarly known. To be sure, psychologists who used to deal with 'only memory for lists and list-making', notes Ulric Neisser, 'now study memory for facts, stories, familiar routines ... and personally experienced events'.[254] But even they devote little attention to the actual past. Their concern is not the contents of memories, but their accuracy, vividness, and emotional force. There are no index entries for 'history' or 'the past' in any recent compendia on everyday or autobiographical memory.

Historians' reliance on the written word reflects the modern discipline's derivation from scriptural chronology and remains hardly less extreme than that of biblical funda-mentalists. 'The art of writing', declared Leopold von Ranke, 'is the basis of historical knowledge', leaving prehistory to theology and science. 'For want of documents the history of immense periods ... is destined to remain for ever unknown', agreed the French authors of an authoritative *fin-de-siècle* manual of history. 'There is no substitute for documents: no documents, no history.'[255] R. G. Collingwood concurred. Only when I confirm that 'I remember writing a letter to So-and-so' by seeing that 'my memory is not deceiving me, because here is his reply', is a statement prioritizing *textual evidence*.[256] The fetish persists. For custodians of history 'yesterday did not exist except on paper', found novelist Stevie Davies. Having lost the note of Davies's telephoned request to visit its rare book collection, the John Rylands Library in Manchester took 'absence of documentation ... as ocular proof that I had made no request. No memo, no event.' Memory meant nothing; 'everything depended on a written record'.[257]

Today's academic fixation on original documents contrasts starkly with prior (and popularly persisting) conflation of oral with written, folkloric with fact-based accounts. If Abbott Ælfric derogated Old English saga as *fabulae* 'which never happened, nor can

[252] Quoted in Miles Orvell, *The Real Thing: Imitation and Authenticity in American Culture, 1880–1940* (North Carolina, 1989), xxiii.

[253] Louis O. Mink, 'Everyman his or her own annalist', in W. J. T. Mitchell, ed., *On Narrative* (Chicago, 1981), 233–9 at 234. See Kerwin Lee Klein, 'On the emergence of memory in historical discourse', *Representations* 69 (2000): 127–50 at 130–1.

[254] Neisser, 'New vistas in the study of memory', 1–10 at 8, and 'What is ordinary memory the memory of?', 356–73, in Neisser and Winograd, eds., *Remembering Reconsidered*.

[255] Leopold von Ranke, *Weltgeschichte: Die Römische Republik und ihre Weltherrschaft* (1881), ix; Charles V. Langlois and Charles Seignobos, *Introduction to the Study of History* (1898; New York, 1904), 17.

[256] R. G. Collingwood, 'Historical evidence', in *The Idea of History* (Oxford, 1946), 249–82 at 252–3.

[257] Stevie Davies, *Impassioned Clay* (London: Women's Press, 1999), 139. See Smail, *On Deep History and the Brain*, 44–46.

ever happen', and praised *historia* as 'things and deeds, which were done in the old days and . . . set down in writing', he like other Anglo-Saxon scholars commonly interwove oral and written sources, popular stories with political and tenurial charters, in a world 'dominated by talk not texts, gossip not parchment'. Indeed, oral transmission was felt to guarantee the reliability of Abbo of Fleury's *Passio sancti Eadmundi* (985–7).[258]

Written history may be denied if it supersedes or conflicts with collective memory. Burgundian villagers shun history as the realm of national matters beyond their control, remote from daily life, menacing to customary routine. They prize orally recounted local heritage laden with enduring and cyclic events, easy to grasp and comfortingly predictable. Much of it is in fact cribbed from local histories in books found in many homes, yet 'never did anyone say to us that they knew something through having read it', reported scholars. 'They knew it from "having heard it said", they knew it "by word of mouth", as if only the spoken word were a true guarantee of the facts'. They concealed the written origin and favoured the spoken word 'to invent a time without blemish or interruption'.[259]

History is deeply reliant on memory; after all, Clio is the daughter of Mnemosyne. Yet they wholly differ, both in how they gain and test knowledge of the past and in how they transmit, preserve, and alter it. We accept our own memory as a premise of knowing; we infer history from evidence mainly of other people's memories. My memory may be flawed, but I must implicitly trust it or surrender any claim to knowing the past. Historical data in principle ultimately require empirical confirmation. Memory is given, history contingent.

Yet ambiguity and overlap confound these distinctions. Memory includes second-hand accounts of the past – that is, history. And history relies on eyewitness recollections – that is, memory. We treat other people's memories much like history, to be tested against evidence; like Everyman, we often have to confirm our own recall. Facts of memory – when things happened, who met whom, what ensued – can often be verified or falsified by records; the prudent memoirist checks his memory against historical sources, and finds, all too often, as Collingwood noted, that he has substituted a subsequent thought or event. But he can rely only on his memory for his *feelings* about those events, for he alone is privy to such knowledge. All he can test those memories against are his own previous accounts.[260] Disparities between what we once reported and what we now recall can be deeply dismaying, as noted in the Bloody Sunday Inquiry (Chapter 7).

But historical reconstruction often impinges on memorial recollection. I treat a bit of history cribbed from someone else as prima-facie true, just like the rest of my memory. If only to avoid acrimony, what spouses and friends tell us happened is usually trusted like our own memories. Only when conflict or patent improbability arouse major doubt do we subject their memory claims to a beady historical eye.

---

[258] Catherine Cubitt, 'Folklore and historiography: oral sources and the writing of Anglo-Saxon history', in Tyler and Balzaretti, eds., *Narrative and History in the Early Medieval West*, 189–223 at 204 (quoting Ælfric's *Grammar*, c. 998), 221 ('talk not texts'), 196–7 (*Passio*).

[259] Françoise Zonabend, *The Enduring Memory: Time and History in a French Village* (Manchester, 1984), 3–4.

[260] R. G. Collingwood, 'History as re-enactment of past experience', in *Idea of History*, 282–302 at 295–6.

Unlike memory, history is intrinsically social. Although my remembered past stems in large part from interacting with others, and is partly shared with and influenced by them, much of it is solely mine. But history is by its very nature collective. Whereas 'an isolated individual could remember no past other than his personal recollections', the historical past is innately sociable. To record and communicate such a past requires enduring associations. Groups validate their identity through history as individuals do through memory. Indeed, historical enterprise is crucial for social preservation. 'Since all societies are organised ... to ensure their own continuity', noted J. G. A. Pocock, saving and handing on history helps to conserve existing arrangements and fosters the feeling of belonging to coherent, stable, and durable institutions.[261]

Endurance privileges historical knowledge. Most memories perish with their holders, but histories long outlive their authors. Indeed, preserving knowledge of the past is one of history's *raisons d'être*: archival records are kept against the lapse of memory and devouring time. And history is less open to alteration than memory. Both undergo change to conform with present needs, but the historical record to some extent resists deformation: writing and especially print can preserve information virtually as it was, even if the original source is defunct. Speech normally involves the speaker's *presence*, writing the writer's *absence*; 'like monuments, writing cheats death by preserving unchanged what has perished'.[262]

While the durability of history today owes most to dissemination in print, much knowledge survives scribal and even oral transmission more or less intact. Notwith-standing manifold copying errors and forgeries, most manuscripts remain essentially true to authors' intent. Oral history cannot be checked against previous records, but residual anachronisms in retold tales show that much persists from narrator to narrator.[263] And those who recount and receive histories – oral, scribal, printed – rely on their being largely stable and faithful records, whereas we *expect* memory often to mislead us.

Hindsight knowledge further distinguishes history from memory. 'Historical under-standing is not remembering', notes Walter Benn Michaels, 'but learning about pasts we've never known' before.[264] To be sure, time-transformed recollections also invent and discover; memory like history reviews the past from the standpoint of present knowledge. But memory revision is usually unselfconscious, whereas historians intentionally reinter-pret the past through subsequent lenses. Both history and memory engender new knowledge, but memory seldom sets out to do so, while history almost always does. Memory makes us; we remake history.

Recent decades have brought memory studies into ever greater prominence, enrich-ing history with data and insights from 'laws and buildings, documents and oral

---

[261] J. G. A. Pocock, 'The origins of the study of the past', *Comparative Studies in Society & History* 4 (1962): 209–46 at 211. See Jeffery Blustein, *The Moral Demands of Memory* (Cambridge, 2008), 183–9.

[262] Charles W. Hedrick, Jr., *History and Silence* (Texas, 2000), 245–6. See Donald R. Kelley, *Foundations of Modern Historical Scholarship* (Columbia, 1970), 215–33; Elizabeth L. Eisenstein, *The Printing Press as an Agent of Change* (Cambridge, 1979; 3rd edn 1991), 112–15.

[263] Joseph C. Miller, 'Listening for the African past', in Miller, ed., *African Past Speaks*, 1–59; Jack Goody and Ian Watt, 'The consequences of literacy' (1963) in Jack Goody, ed., *Literacy in Traditional Societies* (Cambridge, 1968), 27–68 at 28–31, 57–67.

[264] Walter Benn Michaels, 'Race into culture', *Critical Inquiry* 18 (1992): 655–85 at 681n.

tradition', writes a medievalist.[265] Yet memory also threatens to swamp and displace history. Searing personal accounts of monstrous evils make their bearers 'messengers from another world', as is said of Holocaust survivors 'who alone can communicate the incommunicable', thereby salvaging histories otherwise lost.[266] But prevalent uses of such accounts – 'practicing a "therapy of memory" to counter the "pathology of history"' – aim less to tell what happened than to reveal how traumatized victims felt about it. Recollections become sacred relics, venerated not as historical documentation but tragic testimony and potential routes to redemption.[267] 'What makes us authentic ... is our sense of trauma, and thus our status as victims', just as many historians now focus more on 'feelings than doings'. But 'feelings can only be expressed, not discussed', leading either to 'mute acceptance of whatever people wish to say about themselves, or [to] violent confrontations', concludes Ian Buruma. 'You cannot argue with feelings.'[268]

The distinction between facts and feelings reflects divergent approaches to the past. History 'puts the past at a distance', explains a historian, 'help[ing] us understand the weight and complexity of past events'. By contrast, memory 'brings the past into the present. It is ... an affective emotional relation to the past that ... abolishes distance.' Hence 'memory seems more valuable than history'.[269] Memory's attraction lies in 'a poignant immediacy generally absent from history'.[270]

Memory's inherent subjectivity means that we can never ensure its truth or shun its errors. Yet these very 'fallibilities, frailties, and imperfections' lend memory a 'paradoxical strength', argues Oliver Sacks, making it a font of 'flexibility and creativity'. Memory's 'confusion over sources or indifference to them' frees us 'to see and hear with other eyes and ears, to enter into other minds, to assimilate the art and science and religion of the whole culture, to enter into and contribute to ... the general commonwealth of knowledge'.[271] But thus to sift and assimilate the shared past is the supreme role not of frail forgetful memory, but of sturdy source-based history.

'"Memory" is portrayed as wider and somehow more profound and richer', notes history educator Peter Lee, 'than the narrow workings of "academic" history'. This confers equal status on every recall, entitling everyone, informed or ignorant, imperial or indigenous, to assert 'their own versions not only of the past, but of their relationship

---

[265] Matthew Innes, 'Introduction', in Hen and Innes, eds., *Uses of the Past in the Early Middle Ages*, 1–8 at 6–8.

[266] Dominick LaCapra, *History and Memory after Auschwitz* (Cornell, 1998); Christopher R. Browning, *Collected Memories: Holocaust History and Postwar Testimony* (Wisconsin, 2003), 38–9.

[267] Daniel Arasse, *Anselm Kiefer* (Abrams, 2001), 93; Hayden White, 'Afterword', in Jenkins et al., *Manifestos for History*, 230. See Megill, *Historical Knowledge, Historical Error*, 19–21, 30; Klein, 'On the emergence of memory in historical discourse', 137–41; Susannah Radstone, 'Memory studies', *Memory Studies* 1:1 (2008): 31–9.

[268] Ian Buruma, 'The joys and perils of victimhood', *NYRB*, 8 Apr. 1999: 4–9 at 8–9; Phillips, *On Historical Distance*, 178.

[269] Henry Rousso, *The Haunting Past, Memory and Justice in Contemporary France* (1998; PennPress, 2002), 16. See Klein, 'On the emergence of memory in historical discourse', 128–9.

[270] Erik Christiansen, *Channeling the Past: Political History in Postwar America* (Wisconsin, 2013), 23–4.

[271] Oliver Sacks, 'Speak, memory', *NYRB*, 21 Feb. 2013: 19–21 at 21.

with it, and hence what counts as knowledge'. History, by contrast, is 'not the property of any person or group [but] a public form of knowledge' requiring consensual 'standards of validity and relationships to evidence that *anyone* can work with'. Unlike memory, historical knowledge 'constrains what we can assert' about the past, 'however inconvenient or unpalatable such knowledge may be'.[272]

Three decades ago Pierre Nora wrote of history's conquest and virtual eradication of memory; today the emotive immediacy of memory smothers history or relegates it to the margins. How this trend affects our understanding of the past is addressed in my Epilogue. Here it suffices to note, with Nora, that memory and history seem in fundamental opposition. Less 'a stage of progress beyond memory', as it used to be commonly seen, history is more and more 'the antithesis of memory'.[273] Historians find 'an empathic or compassionate response' to traumatic memories without sacrificing critical analysis a daunting challenge.[274] Yet 'emotion-laden memory is inescapable for all of us', wrote historian Bernard Bailyn in the context of the African slave trade, 'and we cannot escape from it by the rational, critical reconstruction of the past'.

Perhaps history and memory in the end may act usefully upon each other. The one may usefully constrain and yet vivify the other. The passionate, timeless memory . . . may be shaped, focused, and informed by the critical history we write, while the history we so carefully compose may be kept alive, made vivid and constantly relevant and urgent by the living memory we have of it. We cannot afford to lose or diminish either.[275]

---

[272] Peter Lee, 'Series introduction', in Mario Carretero et al., eds., *History Education and the Construction of National Identities* (Charlotte, NC: Information Age, 2012), ix–xvi at x–xii.

[273] Nora, 'Entre mémoire et histoire', xviii–xix; Sarah Foot, 'Reading Anglo-Saxon charters: memory, record, or story?', in Tyler and Balzaretti, eds., *Narrative and History in the Early Medieval West*, 39–65 at 65. See Geoffrey Cubitt, *History and Memory* (Manchester, 2007), 46–9, 60, 244.

[274] Dominick LaCapra, 'Resisting apocalypse and rethinking history', in Jenkins et al., eds., *Manifestos*, 160–78 at 173.

[275] Bernard Bailyn, 'Considering the slave trade: history and memory', *William & Mary Quarterly* 58 (2001): 245–52 at 251.

9

Relics

The rolling rock leaves its scratches on the mountain; the river, its channel in the soil; the animal, its bones in the stratum; the fern and leaf their modest epitaph in the coal. The falling drop makes its sculpture in the sand or the stone. Not a foot steps into the snow, or along the ground, but prints ... a map of its march ... The ground is all memoranda and signatures.   Ralph Waldo Emerson, 1850[1]

Most of the marks that man has left on the face of the earth during his 2-million-year career as a litterbugging, meddlesome and occasionally artistic animal have one aspect in common: they are things, they are not deeds, ideas or words.
                                                                                   Glynn Isaac, 1971[2]

When I was a lad, all this was open fields.
         Young Cockney, in London's Charing Cross Underground tunnel, 1982[3]

Myriad traces of natural features and human artefacts long persist as tangible relics. Awareness of such relics conjoins what we know of the past through memory and history. For R. G. Collingwood, experiencing the tangible past was the essential entrée to history.

There is no better way of thinking oneself back into the Roman point of view than to look up on a map a well attested piece of Roman road and follow it for a few miles across country ... Get a Roman road, or, for that matter, any road, under your feet, and you enter the spirit of the men who made it; you see the country through their eyes; you get into your bones a feeling of what they meant to do with the country, and how they meant to do it.[4]

But no physical object or trace is a self-sufficient guide to bygone times; they light up the past only when *thought* to belong to it. 'We cannot know how the flowers in the garden of Epicurus smelled, or how the mountain winds felt in Nietzsche's hair. But we can recreate their thought [about] their original experience.'[5]

   Yet memory and history let us pinpoint only *some* things as relics; the rest may have long been around but suggest little or nothing of the past. Even famed monuments lose reliquary aura as familiarity dims or divests them of their pastness. Historical resonances

---

[1] Ralph Waldo Emerson, 'Goethe: or, the writer' (1850), in *CW*, 4: 261.
[2] Glynn Isaac, 'Whither archaeology?' (1971), in *The Archaeology of Human Origins* (Cambridge, 1989), 397–404 at 397.
[3] Quoted in Michael Dineen, 'The English village re-born', *Observer*, 19 Sept. 1982: 3.
[4] R. G. Collingwood, 'Rome in Britain' (1925), quoted in W. J. van der Dussen, *History as a Science: The Philosophy of R. G. Collingwood* (The Hague: Nijhoff, 1981), 320–1.
[5] R. G. Collingwood, *The Idea of History* (Oxford, 1946), 246–7. See Stein Helgeby, *Action as History: The Historical Thought of R. G. Collingwood* (Exeter: Imprint Academic, 2004); William H. Dray, *History as Re-enactment* (Clarendon Press, 1995).

suffuse Rome's Colosseum and London's Big Ben, but to most modern Romans and Londoners they are simply features of the everyday scene. The tangible past is nonetheless immeasurably voluminous. Few artefacts are entirely new-made; most have recognizable antecedents. Latent reminders are everywhere: they comprise not just ruins and reconstructions but everything marked by age, use, or memorial intent.

These remains form an assemblage incomparably greater than what is only of the present day. What was purposely saved or later found is seldom more than a minuscule fraction of all that was there. 'Above and under the earth', in Rose Macaulay's words, are 'far more ruined than unruined buildings'.[6] The observer of England's living landscape constantly comes 'up against the dead and the dying – prehistoric earthworks, Roman villas, Norman *mottes*, ... decaying towns, deserted villages, nineteenth-century disused railways'.[7] Archaeology inherits the Earth, which contains the debris and inters the memory of innumerable past events.

The most ubiquitous and striking relics are the structures that entomb our forebears and the memorials to their memory – countless pyramids and mausoleums, catacombs and crypts, cemeteries and cenotaphs. No peoples past or present neglect these duties to the dead; inhumation is humanity's signal defining mark. 'To be human means above all to bury', we are reminded. 'The living housed the dead before they housed themselves ... so that their legacies could be retrieved and their afterlives perpetuated.'[8]

Not only human artefacts mark the land and impress the mind; nature too leaves relic features. The polymath Thomas Browne celebrated Earth and cosmos as an inexhaustible cache of things past:

The treasures of time lie high, in urns, coins, and monuments, scarce below the roots of some vegetables. Time hath endless rarities, and shows of all varieties; which reveals old things in heaven, makes new discoveries in earth, and even earth itself a discovery. That great antiquity America lay buried for thousands of years; and a large part of the earth is still in the urn unto us.[9]

Much of that past remains invisible. In Italy, wrote a nineteenth-century observer, 'there is still more, not of antiquity only, but of art, *under* the sod, than *above* it'. Even today 'what has come out of the ground is only a fraction of what is still underneath'.[10] But that visible fraction is itself omnipresent.

Ubiquitous as they are, relics suffer greater attrition than memories or histories, because they are mortal yet irreproducible. Whereas chronicles and recorded memories can be disseminated without limit and are potentially immortal, physical relics continually wear away. However many vestiges may yet be found, resurrected, and deciphered,

[6] Rose Macaulay, *Pleasure of Ruins* (New York: Walker, 1953), xvii.

[7] Glyn Daniel, *The Idea of Prehistory* (Penguin, 1964), 140.

[8] Robert Pogue Harrison, *The Dominion of the Dead* (Chicago, 2003), xi, 39; Zygmunt Bauman, *Mortality, Immortality and Other Life Strategies* (Stanford, 1992), 51.

[9] Thomas Browne, *Hydriotaphia: Urn Burial* (1658), in *Works* (Aalen: Scientia, 1964), 3: 7.

[10] George P. Marsh to Charles Eliot Norton, Rome, April 1881, in George Perkins Marsh Collection, University of Vermont Libraries, Burlington; Elisabetta Povoledo, 'Volunteer archeologists unearth an ancient tomb in Italy', *NYT*, 17 Aug. 2007.

the tangible past is ultimately finite and non-renewable, except as time or faith engender new relics. Earlier structures inexorably give way to subsequent ones, if only because two things cannot occupy the same space at the same time.

Were artefacts like memories, everything ever built might be brought to light again. In Freud's example, Rome would be a city 'in which nothing once constructed had perished, and all the earlier stages of development had survived alongside the latest', like Cornelis van Poelenburgh and Jan Baptist Weenix's seventeenth-century landscapes juxtaposing lost relics with present-day features.

> The palaces of the Caesars and the Septizonium of Septimius Severus would still be rising to their old height on the Palatine and ... the castle of S. Angelo would still be carrying on its battlements the beautiful statues which graced it until the siege by the Goths ... In the place occupied by the Palazzo Caffarelli would once more stand – without the Palazzo having to be removed – the Temple of Jupiter Capitolinus ... not only in its latest shape ... but also in its earliest one, when it still showed Etruscan forms ... Where the Coliseum now stands, we could at the same time admire Nero's vanished Golden House. On the Piazza of the Pantheon we should find not only the Pantheon of to-day ... but, on the same site, the original edifice erected by Agrippa, [and on] the same piece of ground ... the church of Santa Maria sopra Minerva and the ancient temple over which it was built.

But the buildings of the ancient *Roma Quadrata* 'exist no longer ... Their place is taken by ruins, but not by ruins of themselves but of later restorations.'[11] Remote and recent memories may linger alongside present impressions of the same scene, but new artefacts displace the old. The present materializes moth-like, discarding past integuments. Otherwise past and present would blur into unintelligible muddle. The hotchpotch Roman Campagna struck Nathaniel Hawthorne as 'crowded so full with memorable events that one obliterates another, as if Time had crossed and re-crossed his own records'.[12]

Whether abruptly snuffed out by earthquake or flood, war or iconoclasm, or gradually expiring of corrosion, artefacts are ceaselessly effaced. Less of last week survives than of yesterday, less of last year than of last month. 'You can see yesterday; most of it is still left', Jack Finney's time traveller reflected in 1970. 'And there's plenty of 1965, '62, '58. There's even a good deal left of nineteen hundred. And ... of still earlier days ... still-surviving fragments of a clear April morning of 1871, a gray winter afternoon of 1840, a rainy dawn of 1783.' Envisaging future as well as past scenes, William Gibson understood his surroundings 'not as a discrete contemporary tableau but as a hodgepodge of 1910, 1980, 2011 and 2020'.[13]

---

[11] Sigmund Freud, *Civilization and Its Discontents* (1930;) in *CPW* (Hogarth Press, 1966–74), 21: 64–145, at 70. See John Forrester, *Dispatches from the Freud Wars* (Harvard, 1997), 108–10. Freud's Roman fantasy was prefigured in Francisco de Quevedo's *Silva* (from the Spanish poet's 1617 Roman sojourn), modelled on Joachim du Bellay's *Antiquitez de Rome*: 'the bare hills of pre-Roman times coexist with the city of Romulus, the Roman Republic, the conquests of the Roman Empire, and the ruins of the seventeenth century. All the strata of memory have been reactivated at once' (Rodrigo Cacho Casal, 'Memory of ruins', *Renaissance Quarterly* 62 (2009): 1193).

[12] Nathaniel Hawthorne, *The Marble Faun* (1859), in *Works* (Ohio State, 1962–80), 4: 101.

[13] Jack Finney, *Time and Again* (Simon & Schuster, 1970), 56; Pagan Kennedy, 'William Gibson's future is now', *NYT Book Review*, 13 Jan 2012.

But most of the remote past is wholly gone or unrecognizably transformed. 'Could the England of 1685 be, by some magical process, set before our eyes', wrote T. B. Macaulay a century and a half later, 'we should not know one landscape in a hundred or one building in ten thousand. The country gentleman would not recognise his own fields. The inhabitant of the town would not recognise his own street. Everything has been changed, but the great features of nature, and a few massive and durable works of human art.'[14] How much truer now, a century and a half since Macaulay!

Relics succumb by attrition of meaning as well as substance. Our past will lose import for our successors as our present becomes *their* past. 'All our yesterdays diminish and grow dim ... in the lengthening perspective of the centuries', in Carl Becker's phrase; 'even the most striking events ... must inevitably, for posterity, fade away into pale replicas of the original picture, for each succeeding generation losing, as they recede into a more distant past, some significance that once was noted in them, some quality of enchantment that once was theirs'.[15]

Perceiving the tangible past

Born among things there before us, many of which will outlast us, inclines us to view our environs as more durable than ourselves. And our surroundings' relative stability bespeaks endurance.[16] Long-surviving relics simultaneously reflect the past and presume a future. 'Every single thing has its history, its memories', says an elderly Norwegian of his keepsakes. 'When I talk to my things ... I talk to the people I associate them with.' And 'perhaps the future owners will also send me a friendly thought'.[17]

What leads us to identify things as antiquated or ancient varies with locus and history, individual and culture. Certain locales, buildings, furnishings markedly reflect the past – ancient earthworks, ruined cities, memorials to the dead, rooms full of antiques, souvenirs, old family photos. Other places, new, fresh, or provisional, evoke less temporal depth. As in America's pioneer prairies, recently settled locales feel conspicuously empty; they lack the monuments and memorabilia, the cast-offs and hand-me-downs, that invest older ones with a palpable human past.

The felt past is also a function of atmosphere. 'Very much depends on the time of day at which one visits', advises a British antiquities guide. 'A Neolithic barrow seen at high noon in summer-time, surrounded by a spiked Ministry of Works fence, dustbins and warning notices, that seems drained of all mystery, will have an entirely different aspect at sunset when the other visitors have departed.'[18] Weather can augment – or dispel – a sense of history. Autumn fog along the Thames 'may blot out the far hills completely, and the ancient forests of the valley, leaving only the sights and sounds of the harsh industrial jungle', noted that scene's frequenter. But at other times rain over the airport makes 'the

---

[14] T. B. Macaulay, *The History of England from the Accession of James II* (London, 1848), 1: 281.

[15] Carl L. Becker, 'Everyman his own historian', *AHR* 37 (1932): 221–36 at 236.

[16] Paul Connerton, *How Societies Remember* (Cambridge, 1989), 37–8.

[17] Bjarne Rogan, 'Things with a history – and other possessions', *Ethnologia Scandinavica* 28 (1998): 93–107 at 93, 99–100. Two respondents' remarks, conflated.

[18] Eric Newby and Diana Petry, *Wonders of Britain* (Hodder & Stoughton, 1968), xv.

jets invisible and inaudible, while ... Windsor Castle emerges from the mists, ... the sun glittering on the stone battlements and the royal standard straining from the citadel. For a few moments, the landscape becomes in all essentials what the people ... must have glimpsed when Chaucer was still writing.'[19]

Like memories, relics long abandoned or forgotten may become more precious than those in continued use; temporal discontinuity lends them salience, particularly if scarcity or fragility threatens imminent extinction. Many new artefacts of transient and diminishing value soon fall into the limbo of rubbish, later to be resuscitated as cherished and costly collectables. Michael Thompson instances Chippendale chairs and Stevengraph silk pictures, the plastic ducks of their eras.[20]

How far we can or wish to detect antecedents largely determines whether we regard things as relics. We may gaze on ancient stones wholly unaware of their history but invest the new and bare with bygone links. Tribal and traditional cultures often draw no distinction between fresh artefacts and those ancestrally made or long used. In today's throwaway world, instant obsolescence antiquates last year's models into anachronisms born only yesterday. Awareness of relic forms depends less on actual ancient–modern differences than on our being willing and able to recognize such differences.

For example, England's famed lowland tapestry is vaunted as a multigenerational creation. But to appreciate this palimpsest requires W. G. Hoskins's *historically informed* observation. 'I stood on a hill', says Julian Barnes's fictional historian,

and looked down on an undulating field past a copse towards a river and ... a pheasant stirred beneath my feet ... A person passing through would no doubt have assumed that Dame Nature was going about her eternal business. I knew better ... The hill was an Iron Age burial mound, the undulating field a vestige of Saxon agriculture, the copse was a copse only because a thousand other trees had been cut down, the river was a canal and the pheasant had been hand-reared by a gamekeeper.[21]

How much remains of the past – and what should be done with it – also varies with observers' memories. Bombs and redevelopment left 1960s Bloomsbury with so few Georgian remnants that those who could recall the pre-war squares saw little point in saving them from the wrecker. But nostalgic newcomers zealously cherished the few remaining fragments.[22] As souvenirs of an experienced past the relics had small worth; to those newly arrived they were precious reminders of bygone antiquity.

Alterations in ourselves – growth from childhood, decline into old age, or simply accreted experience – imbues unchanged scenes with an aura of time. 'I failed at first to recognise her', Proust's Marcel says on seeing ageless Odette after a lapse of many

---

[19] Paul Johnson, 'London diary', *New Statesman*, 13 Sept. 1968: 314. Far from Chaucerian, Windsor is largely the work of Jeffry Wyattville (1823–40).

[20] Michael Thompson, *Rubbish Theory* (Oxford, 1979), 13–33. See Will Straw, 'Embedded memories', in Charles E. Acland, ed., *Residual Media* (Minnesota, 2007), 3–15.

[21] Julian Barnes, *England, England* (Jonathan Cape, 1998), 60.

[22] Ashley Barker (Surveyor of Historic Buildings, London), interview, 4 May 1978.

years, 'not because she had but because she had not changed'.[23] Old movies reseen seem different not because they but we have altered, through age and exposure to new film technology. The nostalgic haze through which we re-experience black-and-white images and slow-paced dialogue reinforces awareness of archaisms of dress and speech.

Three distinct processes alert us that things stem from or link with the past: ageing, embellishment, and obsolescence. The first, organic decay and wear, was reviewed in Chapters 5 and 6. The second, trappings that memorialize or deliberately call attention to some aspect or person of the past, will be discussed in ensuing chapters. The third, recognizing things outmoded or old-fashioned, treats relics as emanations of a previous age. Moustache cups, vintage cars, classical pediments, open-field traces exhibit or echo outdated styles or modes of life. Some survivals are still useful, others obsolete; some are in the scrapheap, others in the museum. What they have in common is seeming to derive from an earlier epoch: they are incongruously out of date. Consciousness of anachronism calls for historical awareness.

We believe things stem from the past if they seem old-fashioned. They may or may not retain their original functions – watermills sometimes do, oast houses do not. Thatched roofs are still serviceable, and their popularity spawns fireproof fibreglass copies that bear an aura of antiquity because they *look* old-fashioned.

Plant and animal species of hoary antiquity or at an evolutionary dead end likewise seem outdated. The remnant coelacanth, the tuatara, the Joshua tree were plainly more at home in some bygone era. Fossil traces conjure up careers of extinct species, also antiquating the strata that bear them. The very absence of fossils imparts antiquity to Precambrian rocks: devoid of any trace of embedded life, the Canadian Shield feels desolately primordial.

Sounds like substances can appear outdated. Musical themes, tones, and styles termed early or archaic sound 'old'; connoisseurs can locate a work chronologically even if they have never heard it before. A particular key may evoke the musical past: cognoscenti 'cannot hear B minor without our subconscious being stirred by memories of the Kyrie of Bach's Mass, the first movement of the Unfinished Symphony, and Tchaikovsky's *Pathétique*'.[24] The timbre of music can suggest outdatedness. 'The old-fashioned tinny quality' of Philip Larkin's record was 'only partly due to the needle . . . Little empty tricks of syncopation . . . recalled the outmoded dresses of the girls that had danced to it. It was strange to think it had once sounded modern. Now it was like an awning propped in the sun, nearly white, that years ago had been striped bright red and yellow.'[25] Certain instruments produce tones that sound archaic whatever their actual age. We conceive early music as characteristically thin, reedy, quavering, or nasal; it also features acoustical qualities – the castrato voice, for example – rare today. Hearing such sounds, we feel in the presence of the past. The Ukrainian mammoth bones that became Cro-Magnon

[23] Marcel Proust, *Remembrance of Things Past* (1913–27; Penguin, 1983), 3: 990.
[24] Gerald Abraham, *The Tradition of Western Music* (Oxford, 1974), 34–5.
[25] Philip Larkin, *A Girl in Winter* (Faber & Faber, 1975), 118–19.

percussion instruments 20,000 years ago even now yield 'hard, resonant, and musically expressive' tones.[26]

But the presumption of antiquity may be mistaken: Many 'early' instruments are in fact recent copies; some modern music is meant to sound antique and, like Stravinsky's *Lyke-Wake* cantata, is set to antiquated verse. What matters is the presumption of antiquity, not its literal veracity. Deliberate archaisms lend music historical depth even when we know the semblance of age is contrived. Sounds that conjure up previous epochs seem ancient.[27]

To sense anachronism in most realms, however, requires minimal expertise. The veriest tyro in architectural history, unable to tell classical from neoclassical, Queen Anne from Georgian, Tudor from mock Tudor, rightly sees that all these styles have some past connection. Countless clues certify furniture, silverware, clothing, paintings as 'antique', whether actual or repro or fake. The very prevalence of fakes substantiates the point: deceptions persuade by assimilating insignia of antiquity. So too with emulations and imitations – period architecture, retro fashions. Some complain that these debase the true coin, but the objection admits the resemblance and affirms affinity with the past.

Virtues and defects of reliquary knowledge

The supreme merit of tangible remains is the ready access they afford to the past's ubiquitous traces. Relics and remnants viewable by all offer unmediated impressions free to any passer-by. Seeing history on the ground is less self-conscious than reading about it: texts require both an author and our deliberate engagement, whereas relics can come to us seemingly unguided and without conscious effort. 'More open than the written record', in Lewis Mumford's words, 'buildings and monuments and public ways … leave an imprint upon the minds even of the ignorant or the indifferent'.[28] History and memory usually come in the guise of stories we must then filter; physical relics remain directly available to our senses.

This existential concreteness explains their evocative appeal. Noting 'the content a man has to see and handle the very same individual things which were in use so many ages ago', an early-modern antiquary found real proof of the past in engraved coins and medals. 'Would you see a pattern of the … funeral pile burnt at the canonization of the Roman emperors? would you see how the Augur's hat and *lituus* [wand] were made? Would you see true and undoubted models of their temples … ? Repair to old coins, and … there shall you find them excellently and lively represented.'[29] Protestants spurned reputed fragments of the Cross and Judas's pieces of silver as idolatrous frauds, yet venerated classical relics; holding a Corinthian brass nail from Nero's Golden

[26] Sergei N. Bibikov, 'Stone Age orchestra', UNESCO *Courier* 28:6 (1975): 28–31, and *Drevneishii Mukzykalnyi Kompleks iz Kostei Mamonta* (Kiev: Akademiia Nauk, 1981). *Melodiya* (Soviet gramophone) issued a 'hypnotic' recording (Bibikov, [Ancient Musical Ensemble of Mammoth Bones], 1981) of music played on those bones.
[27] See my 'From harmony of the spheres to national anthem', *GeoJournal* 65 (2006): 3–15 at 9–11.
[28] Lewis Mumford, *The Culture of Cities* (Harcourt, Brace, & World, 1938), 4.
[29] Henry Peacham, 'Of Antiquities', in *The Complete Gentleman* (1622; Cornell, 1962), 117–27 at 126–7.

House thrilled a visiting scholar for its intimate contact with antiquity.[30] 'Examination at first hand of surviving monuments is a direct door into the human past', judged Vico, 'and casts a steadier light both on what men were and did, and on their reasons and motives for it, than the stories of later chroniclers and historians'.[31]

Gibbon's visit to Rome, seeing 'each memorable spot where Romulus *stood*, or Tully *spoke*, or Caesar *fell*', lent him vital inspiration: 'On the 15th of October, 1764, as I sat musing amidst the ruins of the Capitol, while the barefooted friars were singing vespers in the Temple of Jupiter ... the idea of writing the decline and fall of the city first started to my mind.'[32] Effigies of French kings in the Musée des Monuments vivified national history for young Michelet.[33] 'The sword of a great warrior, the insignia of a celebrated sovereign', argued the historian Prosper de Barante, in urging the French government to buy the Musée de Cluny collection, were 'relics which people like to see', more stirring than the history book's 'dead letter'.[34]

Romantic evocations such as Shelley's 'Ozymandias' made relics compelling witnesses. Historical training should begin not in town archives, advised a popular historian, but in the quaint old streets where men had lived.[35] The taste, feel, and sight that etch relics into memory vividly conjure up their milieus. 'Picking up for one's self an arrow-head that was dropt centuries ago, and has never been handled since', Hawthorne fancied he had received it 'directly from the hand of the red hunter'. He envisaged 'the Indian village, amid its encircling forest', and recalled 'to life the painted chiefs and warriors, the squaws at their household toil, and the children sporting among the wigwams; while the little wind-rocked papoose swings from the branch of a tree'.[36]

Sites and relics lent special immediacy to classical and scriptural history. Seeing 'the places we know were frequented and inhabited by men whose memory is held in honor, ... stirs us more than hearing the story of their deeds or reading their writings', Montaigne translated Cicero's reactions to his visit to Athens; 'wherever we walk we set our foot on history'.[37] Just as 'one understands better the Greek historians when one has seen Athens with one's own eyes', wrote the fourth-century theologian St Jerome, 'so one understands better the Holy Scriptures when one has seen Judea with one's own eyes'. Holy Land pilgrimages culminated with Ernest Renan's ecstatic Palestinian vision: 'I had before my eyes a fifth Gospel.'[38]

[30] *The Diary of John Evelyn* (1818; Oxford, 1959), 13 & 27 Feb. 1645, 185, 195.
[31] Giambattista Vico, *New Science*, paraphrased in Isaiah Berlin, *Vico and Herder* (Hogarth, 1976), 57.
[32] Edward Gibbon, *Autobiography* (1796; London, 1970), 84–5. Gibbon had not been in the Capitol (long effaced by 1764), but in the Church of the Franciscan friars (Basilica of Santa Maria, Aracoeli).
[33] Jules Michelet, *Ma jeunesse*, 2nd edn (Paris, 1884), 44–6.
[34] Prosper de Barante, 'L'Acquisition du Musée du Sommerard' (1843), in *Études littéraires et historiques* (Paris, 1858): 2: 417–26 at 421.
[35] John Richard Green, *Stray Studies from England and Italy* (London, 1876), 218.
[36] Nathaniel Hawthorne, 'The old manse' (1846), in *Works* (Ohio State, 1962–80), 10: 3–35 at 11.
[37] Cicero, *De finibus honorum et malorum* (390–3), in Margaret M. McGowan, *The Vision of Rome in Late Renaissance France* (Yale, 2000), 249; Montaigne, 'Of vanitie' (1585–88), in *Complete Essays* (Stanford, 1958), 763.
[38] Jerome, *Praefatio in librum Paralipomenon* (387), and Renan, *Life of Jesus*, quoted in Adam G. Beaver, 'Scholarly pilgrims: antiquarian visions of the Holy Land', in Katherine van Liere et al., eds., *Sacred History: Uses of the Christian Past in the Renaissance World* (Oxford, 2012), 267–83, 281, 268.

Archaeological finds in Greece and the Holy Land had by then brought classical and biblical worlds alive to armchair travellers as well. Millions thrilled to Amelia Edwards's necromantic eyewitness tales of Egyptian temples. Each dawn at Abu Simbel 'I saw those awful brethren pass from death to life, from life to sculptured stone', almost believing 'that there must sooner or later come some one sunrise when the ancient charm would snap asunder, and the giants must arise and speak'. And at Karnak 'every breath that wanders down the painted aisles ... seems to echo back the sighs of those who perished in the quarry, at the oar, and under the chariot-wheels of the conqueror'.[39]

Nowadays relics arouse less perfervid responses, but the surge of immersion endures. London's historical intimacy overwhelmed the American writer Helene Hanff: 'I went through a door Shakespeare once went through, and into a pub he knew. We sat at a table ... and I leaned my head back, against a wall Shakespeare's head once touched, and it was indescribable.'[40] Just as palpable original documents vivify the thoughts and events they express – 'nothing seems to bridge the gap of the years so much as the unfolding and reading of ancient letters' – so the shiver of contact with ancient sites brings to mind their lingering barbarity or sanctity.[41]

Authors who visit the scenes of their histories heighten readers' impressions too. George Bancroft trod the Quebec hillside James Wolfe had climbed and 'marked as near as I could the spot where Jacques Cartier may have landed' on the Gaspé Peninsula.[42] Margery Perham's life of Nigeria's imperial ruler Lord Lugard gains verisimilitude from her own Nigerian tour of duty; Bruce Catton intimately knew the Civil War battlefields he describes; Columbus's biographer Samuel Eliot Morison insisted on tracking his voyages by sail.[43]

Tangible cognizance adds visceral immediacy to historical fiction as well. Virgil sought out places visited by Aeneas, Scott reconnoitred the locales his tales describe. 'Does not our sense of that classic struggle between [Sherlock] Holmes and Moriarty quicken if we have seen the Reichenbach Falls?'[44] Even recreated locales help bring history close: Poussin's meticulous models of the Greek and Roman scenes that inspired his Arcadian pictures let him see the past with his own eyes, feel it with his own hands.[45] Sense of place magnified the traveller Robert Wood's sense of the past; steeped in Greek scenes, he felt the closeness of the classics he read there: 'the Iliad has new beauties on the banks of the Scamander'.[46]

[39] Amelia Edwards, *A Thousand Miles up the Nile* (1877; London: Century, 1982), 285, 152.
[40] Helene Hanff, *The Duchess of Bloomsbury Street* (Andre Deutsch, 1974), 30.
[41] C. Veronica Wedgwood, 'A sense of the past' (1957), in *Truth and Opinion* (Collins, 1960), 25.
[42] George Bancroft to his sister, 8 Aug. 1837, quoted in David Levin, *History as Romantic Art* (Stanford, 1959), 17.
[43] Margery Perham, *Lugard* (Collins, 1956–60); Bruce Catton, *Glory Road* (Doubleday, 1952), and *Stillness at Appomattox* (Doubleday, 1953); Samuel Eliot Morison, *Admiral of the Ocean Sea* (Boston, 1942), 1: xvi–xviii.
[44] Robin W. Winks, 'The case of the men who weren't there', in his *The Historian as Detective* (Harper, 1969), 173.
[45] Mario Praz, *On Neoclassicism* (Northwestern, 1969), 28–9.
[46] Robert Wood, *The Ruins of Palmyra, Otherwise Tedmore, in the Desart* (1753; London, 1773), 2.

A past lacking tangible relics seems too tenuous to be credible. Ruskin grumbled that because England had only 'a past, of which there are no vestiges; ... the dead are dead to purpose. One cannot believe they ever were alive, or anything else than what they are now – names in school-books.' By contrast, 'at Verona we look out of [Dante's patron] Can Grande's window to his tomb', and feel 'that he might have been beside us last night'.[47]

To be sure of the past, we need its actual traces. Artefacts redolent of age prove 'that the past really existed once, that it wasn't made up by experts on the basis of archives'.[48] The old chair and table, old oak beams and bench at his rude old tavern in Chester assured Frederick Law Olmsted that the past was real, the date '1539' over the garret window 'TRUE; I can see the sun shine into the figures. Away, then, with your 1850!'[49] To perpetuate memory of the Nazi massacre at Oradour, the town's ruins are preserved intact. As with old houses which 'have stood and watched the processes of change ... you must keep the shells inside which such things happen, in case you forget about the things themselves'.[50]

Synchronic imagination vivifies tangible relics: things old or made to seem old resurrect palpably potent pasts. 'To see the emperors, consuls, generals, orators, philosophers, poets, and other great men ... standing as it were in their own persons before us', wrote an admirer of Roman statues, 'gives a man a cast of almost 2000 years backwards, and mixes the past ages with the present'.[51] The ancient past was present for Amelia Edwards at Philae a century later. 'One forgets for the moment that anything is changed. If a sound of antique chanting were to be borne along the quiet air – if a procession of white-robed priests ... were to come sweeping round between the palms and the pylons – we should not think it strange.'[52]

In a centennial plea to save the site that birthed the Boston Tea Party, the abolitionist Wendell Phillips felt the Revolutionary heroes 'Adams, and Warren, and Otis are to-day bending over us, asking that the scene of their immortal labors shall not be desecrated, or blotted from the sight of men'.[53] Disneyland's moving, speaking model of Abraham Lincoln summoned up the past by making it present, 'not be history *was* but history *is*'.[54] Finding an 1864 volume on Henry Clay in the British Library, its pages still uncut, gave John Updike instant affinity with the reborn past: 'I was the prince whose kiss this book had been awaiting, asleep, for over a century.'[55]

Because artefacts are at once past and present, their historical and modern roles overlap. A flavour of antiquity permeates a row of houses famed for storied architects

[47] John Ruskin, *Modern Painters* (1843–60; New York, 1886), pt. 5, ch. 1, sect. 5, 4: 4–5.

[48] Paul Zweig, 'Paris and Brighton Beach', *American Scholar* 47 (1978): 501–13 at 512.

[49] Frederick Law Olmsted, *Walks and Talks of an American Farmer in England* (New York, 1852), 123.

[50] Sarah Farmer, *Martyred Village: Commemorating the 1944 Massacre at Oradour-sur-Glane* (California, 1999); Penelope Lively, *The House in Norham Gardens* (London: Pan, 1977), 12.

[51] John Northall, *Travels through Italy* (London, 1766), 362.

[52] Edwards, *A Thousand Miles up the Nile*, 207.

[53] Wendell Phillips, *Oration Delivered in the Old-South Meeting House* (1876; Boston, 1884), 10.

[54] Ray Bradbury, 'The machine-tooled happyland: Disneyland', *Holiday* 38:4 (1965): 100–4 at 104.

[55] John Updike, 'Afterword', in *Buchanan Dying* (Knopf, 1974), 256.

and residents, its medley of epochs infusing today's ensemble with depth in time. Landscapes commingling old with new suggest temporal coexistence: the mass of ancient remains on Dorset hills led Thomas Hardy to see himself 'a strange continuator' among ghost upon revenant ghost: 'I seem where I was before my birth, and after death may be ... I am tracked by phantoms having weird detective ways / Shadows of beings who followed with myself of earlier days'.[56]

Yesterday's relics enrich today's landscapes. Long-enduring buildings carry benefits 'over beyond the living group, streaking with different strata of time the character of any single generation'.[57] For Seamus Heaney vestiges of a departed life attested the uncanny oneness of humanity; to 'gaze at an ancient cooking pot or the shoe of a Viking child or a gaming board from the rubble of a Norman keep' is to experience a double sense of great closeness and great distance. '"Old" was not an idea. It was an atmosphere [that] brought you out of yourself and close to yourself all at once'. Digging holes in a field, Heaney unearthed

a hoard of soft red brick and white crumbly mortar ... that even to a six year old meant foundations, meant house, a living but obliterated past. ... The hole ... began to open down and back to a visionary field, a phantom whitewashed cottage with its yard and puddles and hens. The world had been amplified [by] imagining and remembering.[58]

Old relics hand down their stored-up past: rubbing an Elizabethan silk bobbin-boy against her cheeks 'to get the essence of the ancient thing', Alison Uttley's modern heroine finds it 'smooth as ivory, as if generations of people had held it to their faces, and I suddenly felt a kinship with them, a communion through the small carved toy'.[59] For an old man in Ray Bradbury's story, attic keepsakes harbour and enliven the past.

It was indeed a great machine of Time, this attic, ... if you touched prisms here, doorknobs there, plucked tassels, chimed crystals, swirled dust, punched trunk hasps and gusted the vox humana of the old hearth-bellows until it puffed the soot of a thousand ancient fires into your eyes ... Each of the bureau drawers, slid forth, might contain aunts and cousins and grandmamas, ermined in dust.[60]

Along with such objects, pictures and images carry us back. The antiquarian artist C. A. Stothard authenticated medieval costumes to 'arrest the fleeting steps of Time' and enable readers to 'live in other ages than our own'.[61] Historic-site interpreters urge visitors to feel the past alive in the present: docents at prehistoric Amerindian

---

[56] Thomas Hardy, 'Wessex Heights' (1896), in *Collected Poems* (London, 1930), 300. See J. Hillis Miller, 'History as repetition in Hardy's poetry', in *Tropes, Parables, Performances* (Duke, 1991), 107–34; Tim Armstrong, 'Sequence and series in Hardy's poetry', in Keith Wilson, ed., *A Companion to Thomas Hardy* (Wiley-Blackwell, 2009), 378–94 at 381–2.

[57] Mumford, *The Culture of Cities* 4.

[58] Seamus Heaney, 'Place, pastness, poems', *Salmagundi* 68/69 (1985–6), 30–47 at 37, 32.

[59] Alison Uttley, *A Traveller in Time* (1939; Puffin, 1978), 49–50.

[60] Ray Bradbury, 'A scent of sarsaparilla' (1953), in *The Day It Rained Forever* (Penguin, 1963), 196–7.

[61] Charles Alfred Stothard, *Monumental Effigies of Great Britain* (1811–17; London, 1876), ix.

ruins were exhorted 'to convey the notion ... that the ancients who lived there might come back this very night and renew ... the grinding of corn, the cries of children, and the making of love' – though this last dictum 'must not be taken too literally'.[62]

Things thus differ from thoughts and words by their enduring physical existence. Written history demarcates past from present; verbal tense sets off now from then. But artefacts are simultaneously past and present. Their historical connotations coincide with their modern roles, commingling and sometimes conflating them, as in the English National Trust notice 'CHEDWORTH ROMAN VILLA ... COMPLETION DUE AUTUMN 1978'.[63] The tangible past is in continual flux, eroding and accreting, ageing and renewing, always interacting with each new present. Holding a scythe, an age-old tool unchanged for centuries, 'is like grasping the live end of history', muses a countryman. 'You're cutting grass with something as timeless as the lunar crescent'.[64] And as timeful as Father Time, the Grim Reaper who harvests souls.

Locales made famous by great lives and deeds become iconic emblems of national identity. Places answer this purpose better than books, argued the saviours of Washington's headquarters at Newburgh in 1850. 'If our love of country is excited when we read the biography of our revolutionary heroes ... how much more will the flame of patriotism burn in our bosoms when we tread the ground where was shed the blood of our fathers, or when we move among the scenes where were conceived and consummated their noble achievements'.[65] Patristic links fuelled the ardent campaigns for historic preservation discussed in the next chapter.

Yet the material legacy's sheer immediacy also imposes cautions. Relics render the past more compelling but not necessarily better understood. They bring 'a sense of the past' rather than *the* sense of the past.[66] That the tangible past is ubiquitous, directly accessible, and uncontrived in its origins tempts archaeologists to exalt artefactual evidence as the most comprehensive, accurate, and unbiased source of knowledge about the past. Antiquaries aware of textual forgeries, omissions, and corruptions long looked to relics as more reliable witnesses than the ancient historians. Sacred relics in particular were so prized, since by definition they did not decay but indestructibly embodied divine grace.[67] But tangibility lends all physical relics credence. Here we are, they seem to say; you can see us, even touch us; why doubt the reality of your senses? Yet sense impressions are notoriously fickle. And data conveyed by relics are elusive and slippery, ever revised by

---

[62] Freeman Tilden, *Interpreting Our Heritage* (1957; 4th edn North Carolina, 2007), 102.

[63] Still incomplete, Chedworth in 2012 added Romano-British costumed interpreters.

[64] Verlyn Klinkenborg, 'The scythe', *NYT*, 19 July 2013.

[65] Richard Caldwell, *True History of the Acquisition of Washington's Headquarters* ... (1887), quoted in Charles B. Hosmer, Jr., *Presence of the Past* (Putnam, 1962), 36. See Edward P. and Mary Alexander, *Museums in Motion* (1979; 2nd edn AltaMira, 2008), 118–19.

[66] D. S. Carne-Ross, 'Scenario for a new year: 3. the sense of the past', *Arion* 8 (1969): 239, and *Classics and Translation* (Bucknell, 2010), 17.

[67] Eric Cochrane, *Historians and Historiography in the Italian Renaissance* (Chicago, 1981), 432–6; Arnaldo D. Momigliano, 'Ancient history and the antiquarian' (1950), in *Studies in Historiography* (Weidenfeld & Nicolson, 1966), 1–39 at 11–16; Patrick J. Geary, *Furta Sacra: Thefts of Relics in the Central Middle Ages* (1978; Princeton, 1990), 29–33.

new analytic methods, as with the botanical and chemical residues that controversially redate the Turin Shroud.[68]

Although artefacts are now manifestly as easily altered as chronicles, public faith in their veracity endures; a tangible relic seems *ipso facto* authentic. The vivid impress of ancient monumental sites privileges erroneous myth over historical revision. Josephus's tale of mass suicide at Masada is a known bricolage of classical lore, disproved by history and archaeology alike. But Masada's powerful presence makes it still a transcendent reality. Even flagrant fabrications such as the 'Viking' origin of the Kensington Runestone in Minnesota command continuing adherence (see Chapter 12).

Relics are also felt to help correct historians' stress on written, hence usually elite, evidence, along with their partiality for the extraordinary, the grand, the precious. Material-culture scholars often claim that surviving tangible vestiges are truer to the past because more typical and revealing of everyday life.

For the vast majority who have left no archival trace, artefacts can partly redress the bias of written sources, broadening and deepening what is surmised. Populist insights of plebeian relics, consonant with historical fiction's homely virtues, appealed to nineteenth-century scholars. 'We do not understand the ancients', wrote the classicist Bartold Georg Niebuhr, 'unless we form distinct notions of such objects of their everyday life ... under the forms their eyes were accustomed to'.[69] Because the tombs of Thebes depicted familiar scenes of everyday life, the historian George Perkins Marsh termed them 'fraught with richer lore than ever flowed from the pen of Herodotus', just as he felt 'an hour of buried Pompeii is worth more than a lifetime devoted to the pages of Livy'. Marsh urged public display of domestic and artisanal artefacts – agricultural and mechanical tools, furniture, utensils – to reveal the lineaments of typical past lives, anticipating Scandi-navian open-air museums by half a century.[70] Henry Ford, ridiculed for asserting in 1916 that 'history is more or less bunk', retaliated with 'a museum that's going to show industrial history, and it won't be bunk ... That's the only history that is worth observing ... By looking at things people used and that show the way they lived, a better impression can be gained than could be had in a month of reading.'[71]

Seeing the way they lived can cast crucial light on the eminent, too. 'We know them from their houses', declared Virginia Woolf, citing the famously irascible Carlyles' Chelsea home, a half-century after their deaths a National Trust showplace:

One hour spent in 5 Cheyne Row will tell us more about them and their lives than we can learn from all the biographies. Go down into the kitchen. There, in two seconds, one is made acquainted

[68] Mary Virginia Orna, ed., *Archaeological Chemistry* (American Chemical Society, 1996), 223–9, 229–47; William Meacham, *Rape of the Turin Shroud* (Lulu Press, 2005); Ian Wilson, *The Shroud* (Bantam, 2010); James Beresford, 'When faith and science collide', *Minerva* 21:4 (July–Aug. 2010): 42–5; Giulio Fanti, *Il Mistero della Sindone* (Rizzoli, 2013).

[69] Bartold Georg Niebuhr, *History of Rome* (1811–12; Cambridge, 1831), 1: xxiii. See Thomas J. Schlereth, ed., *Material Culture Studies in America* (1981; AltaMira, 1999), 79–92, 101–5, 106–16, 325–37.

[70] George P. Marsh, *The American Historical School* (Troy, NY, 1847), 11; David Lowenthal, *George Perkins Marsh: Prophet of Conservation* (Washington, 2000), 96–9.

[71] Quoted in Roger Butterfield, 'Henry Ford, the Wayside Inn, and the problem of "History is bunk"', *Massachusetts Historical Society Proceedings* 77 (1965): 53–66 at 57.

with a fact that escaped the attention of [their biographer James Anthony] Froude, and yet was of incalculable significance – they had no water laid on. Every drop that the Carlyles used – and they were Scots, fanatical in their cleanliness – had to be pumped by hand, from a well in the kitchen. ... Here, too, is the wide and wasteful old grate upon which all kettles had to be boiled ... and then carried up three flights of stairs. The high old house without water, without electric light, without gas fire, full of books and coal smoke, ...where two of the most nervous and exacting people of their time lived, year in year out, was served by one unfortunate maid. All through the mid-Victorian age the house was necessarily a battlefield where daily, summer and winter, mistress and maid fought against dirt and cold ... The voice of the house ... is the voice of pumping and scrubbing, of coughing and groaning. ... Thus number 5 Cheyne Row is ... the scene of labour, effort, and perpetual struggle ... , bitterness and suffering. Such is the effect of a pump in the basement and a yellow tin bath up three flights of stairs.[72]

That surviving material vestiges faithfully replicate humdrum quotidian reality is far from the case, however. Decay itself discriminates against the ordinary and common-place: imposing and costly remains better withstand attrition, attract protection, encour-age imitation, and draw attention. Because most things built and made for elites outlast Everyman's goods and chattels, material remnants bias how the past is viewed and understood. Efforts to depict Colonial Williamsburg warts and all, including relics of slave life, show how disparate survival subverts historical neutrality, reinforcing class bias. Much of what belonged to Williamsburg's elite endures; exhaustively inventoried for named owners, along with their portraits, it is all on display. But of the slaves – over half the population – virtually nothing material survives. To depict slave life, generic bedding and utensils furnish replica huts and clothe re-enactors. The incongruity is patent. Elites appear in actual, contextualized, explicitly personal detail; faceless, unprovenanced slaves are generalized, undifferentiated, often specified only in terms of market value. The former come across as memorably authentic individuals in specific locales, the latter as depersonalized simulacra in counterfeit milieus, typically seen as 'not even people, [but] one lump of black mass'.[73]

Nor are surviving remnants truly representative of what formerly existed. Because substances differ in durability, what is left warps impressions of past functions and fashions. 'Physical remains from late medieval Europe suggest a society captivated by ceramics' and iron weaponry, but clothing and bed stuffs, of which little survives, dominate household and debt records.[74] Similarly, although pot shards preponderate in many a site, 'no archaeologist ... is liable to conclude that the men and women of the past spent their whole time making and breaking pottery'.[75] Yet many if not most

[72] Virginia Woolf, 'Great men's houses', in *The London Scene* (1932; London: Daunt, 2013), 31–4.
[73] Eric Gable et al., 'On the uses of relativism: fact, conjecture, and black and white histories at Colonial Williamsburg', *American Ethnologist* 19 (1992): 791–805; Richard Handler and Eric Gable, *The New History in an Old Museum* (Duke, 1997), 112–15; Angela da Silva quoted in 'Slave sale reenactment held as part of Civil War anniversary', *Fox2now.com*, 16 Jan. 2011.
[74] Daniel Lord Smail et al., 'Goods', in Andrew Shryock and Daniel Lord Smail, eds., *Deep History* (California, 2011), 219–41 at 227–8.
[75] William St Clair, 'The biographer as archaeologist', in Peter France and William St Clair, eds., *Mapping Lives* (Oxford, 2004), 227.

prehistoric periods and peoples are commonly named after characteristic long-lived materials – Iron and Bronze ages, Beaker folk.

Another deficiency of artefacts is voicelessness. Relics are mute; from them feelings and beliefs can only be conjectured. To know motives and reactions, artefacts must be amplified by accounts or reminiscences. This is a severe handicap, notes a scholar of the Renaissance, for 'thoughts, feelings, actions: these are the stuff of history, not sticks, stones and bombasine'.[76] Unlike history and memory, whose sheer existence presume the past, material relics do not testify on their own. Their reliquary role requires interpreters. Some archaeologists extol relics' explanatory power for cognitive processes.[77] But unaided, their panoramas of the past remain not only deficient but bizarrely contrived, as though 'beaker-folk' or 'Hallstadt Culture' were actual societies. 'When the raw material does not contain traces of thought, the doors to the past remain closed.'[78]

The monuments of southern France inspired the historian Augustin Thierry, though almost blind, 'to see in greater depth and clarity'. But there he saw only the past's material relics; later, while mining data for his *Histoire de la Conquête de l'Angleterre par les Normands* (1825) in the archives and libraries of Paris, he saw 'the past itself, ... vivid and almost naked, as if it were a reality that had not disappeared'.[79]

Relics are also static. Whereas recorded and remembered narratives conjure up sweeps through time, physical survivals (ruins apart) mainly recapture fixed moments. And the arresting visibility of architectural relics leads viewers to overestimate – and often overvalue – past stability. The aura of antiquity in most heritage sites betokens not continuity but a dearth of later innovation. 'Although people walked the pavements, there was a feeling of desertion as though this were a place from which, a long time ago, everyone had gone', Penelope Lively depicts the Cotswold town of Burford. 'Every building was old, many were beautiful: they seemed to be there together in sad abandonment like textbook illustrations of the past.'[80] All the relics felt dead.

To sense a living past demands a 'dynamic tension between what you see and what you know to have existed once and still to exist in some fragmented or symbolic form', suggests Gillian Tindall – a dynamism rare in heavily protected places. She contrasts the ongoing continuity of London's scruffy Kentish Town with the precious and static air of historic showpieces 'that have been socially and architecturally pickled', including most so-called 'historic areas'.

Townscapes which have managed to retain such a homogeneous aspect ... are, by definition, areas which have not suffered the complex social upheavals and physical dislocations that make their history worth studying ... Paradoxically, those places in which local 'concern for the past' is often

---

[76] John Hale, 'Museums and the teaching of history', *Museum International* 21 (1968): 67–72 at 68.
[77] Colin Renfrew, *Towards an Archaeology of Mind* (Cambridge, 1982), 16–23; C. Renfrew, ed., *The Ancient Mind* (Cambridge, 1994); Marc Abramiuk, *The Foundations of Cognitive Archeology* (MIT Press, 2012).
[78] Peter Munz, *The Shapes of Time* (Wesleyan, 1977), 179–80.
[79] Jo Tollebeek, 'Seeing the past with the mind's eye', *Clio* 29:2 (2000): 167–91 at 176, citing Thierry, *Dix ans d'étude historiques* (1834); Jo Tollebeek and Tom Verschaffel, 'The particular character of history', *History & Memory* 4:2 (1992): 69–95 at 69–71.
[80] Lively, *The House in Norham Gardens*, 121.

so marked among successive generations of moneyed and leisured inhabitants, actually tell one less about the past as a whole ... than do more ordinary, battered places.[81]

Places now pickled in aspic may, to be sure, have enjoyed a prolonged equilibrium. But when a huge amount survives from some particular epoch, not much can have happened since; otherwise most of those old things would have been replaced. Early Pompeii endured in its completeness only because there was no later Pompeii. At West Wycombe house in Buckinghamshire 'we get vivid glimpses of how life must have been', the former proprietor maintained, precisely because there 'time appears to have stood still'.[82] But time does not stand still, and to see it so deadens the past.

Interconnections

We live in a world where ... the music that drifts down from the medieval walls into the garden where we sit is an old recording of Vivienne Segal singing 'Bewitched, Bothered and Bewildered'.   John Cheever, 1978[83]

'"The past is here." He touched his heart. "It isn't here." And he pointed at the dusty road'.   V. S. Naipaul, 1979[84]

Memory, history, and relics offer routes to the past best traversed in tandem. Each needs the others to render the journey significant and credible. Relics trigger recollection, which history affirms and extends back over time. History in isolation is barren and lifeless; relics mean only what history and memory tell us they convey. Indeed, many relics originate as witnesses to memory or history. Full awareness demands engagement with previous experience, one's own and others', along all three routes to the past.

Which route we follow at any given moment may be in doubt. Uncertain where memory ends and history begins, we attribute to one what comes from the other, jumbling early memories with stories later heard and read, conflating recent recollections with tales immemorially told. 'Living memory' may include events from long before our birth. Kentish Town residents told their chronicler they 'remembered' farms that had ceased to exist in their grandparents' youth:

I was again and again told 'Cows were grazed at Gospel Oak when I was a girl', or 'It used to be all fields around here, dear; I remember before such-and-such a street was built.' [Yet] reference to a map of the period shows ... every street in central Kentish Town was there before the birth of the oldest person now living ... Regularly reproduced by gullible local newspaper editors, ... these 'reminiscences' [reflect] the fact that people of all ages *wish* to believe ... that these fields still exist in the safety of memory.[85]

---

[81] Gillian Tindall, *The Fields Beneath: The History of One London Village* (1977; Weidenfeld & Nicolson, 2002), 16.

[82] Francis Dashwood, West Wycombe brochure (1977), 1.

[83] 'The Duchess', in *The Stories of John Cheever* (Knopf, 1978), 347–58 at 347.

[84] V. S. Naipaul, *A Bend in the River* (Knopf, 1979), 123.

[85] Tindall, *Fields Beneath*, 129.

The need to confirm memory directs us to history; the desire to vitalize history returns it to memory; relics and re-enactments serve as aides-memoires. Monuments and statues mould collective memory, but changing needs and insights refashion the memories they evoke. Handed down from generation to generation, Incan quipus (knotted cords) preserved socially essential memories.[86] Knocking an English youngster's head against boundary markers ensures memory of their location.

Ritual replays of Exodus make Israelite escape from Egypt personal for each celebrant. In Passover and Seder ceremonies 'both the language and the gesture are geared to spur, not so much a leap of memory as a fusion of past and present', writes Yosef Hayim Yerushalmi. 'Memory here is no longer recollection, which still preserves a sense of distance, but reactualization', as intoned in the dirge:

> A fire kindles within me as I recall – *when I left Egypt*
> But I raise laments as I remember – *when I left Jerusalem.*

'In each and every generation let each person regard himself as though *he* had emerged from Egypt' is the Talmudic dictum. But such calls to 'remember events as if they happened to us' risk confusing the shared moment with a shared memory, mistaking 'a common memorial experience for a common Holocaust experience'. Adopting Israel's national past 'as if it were one's own past' ossifies memory like a material monument.[87]

Potent past legacies are not passively learned but actively felt. 'The force of 4,000 years of history is great if it is alive in our hearts, but if it is merely written in books, then it has no value', said Israel's education minister in 1954. 'If we want to be heirs of the people of Israel, then we must instill those 4,000 years into the heart of every person' by ritual re-performance. Washington's Holocaust Museum heightens empathy by making the horrific legacy intensely personal: each visitor wears the identity tag of a specific victim, a ghostly companion whose persona the visitor adopts and whose fate is disclosed, with haunting impact, at the tour's end.[88]

Some need no rituals to reactivate their history; retrospection is ingrained, habitual. Unassuaged injuries and injustices impel the conflation of remote with recent times, even with the present. For many Irish the Viking invasions, the devastations of Archbishop Laud, the 1840s Famine, the 1916 Easter Rising remain ever near. Irish conflated memory has been likened to historical paintings in which Virgil and Dante converse side by side. The Irish do not 'live in the past', concludes an anthropologist; 'rather, Ireland's history "lives in the present". All previous traitors and all previous heroes remain alive', as in the 'bottomless memory' of a Sean O'Faolain character with

[86] Gary Urton, *Signs of the Inka Khipu* (Texas, 2003); Frank Salomon, *The Cord Keepers: Khipus and Cultural Life in a Peruvian Village* (Duke, 2004).

[87] Yosef Hayim Yerushalmi, *Zakhor* (1982; Washington, 1996), 43–5; James E. Young, 'When a day remembers: performative history of *Yom ha-Shoah*', *History & Memory* 2:2 (1990): 54–75 at 71–2.

[88] Ben Zion Dinur quoted in David N. Myers and Amos Funkenstein, 'Remembering *Zakhor*', *History & Memory* 4:2 (1992): 129–48 at 139–40; Edward T. Linenthal, *Preserving Memory: The Struggle to Create America's Holocaust Museum* (Columbia, 2001).

whom 'one might see, though entangled beyond all hope of unravelling', the entire saga of Irish desolation.[89]

Lineages are telescoped, generations conflated to make the past present. 'Yes, 1852, that was the year ... I fought King Ta'ufa'āhau', asserts a Tongan; but the fighter was his great-great-great-grandfather.[90] West Indians speak of eighteenth-century progenitors as if they were still living or had only recently died; they are 'remembered' in as intimate detail as parents.[91] At dinner parties in Toulouse 'you may hear families solemnly comparing the role of their ancestors in the mediaeval woad trade or the revolt against Richelieu', reported a chronicler of European cities.

'Did your family fight in the First or the Second?' I heard one scion ask another. He was not referring to World Wars, but to the Crusades. Another Toulousain said to me, 'We are all deeply marked here by the Roman Conquest, ...' and then added, 'We're marked by the Nazi Occupation too' – as if the two events were roughly contemporary.[92]

'Our family used to live in Spain before they moved to Turkey', a Ladino-speaking Jew in Sofia told a reporter. 'I asked how long it had been since their family lived there. He said, it was approximately five hundred years, but spoke of those events as though they had occurred a couple of years ago.'[93]

Rekindling sensation can vividly reactivate memory. The sound of a spoon against a glass, the feel of a damask napkin, the uneven paving stones trod in the Guermantes' courtyard, above all aunt Leonie's unforgettable *madeleine* triggered Proust's recapture of the past.

As soon as I had recognised the taste of the piece of madeleine soaked in her decoction of lime-blossom ... immediately the old grey house upon the street, where her room was, rose up like a stage set ... and the whole of Combray and of its surroundings, taking shape and solidity, sprang into being.[94]

Regaining the past through sights, sounds, and smells was a stock Victorian theme. Renewing old sensations recalled the original occasions and their attendant feelings. The scent of violets brought back Tennyson's 'times when I remember to have been / Joyful and free from blame'. A geranium leaf for David Copperfield re-evoked Dora's straw hat, blue ribbons, and curls. For Hardy's reminiscent lover cold water on his bared arm 'Fetched back from its thickening shroud / ... a sense of that time / And the glass we used, and the cascade's rhyme'.[95]

---

[89] Edwin Ardener, 'The cosmological Irishman', *New Society*, 14 Aug. 1975: 362; Sean O'Faolain, *A Nest of Simple Folk* (London, 1933), 39. See Edwin Ardener, *The Voice of Prophecy and Other Essays* (1989 Berghahn, 2007), 135, 234; James M. Cahalan, *Great Hatred, Little Room: The Irish Historical Novel* (Syracuse, 1983), 37, 120; Nuala Johnson, *Ireland, the Great War and the Geography of Remembrance* (Cambridge, 2003).

[90] Marshall Sahlins, *Islands of History* (Chicago, 1985), 47.

[91] David Lowenthal, *West Indian Societies* (Oxford, 1972), 106.

[92] John Ardagh, *A Tale of Five Cities* (Secker & Warburg , 1979), 290.

[93] Claud Cockburn, *Crossing the Line* (MacGibbon & Kee, 1958), 155.

[94] Proust, *Remembrance of Things Past*, 1: 51.

[95] Alfred, Lord Tennyson, 'A dream of fair women' (1832), ll. 79–80, in *Poems* (Longmans, Green, 1969), 440–53 at 445; Charles Dickens, *David Copperfield* (1850; Oxford, 1948), 396; Thomas Hardy, 'Under the waterfall' (1911–12), in *Collected Poems*, 315–16. See Linda M. Austin, *Nostalgia in Transition* (Virginia, 2007), 64–80, 156–96.

Piling history on memory redoubles the past's impact. The medieval personae in William Morris's early poems dream of earlier experiences and look back on what is to *them* the past. The tales in his *Earthly Paradise* are ancient even to their narrators; Guinevere relates her 'Defence' as a recollection; dreams within dreams detach more from less remote pasts.[96] Tennyson's Guinevere 'Went slipping back upon the golden days . . . / moving through the past unconsciously', but Tennyson then imbues her memory with historical consciousness.[97] Friends and lovers revitalize ancient themes in Pre-Raphaelite paintings, deliberate modernisms of dress and gesture highlighting archaistic memory.[98]

Artefacts as metaphors in history and memory

Memory, history, and relics often serve as mutual metaphors. For Plato and Aristotle, sensory images impressed the mind like a signet ring on wax.[99] The writer puzzling out the jigsaw of the past is 'the archaeologist of memory'; recollections are 'artefacts'. For a philosopher 'memory is a repository or reservoir . . . of past events analogous to the records preserved in geological strata'; for a memoirist 'dread and anticipation first soften the tablets of memory, so that the impressions which they bring are clearly and deeply cut, and when time cools them off the impressions are fixed like the grooves of a gramophone record'.[100] The retrieval of memories like goods from storage is a hoary trope.[101] For others the seat of memory became a camera, a recording tape, a compact disc, a website. Among the temporal lobe's nerve cells, in Wilder Penfield's classic phrase sixty years ago, 'runs the thread of time . . . that has run through each succeeding wakeful hour' of our entire past. When 'the neurosurgeon's electrode activates . . . that thread' it responds like 'a wire recorder, or a strip of cinematographic film, on which are registered all those things of which the individual was once aware'.[102]

Archaeological analogies obsessed observers from Petrarch to Freud. Metaphors of unearthing and resuscitating pervaded humanist thought (Chapter 4). Retrieval of antiquity meant resurrecting buried artefacts and texts; excavating relics was likened to

[96] R. C. Ellison, '"The undying glory of dreams": William Morris and the "Northland of old"', in Malcolm Bradbury and David Palmer, eds., *Victorian Poetry* (Edward Arnold, 1972), 139–75 at 148–50.

[97] Alfred, Lord Tennyson, 'Guinevere' (1859), ll. 376–7, in *Poems*, 1724–42 at 1734–5.

[98] Margaret Gent, 'The appeal of the past to the Victorian imagination', 11–35; and Jerome H. Buckley, 'The Pre-Raphaelite past and present', 123–37, in Bradbury and Palmer, eds., *Victorian Poetry*.

[99] John C. Marshall and David M. Fryer, 'Speak, memory!', in Michael M. Gruneberg and Peter Morris, eds., *Aspects of Memory* (Methuen, 1978), 1–25; *Aristotle on Memory and Recollection*, ed. David Bloch (Brill, 2007); Jocelyn Penny Small, *Wax Tablets of the Mind* (Routledge, 1997); Mary Jean Carruthers, *The Book of Memory* (1990; Cambridge, 2008), 18–21; M. J. Carruthers, 'How to make a composition: memory-craft in Antiquity and the Middle Ages', in Susannah Radstone, ed., *Memory: Histories, Theories, Controversies* (Fordham, 2010), 15–29.

[100] Hans Meyerhoff, *Time in Literature* (California, 1955), 20; Oliver Lyttelton, *From Peace to War* (London, 1968), 152.

[101] Aleida Assmann, *Cultural Memory and Western Civilization* (Cambridge, 2011), 137–41, 146–50.

[102] Wilder Penfield, 'Permanent record of the stream of consciousness', *Acta Psychologica* 11 (1955): 47–69 at 68. See Svein Magnussen et al., 'What do people believe about memory?', in Svein Magnussen and Tore Helstrup, eds., *Everyday Memory* (New York: Psychology Press, 2007), 5–26 at 9–15.

restoring classical learning. Deciphering history hidden under visual or verbal surfaces, sub-reading the vestigial forms beneath, 'the reader divines a buried stratum as a visitor to Rome divines the subterranean foundations of a temple'.[103] For humanists this was no mere analogy but actual identity. The world itself was a tissue of words and signs, the Ancients' discourse a faithful mirror of what they described. Visible marks and legible words called for similar interpretation, for what was seen and what was read yielded knowledge of the same order.[104]

Four centuries later Renaissance metaphors became psychoanalytic insights. Like humanists, psychiatrists reconstructed the past from submerged artefacts – patients' repressed memories – 'which had somehow preserved their form and even their life despite their seemingly final disappearance'.[105] Freud repeatedly equated psychoanalysis with excavation. Likening himself to an archaeologist who made dumb stones speak and reveal their forgotten past, he 'unearthed' unconscious memory traces of infantile sexual traumas. Although later recasting them as memories of fantasized rather than actual seductions, Freud retained the archaeological metaphor.[106] 'This fragment might possibly belong to the period about which we are curious but it is . . . not complete' was classic Freudian rhetoric; 'We have to go on digging . . . until we find something more representative.'[107] In restoring what was missing Freud 'follow[ed] the example of those discoverers who . . . bring to the light of day after their long burial the priceless though mutilated relics of antiquity'.[108] An avid collector who kept his trophies in constant view, Freud exulted of one analytic find, 'It is as if Schliemann had dug up another Troy which had hitherto been believed to be mythical.'[109]

Archaeological parlance not only unearthed but also reanimated memory traces. Burying ancient artefacts often preserved them; Pompeii's relics began to decay only after they were exhumed: 'their burial had been their preservation; the destruction of Pompeii was only beginning now that it had been dug up'. Conscious memory similarly wore away, leaving only what was buried and unconscious unchanged. Hence memory fragments were 'often most powerful and most enduring' when unconsciously held. Repressed pathological memories persist 'in such freshness and affective strength because they have been denied the normal wearing-away processes'.[110] (The difference was that

---

[103] Thomas M. Greene, *The Light in Troy* (Yale, 1982), 99.

[104] Michel Foucault, *The Order of Things: An Archaeology of the Human Sciences* (1966; Pantheon, 1970), 33–4, 38–40, 56.

[105] Ernest Jones, *Life and Work of Sigmund Freud* (Basic Books, 1953–7), 3: 318.

[106] Sigmund Freud, 'The aetiology of hysteria' (1896), in *CPW*, 3: 191–222 at 192; J. E. Toews, 'Historicizing psychoanalysis', *Journal of Modern History* 63 (1991): 405–45.

[107] Quoted in Suzanne Cassirer Bernfeld, 'Freud and archeology', *American Imago* 8 (1951): 107–28 at 111. See Peter Gay, 'Introduction: Freud for the marble tablet', in *Berggasse 19* (Basic Books, 1976), 13–54.

[108] Sigmund Freud, 'Fragment of an analysis of a case of hysteria' (1905), in *CPW*, 7: 1–122 at 12.

[109] 21 Dec. 1899, in *The Origins of Psycho-Analysis: Letters to Wilhelm Fliess* (London: Imago, 1954), 305. Freud authenticated his antiquities and discarded any forgeries (Lynn Gamwell, 'The origins of Freud's antiquities collection', in Gamwell and Wells, eds., *Sigmund Freud and Art* (SUNY Press, 1989), 21–32 at 30). But his faith in Heinrich Schliemann, 'whose own autobiography was as fictional as any novel', was as errant as his faith in Sir Arthur Evans (Mary Beard, 'Tablet truths', *TLS*, 12 June 2006: 22).

[110] Sigmund Freud, *Beyond the Pleasure Principle* (1920), in *CPW*, 18: 1–64 at 25, and 'On the psychical mechanism of hysterical phenomena' (1893), in *CPW*, 2: 3–17 at 11.

'every effort was made to preserve Pompeii', whereas Freud's patients were desperate 'to be rid of tormenting ideas'.[111]) And psychoanalysis 'works under more favourable conditions than' archaeology, much of whose crucial evidence has been destroyed; whereas for the Freudian analyst 'all of the essentials are preserved; even things that seem completely forgotten are present somehow and somewhere'.[112]

Made tangible by metaphor, memory became overly determined. Like many scholars of his day, Freud viewed memories both as persisting things – 'engrams' – and as inherited insights verified by history and archaeology. Thus he trusted Arthur Evans's fabulous restorations of 'Minoan' Crete as unimpeachable proof of mother-fixated Bronze Age Mediterranean culture.[113] But while the archaeologist retrieved long-persisting material artefacts, Freudian recovery relied on verbal recall continually deformed by analytic interaction. Patients' utterances were not just memories but new creations, the analyst not just exhuming a past but also refashioning it. The archaeologist ideally sought only to reconstruct; the psychoanalyst aimed to construct anew.

'Like a conscientious archaeologist', Freud claimed, 'I have not omitted to mention ... where the authentic parts end and my constructions begin.' But this implied retrospective omniscience, as though Freud had been privy to, if not an actual eyewitness of, his patients' original experiences. Terms like 'uncovering', 'fragment', and 'reconstruction' presuppose access to the 'true' past, which Freud could not have had. Return to the 'true' past is, to be sure, hardly more possible for archaeologists than for psychoanalysts. But errors and fabrications are easier to detect and correct in dealing with relics of prehistory than of memory.[114]

A childhood memory restored by revivifying Pompeii is the theme of Wilhelm Jensen's novel Gradiva, famously analysed by Freud. For Jensen's protagonist, a reclusive young archaeologist, old 'marble and bronze were not dead, but rather the only really vital thing'. He shuns living women but is entranced by the classical bas-relief of a girl from buried Pompeii. Envisaging his 'Gradiva' striding along the ancient streets, her 'environment rose before his imagination like an actuality. It created for him, with the aid of his knowledge of antiquity, the vista of a long street, ... lively colors, gaily painted wall surfaces, pillars with red and white capitals.'[115]

[111] Sigmund Freud, 'Notes upon a case of obsessional neurosis' (1909), in *CPW* 10: 153–318 at 177.
[112] Sigmund Freud, 'Constructions in analysis' (1937), in *CPW*, 23: 255–70 at 259–60. Unlike the analyst, the archaeologist could not check his constructs with some surviving Trojan or Babylonian (Bertram D. Lewin, *Selected Writings* (New York: Psychoanalytic Quarterly, 1973), 291–2). See Donald Kuspit, 'A mighty metaphor', in Gamwell and Wells, eds., *Sigmund Freud and Art*, 133–51 at 138.
[113] Cathy Gere, 'Cretan psychoanalysis and Freudian archaeology', in Yannis Hamilakis and Nicoletta Momigliano, eds., *Archaeology and European Modernity*, Creta Antica 7 (Padua: Bottego d'Erasmo, 2006), 209–18 at 216–17; E. H. Gombrich, *Abby Warburg* (1970; 2nd edn Phaidon, 1986), 239–59.
[114] Freud, 'Fragment of an analysis of a case of hysteria'. See Donald P. Spence, *Narrative Truth and Historical Truth* (Norton, 1982), 160–1, 165, 176, 267; Kuspit, 'Mighty metaphor', in Gamwell and Wells, eds., *Sigmund Freud and Art*, 139, 146–7.
[115] Wilhelm Jensen, *Gradiva: A Pompeiian Fancy* (1903), in Sigmund Freud, *Delusion and Dream in Jensen's Gradiva* (1906; Boston: Beacon, 1956), 145–235 at 159, 150. The tale was a stock Romantic theme. Théophile Gautier's Faustian 'Arria Marcella: souvenir de Pompeii' (1852), in *Contes fantastiques* (Paris, 1962), 213–51, revives the age of Titus among Pompeii's ruins, his hero seducing a maiden of the period (William Moy S. Russell, 'Time in folklore and science fiction', *Foundation: The Review of Science Fiction,*

Driven to wander among Pompeii's ruins, he realizes that his science had 'merely gnawed at the dry rind of the fruit of knowledge' and taught 'a lifeless, archaeological view'. As he mused 'among the remains of the past ... the sun dissolved the tomb-like rigidity of the old stones, a glowing thrill passed through them, the dead awoke, and Pompeii began to live again'. His beloved Gradiva reappears in the guise of a forgotten childhood friend. 'Can't you remember?' she tries to reawaken his memory. 'It seems to me as if we had eaten our bread together like this once, two thousand years ago ... To think that a person must first die to become alive; but for archaeologists that is necessary, I suppose.'[116] The archaeologist's repressed childhood is excavated from the Vesuvian ashes. Freud lauded this retrieval for neutralizing a regressive traumatic memory. Just as digging up Pompeii had triggered no further eruption of Vesuvius, so would remembering his oppressive past now cease to overwhelm and undermine the analysand.[117]

Freud later saw in the Vatican Museum the Greek prototype of the *Gradiva* relief that had inspired Jensen's story, and hung a plaster cast of it in his consulting room to symbolize the interplay of memory and artefact. As tokens of veneration to their mentor, Freudian analysts commonly hung photos of *Gradiva* in their own offices (Fig. 40).[118] Thus an ancient work of art, reflected as memory and history in Jensen's novel, became for Freud an archaeological emblem of repression and rediscovery, and at length a memorial icon for his followers.[119]

Changing routes to the past

Impressions along all three routes to the past change as we and the world age. Most artefacts that environ and engage the young, like the history they learn, were there before them, with meanings and uses set by others. Growing older, we outdate more of our surroundings; our own past becomes history, of which our lengthened memories encompass more and more, including, by proxy, what ante-dates our own existence.

Modern longevity lengthens remembered pasts and promotes their convergence with history: the very elderly look back over longer stretches of time than ever before. Two

no. 43 (Summer 1988): 5–24 at 17). See Théophile Gautier, 'Pied de momie' (1840), in *Contes fantastiques*, 147–63; Brigitte Gautier, 'Magie de l'art (Gautier, Jensen, Freud)', *Gradiva* 11:1 (2008): 83–94; Sasha Colby, *Stratified Modernism* (Peter Lang, 2009), 9–25 (Gautier), 87–113 (Freud).

[116] Jensen, *Gradiva*, 179, 216, 230.

[117] John Forrester, *Dispatches from the Freud Wars* (Harvard, 1997), 130–1.

[118] Freud, *Delusion and Dream*, Appendix to the 2nd edn, 121; Jones, *Life and Work of Sigmund Freud*, 2: 342; *Berggasse 19*, 58–9, plate 12. While I viewed the *Gradiva* in Freud's London consulting room in 1983, Anna Freud told me about its iconic psychoanalytic role.

[119] Jacques Derrida reiterates my summation in his *Archive Fever* (Chicago, 1996), 85–91. See Richard H. Armstrong, *A Compulsion for Antiquity* (Cornell, 2006), 12, 18–25; Eric Downing, *After Images* (Wayne State, 2006), 87–168, 272–3; Mary Bergstein, 'Delusions and dreams: Freud's "Gradiva" and the photography of ancient sculpture', in *Mirrors of Memory* (Cornell, 2010), 115–204.

Figure 40 Freud's *Gradiva*: archaeology, psychoanalysis, commemoration

centuries ago, when the median Western age was 18 and adult lifespans below 60, few could remember much of the past or had time to spare for it. With a median age nearing 40 and lifespans approaching 80, we now recall a period twice as long and, being older, are more disposed to do so. And more of what we remember also becomes the subject of historical inquiry. At the same time, memory itself becomes a leading topic of historical discourse, alike of personal recall, as in Holocaust testimonies, and of collective memory, from the pioneering work of Maurice Halbwachs to the flood of group-oriented syntheses in the wake of Pierre Nora and his collaborators.[120]

As time distances events beyond personal recall, memory gives way to history, and artefacts gain collective commemorative import. Once events fade past eyewitness recall, their relics look different. When the Founding Fathers were no more, half a century after the Revolution, Americans began to memorialize their nation's birth and to cherish traces and sites of an epoch slipping beyond personal remembrance.[121] As surviving witnesses die off, similar memorial re-emphases feature the Second World War and the Holocaust.

Memory long remained the main highway to the past. Mnemonic devices facilitated the recall of data; 'memory theatres' held keys to tens of thousands of recollectable buildings, landscapes, artefacts, and events. Textual copying and printing facilitated information storage and retrieval, shifting the balance from ephemeral memory towards stable written records.[122] 'If I distrust my memory ... I am able to supplement and guarantee its workings by making a note in writing', as Freud put it; 'I have only to bear in mind the place where this "memory" has been deposited and I can then "reproduce" it any time I like, with the certainty that it will have remained unaltered.'[123]

Writing was anciently feared as a threat to memory. 'This invention will produce forgetfulness in the minds of those who learn to use it', argued Plato, 'Their trust in writing ... will discourage the use of their own memory.'[124] The proliferation of written matter redoubled similar fears. A pioneer printer warned that 'abundance of books makes men less studious', destroying memory and enfeebling the mind.[125] Emerson decried the newspaper as a 'sponge of oblivion'.[126] Internet search engines outsource memory to data banks, obviating need for personal effort.[127]

Freud's recipe for recall makes it clear why history dethroned memory: the brain ceaselessly edits and transforms personal memory, whereas historical records generally stay put. Land-survey techniques exemplify the shift from recalling relics to relying on records. Traditionally, natural features and artefacts – trees, rocks, mountains, rivers, meadows, woodlands, grave sites, buildings – demarcated properties. King Edmund's charter granting Bishop Ælfric land in Northamptonshire in 944 typified the earthy specificity of old-time boundaries: 'Up to the great tumulus beneath the wild garlic wood, then ... along the stone way to the tall crucifix at Hawk Thorn, ... to the third thorn tree

[120] Maurice Halbwachs, *On Collective Memory* (1925; Harper & Row, 1980); Pierre Nora, *Lieux de mémoire* (Gallimard, 1984–92); Kerwin Lee Klein, 'On the emergence of memory in historical discourse', *Representations* 69 (2000): 127–50; Susannah Radstone and Bill Schwarz, eds., *Memory* (Fordham, 2010).

[121] Michael Kammen, *A Season of Youth: The American Revolution and the Historical Imagination* (Knopf, 1973), 21, 163.

[122] Frances A. Yates, *The Art of Memory* (1969; Routledge, 2010); Joshua Foer, *Moonwalking with Einstein: The Art and Science of Remembering Everything* (Penguin, 2011).

[123] Sigmund Freud, 'A note upon the "mystic writing-pad"' (c. 1924), in *CPW*, 19: 227–32 at 227.

[124] Plato, *Phaedrus* (360 BC), in *Works* (Harvard, 1914), 1: 405–579 at 563.

[125] Hieronimo Squarciafico (1477) quoted in Walter J. Ong, *Orality and Literacy* (1982; rev edn Routledge, 2002), 80.

[126] Ralph Waldo Emerson, 'Memory' (1858), in *CW* (1903), 12: 71.

[127] Manfred Osten, *Das Geraubte Gedächtnis* (Frankfurt am Main: Insel, 2004); Nicholas Carr, *The Shallows* (Norton, 2010), 198; Betsy Sparrow et al., Google effects on memory: 'Cognitive consequences of having information at our fingertips', *Science* 333 (5 Aug. 2011), : 776–8. See my 'Archival perils', *Archives* 31 (2006): 49–75.

at bog-myrtle hangar . . . up to the Hill of Trouble, then west to rough lynchet . . . to the heathen burial places'.[128] Regularly perambulating the bounds, landowners and local officials committed such landmarks to memory, and protected them as evidence of possession. Printing, aerial photography, and mathematical cartography have changed all this: boundaries are now traced on an abstract grid and mechanically reproduced, obviating the need either to recall or to retain physical markers.[129] Remote satellites render obsolete the injunction 'Remove not the ancient landmark, which thy fathers have set' (Proverbs 22.28); GIS technology maps all the world's features with spatial precision but is devoid of historical or memorial context.

Pictures along with print augment knowledge of the past and diminish demands on memory. As images of relics become ever cheaper and more precise, relics yield to print in preserving and conveying information; portrayals that once supplemented now displace written words. The very notion of 'seeing' the past gained currency with the flood of book illustrations that began, around 1800, to accustom readers to visually experience the past.[130] Photography made seemingly trustworthy images ubiquitous. Photos became instant antiques, adjuncts to the generalized pathos of looking back. Acquiring a daguerreotype was 'very nearly the same thing as carrying off the palace itself', gloated Ruskin in Venice; 'every chip of stone & stain is here – and, of course, there is no mistake about *proportions*'. Unlike recollections and reports of the past, what the camera captured was exactly replicable – hence the mantra of the documentary film. As noted above photographs gained repute as the *ne plus ultra* of faithful representation.[131] Because 'indifferent to all intermediaries', as Roland Barthes put it, the photo 'does not invent; it is authentication itself . . . an emanation of *past reality*' that made historical truth indubitable. 'Henceforth the past is as certain as the present, what we see on paper is as certain as what we touch'.[132]

From the start, photographers fancied themselves historians recording a vanishing world, and were indeed employed to do just that: Viollet-le-Duc commissioned daguerreotypes of Notre-Dame de Paris before beginning its restoration in 1842.[133] The Depression-era photographer Walker Evans portrayed humdrum domestic artefacts as evocative prospective relics.[134] Family snapshots both goad and amend memory, aligning recall with the depicted past. Viewing them we see that our first home was smaller than

[128] In Margaret Drabble, ed., *A Writer's Britain* (Thames & Hudson, 1979), 17.

[129] John R. Stilgoe, 'Jack-o'-lanterns to surveyors: the secularization of landscape boundaries', *Environmental Review* 1 (1976): 14–31; Tom Greeves, *The Parish Boundary* (Common Ground, 1987).

[130] T. S. R. Boase, 'Macklin and Bowyer', *Journal of the Warburg & Courtauld Institutes* 26 (1963): 148–77 at 170–4; Roy Strong, *And When Did You Last See Your Father? The Victorian Painter and British History* (Thames & Hudson, 1978), 20; Michael Freeman, *Victorians and the Prehistoric* (Yale, 2004), 157–60.

[131] John Ruskin to his father, 7 Oct. 1845, in *Ruskin in Italy: Letters to His Parents*, ed. Harold I. Shapiro (Clarendon Press, 1972), 220. See Stephen Kern, *The Culture of Time and Space 1880–1918* (1983; Harvard, 2003), 38–9.

[132] Roland Barthes, *Camera Lucida* (1980; Hill & Wang, 1982), 87–8.

[133] Eugène Emanuel Viollet-le-Duc, 'Restoration' (1869), cited in Anthony Hamber, 'The use of photography by nineteenth-century art historians', in Helene E. Roberts, ed., *Art History through the Camera's Lens* (Amsterdam, 1995), 89–122 at 96. See Susan Sontag, *On Photography* (Penguin, 1979), 70–80.

[134] James Agee and Walker Evans, *Let Us Now Praise Famous Men* (1936; Houghton Mifflin, 1960); Diana Rathbone, *Walker Evans* (Houghton Mifflin, 1995), 76–89, 226–50, 278, 306.

remembered, our mother younger, our uncle less glamorous. Children poring over the family album join their own pasts with forebears and general bygone times. But as most photos are staged and all are selected, the family album also deceives later viewers with nostalgic fictions of familial fondness and devoted domesticity, 'the Gospel According to Aunt Lizzie' noted in Chapter 7.[135] And at length the picture turns into the memory. 'When you gaze at the same snapshots over and over again . . . the images become part of the recollection itself until the two are interchangeable', notes a novelist. 'Do I really remember standing in front of Big Ben as a child, or do I just remember the photo of me doing so?'[136]

While reducing reliance on written history, audio-visual devices promote other consciousness of the past: television, museum displays, and historic sites substitute visual for verbal images. The British Tourist Authority's 1998 'Movie Map' of Britain lured millions to country-house settings of famed films. Multitudes visit Stoke Poges and Selborne who never read Gray's *Elegy* or Gilbert White's *Natural History*; millions watched TV's *Barchester Chronicles* and *Forsyte Saga* who never turned a page of Trollope or Galsworthy. Film and TV versions of C. S. Forester's Captain Hornblower stories 'dictated the way Napoleonic history is imagined'.[137] 'The time will come', predicted D. W. Griffith a century ago, 'when children in the public schools will be taught practically everything by moving pictures. Certainly they will never be obliged to read history again.'[138] That time is nigh.

Films make history intense and plausible, figures moving and speaking in past-redolent locales more alive than ever. 'Thanks to the cinema, the twentieth century and its inhabitants stand in a different relation to time from any previous age', notes a critic. 'We can conjure up the past, moving [and] talking just like life.'[139] Sights and sounds stored on film and tape increasingly access bygone events, and every passing year lengthens their reach back. They enormously amplify personal memory. A few hundred people may today know your face at 40, but only a few score of these knew it when you were 20, a mere handful when you were 6; by extending access to how we and things around us used to look, snapshots multiply connections with our former selves.[140] So, increasingly, do Internet blogs, MySpace (2003), Facebook (2004), Twitter (2006), and the like.

Today's sensory turn promotes populist takes freed 'from the prison' of elitist history, holds a Swedish ethnologist, to provide 'not so much a testimony about as an entrance to' bygone times. What people glean from viewing and hearing and handling, rather than

---

[135] Marianne Hirsch, ed., *The Familial Gaze* (New England, 1999), xi–xxv. See Marianne Hirsch, *Family Frames* (Harvard, 1997); Martha Langford, *Suspended Conversations: The Afterlife of Memory in Photographic Albums* (McGill-Queen's, 2001).

[136] Lucinda Roseneld, 'Many more images, much less meaning', *IHT* 4 Dec. 2012: 8.

[137] Andrew Higson, *English Heritage, English Cinema* (Oxford, 2003), 58–61; Jerome de Groot, *The Historical Novel* (Routledge, 2009), 81.

[138] D. W. Griffith, 'Five dollar "movies" prophesied' (1915), quoted in Robert Lang, *Birth of a Nation* (Rutgers, 1994), 4.

[139] David Robinson, 'The film immutable against life's changes', *Times*, 7 Dec. 1983: 11.

[140] Michael Lesy, *Time Frames: The Meaning of Family Pictures* (Pantheon, 1980) xiii, 103.

reading, widens the academic–popular gap. History seen rather than read does not have to be translated into the mind's eye or thought about in the context of previous learning; it is immediately accessible to anyone, however unschooled and unskilled. Yet visual and tactile sources tend by their very nature to compromise the past. Their simplified impressions ignore motivation, deny complexity, and banish subtlety. Texts remain the essential comprehensive mode of historical communication. Writers and readers gain imaginative insight into the past through durable linguistic communion.[141]

Such concerns are not new. A similar shift from print to visual delineation was deplored at the *fin de siècle*, when professional historians devoted to scientific objectivity lamented the proliferation of illustrations in journalistic histories. Pictorial matter had been a welcome aid to memory when history mainly told romantic and patriotic stories. But now it bred 'literary degeneration' that undermined scholarly truth. To safeguard the sanctity of the written word and the 'empire of the pen', historians assailed spurious and mendacious depictions of past scenes. When photography, initially exempt from censure owing to its supposed impersonal fidelity, proved supremely prone to falsification – 'every photograph is a fake from start to finish', declared Edward Steichen – the American Historical Association sought to ban all illustrations. Lauded by the man in the street for democratizing history, the camera was condemned by historians for the same reason. Faith in the photographic image encouraged Kodak-toting hordes to imagine they could be historians too, scoffed Albert Bushnell Hart, Harvard's grand old man of American history. Amateur hubris threatened the authority of scholars and trivialized the past.[142]

The Dutch art historian Johan Huizinga lent gravitas to the critique. A pioneer of visual history, he came to fear its popularization. Huizinga's famed *Waning of the Middle Ages* (1919) assailed the resulting perversion of history. 'Most people of today owe their conception of Egypt, Greece or the Middle Ages much more to seeing works of art than to reading.' But the ready availability of pictures seduced viewers to substitute 'artistic for intellectual appreciation'. For most of the past visual evidence was far less complete than literary. Moreover, works of art tended to depict a falsely happy and serene past, whereas 'poets and historians, voicing the endless griefs of life, ... revive the harsh realities of bygone misery'. Thus those who took their history from paintings misgauged the whole tenor of life in past times. Time strengthened Huizinga's animus. 'As more and more visual material for the appreciation of the past became quite generally available, so thinking and writing about the past fell into increasing neglect', and public ignorance grew. Heightened aesthetic receptivity [posed] a great danger for serious historical research. It leads to reading things into history, creating false pictures'.[143]

---

[141] Jonas Frykman, 'Place for something else', *Ethnologia Europaea* 32:2 (2002): 50–1. See David J. Staley, *Computers, Visualization and History* (M. E. Sharpe, 2002), 4–6.

[142] Edward Steichen, 'Ye fakers', *Camera Work* 1 (Jan. 1903): 34; Albert Bushnell Hart (1904) cited in Gregory M. Pfitzer, *Picturing the Past* (Smithsonian, 2002), 179–241; Gregory M. Pfitzer, *Popular History and the Literary Marketplace* (Massachusetts, 2008), 218, 243–4, 287.

[143] Johan Huizinga, *The Waning of the Middle Ages* (1919; Dover, 1999), 222–3; Johan Huizinga, *Dutch Civilisation in the Seventeenth Century* (1941; New York: Ungar, 1958), 9, 241. See Francis Haskell, *History and Its Images* (Yale, 1995), 474, 489–93.

The last few decades' shift from verbal to visual, from print to screen, from reflecting on to 'experiencing' the past, intensifies the disparity that rouses such concerns. Observers note widespread worry that 'visual media ... have become not just a rival of academic history, but in terms of audience, its master [for] just about everybody except academic historians'. As more and more is imbibed from visual media, written history becomes an esoteric pursuit, historians the priests of an arcane outmoded literary cult.[144] Metal detection and museum blockbusters, battle re-enactments and TV's History Channel make the sensate past sensational. Pictorial and visceral participation are royal routes to the past. Children are taught and adults believe that history is what they see, often contrary to what they read about. Pasts felt and touched gain salience and credibility. 'Let your children *experience* history instead of just *reading* about it', declare historic-sites guides, museum brochures, and antiques sales catalogues. 'You will feel the immediacy of events in the pit of your stomach, rather than viewing them from a musty distance', the History Channel touts its French Revolution show.[145] And just as cinematic history became ever more credible than still photos and silent film, so the digital and 3D camcorder remakes yesteryear's Kodak-toter into Everyman's nonstop recorder of the seemingly total past. Yet every increase in data simultaneously distances the past, most digital images soon deleted or stored out of sight.

Self-conscious awareness further set the past apart. An 'anachronism' was initially an error that distorted or misdated things past. But by the nineteenth century the term came to denote *present* survivals or revivals, in the pejorative sense of being outmoded, outliving their time.[146] The better we know the past, the more we outgrow it. 'In earlier ages when there was not enough historical background to project the present against, the present appeared largely inevitable', wrote folklorist Walter Ong. 'Because we [now] have access to so much history ... the present can be examined for Renaissance, medieval, classical, pre-classical, Christian, Hebrew, and countless other elements ... Knowing other cultures' diverse histories informs but does not engage the present.'[147] Looking back with anachronistic misgivings, we shed old memories not merely unwittingly, as people have always done, but with abashed purpose; we recall the past all too well for present comfort. Even last year's or last month's viewpoints, like yesterday's fashions, can seem old hat.

As the past recedes from us, we re-evoke it by multiplying paraphernalia *about* it – souvenirs, mementoes, historical romances, old photos – and by preserving and rehabilitating its relics. These surrogates resemble late Victorian revivals and keepsakes, but while Victorians felt they captured the real past, we suffer postmodern dubiety. Conscious of contriving substitutes, we alter the inherited past even more radically than did our precursors who felt closer to it. These transformations of the past – the modes of effecting them, and the reasons they are made – are the subject of the next section.

[144] Robert A. Rosenstone, *History on Film / Film on History* (Pearson Educational, 2006; 2nd edn 2012), xii; Robert A. Rosenstone, 'History in images / history in words', *AHR* 93 (1988): 1173–85 at 1174.
[145] Hands-on-history homeschooling kits, *handsnhearts.com*; Viktor Wendel et al., 'Seamless learning in serious games', *Proceedings of the CSEDU* [Conference on Computer Supported Education] 1 (2011): 219–24 at 221; History Channel ad., *NYT*, 17 Jan. 2005.
[146] P. B. M. Blaas, *Continuity and Anachronism* (The Hague: Nijhoff, 1978), 29–30.
[147] Walter J. Ong, *Rhetoric, Romance, and Technology* (Cornell, 1971), 326.

PART IV

REMAKING THE PAST

Knowing the past profoundly affects its residues, physical and mental alike. Even safeguarding its integrity transforms historical memory. Historians are inherent revisionists, 'junkies for change', as Philippa Gregory puts it.[1] The ancient truism that not even God can change the past leads sceptics to suspect that She created historians to do it for Her.[2]

Every act of recognition alters what survives. Simply to appreciate a memory or to protect a relic, let alone to embellish or imitate it, skews its form and our impressions. Just as recall modifies memory and subjectivity slants history, handling relics refashions their appearance and meaning. Interaction with the past's residues ceaselessly alters their nature and context, unwittingly if not intentionally.

Such changes can be profoundly disturbing, for they undermine the probity of the past. To validate tradition, to confirm identity, and to make sense of the present requires a securely stable past. 'To tamper with the past', reflects an archaeologist, 'is to bring at times that slipping, sliding, tenuous horror which revolves around all that is done, unalterable, and yet . . . may draw disaster from the air, or make us lonely beyond belief'.[3] Can we trust a past in constant flux, alterable by accident or evolution or at will?

Many take refuge in denying that the past has been or can be fundamentally changed. Scriptural and constitutional literalists cling to these texts' eternal verity and condemn any deviation as heresy. Soviet Communist Party history kept changing every few years, material in textbooks recurrently blotted or excised, while leaders and teachers insisted nothing had altered. 'Participants knew that official history had changed, knew that others knew this, and knew that others knew that they knew this, and yet everyone pretended . . . that nothing of the sort had occurred.' Asked to swear that they had never swerved from the Party line on history, cynics would jest, 'I have deviated only in accordance with the Party.'[4] Bogus claims of consistency are common shields against criticism. When new whole-body imaging machines changed airport scanning in 2010,

---

[1] Philippa Gregory, 'Born a writer: forged as a historian', *History Workshop Journal* 59:1 (Spring 2005): 237–42 at 239.

[2] Samuel Butler, *Erewhon Revisited* (1901; Modern Library, 1927), 468. 'Even God can't change the past / No matter how many tears I've cried / Yes, I thought this dream would last / Yes, I thought this pain would pass' (Rick Nowels, George O'Dowd, and John Themis for Charlotte Church, *Tissues and Issues* (2005).

[3] Loren Eiseley, *All the Strange Hours: The Excavation of a Life* (1975; Nebraska, 2000), 97.

[4] James V. Wertsch, *Voices of Collective Remembering* (Cambridge, 2002), 76–7, 128. See Ronald Hingley, 'That's no lie, Comrade', *Problems of Communism* 11:2 (1962): 47–55; Yale Richmond, 'Vranyo, the Russian fib', in *From Nyet to Da: Understanding the Russians* (1992; London: Brealey, 2003), 127–31; Elena Gorkhova, *A Mountain of Crumbs* (Simon & Schuster, 2009), 51–5, 72.

screeners routinely denied anything was new: 'We have always done this', they insisted; 'The process has always been the same.'[5]

Others strive to retrieve unwanted revisions, like science-fiction time wardens restoring the past to its proper original state. Still others deplore previous alterations but endure them as irreversible, striving instead to steward precious surviving remains against corrosive neglect, perversion, and despoliation. Both aim to stabilize the past, not to change it.

By contrast, many welcome revisions for rectifying or improving past things and thoughts, purposely conforming the past to their own or others' designs. They find solace or take pleasure in altering memories and residues, erasing past errors and unhappy reminders, creating new remnants and recollections to celebrate or bemoan.

Neither stance entirely allays fears that the memorial, historical, and reliquary past is an insecure will-o'-the-wisp. That time continually corrupts its traces and dims our vision, outdating and draining its residues of context, is everywhere ruefully apparent. The passage of centuries thus effaced the original meaning of the medieval hand-linked couple in an ancient church, suggests Philip Larkin.

> Side by side, their faces blurred,
> The earl and countess lie in stone. . . .
> They would not think to lie so long.
> Such faithfulness in effigy
> Was just a detail friends would see:
> A sculptor's sweet commissioned grace
> Thrown off in helping to prolong
> The Latin names around the base. . . .
> Now, helpless in the hollow of
> An unarmorial age . . .
> Only an attitude remains:
> Time has transfigured them into
> Untruth . . .

Yet the hand-in-hand pose was not, in fact, medieval, but a Victorian restoration.[6]

The next three chapters discuss how we affect the residues of the past on the ground and in our minds. Chapter 10 sketches the impact of efforts to save or salvage the past: preserving and protecting its surviving features, and reproducing chosen elements. Chapter 11 discusses efforts to replace what has been lost by restoring artefacts and institutions no longer extant or complete, and by re-enacting past events and activities. Chapter 12 deals with changes deliberately intended to improve or otherwise alter the past, the motives that animate those changes, and their intended and unintended consequences.

---

[5] Joe Sharkey, 'Confusing new procedure is served up with a snarl', *IHT*, 3 Nov. 2010: 18.
[6] Philip Larkin, 'An Arundel tomb' (1956), in *The Whitsun Weddings* (Faber & Faber, 1964), 45–6.

10

Saving the past: preservation and replication

> In a world of concrete and computers, it is vital that we preserve what remains of individuality. If everything were modern, everywhere would look pretty much the same.　　　　　　　　　　　　　　　　　　　　　　Timothy Cantell, 1980[1]

> A civilization which tends to conserve is a civilization in decline.
> 　　　　　　　　　　　　　　　　　　　　　　　　　Pierre Boulez, 1975[2]

> Blessed were the ancients, for they had no antiquities.　　　　　Italian saying[3]

Efforts to save the past as it was, remaining true to its lineaments, take manifold forms. We safeguard material remnants and steward traditional skills and customs. We draw attention to the past with signposts and interpretive markers. We preserve and conserve. We replicate past forms and features in copies and reproductions. We bring back what has been lost, eroded, or corrupted in acts of restoration and resurrection. We seal the past in our hearts and minds by re-enacting and commemorating it.

These devotional endeavours aim to alter what remains as little as possible. The past is holy; changing it is impious, violating its integrity, improperly imposing present concerns. Actual practice mocks such piety: every mode of honouring the past to some extent transforms, even destroys. Yet the desire to keep sacrosanct and intact the pasts we have inherited, discovered, or contrived is potent and pervasive.

Preservation

The urge to preserve derives from several presumptions: that the past informs the present; that its relics are crucial to our identity; and that its cherished remains are fragile and dwindling assets, their loss sped by accelerating change that makes even the recent past irrecoverably remote.

Much preservation sentiment is quite recent. Until a few centuries ago most people lived under much the same circumstances as their forebears, were little aware of historical change, and scarcely differentiated past from present. 'Words and phrases by which we express our sense that the past was not the same, but something different from the present', wrote a scholar a century ago, 'are all of them modern, and most of them, indeed, of very recent introduction'.[4] Few sought to preserve, if only because the sense of the past

---

[1] Timothy Cantell, 'Why care about old buildings?' *Period Home*, 1:3 (1980), 5–8 at 7.
[2] Pierre Boulez, *Conversations with Célestin Deliège* (London: Eulenberg, 1976), 33.
[3] Attributed to Diderot (Stefano Casciani, 'Lo Sgarbi flirioso', *Domus*, No. 851 (Sept. 2002): 153).
[4] Logan Pearsall Smith, *The English Language* (London, 1912), 227.

as a time no longer existing had not yet emerged; to medieval folk the great Gothic architectural works 'did not represent a past state of things, but a present', observed the historian E. A. Freeman.[5] Goths and Vandals left the noble works of antiquity 'wretchedly wounded', while medieval Romans stripped antiquities of bricks and marble for their own walls and buildings.[6]

For all their devotion to the classical past, few Renaissance humanists thought to preserve its physical remnants. Antiquarians strove to safeguard classical manuscripts and inscriptions, but literary concern seldom extended to other remains; the rescue of saintly relics consoled historians for Rome's ruined classical buildings. The past's glories were preserved in lapidary language, not in sculpted stone. Achilles was still remembered through Homer, noted the poet du Bellay, whereas those commemorated only in colossi and pyramids had long been forgotten. Material traces were ephemeral or deeply buried; much was now lost or had crumbled to dust. Montaigne termed Rome's extant remains mere ruins of ruins, 'the least worthy [of] disfigured limbs'.[7]

It was not to salvage ancient fragments that antiquities were disinterred, as shown in Chapter 4, but to bring an exemplary past back to life. The past was not embalmed but refashioned anew. Antiquity's admirers mined ancient temples and sculptures for their own creations: extracting marble from a ruin cost less than quarrying it at Carrara. Rome's marble cutters and lime burners were licensed destroyers of ancient monuments, taxed as such by the Holy See.[8]

The past was creatively reconstructed. A passion for rebuilding Rome along classical lines, not unlike Mussolini's five centuries later, consumed most of what was left of the ancient city. Pope Nicholas V (1447–55) eliminated any vestiges of antiquity that stood in the way of a straightened road or a new church. Although Pius II in 1462 forbade anyone 'to demolish, destroy or reduce to rubble, to dismantle or convert into plaster . . . any ancient building', he himself had many monuments torn down to use their stones in new buildings.[9] Sixtus IV (1471–84) curtailed the export of ancient statues and founded the Vatican antiquities collection but demolished the Temple of Hercules and converted travertine from the Marmorata into cannonballs. Ancient buildings still in use – the Pantheon, Castel Sant' Angelo, the Capitol – might be repaired, but antiquities that lacked utility were neglected. After 1484 even the Arch of Titus (Fig. 71) and the Temple of Vesta were left to decay. The famed first century BC Meta Romuli pyramid made way in 1499 for the new Via Alessandrina; Leo X (1513–21) sacrificed antiquity to straighten the road to the Capitol. Distressed to see 'the corpse of this noble city . . . grievously torn and disfigured', Raphael in

---

[5] Edward A. Freeman, *The Preservation and Restoration of Ancient Monuments* (Oxford, 1852), 15.

[6] 'A report to Leo X', in Dale Kinney, 'Introduction', in Richard Brilliant and Dale Kinney, eds., *Reuse Value: Spolia and Appropriation in Art and Architecture* (Ashgate, 2011), 1–11 at 7. See Michael Greenhalgh, *Marble Past, Monumental Present* (Brill, 2009), 55, 140–67, 530.

[7] Flavio Biondo, *Roma instaurata* (1447), in Roberto Weiss, *The Renaissance Discovery of Classical Antiquity* (Blackwell, 1959), 65–70; Joachim du Bellay, *La Deffence et illustration de la langue francoyse* (1549; Geneva: Droz, 2001), bk. II, ch. 5, 138–44; Michel de Montaigne, *Travel Journal*, 26 Jan. 1581 (San Francisco: North Point, 1983), 79.

[8] Thomas M. Greene, *The Light in Troy* (Yale, 1982), 147–70, 235–6.

[9] Quoted in Wim Denslagen, *Memories of Architecture* (Antwerp: Spinhuis, 2009), 50–1.

1519 gained formal authority to halt destruction, but his powers were nugatory. And even Raphael sought to preserve antiquities less for themselves than for future inspiration, to 'keep alive the examples of the ancients so as to equal and surpass them'.[10]

Demolition continued to defy preservation edicts. Six years after establishing a board to steward ancient monuments, Clement VII in 1640 destroyed the Forum Romanum. In sum, ancient Rome succumbed less to ravages of war and weather than to contractors and stonemasons, papal greed and visionary urban dreams. 'Ironic as it may seem, the Renaissance brought more destruction on the Roman ruins than any other age: the new Rome of the Renaissance meant the annihilation of the old.'[11] The laments of a handful of humanists fell on deaf ears. Not until the eighteenth century did Rome conserve in earnest, even then animated 'not from taste, not from respect for antiquity, but only from avarice', charged a French visitor. Ancient monuments were prized mainly as tourist attractions; Romans 'looked after their ruins for the same reason that beggars look after their sores'.[12] Subsequently the Vatican licensed excavations to entrepreneurs who sold their finds to wealthy collectors.[13]

Concern to preserve artefacts, as distinct from reshaping or emulating them, followed Enlightenment consciousness that history was driven not by constants of human nature, but by manifold contingencies varying with place and period. As every people and each epoch came to seem unique, tangible monuments and physical relics became crucial to historical understanding and empathy. The new premium placed on original and authentic physical remains stimulated their conservation.

Nascent nationalism also promoted preservation: vernacular languages, folklore, material arts, and antiquities became foci of group consciousness in post-Napoleonic Europe's emergent – and perennially beleaguered – nation-states. Prominent relics lent continuity to tradition and became guarantors of national identity:

Nationalism required people to believe that every nation had existed for many centuries even when its existence was not socially and politically noticeable, [hence] the proof for its existence depended on the continuity of its linguistic and cultural coherence. Since not even that coherence was obvious to the naked eye, historians had . . . to demonstrate that the ruins and documents of the past . . . were part of the cultural heritage of each nation, monuments to the existence of cultural continuity.[14]

Cologne Cathedral, restored and completed in old Gothic style by Karl Friedrich Schinkel and his successors (1833–50), was touted as 'the greatest of Germany's bulwarks, which she will either guard or perish, and which will only fall when the blood of the last Teuton has mingled with the waves of Father Rhine'. The state of Hesse's pioneering

---

[10] Weiss, *Renaissance Discovery*, 98–101; Raphael and Baldassare Castiglione to Leo X, in Denslagen, *Memories of Architecture*, 53–6; Leonard Barkan, *Unearthing the Past* (Yale, 1999), 38–40.

[11] Weiss, *Renaissance Discovery*, 205.

[12] Charles-Marguerite Mercier Dupaty, *Lettres sur l'Italie, en 1785*, letter 62 (Paris, 1788), 291–2. See Richard Bosworth, *Whispering City: Rome and Its Histories* (Yale, 2011), 38–44.

[13] Ilaria Bignamini, ed., *Archives and Excavations: Essays on the History of Archaeological Excavations in Rome and Southern Italy from the Renaissance to the Nineteenth Century* (London: British School of Rome, 2004); Ilaria Bignamini and Clare Hornsby, *Digging and Dealing in Eighteenth-Century Rome* (Yale, 2010).

[14] Peter Munz, *The Shapes of Time* (Wesleyan, 1977), 154.

protective decree of 1818 declared that 'the surviving monuments of architecture' attested the nation's 'spiritual roots and public culture', making their preservation a 'patriotic duty'.[15] In France, Victor Hugo hallowed ancient chateaux and abbeys as national shrines and sources of poetic inspiration, and Charles de Montalembert implored the nation to safeguard memorable antiquities, for 'long memories make great peoples'.[16]

Threatened loss or removal fuelled the preservation of antiquities as national icons. The decay of Normandy's ancient abbeys and chateaux, damaged during the Revolution, vandalized and neglected thereafter, energized English antiquarians. 'It is the English alone who labour to preserve the memory of the structures of Normandy, which are doomed to destruction by the disgraceful sloth and ignorance of the French', concluded archivist–historian Francis Palgrave. 'Whilst the owners of these noble structures are dull to their beauties and incapable of appreciating their value, we have made them English property.' Appalled by the English ambassador Lord Stuart de Rothesay's pillage of the Manoir les Andelys and Jumièges Abbey, the archaeologist Arcisse de Caumont founded the Société des Antiquaires de Normandie in 1823, forerunner of François Guizot's French *Service des monuments historiques* .[17]

The Victoria and Albert Museum's 1869 purchase of the 1610–13 rood loft of St John Hertogenbosch (Fig. 41), after that Dutch cathedral had dismantled and sold it to a dealer, caused a scandal that activated Netherlands preservation. American purchasers' dismantling of Tattershall Castle's fifteenth-century fireplaces, threatening the castle's imminent demolition, led the Marquess of Curzon to buy and restore it. Curzon then championed Britain's Ancient Monuments Act of 1913, initiating national protection. Seventy-five years later, alarms re-echoed over similar threats posed by Getty billions. Discussing Yale's Mellon collection of British paintings, an English art historian remarked that 'our so-called heritage never means more to us than when we see it inherited by someone else'.[18] Or aggrieved when neglected by someone else, like 'Cleopatra's Needle', Thutmose III's severely weathered obelisk in Central Park since 1880, its hieroglyphic text worn

---

[15] Karl Friedrich Schinkel et al., *Kölner Dom und Deutschlands Einheit* (1842), quoted in W. D. Robson-Scott, *The Literary Background of the Gothic Revival in Germany* (Clarendon Press, 1965), 288; Ludwig X of Hesse, 22 Jan. 1818, in Miles Glendinning, *The Conservation Movement: A History of Architectural Preservation* (Routledge, 2013), 80. See Arnold Wolff, *Cologne Cathedral* (Cologne, 2003); John Edward Toews, *Becoming Historical: Cultural Reformation and Public Memory in Early Nineteenth-Century Berlin* (Cambridge, 2004), 41–2, 139, 198.

[16] Victor Hugo, 'Bande Noire' (1824), 2: 83–6, and 'Sur la destruction des monuments en France' (1825), 2: 569–74 in *Oeuvres complètes* (Paris, 1967–70); Charles de Montalembert, 'Du vandalisme en France', *Revue des Deux Mondes* 1 (1833): 477–524 at 482.

[17] Francis Palgrave, 'Normandy: architecture of the Middle Ages' (1821), in *Collected Historical Works* (Cambridge, 1922), 10: 363–402 at 402; John Harris, *Moving Rooms: The Trade in Architectural Salvages* (Yale, 2007), 60–3; [Guizot], 'Organisation de fonctionnaires chargés de veiller à la conservation des monuments nationaux', *Revue Normande* 1 (1831): 275–83; Bertrand Monnet, 'The care of ancient monuments in France', *Architectural Association Quarterly* 2:2 (1970): 27–36; Pierre de Lagarde, *La Mémoire des pierres* (Paris: Albin Michel, 1979), 31–3. See Vincent Juhel, ed., *Arcisse de Caumont (1801–1873)*, Mémoires de la Société des Antiquaires de Normande 40 (2004).

[18] Nicholas Penny, 'Constable: an English heritage abroad', *Sunday Times*, 11 Nov. 1983: 43; Charles Avery, 'The rood-loft from Hertogenbosch', *Victoria & Albert Museum Yearbook* 1 (1969): 110–36; Simon Thurley, *Men from the Ministry: How Britain Saved Its Heritage* (Yale, 2013), 73–6.

away by New York City air pollution. 'I have a duty to protect all Egyptian monuments whether they are inside or outside of Egypt', warned Egypt's heritage chief Zahi Hawass. 'If the Central Park Conservancy and the City of New York cannot properly care for this obelisk, I will take the necessary steps to bring this precious artifact home and save it from ruin.'[19]

A major spur to preservation was the acute sense of loss following the French Revolution and the Napoleonic Wars. Vandalized monuments and pillaged art treasures aroused conservation concerns. Notwithstanding Napoleon's wholesale theft of Roman treasures, he termed himself an 'ancient Roman', ordered the preservation of Rome's classical buildings, and helped to defray the cost.[20] Alongside these convulsions came those of the Industrial Revolution, most notably in Britain, where factory and tenement miseries heightened nostalgia for olden rural ways. Religious conflict and monastic dissolution had stunned early-modern observers. But awareness of – and regret for – material loss became widespread by the nineteenth century, when more Europeans than ever were sundered from familiar scenes. Many took solace in recalling, if not revisiting, childhood and ancestral landscapes. And attachment to migrants' past locales stimulated concerns to secure them in their remembered state – and to mourn when they were not.[21]

New-found ancient sites, notably the excavation of Mediterranean cradles of civilization, also ignited preservation sentiment. Widening education and greater leisure spurred interest in the past for its own sake.[22] Viewing ancient sites and collecting antiquities led to calls for their protection. All these early nineteenth-century preservation impulses aroused unprecedented initiatives for safeguarding things past from damage, decay, and expropriation.

That century's end saw a similar mood. Rising doubts about the benefits of progress, unease over social and political instability, a growing sense that the present was utterly alien engendered acute anxiety over the direction and pace of change – an angst exemplified in Brooks Adams's prognosis of imminent social collapse.[23] 'Material, physical, mechanical change in human life' in the century since James Watt's steam engine and Richard Arkwright's spinning frame seemed to an English historian 'greater than occurred in the thousand years that preceded, perhaps even in two thousand years or twenty thousand', and still accelerating. The writer Charles Péguy felt in 1913 that 'the world has changed less since Jesus Christ than it has done in the last thirty years'.[24]

The nostalgia aroused by these ominous portents surfaced in a surge of preservation activity. Country after country enacted laws to protect ancient monuments and set aside ever more bygone structures as cherished memorials. 'I don't like pulling down

[19] Press release, 6 Jan. 2011, *drhawass.com/blog/obelisk-centralpark*.
[20] Derek Linstrum, 'Giuseppe Valadier et l'Arc de Titus', *Monumentum* 25 (1982): 43–71 at 52; Glendinning, *Conservation Movement*, 70–4; Pasquale Paoli and Napoleon in Bosworth, *Whispering City*, 46, 53.
[21] Christopher Salvesen, *The Landscape of Memory* (Edward Arnold, 1965), 1–45, 137–66.
[22] Kenneth Hudson, *A Social History of Archaeology* (Macmillan, 1980), 20, 53, 73–83.
[23] Brooks Adams, *The Law of Civilization and Decay*, 2nd edn (1896; New York, 1955). 292–5, 307–8. See Henry Adams, *The Education of Henry Adams* (1906; Houghton Mifflin, 1918), 486–98.
[24] Frederic Harrison, 'A few words about the nineteenth century' (1882), in *The Choice of Books and Other Literary Pieces* (London, 1886), 417–47 at 424; Charles Péguy, *L'Argent* (Paris, 1913), 10.

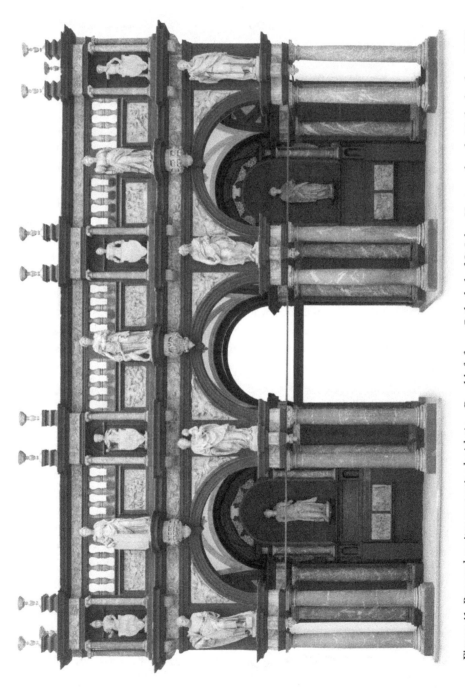

Figure 41 Removal excites protective legislation: Rood loft from Cathedral of St John, Hertogenbosch, Netherlands, c. 1610, purchased by Victoria and Albert Museum, London, 1871

anything ... Keep everything', E. A. Freeman advised.[25] To give the wayfarer 'everything veritable to dwell upon', William Morris's Society for the Protection of Ancient Buildings sought 'to preserve what is left of the past in the most indiscriminate way; whether good or bad, old or new, preserve it all'.[26]

Indiscriminate archival build-up was especially common because it seemed inherently commendable. Judaeo-Christian teaching sanctified the written word, endorsed its accrual, condemned its destruction. Holy books are repositories of God's actual utterances, their preservation divinely ordained. Conserving records and relics became a public duty and a private aspiration, whether against erosion, pollution, avaricious pillage, or iconoclastic spoliation. The archivist's sacred task, in Sir Hilary Jenkinson's canonical dictum, was 'the Conservation of every scrap of Evidence'.[27]

Previously largely confined to limited affairs of state, archives now multiply in every calling. Record-keeping has spread from government and academe to bakeries and beauticians, from heraldry experts to roots-seeking hoi polloi. Wrote Pierre Nora a generation ago:

No epoch has deliberately produced so many archives as ours, due alike to technical advances in reproduction and conservation and to our superstitious respect for these traces. As traditional memory fades, we feel obliged religiously to accumulate the testimonies, documents, images, and visible signs of what was, as if this ever-proliferating dossier should be called on as evidence in some tribunal of history. Hence the inhibition against destroying, the retention of everything. ... In classical times, only great families, the church, and the state kept records; today memories are recorded ... not only by minor actors in history but by their spouses and doctors.[28]

The pace of accretion is exponential: the archives of each American president outnumber those of all his predecessors combined.[29] Storage space, personnel, conservation, and indexing lag ever further behind accessioning. Archivists are besieged by hopelessly contrary diktats: adjured on the one hand to collect only what 'they can afford to responsibly arrange, describe, preserve, and provide access to'; compelled on the other to keep everything dumped on them.[30] No wonder they are sometimes tempted to excise the cancer of accumulation by a root-and-branch clean sweep, to scrap their cluttered holdings for sparse and spacious purity.[31]

Estrangement from the present and pessimism about the future again aggravate today's preservation zeal. Resurgent national and ethnic allegiances sanctify collective heritage.

[25] To Ugo Balzani, 3 Jan. 1886, in W. R. W. Stephens, *The Life and Letters of Edward A. Freeman* (London, 1895), 2: 341.
[26] Nikolaus Pevsner, *Some Architectural Writers of the Nineteenth Century* (Oxford, 1972), 309. See Michael Hunter, 'The fitful rise of British preservation', 1–16, and Chris Miele, 'The first conservation militants', 17–37, both in M. Hunter, ed., *Preserving the Past* (Stroud: Sutton, 1996).
[27] Hilary Jenkinson, 'The English archivist: a new profession' (1947), in *Selected Writings* (London: Alan Sutton, 1980), 236–59 at 258.
[28] Pierre Nora, 'Entre mémoire et histoire', in *Les Lieux de mémoire* (Paris: Gallimard, 1984–92), 1: xxv–xxviii.
[29] John Carlin, 'Records everywhere, but how are they going to survive?' *The Record* [US National Archives] 5:1 (Sept. 1998): 1–3.
[30] Diane Vogt-O'Connor, 'Archives: a primer for the 21st century', *Cultural Resource Management* 22:2 (1999): 4–8 at 7.
[31] See my 'Archival perils', *Archives* 31 (2006): 49–75 at 56–9.

Antiquity's ever more popular yet endangered splendours give heritage tourists and local hosts a prime stake in their survival. Groups devoted to the architectural legacy have multiplied tenfold in the past half century. Preservation in 1960 was still the hobby of a small eccentric elite; by 1980 more than half of American construction involved rehabilitation of old buildings. Half the British population seemed to be seeking converted barns, watermills, oast houses.

Britain protects half a million historic structures – houses and churches, lamp posts and lavatories, phone kiosks and toll booths, mile stones and tombstones. Much of London is included in its almost five hundred conservation areas and thousands of historic listed buildings, much of Italy in its nearly half million formally protected structures. A French heritage once wholly patrician came to include twentieth-century factories and merely familiar locales; 'a simple oven or a village lavatory elicits the patrimonial ardour once given an artistic masterpiece'. The proliferation of the past redoubles the threat of obese excess.[32]

Buildings saved become more various as well. The conserved past now includes structures as recent as the 1990s, typical as well as famed features, homes of the humble along with mansions of the mighty, landmarks cherished for local familiarity besides monuments of global renown. And preservation reaches beyond single structures to embrace neighbourhoods and entire towns. Landscapes are precious relics, Thomas Hardy's imagined 'Egdon Heath' in Dorset, threatened in turn by nuclear power and by wind turbines, is 'as irreplaceable as a Gothic cathedral'.[33] Hundreds of cultural and natural landscapes are among UNESCO's thousand World Heritage Sites of Outstanding Universal Value.[34]

Previously unsung figures and events gain populist stature, their relics newly worth preserving. Thousands of shrines now celebrate industrial history, the arts, and hitherto neglected minority figures. Tourists at antebellum plantations throng restored slave huts once shunned; servants' quarters at stately homes (Fig. 42) and chateaux attract visitors whose parents had eyes only for the sumptuous and the aristocratic. Salvage efforts formerly reserved for renowned remains now extend to commonplace everyday precincts. Preserved factories and tenements are neither pretty nor pleasant. But local residents in industrial New England, as in old England's Pennine factories, proved staunch preservationists. Those Satanic mills 'were part of their entire life story and deeply enmeshed with their sense of place'; their survival validated precious memory.[35] The 1970s historic park

[32] britishlistedbuildings.com; Marc Guillaume, interview, 'La politique du patrimoine ... vingt ans après', *Labyrinthe*, no. 7 (2000): 11–20; Pierre Nora, 'L'ère de la commémoration', in his *Lieux de Mémoire*, III.3: 1000–5.

[33] Christopher Booker, 'The nuclear threat to Hardy's heath', *Times*, 20 Feb. 1982: 6; Ben Webster, 'Wind turbines madden Hardy crowds', *Times*, 4 Nov. 2013: 3. See Richard Bevis, *The Road to Egdon Heath* (McGill-Queen's Press, 1999); Tony Fincham, *Hardy's Landscape Revisited* (Robert Hale, 2010).

[34] *World Heritage Series no. 26 – Cultural Landscapes*; *World Heritage Cultural Landscapes* (UNESCO-ICOMOS Documentation Centre, 2009); *WorldHeritageList*.

[35] Tamara K. Hareven and Randolph Langenbach, *Amoskeag: Life and Work in an American Factory City* (New York: Pantheon, 1978), and their 'Living places, work places and historical identity', in David Lowenthal and Marcus Binney, eds., *Our Past before Us* (London: Temple Smith, 1981), 109–23 at 111–14. See Marcus Binney et al., *Satanic Mills* (SAVE Britain's Heritage, 1979).

Figure 42 The humble past acclaimed: Servants' Hall, Erdigg, Clwyd, Wales

designation of Lowell, Massachusetts, secured inhabitants' collective heritage, for 'our identity lies in this urban industrial past'. Restoring Lowell's defunct textile mills catalysed its half-billion-dollar regeneration, making Lowell a bellwether for historic mill cities from England to eastern Europe, India, and China.[36] From prehistoric sites to postmodern artefacts, preservation has become a world-wide enterprise.

The end result of indiscriminate preservation would be a stultifying museumized world, in which nothing ever made or done was allowed to perish. Failure to winnow is madness. Yet heritage is such a sacred cow that few dare call for its culling. Italy is so stuffed with treasure that only a fraction of it is adequately cared for, let alone accessible. Things are much the same the world over. Everyone knows this, yet no steward publicly affirms it. Rather, they laud the renewal of pride in ancestral roots, the protection of relics threatened by erosion or plunder, the rescue of cherished legacies from purblind greed, the return of every treasure from foreign exile.

Preservation and loss are inherently conjoint and co-dependent, notes Rebecca Solnit.

To imagine both creation and destruction together is to see their kinship in the common ground of change, abrupt and gradual, beautiful and disastrous, to see the generative richness of ruins and the

---

[36] Patrick Mogan quoted in Jane Holtz Kay, 'Lowell, Mass.: new birth for us all', *Nation*, 17 Sept. 1977: 246; *Report of the Lowell Historic Canal District Commission* (1977), 70–84; Carolyn M. Goldstein, 'Many voices, true stories, and the experiences we are creating in industrial history museums', *Public Historian* 22:3 (2002): 129–37.

ruinous nature of all change. . . . Everything is the ruin of what came before. . . . 'The child is the father of the man', wrote Wordsworth, but the man is also the ruin of the child, as . . . the butterfly is the ruin of the caterpillar.[37]

As in David Ely's cautionary *Time Out* (see p. 297 above), salvage demands subtraction.

Archivists, past managers par excellence, limit intake to about 2 per cent of what they are offered and then, perforce, ruthlessly sieve even that.[38] But most cultural property stewards shun the archivists' example. Getting rid of things hurts too much. Viewers of 'Demolition', a 2005 British television series, voted to raze a thousand-odd detested buildings. One of the top 'Dirty Dozen', the 1957–61 brutalist Park Hill Flats in Sheffield, was spared imminent demolition by English Heritage listing in 1997. De-listing is legally difficult, politically fraught, time-consuming, hence rare. Only two World Heritage sites have ever been delisted, Oman's Arabian Oryx Sanctuary in 2007 (both sanctuary and oryx being almost extinct), and Germany's Dresden Elbe Valley cultural landscape in 2009 (occluded by a four-lane bridge).[39]

Consequently, preservation proliferates, cheapening what's kept and cramping creativity. Like Marinetti's Futurists a century ago, Rem Koolhaas's urban visionaries today stress 'not what to keep, but what to give up, what to erase and abandon'. To preserve 'a domain of permanent change' demands wholesale destruction. Rubbishing the 1972 UN World Heritage Convention, their 2010 Convention for the Demolition of the World's Cultural Junk, calls for dossiers of 'artifacts that ought to disappear'.[40]

Other inherent contradictions beset preservation. Protective action invariably alters any site or structure, often to their detriment. Preservation usually inflicts prolonged disturbance. Medieval cathedrals seem forever wrapped in scaffolding and builders' rubble. Protection can debase the ambience of antiquities even when fabric remains intact: Casa Grande, an ancient Amerindian adobe structure in Arizona, is overwhelmed by its 1932 steel protective roof (Fig. 43). The canopy so trivializes Casa Grande that 'it now takes powers of imaginative reconstruction far beyond' anyone's ability 'to see the abode as the great monument of the plain'.[41]

Protected sites become blatantly incongruous. New York City's 1971 air-rights ordinance sold space rights above old buildings to adjacent sites, so that new structures could bypass statutory height and setback requirements by using space 'wasted' above historical landmarks. This saved some old structures from extinction but leaves them dwarfed by

[37] Rebecca Solnit, 'The ruins of memory' (2006), in *Storming the Gates of Paradise* (California, 2007), 351–70 at 351–2, paraphrasing Wordsworth's 'My heart leaps up' (1802).

[38] Carlin, 'Records everywhere', 1–3; Richard J. Cox, *No Innocent Deposits: Forming Archives by Rethinking Appraisal* (Lanham, MD: Scarecrow, 2004), 4–12.

[39] Cheryl Markowsky, 'Pros and cons: de-listing your property', *Country Life*, 25 Feb. 2011; Sophia Labadi, *Unesco, Cultural Heritage, and Outstanding Universal Value* (AltaMira, 2013), 123–4; Douglas Scoch, 'Whose World Heritage?. . . UNESCO's delisting of the Dresden Elbe Valley', *IJCP* 21 (2014): 199–224.

[40] OMA/AMO, 'Venice Biennale 2010: Cronocaos' (*oma.eu/projects*); Teresa Stoppani, 'Altered states of preservation', *Future Anterior* 8:1 (Summer 2011): 96–109 at 104. See Dario Gamboni, *The Destruction of Art* (Reaktion, 1997), 331.

[41] Reyner Banham, 'Preservation adobe', *New Society*, 2 Apr. 1981: 23–4. See Frank G. Matero, 'Lessons from the Great House . . . at Casa Grande Ruins National Monument', *Conservation & Management of Archaeological Sites* 3:4 (1999): 205–24; 'Pre-history meets modernity: Casa Grande Ruins National Monument', 7 Nov. 2009, *eartharchitecture.org/index.php?/archives/679*.

Figure 43 Protection trivializes: Casa Grande Ruins National Monument, Arizona

ever-higher neighbours. Manhattan's Trinity Church, the Old Stock Exchange, and Customs House were made minuscule among nearby giants; the Italianate Villard Houses (Fig. 44) were 'preserved' by the ungainly juxtaposition of a massive hotel tower. Soaring towers loom and cantilever over stultified relics and minuscule plazas in the heart of the city.[42]

Protective measures frequently engender or augment erosive processes, injuring the very relics they aim to preserve. Ancient earthworks fenced off against mechanized agriculture attract burrowing rabbits displaced from ploughed fields. The iron clamps that kept Acropolis columns and caryatids from collapsing became, with expansive corrosion, a major agent of destruction. At the ruins of Babylon, a World Heritage Site, restoration with modern bricks hastens groundwater decay; 'the two together are nearly toxic for the preservation of monuments'.[43]

Admirers literally love the past to death. Devotees wear down old floors, abrade ancient stones, erode prehistoric trackways. Popularity threatens the survival of antiquities

[42] John Costonis, *Space Adrift: Landmark Preservation and the Marketplace* (Illinois, 1974), 54–61; Ada Louise Huxtable, *Kicked a Building Lately?* (New York Times/Quadrangle, 1978), 269–72; Anthony M. Tung, *Preserving the World's Great Cities* (New York: Three Rivers, 2001), 358–64; Charles V. Bagli, '$430 a square foot, for air? Only in New York real estate', *NYT*, 30 Nov. 2005; '$40 million in air rights will let East Side tower soar', *NYT*, 25 Mar. 2013; Raanan Geberer, 'Divine profits: churches, developers, and air rights', *Cooperator: The Co-op & Condo Monthly* 27:1 (Jan. 2007); Robin Finn, 'The great air race', *NYT*, 24 Feb. 2013: BU 8.

[43] Jeff Allen (World Monuments Fund) quoted in Stephen Lee Myers, 'A triage to save the ruins of Babylon', *NYT*, 2 Jan. 2011. See Elizabeth Pye, *Caring for the Past* (London: James & James, 2001) 112–24.

Figure 44 The present dwarfs the past: McKim, Mead, and White, Villard Houses, New York City, 1886

Figure 45 The present dwarfs the past: Memory Lane Lounge beneath Detroit's Renaissance Center

however protected, as with the fading, cracking, and destructive mould on cave paintings at Lascaux and Altamira. Sorely vulnerable to tourism, ancient sites more and more ration access, make visitors don felt overshoes, and replace relics with replicas. Only sandblasting could be more destructive than the humidity, fungi, and dust brought by a near century's thousand tourists a day, staining and peeling the paint off walls of Tutankhamen's tomb.[44] Antique chairs are roped off so they will not be sat on, books pinioned shut against curious hands. Furnishings and fabrics must be shielded against lethal light – curtains installed, blinds kept down, slipcovers added. Watercolours and drawings are held in the dark as much as possible and displayed in the dimmest of light. To see Leonardo's *Last Supper* viewers must first be decontaminated. Ecotourism swamps fragile sites. To protect Galápagos tortoises and birds, an annual ceiling of 12,000 visitors was set three decades ago; this 'ultimate environmental experience' now disastrously lures almost 200,000.[45]

Popularity tarnishes the feel as well as the fabric of the past. 'How one might love it', muses a Henry James protagonist anent a drowsy old English village, 'but how one might spoil it! To look at it too hard . . . was positively to wake it up. Its only safety . . . was to be left still to sleep.'[46] At Kenilworth James frowned on 'a row of ancient pedlars outside the castle wall, hawking twopenny pamphlets and photographs, [and] half a dozen beery vagrants sprawling on the grass'. He lamented not just the numbers but the vulgarity: at 'most romantic sites in England, there is a constant cockneyfication [and] there are always people on the field before you'.[47]

Worse yet, for James, was the fatal embrace of famed past figures. 'There was somebody', remarks the reverential custodian of Shakespeare's birthplace in James's tale. 'But the [tourists] killed Him. And dead as He is, they keep it up, They do it over again, They kill Him every day'.[48] Slaying the precious past may consign the murderer to a similar fate. Umberto Eco's medieval librarian kills himself by devouring the poisoned pages of the volume (Aristotle's lost second book of poetics) he has sought to preserve.[49]

Modern mass tourism blights the aura of all notable relics. In many museums famed pictures can scarcely be seen, viewers herded like cattle to the abattoir. 'I've heard the Mona Lisa is quite a painting', wrote a critic, 'but in all the times I've been to the Louvre, I've never seen it. I have seen the glass box it's housed in, and once I almost caught a glimpse, but I was pushed back to the benches.' Literally mortifying is the Sistine Chapel. Mass tourism in Rome 'has turned what was a contemplative pleasure for Goethe's contemporaries into an ordeal more like a degrading rugby scrum', in Robert Hughes's castigation. 'The crowd of ceiling seekers is streamed shoulder to shoulder

---

[44] Max Hanna, 'Cathedrals at saturation point?' in Lowenthal and Binney, eds., *Our Past before Us*, 178–92; Myra Shackley, 'Costs and benefits: the impact of cathedral tourism in England', *Journal of Heritage Tourism* 1:2 (2006): 133–41; Paul Bahn, 'Killing Lascaux', *Archaeology* 51:3 (2008): 10–12; Cesario Saiz-Jimenez, ed., *Conservation of Subterranean Cultural Heritage* (Leiden: CRC Press, 2014), 139–72, 215–38; Mike Pitts, 'Your last chance to see Tutankhamun's tomb', *Guardian*, 17 Jan. 2011.

[45] Pye, *Caring for the Past*, 85–7; Judith Denkinger and Luis Vinueza, eds., The *Galápagos Marine Reserve* (Springer, 2014), viii.

[46] Henry James, 'Flickerbridge' (1903), in *Complete Tales* (Hart-Davis 1964), 11: 327–50 at 337.

[47] Henry James, *English Hours* (Heinemann, 1905), 124–5.

[48] Henry James, 'The Birthplace' (1903), in *Complete Tales*, 11: 403–65 at 440.

[49] Umberto Eco, *The Name of the Rose* (1980; Harcourt, Brace, 1983), 570.

along a lengthy, narrow, windowless, and claustrophobic corridor in which there is no turning back ... The chapel itself ... scarcely offers room to turn around.' The greatest monuments of the Western world once 'inspired quiet awe, ... but now, like Rome itself, they have been commodified unto death'. Ceasing to inspire, they risk terminal neglect.[50]

The best intentions prove lethal; the more heritage attracts, the sooner it decays or turns to dross. The very act of designating a building worth conserving often endangers it; the owner's fear of mandatory protection triggers hasty demolition to avert the burden of care. Stonehenge, Britain's heritage archetype, typifies dilemmas that bedevil the built legacy. It has long served – and suffered for – myriad purposes. Some locals removed stones for fencing and building, others rented tools to tourists to chip bits off the sarsens – one antiquary grumbled at being 'obliged with a Hammer to labour hard three Quarters of an Hour'.[51]

Nationalization a century ago saved Stonehenge from religious zealots, farmers, and souvenir hunters. But it endures endless custodial folly. Until 2014 access was through a dank concrete tunnel; barbed wire intermittently festooned the stones; car parks, lavatories, a cramped gift shop, a dingy cafe's Sarsen Sandwiches degraded the ambience. 'We've managed to separate the stones from their setting', bragged English Heritage; 'we've surrounded a great monument to the genius of the early British with the worst excesses of the 20th century'. Cult fame and commercial need aggravate these woes. To make Stonehenge seemly for paying visitors, custodians in the 1980s banned New Age sects, hippies, ley-line mystics, and 'Druids'. English Heritage pledged a purified Stonehenge as honeypot and sanctuary. But thirty years on this 'eighth wonder of the world' remained, in its own custodian's words, a 'national disgrace'. The latest rescue from official neglect begot an 'equally ghastly' visitor centre, securing Stonehenge's legacy as a planning disaster.[52]

Stonehenge's woes reflect conundrums common to most famed sites. Popularity degrades Mont-Saint-Michel with tawdry souvenirs. Antiquity bandits machine-gun their way into Angkor Wat, ill-protected even though floodlit and wired like a concentration camp: tourists must evade landmines emplaced to forestall plunder. Art-historical hyping of Cycladic figurines led to the looting of thousands of Dodecanese graves and to a flood of Cycladic fakes. The looting of Bronze Age artefacts at Ban Chiang, smuggled out of Thailand by being passed off as replicas, led Thai villagers to fabricate 'original replicas' of

[50] Celia Brayfield, 'Roll up, roll up, and watch the Mona Lisa weep', *Times*, 19 Feb. 2007: 2: 19; Robert Goldberg, 'Jostling over Mona Lisa', *IHT*, 5–6 July 1980: 8; Robert Hughes, *Rome* (Weidenfeld & Nicolson, 2011), 483; Ingrid D. Rowland, 'The crass, beautiful, eternal city', *NYRB*, 22 Dec. 2011: 20. See Martin Bailey, 'Take your picture and then shove off', *Art Newspaper* 159 (June 2006).

[51] Robert Townson (1799) quoted in Christopher Chippindale, *Stonehenge Complete* (Thames & Hudson, 1983), 91. See Anthony Pace, 'Sustainability in the Management of Archaeological Monuments and Sites' (Ph.D. dissertation, Cambridge University, 2011), 187–90, 211–14, 235–38, 273–5, 286–95, 305–9.

[52] English Heritage chairman Jocelyn Stevens quoted in Alexander Frater, 'The lasting lure of the stones', *Observer on Sunday*, 20 June 1993, 49–50; Clive Aslet, 'Stonehenge's visitor centre is awful – and so is its successor', *Times*, 19 Nov. 2010: 19, 36; Simon de Bruxelles, 'New dawn for a "national disgrace"', *Times*, 1 Oct. 2013: 3; 'Stonehenge visitor centre a £27m flop as it struggles to cope', *Western Daily Press*, 10 Jan. 2014; '"Be patient" plea over new Stonehenge visitor centre', *BBC News*, 14 Jan. 2014.

antique pottery – at the cost of traditional community bonds. 'People destroy the archaeological finds', an observer reflected, and then 'the finds destroy the people'.[53] On the other hand, eBay and the Internet now enable Peruvian villagers to earn much more from mass-produced fakes than they used to get from laboriously unearthing genuine relics, thereby reducing looting. In today's art market, concludes an art historian, 'what is not looted is fake, and what is not fake is looted'.[54]

Hallowing process rather than product, creative act rather than end result is nowadays more and more approved. The primacy accorded to keeping original stone and brickwork, in ICOMOS's Venice Charter of 1964, dismayed many in cultures that do not build or make things to last. For them 'heritage is a bundle of relationships rather than a bundle of economic rights' or tangible objects. They regenerate rather than retain, preserve acts not artefacts.[55] Clinging to old stuff inhibits creative continuity. 'When the product is preserved and venerated, the impulse to repeat the process is compromised', wrote Chinua Achebe of Nigerian art. 'The Igbo choose to eliminate the product and retain the process so that every occasion and every generation will receive its own impulse and kinesis of creation.'[56] A Zuni spokesman concurs. 'Everything for ceremonial, religious, and ritual purposes that my culture makes is meant to disintegrate ... to go back into the ground. Conservation is a disservice to my culture.'[57]

For museums to keep Melanesian sacred artefacts and funerary effigies violates their religious function. And objects fashioned for tribal exchange rituals should be destroyed after use so that new ones can be made. Their presumed life cycle requires reiterated creation and destruction.[58] Intangible legacies of arts and crafts, skills and techniques celebrate handing down not things but ways of doing things – the know-how embodied in UNESCO-designated Living Human Treasures and in English thatching, American lute-making, Japanese temple building, Korean knot-making, Brazilian body painting, Samoan tattooing, and French cuisine.[59]

[53] Debra Weiner, 'Treasures from the Thai earth', *IHT*, 26–27 June 1982: 6. See Jori Finkel, 'Thai antiquities, resting uneasily', *NYT*, 17 Feb. 2008.
[54] Charles Stanish, 'Forging ahead', *Archaeology* 62:3 (June 2009): 23–8; David A Scott, 'Modern antiquities: the looted and the faked', *IJCP* 20 (2013): 49–75 at 65.
[55] Olgierd Czerner, 'Communal cultural heritage in a unified Europe', *ICOMOS News*, 1:1 (March 1991): 25; Erica-Irene A. Daes, *Protection of the Heritage of Indigenous People* (Geneva: United Nations, 1997), 21–2; Folarin Shyllon, 'The right to a cultural past: African viewpoints', in Halina Niec, ed., *Cultural Rights and Wrongs* (UNESCO/Institute of Art & Law, 1998), 103–19 at 110. See Matthew Hardy, ed., *The Venice Charter Revisited* (Newcastle upon Tyne: Cambridge Scholars, 2008).
[56] Chinua Achebe, 'The Igbo world and its art' (1984), in *Hopes and Impediments* (Heinemann, 1988), 64.
[57] Edmund Ladd (1992) quoted in Catherine Sease, 'Code of ethics for conservation', *IJCP* 7 (1998): 98–115 at 106.
[58] Suzanne Küchler, *Malanggan: Art, Memory and Sacrifice* (Berg, 2002), 167–86; Barbara Kirschenblatt-Gimblett, 'Intangible heritage multicultural production', 52–65 at 55, and Mounir Bouchenaki, 'Editorial', 6–11 at 10, both in *Museum International*, special issue, Intangible Cultural Heritage, 56:1–2 (2004); Michael O'Hanlon, 'History embodied: authenticating the past in the New Guinea highlands', in Stanley J. Ulijaszek, ed., *Population, Reproduction and Fertility in Melanesia* (Berghahn, 2005), 182–200.
[59] See Pascal Ory, 'La gastronomie', in Nora, comp., *Lieux de mémoire*, III.2: 822–53; UNESCO Cultural Heritage Sector, 'The gastronomic meal of the French', Decision 6.14 (2010).

But once reverently designated, Living Treasures are ever more apt to be purloined and/or mummified. A UNESCO imprimatur confers on 'Masterpieces of the Oral and Intangible Heritage of Humanity' a fatal promise of eternal life, ossifying things fluid by their very nature into factitious perpetuity. Thus we 'reinforce the notion that heritage is a kind of fortress requiring constant protection', in an African rebuke, and that 'every breach in its walls is one more irreversible step in losing one's culture'.[60]

Nor are intangible traditions the only treasures jeopardized by protocols meant to protect them. Collectors often portray themselves as saviours preserving antiquities that would otherwise remain buried unseen or destroyed by plough and bulldozer. But their unearthing for sale destroys the context in which these cherished relics lived.[61] Yet unenforceable national sanctions against heritage export further aggravate the plunder of ancient sites. To stem parlous loss of historical context, some would consign looted and illegally exported antiquities to a limbo of neglect, neither to be shown nor studied. Thus an ancient Lydian bed from Turkey at the Getty 'is frozen in time, neither displayable nor repatriated . . . a victim of its own uniqueness . . . condemned to be hidden in storage as if it itself was guilty of some transgression'.[62]

This would condemn almost all pre-Columbian Andean gold work in museum collections 'to an unpublishable morass of unprovenanced material of benefit to nobody'.[63] Suspect artefacts should not even be preserved, say archaeological purists, for 'by rendering antiquities more aesthetically pleasing, more durable, and less traceable, the conservator becomes complicit in an illicit trade that obtains the object at the expense . . . of the site', thus colluding in 'destruction of the past'.[64] But, retorts an outraged art historian, 'a conservator who refuses to save an unprovenanced or even an illicitly acquired object is a disgrace to his/her profession, as would be a doctor who refuses to attend to a sick criminal'. Sacrificing baby for bathwater, pearl for oyster, content for context, zealous puritans ditch the remnant past to punish profligate collectors.[65]

Preferring to see the past destroyed to prevent its being abused, these 'conservators' resemble the museum curator in Siegfried Lenz's novel, aghast at the repeated manipulation of his precious artefacts by successive German, Soviet, and Polish nationalists. Only its deliberate destruction secured the beleaguered Masurian past against 'Teutonic' or

---

[60] Sidney Littlefield Kasfir and Labiyi Babalola Joseph Yai, 'Authenticity and diaspora', *Museum International* 56:1–2 (2004): 190–7 at 193–4. See Rosanne Trottier, 'Intellectual property for mystics? Considerations on protecting traditional wisdom systems', *IJCP* 17 (2010): 519–46 at 520; Miranda Forsyth, 'Lifting the lid on "The Community": who has the right to control access to traditional knowledge and expressions of culture?', *IJCP* 19 (2012): 1–31; Krishna Ravi Srinivas, 'Protecting traditional knowledge holders interests and preventing misappropriation', *IJCP* 19 (2012): 401–22.

[61] Hannah Arendt, 'Introduction', in Walter Benjamin, *Illuminations* (New York: Schocken, 1969), 39–45.

[62] Scott, 'Modern antiquities: the looted and the faked', 64.

[63] Ibid., 64, 66.

[64] Kathryn Walker Tubb, 'Shifting approaches to unprovenanced antiquities among conservators', in Lyndel V. Prott et al., eds., *Realising Cultural Heritage Law* (Builth Wells, UK: Institute of Art & Law, 2012), 145–61 at 147. See Einav Zamir, 'The conservation laundering of illicit antiquities', *ArWatchUK* 29 Mar. 2015.

[65] John Boardman, 'Comment on "Irreconcilable differences?"' ['Problems with unprovenanced antiquities', by K. W. Tubb], *PIA* [Papers from the Institute of Archaeology, University College London], 18 (2007): 10–11.

'Slavonic' appropriation. To forestall relics' perversion for propaganda, the curator sets fire to his own museum. When 'the treasured finds have crumbled away, the traces have been obliterated', he will have brought 'the collected witnesses to our past into safety, a final, irrevocable safety, ... where they could never again be exploited for this cause or that'.[66]

In sum, preservation is done 'in the name of no change, but it's all about radical change ... To preserve something is to change it', notes Columbia University's architecture dean. Preservation 'is not about preventing change any more', agrees the president of ICOMOS; 'it is about *managing* change'.[67] And management mandates not just conserving but selective culling.

Identifying, displaying, protecting

Valuing the past leads us to proclaim its existence: here it is, we announce, a previous, original, or ancient feature. And so we mark the site or relic. Designation locates the past and lends it status. Some traces of antiquity are so faint that only contrivance makes them visible. Minus signposts, how many early battlefields would be recognized as such or seen as 'historic'? But for markers, people would pass by most monuments unaware of their antiquity. To be recognized as a worthy destination, a place must be physically labelled as such.[68] One risk of deleting archaeological sites from the British Ordnance Survey, as was proposed, is that landowners discount the value, even doubt the existence, of antiquities no longer pinpointed on maps, thus hastening their extinction.[69]

Historical plaques rescue homes of the famous from obscurity. Except for the rare Monticello or Kelmscott, displaying Jefferson's genius and Morris's memorabilia, few houses are distinctive simply for having sheltered the famed; they become evocative only through subsequent markers. Signposts become imprimaturs. 'How Real Is that Ruin? Don't Ask, the Locals Say' headlined the story on an Inca 'fertility temple' in Chucuito, Peru, whose dubiously ancient stone phalluses brought lucrative tourism. Less the contrivance of antiquity than the absence of a marker distressed one Chucuito visitor: 'You do wonder if it is historical, considering there isn't even a signpost.'[70] Only a *declarative certificate* could confer authenticity.

---

[66] Siegfried Lenz, *The Heritage* (1978; Hill & Wang, 1981), 458. Himself Masurian, Lenz depicts actual East Prussian experience during the Second World War, after which 90 per cent of the 80,000 Masurians were evicted or fled Sovietized Poland into Germany (Andrzej Sakson, 'Masurians – between Polish and German identity', *Ethnologia Polona* 26 (2005): 107–22; Malgorzata Karczewska, '*Cuius regio, eius memoria*. World War I memorials in the territory of former East Prussia, now within Poland', in Józef Niżnik, ed., *Twentieth Century Wars in European Memory* (Frankfurt: Peter Lang, 2012), 231–49).

[67] Mark Wigley, in Francesca von Habsburg et al., 'Debate: preservation, contemporary art, and architecture', *Future Anterior* 4:2 (Winter 2007): 80; Gustavo Araoz, 'Heritage classifications and the need to adjust them to emerging paradigms', in Andrzej Tomaszewski, ed., *Values and Criteria in Heritage Conservation* (Florence: Polistampa, 2008), 167–82 at 170.

[68] Maura Troester, 'Roadside retroscape: history and the marketing of tourism in the middle of nowhere', in Stephen Brown and John F. Sherry, eds., *Time, Space, and the Market* (Armonk, NY: M. E. Sharpe, 2003), 115–40 at 118; Dean MacCannell, *The Tourist* (1976; 3rd edn California, 1999), 110–40, 158–63.

[69] There is 'a firm impression that unless a site of antiquity is shown on an OS map it has no reliable authority for its existence' (Graham Webster, 'Mapping buried history', *Times*, 31 Oct. 1977: 13).

[70] Luke Jerrod Kummer in *NYT*, 21 Mar. 2006.

Figure 46 Restoring and signposting: old iron mine, Roxbury, Connecticut, before renovation

Figure 47 Same, after renovation

Figure 48 Marking the invisible past: Revolutionary conflict, Castine, Maine

Figure 49 Marking the inconsequential past: accident, Harrow on the Hill, Middlesex

A marker may echo the past even if what it points to is not itself old, such as American and Antipodean localities given European names. Knowingly anachronistic street and pub signs in British suburbia – Sylvan Walks, Dells, Hop Poles, Woodmans, Wheatsheafs, Ploughs – evoke a generalized rural past. So do The Coach House, The Barn, The Stables, The Granary, The Brambles, The Sheddings, The Dove Cote, The Harvest Home. Other names recall past holidays – myriad Windermeres and Braemars in 1930s Britain, post-war San Remos and Riminis.[71] A family or functional name more likely identifies a past than present owner or function. 'The Schoolhouse' is a building that *used* to be a school; the sign would be redundant on an existing school. 'The Old Rectory', too grand for the present rector, is an *ipso facto* bygone.

The past thus identified may long antedate present memory. Thousands of American towns attest founders' hunger for the sanction of antiquity; even temporal hybrids – Thermopolis, Minneapolis, Itasca, Spotsylvania – hint of age. Countless Euclid Drives, Appian Ways, and Phaeton Roads suggest ancient felicities; Greek initials bedeck fraternity houses tenanted by unlettered louts to whom Greek is just Greek.[72]

In heralding history, some signs drown it in trivia. Local interest lends notoriety to places that 'marked some event almost too meager to comprehend', such as 'Near this site ... was believed to be ... the original shed where Josiah Dexter, an early settler of Dexterville, hid from four Hessians.'[73] Other traces remain invisible even when well advertised, such as the tree in the Bois de Boulogne purportedly hit by Tsar Alexander II's would-be assassin. Neither bullet nor bullet-hole could be seen, but 'the guides will point it out to visitors for the next eight hundred years', wrote Mark Twain, 'and when it decays and falls down they will put up another there and go on with the same old story'.[74]

Many designations are avowedly speculative. At Top Withens, Emily Brontë's *Wuthering Heights* farm, a sign cautions pilgrims that 'The buildings, even when complete, bore no resemblance to the house she described. But the situation may have been in her mind when she wrote of the moorland setting.' Some markers are gleefully counterfactual – the American Civil War park notice that 'Had General Lee been less troubled by the approach of battle he would have enjoyed the view of this fine pinewood forest'; the sign on a watering-trough that 'This is where Paul Revere would have watered his horse had he come this way'; the neo-Tudor timeshare ad that 'Queen Elizabeth would like to have slept here'; the 'Seed from a lotus plant, that might have been picked by Christopher Columbus, had the American continent not got in the way'; the fanciful English Heritage plaque in Soho memorializing 'Jacob von Hogflume Inventor of time travel 1864–1909 lived here in 2189' (Fig. 50).[75]

[71] Joyce Miles survey cited in 'Favourite house names', *Sunday Times*, 3 Feb. 1980: 49; 'The UK's top 50 house names', Halifax House Name Survey [UK], 2003.
[72] Howard Mumford Jones, *O Strange New World; American Culture* (Viking, 1964), 228; Wilbur Zelinsky, 'Classical town names in the United States', *Geographical Review* 57 (1967): 463–95.
[73] William Zinsser, 'Letter from home', *NYT*, 18 Aug. 1977: C16.
[74] Mark Twain, *The Innocents Abroad* (1869; New American Library, 1966), 101.
[75] *TopWithensPlaque.jpg* 2005-05-18; Marcella Sherfy told me of the Lee sign; Arthur A. Newkirk, 'Artifact or artefact?' *Science*, 180 (1973): 1232; Elmers Court Timeshare, Lymington, Hants., ad, *Sunday Times*, 3 Oct.

Figure 50 Marking the implausible past: plaque to Jacob von Hogflume, time traveller

Familiarity renders some notices invisible, others obtrusive. If we have no need to be shown the way or told the name, should our view be cluttered for the sake of the lazy or ignorant?[76] Yet words can enhance the past. For Americans, European village names conjure up a thousand years of history. Places need not conform to the historical specifics their names imply; a mere impression of *some* past is enough. We do not feel cheated to find Bath more Georgian than Roman, Finchingfield more a Victorian than medieval village, London's Barbican with only scanty Roman traces. Many markers magnify our sense of the past simply by echoing history. More commonly they help, like patina, to validate antiquity. 'That "1537" over the way is TRUE', exulted Frederick Law Olmsted on visiting Chester, England, for 'I can see the sun shine into the figures.'[77] A celebrated sign can make a place-name memorably historic, like Edward Thomas's 'Adlestrop' (1914/17; Fig. 51):

> Yes, I remember Adlestrop –
> The name, because one afternoon
> Of heat the express-train drew up there

1982: 8; *New Scientist*, 28 Oct. 1982: 272; Hogflume in Dave Askwith and Alex Normanton, *Signs of Life* (HarperCollins, 2005).

[76] Elizabeth Beazley, 'Popularity: its benefits and risks', in Lowenthal and Binney, eds., *Our Past before Us*, 193–202 at 201.

[77] Frederick Law Olmsted, *Walks and Talks of an American Farmer in England* (New York, 1852), 88.

Figure 51 'Yes, I remember Adlestrop': this author beneath the railway platform
sign that inspired Edward Thomas

> Unwontedly. It was late June
> The steam hissed. Someone cleared his throat.
> No one left and no one came
> On the bare platform. What I saw
> Was Adlestrop – only the name.[78]

By contrast with bittersweet Adlestrop, mid-century Las Vegas's spectacular neon signs
enriched the tawdry buildings behind them with a fantasized past – the GOLDEN
NUGGET, the HORSESHOE, the LUXOR, EXCALIBUR – making Las Vegas 'the only
town in the world whose skyline' is not of buildings but signs. Salvaged signs in ruinous
disrepair festoon the Neon Museum boneyard, their empty sockets and rusted metal an
'uncanny, sometimes lovely, often haunting' reminder of hustler chutzpah.[79]

All markers unavoidably alter what we see. Awareness of the past is reshaped as well as
sharpened by signs that tell where it is and what it was. Notices touting this or defaming
that relic profoundly influence what we make of them. Labels identifying the keeps,
donjons, and garderobes of ancient castles, the refectories, chapels, and libraries of ruined
monasteries, induce an academic attitude, adjuring viewers to *compare* one ruin with
another, these relics with those. They order antiquities by date, endowing the reliquary

---

[78] Edward Thomas, *Collected Poems* (Clarendon Press, 1978), 71. See Anne Harvey, ed., *Adlestrop Revisited* (Sutton, 1999).
[79] Tom Wolfe, 'Las Vegas (What?) Las Vegas (Can't Hear You! Too Noisy) Las Vegas!!!' (1963), in *The Kandy-Kolored Tangerine-Flake Streamline Baby* (Picador, 2009), 3–28 at 7; Edward Rothstein, 'Where Las Vegas Stardust rests in peace', *NYT*, 1 Feb. 2013.

Figure 52 Marking an intended past: restoring the aboriginal Kansas prairie

Figure 53 Marking a sentiment: honouring the reformer Shaftesbury, Harrow School

past with a chronicle. But just as treasure-hunt questionnaires at museums lead children to focus less on objects than on labels, so historic-site visitors often attend more to markers than to what they designate.

Mere recognition thus transforms the visible past. Identifying and classifying may tell us much about relics but often occludes our view, sacrificing communion with for information about the past. Armed with facts about antique specimens, we 'name and number, appreciate rarity and finally, assign value. This is dangerous knowledge indeed', defining a market for dealing and smuggling, promoting the pillage of the very past being 'protected'.[80] Designation abets loss: just as Britain's historical monuments' inventories became shopping lists for American buyers a century ago, so the act of cataloguing, warns a tribal-rights expert, 'encourage[s] outsiders to think that the heritage of indigenous peoples can be sold'.[81] So popular with GPS-directed tourists is the iconic 1923 'HOL-LYWOOD' sign that beleaguered local residents erect 'NO ACCESS TO THE HOLLY-WOOD SIGN' signs.[82]

Like protective roofs, imposing markers often overshadow the relics they service. Interpretive appendages occlude or deform the historic view. Some structures literally overwhelm the antiquities they enclose: the Lincoln 'birthplace' log cabin (Fig. 54) and Lenin's tomb seem puny and insignificant in their marble temples. Others intentionally clash with the ancient features they display: the geodesic dome over Connecticut's Dinosaur State Park stresses 'the contrast between the very new and the 200 million year old tracks'.[83] But whether blatantly unlike or unobtrusively in keeping, ancillary para-phernalia risk eclipsing actual relics. To be faced, on reaching a historic site, by 'an iron railing and a turnstile' infuriated devotee John Piper.[84] Omnipresent markers, visitor centres, and protective paraphernalia everywhere clutter the heritage landscape. Promo-tional efforts leave their own dubious imprint. Floodlighting was praised for freeing York Minster from visual pollution, but faulted for turning Canterbury Cathedral into Dracu-la's castle.[85]

The displayed past may end up not merely sidelined but utterly subverted. In Massa-chusetts, the Concord–Lexington 1775 combat route in the 1960s became the Minute Man National Historical Park. To display that iconic day's saga, residents were evicted, post-revolutionary houses demolished, sheep and cattle grazing continuous over two centuries terminated. The remaining old houses were boarded up, fields and pastures reverted to brush and second-growth forest; within a few years the route lost all semblance of the revolutionary scene. The visitor centre shows surrogate relics and events of 1775. But outdoors, where the skirmishes actually happened, instead of a living

[80] David Sassoon, '"Considering the perspective of the victim": the antiquities of Nepal', in Phyllis Mauch Messenger, ed., *The Ethics of Collecting Cultural Property* (New Mexico, 1989), 61–72 at 69.
[81] Daes, *Protection of the Heritage of Indigenous People*, paraphrased in Michael F. Brown, *Who Owns Native Culture?* (Harvard, 2003), 210.
[82] Leo Braudy, *The Hollywood Sign: Fantasy and Reality of an American Icon* (Yale, 2011), 6.
[83] Stanley J. Pac, in 'Dinosaur Park dedication', *Connecticut Woodlands* 43:1 (1978): 14.
[84] John Piper, 'Pleasing decay', in *Buildings and Prospects* (London: Architectural Press, 1948), 89–116 at 96.
[85] Cornelius Holtorf, 'The heritage of heritage', *Heritage & Society* 5 (2012): 153–74 at 157, 163; John Shannon, York Civic Trust, and Lois Lang-Sims, Canterbury, interviews 20 Sept., 26 Aug. 1978.

"I was born February 12, 1809...in Kentucky."

Figure 54 Display overwhelms: the Lincoln 'birthplace cabin' in its marble memorial carapace, Hodgensville, Kentucky, 1911

Figure 55 Display denatures: Plymouth Rock, Massachusetts

landscape with past and present visibly and functionally linked, pictorial signs along a wood-chipped trail show the historical views that had largely survived until the National Park Service obliterated them.[86]

Disputes over original intent and use, authenticity, and aesthetics variously affect how antiquity is displayed. London preservationists seek to keep views of St Paul's Cathedral from tower-block obstruction, as it briefly was when wartime bombs flattened all around it, the cathedral 'rising above the wasteland ... restored to its original dominance'. Developers counter that St Paul's was initially meant to be glimpsed intermittently from built-up streets; both camps claim fidelity to different pasts.[87] Against criticism that proposed council houses would destroy a beloved open view of Beverley Minster, local planners retorted that the Minster was not an isolated work of art but integral to the ongoing community that built and sustained it.[88] Love of ivy-clad decay lost out in 1910s and 1920s Britain to dire erosive faults of that 'rank and odious plant'. As romantic ruins were tidied into historical documents, 'the loss to the imagination' was held 'more than repaid by the gain to the intellect'. Defenders of the ivy on Harvard College buildings wished to retain the familiar 'Ivy League' look that unifies the Yard; ivy detractors successfully countered that the costly and damaging ivy only dated from the 1880s; the buildings should be bare, as initially seen.[89]

To show off the past is the obvious aim of identifying it. Labelling a relic affirms its historical significance; displaying it enhances its appeal. But display also segregates. Antiquities in museums are enshrined in glass cases, mounted on velvet, flattered by spotlighting. Relics *in situ* are shorn of unsightly surroundings. *Son-et-lumière* programmes that dramatize the past distance it from nearby excrescences and modern intrusions.

The past displayed is thus displaced. The signpost heralding something of age sets it apart from present-day surroundings. Like a painting mounted in a gallery, the marked antiquity is exhibited to attract attention. The very act of display, like that of protection, detaches surviving past from present-day setting. Ongoing change around them leaves protected relics less and less at home in their surroundings. While the lives of cherished remnants are lovingly extended, everything else is being replaced. The preserved antiquity is ultimately adrift in a modern sea, an isolated feature that stands out because it *alone* is old.

Much as eighteenth-century landscaped parks excluded the workaday world, historic-site managers segregate their patch of the past. Keeping the present out of sight enhances

---

[86] The NPS later planned to recreate 'the landscape which once existed on that momentous day' (Joyce Lee Malcolm, *The Scene of the Battle, 1775: Historic Grounds Report, Minute Man National Historical Park* (NPS, 1983), 6).

[87] Penelope Lively, *Ammonites and Leaping Fish: A Life in Time* (Penguin, 2013), 71–2. 'Protected' views of St Paul's did not save it from being dwarfed by Renzo Piano's seventy-two-storey 'Shard of Glass' (Ross Lydall, 'It's not quite what Wren had in mind 300 years ago', *Evening Standard*, 12 Jan. 2011: 3; Richard Morrison, 'The tower builders are fundamentally altering our skyline', *Times*, 5 Nov. 2010: 2:2).

[88] Ken Powell, *Beverley: Will Housing Sprawl Engulf Minster?* (SAVE Britain's Heritage, 1981).

[89] Thurley, *Men from the Ministry*, 131–43; David Harris Sacks, in *Harvard Magazine*, 84:6 (1982): 96; Allen Freeman, 'The greening of the yard', *Preservation Magazine* 60:1 (Jan.–Feb. 2008): 38–42.

the illusion of being in bygone times. With cement plants, housing tracts, farm machinery screened out, everything within Stones River Battlefield in Tennessee seems 1860s. Even where past and present physically intermingle, interpretation disjoins them. Two-name street signs in Boston and the City of London, the 'Olde Name' beneath the modern, divide attention *between* past and present, urging us to look now at the historical scene, now at the contemporary. Highlighting antique features – furniture, *objets d'art*, souvenirs, framed or otherwise set apart – proclaims their separate historicity. Supervision divorces safeguarded past from surrounding present.

Relics are most segregated where rare. 'We corrupted Old-Worlders are much more sloppy and imprecise with our ancient monuments; we have lived with them for centuries', observed an English historian in America.[90] Compared with the awesome respect accorded scant American antiquities, the English deal casually with their substantial legacy, the French and Italians surfeited by past remains more casually still, noted Ruskin.

Abroad, a building of the eighth or tenth century stands ruinous in the open street; the children play round it, peasants heap their corn in it, the buildings of yesterday nestle about it, and fit their new stones into its rents, and tremble in sympathy as it trembles. No one wonders at it, or thinks of it as separate, and of another time; we feel the ancient world to be ... one with the new.

But 'in England [we] have our new street, our new inn, our green shaven lawn, and our piece of ruin ... – a mere *specimen* of the middle ages put on a bit of velvet carpet', whereas 'on the Continent, the links are unbroken between the past and present'. Ruskin excoriated Walter Scott's hugger-mugger 'Gothic' Abbotsford 'the most incongruous and ugly pile ... ever designed'.[91]

A classical archaeologist commends unselfconscious alterations of antique remains, as both creative and conserving:

The ancient sarcophagus converted into a fountain is not the death of antiquity but its survival. The marble lion ridden to a shine by children, the ancient *putto* worn by the hands of pious women, who believe it to be an angel; the bench fitted together out of spolia for the Homeric *teichoskopia*, the old folks' look-out from the wall of a small Italian city; the Roman milestone in the open landscape used as a bulletin board for local football games and saints' days: these are all *life*.[92]

But past–present links survive unbroken only so long as the past goes unremarked. Imagine a visit to that French ruin by Ruskin's readers. *They* would wonder at it, think it of another time, sketch and photograph it. Villagers would provide lodgings, sell souvenirs, become picturesque likenesses on film. Publicity would swell tourism and require fencing the ruin, stationing guards, charging admission to defray costs. Admiration inevitably estranges antiquity.

---

[90] Reyner Banham, 'Preservation adobe', *New Society*, 2 Apr. 1981: 24.
[91] John Ruskin, *Modern Painters* (1843–60; New York, 1886), pt. 5, ch. 1, sects. 3 and 5, 4: 3–4; pt. 5, ch. 16, sect. 33, 3: 265.
[92] Arnold Esch, 'On the reuse of antiquity', in Brilliant and Kinney, eds., *Reuse Value*, 13–19 at 19.

We think, talk, and act towards the past as a realm of concern essentially apart. Consciousness distances it, underscoring that then is not now. Nations defend or regain relics as icons of present identity, but retrieval and protection then enshrine those relics in a cocoon. Rescuing old buildings from the bulldozer removes them from unremarked present into ostentatious antiquity. So too with self-conscious recall. The child who asks grandmother about olden times may identify with her when she was young, but in so doing makes her now a quaint denizen of a remote time. Labelling family photos refreshes memory but also estranges them by exhibiting their subjects' irretrievable pastness – a pastness reinforced by antiquated clothing and hairstyles, picture frames and sepia prints. Once an artefact, an idea, a memory is recognized and valued as historic, it is severed from the present. The past becomes 'a work of art, free from irrelevancies and loose ends', in Max Beerbohm's words. 'The dullards have all disappeared'.[93]

Manipulation makes the past both less and more like the present: less because set apart; more because marked with our own stamp. Even if we aim to preserve things just as they were or as found, protective and restorative devices mantle them in present trappings.

Removal

Saving or celebrating the past often involves moving relics away from – or back to – sites of origin or discovery. Antiquities as small as a nail or as large as a temple are shifted a few inches or halfway round the world, transported entire or reassembled, broken into segments or reunited from dispersed fragments. So many statues did ancient Romans import that Pliny termed them as numerous as living citizens. Thanks to later imperial sculptors, marble Romans were said to outnumber those of flesh and blood by ten to one.[94]

Many artefacts – books, paintings, bronzes, medals – are created to be portable; others, whose meaning and value derive from and enliven their surroundings, are moved at contextual and ambient loss. Some are removed because everything cognate around them has changed; others, previously uprooted by war, theft, or accident, may go back, often only approximately, to former locales. Should the Elgin Marbles be repatriated, they would not be reattached to the Parthenon but go to the nearby museum. Indeed, the British Museum argues that the present division of the Parthenon frieze – part in Athens, viewable in national context, part in London, viewable in global context, bits in the Louvre and the Vatican – is appropriate in a world of iconoclastic insecurity.[95] Ever more of the world's increasingly portable relics of antiquity are no longer where originally made or found, but on show – or in storage – in museums and private collections.

Dispersed antiquities may be brought together in the mind's eye. Paintings depict far-flung classical monuments in close proximity, often embellished with a fanciful provenance. One artist sets the *Laocoön* before a broken wall to suggest the moment it was unearthed, another amid antique temples by the shores of Troy. The idealized ancient city

[93] Max Beerbohm, *Lytton Strachey* (Knopf, 1943), 17–18.
[94] Pirro Ligorio (late sixteenth century) in Barkan, *Unearthing the Past*, 63.
[95] Neil MacGregor cited in Sharon Waxman, *Loot: The Battle over the Stolen Treasures of the World* (Holt, 2008), 269.

Figure 56 Antiquity rearranged: Pompeo Batoni, *Thomas Dundas*, on the Grand Tour, 1764

in Jean Lemaire's *Roman Senators Going to the Forum* (1645–55) is a Baroque patchwork of well-known ruins – the triumphal arch at Orange, Verona's Porta dei Borsari, the Pantheon portico, the Septizoneum, the Colosseum. A sixteenth-century vestige and a fictitiously ruined Mannerist statue stand alongside the authentic Constantinian Arco di Gione in Jan Baptist Weenix's *Roman Campagna* (c. 1650–5).[96]

Fondness for ruins led eighteenth-century painters to group ancient monuments as decorative accessories. Pompeo Batoni portrayed British Grand Tourists among rearranged classical sculptures and Roman ruins (Fig. 56); a French ambassador commissioned Giovanni Panini's imaginary picture gallery stocked with ancient Rome's scenic treasures.[97] Like family portraits and mantels full of snapshots that gather one's friends together, such pictures let the antiquity lover gaze on all his favourites at once. Modern collages depict historic houses of many epochs cheek by jowl, door-to-door on the same street.

[96] Francis Haskell and Nicholas Penny, *Taste and the Antique* (Yale, 1981), 21; *Gods & Heroes: Baroque Images of Antiquity* (NY: Wildenstein Gallery, 1968), Catalogue nos. 21, 57, plates 28, 51. The statue in Weenix's painting is Giambologna's *Rape of the Sabines* (1583).

[97] Edgar Peters Bowron, 'British patrons and the Grand Tour', in E. P. Bowron and Peter Bjorn Kerber, eds., *Pompeo Batoni* (Yale, 2007), 37–87; Haskell and Penny, *Taste and the Antique*, 84 and fig. 45.

Figure 57 Antiquity dismembered: bisected copy of Trajan's Column, Cast Court

Antiquities are often made adjacent for tourists. Most 'historic' American villages include imported structures: Portsmouth's Strawbery Banke from remote imperilled locales, Mystic Seaport from all over New England. Old Sturbridge Village dates only from 1929, when several dozen old structures were brought together there.[98] Singleton Village in Sussex hosts fourteenth- to nineteenth-century buildings from south-east England. On their new sites these buildings often bespeak pedagogic purpose. To underscore the rise from slavery to freedom and black entrepreneurship, Henry Ford's Greenfield Village clustered together a slave-overseer's log cabin, Abraham Lincoln's Logan County Courthouse, and black educator George Washington Carver's 'Memorial Cabin'.[99]

Replicas of relics are commonly combined. The Victoria and Albert Museum's Cast Court juxtaposes full-scale classical and Gothic copies, with Trajan's Column bisected for easier viewing (Fig. 57). Inserted in the Portico della Gloria from Santiago de Compostela is a copy of the famed bronze doors at San Zeno, Verona, the whole outré twelfth-century

[98] Charles B. Hosmer, Jr., *Preservation Comes of Age* (Virginia, 1981), 1: 108–21, 332–40; Laura E. Abing, 'Old Sturbridge Village' (Ph.D. dissertation, Marquette University, 1997).

[99] Charles Phillips, 'Greenfield's changing past', *History News* 37:11 (1982): 11. See Roger Butterfield, 'Henry Ford, the Wayside Inn, and the problem of "History is bunk"', 53–66; Hosmer, *Preservation Comes of Age*, 75–97, 987–92; Jessica Swigger, '"History is Bunk": Historical Memories at Henry Ford's Greenfield Village' (Ph.D. dissertation, University of Texas, 2008).

Figure 58 National symbols of the Irish Celtic Revival: Pat McAuliffe, Central Hotel facade
Listowel, County Kerry, Eire

Romanesque medley touted as 'a stupendous High Victorian experience'.[100] At Klagenfurt, Austria's, 'Minimundus', 1/25th-scale models of the Tower of London and the Arc
de Triomphe perch bizarrely on opposite sides of Berlin's Brandenburg Gate.[101]
Surrogate-past medleys from Las Vegas to Dubai entice visitors. and purchasers. 'Now
you can own history', a realtor touts houses evoking long-gone towns of the Fertile
Crescent, the cradle of civilization. 'Discover the past and experience . . . a collection of
ancient lost cities. All in one place.'[102] Full-scale replicas of China's famed ancient

[100] Malcolm Baker, *The Cast Courts, Victoria and Albert Museum* (London, 1982); Paul Williamson,
      European Sculpture at the Victoria and Albert Museum (V&A Publications, 1996), 182–5.
[101] Hermann Theodor Schneider, ed., *Minimundus: die kleine Welt am Wörthersee* (1976; Klagenfurt, 1997);
      Daniel Michaels, 'It's a small world, after all; some want it even smaller', *Wall Street Journal*, 26 Sept. 2003.
[102] Nakheel ad, *Times*, 9 Nov. 2004. See Eudore Chand, 'Ancient lost cities revealed by Nakheel at Jebel Ali
      site', *ArabianBusiness.com*, 9 Oct. 2004.

buildings rise side by side in Hengdian World Studios, the world's largest movie lot. Twelve million Chinese came in 2012 to view their country's architectural wonders. Many cities boast new Ming-Qing 'old towns'.[103]

Removal becomes vital to historical salvage. The modern technology that menaces antiquities also moves them out of harm's way. Cut and lifted from Philae in the Nile, the Abu Simbel temples were spared submergence behind the Aswan High Dam. They are more impressive on Agilka's bare rock than in their former palm-tree setting.[104]

Less congruous is John Rennie's 1831 London Bridge, re-erected in the Arizona desert in 1971 alongside lamps cast from Napoleon's cannon and an imitation City of London pub. The sense of context, even of age, is gone, London's sooty patina peeled off the stone arches in the dry desert air. But as a 'Tudor' theme-park centrepiece, the Bridge is Arizona's biggest tourist draw after the Grand Canyon. The fortieth anniversary rededication in 2011 featured plastic heads of four miscreants, from Wat Tyler to Guy Fawkes, who'd fallen foul of the crown – a 'rich European history', said the event's organizer. 'There was struggle and wars and blood associated with it and understanding all that makes you appreciate this bridge even more. It's not just a way to get across the water', diverted from the Colorado River to flow under it. Lake Havasu City is obviously 'the place to be', said Governor Jan Brewer, 'if you want to get A Head in Arizona'.[105]

For many relics, export is the only alternative to terminal decay or demolition. Most transplanted furnishings and period rooms would otherwise have been junked. From some 1,500 lost English houses, John Harris suggests 'at least 4,000 chimneypieces have gone travelling', largely overseas, since 1900. More recently, the stained-glass ceiling of Fulham Free Library, the copper-leaded portals of the Bank of India, the brass doors of London's Café Royal went to American eateries whose patrons hungered for an Olde English ambience. Liverpool Stock Exchange fittings decorate a Beverly Hills restaurant; bits of Morecambe pier adorn a Las Vegas casino; a Middlesbrough convent became a Kansas City cafe.[106]

Also exported are oak beams from fifteenth-century rural structures – historically documented, pest-free, and guaranteed for five more centuries. 'Salvaging those buildings which are just not being cared for', claimed the agent, 'we are preserving the[m] for *mankind* ... rather than letting them deteriorate and vanish'. Such is American appetite for old oak that 'you would have to tear down all of Tudor and Stuart England to meet the demand'. 'Forever England' was a Japanese endeavour to revive Elizabethan carpentry skills with oak imported from Herefordshire. French chateaux otherwise doomed are

[103] Ian Johnson, 'Studio city', *New Yorker*, 22 Apr. 2013, 48–55 at 49; Robert J. Shepherd and Larry Yu, *Heritage Management, Tourism, and Governance in China* (Springer, 2013), 25.

[104] Lennart Berg, 'The salvage of the Abu Simbel temples', *Monumentum* 17 (1978): 25–54; Jill Kamil, *Aswan and Abu Simbel* (Cairo: American University, 1993), 104–33.

[105] E. R. Chamberlin, *Preserving the Past* (Dent, 1979), 127–31; Muriel Bowen, 'Vanishing soot upsets London Bridge buyers', *Sunday Times*, 22 Oct. 1972: 2; Bobbi Holmes, 'Lake Havasu City history', *Havasu Magazine*, 4 Dec. 2009; Marc Lacey, 'A red-letter day, and a party to match', *NYT*, 12 Oct. 2011; Jan Brewer, remarks, 14 Oct. 2011, *azgovernor.gov/dms/upload/GS_101411*. See Travis Elborough, *London Bridge in America* (Jonathan Cape, 2013).

[106] Harris, *Moving Rooms*, 2–5, 94–5, 111–12; 'Where our heritage goes', *Sunday Times*, 20 Oct. 1980: 32; Ronald Faux, 'Transatlantic Steptoe turns to home market', *Times*, 21 Feb. 1983: 3.

dismantled and shipped abroad, some restored integrally, others reshuffled like Lego bricks as trophy fittings for new transatlantic chateaux.[107]

Like sacred and secular eminences whose heads and hearts, toes and fingers, brains and prepuces are separately treasured, historic structures are cut up into keepsakes. After the US Army crossed the Rhine in 1945, chips from piers of Remagen Bridge became paperweight mementoes. Some fragments attest liberation from a dread past. Following the 1789 storming of the Bastille, miniaturized copies along with actual fortress bricks helped defang that prison's noxious memories. Souvenir stone fragments and replicas divested the Berlin Wall of its menacing Cold War aura and invested it with the magic of reunification.[108] New relics are multiplied for devotees; a thousand cross-shaped pieces, authenticated by four bishops, were cut from the carpet on which Pope John Paul II held mass in Cardiff in 1982.

Many benefits accrue from moving remnants. Much otherwise lost is saved, often made more accessible and meaningful. Transplanted relics lend new homes talismanic character. The Washington Monument gains vicarious global antiquity from donated memorials, including a bust from the Temple of Augustus in Egypt, a stone from a Swiss chapel honouring William Tell, and one from a 'Temple of Aesculapius' in Paros.[109] Fragments from ancient structures the world over lend the Chicago Tribune Building a generic historical aura. As long as personal attachments are not jeopardized, people like the tangible past thus manipulated. It is easier to view most relics in museums and public arenas than *in situ*.

Yet such removals exact tolls. Context and provenance are lost: most museumized period rooms, lacking their ceilings, shorn of intrinsic surroundings and social functions, barred to movement, and subservient to paintings and furnishings, are less rooms than treasure caskets.[110] Transport hazards relics. Financial and site constraints deplete or damage antiquities during rebuilding. Aesthetic integrity is a frequent victim. Antiquities are dismembered for ease of transport or, like the huge Tiepolo *Madonna* taken to France by Napoleon, sawn apart to suit later taste. Prudery pruned a Poussin *Venus*, her indelicate legs cut off by a purchaser; avarice dismembered Toulouse-Lautrec canvases. Disjoined pieces are widely scattered: far-flung fragments of a Sienese altarpiece are now to be found in Berlin, Dublin, Paris, Glasgow, Williamstown, Massachusetts, and Toledo, Ohio.[111] The Boston

---

[107] John Durtnell quoted in Ian Ball, 'Barns take US by storm', *Telegraph Magazine*, 17 May 1980: 51, 48; American architect quoted in Ian Ball, 'US imports old British farmhouses', *Telegraph*, 2 Aug. 1979: 19; Christine Webb, 'A yen for ye olde English joiste', *Times*, 10 Mar 1993: 39; Max Rosenberg, '19 chateau-style mansions that will make you feel like you live in France', *Business Insider*, 18 Feb. 2013.

[108] Hans-Jürgen Lüsebrink and Rolf Reichardt, *The Bastille* (1990; Duke, 1997); Polly Feversham and Leo Schmidt, *The Berlin Wall Today* (Berlin: Bauwesen, 1999).

[109] Frederick L. Harvey, *History of the Washington National Monument*, 57 Cong. 2 Sess., Sen. Doc. 224 (Washington, DC, 1903). 48; George J. Olszewski, *History of the Washington Monument* (Washington, DC: NPS, 1971), 12–13.

[110] Harris, *Moving Rooms*, 3–7.

[111] On Tiepolo, Robert Adams, *The Lost Museum: Glimpses of Vanished Originals* (Viking, 1980), 12, 142–5, and Franco Renzo Pesenti, 'Italian painting', 18–51 at 25, 48–51; on Nicolas Poussin, Jacques Thuillier, 'French painting', 88–115 at 90–1, both in UNESCO, *Illustrated Inventory of Famous Dismembered Works of Art* (Paris, 1974).

Museum of Fine Arts' return of the looted 1,800-year-old *Weary Herakles* bust, to be rejoined with the statue's legs and torso in Antalya, Turkey, enabled a rare reunification.[112]

Not every dispersal is contemptible; nor do all dismembered relics merit reunification. Being moved, even split up, may infuse relics with new life, adding decor or meaning, as with medieval dispersal of Christian relics, notably body parts.[113] Restoring treasures to Russian churches may please priests, but the aesthetic loss is parlous; back where it came from in the Kremlin Cathedral of the Annunciation, an exquisite painting of Theophanes the Greek is barely discernible even through binoculars.[114] A niche showing books and other objects in *trompe l'œil*, cut from a panel of Barthélemy d'Eyck's *Aix Annunciation* (1441–5) in the eighteenth century, gained fame as an early French still life, its very mutilation lending it scholarly and aesthetic repute. It is often too late to rejoin what was sundered, subsequent mishaps to segments precluding re-amalgamation. The clumsily restored fragment of Poussin's *Venus and the Liberal Arts* (c. 1627–31) at Dulwich would mar rather than enhance the main canvas in the Louvre, which is missing other important pieces as well.[115]

Fragmentation diminishes collections meant to be integral; dispersing an artist's oeuvre can reduce the worth of the whole. Divided between two inheritors, half of the Flemish painter Justus of Ghent's twenty-eight portraits of *Famous Men* are in Urbino, the rest in the Louvre.[116] So with the dispersal of furnishings designed for a particular home. 'Separated from each other, out of context, they lose two-thirds of their meaning', a critic scored the sale of baroque furniture commissioned for St Giles House, Dorset. Family portraits meaningful when viewed together on their own walls lose significance when disassembled: 'considered on its own merits, each piece becomes [a] boring conventional portrait'. Antiquities long gathered together accrue historicity as an ensemble. The 1980 break-up of the Castle Ashby Greek vases collected in the 1820s was held to blot out 'part of the collective memory of a nation': the nation referred to was not Greece but Britain, the memory not of the vases themselves but of the passion for collecting them.[117]

A grievous effect of dispersing antiquities is loss of environmental context. The removal of relics whose lineaments are indissolubly of their place annuls their testamentary worth and forfeits ties with place. The true merit of many relics, man-made and natural alike, inheres in their locale; the landmark must stay put if it is to mark the land. 'It's a dreadful thing to do', says Lucy Boston's *Green Knowe* child when the local Standing Stones are carted off to a museum. 'They were in their own place. Out of it they will be dead.'[118] Those who move antiquities may try to retain context by lifting the

---

[112] Alexander Christie-Muller, 'Victory in campaign to seize back priceless artefacts lost to the world', *Times*, 22 July 2011: 29.

[113] Caroline Walker Bynum, *The Resurrection of the Body in Western Christianity* (Columbia, 2005), 104–8.

[114] Irina Danilova, 'Russian painting', in UNESCO, *Illustrated Inventory*, 175–87 at 178.

[115] Thuillier, 'French painting', 90–3, 98–103; Jacques Lavalleye, 'Flemish painting', in UNESCO, *Illustrated Inventory*, 52–87 at 55.

[116] Lavalleye, 'Flemish painting', in UNESCO, *Illustrated Inventory*, 52, 62–3.

[117] *St Giles House, Dorset, Sale: Highly Important English Furniture and Sculpture*, Christie's sale catalogue, London: 26 June 1980; Souren Melikian, 'Collection lost forever', *IHT*, 5–6 July 1980: 8.

[118] Lucy Boston, *The Stones of Green Knowe* (Penguin, 1979), 120.

whole locale, as Henry Ford did at Greenfield Village with Thomas Edison's famous laboratory:

Before he moved the [Menlo Park] laboratory here, he went out to New Jersey – the land where the building was originally – and dug up tons of dirt, just tons of it. Then he had it all carted out here and dumped it all over this site before they stuck the building down on top of it. That was his idea of complete restoration. This place had been built on New Jersey soil, so it should be restored on New Jersey soil. Stuff like that drove the experts crazy.[119]

Indeed, Ford moved not only Edison's lab site but old Edison himself, brought to Greenfield on the fiftieth anniversary to play himself turning on the first electric bulb.[120]

Moving remnants and reminders can vitally affect national and cultural identity. Removal may desecrate if a sacred symbol is at stake. When Phineas T. Barnum bid to buy Shakespeare's birthplace, *The Times* envisaged his 'trundling it about on wheels like a caravan of wild beasts, giants, or dwarfs'.[121] Ripping the Assyrian statues of winged beasts from Nimrod's palace 'seemed almost sacrilege' to A. H. Layard, the archaeologist–diplomat responsible. 'They were better suited to the desolation around them; for they had guarded the palace in its glory, and it was for them to watch over it in its ruin.'[122] Lord Elgin's dismemberment of the Parthenon may have spared the frieze some further mishaps but impoverished the temple and deprived the Greek nation of its supreme emblem of identity – although the Parthenon Marbles in fact became such only after being taken away.[123] In like fashion, the *Mona Lisa* become a famed iconic treasure only after its 1911 theft, when thousands who had never visited the Louvre or seen the painting thronged to view the empty space where it had hung.[124]

Whatever the motive for moving relics, removal accentuates their difference from the surrounding or neighbouring present. This reinforces the view of the past as a foreign precinct if not a foreign country. Relics in museums are remoulded solely for display; appreciative regard distinguishes the functionally useless but attractive past from the workaday present. 'On one side plastic, formica, gadgets, nothingness; on the other beauty and culture, mummified.'[125] With 'lustre cream pitchers that held no cream, the Dutch oven that held no bread, chairs with tapes across where no one could sit, pineapple-post beds where no one slept, and the rooms that no one lived in', museums devitalize the past. Historic house interiors lose the life and warmth of occupancy.[126]

[119] Interpreter in Phillips, 'Greenfield's changing past', 10.

[120] William S. Pretzer, 'Introduction', in *Working at Inventing: Thomas A. Edison and the Menlo Park Experience* (1989; Johns Hopkins, 2002), 25; Kerstin Barndt, 'Fordist nostalgia', *Rethinking History*, special issue, Reenactment, 11:3 (2007): 379–410 at 380.

[121] 21 July 1847, quoted in Kim C. Sturgess, *Shakespeare and the American Nation* (Cambridge, 2004), 185. See Julia Thomas, *Shakespeare's Shrine: The Bard's Birthplace and the Invention of Stratford-upon-Avon* (PennPress, 2012), 53–6, 148.

[122] A. H. Layard, *Nineveh and Babylon* (London, 1853), 67. See Mogens T. Larsen, *The Conquest of Assyria* (Routledge, 1996), 88–98.

[123] Yannis Hamilakis, *The Nation and Its Ruins* (Oxford, 2007).

[124] Darian Leader, *Stealing the Mona Lisa* (Faber, 2002).

[125] Bernard Marrey, *Les Grands Magasins des origines à 1939* (Paris, 1979), 246.

[126] Sally Benson, 'Spirit of '76', *New Yorker*, 25 Dec. 1954: 20–5 at 24.

Sheer classification distances and diminishes the past, as with old documents being sorted for archival storage: 'The piles of paper dwindled slowly into their classes, losing personality as they gained the pale immortality of a Special Collection.'[127]

Many antiquities are much more accessible in a gallery or museum, to be sure, than in initial cathedral or remote jungle settings. But if bringing relics within walls makes them easier to see it also abridges temporal awareness. In an antique building or landscape one moves in time among survivals; in a museum they are shorn of duration, 'and how singularly lifeless the loveliest things appear'.[128] The most artful placement, the most breathtaking proximity, cannot overcome that detachment.

Yet removal, often mandated by safety or conservation, may more than compensate on aesthetic grounds as well. Works of art can benefit by being freed from contexts of time and place, as many creators intended and collectors constantly contend. 'Our age', noted Proust a century ago, 'is infected with a mania for showing things only in the environment that properly belongs to them, thereby suppressing the essential thing, the act of mind which isolated them from that environment' in the first place. A masterpiece contemplated 'in the midst of furniture, ornaments, hangings of the same period, stale settings ... does not give us the exhilarating delight that we can expect from it only in a public gallery', whose neutral and uncluttered background accords far better with 'those innermost spaces into which the artist withdrew to create it'.[129] Whatever the merits of these rival views, wholesale migrations of peoples, climates, and institutions involve migration of legacies as well, revaluing content and context.

Copying and replicating

Pasts that fascinate are much copied. Every enterprise and all the arts recycle bygone forms and features. Now inspired emulation, now faithful imitation, now kitsch or fake, recycling serves three distinct purposes. Duplicates and copies replicate existing or lost originals; forgeries masquerade as originals; facsimiles reproduce prototypes in other locales. But practice smudges these distinctions. Like 'home-cooked' pub food, traditionally crafted facsimiles pass muster. Nowell's modern 'Victorian' furnishings can't be told from the originals because 'we make them one at a time by hand, exactly the way the originals were made, and ... of exactly the same materials. And we make them well enough to hang right next to period originals without looking out of place.'[130]

Antiquity scarcely distinguished copying from creative innovation: all art and architecture were copied from nature or the human form. Late Roman and Hellenistic copies were held masterpieces; medieval artists and craftsmen copied prototypes with no concern for being original. Humanist historical awareness made copying more self-conscious but no less praiseworthy. Renaissance architects and sculptors copied works of antiquity (or their Hellenistic copies); artists copied one another. In non-Western

---

[127] Chamberlin, *Preserving the Past*, 107.
[128] John Betjeman, 'Antiquarian prejudice' (1937), in *First and Last Loves* (London, 1960), 54–72 at 69.
[129] Marcel Proust, *Remembrance of Things Past* (1913–27; Penguin, 1983), 1: 693–4.
[130] *Preservation News* 20:4 (1980): 9.

cultures the distinction is often erased entirely. For many Chinese engravings no original exists. None of the famed calligrapher Wang Xizhi's work survives, and objects revered as his for seventeen centuries are copies of copies and valued as such .[131] For Zuni Indians, as for many tribal peoples, 'there is no such thing as a "replica" or "model"'; every *Ahayu:da* copy is a genuine sacred original.[132] There are several slightly different copies of the Vietnamese painter Nguyen Tu Nghiem's *New Year's Eve on Ho Guom Lakeshore* (1957); 'perhaps they are all forgeries, or perhaps they can all be considered originals'.[133] Told that the USS *Constellation* in Baltimore, supposedly the oldest (1797) frigate afloat, was in fact an 1850s replica, a visitor was unfazed: 'So it wasn't the original one, so what? How many things in life are original anyway?'[134]

Past connoisseurs knew famed art largely through copies. Most antiquities, privately held or difficult of access, were experienced mainly through reproductions and descriptions. Replicas of the Church of the Holy Sepulchre were in high demand during the Crusades.[135] Only recently have public museums and mass travel enabled direct familiarity with originals. Plaster casts of antique sculptures vied in popularity with bronze, ceramic, and lead copies. Woburn Abbey housed sixteen marble copies of the first century AD *Medici Vase*, also found in cast iron at Alton Towers. Immortalized in Byron's *Childe Harolde's Pilgrimage* (1812/18), the *Dying Gladiator* (230–220 BC) figured in stone at Rousham, in marble at Wilton, in bronze at Syon. The *Apollo Belvedere* in affordable Parian ware (unglazed porcelain) (Fig. 60) adorned thousands of Victorian homes.[136]

Copies were miniaturized for mass markets from the mid-eighteenth century – small Italian bronzes of antique sculptures, dwarf statues in Tuscan alabaster, Staffordshire earthenware figurines. Architectural copies were often three-fifths the originals, large enough to feel like real buildings, small enough to be quaint. Period revival and retro structures can seem miniature even when full-scale. In Norman Shaw's 'seventeenth-century' Bedford Park Village (1875–), W. B. Yeats felt 'we were living among toys', much as today's visitor feels large and gawky amid small things of the past's smaller folk.[137] A three-quarter-size replica of William Lethaby's 1902 thatched All Saints Church in Brockhampton, England, on the twenty-first floor of a tower block in Osaka, Japan, caters Western-style weddings (honeymoon suites on the floor above).[138] Some replicas are

---

[131] Craig Clunas, *Art in China*, 2nd edn (Oxford, 2009), 137–40. See Shepherd and Yu, *Heritage Management ... in China*, 2, 36, 40–1.

[132] Gwyneira Isaac, 'Whose idea was this? Museums, replicas and the reproduction of knowledge', *Current Anthropology* 52 (2011): 211–33 at 219.

[133] Seth Mydans, 'A legacy of war: fake art in Vietnam', *NYT*, 31 July 2009.

[134] Quoted in Ada Louise Huxtable, *The Unreal America: Architecture and Illusion* (New York: New Press, 1997), 182–3.

[135] Annabel Jane Wharton, *Selling Jerusalem: Relics, Replicas, Theme Parks* (Chicago, 2006), 50.

[136] Haskell and Penny, *Taste and the Antique*, 16, 35–9, 87–93, 136–40, 148–51, 184–7, 252–5, 316; Francis Haskell and Nicholas Penny, *The Most Beautiful Statues* (Oxford: Ashmolean Museum, 1981), xii; Dennis Barker, *Parian Ware* (Aylesbury: Shire, 1998); Hillel Schwartz, *The Culture of the Copy* (New York: Zone, 1996), 211–320.

[137] William Butler Yeats, *Reveries over Childhood and Youth* (Macmillan, 1916), 47. See Nicholas Taylor, *The Village in the City* (London: Temple Smith, 1973), 60.

[138] David Wilkes, 'Room with a pew: businessman builds replica of Herefordshire church', *MailOnline*, 24 Oct. 2009.

Figure 59 Antiquity multiplied and miniaturized: Classical replicas,
Robert Adam entrance hall, Syon House, Middlesex

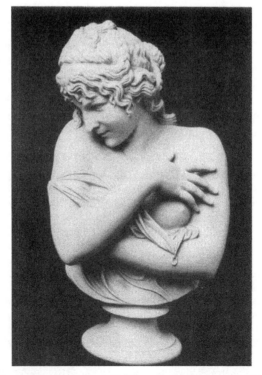

Figure 60 *Venus*, after Clodion, in Parian ware, *c.* 1862

Figure 61 St Basil's Cathedral, Thorpe Park, Surrey

doll's-house size. At Thorpe Park near London (Fig. 61), the Uffington White Horse in concrete was one-fifth size, the Taj Mahal, the Temple of Artemis, the Great Pyramid, Bodiam Castle a few feet high, among life-size flowers that made them still more toy-like.

Smaller miniatures become tourist souvenirs. Anne Hathaway's cottage (Fig. 63) and snow-stormed Eiffel Towers adorn millions of mantels and countless key rings. 'Lilliput Lane' and 'Lilliput Land' vivify myriad antiques collectors' clubs.[139] 'Limited-edition' replicas vaunt the trivial precision mocked in Bruce McCall's 'miniature pewterine reproductions, authenticated by the World Court at The Hague, of the front-door letter slots of Hollywood's 36 most beloved character actors and actresses'.[140] Paper and cardboard replicas of mansions, luxury handbags, and banknotes accompany deceased Chinese. The arrest of a New York City funeral supplier for selling 'fakes' outraged – and amused – the Chinese community long at home with copies in all walks of life.[141]

Copied foreign pasts today pervade urban China. Hundreds of new suburbs mimic Western period styles. Millions inhabit locales patterned wholesale on Olde Worlde exemplars – Shenyang's New Amsterdam, Weimar Villas in Anking, Champs Elysée

---

[139] 'Walk down Lilliput Lane' (1999), in Susan M. Pearce and Paul Martin, eds., *The Collector's Voice*, vol. 4: *Contemporary Voices* (Ashgate, 2002), 27–9.

[140] Bruce McCall, 'Rolled in rare Bohemian onyx, then vulcanized by hand', *New Yorker*, 21 Dec. 1981: 39.

[141] Jeffery E. Singer and Corey Kilgannon, 'Yes, officer, they're fakes – but that is what they're supposed to be', *IHT*, 26 Aug. 2011: 18.

Square in Hangzhou's 'Oriental Paris' (with a three-quarter replica Eiffel Tower), Shanghai's 'Dream of England, Live in Thames Town'. Omitting tangled narrow squalid streets to ensure good *feng shui*, these historical pastiches exaggerate iconic details like towers and clocks.

Whereas earlier Maoists showcased Soviet modernism, today's Western models are openly reactionary. Contrary to modernization elsewhere, antiquarian quaintness is de rigueur. Simulacra of monumental luxury that once spelled civilization now spell success for parvenu moguls. Aping the foreign past affirms present superiority. And Chinese policy transcends architectural mimicry, immersing these enclaves in imported street names, statues, foodstuffs and festivals. Only this foreign past is chic; the native past still calls to mind China's poverty and backwardness.[142]

In the West, the word 'copy' first got a bad name when Romantic poets began to contrast it with originality as the sine qua non of creative genius. But in visual arts copying long remained de rigueur, plaster casts of antiquities canonical. Painters reproduced and reinterpreted precursors. Copies of classical and Gothic prototypes featured architectural revivals that dominated the built environment of the Western world until Modernists scrapped the past.

Antiquities were also copied against risks of erosion, pollution, and theft. A facsimile of Michelangelo's *David* (moved into the Accademia in 1873) has stood outside Florence's Palazzo Vecchio since 1910; in November 2010 a fibreglass replica was briefly hoisted onto the cathedral roof.[143] Fibreglass copies replace Venice's (originally Constantinople's) Byzantine bronze horses in Piazza San Marco. Replicas replace parts of five Gothic abbeys shipped from France in the 1930s to become New York's Cloisters. During the summer of 2004 a lone iconoclast wielding only a wrench and a screwdriver wreaked havoc in Venice with impunity; to safeguard the city's heritage would require putting the whole of it behind glass or replacing every piece of marble, stone, and plaster with a copy.[144]

Viewers often fail to realize, or soon forget, that they are seeing facsimiles rather than original relics. Natives who actually saw old buildings torn down in Sudbury, Suffolk, years later insisted the rebuilt facades were the originals.[145] So quickly and comprehensively was Warsaw's war-destroyed 'medieval' core restored that within a decade, wrote its restorer, 'even the elders do not realize in their everyday life that this town, which appears old, is to a great extent new' (Figs. 5 and 6). Knowing its true history can disconcert. 'The house I was born in was destroyed violently thirty-six years ago – but I can go into the bedroom I had as a boy, look out of the exact same window at the exact same house across the courtyard', avers an architect. 'There's even a lamp bracket with a curious twist in it hanging in the same place. . . . Is it "real" or isn't it?'[146]

[142] Bianca Bosker, *Original Copies: Architectural Mimicry in Contemporary China* (Hawai'i, 2013).

[143] Rossella Lorenzi, 'Michelangelo's David as it was meant to be seen', *Discovery News*, 12 Nov. 2010.

[144] Charles Freeman, *The Horses of St Marks* (Little Brown, 2004); Elisabetta Povoledo, 'Venice shaken by vandalism spree', *IHT*, 3 July 2004.

[145] John Popham, Suffolk Preservation Society, interview, 15 June 1978.

[146] Stanislaw Lorentz, 'Reconstruction of the old town centers of Poland', in *Historic Preservation Today* (1966), 43–72 at 52; Piotr Ziolkowski quoted in Chamberlin, *Preserving the Past*, 8–9. See Tung, *Preserving the World's Great Cities*, 4, 73–83.

Fake replicas masquerade as lost or undiscovered originals. Scarce antiquities have long made forgery a major enterprise. During the 1910s and 1920s André Mailfert's Paris workshop produced 50,000 pieces of 'antique' furniture and thousands of fake paintings. Insatiable demand gave rise to 'Valamasters' – photographs of Old Master paintings with brushstrokes hand-applied in a transparent glaze.[147] Forgeries amplify as well as debase valued legacies. Fakes of lost originals seem to restore to life what once existed; fakes of imaginary originals add to an artist's supposed oeuvre or augment an epoch's output. In line with the adage that a forgery can be distinguished from an original because it looks more genuine, fakes reflect credit on their exemplars. Notwithstanding their spurious antiquity, Han van Meegeren's forgeries of Vermeer now fetch sums far beyond what Vermeer himself ever received, and Tom Keating's forged Constables are now themselves faked as Keating originals.[148] Finding that Norman Rockwell's famed *Breaking Home Ties* (1954) was a copy faked by its owner raised the original's auction sale to a Rockwell record. 'Fakes are arguably the most authentic' modern masterpieces, declares conceptual artist Jonathon Keats, instancing Lothar Malskat's famed 'medieval' church murals in Schleswig and Lübeck; and 'forgers are the foremost artists of our age'.[149]

Like filmmakers who claim to bring true history to life, many copyists have utter faith in their empathetic expertise. No deceptive intent taints Britain's Palladian villas or America's Independence Hall replicas. Yet replicas however faithful inevitably diverge from prototypes. Unlike the originals, they are self-consciously past, and that intention cannot help but show. And temporal distance brings other telltale differences.

Nashville's 1920s reinforced-concrete Parthenon is a case in point (Fig. 62). Unlike Phidias' decayed and vandalized ruin in Athens, the model is complete. Plaster casts of the Elgin Marbles, supplemented by sculptures of live models posing as described in Pausanias' *Periegesis* (second century AD), supply the east pediment's missing figures. So 'authentic' was the replica, builders boasted, that to restore the original Greeks would have to come to Nashville. Together with the 1855 Greek Revival state capitol, the Parthenon replica made Nashville the proud 'Athens of the South'. But verisimilitude ended at the portico. Nashville's Parthenon dispensed with the steep rise up to the Acropolis because 'the effort needed to climb the hill might discourage visitors'. More like Athens is the unfinished Cockerell–Playfair 1820s Parthenon replica on Calton Hill, Edinburgh (Fig. 82).[150]

[147] André Mailfert, *Au Pays des antiquaires: confidences d'un 'maquilleur' professionnel* (Paris: Flammarion, 1935), 23, 145; Leo Vala, interview, 13 Jan. 1984.
[148] Adolf Rieth, *Archaeological Fakes* (London: Barrie & Jenkins, 1970), 7; Mark Sagoff, 'The aesthetic status of forgeries' (1976), in Denis Dutton, ed., *The Forger's Art* (California, 1983), 131–52; Jonathan Lopez, *The Man Who Made Vermeers* (Harcourt, 2008); Edward Dolnick, *The Forger's Spell* (HarperCollins, 2008); Scott, 'Modern antiquities', 69.
[149] Carol Vogel, '$15.4 million at Sotheby's for a Rockwell found hidden behind a wall', *NYT*, 30 Nov. 2006; Jonathon Keats, *Forged* (Oxford, 2013), 4–5, 31–49.
[150] Wilbur F. Creighton, Jr., and Leland R. Johnson, *The Parthenon in Nashville* (1968; rev. edn Nashville: JM Productions, 1989), 22, 48; Christine Kreyling et al., *Classical Nashville* (Vanderbilt, 1996), 40–4, 124–49. See André Retzler, *Les Nouvelles Athènes* (Gollion, Switzerland: Infolio, 2004).

Figure 62 Replication: the Nashville Parthenon, 1922-32

Figure 63 Replication: Anne Hathaway's Cottage, Victoria, British Columbia

Copies are often preferred. When Francis I of France envied the papacy's *Laocoön*, Baccio Bandinelli promised to make a copy even more perfect than the original.[151] Pictorial surrogates are often less costly, easier to move and conserve, more nostalgically tasteful than originals. Pictures of and antiquarian tracts about lost gates and towers were sold as souvenirs to the Victorian merchants who had had them torn down. In the 1950s and 1960s Taunton, Somerset, shed many old buildings as scruffy relics; soon afterwards postcards and tea towels portraying these vanished landmarks became locally popular. Like Italo Calvino's revamped 'Maurilia', whose 'lost grace … can be appreciated only now in the old post cards', L. S. Lowry's paintings became popular only after the industrial scenes they portrayed were safely gone.[152]

The old maxim that 'a happy imitation is of much more value than a defective original' chimes with Walt Disney's boast that Disneyland's 'Vieux Carré' was just like New Orleans's 1850s original, but 'a lot cleaner'. Dubrovnik restored was held just as it had been, but 'older'. The California coast boasts seven waxwork 'Last Suppers' (Fig. 65), all touted as superior to Da Vinci's Milan original, noted Umberto Eco. For the painting in Milan is 'by now so ruined, almost invisible, unable to give you the emotion you [get] from the three-dimensional wax, which is more real, and there is more of it'.[153] So fast has the 1916 reinforced concrete replica Stonehenge at Maryhill, Washington, decayed that it seems more ancient than the Salisbury Plain original.

Yet the clone lacks living intimacy. 'A child dies, leaving behind a worn, dirty, and much-hugged teddy bear. Would a molecular reproduction, known to be such, have the same value to the parents?' No; it would not be the bear that child had hugged (Fig. 66).

When a child loves you for a long, long time, not just to play with, but REALLY loves you, then you become Real. … It doesn't happen all at once. … It takes a long time. … Generally, by the time you are Real, most of your hair has been loved off, and your eyes drop out and you get loose in the joints and very shabby.[154]

Similarly deficient would be a replica Grand Canyon in, say, New Jersey. 'What we respond to in hiking down the Bright Angel Trail is the way in which the canyon has been whittled, particle by particle, by water and wind: we do not have this experience in the Bayonne [New Jersey] Grand Canyon, however, because it was fabricated quite mechanically, all at once'.[155] Ascending worn steps to an ancient cathedral or touching smoothed

[151] Giorgio Vasari, *Lives of the Most Eminent Painters, Sculptors & Architects* (1550/1568; London, 1850), 4: 244–5. See Haskell and Penny, *Most Beautiful Statues*, xiii; Barkan, *Unearthing the Past*, 10.

[152] Chris Miele, 'Conservation and the enemies of progress', in his, ed., *From William Morris* (Yale, 2005), 1–29 at 15–16; Somerset County planning officers, Taunton, personal communication, 3 Mar. 1978; Robin Bush, *The Book of Taunton* (Chesham: Barracuda, 1977); Italo Calvino, *Invisible Cities* (1972; Vintage, 1997), 26–7; John Berger, 'Lowry and the industrial North' (1966), in *About Looking* (London, 1980), 87–95 at 90–3.

[153] James Dallaway, *Anecdotes of the Arts in England* (London, 1800), 156–9; 'New scene at Disneyland simulates New Orleans', *NYT*, 26 July 1966: 25; J. Mark Souther, 'The Disneyfication of New Orleans', *Journal of American History* 94 (2007): 804–11; Cornelius Holtorf, *From Stonehenge to Las Vegas* (AltaMira, 2005), 122; Umberto Eco, *Faith in Fakes: Travels in Hyperreality* (1973; Harcourt, 1986), 17–18.

[154] M. P. Battin, 'Exact replication in the visual arts', *Journal of Aesthetics and Art Criticism* 38 (1979): 153–8 at 154; Margery Williams, *Velveteen Rabbit or How Toys Become Real* (London, 1922), unpaginated.

[155] Battin, 'Exact replication', 155.

Figure 64 Mission models, San Gabriel Mission courtyard, California

Figure 65 *The Last Supper*, Bibleland, Santa Cruz, California

Figure 66 Precious authenticity: seventy-year-old 'Harry White', deaf in one ear

banisters in an old house links visitors with the long histories that wore and smoothed them – histories no known replica could convey.[156]

The architectural critic Ada Louise Huxtable penned a classic Ruskinian censure:

> To equate a replica with the genuine artifact . . . cheapens and renders meaningless its true age and provenance . . . An authentic reproduction is a genuine oxymoron . . . Preservation 'enclaves' are . . . developer-dispossessed fragments given a new 'olde' name after having been moved from places where they were inconveniently interfering with profitable new construction . . . Everything is made to resemble what it might have been once – only better. . . . Inventions and simulacra, of things that existed and things that did not, [are] value[d] more than the shabby, incomplete survivals [but] they wipe out all the incidents of life and change. The worn stone, the chafed corner, the threshold low and uneven from many feet, the marks on walls and windows that carry the presence and message of remembered hands and eyes – all of these accumulated, accidental, suggestive and genuine imprints that imbue the artifact with its history and continuity . . . are absent or erased There is nothing left . . . that palpably joins the past to the present.[157]

Felt links with teddy bears, buildings, or landscapes may need authentic originals. But newly minted replicas can convey historical immediacy. The heavy greasy chain-mail armour available to try on at the Wallace Collection weightily impressed my family. 'The boy or girl of today may be denied the undoubted thrill of putting on the actual garment of a former age', but a substitute can 'recreate the feeling which the first wearer may have felt', a teacher writes. 'Who is to say that wearing the copy affords any less of a true historical experience than putting on the original?'[158] The sheer effort of replication can bring the original's history to life – as with Knott's Berry Farm's 'Liberty Bell' frozen in dry ice and then 'authentically cracked' to resemble the original.[159] So too in 'Old Town' Warsaw, which once again looks old thanks to five decades of grime, but where visitors (unlike the post-war residents mentioned above) 'are constantly reminded that what they're seeing is not historically original but a defiant reproduction. Postcards at every souvenir stand juxtapose 1945 photos of bombed-out buildings and squares with their elegant reincarnations'.[160]

Cognoscenti deem reproductions *ipso facto* inferior because unoriginal. 'Genuineness is the real thing', insisted an architectural purist. 'It puts us in the presence of what was – the experience of history – not a later impression of what something looked like.' Without actual bits of the past, our 'ability to judge the real from the fake is damaged – or worse, never developed'.[161] But just as most know the *Iliad* and the Bible only through translation, so the tangible past is mostly known from copies, reflections, and subsequent impressions. Not only can we seldom tell originals from replicas, we are often more

---

[156] Kevin Lynch, *What Time Is This Place?* (MIT Press, 1972), 44; Walter Benjamin, 'The work of art in the age of mechanical reproduction' (1936), in *Illuminations*, 217–51 at 222–4.

[157] Huxtable, 'The way it never was', in *Unreal America*, 18–27.

[158] John A. Fairley, *History Teaching through Museums* (Longman's, 1977), 127–8.

[159] John Maass, 'Architecture and Americanism or pastiches of Independence Hall', *Historic Preservation* 22:2 (1970): 17–25 at 24–5.

[160] Deborah Tall, 'Memory's landscapes' (1998), in Robert L. Root, ed., *Landscapes with Figures* (Nebraska, 2007), 283–92 at 284.

[161] Ben Thompson quoted in Alexandra Lange, 'Rebooting the festival marketplace', *Design Observer*, 9 Feb. 2009.

pleased with the latter. Las Vegas and Disneyland's facsimiles appeal by not requiring the solemn awe owed the originals. Remoteness from prototypes endears their images. As with Taunton's bygone tenements, old photos substitute for ancestors estranged by the erosion of family coherence; pictures of tanned peasants or careworn peddlers bespeak their temporal and hence emotional distance.[162]

Replicas' sheer existence alters how originals are seen. Extant relics are profoundly affected by being copied and depicted, becoming not only better but *differently* known. The visitor sees Rome through centuries of Grand Tour Piranesi-shaped expectations, Philadelphia's Independence Hall through the lens of familiarity with dozens of replicas, the Eiffel Tower through countless travel posters.[163]

Pictorial likenesses have dominated perceptions of things past at least since the printing press. Sacred texts and images have been replicated by woodblock printing in China since the third century, their fame enhanced by numerousness, as with the million copies of Buddhist charms ordered by an eighth-century empress.[164] Prints of classical sculpture were hawked in Rome soon after 1500; Bernard de Montfaucon's *L'Antiquité expliquée et représentée en figures* (1719–24) contained thirty thousand copperplate engravings of ancient art; Stuart and Revett's sketches made Greek antiquities the lodestar for neoclassical architecture. Well into the nineteenth century, fine engravings were often more valuable than their source paintings, both as works of art in their own right and as producers of prints.[165] Pictorial availability shaped what people knew and thought of the past; readers of history began to 'see' the past visually.

Until recently, replication was felt to benefit originals. Multiplying copies of ancient masterpieces would help 'prevent the Return of Ignorant and barbarous Ages', Josiah Wedgwood assured potential customers. Copies diffused good taste, instructed the public eye, and improved the arts while enhancing the prototype. 'The more Copies . . . of the Venus Medicis for instance, the more celebrated the Original will be'.[166] The poet Samuel Rogers extolled Wedgwood's mass-produced cameos and intaglios as aids to antique appreciation:

> Be mine to bless the more mechanic skill,
> That stamps, renews, and multiplies at will;
> And cheaply circulates, thro' distant climes,
> The fairest relics of the purest times.[167]

The 'noble enterprise' of copying culminated in an 1867 pan-European Convention for Promoting Universally [the] Reproduction of Works of Art for the Benefit of Museums of All Countries.[168]

---

[162] Julia Hirsch, *Family Photographs* (Oxford, 1981), 119.

[163] Michael Taussig, *Mimesis and Alterity: A Particular History of the Senses* (Routledge, 1993), 407–8.

[164] Clunas, *Art in China*, 109.

[165] James Stuart and Nicholas Revett, *The Antiquities of Athens* (1762–1816; Princeton Architectural Press, 2007); Haskell and Penny, *Taste and the Antique*, 17–21, 43; Helena E. Wright, *The First Smithsonian Collection* (Smithsonian Institution, 2015), 35–8, 115–17, 124–5, 178–88.

[166] Wedgwood & Bentley 1779 catalogue, in Wolf Mankowitz, *Wedgwood* (Batsford, 1953), 253, 229.

[167] Samuel Rogers, 'Epistle to a Friend', ll. 65–8 (1799), in *Pleasures of Memory* (1802), 91–131 at 103–4. See Mankowitz, *Wedgwood*, 104–7, 214–15, 221–3.

[168] Scott, 'Modern antiquities', 67–8.

As plaster-cast makers, marble workshops, and bronze foundries multiplied replicas, their quality declined. Wedgwood to the contrary, *Venus de' Medici*'s repute began to wane as she was multiplied. The prestige of ancient masterpieces had stemmed partly from their uniqueness and remoteness; over-exposure dimmed distinction, turning touchstones into clichés, devotees into sceptics. Made aware by the work of Winckelmann and Anton Raphael Mengs that most of the admired statues in Roman collections could not be originals, eighteenth-century connoisseurs no longer asked of an ancient statue 'Why is it so sublime?' but 'What lost work may it reflect?'[169] Each find that more accurately detailed antiquity reduced the aesthetic worth of the plethora of copies.

Replicas seem more acceptable as one-off insurance against harm to the original than when mass-marketed. Nelson Rockefeller claimed that cheap replicas of his collection helped make art 'for the first time the common heritage of all mankind', but art dealers complained that they were 'sold as substitutes for, rather than reminders of, "the real thing"'. Indeed, museum-shop replicas enable many to come solely to buy 'without the expense or bother' of seeing the originals at all.[170] Kitsch replication further tarnishes relics' repute. Shakespeare is demeaned, a visitor to Stratford complained, when one eats an omelette or stubs out a cigarette on a portrait of the Bard'.[171]

Duplication was increasingly felt to dislocate, alienate, and devalue the original. When a second copy of a rare book he owns turns up, a collector buys and notarizes its destruction, restoring the unique value of his sole copy. Viewers throng to the *Mona Lisa*, as they goggle at film stars, mainly because its likeness is familiar. 'Oh my, it was beautiful', enthused a Louvre viewer. 'It was just like all those copies I've seen'.[172] Antique costumes remind viewers not of their historical wearers but of entertainers portraying them. A guide book identifies the sixteenth-century Duke of Norfolk, entombed in Framlingham church, Suffolk, as figuring prominently in the TV series, *The Six Wives of Henry VIII*. Castle Howard is touted – and largely visited – as the locale of *Brideshead Revisited* (1981 and 2008) and other films. Relics become simulacra of their own offshoots, like Harold Bloom's anxious poets reversing the direction of influence from successor to forerunner.

Humdrum originals spoil the picture in the mind's eye. Proust's Marcel finds the statue of the Virgin at Balbec, long adored in his imagination, 'reduced now to its own stone semblance ... coated with the same soot as defiled the neighbouring houses ... transformed, as was the church itself, into a little old woman whose height I could measure and whose wrinkles I could count'.[173] Anticipatory depiction detracts from

---

[169] Ernst H. Gombrich, 'Worship of ancient sculpture' (1981), in *Reflections on the History of Art* (Oxford: Phaidon, 1987), 103.

[170] Grace Glueck, 'Dealers take on Rockefeller', *IHT*, 8 Dec. 1978; Margaret P. Battin, 'Cases for kids: using puzzles to teach aesthetics to children', *Journal of Aesthetic Education* 28 (1994): 89–104 at 96; Benjamin, 'Work of art in the age of mechanical reproduction', 220–3; Huxtable, *Unreal America*, 84.

[171] Grigori Kozintsev, *Shakespeare* (London: Dobson, 1967), 7; Gillo Dorfles, *Kitsch* (London: Studio Vista, 1969), 31–2, 94–7.

[172] Maurice Rheims, *La Vie étrange des objets* (Paris: Plon, 1959), 48; Robert Goldberg, 'Jostling over Mona Lisa', *IHT*, 5–6 July 1980: 8. See Susan Stewart, *Crimes of Writing* (Oxford, 1991), 17, 104–5, 152, 189–96, 200, 276, 287; Dana Arnold, 'Facts or fragments?' *Art History* 25 (2003): 450–68.

[173] Proust, *Remembrance of Things Past*, 1: 709–10.

seeing originals, depriving the viewer of a fresh unmediated experience. Screening out irrelevance and showing ancient monuments at awe-inspiring angles, coffee-table reproductions arouse anticipations often disappointed. Expecting solemn majesty at the Parthenon and columnar splendour at Persepolis, the visitor is shocked 'to see that these are isolated survivors arising out of something like a builder's yard'. The actual antiquity is often a comedown: 'It was much smaller than I expected', 'It was all broken up – I couldn't make head or tail of it', 'It was sort of scruffy'.[174]

Just as live performances sound thin to ears jaded by souped-up recordings, and baroque violins and cellos are scarcely audible to audiences accustomed to modern strings on steroids, so do glossy art-book reproductions corrupt the eye, doing down gentler originals.[175] Media perversion further dims old masterpieces in modern eyes. At first a prototype of naturalistic realism, the *Mona Lisa* came in the nineteenth century to stand for enigmatic seduction; twentieth-century copies made it common coin. The beard and moustache in Marcel Duchamp's *L.H.O.O.Q.* (1919) are now themselves archetypal accoutrements.[176]

Famed portrayals transform perceptions of the history they portray. Emanuel Leutze's *Washington Crossing the Delaware* (1851) elevated a minor episode of the American Revolution to a mythic event, now reduced to a patriotic cliché. Films recurrently alter the message of Custer's Last Stand, the most reproduced event in American history.[177] Archibald Willard's *Spirit of '76* (originally *Yankee Doodle*) changes meaning with every national crisis (Figs. 67, 68). Staged parallels with Willard's figures made the Iwo Jima flag scene an icon of American fortitude in the Second World War. During the bicentennial the *Spirit of '76* lent lustre to Budget Rent-a-Car, Sesame Street, the American Chiropractic Association, Kentucky Fried Chicken, and Disneyland. Down 'Main Street, USA', in the heart of Disney World, came America on Parade, and 'at the head of the parade, bearing drum and fife … and patched with bandages, stand the three symbols of the American Revolution: Mickey Mouse, Donald Duck, and Goofy'.[178] Copies of things past gain careers of their own, derailing or submerging their prototypes'. Whether replication reinvigorates or degrades the past, its remnants are profoundly altered.

Ultimately the replica effaces and replaces the original past. In Boston, fumes a critic, everything 'which was actually old has been made Olde instead; historical facades and interiors have been restored not to how they used to look, but to how (city planners

---

[174] Chamberlin, *Preserving the Past*, 66.

[175] Sarah Walden, *The Ravished Image* (1985; 2nd edn London: Gibson Square, 2004), 6.

[176] George Boas, 'Mona Lisa in the history of taste', *JHI* 1 (1940): 207–24; Harold Rosenberg, 'The Mona Lisa without a mustache', *Art News* 75:5 (1976): 47–50 at 48; Mary Rose Storey, *Mona Lisas* (Constable, 1980); Richard Ducousset, 'Epidémie des parodies', *Connaissance des Arts*, no. 281 (July 1975): 66–73; Donald Sassoon, *Becoming Mona Lisa* (Harcourt, 2001).

[177] Michael Kammen, *A Season of Youth* (Knopf, 1973), 81–3; Ann Hawkes Hutton, *Portrait of Patriotism: Washington Crossing the Delaware* (Philadelphia, 1959); David Hackett Fischer, *Washington's Crossing* (Oxford, 2004); Michael A. Elliott, *Custerology* (Chicago, 2007).

[178] Thomas H. Pauly, 'In search of "The Spirit of '76"' (1976), in Leila Zenderland, ed., *Recycling the Past* (PennPress, 1978), 29–49; Dick Schaap, 'Culture shock: Williamsburg and Disney World, back to back', *NYT*, 28 Sept. 1975: TR1; Guy Westwell, 'One image begets another', *Journal of War and Cultural Studies* 1 (2008): 325–40.

Figure 67 Updating the patriotic past: Archibald M. Willard, *Spirit of '76*, 1876

imagine) tourists want them to look; every incident of (family-friendly) historical importance which has ever transpired within city limits is now re-enacted in an entirely Disneyfied manner'.[179]

---

[179] Joshua Glenn, 'Fake authenticity' (1999), in *HiLoBrow*, June 1, 2010.

Figure 68 Updating the patriotic past: Sheraton Hotels advertisement, 1976

But that is precisely why the replica is preferred – it subdues the original, domesticating the foreign past by banishing 'the profound atavistic fear we experience when we are face to face with the original', says Julian Barnes's art-history guru. Threatened by the past's powerful reality, 'we must demand the replica, since the reality, the truth, the authenticity of the replica is the one we can possess, colonise, reorder, find *jouissance* in, and finally . . . confront and destroy'.[180]

---

[180] Julian Barnes, *England, England* (Jonathan Cape, 1998), 54–5.

11

Replacing the past: restoration and re-enactment

'These old offices of ours, such as the Badgeries, are much more important as rituals than they were as realities. Like old churches, they are nostalgic, photogenic, and give a sense of security. Centuries ago, the Co-Wardens held every badger in the land, and they still do, technically, but with no badgers involved any more.'

'Is there no immediate badger whatever? An occasional glimpse of one would serve as a foundation, though I admit that invisibility is a higher and more splendid challenge.'

'There is a token badger maintained by the Yeomen of Hertford Forest. It is a stuffed one, of course.'

'I suppose they let us take it on ceremonial occasions.'

'Not the actual, token badger, except on the death of the Lord Royal. Normally, you get a clip of artificial fur set in an osier staff. This is an emblem of the token. A symbolic dog-rose [is] presented to you annually by the Knights of Egham.'

'In short, what is not symbolic is emblematic?'

'Except when it is token. Then, it is stuffed.'

'Which of these – token, symbolical, or emblematical – applies to our annual ritual of Easing the Badger?'

'All three. The stuffed, or token, boar-badger is inserted into a symbolic den and then eased out with your symbolical gold spade. In this way, there is no need actually to disturb any living badger.' Vinson represented the spirit of English history and institutions. Carrying his token spade, he stood for everything whose demise was beyond dispute.
                                                                    Nigel Dennis, 1955[1]

What if the past's demise is indisputable? What if its forms and features are no more? Is there any way to bring them back? Can pasts that survive only in memory and memoir somehow be retrieved? History is full of efforts to recover bygone things and thoughts. Attempts to replace what has been lost are legion. Two types of retrieval are paramount. One is to restore what was once there; the other is to travel back to how things used to be.

Yearning for departed ancestors and bygone things takes two main routes, restoration and re-enactment. Both aim, as faithfully as possible, to reconstitute what has been recalled and recorded. Although the actual past remains unreachable, such simulacra may become laudable substitutes. Indeed, as the offspring of our own efforts, they may even feel superior to the original past they ostensibly replicate.

---

[1] Nigel Dennis, *Cards of Identity* (1955; Weidenfeld & Nicolson, 1974), 125–7, 134 (conflated).

Restoration

Come again, / Come back, past years. ... The golden age, the golden age come
back   William Morris, 1868[2]

Can't repeat the past? ... Why of course you can!   F. Scott Fitzgerald, 1925[3]

'O! call back yesterday, bid time return', cries Salisbury in Shakespeare's *Richard II*, bearing the king dire news. Craving restoration is age-old. So is faith that it will come to pass. 'Every city and village and field will be reconstituted as before, again and again', forecast a fourth-century ecclesiastic.[4] From divine fulfilment, restoration devolved into human agency. Someday, mused H. G. Wells, as noted in Chapter 2, we would learn how to restore the whole of the past.[5]

Restoration implies return to an earlier condition, typically the pristine original. The previous is held better – healthier, safer, purer, truer, more enduring, beautiful, or authentic – than what now exists. Whether with lost or stolen property, damaged paintings, depleted health, sullied reputations, or undermined trust, the aim is to retrieve the lost good.[6] To restore is to make whole again, in defiance of 'All the king's horses, and all the king's men [who] couldn't put Humpty together again'. We cannot do so in any realm. 'One can no more restore an area of natural beauty or a painting to its original state', writes a biologist, 'than one can turn women into the little girls they once were'.[7]

Yet hugely popular restoration efforts are legion. The BBC's *Restoration* series featured buildings, furnishings, and works of art that viewers wanted restored. *Restoration Roadshow* (2009–11) featured heirloom furniture, paper and books, clocks, ceramics, paintings, and gilding. Image restoration ranges from digital repair of faded photos to public-relations recovery of the repute of tarnished countries or corporations, priests or presidents. The restoration of memory, of classical culture, of paintings and buildings, and of Christian tradition was discussed in previous chapters. Here I review all modes of recouping the past.

The urge to restore is instinctive. For toddlers nothing irretrievably wears out, no act is irreversible; restorative power can rejoin things broken, rejuvenate the old, return the dead to life. Indeed, restoration is obligatory. The child feels responsible for the breakage and must make amends – reparation.[8] Growing up we sadly learn that there

[2] William Morris, *The Earthly Paradise* (London, 1868), 216, 124.
[3] F. Scott Fitzgerald, *The Great Gatsby* (1925; Scribners, 1953), 89.
[4] Nemesius, Bishop of Emesa, *On the Nature of Man* (late fourth century; Liverpool, 2008), 193.
[5] H. G. Wells, *The Dream* (Collins, 1929), 236.
[6] R. A. Duff, 'Restorative punishment and punitive restoration', in Lode Walgrave, ed., *Restorative Justice and the Law* (Cullompton: Willan, 2002), 82–100; Brian A. Weiner, *Sins of the Parents: The Politics of National Apologies in the United States* (Temple, 2005), 116; Charles S. Maier, 'Overcoming the past? Narrative and negotiation, remembering and reparation', in John Torpey, ed., *Politics and the Past: On Repairing Historical Injustices* (Rowman & Littlefield, 2003), 295–304. See my 'Restoration', in Stephen Daniels et al., eds., *Envisioning Landscapes: Making Worlds: Geography and the Humanities* (Routledge, 2011), 209–26.
[7] Midas Dekkers, *The Way of All Flesh* (1997; London: Harvill, 2000), 94.
[8] Jean Piaget, *The Child's Conception of the World* (1929; Routledge, 1998), 361–7; Virginia Slaughter et al., 'Constructing a coherent theory: children's biological understanding of life and death', in Michael Siegal and

are limits to our own and others' restorative powers. Hence the compelling regressive urge: 'Backward, turn backward, O Time, in your flight, / Make me a child again just for to-night!'[9]

Restorative cycles in human and terrestrial history

We sense time both as circle and as arrow. Time's circle promises restoration; time's arrow forbids it. In traditional societies, lived time was more circle than arrow, lived annals overwhelmingly repetitive, human nature enduringly the same. There was no new thing under the sun (Ecclesiastes 1:9). Although Judaeo-Christianity posited a flow of time in which events happened only once, repetitive resurrection and re-enactment suffused religious faith. Politics too were recurrently repetitive. As in Polybius's universal history, monarchy led to tyranny, then to aristocracy, oligarchy, democracy, and anarchy, circling back again to monarchy.[10]

Restorative cycles likewise governed geological history. Because providence 'loves to recover what was lost or decayed ... and what was originally good and happy, to make it so again', Thomas Burnet's restored primordial Earth had 'not a wrinkle, scar or fracture in all its body'.[11] James Hutton limned Earth's saga 'as a stately series of strictly repeating events, the making and remaking of continents as regular as the revolution of planets'. Hutton's terrestrial uplift, erosion, deposition, back to uplift mirrored the monarchy-back-to-monarchy political cycle.[12] Charles Lyell depicted Earth as eternally cyclic, positing wholesale restoration. When global warming resumed, 'then might those genera of animals return, of which the memorials are preserved in the ancient rocks ... The huge iguanodon might reappear in the woods, and the ichthyosaur in the sea, while the pterodactyl might flit again through the umbrageous groves of tree-ferns.'[13]

But new finds undermined restoration faith. Earth's cyclic regularities were warped into novel trajectories by episodic catastrophes: asteroid impacts, tsunamis, heat-occluding volcanic eruptions. Unique and unrepeatable natural history mirrored unique and unrepeatable biblical history, shedding perennial regularities for sporadic singularities.[14] Evolutionary biology, showing old life forms continually extinguished, new forms engendered, dimmed restorative hopes. Nothing dismayed Darwin more forcibly than the absence, amid teeming extant species, of virtually all previous ones.

Candida Peterson, eds., *Children's Understanding of Biology and Health* (Cambridge, 1999), 71–96; Brandon Hamber, 'Narrowing the micro and the macro: a psychological perspective on reparations', in Pablo de Greiff, ed., *The Handbook of Reparations* (Oxford, 2006), 560–88 at 562–3; Sandra Rafman, 'Restoration of a moral universe: children's perspectives on forgiveness and justice', in Wanda Malcolm et al., eds., *Women's Reflections on the Complexities of Forgiveness* (Routledge, 2007), 215–34.

[9] Elizabeth Akers Allen, *Rock Me to Sleep, Mother*, ll. 1–2 (1859; Boston, 1883).

[10] Polybius, *The Histories* (after 146 BC; London, 1889), bk. VI.

[11] Thomas Burnet, *The Sacred Theory of the Earth* (1684–90; Southern Illinois, 1965), 53, 64.

[12] James, Hutton, *Theory of the Earth* (Edinburgh, 1795); Stephen Jay Gould, *Time's Arrow, Time's Cycle* (Harvard, 1987), 77–9, 129.

[13] Charles Lyell, *Principles of Geology* (1830; London, 1840), 1: 193; Gould, *Time's Arrow*, 105–45.

[14] Martin J. S. Rudwick, *Bursting the Limits of Time* (Chicago, 2005), 188–93, 642–51.

He dolefully concluded that 'not one living species will transmit its unaltered likeness to a distant futurity'.[15]

Darwin's 'intolerable thought that [man] and all other sentient beings are doomed to complete annihilation' was echoed, the very year of *On the Origin of Species*, in Edward FitzGerald's *Rubaiyat*: 'One thing is certain and the Rest is Lies; / The Flower that once has blown forever dies'.[16] Most sobering was the fadeout of the entire universe, beginning with the Sun's impending heat death. 'Within a finite period', Kelvin warned of entropy's grim implacability, Earth would become uninhabitable. Fears of the Sun's non-reappearance underlay enduring myth. Humanity's age-old terror lest daylight not be restored endures in the modern mindset.[17]

Cyclical regularity gave way to distressing uncertainty in human affairs too (see Chapter 8). Such fears intensified nostalgia for earlier times, when historical change was slow, cyclic, or imperceptible. Haunted by Mircea Eliade's 'terror of history', men hungered for past certitudes. Against fearsome revolution in regicidal England and France, Stuart and Bourbon monarchical restoration promised time-honoured security.[18]

Restoration in the arts

Restoration in art and architecture likewise grew problematic. Early-modern efforts to recover original or idealized perfection shifted, as shown in Chapter 6, to Romantic and Victorian fondness for fragments, delight in decay, and rejection of restoration as impious fraud. A major factor was revulsion against ecclesiastical renovators who transformed while claiming to conserve. 'To restore a building', recognized Eugène Viollet-le-Duc, 'is to reinstate it in a condition of completeness that could never have existed at any given time'.[19] His approval of such action horrified those for whom virtuous truth lay in inviolate original structures. 'Restoration is impossible', inveighed historian–archivist Francis Palgrave.

You cannot grind old bones new. You may repeat the outward form (though rarely with minute accuracy), but you cannot the material ... the bedding and laying, and above all the tooling ...

---

[15] Charles Darwin, *On the Origin of Species by Means of Natural Selection* (1859; Oxford, 1998), 395.

[16] *The Autobiography of Charles Darwin 1809–1882* (Norton, 1958), 92; *The Rubáiyàt of Omar Khayyám* (c. 1100; London, 1859), quatrain 26, lxiii.

[17] Lord Kelvin, 'On a universal tendency in nature to the dissipation of mechanical energy', *Proceedings of the Royal Society of Edinburgh*, 18 Apr. 1852; Gillian Beer, '"The death of the sun"', in J. B. Bullen, ed., *The Sun Is God* (Clarendon Press, 1989), 159–80; Paul T. Davies, *The Last Three Minutes: Conjectures about the Ultimate Fate of the Universe* (Basic Books, 1994), 9–13; 'Rotation of Earth plunges entire North American continent into darkness', *Onion*, 27 Feb. 2006: 1.

[18] Mircea Eliade, *The Myth of the Eternal Return* (1949; Princeton, 1994); Edmund Burke, *Reflections on the Revolution in France* (1790; Yale, 2003), 170, 181–5; Geoffrey Cubitt, 'The political uses of seventeenth-century English history in Bourbon Restoration France', *Historical Journal* 50:1 (2007): 73–95.

[19] Eugène Viollet-le-Duc, 'Restauration', in *Dictionnaire raisonné de l'architecture française du XIe au XVIe siècle* (Paris, 1866), 8: 14–34 at 14. See M. F. Hearn, ed., *The Architectural Theory of Viollet-le-Duc* (MIT Press, 1990), 269–86.

There is an anachronism in every stone ... The sensation of sham is invincible ... In the most perfect resuscitation of Henry the Third's 'Early English', the tooling of the well-tempered town-made chisel inscribes 'Victoria and Albert' upon every stone.[20]

In restoration's 'double process of destruction and addition', pronounced William Morris, 'the appearance of antiquity is taken away from such old parts of the fabric that are left', and the final result is 'a feeble and lifeless forgery'. Ancient buildings were 'monuments of a bygone art, created by bygone manners, that modern art cannot meddle with without destroying'. Old edifices like living beings called for daily care, not artificial rejuvenation.[21]

Anti-restoration tenets set forth by Ruskin and Morris long swayed European art and architecture though more in precept than in practice (see pp. 498–9 below). Honouring the initial structure meant expunging traces of previous ill-conceived restorations. Unavoidable replacements required contrasting textures and colours utterly distinct from the old. But these glaring disjunctions destroyed aesthetic unity and abolished the aura of antiquity. Hence some later restorers opted to stress 'original' *aesthetic* qualities, stripping off marks of age and wear, while others emphasized *venerableness*, antiquating paintings with patinas of varnish, buildings with lichen. Replacements chosen to match, rather than clash with, original elements were detectable as new only by close inspection of tooling on stonework, dates on stained glass, tints slightly differing.

The history of Giotto's fourteenth-century *Life and Miracles of St Francis*, in Santa Croce, Florence, typifies ever-changing restoration aims. Partly destroyed and white-washed over in the eighteenth century, the frescoes were restored in the mid-nineteenth by repainting Giotto's scenes, with Giottoesque figures added in lacunae. Twentieth-century restorers expunged these 'forgeries' so as to highlight original remnants and reveal Giotto's original intent. This purist restoration was in turn repudiated as 'optically disruptive'. Aiming at Cesare Brandi's 'visible dialogue between past and present', 1970s restorers sought to recover the frescoes' original significance as 'Franciscan stories with deep Christian meaning'.[22]

Devotion to material authenticity seems ever more historically illusory and aesthetic-ally unappealing. 'Designed to open people's eyes to how things were in the past', the restored Elizabethan garden at Kenilworth Castle is lauded as archaeologically authentic,

[20] To Dawson Turner, 19 July 1847, in R. H. Inglis Palgrave, 'Biographical memoir of Sir Francis Palgrave, KH', in Francis Palgrave, *Collected Historical Works* (Cambridge, 1922), 1: xi–lvi at xlv; Francis Palgrave, *The History of Normandy and England* (London, 1851–64), 1: xxix. See Alessandra Melluco Vaccaro, 'Restoration and anti-restoration', in Nicholas Stanley Price et al., eds., *Historical and Philosophical Issues in the Conservation of Cultural Heritage* (Getty, 1996), 308–13.

[21] William Morris, 'Manifesto of the Society for the Protection of Ancient Buildings' (1877), in Price et al., *Historical and Philosophical Issues*, 319–21; Stephan Tschudi-Madsen, *Restoration and Anti-Restoration*, 2nd edn (Oslo: Universitetsforlaget, 1976); Charles Harvey and Jon Press, *William Morris* (Manchester, 1991), 118; John Ruskin, *The Seven Lamps of Architecture* (1849; New York: Noonday, 1961), 178, 183.

[22] Cathleen Sara Hoeniger, 'Aesthetic unity or conservation honesty? Four generations of wall-painting restorers in Italy and the changing approaches to loss, 1850–1970', in Andrew Oddy and Sandra Smith, eds., *Past Practice – Future Prospects* (British Museum Occasional Paper 145, 2001), 115–22.

Figure 69 Antiquity reconstituted: St Albans Cathedral west front, before restoration

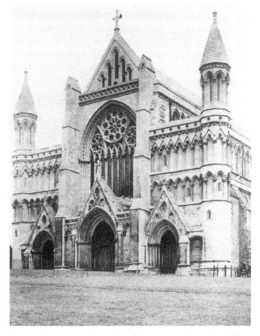

Figure 70 Antiquity reconstituted: after restoration by Edmund Beckett,
1st Baron Grimthorpe in 1879

although the flowers are largely conjectural or modern hybrids, the aviary has tame
instead of wild birds, and the lawn-fringed paths are wholly anachronistic. But the main
defect is that 'it is not beautiful', complained a viewer. 'The aviary is too big. ... The
obelisks are too high', all the features 'out of scale with each other. It does not have
the charm of a medieval garden or the dignity of a renaissance garden'. Meticulous

Figure 71 Antiquity sustained: Arch of Titus, before restoration by Giuseppe Valadier, 1820s: Giovanni Battista Piranesi, *Vedute dell'Arco di Tito, c.* 1760

Figure 72 After restoration: Arch of Titus at the end of the nineteenth century

Figure 73 Renewing antiquity: the ragged Roman regiment around the Sheldonian Theatre, Oxford (1868 restorations of seventeenth-century originals), photo 1965

Figure 74 The heads replaced, Michael Black, sculptor, 1972

restoration missed the romantic magic of earlier 'Shakespeare' gardens.[23] As Marguerite Yourcenar remarks of antique sculptures, 'Our ancestors restored statues; we remove from them their false noses and prosthetic devices. ... The great lovers of antiquity restored out of piety. Out of piety, we undo what they did'. More censorious is Alan Bennett's history master. The ancients 'venerated strenuous piety, we venerate supine antiquity. ... Things matter to us more than people.'[24]

Conflicting aims continue to embroil conservators, curators, and the public. Restorers lauded the 1990s renovation of the Sistine Chapel and Michelangelo's *Last Judgement* for freeing the frescoes from five centuries' accumulated grime and earlier restorers' darkened glue, and for revealing Michelangelo's colouristic genius. But critics termed it a disaster, voiding the frescoes of inspiration and corrupting their essence. For restorers, removing the veil of time recovered Michelangelo's 'full chromatic effects'. For critics, the expunged veil contained Michelangelo's intended *a secco* shadow-and-chiaroscuro finishing, and balanced tinting – *colorito* – quite unlike today's sense of colour.[25]

Moreover, artists' aims change as they go on, and often again after finishing. Did restoration reveal Michelangelo's first creative burst at the expense of his later views? 'Any artist's intention', warns an art historian, is 'a complex and shifting compound of conscious and unconscious aspirations, adjustments, re-definitions, acts of chance and evasions'. Nor is all ageing planned. 'Where does the *sfumato* [shading] stop', wonders a viewer of Leonardo's ravaged *Salvator Mundi*, 'and the corrosion begin?'[26]

These paradoxes in restoration philosophy reflect changing presuppositions summarized by Leonard Barkan. Up to the early nineteenth century neoclassical taste mandated restoring back to supposed original condition. Later, conservators simultaneously believed it possible to retrieve art works' original form but 'refuse[d] to lay a finger on them'. Now we respect 'the different privileges of works that remain in their original pristine condition, of works that have a long and familiar history in some altered state, and of works that are technologically returned to some condition that we can only guess at'.[27]

Restoration tenets increasingly respect art and artefacts' total history. Past worth inheres not only in original materials, forms, and intentions, but in time's attritions

---

[23] Rebecca W. Bushnell, 'Gardens, memory, and history: the Shakespeare and modern Elizabethan garden', *Change over Time* 3:1 (Spring 2013): 64–81 at 78.

[24] Marguerite Yourcenar, *That Mighty Sculptor, Time* (Macmillan, 1993), 57–62 at 60; Alan Bennett, *The History Boys* (Faber & Faber, 2006), 62–3.

[25] Carlo Pietrangeli et al., *The Sistine Chapel: A Glorious Restoration* (Abrams, 1999); Peter Layne Arguimbau, 'Michelangelo's Sistine Chapel cleaned with oven cleaner' (2011), online; James Beck with Michael Daley, *Art Restoration* (Norton, 1996), 88–100; Paul Eggert, *Securing the Past: Conservation in Art, Architecture and Literature* (Cambridge, 2009), 90–3; Andrew Graham-Dixon, *Michelangelo and the Sistine Chapel* (Weidenfeld & Nicolson, 2008); Michael Daley, 'Michelangelo's watery grave', *ArtWatch UK* 27 (Spring 2011): 21–3; Charles Hope, 'The National Gallery cleaning controversy', *ArtWatch UK* 28 (Winter 2012): 15.

[26] Martin Kemp, 'Looking at Leonardo's *Last Supper*', in Peter Booth et al., eds., *Appearance, Opinion, Change: Evaluating the Look of Paintings* (London: UK Institute for Conservation, 1990), 14–21 at 18; Julian Bell, 'Cosmic dreams', *TLS*, 25 Nov. 2011: 5. See Mansfield Kirby Talley, 'The original intent of the artist', in Price et al., eds., *Historical and Philosophical Issues*, 162–75.

[27] Leonard Barkan, *Unearthing the Past* (Yale, 1999), 187.

and the interventions of collectors, curators, conservators, and restorers. Objects ever accrue new meanings and values, altering or replacing previous ones.[28] Rigid restoration strictures become ever less tenable. Injunctions about original structures, original intent, original anything are fast eroding. That no assemblage, no structure, no image, can be returned to an original or any previous state is ever more evident. Restorations at best approximate or suggest what once was. And every restoration is filtered through and tinctured by irremediably modern minds, making anachronism unavoidable.

Early-music restoration is a case in point. Enraptured by rediscovered melodic marvels, 1920s and 1930s devotees retrieved original scores, instruments, acoustics, performance modes, audience habits. Some claimed to perform pre-classical music as it had been played, others as it *should* have been. Whether authentic notation, original instruments, composers' intentions, or listeners' expectations mattered most was hotly debated; any choices cost some of the past. Period recitals could never fully replicate past circumstances. Vocal restorations would require modern castrati, gelded in childhood, and boy sopranos with voices still unbroken at sixteen, yet mature enough both to master early-music complexity and to be at home in 'the spiritual world of their forebears five centuries ago'. Return to any *Ur* condition came to seem impossible, restoring *in toto* preposterous. However faithful a recital to its origins, modern ears, accustomed to modern sounds and unused to the older ones, necessarily hear music differently. One might reconstruct, revive, rebuild, but not restore the musical past.[29]

Museum visitors like musical audiences are ineluctably of their own epoch. What they make of what they see is shaped by creations and viewing habits that post-date the relics they observe. Time's erosions and accretions are bound to alter viewers' perceptual frameworks along with the objects themselves. We cannot see the spinning wheel displayed as those who used it did. For us it is not a new tool, but a *former* tool, left stranded in the present by the tides of industrial change. Its proper role today is that of antique décor in some atavized locale. For people to see spinning wheels as they were once seen, the whole subsequent history of spinning jennies, Crompton mules and so forth would have to be unknown to them.

Recovering nature

Restoring nature gained favour in Victorian reaction to industrial blight and urban squalor. But like biblical Eden, 'nature' thus redeemed was intensely managed, agrarian or emparked or gardenesque. Idealized in the canvases of Claude and Poussin, the verses of Goldsmith and Wordsworth, bucolic nature was cultivated and controlled.

---

[28] Jerry Podany, 'Restoring what wasn't there', in Andrew Oddy, ed., *Restoration* (British Museum Occasional Paper 99, 1994), 9–16; Alessandra Melluco Vaccaro, 'The emergence of modern conservation theory', 202–11, and 'The idea of patina', 366–71, in Price et al., *Historical and Philosophical Issues*.

[29] Richard Taruskin, 'The pastness of the present and the presence of the past', in Nicholas Kenyon, ed., *Authenticity and Early Music* (Oxford, 1988), 137–207; John Butt, *Playing with History: The Historical Approach to Musical Performance* (Cambridge, 2003), 43; Stan Godlovitch, 'Performance authenticity', in Salim Kemal and Ivan Gaskell, eds., *Performance and Authenticity in the Arts* (Cambridge, 1999), 154–74. See my 'From harmony of the spheres to national anthem', *GeoJournal* 65 (2006): 3–15 at 8–9.

Untouched nature was first exalted by *fin-de-siècle* Americans, aghast at their land's lost purity and vanishing wilderness.[30] Nature restoration came to mean bringing back not Thoreauvian but pre-industrial or even Adamic landscapes. Restoration as re-wilding featured in a 1908 best-seller set in Tennessee's Cumberland Gap. Fouled by soulless loggers, a once crystal-clear stream is now 'black as soot' and choked with sawdust. Tree-felling was 'the cruel deadly work of civilization'. Our hero, a mining engineer turned nature-lover, vows to restore Lonesome Cove:

> 'I'll tear down those mining shacks, . . . stock the river with bass again. And I'll plant young poplars to cover the sight of every bit of uptorn earth . . . I'll bury every bottle and tin can in the Cove. I'll take away every sign of civilization . . .'
> 'And leave old Mother Nature to cover up the scars', says his fiancée, June.
> 'So that Lonesome Cove will be just as it was.'
> 'Just as it was in the beginning', echoes June.
> 'And shall be to the end.'[31]

Restoration redeems all: corporate greed vanquished, machine-age poisons excised, nature left to heal itself, Edenic plenitude in everlasting tranquillity.

Restoration ecology's redemptive bent reflects biblical tradition. In Burnet's second Golden Age, all lands will be 'restored to the same posture they had at the beginning . . . before any disorder came into the natural or moral world'. Two centuries later, another English cleric took heart that St John's Revelation placed 'the restoration of man and the restoration of nature . . . side by side'. Responding to Lynn White's 1967 tirade against Judaeo-Christian environmental abuse, today's ecological theologians bid us to bring the Earth as close as possible to God's destined final restoration.[32]

Nature restorers are fond of medical analogies, likening ecosystem repair to health care. Just as a prosthetic limb aims 'to rehabilitate the function of leg rather than to recompose original flesh and bones', the restoration ecologist aims at ecosystem function, not composition – 'not just certain species, communities, or habitats, but all natural and anthropogenic flow processes'.[33] Human like natural agencies are organically interactive. 'Environment is not something to be passively fixed like a car but . . . actively healed like the human body.' Radical ecosystem intervention is major surgery; raking up stream and shore debris resembles aspirins for headaches, Band-Aids for cuts.[34] Psychologists credit regaining psychic health to relaxing natural scenes. And those so restored in turn promote nature restoration.

Most revealing are analogies with art. As guardians of culture shifted from remaking things whole, to revering original fragments, to recreating palimpsests, analogous

---

[30] Carolyn Merchant, *Reinventing Eden* (Routledge, 2003), 5–10, 86–7, 137–43.
[31] John Fox, Jr., *The Trail of the Lonesome Pine* (New York, 1908), 201–2.
[32] Burnet, *Sacred Theory of the Earth*, 376, 257; Brooke Foss Westcott, *The Gospel of Life* (Macmillan, 1892), 243; Lynn White, Jr., 'The historical roots of our ecologic crisis', *Science* 155 (1967): 1203–7; Douglas J. Moo, 'Nature in the new creation: New Testament eschatology and the environment', *Journal of the Evangelical Theological Society* 49 (2006): 449–88.
[33] Young D. Choi, 'Restoration ecology to the future', *Restoration Ecology* 15 (2007): 351–3.
[34] Valentin Schaefer, 'Science, stewardship, and spirituality: the human body as a model for ecological restoration', *Restoration Ecology* 14:1 (2006): 1–3.

impulses led environmental stewards from regenerating gardens, to restoring degraded landscapes, to re-wilding, and to concern for ecological processes. Art and architecture lent admonitory cautions. 'Just as faked art is less valuable than authentic art', warned an environmentalist, 'faked nature is less valuable than original nature'.[35] The Sierra Club's charismatic David Brower likened US Bureau of Reclamation plans to dam the Grand Canyon for visitor access to 'flood[ing] the Sistine Chapel so tourists can get nearer to the ceiling'. How far damaged landscapes can or should be returned to their 'original' state is called the 'Sistine Chapel Debate'.[36]

But differing restoration aims and assumptions make the analogy dubious. Paintings, creeds, legal codes get restored back to whenever most new and fresh, effective, intelligible, admired, or sacred. In contrast, natural landscapes are restored to when least deranged by human action, most ecologically diverse, or most stable and sustainable. Cultural relics are cherished mainly as unique features – Lascaux, Stonehenge, Parthenon, Chartres, Monticello, Gettysburg, *Mona Lisa*, a First Folio. But nature is valued for composite amalgams: clusters, swarms or herds, species, genera or ecosystems, or natural selection in general.[37]

Unlike paintings, landscapes have no 'original state'; they ceaselessly evolve. And efforts to restore pre-human circumstances are in essence self-contradictory, for nature restored becomes a human artefact. To be sure, most restorations aim to repair already degraded nature; no place on Earth remains untouched by human agency. 'What we now regard as a pristine landscape was actually fashioned by perhaps a hundred thousand years of our forebears' intervention.'[38] But we readily imagine pre-disturbance conditions and exalt nature freed from human impress.[39] Lauding the restoration of a previously canalized Montana waterway, a delighted celebrant 'couldn't tell that man had been at work – not in the past five years and not in 1951. And neither could the birds and the fish.'[40] In nature restoration, human agency is the passion that dare not speak its name, human mastery omnipresent but unseen.

That nature can and should repair itself – an idle fancy for humans dependent on agriculture, architecture, antibiotics, reservoirs, sewage systems – is also scientifically untenable. Ecology a half century ago abandoned equilibrium models that equated non-interference with environmental health and stable climaxes Yet many ecologists still elevate nature over culture, deploring humanity's imprint as retrogression from the untouched fundament.[41] Public faith in the beneficent stability of untamed nature

---

[35] Robert Elliot, *Faking Nature* (1982; Routledge, 1997), vii.

[36] Sierra Club, June 1966, quoted in Marcus Hall, *Earth Repair* (Virginia, 2005), 1–2, 13–15; Peter Losin, 'Faking nature', and 'Sistine Chapel debate', *Restoration & Management Notes* 4 (1986): 55, and 6 (1988): 6.

[37] See my 'Natural and cultural heritage', in Kenneth R. Olwig and David Lowenthal, eds., *The Nature of Cultural Heritage and the Culture of Natural Heritage* (Routledge, 2006), 79–90.

[38] Gregory Benford, *Deep Time: How Humanity Communicates across Millennia* (Harper, 2000), 171–3; William M. Denevan, 'The "Pristine Myth" revisited', *Geographical Review* 101 (2011): 576–91.

[39] Eric Katz, 'The big lie: human restoration of nature', *Research in Philosophy and Technology* 12 (1992): 231–41 at 235; Elliot, *Faking Nature*, 111–12.

[40] Verlyn Klinkenborg, 'Restoring a Montana spring creek', *IHT*, 10–11 July 2010: 7.

[41] Bernd von Droste et al., eds., *Cultural Landscapes of Universal Value* (Jena: Gustav Fischer/UNESCO, 1995).

persists in denial of all experience of human improvement and natural disaster. Hence the contrariness of re-wilding devotees who prefer nature restored with all sullying trace of human agency concealed. No wonder nature conservation is so expensive: 'many human hands are needed to make nature look untouched by human hands'.[42]

In ecology, as in art, what restorers do is often at odds with what they say. River restoration practitioners and stakeholders worldwide were asked what restoration meant. Four out of five named the strict canonical definition, 'complete structural and functional return to a predisturbance state'. But most of them actually *improved, enhanced,* and *created*, to make 'something new and more valuable than what was there originally'. Despite declaring adherence to 'the most ... widely accepted definition in the restoration literature', practitioners continually transgressed it.[43] Although obviously manipulating, like Victorian architectural restorers they are reluctant to admit that they do so. 'We bury our efforts beneath an ecological cover', concludes a leading restorer, 'and pretty quickly a landscape that depends on or originates in extensive human contrivance becomes naturalized'.[44] Hence landscape restoration is vilified as 'gardening dressed up with jargon to simulate ecology', or 'agriculture in reverse', or simply 'a fiction'.[45] In actuality 'restoration is fencing, planting, fertilizing, tilling, and weeding the wildland garden: succession, bioremediation, reforestation, afforestation, fire control, prescribed burning, crowd control, biological control ... and much more'.[46]

Restoring what was in nature, even more than in culture, is an unreachable Holy Grail. Those who seek it, like those who seek to preserve, willy-nilly retrieve a much-altered past. On the land as in the arts, restoration is at best 'a necessary evil', judged a connoisseur: 'The business of the restorer is the most thankless one imaginable.' If he does his work well he is a forger, if badly he is despised as a destroyer.[47]

Yet restoration has long been praised as divinely ordained. God created; repentant humans restore, not only repairing losses caused by the sinful corruption of nature, but improving on original nature. Indeed, 'the works of restoration are much worthier than the works of creation', argued the twelfth-century theologian Hugh of St Victor, for 'restoration heals and reveals, illuminates and demonstrates'. Restoring 'things which had been laid waste' or 'fallen into ruin' perfected them – 'the water of creation reformed into

---

[42] Dekkers, *Way of All Flesh*, 92. See Eric Katz, 'Further adventures in the case against restoration', *Environmental Ethics* 34 (2012): 67–97; Jan E. Dizard, *Going Wild*, rev. edn (Massachusetts, 1999); Hall, *Earth Repair*, 11–13, 138–49, 195–9. See my 'Environment as heritage', in Kate Flint and Howard Morphy, eds., *Culture, Landscape, and the Environment* (Oxford, 2000), 198–217.

[43] Joseph M. Wheaton et al., 'Does scientific conjecture accurately describe restoration practice? Insight from an international river restoration survey', *Area* 38 (2006): 128–42; John Cairns, Jr., 'The status of the theoretical and applied science of restoration ecology', *The Environmental Professional* 13 (1991): 186–94 at 187; Anthony D. Bradshaw, 'Alternative endpoints for reclamation', in John Cairns, Jr., ed., *Rehabilitating Damaged Ecosystems* (Boca Raton, FL: CRC Press, 1988), 2: 69–85.

[44] Eric Higgs, 'Restoration goes wild', *Restoration Ecology* 14 (2006): 500–3 at 502.

[45] Peter Del Tredici, 'Neocreationism and the illusion of ecological restoration', *Harvard Design Magazine*, no. 20 (2004): 87–9; William R. Jordan, III, 'Restoration, community, and wilderness', in Paul H. Gobster and R. Bruce Hull, eds., *Restoring Nature* (Island Press, 2000), 21–36 at 27; Mark A. Davis, '"Restoration" – a misnomer?' *Science* 287 (2000): 1203 (letter).

[46] Daniel Janzen, 'Gardenification of wildland nature and the human footprint', *Science* 279 (1998): 1312–13.

[47] Max J. Friedländer, *On Art and Connoisseurship* (1942; Boston, 1960), 267.

the wine of restoration'.[48] Four centuries on, Erasmus, restoring the New Testament to the heavenly founder's supposed intent, praised Pope Leo X, as a second Esdras restoring Rome as the prophet Ezra had Jerusalem. And 'to restore great things', added Erasmus, 'is sometimes not only a harder but a nobler task than to have introduced them'.[49]

Divine restoration demands human agency. This reading of the Fortunate Fall, Adam's sin leading to a ' wonderful' greater good, is prefigured in Milton's *Areopagitica*. Wicked deceivers had hewed 'the virgin Truth's lovely form into a thousand pieces, and scatter'd them to the four winds'. Just as Isis had sought 'the mangled body of Osiris', Truth's grieving disciples gathered up 'dissevered pieces' to restore Truth limb by limb.[50] As I have shown, restoration is unattainable. But the mission is morally compelling, as Paul Auster's Stillman observes of his collection of smashed and fragmented artefacts. 'The world is in fragments. And it's my job to put it back together again.' But Stillman is Everyman, Adam as Humpty Dumpty:

Man is a fallen creature – we know that from Genesis. Humpty Dumpty is also a fallen creature. He falls from his wall, and no one can put him back together again. . . . But that is what we must all now strive to do. It is our duty as human beings: to put the egg back together again. For each of us . . . is Humpty Dumpty.[51]

And however flawed, the restorative effort can be intensely rewarding. 'He who calls departed ages back into being', affirmed a famed chronicler of ancient Rome, 'enjoys a bliss like that of creating'.[52]

Re-enactment

Like restorers, re-enactors seek to retrieve a vanished past. Sharing similar aims, they are shadowed by the same limitation: the impossibility of repeating the past. Like restorers, re-enactors start with what's known or believed and fill in the gaps with the probable, the possible, the plausible, or the risible. Just as the restored past is never the same, no re-enactment duplicates the original act. But re-enactors like restorers strive to get as close to past reality as possible, if not to improve on it. Many famed historical depictions, such as Matthew Brady's Civil War scenes and Joe Rosenthal's iconic Iwo Jima flag-raising photo (1945), were not of the actual events but painstakingly restaged for dramatic effect.[53]

Re-enactment originated and is continued in religious and political rituals.[54] Evocations of Exodus make ancient Israelites' escape from Egypt a personal experience for

---

[48] *Sententiae divinitatis* (1145–50), quoted in Boyd Taylor Coolman, *The Theology of Hugh of St Victor* (Cambridge, 2010), 12–15, 99, 132, 144, 172, 205, 218. See Paul Rorem, *Hugh of Saint Victor* (Oxford, 2009), 27, 31, 66.

[49] Erasmus to Leo X, 1 Feb. 1516, letter 384, in *Correspondence . . . (1514–1516)* in *CW*, vol. 3 (1976), 221–2. See Ch. 4 above on Erasmus's claims to restore when he instead created.

[50] John Milton, *Paradise Lost*, XII: 472–4; and *Areopagitica* (1644; Cambridge, 1918), 48.

[51] Paul Auster, *City of Glass* (Los Angeles: Sun & Moon, 1985), 119, 128.

[52] Barthold Georg Niebuhr, *The History of Rome* (1811–12; Cambridge, 1831), 1: 5.

[53] Barry Misenheimer, 'The stage of war', *New Yorker*, 7 Feb 2011: 7.

[54] Emile Durkheim, *The Elementary Forms of Religious Life* (1912; Free Press, 1995), 416–17; Meyer Fortes, 'Rituals and office in tribal society', in Max Gluckman, ed., *Essays on the Ritual of Social Relations*

modern celebrants, while Passover ceremonies annually fuse past with present. The Eucharist re-enacts the Last Supper, communion bread and wine Christ's flesh and blood. Anti-Semitism, from Passion Plays and choral masses to blood-rite hysteria and murderous pogroms, re-enacts vengeance for Christ's killing.[55] Good Friday scourging rituals in Calabria continue penitential medieval performances. Philippine villagers re-enact 'Roman centurions dragging Jesus to Golgotha, with a few men briefly crucified. If performing Jesus is painful, re-enacting Judas is a lasting curse, his impersonators jeered and cursed for life.[56]

Varieties of replay

Re-enactment takes many forms. Role-players at historic sites and commemorative events repeat what past people might have done or said. Theatrical restaging ranges from weekly transubstantiations and annual Nativity plays to once-in-a-lifetime spectacles, such as the late Shah of Iran's 1971 pageant in reconstructed Persepolis celebrating Cyrus's founding of the Persian Empire 2,500 years earlier.[57]

Repeat performances are common fare. A Western desperado is shot every hour at Old Fort Dodge; Redcoats again and again confront rebel militia at Concord's Old North Bridge; 'three to four times an hour you can experience a hazardous voyage with Leif Eiriksson at the helm' at Norway's Viking Farm; Confederate infantrymen at Stones River Battlefield daily recount Civil War exploits. Battle buffs exhibit the traumatic obsession of Tristram Shandy's Toby and Trim, replaying old military sieges.[58] Repetitive re-enactors resemble post-traumatic stress sufferers who expose themselves over and over to horrific reminiscence, like the trench-warfare victims in Pat Barker's *Regeneration* trilogy (1991–5).[59] Modern media foment endless replay. The 1976 *Eternal Frame* videotapers of Kennedy's 1963 assassination re-enacted the Zapruder filming of the event; 'just as the

(Manchester, 1962), 53–88; Jan Assmann, *Cultural Memory and Early Civilization* (Cambridge, 2011), 3–4, 70–4, 81–6; Janeen A. Costa and Gary J. Bamossy, 'Retrospecting retroscapes', in Stephen Brown and John F. Sherry, eds., *Time, Space, and the Market* (Armonk, NY: M. E. Sharpe, 2003), 253–70 at 260–1.

[55] Helmut Walser Smith, 'Anti-Semitic violence as reenactment', *Rethinking History* 11:3 (2007): 335–51.

[56] Giovanni Orlando Muraca, 'Scourging rituals in southern Italy', in George Mifsud-Chircop, ed., *SIEF Working Group on the Ritual Year . . .: Proceedings* (San Gwann, Malta: PEG, 2006), 420–5; Roberto Deri, 'The largest self-punishment rite in the Western world', *DEMOTIX.com/news/419737* (22 Aug. 2010); Kathy Marks, 'Dozens ignore warnings to re-enact crucifixion', *Independent on Sunday*, 22 Mar. 2008; Barbara Mae Dacaney, 'Crucifixion ritual suffers as nobody is willing to play the part of Judas', *Gulfnews. com* (13 Apr. 2008). A replica Jesus is crucified and resurrected twice a day (following ten daily Last Suppers) at Disney's Holy Land Experience in Orlando, Florida.

[57] E. R. Chamberlin, *Preserving the Past* (Dent, 1979), 18–24; Vesta Sarkhosh Curtis, 'The legacy of ancient Persia', in John F. Curtis and Nigel Tallis, eds., *Forgotten Empire* (California, 2006), 250–64 at 257.

[58] K. M. Hjemdahl, 'History as a cultural playground', *Ethnologia Europaea* 32:2 (2002): 105–24 at 107; Laurence Sterne, *The Life and Opinions of Tristram Shandy* (1759; Penguin, 2003), 184–90, 510–11; Simon During, 'Mimic toil', *Rethinking History* 11:3 (2007): 320–6.

[59] John Brannigan, 'Pat Barker's *Regeneration* trilogy', in Richard J. Lane et al., eds., *Contemporary British Fiction* (Polity, 2003), 13–26 at 21–3; Bessel A. Van der Kolk, 'The compulsion to repeat the trauma', *Psychiatric Clinics of North America* 12 (1989): 389–411. See Robert C. Scaer, *Body Bears the Burden* (Haworth Medical, 2007), 129–40.

image had been rerun again and again, the artists drove through the plaza again and again', a cathartic reliving that spectators found 'so real ... a beautiful re-enactment'.[60]

Along with replay of specific events, usually battles, go vignettes of everyday life. While men re-fight the Wars of the Roses or the Battle of Gettysburg, women perform bygone domestic tasks. At historic sites coopers make barrels for salt pork, pumpkin rinds are hung out to dry, sorghum boiled. These are activities 'typical of the nineteenth century', time travellers to Olde Illinois are told, 'yet you are experiencing them today!' Imbibing such sights and smells is a pedagogic vogue, 'reliving the past the best way to learn about it'.[61] Week-long visitors to Lejre in Denmark who relive the Iron Age 'with all their senses and through their own bodies' gain empathy with prehistory through 'performative authenticity'.[62] The stench and din of servants' life below stairs re-evokes Edwardian working-class life.[63] Bygone contact lends visceral assurance of the past's reality, and re-enactors claim it their duty to convey that reality. To act as 'the mirror image of our forefathers', says a Civil War player, is something 'we owe to posterity'.[64]

Time-travel illusion varies with the type of role play. 'Third-person' interpreters dress and work in period style but do not pretend to be past people. Speaking with today's words and know-how, they stress the past's difference and distance. 'Second-person' replay cajoles visitors to take on bygone tasks, churning butter or making soap, saddling horses or shooting arrows. Living-history sites restage historical episodes with visitors enacting past personae.[65] 'First-person' character imposters feign previous folk 'from outward appearances to innermost beliefs and attitudes'. Pretending to know nothing of later events, they engage with modern visitors in antiquated ways. Those at Plimoth Plantation's replica village ape the dialect and perspectives of William Brewster and other inhabitants of 1627. To avoid confusion with period actors, visitors are asked to dress normally – a precaution confounded by a busload of Mennonites who looked uncannily like Massachusetts Pilgrims.[66]

Animated replay is ever more popular; manuals, journals, and websites cater for hosts of hobbyists. Tens of thousands re-perform battles, often before spectators who help finance such events but cloud their authenticity. Professional–amateur and first-, second-, and third-person distinctions are often blurred: guests at Conner Prairie's '19th-century' baseball games are asked to cheer in period lingo (but no profanity). Tourists spending

[60] Patricia Mellencamp, *High Anxiety* (Indiana, 1992), 99–103; Marita Sturken, *Tangled Memories* (California, 1997), 29–31. *Eternal Frame* was itself replayed by Oliver Stone's *JFK* (1991).
[61] James Allen, 'Living the past in Illinois', *Historic Illinois* 1:4 (1978): 3; Vicky Middlesworth, 'History and hardtack: a museum workshop program for Kentucky teachers', *Journal of American Culture* 12:2 (Summer 1989): 87–91.
[62] Kristi Mathiesen Hjemdahl, 'History as a cultural playground', *Ethnologia Europaea* 32:2 (2002): 105–24 at 107–10; Cornelius Holtorf, 'The time travellers' tools of the trade: some trends at Lejre', *International Journal of Heritage Studies* 19:5 (2013): 1–16 at 10.
[63] Lucy Delap, *Knowing Their Place: Domestic Service in Twentieth-Century Britain* (Oxford, 2011), 224, 229.
[64] Cathy Stanton, *Reenactors in the Parks* (Boston: NPS, 1999), 22.
[65] Carl Weinberg, 'The discomfort zone: reenacting slavery at Conner Prairie', *Magazine of History* 23:2 (Apr. 2009): 62–4.
[66] Steven Eddy Snow, *Performing the Pilgrims: ... Plimoth Plantation* (Mississippi, 1993), 156; Scott Magelssen, 'Recreation and re-creation ... at Plimoth Plantation', *Journal of Dramatic Theory and Criticism* 17 (2002): 107–26.

Figure 75 Re-enacting the past: Plimoth Plantation as of 1627

Figure 76 Re-enacting the past: visitors to the Stone Age, Stockholm, 2006

the night in Newport mansions or Badlands homesteaders' cabins relive America's 'geeky, gaudy, mystical, majestic, tough and tragic roots'.[67] Like history teachers, museums find that for today's interactive visitors 'it is no longer enough merely to be told about times past. They are fully satisfied only if they live it – feel it – experience it'. At Colonial Williamsburg they want to 'join in the action of the story being told' and share the joys and sorrows of the historical figures they meet there.[68]

Archaeologists repeat bygone toils to learn something new. Egyptian pyramids, replica Stonehenges, medieval siege engines are constructed, archaic crops planted and harvested to test historical conjectures. At Butser Ancient Farm in England, Lejre in Denmark, L'Esquerda in Catalonia, work with facsimile tools and bred-back livestock confirm or deny conjectural pasts.[69] Bonding with the past accompanies learning about it. Sailing replica double-hulled canoes helps explain ancient voyaging, at the same time instilling pride in Polynesian forebears who navigated vast distances and colonized far-flung islands without modern tools.[70]

Inspired by 1960s Civil War centennial replays, re-enactors repeated every American revolutionary skirmish during the 1976 bicentenary. Many revolutionary replays were barefaced contrivances. That not every locality had hosted one of Washington's tactical withdrawals was no bar to re-enactment. 'You give us the Bicentennial, we'll provide the battle', promised celebrants in New York. Baltimore staged a mythical War of 1812 battle, with British soldiers arresting city fathers. 'So what?' retorted officials chided for the fiction. 'Just because it never happened doesn't detract from it.'[71]

While those replaying 'Americans' complained that 'British' soldiers went 'too far in pursuit of authenticity', the 'British' scorned 'ragtag colonials' makeshift uniforms and harum-scarum drill. 'They started as a rabble in 1775', sneered a 'British' officer, 'and now they are authentically portraying a rabble'.[72]

[67] Jay Anderson, *Time Machines* (AASLH, 1984), 43–52; Scott Magelssen, *Living History Museums* (Scarecrow Press, 2007), 138–54; 'Twelve unexpected history trips', *NYT*, 12 July 2010: TR1. Manuals include Stacy F. Roth, *Past into Present* (1988); F. L. Watkins and Julia K. Watkins, *The Persona Handbook* (1992); R. Lee Hadden, *Reliving the Civil War* (1996); and B. C. Kemmer and K. M. Kemmer, So, *Ye Want to Be a Reenactor?* (2001).
[68] Cary Carson, 'The end of history museums?' *Public Historian* 30:4 (2008): 9–27 at 18.
[69] Alexander Cook, 'The use and abuse of historical reenactment', *Rethinking History* (2007): 487–96 at 487–8; Peter J. Reynolds *Iron-Age Farm: The Butser Experiment* (British Museum, 1979), and 'The nature of experiment in archaeology', in A. F. Harding, ed., *Experiment and Design in Archaeology* (Oxbow, 1999), 156–62; Carmen Cubero i Corpas et al., 'From the granary to the field: archaeobotany and experimental archaeology at l'Esquerda (Catalonia, Spain)', *Vegetation History & Archaeobotany* 17:1 (2008): 85–92; Anderson, *Time Machines*, 85–131; Dana C. E. Millson, ed., *Experimentation and Interpretation* (Oxford: Oxbow, 2010); Stephen C. Saraydar, *Replicating the Past* (Long Grove, IL: Waveland Press, 2008).
[70] Greg Dening, *Beach Crossings* (PennPress, 2004), 176–83; Greg Dening, 'Voyaging the past, present and future: historical reenactments on HM Bark *Endeavour* and the voyaging canoe *Hokule'a* in the sea of islands', in Felicity A. Nussbaum, ed., *The Global Eighteenth Century* (Johns Hopkins, 2005), 309–24; Polynesian Voyaging Society, *pvs.kcc.hawaii.edu*.
[71] Murray Schumach, 'Queens gets battle of '76 at last', *NYT*, 28 May 1976: C1–2; 'Undeterred', *IHT*, 24 June 1975: 14; see my 'The bicentennial landscape', *Geographical Review* 67 (1977): 253–67.
[72] Betty Doak Elder, 'War games: recruits and their critics draw battle lines over authenticity', *History News* 36:8 (1981): 8–12; Tim Clark, 'When the paraders meet the button-counters at Penobscot Bay', *Yankee* (July 1980): 44–9, 129–43 at 49, 134–5.

Patent errors and anachronisms led historians to condemn replay as demeaning sham. Censuring carnivalesque 'enjoyment out of what was literally a human tragedy', and fearing costly lawsuits in case of accidents, the US National Park Service banned battle re-enactments on its sites. Subsequent replays became bizarrely incongruous. The 'Battle Road 2000' commemorative at Minute Man National Historical Park redid the clash that ignited the Revolution with no hint of combat.[73]

Tower of London Beefeaters aside, Britain was slower to embrace re-enactment. Actors in period dress seemed superfluous where *real* history was plentiful. Historic-house grandees 'creaking in armour with swords dripping in blood or in wigs and crinolines armed with smoking warming pans' would be ludicrous. Were Sir Francis Dashwood to re-enact his eighteenth-century forebear's orgies at Hell Fire Caves, modern High Wycombe could never 'supply enough virgins' to meet the demand. A 2006 pagan revel at the caves was confined to decorous feasting.[74] Compared with spirited American shows, Britain's past remained largely passive.

American advice at Tatton Park in Cheshire, a National Trust property, typified the contrast. The kitchen needed a 'worked-in' look; guides should stress the 'common humanity shared by today's visitor and Tatton's medieval residents'. A peasant family (with livestock) should inhabit an 'authentic' cottage. Reanimated Tatton Park now hosts Viking Sundays, World War II Weekends, annual Medieval Fayres, even American Civil War battles.[75]

In recent decades England has embraced re-enactment, reviving ancient fanciful customs. But while earlier replay was exclusively elite, today's is all-embracing and populist. Kentwell Hall, Suffolk, annually recreates Tudor domestic life.[76] English Heritage events – Roman military manoeuvres, medieval tile painting, darning socks with a '1940s' housewife – drew 620,000 participants in 2009. Blending the showmanship of Heinrich Schliemann and P. T. Barnum, York's Jorvik Viking Centre (founded in 1984) has attracted 20 million visitors; 'Get face to face with Vikings' includes 'best-bearded' barbarian competitions. From rats in the scullery and urine in the bedroom in Dennis Severs's Spital-fields Huguenot weavers' house, to a debauched Regency dinner party, the hostess collapsed on the dining table, at Port Eliot, Cornwall, re-enacting is now de rigueur. 'Shamefully lowbrow . . . queasy voyeurism' is said to Disneyfy the once-elitist National Trust's embrace of the seedy and disreputable.[77] The continent has followed suit. A generation ago history was 'beautifully embalmed, but dead'. Now all Europe enjoys American-style animation.[78]

---

[73] Elder, 'War games', 9, 11; Dwight F. Rettie, *Our National Park System* (Illinois, 1996), 47, 60n16; Cathy Stanton, 'Battle road 2000', *Journal of American History* 8 (2000): 992–5, and *Reenactors in the Parks*, 21–3.

[74] Duke of Bedford, 'Historic homes', *Times*, 9 Sept. 1976: 15; *ukpaganlinks.co.uk/article.php?n=113&page=1*.

[75] US NPS, *Tatton Park Interpretive Study* (Countryside Commission [UK] 1975), 31–4, App. II, pp. ii, x; Dolly Pile, 'Interpreting Old Hall, Tatton Park', *Interpretation*, no. 17 (1981): 3–5; *tattonpark.org.uk*.

[76] Kentwell's Great Annual Re-Creation of Tudor Life, onthetudortrail.com.

[77] Emily Burns, 'Re-enacting history', 8–9, and Simon Jenkins, interview, 'Popularising the past', 3–5, in EH *Conservation Bulletin*, no. 64 (Summer 2010); Stephen Bayley, 'Stop this Disneyfication of the National Trust', *Times*, 18 Oct. 2010: 20; Alan Bennett, *People* (Faber & Faber, 2012), ix–xi.

[78] Judith Schlehe et al., eds., *Staging the Past* (Bielefeld: Transcript, 2010). On earlier European reluctance to animate the past, see Magelssen, *Living History Museums*, 2–4, 194–6.

The pious presentism of American and the (previously) prissy reserve of British re-enactments are riotously subverted in Australian replays. Spectators hijacked the 1951 federation semi-centenary by lampooning history. At the rerun of Charles Sturt's epic expedition down the Murray River, Hollywood-style cowboys and Indians ambushed the 'explorers' and fed them 'roasted snake' (sausage) and 'witchety grubs' (cake icing).[79] Six million visitors to 'Old Sydney Town', an hour's drive north of actual Sydney, joined actors in inventing comic anachronisms during the theme park's three decades (1975–2003). Sentenced to a thousand lashes, a 'convict''s last wish is chloroform. 'But chloroform hasn't been invented yet!' says the 'flogger'. 'Never mind; I'll wait.' Shooting a fleeing convict, a militiaman yells, 'Go on, kiddies; see if you can pick the bullets out of his belly.'[80] No British or American re-enactment thus violates bygone sanctities, or casually lampoons time travel.

Enduring the past's authentic hardships

Grubby authenticity is a mantra of replay. 'Sink your "teeth" into living history!' American Civil War players can chomp on stained, chipped, and snaggled dentures styled in 'Tavern sot', 'Lick spittle', 'Village idiot', 'Gin lane', or 'Jackanape'. These re-enactors range from 'farbs' (ignorant novices or feckless casuals), to 'canvas cowboys' prone to minor defects, to 'pards' (perfectionists).[81] Marching toward Gettysburg, a hard-core pard's uniform must be 'gray cloth with just the right amount of dye and the exact number of threads. It's like ... the Holy Grail.' Refusing to fall in with the 17th Kentucky Regiment, the 6th Tennessee vented 'Hell no ... bunch of farbs ... look at the crap they're wearing.'[82]

Mocked as 'button pissers' or 'stitch Nazis', authenticity gurus pen 'unreadable articles on the "Color, Type and Efficacy of Seam Threads Used in Federal Issue Trousers of the Trans Mississippi from May 1862–Aug 1863"'. They deride farbs' egregious gaffes: a 'ghost' is a dead re-enactor who resurrects himself too soon, a 'Kevlar reenactor' won't die no matter how often shot.[83] Yet 'nobody wants to drive three hours and spend the day lying on cowpies' tormented by fire ants, as one buff found when tempted by heat and fatigue to die on the spot.[84] But no actual casualty could experience a

---

[79] Stephen Gapps, 'Blacking up for the explorers of 1951', in Vanessa Agnew and Jonathan Lamb, eds., *Settler and Creole Re-Enactment* (Palgrave Macmillan, 2010), 208–20.

[80] I visited Old Sydney Town in 1987. See my 'Tombs or time-machines? Antipodean and other museums', in Donald F. McMichael, ed., *Australian Museums* (Canberra, 1991), 9–21.

[81] Kip M. Grunska, *From Fard to Pard: A Story of Civil War Reenactment* (Lincoln, NE: iUniverse, 2003); M. D. Strauss, 'Pattern categorization of male U.S. Civil War reenactment images', *Clothing and Textiles Research Journal* 20 (2002): 99–109.

[82] Tony Horwitz, *Confederates in the Attic* (Pantheon, 1998), 387–8; M. D. Strauss, 'A framework for assessing military dress authenticity in Civil War reenacting', *Clothing and Textiles Research Journal* 19:4 (2001): 145–57 at 150.

[83] Jenny Thompson, *War Games: Inside the World of 20th-Century War Reenactors* (Smithsonian, 2004); Jonah Begone, "Seven annoying reenacting types', and 'Who was the founding father of farb?' *Camp Chase Gazette* 20:10 (Sept. 1993), and 26:10 (Sept. 1999).

[84] Horwitz, *Confederates in the Attic*, 133; Jack Barth, 'The red badge of make-believe courage', *Outside* (Mar. 1996), 88–92.

Union army re-enactor's spooky thrill when Confederates stepped on his dead body and ransacked his haversack.[85]

Authentic concern is most intense for events that still elicit strong feelings. In the US the Civil War tops the list. Participants stress truth in dress, drill, chow, and speech even as they defend their side's original aims – 'I do this because I believe in what they believed in … The real pure hobby is not just looking right; it's thinking right.' But right thinking ignores past horror, celebrating valour and chivalry, not slavery or gangrened amputations. Impassioned attachment to states' rights and the Lost Cause inhibits 'galvanizing' (switching from Rebel to Union garb to rectify the usual battle imbalance). One Southerner claimed that his horse refused to let him into the saddle until he put away his Yankee blue.[86] 'Most of us', confesses the flagship journal's publisher, 'blur the line between Civil War reenacting and personal political agendas'. Buffs who 'honor those who fought for their beliefs' are really enacting their own beliefs.[87] Bavarian role-playing Confederates are said to act out Nazi fantasies of racial superiority. Tarred with the same brush, an Ohio congressional candidate who often donned Waffen SS uniforms for Second World War replays failed to persuade critics that he was simply 'educating the public about an event that happened'.[88]

No enduring Lost Cause afflicts 'Patriots' or 'Tories' at American revolutionary replays. Rules are relaxed because authentic gear and know-how are harder to come by and re-enactors are longer in the tooth: Civil War average age 29, Revy War 104.[89] Britain's Tudor Group preaches period accuracy, but indulges members' common bent to hide any anachronism by covering it with hessian cloth.[90]

Earlier epochs evoke still less fidelity to more fugitive fact. Aiming to be 'medievalish' rather than authentically medieval, the Society for Creative Anachronism sanctions a 'Celtghanistan' medley of costumes and personas. Availability constrains authenticity. 'I know they wore wool … because that's what was available to them', said a perspiring American medievalist. 'But if they were in North America … they would have worn cotton, because it's what would have been available'. Comments an SCA leader, 'you can justify almost anything with the if-they-had-it-they-would-have-used-it argument'. The SCA motto is 'The middle ages not as they were, but as they should have been'. Members

[85] Randal Allred, 'Catharsis, revision, and re-enactment: negotiating the meaning of the American Civil War', *Journal of American Culture* 19:4 (1996): 1–13 at 6; Jonah Begone, 'Do something new!' *Camp Chase Gazette* (Oct. 1995).

[86] Patrick McDermott (1988) quoted in Allred, 'Catharsis, revision, and re-enactment', 4; James Oscar Farmer, 'Playing rebels: reenactment as nostalgia and defense of the Confederacy in the Battle of Aiken', *Southern Cultures* 11:1 (2005): 46–73 at 50.

[87] Bill Holschuh in *Camp Chase Gazette* 28:4 (2001): 71, quoted in M. D. Strauss, 'Identity construction among Confederate Civil War reenactors', *Clothing and Textiles Research Journal* 21:4 (2003): 149–61 at 155, 160; Jonah Begone, '10 bad reasons to reenact', *Camp Chase Gazette* 18:8 (July 1991).

[88] 'Germany reenacting!!', *angelfire.com/me/cwcontact/Germany.html* (1 Feb. 2012); Horwitz, *Confederates in the Attic*, 187; Rich Iott quoted in 'Candidate rejects criticism of Nazi uniform', *Washington Post*, 12 Oct. 2010. See Thompson, *War Games*; Eva Kingsepp, 'Hitler as our devil? Nazi Germany in mainstream media', in Sara Buttsworth and Maartje Abbenhuis., eds., *Making Monsters* (Praeger, 2010), 29–52 at 45–7.

[89] Jonah Begone, 'Differences between Civil War & Revolutionary War reenacting', *Camp Chase Gazette* 17:9 (Aug. 1990).

[90] Mark Goodman, 'Re-enactment: is it still a hobby?' in *Echoes of the Past* ([BBC], 2000; repr. Tudor Group, 2009).

'build armor that articulates, cook feasts that taste good, build happy, prosperous kingdoms'.[91] The SCA's idealized past resembles Skansen's nineteenth-century Swedish village, a 'very nice place', assures a hostess, 'no bad things happen here – ever'. The grim crop failures that exiled 1.3 million starving Swedes to America go unmentioned.[92]

Re-enactment offers a sense of purpose felt lacking in the humdrum present. 'Most of us lead crappy little lives', says a Civil War buff; we are 'truer to our real selves' in the past.[93] Like sci-fi time travellers, re-enactors feel fulfilled back then. Playing a Civil War 'chaplain', a cleric found his truest ministry in bringing his bygone regiment to Jesus. 'If I could trade places with my great-great-grandpappy', said the scion of his thrice-wounded Civil War ancestor, 'I'd do it in a second. Life was harder then but . . . simpler. He didn't have to pay phone bills, put gas in the car, worry about crime. And he knew what he was living for.'[94]

Many link bygone seemliness with clear-cut gender roles. A woman washing clothes in a Union army tub romanticizes an era when 'men were men and women were women. No one's that polite in real life anymore.'[95] The re-enactor playing the butler in *Edwardian Country House* 'inhabited the world that my grandparents inhabited and they can be proud of their grandson, because I behaved like an Edwardian'. Three months back then alienated him from today's world: 'I don't . . . like the 21st century . . . nothing whatsoever to do with my modern life'.[96] Those enlivened by bygone personas find it hard to quit the past. 'Reenactors don't experience relief when we get back to the present. We experience depression!' when 'the twentieth century starts flooding in again'.[97]

The past is adored for being not just different but *past*, with a finished coherent truth absent in the messy ongoing here and now. 'Kerry and I are always saying we wish we lived in the olden days', said an Australian 'ex-convict' in *The Colony*. 'Life now . . . well, everything seems so false.'[98] Even olden miseries attract devotees. Shipped to the

---

[91] Stephanie K. Decker, 'Being period: an examination of bridging discourse in a historical reenactment group', *Journal of Contemporary Ethnography* 39:3 (2010): 273–96 at 289–90; David D. Friedman, 'A dying dream' (1986), 189–91, 'Concerning the "C" in "SCA"' (1988), 201–2, and 'Medieval vs. medievalish', 207–10, in David D. Friedman and Elizabeth Cook, *Cariadoc's Miscellany* (San Jose, CA, 2000).

[92] Scott Magelssen, 'Performance practices of [living] open-air museums (and a new look at "Skansen" in American living museum context)', *Theatre History Studies* 24 (June 2004): 125–49 at 146.

[93] Strauss, 'Framework for assessing military dress authenticity', 150.

[94] Clifford Pierce, *Life and Times of a Civil War Reenactor* (Palm Coast, FL: Backintyme, 2008), i, 4; Horwitz, *Confederates in the Attic*, 133.

[95] Horwitz, *Confederates in the Attic*, 134. The NPS barred Lauren Cook Burgess from an Antietam battle re-enactment for 'lack of authenticity . . . caused by her gender'; after she won a sex discrimination suit, the number of cross-dressing women re-enactors 'has steadily grown' (Elizabeth Young, *Disarming the Nation: Women's Writing and the American Civil War* (Chicago, 1999), 287–8).

[96] *The Edwardian Country House*, Channel 4, Episode 6, 28 May 2002, quoted in Jerome de Groot, *Consuming History* (Routledge, 2009), 179.

[97] Jonah Begone, 'Reenacting: a hobby for every generation', *Camp Chase Gazette* 24:2 (Nov.–Dec. 1996); Horwitz, *Confederates in the Attic*, 139. See Rory Turner, 'Bloodless battles: the Civil War reenacted', *Drama Review* 34:4 (1990): 123–36 at 126; Dennis Hall, 'Civil War reenactors and the postmodern sense of history', *Journal of American Culture* 17:3 (1994): 7–11 at 11; Vanessa Agnew, 'Introduction: what is reenactment?' *Criticism* 46:3 (2004): 327–40 at 330.

[98] Belinda Gibbon (2005) quoted in Michelle Arrow, '"That history should not ever have been how it was": *The Colony, Outback House*, and Australian history', *Film & History* 37:1 (2007): 54–66 at 59.

thirteenth century as a crippled peasant, Douglas Coupland's identity seeker gets to 'be real and hang with real people having real lives'.[99]

Pain and privation enforce authenticity. Dour jokes are traded about today's tweedy toffs on the treadmill, picking oakum and crushing lime at the National Trust's South-well, Nottinghamshire, workhouse, to experience how former inmates lived.[100] A Maine farm set in the 1870s conveys past midwinter hardships; kids 'go to the outhouse, and it's *icy*. Those kids were feeling history right in the seat of their pants.'[101] Catching ticks and lice in Civil War replay, 'I'd know what it felt like to scratch my head all day long'.[102] American Mountain Men 'reliving' arduous early Western frontier days eschew 'so-called creature comforts' for primitive 'techniques a thousand times better'. They recruit only those ready 'to live life as man was meant to live it, a Free Individual, a true Son of the Wilderness, using only what nature has to offer to survive alone, under any circumstances'.[103]

The visceral past agenda has a renowned pedigree, Collingwood's 'Roman road under your feet' (p. 383 above).[104] 'The business of the local historian', wrote their doyen a generation later, is 'to re-enact in his own mind, and to portray for his readers, the Origin, Growth, Decline and Fall of a Local Community'.[105] Among the period techniques used to recreate a thirteenth-century French castle was a human treadmill. 'I don't have to eat mammoths or think the world is flat to build a castle. But I have to think my way into the authenticity of the process', said the architect. 'Forced to our knees by slave drivers', visitors playing escaped slaves at Conner Prairie felt their 'bodies surrogated for those of our historical subjects, becoming … authentic witness to events of the past more powerful than the book or the archive'.[106] Indeed, the re-enactor comes to *possess* the past. The experience 'is something you can actually collect and show off', says a Second World War buff, 'as an intrinsic part of yourself'.[107]

Enduring past privations is an immersion bona fide. 'The most intense manifestation of suffering [is] the most authorized to occupy the voice of history'. Reliving the Blitz, participants in *The 1940s House* (2001) insisted 'we are going to be real people experiencing those hardships … we'll discover something of the psychology of people subjected

[99] Douglas Coupland, *Generation A* (London: Windmill, 2010), 269.
[100] T. A. J. Knox, 'Et in Arcadio ego', in N. S. Baer and F. Snickars, eds., *Rational Decision-Making in the Preservation of Cultural Property* (Berlin: Dahlem, 2001), 83–99 at 96.
[101] Billie Gammon quoted in Tracey Linton Craig, 'Retreat into history', *History News*, 38:6 (1983): 10–19 at 15.
[102] Civil War buff in Horwitz, *Confederates in the Attic*, 16.
[103] Dick 'Beau Jacques' House, 'Introduction', in William H. Scurlock, ed., *The Book of Buckskinning* (1981), quoted in R. W. Belk and J. A. Costa, 'The Mountain Man myth', *Journal of Consumer Research* 25 (1998): 218–40 at 222, 232; 'The Mountain Man Rendezvous', *over-land.com/rendez.html* (22 Feb. 2001), AMM Bylaws: 'Methods of and Requirements for ACCEPTANCE INTO MEMBERSHIP', website.
[104] R. G. Collingwood, 'Rome in Britain' (1925): 7, quoted in W. J. van der Dussen, *History as Science: The Philosophy of R. G. Collingwood* (The Hague: Nijhoff, 1981), 321.
[105] R. G. Collingwood, 'History as re-enactment of past experience', in *The Idea of History* (Oxford, 1946), 282–302; H. P. R. Finberg, *The Local Historian and His Theme* (Leicester, 1952), 9.
[106] Steve Erlanger, 'A labor of love, ye olde way', *IHT*, 2 Aug. 2010: 2; Scott Magelssen, '"This is a drama. You are characters": the tourist as fugitive slave in Conner Prairie's "Follow the North Star"', *Theatre Topics* 16:1 (Mar. 2006): 19–36 at 19–22.
[107] Jenny Thompson, 'Playing wars whose wounds are fresh', *NYT*, 5 June 2004: 1, 17.

to extreme circumstances'. Crew re-enacting Cook's famed voyage on a replica HMS *Endeavour* deplored their anachronistic anti-malarials and sunscreens, regretted that safety harnesses in the rigging lessened the past's true terrors, and suggested that they should have been flogged. To become convincingly emaciated or myopic, Civil War players starve or shed spectacles.[108]

Horrific re-creations – antique torture devices, high-decibel simulation of the FBI assault on Branch Davidians in Waco, Texas, Jim Jones's sermon ordaining his cult's mass suicide in the Guyanese jungle, Stanley Milgram's infamous 'experimenters' obediently 'shocking' victims – are an artist's signature stock in trade.[109] Visitors to Washington's Holocaust Museum role-play doomed Jews. Replicating horrors seems widely acceptable, though not to victims' descendants. Tribal Caribs on Dominica assailed Disney's *Pirates of the Caribbean* for perpetuating the myth of Carib cannibalism. Japanese were outraged when *Enola Gay* pilot Paul Tibbets's replica Hiroshima bomb unleashed a mushroom cloud at a 1976 Texas airshow.[110]

But since painful and hazardous past circumstances are by their very nature unrepeatable, reruns in the end seem inauthentic. 'We can never be Them', concluded a latter-day 'Captain Cook' sailor; awareness of 'the world beyond our temporary cage inflects all our responses'.[111] The Civil War re-enactor enjoys 'being very dirty but knowing you will be clean again'. The slave re-enactor knows his griefs are transient; to 'get even the faintest feel for what slave labor would be like would require subjecting oneself to interminable repetition of the historic task'.[112] Tours of South Africa's Robben Island offer 'no prerecorded screams of prisoners', nor even a two-minute taste of what solitary confinement would have been like for two weeks, two years, two decades.[113]

Excruciatingly authentic is film director Ilya Khrzhanovsky, whose acting-crew for *Dau* wore Stalin-era clothes and ate Soviet-style food for five years; 'when the cleaning lady had to mop the same toilet floor every day for two years', he explains, 'she will do it differently when she's doing it on camera'.[114] But few today can imagine being in a lynch mob or among Daniel Goldhagen's enthusiastic German executionists.[115] And only those ignorant of actual battle replay 'wargasm'. 'If they knew what a war was like', said a

---

[108] *The 1940s House*, quoted in De Groot, *Consuming History*, 177; Vanessa Agnew, 'Introduction: What is reenactment?', *Criticism*, special issue, Extreme and Sentimental History, 46:3 (2004): 327–40 at 331–2.

[109] Robert Blackson, 'Once more … with feeling: reenactment in contemporary art and culture', *Art Journal* 66:1 (Spring 2007): 28–40; artist Rod Dickinson cited in Sean O'Hagan, 'It's simply shocking', *Observer*, 10 Feb. 2002; Thomas Blass, *The Man Who Shocked the World: The Life and Legacy of Stanley Milgram* (Basic Books, 2004); Steve Rushton, ed., *The Milgram Re-Enactment* (Berlin: Kellerrevolver, 2004); Adam Kargman film *Atrocity* (2006).

[110] Adam Sherwin, 'Film pirates sunk by the real thing', *Times*, 25 Nov. 2005: 21; Peter J. Kuznick, 'Defending the indefensible: a meditation on the life of Hiroshima pilot Paul Tibbets, Jr.', *Asia-Pacific Journal: Japan Focus*, 22 Jan. 2008.

[111] Cook, 'Use and abuse of historical reenactment', 487–9.

[112] Rory Turner, 'Bloodless battles', *Drama Review* 34:4 (1990): 130; Magelssen, '"This is a drama"', 24.

[113] Annie E. Coombs, *History after Apartheid: Visual Culture and Public Memory in a Democratic South Africa* (Duke, 2003), 73.

[114] Michael Idov, 'The movie set that ate itself', *GQ Magazine*, Nov. 2011: 190–3.

[115] Karsten R. Stueber, 'The psychological basis of historical explanation: reenactment, simulation, and the fusion of horizons', *History and Theory* 41:1 (2002): 25–42 at 41.

Second World War combat veteran, 'they'd never play at it'.[116] Above all, re-enactment departs from the past in that actors and audiences, like historians, know the *future* of the past portrayed. In English Civil War replays Cromwell looks smug and Charles I glum because their fate is foreordained.[117]

Disparate physiques, lifestyles, and outlooks leave re-enactors aware how little they can truly replicate. 'Way too much blubber; the whole unit needs liposuction', a Civil War outfit is critiqued.[118] 'Our bowels and taste buds rebelled against the fare [ships biscuits, salt pork, sauerkraut] that Cook's men had found wholesome', said *Endeavour* re-enactors, deprived, moreover, of fresh fish plentiful in Cook's day.[119] In a year-long attempt to relive the Iron Age at Butser Ancient Farm, 1980s needs proved insuperable obstacles. Re-enactors could not do without pen and paper, Tampax, condoms, antibiotics; they endlessly disputed whether it was authentic or anachronistic to use an old ploughshare as a pot holder, a shard of glass as a mirror.[120] A 2000 BBC Iron Age re-enactment in a Welsh hill fort dramatized breaches of authenticity when food-poisoned volunteers needed modern medicine.[121]

Period corsets made actresses feel ladylike in Living History Farms' 1875 Iowa, but cut their lung capacity to fainting-point.[122] 'I've had enough', declared a Aussie 'pioneer' at *Outback House*, after days with a batch of lambing ewes. 'I'm filthy, I reek, the flies won't leave me alone, my feet are killing me ... I'm not tough enough.'[123] Colonial Williamsburg guides should be toothless and ready to admit that 'if we were really colonial people, most of us would be dead on account of the short life span'.[124]

Even a comfy recent past can feel daunting. Assigned to live for a week thirteen years back, an American 13-year-old found 1992 'a very confusing, difficult time ... Having to use landlines and eat carbohydrates were hardships for the people to endure ... I'm so grateful to live in 2005!' Little Danae in Wiley Miller's comic strip can't install her 'Anti-social network', because the Internet's fail-safe system shuts down her laptop. 'Conflicting social networks would cause a temporal vortex to open, sending us all back to the stone age.' 'Y-y-you mean ... back to the 1980s?!' 'Worse ...The pre-cable TV 70's'.[125]

Compromise is inevitable. Families who overnight in Plimoth Plantation's earth-floor hut with outdoor privies and no running water find 1627 mornings cheerlessly coffee-less

---

[116] Joseph B. Mitchell quoted in Rita Mae Brown, 'Fighting the Civil War anew', *NYT*, 12 June 1988.

[117] Robert Westall, *The Devil on the Road* (Macmillan, 1978), 7.

[118] Horwitz, *Confederates in the Attic*, 141.

[119] Iain McCalman, 'Little ship of horrors', *Criticism* 46:3 (2004): 477–86 at 479–80; BBC, *The Ship*, 2001.

[120] John Percival, *Living in the Past* (BBC, 1980), 16, 25–6, 37, 111–27; Coles, *Experimental Archaeology*, 249.

[121] Peter L. Firstbrook, *Surviving the Iron Age* (BBC, 2001); Katie King, *Networked Reenactments* (Duke, 2011), 147–51. Two months simulating Stone Age Bodensee for TV in 2006 left six adults and seven children cold, wet, muddy, and footsore (Rolf Schlenker and Almut Bick, *Steinzeit: Leben wie vor 5000 Jahren* (Stuttgart: Theiss, 2007); Gunter Schöbel, 'Steinzeit – das Experiment, das hat noch gefehlt – Steinzeit als Doku-Soap?' *Plattform* 15/16 (2008): 4–44).

[122] Colleen Gau, 'Physiologic effects of wearing corsets: studies with reenactors', *Dress: Costume Society of America* 26 (1999): 63–70 at 67.

[123] Arrow, '"That history should not ever have been how it was"', 250.

[124] Dave Barry, 'Why I like old things', *Historic Preservation* 35:1 (1983): 50.

[125] Billy Frolick, '1992 House', *New Yorker*, 17 Jan 2005: 49; Wiley Miller, 'Non sequitur', *IHT*, 15 Jan. 2011.

and make a beeline for the museum cafe. Warned that 'you won't take a shower for three days, you'll sleep on a cornhusk mattress in the dead of winter', visitors to 1870s Maine baulked at the absence of window screens in summer and toilet paper year round.[126] Toilets in Norway's Viking Land are 'built the way you would imagine toilets would be like if they had in fact existed back then, in apparently old and uneven timbers, with a turf roof', and provocative queries along with the toilet paper – 'What did the Vikings do? . . . Did they use moss? Or a sprig of spruce? Perhaps wet new snow.' Civil War players 'not willing to suffer enough' (sleeping in tents, cushioned insoles in their period boots) greatly outnumber hard-core zealots.[127]

No re-enactors transcend 'vaccinated time travel', in Douglas Coupland's phrase, 'going back into the past for everything but the plagues, nasty infections, and bullet wounds'.[128] 'I wouldn't . . . fight in that war unless I could do it in an [1970s] F-15 and with a pocket full of penicillin', said a realist, of the 1864 Battle of the Wilderness. 'The only Scarlett they knew back then was fever, not O'Hara.' Hard-cores who brag, '"We're doing it just like they did" [are] thankful that we don't get shot like they got shot, get sick like they got sick'.[129] No one remains in 'first-person' for an entire event. 'We are all farbs, some just farbier than others.' Credulous spectators elicit self-mockery. 'Do y'all use real bullets?' 'We used to, but we started running low on reenactors.'[130]

Forbidden to forgo modern health and safety, re-enactors cannot even begin to shed today's ethical mantras. Volunteers in reality television history eager to escape meretricious modernity end up unable to cope (except for lords and ladies pleased with their perks) with rigid past codes of authority, hierarchy, gender, and race. Violating the rule that junior servants never address their master directly, 'Antonia' in the Edwardian *Manor House* (PBS, 2003) challenges Sir John's orders: 'I tried it their way but it was impossible'. She was 'just too 21st century'. In *Colonial House* (PBS 2002–), set in 1628 New England, volunteers who defied Sabbath or community strictures were 'branded' with scarlet letters, 'but the transgressors openly mock these penalties for misconduct, flaunting modern individualism and rejection of seventeenth-century civic and moral codes'. The 'colonists' fall afoul of 'the 17th century social hierarchy in which one's status, rights, and duties are determined at birth'. And they refuse to cheat Native American trading partners, sacrificing community survival needs to their guilt over past racial abuses.[131]

[126] Jane Margolies, 'Plymouth, Mass.: live as a Pilgrim', *NYT*, 12 July 2010: TR; Billie Gammon in Craig, 'Retreat into history', 15.

[127] Hjemdahl, 'History as a cultural playground', 117–18; Strauss, 'Framework for assessing military dress authenticity', 150–2.

[128] Douglas Coupland, *Generation X* (St Martin's Press, 1991); Jonah Begone, 'Time's arrow', *Camp Chase Gazette* 28:4 (Mar. 2001).

[129] Horwitz, *Confederates in the Attic*, 138; Jeff Hendershott, 'Annoying reenacting types (Part II)', *Camp Chase Gazette*, c. 2006.

[130] Jeff Hendershott, 'Things I'll never understand about Civil War reenacting', *Camp Chase Gazette*, n.d.; re-enactors quoted in Farmer, 'Playing rebels', 68.

[131] Julie Anne Taddeo and Ken Dvorak, 'The PBS Historical House series: where historical reality succumbs to reel reality', *Film & History* 37:1 (2007): 18–28 at 18, 20, 25.

Australian time-travellers repeatedly anachronize their seedy colonial saga. In New South Wales' 1804 'frontier village', actors in *The Colony* (2004) rejigged the violent racist past to suit their own classless and pacifist values.[132] In *Outback House*, an 1860s' reality show, 'squatters' who conformed to hierarchical past norms were forced to quit. Actors wanted the past 'to represent what we believe in'. When Aborigines were told to stop fraternizing with whites, both rebelled. 'I don't give a shit what the history man says', said a 'squatter'.[133] Present rectitude could not stomach past reality.

'Period rush' vs. rectifying the past

Re-enactments are thus patent anachronisms. But devotees feel they truly experience bygone times. Absorbed in 'period rush', they become mobile monuments in a reborn past.[134] 'Time warp' in a Pickett's Charge replay gave one scholar–soldier 'a consciousness of history that passeth all understanding. [As] I lay dead and still ... I thought, "So that's what it was like."' But of course it wasn't; only a modern actor could have such a thought. Re-enacting 'entails a distinctive consciousness – of the past *as a past worthy of being relived* – that could not have been present in the minds of those historical others whom one simulates'.[135] The father at Gettysburg in the Civil War episode of *Everybody Loves Raymond* mocks re-enactors' zeal. There's camaraderie here. There's spirit ... You have no idea what it feels like to stand on a battlefield pretending to fight for something you believe in.'[136]

A too-vibrant past afflicts present reality. A Second World War paratroop re-enactor found it all too easy 'to get re-enacting and real life confused'. At Lejre, Denmark, 'medieval' experimental staff wore modern clothing lest they begin fantasizing themselves Vikings. Archaeologists resurrecting the Amerindian past in tidewater Virginia took similar precautions.[137] All those hired as soldiers in a Napoleonic Wars film got the same pay, but soon 'the officers of this celluloid army began to eat at a separate table from the mere privates and NCOs', historian Emmanuel Le Roy Ladurie reported; 'later on, an actual partition was put up to divide the "officers' mess" from the *vulgum pecus*'[138] 'It is curious', said a participant in *The Edwardian Country House* (2002), 'if people treat you like Milady how you grow in to the position'. 'Sir' John Olliff-Cooper, Bt., admitted that 'we do things within the house that conscience would not allow us to do in 2001'.[139]

[132] Gapps, 'Blacking up for the explorers of 1951', 208–20; Baz Kershaw, *The Radical in Performance* (Routledge, 1999), 140–43; Stephen Gapps, 'Adventures in *The Colony*', *Film & History* 37:1 (2007): 67–72.

[133] Arrow, 'That history should not ever have been how it was', 59, quoting Tracy Hohnke, 63.

[134] Stephen Gapps, 'Mobile monuments', *Rethinking History* 11:3 (2007): 395–407 at 407; Richard Handler and William Saxton, 'Dyssimulation: reflexivity, narrative, and the quest for authenticity in "living history"', *Cultural Anthropology* 3 (1988): 242–60.

[135] Richard Handler, 'Overpowered by realism: living history and the simulation of the past', *Journal of American Folklore* 100:397 (1987): 337–41 at 340.

[136] CBS 1998 Season Two, Civil War 13:55, quoted in Iain McCalman and Paul A. Pickering, 'From realism to the affective turn', in their, eds., *Historical Reenactment* (Palgrave Macmillan, 2009), 1–17 at 11.

[137] Quoted in Anderson, *Time Machines*, 155, 86, 95; Coles, *Experimental Archaeology*, 214.

[138] Emmanuel Le Roy Ladurie, 'Democracy and modernity', *London Review of Books*, 3–17 Feb. 1983: 10.

[139] Quoted in De Groot, *Consuming History*, 179–80.

Battle time warps can be dangerous; weapons pose hazards when re-enactors get caught up in the past. 'Participants sometimes lose sight of the fact that it is all in play, and feel the same emotions their ancestors felt'; Battle of Manassas (Bull Run) re-enactors ended up clubbing each other with rifle butts.[140] Following a spate of accidents, unsheathed swords and replica guns were banned in Britain.[141]

Simulated history time-warps spectators, too. 'British' troops were brutally assaulted at Revolutionary bicentenaries in Boston. 'We could have been wearing Nazi uniforms, for the reaction – there was the same feeling of hatred as 200 years ago.' Militia at a Penobscot Bay 'tarring-and-feathering' 1770 reprise had to protect a 'British sympathizer' from vengeful onlookers. Watching his children re-enact a seventeenth-century hanging curtailed their father's zest for history: 'they take authenticity too far'.[142] At Conner Prairie, visiting 'fugitive slaves' became so immersed in the past that they panicked and attacked 'bounty hunters'. The filming of *Pirates of the Caribbean* suffered raids by actual brigands in Grand Bahama; robbed of their laptops, replay 'pirates' fled.[143]

Re-enactments necessarily enliven the past for present needs. Just as literal archival recapitulation would deaden any historical narrative, so undiluted replay would be unbearably tedious. 'You can't reenact a siege. Everybody would get bored and go home.'[144] Restaged battles are selectively action-packed. A dramatist enlivens Cromwell's Levellers' Masque by having a colonel's wife tearfully recognize a prisoner as her lover. But 'it didn't happen', she is told. 'So it didn't. But it might have done ... No way do I rehearse that scene again like it was. It's dull dull dull.'[145] So too with films. 'Medieval warfare was sedate. Weighted down by chain mail, two knights hacked at each other in slow-motion, ... fighting in a lake of treacle.' But no one would now watch this. In Ridley Scott's *Robin Hood* (2010) warriors used lightweight aluminium chain mail and plastic shields filled with uncooked lasagne that shattered dramatically on impact.[146]

Some re-enactments seek to rectify past injustice or outcome. Jeremy Deller's 2001 *Battle of Orgreave* recast the 1980s British miners' strike to controvert media reports that vilified the miners.[147] Participants on the losing side – Southerners in the American Civil War, Cavaliers in the English – demand counterfactual replay. 'Not this year! This year belongs to the Confederacy!' cries 'Robert E. Lee' in *South Park*'s 'The Red Badge of Gayness' (1999). 'We took over Fort Sumter by force once before', declared a re-enactor,

---

[140] Clark, 'When the paraders meet the button-counters', 138–41; Elder, 'War games', 10.
[141] Michael Horsnell and Liz Chong, 'Blade fells martial arts warrior in Wars of the Roses', *Times*, 28 June 2005: 2; Thair Shaikn, 'Battle cry to save history from ban on replica guns', *Times*, 9 May 2005: 16.
[142] Quoted in Clark, 'When the paraders meet the button-counters', 135, 141; Tom Forester, 'Weekend warriors', *New Society*, 10 Sept. 1981: 418.
[143] Magelssen, '"This is a drama"', 24–5; Magelssen, *Living History Museums*, 9–11; Adam Sherwin, 'Film pirates sunk by the real thing', *Times*, 25 Nov. 2005: 21.
[144] Quoted in Elder, 'War games', 12. See Jeremy D. Popkin, *History, Historians, and Autobiography* (Chicago, 2005), 170.
[145] Penelope Lively, *Judgement Day* (Heinemann, 1980), 138.
[146] Alex von Tunzelmann, 'Reel history special: Ridley Scott's Robin Hood: wide of the mark?' *Guardian*, 23 Sept. 2010.
[147] Blackson, 'Once more ... with feeling', 32; Katie Kitamura, '"Recreating chaos": Jeremy Deller's *The Battle of Orgreave*', in McCalman and Pickering, eds., *Historical Reenactment*, 39–49.

as a looming federal shut-down threatened the sesquicentennial replay of the Union surrender that launched the Civil War, 'and we can do it again'.[148]

Needs for retrospective success reshaped the American bicentenary. Americans actually lost many battles along the way to victory. But in 1976 replays they always emerged with glory. Defeats became draws, routs tactical withdrawals. 'To hear them talk about it now in Conshohocken, Lafayette's decision to cross the [Schuylkill] river to escape from superior forces was the greatest victory in American history.' Of the disastrous Battle of Penobscot Bay a spectator grumbled, 'Why couldn't they at least do one that we win?'[149] Sore historical losers are legion. To propitiate French viewers mock Battles of Waterloo let France 'win' on one day; in 2010 a Bonaparte heir (Louis-Napoleon Bonaparte-Wyse) urged a replay of the Battle of Ligny, Napoleon's last victory. Rebel troops at the 125th anniversary of Lee's doomed Pickett's Charge plotted to change history by breaching the Union line.[150] Revolutionary re-enactors dreamed of '18th-century war games, where British and American units can test their mettle in combat situations without foreordained conclusions'. Leaving the outcome of the past up to the player is a common feature of video games.[151]

Interactive history discomfits many. 'Busy as they are, the villagers are always eager for conversation', welcomes Plimoth Plantation. 'You are invited to explore their community, to ask about their lives … to examine their possessions, habits and values.' But prying annoys or intimidates reticent visitors. 'Do I have to talk to these strange people?' ask shy Minnesotans at Old Fort Snelling.[152] Tongue-tied beyond technical queries about skills, crops, and beverages, they are reluctant to 'share a riddle, a joke, a bit of gossip' with these 'friendly' but alien folk. Sightseers feel it rude to enter 'Lincoln's log cabin' while a period meal is being eaten.[153] The rumpled garb and rude ways of militiamen at Canada's restored Louisbourg Fortress upset even tourists told that they were slovenly and demoralized because that was how they *had* been, back then.[154]

---

[148] Anja Schwarz, '"Not this year!": Reenacting contested pasts aboard *The Ship*', *Rethinking History* 46 (2004): 427–46; 'Lee' quoted in Ashley E. Bowen, '"Old Times There Are Not Forgotten": Civil War Re-enactors and the Creation of Heritage' (MA thesis, Georgetown University, 2009), 127; Mike Short quoted in Sam Dillon, 'All of a war's trappings, with accuracy at stake', *NYT*, 10 Apr. 2011: 24. See Stephen Gapps, 'On being a mobile monument: historical reenactment and commemoration', in McCalman and Pickering, eds., *Historical Reenactment*, 50–62.

[149] Oran Henderson quoted in Israel Shenker, 'U.S. bicentennial cures history's warts', *IHT*, 5–6 July 1975: 5; Penobscot spectator in Clark, 'When the paraders meet the button-counters', 44.

[150] Allred, 'Catharsis, revision, and re-enactment', 9–10; Jack Malvern, 'One of these days we're going to win, say the French as weekend warriors replay Waterloo', *Times*, 21 June 2010: 19. 'In terms of his historical importance', said Napoleon's bicentenary re-enactor, 'it's clear that he won' (Frank Samson quoted in Adam Page, 'Crafty French back their man to win at Waterloo, part deux', *Times*, 28 Jan. 2015: 3).

[151] Clark, 'When the paraders meet the button-counters', 143; Brian Rejack, 'Toward a virtual reenactment of history: video games and the recreation of the past', *Rethinking History* 11:3 (2007): 411–25.

[152] Plimoth Plantation 1981 brochure, *Have the Time of Their Life*; Minnesota Historical Society study quoted in Magelssen, *Living History Museums*, 152.

[153] Snow, *Performing the Pilgrims*, 62, 173; Tom Vance, 'History lives at Lincoln's log cabin', *Historic Illinois* 1:4 (1978): 10.

[154] John Fortier, 'Louisbourg: managing a moment in time', in Peter E. Rider, ed., *The History of Atlantic Canada: Museum Interpretations* (Ottawa, 1981), 91–123; Dan Proudfoot, 'How Louisbourg restored looks today', *Canadian Geographical Journal* 93:1 (1976): 28–33; Charley Fawkes quoted in 'Fortress of Louisbourg awaits Wolfe's redcoats one more time', *Canwest News Service*, 21 June 2008.

First-person role-play risks arousing rage rather than reflection, especially with unsavoury pasts. Starting to protest a 1994 'slave auction' at Colonial Williamsburg as an affront to black dignity, NAACP chief Jack Gravely stayed to laud the event for raising historical awareness, black and white: 'Pain had a face, indignity had a body, suffering had tears.'[155] But restaging the horrendous imperils historical distance; spectators were barely restrained from freeing the auctioned 'slaves'.

Yet replay can foster access to otherwise inaccessible pasts. At Plimoth Plantation I watched 'William Bradford' engage a Midwestern booster. This visitor believed the Pilgrim Fathers true begetters of his own free-enterprise individualism. But Bradford was a devotee of sacred community to whom capitalism was blasphemous, self-serving individualism anathema. Seething with indignation, the visitor could not dismiss pious Bradford as a crank or a communist. In the present he would have spurned or even struck him, but the historic-site venue demands tolerant colloquy, facing up to difference. Perhaps for the first time, he had to engage with a world view fundamentally at odds with his own. One wonders how other visitors react when 'Pilgrims', 'aghast' at their cameras and cell phones, accuse them of consorting with the devil.[156] The pedagogic value of confronting alien and abhorrent creeds induces schools in Alabama to replay slave escapes. Simulating Nazi anti-Semitism, South Carolina sixth graders switched roles between teacher-pet Germans and shunned Jews. But experiencing prejudice may induce more desire for privilege than empathy with the underdog. 'I'm glad I'm a German today', said one eleven-year-old.[157]

Re-enactments enliven history for millions who turn a blind or bored eye on monuments and museums. One reason is that, more than in most efforts to retrieve the past, re-enactors willy-nilly stray from it. They either 'hallucinate a past as merely the present in fancy dress' or contrive a comforting in place of a contested or unpalatable past.[158] Replay pageantry transports them to a crypto-past where they act out fantasies denied in the here and now.

But that consigns others to indulge their time-travel fancy. Many re-enact not out of nostalgia but need. 'You'll work down the Heritage Museum, like your mother and me', a Welsh miner tells his sulky son, in Chris Glynn's cartoon.[159] Villagers in much-filmed picturesque Lacock, Wiltshire, fear gentrified National Trust erosion of local identity, noting that 400,000 visitors annually 'want to come to a real English village full of real

[155] Quoted in Cary Carson, 'Colonial Williamsburg and the practice of interpretive planning in American history museums', *Public Historian* 20 (1998): 11–51 at 51. See Timothy W. Luke, *Museum Pieces* (Minnesota, 2002), 16, 36.

[156] Barbara Kirschenblatt-Gimblett, *Destination Culture: Tourism, Museums, and Heritage* (California, 1998), 199.

[157] Noelle Phillips, 'Simulation teaches Holocaust lesson', *The State: South Carolina's Homepage* (21 Jan. 2011). But Albany, NY, high school students in April 2013 were appalled at being asked to imagine simulating Nazi anti-Semitism; the school apologized and suspended the teacher.

[158] Greg Dening, *Mr Bligh's Bad Language* (Cambridge, 1992), 4; Kent Courtney, *Returning to the Civil War* (Salt Lake City: Peregrine, 1997), 40–1; George Lipsitz, *Time Passages* (Minnesota, 1990), 233–56; Tom Dunning, 'Civil War re-enactments', *Australasian Journal of American Studies* 21 (2002): 63–72 at 68–71.

[159] See Ian Buruma, 'Shut up and deal', *Spectator*, 30 Apr. 1993: 34.

villagers, not a Disney-style theme park of people putting on a show'. Lacock is 'still like a proper community . . . like what people imagine England to be'. Indeed, the past people imagine proves irresistible. 'It would be a shame if we all ended up dressed in 16th century costumes', said a parish councillor. 'But if the National Trust had not taken over the village, it would be like that already.'[160]

Tourists enjoy Croatia as 'the Mediterranean As It Once Was'; inhabitants complain that 'we are supposed to live in that place as it used to be'. Residents in Djenné, Mali, a UNESCO World Heritage site, are forbidden to modernize their cramped mud-floored mud-brick houses. 'This is not a room', an inhabitant growls, 'It is a grave.'[161] Frozen in heritage time, the denizens of brothel-famed Pelourinho, in Bahia, Brazil, become patrimonialized property, 'living human treasures' refashioned into symbolic ancestors of themselves.[162]

Life in the replica 1840s Indiana frontier village of Margaret Haddix's novel is nasty, short, and mean. Corralled by tourist entrepreneurs, they are confined to their historical enclave, denied modern medicines, forced to forget the modern world outside.[163] But some willingly exchange inherited for lucrative invented pasts. Painted entirely blue to film *The Smurfs* in 2011, the Spanish village of Júzcar, formerly a famed *pueblo blanco*, opted by a vote of 141 to 33 to remain blue, even to its gravestones, after a 250-fold increase in tourism. Their fiftieth anniversary in 2008 made the Smurfs a treasured legacy, reinforced by the 2013 inaugural preview of *Smurfs2*. 'We love the Smurfs', said a Júscarene. 'It reminds me of when I was a kid.'[164]

Conclusion

All these efforts to save and salvage things past – to retain, preserve, reveal, reproduce, restore, and re-enact – exhibit two conflicting traits. The first couples ardent attachment to how things actually were with faith in resuming it. The second is that goal's utter hopelessness. It is impossible not only because the past is irretrievable and irreproducible, but because we are not past but present people, with experience, knowledge, feelings, and aims previously unknown. Today's outlooks constantly refashion professed preservative

---

[160] David Lowenthal, *The Heritage Crusade and the Spoils of History* (Cambridge, 1998), 101; David Brown, 'Ye olde English village with very modern cost of living', *Times*, 22 Oct. 2011: 16–17; John Urry, *The Tourist Gaze* (Sage, 1990; 2nd edn 2002), 131.

[161] Dinko Peracic in Francesca von Habsburg et al., 'Debate: Preservation, contemporary art, and architecture', *Future Anterior* 4:2 (Winter 2007): 70–85 at 78.; Mahamame Bamoye Traoré quoted in Neil Macfarquhar, 'Frozen in time, and resenting it', *IHT*, 10 Jan. 2011: 2. 'The inhabitants . . . have the impression of living in a protected area where . . . nothing is allowed' (World Heritage Committee Report, 30th Session, item 38 (Paris: UNESCO, 2006), 96–8); Charlotte L. Joy, *The Politics of Heritage Management in Mali: From UNESCO to Djenné* (Walnut Creek, CA: Left Coast Press, 2013).

[162] John Collins, '"But what if I should need to defecate in your neighborhood, Madame?": Empire, redemption, and the "Tradition of the Oppressed" in a Brazilian World Heritage Site', *Cultural Anthropology* 23 (2008): 279–328.

[163] Margaret Peterson Haddix, *Running Out of Time* (Simon & Schuster, 1995).

[164] Graham Keeley, 'Village will vote on staying Smurf', *Times*, 15 Dec. 2011: 38; 'Spanish village of Juzcar votes to stay blue', *Telegraph*, 19 Dec. 2011.

and restorative aims. However faithfully kept or impeccably brought back, the past is transformed by filtering through modern minds and senses.

A common reaction to this distressing disconnect is to deny it, to wish it away, to resist awareness that the past can at most be fancifully and fallibly regained. Hence the restorer insists that he seeks only to return to a known previous state, the builder contends that his replica is truer to the original than what survives of it, the re-enactor claims that 'period rush' truly resurrects what life was really like. Present needs push us to proclaim fidelity to the past's material remnants or unrealized aims. Hence Victorians built finer Gothic than their medieval precursors, ecologists restore ecosystems more stable than unaided nature's, literary compilers opt for *Ur*-texts unrecognizable to original authors, re-enactors boast of battle outcomes or sailing achievements their ancestors might have desired, reality-show actors cope better with Australian frontier hardship than the original settlers did.

The more present-day aims and agendas encroach, the more their corrupting influence is denied. Hence Victorian restorers' insistence that they sought only to save, not alter, past ecclesiastical structures. Hence ecologists' reversion to whatever – species, ecosystems, or evolutionary processes – is denoted 'natural', against any suspicion of meddling with nature. Hence hard-core Civil War re-enactors claim they 'fight' not out of sympathy with Confederate causes but only from devotion to civic truth. Hence Colonial Williamsburg's insistence that the patriotic pride its displays inspire is uncontrived, a happy fortuitous result of flawless entrepreneurial fidelity to truth.

Disclaimers of tampering all presume the virtue of authenticity, the real thing, the true not the false or fake.

The past is unarguably authentic. The past is a world that already existed before Disney and Murdoch ... and all the other shapers of the present day. ... *And this will make the past unbelievably attractive.* People ... want to visit not other places, but other times ... medieval walled cities, Buddhist temples, Mayan pyramids, Egyptian necropolises ... the vanished world. And they don't want it to be fake. They don't want it to be made pretty, or cleaned up. They want it to be authentic.[165]

Hence heritage tourism fosters illusions of actual discovery and visceral participation in pasts on display. Hence re-enactors' 'desperate search for the real thing by borrowing the personas and accoutrements' of bygone folk 'whom modern mythology defines as quintessentially real'.[166]

The authentic past moreover comes in competing guises. For material artefacts, choices must be made between authenticity of material or form, original intent or subsequent adaptation, pristine newness or wear or decay. Visitors to restored New Salem, Illinois, Abraham Lincoln's home in the 1830s, are assured of its authenticity on several grounds. Some buildings are in part original; others have original furnishings. The whole looks so 'true' that an 1830s person coming back would find it real. That claim can't be tested. But New Salem does conform to visitors' *present* 1830s expectations. Moreover, authenticity

---

[165] Michael Crichton, *Timeline* (Knopf, 1999), 436.
[166] Handler, 'Overpowered by realism', 340.

is officially authorized by the State of Illinois.[167] In sum, New Salem is authentic because it *is* real, or looks real, or might look real, or simply because its custodians say so.

Purveyors claim to cleave to the true past even while subverting it. Such duplicity takes several forms. One is to stress mistreatment due to previous ignorance or bias, like repainting Colonial Williamsburg houses all over, instead of only in front; this implies that knowing better we recreate more truly. Another is to point out obligatory anachronisms – litter bins or portapotties behind the foliage, mandatory non-leaded roofing and fire extinguishers, tools unlike no-longer procurable originals. Back then, explains Old Sturbridge, the flag ritual involved no allegiance pledge, shoemakers used other tools, and carpenters' sawdust today bagged was dumped in the river. A third strategy is to blame customers themselves for lamentable lapses. The leafy old trees lining Colonial Williamsburg streets are post-colonial additions that cannot now be uprooted because modern visitors could not tolerate unshaded summer sun.[168]

The underlying message is that the authentic past, however subverted in detail, is *essentially* recovered. Delinquencies are minor and trivial, their very admission an assurance of trustworthy legitimacy. Increasingly cynical audiences, only too apt to suppose a historic site artificial, must be 'coached to recognize the residues of authenticity'. For 'any time you have a break in your credibility, then everything . . . is called into question', stressed a Colonial Williamsburg manager, because visitors then 'fear that history is . . . concocted'. Frank admission of minor anachronisms suggests a self-critical honesty that bolsters illusions of fidelity. Colonial Williamsburg continues to peddle traditional coffee-table chic alongside interpreters' revisionist dust-dirt-and-slave history, on the constructivist tenet that the 'true' past is an ever-changing target. Transitory and fleeting current truths are overlain with morally uplifting myths that celebrate time-honoured American values.[169] What is deeply deceitful is pretended adhesion to an invented enduring verity. 'Historical authenticity resides not in fidelity to an alleged past', cautions an anthropologist, but in being honest about how the present 're-presents that past'.[170]

In sum, every effort to save, to celebrate, to resurrect, even to study the past, however untainted the aim, revises its remnants, its appearance, and its remembrance. Moreover, almost all salvage efforts are suffused with other purposes, openly avowed or subconsciously held, but usually passionately denied. These alterations, and the aims that animate them, are the subject of the final chapter.

---

[167] Edward M. Bruner, 'Abraham Lincoln as authentic reproduction', *American Anthropologist* 96:2 (1994): 397–415 at 400–1.

[168] Magelssen, 'Performance practices of [living] open-air museums', 143; Eric Gable and Richard Handler, 'After authenticity at an American heritage site', *American Anthropologist* 98:3 (1996): 568–78 at 572–4.

[169] Eric Gable and Richard Handler, 'Deep dirt: messing up the past at Colonial Williamsburg', *Social Analysis* 34 (1993): 3–16 at 8; Richard Handler and Eric Gable, *New History in an Old Museum: Creating the Past at Colonial Williamsburg* (Duke, 1997), 6–7, 35, 45–6.

[170] Michel-Rolph Trouillot, *Silencing the Past* (Beacon, 1997), 148.

12

Improving the past

We must add to our heritage or lose it.   George Orwell, 1941[1]

You don't like the past? Then fiddle the books ... How easy it is, as long as it's just
paper and fallible memory.   Robert Goddard, 1986[2]

If we need another past so badly, is it inconceivable that we might discover one, that
we might even invent one?   Van Wyck Brooks, 1918[3]

The Byzantine Queen Helena [was] the most successful archaeologist in history.
Whatever she looked for she promptly found hundreds of years after the event: the
stable where Mary had given birth to Christ, the twelve stations of the cross, Calvary,
the true cross, the nails, the lancet, the Holy Sepulchre and so on and on.
                               Yigael Yadin, quoted in Amos Elon, 1994[4]

Societies which cannot combine reverence to their symbols with freedom of revision
must ultimately decay either from anarchy, or from the slow atrophy of a life stifled by
useless shadows.   Alfred North Whitehead, 1927[5]

This chapter reviews why and how we change the past. We may be fully conscious, hazily
cognizant, or wholly unaware of what impels us to revision. As shown in Chapters 10 and
11, efforts to save or retrieve the past are bound to alter it, no matter how much we strive
to keep it as it was. Many seriously impact the past with no intent of doing so. Admirers
of antiquity unwittingly mar its relics. Visitors who wear down the floor of Canterbury
Cathedral seldom consider the cumulative impact of thousands of feet. Viewers whose
breath and body heat imperil Lascaux's prehistoric drawings ignore the corrosive effect of
their presence.

Flawed expertise has dire consequences: conservators who secured Parthenon pillars
with iron bolts never dreamt that rust and metal expansion would do more harm than
they allayed. Few who signpost antiquities, copy Old Masters, or emulate period building
styles realize that these appreciative acts deform how the originals are seen. Those who
recycle ancient remnants discount the corollary damage, if they consider it at all. Later
Romans who quarried marble from imperial temples and statuary, contractors who
demolish prehistoric sites, farmers who plough over medieval traces seldom note or little

---

[1] George Orwell, *The Lion and the Unicorn* (1941), in *Collected Essays* (Secker & Warburg, 1968), 2: 109.
[2] Robert Goddard, *Past Caring* (London: Robert Hale), 342.
[3] Van Wyck Brooks, 'On creating a usable past', *Dial* 64 (1918): 337–41 at 339.
[4] Amos Elon, 'Politics and archaeology', in N. A. Silberman and D. B. Small, eds., *The Archaeology of Israel* (Sheffield: Academic Press, 1997), 34–47 at 37.
[5] Alfred North Whitehead, *Symbolism* (Cambridge, 1927), 104.

care what they expunge. Others, however, deliberately purge or refashion pasts they find inglorious, shameful, inadequate, or simply unsuited to present purposes. Indeed, most of us do all these things in turn. At various times we are hands-off preservers and restorers, unconscious meddlers, and forthright improvers.

Those who knowingly change the past often claim to remake its real essence. Far from tampering with bygone truth, they expose lies and expunge fabrications to redeem historical fidelity from previous perversion. But just as those who falsify history rarely confess except under compulsion, so those who revise to rectify are blind to their own biases. As most perpetrators of change are unaware or unrepentant, many alterations never come to light. How much intervention our legacy has undergone is incalculable.

Relics are often reshaped and history rewritten to become what they would have been but for attrition or prior interference. We feel impelled to right past wrongs and repair past crimes and errors. Wanton destruction such as Nazi eradication of Poland's old city centres; untoward revision animated by aesthetic morality such as Victorian Gothic church fittings; ill-informed or ineptly executed previous restorations are zealously amended. Some thereby expiate their own complicity; Henry Ford's Greenfield Village re-created an artisanal America that his automobiles had done much to unmake.[6] The rectified past aims to be seen as the true original. 'Historic' villages that expunge previous pedagogic and patriotic invention now boast archaeological authenticity. And because the up-to-date truth they profess is a point of professional pride, doubts are disregarded. Seemingly laudable, 'setting the record straight' begets massive self-deception. Certain *they* see the past in its true light, rectifiers of previous accretions and deceptions remain oblivious to their own.

The more strenuously we contrive a desired past, the more forcefully we assert that things really were that way; what *ought* to have been becomes what *was*. Professing to correct precursors' prejudices and to recover pre-existing truths, we fail to see how much of today we put in the past. Faith in its durable resilience buttresses belief that sloughing off previous alterations retrieves what actually was. Insisting that the past originally existed in the form we now devise, we deny our own inputs. Like Orwell's Ministry of Truth and Soviet textbooks, which continually revised the past to show that the Party had always been right, we persuade ourselves that we unearth what in fact we fabricate.

Thus the Victorian architect George Gilbert Scott, who substituted his own 'Gothic' for surviving Norman and other styles, discounted the wholesale changes he introduced. Terming 'an original detail [however] decayed and mutilated infinitely more valuable than the most skilful attempt at its restoration', Scott claimed he had sought 'the least possible displacement of old stone', replacing only those 'features which have actually been destroyed by modern mutilation'. Persuaded 'in an evil hour' to restore the dilapidated Chantry Chapel of St Mary the Virgin on the medieval bridge at Wakefield, Scott later 'wonder[ed] how I ever was induced to consent to it at all, as it was contrary to

---

[6] George E. Vaillant, *The Wisdom of the Ego* (Harvard, 1992), 191. 'Ford built this place out of guilt' (quoted in Charles Phillips, 'Greenfield's changing past', *History News* 37:11 (1982): 11). Greenfield is 'preservation by expiation', akin to 'mourning for what one has destroyed' (Renato Rosaldo, *Culture and Truth* (Beacon Press, 1989), 67–71).

the very principles of my own report ... I think of this with the utmost shame and chagrin.'[7] Practice similarly flouted precept with George Edmund Street. He reproached restorers of Burgos Cathedral and St Mark's, Venice, for the same historical insensitivity ('when we find old work ... we cannot be wrong in letting well alone') that later led Street himself to replace the fourteenth-century choir of Dublin's Christ Church Cathedral with a 'pastiche' of the 'original'. Leaving the past alone was for both a dogma they so unhappily breached they seldom knew it.[8]

Fabricated pasts

Those who remake what *ought* to have been are at least aware of altering residues. They purposely improve history, memory, and relics to reveal the past's 'true' nature better than could be done in its own time. African chroniclers transmute received oral accounts lest untoward facts about the past undermine ruling elites: official Akan history holds that the ruling class was indigenous, though members of the royal clan know well that they were immigrants.[9] Contrariwise, Anglo-Saxon charters were often deliberately fabricated to supersede inconvenient oral memory. They in turn might suffer the same fate. In late medieval England 'a charter was inaccurate and should be corrected if it failed to give the beneficiary a privilege which the author had obviously intended it to have, had he still been alive to express his wishes', concludes Michael Clanchy. Obsolescence drove other change: 'An authentic charter of an early Anglo-Saxon king might be rejected by a court of law because it seemed strange, whereas a forged charter would be acceptable because it suited contemporary notions of what an ancient charter should be like.'[10]

Refashioned antiquity realizes supposed aims originally unachieved for lack of resources or skills. Disciples of Vitruvius 'corrected' architectural deviations thought due to early imperfect knowledge. Upgrading sixteenth-century English Gothic, the architect Ralph Adams Cram sought 'not to turn back the clock so much as to set a much finer clock ticking again'.[11] In copying old pictures, Nathaniel Hawthorne's Hilda does 'what the great Master had conceived in his imagination, but had not so perfectly succeeded in putting upon canvas'; Hilda is 'a finer instrument ... by the help of which

---

[7] George Gilbert Scott, *A Plea for the Faithful Restoration of Our Ancient Churches* (London, 1850), 21, 126, and *Personal and Professional Recollections* (1879; Paul Watkins, 1995), 102.

[8] George Edmund Street, *Some Account of Gothic Architecture in Spain* (London, 1865), 27n; Roger Stalley, ed., *George Edmund Street and the Restoration of Christ Church Cathedral, Dublin* (Dublin: Four Courts, 2000), 106–9.

[9] Jan Vansina, *Oral Tradition* (1961; Aldine, 2006), 76–85; J. D. Y. Peel, 'Making history: the past in the Ijesha present', *Man* 19 (1984): 111–32 at 124–7, and *Religious Encounter and the Making of the Yoruba* (Indiana, 2000), 22, 58, 279, 361n85.

[10] Sarah Foot, 'Reading Anglo-Saxon charters', in Elizabeth M. Tyler and Ross Balzaretti, eds., *Narrative and History in the Early Medieval West* (Turnhout: Brepols, 2006), 39–65 at 65; M. T. Clanchy, *From Memory to Written Record: England, 1066–1307* (Harvard, 1979), 253, 249.

[11] Walter C. Kidney, *The Architecture of Choice* (Braziller, 1974), 39. See Douglass Shand-Tucci, *Ralph Adams Cram* (Massachusetts, 2005), 23–64.

the spirit of some great departed Painter now first achieved his ideal'.[12] Evelyn Waugh's Forest Lawn replica of Oxford's 'St Peter-without-the-walls' is what 'the first builders dreamed of', an inspired realization of 'what those old craftsmen sought to do, with their rude implements of bygone ages'.[13]

The 'Tudor' cottages in Potton's 'Heritage' range fulfilled these fictions. 'We *have* turned the clock back', boast the modern builders, and 'if Oliver Cromwell or even Inigo Jones walked into the house they wouldn't find a brick or an oak beam out of place', a critic observed – except that the beams aren't oak but Canadian Douglas fir. Thwarted in their pre-scientific day by wormwood, mould, and rot, Tudor builders' aims are at last achieved in our enlightened time. Potton's self-build Heritage Barn (launched 1998) 'boasts all the charm of an old-world house' with all the comforts of the new.[14]

Rather than idealizing the past to its supposed best, others cook up evidence to skew it. Some falsify the past because what actually happened shames or beggars or scares them; others forge paintings or salt sites with fake antiquities to gain wealth or to perpetrate a hoax; still others invent history for pride or patriotism. Providentialist theology – the belief that God's will is evident in all that happens – made Annius of Viterbo's forgery of the Donation of Constantine a laudable act that sustained papal claims to temporal power and underpinned faith in unbroken Church continuity. Cardinal Cesare Baronio's *Annales Ecclesiastici* (1588–1607) skewed documents to prove that the Church had never fundamentally changed.[15] James Macpherson's 'Ossian' transcribed Homeric tradition into heroic Gaelic antiquity. As early as the fifteenth century forgeries were so common that some scholars dismissed all historical chronicles as mendacious.[16] Seemingly unaware that physical relics were forged with equal ease, antiquaries put misplaced faith in material remains.

Irked by an evangelical preacher's oft-intoned 'There were giants in the earth in those days' (Genesis 6.4), a nineteenth-century cynic carved a ten-foot block of gypsum in his own likeness and buried it near Cardiff, New York, to be 'discovered' by well-diggers the following year. Some sightseers thought the Cardiff Giant a petrified body, others a work of ancient art. A Yale professor found 'Phoenician inscriptions' on its right arm; Oliver Wendell Holmes saw 'anatomical details' through a hole bored in its head. 'Giant Saloons' and 'Goliath Houses' refreshed tourists, more numerous after the hoax was revealed. Barnum had it copied; the imitation outdrew the real humbug. In Mark Twain's 'A ghost story' (1870), the Giant's confused ghost haunts the Barnum likeness by mistake.[17]

---

[12] Nathaniel Hawthorne, *The Marble Faun* (1859), in *Works* (Ohio State, 1962–80), 4: 59.

[13] Evelyn Waugh, *The Loved One* (1948; London, 1965), 64–5.

[14] Potton 1982 catalogue, 3; Robert Troop, 'Buy yourself a date in history', *Sunday Times*, 28 Mar. 1982: 19; Helen Liddle, 'Kay and Peter Baldwin', 15 July 2009, *potton.co.uk/self-build/case-studies*.

[15] Nick Temple, 'Heritage and forgery: Annio da Viterbo and the quest for the authentic', *Public Archaeology* 2 (2002): 151–62; Anthony Grafton, *Bring Out Your Dead: The Past as Revelation* (Harvard, 2001), 56.

[16] Julian H. Franklin, *Jean Bodin and the Sixteenth-Century Revolution in the Methodology of Law and History* (Columbia, 1963), 89–101, 121–2; Ludovic Desmedt and Jérôme Blanc, 'Counteracting counterfeiting?', *History of Political Economy* 42 (2010): 323–60.

[17] James Taylor Dunn, 'The Cardiff Giant hoax, or the American Goliath', *New York History* 29 (1948): 367–77; Edmund Wilson, *Upstate: Records and Recollections of Northern New York* (New York, 1971), 33;

Like the Cardiff Giant, many hoaxes are intended to be soon unmasked, such as the 'runic' inscription at Mullsjö, Sweden, 'found' in 1953: 'Joe Doakes went East 1953. He discovered Europe. Holy smoke!'[18] But scholarly reputation can delay truth indefinitely. The Piltdown forgery was 'at first ... merely a delicious joke to see how far a gullible professional could be taken' in, but the experts 'tumbled too fast and too far' for the hoaxer to find a moment when the truth could safely be told.[19]

From medieval times on, the proliferation of sacred relics from the Holy Land so taxed credulity that, notwithstanding faith in divine multiplication, they became increasingly the butt of sacrilegious dubiety (see below, pp. 501–2). An efficacious alternative was to proclaim the possession of non-existent relics. One such fabrication was the Magi. In 1162, Milan fell to Frederick Barbarossa. As a reward to archbishop-elect Rainald of Cologne for his help in the conquest, he pillaged Milan's relics. Rainald's most notable coup was the remains of the Magi, legendarily brought from Constantinople (thanks to the emperor Constantine) to Milan by St Eustorgio in an ox-cart in 344.

Now the Magi were on the move again. Although waylaid en route by minions of Pope Alexander III, the three coffins with their sacred booty reached Cologne unharmed. In Nicolas of Verdun's splendid golden shrine (*c.* 1200), they become Cologne's iconic patrons. By the thirteenth century the Three Kings were a royal cult, emperors coming to venerate them after being crowned in Aachen. Otto IV of Brunswick had himself portrayed on the reliquary as the Fourth King. Belatedly, the Milanese lamented the theft. The sixteenth-century archbishop St Carlo Borromeo campaigned for their return; in 1909 a few Magi fragments were actually sent from Cologne to Milan.

But they were *not* sent *back*; they had never been in Milan. The whole story – Constantine, Eustorgio, removal to Cologne – had been fabricated by Rainald. Every mention of the Magi in Milan traces to the archbishop's own self-serving account. No wonder the Milanese were tardy in recognizing the theft; only in the late thirteenth century did Rainald's tale reach them. Milan then mourned the loss of relics it had never had: 'Oh shame Oh pain ... the bodies of the Magi were stolen from the city by the enemies of the church.'[20]

Rainald's purpose was clear: to promote the power of the emperor and the glory of Cologne. Relics of the Saviour were the most precious the Franks got from Italy and the Holy Land. As symbols of Christ's lordship and of divine kingship, the Magi trumped vestiges of Church Fathers and Roman martyrs. But they needed a pedigree; a legacy of veneration was vital to their efficacy in Cologne. Hence Constantine, the ox-cart, stewardship in Milan, their incorruptible state en route. And it worked. It worked even in Milan, where Visconti patronage of the lamented Magi helped scuttle both republicanism and rivals accused of exposing the Magis' hiding place to Frederick Barbarossa.

Mark Twain, 'A ghost story' (1870), in *Sketches, New and Old* (Hartford, CT, 1875), 215–21. See Scott Tribble, *A Colossal Hoax* (Rowman & Littlefield, 2009).

[18] Thierry Lenain, *Art Forgery* (Reaktion, 2011), ch. 1; Glyn Daniel, 'The Minnesota petroglyph', *Antiquity* 32 (1958): 264–7 at 267n.

[19] Stephen Jay Gould, 'Piltdown revisited', *Natural History* 88:3 (Mar. 1979): 86–98 at 98.

[20] Patrick J. Geary, *Living with the Dead in the Middle Ages* (Cornell, 1994), 251–55; Richard C. Trexler, *Journey of the Magi* (Princeton, 1997), 54–91, quoting Bonvesin de la Riva (Milan, 1288), 88.

This fabrication was multiply worthy. It confirmed the Holy Roman Empire's sacred roots. It updated and enlarged a useful biblical legend (little before was known of the Magi, even how many they were). It benefited Milan and later Florence, where the Medici became patrons of the Magi. The legend and the loss spurred both cities to *festae dei magi*, opulent spectacles of exotic splendour in the fourteenth and fifteenth centuries. It became an exemplar of other sacred translations: fragments of bone and dust that were easy to fake, easy to steal, easy to move, easy to reassign to new saints as needed. It begot great value from wishful fantasy. It destroyed nothing, not even faith when the fake was found out.

At its best, historical fabrication is both creative art and act of faith. By means of it we tell ourselves who we are, where we came from, and to what we belong. Ancestral loyalties rest on fraud as well as truth and foment peril along with pride. We cannot escape dependency on this motley and peccable past. We need to remember that its fictions are integral to its strengths, while at the same time not forgetting that they are indeed fictions.

Possessive and partisan pasts

Everyone revises the past to make it *theirs*. Retooling the past to our needs and desires, we merge into it, conform it with ourselves, and ourselves with it, matching our self-images and aspirations. Rendered grand or homely, magnified or tarnished, the past is continually recast to promote personal or group agendas. To that end the less well we know it the better; historical ignorance is heritage insight. A smattering will do, the vaguer the better. 'Heroes and founding fathers . . . must be mythical characters like Romulus and Remus or King Arthur, obscured in the mists of the distant past', argues Gordon Wood; 'they cannot be, like Jefferson and other "founding fathers," real human beings' about whom too much is known not to tarnish their legend.[21]

Ignorance safeguards heritage against harsh scrutiny. When Prince Edward Islanders refer to their Hebridean origins after the Clearances, or to the Glencoe Massacre, it does not matter that they know little about these events; 'the mere sound of the words arouses a homing instinct, a feeling of belonging'.[22] They belong to the Hebrides in a way that explicit knowledge would only weaken. 'We have a history here, you know', say Greek villagers content to leave its details to scholars.[23] 'We don't know what sort of history Adamsville has had', implies a Rhode Island village roadside display, 'but we feel certain that it had a history'.[24]

What do we infuse into our inheritance? We improve it – exaggerating its virtues and beauties, celebrating what makes us proud, playing down the ignoble and shameful, antiquating what's not old enough or updating to current perspectives. Memories, annals, and monuments highlight triumph and victory, or, increasingly nowadays, defeat and

---

[21] Gordon Wood, 'Jefferson at home', *NYRB*, 13 May 1993: 6–9.

[22] Stephen B. Maly, 'The Celtic fringe', Institute of Current World Affairs newsletter SM-10, 31 Apr. 1990.

[23] Roger Just, 'Cultural certainties and private doubts', in Wendy James, ed., *The Pursuit of Certainty: Religious and Cultural Formulations* (Routledge, 1995), 285–308 at 294.

[24] Kent C. Ryden, *Mapping the Invisible Landscape* (Iowa, 1993), 6. Adamsville is the reputed 1854 birthplace of the state bird, the Rhode Island Red chicken.

tragedy. Mostly we crave a legacy that is long, honourable, distinguished, manifesting continuity or reversion to first principles, revering ancestral precepts yet harmonizing with the present's best impulses. If missing or scanty in extant remains, these desiderata abound in subsequent additions to records and relics and in works of emulation and commemoration.

Reanimation renders the past pertinent. That classical splendour still suffuses Greece, patriots proudly assert, is thanks to modern care. 'When you are born, they talk to you about the Parthenon, the Acropolis', said culture minister Melina Mercouri. 'Everyone in Greece thinks they have built it with their own hands.' A living legacy needs constant nourishment; celebrating ancestors, Greeks build open-air theatres, cherish ancient place-names, launch replica triremes, copy classical facades. A century ago at Mount Pentelikon Virginia Woolf sardonically noted that 'dirty peasant boys' no longer spoke their own language 'as Plato would have spoken it had Plato learned Greek at Harrow'. Faith that if you spoke like Plato you might begin to think like him fuelled attachment to the ancient tongue.[25]

Collective memory like autobiography must seem our own. Only a past clearly ours feels worth having. Like family heirlooms, group heritage is a sacred possession to be handed on inviolate generation to generation. 'The issue is ownership and control', says an American civil-rights veteran battling for stewardship of the movement's sites. 'If we don't tell the story or control the telling, then it's no longer about us.'[26]

How history is bent reflects partisan concerns that distinguish *us* from *others*. Portrayals of bygone folk and affairs necessarily reflect present viewpoints. When Britain's National Maritime Museum demoted slave-trader Sir Francis Drake to a minor slot in its 1988 Armada show (to mollify both Spain and black Britons), Plymouth notables were outraged. Drake *was* the Armada; 'what Robin Hood is to Nottingham and Mickey Mouse to Disneyland, Francis Drake is to Plymouth' – sacred legacy and crux of local tourism. 'If you've got something to sell, then package it up and sell it', said Plymouth's Armada spokesman; 'What's history if you can't bend it a bit?'[27]

Treating the past as our own possession profoundly affects what we learn and how we alter what we gain or crave from former times. We may admire or venerate an untouched relic or recollection, but we feel more at home with it by putting our own stamp on it. Domesticating the past makes it truly ours. However pleasing the impress of history, occupants of old or ancestral houses commonly need to exorcise some imprint of previous inhabitants, replacing precursors' brand with their own. 'Heirs to the collections they own', writes a British museum director, must feel 'free to decide for themselves what

[25] Virginia Woolf, 'A dialogue upon Mount Pentelicus' (1906), *TLS*, 11–17 Sept. 1987: 979; Elizabeth Kastor, 'Melina Mercouri: dramatizing culture', *IHT*, 3 Feb. 1988; Michael Herzfeld, *A Place in History: Social and Monumental Time in a Cretan Town* (Princeton, 1991), 15–17, 34–5, 57.

[26] David W. Blight, 'If you don't tell it like it was, it can never be as it ought to be', in James O. and Lois E. Horton, *Slavery and Public History* (New Press, 2006), 19–34 at 24; David Dennis quoted in Ronald Smothers, 'Issue behind King Memorial: who owns history?' *NYT*, 16 Jan. 1995: A1.

[27] Quoted in Alan Hamilton and Ruth Gledhill, 'Plymouth defends Drake against new Armada, *Times*, 17 Sept. 1987: 5, 11. See my 'The timeless past', *Journal of American History* 75 (1989): 1263–80 at 1274.

they are going to do with the past'. Dresdeners rebuilding their carpet-bombed city not only restored but also rewrote their past; 'that which was complete was carefully broken into pieces, while that which was in pieces was carefully put together'.[28]

Acquiring the past, we also become part of it, revising history to play a role in it. As noted in Chapter 7, people commonly 'remember' being present at historic events they were nowhere near. Sixteen years after the 1929 banquet commemorating the invention of the electric light, Henry Ford commissioned Irving Bacon's painting, based on photos of the event; Ford insisted that Bacon add likenesses of his grand-sons, who 'couldn't be at the party because they were ill, [but] this is our picture, and they should ... be in there'.[29] Like hospital and museum benefactors, we are gratified to be memorialized, our names inscribed and our features framed in rever-ential perpetuity.

Graffitists avid for nominal immortality defaced monuments in ancient Greece and Pompeii, as did Renaissance scribblers in the Catacombs. The temptation seems irresist-ible; at Persepolis the eighteenth-century painter Robert Ker Porter added his own name alongside those he had scolded for doing the same thing.[30] Restorers add their carved initials to historic stonework. 'The architects get furious and call us vandals', said a Westminster Abbey mason. 'They do it, of course – but that's called signing their work.' The words 'Tolfink carved these runes in this stone', inscribed in Carlisle Cathedral, attest 'the existence of Tolfink, a human being unwilling to dissolve entirely into his surroundings'.[31]

The crudest disfigurements eventually embellish history, the carver's name adding a homely time-worn aura. Even as he censured Canadian troops for cutting names and addresses in James Paine's 1770s bridge at Brocket Park, Hertfordshire, James Lees-Milne reflected 'what an interesting memorial this will be thought in years to come, ... like the German mercenaries' names scratched in 1530 on the Palazzo Ducale in Urbino'. Newly uncovered prisoners' graffiti were the prime draw for Victorian tourists to the Tower of London.[32] 'John Scott 2010' carved on my gatepost is an outrage, writes a historian; 'JohnScot 1790' is charming; 'IohanScotus MCCCCXC' is a treasure. Footprints of Hollywood stars lend Sid Grauman's Chinese Theatre historic fame.[33] The obscene graffiti at the Sex Pistols' 1970s Soho premises, penned when Johnny Rotten felt the

[28] Neil MacGregor, 'Scholarship and the public', *Journal of the Royal Society of Arts* 139 (1991): 191–4; Neal Ascherson, 'A time to break down and a time to build up', *Independent on Sunday*, 23 Feb. 1992: 25.

[29] Quoted in Michael Wallace, 'Visiting the past: history museums in the United States', *Radical History Review* 25 (1981): 63–96 at 74–5.

[30] Erwin Panofsky, *Renaissance and Renascences in Western Art* (1960; Paladin, 1970), 173; Robert Ker Porter, *Travels in Georgia, Persia, Armenia, Ancient Babylonia* (1823), cited in Rose Macaulay, *Pleasure of Ruins* (New York: Walker, 1953), 145–6.

[31] Mason in E. R. Chamberlin, *Preserving the Past* (Dent, 1979), 190; Tolfink in Ursula K. Le Guin, 'It was a dark and stormy night', *Critical Inquiry* 7:1 (1980): 191–9 at 198.

[32] James Lees-Milne, diary 7 Jan. 1942, in *Ancestral Voices* (Chatto & Windus, 1975), 5; Simon Thurley, *Men from the Ministry* (Yale, 2013), 28–9.

[33] Michael R. G. Spiller, letter, *Times* 9 Apr. 1990: 13; Stacey Endres and Robert Cushman, *Hollywood at Your Feet* (Los Angeles: Pomegranate, 1992).

rooms 'too posh', are extolled for visceral immediacy in the true spirit of punk. The 2011 London find was likened to Tutankhamen and Lascaux.[34]

To leave his own mark on the past, Robert Rauschenberg all but expunged a Willem de Kooning drawing. Persuaded that deliberate erasure would lend salutary emphasis to time's inexorable erosion, de Kooning handed over a work to be effaced. 'The drawing was done with a hard line, and it was greasy, too, so I had to work very hard on it, using every sort of eraser. But in the end', said Rauschenberg, 'I felt it was a legitimate work of art.' Below the barely detectable original lines the inscription reads:

ERASED DE KOONING DRAWING
ROBERT RAUSCHENBERG
1953

Heralded as 'the first . . . exclusively art-historical artwork', *Erased de Kooning* exemplifies the wish for personal involvement that moves many to alter, add to, or cull the past.[35]

Like individuals, groups transform legacies to which they lay claim. Indeed, the claim *requires* the revision, for the past can only be securely our own if its lineaments are uniquely suited to us, hence alien and inaccessible to others. Such pasts, made usable by partisan manipulation, are 'heritage' as opposed to more widely agreed history. Groups reify collective memories ('partial histories') to cement the bonds that further their own aims. History is for all, heritage for us alone.[36]

The past as heritage transmits exclusive myths of origin and continuance, endowing an elect group with prestige and common purpose. History is never perfectly open – scholars hoard sources, archives get locked away, critics are denied access to records, misdeeds are hidden. But historians condemn concealment. In contrast, the heritage past is confined to the in-group. Tribal rules make it a restricted, secret possession. Created to generate and protect group interests, it benefits them only if withheld from others. Secrecy is power. Sharing or even showing a legacy to outsiders vitiates its virtue and potency; like Pawnee Indian 'sacred bundles', its value inheres in being opaque to outsiders. White Australian embrace of Aboriginal 'dreamtime' landscapes demeans their worth in tribal eyes.[37]

---

[34] Paul Graves-Brown and John Schofield, 'The filth and fury: 6 Denmark Street (London) and the Sex Pistols', *Antiquity* 85: 330 (2011): 1385–1401; 'Rotten drawings "the equal of World Heritage cave art"', *Times*, 11 Nov. 2011: 16.

[35] Quoted in Calvin Tomkins, 'Moving out' (1964), in *Off the Wall: A Portrait of Robert Rauschenberg* (Macmillan, 2005), 88; Harold Rosenberg, 'American drawing and the academy of the Erased de Kooning', *New Yorker*, 2 Mar. 1976: 106–10 at 108; Vincent Katz, 'A genteel iconoclasm', *Tate Etc.*, no. 8 (Autumn 2006). But when Rauschenberg exhibited *Erased de Kooning*, de Kooning was deeply distressed; he felt that the work should have been destroyed (Mark Stevens and Annalyn Swan, *De Kooning* (Knopf, 2004), 258–60).

[36] Maurice Halbwachs, *On Collective Memory* (1925; Harper & Row, 1980), 84.

[37] Bahar Aykan, 'How participatory is participatory heritage management? The politics of safeguarding the Alevi ritual as intangible heritage', *IJCP* 20 (2013): 381–406 at 392–3, 397; Roger O'Keefe, 'World cultural heritage: obligations to the international community as a whole?' *International and Comparative Law Quarterly* 53 (2004): 189–209; Lynn Meskell, 'Unesco and the fate of the World Heritage Indigenous Peoples Council of Experts (WHIPCOE)', *IJCP* 20 (2013): 155–74 at 168–9.

Fearing exploitation, ethnic and religious minorities as well as tribal indigenes seek 'security through obscurity', reprobating all external knowledge of their heritage. 'Why [does] our *Semah* become the world's concern?' inveighs an Alevi Turk against UNESCO designation of his religious ritual as 'folkloric' heritage. 'This is an issue between me and my God, why does the world wish to interfere in it?' The act seemed a Turkish mainstream Muslim ploy to delegitimize Alevi worship. 'If the state or the government is doing something for us, we automatically suspect something fishy behind it.' Ignored and misled during the 'consultation' process, the Alevi 'don't want to be protected, defined, or interfered with in any way'. Global vows to protect 'imalienable' indigenous heritage remain toothless pieties, as in UNESCO, where only nation-states can nominate world heritage sites and statism routinely stifles tribal advocacy.[38]

Ignorance about others reinforces pride in our own past. Britons gloried in insularity, so sure of their pre-eminence, wrote Emerson, as to be 'provokingly incurious about other nations'. Foreign admirers of English heritage were dismissed by a National Trust chairman as folk with 'funny names [from] silly countries'.[39] After all, 'if people feel proud of their identity and rich in their cultural inheritance', in a characteristic reaction, 'why should they ... spend time learning about those of others?'[40] Teaching children 'a patriotic narrative of British history as a way of cementing national identity', charges Cambridge's Regius history professor, dominates government thinking. Although 'world' history gets a cursory nod, European history goes unmentioned – no Habsburg Empire, imperial Germany, French or Russian revolutions. Meanwhile in Welsh schools' history curriculum 'the other Britain let alone Europe hardly exist[s]'.[41]

Throughout Europe the focus on national history intensifies to the detriment of continental, let alone global, perspectives: as in the wake of Napoleon and of the First World War, the end of Soviet hegemony in eastern Europe spurred nationalist history-making. Even the traditionally cosmopolitan Netherlands now stresses a Dutch history

[38] Diane L. Good, 'Sacred bundles: history wrapped up in culture', *History News* 45:4 (July–Aug. 1990): 13–14, 27; Howard Creamer, 'Aboriginal perceptions of the past', in Peter Gathercole and David Lowenthal, eds., *The Politics of the Past* (Unwin & Hyman, 1990), 130–40; Michael F. Brown, 'Heritage trouble: recent work on the protection of intangible cultural property', *IJCP* 12 (2005): 40–61 at 46–9; Rosanne Trottier, 'Intellectual property for mystics? Considerations on protecting traditional wisdom systems' *IJCP* 17 (2010): 519–46 at 524; Gwyneira Isaac, 'Whose idea was this? Museums, replicas and the reproduction of knowledge', *Current Anthropology* 52 (2011): 211–33. See Miranda Forsyth, 'Lifting the lid on "The Community": who has the right to control access to traditional knowledge and expressions of culture?', *IJCP* 19 (2012): 1–31; Marianna Bicskei et al. 'Protection of cultural goods', *IJCP* 19 (2012): 97–118; W. F. Merrill and R. E. Ahlborn, 'Zuni archangels and ahayu:da', in Amy Henderson and Adrienne L. Kaeppler, eds., *Exhibiting Dilemmas* (Smithsonian, 1997), 176–205; Martha Royce Blaine, *Some Things Are Not Forgotten: A Pawnee Family Remembers* (Nebraska, 1997), 181–99.

[39] Ralph Waldo Emerson, 'English traits' (1856), in *The Portable Emerson* (Viking, 1946), 353–488 at 425; Lord Chorley quoted in Paula Weideger, *Gilding the Acorn: Behind the Façade of the National Trust* (Simon & Schuster, 1994), 163–4.

[40] James Murphy quoted in *Observer*, 10 Dec. 1989: 16.

[41] Richard J. Evans quoted in Lorien Kite and Chris Cook, 'Mantel attacks "pernicious" Gove reforms', *Financial Times*, 19 Oct. 2012; Richard J. Evans, 'Myth-busting', *Guardian*, 11 Aug. 2013: Review, 2; Joke van der Leeuw-Roord, 'Education for inclusion, awareness and tolerance', in Semih Aktekin et al., eds., *Teaching History and Social Studies for Multicultural Europe* (Ankara: Harf, 2009), 127–40 at 131.

canon mandated to strengthen national collective memory. In a backlash against multi-culturalism, narrowly chauvinist school history is widely resurgent.[42]

Each of the world's seven thousand-odd languages is both a vehicle of communication that unites its speakers and a bulwark against non-conversant outsiders. Babel's curse of incoherence became a club for like-minded monolinguals whose distinct tongues embody, express, and inflate pride in their own ways and contempt for alien others. The foreign country of the past is made most alien by linguistic exclusion and denigration.[43]

Many American students 'work all too hard to avoid pronouncing foreign words and names the way the foreigners intended', out of 'a belief that anything not clearly American is unworthy of bother or is even a little, or a lot, suspect', reported their history professor.[44] 'I don't need to visit other countries', said a proudly provincial Florida school board head, 'to know that America is the best country in the world'.[45] That 'America is simply the most extraordinary nation in history … is not a statement of nationalist hubris', contended presidential candidate Newt Gingrich, but 'an historic fact'.[46] For declaring 'I believe in American exceptionalism', but then adding, 'just as I suspect that the Brits believe in British exceptionalism and the Greeks believe in Greek exceptional-ism', President Obama was charged by Republicans with craven un-Americanism.[47]

Claims of past pre-eminence offensive to others keep outsiders at bay. We exalt our own past not as demonstrably true but because it *ought* to be. A partisan past cannot be universally true; to those beyond the pale its tenets must defy reason. Empirical error and irrational argument render our past opaque or erroneous to outsiders, clear and tenable only to us – like the famed Slav soul, hidden and enigmatic, yet irrefutable.[48] In treating its sacred past as distinctive and its distinctive past as sacred, each nation is a 'chosen people'. Thus America, as president-to-be George W. Bush echoed Herman Melville, 'is

---

[42] Joke van der Leeuw-Roord, 'Yearning for yesterday', in Linda Symcox and Arie Wilschut, eds., *National History Standards* (Charlotte, NC: Information Age, 2007), 73–95 at 79, 86; Siep Stuurman and Maria Grever, 'Introduction: old canons and new histories', in M. Grever and S. Stuurman, eds., *Beyond the Canon: History for the Twenty-First Century* (Palgrave Macmillan 2007), 1–16 at 2–3; Mario Carretero et al., 'Students' historical narratives and concepts about the nation', in M. Carretero et al., eds., *History Education and the Construction of National Identities* (Charlotte, NC: Information Age, 2012), 153–70 at 153–7. See Mario Carretero, *Constructing Patriotism: Teaching History and Memory in Global Worlds* (Charlotte, NC: Information Age, 2011).

[43] See my 'Heritage care: from the Tower of Babel to the ivory tower', *Change over Time* 1 (2011): 130–6; Mark Pagel, *Wired for Culture: The Natural History of Human Cooperation* (Penguin, 2012), 275–303.

[44] Victoria Chandler, 'What we can learn from "Chuck Oozo"', AHA *Perspectives* 24:7 (Oct. 1986): 24–7 at 26.

[45] Quoted in Larry Rohter, 'Battle over patriotism curriculum', *NYT*, 15 May 1994: 1: 22.

[46] Newt Gingrich, *A Nation like No Other: Why American Exceptionalism Matters* (Regnery, 2011), 13. See Michael Kammen, 'The problem of American exceptionalism', in *In the Past Lane* (Oxford, 1997), 169–98; and Daniel T. Rogers, 'Exceptionalism', in Anthony Molho and Gordon S. Wood, eds., *Imagined Histories* (Princeton, 1998), 21–36.

[47] Barack Obama (April 2009) quoted in James Carroll, 'The harsh truth of the "City on a Hill"', *IHT*, 29 Nov 2011: 6. See Jerome Karabel, '"American exceptionalism" and the battle for the presidency', *Huffington Post*, 22 Dec. 2011.

[48] Mary Garrison, 'The Franks as the new Israel?', 114–61 at 116, 157, and Rosamond McKitterick, 'Political ideology in Carolingian historiography', 162–74 at 174, in Yitzak Hen and Matthew Innes, eds., *The Uses of the Past in the Early Middle Ages* (Cambridge, 2000); Aleksandr Ivanovich Kuprin, *A Slav Soul* (Constable, 1916).

chosen by God and commissioned by history to be a model to the world'.[49] Extolling
American imperialism a century ago, Indiana senator and historian Albert J. Beveridge
was more magisterial: 'Almighty God ... has marked us out as His chosen people,
henceforth to lead in the regeneration of the world.'[50]

Out of some legendary kernel of history, every group harvests a crop of delusory faiths –
faiths nutritive not *despite* but *thanks to* their flaws. Partisan needs actuate a mass of false
information about the past that sustains all societies, as Émile Durkheim demonstrated.
Like individuals, Freud posited, 'mankind as a whole has developed delusions which are
inaccessible to logical criticism and which contradict reality'. Such arcana cannot be
exposed to sceptical scrutiny, lest 'critical thinking', anathematized by conservative Texans
in 2012, undermine 'fixed beliefs' and subvert parental authority. The bad effects of wrong
beliefs are more than compensated by the bonding they confer and the barriers they erect.
From childhood on, social bonding and dread of ostracism induce adhesion to group
norms – the more nonsensical and irrational the better – to reflect group values, to
demonstrate shared commitments, and to exclude others who fail to imitate that behaviour. Shared *mis*information bans those whose own legacy encodes different catechisms.
'Correct' history could not so serve, because it is open to all, alien and domestic alike; only
a distorted past can be a gauge of exclusion.[51] Partisan needs mandate *mis*reading the past.

Misreadings become cherished myths. Steelworkers in 1970s Terni, Italy, 'remembered'
things done and said by 1940s anti-fascists that never happened (but should have).[52] It is
well known that 'the two absolute facts on which [Londonderry] is built actually didn't
happen'; it was not founded by St Columba, and the famed 1689 'siege' was a mere blockade.
But Derry folk dote on these founding fables all the more because they *are* fabulous.[53]

Plato's *Republic* shows the civic value of such 'noble lies'. To instil loyalty, Socrates
contrived a 'magnificent myth that would carry conviction to our whole community'. He
aimed to persuade them that they had been 'fashioned and reared in the depths of the earth,
and Earth herself, their mother, brought them up into the light of day; so now they must
think of the land in which they live as their mother and protect her if she is attacked'.[54]

Sacred origins still sanction obscure credos. You are asked if you 'believe in the Monroe
Doctrine', in an early example. 'You do not dare to say that you do not know what it is,

[49] Anthony D. Smith, *Chosen Peoples* (Oxford, 2003), 255–61; George W. Bush, Remarks at Simon Wiesenthal
     Center, Los Angeles, 6 Mar. 2000; Herman Melville, *White-Jacket* (1850; Northwestern, 1970), 179.
[50] Albert J. Beveridge, 'In support of an American empire', US Senate, 9 Jan. 1900, *Cong. Record* 56th
     Congress, 1st sess. 704–12 at 704.
[51] Emile Durkheim, *The Elementary Forms of Religious Life* (1912; Free Press, 1995), 134–8; Sigmund Freud,
     'Constructions in analysis' (1937), in *CPW*, 23: 255–70 at 268–9; 2012 Republican Party of Texas, *Report of
     Platform Committee and Rules Committee*, 'Educating our children', 12; Peter Munz, *Our Knowledge of the
     Growth of Knowledge* (Routledge, 1985), 282–302; Cristine H. Legare and Rachel E. Watson-Jones, 'The
     evolution and ontogeny of ritual', in David M. Buss, ed., *The Handbook of Evolutionary Psychology*, vol. 2:
     Applications 2nd edn (Wiley, 2015, in press) Chapter 34.
[52] Alessandro Portelli, 'The time of my life: functions of time in oral history', *International Journal of Oral
     History* 2 (1981): 162–80, and 'Uchronic dreams: working-class memory and possible worlds', in Raphael
     Samuel and Paul Thompson, eds., *Myths We Live by* (London, 1990), 143–60.
[53] Brian Lacey quoted in Simon Tait, 'Not afraid to face up to the facts', *Times*, 25 Oct. 1995. See Brian Lacey,
     Siege City: The Story of Derry and Londonderry (Belfast: Blackstaff, 1990), 128–31.
[54] Plato, *The Republic* (360 BC), 414c–415d (Penguin, 1974), 181–2.

because you understand that ... every good American is bound to believe in' it. 'To tamper seriously with America's received story of its past is dangerous', notes a modern historian, because 'it disturbs the fixed version of the sanctified past that makes the present bearable'.[55]

Society thrives on persisting error about the past. 'Getting its history wrong is crucial for the creation of a nation', Ernest Renan comforted French chauvinists; the need for amnesia and error made historical truth a danger to national unity. English historians praise precursors' muddled thinking as a national virtue. 'We made our peace with the Middle Ages by misconstruing them; "wrong" history was one of our assets', exulted Butterfield. 'Precisely because they did not know the Middle Ages, the historians of the time gave the 17th century just the type of anachronism that it required' – they mistook England's new constitution for a restoration of ancient liberties. Useful *because* mistaken, this fable became a pillar of national heritage; 'whatever it may have done to our history, it had a wonderful effect on English politics'.[56]

The British still revel in unreason. Opposing a 1993 bill in the House of Lords to let daughters inherit noble titles, the historian Hugh Trevor-Roper (Lord Dacre) lauded male primogeniture for its 'traditional irrationality'. The Duke of Norfolk refused to tamper with Richard II's original intent (1299): 'Who are we to change that now, centuries later? This is interfering with history and I don't like it'.[57] The finding of a sixth-century stone inscribed 'Artognov' (Arthur) at Tintagel roused a spirited defence of 'a myth that has survived so long without historical legs ... The myth and the man shouldn't come too close together. Sometimes truth needs to be kept at a distance – so memories can live on.'[58]

The Swiss similarly vaunt their mythic past. Since history was 'a school of patriotism', warned an educator in 1872, its errors should be uncorrected. To question traditions that 'symbolize liberty, independence, and republican virtues' would corrode public patriotism; historical niceties were 'not the concern of the masses'. William Tell's defiance of Habsburg oppression is a notorious fiction, but the infallible archer, the apple, and the cap are pivotal to Swiss identity. A 1994 Lausanne exhibition that debunked Tell and other 'pseudo-historical' icons of Swiss virtue was savagely abused, its authors sent death threats.[59]

---

[55] William Graham Sumner, 'War' (1903), in *War and Other Essays* (Yale, 1919), 3–40 at 36; Donna Merwick, 'Comment [on James Hijaya, 'Why the West is lost']', *William & Mary Quarterly* 51 (1994): 736–9 at 736.

[56] Ernest Renan, *Qu'est-ce qu'une nation?* (1882; Paris: Bordas, 1991), 38; Herbert Butterfield, *The Englishman and His History* (Cambridge, 1944), 7–9.

[57] Hugh Trevor-Roper in *Times*, 8 Mar. 1994; Duke of Norfolk, in 'Lords shut the door on breeze of change', *Commonwealth Law Review* 18 (Jan. 1993): 411.

[58] 'Arthur's slate: is he better as fact or fiction?' *Guardian* leader, 7 Aug. 1998: 15. See R. J. Higham, *King Arthur: Myth-Making and History* (Routledge, 2002), 16–20, 79, 95, 268–9.

[59] Alexandre Daguet (1872) quoted in Geneviève Heller, *D'un pays et du monde* (Yverdon-les-Bains, Switzerland, 1993), 38; Charles Heimberg, *Un étrange anniversaire: le centenaire du premier août* (Geneva, 1990), 61–3; Werner Meyer, *1291: L'histoire: Les prémices de la Conféderation suisse* (Zurich, 1991); Werner Meyer, *Nos ancêtres les Waldstaetten* (Musée Historique de Lausanne, 1994), 48; Olivier Pavillon, 'Du débat à l'anathème', *Revue Suisse d'Histoire* 44 (1994): 311–14; Oliver Zimmer, *A Contested Nation: History, Memory and Nationalism in Switzerland* (Cambridge, 2003), 235–40.

Remade pasts unashamedly annex those of rivals. To emphasize Jewish acumen and ridicule Gentile rulers, Hellenistic Jews magnified their own heroes, religious superiority, and military prowess. Enhancing rather than questioning scriptural stories, they expanded King David's conquests and Solomon's sway, blended Babylonian and Greek legends with Abrahamic, appropriated Egyptian myth, and made Moses a pan-Mediterranean mentor.[60]

Chauvinism everywhere reshapes the past. Poles favour Slavonic antiquities, neglecting or reattributing those of Teutonic provenance. To denigrate a rival heritage its relics are hidden or demolished. The Mexican emperor Itzcoatl destroyed an earlier Náhuatl codex so as to leave the Aztec version of history uncontested; the Spanish concealed the imposing Inca masonry at Cuzco lest observers doubt that the Indians were a 'depraved' and 'idle' race. White Rhodesia displayed the Great Zimbabwe ruins as a European creation.[61] The British razed Irish churches 'to destroy evidences of past civilisation in order to' show, the Irish charged, that 'we are "a people without a history"'. And Britain left records of its Ordnance Survey of Ireland unpublished for fear they would generate interest in antiquities and excite Irish nationalism.[62] Once sovereign, the Irish pulled down Georgian buildings as symbols of English oppression, to be replaced by the 'peasant–Gaelic' architecture of independent Eire. 'I was glad to see them go', said Ireland's minister of culture in 1961; 'they stand for everything I hate'.[63]

Ireland's canonical epic is 'a beneficent legacy, its wrongness notwithstanding', writes historian Brendan Bradshaw. Puncturing Gaelic origin legends would forfeit their 'positive dynamic thrust'; denuding history of heroes of national liberation would 'make the modern Irish aliens in their own land'. The grand tale of tribulations overcome is crucial to Irish identity. 'They all know it's not true', says an Ulster Catholic of a saga

---

[60] Erich S. Gruen, *Heritage and Hellenism: The Reinvention of Jewish Tradition* (California, 1998), xvi–xix, 71, 292–6.

[61] Miguel Léon-Portilla, *Pre-Columbian Literature of Mexico* (Oklahoma, 1969), 119; Peter S. Garlake, 'Prehistory and ideology in Zimbabwe', in J. D. Y. Peel and Terence Ranger, eds., *Past and Present in Zimbabwe* (Manchester, 1983), 1–19 at 11, 14–16; Peter S. Garlake, *The Early Art and Architecture of Africa* (Oxford, 2002), 23–5.

[62] Samuel Ferguson, 'Architecture in Ireland' (1846) quoted, and Patrick McSweeney, *A Group of Nation Builders* (1913) cited, in Jeanne Sheehy, *The Rediscovery of Ireland's Past: The Celtic Revival* (Thames & Hudson, 1980), 58, 20; Rachel Hewitt, *Map of a Nation: A Biography of the Ordnance Survey* (Granta, 2010), 286–7. For the Ordnance Survey's impact on the Irish, see Hewitt, *Map of a Nation*, 242–88, and Brian Friel, *Translations* (Faber & Faber, 1981).

[63] Desmond Guinness (1961), quoted in K. C. Kearns, 'Preservation and transformation of Georgian Dublin', *Geographical Review* 72 (1982): 270–90 at 273. Irish hostility to Ascendancy structures – 'no one wanted these walls of memories around. The sooner they go, the better' (Duncan McLaren, *Ruins: The Once Great Houses of Ireland* (Knopf, 1980), ii); 'these "symbols of oppression" should be swept away to be replaced by the bright new architecture of an independent Ireland' (Kevin B. Nowlan et al., eds., *Dublin's Future* (Country Life/An Taisce, 1980), 8), gave way to pride in Georgian work by Irish craftsmen. In 1962 architecture students carried banners proclaiming 'Dublin must not be a museum'; in 1969 they occupied threatened historic buildings to prevent their destruction (K. C. Kearns, *Georgian Dublin* (David & Charles, 1983), 76–7). A law requiring towns in the Gaeltacht to restore their Gaelic names was rejected in An Daingeau, the Anglicized name 'Dingle' having become its touristic lifeblood ('Dingle votes overwhelmingly for a return to the Anglicized past', *Times*, 21 Oct. 2006: 41).

of Protestant infamy, 'but that won't stop them believing it. In a few years it will be gospel'.[64]

For Finnish patriots the *Kalevala* though 'a clear counterfeit' is nonetheless a holy book that reflects their deepest being; 'if a Finn ridicules the Kalevala . . . that is a sin against the Holy Ghost'.[65] It is a sacrosanct Greek credo that secret schools run by Orthodox monks kept Hellenic culture alive under Turkish oppressors. In fact, Greek schooling was widely tolerated during Ottoman rule, but it is forbidden to say so. A 1960s teacher was pilloried for questioning the legend. 'Even if the *krypha skholeia* [secret schooling] was a myth', asserts a spokesman, 'it should still . . . be propagated, for such myths are an essential element in the national identity'.[66]

Conversely, nations on occasion promote myths of cosmopolitan diversity in place of once-rejected pasts. In drearily homogeneous 1980s Poland many told me wistfully of lamented 'Lithuanian heritage' and 'Jewish grandmothers', a multi-ethnic nostalgia since augmented by its conformity with European Union ideals.[67] Suppressed over five centuries, Spain's Jewish past lately became an object not only of curiosity but of longing. 'I don't go a week without someone calling and asking me if their last name has Jewish roots', says a specialist. 'People are . . . creating a Jewish patrimony that never existed', inventing old Jewish quarters and 'medieval synagogues that are hardly medieval, if they ever functioned as synagogues at all'.[68]

Defining Native Americans as wandering nomads was a useful American fiction. That many tribes were settled farmers was ignored in rationalizing their forced removal. 'If the author of [a much-used text] cannot remember from one chapter to the next that the Indians didn't need to settle down' because they already *were* settled, 'we can hardly expect his readers to', comments a critic. 'The story is too powerful an archetype' to relinquish. A Tennessee Tea Party leader in 2011 demanded that schools stop teaching 'an awful lot of made-up criticism about . . . the founders intruding on the Indians or having slaves'.[69]

Fiction persists as fond heritage. Parson Weems's Washington fables have been 'shattered again and again, but they live on in the popular mind, and nothing can extirpate them,

---

[64] Brendan Bradshaw, 'Nationalism and historical scholarship in modern Ireland', *Irish Historical Studies* 26 (1989): 329–51 at 348–9; Colm Tóibín, 'New ways of killing your father', *London Review of Books*, 18 Nov. 1993: 3–6; Briege Duffaud, *A Wreath upon the Dead* (Dublin: Poolbeg, 1993), 445.

[65] *c.* 1917 quoted in William A. Wilson, *Folklore and Nationalism in Modern Finland* (Indiana, 1976), 76–9.

[66] Quoted in Richard Clogg, 'The Greeks and their past', in Dennis Deletant and Harry Hanak, eds., *Historians as Nation-Builders* (Macmillan, 1988), 16–28 at 28. See Anna Collard, 'Investigating "social memory" in a Greek context', in Elizabeth Tonkin et al., eds., *History and Ethnicity* (Routledge, 1989), 89–103. On the risks of dispelling Greek myths, see Keith S. Brown and Yannis Hamilakis, eds., *The Usable Past: Greek Metahistories* (Lexington Books, 2003), notably Philip Carabott, 'Monumental visions', 23–37, Yannis Hamilakis, 'Learn history!' 39–68, Patrick Finney, 'The Macedonian question', 87–104, and Loring Danforth, 'Afterword', 211–19.

[67] 'Introduction' to John-Paul Himka and Joanna Beata Michlic, eds., *Bringing the Dark Past to Light* (Nebraska, 2013), 1–24 at 8, 13.

[68] Javier Castaño in Renwick McLean, 'Spain digs for its once-hidden Jewish heritage', *NYT*, 5 Nov. 2006.

[69] James W. Loewen, *Lies My Teacher Told Me* (New York: New Press, 1995), 123; Hal Rounds quoted in Richard Locker, 'Tea Parties issue demands to Tennessee legislators', Memphis *Commercial Appeal*, 13 Jan. 2011.

Figure 77 George Washington and the cherry tree: the original myth. Grant Wood, *Parson Weems' Fable*, 1939

Figure 78 George Washington and the cherry tree: a modern explanation. 'Give a kid a hatchet, he's going to chop things' (Robert Kraus, *New Yorker*, 25/1/1969, p. 28)

Figure 79 George Washington and the cherry tree: technology tarnishes the fable.
'Father, I cannot tell a lie' (Dana Fredon, *New Yorker*, 13/5/1972, p. 45)

however much they are mocked'.[70] The saga of Rhondda Valley miners shot down by British troops in 1910 is an outrage the Welsh will never forget, yet 'every single man who was there knows that the story is nonsense', wrote Josephine Tey a generation later. Nonetheless 'it has never been contradicted. It will never be overtaken now.'[71] The 'ancient' folklore classic *Barzaz-Breiz*, long exposed as a nineteenth-century pastiche, remains the 'authentic' Breton voice because six generations have used it to express that voice. 'What matter if learned hands have harmonised a few lines in places', writes a defender. 'They could not have invented ... fifteen centuries [of] collective genius.' Breton heritage 'is not what history bequeathed them, but what romantic reconstruction' led them to build.[72]

Commending past error is the theme of Joseph Roth's *Radetzky March*, whose protagonist, Joseph Trotta, rescues Emperor Franz Joseph at the battle of Solferino in 1859. Years later, Trotta reads a gushy version of the episode in his son's school text. 'It's a pack of lies', he yells. 'Captain, you're taking it too seriously', says a friend. 'All historical events are modified for consumption in schools. And quite right, too. Children need examples which they can understand, which impress them. They can learn later what actually occurred.'

[70] Henry Cabot Lodge, 'An American myth', in *The Democracy of the Constitution* (Scribners, 1915), 208–19. See Michael Kammen, *The Mystic Chords of Memory* (Knopf, 1991), 484.

[71] Josephine Tey, *The Daughter of Time* (London, 1954), 95. See Gwyn Evans and David Maddox, *Tonypandy Riots 1910–11* (Plymouth University Press, 2010).

[72] Morvan Lebesque, *Comment peut-on être Breton?* (Paris: Seuil, 1970), quoted in Ellen Badone, 'Folk literature and the invention of tradition: ... the *Barzaz-Breiz*', American Anthropological Association meeting, San Francisco, Dec. 1992; Jean-Yves Guiomar, 'Le *Barzaz-Breiz* de Théodore Hersart de La Villemarqué', in Pierre Nora, *Lieux de mémoire* (Paris: Gallimard 1984–92), III.2: 526–65 at 554.

The emperor himself rejects literal truth. 'It's a bit awkward', he admits to the now ennobled Trotta, 'but neither of us shows up too badly in the story. Forget it.'[73]

Such falsifying appals scholars, apt to judge their own jingoists uniquely perverted. 'In no other European country', charged Spain's Royal Academy of History, 'is ignorance of history used with the political aim of distortion'.[74] To the contrary, nationalists the world over thrive on, even require, historical ignorance and error. Falsified pasts are integral to group bonding. Those who seek a past as sound as a bell forget that bells *need* built-in imperfections to bring out their crucial special resonances.

Altering past scene and substance

Adaptations

To look or function better in today's world, the past is variously enhanced. We rectify or amplify surviving materials and memories, purifying or discarding what is now unwanted. We antiquate or modernize our legacy to make it more exotic or more familiar, endowing the past with present desiderata or the present with idealized traits of earlier times. We ameliorate our yesterdays by augmenting or shedding their physical and mental remains, either distancing or domesticating what we retain and reshape.

Without adaptive reuse most artefacts and memories would soon perish; altering records and relics to present-day purposes prolongs their existence. 'New uses preserve; only what later eras can appropriate has a chance of survival.' Had the Parthenon not served as a mosque, a harem, even a gunpowder repository, it would have succumbed to plunder and erosion. Enduring icons over time accrue many different resonances. The Paris Panthéon was successively cherished as Christian shrine, Enlightenment emblem, icon of national unity, and temple of humanity.[75] As change outdates earlier functions, survival demands other uses. Later technology made obsolete the defence of the realm at the Tower of London; Christian worship alone cannot now sustain ancient cathedrals. Eighteenth-century jails no longer serve as prisons, nor workhouses as indigent abodes; convicts and the poor are now otherwise housed. Old dwellings are uninhabitable unless modernized, doomed by current demands of comfort, safety, and decor.

Adaptive change is contentious. Violating the modernist creed that 'form ever follows function', new uses may seem sacrilege. Rather than demean redundant churches by secular misuse, traditionalists prefer vacant spiritual shrines.[76] But others delight in malleability: the chequered past of Washington's Lafayette Square as cherry orchard, racetrack, graveyard, zoo, militia camp, Andrew Jackson's inaugural site, slave market,

---

[73] Joseph Roth, *The Radetzky March* (1932; London, 1974), 7–10.

[74] Quoted in Giles A. Tremlett, *Ghosts of Spain* (New York: Walker, 2006), 14, 23.

[75] Arnold Esch, 'On the reuse of antiquity', in Richard Brilliant and Dale Kinney, eds., *Reuse Value* (Ashgate, 2011), 13–19 at 15; Edward Hollis, *The Secret Lives of Buildings* (London: Portobello, 2009); Mona Ozouf, 'Le Panthéon', in Nora, *Lieux de mémoire*, 1 (1984): 139–66. See Richard Wrigley and Matthew Craske, eds., *Pantheons* (Ashgate, 2004).

[76] Louis Henri Sullivan, 'The tall office building artistically considered', *Lippincott's Magazine* (Mar. 1896): 403–9; 'New uses for redundant churches opposed', *Times*, 8 Sept. 1977: 14; Matthew Saunders, *Saving Churches: Friends of Friendless Churches* (London: Frances Lincoln, 2010).

sheep pasture, now a park with 'the densest squirrel population known to science'.[77] 'A heritage is something to be preserved', said the curator of the exhibition *Hier pour Demain* (Yesterday for Tomorrow), 'but also to be modified to meet the needs of a changing world'.[78] Developers ratify reuse with nostalgia. A cartoonist envisioned the Statue of Liberty remade into luxury flats whose residents would 'sleep in the splendor of a national monument', with doormen 'dressed in the native costumes of their [immigrant] grandparents'.[79]

Relics' penultimate reuse is decorative or pedagogic. Like a 'discarded hubcap ... launched on a second life as a planter for a nice cactus assortment', their workaday function ceases when acquired by collectors or museums. A sword begins as a warrior's weapon; at his death it becomes a sacred ceremonial object; next it is looted as a souvenir of conquest; reclaimed by curators it goes on display. But only successive retention as weapon, holy relic, and treasure enabled this sword to survive to the museum stage, while other swords rusted, rotted, and vanished from view.[80]

Display may not be antiquities' final role, as Rome's frequent rebirth from ancient ruins attests. Periodic reuse features Italo Calvino's Clarice, a city whose inhabitants recycle relics during recurrent epochs of ruin and regeneration. At Clarice's decline and imminent collapse, its survivors

grabbed everything that could be taken from where it was and put it in another place to serve a different use: brocade curtains ended up as sheets; in marble funerary urns they planted basil; wrought-iron gratings torn from the harem windows were used for roasting cat-meat on fires of inlaid wood.

When Clarice prospers again the artefacts are remembered as relics of a better past; 'shards of the original splendor that had been ... adapt[ed] to more obscure needs, ... were now preserved under glass bells, locked in display cases, set on velvet cushions' so that citizens could reconstruct the previous Clarice in their minds' eye.[81] Each successive stage reshuffles remnants of former uses, sacred or profane, now functional, now decorative.

As time or travail disqualify previous alterations, new needs and outlooks remould the past over and over. Revered American founding fathers debunked in the 1920s were rehabilitated in the 1940s and '50s, deflated again in the '60s, restored to favour in the '80s, purged by the politically correct '90s, made Tea Party apostles in 2010. The novelist Siegfried Lenz charts the shifting repute of folk relics in a Masurian borderland museum under successive Russian and German rule. Things that local people 'had previously thought poignant they now saw as tasteless or even incriminating', those once derogated

---

[77] Architour, *Architectural Tour of Lafayette Square* brochure, *c.* 1979; David A. Fahrenhold, 'An exotic evolution', *Washington Post*, 19 May 2005.

[78] Jean Cuisenier quoted in Michael Gibson, 'Preserving France's heritage from before the (Industrial) Revolution', *IHT*, 5–6 July 1980: 8.

[79] Bill Day, *Preservation News* 20:8 (1980): 4.

[80] Charlie Haas, 'The secret life of the American tourist', *New West* 5:16 (1980): 13–29 at 14, 21; Philip Fisher, 'The future's past', *New Literary History* 6 (1975): 587–606.

[81] Italo Calvino, *Invisible Cities* (1972; Vintage, 1997), 106–7.

newly admired.[82] Relics formerly beyond the pale may gain modern favour. Architecturally touted, a once-repudiated Arkansas brothel acquired a new social pedigree to match. 'It wasn't just the transients who came here', said a local booster. 'Some very prominent people frequented Miss Laura's House.' Populism converted General Sam Houston's Greek Revival Texas mansion into a rough-hewn log cabin that Houston would have disdained.[83]

Rivalry between homely and handsome pasts embroiled historians at the Lyndon B. Johnson National Historic Site in Texas. While president, Johnson in 1964 built a new house at his birthplace, furnishing it with memorabilia from his whole career. After his death, the National Park Service replaced Johnson's version with a facsimile of the unadorned original. Others demurred: what Johnson thought his birthplace *ought* to have been mattered more than a conjectural facsimile. So the Birthplace Cottage was restored back to how it looked from 1964 to 1972.[84]

Ethnic relics and records emerge, vanish, and resurface in line with changing stereotypes. American Indians degenerated from implacable foes into cigar-store-and-movie buffoons in the 1920s and '30s, faded from public view in the '40s and '50s, re-emerged in the '60s and '70s as victims of racist oppression, and figure today as restitution claimants, savvy ecologists, and crafty casino entrepreneurs.

Additions

We alter the past not only by changing its surviving lineaments but by copying and embellishing them. A dwindling array of original fragments is embedded among myriad substitutes. Some additions replace antiquities too fragile to withstand erosion or fond attention; others are surrogates for what has been or is likely to be lost; still others remake past motifs in modern dress. We inherit this congeries of later creations along with original and remade relics. Acts of emulation and commemoration transform the impact of surviving residues. And our changing sense of the past reflects the entire chain of things ever remade.

All additions are in some sense novel, yet none of this host of novelties is altogether new. 'Everything made now is either a replica or a variant of something made a little while ago', noted anthropologist George Kubler, 'and so on back without break to the first morning of human time'.[85] But if no addition is wholly new, neither are any wholly old. Those who recall or re-enact the past or imitate its products strive in vain for faithful replication; painters of memory and history claim fidelity to, yet creatively elaborate on,

---

[82] Siegfried Lenz, *The Heritage* (1978; Hill & Wang, 1981), 452.

[83] Julia Yadon quoted in Patricia Leigh Brown, 'The problem with Miss Laura's house', *Historic Preservation* 32:5 (1980): 16–19, subsequently Miss Laura's Whorehouse and Tourist Welcome Center (*NYT*, 27 Nov. 1997: F8); Ben Boulden, *Hidden History of Fort Smith* (Charleston, SC: History Center, 2012), 27–9, 72–5; Michael Leccese, 'Sow's ear from silk purse? Texas landmark endangered', and 'Epilogue: cabin conversion complete', *Preservation News* 20:12 (1980): 1, 10 and 22:6 (1982): 12.

[84] Edwin C. Bearss, *Furnishing Study: Lyndon B. Johnson National Historic Site* (NPS, 1979), 3; Robert M. Utley and E. C. Bearss, interviews, 2 Aug. 1978 and 25 Apr. 1984.

[85] George Kubler, *The Shape of Time* (1962; Yale, 2008), 2.

exemplars; emulators avowedly mine the past for new inspiration; monuments and memorials are fashioned in unavoidably modern guise. Many additions to surviving relics are free, even fanciful, readaptations. But it is in self-conscious period revivals – devoted yet innovative reworkings – that the past is most pervasively altered.

Revivals are bound to reflect their own time; the most faithful followers cannot avoid modern influence. Seeing J. E. Carew's toga-clad statue of William Huskisson (1770– 1830) in Chichester Cathedral roused a conservator to defend pastiche: 'Artists should never be afraid of their work appearing derivative and unoriginal, for whatever they produce inevitably retains the flavour of their [own] epoch.'[86] Fidelity to history did not prevent Victorians from gilding Greek or Gothic Revival buildings; nostalgia and religiosity begot 'medieval' architecture that was nonetheless manifestly Victorian. 'Under the guise of "revival"', remarks a chronicler of Pugin and Morris, they 'were in fact being highly original and inventive'.[87]

Yet revivals also augment appreciation of emulated epochs. Indeed, artefacts inspired by past exemplars loom larger in the landscape than do the originals. Not only are emulations more numerous; many a legacy now survives only or mainly in subsequent refractions of it. Awareness of all but the most recent past derives less from its own remains than from subsequent works. Images of 'classical' depend far less on actual Greek and Roman survivals than on Hellenistic and later evocations. And present-day notions of Gothic owe less to sparse medieval remains than to later additions that reflect and rework Gothic style or spirit. Jacobean nostalgia led to neo-medieval chivalry and battlements, vaulted halls, ogee-arched fireplaces. Gothick forts date from the age of gunpowder, not the days of pikes. The prototype fairy-tale castle that now spells 'Gothic' – central keep and rectangular ramparts with corner turrets – is a picturesque amalgam of Palladian with faux-medieval. But 'Gothic may lose *all* those features by which we know it', remarked a Victorian architect, 'and yet for our purposes be Gothic in the truest sense after all', changing the letter to better reflect the spirit.[88]

However unlike original Gothic, revivals are now *echt* Gothic. Medieval ruins, Tudor castles, Romantic Gothick follies, ecclesiological and municipal Gothic, and Salvation Army battlements comprise a composite medley seldom disaggregated. Similarly, few admirers of the classical can tell Roman from Grecian, let alone Hellenistic. Commonly mistaken for survivals, revivals by and by engulf them. The passage of time dissolves distinctions, originals and emulations becoming confluent.

Indeed, a past that lacks such additions can seem implausible. To be credible historical witnesses, antiquities must conform with modern stereotypes. Unless medieval forts are castellated and castles moated, New England 'Colonials' furnished with candlesticks and spinning-wheels, Victorian Gothic churches made 'church-like' with encaustic tiles and canopied sedilia, steeples and neo-Gothic windows, they disappoint expectations. In England 'the Tudor we now look upon is not sixteenth century Tudor but Tudor made

---

[86] James Lees-Milne, diary, 24 Mar. 1942, in *Ancestral Voices*, 40.

[87] Nicholas Taylor, *The Village in the City* (Temple Smith, 1973), 32.

[88] T. G. Jackson, *Modern Gothic Architecture* (London, 1873), 113. See J. Mordaunt Crook, 'Introduction', in Charles L. Eastlake, *History of the Gothic Revival* (1872; Leicester, 1978), 13–57 at 50–3.

Figure 80 The classical: the Pantheon, Rome, 27 BC, rebuilt AD 117–125

in the image of what twentieth century builders think Tudor ought to look like'.[89] And in conforming to current fancy renovators claim to supply a *more* faithful past than what then existed, knowing bygone buildings better than did their denizens.

Revivals based on modern views of supposed past intentions seem more 'correct' than their prototypes. Los Angeles's Getty Museum was said to recreate Pompeian villas 'with an accuracy ... greater than the original'.[90] The genius of the past is only scantily manifest in its surviving remnants. The revivalist perfects it in the spirit of his own time. It was because certain seventeenth-century stained glass seemed *too* correctly Gothic that Nikolaus Pevsner suspected it had undergone Victorian alteration.[91]

Modernists censure commingling originals and derivatives. The purist ideology enshrined in the 1964 Venice Charter mandated total segregation: the new must bear an entirely contemporary stamp without any stylistic trace of the old.[92] Harrow's Conservation Area planners told developers to avoid revival styles that would 'devalue the merits of the existing genuine buildings'. Neo-Georgian was long disowned by the Georgian

[89] Hugh C. Prince, 'Reality stranger than fiction', *Bloomsbury Geographer* 6 (1973): 2–22 at 14.
[90] Charles Jencks, ed., *Post-Modern Classicism*, special issue, *Architectural Design* 50:5/6 (1980): 10.
[91] Cited in Robert Adams, *The Lost Museum* (Viking, 1980), 88. See Peter Faulkner, 'Pevsner's Morris', *Journal of William Morris Studies* 17:1 (Winter 2006): 49–72.
[92] Matthew Hardy, ed., *The Venice Charter Revisited* (Newcastle upon Tyne: Cambridge Scholars, 2008), xv–xviii at xvi–xvii.

Figure 81 Classical derivatives: John Soane, Dairy, Hamels Park, Hertfordshire, 1783 (demolished), sketch by G. Richardson

Figure 82 National Monument, Calton Hill, Edinburgh, by C. R. Cockerell and W. H. Playfair, 1822-9

Figure 83 Forest Lawn Memorial Park mortuary, Glendale, California, 1920s

Figure 84 G. P. W. Custis residence, Arlington, Virginia, by George Hadfield, 1820

Figure 85 Bank facade Madison, Wisconsin, 1972

Group, lest the offspring's vulgar excess diminish the parent's prestige.[93] Demoting the University of Pennsylvania's medieval-Romanesque-Jacobean-Georgian eclectic *mélange*, current architectural guidelines allow 'no historical styles'.[94]

But public taste is far more catholic. For most people adaptations merge companionably with prototypes. London suburbanites fought as hard to save Edwardian half-timbering and thatched roofs as for rare surviving originals. John Betjeman's bogus Tudor 1930s pubs and Osbert Lancaster's Stockbrokers' and Roadhouse Tudor took on the sacred aura nostalgically evoked in Richard Thompson's 1999 'Mock Tudor' album. Like Marmite, mock-Tudor's current comeback reflects a cottagey familiarity popular everywhere from country-house piles to mass-market flats.[95]

The eclectic mix of revival styles reconfigures the broader past. The 'infernal amalgam [of] quaint gables culled from Art Nouveau ... twisted beams and leaded panes of Stockbrokers Tudor', Pont Street Dutch terracotta plaques, Wimbledon Transitional porch, and vaguely Romanesque red-brick garage that comprised Osbert Lancaster's immortal Bypass Variegated (Fig. 96) reinvigorated England's urban heritage. Jacobethan

[93] London Borough of Harrow, 'Advice on new buildings', *Conservation Areas* (1983); Eleanor Murray, Georgian Group, interview, 15 May 1978.
[94] Witold Rybczynski, 'The spirit of campus past', *Change over Time* 3:1 (Spring 2013): 56–63 at 58, 62.
[95] Matthew Saunders, 'Metroland: half-timbering and other souvenirs in the Outer London suburbs', in David Lowenthal and Marcus Binney, eds., *Our Past before Us* (London: Temple Smith, 1981), 165–74; Susan Emmett, 'The revival of mock-Tudor homes', *Timesonline*, 5 Mar. 2009; Andrew Ballantyne and Andrew Law, *Tudoresque* (Reaktion, 2011). A new ramparted folly fell foul of Surrey planners (Tom Peck, 'Fate of farmer's hidden castle is sealed', *Independent*, 4 Feb. 2010).

Figure 86 The Gothic: Bodiam Castle, Sussex, 1386

Figure 87 Gothic derivatives: James Malton, design for a hunting-lodge, *c.* 1802

Figure 88 Capitol, Baton Rouge, Louisiana, by J. H. Dakin, 1847

gems became icons of reverential preservation for the Twentieth Century Society, Britain's latest amenity group.[96]

Revival structures often serve commemorative intents or results. Reminders of ancient Greece so suffused the American scene that to 'separate ourselves entirely from the influence of all those memorials', remarked Daniel Webster in the US House of Representatives in 1824, we would have to abandon most of 'the scenes and objects which here surround us'. Urging American recognition of Greek independence, he noted that 'even the edifice in which we assemble, these proportioned columns, this ornamented architecture, all remind us that Greece has existed, and that we, like the rest of mankind, are greatly her debtors'.[97] Many edifices are expressly built as reminders of some past. To these consciously contrived memorials I now turn.

---

[96] Osbert Lancaster, *Here, of All Places* (Houghton Mifflin, 1958), 152; Marcus Field and Jane Hughes, '... Even the humble semi goes through the roof', *Independent*, 5 Mar. 2000.
[97] Daniel Webster, 'The revolution in Greece' (1824), in *Writings and Speeches* (Boston, 1903), 5: 60–93 at 61.

Figure 89 'Lyndhurst', Tarrytown, New York, by Alexander Jackson Davis, 1838-65

Commemorations

Monuments embellish the past by evoking some epoch's splendour, some person's power or genius, some glorious or piteous occasion. Created after the event, they honour the past in later guise. Memorial forms and features bear little resemblance to those of the

Figure 90 Strawberry Hill, Twickenham, by Horace Walpole, *c.* 1760

Figure 91 William Burges, design for Church of St Mary, Alford-cum-Studley, Yorkshire, *c.* 1872

Figure 92 Oxfordshire County Hall, by John Plowman, 1840-1

Figure 93 Salvation Army, Poole, Dorset

Figure 94 Mortuary, Encinitas, California

times they celebrate. They may draw upon antique motifs, but monuments emphatically reflect the iconographic fashions of their own day. Seventeenth-century effigies loll on their elbows among cherubs, skulls, scythes, and twisted columns, then-popular icons of death and immortality; eighteenth-century mania for things Egyptian filled the funerary scene with pyramids, obelisks, sphinxes, and sarcophagi.[98]

Heroes are commonly memorialized in anachronistic garb echoing long-gone eras. George Washington's toga, in Antonio Canova's 1821 Raleigh, North Carolina, statue, denoted the republican virtues of ancient Rome, but semi-nudity soon became unacceptable to Americans. Commissioned for the US Capitol, Horatio Greenough's 1841 loin-clothed Washington, 'the most reviled public statue ever erected', was a ridiculed embarrassment. The decorous Father of his Country, it was said, must have emerged fully dressed from the womb.[99]

Turning Mario Rutelli's equestrian tribute to Anita Garibaldi into a symbol of heroic womanhood (gun in right hand, infant Menotti on her left arm), Mussolini commissioned an anachronistic harbinger of fascist femininity.[100] Israel's one-armed legendary hero Yoseph Trumpeldor is commonly pictured brandishing twin Zionist settler/warrior icons, plough and gun; most thus disabled would have trouble wielding either, but

[98] James Stevens Curl, *The Egyptian Revival* (Routledge, 2005), xxvii–xxix, 22–9, 39–40, 143–247.
[99] Margaret French Cresson, 'First in toga, first in sandals – ', *American Heritage Magazine* 8:2 (Feb. 1957): 46–7; Kirk Savage, *Monument Wars: Washington, D.C.., the National Mall, and the Transformation of the Memorial Landscape* (California, 2009), 49–51.
[100] Claudio Fogu, *The Historic Imaginary: Politics of History in Fascist Italy* (Toronto, 2003), 79–82.

Figure 95 Post-modern classical: Charles Moore, Piazza d'Italia, New Orleans, 1978

Trumpeldor excelled at both at once.[101] Pakistan's founding father Mohammed Ali Jinnah, a fastidious Westerner in dress, was from 1982 depicted by government order in the close-fitting, high-buttoned *sherwani* later nationally de rigueur.[102] Feeling that a memorial should attest 'the good taste and judgment of those who erect it', Massachusetts worthies wanted Washington and Bunker Hill monuments both to call to mind the Revolutionary struggle *and* to show posterity 'that the people of Massachusetts of *this* generation' had thought to do so.[103]

[101] Yael Zerubavel, *Recovered Roots: Collective Memory and the Making of the Israeli National Tradition* (Chicago, 1995), 39–47, 84–95, 147–77.
[102] 'Times diary: Redressing history', *Times*, 29 Mar. 1982: 6.
[103] William Tudor (1816) quoted in Blanche M. G. Linden, *Silent City on a Hill* (1989; rev. edn Massachusetts, 2007), 228; Edward Everett, 'Speech delivered in Faneuil Hall, May 28th, 1833, on … the Bunker Hill Monument', in *Orations and Speeches* (Boston, 1836–70), 1: 332–42 at 333 (my italics).

Figure 96 The eclectic past: Osbert Lancaster, 'Bypass Variegated'

Monuments are more numerous and imposing in the Old World than the New, memorial purposes more didactic. By the nineteenth century 'a thickening forest of monuments' to past national glories 'threatened to choke the city squares and picturesque sites of Europe'.[104] Today, laments a critic, 'in every Scottish village, harbour head and mountain top, there is a memorial to someone', turning the entire landscape into a necropolis, and 'littering everyday life with what properly belongs in the church and the graveyard'.[105] An American grumbled that 'every tacky little fourth-rate déclassé European country has monuments all over the place and one cannot turn a corner without banging into an eighteen-foot bronze of Lebrouche Tickling the Chambermaids at Vache while Planning the Battle of Bledsoe, or some such'.[106] Indeed, so crowded is European history that most public sites cater for multiple memorials, the whole continent seemingly 'one vast time-share arrangement for the simultaneous remembrance of different . . . strands in its past'.[107]

---

[104] Marvin Trachtenberg, *The Statue of Liberty* (Penguin, 1977), 100.

[105] J. G. Graham, 'Too many memorials', *Times*, 16 Nov. 2009: 27. See Philippe Ariès, *The Hour of Our Death* (1977; Penguin, 1983), 215, 230, 235; Ivor Hall, 'Glut of memorials', *Times*, 16 July 2011: 23.

[106] Donald Barthelme, 'Monumental folly', *Atlantic Monthly* 237:2 (1976): 33–40 at 33.

[107] Joep Leerssen, 'Introduction', in Lotte Jensen et al., eds., *Free Access to the Past* (Brill, 2010), xv–xxii at xxi.

Figure 97 Commemorative motifs from Egypt: Grove Street Cemetery,
New Haven, Connecticut, by Henry Austin, 1845-6

Figure 98 Commemorative and contemporary: Milford, Connecticut

Figure 99 Unique and apposite commemoration: concrete and stone tent, mausoleum of
Richard F. Burton of *The Arabian Nights*, Mortlake, Surrey, 1890

Figure 100 Collective and generic commemoration: monument
to soldiers of successive wars, Hartland, Vermont

By contrast, Americans 'pile up a few green cannon balls next to a broken-down mortar and forget about it'. Yet after the Civil War and the First World War, a plague of 'statues of men, each one uglier than the other', was already held to be 'ruining every city in the United States'.[108] But latterly, in the wake of repeated sorrows and failures and regrets for past iniquities, American commemoration has turned relentlessly remorseful. Memorials to executed witches, enslaved Africans, dead astronauts, aborted foetuses, murdered teenagers, civil rights activists, cancer survivors, organ donors reflect a sorrowful compound of shame, anger, fear, and grief. The entire Washington Mall is now saturated with monumental recollection, the Lincoln and Jefferson memorials framing sites of mourning for the victims of every American war, every victimized ethnic group, Amerindian, now African-, and next Latino-American. To be relegated off the Mall would mortify anew.[109]

Earlier monuments reminded people what to believe and how to behave. By the end of the nineteenth century, remembrance replaced exhortation. The contrast between Lincoln's Gettysburg Address (1863) and that battlefield's designation as a national park (1895) exemplifies the change. Lincoln dedicated 'us the living ... to the unfinished work which they who fought here have ... so nobly advanced'. He thus implied, in J. B. Jackson's gloss, that 'a contract was entered into, a covenant was made, and the monument is to remind us of that contract; just as it confers a kind of immortality on the dead, it determines our actions in years to come'. After the Civil War, Gettysburg became its own monument, the place its own memorial. 'It was no longer a reminder; it no longer told us what to do; it simply explained the battle.'[110]

Celebration then took over. Gettysburg's 1,400 statues and edifices, installed by veterans' descendants between 1870 and 1920, swamped Lincoln's admonitory message in marmoreal tributes to valour, courage, and reunion, in line with the North–South reconciliation then sought. They explained nothing. 'A few commemorate the preservation of the Union. Not one commemorates the ending of slavery', or even mentions slavery. The latest (1963) memorial declares that 'dedicated South Carolinians stood ... for their heritage and convictions', their creed 'abiding faith in the sacredness of states rights'.[111] The historical fable thus intoned was invoked, a century after the Civil War, to fend off racial integration. Not until 1998 did the National Park Service begin to address the meanings of Gettysburg embodied in Lincoln's Address. Even then, it muted causes and consequences and the vision of emancipation. The park's monuments and markers

[108] Barthelme, 'Monumental folly', 33; Janet Scudder (1925) quoted in Erika Doss, Memorial Mania (Chicago, 2010), 28–30.

[109] Doss, Memorial Mania, 1; James S. Russell, 'Crowding the Mall', Harvard Design Magazine (Fall 1999): 32–7; Savage, Monument Wars, 2–7, 257–9, 309–10; Kate Taylor, 'The thorny path to a national Black museum', NYT, 22 Jan. 2011.

[110] Abraham Lincoln, 'Gettysburg Address', 19 Nov. 1863, in CW, 7: 20; J. B. Jackson, The Necessity for Ruins (Massachusetts, 1980), 93.

[111] John Latschar, 'Coming to terms with the Civil War at Gettysburg National Military Park', CRM: Journal of Heritage Stewardship 4:2 (Summer 2007): 7–17 at 12; James W. Loewen, Lies across America: What Our Historic Sites Get Wrong (New York: New Press, 1999), 371–7. See Jim Weeks, Gettysburg (Princeton, 2003).

continue to tell the veterans' old story, reminders of the endeavour and cost of warfare.[112] We increasingly commemorate, as we restore and re-enact, neither to heed an example nor to explain the past but simply to celebrate or mourn.

We also recall more generically. Post-Civil War America memorialized not just generals but all participants, erecting statues to literally unknown soldiers. Other unknowns soon followed: after Daniel Chester French's 1876 *Minute Man* at Concord came monuments to prototypical trades – the anonymous cowboy, newsboy, fishermen, even boll weevil.[113] Across the Atlantic, late eighteenth-century monuments to fallen soldiers prefigured First World War mass-produced French 'Mariannes' and British 'Tommies', for the 'intolerable nameless names' of Siegfried Sassoon's fifty-five thousand 'unheroic Dead".[114] The scale of World War slaughter mandated collective memorials, even when, as in Maya Lin's Vietnam War Memorial and various Holocaust museums, inscribed names of victims dominate their decor and lend them their pathos.

Monuments may be remote from dedicatees in space as well as style, distancing funerary statues from entombed remains. Memorials adorn locales unconnected with the celebrated person or event: Poets' Corner in Westminster Abbey, Nelson's Column at Trafalgar Square. Rulers' statues grace places half a world away. Caesar is commemorated far beyond the former Roman Empire; Washington bestrides a horse in countless far-flung squares; Victoria oversees traffic in Benares and Berbice, Melbourne and Mumbai.

The famed seem most suitably recalled where they lived or worked or vitally affected.[115] Yet origins and endings also arouse memorial interest. Where some pioneer or pop star was born or died may have no bearing on their fame, but we nonetheless expect those sites to be marked. The memorial act itself implies termination. Save for totalitarian idolatry, states erect few monuments to living heroes. Being commemorated alive makes us queasy. Back home in Pennsylvania, John Updike's protagonist finds himself enshrined in old pictures, schoolboy medals, certificates 'permanized' in plastic, 'so abundantly memorialized it seemed I must be dead'. Updike fell victim to his own quasi-fictional memorial: a 1982 BBC show had him read *Of the Farm* in the very room, the camera picking out the very mementoes, that the book describes.[116]

Tombstones dominate memorial scenes. Graveyards do double duty as fields of remembrance for the living and repositories of the dead, whose place of burial loses consequence as they moulder into dust or are removed to make way for others. Massed crosses and anonymous graves in military cemeteries recall not individual soldiers but

---

[112] John Latschar, personal communication, 30 May 2008.

[113] Jackson, *Necessity for Ruins*, 94–5; Barry Schwartz, *Abraham Lincoln and the Forge of National Memory* (Chicago, 2000).

[114] Ariès, *Hour of Our Death*, 547–9; Eric Hobsbawm, 'Mass-producing traditions', in his and Terence Ranger, eds., *The Invention of Tradition* (Cambridge, 1983), 263–307 at 271–2; Reinhart Koselleck, 'War memorials: identity formations of the survivors', in *The Practice of Conceptual History* (1979; Columbia, 2004), 285–326; Siegfried Sassoon, 'On passing the new Menin Gate' (1927–8), *Collected Poems* (Viking, 1949), 188. See Stefan Goebel, *The Great War and Medieval Memory* (Cambridge, 2006); John Gillis, ed., *Commemorations* (Princeton, 1994), pt. 3, 'Memories of war and wars over memory', 125–211.

[115] Emily Cole, ed., *Lived in London: Blue Plaques and the Stories behind Them* (Yale, 2009).

[116] John Updike, *Of the Farm* (Fawcett, 1965), 17; Valentine Cunningham, 'Authenticating the poet', *TLS*, 5 Feb. 1982: 134.

general carnage. Old graveyards lose specificity. The personal significance of the interred dwindles, headstones recalling particular forebears less than collective ancestors.[117]

Perdurable monuments accrue their own reputable antiquity; in a poet's words, 'Monuments themselves Memorials need'.[118] Their patinated surfaces, the archaistic content and calligraphy of their graven texts, add new historical resonance. People 'saw their chronicles upon the marble', wrote an early Victorian of ancient inscriptions. 'The lines were read by the fathers, the children, and grandchildren, and after the lapse of ages, the moss-grown characters add the most powerful charms to the majestic ruin.'[119] The accumulated aura of antiquity merges commemorative sites with other additions to the past. Monuments from the 1876 Revolutionary centennial adorn Concord's reconstructed Old North Bridge, overlooked by Hawthorne's Old Manse. In James Russell Lowell's lines against tyranny, a tablet ironically memorializes the British dead, who 'came three thousand miles, and died, / To keep the Past upon its throne'.[120]

As original relics perish, commemorative creations, made durable precisely for perpetual recall, may become the past's sole physical reminders. Semblances of Ireland's early architecture – a Romanesque chapel, a Celtic cross, a round tower – festooned George Petrie's proposed tomb for Daniel O'Connell, so that even when 'the wreck of time and the devastations of ignorance' had wasted all other vestiges, the memorial would keep alive the forms and features that recalled Ireland's famed Liberator.[121] Enriching the landscape with old and new medleys of funerary and hortatory symbols, monuments not only remind us of the past, but move us to dwell on its significance and our loss.

Aggrandizing and abridging

The past embellished and amplified

The past is vivified by our focus on its grandest residues. 'Even the most faithful histories', wrote Descartes, 'that neither change nor augment the significance of things to make them more readable, almost always omit the most commonplace and least striking events, thereby distorting what they leave in'.[122] Jettisoning the humdrum dross of which the present shows us quite enough, historical romance still fits an 1845 Scottish historian's goal: it 'discards from

---

[117] W. Lloyd Warner, *The Living and the Dead* (Yale, 1959), 319; Gavin Stamp, *Silent Cities: An Exhibition of the Memorial and Cemetery Architecture of the Great War* (London: RIBA, 1977); Robert Pogue Harrison, *The Dominion of the Dead* (Chicago, 2003); Antonius C. G. M. Robben, ed., *Death, Mourning and Burial* (Wiley-Blackwell, 2004).

[118] George Crabbe, *The Borough* (1810; London, 1916), 18. Crabbe's is a gloss on Juvenal's 'sepulchres, too, have their allotted fate' (Satire 10, line 146, in Juvenal, *Satires* (late 1st-2nd century AD; 1958), 210).

[119] 'Application and intent of the various styles of architecture', *The Civil Engineer and Architect's Journal* 2 (July 1839): 247–52 at 249.

[120] James Russell Lowell, 'Lines suggested by the graves of two English soldiers on Concord battle-ground' (1849), in *CW*, 9: 271–2.

[121] 'Report to the Committee of the O'Connell Monument' (1851), in William Stokes, *The Life and Labours in Art and Archaeology of George Petrie* (London, 1868), 434.

[122] René Descartes, *Discours de la méthode pour bien conduire la raison et cherchez la vérité dans les sciences* (1637; Paris, 1947; Indianapolis: Hackett, 1998), 51–2.

human annals their years of tedium, and brings prominently forward their eras of interest, giving us the truth of history without its monotony'.[123]

Trendy down-to-earth populism today partly reverses bias towards elite splendour. But selective preservation and attention continue to make the distant past more vivid than it was, and more spectacular than our mundane present and tawdry yesterday. 'The thirteenth century is celebrated as if it were summed up by St Thomas Aquinas, Dante, and the Virgin of Chartres', wrote an historian in 1952, 'while the twentieth century is reduced to Hitler, Hearst, and the sex queens of Hollywood'.[124] Like Italian painters who depicted the Nativity in Renaissance palaces, we colour bygone events sumptuous or seemly. Great victories and glorious deeds dominate our histories, aristocratic forebears our ancestries, castles and cathedrals our reliquary landscapes.

The past is habitually reshaped by the criteria of a Henry James duchess, unsure if 'Stories from English History' is suitable for her little niece:

'Is it all right?'
'I don't know ... There have been some horrid things in English history.'
'Well, darling, Mr. Longden will recommend to you some nice historical work – for we love history, don't we? – that leaves the horrors out. We like to know ... the cheerful, happy, *right* things. There are so many, after all.'[125]

The right things make the past virtuous, successful, beautiful. Like Ramesses II, who despite his peace with the Hittites (1258 BC) termed himself their conqueror in monumental inscriptions, we augment relics and records that evince desired deeds and traits and ignore or erase contrary evidence. 'We want to know the beautiful or useful things that were built and the originality that was shown', intoned an American panegyrist, 'the grace-notes to life that were sounded'. History becomes a saga of progress interrupted by only minor setbacks; quaint serenity softens gritty past reality.[126]

Modern parents still emulate Henry James's duchess. 'We take the children to Stonehenge', writes Penelope Lively, 'but ... shrink from exposing them to a candid account of Bronze Age beliefs and practices. We like the past gutted and nicely cleaned up.'[127] Absent are the filth and stench of early town life, the foraging of pigs in city streets, the din of horse-drawn vehicles on cobblestones, the terror of pain before modern anaesthesia.[128] Atypical was the docent in Mystic Seaport's olde apothecary shop, whom I overheard detailing the dire effects of tight corsets, arsenic, and leeches, and concluding: 'Aren't you really glad you're living *today*?'

---

[123] Archibald Alison, 'The historical romance', *Blackwood's Magazine* 58 (1845): 341–56 at 346.

[124] Herbert J. Muller, *The Uses of the Past* (Oxford, 1952), 23.

[125] Henry James, *The Awkward Age* (1899; Penguin, 1966), 180.

[126] John Van Seters, *In Search of History: Historiography in the Ancient World* (Yale, 1983; Eisenbraun, 1997) 177; K. A. Kitchen, *Ramesside Inscriptions* (Blackwell, 1999–2008), 2: 167–8; Sidney Hyman, 'Empire for liberty', in Byrd Wood, ed., *With Heritage So Rich* (1966; Washington: National Trust for Historic Preservation, 1999), 1–27 at 1.

[127] Penelope Lively, 'Children and the art of memory', *Horn Book Magazine* 54 (1978): 17–23, 197–203 at 201.

[128] Walter M. Whitehill, '"Promoted to glory": the origin of preservation in the United States', in Wood, ed., *With Heritage So Rich*, 35–44 at 43.

An embellished past conforms to our expectations, for jaded modern perceptions require stimuli that no unadorned past could supply. As restored in the 1980s, the century-old Statue of Liberty carried a flamier (and more phallic) torch – not sexy enough, though, for the US Postal Service, whose 2011 stamp instead reproduced the gussied-up replica Liberty from a Las Vegas gambling resort, the first casino so honoured.[129] Habituated to a far wider range of artefacts and locales than our forebears, accustomed to vivid light and colour, sound, and speed, we would barely notice the dim and dingy particulars of previous epochs. What is known about the past patently conflicts with how it is usually purveyed. Pre-Gutenberg books conjure up a world of splendid illuminated manuscripts, yet such work was scanty, seen by far fewer than are nowadays used to lurid ads and tabloids. Everyday medieval life for most was hard and poor, drab, and dreary – little like the castellated glitter of popular romance. *Doctor Who*'s modern lass chides her medieval captors for their overly authentic reek of savagery: 'I know things were pretty scruffy in the middle ages, but really! You might leave the tourists a bit of glamour and illusion.'[130] Envisaging the past as either blood-drenched or rose-coloured flouts ordinary historical reality.

Just as modern demands of comfort reshape restored and re-enacted pasts, so modern tenets of taste alter what is displayed. Forced to compromise 'between what we believe to be accurate and what we presume [visitors] want to see', curators ditch the commonplace for museum-worthy *crème de la crème* and imaginary serenity. At most historic sites piety or nostalgia pay the bills, so 'even the less appalling unpleasantnesses that we know were part of daily life – the lack of fuel for heat, the smells of spoiling food, then common diseases' – can't be shown. Warwick Castle's Dungeon Experience abridges 'the more gruesome aspects of our historic past in an appealing and fun manner'.[131]

Replica relics usually appear to pristine advantage. Grist mills function faultlessly, print shops unfailingly churn out facsimile broadsides, medieval herb gardens seem invariably fruitful; 'nothing needs to be fixed, raked, painted: there is no dung, no puddles, no weeds'. Nature's normal vicissitudes and mankind's customary tribulations seldom afflict bygone life as portrayed. Later views of early Bruges gloss over the seamy side, bathing the city in sunshine. 'Paintings were commissioned by rich men for their drawing rooms. They didn't want to look at snivelling wretches in the rain.'[132]

Like Victorian Gothic and vernacular revival furnishings, 'Colonial Revival' houses were far more sumptuous than actual colonial America. In place of bare floors and windows and untreated or whitewashed walls, nostalgic comfort mandated rugs and curtains, panelling and wallpaper, along with Hawthorne's 'Grandfather's Chair' (1840)

---

[129] Dean MacCannell, *Empty Meeting Grounds: The Tourist Papers* (Routledge, 1992), 153–5; 'This lady Liberty is a Las Vegas teenager', *NYT*, 14 Apr. 2011.

[130] Terrance Dicks, *Doctor Who and the Time Warrior* (London: W. H. Allen, 1978), 64.

[131] Mary Lynn Stevens, 'Wistful thinking: the effect of nostalgia on interpretation', *History News* 36:12 (1981): 10–13; Georgina Kelly, 'Warwick Castle', *EH Conservation Bulletin*, no. 64 (Summer 2010): 23–5.

[132] Mark P. Leone, 'The relationship between artifacts and the public in outdoor history museums', *Annals of the New York Academy of Sciences* 376 (Dec. 1981): 301–13 at 301; Bruno Van Dycke quoted in Rona Dobson, 'Through new/old Bruges', *IHT*, 12–13 July 1980: 9.

and Longfellow's 'Old Clock on the Stairs' (1845). The Philadelphia 1876 Centennial Exhibition popularized huge 'colonial' hearths anachronistically festooned with guns and powder horns, which had been fire hazards sedulously avoided.[133]

In the sanitized American past not even slaves are wretched: added porch columns and chimneys raise restored slave quarters to the standard of overseers' dwellings. 'If slaves were so cruelly treated', doubts a high school student, 'why do they always have such pretty teeth in the movies?'[134] Restored Port Arthur, Tasmania's notorious prison, long made convicts seem lucky to be jailed in so idyllic a setting. The bullpen in Colonial Williamsburg 'looked so freshly cleaned and sterilized that it seemed impossible to imagine a drunk had ever committed a nuisance in its virgin space'.[135] Boosters in Arizona's revived Old Jerome, once 'the wickedest town in the West' and since 1967 a National Historic Landmark, looked askance at the ghost-mine city's messier human vestiges. 'The only thing that's holding us back is some of those old relics who live in town.'[136]

Faced with the reality of early New England – 'Stark. Bleak. No trees, only stumps. Cowpats. Horse dung. Pig manure. Smoke-blackened rooms. Unwashed illiterate people huddled against the cold. Trampled dirt around the house' – modern preservationists in Jane Langton's tale are

shocked by this perversion of their common vision of the past, with its butter-churning, candle-making, musket-seizing forefathers – those large comfortable families beaming around their jolly hearthsides where great black pots were bubbling over blazing logs; the women bustling around the kitchen in aprons and ruffled mobcaps; ... and then at bedtime everyone picking up those little pewter candlesticks – that nice gift shop in Concord had some just like them – and climbing the stairs to their plump featherbeds.[137]

Retrofitted facts sustain the feather-bed past. As 'reconstructed', Hugo Reid's crude adobe pioneer Los Angeles home (not the actual one) was tricked out with a tile floor and roof, rich furnishings, and a Spanish patio, becoming a rich Don's ranch.[138]

The preferred past is that of the wealthy, the well born, the powerful. 'Build a kingdom. Rule the Nile. Live Forever', advertises the computer game *Pharaoh* (1999). 'Pass along your legacy from generation to generation, creating an empire and a bloodline built only for a Pharaoh.'[139] Like the renowned or rich pre-incarnates chosen by time travellers, popular past avatars were an Indian chief, Queen Elizabeth, a noble lady in

---

[133] Marilyn Casto, 'Colonial Revival: reinvention interiors', *Old-House Journal* 31:1 (Jan.–Feb. 2003): 52–7, and 'The concept of hand production in Colonial Revival interiors', in Richard Guy Wilson et al., eds., *Re-creating the American Past: Essays on the Colonial Revival* (Virginia, 2006), 321–35. See p. 203 above.

[134] Quoted in Tony Horwitz, *Confederates in the Attic* (Pantheon, 1998), 373.

[135] E. Graeme Robertson, *Early Buildings of Southern Tasmania* (Routledge, 1970), 2: 368–76; Albert Eide Parr, 'History and the historical museum', *Curator* 15 (1972): 53–61 at 58.

[136] Quoted in Haas, 'Secret life of the American tourist', 24. See Madge Steuber, *Jerome* (Arcadia, 2008), 8, 52, 63, 109.

[137] Jane Langton, *Natural Enemy* (Penguin, 1982), 61–2.

[138] Robert Schuyler, 'Images of America', *Southwestern Lore* 42 (1976): 27–39 at 30; Bill Peters, 'Arboretum's shocking revelation' *Arcadia* [CA] *Weekly*, 8 Oct. 2009.

[139] Lauren E. Talalay, 'The past as commodity', *Public Archaeology* 3 (2004): 205–16 at 211.

sixteenth-century Dubrovnik, a Viennese aristocrat, an English squire. 'Being a poor person "ain't much fun".'[140]

Historical annals are likewise upgraded. Exaggerating ancient chivalry and elevating Arthurian legend into fact, Victorians depicted medieval life in their own self-image. Nineteenth-century Americans imbued Revolutionary history with genteel domestic tone and salutary guerrilla flavour.[141] Ignoring Christianity's role as Rome's official faith, novelists laid the empire's fall to pagan immorality. To sanctify the classical past, Greek myth gained biblical sanction; evidence that threatened Homer's suitability for Victorian readers was disregarded.[142] Dante's *Divine Comedy* became a pious tract of character formation, medieval Catholics morphing into proto-Protestant apostles.[143]

Bygone heroes are anachronistically praised. Admired forebears acquire qualities esteemed today, what are now deemed faults concealed or palliated. The plantation homes of the nation's Founding Fathers – Washington's Mount Vernon, Jefferson's Monticello, Monroe's Ash Lawn – are still presented as models of social propriety, suggesting that slavery was benignly paternalistic. Slave descendants who manage Mount Vernon portray an 'antebellum Eden, complete with happy, welcoming slaves'. Washington's vows to buy no more slaves and to manumit those he held are stressed; his later slave purchases and his failure to free them shrouded in silence. Martin Luther, who had fought against peasant reform, was lauded in Communist East Germany as a champion of the proletariat.[144] The great are presumed good. We are exhorted, observed Lord Acton, 'to judge Pope and King unlike other men, with a favourable presumption that they did no wrong' – a doctrine detestable to that historian, for whom 'great men are almost always bad men'.[145]

Past discord is played down, times of violent strife becoming benign and orderly. Mount Vernon was later saved as a symbol of early American concord quite absent in Washington's own day. D. W. Griffith's *The Birth of a Nation* (1914) depicted the North and the South as virtually identical fraternal folk, the Civil War without clear cause. From pallid histories in which both sides figure 'as perfectly reasonable people without strong

---

[140] 'The century game', *Harvard Bulletin* 75:6 (1973): 3, 21–9; R. H. Griffiths (1983) quoted in Jay Anderson, *Time Machines* (AASLH, 1984), 187; Hannah Betts, 'Why I wish the 15th century had lasted forever', *Times* 2, 21 Aug. 2013: 2.

[141] Mark Girouard, *The Return to Camelot* (Yale, 1981); Charles Dellheim, *Face of the Past* (Cambridge, 1982); Michael Kammen, *A Season of Youth* (Knopf, 1973), 186–220.

[142] Edward Bulwer-Lytton, *Last Days of Pompeii* (1834), Charles Kingsley, *Hypatia* (1853), Lew Wallace, *Ben Hur* (1880), Henryk Sienkiewicz, *Quo Vadis?* (1896). See Gilbert Highet, *The Classical Tradition* (Clarendon Press, 1949), 462–3; Frank M. Turner, *The Greek Heritage in Victorian Britain* (Yale, 1981); Isobel Hurst, 'Victorian literature and the reception of Greece and Rome', *Literature Compass* 7 (2010): 484–95.

[143] T. J. Jackson Lears, *No Place of Grace* (Pantheon, 1981), 158–9.

[144] Merrill Peterson, *The Jeffersonian Image in the American Mind* (Oxford, 1962); J. O. Horton and S. R. Crew, 'Afro-Americans and museums', in Warren Leon and Roy Rosenzweig, eds., *History Museums in the United States* (Illinois, 1989), 215–36 at 230–1; 'National symbols: presidential homes', *History News* 45:1 (Jan.–Feb. 1990): 8–17; Scott E. Casper, *Sarah Johnson's Mount Vernon* (Hill & Wang, 2008); Scott E. Casper, 'Rebranding Mount Vernon', *NYT*, 21 Feb. 2011: A17; Gordon R. Mork, 'Martin Luther's left turn', *History Teacher* 16:4 (Aug. 1983): 585–95; Robert F. Goeckel, 'The Luther anniversary in East Germany', *World Politics* 37 (1984): 112–33.

[145] Lord Acton to Mandell Creighton, Apr. 1887, 'Acton–Creighton correspondence', in *Essays on Freedom and Power* (Boston, 1948), 357–73 at 364.

prejudices', concluded a later historian, no one could 'infer from any text ... the passions that animated the war'.[146]

Those fearing loss of power or disheartened by a sorry present draw solace from a romantically enhanced past. Faced with upstart entrepreneurs, eighteenth-century England's old gentry harked back to when their forebears' status was supposedly unquestioned. Fearful of uncouth immigrants and industrial populism, *fin-de-siècle* New England Brahmins repeopled the colonial past with upright, frugal forebears, invoking idealized virtues to censure modern evils.

Patriotic selectivity is ubiquitous and unabashed. It was 'objectionable', held a French director of education in Senegal, to reveal 'the mistakes we made before arriving at the stage of civilization we have attained'. Former President Nicolas Sarkozy's prospective museum to celebrate French nationalist history was jettisoned because France's past was too notoriously divisive to be touted as consensual.[147] Chiding the Cassandras who defame 'our heritage and our past', Prime Minister Margaret Thatcher termed Britain's legacy wholly laudable. 'In Thatcher's eyes there is no such thing as a bad heritage. Everything the government calls heritage is holy.'[148] President Ronald Reagan admired American history as the triumphal saga of 'why the Pilgrims came here, who Jimmy Doolittle was, and what those 30 seconds over Tokyo meant'.[149] 'Take a look in your history book', ran Irving Berlin's popular song, 'And you'll see why we should be proud.'[150]

Chauvinism aborted the Smithsonian's *Enola Gay* exhibition, 'The Atomic Bomb and the End of World War II'; patriotic insistence on a feel-good past scuttled plans to show disputed versions of why the bomb was dropped (to shorten the war, to save American lives, to preclude Soviet involvement). Curators who sought to show history in its agonizing complexity were overruled by those for whom the bomb meant victory. Veterans celebrating its semi-centennial 'were not looking for analysis' but for admiration. 'I don't want sixteen-year-olds walking out of there thinking badly of the U.S.', declared a Massachusetts congressman. A Smithsonian regent was more explicit: 'We've got to get patriotism back into the Smithsonian. We want the Smithsonian to reflect real America and not something that a historian dreamed up.'[151]

---

[146] Frances FitzGerald, *America Revised* (Random House, 1980), 156. See Charles B. Hosmer, Jr., *Presence of the Past* (Putnam, 1965), 41–62; Pierre Sorlin, *The Film in History* (Blackwell, 1980), 91–5; David W. Blight, *Race and Reunion: The Civil War in American Memory* (Harvard, 2001), 2–5.

[147] Garrigues (Senegal, 1898) quoted in Merc Ferro, *The Use and Abuse of History, or How the Past Is Taught* (1981; Routledge, 2003), 26; Kelly D. Bryant, *Education as Politics: Colonial Schooling and Political Debate in Senegal* (Wisconsin, 2015), 99; Adam Sage, 'Museum is guillotined because French past is too divisive', *Times*, 5 Jan. 2013: 45.

[148] James Bishop interview, 'Programme for the 1980s', *Illustrated London News*, May 1983, 23–5; Neal Ascherson, 'A time to break down and a time to build up', *Independent on Sunday* 23 Feb. 1992: 25.

[149] Ronald Reagan, Farewell Address to the Nation, 11 Jan. 1989. The 18 April 1942 Doolittle Raid, heavily fictionalized in the 2001 film *Pearl Harbor*, restored American wartime morale.

[150] 'This is a great country', in *Mr President* (1962). 'We Americans know that our country is great, better than we know why it is great': *Report of the Committee of Ten on Secondary School Studies* (New York: National Educational Association, 1894), 169.

[151] Smithsonian Secretary I. Michael Heyman, 30 Jan. 1995, in Martin Harwit, *An Exhibit Denied: Lobbying the History of Enola Gay* (Springer, 1996), 396; Peter I. Blute and Sam Johnson quoted in Edward T. Linenthal, 'Struggling with history and memory', *Journal of American History* 82 (1995): 1100.

The past concealed and expurgated

Distressing and distasteful pasts are hidden or whitewashed. In nations as in families, forgetting is a common prelude to forgiving. 'Come back, my boy', the Alzheimer-ridden father tells his prodigal son; 'all is forgotten'. Amnesia furthers amnesty. Acclaiming the shredding of East Germany's Stasi files, a philosopher echoes Hobbes: nations should 'foster forgetting as much as remembering'.[152] Devotion to heroes is fortified 'by mercifully forgetting those weaknesses ... which seem irrelevant to their fame', held an American educator.[153]

Viewpoints repugnant to national pride are routinely purged. 'We've made practically no movies about our defeats', said a French cultural spokesman. 'We don't want to be told we were not so great in Algeria or Vichy. We were taught in history class that the French Empire was all about spreading civilization. We aren't going to make movies that call that into question, even if we know that what really happened was profoundly different.'[154] Tweaking the past out of loyalty is standard practice, historians concede; it is not 'sinister to ... manipulate national history, as we all do with our own lives'.[155]

Americans who see their history as inspirational shun reminders of anything shameful or demeaning. Republicans reading out the constitution in the House of Representatives in January 2011 omitted its original acceptance of slavery. Tea Party devotee Michele Bachmann credited the founding fathers with emancipation: the 'founders worked tirelessly until slavery was no more'.[156] The only villains compatible with past virtue are Western outlaws. But American history 'is still so full of heroes that it is a mighty relief to see a few treated, however clumsily, with the disrespect they deserve', suggested a reviewer of E. L. Doctorow's *Ragtime* (1975). By contrast, British deprecation, 'which results in half our national figures being better known for their foibles than for ... their achievements, has disrespect built into it'.[157] But like Margaret Thatcher, Little Englanders still echo the Leeds manufacturer who told a historian, 'If history does not make young men proud of their country, the less they learn of it the better.'[158]

Amnesiac motives are diverse. Some invoke accord with divine judgement, expunging at the altar the names of those excommunicated. Others wipe out memory of rivals to immortalize themselves: Herostratos torched the temple of Artemis at Ephesus in 356 BC to make posterity forget her name and remember his own; Pausanias of Orestis assassinated Philip of Macedon on being assured that 'if he killed an illustrious man that man's glory would redound to himself'. Besotted with the classical glories that inspired northern

[152] Avishai Margalit, *The Ethics of Memory* (Harvard, 2002), 13.
[153] John Erskine, 'The centurion' *Century Magazine*, (Feb. 1927): 501.
[154] André-Marc Delocque-Fourcaud quoted in Ronald Koven, 'National memory', *Society* [New Brunswick] 32:6 (1995): 52–8 at 57. See Alison Castle, ed., *Stanley Kubrick's 'Napoleon': The Greatest Movie Never Made* (Cologne: Taschen, 2011).
[155] Joyce Appleby et al., *Telling the Truth about History* (Norton, 1994), 107.
[156] Michele Bachmann speech, Des Moines, Iowa, 21 Jan. 2011; National Association of Outlaw and Lawman History (NOLA), *outlawlawman.com*.
[157] Russell Davies, 'Mingle with the mighty', *TLS*, 23 Jan. 1976: 77.
[158] J. F. Ransome to T. F. Tout, 1893, quoted in R. I. Moore, 'A toxic waste dump?' *TLS*, 15 Mar. 2002: 4.

neo-Hellenism, Greeks after independence deliberately destroyed later monuments to 'purify' their legacy of 'remnants of barbarism'. Victors conceal legacies of the vanquished to discourage revanchism: Austro-Hungarians quelled nascent Bosnian nationalism by hiding Bogomil royal graves. American occupation forces in Japan after 1945 deconsecrated imperial sacred sites to quash emperor worship.[159] Other iconoclasts would destroy anything built, crafted, or written in a bad cause.

Changing standards of taste and truth curtailed the nature and number of Roman Catholic icons. In medieval and early-modern times the transcendent value attached to the relics of Christ, the Virgin Mother, and the saints led to their multiplication, to their relocation by purchase, conquest, or theft, and to competing claims of authenticity. Contestations were most intense for body parts, as among the reputed heads of St John the Baptist at Amiens, Nemours, St-Jean d'Angeli (France), San Silvestro in Capite (Rome), and Emesa (Phoenicia). To quiet Cistercian and Dominican rivalry, Pope Urban V gave each order a head of St Thomas Aquinas. Most problematic, given the lack of distinctive features, were manifold claims of Christ's foreskin, long venerated as His most conspicuous earthly remnant (save by Vatican librarian Leo Allatius, who contended that the foreskin had ascended to heaven with Jesus, to become the rings of Saturn). Places with holy prepuces included Poitiers, Coulombs, Charraux, Hildesheim, Puy-en-Velay, Antwerp, and Rome's Church of St John Lateran. The last was declared authentic in the sixteenth century, only to be stolen and taken to the Church of SS Cornelius and Cyprian in Calcata, near Viterbo. Calcata became a prime pilgrimage destination, worth ten years' indulgence.[160]

The prepuce was especially cherished because it was already what bread became only by transubstantiation. Hence it was famed for its flavour (authenticated by a *croque-prépuce*). 'So great was the sweetness at the swallowing of His membrane', exulted the fourteenth-century St Birgitta, 'that it transformed her entire being. At St Catherine of Siena's 'mystical marriage' to Christ, His foreskin became her wedding ring. Scores of paintings depict the infant Jesus' circumcision, celebrated also in Jan Dismas Zelenka's D minor *Missa Circumcisionis* (1728). 'Nothing', declared Jansenist Adrien Baillet in 1703, 'is more worthy of our veneration'.[161]

Foreskin veneration endured for two more centuries, though increasingly repressed as a too-Jewish 'irreverent curiosity'. A papal decree of 1900 confined public display at Calcata to the annual Feast of the Circumcision, excised it from Italian Touring Club

[159] Albert Borowitz, *Terrorism for Self-Glorification: The Herostratos Syndrome* (Kent State, 2005), xiv, 6–7, citing Valerius Maximus, *Factorum ac dictorum memorabilium libri, c.* AD 31; Jacques Le Goff, *History and Memory* (1977; Columbia, 1992), 73; Daphne Voudouri, 'Law and the politics of the past: legal protection of cultural heritage in Greece', *IJCP* 17 (2010): 547–68 at 550–1; Marian Wenzel, 'Bosnian history and Austro-Hungarian policy', *Museum Management & Curatorship* 12 (1993): 127–42; Jonathan Watts, 'Japan's revisionists turn emperor into a god once more', *Guardian*, 21 Aug. 2002.

[160] Sébastien Le Nain Tillemont, *Ecclesiastical Memoirs of the First Six Centuries* (1693; London, 1733), 1: 85–6, 407–17; Leo Steinberg, *The Sexuality of Christ in Renaissance Art and in Modern Oblivion* (Pantheon, 1983), 159, 202.

[161] Marc Shell, 'The holy foreskin', in Jonathan and Daniel Boyarin, eds., *Jews and Other Differences* (Minnesota, 1997), 345–60 at 345–7, 354. See Amy G. Remensnyder, 'Legendary treasure at Conques: reliquaries and imaginative memory', *Speculum* 71 (1996): 884–906 at 894–6.

guides, and decreed excommunication for speaking or writing of it. The Second Vatican Council (1962–5) deleted the Feast of the Holy Circumcision from the church calendar. In 1984 the Calcata prepuce was stolen from the home of the parish priest, its loss relieving the Church of further embarrassment.[162]

Multicephalous saints have since followed the Holy Foreskin into Catholic oblivion. Outdated is the papacy that turned a blind eye to, or even encouraged the duplication of, St Stephen's thirteen arms, John the Baptist's fifty fingers, St Agatha's five breasts. In 1988 Vicar-General Monsignor van Lierde asked scientists to help expose fake relics, for 'the church is eager to go into the 21st century with two-legged, two-armed and one-headed saints'.[163] Modern faith increasingly forswears the tangibly incredible.

Museums are prone to reject unsavoury pasts. Dislike of a legacy at odds with 'the self-portrait Swedes would like to draw' explained the two-century hiatus after the Vasas (1523–1654) in Stockholm's historical museum. Chiding this 'liquidation of their own history', a Norwegian asks, 'How can such an old nation know what it's doing if it doesn't know what it has inherited?'[164] In fact, Swedes do *know*; it is in their history books. But it is not a legacy they *celebrate*. Brazil's museums dwell almost exclusively on imperial and religious history, slighting Indian indigenes, slavery, and post-colonial decline. New York's Museum of Immigration on Ellis Island ignores the underworld of Sicilian mafiosi and Jewish prostitutes. 'Let's not perpetuate the memory of such dishonorable events by erecting monuments to them', argued a Vietnam War veteran against Maya Lin's memorial. Animal rightists damned a proposed museum of British hunting as glorifying 'part of our heritage we ought to eradicate altogether from our minds'.[165]

History texts are truncated (and sometimes even aborted) lest exposure to the unto-ward nip patriotism in the bud. 'I shall not undeceive future generations', the secretary of the Continental Congress explained why he would not chronicle the American Revolu-tion. 'I could not tell the truth without giving great offense. Let the world admire our patriots and heroes. Their supposed talents and virtues ... will serve the cause of patriotism.'[166] Were children told what really went on, civic allegiance would wither. 'Away with such skepticism!' an American magazine of 1908 denounced muckraking revision. Sacred myths were 'the very soul of our history ... To take them away would

---

[162] David Farley, *An Irreverent Curiosity* (New York: Gotham Books, 2009).

[163] Quoted in Uli Schmetzer, 'Tests of faith', *Chicago Tribune*, 24 May 1988.

[164] Quoted in Hans Magnus Enzensberger, *Europe, Europe* (Random House, 1989), 26–7. By my 2012 museum visit, the post-Vasa era had become an age of liberty, science, art, and poverty.

[165] John P. Dickenson, 'Nostalgia for a gilded past? Museums in Minas Gerais, Brazil', in Flora E. S. Kaplan, ed., *Museums and the Making of 'Ourselves'* (Leicester, 1994), 221–45; Ghislaine Lawrence, 'Object lessons in the museum medium', in Susan Pearce, ed., *Objects of Knowledge* (Athlone, 1990), 103–24; Mike Wallace, 'Razor ribbons, history museums, and civic salvation', in *Mickey Mouse History and Other Essays on American Memory* (Temple, 1996), 33–54 at 44; Robert Wagner-Pacifici and Barry Schwartz, 'The Vietnam Veterans Memorial', *American Journal of Sociology* 97 (1991): 376–420 at 388n; *Times*, 31 May 1990: 5 [museum of British hunting].

[166] Charles Thomson quoted in *The Autobiography of Benjamin Rush* (Princeton, 1948), 155; and Charles Thomson to Hannah Thomson (1783), in John Murrin, ed., *Congress at Princeton* (Princeton, 1985), xxii.

now be a baneful disorganization of the national mind.'[167] The American Legion faulted 1920s history texts for 'placing before immature pupils the blunders, foibles, and frailties of prominent heroes and patriots'. A Daughter of Colonial Wars censured social studies textbooks that

tried to give the child an unbiased viewpoint instead of teaching them real Americanism. All the old histories taught 'my country, right or wrong'. That's the point of view we want our children to adopt. We can't afford to teach them to be unbiased and let them make up their own minds.[168]

Banning President Harding's newly found love letters from public view for sixty years, a judge in 1964 argued that 'anything damaging to the image of an American president should be suppressed to protect the younger generation'. Whatever the facts, showing 'national heroes in an uncomplimentary fashion' offends propriety. History lessons that encourage scepticism about British heroes and heroines, sullying the reputations of Florence Nightingale, Horatio Nelson, or Alfred the Great, are similarly proscribed.[169]

  Profit if not piety sways publishers to expunge the infamous, the awkward, even the debatable. 'Are you going to tell kids that Thomas Jefferson didn't believe in Jesus?' a textbook editor harangued a history teacher. 'Not me!' A publisher reasoned that 'if there's something that is controversial it's better to take it out'. Another would omit not only 'controversial' notables such as Roosevelt and Nixon, but any 'living people who might possibly become infamous'.[170]

  Memories of ill repute are expunged, disreputable events deleted from anniversaries. Newburyport's tercentenary celebrants 'ignored this or that difficult period of time or unpleasant occurrence or embarrassing group of men and women; they left out awkward political passions ... to express today's values'.[171] Tarrytown long refused to honour A. J. Davis's Gothic Revival 'Lyndhurst' (Fig. 89) as the home of the reprehensible tycoon Jay Gould.[172] The traitor Benedict Arnold was totally ignored in the bicentenary of his Norwich, Connecticut, birthplace. 'What can you do when what you've got is Benedict Arnold?' sighed the organizer. 'If only he'd gotten killed before going bad. Then we'd have a hero and it would all be so much easier' (Fig. 101). A tableau depicting Arnold's 1775 expedition to Canada, bizarrely allocated to Norwich's Jewish community, was withdrawn as suggestive of Judas's betrayal of Jesus.[173]

---

[167] Quoted in Ray Raphael, *Founding Myths: Stories That Hide Our Patriotic Past* (New York: New Press, 2004), 263.

[168] Mrs Ellwood J. Turner (1940) quoted in Ronald W. Evans, *This Happened in America: Harold Rugg and the Censure of Social Studies* (Charlotte, NC: Information Age, 2007), 195.

[169] Edward Ruzzo quoted in Loewen, *Lies My Teacher Told Me*, 289; Nicholas Tate in *Times*, 18 Sept. 1995.

[170] Loewen, *Lies My Teacher Told Me*, 172; Holt, Rinehart & Winston editor (1982) in Joan DelFattore, *What Johnny Shouldn't Read* (Yale, 1992), 131–2; publisher quoted in Diane Ravitch, 'Decline and fall of teaching history, *NYT Magazine*, 17 Nov. 1985: 56.

[171] Warner, *Living and the Dead*, 110.

[172] 'Tarrytown urging U.S. to cancel law for a Gould shrine', *NYT*, 16 Sept. 1964: 33; Thomas W. Ennis, 'Jay Gould mansion: Hudson's Gothic castle', *NYT*, 19 Nov. 1964: 41.

[173] Marian O'Keefe quoted in Michael Knight, 'Benedict Arnold: a bicentennial nonperson', *IHT*, 8 Mar. 1976: 3; Warner, *Living and the Dead*, 119, 200–3.

In American and Australian re-enactments, tribal members and slave descendants shun impersonating victimized forebears.

Evil associations jeopardize relics. An ancient Greek Venus unearthed in fourteenth-century Siena was destroyed out of fear of pagan malevolence. English churchmen fulminated against Avebury's neolithic stone circle as a relic of black magic.[174] A memorial to the 'world's oldest profession' – prostitutes who serviced California gold-rushers – was demolished by embarrassed local worthies. Even fictional echoes may be too loud. Until George III died in 1820, *King Lear* was banned from the London stage for madness too close to the royal bone. 'Aunt Jemima', the ex-slave whose secret recipe and rapturous smile enriched Quaker Oats, was banished even from Disneyland, where her semblance had once signed autographs all day long. Gone are Redskins, Mexicans, frontier dentists, and others of whom any portrayal might now be deemed offensive.[175] At Dartmouth College, founded to convert Indians to Christianity, the 1930s dining-room mural of unfrocked squaws was boarded over, the Indian head emblazoned on the basketball court sanded down, cheers of 'Scalp me' and 'Wah-hoo-wah' silenced. All over America the very name 'Indian', along with place-names such as 'Squaw Peak' and 'Squaw Valley', are consigned to oblivion.[176]

Remembering great evil saddles descendants with ancestral guilt. Germans still veer between forcibly recalling and wishing fervently to forget Nazi atrocity. Counter-monuments (*Gegen-Denkmale*) to Nazi victims in Hamburg and Kassel, obelisks slowly submerging underground, are reminders of shame that Germans hope will fade away. Because Holocaust recall still looms large, other tragic events remain unsung. The 150,000 German dead at Stalingrad lie in oblivion, a legacy Germans have only begun to confront.[177] Laden with Marxist-Leninist kitsch, the East German historical museum on Unter den Linden was closed after reunification for 'forty years of lying about history'.[178]

Commands to forget coexist with zeal to commemorate. Those who deny the Holocaust, no less than its mourners, attest its enduring potency. Far from expunging all memory of Jews, Nazis planned a museum of former Jewish life to celebrate the Final Solution. 'The Jews were not to be annihilated and then forgotten, but annihilated and then remembered forever', Germans masters not just of Jewish lives but afterlives. Their

---

[174] Aubrey Burl, *Prehistoric Avebury* (Yale, 1979), 36–40.

[175] Jon Wiener, 'Tall tales and true', *Nation*, 31 Jan. 1994: 133–5; Jackie Young, *Black Collectibles: Mammy and Her Friends* (Atglen, PA: Schiffer, 1988); Thomas C. Holt, 'Marking: race, race-making, and the writing of history', *AHR* 100 (1995): 1–20.

[176] FitzGerald, *America Revised*, 90–93; Gretchen M. Bataille and Charles L. P. Silet, eds., *The Pretend Indians* (Iowa State, 1980); Mark Monmonier, *From Squaw Tit to Whorehouse Meadow* (Chicago, 2006); Colin G. Calloway, *The Indian History of an American Institution: Native Americans and Dartmouth* (New England, 2010).

[177] James E. Young, *The Texture of Memory: Holocaust Memorial and Meaning* (Yale, 1993), 27–48; Thomas Stubblefield, 'Do disappearing monuments simply disappear?', *Future Anterior* 8:2 (2011): 1–11; Timothy W. Ryback, 'Stalingrad: letters from the dead', *New Yorker*, 1 Feb. 1993: 58–71.

[178] Jane Kramer, *The Politics of Memory: Looking for Germany in the New Germany* (Random House, 1996), 274. See Susan A. Crane, 'Memory, distortion, and history in the museum', in Bettina Messias Carbonell, ed., *Museum Studies* (Blackwell, 2012), 303–16 at 309–10.

'eternal death was not to be oblivion, but the torture of being eternally remembered by their persecutors'. As Walter Benjamin presciently predicted, '*even the dead* will not be safe from the enemy if he wins'.[179]

New proprieties habitually fig-leaf no longer seemly pasts. As decreed by the Council of Trent (1564), loincloths were painted over torsos in Michelangelo's *Last Judgement* (1536–41). 'Ee!' said a young viewer, of a painted Canovaesque maiden with her hand demurely hiding her crotch, 'If I'd felt like that about it, I'd've kept me knickers on.' A phallic Greek pot in Oxford's Ashmolean Museum long passed genteel muster by being labelled 'vase with a peculiar foot'.[180] More rarely, heritage endorses genitalia: Mexican War commander Winfield Scott's grandchildren regendered the statue of the old mare the ageing general actually rode into a more suitable stallion. Genitals of the *Hercules* carved for London's Great Exhibition of 1851, sawn off in 1883, were reattached in 1977.

Replicas of Michelangelo's *David* are variously scorned, celebrated, and castrated: Orthodox zealots forced Jerusalem to refuse a 'pornographic' *David*, a Florentine gift to mark the 3,000th anniversary of King David's conquest. On the face-down fragmented Cal State Fullerton campus replica, kissing the upturned buttocks gives students luck. The Victoria & Albert's 1857 study replica gained a detachable fig leaf to spare the blushes of Queen Victoria and other female viewers. The oversized testicles on Jacob Epstein's *Tomb of Oscar Wilde* (1912), in Père Lachaise Cemetery, were hacked off by indignant English ladies in 1961. The glass partition erected in 2011 to protect Wilde's tomb and statue from lipsticked admirers' kisses was itself soon kiss-spotted.[181]

Diplomatically offensive legacies elicit sporadic concealment. For Georges Pompidou's visit to the House of Lords, the huge canvases of French defeats at Trafalgar and Waterloo in the anteroom were said to have been draped in muslin. Lord St John of Fawsley in 1994 concealed the portrait of Oliver Cromwell above the high table at Sidney Sussex College, Cambridge, to spare Princess Margaret having to dine under the gaze of the 'executor' of her forebear Charles I.[182]

Modern health fetishes are backdated. Today's anti-smoking crusade excises tobacco from past as well as present. Cigarettes are brushed out of portraits of bluesman Robert Johnson on US stamps, of Enver Hoxha when dictator of Albania, of Stalin shown with Ribbentrop, and of Mao, though Mao's shadow still visibly puffs away. Yet Churchill's dogged cigar and Roosevelt's debonair cigarette remain intrinsically durable. And although the 2006 statue of Isambard Kingdom Brunel ditched his iconic cigar, Kenneth Branagh playing Brunel restored it in opening the 2012 Olympics. Whether Roosevelt's

[179] Elisabeth Domansky, '"Kristallnacht", the Holocaust and German unity', *History & Memory* 4:1 (1992): 60–94 at 60; Walter Benjamin, 'Theses on the philosophy of history', in *Illuminations* (New York: Schocken, 1969), 253–64 at 255. See Deborah Lipstadt, *Denying the Holocaust* (Free Press, 1993); Stephen Greenblatt, 'Resonance and wonder', in Ivan Karp and Steven D. Lavine, eds., *Exhibiting Cultures* (Smithsonian, 1991), 46–8.
[180] 'Canny judges of heritage', *Times*, 5 Nov. 1994; Philip Howard, *Times*, 14 Dec. 1991: 14.
[181] Dario Gamboni, *The Destruction of Art* (Reaktion, 1997), 149–54; John Tagliabue, 'Sealed with a kiss in Paris', *IHT*, 17 Dec. 2011: 2.
[182] Georges Pompidou in Matthew Parris, *Times*, 11 Nov. 1992 (Parris later told me this had proved to be a myth, but he would continue to dine out on it); St John of Fawsley in *Times*, 14 Nov. 1994.

new Washington memorial should show FDR crippled (as the disabled demanded) or conceal his crutches and wheelchair (as he himself usually did) was hotly contested. (He ended up lamed but nicotine-free.) Animal rightists 'corrected' Eleanor Roosevelt's hallmark fox fur to a cloth coat.[183]

Forgetting what displeases is made easier by the natural oblivion of time, which liquidates much that shames. Washington tour guides still point out where the Watergate scandal began, but forty years later that ignoble episode now survives mainly as a label for any sleazy fix. 'Where are the preservationists who usually rally to the salvation of historic bars and battlefields?' wondered a columnist when the Watergate plumbers' headquarters literally disappeared. Heritage fanciers 'metaphysically denied' this infamous shrine until 2013, when the National Trust for Historic Preservation, pledged to protect 'important places from every era of American history', announced its own impending move to Watergate.[184]

Unfamiliarity dooms other legacies. When classical motifs no longer convey their allegorical intent, past public statuary becomes obnoxious. Frederick MacMonnies's 22-ton 1922 'Civic Virtue Triumphant over Unrighteousness' was banished in 1941 from New York's City Hall Park to the boondocks (near Queens Borough Hall), because viewers ignorant or disdainful of mythology took offence at a man trampling women representing vice. Unloved in Queens, 'Civic Virtue' has been consigned to Brooklyn's Green-Wood Cemetery.[185] Obsolete language too consigns past work to oblivion. Well into the eighteenth century the stomach, not the heart, was the seat of emotions. We still 'stomach' things and speak of 'gut feelings', but John Wesley's great hymn, 'How blest the man whose bowels move', is today quite unsingable.[186]

Decorum conceals the unspeakable, the unpalatable, and the outdated. To sanitize a seamy past is preferred to laying it bare. Victorians viewed Thomas Bowdler's expurgations of Shakespeare and Gibbon as 'a reflection of moral progress'; the reason 'people in the eighteenth century, and earlier, didn't take offense at coarse passages [was] because they were coarse themselves'.[187] A Victorian drawing-room 'could no more suffer ... a fine gentleman or fine lady of Queen Anne's time, or hear what they heard and said', Thackeray warned squeamish readers, 'than you would receive an ancient Briton'.[188]

---

[183] Paul Freund, 'Snuffing out the smokes of the great and famous', *IHT*, 7 Oct. 1994: 5; Sally Feldman, 'Wild things', *New Humanist* 121:5 (Sept.–Oct. 2006), 26–8; Doss, *Memorial Mania*, 34–6. A Churchill cigar stub went for £1,340, Brunel's cigar case for £26,400, at a 19 Jan. 2011 Bonhams auction.

[184] William Safire, 'Great mystery in Washington: where is the sinister room 16?' *NYT*, 15 Sept. 1989; Stephanie K. Meeks quoted in 'National Trust for Historic Preservation moving offices to the Watergate', *Washington Post*, 27 June 2013. See Michael Schudson, *Watergate in American Memory* (Basic Books, 1992), 59; Jessica Gresko, 'Forty years on, Watergate crime scene is forgotten', *Associated Press*, 18 June 2012.

[185] Michele H. Bogart, *Public Sculpture and the Civic Ideal in New York City, 1890–1930* (Chicago, 1989), 266–8; Joyce Purnick, 'Women seen, or just used, through art', *NYT*, 14 Oct. 1996: B1; NYC Dept. of Parks & Recreation, *Civic Virtue*, 1 Feb. 2002, nycgovparks.org/sub_your_park/historical_signs....php?id=13093; Sarah Maslin Nir, 'Little-loved statue may be exiled to a Brooklyn cemetery', *NYT*, 21 July 2012.

[186] Samuel Wix, reviser, *New Week's Preparation for a Worthy Receiving of The Lord's Supper* (London, 1827), 111. See 'Blest the man whose bowels move', in Isaac Watts, *Hymns and Spiritual Songs* (London, 1707), no. 46.

[187] Noel Perrin, *Dr. Bowdler's Legacy: A History of Expurgated Books* (1969; Boston: Godine, 1992), 7.

[188] William Makepeace Thackeray, *English Humourists of the Eighteenth Century* (New York, 1953), 96–7.

Race now supplants sex as the prime arena of polite concealment. Modern racial sensitivity suppresses old lyrics that would grossly offend. Now never sung is the second verse of Stephen Foster's legendary 'Oh Susannah' (1847):

> I jump'd aboard de telegraph,
> And trabbled down de ribber,
> De lecktric fluid magnified,
> And killed five hundred Nigga.

These lines would effectively deafen modern hearers, just as the stench of a functioning ancient privy would cause visitors to flee. A new edition of Mark Twain's *Huckleberry Finn* replaces 'nigger' with 'slave' (and injun with Indian); not even graduate students can tolerate 'textual encounters with this racial appellative'.[189] Presidential aspirant Texas governor Rick Perry's campaign suffered a serious setback when it was revealed that his hunting lodge had been named 'Niggerhead'.[190]

'All I want is the truth', sang John Lennon in 1971. 'Just gimme some truth.' But truth can hurt too much. 'Should we censor *Birth of a Nation* or *Jud Süss* because of their racist messages?' asks a historian. 'Of course, no.' But they are not easily shown. Griffith's rabidly racist 1915 movie (lauded by President Woodrow Wilson as 'all so terribly true'), is a cinematic classic, 'perhaps the single most important film ever made'. But it was left out of the Library of Congress's 1993 film centenary because Griffith's depiction of the Ku Klux Klan as heroes and blacks as leering rapists would have drowned out its cinematic merits.[191] A period-costumed 'secession gala' in Charleston opened South Carolina's sesquicentennial celebration in December 2010. Revellers were rebuked: 'the South's break with the Union [held] a milestone to be marked with sorrow and honesty, not with historical denial and fancy-dress balls'. But when Charleston's mayor declared that the South had seceded to protect slavery he was called a liar.[192]

A despicable past can be stood on its head. *Uncle Tom's Cabin*, written to expose slavery's oppressive cruelty, was inverted in the novels of Joel Chandler Harris and Thomas Nelson Page to limn compassionate slaveholders and contented slaves. Abraham Lincoln's uncouth Midwestern background, a handicap young Abe struggled to overcome, became estimable after Frederick Jackson Turner lauded the frontier as the seedbed of democracy. Once a 'dung-hill', New Salem, Illinois, became a 'sacred spot' that shaped Lincoln's character.[193] In Peter Hunt's film *1776* (1972) Thomas Jefferson's

---

[189] Alan Gribben quoted in Julie Bosman, 'Publisher tinkers with Twain', *NYT*, 4 Jan. 2011. Perrin's 1992 afterword (*Dr. Bowdler's Legacy*, 264–88) details the shift from sex/religion to race/ethnicity.

[190] Steven Thrasher, 'Rick Perry and the curious case of "Niggerhead" ranch', *Village Voice*, 2 Oct. 2011.

[191] Alon Confino, 'On Disney's America', AHA *Perspectives* 33:3 (Mar. 1995): 10; Loewen, *Lies My Teacher Told Me*, 18; Leon F. Litwack, 'Birth of a Nation', in Mark C. Carnes, ed., *Past Imperfect: History According to the Movies* (New York: Henry Holt, 1995), 136–41; Pat Laughney (Library of Congress film centenary), *IHT*, 30–31 Oct. 1993, 3; Melvyn Stokes, *D. W. Griffith's The Birth of a Nation* (Oxford, 2007); Eric M. Armstrong, 'Revered and reviled', *Moving Arts Film Journal*, 26 Feb. 2010.

[192] Jeff Jacoby, 'Denying an ugly past', *IHT*, 6 Jan. 2011: 7.

[193] Thomas P. Riggio, '*Uncle Tom* reconstructed', in Leila Zenderland, ed., *Recycling the Past* (PennPress, 1978), 66–80; Richard S. Taylor, 'How New Salem became an outdoor museum', *Historic Illinois* 2:1 (1979): 2; Ralph Gary, *Following in Lincoln's Footsteps* (Basic Books, 2002), 91–100.

Figure 101 A turncoat returned to favour in London: Benedict Arnold, 'American patriot'

'scandalous' behaviour angers John Adams, who exclaims: 'What will people think?'
'Don't worry, John', says Benjamin Franklin; 'the history books will clean it up'.[194] In
London, Benedict Arnold's betrayal is recast as heroism (Fig. 101).

Other divisive pasts are defanged by marinating in time-free trivia. In the laser show at
Stone Mountain, Georgia, a long-time Confederate shrine, clichéd images of Scarlett
O'Hara, peaches, and plantations give way to mishmashes of South and North, Jeff Davis
and Abe Lincoln, Elvis Presley and Martin Luther King, 'Dixie' and 'God Bless America' –
'a puddle of political correctness', felt Tony Horwitz. 'Why debate who should or
shouldn't be remembered and revered when you could just stuff the whole lot in a
blender and spew it across the world's biggest rock?'[195]

The errant past deplored and displayed

Celebrating the past nowadays stresses the sad and the seedy as well as the seemly.
History 'fumigate[s] experience, making it safe and sterile', commented an observer a
generation ago. 'The past, all the parts of it that are dirty and exciting and dangerous and

---

[194] Alex von Tunzelmann, '1776: spinning the Congressional record', *Guardian*, 12 Aug. 2010.
[195] Horwitz, *Confederates in the Attic*, 287–8.

uncomfortable and real ... undergoes eternal gentrification.'[196] No longer. Underscoring a sordid or shaming legacy suggests a regard for truth at any cost, a frank avowal of guilt, a wish to make amends. Hence the global spate of apologies. Lamentations for the slaughter of innocents go back many millennia, but widespread public contrition is a recent phenomenon. Pope John Paul II's manifold apologies for past faults were papally unprecedented; no previous Jubilees, noted a 1999 'Purification of Memory' report, had shown awareness 'of any faults in the Church's past, nor of the need to ask God's pardon'.[197]

Apologies and regrets for slavery issued by North Carolina, Alabama, Virginia, Maryland, New Jersey, and Florida in 2007–8 were undreamed of a mere generation ago. The 1907 centenary of the abolition of the slave trade had gone virtually unremarked in Britain; the 2007 bicentenary saturated media, museums, and public events.[198] Lifeline Expedition followers – 'healing the past, transforming the future' – lamented their ancestors' role in the Atlantic slave trade in West African and Caribbean reconciliation ceremonies. A descendant of slave-trader Sir John Hawkins, his T-shirt inscribed 'So Sorry' and 'Pardon', knelt in chains before 25,000 Gambians in Banjul, asking forgiveness for his forebear's crimes. Joining in contrition, the presidents of Benin and Ghana begged forgiveness for the 'shameful' and' abominable' role of Africans themselves in the slave trade.[199]

Slavery is by no means the only ancestral iniquity nowadays deplored. Britain's prime minister apologized for the Irish Famine, the pope for the Fourth Crusade's sacking of Constantinople and for the Inquisition. Australia declared a 'National Sorry Day' for past mistreatment of Aborigines; Canada issued formal apologies to its tribal peoples. A Fijian apology for eating the Reverend Thomas Baker in 1867 came with apposite amends: the cannibals' descendants cooked a cow for the missionary's offspring.[200]

The International Center for Transitional Justice's thousand-page *Handbook of Reparations* chronicles efforts to rectify the past century's state wrongs.[201] As for the remote past, one wag suggests apologies are due from 'every human being who ever lived' to Neanderthal Man for his extinction thirty thousand years ago.[202] An Egyptian law school dean is suing all the world's Jews for reparations for the clothing, cooking

---

[196] 'Notes and comment', *New Yorker*, 24 Sept. 1984: 39.

[197] Catholic Church, International Theological Commission, *Memory and Reconciliation* (St Paul's Publications, 2000), 11. See my 'On arraigning ancestors: a critique of historical contrition', *North Carolina Law Review* 87 (2009): 901–66 at 909–14, 919–20.

[198] Cora Kaplan, 'Commemorative history without guarantees', *History Workshop Journal* 64 (2007): 389–97; James Walvin, 'The slave trade, abolition and public memory', *Transactions of the Royal Historical Society*, 6th ser., 19 (2009): 139–49.

[199] Alan Hamilton, 'Slaver's descendant begs forgiveness', *Times*, 22 June 2006: 9; Henry Louis Gates, Jr., 'Ending the slavery blame game', *NYT*, 23 Apr. 2010.

[200] Nick Megoran, 'Towards a geography of peace: pacific geopolitics and evangelical Christian Crusade apologies', *Transactions of the Institute of British Geographers* 35 (2010): 382–98; 'Sorry Day and the Stolen Generations', 26 May 1998, *australia.gov.au*; Graeme Davison, *The Use and Abuse of Australian History* (Allen & Unwin, 2000), 4–9; Canadian government apologies, *CBCNews*, 6 Jan. 1998, 11 June 2008; Gorman Beauchamp, 'Apologies all', *American Scholar* 76:4 (Autumn 2007): 83–93 at 84.

[201] Pablo De Greiff, ed., *The Handbook of Reparations* (Oxford, 2006), 1.

[202] Giles Coren, 'Three grunts for those Neanderthal geniuses', *Times*, 30 Aug. 2008: 16.

utensils and 300 tons of gold stolen during Exodus, at compound interest since 1230 BC; Jews countered with demands for reparations for four hundred years of involuntary servitude in Egypt.[203] Citing the papal revocation of Joan of Arc's conviction, a Kenyan lawyer has petitioned the International Court of Justice to nullify Pontius Pilate's death sentence against Jesus as a violation of His human rights, which if upheld would have troubling consequences for Christian doctrine.[204] Remorse is bestowed even on places: John Betjeman's daughter said sorry to Slough, a byword for English urban blight, for the poet's 1937 ditty, 'Come, friendly bombs, and fall on Slough / It isn't fit for humans now'.[205]

Remorseful excess inevitably incurs a backlash. 'I repent, we repent [is] currently the most common verb in the French language', grumbled a diplomat-scholar at the deluge of Vichy apologies in the wake of Prime Minister Jacques Chirac's official contrition: 'The churches, the doctors, and the police parade and contrive. We are now waiting for the postmen, the train conductors, and the truck drivers to join the great self-flagellating movement ... Me, too, I ask for forgiveness. Forgiveness for not wanting to repent.'[206] Contrition chic is reviled as 'a bargain-basement way to gain publicity, sympathy, and even absolution'. Errant forebears serve as surrogates for our former selves; 'people eager to be praised as the salt of the earth are apologizing for the low-lifers they used to be'.[207] Apology sinks into self-service.

When forgiveness becomes the public rallying cry, played out on daytime-television soap operas, encouraged by civic and religious leaders, and praised far and wide for its power to heal, its slide into confusion and vulgarity is almost inevitable. It becomes identified with 'closure', it is sentimentalized and transformed into therapy.[208]

'Apologizing for something you didn't do to people to whom you didn't do it (in fact, to people to whom it wasn't done)' is a self-righteous bow to history deployed as a weapon in the arsenal of image restoration in business, politics, and religion.[209]

Seen in this light, present contrition for ancient crimes is hypocrisy. British deserters in the Great War were recently granted posthumous pardons, on the ground that military tribunals in those benighted days knew nothing about post-traumatic stress. In 2013 codebreaker Alan Turing was given a posthumous royal pardon for conviction in 1952 of 'gross indecency'. How far back can the past thus be rectified? 'Should Oscar Wilde be

[203] Nabil Hilmi, interview 9 Aug. 2003, *Al-Ahram Al-Arabi*, 9 Aug. 2003; Ted Olsen, 'The world's most outrageous biblical lawsuit', *Christianity Today*, 1 Sept. 2003.
[204] Fredrick Nzwili, 'Kenyan lawyer on quixotic quest to nullify trial of Jesus', *National Catholic Reporter* Religion News Service 30 July 2013.
[205] John Betjeman, 'Slough' (1937), in *Collected Poems* (Farrar, Straus & Giroux, 2006), 20–1; 'Despond of Slough lifts after Betjeman apology', *Times*, 16 Sept. 2006: 18.
[206] Philippe Moreau Defarges (2000) quoted in Julie Fette, 'The apology moment: Vichy memories in 1990s France', in Elazar Barkan and Alexander Karn, eds., *Taking Wrongs Seriously* (Stanford, 2006), 259–85 at 274.
[207] Jean Bethke Elshtain, 'Politics and forgiveness', in Nigel Biggar, ed., *Burying the Past* (Georgetown, 2003), 45–64 at 45; Russell Baker, 'No time for the future', *NYT*, 7 Oct. 1997: A27.
[208] Charles L. Griswold, *Forgiveness: A Philosophical Exploration* (Cambridge, 2007), 182.
[209] Walter Benn Michaels, *The Trouble with Diversity* (Holt, 2006), 122.

posthumously pardoned because we now think the laws under which he was convicted were unjust?' Should we retrospectively exonerate all those charged in centuries past with attempted suicide, witchcraft, or Catholicism?[210] To try to repair all past wrongs is futile. 'Contrition and congratulation are both strictly non-transferable. Hereditary guilt makes no more sense than hereditary honors.'[211] Yet the 1992 Columbus quincentenary unleashed a torrent of anachronistic reproach. A San Diego State University history instructor castigated a visiting Spanish naval officer, a descendant of Christopher Columbus, for his ancestor's rape of the New World.[212]

Why is the world, especially the developed West, now swamped in collective remorse? The reasons are multiple. Some stem from the failure of roseate post-war hopes. The collapse of pledges to end poverty, famine, disease, and injustice eroded faith in technological and economic panaceas. As Enlightenment optimism has come to seem a cruel illusion, visions of a better tomorrow give way to righting past wrongs. Others cite Internet websites – ThePublicApology.com, PerfectApology.com – that facilitate quests for personal absolution.[213] But above all, what ushered in 'a fin de millénaire fever of atonement' was dawning awareness of Holocaust horrors and ensuing amends to its survivors and descendants.[214] Coming to terms with the past became a major preoccupation first in post-war Germany. Chancellor Konrad Adenauer saw Wiedergutmachung, 'making good again', as not only a necessary act of atonement but also essential to rehabilitate Germany in the global community. Hence the most substantial reparations ever implemented were paid to the state of Israel and to individual Jewish sufferers.[215]

The Holocaust example fuelled reparations campaigns the world over. Claimants in South Africa, Namibia, Argentina, Brazil, and Chile, Australian Aborigines, Native Americans, Japanese-Americans and African-Americans all deployed the same rationales and rhetoric, the same legal instruments and expertise, often the same lawyers and publicists, as had victimized Jews. And just as global Holocaust attention helped revitalize Jewish group identity, memories of Armenian slaughter sustained adherence to national identity among Armenians abroad, the Nanking massacre among overseas Chinese.[216] Launched in 2002, an International Coalition of Historic Site Museums of Conscience embraces locales of slavery and mass slaughter, the Irish Famine, the Holocaust, the

---

[210] Matthew Parris, 'A clever trick: say sorry, condemn the past and look good, with no cost', Times, 26 Aug. 2006: 21. See Fran Yeoman and Marcus Leroux, 'War pardon will clear rogues and innocents', Times, 9 Sept. 2006: 16.

[211] Peter Manning, 'Slavery, abolition and apologies', Guardian, 24 Mar. 2007: 37.

[212] Gary B. Nash et al., History on Trial (Knopf, 1997), 123.

[213] John Torpey, Making Whole What Has Been Smashed: On Reparations Politics (Harvard, 2006), 36, 160; Elizabeth Bernstein, 'Who's sorry now? Nearly everyone', Wall Street Journal, 13 Jan. 2010.

[214] Wole Soyinka, The Burden of Memory, the Muse of Forgiveness (Oxford, 1999), 90; A. O. Scott, 'Why so many Holocaust films now, and who benefits?' IHT, 23 Nov. 2008: 1, 7.

[215] Ariel Colonomos and Andrea Armstrong, 'German reparations to the Jews after World War II', in De Greiff, ed., Handbook of Reparations, 390–419 at 393, 408; Constantin Goschler, Wiedergutmachung (Munich: Oldenbourg, 1992); Karl Jaspers, The Question of German Guilt (1946; Fordham, 2000); Elazar Barkan, The Guilt of Nations (Norton, 2000), 8–15.

[216] Alfred L. Brophy, Reparations Pro and Con (Oxford, 2006), 55–62; Torpey, Making Whole What Has Been Smashed, 21, 161.

Gulag, tenement slums, prisons, and workhouses.[217] Echoing Maya Lin's Vietnam War Memorial in Washington, the Monument to the Victims of State Terrorism in Buenos Aires's Memory Park attests not just Argentinian but global anguish. Like re-enactments of suffering and deprivation, tourist visits to such memorial sites reflect needs to overcome trauma by re-experiencing it.[218]

Practicing self-blame in place of self-praise, museums now 'highlight what was once lacking by minimizing what was once venerated'. Thus the 2013 National Archives 'Records of Rights' exhibition of America's most sacred documents – the Declaration of Independence, the Constitution, the Bill of Rights – focuses on how their ideals have *not* been fulfilled.[219]

Popular media more commonly trivialize and defang lamented pasts, as in *The Definitive Chronicle of History's 100 Worst Atrocities*.[220] Purging memories of lost partners, the Zagreb Museum of Broken Relationships, the prize-winning European Innovative Museum of 2011, exhibits mementoes donated by forsaken lovers, such as a prosthetic limb that 'lasted longer than love, as it was made of better material'.[221] Launched in 1993, Terry Deary's *Horrible Histories* for children – *The Rotten Romans, The Smashing Saxons, The Slimy Stuarts, The Terrible Tudors, The Vicious Vikings, The Vile Victorians* – have sold more than 25 million copies. Like their American spin-offs – *Cranky Colonials, Revolting Revolutionaries, Westward, Ha-Ha!* – they purvey the opposite of Henry James's seemly past, 'no more nice guy nonsense' but history 'like it is – a sickening saga of dire disasters, brainless blunders and terrible twists – history with the nasty bits left in'.[222]

Nasty becomes nauseating. In the History Channel's *Barbarians* (2004), Vikings, Huns, and Goths 'transformed themselves into world dominance . . . gained by the use of terror. Their calling card was annihilation. . . . They resembled nothing we identify as human, living deeply buried in inhumanity, below the lowest level of depravity'. Horror is then made all too pertinent: 'Allow 1,000 years of bestial behavior, of passion deformed and corrupted, to burn itself into your memory . . . In 2004 the weapons may have changed, but the calling card remains the same.' The horrific past is unbelievable yet exemplary. Infamy dominates today's past. 'The bullying, the backpedaling. The backstabbing. The bloodletting', trumpets *American Heritage* magazine. 'That's what history is about.' The archaeological record of the ancient Anasazi in the American Southwest 'reads like a

[217] Mary Alexander, 'Do visitors get it? A sweatshop exhibit', *Public Historian* 22:3 (Summer 2000): 85–94; Liz Ševčenko and Maggie Russell-Ciardi, 'Foreword', *Public Historian*, special issue, Sites of Conscience, 31:1 (Winter 2008): 9–15; Ruth J. Abram, 'Kitchen conversations: . . . at the Lower East Side Tenement Museum', *Public Historian* 29:1 (Winter 2007): 59–76 at 65. See William Logan and Keir Reeves, eds., *Places of Pain and Shame* (Routledge, 2009).

[218] Andreas Huyssen, 'Memory sites in an expanded field: the Memory Park in Buenos Aires', in *Present Pasts* (Stanford, 2003), 94–109; Laurie Beth Clark, 'Never again and its discontents', *Performance Research* 16:1 (2011): 68–79.

[219] Edward Rothstein, 'New insights may skew big picture', *NYT*, 20 Mar. 2014, F1, 28.

[220] Matthew White, *The Great Big Book of Horrible Things* (Norton, 2011).

[221] Bojan Pancevski, 'Your broken CDs and torn suits are in the museum', *Times2*, 30 Oct. 2007: 2; Ben Hoyle, 'On the shelf: relics of broken romances', *Times*, 15 Aug. 2011: 11. See Olinka Vističa and Drazen Grubisič, *Museum of Broken Relationships* (Zagreb: Hulahop, 2010).

[222] Jerome de Groot, *Consuming History* (Routledge, 2009), 22, 39; *Horrible Histories* TV Tie-in Pack.

Figure 102 Cashing in on an evil past: witch postcard, Salem, Massachusetts

war crimes indictment'. Naming the top British villains of the past thousand years – King John, Titus Oates, Jack the Ripper, Oswald Mosley – historians feed public hunger for 'the worst we did, not the best'.[223]

In modern views of past misery, warts-and-all often becomes warts alone. Helsinki's Worker Housing Museum shows life among poor labourers over a 150-year period; home to a nineteenth-century family of twelve, one room held little but beds. 'This doesn't look how it should – it isn't bad enough!' a journalist told me at the museum's 1991 opening. He sought squalid disarray, smashed toys and dishes on the floor, shit-smeared walls. That toys were then rare and tidiness a fetish does not fit today's image of yesteryear's downtrodden.

Warts-and-all turns off the past's habitual clientele. Period actors in newly gritty Plimoth Plantation struck conservative visitors as more like modern hippies than Pilgrim Fathers. Early-American design devotees, Colonial Williamsburg's customary consumers, were distressed by the dreary realism of garbage-strewn walkways and dung-laden streets, mandated by 1980s authenticity: 'We can see all the dust and lint balls we want without ever leaving home.'[224] Colonial Williamsburg's craftspeople were angered by being

---

[223] History Channel ads, 18 and 19 Jan. 2004; *American Heritage* ad, 2004; Craig Childs, *House of Rain: Tracking a Vanished Civilization across the American Southwest* (Little, Brown, 2006), 156 [Anasazi]; 'True infamy', *BBC History Magazine*, 26 Dec. 2005; P. D. James, *The Lighthouse* (2005), 308–9 ['the worst'].

[224] Michael Olmert, 'New, no-frills Williamsburg', *History News* 37:5 (Oct. 1985): 26–33; Warren Leon and Margaret Piatt, 'Living-history museums', in Warren Leon and Roy Rosenzweig, eds., *History Museums in the United States* (Illinois, 1989), 64–97 at 75.

'deskilled', forced to make shoddy replicas true to supposed originals.[225] A newly found homely photo of Charlotte Brontë will not oust George Richmond's flattering portrait in the Brontë Parsonage souvenir shop. 'People would rather buy a pretty Charlotte', says the director. 'We've always known she wasn't very attractive', commented a Brontë scholar. 'We just don't want to believe it.'[226] Nicety outbids naked truth.

Changing public expectations keep altering portrayals of the past. When *The Return of Martin Guerre* (1982) was first filmed, viewers complained that the sixteenth-century Languedoc village 'was too neat, that there was not enough refuse and swill in the streets, that the peasants looked rather too scrubbed'. But twenty years later even media-studies majors found it 'oppressively filthy and primitive'.[227] Centenary *Titanic* commemorations in 2012 included cruise ship re-enactments of the disastrous maiden voyage – wining, dining, dancing – and then wreath-laying where the ship went down. Belfast's *Titanic* visitors' centre tells the ship's whole story – making, launching, loss, remembrance – with a somewhat perverse memorial to the city's high-tech past, 'the biggest new product failure of all time'.[228]

In sum, we use heritage to improve the past, making it better by modern lights. We do so by hyping its glories (like Thatcher and Reagan), by divesting its exemplars of current anathemas (slaveholders, smokers), by banning demeaning clichés, by fig-leafing, and by improvising former splendour.

Anachronizing the past

Antiquating

> My people were civilized before your people. Or better still, my people *civilized* your
> people.   Bernard Wailes and Amy L. Zoll, 1995[229]

Like many prized 'antiques', venerated pasts are customarily antiquated. Indeed, the Greek word for conserving or preserving, *anapaleosi*, literally means remaking something old, 'reinfusing a house with antiquity, the architectural equivalent ... of *Katharevousa*, the "purified" language that made the new Greek nation neoclassical.[230] Antiquating is ubiquitous, if seldom so far back as a publisher's claim to purvey 'human history from

---

[225] Richard Handler and Eric Gable, *The New History in an Old Museum* (Duke, 1997), 193–4.

[226] Charlotte Cory, 'A friend of Charlotte's', *Independent Magazine*, 13 Nov. 1993; Jane Sellars and Marilyn Butler, *Times*, 11 Jan. 1994. See Christine Alexander and Jane Sellars, *The Art of the Brontës* (Oxford, 1995), xxvi, 307.

[227] Robert A. Rosenstone, 'The reel Joan of Arc', *Public Historian* 25:3 (Summer 2003): 61–77 at 71.

[228] Stephen Brown, 'Retro from the get-go', *Journal of Historical Research in Marketing* 5 (2013): 521-36. See Steven Biel, *Down with the Old Canoe: A Cultural History of the Titanic Disaster* (1996; Norton, 2012), 221–34.

[229] Bernard Wailes and Amy L. Zoll, 'Civilization, barbarism, and nationalism', in Philip Kohl and Clare Fawcett, eds., *Nationalism, Politics, and the Practice of Archaeology* (Cambridge, 1995), 21–38 at 24.

[230] Patricia Storace, *Dinner with Persephone: Travels in Greece* (Granta, 1997), 130. See Peter Mackridge, *Language and National Identity in Greece* (Oxford, 2009), 102–25, 319–22.

500 million BC to the present day'.[231] Many who glorify their past amplify its age. Relics and records that antedate rival claims to power, prestige, or property are treasured; antecedent envy lengthens family, faith, and national pedigrees.

In the 'conceit of nations' reviled by Vico, all peoples exaggerate their territorial or cultural antiquity or conceal its recency.[232] English antiquaries dated Oxford from Alfred the Great, Parliament from the Romans, Christianity from Joseph of Arimathea bringing the Grail to Glastonbury. Olaus Rudbeck's *Atlantica* (1679) made ancient Sweden the fount of modern culture; Germans and then the English and Americans ascribed the roots of democracy to early Goths; African arts are said to antedate Assyrian.[233] Only chauvinists' own antiquity counts. The French denied 'Lucy', long the oldest hominid found, as an alien African. Greeks dismiss English prehistory as irrelevant. So what if Stonehenge antedates the Acropolis; *their* history goes back two and half millennia, while England had no 'real' history before 1066. 'When we were writing philosophy and building the Parthenon, you were swinging from the trees'.[234]

Charisma of precedence fuels many fabrications. Medieval forgeries buttressed ecclesiastical rule with the halo of antiquity. Prehistoric finds revealing Teutonic backwardness dismayed Hitler: 'Why do we call the whole world's attention to the fact that we have no past?' While Himmler enthused over every potsherd and stone axe, Hitler grumbled that 'all we prove by this is that we were still throwing stone hatchets and crouching over open fires when Greece and Rome had already reached the highest point of culture. We really should ... keep quiet about this past.' To validate Nordic mystique, Nazi archaeologists fabricated a Germanic lineage antedating Romans, Celts, and Slavs.[235]

Illusory antiquity bolsters countless causes. From Diocletian's third-century edicts to a fifteenth-century carving that transformed a contest between Athene and Poseidon into a portrayal of the Fall, a halo of forged and borrowed ancientness has enshrined Christian claims. The Turks were 'the first cultured peoples of the world', insisted Ataturk's historians, their saga not 'of a tribe of four hundred tents, but ... a great nation' founded twelve centuries before Christ. Retrospective glory birthed the 1908 Turkish Revolution.[236] Piltdown Man was touted as proof of Britain's humanoid antiquity, trumping

[231] PenguinHutcheon CD-Rom, *New Scientist*, 17 Aug. 2004: 88.

[232] Giambattista Vico, *New Science* (1744; Cornell, 1948), paras 125–6, 55. See Leon Pompa, *Vico: A Study of the New Science* (1975; Cambridge, 1990), 8–9; Grafton, *Bring Out Your Dead*, 265.

[233] Joan Evans, *A History of the Society of Antiquaries* (Oxford, 1956), 11; Samuel T. Kliger, *The Goths in England* (Harvard, 1952), 1–13, 22, 59, 87, 119–23, 140–1, 170, 254; John Michell, *Megalithomania* (Thames & Hudson, 1982), 42–3; David Lowenthal, *George Perkins Marsh, Prophet of Conservation* (Washington, 2000), 55, 59–63; David Levin, *History as Romantic Art* (Stanford, 1959), 74–92; Dorothy Ross, 'Historical consciousness in nineteenth-century America', *AHR* 89 (1984): 909–28 at 918–21; Edward Wilmot Blyden, *The Negro in Ancient History* (Washington, DC: Methodist Episcopal Church, 1869).

[234] Suzanne Citron, *Le mythe national: L'histoire de France en question revisitée* (1989; rev. edn Paris: L'Atelier, 2008), 96; Just, 'Cultural certainties and private doubts', 295; Mackridge, *Language and National Identity in Greece*, 332.

[235] Hitler quoted in Albert Speer, *Inside the Third Reich* (1969; Simon & Schuster, 1997), 141; W. J. McCann, '"Volk und Germanentum"', in Gathercole and Lowenthal, eds., *Politics of the Past*, 74–88 at 81–3.

[236] Tekin Alp, 'Restoration of Turkish history' (1937), in Kedourie, ed., *Nationalism in Asia and Africa*, 207–24 at 210; Kemal H. Karpat, ed., *Ottoman Past and Today's Turkey* (Brill, 2000), vii–xv, 1–27, 150–78.

Cro-Magnon France. Moreover, Piltdown spelt racial primacy, for this 'earliest English-man was the progenitor of white races', proving that whites attained 'full humanity long before other people ... As longer residents in this exalted state, whites must excel in the arts of civilization.'[237]

The monarchy generates popular fables of British antiquity. At George VI's 1937 coronation, pomp and ceremony new-made for Edward VII's coronation in 1902 was already 'immemorial: I might be watching something that happened a thousand years before. In all that time there has been no major change in our Coronations', said a BBC presenter; neophyte Americans 'must wait a thousand years before they can show the world anything so significant'. The 'ancient continuity' of recently crafted royal ritual hyped the Queen Mother's funeral in 2002 and Prince William's wedding in 2011.[238] 'Our tradition of instant heritage is a wonderful thing', remarked a journalist. 'To watch the introduction of a life peer' into the House of Lords in 1994 'is to witness a pageant whose origins are all but lost in the mists of time' (way back in 1958).[239]

Pre-Columbian misattributions lent New World civilization respectable venerabil-ity. To compensate for 'an empty land peopled only by naked wandering savages', longed-for traces of Old World precursors were imagined. Hebrews, Greeks, Persians, Romans, Vikings, Hindus became fancied builders of Indian mounds in the Ohio and Mississippi valleys; meteor fragments mistaken for cast iron showed that 'ancient millions of mankind had their seats of empire in America'.[240] It suited those dispossessing Indians to suppose them savage interlopers who had brutally shat-tered an earlier high civilization. A reviewer of E. G. Squier and E. H. Davis's lavish *Ancient Monuments of the Mississippi Valley* (1848) rejoiced that Americans could now refute

the reproach [of] the excessive modernness and newness of our country ... as being bare of old associations as though it had been made by a journeyman potter day before yesterday ... We have here, what no other nation on the known globe can claim: a perfect union of the past and present; the vigor of a nation just born walking over the hallowed ashes of a race whose history is too early for a record.[241]

[237] Gould, 'Piltdown revisited', 95–6, paraphrasing Arthur Smith Woodward, *The Earliest Englishman* (1948). See Paul Craddock, *Scientific Investigation of Copies, Fakes and Forgeries* (Butterworth-Heinemann, 2009), 475–96.

[238] David Cannadine, 'Context, performance and meaning of ritual', in Hobsbawm and Ranger, eds., *Invention of Tradition*, 101–64; Richard Dimbleby, 'My coronation commentary' (1953), in Leonard Miall, *Richard Dimbleby: Broadcaster* (BBC, 1966), 83–5; Steve Reicher, 'Making a past fit for the future', in Fabio Sani, ed., *Self Continuity* (New York: Psychology Press, 2008), 148-58 at 145–6; Philip Collins, 'Keep the monarchy, but update the rituals', *Times*, 19 Nov. 2010: 35.

[239] Matthew Parris, *Times*, 27 Oct. 1994.

[240] Josiah Priest, *American Antiquities, and Discoveries in the West* (1833), quoted in Robert Silverberg, *The Mound Builders* (New York: Ballantine, 1974), 42; see also 1, 5, 30, 34–5.

[241] 'The Western mound builders', *Literary World* (1848) in Terry A. Barnhart, *Ephraim George Squier and the Development of American Anthropology* (Nebraska, 2005), 98. See Stephen Williams, *Fantastic Archaeology* (PennPress, 1991), 80–97, 180–9; Andrew Lawler, 'America's lost city', *Science* 334 (23 Dec. 2011): 1618–23.

Figure 103 Cashing in on a fraudulent past: Viking logo in Alexandria, Minnesota

A cult of antique origins inspired the Church of the Latter Day Saints. According to the fabulous tablets Joseph Smith unearthed in 1823, Jaredites and Nephites came from the Old World between *c.* 2000 and *c.* 600 BC, and the great mounds are relics of their civilization.

Invented antiquity aggrandizes. Tracing lineages to Rome and Troy, with Noah and Adam as certified forebears, legitimated European aristocracies. Long proven fraudulent, the '1362' Kensington Runestone unearthed in 1898 in Alexandria, Minnesota, remains a fixture of Scandinavian-American faith and local tourism; a replica twelve times the size of the original and 'the world's largest Viking' (Fig. 103) grace this 'Birthplace of Civilization'.[242] Antiquarian lust outlasts historical evidence. The Viking relic remains as veracious as the old stone inscribed

B I L S T

U M

P S H I

S. M.

A R K

in Dickens's *Pickwick Papers* (Bil Stumps, his mark').[243]

---

[242] Erik Wahlgren, *The Kensington Stone* (Wisconsin, 1958); Barry Fell, *America B.C.* (1976); Alice Beck Kehoe, *The Kensington Runestone* (2005). Richard Nielsen and Scott F. Wolter, *Kensington Rune Stone* (2005); and Scott F. Wolter, *Hooked X: Key to the Secret History of North America* (2009) typify unquenchable yearning for pre-Columbian origins. See Larry J. Zimmerman, 'Unusual or "extreme" beliefs about the past', in Chip Colwell-Chanthaphonh and T. J. Ferrguson, eds., *Collaboration in Archaeological Practice* (Walnut Creek, CA: AltaMira, 2008), 55–86.
[243] Charles Dickens, *The Pickwick Papers* (1836–7; Oxford, 1998), 126–38. See Angus Vine, *In Defiance of Time: Antiquarian Writing in Early Modern England* (Oxford, 2010), 1–2.

Figure 104 'Earlying up' the past: G. E. Moody cartoon, *Punch*, 28 Sept. 1938, p. 344

Lust for antiquity forfeits more recent relics. Some restorers virtually raze buildings to return them to their supposed original state. Style and decor attributed to earlier times replace what is disparaged as later: *fin-de-siècle* English terraced houses accrete simulated Tudor and Georgian facades; American towns 'early-up' Victorian centres to look 'Colonial'. Medieval walled Carcassonne is largely the nineteenth-century creation of Viollet-le-Duc. Baroque Bologna was medievalized in the early twentieth century.[244]

Post-Napoleonic chauvinists 'dated' primordial moments when 'their' peoples, arriving in the ruins of the Roman Empire, established their sacred territory and national identity. Linguistic and archaeological claims link modern Germans, French, Serbs, Slovenes, and others with remote pre-literate ancestors. Lost in the mists of antiquity, these origins antedate historical awareness. 'The people was a people, in other words, before it knew itself.' Bound by 'immutable' language, customs, and national character, each people ardently avers rights to a realm defined by ancient settlements, no matter who lives there now. But 'congruence between early medieval and contemporary "peoples" is a myth', notes historian Patrick Geary:

The history of European peoples [is] a history of constant change, of radical discontinuities. . . . Franks 'born with the baptism of Clovis' are not the Franks of Charlemagne or those of the French people [of] Jean Le Pen. The Serbs . . . in the decaying remnants of the Avar Empire were not the people defeated at the battle of Kosovo in 1389, and neither were they the Serbs called to national aggrandizement by Slobodan Milosevic.

Claims that '"we have always been a people" actually are appeals to *become* a people – appeals not grounded in history, but rather attempts to create history'.[245]

Factitious ancient fame salves the sorrows of the subjugated and boosts the pride of the newly sovereign. Hellenized Jews remade ancient Hebrews from expatriate victims into masters of Egypt. For Muslim panegyrists Islamic Iberia is the wellspring of Western science; Turkish schoolchildren learn that civilization began in Anatolia; murals in Accra show Ghanaians inventing the alphabet and the steam engine. Teutonic and Anglo-Saxon admiration of classical Greece led Greek nationalists to emulate ancient Athenians and pen their 1822 charter (the Constitution of Epidaurus) in language so archaic few could fathom it, while cleansing Greek folklore of later tales to stress continuity with classical precepts.[246] Early Christian conversion and ancient Erse freedom braced the Irish quest for liberty. And 'since the ancient Celtic past was a thinly-disguised version of the British imperial present', it presaged 'a restoration of former Irish glories'.[247]

Antiquation is legion. Pride in being Europe's most ancient people and oldest sovereignty underpins modern Basque separatism. Although 'Pakistan' was coined only in 1932 (from Punjab, Afghan, Kashmir, Sind, and Baluchistan), its 'authorized' history is

---

[244] Gabriele Tagliaventi, 'The eternal youth of imitation in architecture', in Hardy, ed., *Venice Charter Revisited*, 503–11.

[245] Patrick Geary, *The Myth of Nations* (Princeton, 2002), 32–3, 37, 156–7, 174.

[246] Gruen, *Heritage and Hellenism*, 293; Bernard Lewis, *History Remembered, Recovered, Invented* (Princeton, 1975), 74–7, 38–9; Michael Herzfeld, *Ours Once More: Folklore, Ideology, and the Making of Modern Greece* (Texas, 1982), 6, 20, 85–6.

[247] Declan Kiberd, *Inventing Ireland* (Harvard, 1995), 625–7.

titled *Five Thousand Years of Pakistan*. President Sukarno used to harp on the 350 years of colonialism endured by 'Indonesia', a twentieth-century innovation. In the Caucasus, Georgian and Armenian 'revisionist dismissal of Johnny-come-lately Ossetians' stress the shortfall of 'a history that only stretches back to medieval times'.[248]

The subjugated Welsh glorified their lost nationhood by antiquating the eisteddfod and choral singing. English songs translated into Welsh in the late eighteenth century became ancient Celtic melodies, the recent musical tradition attributed to hoary antiquity. Druids were upgraded from barbarous cranks to proto-Hellenic sages; William Owen re-created modern Welsh as a copious tongue of patriarchal purity; legendary sites such as the 'grave of Gelert' cairn (ascribed to Llewellyn the Great, 1172–1240) were fabricated for tourist consumption. And purported ancient Welsh remnants among Amerindian tribes spurred Welsh overseas emigration.[249]

Reborn nations typically claim ancient paragons – revolutionary France, the American republic, imperial Germany, and Mussolini's Italy harked back to classical prototypes. Bygone autonomy is antiquated to justify its rebirth; feats admired as primordial legitimize freedom crusades. As embattled Finnish patriots said of the *Kalevala* in 1910, 'a nation able in early times to create such a work of genius cannot succumb'.[250]

Primordial yearnings antiquated English folk-life revivals. Since only the most ancient elements were 'authentic', folklorists exhorted villagers to strip away subsequent corruptions and restore original pagan rites. Few locals had heard of these 'ancient fertility rituals', but they deferred to the experts. The annual 'Souling' play at Antrobus adopted Arnold Boyd's reincarnation of ancestral Halloween ghosts; Violet Alford in the 1930s revived Marshfield Mummers' perambulation as a 'magic circle'. Castleton's Garland Day, celebrating the Stuart Restoration, was reinterpreted as a Celtic sacrificial rite. To understand present-day British folklore, one must retrace the routes of persuasive folklorists who conned villagers into archaist revision.[251]

Origin beliefs derive in large measure from later findings and fabulations. Pacific islanders accrete insights (and errors) from imperial conquerors, missionaries, and ethnographers. Conflating ancient with recent, endemic with exotic, local legends manufactured for outside consumption soon become traditional. Anthropologist Ernest Beaglehole, revisiting a Polynesian atoll in 1935, was disappointed to find Pukapukan islanders, Christianized since 1823, about to stage their annual biblical play. 'Why not play for a change old Pukapukan stories, the story of Malotini for example, or the Eight

[248] R. E. M. Wheeler, *Five Thousand Years of Pakistan* (1950; Karachi, 1992); Benedict Anderson, *Imagined Communities* (1983; 2nd edn Verso, 1991), 11n4 [Sukarno]; Margarita Diaz-Andreu, 'Archaeology and nationalism in Spain', 39–56 at 52, and P. L. Kohl and Gocha R. Tsetskhladze, 'Nationalism, politics, and the practice of archaeology in the Caucasus', 149–76 at 160–1, in Kohl and Fawcett, eds., *Nationalism, Politics, and the Practice of Archaeology*.

[249] Prys Morgan, 'From a death to a view: the hunt for the Welsh past in the Romantic period', in Hobsbawm and Ranger, eds., *Invention of Tradition*, 43–100 at 72–9, 86–7; Gwyn A. Williams, *Madoc* (Eyre Methuen, 1979); Caroline Franklin, 'The Welsh American dream', in Gerald Carruthers and Alan Rawes, eds., *English Romanticism and the Celtic World* (Cambridge, 2003), 69–84.

[250] Quoted in Wilson, *Folklore and Nationalism in Modern Finland*, 59–60.

[251] Georgina Boyes, 'Cultural survivals theory and traditional customs', *Folk Life* 26 (1987–8): 5–11, and *The Imagined Village: Culture, Ideology and the English Folk Revival* (Manchester, 1993), 10, 64, 104–5.

Men of Ngake, or the Slaughter of the Yayake people?' implored Beaglehole. 'The acting of them would help us to remember them more vividly when we came to write them down.' Compliant islanders jettisoned David and Goliath for long-abandoned native legends. Seventy years on, these are performed in tandem with the biblical tales on Pukapuka Gospel Day.[252]

The past is everywhere antiquated in ways that people soon forget. In the Italian village of Ripacandida, impoverished peasants used to dress children as abstemious monks in festivals for St Anthony of Padua. In the 1950s, to honour the martyred local bishop St Donatus of Arezzo, they switched to richer garments; the shift from humble monk to sumptuous bishop was paid for by rising pensions and emigrant remittances. Conflating their own twelfth-century patron saint with the earlier Donatus, villagers now insist that their children have dressed as St Donatus ever since the fourth century.[253] Once popularly enshrined, spurious antiquity becomes ineradicable, like the Plymouth Pilgrim origin of Thanksgiving, in fact 'a 19th-century celebration that was in search of some history, so it glommed onto 1621'.[254]

Modernizing

We extend the past forwards as well as backwards, renovating in line with current predilections. Refashioned in present garb, the past becomes more comprehensible or congenial. Indeed, a present guise is generally needed to convey things past. In oral transmission, updating is routine if no past witnesses or writings survive to gainsay it. Tiv tribesmen in Nigeria disowned genealogies British scribes had recorded for them fifty years back because they no longer accorded with the ancestry the Tiv *now* required.[255]

Besides clarifying and uplifting the past, updating bonds it to us. Like memories retrieved by analysis, history is less a record of the past than a template of present beliefs and wishes. Presentism is integral to England's Whig legacy. Long accretion proves that this heritage was 'formed with a wish to deal with Englishmen as they are', not just as they were, historian Mandell Creighton assured readers. Its potency derived from being both ancient *and* responsive to present needs. Praising the *process* of forging a usable past, the English ensured both its continuance and its openness to ongoing change.[256]

Geary shows how medieval monastic orders revised their origins and benefactions to secure their survival when founders' dynasties crumbled. Since new alliances required a

---

[252] Ernest Beaglehole, *Islands of Danger* (1944), quoted in Robert Borofsky, *Making History: Pukapukan and Anthropological Constructions of Knowledge* (Cambridge, 1987), 142–3. See Allan Hanson, 'The making of the Maori', *American Anthropologist* 91 (1989): 890–902; Bernard S. Cohn, 'Anthropology and history in the 1980s' (1981), in *A Bernard S. Cohn Omnibus* (Oxford, 2004), ch. 3.

[253] Thomas Hauschild, 'Making history in southern Italy', in Kirsten Hastrup, ed., *Other Histories* (Routledge, 1992), 29–44 at 32–6; T. Hauschild, *Power and Magic in Italy* (2002; Berghahn, 2011).

[254] Kathleen Wall quoted in Neil Genzlinger, 'Thanksgiving re-enactments, from Utah to Plymouth, Mass', *NYT*, 17 Nov. 2011.

[255] Jack Goody, 'The time of telling and the telling of time in written and oral cultures', in John Bender and David E. Wellbery, eds., *Chronotypes* (Stanford, 1991), 77–96 at 94.

[256] W. Walter Menninger, 'Memory and history: what can you believe?' *Archival Issues* 21:2 (1996): 97–106; Mandell Creighton, *The English National Character* (London, 1896), 8, 11, 14–18, 23.

Carolingian ancestry, the Camargue monastery of Montmajour, founded in 949 in memory of King Hugo of Italy, was reattributed to a fictional victory by Charlemagne.

> The memory of Hugo … meant nothing. What mattered was the counts' relationship to a new family. … The expulsion of the Saracens by Charlemagne and his subsequent support of the monastery as a burial place for his fallen warriors is the archetype for the role the new counts played. That this memory did not correspond with the 'facts' of the past is much less important than that it corresponded to the circumstances of the present.

Early chroniclers had Charlemagne attacked by Basques at Roncevaux in 778; Crusaders turned the Basques into Saracens.[257] Similarly, after Capetians ousted the French king Charles the Simple in the early tenth century, chroniclers expunged his reign's achievements, made him a figure of weakness and folly, and backdated his monastic benefactions to his grandfather Charles the Bald or updated them to his grandson Charles of Lorraine.[258] Fourteenth-century canons of eighth-century Beverley Minster fended off Archbishop Richard Neville of York by forging a charter in the name of King Aethelstan (924–39), and on the basis of this supposed royal foundation secured Richard II's support.[259]

Updating recurrently conforms New World legacies to later needs. Originally penned to confirm Pilgrim control of the new colony, the Mayflower Compact of 1620 was successively recycled as an emblem of revolutionary freedom, a *fin-de-siècle* anchor of Anglo-Saxon cohesion, a WASP genealogical bona fide, a hallmark of community self-help, and a vainglorious myth of American exceptionalism.[260] In making the past usable, noted a leading historian, Americans were especially prone to confuse 'forebears with descendants' and homogenize 'time past with time present'.[261]

Past genres now obnoxious are redefined. Feminist diktat in 1993 gave the Calvert family maxim and Maryland state motto, *Fatti maschii, parole femine* (manly deeds, womanly words) a gender-free translation: 'Strong deeds, gentle words'. Inscribed below George Grey Barnard's 1918 Abraham Lincoln statue in Manchester, England, is Lincoln's letter thanking cotton-factory workers for downing tools in support of the Union during the Civil War. Renovation in 1986 revealed an altered text on the plinth: Lincoln's 'workingmen' had become 'working people', his 'men' 'men and women' (given widespread child labour, 'children' might have been added). Manchester councillors had found Lincoln's 'sexist' language unbearably discordant with the Great Emancipator as

---

[257] Patrick J. Geary, *Phantoms of Remembrance* (Princeton, 1994), 135–46. See F. de Marin Carranrais and D. Chantelou, *L'Abbaye de Montmajour* (Marseilles, 1877).

[258] James Fentress and Chris Wickham, *Social Memory* (Blackwell, 1992), 59, 73; Geary, *Phantoms of Remembrance*, 147–53.

[259] David Woodman, 'Forging the Anglo-Saxon past: Beverley Minster in the 14th century', *British Academy Review* 17 (2011): 23–5.

[260] Mark L. Sargent, 'The conservative covenant: the rise of the Mayflower Compact in American myth', *New England Quarterly* 61 (1988): 233–51; Arthur Kroker, *Born Again Ideology* (C Theory, 2006); Newt Gingrich, *A Nation like No Other: Why American Exceptionalism Matters* (Washington, DC: Regnery, 2011).

[261] C, Vann Woodward, 'The future of the past', *AHR* 75 (1970): 711-26 at 725.

an apostle of freedom.[262] In like fashion, 'you'll be a Man, my son!' in Kipling's 'If' (1895) became 'you'll be grown up, my child!' and Bob Dylan's 'How many roads must a man walk down / Before you call him a man?' (1963) is atrociously neutered to 'How many roads must an individual walk down before you can call them an adult?'[263]

Past enjoyment of privilege distresses today's egalitarians. An early portrait of founder Elihu Yale with a dark-skinned servant kneeling at his feet was removed from Yale University's corporate boardroom because bygone elites' penchant for being painted with menials now embarrasses. 'Depictions of servants and slaves in portraits of their employers and owners', says an art historian, 'can be shocking to modern audiences'.[264] Yet today's sanitizers live with grosser inequalities, the super-rich waited on by a phalanx of invisible underlings. Forebears openly flaunted their superior status; we hide our unseemly privileges even from ourselves.

Much presentism is politically motivated. The heroic traits Margaret Thatcher saw in the sixteenth-century crew of Henry VIII's recently exhumed *Mary Rose* served as a mirror for the Falklands. 'Just as the recovery of the *Mary Rose* was presented as giving "us" something back, the Falklands war proved that "we" are . . . still capable of rallying to one flag with confidence and moral righteousness'.[265] The new American Tea Party transmutes colonial corporate settlers into egalitarian individualists, slave-owning Founding Fathers into freedom-loving abolitionists. 'Once you got [to America] we were all the same', as newly elected Representative Bachmann rewrote the American past. 'It didn't matter the colour of their skin, it didn't matter their language, it didn't matter their economic status.'[266]

Current ecological pieties masquerade as indigenous tradition. The nonpareil anachronism is Chief Seattle, whose 1854 letter to President Franklin Pierce, 'Brother Eagle, Sister Sky', is recited at many an Earth Day powwow:

The earth is our mother. I have seen a thousand rotting buffaloes on the prairies left by the white man who shot them from a passing train. What will happen when the buffalo are all slaughtered? The wild horses tamed? . . . when the secret corners of the forest are heavy with the scent of many men and the view of the ripe hills is blotted by talking wires?

But no buffalo had roamed within six hundred miles of Chief Seattle's Puget Sound home; the railroad first crossed the Plains in 1869, three years after he died; the infamous buffalo slaughter came a decade later; the prose is Pretend Indian. The letter that made Chief Seattle an ecological guru was penned in 1971 by screenwriter Ted Perry. 'The environmental awareness was based on my own feelings', Perry later admitted; he hadn't 'the slightest knowledge of Indian views on the environment'. Rueful, he termed the episode 'typical of the way we want to patronize and idealize Indians'. But for Susan

---

[262] *IHT*, 8–9 May 1993 [Maryland]; Public Monument and Sculpture Association National Recording Project, *pmsa.cch.kcl.ac.uk/MR/MR-MCR09.htm*. See my *Heritage Crusade and the Spoils of History* (Cambridge, 1998), 150.

[263] Diane Ravitch, *The Language Police* (Knopf, 2003), 175 (Bod Dylan, 'Blowin' in the Wind').

[264] John Marciari quoted in Tyler Hill, 'University to retire "racist" portrait', *Yale Daily News*, 7 Feb. 2007: 1.

[265] Patrick Wright, *On Living in an Old Country* (1985; Oxford, 2009), 148–9.

[266] Michele Bachmann, speech, Des Moines, Iowa, 21 Jan. 2011.

Jeffers, whose children's book of the speech has sold 400,000 copies, Chief Seattle incarnated the creed that 'every creature and part of the earth was sacred … Basically, I don't know what he said – but I do know that the Native American people lived this philosophy, and that's what is important'.[267] This modern virtue deserves that ancestry.

Today's rectitudes are likewise invoked to 'explain' prehistory. Native American artefacts in a Connecticut museum 'prove' that 'there never was oppression and colonization without native resistance'. The many female figurines in Shantok Indian pottery show that women were 'leaders in a movement to reject the values, desires, and laws of the [English] colonists'. Those who ascribe today's Indianist and feminist credos to early indigenes update as blatantly as Hollywood's *Last of the Mohicans* (1992) or Disney's *Pocahontas* (1995).[268] The past is made compliantly modern.

Yet like upgrading, most updating is done in the name of truth. Summoning up a past that suits us, we come to credit its actuality; our faithful adherence then attests its integrity. Into Magna Carta later generations 'read back … whatever political maxim or precedent they required', taking for granted it was in the original. An American jurist in 1845 marvelled at 'how easily men satisfy themselves that the Constitution is exactly what they wish it to be'.[269] Since then it has become an epitome of eternal verities, its authors reborn as American Moseses, its ever-updated tenets fixed on tablets of stone.

Paths to preferred pasts are potholed with heedless anachronisms. Period drama perfects the look of the past but ignores the lingo; actors in stovepipe hats and periwigs mouthing 'you know what I mean' and 'for starters'.[270] Early-music authenticity often bespeaks its modern origins. 'Recreating the music of Bach or Handel as the composer himself might have heard it' is a promise never fulfilled; instead, performers 'are actually recreating it in the high-tech, precise, pristine style that chimes with modern taste'.[271] Old Master paintings are 'restored' to a sumptuous radiance less in line with their original appearance than with expectations based on Impressionist and subsequent art. Many modern eyes, prefer a Michelangelo to look like a Matisse.[272]

[267] Ted Perry quoted in John Lichfield, *Independent on Sunday*, 26 Apr. 1992, 13; Susan Jeffers, *Brother Eagle, Sister Sky: A Message from Chief Seattle* (Dial, 1991; Puffin, 2008); Jeffers quoted in Timothy Egan, 'Mother Earth? From the film, not the Indian', *IHT*, 22 April 1992: 2. See Mary Murray, 'The little green lie', *Reader's Digest*, May 1993: 100–4; David Rothenberg, *Always the Mountains* (Georgia, 2002), 53–61.
[268] Exhibit captions, American Indian Archaeological Institute (now Institute for American Indian Studies), Washington, CT, July 1987; Russell G. Handsman, 'Material things and social relations', *Conference on New England Archaeology Newsletter* 6:2 (1987): 9–19; R. G. Handsman and T. L. Richmond, 'Confronting colonialism' (1995), in Robert W. Preucel and Stephen A. Mrozowski, eds., *Contemporary Archeology in Theory*, 2nd edn (Wiley, 2010), 445–58; Richard White, 'The last of the Mohicans', in Carnes, ed., *Past Imperfect*, 82–5. See Michael S. Nassaney, 'An epistemological enquiry into some archaeological and historical interpretations of 17th century Native American–European relations', in Stephen J. Shennan, ed., *Archaeological Approaches to Cultural Identity* (Unwin Hyman, 1989), 76–93.
[269] Anne Pallister, *Magna Carta: The Heritage of Liberty* (Clarendon Press, 1971), 62; Joseph Story to Simon Greenleaf, 16 Feb. 1845, in William W. Story, ed., *Life and Letters of Joseph Story* (Boston, 1851), 2: 514.
[270] Giles Coren, 'Wicked stovepipe hat you've got there, bruv', *Times*, 8 Jan. 2011: 26.
[271] Robert P. Morgan, 'Tradition, anxiety, and the current musical scene', in Nicholas Kenyon, ed., *Authenticity and Early Music* (Oxford, 1988), 57–82; Harry Haskell, *The Early Music Revival* (Thames & Hudson, 1988), 184.
[272] Hilary Spurling, *Matisse the Master* (Hamish Hamilton, 2005), 248, 281; Claudia Beltramo Ceppi Zevi, ed., *Matisse: La seduzione di Michelangelo* (Florence: Giunti, 2011).

Against presentist warping critics rail in vain. 'Would you like to see machine guns inserted into Uccello's "Battle of San Romano"?' carps a purist. 'Or a reference to AIDS into Shakespeare's famous sonnet about lust? Or a psychoanalyst into *Oedipus Rex*?'[273] Yet art, like other things, is ever thus updated. Chastised for playing *King Lear* with the happy ending substituted by Nahum Tate in 1681, Edmund Kean in 1826 replied that 'a large majority of the public – whom we like to please, and must please to be popular – liked Tate better than Shakespeare'. Morality sanctioned Tate's corruption: Shakespeare killed Lear and Cordelia 'without reason and without fault', but Tate rewarded their virtue, restoring Lear for his throne and giving Cordelia a wedding.[274]

Promoters cater for popular misdatings. 'Medieval' performers play Renaissance melodies on sixteenth-century shawms and regals because these later sounds and instruments fit what audiences now mistake for medieval. Adolph Zukor's 1934 film of Catherine the Great, *The Scarlet Empress*, replaced St Petersburg's elegant classical palaces with neo-Gothic monstrosities, Baroque harpsichord delicacies with lush Wagner and Tchaikovsky – what palaces and Russia conjured up in the popular mind.[275]

A 1990s BBC play showed Vita Sackville-West dining with her mother at Knole, the family seat, in 1910, 'both in full evening dress, sitting at opposite ends of a long table … Two footmen in livery and a butler in tails … stood impassively … while Vita and her mother discussed sex.' The tableau was doubly anachronistic. 'In 1910 mothers did not discuss sex with their daughters, let alone in front of the servants', objected Vita's son Nigel Nicolson; 'they would not be wearing evening dress, nor the footmen livery; they would be sitting side by side at a much smaller table'. The director was unregenerate: 'The scene needed highlighting in a way that the audience expected. It was more truthful than actuality.' Quaint period dress and manners apart, films 'make the past accessible by collapsing it into the present. … We don't get to know people in their strangeness but get rid of the strangeness by making people in the past similar to us.'[276]

Advertisers routinely modernize. An 'authentic period recipe' for Plimoth Rock Ale was 'updated for today's tastes'. Again updated, Mayflower Golden Anniversary Ale remains an 'authentic taste of American history'.[277] A 1990s 'authentic facsimile' of the 1942 *Rupert Annual* unblushingly owned that wording 'has been changed or deleted [in] line with present day sensibility'. Changes cater to the jaded as well as the squeamish; the BBC's *The Buccaneers*, based on Edith Wharton's unfinished 1938 novel, gained relevance for 1995 viewers with a rape and a homosexual encounter.[278] *Any* past seriously unlike the present is now apt to be axed.

Improvers revise past aesthetics to their own taste – classical statuary and architecture to the 'purity' of whiteness, as with Lord Duveen's scouring of the Elgin Marbles in the

[273] Benedict Nightingale, 'Changes for the worse', *Times*, 14 Apr. 1993: 19.
[274] Theatregoer quoted in Lawrence W. Levine, 'William Shakespeare and the American people' (1984), in his *The Unpredictable Past* (Oxford, 1993), 139–71 at 160–1.
[275] Carolly Erickson, 'The scarlet Empress', in Carnes, ed., *Past Imperfect*, 86–9 at 88.
[276] Nigel Nicolson, 'Upstairs, downstairs', *Spectator*, 18 Mar. 1995, 46; Rosenstone, 'Reel Joan of Arc', 69.
[277] James A Merolla, 'The toast of 1620', Attleboro, MA, *Sun Chronicle*, 6 May 2007.
[278] Jabeen Bhatti, 'How did a Wharton mini-series end up with such a happy ending?' *Current* [public TV & radio], 11 Sept. 1995.

1930s, or medieval triptychs shorn of their side panels and tops to conform with the gallery image of a 'picture'.[279] Modern taste trumps previous truth. In period interiors the formal 'stilted' line-up of chairs customary in eighteenth-century salons is rejected for casual layouts with a 'lived-in' look. Historical wallpaper is chosen to conform with today's aesthetics. 'Often, after professional research reveals the actual paper that was used in a room, the results are ignored', the paper judged 'ugly and therefore "inappropriate"'. Colonial Williamsburg restorers justified paints and fabrics brighter than colonial gentry ever had on the ground that they would surely have used such colours had they found them.[280]

'Christmas' at Conner Prairie Pioneer Settlement triggered a salient updating squabble. Since the 1930s, visitors had enjoyed 'traditional' celebrations at this Indiana replica frontier site. But in 1978, when curators learned that Christmas was little known in pioneer days, they treated it like any old winter day, featuring hog butchering. Customers were outraged 'that we actually had dropped the "true", early-American Christmas' they had come for. Falling revenue forced reversion: every December day became 'Christmas Eve' 1836, adjusting settlers to suit. A family from upstate New York was shifted eastward 'to acquire sufficient Dutch influence to have come across . . . St. Nicholas. Remaking the Presbyterian doctor's wife Episcopalian enabled 'Christmas greens to slip into their house'.[281]

Exorcizing forerunners' now dismaying foibles, we foist on them our own moral standards. Revising the past to embody their own virtues was a major Victorian enterprise. The classicist Benjamin Jowett insisted that apparent homosexuality in *Phaedrus* was actually heterosexual; had Plato 'lived in our times he would have made the transposition himself'.[282] Modernizing the Greeks while archaizing themselves, Victorians fancied the ancients as living contemporaries.[283] Whig historians transplanted into Anglo-Saxondom their own 'enthusiasm for democracy or freedom of thought or the liberal tradition'. Outdoing English medievalists who romanticized the Great Hall as a locus of classless camaraderie, *fin-de-siècle* Americans idealized the Middle Ages as a principled time of forthright candour. Revivalists dreamed of replacing present with past, but ended up conforming past to present.[284]

Presentism strews similar anachronisms throughout the American past. DuPont's radio and TV series *Cavalcade of America* (1935–57) portrayed the Pilgrim Fathers as archetypes of rugged individualism and free enterprise. Just as Indian- and wilderness-besieged Pilgrims stuck it out rather than return to England, so dust-storm- and grasshopper-besieged midwestern farmers in the 1930s remained steadfast. For American

---

[279] William St Clair, *Lord Elgin and the Marbles* 3rd edn (Oxford, 1998), 283, 289–90, 299.

[280] Catherine Lynn Frangiamore, *Wallpapers in Historic Preservation* (1977; University Press of the Pacific, 2005), 2; Daniel Boorstin, *America and the Image of Europe* (New York: Meridian, 1960), 94.

[281] Robert Ronsheim, 'Christmas at Conner Prairie', *History News* 36:12 (1981): 14–17.

[282] Benjamin Jowett, 'Introduction', *Phaedrus* (1875), in *Dialogues of Plato* (Oxford, 1892), 1: 370–95 at 380; Turner, *Greek Heritage in Victorian Britain*, 424–7.

[283] Richard Jenkyns, *The Victorians and Ancient Greece* (Blackwell, 1980), 316–17. See Turner, *Greek Heritage in Victorian Britain*, xii, 8, 229, 263, 383.

[284] Herbert Butterfield, *The Whig Interpretation of History* (London, 1931), 96; J. W. Burrow, *A Liberal Descent: Victorian Historians and the English Past* (Cambridge, 1981), 224–8; Lears, *No Place of Grace*, 149, 163.

perseverance and self-reliance were 'as necessary in 1935 as three hundred years before'.[285] The Founders' hardihood and love of liberty are traits that we, their inheritors, should live up to.[286] But these are modern merits, not those of earlier times. Beneath period veneer, faces and behaviour in historical film and fiction are likewise emphatically of our time. 'In Louis L'Amour's West', boasts the publisher of best-selling frontier romances, 'women walk beside men, not behind them'; L'Amour has given the past what readers applaud in the present, in the comforting mystique that American 'people, institutions, and structures are fundamentally the same across the centuries, and what once was true is equally true now and forever'.[287]

Stressing ancestral traits and values that accord with our own coalesces past with present. 'In the youth of a land barren of visible memorials of former times', America's first art historian, Charles Eliot Norton, aimed 'to quicken ... the sense of connection with the past and of gratitude for the efforts ... of former generations'.[288] Viewed with civic intent, the foreign country of the past becomes cosily familiar.

A common device for linking past to present is to highlight everyday familiar things. A wooden darning egg, a needle holder, a detachable pocket, and an old comb were displayed at Minute Man National Park with the legend: 'Life was a daily thing. Battles only temporary. But both went on while colonists waited out the war'. Valley Forge, Washington's 1777–8 headquarters, offers clichéd timeless values; the soldiers encamped there 'demonstrated the universal desire of the human spirit ... for freedom and self-determination'.[289] Unlike sites that reactivate bygone cherished crafts, Minute Man and Valley Forge highlight workaday legacies that comfort by continuance.

Common traits based on English descent 'preserved our national character throughout the ages', contended Eton's historian and royal tutor in 1905. 'The mediaeval, the Elizabethan, and, we hope, the modern Englishman all show the same individuality ... , the same initiative ... , the same independence ... , the same practical sagacity.'[290] Americans past and present are likewise held to face similar perils. 'People in all our communities today have serious problems, just as slaves had problems before the Civil War', asserts a schoolbook.[291] Being similarly 'serious' softens slavery from enormity to mere nuisance. Struck by the seeming 'innateness, depth, and historical rootedness of modern American problems', historians look to some timeless strain 'that has always led to these kinds of problems', and to their solutions. Tea-Party Constitution lovers contend that 'the Founding Fathers have answers to nearly every problem we have in America today'.[292] A Xerox ad entitled 'Ancient Dilemma' pictures long-lost parchments (the

---

[285] Erik Christiansen, *Channeling the Past: Politicizing History in Postwar America* (Wisconsin, 2013), 58.
[286] Jill Lepore, *The Whites of Their Eyes: The Tea Party's Revolution and the Battle over American History* (Princeton, 2010).
[287] Bantam Books ad, 1982; Christiansen, *Channeling the Past*, 223.
[288] To Thomas Carlyle, 7 May 1874, in *Letters of Charles Eliot Norton* (London, 1913), 2: 44.
[289] Lowenthal, 'Timeless past', 1267.
[290] C. H. K. Marten, 'The study of history in public schools', *Twentieth Century* 58 (1905): 583–99 at 586.
[291] Edwin Fenton, *The Americans* (American Heritage, 1970), 192.
[292] Bernard Bailyn, *On the Teaching and Writing of History* (NEUP, 1994), 41–2; Paul Taylor quoted in Krissah Thompson, 'Conservative class on Founding Fathers' answers to current woes gains popularity', *Washington Post*, 7 June 2010.

Figure 105 Domesticating classical antiquity: Lawrence Alma-Tadema, *A Favourite Custom*, 1909

Figure 106 Manipulating the medieval: British recruiting poster,
First World War (Art. IWM PST 0408)

Dead Sea Scrolls?) in an antique vase, showing that back then, just as now, people struggled to organize data.[293]

Perceived parallels enable 'people of today to make contact with people of the past', avers an American museum head. 'The stage is different, the stakes are different, but the story is that of the human condition.'[294] Deep down we are one with our forebears. Sharing ancestral desires, foibles, and strengths, our own viewpoints seem congruent with national character or human nature. A Morris dancer becomes living proof of timeless feeling: 'Our dances are what they were and what they'll always be.' The celebrant who claims that Padstow's Hobby-Horse festival 'still means the same to us as a thousand years ago' voices a common faith in continuity.[295] Linking past with present sustains hoary unbroken tradition. 'Under the watchful gaze of St Mary's Church', blurbs a local realtor, 'groundsmen lovingly tend Harrow School's cricket pitch, living figures in a scene which could have been plucked out of any decade in Harrow's history'. The monarchy is touted as enduring: it is a thrill 'to visit the home of the Queen – not that of some monarch of the distant past, as in other countries, but of the present occupant of the throne'.[296]

Resonance across a temporal gulf, like Renaissance veneration of classical learning, or Henry Adams's devotion to the Virgin of Chartres, strips away what lies between the newly revered past and the present. Identifying with imperial classical Rome, Mussolini demolished later buildings to underscore the parallel grandeur of antiquity and modern fascism – although he was not shy of excising antiquity, too, when it stood in the way of his own imperial megalomania. The present is not just the past's inheritor but its active partner, reanimating the sleeping, excavating the buried, arousing legatees to their legacies.

Scripture serves endless later uses. Biblical personae and scenes prefigured Frankish figures and events: rulers became Joshuas, battles Jerichos. The Old Testament hallowed both Pippin II and Charlemagne as 'David', Israelite heirs to royal blood; Bede compared Æthelfrith with Saul.[297] Just as Virgil had traced Rome's founders back to Troy, so the Franks made their rulers descendants of Aeneas. By the twelfth century all French nobles were Trojans; later 'scholars who denied the Trojan origins of the Franks literally lost their heads'.[298]

---

[293] Talalay, 'Past as commodity', 213.

[294] Michael J. Smith, 'Looking out and looking in' *History News* 45:6 (1990): 8.

[295] Boyes, *Imagined Village*, 44–5; 'The future of the past', Channel 4 (UK) TV, 22 June 1986.

[296] Simon Harrison, 'Back to the future: when Victorians travelled in space', *Observer*, 6 June 1993: 65; Mike Richardson, English Tourist Board, *Times*, 1 May 1993.

[297] Janet L. Nelson, 'The Lord's anointed and the people's choice: Carolingian royal ritual' (1987), in *The Frankish World: 750–900* (Hambledon, 1996), 99–132; Garrison, 'Franks as the new Israel?' 114–61; Yitzhak Hen, 'The annals of Metz and the Merovingian past', 175–90 at 178, and Mayke De Jong, 'The empire as *ecclesia*', 191–226, in Hen and Innes, eds., *Uses of the Past*.

[298] Jean Dunbabin, 'Discovering a past for the French aristocracy', in Paul Magdalino, ed., *Perception of the Past in Twelfth-Century Europe* (Hambledon, 1992), 1–14 at 3; Matthew Innes, 'Teutons or Trojans?', in Hen and Innes, eds., *Uses of the Past*, 248–9. See Marie Tanner, *The Last Descendant of Aeneas* (Yale, 1993), 107; Rosamund McKitterick, 'Political ideology in Carolingian historiography', in Hen and Innes, eds., *Uses of the Past*, 162–74 at 163, 174.

A millennium after Charlemagne, Americans termed the New World a New Israel, harnessing ideals and independence to the biblical covenant. England and George III were Egypt and the Pharaoh, the Founding Fathers ancient Hebrews. Washington, 'the American Moses', gave up domestic ease to liberate his people from servitude. His Farewell Address was a Mosaic legacy, his death, on the verge of the move to a new capitol, likened to Moses succumbing en route to Canaan.[299] The 1894 Fredericksburg, Virginia, obelisk to 'Mary the Mother of Washington' implies Christ-like congruence – not mere analogy, but identity reincarnate. The paired Jesus-and-George life histories in the stained-glass windows of the Valley Forge Memorial Chapel sacralized the analogy.[300]

Following Washington, Lincoln became 'God's chosen one ... For fifty years God rolled Abraham Lincoln through His fiery furnace', declared Lincoln's former law partner, 'making him *the noblest and loveliest character since Jesus Christ*', and like Him martyred for having cleansed His people of their sin. An Old Testament epic in New Testament garb, Steven Spielberg's 2012 *Lincoln* hews closely to self-image as 'guided by an omnipotent moral hand toward a transcendent goal ... Swept away by a great story, ... a careful analysis of the historical facts no longer seems so important, ... though we are left wondering what it means for a nation to continue remembering its own history as if that history were a Bible story'.[301]

Conflation

Imbuing the past with present-day intention and artifice homogenizes it as '*the* Past', rather than the congeries of different pasts that actually were. Whether antiquated or modernized, idealized or domesticated, the past gets set apart as an indiscriminate whole. Its multiform segments become more and more alike.

To be sure, much that is past has a natural family likeness. Things of similar material weather in roughly similar ways whatever their age; an Attic temple and the Albert Memorial decay in the same general fashion, though agency and pace differ with local pollution. Obsolescence also homogenizes; relics now functionally useless are alike anachronistic, ten years out of date or ten centuries. But above all our own intervention makes the past seem essentially one. The diversity of previous things and people is reduced to a few themes within a narrow time span or flattened into uniformity, as with the generic aura of pastness in grainy old photos.

Such conflation seems counter-intuitive; for scholarship reveals ever more remote and unlikely pasts, while technology – textual analysis, radiocarbon dating, DNA – ever more keenly discriminates age and style. Yet we tend to minimize past distinctiveness, unite former folk as alike 'old', impart the same vintage aroma to relics and memories. Revived

---

[299] Barry Schwartz, 'The character of Washington', *American Quarterly* 38 (1986): 202–22; Bruce Feiler, *America's Prophet* (HarperCollins, 2009), 73–86, 98–105, 199, 205, 243.

[300] Shelley Adair Perdue, 'The Washington Memorial Chapel' (M.Sci. thesis, University of Pennsylvania, 2005), 6–7.

[301] William Henry Herndon, in Sherwood Eddy, *The Kingdom of God and the American Dream* (Harper, 1941), 162; Ira Chernus, '"Lincoln": Jesus Christ! God Almighty!' *Huffington Post*, 28 Nov. 2012.

and surviving pasts collapse into a single realm, temporal specifics yield to a blurred continuum 'without the trivial and reachable individuality of a year attached to it', in Robert Harbison's phrase.[302] To most the specific dates of Stonehenge's construction or Pompeii's ruination are of no consequence; both just grandly convey 'the past'.

Tourist media amalgamate medieval, Renaissance, and early-modern into a single prototypical past. Hampton Court Palace and the Tower of London merge as Tudor-bethan bastions of tragic queens and bloody axes. Museums guide viewers down the centuries from BC to AD, ending up much the same to most. Nostalgic fashion hypes anything fancied from any bygone time. Retro icons from congeries of centuries – half-timbering, cut-glass pub windows, signposted castles, steam engines – betoken bygones in general.

Conforming past relics and records accentuates homogeneity. The reworked heritage acquires a studied air of coherent uniformity utterly unlike the inviolate past's discrepant nature, let alone the ramshackle detritus that unaided time bequeaths us. With 'charming and rich effects suitable to ... today's decorator taste', observed an architectural critic, 'most restored houses look as if they'd had the same decorator. They are all ... Williamsburged.'[303] Historic docents seem cloned from Galsworthy's 1960s *Forsyte Saga* or Laura Ingalls Wilder's 1970s *Little House on the Prairie* TV series. New historical sites copy older ones. Present-day demands and techniques impose a uniform gloss on refitted historical structures. Whether an old-time precinct is purportedly neolithic, medieval, or Edwardian, the visitor is apt – and expects – to see it tricked out in much the same way. Standard display and restoration practices apply today's veneer to relics of all epochs.[304]

Preservation from a single period, as at Williamsburg, makes the past decidedly unlike the present. When everything dates from one selected time and nothing from any other, the effect is peculiarly static, wholly unlike present-day scenes where new and old everywhere commingle. Temporally arrested, such displays banish the present altogether. Even temporal *mélanges* that stress change somehow feel lifelessly homogeneous. When each room in a historic house is restored to its own peak period, these stylistic epochs seem coexistent rather than successional. And the peaks of perfection all bear a family likeness, similarly capstones of achievement.

Like shopping malls, revamped old markets are purposely alike. 'Blindfold a tourist and drop him in Canal Square in Washington or Ghirardelli Square in San Francisco or Quincy Market in Boston' and he'd hardly spot the difference, for they 'use their histories as an excuse to become more and more like each other, to the reassurance of their tourist audience'. Even those that try to be different succumb to the mould; the Schoolhouse

[302] Robert Harbison, *Deliberate Regression* (Knopf, 1980), 161.

[303] Ada Louise Huxtable, 'The old lady of 29 East Fourth St.', *NYT*, 28 June 1972, 2: 22. See her *The Unreal America: Architecture and Illusion* (New York: New Press, 1997), ch. 1.

[304] Calvin Trillin, 'Thoughts brought on by prolonged exposure to exposed brick', *New Yorker*, 16 May 1977: 101–7; Richard Handler and William Saxton, 'Dyssimulation: reflexivity, narrative, and the quest for authenticity in "living history"', *Cultural Anthropology* 3 (1988): 242–60; Edward M. Bruner, 'Abraham Lincoln as authentic reproduction', *American Anthropologist* 96 (1994): 397–415 at 403–4.

Figure 107 The past as *mélange*: Disneyland, Anaheim, California

complex in Old Jerome 'precisely duplicates the appearance and merchandise' of its Ghirardelli–Quincy precursors.[305]

Remade past uniformity is far from new. In medieval French pedigrees, generation after generation of ancestors seem numbingly alike. The genealogist portrays

imagined beings whose attitudes and dress reproduce those of the masters for whom he writes, those masters who wish their mores to be the model, from the virtues they profess to the failings of which they are proud . . . These supple unfurlings then stretch back toward the present life, binding it to a reflection of what the living would wish to be.

Over several centuries 'all wear the same costume, parade in the same figures, [exhibit] the behaviour judged fitting, at the moment when this narration was written, by those who ordered its composition'.[306] The normative features of the present become imprinted on the whole length of the narrated past.

[305] Andrew Kopkind, 'Kitsch for the rich', *The Real Paper* (Cambridge, MA), 19 Feb. 1977: 22; Haas, 'Secret life of the American tourist', 22, 24. See Jeffrey S. P. Hopkins, 'West Edmonton Mall', *Canadian Geographer* 34:1 (1990): 2–17; Russell W. Belk, 'Las Vegas as farce', *Consumption, Markets, & Culture* 4:2 (2000): 101–23.

[306] Georges Duby, 'Memories with no historian' (1977), *Yale French Studies*, no. 59 (1980): 7–16 at 12, 14.

In popular recall today the Gauls come close to de Gaulle, Elizabeth I joins Elizabeth II, Salem witches and Watergate twisters tread the same American stage. Tradition conflates Hellenic culture to an all-embracing entity from Homer on. For most Americans, 'there's the present and then there's this dumpster of undifferentiated synchronic trivia called "history". Ask a kid which happened first, the Peloponnesian Wars or the Korean War – no clue.'[307] An English boy asks, 'When you were young, Mummy, was that ... the Olden Days?' To be sure, Olden Days also jumbled epochs, as with historical paintings showing Dante holding hands with Virgil, Charlemagne chatting with Napoleon, Balzac's depiction of Napoleon on a Sèvres vase next to a sphinx dedicated to Sesostris, the beginnings of creation and yesterday's events grotesquely conjoined.[308] But these implied affinity *across* epochs, not the anachronistic conflation of Stanley Kubrick's *Spartacus* (1960), dubbing in the dead and the unborn to give the film as many famous Romans as possible. In counterfactual fiction Caesar duels with Napoleon, Euclid proves Fermat's last theorem, and Columbus shares exploits with Dumas's d'Artagnan. Everything that is not present is 'past'.[309]

Public memory normally conflates in just this way. Washington gets twinned with Lincoln – the Father of his Country with its Saviour. The aloof, aristocratic Washington earlier venerated was made over into the folksy Lincolnesque icon later needed. Jean Leon Gerome Ferris's popular *The American Cincinnatus* (1919) incongruously depicts Washington as a blacksmith wearing the apron of a slave he is relieving at the forge.[310]

Thus we lump together all the past, commingling epochs with small regard to calendar or context. Few who spend a week in prehistoric Lethra at Lejre distinguish the Stone from the Iron Age, Viking times from the comic Asterix; all periods merge into one generic past. At Genesis Farm in New Jersey, Dominican nuns raise organic crops in a setting variously evocative of the First Creation, Native American husbandry, medieval pilgrimage, and New Age eco-theology. Indifferent to chronology, popular memory assigns events to generalized good old days (or bad old days) or to storytellers' 'once upon a time'. 'Living history' favours period crafts over particular events, as if one were at Bread-Baking or Barrel-Making National Historic Site.[311] Places are homogenized as cavalierly as periods. In Israel specific kibbutz histories are storyfied into a generic kibbutz saga. 'Well, it may not have happened in Ein Shemer, perhaps it was in Ein

---

[307] Mark Leyner, 'Eat at Cosmo's', *New Yorker*, 7 Mar. 1994: 100.

[308] Honoré de Balzac, *La Peau de chagrin* (1831; Penguin, 1977), 34. See Didier Maleuvre, *Museum Memories* (Stanford, 1999), 193, 277.

[309] Umberto Eco, *Six Walks in the Fictional Woods* (Harvard, 1994), 109.

[310] Kammen, *Mystic Chords of Memory*, 129; Barry Schwartz, 'Social change and collective memory: the democratization of George Washington', *American Sociological Review* 56 (1991): 221–36 at 225–7, and 'George Washington', in Barbara J. Mitnick, ed., *George Washington: American Symbol* (New York: Hudson Hills, 1999), 127–36.

[311] Colman McCarthy, 'In NJ, nuns cultivate a spiritual ecological link on Genesis Farm', *Washington Post*, 2 Oct. 1993: B6; Sarah M. Taylor, *Green Sisters: A Spiritual Ecology* (Harvard, 2007), 51, 94–9, 181–4, 198–202, 212, 227, 254–5; Cornelius Holtorf, 'The time travellers' tools of the trade: some trends at Lejre', *International Journal of Heritage Studies* 19:5 (2013): 1–16 at 5–6; Christina Cameron, 'Commemoration: a moving target?', in *The Place of History: Commemorating Canada's Past* (Ottawa: Royal Society of Canada, 1997), 27–39.

Harod', says the guide; 'but it did happen someplace, so what difference does it make?'[312] The nostalgically generalized 'Hill Valley' in *Back to the Future* (1985) could be any American 1950s small town.[313]

Two centuries after the *Mayflower* Pilgrims' landing, the town of Plymouth installed a suitable Rock on which they ought to have stepped ashore, later given a protective neo-classical canopy (Fig. 55). That the site is manifestly mythic is clear from tourist queries: 'Why doesn't the rock say "1492?"' 'Where is the sword that should be in the stone?' The nearby *Mayflower* replica, where re-enactors read from Moses (Exodus 14), reinforces Columbian and Noahite connections. 'Where are the *Nina* and the *Pinta*?' ask visitors. 'How did he get all those animals on that little boat?'[314] All the past is one, the Planting of the Promised Land merged not merely with the Discovery of America but with medieval legend and biblical lore. The Rock and the *Mayflower* stand for all beginnings, all voyages to new worlds, all paths to new ways.

Enlarged or diminished, embellished or purified, lengthened or abbreviated, the past becomes ever more alien, even though increasingly tinted in present-day colours. Despite its modern overlay, the altered past retreats from the present more rapidly than the untouched past, and suffers earlier extinction. Only continual accretion of the recent prevents the revised past from becoming totally estranged.

Our alterations homogenize reminiscences along with relics. Reshaped to present-day images, retrospections become more and more similar. Whereas an unrevised past elicits diverse reactions and explanations, a past reformed to received views curtails historical experience and reduces perspectives. Less idiosyncratically encountered, the remade past is more monolithically seen, for its guides fit us all with the same distorting lenses.

History tailored to our misconceptions becomes more and more a collective enterprise; your past resembles mine not only because we share a common heritage but also because we have changed it in concert. But this fabricated consensus is highly evanescent. History becomes outdated with increasing speed; even quite recent views of the past, available in voluminous detail on tape and film, now seem unbelievably strange. Textbooks bring the 'truth' about American history quickly up to date, but because each generation of schoolchildren reads only one such version of the past, notes Frances FitzGerald, 'that transient history is those children's history forever'.[315] A past remoulded in the image of the ever-changing present may enable a whole age group to share perspectives, but cuts them off entirely from those historical perspectives that preceded and will follow them.

Incessant revision makes our predecessors' sense of the past inaccessibly remote We lose parents' and grandparents' views of history, not to mention earlier views, not merely because time interpolates new pasts and alters what we know of older ones, but also because each new consensus outdates the structure and syntax of previous history.

---

[312] Tamar Katriel, 'Remaking place: cultural production in an Israeli pioneer settlement museum', *History & Memory* 5:2 (1993): 104–35 at 113. See T. Katriel, *Performing the Past* (Mahwah, NJ: Erlbaum, 1997).
[313] Vivian Sobchack, *Screening Space: The American Science Fiction Film* (New York: Ungar, 1987), 274; Andrew Shail and Robin Stoate, *Back to the Future* (Plagrave Macmillan, 2010), 81.
[314] John McPhee, 'Travels of the Rock', *New Yorker*, 26 Feb. 1990, 108–17. See Feiler, *America's Prophet*, 3.
[315] FitzGerald, *America Revised*, 17.

Acceptability

The past is profoundly biddable. Since few from yesteryear can answer back, it offers scope for invention too risky in the present. Take Doctorow's rejoinder to an elderly Texan who challenged his novel *Welcome to Hard Times* (1960), set in nineteenth-century Dakota Territory. "'Young man,' she wrote, "when you said that Jenks enjoyed for his dinner the roasted haunch of a prairie dog, I knew you'd never been west of the Hudson. Because the haunch of a prairie dog wouldn't fill a teaspoon." She had me. I'd never seen a prairie dog. So I did the only thing I could. I wrote back and I said, "Ma'am, that's true of prairie dogs today, but in the 19th century they were much bigger.""[316]

Alterations of the past have long been unashamedly advanced and readily welcomed.

Hellenistic Jews found no inconsistency between regarding the Scriptures as Holy Writ and rewriting them to their own taste. Some ... sought simply to explain incongruities, others to abbreviate tales, thus making them more pointed or omitting unpalatable matters. Some ... improved the behavior of their ancestors, ... portraying them in the form of epic poetry or tragic drama. ... Inventive writers added episodes to received texts, adapted pagan folktales and inserted amusing stories into the books of Ezra and Daniel.[317]

Early-modern English genealogists created pedigrees for wannabe nobles based on 'garbled records of perfectly genuine documents, ... alleged transcripts of wholly imaginary documents, ... actual forgeries expressly concocted for the purpose', and 'sheer fantastic fiction'.[318]

Those who openly deploy the past for partisan purposes, mercenary, chauvinist, or touristic, disdain historians' truth fetishes. 'It is our culture and history', say Nez Perce tribal spokesmen, 'and we do not have to prove it to anyone by footnoting'. An Iowa senator was incensed when the state historical society vetoed a bogus memorial to his bailiwick's patron. 'All they care about are the historical facts', he fumed. 'I don't care if he lived in it or not; I just want a memorial ... Just put up a plaque, say Ansel Briggs lived here, and who would know the difference?'[319]

A knowingly manipulated or adulterated past can coexist easily with unaltered relics. In historic-village compounds, old houses *in situ* nestle side by side with others brought in from far and wide, with replicas of extinct local buildings, and with generic antiquities. Even when signs and guidebooks specify which is which, visitors soon forget, if they ever note, differences between authentic and imitated, untouched and restored, fact and fabrication. 'I don't know how many times a day I hear somebody say, "Why, I never realized Henry Ford, Thomas Edison, Noah Webster and the Wright Brothers all lived in the same town"', said a Greenfield Village docent forced to admit that none of them

---

[316] Catherine O'Neill, 'Music in Doctorow's head' (1979), in Christopher D. Morris, ed., *Conversations with E. L. Doctorow* (Mississippi, 1999), 53–8 at 56.

[317] Gruen, *Heritage and Hellenism*, xix.

[318] J. Horace Round, *Family Origins and Other Studies* (Constable, 1930), 170–1.

[319] Allen P. Slickpoo, Sr., and Deward E. Walker, Jr., *Noon-Nee-Me-Poo* (Nez Perces Tribe of Idaho, 1973), viii; Senator Richard Norpel quoted in Charles Phillips, 'The politics of history', *History News* 40:9 (Sept. 1985): 16–20. Ansel Briggs was Iowa's first governor (1846–50).

had.[320] Few historic village visitors distinguish original from reconstructed buildings, and most regard them as equally authentic. In any case, the buildings all get much the same custodial and interpretive treatment owing to cost, convenience, or desire for coherence. Commingling originals with fabrications no more distresses proprietors than publics.

Films routinely pervert the past, paying 'lip service to the historical record before either ignoring or butchering it to public satisfaction'. Told there had only been six modestly attired vestal virgins, Josef von Sternberg, casting for *I, Claudius*, retorted, 'I want 60 and I want them naked!'[321] In Hollywood's breezily cavalier heyday, few knew or cared where fact ended and fiction began, like Nicholas Bentley's clerihew of Cecil B. de Mille, who 'Much against his will / Was persuaded to leave Moses / Out of *The Wars of the Roses*' (but made him a Cold War hero in *The Ten Commandments* (1956)). An adviser who disputed invented episodes in the 1970 film *Cromwell* was 'told that most people wouldn't know that such events hadn't happened, so it wouldn't matter'.[322] It would hardly have mattered had they known.

Perversions purveyed to tourists are much mocked but seldom scrapped. If Oliver Goldsmith was appalled by the lies pitchmen rattled off at Westminster Abbey's Poets' Corner, most neither crave veracity nor mind its absence. Echoing Washington Irving's indulgence of spurious Shakespeare relics at Stratford, we are 'ever willing to be deceived, where the deceit is pleasant, and costs nothing. What is it to us, whether these stories be true or false, so long as we can persuade ourselves into the belief of them?'[323] Irving himself was a practised spinner of historical yarns. They could be valued even without being believed. Jane Austen's Eleanor Tilney is 'fond of history – and am very well contented to take the false with the true ... I like embellishments as such ... If a speech be well drawn up, I read it with pleasure, by whomsoever it may be made – and probably with much greater, if the production be of Mr. [David] Hume or Mr. [William] Robertson, than if the genuine words of Caractacus, Agricola, or Alfred the Great.'[324]

Like the surrealists Magritte and Dali, fabricators of the past take pride in their concoctions. 'It is always flattering', concludes a do-it-yourself reproduction furniture ad, 'to have your own creations mistaken for originals'. Those 'tired' of their modern furniture are urged: 'Let us antique it for you. Send for our illustrated booklet showing pieces we have Chippendaled, Sheratoned, etc.'[325] The Hampshire hobbyist who built a

---

[320] Phillips, 'Greenfield's changing past', 11.

[321] Ben Macintyre, 'At last Hollywood history is no longer bunk', *Times*, 18 Jan. 2011: 21; Philip Kemp, 'Book of the week: Hollywood's ancient worlds', *Times Higher Education*, 25 Sept. 2008. Aborted in 1937, *I, Claudius* became a BBC TV series in 1976 (Brian McFarlane, 'Rome-on-the-Colne: the aborting of *I, Claudius*', in Dan North, ed., *Sights Unseen: Unfinished British Films* (Newcastle: Cambridge Scholars, 2008), 19–32).

[322] Aubrey Dillon-Malone, *Sacred Profanity: Spirituality at the Movies* (Greenwood, 2010), 18; letter, *Times*, 23 Mar. 1994: 19.

[323] Ian T. Ousby, *The Englishman's England: Taste, Travel, and the Rise of Tourism* (Cambridge, 1990), on Goldsmith (1760), 28–9, on Shakespeare frauds, 39–55; Washington Irving, 'Stratford-on-Avon' (1815), in *The Sketchbook of Geoffrey Crayon, Gent.* (London, 1822), 145–84 at 152. See Erik Cohen, 'Authenticity and commoditization in tourism', *Annals of Tourism Research* 15 (1988): 371–86 at 377, 383.

[324] Jane Austen, *Northanger Abbey* (1818; Penguin, 1995), 97–8. See William H. Galperin, *The Historical Austen* (PennPress, 2003).

[325] *Cohasset Colonials*, Hagerty catalogue, 1967; the Spring 2013 catalogue listed ten 'authentic' and five 'antiqued' reproductions.

Figure 108 Original and 'authentic': Harrow School building, by Mr Sly, 1608-15 (left), modified
by Samuel and C. R. Cockerell to conform with their matching right wing, 1820

full-scale 'Hursley railway station', complete with tarnish and soot, was delighted by an
unwitting visitor's accolade: 'Do you know, my grandfather used to work in that very
signal-box?' An autobiographer is elated by his sister's response to his invented tale about
shielding her from childhood bullies: 'I'm so glad you put that in, I'd forgotten all about
it. Now I remember it perfectly'.[326] F. Scott Fitzgerald's Gatsby gains kudos for the actual
books in his oak-panelled Gothic library, lifted from some English ruin:

'They're real . . . have pages and everything. I thought they'd be a nice durable cardboard. Matter of
fact, they're absolutely real. Pages and – Here! Lemme show you'. . . . He rushed to the bookcases
and returned with Volume One of the 'Stoddard Lectures'. 'See! . . . It's a bona fide piece of printed
matter. It fooled me. . . . What thoroughness! What realism! Knew when to stop, too – didn't cut
the pages.'[327]

Finding that revered tradition is recent invention leaves most unfazed. Rather than
disdain Geoffrey of Monmouth's *Historia Regum Britanniae* (1136) as the palpable fiction
it largely was, undeceived medieval readers mined it for their own imitative fictions.[328]
From the Donation of Constantine to the Protocols of the Elders of Zion, preconceptions
that induce fakes in the first place sustain faith in them long after their exposure. Indeed,

---

[326] Martyn Welch quoted in George Hill, 'A train not arriving at platform 2', *Times*, 25 Oct. 1990; *Modern
Railway Journal*, no. 40, 1970; Jean Little, *Little by Little: A Writer's Education* (Penguin, 1987), 103–4.
[327] F. Scott Fitzgerald, *The Great Gatsby* (1925; Scribners, 1953), 46.
[328] Monika Otter, 'Functions of fiction in historical writing', in Nancy Partner, ed., *Writing Medieval History*
(Hodder Arnold, 2005), 109–30 at 118–21.

dubious origins enhance many a tradition. Exposing 'Ossian' as James Macpherson's forgery rather than discovery did not douse but inflamed the Scottish nationalism it had ignited. Querying the authenticity of 'medieval' manuscripts found in Bohemia in 1817–18 kindled Czech chauvinism; philologist Václav Hanka gained more acclaim as their forger than when thought their finder.[329]

Similarly, Vladimir Putin gained rather than lost repute by his incredible historical find, reminiscent of the sainted Helena. The prime minister was shown on TV in August 2011 walking out of the Black Sea in wetsuit with oxygen tank on his back, as if he had gone to great depths, clutching two suspiciously moss-free ancient Greek amphorae, sought by archaeologists for decades. 'The picture had everything to make our hearts flutter with patriotic pride: a strongman defying time and human limitations.' But as with Party-line Soviet history (Chapter 10), few were actually fooled by this patent fabrication.

Thousands of Russians were smirking in recognition of the old pretending game: Putin was lying to us, we knew he was lying, he knew we knew he was lying, but he kept lying anyway, and we pretended to believe him. ... The Putin Black Sea dive was a setup. The ancient amphorae had been found during an archaeological dig and placed in six feet of water. Putin didn't need a wet suit. All he needed to do was bend down, wrap his fingers around the handles and look into the camera.[330]

Israel still deploys Masada (Chapter 9) as a prime national symbol, though literary and material evidence totally discredit the myth of first-century self-sacrifice there ('rather than be taken as slaves, 967 zealots committed suicide; only one family survived to tell the tale'). On ritual occasions, scouts gather around camp fires intoning Yitzhak Lamdan's 'Masada Shall not Fall Again', while guides read aloud the speech Josephus concocted for the last Jewish survivor. Just as the Donation of Constantine lost little potency after being shown fraudulent, fabled history leaves Masada no less gripping than if true. Visitors come not for tangible proof of the ancient legend but for a passion play of national rebirth.[331] In similar spirit, earlier tourists went to Kenilworth Castle 'not to see a place where the acts of history had really happened long ago but ... where the deeds of fancy were fictionally recurring forever'.[332]

Sites artfully contrived often serve better than those faithfully preserved. Knowing that 'authentic Old Tucson' was actually built in 1939 as the film set for *Arizona* increases rather than impairs viewers' enjoyment. A visitor to Beatrix Potter's Hilltop Farm in the Lake District exclaims, 'This is how I always imagined it!'[333] That Scotland, rather than

[329] Andrew Lass, 'Romantic documents and political monuments: the meaning-fulfillment of history in 19th-century Czech nationalism', *American Ethnologist* 15 (1988): 456–71.

[330] Elena Gorkhova, 'From Russia with lies', *IHT*, 25 Oct. 2011: 7.

[331] Zerubavel, *Recovered Roots*, 48–76, 96–144; Barry Schwartz et al., 'The recovery of Masada', *Sociological Quarterly* 27 (1986): 147–64; Neil Asher Silberman, *Between Past and Present* (Henry Holt, 1989), 87–101; Elon, 'Politics and archaeology', 34–47; Silberman and Small, *Archaeology of Israel*; Robert Paine, 'Masada', *History and Anthropology* 6 (1994): 371–409; Nachman Ben-Yehuda, *The Masada Myth* (Wisconsin, 1995).

[332] Christopher Mulvey, *Anglo-American Landscapes: A Study of Nineteenth-Century Anglo-American Travel Literature* (Cambridge, 1983), 18.

[333] Donna Morganstern and Jeff Greenberg, 'Influence of a multi-theme park ... the myth of the Old West', *Journal of Applied Social Psychology* 18 (1988): 584–96; Adrian Mellor, 'Enterprise and heritage in the

the Lake District, had inspired Peter Rabbit makes no difference; hers was the fulfilment not of fact but of fancy. Many enjoy knowledge of contrivance. Renovated relics seem superior to untouched antiquities because they *are* remade for *us*; we are comfortable with an invented past because it is partly a product of the present, of people like us – not wholly the work of strange folk of long ago, with their weird and outlandish ways.

Media-fabricated pasts seem truer because more probable. *Mutiny on the Bounty* (1935) made Charles Laughton's Captain Bligh a sadist for the sake of 'a strong, close-knit, comprehensive' portrayal; the actual story 'might have confused the issue'.[334] *Pocahontas*, a 1995 hit, got Indian consultants to endorse Disney's fictions as acceptable despite being historically wrong, for 'getting th[ings] wrong is quicker, simpler and usually makes a better story than getting them right'.[335] Eager to film Slavomir Rawicz's *The Long Walk* (1956), Peter Weir found that Rawicz was a fraud, and said 'I can't do it if it's not true'. But he did it anyway (*The Way Back*, 2010) on the ground that 'even if Rawicz didn't do the walk, someone else did'.[336] A Viking movie (*Pathfinder*, 2007) had to reckon with 'the common perception of what a Viking looked like. If people these days looked at Vikings the way they were, they'd almost be a little quaint ... A Viking horse was tiny ... We needed to ramp it up. For the impact of our film we wanted these rampaging monsters.' At least the director knew the truth before subverting it. 'I don't care about historical accuracy, but ... you have to know what it is before you decide not to do it.'[337]

Visitors thronged the Alamo when its memorial mural replaced the actual heroes with actors from the 1960 film; Davy Crockett was more recognizable as John Wayne than as himself. The *Spirit of St Louis* that Lindbergh flew across the Atlantic, enshrined at the Smithsonian in Washington, awes fewer than the plane in Dearborn's Ford Museum that Jimmy Stewart 'flew' in the movie; it was the Hollywood plane that people '*saw* crossing the ocean'.[338] When the home of Mark Twain's childhood sweetheart Laura Hawkins became 'Becky Thatcher's' house in Hannibal, Missouri, the elderly Laura co-opted her fictional identity; 'BT' is inscribed on her headstone.[339]

The Cokes, Marlboros, and Mercedes in Alex Cox's *Walker* (1987), a film about American freebooters in nineteenth-century Nicaragua, were lauded as *creative* anachronisms, stressing how present vision permeates *all* perception of past scenes.

dock', in John Corner and Sylvia Harvey, eds., *Enterprise and Heritage* (Routledge, 1991), 93–115; Shelagh Squire, 'The cultural values of literary tourism', *Annals of Tourism Research* 21 (1994): 103–20 at 114–16.

[334] Producers quoted in Greg Dening, 'Mutiny on the Bounty', in Carnes, ed., *Past Imperfect*, 98–103 at 100; see Greg Dening, *Mr Bligh's Bad Language* (Cambridge, 1992), and 'Hollywood makes history' (1993), in *Performances* (Melbourne University Press, 1996), 168–90.

[335] Feiler, *America's Prophet*, 4; Hanay Geiogamah quoted in 'Disney assailed for Pocahontas portrayal', *IHT*, 27–28 May 1995.

[336] Henry FitzHerbert, 'Peter Weir leads the way back to intelligent cinema', *Daily Express*, 26 Dec. 2010; Hugh Levinson, 'How the long walk became "The Way Back"', *BBC News*, 4 Dec. 2010.

[337] Quoted in Mark Olsen, 'How to build a Viking. A very, very big Viking', *NYT*, 7 May 2006: MT5.

[338] Wallace, *Mickey Mouse History*, 111; Garry Wills, *Reagan's America* (Doubleday, 1987), 375.

[339] James R. Curtis, 'The most famous fence in the world: fact and fiction in Mark Twain's Hannibal', *Landscape* 28:3 (1985): 8–13; William Zinsser, 'They keep mixing fact and fiction in Hannibal, Missouri', *Smithsonian* 9:7 (Oct. 1978): 155–63.

A Knight's Tale (2001) inserted anachronisms so blatant (an MTV reference; the modern fan gesture 'the Wave'; segueing from medieval recorder to modern rock with electric guitars) 'that nobody could mistake them for an actual historical reference', but would revel in erotic fun common to past and present.[340] After all, jested director Brian Helgeland in the DVD commentary, the 1370s and the 1970s were not all that different. Regardless of century, 'the seventies are always the same'. BBC's *Life on Mars* (2006–7) was laden with anachronisms intended to leave viewers uncertain whether the time-travelling protagonist was insane, in a coma, or really back in 1973.[341]

Bogus pasts are often felicitous. In 1993 six missing Haydn sonatas were unearthed – and then exposed as modern fakes. Haydn expert H. C. Robbins Landon, who had vouched for their authenticity, was unrepentant. 'It's the most brilliant fraud', he said. 'I don't mind being taken in by music this good – what Haydn would have written at this time.' The art forger Han van Meegeren is now lauded for 'pictures the old masters ought to have painted, the pictures we wish they had painted'.[342]

At Cana in 1929 a girl peddled wine jars as true relics of Christ's miracle; if Evelyn Waugh preferred smaller jars, she assured him these too were authentic. Waugh saw ignorance and cupidity. Today, the tale suggests shrewd irony. The guide who tells tourists, 'This is a piece of Noah's Ark; or maybe it's just a symbol', and 'Here is the spear that pierced Christ's side. Though maybe it's a copy, who knows?' would once have been rebuked for libelling sacred history; nowadays he is admired for deconstructing it. Leading a group of nuns in Christ's footsteps, a tour conductor says, 'This isn't the way He actually came. But it's a more interesting route'; he is not mocking but improving the Via Dolorosa.[343]

These modern guides follow the lead of Henry James's Bardolatrous 'Birthplace' curator. A Shakespeare devotee, he initially refuses to lard the fragmentary facts, thus discouraging visitors – and reducing profits. Warned to improve his pitch or lose his job, the curator veers to the opposite hyperbole:

Across that threshold He habitually passed; through those low windows, in childhood, He peered out into the world that He was to make so much happier by the gift to it of His genius; over the boards of this floor – that is over *some* of them, for we mustn't be carried away! – his little feet often pattered. ... In this old chimney corner [is] where His little stool was placed, and where, I dare say, if we could look close enough, we should find the hearth-stone scraped with His little feet.

Far from such subversion getting him sacked, visitors lap it up. 'Don't they want then *any* truth? – even for the mere look of it?' asks an appalled friend. 'The look of it', says the

---

[340] Robert A. Rosenstone, *Visions of the Past: The Challenge of Film to Our Idea of History* (Harvard, 1995), 148–9, 206–7; Rosenstone, 'Reel Joan of Arc', 68–9.
[341] James Donaghy, 'Is there life after Life on Mars?' *Guardian*, 11 Apr. 2007.
[342] Michael Beckerman, 'Classical view: all right, so maybe Haydn didn't write them. So what', *NYT*, 15 May 1994; Alex Danchev, 'Tales of a master forger', *TLS*, 30 Aug. 2006: 32.
[343] Evelyn Waugh, *Labels: A Meditrranean Journal* (Duckworth, 1930), 64; David Remnick, 'Armenia's struggle to endure', *IHT*, 13 Sept. 1988: 4; Stephen Pile, 'The past is another load of old cobblers', *Sunday Times*, 20 Mar. 1988: A13.

curator, 'is what I give!'[344] The look of it equally suffices filmgoers. 'If historical accuracy were the thing people went to the movies for', says a director, 'historians would be the vice presidents of studios'.[345]

Yet public like producers require a *semblance* of accuracy, historical films 'based on a true story'. But that story need adhere only to 'truthiness', the appearance of truth, as at Colonial Williamsburg. 'Authenticity has been virtually [our] religion', avowed Colonial Williamsburg's director in 1941; 'sacrifices have been offered before its altar. Personal preferences, architectural design, time, expense … even the demands of beauty have given way to the exacting requirements of authenticity.'[346]

Fifty years on Williamsburg staff saw that it was all wrong back then – and were confident that they were *now* getting it right. The toll-free telephone number, 1–800-HISTORY, suggests devotion to truth. Staff proudly purvey real history, as opposed to Disneyland fiction. Fearing a prospective Disney history theme park in their back yard, they were shocked to find that the public saw little difference. Panel discussants agreed that Williamsburg was authentic.

'And Disneyland?' and without a pause, every one of them said, 'Oh yes, yes, Disneyland is authentic too'. [The moderator] asked 'How can this be? We all know that Disney's America … is going to be totally made up. It isn't even a real historical site. Everything will be artificial. And you all know that Colonial Williamsburg is a real place, even if much restored.' 'Sure', they said, but … 'Disney always does things first-class, and if they set out to do American history, they'll hire the best historians money can buy … to create a completely plausible, completely believable appearance of American history.'[347]

Appearance beats truth, and historians are worthy of their hire. A trusted venue confers credibility on recognized contrivance. 'Authentic' is used seventeen times in the Disney Holy Land Experience Fact Sheet, to describe the shrunken Damascus Gate, the 25-foot model of Jerusalem in AD 66, and the North London Jewish Renaissance Temple.[348]

But not all venues are trusted to be truthful, or even truthy. The pasts reimagined at Las Vegas are not meant to be taken seriously; souped-up or parodic extravaganzas invite laughter. Consider the contrast between the Hotel Luxor's Egyptiana and Cairo's Egyptian Museum. In Cairo 'authenticity is unquestioned, … reverent decorum' enjoined, whereas the Luxor's 'patent falsity' playfully 'combine[d] extravagant spectacle and comic farce'. The Luxor's Egyptologist aimed 'not so much to assure authenticity as to assure that the hieroglyphics displayed throughout the hotel' were meaningless, hence inoffensive. As all over Las Vegas, 'farcical architecture and spectacles encourage[d] a playful

[344] Henry James, 'The Birthplace', in *Complete Tales* (Scribners, 1908–9), 11: 403–65; Andrea Zemgulys, 'Henry James in a Victorian crowd: "The Birthplace" in context', *Henry James Review* 29:3 (2008): 245–56. See Julia Thomas, *Shakespeare's Shrine* (PennPress, 2012), 104–6.
[345] Eric Foner and John Sayles, 'A conversation', in Carnes, *Past Imperfect*, 11–29 at 22.
[346] Kenneth Chorley (1941) quoted in Kammen, *Mystic Chords of Memory*, 373n.
[347] Sheldon Hackney, 'Who owns history? Conversations with William Styron and Cary Carson', *Humanities* 16:1 (Jan.–Feb. 1995): 8–11, 50–3 at 9.
[348] Annabel Jane Wharton, *Selling Jerusalem: Relics, Replicas, Theme Parks* (Chicago, 2006), 191–5; Tanya Gold, 'The Holy Land Experience: Florida's Christian theme park', *Guardian*, 23 Dec. 2011.

mood of irreverent disregard'.[349] The Luxor's aim was reminiscent of old-time kitsch – the wax mannequins, schlocky souvenirs, and crude jokes that cocked a snook, clearly distinguishing the lived past from its representation, never trying to fool the visitor into believing it was real. The vacationing audience still 'wants fun, wants nostalgia and sentiment. It does not want significant discomfort or images and text that challenge its notions of the past.'[350]

A shift of venue can sanctify what was previously fake, however kitschy. A British Museum exhibition on fakes juxtaposed pairs of objects – paintings, sculpture, ceramics, manuscripts – the authentic and the fraudulent side by side. Awed by the sumptuous precinct and display, audiences viewed the false and the true with equal veneration; the museum aura dispelled any frisson of pleasure in seeing experts fooled.[351] So too in Las Vegas. Most of the Luxor's Egyptiana – wacky hieroglyphics, talking camels, 'Nile' boat ride around the casino – was dismantled in 2008 (though the ten-storey Sphinx still guards valet parking). Donated with the rest of the replicas to the Las Vegas Natural History Museum, 'King Tut's sarcophagus is no longer just a fake Egyptian artifact, it's now a *real* artifact from a pyramid-shaped Las Vegas casino' offering 'hands-on mummy rendering technology [with] real-life medical images'.[352]

Salutary deceit was the *raison d'être* of the 1987 London hit *Lettice and Lovage*. Peter Shaffer's eponymous tour guide thrills historic-house visitors with flights of fancy that bring 'Fustian Hall' to life as bald facts failed to do. 'Enlarge – enliven – enlighten' is her maxim; 'fantasy floods in where fact leaves a vacuum'. Such tales not only delight in heritage hype, they suggest a *need* for fantasy. Hungry for false facts, we bring to the most improbable past an 'immense assumption of veracities and sanctities, of the general soundness of the legend', noted Henry James.[353] Like Washington Irving at Stratford, we swallow the reliquary shell's 'preposterous stuffing' almost whole.

But not *quite* whole, for we know we are being fed this past by partisans. As playwright Alan Bennett says, 'Scepticism about one's heritage [is an] essential part of that heritage.' Yet legend, even if deceptive, remains salutary. When the historian Nell Irvin Painter found that her revisionist portrait of the ex-slave abolitionist Sojourner Truth distressed her admirers, she conceded that 'the symbol of Sojourner Truth is stronger and more essential in our culture' than the complex history. 'The symbol we require in our public life still triumphs over scholarship'. Heritage trumps history.[354]

While altering and enlarging earlier legacies, we never wholly supplant them. Doctor-ow's prairie dog remains a recognizable prairie dog. New-minted memories coexist with

---

[349] Richard Wolkomir, 'Las Vegas meets la-la land', *Smithsonian* 26:7 (Oct. 1995): 50–9; Belk, 'Las Vegas as farce'.

[350] Scott Magelssen, 'In search of kitsch at U.S. living history museums', *InterCulture* 3:3 (Fall 2006), online.

[351] Mark Jones, ed., *Fake? The Art of Deception* (British Museum Press, 1990).

[352] 'Luxor gutted, treasures to museum', *RoadsideAmericana.com*, 30 June 2008. The museum veers from authenticity to farce: 'its replicas are … authorized by the Egyptian Ministry of Antiquities', but its 'Pharaoh's Tomb' maze features Boris Karloff's classic 1932 horror film *The Mummy* (lvnhm.org/).

[353] Peter Shaffer, *Lettice and Lovage* (André Deutsch, 1988), 25; James, 'Birthplace', 422–5, 442–3.

[354] Alan Bennett, *Writing Home* (Faber & Faber, 1994), 211; Nell Irvin Painter, *Sojourner Truth* (Norton, 1996), 287; Gordon S. Wood, 'No thanks for the memories', *NYRB*, 13 Jan. 2011: 40–2.

inherited ones; the present retains as well as reconstructs the past. Though Washington and Lincoln become radically transformed in the public eye, they are not mistaken for each other or for other men; their identities survive the conversions.[355] We sustain traditional perspectives notwithstanding each generation's rift with the previous.

We conflate as we create, keeping menacing breaches at bay by making the new seem old and the old feel new. History thus transformed merges intention with performance, ideal with actuality. Acting out a fantasy our own time denies us, we convert the past into an epoch much like the present – except that it does not constrain us with daily demands. The present cannot be moulded to such desires, for we share it with others; the past is malleable because its inhabitants – denizens for whom it was their present – are no longer here to contest our manipulations.

Yet, I suggest in the Epilogue, as creatures and creators of the past, we moderns remain responsible for what we inherit, inhabit, and inaugurate.

---

[355] Schwartz, 'Democratization of George Washington', 222, 232–4; Barry Schwartz, *Abraham Lincoln and the Forge of National Memory* (Chicago, 2000), 56, 87, 138–40, 169, 232–5, 304.

Epilogue: the past in the present

> We live in the age of speed, immediacy, and the instantaneous. The value of a bit of information is measured not in terms of its reliability but in terms of its rapidity ... The very notion of duration appears to have become unbearable. Thus, the past seems to slip away, which in turn provokes the desire to bring it back into the present.
>
> Henry Rousso, 1998[1]

> The life of the past, persisting in us, is the business of every thinking man and woman ... A lifetime's study will not make accessible to us more than a fragment of our own ancestral past, let alone the aeons before our race was formed. But that fragment we must thoroughly possess and hand on.
>
> A. S. Byatt, 1990[2]

How is the past now seen? By what means and media is it accessed? Is it prized more or less than previously? Is it better or less well understood, clearer or more opaque? Is it more treasured or trashed, venerated or violated? Are the revisions that alter it felt desirable or deplorable? What has been expunged or invented, and why?

To generalize about global attitudes invites incredulity. If nothing else, this book has shown the overwhelming diversity of responses to what has happened, to what is inherited, to remnants and memories championed or cherished, regretted or resented.[3] Indeed, the very facts of the past seem less and less consensual. 'Not just polarized opinion but polarized knowledge' spawns 'wildly divergent accounts of the past', observes a historian. 'I have my past, and you have yours, and never the twain shall meet.'

'Never look back', advised an ageing baseball star, asked the secret of his durability; 'something might be gaining on you'.[4] For looking back while fleeing Sodom, Lot's wife was turned into a pillar of salt; Orpheus left Hades deprived of Eurydice. But despite such dire portents, few resist the temptation to look back, whether homeward- or hitherto-bound. Our cumulative backward glances disclose countless pasts. Some are crippling or soul-destroying, as when Oedipus learned his parentage. Others are joyous or enlightening, as for mystic Thomas de Quincey and historian Jules Michelet. Much retrospection is obligatory – essential in facing the future. 'People will not look forward to posterity', counselled Edmund Burke, 'who never look backward to their ancestors'.[5]

---

[1] Henry Rousso, *The Haunting Past* (1998; PennPress, 2002), 16.
[2] A. S. Byatt, *Possession* (Random House, 1990), 116.
[3] Erik Christiansen, *Channeling the Past* (Wisconsin, 2013).
[4] Mark Ribowsky, *Don't Look Back: Satchel Paige in the Shadows of Baseball* (Simon & Schuster, 1994), 11, 18, 302. 'Never look back / At that Devil behind you / Never look back / Or the Devil may catch you' (Howard Scott Pearlman, 'Never look back' 2003).
[5] Edmund Burke, *Reflections on the Revolution in France* (1790; Yale, 2003), 47–8.

Outlooks on the past are as multiform as Renato Rosaldo's metaphorical takes on history:

It makes a great deal of difference ... whether one speaks about history as a river running slowly to the sea or as the fierce gales of change, an irretrievably lost moment, a seed grown into a blossoming flower, the good old days, an ugly duckling become a swan, a green betel quid chewed into red saliva, a walk along the path of life, or an oscillation between the focus of inward movement and the diffusion of outward dispersal ... attitudes as distinctive as soulful nostalgia versus equally deep indifference, and conceptions as divergent as cyclic repetition versus linear change for the better or the worse.[6]

The foreign country of the past here revisited now seems to me more and more domesticated. This seeming paradox reflects two concurrently pervasive – and strikingly contradictory – perspectives. One is to be engrossed by the past, the other to dispense with it.

The omnipresent past

Many take refuge in the past as an antidote to present disappointments and future fears. They hark back to the fancied benefits, even to the fearsome burdens, of times of lost purity and simplicity, lapsed immediacy and certitude, in some Golden Age of classical serenity, Christian faith, pastoral plenitude, or childhood innocence. Sojourning in or sifting through the past solaces the malaise of the present.[7] 'Scrapbooking', a craze of consummate devotion to family history, has become a lucrative industry. Creativememories.com serves popular fixation with voyeuristic navel-gazing. Today's children seem destined to be swamped by their pasts. 'My kid', says a mother who devotes hundreds of hours to her albums, 'already at age 5 has 10 times as much information about her life' than she herself had. Of American children under two, 92 per cent had an online presence in 2010, one in four while still in the womb. 'For the generation that begat reality television ... not a tale from the crib (no matter how mundane or scatological) is unworthy of narration.'[8]

Yet scrapbooks are already said to be 'things of the past, relics of an era before the smartphone'. Mementoes are now increasingly scattered among various apps.[9] Digital archivists promise a past 'malleable with a new viscosity' and 'rich interiority', hence 'much more, and in many more ways, present in our lives'. We deposit so many traces that we can recover virtually our entire personal life. An Internet expert delights in vastly elaborated 'access to my fleeting thoughts of previous years'. It is now 'so easy to leave and to assemble traces, that we are developing a kind of universal prosthetic

---

[6] Renato Rosaldo, *Ilongot Headhunting 1883–1974* (Stanford, 1980), 54–5.

[7] 'Sins of the fathers', *Times* leader, 5 Jan. 2003.

[8] Ginia Bellafante, 'Trafficking in memories (for fun and profit)', *NYT*, 27 Jan. 2005: D: 1, 8; Kate Burt, 'Fancy a scrap? Then join the club', *Times*, 1 July 2005: T2: 6–7; AVG Security study, 'Digital birth: welcome to the online world', *businesswire.com*, 6 Oct. 2010; David Hochman, 'Mommy (and me)', *NYT*, 30 Jan. 2005: 9: 1, 6. See Stephanie R. Medley-Rath, 'Scrapworthy Lives', PhD dissertation, Georgia State University, 2010; *obsessedwithscrapbooking.com*.

[9] Jenna Wortham, 'Outsource your memory, with an app', *NYT*, 18 Sept. 2013, and 'Life as an instant replay, over and over again', *NYT*, 21 Sept. 2013.

memory'. As with Tristram Shandy, obsessive self-tracking risks mattering more, and taking longer, than the activities being recorded.[10]

Moreover, such memory is mired in self-referential trivia. 'Recording absolutely everything that ever happens to you' gives computer scientist Gordon Bell a 'tremendous feeling of freedom – and of security. By having everything in e-memory you don't have to remember any more.' But he admits that most of the moments he records are 'mind-numbingly dull, trite, predictable, tedious and prosaic'.[11]

Far from enhancing knowledge, this avalanche of raw data imperils it. It forces us to spend ever more time with 'information as garbage, information divorced from purpose and even meaning' – not just 'more statements about the world than we have ever had', but 'more *erroneous* statements than we have ever had'.[12] Bereft of cataloguing aids, Internet users cannot evaluate the glut they face and, worse still, have no idea what may be missing. Unstructured data 'is a growing tumour that will kill enterprises', warns a software expert. 'The cost of storing and managing it eats up the entire IT budget. Companies are being choked by floods of data.'[13] The Internet user is Stanislaw Lem's robot, devouring 'the sizes of bedroom slippers available on the continent of Cob, ... six ways to cook cream of wheat ... and the names of all citizens of Foofaraw Junction beginning with the letter M'. At last he cries 'enough', but 'information had so swathed and swaddled him in its three hundred thousand tangled paper miles, that he couldn't move and had to read on' and on and on, suffocated in nonsense. The crush of fatuous Internet fodder – the latest in the lives of the reality TV Kardashian family, the brouhaha over Lupita Nyong'o's stolen $150,000 dress for the Oscar awards – inundates social media junkies.[14]

Glut makes the collective built heritage similarly pervasive. Critics hold it crushingly voluminous, backward looking, crippling present enterprise. Fifty years ago a famed modernist condemned 'the load of obsolete buildings that Europe is humping along on its shoulders [as] a bigger drag on the live culture of our continent than obsolete nationalisms or obsolete moral codes'.[15] The load is now heavier. In much of England one feels hardly ever out of sight of a listed building, a protected archaeological site, a museumized work of art. 'There is now no place in the country without a heritage of some kind or other', complains an architectural historian, 'and, worse, no heritage which is beyond keeping', all alike promiscuously precious. So toxic by 1997 was the word heritage that the Department of National Heritage was renamed Culture, Media and

---

[10] Geoffrey C. Bowker, 'The past and the Internet', in Joe Karaganis, ed., *Structures of Participation in Digital Culture* (New York: Social Science Research Council, 2007), 20-37 at 24. See Mary Carless, 'Keeping track', *New Scientist*, 25 Aug. 2012: 32.

[11] Quoted in Alun Anderson, 'Dear diary, who am I really?' *New Scientist*, 1 Jan. 2012: 36. On the risks of having 'all our past activities ... always present', see Viktor Mayer-Schönberger, *Delete: The Virtue of Forgetting in the Digital Age* (Princeton, 2009), 5.

[12] Neil Postman, *Building a Bridge to the Eighteenth Century* (Knopf, 1999), 89–92.

[13] Phil Tee, 'Useless information', *Times*, 29 June 2005: BusIntellSupp.

[14] Stanislaw Lem, *The Cyberiad* (1967; New York: Harvest, 1985), 157–9; Laura M. Holson, 'Far from the madding crowd (and its memes)', *NYT*, 29 Mar. 2015: 11.

[15] Reyner Banham, 'The embalmed city', *New Statesman*, 12 Apr. 1963: 528–30.

Sport. Prime Minister Tony Blair's minders kept him sedulously out of sight of antiquities, lest any taint of elite tradition tarnish New Labour as old hat.[16]

The treasured past is said to overwhelm French culture and politics. 'Everything is
indiscriminately conserved and archived', notes a historian of the patrimony. 'We no
longer make history', charges the philosopher Jean Baudrillard. 'We protect it like an
endangered masterpiece.'[17] The Dutch architect Rem Koolhaas calls preservation a
'dangerous epidemic' spread by 'clueless preservationists who, in their zeal to protect
the world's architectural legacies, end up debasing them', gentrifying and sanitizing
historic urban centres. Noting that UNESCO and similar bodies sequester one-sixth of
the earth's surface, with more to come, he terms heritage a 'metastasizing cancer'.[18]

Heritage is commonly faulted as socially regressive, created for Ozymandian self-
aggrandizement. The world's most imposing monuments were built in a bad cause: the
pyramids reek of incest and slavery, the Arch of Titus of imperial arrogance, Versailles of
absolutism, Georgian London's civic splendours of Caribbean slave labour. So too with
sacred texts: the Old Testament and the Koran were born of tribal blood lust and misogyny.

The global legacy's regressive nature is satirized in a salute to 'the most colossal and
enduring of mankind's creations – the Gap between the Rich and the Poor'.

Of all the epic structures the human race has devised, none is more staggering or imposing. . . . And
thanks to careful maintenance through the ages, this massive relic survives intact ... The vast
chasm of wealth, which stretches across most of the inhabited world, [is] by far the largest man-
made structure on Earth. 'The original Seven Wonders of the World pale in comparison to this,'
said a World Heritage Committee member. 'It is an astounding feat of human engineering that
eclipses the Great Wall of China, the Pyramids of Giza, and perhaps even the Great Racial
Divide.' ... Untold millions of slaves and serfs toiled their whole lives to complete the gap. . . .
Its official recognition as the Eighth Wonder of the World marks the culmination of a dramatic
turnaround from just 50 years ago, when popular movements called for the gap's closure. However,
owing to a small group of dedicated politicians and industry leaders, vigorous preservation efforts
were begun around 1980 to restore – and greatly expand – the age-old structure. 'It's breathtaking,'
said Goldman Sachs CEO Lloyd Blankfein, a long-time champion and benefactor of the rift's
conservation. 'There's no greater privilege than watching it grow bigger and bigger each day.'[19]

The eviscerated past

The popular alternative to wallowing in the past is to dismiss it entirely. The past has
ever-diminishing salience for lives driven by today's feverish demands. The sensory-

---

[16] Chris Miele, 'Conservation and the enemies of progress?' in his, ed., *From William Morris* (Yale, 2005),
1–29 at 3, 7; Mark Fisher, 'Objections to the object', *TLS*, 22 Mar. 2002: 13–14.

[17] François Hartog, 'Time and history', *Museum International* 57/227 (2005): 7–18; Marc Guillaume,
interview, '*La politique du patrimoine* [Paris: Galilée, 1980] ... vingt ans après', *Labyrinthe*, no. 7 (2000):
11–20; Jean Baudrillard, 'The illusion of the end' (1992), in *Selected Writings*, 2nd edn (Polity, 2001), 254–
65 at 261.

[18] OMA/AMO, 'Venice Biennale 2010: Cronocaos' (*oma.eu/projects*); Teresa Stoppani, 'Altered states of
preservation', *Future Anterior* 8:1 (Summer 2011): 96–109 at 101–6.

[19] 'Gap between rich and poor named 8th wonder of the world', *Onion*, 47-04, 24 Jan. 2011.

laden thrill of the moment in computer gaming, coupled with the rise of attention-deficit hyperactivity disorder, betoken a here-and-now environment dominated by raw sensations, in which 'we live perpetually in the present', suggests an authority on the brain.[20] Being up-to-date now not only matters most, it is *all* that matters; knowing or understanding the past is an impediment in the present rat-race.

The dwindling of history was already clear in the rapidly modernizing 1960s, when the past seemed of 'very limited use', and history a burden hampering renewal.[21] In the 1990s Eric Hobsbawm noted an alarming loss of familiarity with bygone times:

> For historians of my generation and background, the past['s] public events are part of the texture of our lives. ... The destruction of ... the social mechanisms that link one's contemporary experiences to that of earlier generations, is one of the most characteristic and eerie phenomena of the late twentieth century. Most ... grow up in a sort of perpetual present lacking any organic relation to the public past of the times they live in.[22]

American high-school history students surveyed in the 1990s shared 'no common ground, no common stories, no common knowledge; fewer than one in four could come up with a single event from the wider past that affected them'. Their 'overriding motive for going to the past [was] to find out where they came from', and they defined their 'personal identity only by their own psyche and lineage, excluding the Depression and the shtetl and the potato famine'.[23] In this they echoed television's 'inveterate tendency towards person-alizing all' history. And because *'television is the principal means by which most people learn about history'*, the remembered past is in considerable part what television has chosen to recall and represent. Just as it foregrounds personal remembrance, the media selects and shapes public memory.[24] As John Lukacs concluded a generation ago, history had entered the American blood but had little place in the American mind. Nor had it in other minds. Family history, not local, national, or global history, excited interest among fourteen- to eighteen-year-olds surveyed in Britain and the Netherlands. Asked 'What's the most important thing that's happened in the last thirty years?' young visitors to the Stockholm Historical Museum overwhelmingly responded, 'I was born!'[25]

For kids in school today, the Holocaust ranks alongside the Massacre of Glencoe and the Pilgrimage of Grace, and that bloke who got an arrow in his eye and let in William the Conqueror.

---

[20] Susan Greenfield, 'Are video games taking away our identities?' *Times*, 5 Nov. 2011: 30, quoting her *You and Me: The Neuroscience of Identity* (Notting Hill, 2011).

[21] Linda Symcox and Arie Wilschut, eds., *National History Standards* (Charlotte, NC: Information Age, 2007), 1–11 at 2.

[22] E. J. Hobsbawm, *The Age of Extremes: The Short Twentieth Century* (Michael Joseph, 1994), 3–4.

[23] Michael Zuckerman, 'The presence of the present, the end of history', *Public Historian* 22:1 (2000): 19–22, review of Roy Rosenzweig and David Thelen, *The Presence of the Past: Popular Uses of History in American Life* (Columbia, 1998), 12, 31, 111, 113, 129, 191, 210.

[24] Gary R. Edgerton, 'Television as historian: a different kind of history altogether', in Edgerton and Peter C. Rollins, eds., *Television Histories* (Kentucky, 2001), 1–16 at 1–2; Barbie Zelizer, *Covering the Body* (Chicago, 1992), 214.

[25] John Lukacs, 'Obsolete historians', *Harper's Magazine* 261 (Nov. 1980): 80–4 at 82; Maria Grever et al., 'Identity and school history: the perspective of young people from the Netherlands and England', *British Journal of Educational Studies* 56 (2008): 76–94 at 85, 91. Stockholm museum survey, Sept. 2012.

None of these things has anything to do with us, because they happened a long time ago, and things that have happened a long time ago are 'History', and the most obvious thing about History is that it is over.[26]

Not only schoolchildren disown the 'distant' past. Reviewing this book's precursor, the historian Peter Laslett contended that unlike me, an American, he was 'quite unconscious' of his British past. 'Nothing whatsoever in my present life depends upon' who won the Civil War. 'Magna Carta means even less to me ... The Norman Conquest took place so long ago that it can't possibly count in my experience.'[27]

In today's digital age, 'the intellectual legacy of the past' has little relevance in schooling notes a sociologist. Hence the 'growing tendency to flatter children ... that their values are more enlightened than those of their elders because they are more tuned in to the present' than to the outdated and irrelevant past.[28] Scholars – geologists and geneticists, archaeologists and historians – know more and more about manifold pasts, but broad historical expertise is increasingly rare. 'It is sometimes assumed that people in the twenty-first century know more than the benighted people of the seventeenth century, but in many ways the opposite is true', concludes Gordon Campbell, instancing the committee that produced the King James Bible four centuries ago. We 'live in a world with more knowledge, but it is populated by people with less knowledge.' With a thousand-fold as many 'educated' today, 'it would be difficult now to bring together a group of more than fifty scholars with the range of languages and knowledge of other disciplines that characterised the KJV translators'. The King James Version preface affirms 'that the Syrian [Syriac] translation of the New Testament is in most learned men's libraries ... and the Psalter in Arabic is with many', hardly the case with any equivalents today.[29] 'Great scholars are now as little nourished by the past', charged C. S. Lewis, 'as the most ignorant mechanic who holds that "history is bunk"'.[30]

Still less is the past known by the quasi-educated public, bereft of an enduring social framework grounded in shared cultural references. To be sure, historical illiteracy is lamented by every passing generation. American students today are termed 'woefully ignorant', lacking 'even a basic knowledge of American history'. But 'a century of history testing' provides no evidence for '*growing* historical ignorance', concludes Sam Wineburg. 'The only thing growing seems to be our amnesia of past ignorance.'[31] Pundits who bemoan British students' lack of history are likewise unaware of the 'wide range of ignorance' among 1950s teenagers 'for that long time before they were born'.[32]

What is new is *admiration* of ignorance. 'Idiocy is our new national goal', a former poet laureate concludes of American notions of the past. 'It took years of indifference and stupidity to make us as ignorant as we are today ... In the past, if someone knew

---

[26] Bernard Levin, 'Compounding the evil', *Times*, 25 June 1993: 16.
[27] Peter Laslett, 'The way we think we were', *Washington Post*, 30 Mar. 1986: Book World: 5.
[28] Frank Furedi, 'Let's give children the "store of human knowledge"', *spiked.online.com*, 18 Nov. 2009.
[29] Gordon Campbell, *The Bible: The Story of the King James Version 1611–2011* (Oxford, 2011), 55.
[30] C. S. Lewis, *The Screwtape Letters* (1942; HarperCollins, 2009), 151.
[31] Samuel S. Wineburg, 'Crazy for history', *Journal of American History* 90:4 (Mar. 2004): 1401–14 at 1404–6.
[32] *Times Educational Supplement*, 21 July 1950.

nothing and talked nonsense, no one paid any attention ... Now such people are courted and flattered.'[33] In some previous epochs oblivion was accounted a blessing. To heal Civil War wounds, seventeenth-century English parliaments enacted Acts of Oblivion; Alexander Pope's *Dunciad* (1728) mocked what some thought an enlightened age; French Revolutionaries strove to expunge all memory of the past; pioneers exhorted Americans never to look back. Today the past is not shrugged off or deemed valueless. Only *knowledge* of the past is eschewed, while empathetic feeling is exalted. For that, being ill-informed, even uninformed, is a positive aid.

Like ignorance, the fading away of familiar terms of historical discourse is a complaint recurrently voiced and, perhaps, unavoidable. For consensual knowledge of the past dwindles in inverse proportion to how much is known *in toto*. In oral societies history is meagre and sometimes hoarded as secret, yet most knowledge of the past is widely shared. In literate societies texts are widely disseminated, but most knowledge of the past is confined to a few specialists, the shared past shrunk to a thin veneer. 'The mere size of the literate repertoire means that the proportion of the whole which any one individual knows must be infinitesimal', concluded Jack Goody and Ian Watt fifty years ago. 'Literate society, merely by having no system of elimination ... prevents the individual from participating fully in the total cultural tradition.'[34] But today's media, notably television, lend the charge new cogency. 'The more "collective" the medium', concludes an historian, the less its take on the past will reflect or consolidate its vast and heterogeneous audience's collective memory. Consequently, the monuments, books, and films that best convey collective memory 'can quickly pass into oblivion without shaping the historical imagination of any individuals or social groups'.[35] Indeed, research shows that once memorable people, events, and idioms ebb ever sooner into oblivion.[36]

A confrontation in Paris left the erudite Alethea Hayter fearful that historical consciousness would soon 'be not merely eclipsed but extinguished'. An Anglophone visitor at Sainte Chapelle asked her what the place was about.

'Well, it was built by Saint Louis ...' 'Saint Louis?' was her puzzled reply ... 'Yes, it was built by a king of France who went on a crusade ...' 'Crusade?' she asked, bewildered. Despairingly I persevered. 'Yes, he went on a journey to the Mediterranean, and brought back a sacred relic, the Crown of Thorns ...' 'Crown of Thorns?' she queried, still more at sea. At that point I gave up; I felt unable to insert any idea of the significance of the Sainte Chapelle into a mind which had been given no context of European history or Christian belief at all.[37]

Hayter's experience is far from unique. In 1947 Dorothy L. Sayers undertook to translate the *Divine Comedy*, in order to make Dante intelligible to a 'public which knows no

---

[33] Charles Simic, 'Age of ignorance', *NYRB* blog, 20 Mar. 2012.

[34] Jack Goody and Ian Watt, 'The consequences of literacy' (1963), in Jack Goody, ed., *Literacy in Traditional Societies* (Cambridge, 1968), 27–68 at, 57.

[35] Wulf Kansteiner, 'Finding meaning in memory: a methodological critique of collective memory studies', *History & Theory* 41 (2002): 179–97 at 192–3.

[36] Jean-Baptiste Michel et al., 'Quantitative analysis of culture using millions of digitized books', *Science* 331: 6014 (14 Jan. 2011): 176–82. See my 'Archival perils', *Archives* 31 (2006) 49–75.

[37] Alethea Hayter, 'The rise and fall of Clio', *Spectator*, 18 July 1998: 38.

History, no Classics, no Theology and has almost forgotten its Bible'. Two-thirds of a century later, public awareness of *The Divine Comedy* is largely confined to scores of rock bands, video games, restaurants, and hot sauces and Dan Brown's *Inferno*.[38]

Because 'our entire collective subjective history . . . is encoded in print', a literary critic suggests that the shift from print to electronic data 'has rendered a vast part of our cultural heritage utterly alien'.[39] Finding that 'hardly a day goes by when I don't make an allusion (Greta Garbo, Proust's madeleine) that prompts my [Princeton] students to stare at me as if I just dropped in from the Paleozoic era', a 49-year-old teacher senses, beyond generational disconnect, a 'Balkanization of experience'.

In a wired world with hundreds of television channels, countless byways in cyberspace, and . . . technological advances that permit each of us to customize his or her diet, . . . everyone's on a different page. With so very much to choose from, a person can stick to one or two preferred micro-genres and subsist entirely on them, while other people gorge on a completely different set of ingredients.

As the personal niche supplants the cultural sphere, common points of reference dwindle.[40]

Jettisoned with once familiar modes of apprehension is the very fabric of the past. While the range of historical scrutiny expands to include folk and aspects of life hitherto little known, we have lost the ready familiarity with the classical and biblical heritage that long imprinted European culture and environment. The breach with that legacy leaves us surrounded by monuments and relics we can barely comprehend and scarcely feel are ours. The rage to preserve is in part a reaction to anxieties generated by modernist amnesia. We preserve because the pace of change and development has attenuated a legacy integral to our identity and well-being. But we also preserve, I suggest, because we are no longer intimate enough with that legacy to rework it creatively. We admire its relics, but they seldom inspire our own acts and works. Past remains survive not to educate or emulate but only to be saved. Precisely because preservation has become a prime end in itself, it tends to preclude other uses of the past. Thus Proust's Vinteuil forgoes imposing on a precious friendship, 'so as to have the wholly Platonic satisfaction of preserving it'.[41]

'Not to know what happened before one was born is always to be a child', warned Cicero.[42] Yet for most teenagers, notes an English educator, 'the past that antedates their own lived experiences . . . is "dead and gone" and therefore irrelevant . . . They assume the past to be a "foreign country" . . . disconnected from their own country, the present.'

---

[38] Dorothy L. Sayers to the Dean of Chichester, quoted in *TLS*, 17 Dec. 1999: 12–13. Her translation (London: Penguin): *Hell*, 1949; *Purgatory*, 1955; *Paradise*, 1962. Dante today: Citings & sightings of Dante's works in popular culture, *learn.bowdoin.edu/italian/dante*.

[39] Sven Birkerts, *The Gutenberg Elegies* (1994; Faber, 2006), 19–20.

[40] Frank Bruni, 'The water cooler runs dry', *NYT*, 8 April 2014: A21.

[41] Graham Fairclough, 'Conservation and the British', in John Schofield, ed., *Defining Moments: Dramatic Archaeologies of the Twentieth Century* (Oxford: Archaeopress, 2009), 157–64 at 158; Cornelius Holtorf, 'The heritage of heritage', *Heritage & Society* 5 (2012): 153–74 at 159; Marcel Proust, *Remembrance of Things Past* (1913–27; Penguin, 1983), 1: 163.

[42] Cicero, *De oratore* (c. 55 BC) (Harvard, 1942).

Up to their own arrival on the scene history contains only picturesque, not meaningful, information, and is inhabited by storybook not real people.[43] Dwelling more and more on the present, 'we are forgetting our past faster with each passing year', as shown by the ever speedier demise of historical keywords between 1800 and 2000. Personal fame likewise fades ever faster; 'the more transient the media, the more transient the fame'. If not as short-lived as Andy Warhol's prophetic fifteen minutes, the brevity of public renown may deter a legacy-bent benefactor warned that 'donor intent cannot realistically be guaranteed beyond a generation'.[44]

To be sure, some communal memories persist; mass-media consumers share extensive repertoires about celebrities in sports, music, fashion, and film. But that store of data is trivial, inchoate, and ephemeral; it nourishes no discourse beyond its own short-lived icons; its substance is too thin to support a meaningful social fabric; it links devotees with only a very recent past. Pop culture does not compensate for 'the loss of the historical frame of reference, the amputation of the time dimension from our culture'. To be 'in the swim', noted Ernst Gombrich, is not equivalent to 'being in the culture'.[45]

Gamesters like time-travellers gleefully replace the actual past with counterfactual fantasy. 'Every person can already create their own private historical narratives', exults an ultra-modern historian, and 'they will soon also be able to invent . . . a whole historical culture consisting of a past, various interpretations of that past, and a social community that believes and cherishes those interpretations'.[46] But such fictitious histories further the demise of the credible and creditable past. 'Cultural memory as an embedded and lived practice', charges an historian of the genre, has 'ceased to exist in modern Western societies'. Because 'everything appears to be available everywhere anytime', we instead engage ideologically or nostalgically with 'fleeting and passing . . . media events, art and fashion phenomena' that 'encourage, indeed require, forgetfulness'.[47]

Some contend that the ease and speed of modern information retrieval makes cultural memory redundant: why store in the mind names and dates readily found on the Internet? But references at our fingertips are not the same as having them in our heads. To converse, to compare, to contrast, even to consult an encyclopaedia requires a stock of common knowledge not merely on tap but ingrained in communal awareness. That is why great classics remain canonical: their enduringly resonant words and allusions bridge barriers of time and culture. 'It is the destiny of those grave, restrained and classic

---

[43] Denis Shemilt, 'Drinking an ocean and pissing a cupful: how adolescents make sense of history', in Symcox and Wilschut, eds., *National History Standards*, 176, 183.

[44] Michel et al., 'Quantitative analysis of culture using millions of digitized books', 178–80; Leo Braudy quoted in Alex Williams, '15 minutes of fame? More like 15 seconds of nanofame', *NYT*, 6 Feb. 2015; Foundation head James Piereson quoted in Patricia Cohen, 'Gifts of art, tangled in strings', *IHT*, 7 Feb. 2013: 9. See Leon Levy, p. 24 above.

[45] Katherine Nelson, 'Self and social functions', *Memory* 11 (2003): 125–36 at 133; Ernst H. Gombrich, 'The tradition of general knowledge' (1962), in *Ideals and Idols* (Phaidon, 1979), 9–23 at 21, 14.

[46] Wulf Kansteiner, 'Alternate worlds and invented communities', in Keith Jenkins et al., eds., *Manifestos for History* (Routledge, 2007), 131–48 at 141.

[47] Philipp Wolf, 'The anachronism of modern cultural memories', in Herbert Grabes, ed., *Literature, Literary History, and Cultural Memory* [*REAL: Yearbook of Research in English and American Literature 21*] (Tübingen: Gunter Narr, 2005), 331–47 at 331, 334.

writers', wrote Robert Louis Stevenson, 'to pass into the blood and become native in the memory'.[48] Lacking the collective creative past we are 'untethered, adrift in time'.[49]

The past made present

Thus, for some the past becomes the only worthwhile time, while for others it seems of little if any account.[50] Yet these two takes, which seem utterly at odds, reflect the same overriding tendency to fold past within present. Both nostalgists and amnesiacs smudge the line between then and now to virtual invisibility. Whether all-consuming or over-looked, betokening everything or nothing, the past is less and less distinguishable from the present.

For the general public, to be sure, the past was never a foreign country. Significantly, the film-script of Hartley's book omits his second clause, 'they do things differently there', and shuns its implications. In the film the past is not foreign or different. History vanishes; change becomes nothing but life-cycle nostalgia.[51] So too with most docu-dramas. Beyond their costumes, characters differ only in age and gender and status; the same motives and mentalities animate medieval as modern folk, elemental passions enacted on a timeless stage.

But today the past is ever more comprehensively domesticated. 'Just as easy travel eroded the differences between one country and another, and between one world and another', say Douglas Adams's time travellers, so we are now 'eroding the differences between one age and another. The past ... is now truly like a foreign country. They do things exactly the same there.'[52] Fiction that mimics history without being historical – Michael Cunning-ham's *The Hours* (1999), David Mitchell's *Cloud Atlas* (2004), Hari Kunzru's *Gods without Men* (2011) – 'inserts the contemporary reader into other locations and times, while leaving no doubt that its viewpoint is relentlessly modern and speaks entirely of our extreme present', judges Douglas Coupland. In the Internet of electronic recall, 'All the past of recent memory ... floods our ever-broadening present', with yesteryear's mores and music, fads and fashions, swallowed up in our all-engulfing shallow 'now'.[53]

The past is increasingly spoken of in the present tense. Present-tense narration is now taken for granted by many fiction readers because everything they read, from Internet news to texting, is in the present tense. The past is more and more portrayed as if just happening – 'Caesar is eager to cross the Rubicon.' A bogus sense of immediacy disre-gards pastness and disconnects causal sequence. 'The present tense is a narrow-beam

---

[48] Robert Louis Stevenson, *The Ebb-Tide* (1894; Heinemann, 1912), 3.

[49] Penelope Lively, *Ammonites and Leaping Fish: A Life in Time* (Penguin, 2013), 138.

[50] Michael Kammen notes a similar 'pattern of historical indifference and ignorance in an age of escapist nostalgia' ('History is our heritage: the past in contemporary American culture', in *In the Past Lane* (Oxford, 1997), 214).

[51] L. P. Hartley, *The Go-Between* (1953; NYRB Classics, 1962, 2002). See my 'The past is a foreign country', in Tim Ingold, ed., *Key Debates in Anthropology* (Routledge, 1996), 206–12.

[52] Douglas Adams, *Life, the Universe, and Everything* (1982; Del Rey, 1995), 116.

[53] Douglas Coupland, 'Convergences', *NYT Book Review*, 11 Mar. 2012: 1, 10; Hans Ulrich Gumbrecht, *Our Broad Present: Time and Contemporary Culture* (Columbia, 2014), xiii.

flashlight in the dark, limiting the view to the next step – now, now, now', concludes Ursula Le Guin; 'The world of the infant, of the animal'. The false nowness reflects the extinction of the past tense requisite in film and TV.[54]

But 'television's unwavering allegiance to the present tense' is not merely a 'grammatical imperative', it is built into the medium's presentist bent. Shown from the purview of its denizens, who are necessarily devoid of historical hindsight, the past becomes more and more like the ongoing present: messy, inchoate, and inconclusive. 'You are not learning about history', as film producer David Grubin put it; 'you feel like you're experiencing it'. Seeking to emulate filmic immediacy and intimacy, many popular historians likewise stress actor and eyewitness testimony.[55]

Whereas previous purveyors of history sought to order and explain, bringing coherence that made the past quite unlike the present, recent historiography stresses complexity and contradiction, disparate viewpoints, inherent uncertainties much like those that afflict times today. The past in film resembles the present not only in its intimate immediacy, however, but also in its wholesale hijacking of present concerns and values. 'Concentrating only on those people, events, and issues that are most relevant to themselves and their target audiences', and stressing current concerns, makes film and TV history hugely popular and lucrative.[56]

Our precursors identified with a simplified unitary antiquity whose vestiges became models for their own creations. Our own more numerous and exotic pasts, prized as vestiges, are divested of the iconographic meanings they once embodied. Now an exotic terrain with a booming tourist trade, the past has undergone the usual consequences of popularity. The more it is appreciated for its own sake, the less real or relevant it becomes. No longer revered or feared, the past is swallowed up by the ever-expanding present; we enlarge our sense of the contemporary at the expense of dissevering it from the past. 'We are flooded with disposable memoranda from us to ourselves', held historian Daniel Boorstin, but 'we are tragically inept at receiving messages from our ancestors'.[57]

For historians the past grows ever more foreign. But the public at large cannot tolerate an alien past and strenuously domesticates it, imputing present-day aims and deeds to earlier times, clothing previous folk in their own mental garb, praising them for echoing their own precepts or damning them for failing to conform to them. The foreign past gets reduced to exotic sites of tourism or filmic period fantasy; the past cherished at home becomes a haunt of chauvinist heritage, nostalgic tribalism, and retro remakes. In popular media, at historical sites and museums, human nature remains constant, people unchanged from age to age. Legends of origin and endurance, of victory or calamity, project the present back, the past forward. Rather than a foreign country, the past becomes our sanitized own.[58]

[54] Ursula K. Le Guin, 'A whopper of a story', *Guardian Review*, 6 Sept. 2014: 8. See Douglas Rushkoff, *Present Shock: When Everything Happens Now* (Penguin, 2013), 197–242.

[55] Edgerton, 'Television as historian', 3–4.

[56] Ibid. 4–6.

[57] Daniel J. Boorstin, 'America and the world experience: the enlarged contemporary' (Reith Lectures, 1975), *Listener*: 11 Dec. 1975: 786–9 at 787 (repr. in *The Exploring Spirit* (BBC, 1976)).

[58] See my 'The timeless past', *Journal of American History* 75 (1989): 1263–80.

And history is no longer the privileged mode of access to the past it used to be. Memory's emotional immediacy dethrones history's aloof sobriety and reclaims the past as a resource for identity politics.[59] History's sober distance is not only boring, it challenges our possession of the past, which memory enables us to select. No longer what elites and experts tell us it was, the past becomes what Everyman chooses to accept. Personal preference trumps objective knowledge – Doonesbury's 'MyFACTS, privatizing the truth since 2003'.[60] 'It used to be, everyone was entitled to their own opinion, but not their own facts. But that's not the case any more. Facts matter not at all. Perception is everything . . . "What I say is right". . . It's not only that I *feel* it to be true, but that *I* feel it to be true.'[61] Long averse to egg-head elites, Americans today 'are no longer willing to defer to professional historians', writes one of them. 'We are not credible.'[62]

'Fifty years ago, the past seemed to belong only to those who . . . acquire[d] the skills to tell it', recalled Greg Dening, a historian of Oceania. 'Now it belongs to all those on whom it impinges.' Dening praised 'such a history . . . for being inclusive. Each side can only tell its history by also telling the other's, [and so] disempower itself.'[63] But few do so. Possession instead privileges one's own view. Other viewpoints, especially those of bygone people whom death and absence has silenced, are dismissed as mistaken, barbarous, iniquitous. Like C. S. Lewis's devil's disciple, who 'feels superior and patronizing to the ones he has emerged from, . . . simply because they are in the past', we disdain 'the ancient writer as a possible source of knowledge', thus avoiding the risk of confronting disturbing truths.[64]

Emboldened by self-righteous solipsism, Everyman today constrains the past to his own image, denying its difference and demanding its likeness to his prejudices. Thus, is resuscitated the sense of history long previously held, by the learned as well as the laity, that people of all epochs are basically alike, human nature changeless, past and present essentially the same.[65]

A major consequence of thus folding past into present is a growing inability to accept that bygone folk held other principles and viewpoints – that the Zeitgeist alters over time. 'The inability or unwillingness of people in public affairs to consider the events of another period in the context of the beliefs and prejudices of that time' strikes a political pundit as a growing problem in international relations.[66] Unaware that preceding generations judged things by standards unlike their own, right-thinking youngsters confront such evidence with outraged incredulity. 'I don't believe you!' explodes a teenager told of Oscar

[59] Aleida Assmann, 'Transformations between history and memory', *Social Research* 75 (2008): 49–72 at 54, 57; Andreas Huyssen, *Twilight Memories: Making Time in a Culture of Amnesia* (New York: Psychology Press, 1995), 5–8; Geoffrey Cubitt, *History and Memory* (Manchester, 2007), 60.
[60] G. B. Trudeau cartoon, *IHT*, 8 Feb. 2012.
[61] Stephen Colbert interview by Nathan Raban, 16 Jan. 2006, avclub.com/content/node/44705
[62] Johann N. Neem, 'Taking historical fundamentalism seriously', *Historically Speaking* 12:5 (2011): 2–5 at 4.
[63] Greg Dening, *Beach Crossings: Voyaging Across Times, Cultures, and Self* (PennPress, 2004), 13.
[64] Lewis, *Screwtape Letters*, 46, 140.
[65] Learning to perceive the past's otherness, to recognize that moral principles change demands 'enormous efforts' (Jörn Rüsen, 'The development of narrative competence in historical learning', *History & Memory* 1:2 (1989): 26–60 at 53).
[66] William Pfaff, 'The danger of seeing the past through today's prism', *IHT*, 6 June 1998.

Wilde's scandal, trial, and imprisonment. 'He was sent to prison because he was *gay!*'[67] Modern egalitarians find it incredible that slavery, genocide, and gross inequality, far from being evil aberrations, were habitual practices, sanctioned by moral philosophers from Aristotle to Machiavelli and Montesquieu.[68]

Early-modern belief in witchcraft is likewise censured as superstitious ignorance. Dismissing pre-modern fears as illogical, implausible, and contrary to empirical evidence, young Americans remain blind to the 'leaps of faith that undergird' their own unsubstantiated assumptions. Nor can they imagine 'any substantial argument in favor of aristocracy or monarchy, [those] inexplicable follies of the past'.[69] Stanford history students felt aggrieved to have to discuss the aims of kings, aristocrats, and other 'inherently repulsive ... antiquated beings'.[70] Student presentism is not surprising, since publishers now ban gender terms and differences and require depictions of the past to replace women passengers on sailboats with women hoisting the sails, women nurses and secretaries with women doctors and managers. McGraw-Hill's textbook pretence that the modern ideal of gender equality 'was a customary condition' in previous centuries perverts the past into an idealized egalitarian utopia.[71]

Young Europeans are equally blind to the otherness of the past, incapable of accepting its alterity. Seemingly unaware that people viewed things differently five centuries ago, 15-year-old history students 'argue only from their modern viewpoint of individualism, secularism and autonomy'. Unable to envision 'pre-modern reality and morality, even in theory', they rely solely on human rights philosophy 'for an era before the invention of human rights'.[72]

When the contradiction becomes patent, moral righteousness trumps historical reason. Faced with the illogicality of calling aboriginal Indians the first Argentinians while simultaneously terming Argentina a nineteenth-century-born nation (that moreover excluded and extirpated the indigenes), University of Buenos Aires first-year students could not reconcile their ingrained patriotism with their devotion to universal human rights. So both became mythic, ahistorical, immutable essences: Argentina had existed before the European discovery, inhabited by natives who didn't know they were Argentinian, and whose subsequent persecution had to be expiated by endowing them with ancestral nationality.[73]

---

[67] Lively, *Ammonites and Leaping Fish*, 117.

[68] Joyce Appleby, *A Restless Past: History and the American Public* (Rowman & Littlefield, 2005), 74. See Louis Dumont, *Homo Hierarchicus* (Chicago, 1980), and my 'On arraigning ancestors', *North Carolina Law Review* 87 (2009): 901–66 at 930–5.

[69] Richard Godbeer, '"How could they believe that?": Explaining to students why accusations of witchcraft made good sense in seventeenth-century New England', OAH *Magazine of History* 17:4 (2003): 28–31 at 31; Allan D. Bloom, *The Closing of the American Mind* (Simon & Schuster, 1987), 90.

[70] Daniel Gordon, 'Teaching Western history at Stanford', in Lloyd Kramer et al., eds., *Learning History in America* (Minnesota, 1994), 44–52 at 52.

[71] Diane Ravitch, *The Language Police* (Knopf, 2003), 38–44, 63, citing McGraw-Hill's *Reflecting Diversity: Multicultural Guidelines* (1993).

[72] Andreas Körber, 'Can our pupils fit into the shoes of someone else?' in Joke van der Leeuw-Roord, ed., *The State of History Education in Europe* (Körber-Stiftung, 1998), 123–38 at 136.

[73] Mario Carretero and Miriam Kriger, 'Historical representations and conflicts about indigenous peoples as national identities', *Culture & Psychology* 17 (2011): 177–95; Mario Carretero et al., 'Students' historical

Nor are the young today's only innocents astounded by wicked ancestral ways. Of the transatlantic slave trade, British Prime Minister Blair found it 'hard to believe that what would now be a crime against humanity was legal at the time'.[74] Yet until recently many denounced not slave but free labour, at the mercenary mercy of avaricious employers.[75] So too with other aspects of the past. 'We mislead our readers into believing that nothing has ever been different from right now, [that] there's nothing new under the sun', asserts a historical novelist. On the contrary, 'the sun never rises twice on the same human sentiments ... We must remember that until the twentieth century the condescension of the upper class and the submissiveness of the working class were considered normal and even admirable.'[76]

Few memorials reveal that bygone heroes lived by principles unlike those of today. A rare instance is New Orleans's Liberty Monument statue, erected in 1891 to honour eleven men 'who fell in defense of liberty and home rule' in September 1874, when white paramilitaries overcame police and state militia and ousted 'carpetbag' Republicans from the state capitol. Federal troops 'reinstated the usurpers', but the 1876 national election 'recognized white supremacy and gave us [back] our state', according to a 1935 plaque. After the Civil Rights movement a 1976 plaque gainsaid this, saying the 'white supremacy' sentiments previously expressed 'are contrary to the philosophy and beliefs of present-day New Orleans'.[77] That recognition of mutability incurred racist retaliation, the monument defaced with swastikas and faeces.

The past held to blame

A century ago, Italian Futurists assailed the past as an incubus stifling present enterprise. They consigned the relics of antiquity – ancient monuments, museum collections, ancestral veneration – to the flames.[78] In the wake of Futurism came Modernism, similarly dedicated to all that was new, eager to shed the shackles of the burdensome past. As noted above, architects and artists flaunted contempt for tradition by jettisoning plaster casts of classical and Renaissance structures and by eliminating history from students' training. Emulation was passé, innovation obligatory.

Today the past is again under assault. But the cause and the context are utterly different. Unlike Futurists and Modernists, we do not reprobate the past's material and aesthetic achievements; quite to the contrary, we cherish them. Instead, we condemn precursors' wicked misdeeds and immoral institutions. Our racist, sexist, elitist forebears

---

narratives and concepts', in Carretero et al., eds., *History Education and the Construction of National Identities* (Charlotte, NC: Information Age, 2012), 155–70 at 158–68.

[74] David Smith, 'Blair, Britain's sorrow for shame of slave trade', *Observer* 26 Nov. 2006: 1.

[75] Two centuries ago 'the overwhelming majority of civilized, decent people' thought 'free labor ... alarming' (Elizabeth Fox-Genovese and Eugene D. Genovese, *The Mind of the Master Class* (Cambridge, 2005), 2).

[76] Edmund White, 'The new historical novel', in *Arts and Letters* (San Francisco: Cleis, 2004), 20–34 at 25, 27.

[77] Sanford Levinson, *Written in Stone: Public Monuments in Changing Societies* (Duke, 1998), 45–50.

[78] F. T. Marinetti, 'Founding and manifesto of Futurism' (1909), in Umbro Apollonio, comp., *Futurist Manifestos* (Viking, 1973), 19–23.

are anathematized as cruel and avaricious hierarchs, and hypocrites to boot. For the likes of that apostle of liberty Patrick Henry, who confessedly kept slaves owing to the 'general inconvenience of living without them',[79] there seems no excuse. Other Founding Fathers who fall short of contemporary morality are refashioned, as shown in Chapter 12, to reflect current pieties. American history textbooks previously portrayed slavery without anger, for there was no one to be angry *at*: 'somehow we ended up with four million slaves in America but no owners!'[80]

Critics decry such cover-ups. 'If we are interested in history more than enshrinement', grumbles a historian, 'the apologies offered for slavery at [presidential] sites . . . suggest a shallow faith in the greatness of these men'.[81] But these sites *are* shrines. It is their custodians' function to regret slavery yet salvage their owners' reputations, like the Alabaman who assured Jonathan Raban that her Civil War ancestor 'did not *believe* in slavery. He had a *very* few, only about sixteen or twenty'.[82] Portraying forebears as reluctant or marginal accessories mitigates what is newly unconscionable.

We lack the appreciation of temporal distance that led antebellum abolitionist Wendell Phillips to say, of America's Founding Fathers, 'I love these men; I hate their work. I respect their memory; I reject their deeds. I trust their hearts; I distrust their heads.'[83] Few today would join Harriet Beecher Stowe in praising North Carolina Judge Thomas Ruffin's self-reproach that the law compelled him to exonerate a hirer's brutality towards a slave; his harsh verdict in *State v. Mann* was inherent in 'the curse of slavery', for 'the duty of the magistrate' must prevail over 'the feelings of the man'. Ruffin's words left Stowe 'feeling at once deep respect for the man and horror for the system'.[84]

Stowe's distinction between 'the man' and 'the system' now goes unrecognized; blindness to past complexity mires us in cognitive dissonance. Unaware that the Constitution's authors anticipated its continual revision as essential, Americans now venerate it as a sacred compact never to be altered, while simultaneously censuring the Founding Fathers who wrote it as Dead White Male slave owners.[85] Similarly, in newly penitential Australia, 'the White nation appears not to want to understand its [pioneer settler] forebears', writes an anthropologist. It is far easier to 'disinherit them, than to try to unravel the uncomfortable fact that it was mostly reasonable and humane men and women who took part in the processes and policies that we now see as repugnant'.[86]

---

[79] Patrick Henry to Robert Pleasants, 18 Jan. 1773, in Moses Coit Tyler, *Patrick Henry* (Boston, 1887), 209.

[80] James W. Loewen, *Lies My Teacher Told Me* (New York: New Press, 1995), 138.

[81] Mark Bograd, 'Apologies accepted: facing up to slave realities at historic house museums', *History News* 47:1 (Jan.–Feb. 1992): 20–1.

[82] Jonathan Raban, *Hunting Mister Heartbreak: A Discovery of America* (Pan Macmillan, 1991), 218.

[83] Wendell Phillips, speech, 12 May 1848, quoted in George B. Forgie, *Patricide in the House Divided* (Norton, 1979), 130. See my 'On arraigning ancestors', 903–5, 928–9.

[84] Thomas Ruffin, *State v. Mann*, 13 N.C. (2 Dev.) (1829), 263–7 at 264, 266; Harriet Beecher Stowe, *A Key to Uncle Tom's Cabin* (Boston, 1853), 78–9. See Mark V. Tushnet, *Slave Law in the American South: State v. Mann in History and Literature* (Kansas, 2003).

[85] Elazar Barkan, *The Guilt of Nations* (Norton, 2000), xxxi; Michael Kammen, *A Machine That Would Go of Itself* (1986; Transaction, 2006), 3, 316; François Furstenberg, *In the Name of the Father* (Penguin, 2006), 230.

[86] Gillian K. Cowlishaw, 'Cultures of complaint', *Journal of Sociology* 42:4 (2006): 429–45 at 442.

In 1996 William Pfaff noted that 'every figure from the past is held accountable for not thinking and acting as right-minded people do today'. Ancestor-bashing has since intensified (see Chapter 12). We preen ourselves on being better than our precursors. 'Sorry, folks, for the brutality of our morally inferior ancestors. If it had been us in charge, with our enlightened new-age sensitivity, instead of those immoral old-timers, it would never have happened'.[87]

Shifting morality, as Wendell Phillips realized, leaves our hearts at odds with our heads. 'We are all convinced that enslaving human beings is bad. How shall we characterize the once universal teaching that you acquire a slave baby lawfully by owning the baby's mother?' asks jurist John Noonan. 'Can anyone today contemplate the slave trader and slaveholder without a shudder of disgust? Can anyone empathize with the bigot putting a torch to the stake where the condemned heretic will be incinerated? Abstractly, we may concede that the slave owner and the persecutor thought that they acted justly. In our bones we experience repugnance and even righteous rage.'[88]

Some feel obliged to arraign the deceased. 'Think not that morality is ambulatory; that vices in one age are not vices in another', cautioned Thomas Browne.[89] Lord Acton famously inveighed against historical apologists who claimed 'we have no common code; our moral notions are always fluid; and you must consider the times, the class from which men sprang, the surrounding influences, the masters in their schools, the preachers in their pulpits, the movement they obscurely obeyed, and so on, until . . . not a culprit is left for execution'. Acton approved the French statesman Albert de Broglie's maxim, 'Beware of too much explaining, lest we end by too much excusing'. To be sure, Acton added, 'opinions alter, manners change, creeds rise and fall, but the moral law is written on the tablets of eternity'. Because modern historians could be 'rigidly impersonal, disinterested and just', they should 'look with remorse upon the past'.[90] He faulted H. C. Lea's *History of the Inquisition of the Middle Ages* (1887) for denouncing persecution but absolving the persecutors: 'crime without a culprit, the unavenged victim who perishes by no man's fault, law without responsibility, the virtuous agent of vicious cause'.[91]

Acton's colleagues and subsequent historians have mostly dissented. 'The men who conscientiously thought heresy a crime may be accused of an intellectual mistake, not

---

[87] William Pfaff, 'Too bad for them, they should have been more like us', *Baltimore Sun*, 18 July 1996; Russell Baker, 'Sorry about that', *NYT*, 1 July 1997: A21.

[88] John T. Noonan Jr., *A Church That Can and Cannot Change: The Development of Catholic Moral Teaching* (Notre Dame, 2005), 201, 197.

[89] Thomas Browne, *Christian Morals* [1670s], in *Works* (1852; London, 1928), 3: 83–146 at 93.

[90] Lord Acton, 'Inaugural lecture on the study of history' (1895), in *Lectures on Modern History* (Macmillan, 1906), 1–30 at 25–8, quoting Albert de Broglie, *Discours . . . pour la réception de M. Albert Sorel* (1895). Acton's plaint was anticipated a generation earlier: 'Our monsters of tyranny and iniquity come forth . . . restored to human shape; . . . there has been a perpetual rehabilitation of the damned of history, till very soon we may expect to be left without a time-dishonoured villain' (Frances Power Cobbe, 'Fallacies of memory' (1866), in *Hours of Work & Play* (London, 1867), 87–113 at 91).

[91] Lord Acton, 'A history of the inquisition of the Middle Ages. By Henry Charles Lea' (1888), in *The History of Freedom and Other Essays* (Macmillan, 1922), 551–74 at 572. See Perez Zagorin, 'Lord Acton's ordeal: the historian and moral judgement', *Virginia Quarterly Review* 74:1 (Winter 1998): 1–17, and *How the Idea of Religious Toleration Came to the West* (Princeton, 2003), 14–18.

"The past, Your Honor, is a foreign country, and we did things differently there."

Figure 109 The culpable past (Charles Barsotti, *New Yorker*, 17/5/2010)

necessarily of a moral crime', countered Bishop Mandell Creighton.[92] Acton assumed 'that absolute knowledge of right and wrong which enables us to pass final judgment on the men of the past, secure that we make no mistake when we measure them by our own moral yardstick', said Lea. 'Every foregone age has similarly flattered itself with the same illusion. But 'there is scarce a sin condemned in the Decalogue [Ten Commandments] which has not been or may not now be regarded rather as a virtue'.

We are unable to conceive of vicarious punishment as justifiable, yet Hammurabi ... slays the innocent son and lets the guilty father go scatheless. To us the idea of levirate marriage is abhorrent, but it has been regarded as legally a duty by ... the Hebrew and the Hindu. ... No character in medieval history stands forth with greater lustre than the good St. Louis of France, yet ... he fostered the nascent Inquisition and ... enrich[ed] his treasury with the confiscations resulting from the burning of heretics. ... Who among us would feel justified in ... condemning the Hebrew or St. Louis?

The historian who 'aspires to be a judge ... should not try a case by a code unknown to the defendant'.[93]

Indeed, 'elementary justice demands that he who is to be judged should have a hearing: the dead are powerless to defend themselves', concurs a modern judge. 'It may make a

---

[92] Mandell Creighton to Acton, 9 Apr. 1887, in Acton, *Essays on Freedom and Power* (Free Press, 1942), 372.
[93] Henry Charles Lea, 'Ethical values in history', *AHR* 9 (1904): 233–46 at 234–9.

historian swell with pride to ... set down Thomas More as a persecutor or Abraham Lincoln' as a racist. But 'no figure of the past will meet the standards of the present'. Should we condemn Augustine and Aquinas for defending slavery and religious persecution? Adjudge Washington, Jefferson, and Madison evil because they owned slaves? Rebuke Supreme Court icons Brandeis, Holmes, and Hughes for upholding racial segregation in the schools in 1926? 'If each generation is free to measure its predecessors morally, using the criteria now accepted, no one will escape condemnation'.[94] Censuring predecessors puts us at the like mercy of posterity. 'The future has no right to rehear past judgments in the light of altered morality. To deny our ancestors autonomy in the judgments they reached is to cede our own moral authority to our successors.'[95] 'As we would have our descendants judge us, so we ought to judge our fathers', advised T. B. Macaulay. 'To form a correct estimate of their merits, we ought to place ourselves in their situation, to put out of our minds, for a time, all that knowledge which they could not have, and which we could not help having.'[96]

The antidote to presentist misjudgement is historical understanding. 'The follies, the crimes, and the wilfulnesses that were unspeakable will not be turned into virtues but at least will become humanly understandable', reasoned Herbert Butterfield. It was useless to say 'We cannot enter imaginatively into this particular case because Catherine de' Medici was wicked beyond all imagination'; we should instead remedy our deficiency of imagination. Amid ongoing atrocities, to be sure, 'one cannot – what is more, one must not – understand what happened', argued Primo Levi in the wake of Auschwitz, for 'it is desirable that [they] cannot be comprehensible to us. They are nonhuman words and deeds, really counter-human, without historic precedents'. All the more essential, then, to try to understand them historically.[97]

It is one thing to deplore past injustice, quite another to blame its perpetrators for not living up to today's ethical code. Following John Paul II's profuse contrition for previous Church misdeeds, theological observers found 'something repellent, as well as profoundly unhistorical, about judging the past by the standards and prejudices of another age'.[98] A Catholic scholar envisages a bimillennial 'heavenly choir ... made up of former slaves ... and of slaveholders such as Popes Gregory the Great, Pius V, Pius VII', countless saints, Dominican and Jesuit missionaries, and Augustinian and Carmelite nuns. Who would 'retroactively disqualify from this assembly those who had owned human beings?'[99]

---

[94] Noonan, *Church That Can and Cannot Change*, 200.

[95] Matthew Parris, 'A clever trick: say sorry, condemn the past and look good, with no cost', *Times*, 26 Aug. 2006: 21.

[96] T. B. Macaulay, 'Sir James Macintosh' (1835), in *Critical and Historical Essays* (London, 1903), 2: 49–114 at 68.

[97] Herbert Butterfield, *History and Human Relations* (Collins, 1951), 120, 124–5; Primo Levi interview, *New Republic*, 17 Feb. 1986.

[98] Paul Johnson, 'When is God going to apologise for raining fire and brimstone on Sodom?' *Spectator*, 8 Nov. 1997: 28. See Avery Cardinal Dulles, 'Should the Church repent?' (1988), in *Church and Society* (Fordham, 2008), 262–75 at 266–70.

[99] Noonan, *Church That Can and Cannot Change*, 200.

Accepting the past

Six centuries ago, Reformation clerics condemned Church practices then abhorrent. Demanding a return to patristic virtue, radical reformers excoriated subsequent corruptions. Countering Protestants' root-and-branch extirpations, Catholic improvers counselled toleration of inherited abuses, lest the entire fabric of Christendom be lost. Erasmus warned Luther that his iconoclastic cure might be more dangerous than the disease. Ten centuries of accrued degeneration could not be removed at once. The ideal church that reformers sought was a chimera; evil had existed at all times and always would; error might be mitigated but never wholly removed.[100]

Instead of thundering abominations against 'those who exhibit doubtful relics for authentic ones, who attribute to them more than is proper, and basely make money by them', Erasmus advised forbearance and humour. That medieval saints' annals were suffused with skulduggery did not justify wholesale destruction of their shrines and relics.[101] Reformers' scorn might 'work great harm among the simple and uninstructed'. Showy piety was 'necessary for children in Christ . . . until they have become a little more mature'. Since men 'cannot without external means be raised easily to meditation on divine things', ceremonial ritual must excite 'the minds of the faithful'. Hence Erasmus 'reproached those who . . . have thrown all images out of the churches'.[102]

Rather than rage and bitterness, Erasmus deployed satire and pity. 'A Pilgrimage for Religion's Sake' mocks the proliferation of sacred images, trinkets, knickknacks, and gewgaws, the ecclesiastical greed that made the numinous numismatic.[103] At Walsingham Abbey he scoffed at the supposed 'Milk of the blessed Virgin':

Oh mother most imitative of her Son! He has left us so much of his Blood upon earth; she so much Milk, as it is scarcely credible . . . [Fearing] that many such things are fabricated for lucre, [I asked the canon] 'by what proofs he was assured that this was the Milk of the Virgin'. . . . 'What need to ask such questions, when you have the authenticated inscription?' And he seemed ready to turn us out as heretics, if a few pence had not smoothed down the man's ferocity. . . . I was ashamed that I had at all hesitated, so plainly was the whole thing stated – the name, the place, the mode of transaction. . . . [As for] Saint Bernard . . . whose good fortune it was to taste the Milk from the very same breast which was sucked by the child Jesus, . . . I am surprised he is styled the mellifluous Bernard and not the lactifluous.[104]

---

[100] Erasmus, *Hyperaspistes II* (1527) and *De recta . . . pronuntiatione* (1528), cited in István Bejczy, *Erasmus and the Middle Ages: The Historical Consciousness of a Christian Humanist* (Brill, 2001), 176–9. See Zagorin, *How the Idea of Religious Toleration Came to the West*, 46–68.

[101] Erasmus, *De utilitate colloquiorum* (1526), in *Colloquies*, CW, 39: 1095–118 at 1104; *Peregrinatio religionis ergo* (c. 1512/26), cited in Gary Waller, *Walsingham and the English Imagination* (Ashgate, 2011), 72–3.

[102] Erasmus, *Enchiridion militis Christiani* (1503), quoted in Jan van Herwaarden, *Between Saint James and Erasmus* (Brill, 2003), 194–5; Erasmus, *De utilitate colloquiorum*.

[103] Waller, *Walsingham*, 82; Walter M. Gordon, *Humanist Play and Belief: The Seriocomic Art of Desiderius Erasmus* (Toronto, 1990), 102–4, 117.

[104] Erasmus, *Pilgrimages to Saint Mary of Walsingham and Saint Thomas of Canterbury*, (c. 1512/1526; Westminster, 1849), 19–32. When Henry VIII turned Protestant, he invoked Erasmus's satire to devastate Walsingham Abbey (1538).

Over the next four centuries relic proliferation continued to gratify pilgrims, enrich the Church, and amuse sceptics. Erasmus's jesting at multiplied relics, like his ambiguity in pretending merely to restore what he deliberately modernized, is mirrored in the duplication of his own mortal remains. In excavating Erasmus's grave in Basle in 1928, two skulls were found, and much labour was devoted to deciding which was his. But 'did no one consider the possibility', asked Johann Huizinga, another playful Dutch scholar, 'that Erasmus could have had two heads? That would certainly explain a great many aspects of his personality'.[105] Erasmus himself joked that he did not know whether he was 'Gallus' [French] or 'Germanus' and hence could be considered 'two-headed'.[106]

Erasmus regarded himself and his generation as accountable for the entirety of Christian history – even those deplorable centuries when literary culture was destroyed – along with all the evils and errors of the Church. Only by accepting responsibility for what went wrong could one redeem the past.[107] He deplored the ahistoricism of humanists and Protestants, who distanced themselves from medieval decline, claiming direct descent from early Christianity untouched by intervening centuries.

Little honoured in his own era, Erasmian inclusivity is still seldom practised. Many who no longer selectively praise the past instead totally disown it. Thomas Paine's *Rights of Man* advised washing one's hands of ancestral deeds and misdeeds. 'Those who have quitted the world, and those who are not arrived yet at it, are as remote from each other as the utmost stretch of mortal imagination can conceive: what possible obligation then can exist between them ... that the one should control the other to the end of time?'[108]

Collective responsibility for the past

Perdurable social continuity was the legendary credo of Thomas Paine's arch-antagonist, Edmund Burke. Burke condemned the wholesale erasures of the French Revolution for expunging their entire legacy. 'Unmindful of what they have received from their ancestors, or of what is due to their posterity', they risk breaking 'the whole chain and continuity of the commonwealth'. Obeisance to lasting tradition was indispensable. Otherwise 'no one generation could link with the other. Men would become little better than flies of a summer.'

[Society] is a partnership in all science; a partnership in all art; a partnership in every virtue, and in all perfection. As the ends of such a partnership cannot be obtained in many generations, it

---

[105] Johan Huizinga, *Briefwisseling* (1989–91), quoted in Bejczy, *Erasmus and the Middle Ages*, 194n3. Erasmus's broadminded eclecticism echoes St Augustine's reconciliation of seemingly incompatible elements of faith, 'the idea that the Old Testament was at once true and superseded' (Carlo Ginzburg, *Wooden Eyes* (Columbia, 2001), 147–8). See pp. 343–4.

[106] Erasmus to Louis Ruzé (1519), in *Opus Epistolarum des Erasmi Roterdam* (Oxford, 1913), 3: 511. See J. J. Poelhekke, 'The nameless homeland of Erasmus', *Acta Historiae Neerlandicae* 7 (1974): 54–87.

[107] Erasmus, *Antibarbari* (1500–20), in *CW*, 23: 1–122; Bejczy, *Erasmus and the Middle Ages*, 8–12, 185–7.

[108] Thomas Paine, *Rights of Man* (1791–2), in *CW* (Library of America, 1995), 433–664 at 439.

becomes a partnership not only between those who are living, but between those who are living, those who are dead, and those who are to be born.[109]

Burke's reverence for tradition was long assailed as a reactionary defence of the *ancien régime*. 'Hardly any American then or now', contends an eminent historian, 'would side with Burke in his famous exchange with Thomas Paine'. Freedom from past precedents, prior promises, and ancestral customs strikes another historian as a *sine qua non* of modern sovereignty and citizenship.[110] Yet Burke is now often invoked to justify enduring accountability.[111] 'Each generation must … preserve the gains of culture and civilization, and maintain intact those just institutions that have been established', asserts the philosopher John Rawls.[112] 'I inherit from the past of my family, my city, my tribe, my nation, a variety of debts, inheritances, rightful expectations and obligations', echoes Alasdair MacIntyre.[113]

Burke demurred at holding the present responsible for rectifying past injustice, because like Erasmus he feared reformers inventing or inflating historical crimes. They 'think they are waging war with [past] intolerance, pride, and cruelty, whilst, under colour of abhorring the ill principles of antiquated parties, they are authorizing and feeding the same odious vices in different factions … It is not very just to chastise men for the offenses of their natural ancestors: but to take the fiction of ancestry in a corporate succession, as a ground for punishing men who have no relation to guilty acts … is [deeply unjust]. Corporate bodies are immortal for the *good* of their members, but not for their *punishment*.'[114]

But Burke's distinction seems untenably inconsistent. To be sure, 'keeping an agreement made by our predecessors forces us to bear burdens that we had no say in incurring'.[115] Paying for wrongs we ourselves did not commit smacks of outworn biblical injunctions – 'In Adam's fall, we sinnèd all'.[116] Repairing historical injustices risks visiting sins on innocent descendants, implying that moral pollution stains entire communities over generations.[117] Nowadays 'public confessions, official apologies, and ritual reflections on their sinful nature [are required] not only of the generation of sinners, but also of the children and grandchildren who inherited the mark of Cain'.[118]

---

[109] Burke, *Reflections on the Revolution in France*, 81–2. John Stuart Mill (*Considerations on Representative Government* (1861), in *CW*, 19: 371–578 at 546) echoed Burke's union with the dead and the yet-to-be-born as a 'community of recollections' essential to collective political identity; see W. James Booth, *Communities of Memory* (Cornell, 2006), 22, 55, 122.

[110] Joyce Appleby, 'To the G.O.P.: who moved my party?' letter, *NYT*, 9 Oct. 2007; Constantin Fasolt, *The Limits of History* (Chicago, 2004), 7–9.

[111] Christopher Kutz, 'Justice in reparations', *Philosophy and Public Affairs* 32 (2004): 277–312 at 310.

[112] John Rawls, *A Theory of Justice* (1971; Oxford, 1999), 252. See my 'On arraigning ancestors', 946–53.

[113] Alasdair MacIntyre, *After Virtue* (1981; Notre Dame, 2007), 220. See Bruce James Smith, *Politics and Remembrance* (Princeton, 1985), 102–30; Alexander Gillespie, *International Environmental Law, Policy, and Ethics* (Clarendon Press, 1997), 115–16.

[114] Burke, *Reflections on the Revolution in France*, 118, 120 (my emphasis).

[115] Janna Thompson, *Taking Responsibility for the Past: Reparation and Historical Injustice* (Polity, 2002), 25.

[116] Benjamin Harris, *The New England Primer* (1690; Albany, NY, 1805), 14–16.

[117] George P. Fletcher, *Romantics at War: Glory and Guilt in the Age of Terrorism* (Princeton, 2002), 187–92; Booth, *Communities of Memory*, 17.

[118] Ian Buruma, 'War guilt, and the difference between Germany and Japan', *NYT*, 29 Dec. 1998: A19.

But beneficiaries of corporate precursors are by the same token bound to amend their wrongs. 'Recent immigrants or descendants of the guiltless may not . . . feel guilt or shame', reasons a political philosopher, but they are nonetheless responsible as citizens, whether by birth and tacit consent or by positive choice, for trying to set things right.[119] Children of twentieth-century American immigrants 'can and do feel guilt' for nineteenth-century slavery; identity as citizens requires them 'not only to feel pride' in America, holds a legal authority, 'but also to recognize the crimes of the American nation and to accept the guilt that follows from wrongdoing', a collective legacy manifest in qualms over politically incorrect speech.[120]

For the sake of peace and comity, national treaties bind future generations. Similarly, state misdeeds should be expiated by subsequent state agents. Heirs and ancestors share collective entities. Legal statutes routinely presume us beholden to ancestral deeds, bound to honour ancestral commitments. Court judgments refer to a temporally inclusive 'we', embracing the lasting juridical institution, not just today's judges. 'They are part of an ongoing enterprise', notes Stanley Fish, 'responsible for its history, [and] charged with the duty of carrying on a project that precedes them and will survive them'.[121]

As with past promises, so with past injustices. 'A responsible government', reasons a philosopher, 'wants to clean up a mess not of its own making, [to] try to repair the injuries of its predecessor'.[122] 'We are all guilty', declared Russian President Boris Yeltsin, apologizing on behalf of the Soviet state for massacring the Romanov family eighty years back.[123] 'European Americans received the fruits of the slave trade', said President Bill Clinton in 1998, 'and *we* were wrong in that'.[124] 'When we say that "the American slave system was wrong" . . . we acknowledge past enslavement as *our* wrong.'[125] Australian Prime Minister Paul Keating assumed accountability for past settler injuries to Aborigines. '*We* took the traditional lands and smashed the traditional ways of life. *We* brought the diseases. *We* committed the murders. *We* took the children from their mothers. *We* practiced discrimination and exclusion. It was *our* ignorance and *our* prejudice. And *our*

[119] Peter Laslett, 'Is there a generational contract?' in his and James S. Fishkin, eds., *Justice between Age Groups and Generations* (Yale, 1992), 24–47 at 41–2. Nations, corporations, churches 'capable of making and keeping transgenerational commitments' should be held responsible for past misdeeds (Thompson, *Taking Responsibility for the Past*, 36–7). Some also consider families collectively responsible (Jeffrey Blustein, *The Moral Demands of Memory* (Cambridge, 2008), 145–69). Eric A. Posner and Adrian Vermeule, 'Reparations for slavery and other historical injustices', *Columbia Law Review* 103 (2003): 689–748 at 707, discuss whether corporate groups of perpetrators and victims are persons for moral purposes.
[120] Fletcher, *Romantics at War*, 207–8. See Anne Norton, 'The virtues of multiculturalism', in Arthur Melzer et al., eds., *Multiculturalism in American Democracy* (Kansas, 1998), 130–8 at 131.
[121] Stanley Fish, 'But I didn't do it!' *NYT*, 21 Mar. 2007: A21. See Avishai Margalit, *The Ethics of Memory* (Harvard, 2002), 96.
[122] P. E. Digeser, *Political Forgiveness* (Cornell, 2001), 166.
[123] 'Address at the Romanov reburial ceremony', 17 July 1998, quoted in Timothy Colton, *Yeltsin* (Basic Books, 2008), 393.
[124] Quoted in Alfred L. Brophy, *Reparations Pro and Con* (Oxford, 2006), 13.
[125] W. James Booth, '"From this far place": Justice and absence', *American Political Science Review*, 105:4 (2011): 750–64 at 757.

failure to imagine these things being done to *us*.'[126] The Swiss canton of Glarus apologized for the 1782 execution of a maid framed as a 'witch'; '*we* were the last to murder a 'witch', and *we* should be the first to pardon one'.[127] 'We' for Yeltsin and Clinton and Keating and the Swiss was a profession not of *personal* complicity or guilt but of continuing *collective responsibility.*

So too with other entities. Repenting their misdeeds acknowledges our corporate implication, our standing 'in some kind of solidarity' with those who did what is now seen as wrong.[128] The Bureau of Indian Affairs (BIA) had long done manifold harm to the tribes in its care, acknowledged a contrite BIA spokesman (himself Indian) in 2000. Although 'BIA employees of today did not commit these wrongs', they must 'acknowledge that the institution [they] serve did, [and] accept ... this legacy of racism and inhumanity. And [take on] the responsibility of putting things right.'[129] Apologizing to African-Americans and pledging aid to black students, J. P. Morgan Chase accepted culpability for predecessor banks that had financed the slave trade and held slaves as collateral on loans.[130] Although not responsible for the criminal 'thoughts and actions of those long deceased', the University of Alabama senate apologized to descendants of slaves forced to construct campus buildings. The institution was organically 'the same', its past and present faculty linked, hence accountable.[131]

'Collective *guilt* across generations may be a morally dangerous idea', concedes a theologian, but 'collective *responsibility* across generations [is] morally necessary ... Old sins will continue to haunt us if we try to forget them or deny that they *were* sins.'[132] It is a contemporary credo that 'a society will not be able to successfully pass into the future until it somehow deals with its demons from the past'.[133] Apologizing on behalf of the once-slaveholding Church of England, the Archbishop of Canterbury declared 'we ... share the shame and sinfulness of our predecessors'.[134] He echoed German President Richard von Weizsäcker's 1985 Bundestag warning that anyone who 'does not wish to remember inhumanity becomes susceptible to ... new infection'. It is essential to 'recognize our continuity with those in the past who ... routinely said and did things that we would today regard as unthinkable'.[135]

[126] Quoted in James Curran, *The Power of Speech: Australian Prime Ministers Defining National Identity* (Melbourne, 2004), 232.
[127] Swiss journalist Walter Hauser quoted in Bojan Pancevski, 'MPs seek pardon for maid framed by rich lover and executed as witch', *Times*, 7 Nov. 2007: 39 (my emphases throughout paragraph).
[128] Dulles, 'Should the Church repent?', 268–70.
[129] Kevin Gover in Rebecca Tsosie, 'The BIA's apology to Native Americans', in Elazar Barkan and Alexander Karn, eds., *Taking Wrongs Seriously* (Stanford, 2006), 185–212 at 193.
[130] Steven Deyle, *Carry Me Back: The Domestic Slave Trade in American Life* (Oxford, 2005), 144.
[131] Charles L. Griswold, *Forgiveness* (Cambridge, 2007), 148–9, and 148n12 (quoting University of Alabama Senate Minutes, 20 April 2004).
[132] Donald W. Shriver, Jr., 'Is there forgiveness in politics?' in Robert D. Enright and Joanna North, eds., *Exploring Forgiveness* (Wisconsin, 1998), 131–49 at 141–2 (my emphasis).
[133] Rhoda E. Howard-Hassmann and Mark Gibney, 'Introduction: apologies and the West', in Mark Gibney et al., eds., *The Age of Apology* (PennPress, 2008), 1–9 at 1.
[134] Rowan Williams, quoted in 'Church apologises for slave trade', *BBC News*, 8 Feb. 2006..
[135] Shriver, 'Is there forgiveness in politics?' 142; Fletcher, *Romantics at War*, 209.

These minatory cautions derive from axiomatic precepts about personal trauma: Freud famously taught that repressing the past came at huge psychic cost. The collective costs of repression are arguably no less onerous.[136] 'When nations, like individuals, try to … ignore [the past's] impact', writes an authority on Korea, 'they are likely to become sick, and their affirmations to become obsessions'.[137] Hence the widespread consensus about confronting horrific histories. 'Nations, like individuals, need to face up to … traumatic past events before they can put them aside and move on to normal life.'[138]

Yet for all the pious talk such confrontation remains rare. The historical hair shirt on the German landscape, if not on the German psyche, more than two generations after the Holocaust, is virtually unique. Exhortations to atone for the last century's manifold horrors, lest the poisons of the past reinfect the body politic, have had only limited success. Few nations have faced up to discreditable pasts. Hiroshima and Nagasaki enabled the Japanese to feel more victimized than victimizers.[139] Seldom (save for works of art) called on to make restitution and long exempt from war-crimes trials, Austrians denied Holocaust complicity until the Waldheim Affair of 1985, and still fancy themselves primarily *victims* of Nazism.[140] The Spanish 1936–9 civil war remained undiscussed by common consent until a 'law of historical memory' was enacted in 2007. But this largely toothless act was an unspoken pact to go on letting the past alone, as one legislator put it, 'forgetting by everyone for everyone', or worse, settling scores, distorting memory, installing new myths that glorify what was once demonized.[141]

Few Russians feel, let alone own up to, complicity in Gulag atrocities. 'We need to do a great deal to ensure [the Soviet Great Terror] is never forgotten', declared President Vladimir Putin.[142] But to most Russians, Stalin's triumphs more than compensate for his cruel tyranny; a 2012 poll held him the greatest figure in Russian history displacing

[136] Sigmund Freud, *Civilization and Its Discontents* (1930), in *CPW*, 21: 64–145; Susan Rubin Suleiman, *Crises of Memory and the Second World War* (Harvard, 2006), 222–5.

[137] Paul M. Edwards, *To Acknowledge a War: The Korean War in American Memory* (Greenwood, 2000), 18.

[138] Tina Rosenberg, *The Haunted Land: Facing Europe's Ghosts after Communism* (Vintage, 1995), xviii. But Rosenberg realizes (xxiv) that states often recall past injustice to justify reprisals.

[139] Ian Buruma, *The Wages of Guilt: Memories of War in Germany and Japan* (Jonathan Cape, 1994), 92–111; Elizabeth S. Dahl, 'Is Japan facing its past?', in Gibney et al., eds., *Age of Apology*, 241–55.

[140] Günter Bischof and Anton Pelinka, eds., *Austrian Historical Memory and National Identity* (Transaction, 1997), 8, 69–95, 106, 114, 119–23, 305–15, 324; Günter Bischof et al., eds., *New Perspectives on Austrians and World War II* (Transaction, 2009), 5, 14–25, 58–9, 182, 192, 333–4, 377; Heidemarie Uhl, 'From victim myth to co-responsibility thesis: Nazi rule, World War II, and the Holocaust in Austrian memory', in R. N. Lebow et al., eds., *The Politics of Memory in Postwar Europe* (Duke, 2006), 40–72; Heidemarie Uhl, *Transformationen des österreichischen Gedächtnisses: Nationalsozialismus, Krieg und Holocaust in der Erinnerungskultur der Zweiten Republik* (Studien Verlag, 2013); Eric R. Kandel, *In Search of Memory* (Norton, 2006), 405–6.

[141] Giles A. Tremlett, *Ghosts of Spain* (New York: Walker, 2006), 70, 79; Felipe Fernandez Armesto, 'After the Generalissimo', *TLS*, 15 Nov. 2013: 10. See Paloma Aguilar Fernández, *Memory and Amnesia* (Berghahn, 2002); Peter Burbidge, 'Waking the dead of the Spanish Civil War', *Journal of International Criminal Justice* 9:3 (2011): 753–81.

[142] Putin at Butovo Memorial Site, 30 Oct. 2007, in Thomas de Waal, ed., *The Stalin Puzzle: Deciphering Post-Soviet Public Opinion* (Washington, DC: Carnegie Endowment for International Peace, 2013), 19.

Lenin (1989), Peter the Great (1994), and Pushkin (2008).[143] Avoided out of fear or apathy, the past for the vast majority is 'simply not interesting', says a chronicler of the horrors of Leningrad's siege; there is a widespread 'desire to forget about everything'.[144]

Forgetting their own involvement in persecuting Jews, Eastern Europeans in Sovietized regimes blamed Germany for all wartime atrocities. Despite massive archival and other evidence of Holocaust participation, most continue to claim guilt-free innocence or ignorance. 'Too much truth' about the past would subvert 'positive collective self-image and soothing national myths'.[145] Balkan failures to come to terms with the past stem from a surfeit of selective memory, obsessive preoccupation with ancient wrongs and enmities.[146] Given that so many nations repress the past 'with psychological impunity', it would seem that 'collective memories can be changed without a "return of the repressed"'.[147]

Burke's compact between the dead, the living, and the unborn works well only where members – citizens or co-religionists – have long felt at home with their institutions. Just as collective apology requires collective agency, collective agency requires 'corporate identity over time and a network of duties assumed and rights conferred'.[148] For historical contrition to be useful also requires consensual faith that moral progress is possible. Absent such hope, apology is 'reduced to a political stratagem', or, concludes Charles Griswold bleakly, 'assuming that wrong-doing was as pervasive in human life as we know it to be', would simply justify 'revenge for never-to-be-forgotten insults and injuries'.[149]

Yet we remain willy-nilly accountable, avers a political scientist, for the whole of our collective pasts:

Our past ... is at the center of our identity in its entirety. An American memory with Emerson but without slavery would scarcely be intelligible; a German memory with Goethe but without the National Socialist years ... unthinkable. [The past] is something given to us into which we are 'thrown', ... a fact at once non-elective and unalterable ... We think back to that past, commemorate it in public, atone for it, and, occasionally, try to forget it. ... [But] it is with us always.[150]

The past's 'attendant injuries and injustices are also a part of that memory, ... woven into what we are as a political community ... even if they are not always at the forefront of our consciousness'.[151] The past is integral to our being. We learn to live courageously with its

---

[143] De Waal, ed., *Stalin Puzzle*, 16, 29–30, 34, 37–8; Andrew E. Kramer, 'New Russian history: yes, people died, but ... ', *IHT*, 16 Aug. 2007: 2.

[144] Yelena S. Chizhova quoted in Ellen Barry, 'A writer invites Russia to engage its painful past', *NYT*, 5 Mar. 2010: A7; De Waal, *Stalin Puzzle*, 43.

[145] John-Paul Himka and Joanna Beata Michlic, eds., *Bringing the Dark Past to Light* (Nebraska, 2013), 'Introduction', 1–24 at 2.

[146] Allan Megill, *Historical Knowledge, Historical Error* (Chicago, 2007), 23–4.

[147] Wulf Kansteiner, 'Finding meaning in memory', *History and Theory* 41 (2002): 179–97 at 186. Expressions of national contrition risk fuelling enmity rather than aiding reconciliation (Jennifer Lind, *Sorry States* (Cornell, 2008)).

[148] Roger Scruton, 'Sorry!' *TLS*, 14 Dec. 2007: 5; Stanley Fish, 'But I didn't do it!' *NYT*, 21 Mar. 2007: A21.

[149] Griswold, *Forgiveness*, 192.

[150] Booth, *Communities of Memory*, 62–3.

[151] W. J. Booth, 'The work of memory: time, identity, and injustice', *Social Research* 75 (2008): 237–62 at 250.

totality, as aware of and alert to its defects and malfunctions as to its glories and virtues, history's farces along with its tragedies.[152] 'There is no document of civilization', Walter Benjamin reminds us, 'which is not at the same time a document of barbarism'.[153] Like Erasmus we need to embrace the vile along with the valiant, the evil with the eminent, the sordid and sad as well as the splendid. For the whole of the past is our legacy.

We do well to retain reminders of actions and agents once acclaimed but since reviled, as lessons in the transience of fame, the fallibility of repute, and the risks of hero worship. Pennsylvania State University has stored out of sight the statue of its once-idolized football coach Joe Paterno, shown to have connived at concealing child abuse. Administrators feared 'its looming presence' would be a 'recurring wound' to victims, triggering 'a visceral, incapacitating memory'. But removing the Paterno statue lets the university forget 'its own culpability in its ruthless pursuit of glory ... Memorial statues are not simply comments on their subjects, but comments on their makers.' Better to have kept the statue, inscribing on it an account of the crimes, to caution those 'who would turn a pastime into a god and elect a mortal man as its avatar'.[154] Or install a 'darkly alluring statue behind Paterno, whispering in his ear, "Mephistopheles". For ... the saint in black cleats sold his soul, and Satan leads the dance'.[155]

Yet our legacy, divine and diabolical alike, is not set in stone but simmers in the incipient flux of time. Far from inertly ending, the ongoing past absorbs our own creative agency, replenishing that of countless precursors. I conclude as I began, with Václav Havel, 'convinced that my existence – like everything that has ever happened – has ruffled the surface of Being, and that after my little ripple, however marginal, insignificant, and ephemeral it may have been, Being is and always will be different from what it was before'.[156]

---

[152] Karl Marx, *The Eighteenth Brumaire of Louis Napoleon* (1852; New York, 1972), 5.

[153] Walter Benjamin, 'Theses on the philosophy of history' (1936), in *Illuminations* (New York: Schocken, 1969), 253–64 at 256.

[154] Ta-Nehisi Coates, 'Leave the statue, to remember', *NYT*, 17 July 2012; Ta-Nehisi Coates, 'The Paterno statue comes down', *Atlantic*, 22 July 2012.

[155] Maureen Dowd, 'Paterno sacked off his pedestal', *NYT*, 21 July 2012.

[156] Václav Havel, *To the Castle and Back* (Knopf, 2007), 330.

SELECT BIBLIOGRAPHY

For university presses, well-known and global publishers place of publication is omitted. For other recent works both place and publisher are given, for older works place only.

Acton, John Emerich Edward Dalberg, Lord, *Essays on Freedom and Power* (Boston, 1948).
    Lectures on Modern History (Macmillan, 1906).
Adams, Douglas, *Life, the Universe, and Everything* (1982; Del Rey, 1995).
Adams, Henry, *Mont-Saint-Michel and Chartres* (1912; Constable, 1950).
Adams, Timothy Dow, *Telling Lies in Modern American Autobiography* (University of North Carolina Press, 1990).
Agee, James, and Walker Evans, *Let Us Now Praise Famous Men* (1936; Houghton Mifflin, 1960).
Alexander, Michael, *Medievalism: The Middle Ages in Modern England* (University of California Press, 2007).
Anderson, Jay, *Time Machines: The World of Living History* (AASLH, 1984).
Anderson, Poul, *Guardians of Time* (London: Pan, 1977).
Ankersmit, Frank, *Sublime Historical Experience* (Stanford University Press, 2005).
Appleby, Joyce, *A Restless Past: History and the American Public* (Rowman & Littlefield, 2005).
Ariès, Philippe, *The Hour of Our Death* (1977), trans. Helen Weaver (Penguin, 1983).
Arnau, Frank [Heinrich Schmitt], *Three Thousand Years of Deception in Art and Antiques* (Jonathan Cape, 1961).
Arthuriana, 'Victorian Arthuriana', 21:2 (Summer 2011): 3–124.
Assmann, Aleida, *Cultural Memory and Western Civilization: Functions, Media, Archives* (Cambridge University Press, 2011).
Assmann, Jan, *Cultural Memory and Early Civilization: Writing, Remembrance, and Political Imagination* (Cambridge University Press, 2011).
Aston, Margaret, *England's Iconoclasts: Laws against Images* (Oxford University Press, 1988).
Atwood, Margaret, *Writing with Intent* (New York: Carroll & Graf, 2005).
Augustine of Hippo, *The City of God* (413–426), trans. Marcus Dods (New York, 1886).
Austin, Linda M., *Nostalgia in Transition, 1780–1917* (University of Virginia Press, 2007).
Babbage, Charles, *The Ninth Bridgewater Treatise: A Fragment* (1837; 2nd edn 1838), in *Works*, 11 vols. (New York University Press, 1989), vol. 9.
Bacon, Francis, *The Advancement of Learning, Book I* (1605; Clarendon Press, 1885).
    The New Organon (1620), ed. Lisa Jardine and trans. Michael Silverthorne (Cambridge University Press, 2000).
Bailyn, Bernard, *On the Teaching and Writing of History* (University Press of New England, 1994).
Baldwin, Stanley, *On England and Other Addresses* (1927; London, 1971).
Bann, Stephen, *The Clothing of Clio: A Study of the Representation of History in Nineteenth-Century Britain and France* (Cambridge University Press, 1984).
Barkan, Elazar, *The Guilt of Nations: Restitution and Negotiating Historical Injustices* (Norton, 2000).
Barkan, Elazar, and Alexander Karn, eds., *Taking Wrongs Seriously: Apologies and Reconciliation* (Stanford University Press, 2006).

Barkan, Leonard, *Unearthing the Past: Archaeology and Aesthetics in the Making of Renaissance Culture* (Yale University Press, 1999).

Barnes, Julian, *England, England* (Jonathan Cape, 1998).

Baron, Hans, *The Crisis of the Early Italian Renaissance: Civic Humanism and Republican Liberty in an Age of Classicism and Tyranny* (1955; rev. edn Princeton University Press, 1966).
'The *Querelle* of the Ancients and the Moderns as a problem for Renaissance scholarship', *JHI* 20 (1959): 3–22.

Bartlett, Frederic C., *Remembering: A Study in Experimental and Social Psychology* (1932; Cambridge University Press, 1995).

Basile, Giambattista, *The Tale of Tales, or Entertainment for Little Ones* (1634), trans. Nancy L. Canepa (Wayne State University Press, 2007).

Bate, Walter Jackson, *The Burden of the Past and the English Poet* (1971; Harvard University Press, 1991).

Bator, Paul M., *The International Trade in Art* (University of Chicago Press, 1983).

Bauer, Patricia J., et al., 'Working together to make sense of the past: mothers' and children's use of internal states language in conversations about traumatic and nontraumatic events', *Journal of Cognition and Development* 6 (2005): 463–88.

Bauman, Zygmunt, *Mortality, Immortality and Other Life Strategies* (Stanford University Press, 1992).

Baxandall, Michael, *Patterns of Intention: On the Historical Explanation of Pictures* (Yale University Press, 1985).

Baycroft, Timothy, and David Hopkin, eds., *Folklore and Nationalism in Europe during the Long Nineteenth Century* (Brill, 2012).

Beauvoir, Simone de, *Old Age* (1970), trans. Patrick O'Brian (Penguin, 1977).

Beaver, Adam G, 'Scholarly pilgrims', in Katherine Van Liere et al. eds., *Sacred History: Uses of the Christian Past in the Renaissance World* (Oxford University Press, 2012), 267–83.

Beck, James, with Michael Daley, *Art Restoration: The Culture, the Business and the Scandal* (Norton, 1996).

Becker, Carl L., 'Everyman his own historian', *AHR* 37 (1932): 221–36.

Beerbohm, Max, *Seven Men and Two Others* (1919; Oxford University Press, 1966).

Bejczy, István, *Erasmus and the Middle Ages: The Historical Consciousness of a Christian Humanist* (Brill, 2001).

Belk, Russell W., 'Las Vegas as farce, consumption as play', *Consumption, Markets, & Culture* 4:2 (2000): 101–23.

Beneš, Barton Lidice, *Curiosa: Celebrity Relics, Historical Fossils, & Other Metamorphic Rubbish* (Abrams, 2002).

Benjamin, Walter, *Illuminations*, trans. Harry Zohn (New York: Schocken, 1969).

Bennett, Alan, *The History Boys* (Faber & Faber, 2006).
People (Faber & Faber, 2012).

Bennett, Andrew, *Romantic Poets and the Culture of Posterity* (Cambridge University Press, 1999).

Berger, Peter L., *Invitation to Sociology: A Humanistic Perspective* (Penguin, 1966).

Berggasse 19: Sigmund Freud's Home and Offices, Vienna 1938 (Basic Books, 1976).

Bergstein, Mary, *Mirrors of Memory: Freud, Photography, and the History of Art* (Cornell University Press, 2010).

Berlin, Isaiah, *Vico and Herder: Two Studies in the History of Ideas* (Hogarth, 1976).

Bester, Alfred, 'Hobson's choice' (1952), in *Starburst* (New York: Signet, 1958), 133–48.

Betjeman, John, 'Antiquarian prejudice' (1937), in *First and Last Loves* (London, 1960), 54–72.

Bettella, Patrizia, *The Ugly Woman: Transgressive Aesthetic Models in Italian Poetry from the Middle Ages to the Baroque* (University of Toronto Press, 2005).

Bignamini, Ilaria, and Clare Hornsby, *Digging and Dealing in Eighteenth-Century Rome* (Yale University Press, 2010).

Billig, Michael, *Talking of the Royal Family* (1992; rev edn Routledge, 1998).

Binney, Marcus, et al., *Satanic Mills: Industrial Architecture of the Pennines* (SAVE Britain's Heritage, 1979).

Blaas, P. B. M., *Continuity and Anachronism: Parliamentary and Constitutional Development in Whig Historiography and in the Anti-Whig Reaction between 1890 and 1930* (The Hague: Nijhoff, 1978).

Blair, Ann M., *Too Much to Know: Managing Scholarly Information before the Internet* (Yale University Press, 2010).

Bloch, Ernst, *Traces (1910–26),* trans. Anthony A. Nassar (Stanford University Press, 2006).

Bloom, Harold, *The Anxiety of Influence: A Theory of Poetry* (1975; 2nd edn Oxford University Press, 1997).

Blustein, Jeffrey, *The Moral Demands of Memory* (Cambridge University Press, 2008).

Blythe, Ronald, *The View in Winter: Reflections on Old Age* (Allen Lane, 1979).

Boardman, John *The Archaeology of Nostalgia: How the Greeks Re-created Their Mythical Past* (Thames & Hudson, 2003).

Boase, T. S. R., *Death in the Middle Ages: Mortality, Judgment and Remembrance* (Thames & Hudson, 1972).

Bodnar, John, *Remaking America: Public Memory, Commemoration, and Patriotism in the Twentieth Century* (Princeton University Press, 1992).

Bolingbroke, Henry St John, *Letters on the Study and Use of History,* 2 vols., rev. edn (1735; London, 1752).

Boorstin, Daniel, *America and the Image of Europe: Reflections on American Thought* (New York: Meridian, 1960).

Booth, W. James, *Communities of Memory: On Witness, Identity, and Justice* (Cornell University Press, 2006).

Borges, Jorge Luis, *Labyrinths* (Penguin, 1970).
  Other Inquisitions 1937–1952 (University of Texas Press, 1964).
  A Personal Anthology (Jonathan Cape, 1967).

Bosworth, R. J. B., *Whispering City: Rome and Its Histories* (Yale University Press, 2011).

Botton, Alain de, *The Architecture of Happiness* (Penguin, 2007).

Boulez, Pierre, *Conversations with Célestin Deliège* (1975), trans. B. Hopkins (London: Eulenberg, 1976).

Bowler, Peter J., *The Invention of Progress: The Victorians and the Past* (Blackwell, 1989).

Bowron, Edgar Peters, and Peter Bjorn Kerber, *Pompeo Batoni: Prince of Painters in Eighteenth-Century Rome* (Yale University Press, 2007).

Boyes, Georgina, *The Imagined Village: Culture, Ideology and the English Folk Revival* (Manchester University Press, 1993).

Boym, Svetlana. *The Future of Nostalgia* (Basic Books, 2002).

Bracker, Alison, and Alison Richmond, eds., *Conservation: Principles, Dilemmas, and Uncomfortable Truths* (Elsevier, 2009).

Bradbury, Malcolm, and David Palmer, eds., *Victorian Poetry* (Edward Arnold, 1972).

Bradshaw, Brendan, 'Nationalism and historical scholarship in modern Ireland', *Irish Historical Studies* 26 (1989): 329–51.

Briggs, Martin S., *Goths and Vandals: A Study of the Destruction, Neglect and Preservation of Historical Buildings in England* (Constable, 1952).

Brilliant, Richard, and Dale Kinney, eds., *Reuse Value: Spolia and Appropriation in Art and Architecture, from Constantine to Sherrie Levine* (Ashgate, 2011).

Brockelman, Paul, 'Of memory and things past', *International Philosophical Quarterly* 15 (1975): 309–25.

Bromley, Roger, *Lost Narratives: Popular Fictions, Politics and Recent History* (Routledge, 1988).

Brophy, Alfred L. *Reparations Pro and Con* (Oxford University Press, 2006).

Brown, George Baldwin, *The Care of Ancient Monuments* (Cambridge University Press, 1905).

Brown, Keith S., and Yannis Hamilakis, eds., *The Usable Past: Greek Metahistories* (Lexington Books, 2003).

Brown, Michael F., 'Heritage trouble: recent work on the protection of intangible cultural property', *IJCP* 12 (2005): 40–61.

    Who Owns Native Culture? (Harvard University Press, 2003).

Brown, Stephen, *Marketing: The Retro Revolution* (Sage, 2001).

Brown, Stephen, and John F. Sherry, Jr., eds., *Time, Space, and the Market: Retroscapes Rising* (Armonk, NY: M. E. Sharpe, 2003).

Browne, Thomas, *Miscellaneous Works of Sir Thomas Browne* (Cambridge, 1831): *Pseododoxia epidemica* (1646), 271–394.

    Works, 6 vols. (1852; London, 1928): *Hydriotaphia: Urn Burial* (1658), 3: 1–50; *Religio medici* (1635), 1: 9–93.

Bruner, Edward M., 'Abraham Lincoln as authentic reproduction', *American Anthropologist* 96 (1994): 397–415.

Bryden, Inga, *Reinventing King Arthur: The Arthurian Legends in Victorian Culture* (Ashgate, 2005).

Buckley, Jerome Hamilton, *The Triumph of Time: A Study of Victorian Concepts of Time, History, Progress, and Decadence* (Harvard University Press, 1967).

Burke, Edmund, *Reflections on the Revolution in France* (1790; Yale University Press, 2003).

Burke, Peter, *The Renaissance Sense of the Past* (Edward Arnold, 1969).

Burnet, Thomas, *The Sacred Theory of the Earth* (Latin 1681–9; English 1684–90, 6th edn 1726; 1752; University of Southern Illinois Press, 1965).

Burrow, J. A., *The Ages of Man: A Study in Medieval Writing and Thought* (Clarendon Press, 1986).

Burrow, J. A., and Ian P. Wei, eds., *Medieval Futures: Attitudes toward the Future in the Middle Ages* (Boydell, 2000).

Burrow, J. W., *A Liberal Descent: Victorian Historians and the English Past* (Cambridge University Press, 1981).

    'The sense of the past', in Laurence Lerner, ed., *The Victorians* (Methuen, 1978), 120–38.

Buruma, Ian, *The Wages of Guilt: Memories of War in Germany and Japan* (Jonathan Cape, 1994).

Butt, John, *Bach's Dialogue with Modernity* (Cambridge University Press, 2010).

    Playing with History: The Historical Approach to Musical Performance (Cambridge University Press, 2003).

Butterfield, Herbert, *The Englishman and His History* (Cambridge University Press, 1944).

    The Historical Novel (Cambridge University Press, 1924).

    Man on His Past: The Study of Historical Scholarship (Cambridge University Press, 1969).

    The Whig Interpretation of History (London: G. Bell, 1931).

Butterfield, Roger, 'Henry Ford, the Wayside Inn, and the problem of "History is bunk"', *Massachusetts Historical Society Proceedings* 77 (1965): 53–66.

Bynum, Caroline Walker, *The Resurrection of the Body in Western Christianity, 200–1336* (Columbia University Press, 2005).

Cabinet Magazine, issue 20, Ruins (Winter 2005/6).

Cacho Casal, Rodrigo, 'The memory of ruins: Quevedo's *Silva* to "Roma antigua y moderna"', *Renaissance Quarterly* 62 (2009): 1167–1203.

Calvino, Italo, *Invisible Cities* (1972), trans. William Weaver (Vintage, 1997).

Campbell, Gordon, *The Bible: The Story of the King James Version 1611–2011* (Oxford University Press, 2011).

Caple, Chris, *Conservation Skills: Judgement, Method and Decision Making* (Routledge, 2000).

Carlyle, Thomas, *Critical and Miscellaneous Essays*, 4 vols. (London, 1888).

Carne-Ross, D. S., 'Scenario for a new year: 3. the sense of the past', *Arion: A Journal of the Humanities and the Classics* 8 (1969): 230–60.

Carnes, Mark C., ed., *Past Imperfect: History According to the Movies* (New York: Henry Holt, 1995).

Carr, John Dickson, *The Devil in Velvet* (Penguin, 1957).

Carretero, Mario, et al., eds., *History Education and the Construction of National Identities* (Charlotte, NC: Information Age, 2012), 153–70.

Carroll, Peter N., *Keeping Time: Memory, Nostalgia, and the Art of History* (University of Georgia Press, 1990).

Carruthers, Mary Jean, *The Book of Memory: A Study of Memory in Medieval Culture* (1990; Cambridge University Press, 2008).

Carson, Cary, 'Colonial Williamsburg and the practice of interpretive planning in American history museums', *Public Historian* 20 (1998): 11–51.

Cave, Terence, *The Cornucopian Text: Problems of Writing in the French Renaissance* (Clarendon Press, 1979).

Chamberlin, E. R., *Preserving the Past* (Dent, 1979).

Chateaubriand, François-René de, *The Genius of Christianity; or, the Spirit and Beauty of the Christian Religion* (1802), trans. Charles I. White (Baltimore, 1871).

Cheever, John, *The Stories of John Cheever* (Knopf, 1978).

Choay, Françoise, *L'Allegorie du patrimoine* (1992; Paris: Éditions du Seuil, rev. edn 1999).

Christian, David, 'A single historical continuum', *Cliodynamics* 2 (2011): 6–26.

Christiansen, Erik, *Channeling the Past: Politicizing History in Postwar America* (University of Wisconsin Press, 2013).

Citron, Suzanne, *Le mythe national: L'histoire de France en question* (1989); *Le mythe national: L'histoire de France en question revisitée* (Paris: L'Atelier, 2008).

Clanchy, M. T., *From Memory to Written Record: England, 1066–1307* (Harvard University Press, 1979).

Clarendon, Edward Hyde, First Earl of, *Of the Reverence Due to Antiquity* (1670), in *A Collection of Several Tracts . . .* (London, 1727), 218–40.

Clark, Tim, 'When the paraders meet the button-counters at Penobscot Bay', *Yankee* (July 1980): 44–9, 129–43.

Clarke, Arthur C., *2001: A Space Odyssey* (1968; New American Library, 1999).

Classen, Albrecht, ed., *Old Age in the Middle Ages and the Renaissance* (De Gruyter, 2007).

Classen, Constance, et al., *Aroma: The Cultural History of Smell* (1994; Routledge, 2002).

Cobbe, Frances Power, 'Fallacies of memory' (1866), in *Hours of Work and Play* (London, 1867), 87–113.

Cochrane, Eric, *Historians and Historiography in the Italian Renaissance* (University of Chicago Press, 1981).

Cohen, Gillian, and Martin A. Conway, eds., *Memory in the Real World*, 3rd edn (New York: Psychology Press, 2008).

Cohen, Kathleen, *Metamorphosis of a Death Symbol: The Transi Tomb in the Late Middle Ages and the Renaissance* (University of California Press, 1973).

Cole, Thomas R., and Sally Gadow, eds., *What Does It Mean to Grow Old? Reflections from the Humanities* (Duke University Press, 1986).

Coleman, Janet, *Ancient and Medieval Memories: Studies in the Reconstruction of the Past* (Cambridge University Press, 1992).

Coles, John, *Experimental Archaeology* (London: Academic Press, 1979).

Collingwood, R. G., *The Idea of History* (Oxford University Press, 1946).

Compton-Burnett, Ivy, *A Father and His Fate* (Gollancz, 1957).

   A Heritage and Its History (1959; Virago, 1992).

Connerton, Paul, *How Modernity Forgets* (Cambridge University Press, 2009).

   How Societies Remember (Cambridge University Press, 1989).

Constable, John, *John Constable's Discourses* (Suffolk Records Society, 1970).

Conway, Martin A., ed., *Recovered Memories and False Memories* (Oxford University Press, 1997).

Cornford, Francis M., *Microcosmographia Academica* (1908; Cambridge University Press, 1953).

Corzo, Miguel Angel, ed., *Mortality Immortality? The Legacy of 20th-Century Art* (Getty Conservation Institute, 1999).

Coupland, Douglas, *Generation A* (London: Windmill, 2010).

   Generation X (St Martin's Press, 1991).

Cowlishaw, Gillian K., 'Cultures of complaint: an ethnography of rural racial rivalry', *Journal of Sociology* 42:4 (2006): 429–45.

Crabbe, George, *The Borough* (1810; London, 1916).

Craddock, Paul, *Scientific Investigation of Copies, Fakes and Forgeries* (Butterworth-Heinemann, 2009).

Creighton, Mandell, *The English National Character* (London, 1896).

Crichton, Michael, *Timeline: A Novel* (Knopf, 1999).

Criticism, Extreme and Sentimental History, 46:3 (2004): 327–496.

Crook, J. Mordaunt, *William Burges and the High Victorian Dream* (London: Murray, 1981).

Csikszentmihalyi, Mihaly, and Eugene Rochberg-Halton, *The Meaning of Things: Domestic Symbols and the Self* (1981; Cambridge University Press, 2002).

Cubitt, Geoffrey, *History and Memory* (Manchester University Press, 2007).

Curl, James Stevens, *A Celebration of Death* (Constable, 1980).

   The Egyptian Revival (Routledge, 2005).

   The Victorian Celebration of Death (Sutton, 2000).

Dames, Nicholas, *Amnesiac Selves: Forgetting, Nostalgia, and British Fiction, 1810–1870* (Oxford University Press, 2001).

Davies, Gordon L., *The Earth in Decay: A History of British Geomorphology 1578–1878* (London: Macdonald, 1969).

Davis, Fred, *Yearning for Yesterday: A Sociology of Nostalgia* (Free Press, 1979).

Davison, Graeme, *The Use and Abuse of Australian History* (Allen & Unwin, 2000).

De Greiff, Pablo, ed., *The Handbook of Reparations* (University of Oxford Press, 2006).

De Groot, Jerome, *Consuming History: Historians and Heritage in Contemporary Popular Culture* (Routledge, 2009).

   The Historical Novel (Routledge, 2010).

DeJean, Joan, *Ancients against Moderns: Culture Wars and the Making of a Fin de Siècle* (University of Chicago Press, 1997).

Dekkers, Midas, *The Way of All Flesh: A Celebration of Decay* (1997), trans. Sherry Marx-MacDonald (London: Harvill, 2000).

Delap, Lucy, *Knowing Their Place: Domestic Service in Twentieth-Century Britain* (Oxford University Press, 2011).

Deletant, Dennis, and Harry Hanak, eds., *Historians as Nation-Builders: Central and South-Eastern Europe* (Macmillan, 1988).

Dellheim, Charles, *The Face of the Past: The Preservation of the Medieval Inheritance in Victorian England* (Cambridge University Press, 1982).

Dening, Greg, *Beach Crossings: Voyaging Across Times, Cultures, and Self* (University of Pennsylvania Press, 2004).

Mr Bligh's Bad Language: Passion, Power and Theatre on the Bounty (Cambridge University Press, 1992).

Performances (Melbourne University Press, 1996).

Dennis, Nigel, *Cards of Identity* (1955; Weidenfeld & Nicolson, 1974).

Denslagen, Wim, *Memories of Architecture: Architectural Heritage and Historiography in the Distant Past*, trans. Donald Gardner (Antwerp: Spinhuis, 2009).

Romantic Modernism: Nostalgia in the World of Conservation, trans. Donald Gardner (Amsterdam University Press, 2009).

De Quincey, Thomas, *Confessions of an English Opium-Eater* (1822) (1–145); ... *Suspira de Profundis* (1845–54) (229–79) (London: Constable, 1927).

De Waal, Thomas, ed., *The Stalin Puzzle: Deciphering Post-Soviet Public Opinion* (Washington, DC: Carnegie Endowment for International Peace, 2013).

Descartes, René, *Discours de la méthode pour bien conduire la raison et cherchez la vérité dans les sciences* (1637; Paris: Vrin, 1989).

Dickens, Charles, *The Pickwick Papers* (1836–1837; Oxford University Press, 1998).

The Uncommercial Traveller (1860; Macmillan, 1925).

Diderot, Denis, *Ruines et paysages III: Salons de 1767* (Paris: Presses Internationales Polytechnique, 1995).

Salons, critique d'art (1759–81), ed. Jean Seznec and Jean Adhémar, 4 vols. (Clarendon Press, 1957–67).

Dietler, Michael, '"Our ancestors the Gauls": archaeology, ethnic nationalism, and the manipulation of Celtic identity', *American Anthropologist* 96 (1994): 584–605.

Digeser, P. E., *Political Forgiveness* (Cornell University Press, 2001).

Dillon, Brian G., ed., *Ruins* (MIT Press, 2011).

Ditchfield, Simon, *Liturgy, Sanctity and History in Tridentine Italy* (Cambridge University Press, 1995).

Donne, John, *Poetry of John Donne*, vol. 2: *The Elegies* (University of Indiana Press, 2000).

Doss, Erika, *Memorial Mania: Public Feeling in America* (University of Chicago Press, 2010).

Draaisma, Douwe, *The Nostalgia Factory: Memory, Time and Ageing* (Yale University Press, 2013).

Why Life Speeds Up as You Get Older: How Memory Shapes Our Past (2001), trans. A. and E. Pomerans (Cambridge University Press, 2004).

Dray, William H., *History as Re-enactment: R. G. Collingwood's Idea of History* (Clarendon Press, 1995).

Dryden, John, *The Works of John Dryden*, 20 vols. (University of California Press, 1956–79).

du Bellay, Joachim, *La Deffence et illustration de la langue francoyse* (1549; Geneva: Droz, 2001).

'The Regrets', with 'The Antiquities of Rome' [1558], *Three Latin Elegies, and 'The Defence and Enrichment of the French Language'*, trans. Richard Helgerson (University of Pennsylvania Press, 2006).

Dubin, Nina L., *Futures & Ruins: Eighteenth-Century Paris and the Paintings of Hubert Robert* (Getty Research Institute, 2010).

Dulles, Cardinal Avery, *Church and Society: The Lawrence J. McGinley Lectures, 1988–2007* (Fordham University Press, 2008).

du Maurier, Daphne, *The House on the Strand* (1969; London: Pan, 1979).

Durkheim, Émile, *The Elementary Forms of Religious Life* (1912), trans. Karen Fields (Free Press, 1995).

Dussen, W. J. van der, *History as a Science: The Philosophy of R. G. Collingwood* (The Hague: Nijhoff, 1981).

Dvořák, Max, *Katechismus der Denkmalpflege* (Vienna, 1916).

Eco, Umberto, *Faith in Fakes: Travels in Hyperreality* (1973), trans. William Weaver (Harcourt, 1986).
  Mouse or Rat: Translation as Negotiation (London: Phoenix, 2004).
  Six Walks in the Fictional Woods (Harvard University Press, 1994).

Eco, Umberto, comp., *On Ugliness*, trans. Alastair McEwen (London: Harvill Secker, 2007).

Edensor, Tim, *Industrial Ruins: Spaces, Aesthetics and Materiality* (Berg, 2005).

Edgerton, Gary R., and P. C. Rollins, eds., *Television Histories: Shaping Collective Memory in the Media Age,* (University Press of Kentucky, 2001).

Edwards, Amelia, *A Thousand Miles up the Nile* (1877; reprint of 1888 edn London: Century, 1982).

Eggert, Paul, *Securing the Past: Conservation in Art, Architecture and Literature* (Cambridge University Press, 2009).

Eiseley, Loren, *All the Strange Hours: The Excavation of a Life* (1975; University of Nebraska Press, 2000).

Eisenstein, Elizabeth L., 'Clio and Chronos', *History and Theory* 6 (1966): 36–64.
  The Printing Press as an Agent of Change: Communications and Cultural Transformations in Early-Modern Europe (Cambridge University Press, 1979; 3rd edn 1991).

Elder, Betty Doak, 'War games: recruits and their critics draw battle lines over authenticity', *History News* 36:8 (1981): 8–12.

El-Haj, Nadia Abu, *The Genealogical Science: The Search for Jewish Origins and the Politics of Epistemology* (University of Chicago Press, 2012).

Eliade, Mircea, *Myth and Reality*, trans. Willard R. Trask (Allen & Unwin, 1964).
  The Myth of the Eternal Return (1949), trans. Willard R. Trask (Princeton University Press, 1994).

Eliot, T. S., *Selected Essays* (Faber & Faber, 1934).

Elliot, Robert, *Faking Nature: The Ethics of Environmental Restoration* (1982; Routledge, 1997).

Ellison, Ralph, et al., 'The uses of history in fiction', *Southern Literary Journal* 1:2 (Spring 1969): 57–90.

Elon, Amos, 'Politics and archaeology' (1994), in Neil Asher Silberman and David B. Small, eds., *The Archaeology of Israel: Constructing the Past, Interpreting the Present* (Sheffield: Academic Press, 1997), 34–47.

Elsner, John, and Roger Cardinal, eds., *The Cultures of Collecting* (Reaktion, 1994).

Elson, Ruth Miller, *Guardians of Tradition: American Schoolbooks of the Nineteenth Century* (University of Nebraska Press, 1964).

Ely, David, *Time Out* (Secker & Warburg, 1968).

Emerson, Ralph Waldo, *The Complete Works*, 12 vols. (Boston: Houghton Mifflin, 1904–12).
  The Portable Emerson (Viking, 1946).

Emery, Elizabeth, and Laura Morowitz, *Consuming the Past: The Medieval Revival in Fin-de-Siècle France* (Ashgate, 2003).

Erasmus, Desiderius, *Collected Works* (University of Toronto Press, 1999).
  Pilgrimages to Saint Mary of Walsingham and Saint Thomas of Canterbury (c. 1512–1526), trans. John Gough Nichols (Westminster, 1849).
  The Praise of Folly (1509), trans. John Wilson (University of Michigan Press, 1958).

Everett, Edward, *Orations and Speeches on Various Occasions*, 3 vols. (Boston, 1836–1870).

Farmer, James Oscar, 'Playing rebels: reenactment as nostalgia and defense of the Confederacy in the Battle of Aiken', *Southern Cultures* 11:1 (2005): 46–73.

Fasolt, Constantin, *The Limits of History* (University of Chicago Press, 2004).

Feiler, Bruce, *America's Prophet: Moses and the American Story* (HarperCollins, 2009).

Ferguson, Margaret, 'The exile's defense: Du Bellay's *La Deffence et illustration de la langue francoyse*', *PMLA* 93 (1978): 275–89.

Fernyhough, Charles, *Pieces of Light: The New Science of Memory* (London: Profile, 2012).

Ferro, Marc, *The Use and Abuse of History, or How the Past Is Taught* (1981; Routledge, 2003).

Film & History, Reality television, 37:1 (2007), 16–72.

Finney, Jack, *Time and Again* (Simon & Schuster, 1970).

Fischer, David Hackett, *Washington's Crossing* (Oxford University Press, 2004).

Fitzgerald, F. Scott, *The Great Gatsby* (1925; Scribners, 1953).

FitzGerald, Frances, *America Revised: History Schoolbooks in the Twentieth Century* (Random House, 1980).

Fletcher, George P., *Romantics at War: Glory and Guilt in the Age of Terrorism* (Princeton University Press, 2002).

Fliegelman, Jay, *Prodigals and Pilgrims: The American Revolution against Patriarchal Authority, 1750–1800* (Cambridge University Press, 1982).

Fontenelle, Bernard, *Entretiens sur la pluralité des mondes & Digression sur les Anciens et les Modernes* (1688; Clarendon Press, 1955).

Foote, Bud, *The Connecticut Yankee in the Twentieth Century: Travel to the Past in Science Fiction* (Greenwood, 1991).

Forgie, George B., *Patricide in the House Divided: A Psychological Interpretation of Lincoln and His Age* (Norton, 1979).

Fornara, Charles William, *The Nature of History in Ancient Greece and Rome* (University of California Press, 1983).

Forty, Adrian, and Susanne Küchler, eds., *The Art of Forgetting* (Berg, 1999).

Foucault, Michel, *The Order of Things: An Archaeology of the Human Sciences* (1966; Pantheon, 1970).

France, Peter, and William St Clair, eds., *Mapping Lives: The Uses of Biography* (Oxford University Press, 2004).

Frederiksen, Rune, and Eckart Marchand, eds., *Plaster Casts: Making, Collecting and Displaying from Classical Antiquity to the Present* (De Gruyter, 2011).

Freedberg, David, *Iconoclasts and Their Motives* (Maarssen, Netherlands: Gary Schwartz, 1985).

Freeman, Charles, *Holy Bones, Holy Dust: How Relics Shaped the History of Medieval Europe* (Yale University Press, 2011).

Freeman, Edward A., *The Preservation and Restoration of Ancient Monuments* (Oxford, 1852).

Freeman, Michael, *Victorians and the Prehistoric: Tracks to a Lost World* (Yale University Press, 2004).

Freud, Sigmund, *Civilization and Its Discontents* (1930), in *CPW*, 21: 64–145.

The Complete Psychological Works (Hogarth Press/Institute of Psycho-Analysis, 1966–74).

Delusion and Dream in Jensen's Gradiva (1906), and Appendix to 2nd edn (1911), in *CPW*, 9: 7–95 [pagination from *Delusion and Dream and Other Essays* (Boston: Beacon, 1956), 25–118, 119–21].

Friel, Brian, *Translations* (Faber & Faber, 1981).

Fritzsche, Peter, *Stranded in the Present: Modern Time and the Melancholy of History* (Harvard University Press, 2004).

Frye, Northrop, *The Great Code: The Bible and Literature* (Routledge, 1983).

Fuglestad, Finn, *The Ambiguities of History: The Problem of Ethnocentrism in Historical Writing* (Oslo: Academic Press, 2005).

Fumaroli, Marc, 'Les abeilles et les araignées', in Anne-Marie Lecoq, ed., *La Querelle des Anciens et des Modernes XVIIème–XVIIIème siècles* (Paris: Gallimard, 2001), 7–218.

Furstenberg, François, *In the Name of the Father: Washington's Legacy, Slavery, and the Making of a Nation* (Penguin, 2006).

Gable, Eric, Richard Handler, and Anna Lawson, 'On the uses of relativism: fact, conjecture, and black and white histories at Colonial Williamsburg', *American Ethnologist* 19 (1992): 791–805.

Gamboni, Dario, *The Destruction of Art: Iconoclasm and Vandalism since the French Revolution* (Reaktion, 1997).

Gamwell, Lynn, and Richard Wells, eds., *Sigmund Freud and Art: His Personal Collection of Antiquities* (SUNY Press/Freud Museum, 1989).

García Márquez, Gabriel, *One Hundred Years of Solitude* (1967), trans. Gregory Rabassa (Penguin, 1972).

Gathercole, Peter, and David Lowenthal, eds., *The Politics of the Past* (Unwin Hyman, 1990).

Geary, Patrick J., *Furta Sacra: Thefts of Relics in the Central Middle Ages* (1978; rev. edn Princeton University Press, 1990).

 Living with the Dead in the Middle Ages (Cornell University Press, 1994).

 The Myth of Nations: The Medieval Origins of Europe (Princeton University Press, 2002).

 Phantoms of Remembrance: Memory and Oblivion at the End of the First Millennium (Princeton University Press, 1994).

Giamatti, A. Bartlett, *Exile and Change in Renaissance Literature* (Yale University Press, 1984).

Gibbon, Edward, *The History of the Decline and Fall of the Roman Empire*, 3 vols. (1776–88; Allen Lane, 1994).

Gibney, Mark, et al., eds., *The Age of Apology: Facing up to the Past* (PennPress, 2008).

Gildea, Robert, *The Past in French History* (Yale University Press, 1994).

Gill, A. A., *The Angry Island: Hunting the English* (London: Phoenix, 2006).

Gilmore, Myron P., *Humanists and Jurists: Six Studies in the Renaissance* (Harvard University Press, 1963).

Gilpin, William, *Observations on the River Wye, and Several Parts of South Wales, &c, relative chiefly to Picturesque Beauty; Made in . . . 1770*, 3rd edn (London, 1792).

 Observations, relative chiefly to Picturesque Beauty, Made in the Year 1772, on . . . the Mountains, and Lakes of Cumberland, and Westmoreland, 2 vols. (London, 1796).

 Remarks on Forest Scenery and Other Woodland Views . . . , 3 vols. (London, 1794).

Gingrich, Newt, *A Nation like No Other: Why American Exceptionalism Matters* (Regnery, 2011).

Ginsberg, Robert, *The Aesthetics of Ruins* (Rodopi, 2004).

Ginzburg, Carlo, *Wooden Eyes: Nine Reflections on Distance* (1998), trans. Martin Ryle and Kate Soper (Columbia University Press, 2001).

Girouard, Mark, *The Return to Camelot: Chivalry and the English Gentleman* (Yale University Press, 1981).

Glassberg, David, *American Historical Pageantry* (University of North Carolina Press, 1990).

Glendinning, Miles, *The Conservation Movement: A History of Architectural Preservation* (Routledge, 2013).

Godkin, E. L., 'The Constitution, and its defects', *North American Review* 99 (1864): 117–45.

Goebel, Stefan, *The Great War and Medieval Memory: War, Remembrance and Medievalism in Britain and Germany, 1914-1940* (Cambridge University Press, 2006).

Goethe, Johann Wolfgang von, *Gedenkausgabe der Werke, Briefe, und Gespräche*, 24 vols. (Zurich: Artemis, 1948–71).

 Goethe: Conversations and Encounters, trans. David Lake and Robert Pick (Regnery, 1966).

Goldhill, Simon, *Victorian Culture and Classical Antiquity* (Princeton University Press, 2011).

Goldsmith, Oliver, *The Deserted Village* (London, 1770).

Goldwater, Robert, *Primitivism in Modern Art* (Harvard University Press, 2003).

Gombrich, Ernst H., *Norm and Form: Studies in the Art of the Renaissance* (Phaidon, 1966).
  Reflections on the History of Art: Views and Reviews (University of California Press, 1987).
Goody, Jack, and Ian Watt, 'The consequences of literacy' (1963), in Jack Goody, ed., *Literacy in Traditional Societies* (Cambridge University Press, 1968), 27–68.
Gosse, Edmund, *Father and Son: A Study of Two Temperaments* (1907; Heinemann, 1964).
Gosse, Philip Henry, *Omphalos: An Attempt to Untie the Geological Knot* (London, 1857).
Gould, Stephen Jay, *The Flamingo's Smile: Reflections in Natural History*, (Norton, 1985).
  'Piltdown revisited', *Natural History* 88:3 (Mar. 1979): 86–98.
  Time's Arrow, Time's Cycle: Myth and Metaphor in the Discovery of Geological Time (Harvard University Press, 1987).
Grafton, Anthony T., *Bring Out Your Dead: The Past as Revelation* (Harvard University Press, 2001).
  Forgers and Critics: Creativity and Duplicity in Western Scholarship (Princeton University Press, 1990).
  What Was History? The Art of History in Early Modern Europe (Cambridge University Press, 2007).
Green, Christopher, and Jens M. Daehner, eds., *Modern Antiquity: Picasso, de Chirico, Léger, Picabia* (J. Paul Getty Museum, 2011).
Greenberg, Jeff, Jeff Schimel, and Andy Martens, 'Ageism: denying the face of the future', in Todd D. Nelson, ed., *Ageism: Stereotyping and Prejudice against Older Persons* (MIT Press, 2002), 27–48.
Greene, Thomas M., *The Light in Troy: Imitation and Discovery in Renaissance Poetry* (Yale University Press, 1982).
Greenfield, Jeanette, *The Return of Cultural Treasures* (1989; 2nd edn Cambridge University Press, 1996).
Griffiths, Tom, *Hunters and Collectors: The Antiquarian Imagination in Australia* (Cambridge University Press, 1996).
Griswold, Charles L., *Forgiveness: A Philosophical Exploration* (Cambridge University Press, 2007).
Gross, David, *Lost Time: On Remembering and Forgetting in Late Modern Culture* (University of Massachusetts Press, 2000).
Gruen, Erich S., *Heritage and Hellenism: The Reinvention of Jewish Tradition* (University of California Press, 1998).
Grunska, Kip M., *From Fard to Pard: A Story of Civil War Reenactment* (Lincoln, NE: iUniverse, 2003).
Gubser, Michael, *Time's Visible Surface: Alois Riegl and the Discourse on History and Temporality in Fin-de-Siècle Vienna* (Wayne State University Press, 2006).
Guffey, Elizabeth F., *Retro: The Culture of Revival* (Reaktion, 2006).
Guillaume, Marc, interview, '*La politique du patrimoine* . . . vingt ans après', *Labyrinthe*, no. 7 (2000): 11–20.
Gullette, Margaret Morganroth, *Aged by Culture* (University of Chicago Press, 2004).
Gurevitch, Aron J., *Categories of Medieval Culture* (1972; Routledge, 1985).
Haas, Charlie, 'The secret life of the American tourist', *New West* 5:16 (1980): 13–29.
Haggard, H. Rider, *She: A History of Adventure* (1887; London: Macdonald, 1948).
Hakewill, George, *An Apologie or Declaration of the Power and Providence of God in the Government of the World Consisting in an Examination and Censure of the Common Errour Touching Nature's Perpetuall and Universal Decay* (1627; 3rd edn, 2 vols., Oxford, 1635).
Halbwachs, Maurice, *On Collective Memory* (1925), trans. F. J. and V. Y. Ditter (Harper & Row, 1980).

Hall, Marcus, *Earth Repair: A Transatlantic History of Environmental Restoration* (University of Virginia Press, 2005).

Hamilakis, Yannis, *The Nation and Its Ruins: Antiquity, Archaeology, and National Imagination in Greece* (Oxford University Press, 2007).

Hamilakis, Yannis, and Nicoletta Momigliano, eds., *Archaeology and European Modernity: Producing and Consuming the 'Minoans'*, Creta Antica 7 (Padua: Bottego d'Erasmo, 2006).

Hamlin, Talbot, *Greek Revival Architecture in America* (1944; Dover, 1964).

Handler, Richard, and Eric Gable, *The New History in an Old Museum: Creating the Past at Colonial Williamsburg* (Duke University Press, 1997).

Handler, Richard, and Willam Saxton, 'Dyssimulation: reflexivity, narrative, and the quest for authenticity in "living history"', *Cultural Anthropology* 3 (1988): 242–60.

Harbison, Robert, *The Built, the Unbuilt and the Unbuildable* (MIT Press, 1991).

  Deliberate Regression (Knopf, 1980).

Hardy, Matthew, ed., *The Venice Charter Revisited: Modernism, Conservation and Tradition in the 21st Century* (Newcastle upon Tyne: Cambridge Scholars, 2008).

Hardy, Thomas, *Collected Poems*, 4th edn (Macmillan, 1948).

  Jude the Obscure (1895; Oxford University Press, 1998).

  A Laodicean (1881; London, 1912).

Harris, Alexandra, *Romantic Moderns: English Writers, Artists and the Imagination from Virginia Woolf to John Piper* (Thames & Hudson 2010).

Harris John, *Moving Rooms; The Trade in Architectural Salvages* (Yale University Press, 2007).

Harris, Victor, *All Coherence Gone: A Study of the Seventeenth Century Controversy over Disorder and Decay in the Universe* (University of Chicago Press, 1949).

Harrison, Robert Pogue, *The Dominion of the Dead* (University of Chicago Press, 2003).

Harrisson, Tom, *Living through the Blitz* (Collins, 1976).

Hartley, L. P., *The Go-Between* (1953; NYRB Classics, 2002).

Harvey, John, *Conservation of Buildings* (London: John Baker, 1972).

Haskell, Francis, *History and Its Images: Art and the Interpretation of the Past* (Yale University Press, 1995).

  Rediscoveries in Art: Some Aspects of Taste, Fashion and Collecting in England and France, 2nd edn (Phaidon, 1976).

Haskell, Francis, and Nicholas Penny, *The Most Beautiful Statues: The Taste for Antique Sculpture 1500–1900* (Oxford: Ashmolean Museum, 1981).

  Taste and the Antique: The Lure of Classical Sculpture 1500–1900 (Yale University Press, 1981).

Hastrup, Kirsten, ed., *Other Histories* (Routledge, 1992).

Hatherley, Owen, *Militant Modernism* (Ropley: 0 Books, 2008).

Havel, Václav, *To the Castle and Back*, trans. Paul Wilson (Knopf, 2007).

Hawthorne, Nathaniel, *Doctor Grimshawe's Secret* (Boston: Houghton Mifflin, 1883).

  The English Notebooks (New York: [P]MLA, 1941).

  The House of the Seven Gables (1852), in *Works*, 2.

  The Marble Faun; or, The Romance of Monte Beni (1859), in *Works*, 4.

  Works, Centennial edn, 23 vols. (Ohio State University Press, 1962–80).

Hazlitt, William, *Complete Works*, 21 vols. (Dent, 1930–4).

Heaney, Seamus, 'Place, pastness, poems: a triptych', *Salmagundi* no. 68/69 (1985/6), 30–47.

Hedrick, Charles W., Jr., *History and Silence: Purge and Rehabilitation of Memory in Late Antiquity* (University of Texas Press, 2000).

Hell, Julia, and Andreas Schönle, eds., *Ruins of Modernity* (Duke University Press, 2010).

Hen, Yitzhak, and Matthew Innes, eds., *The Uses of the Past in the Early Middle Ages* (Cambridge University Press, 2000).

Henket, Hans-Hubert, and Hilde Heynen, eds., *Back from Utopia: The Challenge of the Modern Movement* (Rotterdam: 101 Publ. 2002).

Herder, Johann Gottfried von, *On World History: An Anthology*, ed. Hans Adler and trans. Ernest A. Menze (Armonk, NY: M. E. Sharpe, 1997).

Reflections on the Philosophy of the History of Mankind (1784–91), abridged trans. T. O. Churchill (University of Chicago Press, 1968).

Hewison, Robert, *The Heritage Industry: Britain in a Climate of Decline* (Methuen, 1987).

Hewitt, Rachel, *Map of a Nation: A Biography of the Ordnance Survey* (Granta, 2010).

Hexter, J. H., 'The rhetoric of history', in *International Encyclopedia of the Social Sciences* (Macmillan, 1968), 6: 368–94.

Highet, Gilbert, *The Classical Tradition: Greek and Roman Influences on Western Literature* (Clarendon Press, 1949).

Himka, John-Paul, and Joanna Beata Michlic, eds., *Bringing the Dark Past to Light: The Reception of the Holocaust in Postcommunist Europe* (University of Nebraska Press, 2013).

Hirsch, Marianne, *The Generation of Postmemory: Writing and Visual Culture after the Holocaust* (Columbia University Press, 2012).

Hirsch, Marianne, ed., *The Familial Gaze* (University Press of New England, 1999).

Historic Preservation Today (Charlottesville, VA: National Trust for Historic Preservation/Colonial Williamsburg, 1966).

History and Theory, Historical Distance: Reflections on a Metaphor, 50:4 (Dec. 2011).

Hjemdahl, Kirsti Mathiesen, 'History as a cultural playground', *Ethnologica Europaea* 32:2 (2002): 105–24.

Hobsbawm, Eric J., and Terence Ranger, eds., *The Invention of Tradition* (Cambridge University Press, 1983).

Hofer, Johannes, 'Medical dissertation on nostalgia' (1688), trans. Carolyn Kiser Anspach, *Bulletin of the Institute of the History of Medicine* (Aug. 1934): 376–91.

Hoffman, Eva, *After Such Knowledge: Memory, History, and the Legacy of the Holocaust* (New York: Public Affairs, 2004).

Holtorf, Cornelius J., *From Stonehenge to Las Vegas: Archaeology as Popular Culture* (AltaMira, 2005).

'The heritage of heritage', *Heritage & Society* 5 (2012): 153–74.

'On pastness: a reconsideration of materiality in archaeological object authenticity', *Anthropological Quarterly* 86 (2013): 427–44.

'The time travellers' tools of the trade: some trends at Lejre', *International Journal of Heritage Studies* 19:5 (2013): 1–16.

Homer, *The Odyssey*, trans. Robert Fagles (Penguin, 1996).

Hope, Charles, 'The National Gallery cleaning controversy', *ArtWatch UK* 28 (Winter 2012): 4–15.

Horwitz, Tony, *Confederates in the Attic: Dispatches from the Unfinished Civil War* (Pantheon, 1998).

Hosmer, Charles B., Jr., *Presence of the Past: A History of the Preservation Movement in the United States before Williamsburg* (Putnam, 1965).

Preservation Comes of Age: From Williamsburg to the National Trust, 1926–1949, 2 vols. (University of Virginia Press, 1981).

Housman, A. E., *A Shropshire Lad* (1896; London, 1956).

Hubbard, L. Ron, *Dianetics: The Modern Science of Mental Health* (1950; Church of Scientology, 1979).

Typewriter in the Sky (1940; London: Fantasy, 1952).

Hudson, Kenneth, *A Social History of Archaeology: The British Experience* (Macmillan, 1980).

Hugo, Victor, *Oeuvres complètes*, 18 vols. (Paris, 1967–70).

Huizinga, Johan *The Waning of the Middle Ages* (1919), trans. Frederik Jan Hopman (Dover, 1999).

Humboldt, Wilhelm von, 'On the historian's task' (1822), trans. Louis O. Mink, *History and Theory* 6 (1967): 57–71.

Hume, David, *An Enquiry Concerning Human Understanding* (1748), *Philosophical Works*, 4: 3–135.

    The Philosophical Works, 4 vols. (repr. edn 1886; Aalen: Scientia, 1964).

Humphrey, Chris, and W. M. Ormrod, eds., *Time in the Medieval World* (York Medieval Press, 2001).

Hunter, Michael, ed., *Preserving the Past: The Rise of Heritage in Modern Britain* (Stroud: Sutton, 1996).

Hussey, Christopher, *The Picturesque: Studies in a Point of View* (1927; London: Cass, 1967).

Huxtable, Ada Louise, *The Unreal America: Architecture and Illusion* (New York: New Press, 1997).

Huyghe, René, 'The Louvre Museum and the problem of cleaning old pictures', *Museum International* 3 (1950): 191–206.

Huyssen, Andreas, *Present Pasts: Urban Palimpsests and the Politics of Memory* (Stanford University Press, 2003).

Isaac, Gwyneira, 'Whose idea was this? Museums, replicas, and the reproduction of knowledge', *Current Anthropology* 52 (2011): 211–33.

Jackson, John Brinckerhoff, *The Necessity for Ruins, and Other Topics* (University of Massachusetts Press, 1980).

Jalland, Pat, *Death in the Victorian Family* (Oxford University Press, 1996).

James, Henry, *The American Scene* (1907; University of Indiana Press, 1968).

    The Awkward Age (1899; Penguin, 1966).

    The Complete Tales, 12 vols. (Hart-Davis, 1964): 'The Birthplace' (1903), 11: 405–65.

    English Hours (Heinemann, 1905): 'Abbeys and castles' (1877), 225–43; 'In Warwickshire' (1877), 197–223.

    Hawthorne (Macmillan, 1879).

    Novels and Tales, 24 vols. (Scribners, 1908–9).

    The Outcry (1911; New York: H. Fertig, 1982).

    The Sense of the Past (Scribners, 1917), with 'Notes', 289–358.

    A Small Boy and Others (1913), *Autobiography* (London: W. H. Allen, 1956), 3–236.

    The Spoils of Poynton (1897; Penguin, 1963).

Jencks, Charles, ed., *Post-Modern Classicism: The New Synthesis* (Wiley, 1980).

Jenkins, Keith, et al., eds., *Manifestos for History* (Routledge, 2007).

Jenkyns, Richard, *The Victorians and Ancient Greece* (Blackwell, 1980).

Jones, Mark, ed., *Fake? The Art of Deception* (British Museum Press, 1990).

Jones, Richard Foster, *Ancients and Moderns: A Study of the Rise of the Scientific Movement in Seventeenth-Century England*, 2nd edn (University of California Press, 1965).

Jupp, Peter C., and Clare Gittings, eds., *Death in England* (Manchester University Press, 1999).

Just, Roger, 'Cultural certainties and private doubts', in Wendy James, ed., *The Pursuit of Certainty: Religious and Cultural Formulations* (Routledge, 1995), 285–308.

Juvenal, *The Satires* (early second century AD), trans. Rolfe Humphries (University of Indiana Press, 1958).

Kahneman, Daniel, *Thinking, Fast and Slow* (Penguin, 2011).

Kames, Henry Home, Lord, *Sketches of the History of Man* (1734), rev. edn, 4 vols. (Edinburgh, 1788).

Kammen, Michael, *In the Past Lane: Historical Perspectives on American Culture* (Oxford University Press, 1997).

    A Machine That Would Go of Itself: The Constitution in American Culture (1986; Transaction, 2006).

Mystic Chords of Memory: The Transformation of Tradition in American Culture (Knopf, 1991).

A Season of Youth: The American Revolution and the Historical Imagination (Knopf, 1973).

Kandel, Eric R., *In Search of Memory: The Emergence of a New Science of the Mind* (Norton, 2006).

Katriel, Tamar, *Performing the Past: A Study of Israeli Settlement Museums* (Mahwah, NJ: Erlbaum, 1997).

Katz, Eric, 'Further adventures in the case against restoration', *Environmental Ethics* 34 (2012): 67–97.

Kearl, Michael C., The proliferation of postselves in American civic and popular culture, *Mortality* 15:1 (2010): 47–63.

Keats, Jonathon, *Why Fakes Are the Great Art of Our Age* (Oxford University Press, 2013).

Kedourie, Elie, ed., *Nationalism in Asia and Africa* (Weidenfeld & Nicolson, 1971).

Keene, Donald, *The Pleasures of Japanese Literature* (Columbia University Press, 1988).

Kelley, Donald R., *Foundations of Modern Historical Scholarship: Language, Law, and History in the French Renaissance* (Columbia University Press, 1970).

Kemp, Anthony, *The Estrangement of the Past: A Study in the Origins of Modern Historical Consciousness* (Oxford University Press, 1991).

Kendig, Frank, and Richard Hutton, *Life-Spans or How Long Things Last* (Holt, Rinehart and Winston, 1979).

Kenyon, Nicholas, ed., *Authenticity and Early Music* (Oxford University Press, 1988).

Kern, Stephen, *The Culture of Time and Space 1880–1918* (1983; Harvard University Press, 2003).

Kewes, Paulina, ed., *The Uses of History in Early Modern England* (University of California Press, 2006).

Kiberd, Declan, *Inventing Ireland: The Literature of a Modern Nation* (Harvard University Press, 1995).

King, Stephen, *11.22.63: A Novel* (Scribner, 2011).

Kinser, Samuel, 'Ideas of temporal change and cultural process in France, 1470–1535', in Anthony Molho and John A. Tedeschi, eds., *Renaissance Studies in Honor of Hans Baron* (University of Northern Illinois Press, 1971), 713–55.

Kirschenblatt-Gimblett, Barbara, *Destination Culture: Tourism, Museums, and Heritage* (University of California Press, 1998).

Klein, Kerwin Lee, 'On the emergence of memory in historical discourse', *Representations* 69 (2000): 127–50.

Knight, Richard Payne, *An Analytical Inquiry into the Principles of Taste*, 3rd edn (London, 1805).

Kohl, Philip L., and Clare Fawcett, eds., *Nationalism, Politics, and the Practice of Archaeology* (Cambridge University Press, 1995).

Koriat, Asher, Morris Goldsmith, and Ainat Pansky, 'Toward a psychology of memory accuracy', *Annual Review of Psychology* 51 (2000): 481–537.

Koselleck, Reinhart, *Futures Past: On the Semantics of Historical Time* (1979), trans. Keith Tribe (Columbia University Press, 2004).

The Practice of Conceptual History, trans. Todd Samuel Presner et al. (Stanford University Press, 2002).

Kracauer, Siegfried, *History: The Last Things before the Last* (1969), rev. edn., completed by Paul Oscar Kristeller (Princeton, NJ: Markus Wiener, 1995).

Kubler, George, *The Shape of Time: Remarks on the History of Things* (1962; Yale University Press, 2008).

Labadi, Sophia, *Unesco, Cultural Heritage, and Outstanding Universal Value* (AltaMira, 2013).

Lancaster, Osbert, *Here, of All Places* (Houghton Mifflin, 1958).

Lang, Robert, ed., *The Birth of a Nation: D. W. Griffith, Director* (Rutgers University Press, 1994).

Laumer, Keith, *The Great Time Machine Hoax* (Grosset & Dunlap, 1963).

Lears, T. J. Jackson, *No Place of Grace: Antimodernism and the Transformation of American Culture 1880–1920* (Pantheon, 1981).

Lebow, Richard Ned, Wulf Kansteiner, and Claudio Fogu, eds., *The Politics of Memory in Postwar Europe* (Duke University Press, 2006).

Lees-Milne, James, *Ancestral Voices* (Chatto & Windus, 1975).
  Caves of Ice (Chatto & Windus, 1983).
  People and Places: Country House Donors and the National Trust (London: Murray, 1992).

Leeuw-Roord, Joke van der, 'Beyond the doorstep: the nature of history teaching across Europe', 155–76, and 'Education for inclusion, awareness and tolerance', 127–40, in Semih Aktekin et al., eds., *Teaching History and Social Studies for Multicultural Europe* (Ankara: Harf, 2009).
  The State of History Education in Europe: Challenges and Implications of the Youth and History Survey (Hamburg: Koerber, 1998).

Le Goff, Jacques, *History and Memory*, trans. Steven Rendall and Elizabeth Claman (1977; Columbia University Press, 1992).

Lejeune, Philippe, *On Autobiography*, transl. Katherine Leary (University of Minnesota Press, 1989).
  On Diary, ed. Jeremy D. Popkin & Julie Rak (University of Hawai'i Press, 2009).

Lenain, Thierry, *Art Forgery: The History of a Modern Obsession* (Reaktion, 2011).

Lenz, Siegfried, *The Heritage*, trans. Krishna Winston (1978; Hill & Wang, 1981).

Leon, Warren, and Roy Rosenzweig, eds., *History Museums in the United States* (University of Illinois Press, 1989).

Leonard, Mark, ed., *Personal Viewpoints: Thoughts about Paintings Conservation* (Getty Conservation Institute, 2003).

Leonard, Mark, and David Bomford, eds., *Issues in the Conservation of Paintings* (Getty Conservation Institute, 2004).

Le Poidevin, Robin, *The Images of Time: An Essay in Temporal Representation* (Oxford University Press, 2007).

Le Roy Ladurie, Emmanuel, *Montaillou: Cathars and Catholics in a French Village 1294–1324*, trans. Barbara Bray (1975; London: Scolar, 1978).

Lesy, Michael, *Time Frames: The Meaning of Family Pictures* (Pantheon, 1980).

Levin, David, *History as Romantic Art: Bancroft, Prescott, Motley, and Parkman* (Stanford University Press, 1959).

Levine, Joseph M., *The Battle of the Books: History and Literature in the Augustan Age* (Cornell University Press, 1991).
  Between the Ancients and the Moderns: Baroque Culture in Restoration England (Yale University Press, 1999).
  Re-enacting the Past: Essays on the Evolution of Modern English Historiography (Ashgate, 2004).

Lewis, C. S., *Out of the Silent Planet* (1938; Scribner, 2003).
  The Screwtape Letters (1942; HarperCollins, 2009).

Lewis, Clarence Irving, *An Analysis of Knowledge and Valuation* (1946; Read Books, 1998).

Lincoln, Abraham, *Collected Works*, 8 vols. (Rutgers University Press, 1953).

Lindgren, James M., *Preserving Historic New England: Preservation, Progressivism, and the Remaking of Memory* (Oxford University Press, 1995).

Linenthal, Edward T., *Preserving Memory: The Struggle to Create America's Holocaust Museum* (Columbia University Press, 2001).

Lipsitz, George, *Time Passages: Collective Memory and American Popular Culture* (University of Minnesota Press, 1990).

Liu, Alan, *Local Transcendence: Essays on Postmodern Historicism and the Database* (University of Chicago Press, 2008).

Lively, Penelope, *According to Mark* (Heinemann, 1984).
  Ammonites and Leaping Fish: A Life in Time (Penguin, 2013).
  'Children and the art of memory', *Horn Book Magazine* 54 (1978): 17–23, 197–203.

The House in Norham Gardens (London: Pan, 1977).

The Road to Lichfield (Heinemann, 1977).

Locke, John, *Two Treatises of Government* (1690; New York, 1947).

Loewen, James W., *Lies My Teacher Told Me: Everything Your American History Textbook Got Wrong* (New York: New Press, 1995).

Longfellow, Henry Wadsworth, *The Writings*, 11 vols. (London, 1886–93).

Lowenthal, David, 'Archival perils', *Archives* 31 (2006): 49–75.

George Perkins Marsh: Prophet of Conservation (University of Washington Press, 2000).

The Heritage Crusade and the Spoils of History (Cambridge University Press, 1998).

'On arraigning ancestors: a critique of historical contrition', *North Carolina Law Review* 87 (2009): 901–66.

The Past Is a Foreign Country (Cambridge University Press, 1985).

'The timeless past: some Anglo-American historical preoccupations', *Journal of American History* 75 (1989): 1263–80.

Lowenthal, David, and Marcus Binney, eds., *Our Past before Us: Why Do We Save it?* (London: Temple Smith, 1981).

Lowry, Lois, *The Giver* (1993; HarperCollins, 2003).

Lukács, Georg, *The Historical Novel*, trans. H. and S. Mitchell (1937; Penguin, 1981).

Lumley, Robert, ed., *The Museum Time-Machine: Putting Cultures on Display* (Routledge, 1988).

Luzzi, Joseph, *Romantic Europe and the Ghost of Italy* (Yale University Press, 2008).

Lynch, Kevin, *What Time Is This Place?* (MIT Press, 1972).

McCalman, Iain, and Paul A. Pickering, eds., *Historical Reenactment: From Realism to the Affective Turn* (Palgrave Macmillan, 2010).

Macaulay, Rose, *Pleasure of Ruins* (New York: Walker, 1953).

Macaulay, Thomas Babington, *Critical and Historical Essays Contributed to the Edinburgh Review*, 5 vols. (London, 1903).

The History of England from the Accession of James II, 5 vols. (London, 1848).

McGowan, Margaret T., *The Vision of Rome in Late Renaissance France* (Yale University Press, 2000).

McKenna, Terence, *The Archaic Revival* (Harper & Row, 1992).

McKitterick, Rosamond, *History and Memory in the Carolingian World* (Cambridge University Press, 2004).

Mackridge, Peter, *Language and National Identity in Greece, 1766–1976* (Oxford University Press, 2009).

Magdalino, Paul, ed., *Perception of the Past in Twelfth-Century Europe* (London: Hambledon Press, 1992).

Magelssen, Scott, *Living History Museums: Undoing History through Performance* (Scarecrow Press, 2007).

'Performance practices of [living] open-air museums (and a new look at "Skansen" in American living museum context)', *Theatre History Studies* 24 (June 2004): 125–49.

'"This is a drama. You are characters": The tourist as fugitive slave in Conner Prairie's "Follow the North Star"', *Theatre Topics* 16:1 (Mar. 2006): 19–36.

Magnussen, Svein, and Tore Helstrup, eds., *Everyday Memory* (New York: Psychology Press, 2007).

Malamud, Margaret, *Ancient Rome and Modern America* (Wiley-Blackwell, 2009).

Mankowitz, Wolf, *Wedgwood* (Batsford, 1953).

Margalit, Avishai, *The Ethics of Memory* (Harvard University Press, 2002).

Marsh, George P., *Man and Nature; or, Physical Geography as Modified by Human Action* (1864; Harvard University Press, 1965).

Marx, Karl, *The Eighteenth Brumaire of Louis Napoleon* (1852), trans. Saul K. Padover (New York, 1972).

Matt, Susan J., *Homesickness: An American History* (Oxford University Press, 2011).

Mazzocco, Angelo, 'The antiquarianism of Francesco Petrarca', *Journal of Medieval and Renaissance Studies* 7 (1977): 203–24.

Mazzocco, Angelo, ed., *Interpretations of Renaissance Humanism* (Brill, 2006).

Mazzotta, Giuseppe, *The New Map of the World: The Poetic Philosophy of Giambattista Vico* (Princeton University Press, 1999).

   The Worlds of Petrarch (Duke University Press, 1993).

Meckler, Michael, ed., *Classical Antiquity and the Politics of America from George Washington to George W. Bush* (Baylor University Press, 2006).

Megill, Allan, *Historical Knowledge, Historical Error* (University of Chicago Press, 2007).

Melville, Herman, *White-Jacket: or, The World in a Man-of-War* (1850; Northwestern University Press, 1970).

Menninger, W. Walter, 'Memory and history: what can you believe?', *Archival Issues* 21:2 (1996): 97–106.

Merryman, John Henry, 'A licit international trade in cultural objects', *IJCP* 4 (1995): 13–60.

Merton, Robert K., *On the Shoulders of Giants: A Shandean Postscript* (Harcourt Brace Jovanovich, 1965).

Meyer, Karl E., *The Plundered Past* (Atheneum, 1973).

Michaels, Walter Benn, *The Trouble with Diversity: How We Learned to Love Identity and Ignore Inequality* (Holt, 2006).

Miele, Chris, ed., *From William Morris: Building Conservation and the Arts and Crafts Cult of Authenticity, 1877–1939* (Yale University Press, 2005).

Mill, John Stuart, *The Collected Works*, 33 vols. (University of Toronto Press, 1963–91).

Miller, J. Hillis, 'History as repetition in Thomas Hardy's poetry: the example of "Wessex Heights"' (1972), in *Tropes, Parables, Performatives: Essays on Twentieth-Century Literature* (Duke University Press, 1991), 107–34.

Miller, Joseph C., ed., *The African Past Speaks: Essays on Oral Tradition and History* (Folkestone: Dawson, 1980).

Mills, Gary B., and Elizabeth Shown Mills, 'Roots and the new "faction": a legitimate tool for Clio?' *Virginia Magazine of History and Biography* 89:1 (Jan. 1981): 3–26.

Milton, John, *Paradise Lost* (1667; London, 1821).

Mink, Louis O., 'Everyman his or her own annalist', in W. J. T. Mitchell, ed., *On Narrative* (University of Chicago Press, 1981) 233–9.

Minkowski, Eugène, *Lived Time: Phenomenological and Psychopathological Studies* (1933; Northwestern University Press, 1970).

Molho, Anthony, and Gordon S. Wood, eds., *Imagined Histories: American Historians Interpret the Past* (Princeton University Press 1998).

Momigliano, Arnaldo D., 'Ancient history and the antiquarian' (1950), in *Studies in Historiography* (Weidenfeld & Nicolson, 1966), 1–39.

   Essays in Ancient and Modern Historiography (Blackwell, 1977).

   Paganism and Christianity in the Fourth Century (Clarendon Press, 1963).

Monmonier, Mark, *From Squaw Tit to Whorehouse Meadow: How Maps Name, Claim, and Inflame* (University of Chicago Press, 2006).

Montaigne, Michel de, *The Complete Essays*, trans. Donald Frame (Stanford University Press, 1958).

Moore, Brian, *The Great Victorian Collection* (Jonathan Cape, 1975).

Moore, Ward, *Bring the Jubilee* (1955; London, 1976).

Morris, William, *Collected Works* (Longmans, Green, 1910–1915).

   The Earthly Paradise (London, 1868).

Mortier, Roland, *Le poétique des ruines en France: ses origines, ses variations de la Renaissance à Victor Hugo* (Geneva: Droz, 1974).

Muller, Jeffrey M., 'Rubens's theory and practice of the imitation of art', *Art Bulletin* 64 (1982): 229–47.

Mumford, Lewis, *The Culture of Cities* (Harcourt, Brace & World, 1938).

Munz, Peter, *Our Knowledge of the Growth of Knowledge: Popper or Wittgenstein?* (Routledge, 1985).
The Shapes of Time: A New Look at the Philosophy of History (Wesleyan University Press, 1977).

Murphy, Cullen, *God's Jury: The Inquisition and the Making of the Modern World* (Houghton Mifflin Harcourt, 2012).

Museum International, Intangible Cultural Heritage, 56:1–2 (May 2004).

Myrberg, Nanouschka, 'False monuments? On antiquity and authenticity', *Public Archaeology* 3 (2004): 151–61.

Nabokov, Vladimir, *Speak, Memory: An Autobiography Revisited* (1951; Putnam, 1966).

Nahin, Paul J., *Time Machines: Time Travel in Physics, Metaphysics, and Science Fiction*, 2nd edn (Springer, 1999).

Naipaul, V. S., *A Bend in the River* (Knopf, 1979).

Naqvi, Nauman, *The Nostalgic Subject: A Genealogy of the 'Critique of Nostalgia'*, Working Paper 23 (Messina: Università degli Studi, 2007).

Nash, Gary B., Charlotte Crabtree, and Ross E. Dunn, *History on Trial: Culture Wars and the Teaching of the Past* (Knopf, 1997).

Neiger, Motti, Oren Meyers, and Eyal Zandberg, eds., *On Media Memory: Collective Memory in a New Media Age* (Palgrave Macmillan. 2011).

Neisser, Ulric, ed., *Memory Observed: Remembering in Natural Contexts* (San Francisco: Freeman, 1982).

Neisser, Ulric, and Robyn Fivish, *The Remembering Self: Construction and Accuracy in the Self-Narrative* (1994; Cambridge University Press, 2008).

Neisser, Ulric, and Ira E. Hyman, Jr., eds., *Memory Observed*, 2nd edn (New York: Worth, 2000).

Neisser, Ulric, and Eugene Winograd, eds., *Remembering Reconsidered* (Cambridge University Press, 1988).

Nelson, Katherine, 'Self and social functions: individual autobiographical memory and collective narrative', *Memory* 11 (2003): 125–36.

Newell, William H., ed., *Ancestors* (The Hague: Mouton, 1976).

Nicholls, Peter, ed., *Encyclopedia of Science Fiction* (Granada, 1979); rev. edn with John Clute (Orbit, 1993).

Nicolson, Adam, (Harper, 2008).

Nicolson, Marjorie Hope, *Mountain Gloom and Mountain Glory: The Development of the Aesthetics of the Infinite* (Cornell University Press, 1959).

Niebuhr, Barthold Georg, *The History of Rome* (1811–12), 4th edn, 2 vols., trans. J. C. Hare and Connop Thirlwall (Cambridge, 1831).

Nietzsche, Friedrich, *The Use and Abuse of History* (1874), trans. Adrian Collins (Bobbs-Merrill, 1957).

Ní Fhlainn, Sorcha, ed., *The Worlds of Back to the Future: Critical Essays on the Films* (London: McFarland, 2010).

Noble, Louis Legrand, *The Life and Works of Thomas Cole* (1853; Harvard University Press, 1964).

Noonan, John T., Jr., *A Church That Can and Cannot Change: The Development of Catholic Moral Teaching* (University of Notre Dame Press, 2005).

Nora, Pierre, comp., *Les Lieux de mémoire*, I, II (3 vols.), III (3 vols.) (Paris: Gallimard, 1984–92).

Novick, Peter, *That Noble Dream: The 'Objectivity Question' and the American Historical Profession* (Cambridge University Press, 1988).

Oddy, Andrew, ed., *Restoration: Is It Acceptable?* (British Museum Occasional Paper 99, 1994).

Oddy, Andrew, and Sara Carroll, eds., *Reversibility: Does It Exist?* (British Museum Occasional Paper 135, 1999).

Oddy, Andrew, and Sandra Smith, eds., *Past Practice – Future Prospects* (British Museum Occasional Paper 145, 2001).

Ofshe, Richard, and Ethan Watters, *Making Monsters: False Memories, Psychotherapy, and Sexual Hysteria* (Scribners, 1994).

Olmsted, Frederick Law, *Walks and Talks of an American Farmer in England* (New York, 1852).

Ong, Walter J., *Orality and Literacy: The Technologizing of the Word* (1982; rev. edn Routledge, 2002).

Orlando, Francesco, *Obsolete Objects in the Literary Imagination: Ruins, Relics, Rarities, Rubbish, Uninhabited Places, and Hidden Treasures*, trans. Gabriel Pihas and Daniel Seidel (1994; Yale University Press, 2006).

Orvell, Miles, *The Real Thing: Imitation and Authenticity in American Culture, 1880–1940* (University of North Carolina Press, 1989).

Orwell, George, *The Collected Essays, Journalism and Letters*, 4 vols. (Secker & Warburg, 1968).
    Nineteen Eighty-Four (1948; Penguin, 1954).

Otter, Monika, *Inventiones: Fiction and Referentiality in Twelfth-Century English Historical Writing* (University of North Carolina Press, 1996).

Ozment, Steven E., *Ancestors: The Loving Family in Old Europe* (Harvard University Press, 2001).

Page, Max, and Randall Mason, eds., *Giving Preservation a History* (Routledge, 2004).

Paine, Thomas, *The Political Writings of Thomas Paine*, 2 vols. (New York, 1830).
    Rights of Man (1791–2), in *The Collected Writings* (Library of America, 1995), 433–664.

Palgrave, Francis, *Collected Historical Works*, 10 vols. (Cambridge University Press, 1922).

Panofsky, Erwin, *Meaning in the Visual Arts* (1955; Penguin, 1993).
    Renaissance and Renascences in Western Art (1960; Paladin, 1970).
    Tomb Sculpture: Its Changing Aspects from Ancient Egypt to Bernini (Thames & Hudson, 1964).

Partner, Nancy, ed., *Writing Medieval History* (Hodder Arnold, 2005).

Pater, Walter, *Marius the Epicurean: His Sensations and Ideas*, 2nd edn, 2 vols. (London, 1885).

Peacock, Thomas Love, *Peacock's Four Ages of Poetry; Shelley's Defence of Poetry*, ed. H. F. Brett-Smith (Blackwell, 1921), 1–19.

Pearce, Susan, and Paul Martin, eds., *The Collector's Voice*, vol. 4: *Contemporary Voices* (Ashgate, 2002).

Pearcy, Lee T., *The Grammar of Our Civility: Classical Education in America* (Baylor University Press, 2005).

Penfield, Wilder, 'The permanent record of the stream of consciousness', *Acta Psychologica* 11 (1955): 47–69.

Perrault, Charles, *Paralèlle* [sic] *des anciens et des modernes, en ce qui regarde les arts et les sciences* (Paris, 1693).

Perrin, Noel, *Dr. Bowdler's Legacy: A History of Expurgated Books in England and America* (1969; Boston: Godine, 1992).

Petrarch, Francesco, *Letters from Petrarch*, ed. Morris Bishop (University of Indiana Press, 1966).
    Petrarch's Letters to Classical Authors, trans. Mario Emilio Cosenza (University of Chicago Press, 1910).

Petzet, Michael, *International Principles of Preservation* (Paris: ICOMOS, 2009).

Pevsner, Nikolaus, *Some Architectural Writers of the Nineteenth Century* (Oxford University Press, 1972).

Pfitzer, Gregory M., *Picturing the Past: Illustrated Histories and the American Imagination, 1840–1900* (Smithsonian, 2002).
    Popular History and the Literary Marketplace (University of Mississippi Press, 2006).

Phillips, Charles, 'Greenfield's changing past', *History News* 37:11 (1982): 9–14.

Phillips, Mark Salber, *On Historical Distance* (Yale University Press, 2013).

Piaget, Jean, and Bärbel Inhelder, *Memory and Intelligence*, trans. Arnold J. Pomerans (1968; Routledge, 1973).

Piccini, Angela, 'Faking it: why the truth is so important for TV archaeology', in Timothy Clack and Marcus Brittain, eds., *Archaeology and the Media* (Walnut Creek, CA: Left Coast Press, 2009), 221–36.

Pigman, G. W., III, 'Imitation and the Renaissance sense of the past: the reception of Erasmus' Ciceronianus', *Journal of Medieval and Renaissance Studies* 9 (1979): 155–77.

  'Versions of imitation in the Renaissance', *Renaissance Quarterly* 33 (1980): 1–32.

Piper, John, 'Pleasing decay' (1947), in *Buildings and Prospects* (London: Architectural Press, 1948), 89–116.

Plato, *The Republic* (360 BC), trans. Desmond Lee (Penguin, 1974).

Plumb, J. H., *The Death of the Past* (1969; Penguin, 1973).

Pocock, J. G. A., 'The origins of the study of the past', *Comparative Studies in Society & History* 4 (1962): 209–46.

Polybius, *The Histories* (after 146 BC), trans. Evelyn Shuckburgh 2 vols. (London, 1889).

Pompa, Leon, *Human Nature and Historical Knowledge: Hume, Hegel and Vico* (Cambridge University Press, 1990).

Popkin, Jeremy D., *History, Historians, and Autobiography* (University of Chicago Press, 2005).

Porciani, Ilaria, and Jo Tollebeek, eds., *Setting the Standards: Institutions, Networks and Communities of National Historiography* (Palgrave Macmillan, 2012).

Posner, Eric A., and Adrian Vermeule, 'Reparations for slavery and other historical injustices', *Columbua Law Review* 103 (2003): 689–748.

Poulet, Georges, *Studies in Human Time* (1949), trans. Elliott Coleman (Johns Hopkins University Press, 1956).

Price, Nicholas Stanley, Mansfield Kirby Talley, and Alessandra Melluco Vaccaro, eds., *Historical and Philosophical Issues in the Conservation of Cultural Heritage* (Getty Conservation Institute, 1996).

Price, Uvedale, *Essays on the Picturesque, as Compared with the Sublime and the Beautiful*, 3 vols. (London, 1810).

Prott, Lyndel V., et al., eds., *Realising Cultural Heritage Law: Festschrift for Patrick O'Keefe* (Builth Wells, UK: Institute of Art & Law, 2012).

Proust, Marcel, *Remembrance of Things Past* (1913–27), trans. C. K. Scott-Moncrieff and Terence Kilmartin, 3 vols. (Penguin, 1983).

Pye, Elizabeth, *Caring for the Past: Issues in Conservation for Archaeology and Museums* (London: James & James, 2001).

Radstone, Susannah, and Bill Schwarz, eds., *Memory: Histories, Theories, Debates* (Fordham University Press, 2010).

Raphael, Ray, *Founding Myths: Stories That Hide Our Patriotic Past* (New York: New Press, 2004).

Ravitch, Diane, *The Language Police: How Pressure Groups Restrict What Students Learn* (Knopf, 2003).

Renan, Ernest, *Qu'est-ce qu'une nation?* ed. Philippe Forest (Paris: Bordas, 1991).

Rethinking History, Reenactment, 11:3 (2007): 299–462.

Ricoeur, Paul, *Memory, History, Forgetting*, trans. Kathleen Blamey and David Pellauer (University of Chicago Press, 2004).

Riegl, Alois, *Der moderne Denkmalkultus* (Vienna, 1903).

Rigney, Ann, *Imperfect Histories: The Elusive Past and the Legacy of Romantic Historicism* (Cornell University Press, 2001).

Rítívoí, Andreea Decíu, *Yesterday's Self: Nostalgia and the Immigrant Identity* (Rowman & Little-field, 2002).

Rogers, Samuel, *The Pleasures of Memory, with Other Poems* (1792; London, 1802).

Rosenberg, Daniel, and Anthony Grafton, *Cartographies of Time: A History of the Timeline* (Princeton Architectural Press, 2010).

Rosenberg, John D., *Elegy for an Age: The Presence of the Past in Victorian Literature* (London: Anthem, 2005).

Rosenblum, Robert, *Transformations in Late Eighteenth Century Art* (Princeton University Press, 1967).

Rosenstone, Robert A., *History on Film / Film on History* (Pearson Educational, 2006; 2nd ed. 2012).

    'The reel Joan of Arc: reflections on the theory and practice of the historical film', *Public Historian* 25:3 (Summer 2003): 61–77.

Rosenzweig, Roy, 'Scarcity or abundance? Preserving the past in a digital era', *AHR* 108 (2003): 735–62.

Rosenzweig, Roy, and David Thelen, *The Presence of the Past: Popular Uses of History in American Life* (Columbia University Press, 1998).

Ross, Dorothy, 'Historical consciousness in nineteenth-century America', *AHR* 89 (1984): 909–28.

Roth, Joseph, *The Radetzky March* (1932), trans. Eva Tucker (London, 1974).

Roth, Michael S., *Memory, Trauma, and History: Essays on Living with the Past* (Columbia University Press, 2011).

Rousso, Henry, *The Haunting Past: History, Memory and Justice in Contemporary France* (1998), trans. Ralph Schoolcraft (University of Pennsylvania Press, 2002).

Rowan, Yorke, and Uzi Baram, *Marketing Heritage: Archaeology and the Consumption of the Past* (AltaMira, 2004).

Rowland, Ingrid D., *The Scarith of Scornello: A Tale of Renaissance Forgery* (University of Chicago Press, 2004).

Rowles, Graham D., and Habib Chaudhury, eds., *Home and Identity in Late Life: International Perspectives* (Springer, 2005).

Rudwick, Martin J. S., *Bursting the Limits of Time: The Reconstruction of Geohistory in the Age of Revolution* (University of Chicago Press, 2005).

Rüsen, Jörn, ed., *Western Historical Thinking: An Intercultural Debate* (Berghahn, 2002).

Ruskin, John, *Complete Works*, ed. E. T. Cook and Alexander Wedderburn, 39 vols. (London: George Allen, 1903–12).

    Modern Painters, 5 vols. (1843–1860; New York, 1886).

    Ruskin in Italy: Letters to his Parents, ed. Harold I. Shapiro (Clarendon Press, 1972).

    The Seven Lamps of Architecture (1849; New York: Noonday, 1961).

Russell, Bertrand, *The Analysis of Mind* (Allen & Unwin, 1921).

Ryckmans, Pierre, 'The Chinese attitude towards the past' (1986), [as Simon Leys], in *The Hall of Uselessness: Collected Essays* (NYRB, 2013), 285–301.

St Clair, William, *Lord Elgin and the Marbles* (1967; 3rd edn Oxford University Press, 1988).

Salvesen, Christopher, *The Landscape of Memory: A Study of Wordsworth's Poetry* (Edward Arnold, 1965).

Samuel, Raphael, *Patriotism: The Making and Unmaking of British National Identity*, vol. I: *History and Politics* (Routledge, 1989).

Sanders, Andrew, *In the Olden Time: Victorians and the British Past* (Yale University Press, 2013).

Sani, Fabio, ed., *Self-Continuity: Individual and Collective Perspectives* (New York: Psychology Press, 2008).

Santesso, Aaron, *A Careful Longing: The Poetics and Problems of Nostalgia* (Associated University Presses, 2006).

Santmyer, Helen, *Ohio Town* (1962; Harper & Row, 1984).

Savage, Kirk, *Monument Wars: Washington, D.C., the National Mall, and the Transformation of the Memorial Landscape* (University of California Press, 2009).

Scanlan, John, *On Garbage* (Reaktion, 2005).

Schachtel, Ernest G., *Metamorphosis: On the Development of Affect, Perception, Attention, and Memory* (New York: Basic Books, 1959).

Schacter, Daniel L., *The Seven Sins of Memory: How the Mind Forgets and Remembers* (Houghton Mifflin, 2001).

Schacter, Daniel L., ed., *Memory Distortion: How Minds, Brains, and Societies Reconstruct the Past* (Harvard University Press, 1995).

Schacter, Daniel L., and Elaine Scarry, eds., *Memory, Brain, and Belief* (Harvard University Press, 2000).

Schafer, R. Murray, *The Soundscape: Our Sonic Environment and the Tuning of the World* (1977; Rochester, VT: Inner Traditions, 1993).

Schechtman, Marya, 'Stories, lives, and basic survival: a refinement and defense of the narrative view', *Royal Institute of Philosophy*, supplement 60 (2007): 155–78.

Scheffer, John D., 'The idea of decline in literature and the fine arts in eighteenth-century England', *Modern Philology* 34 (1936–7): 156–78.

Schiavone, Aldo, *The End of the Past: Ancient Rome and the Modern West* (1996; Harvard University Press, 2000).

Schiffman, Zachary Sayre, *The Birth of the Past* (Johns Hopkins University Press, 2011).

Schlanger, Judith E., *Les Métaphores de l'organisme* (1971; Paris: L'Harmattan, 1995).

Schlehe, Judith, et al., eds., *Staging the Past: Themed Environments in Transcultural Perspectives* (Bielefeld: Transcript, 2010).

Schochet, Gordon J., *Patriarchalism in Political Thought: The Authoritarian Family and Political Speculation and Attitudes Especially in Seventeenth-Century England* (Blackwell, 1975).

Schopenhauer, Arthur, *Parerga and Paralipomena* (1851), trans. E. F. J. Payne, in *Short Philosophical Essays*, 2 vols. (Oxford University Press, 1974).

Schudson, Michael, *Watergate in American Memory: How We Remember, Forget, and Reconstruct the Past* (New York: Basic Books, 1992).

Schwartz, Barry, *Abraham Lincoln and the Forge of National Memory* (University of Chicago Press, 2000).

  'Social change and collective memory: the democratization of George Washington', *American Sociological Review* 56 (1991): 221–36.

Scott, David A., 'Modern antiquities: the looted and the faked', *IJCP* 20 (2013): 49–75.

Scott, George Gilbert, *Remarks on Secular & Domestic Architecture Present & Future* (1857; Nabu Press, 2010).

Scott, Walter, *The Antiquary* (1816; London: Dent, 1907).

  Ivanhoe (1820; Boston, 1834).

Segal, Daniel A., '"Western Civ" and the staging of history in American higher education', *AHR* 105 (2000): 770–805.

Seixas, Peter, ed., *Theorizing Historical Consciousness* (University of Toronto Press, 2004).

Shaffer, Peter, *Lettice and Lovage* (André Deutsch, 1988).

Shahar, Shulamith, *Growing Old in the Middle Ages* (Routledge, 1997).

Shail, Andrew, and Robin Stoate, *Back to the Future* (Palgrave Macmillan, 2010).

Shattuck, Roger, *Forbidden Knowledge* (St Martin's Press, 1996).

Proust's Binoculars: A Study of Memory, Time, and Recognition in 'A la recherche du temps perdu' (Random House, 1963).

Shaw, Christopher, and Malcolm Chase, eds., *The Imagined Past: History and Nostalgia* (Manchester University Press, 1989).

Sheehy, Jeanne, *The Rediscovery of Ireland's Past: The Celtic Revival 1830–1930* (Thames & Hudson, 1980).

Sheen, Mercedes, Simon Kemp, and David C. Rubin, 'Twins dispute memory ownership: a new false memory phenomenon', *Memory & Cognition* 29 (2001): 779–88.

Shemilt, Denis J., 'Adolescent ideas about evidence and methodology in history', in Christopher Portal, ed., *The History Curriculum for Teachers* (Lewes, Sussex: Falmer, 1988), 39–61.

Shepherd, Robert J., and Larry Yu, *Heritage Management, Tourism, and Governance in China: Managing the Past to Serve the Present* (Springer, 2013).

Shryock, Andrew, and Daniel Lord Smail, eds., *Deep History: The Architecture of Past and Present* (University of California Press, 2011).

Silberman, Neil Asher, *Between Past and Present: Archaeology, Ideology, and Nationalism in the Modern Middle East* (Henry Holt, 1989).

Silverman, Helaine, ed., *Contested Cultural Heritage: Religion, Nationalism, Erasure, and Exclusion* (Springer, 2011).

Simak, Clifford D., *Catface* [US title *Mastodonia*] (1973; Methuen, 1978).

Simons, Daniel J., and Christopher F. Chabris, 'What people believe about how memory works: a representative survey of the US population', *PloS One* 6.8 (2011): e22757.

Skinner, Quentin, 'Meaning and understanding in the history of ideas', *JHI* 8 (1969): 3–53.

Slade, Giles, *Made to Break: Technology and Obsolescence in America* (Harvard University Press, 2006).

Slavery & Abolition, Remembering Slave Trade Abolitions, 30:2 (2007): 161–338.

Smail, Daniel Lord, *On Deep History and the Brain* (University of California Press, 2008).

Small, Jocelyn Penny, *Wax Tablets of the Mind: Cognitive Studies in Memory and Literacy in Classical Antiquity* (Routledge, 1997).

Smith, Anthony D., *Chosen Peoples: Sacred Sources of National Identity* (Oxford University Press, 2003).

Smith, Mark M., *Sensing the Past: Seeing, Hearing, Smelling, Tasting and Touching in History* (University of California Press, 2007).

Snow, Steven Eddy, *Performing the Pilgrims: A Study of Ethnohistorical Role-Playing at Plimoth Plantation* (University of Mississippi Press, 1993).

Sophocles, *Oedipus at Colonus*, trans. Robert Fitzgerald (Harcourt, Brace, 1941).

Sorlin, Pierre, *The Film in History: Restaging the Past* (Blackwell, 1980).

Southern, R. W., *History and Historians: Selected Papers* (Blackwell, 2004).

Spence, Donald P., *Narrative Truth and Historical Truth: Meaning and Interpretation in Psychoanalysis* (Norton, 1982).

Spender, Stephen, *Love–Hate Relations: A Study of Anglo-American Sensibilities* (Hamish Hamilton, 1974).

Spiegel, Gabrielle M., *The Past as Text: The Theory and Practice of Medieval Historiography* (Johns Hopkins University Press, 1997).

Romancing the Past: The Rise of Vernacular Prose Historiography in Thirteenth-Century France (University of California Press, 1993).

Stanton, Cathy, *Reenactors in the Parks: A Study of External Revolutionary War Reenactment at National Parks* (Boston: NPS, 1999).

Starobinski, Jean, 'The idea of nostalgia', *Diogenes* 54 (June 1966): 81–103.

Stegner, Wallace, *Wolf Willow: A History, a Story, and a Memory of the Last Plains Frontier* (1962; Penguin, 2000).

Sterne, Laurence, *The Life and Opinions of Tristram Shandy, Gentleman* (1759; Penguin, 2003).

Stokes, Melvyn, *D. W. Griffith's The Birth of a Nation* (Oxford University Press, 2007).

Storace, Patricia, *Dinner with Persephone: Travels in Greece* (Granta, 1997).

Straub, Jürgen, ed., *Narration, Identity and Historical Consciousness* (Berghahn, 2005).

Stuart, James, and Nicholas Revett, *The Antiquities of Athens* (1762–1816; Princeton Architectural Press, 2007).

Strawson, Galen, ed., *The Self?* (Blackwell, 2005).

Summerson, John, *Heavenly Mansions and Other Essays on Architecture* (Norton, 1963).

Sweet, Rosemary, *Antiquaries: The Discovery of the Past in Eighteenth-Century Britain* (Hambledon and London, 2004).

Swift, Jonathan, 'The battle of the books' (1698), in *A Tale of the Tub and Other Satires* (Dent, 1975), 37–65.

   Gulliver's Travels (1726; Penguin, 1967).

Symcox, Linda, and Arie Wilschut, eds., *National History Standards: The Problem of the Canon and the Future of Teaching History* (Charlotte, NC: Information Age, 2007).

Tanizaki, Junichiro, *In Praise of Shadows* (1933–4), trans. T. J. Harper and E. G. Seidensticker (Vintage, 2001).

Tarlow, Sarah, and Susie West, eds., *The Familiar Past: Archaeologies of Later Historical Britain* (Routledge, 1999).

Tennyson, Alfred, Lord, *The Poems* (London, 1969).

Tey, Josephine, *The Daughter of Time* (London, 1954).

Thane, Pat, ed., *The Long History of Old Age* (Thames & Hudson, 2005).

Thomas, Sophie, *Romanticism and Visuality: Fragments, History, Spectacle* (Routledge, 2008).

Thompson, Janna, *Taking Responsibility for the Past: Reparation and Historical Injustice* (Polity, 2002).

Thompson, Jenny, *War Games: Inside the World of 20th-Century War Reenactors* (Smithsonian, 2004).

Thompson, Michael, *Rubbish Theory: The Creation and Destruction of Value* (Oxford University Press, 1979).

Thoreau, Henry David, *Walden* (1854; Modern Library, 1937).

Thurley, Simon, *Men from the Ministry: How Britain Saved Its Heritage* (Yale University Press, 2013).

Tilden, Freeman, *Interpreting Our Heritage: Principles and Practices for Visitor Services in Parks, Museums, and Historic Places* (1957; 4th edn University of North Carolina Press, 2007).

Tilmans, Karin, et al., eds., *Performing the Past: Memory, History, and Identity in Modern Europe* (Amsterdam University Press, 2010).

Tindall, Gillian, *The Fields Beneath: The History of One London Village* (1977; Weidenfeld & Nicolson, 2002).

Tintner, Adeline R., *The Twentieth-Century World of Henry James* (Louisiana State University Press, 2001).

Tocqueville, Alexis de, *Democracy in America* (1834–40), trans. Henry Reeve, 2 vols. (Cambridge, MA, 1863).

Tollebeek, Jo, 'Seeing the past with the mind's eye: the consecration of the romantic historian', *Clio* 29:2 (2000): 167–91.

Tomasello, Michael, *The Cultural Origins of Human Cognition* (Harvard University Press, 1999).

Tonkin, Elizabeth, *Narrating Our Pasts: The Social Construction of Oral History* (Cambridge University Press, 1992).

Tonkin, Elizabeth, et al., eds., *History and Ethnicity* (Routledge, 1989).

Torpey, John, *Making Whole What Has Been Smashed: On Reparations Politics* (Harvard University Press, 2006).

Trevelyan, George Macaulay, 'Autobiography of an historian', in *An Autobiography & Other Essays* (Longmans, Green, 1949), 3–17.

Trexler, Richard G., *The Journey of the Magi: Meanings in History of a Christian Story* (Princeton University Press, 1997).

Tribble, Scott, *A Colossal Hoax: The Giant from Cardiff That Fooled America* (Rowman & Littlefield, 2009).

Trigg, Dylan, *The Aesthetics of Decay: Nothingness, Nostalgia, and the Absence of Reason* (New York: Peter Lang, 2006).

Trompf, Garry W., *The Idea of Historical Recurrence in Western Thought: From Antiquity to the Reformation* (University of California Press, 1979).

Trouillot, Michel-Rolph, *Silencing the Past: Power and the Production of History* (Beacon, 1997).

Tschudi-Madsen, Stephan, *Restoration and Anti-Restoration: A Study in English Restoration Philosophy*, 2nd edn (Oslo: Universitetsforlaget, 1976).

Tucker, Aviezer, *Our Knowledge of the Past: A Philosophy of History* (Cambridge University Press, 2004).

Tulving, Endel, 'Episodic memory: from mind to brain', *Annual Review of Psychology* 53 (2002): 1–25.

Tunbridge, J. E., and Gregory J. Ashworth, *Dissonant Heritage: The Management of the Past as Conflict* (Wiley, 1996).

Turner, Frank M., *The Greek Heritage in Victorian Britain* (Yale University Press, 1981).

Twain, Mark, *A Connecticut Yankee in King Arthur's Court* (1889; University of California Press, 1983).

   The Innocents Abroad, or the New Pilgrim's Progress (1869; New American Library, 1966).

   Sketches, New and Old (Hartford, CT, 1875).

Tyler, Elizabeth M., and Ross Balzaretti, eds., *Narrative and History in the Early Medieval West* (Turnhout: Brepols, 2006).

UNESCO, *An Illustrated Inventory of Famous Dismembered Works of Art: European Painting* (Paris, 1974).

Updike, John, *Buchanan Dying: A Play* (Knopf, 1974).

Uttley, Alison, *A Traveller in Time* (1939; Puffin, 1978).

Vansina, Jan, *Oral Tradition: A Study in Historical Methodology* (1961), trans. H. M. Wright (Aldine, 2006).

Vasari, Giorgio, *The Lives of the Most Eminent Painters, Sculptors, and Architects* (1550/1568), trans. Mrs. Jonathan Foster, 5 vols. (London, 1850).

Vico, Giambattista, *The New Science*, trans. T. G. Bergin and M. H. Frisch (1725, 3rd edn 1744; Cornell University Press, 1948).

   On the Study Methods of Our Time, trans. Elio Gianturco (1709; Bobbs-Merrill, 1965).

Volney, Constantin-François, Comte de, *The Ruins: or, A Survey of the Revolutions of Empire* (1789; 5th edn London, 1807).

Walden, Sarah, *The Ravished Image* (1985; 2nd edn London: Gibson Square, 2004).

Wallace, Mike, *Mickey Mouse History and Other Essays on American Memory* (Temple University Press, 1996).

Wang, Ban, *Illuminations from the Past: Trauma, Memory, and History in Modern China* (Stanford University Press, 2004).

Wang. Zheng, *Never Forget National Humiliation: Historical Memory in Chinese Politics and Foreign Relations* (Columbia University Press, 2012).

Warner, W. Lloyd, *The Living and the Dead: A Study of the Symbolic Life of Americans* (Yale University Press, 1959).

Webster, Daniel, *The Writings and Speeches*, 18 vols. (Boston, 1903).

Webster, Noah, Jr., *A Collection of Essays and Fugitive Writings* (Boston, 1790).

Wedgwood, C. Veronica, *Truth and Opinion: Historical Essays* (Collins, 1960).

Weil, François, *Family Trees: A History of Genealogy in America* (Harvard University Press, 2013).

Weinrich, Harald, *Lethe: The Art and Critique of Forgetting*, trans. Stephen Rendall (1997; Cornell University Press, 2004).

Weiss, Roberto, *The Renaissance Discovery of Classical Antiquity* (Blackwell, 1959).

Wells, H. G., *The Dream* (Collins, 1929).

The Time Machine (1895; Signet, 2002).

Welzer, Harald, Sabine Moller, and Karoline Tschuggnall, *'Opa war kein Nazi': National-sozialismus und Holocaust in Familiengedächtnis* (Frankfurt: Fischer, 2002).

Wertsch, James V., *Voices of Collective Remembering* (Cambridge University Press, 2002).

Wharton, Annabel Jane, *Selling Jerusalem: Relics, Replicas, Theme Parks* (University of Chicago Press, 2006).

Wharton, Glenn, *The Painted King: Art, Activism and Authenticity in Hawai'i* (University of Hawai'i Press, 2011).

Whately, Richard, *Historic Doubts Relative to Napoleon Buonaparte* (1819; 7th edn London, 1841).

White, Hayden, *The Content of the Form: Narrative Discourse and Historical Representation* (Johns Hopkins University Press, 1987).

Wiener, Martin J., *English Culture and the Decline of the Industrial Spirit, 1850–1980* (1981; Cambridge University Press, 2004).

Wilde, Oscar, *The Picture of Dorian Gray* (1891; London: Dent, 1930).

Willis, Connie, *Doomsday Book* (Bantam, 1992).

Wilson, Richard Guy, et al., eds., *Re-creating the American Past: Essays on the Colonial Revival* (University of Virginia Press, 2006).

Wineburg, Samuel S., 'Crazy for history', *Journal of American History* 90:4 (Mar. 2004): 1401–14.

Historical Thinking and Other Unnatural Acts: Charting the Future of Teaching the Past (Temple University Press, 2001).

Winter, Alison, *Memory: Fragments of a Modern History* (University of Chicago Press, 2012).

Wolin, Sheldon S., *The Presence of the Past: Essays on the State and the Constitution* (Johns Hopkins University Press, 1989).

Wood, Byrd, ed., *With Heritage So Rich* (1966; Washington: National Trust for Historic Preservation, 1999).

Wood, Gordon S., *The Purpose of the Past: Reflections on the Uses of History* (Penguin, 2008).

The Radicalism of the American Revolution (Knopf, 1992).

Woodward, C. Vann, *The Future of the Past* (Oxford University Press, 1989).

Woodward, Christopher, *In Ruin: A Journey through History, Art, and Literature* (Pantheon, 2001).

Woolf, Virginia, *Moments of Being* (Chatto & Windus/Sussex University Press, 1976), 61–139.

Orlando (1928; New American Library, 1960).

Wordsworth, William, *The Poetical Works*, 5 vols. (Clarendon Press, 1940–66).

Wotton, William, *Reflections upon Ancient and Modern Learning* (London, 1694).

Wright, Lawrence, *Remembering Satan: A Tragic Case of Recovered Memory* (Knopf, 1994).

Wright, Patrick, *On Living in an Old Country: The National Past in Contemporary Britain* (1985; Oxford University Press, 2009).

Yablon, Nick, *Untimely Ruins: An Archaeology of American Urban Modernity, 1819–1919* (University of Chicago Press, 2010).

Yates, Frances A., *The Art of Memory* (1969; Routledge, 2010).

Yerushalmi, Yosef Hayim, *Zakhor: Jewish History and Jewish Memory* (1982; University of Washington Press, 1996).

Young, Edward, *Conjectures on Original Composition*, 2nd edn (1759; Manchester University Press, 1918).

Young, Terence, and Robert Riley, eds., *Theme Park Landscapes* (Dumbarton Oaks, 2002).

Yourcenar, Marguerite, *That Mighty Sculptor, Time*, trans. Walter Kaiser (1983; Macmillan, 1993).

Zagorin, Perez, 'Lord Acton's ordeal: the historian and moral judgement', *Virginia Quarterly Review* 74:1 (Winter, 1998): 1–17.

Zenderland, Leila, ed., *Recycling the Past: Popular Uses of American History* (University of Pennsylvania Press, 1978).

Zerubavel, Eviatar, *Ancestors and Relatives: Genealogy, Identity, and Community* (Oxford University Press, 2012).

  Time Maps: Collective Memory and the Social Shape of the Past (University of Chicago Press, 2004).

Zerubavel, Yael, *Recovered Roots: Collective Memory and the Making of the Israeli National Tradition* (University of Chicago Press, 1995).

INDEX

639

CPSIA information can be obtained
at www.ICGtesting.com
Printed in the USA
LVHW041824271118
598428LV00012B/219/P